AUFSTIEG UND NIEDERGANG DER RÖMISCHEN WELT

II.19.2

AUFSTIEG UND NIEDERGANG DER RÖMISCHEN WELT

GESCHICHTE UND KULTUR ROMS IM SPIEGEL DER NEUEREN FORSCHUNG

II

HERAUSGEGEBEN
VON
HILDEGARD TEMPORINI
UND
WOLFGANG HAASE

WALTER DE GRUYTER · BERLIN · NEW YORK
1979

PRINCIPAT

NEUNZEHNTER BAND
(2. HALBBAND)

RELIGION
(JUDENTUM: PALÄSTINISCHES JUDENTUM
[FORTS.])

HERAUSGEGEBEN
VON
WOLFGANG HAASE

WALTER DE GRUYTER · BERLIN · NEW YORK
1979

Herausgegeben mit Unterstützung der Robert Bosch Stiftung, Stuttgart

CIP-Kurztitelaufnahme der Deutschen Bibliothek

Aufstieg und Niedergang der römischen Welt:
Geschichte u. Kultur Roms im Spiegel d. neueren Forschung / hrsg. von Hildegard Temporini u. Wolfgang Haase. — Berlin, New York: de Gruyter.
NE: Temporini, Hildegard [Hrsg.];
2. Principat.
Bd. 19.
2. Halbbd. / Hrsg. von Wolfgang Haase. — 1. Aufl. — 1979.
ISBN 3-11-007969-0
NE: Haase, Wolfgang [Hrsg.]

Printed in Germany
Satz und Druck: Walter de Gruyter & Co., Berlin 30
Einbandgestaltung und Schutzumschlag: Rudolf Hübler
Buchbinder: Lüderitz & Bauer, Berlin
Klischees: Union Klischee, Berlin

Vorbemerkung

Aus technischen Gründen erscheint der zweite Halbband des Bandes II 19 von ANRW vor dem ersten; der erste Halbband wird ihm innerhalb weniger Monate im Sommer 1979 folgen.

Tübingen, im März 1979 W. H.

Inhalt

RELIGION (JUDENTUM: PALÄSTINISCHES JUDENTUM [FORTS.])

Band II.19.2:

RELIGION

(JUDENTUM: ALLGEMEINES; PALÄSTINISCHES JUDENTUM [FORTS.])

The Formation of Rabbinic Judaism: Yavneh (Jamnia) from A. D. 70 to 100

by JACOB NEUSNER, Providence, R. I.

Table of Contents

I. The Nature of the Sources

Rabbinic Judaism[1] took shape in the century from 70 to 170, making use of the antecedent heritage of the Old Testament as well as of the 'traditions of the fathers' associated with Pharisaism and of certain convictions and procedures of scribism. An amalgam of Pharisaism, Scribism, and yet its own distinctive interests shaped in the crucible of the destruction

[1] The term is defined below, part III. This paper is intended to summarize my research, cited in notes 3—5, on the nature of the sources pertinent to earlier Rabbinic Judaism and the way in which those sources are to be used for the historical enterprise. In the cited works, the sources are translated and fully analyzed from various perspectives. Merely citing an unanalyzed pericope in the present paper would serve no useful purpose, since without full discussion of the relationship of said pericope to all other evidence, the meaning and historical usefulness of the item are hardly going to be self-evident. That is why I refer the reader to the complete compendia of pertinent materials and their analysis. Here are given only the results of much more extensive work.

of the Jerusalem Temple, Rabbinic Judaism left behind an immense literary corpus. The use of this literature for historical and religious-historical purposes, in particular for the examination of the history of the major ideas and mythic motifs of Rabbinic Judaism, is exceedingly complex. Since the present paper is addressed to scholars well aware of equivalent difficulties in the use of evidence pertinent to other philosophico-religious groups in ancient times, it is best to lay out, at the outset, the methodological alternatives under consideration and debate at the present time. Then, having argued in favor of one available alternative, I shall present the primary results attained thereby. These results, as the title makes clear, pertain solely to the earliest stages of Rabbinic Judaism. But they should serve to illustrate what is to be expected from the nascent methodological approaches undertaken by this writer in the past decade.

II. Two Approaches to the Use of Sources of Rabbinism: Traditional and Critical

The established, traditional and Orthodox conceptions on the use of the rabbinical literature for historical purposes are admirably illustrated in a current and important work by EPHRAIM URBACH[2]. Through the analysis and criticism of that work, I propose to indicate how and why these conceptions fail to accord with contemporary and correct criticism and to spell out the real problems and their methodological solutions. The established approach is called 'traditional' because it stands wholly within the presuppositions of the texts it proposes to use for historical purposes and because, for obvious reasons, it is staunchly espoused and defended within Orthodox Jewish circles, particularly in the State of Israel, where credulous traditionalism is deemed historical, and truly critical efforts are dismissed unread.

EPHRAIM E. URBACH, professor of Talmud at the Hebrew University and author of numerous articles and books on the Talmud and later rabbinic literature, in 'The Sages' presents a compendious and in many ways definitive work intended "to describe the concepts and beliefs of the Tannaim and Amoraim and to elucidate them against the background of their actual life and environment". When published in Hebrew, in 1969, the work enjoyed immediate success, going into a second edition within two years. URBACH is an imposing figure in Israeli scholarly and religious-political circles, serving as president of the Israel Academy of Sciences and Humanities and running for the presidency of the State of Israel as candidate of the

[2] The Sages. Their Concepts and Beliefs. By EPHRAIM E. URBACH. Translated from the Hebrew by ISRAEL ABRAHAMS. Jerusalem: The Magnes Press. The Hebrew University, 1975. Two volumes. I. Text, pp. xxii and 692; II. Notes, pp. 383.

right-wing and 'religious' political parties. Within Orthodox Judaism URBACH derives from the German stream, which proposes to combine piety with academic learning. The work before us has been accurately described by M. D. HEER (Encyclopaedia Judaica 16, 1971, 4): "He [URBACH] outlines the views of the rabbis on the important theological issues such as creation, providence, and the nature of man. In this work URBACH synthesizes the voluminous literature on these subjects and presents the views of the Talmudic authorities." The topics are as follows: belief in one God; the presence of God in the world; "nearness and distance — Omnipresent and heaven"; the power of God; magic and miracle; the power of the divine name; the celestial retinue; creation; man; providence; written law and oral law; the commandments; acceptance of the yoke of the kingdom of heaven; sin, reward, punishment, suffering, etc.; the people of Israel and its sages, a chapter which encompasses the election of Israel, the status of the sages in the days of the Hasmoneans, Hillel, the regime of the sages after the destruction of the Temple, and so on; and redemption. The second volume contains footnotes, a fairly brief and highly selective bibliography, and alas, a merely perfunctory index. The several chapters, like the work as a whole, are organized systematically, consisting of sayings and stories relevant to the theme under discussion, together with URBACH's episodic observations and comments on them.

In the context of earlier work on Talmudic theology and religion, URBACH's contribution is, as I said, definitive, a distinct improvement in every way. Compared to a similar, earlier compendium of Talmudic sayings on theological subjects, A. HYMAN's Oṣar divré hakhamin ufitgamehem (Tel Aviv 1934), a collection of sayings laid out alphabetically, according to catchword, URBACH's volumes have the advantage of supplying not merely sayings but cogent discussions of the various sayings and a more fluent, coherent presentation of them in essay form. SOLOMON SCHECHTER's Some Aspects of Rabbinic Theology (New York 1909, based on essays in the 'Jewish Quarterly Review' printed in 1894—1896) covers exactly what it says, some aspects, by contrast to the much more ambitious dimension of the present work. The comparison to GEORGE FOOT MOORE's Judaism in the First Centuries of the Christian Era: The Age of the Tannaim (Cambridge 1927—1930) is somewhat more complex. MOORE certainly has the advantage of elegant presentation. URBACH's prose, in I. ABRAHAM's English translation, comes through as turgid and stodgy, while MOORE's is the opposite. MORTON SMITH comments on MOORE's work, "Although it too much neglects the mystical, magical, and apocalyptic sides of Judaism, its apology for tannaitic teaching as a reasonable, humane, and pious working out of biblical tradition is conclusive . . . " (Encyclopaedia Judaica 12, 1971, 293—294; compare Harvard Library Bulletin 15, 1967, pp. 169—179). By contrast to MOORE, URBACH introduces sayings of Amoraim into the discussion of each category, and, since both URBACH and MOORE aim to present a large selection of sayings on the several topics, URBACH's work is on the face of it a more comprehensive collection.

URBACH's comments on his predecessors (I, pp. 5—18) underline the theological bias present in most, though not all, former studies. WILHELM BOUSSET and HUGO GRESSMANN, Die Religion des Judentums im späthellenistischen Zeitalter (Leipzig 1926; repr. [Tübingen 1966[4]]) is wanting because rabbinic sources are used sparingly and not wholly accurately and because it relies on "external sources", meaning apocryphal literature and Hellenistic Jewish writings. URBACH's own criticism of MOORE, that "he did not always go deeply enough into the essence of the problems that he discussed", certainly cannot be leveled against URBACH himself. His further reservation is that MOORE "failed to give an account of the origin of the beliefs and concepts, of their struggles and evolution, of their entire chequered course till their crystallization, of the immense dynamism and vitality of the spiritual life of the Second Temple period, of the tension in the relations between the parties and sects and between the various sections of the Sages themselves". This view underlines the historical ambition of URBACH's approach and emphasizes his view of his own contribution, cited at the outset: to elucidate the concepts and beliefs of the Tannaim and Amoraim against the background of their actual life and environment. Since that is URBACH's fundamental claim, the work must be considered not only in the context of what has gone before, in which, as I said, it emerges as a substantial step forward, but also in the setting of its own definition and understanding of the historical task, its own theory of how Talmudic materials are to be used for historical knowledge. In this regard it is not satisfactory.

There are some fairly obvious problems, on which we need not dwell at length. URBACH's selection of sources for analysis is both narrowly canonical and somewhat confusing. We often hear from Philo, but seldom from the Essene Library of Qumran, still more rarely from the diverse works assembled by R. H. CHARLES as the 'Apocrypha and Pseudepigrapha of the Old Testament' (Oxford 1913), and the like. If we seek to describe the Talmudic rabbis, surely we cannot ask Philo to testify to their opinions. If we listen to Philo, surely we ought to hear — at least for the purpose of comparison and contrast — from books written by Palestinian Jews of various kinds. The Targumim are allowed no place at all because they are deemed 'late'. (The work of historians of traditions, e. g., JOSEPH HEINEMANN, and of comparative Midrash, e. g., RENÉE BLOCH and GEZA VERMES, plays no role at all in this history!) But documents which came to redaction much later than the several Targumim (by any estimate of the date of the latter) make rich and constant contributions to the discussion. Within a given chapter, the portrayal of the sources will move rapidly from biblical to Tannaitic to Amoraic sources, as though the line of development were single, unitary, and harmonious, and as though there were no intervening developments which shaped later conceptions. Differentiation among the stages of Tannaitic and Amoraic sayings tends to be episodic. Commonly, slight sustained effort is made to treat them in their several sequences, let alone to differentiate among schools and circles within a given period. URBACH takes with utmost seriousness his title, 'The sages, their concepts and beliefs', and his 'history', topic by topic, reveals remarkably little variation, development, or even movement. It would not be fair to URBACH to suggest that all he has done is publish his card-files. But I think his skill at organization and arrangement of materials tends to outrun his interest in differentiation and comparison within and among them, let alone in the larger, sequential history of major ideas and their growth and coherent development over the centuries. One looks in vain for URBACH's effort to justify treating 'the sages' as essentially a coherent and timeless group.

Let us turn, rather, to the more fundamental difficulties presented by the work, because, as I said, it is to be received as the definitive and (probably) final product of a long-established approach to the study of Talmudic religion and history. URBACH has certainly brought to their ultimate realization the methods and concepts of his predecessors.

First, let us ask, does the world-view of the Talmudic sages emerge in a way which the ancient sages themselves would have recognized? From the viewpoint of their organization and description of reality, their world-view, it is certain that the sages would have organized their card-files quite differently. We know that is the case because we do not have, among the chapters before us, a single one which focuses upon the theme of one of the orders, let alone tractates, within which the rabbis divided and presented their various statements on reality, e. g., Seeds, the material basis of life; Seasons, the organization and differentiation of time; Women, the status of the individual; Damages, the conduct of civil life including government; Holy Things, the material service of God; and Purities, the immaterial base of divine reality in this world. The matter concerns not merely the superficial problem of organizing vast quantities of data. The Talmudic rabbis left a large and exceedingly complex, well-integrated legacy of law. Clearly, it is through that legacy that they intended to make their fundamental statements upon the organization and meaning of reality. An account of their concepts and beliefs which ignores nearly the whole of the *halakhah* surely is slightly awry.

In fairness to URBACH, I must stress that he shows himself well-aware of the centrality of *halakhah* in the expression of the world-view of the Talmudic rabbis. He correctly criticizes his predecessors for neglecting the subject and observes, "The Halakha does not openly concern itself with beliefs and concepts; it determines, in practice, the way in which one should walk . . . Nevertheless beliefs and concepts lie at the core of many Halakhot; only their detection requires exhaustive study of the history of the Halakha combined with care to avoid fanciful conjectures and unfounded explanations." URBACH occasionally does introduce halakhic materials. But, as is clear, the fundamental structure of his account of Talmudic theology is formed in accord not with the equivalent structure of the Talmud — the *halakhah* — but with the topics and organizing rubrics treated by all nineteenth and twentieth century Protestant historical studies of theology: God, ethics, revelation, and the like. That those studies are never far from mind is illustrated by URBACH's extensive discussion of whether Talmudic ethics was theonomous or autonomous (I, pp. 320ff.), an issue important only from the viewpoint of nineteenth-century Jewish ethical thought and its response to KANT. But URBACH's discussion on that matter is completely persuasive, stating what is certainly the last word on the subject. He can hardly be blamed for criticizing widely-held and wrong opinions.

Second, has URBACH taken account of methodological issues important in the study of the literary and historical character of the sources? In particular, does he deal with the fundamental questions of how these particular sources are to be used for historical purposes? The answer is a qualified negative. On many specific points, he contributes sporadic philological observations, interesting opinions and judgments as to the lateness of one saying as against the antiquity of another, subjective opinions on what is more representative or reliable than something else. If these opinions are not systematic and if they reveal no uniform criterion, sustainedly applied to all sources, they nonetheless derive from a mind of immense learning and cognitive experience. Not all judgment must be critical, and not all expression of personal taste systematic. The dogmatic opinions of a man of such self-evident mastery of the tradition, one who, in addition, clearly is an exemplar of the tradition for his own setting, are important evidence for the study and interpretation of the tradition itself, particularly in its modern phase.

Yet we must ask, if a saying is assigned to an ancient authority, how do we know that he really said it? If a story is told, how do we know that the events the story purports to describe actually took place? And if not, just what are we to make of said story and saying for historical purposes? Further, if we have a saying attributed to a first-century authority in a document generally believed to have been redacted five hundred or a thousand years later, how do we know that the attribution of the saying is valid, and that the saying informs us of the state of opinion in the first century, not only in the sixth or eleventh in which it was written down and obviously believed true and authoritative? Do we still hold, as an axiom of historical scholarship, *'ain muqdam ume'uhar* (Chronology does not apply) in the Talmud?! And again, do not the sayings assigned to a first-century authority, redacted in documents deriving from the early third century, possess greater credibility than those first appearing in documents redacted in the fifth, tenth, or even fifteenth centuries? Should we not, on the face of it, distinguish between more and less reliable materials? The well-known tendency of medieval writers to put their opinions into the mouths of the ancients, as in the case of the Zohar, surely warns us to be cautious about using documents redacted, even formulated, five hundred or a thousand or more years after the events of which they speak.

There is yet a further, equally simple problem. The corpus of evidence is simply huge. Selectivity characterizes even the most thorough and compendious accounts, and I cannot imagine one more comprehensive than URBACH's. But should we not devise means for the filtering downward of some fundamental, widely- and well-attested opinions, out of the mass of evidence, rather than capriciously selecting what we like and find interesting? We have few really comprehensive accounts of the history of a single idea or concept. URBACH himself has produced some of the better studies which we do have. It seems somewhat premature to describe so vast a world in the absence of a far more substantial corpus of *Vorstudien* of specific ideas and the men who held them than is available. Inevitably, one must characterize the treatment of one topic after another as unhistorical and superficial, and this is despite the author's impressive efforts to do history and to do it thoroughly and in depth.

After all, URBACH has done this great work without the advantage of studies of the history of the traditions assigned over the centuries to one authority or another. He has at hand scarcely any critical work comparing various versions of a story appearing in successive compilations. He has no possibility of recourse to comprehensive inquiries into the Talmud's forms and literary traits, redactional tendencies, even definitive accounts of the date of the redaction of most of the literature used for historical purposes. He cannot consult works on the thought of any of the individual Amoraim or on the traits of schools and circles among them, for there is none of critical substance. Most collections which pass as biographies even of Tannaim effect no differentiation among layers and strata of the stories and sayings, let alone attempting to describe the history of the traditions on the basis of which historical biography is to be recovered. The laws assigned, even in 'Mishnah-Tosefta', to a given Tanna have not been investigated as to their underlying presuppositions and unifying convictions, even their gross thematic agendum. If URBACH speaks of "the rabbis" and differentiates only episodically among the layers and divisions of sayings, in accord either with differing opinions on a given question or with the historical development of evidently uniformly-held opinions, he is hardly to be criticized. The episodic contributions he himself makes in large measure constitute such history of ideas as presently is in hand. And, as I said, even that history is remarkable for the pre-critical methods and uncritical presuppositions upon which it is based.

Nor have I alluded to the intractable problems of internal, philosophico-theological analysis of ideas and their inner structures, once their evident historical, or sequential, development, among various circles and schools of a given generation and over a period of hundreds of years, has been elucidated. That quite separate investigation, analysis of the logic and meaning of the concepts and beliefs of the sages, requires definition in its own terms, not in accord with the limited and simple criteria of working historians. If URBACH does not attempt it, no one else has entirely succeeded either. In this regard, URBACH's cavalier dismissal of the work of MARMORSTEIN, HESCHEL, and KADUSHIN, among others, is not heartening. While they may not have 'persuaded' URBACH of the correctness of their theses, while they may have been wrong in some of their conclusions, and while their methods may have been unrefined, they at least have attempted the task which URBACH refuses even to undertake. One of the less fortunate aspects of URBACH's book, which makes for unpleasant reading, is the way in which he treats the work of other scholars. In the case of the above named, this is not only disgraceful, it also is disastrous for URBACH's own undertaking. And since the whole opinion on works of considerable scholarship is the single word 'worthless' or 'unpersuasive', it may be observed that there is a certain subjectivity which seems to preclude URBACH's reasoned discussion of what he likes and does not like, in the work of many others and to prevent any sort of rational exchange of ideas.

URBACH's work, as I said, in the balance majestically and magnificently brings to their full realization the methods and suppositions of the past hundred years. I cannot imagine that anyone again will want, from these perspectives, to approach the task of describing all of "the concepts and beliefs of the Tannaim and Amoraim", of elucidating all of them "against the background of their actual life and environment". So far as the work can be done in accord with established methods, here it has been done very competently indeed. Accordingly, we may well forgive the learned author for the sustained homiletical character of his inquiry and its blatantly apologetic purposes: "The aim of our work is to give an epitome of the beliefs and concepts of the Sages as the history of a struggle to instill religious and ethical ideals into the everyday life of the community and the individual, while preserving at the same time the integrity and unity of the nation and directing its way in this world as a preparation for another world that is wholly perfect . . . Their eyes and their hearts were turned Heavenward, yet one type was not to be found among them . . . namely the mystic who seeks to liberate himself from his ego and in doing so is preoccupied with himself alone. They saw their mission in work here in the world below. There were Sages who inclined to extremism in their thoughts and deeds, and there were those who preached the way of compromise, which they did not, however, determine on the basis of convenience. Some were severe and exacting, while others demonstrated an extreme love of humanity and altruism. The vast majority of them recognized the complexities of life with its travail and joy, its happiness and tragedy, and this life served them also as a touchstone for their beliefs and concepts." All of this may well be so, but it remains to be demonstrated as historical fact in the way in which contemporary critical historians generally demonstrate matters of fact. It requires analysis and argument in the undogmatic and unapologetic spirit characteristic of contemporary studies in the history of ideas and of religions. But in the context in which these words of URBACH are written, among the people who will read them, this statement of purpose puts forth a noble ideal, one which might well be emulated by the 'sages' — exemplars and politicians of Orthodox Judaism — to whom, I believe, URBACH speaks most directly and persuasively, and by whom (alone) his results certainly will be taken as historical fact. The publishing success of the book and the well-merited recognition accorded its learned author are hopeful signs that the ideal of the sages of old indeed has not been lost upon their most recent avatars. It is by no means a reduction of learning to its sociological and political relevance to say that, if it were only for his advocacy of the humane and constructive position just now quoted, URBACH has made a truly formidable contribution to the contemporary theological life of Orthodox Judaism.

To respond to a work of such importance as URBACH's, it will not suffice to outline problems of method which await solution. Having stressed, for example, the importance of beginning the inquiry into the world-view of the Talmudic rabbis with the study of the law, in particular of the earliest stratum, faithfully represented by 'Mishnah-Tosefta', I have now to propose the sorts of work to be done. Since I have raised the question of how we know what is assigned to a person was really said by him, and since by implication I have suggested that we cannot affirmatively answer that question, what sort of inquiry do I conceive to be possible, and upon what historical-epistemological basis? Let me here present very briefly an alternative conception of how to define and approach the formidable task accomplished by URBACH, in accord with the prevailing methods and within established suppositions about the detailed and concrete historicity of Talmudic evidences: the description of the world-view of 'our sages'.

The problems that lie ahead and the line of research leading to their solution are now to be specified. Let us begin with the matter generally regarded as settled: the meaning of the texts. While philological research by Semitists and archaeological discoveries self-evidently will clarify the meanings of words and the identification of objects mentioned in the rabbinical literature, there is yet another task, the fresh exegesis of the whole of rabbinical literature within the discipline of contemporary hermeneutical conceptions. The established exegesis takes for granted an axiom which is simply false: that all texts are to be interpreted in the light of all other texts. Talmudic discussion of Mishnah and its meanings invariably shape the received interpretation of Mishnah, for example. If 'Tosefta' — itself a commentary — supplies a conception of Mishnah's principle or rule, then 'Tosefta' places the imprint of its interpretation upon the meaning of Mishnah.

Now no one would imagine that the original meaning of *Tanakh* is to be uncovered in the pages of Midrash or in the medieval commentaries to the Scriptures. On the contrary, everyone understands that *Tanakh* has been subjected to a long history of interpretation, and that that history, while interesting, is germane to the original meaning of *Tanakh* only when, on objective and critical grounds, we are able to affirm it by historical criteria. By contrast, discussion of Mishnaic pericopae in Talmud and medieval commentaries and codes invariably exhausts the analysis of the meaning of Mishnaic pericopae. It is to the credit of H. ALBECK that his excellent commentary to Mishnah makes the effort at many points deliberately to exclude considerations introduced only later on. This is done not merely to facilitate a simple and popular interpretation, though ALBECK admirably succeeds in doing just that, but also to present what ALBECK considers to be the primary and original meaning of the law. It is no criticism of ALBECK, limited as he was by his form, a commentary of the most abbreviated sort, to say that the discussion of the primary meaning of Mishnah has to begin.

What is meant is simply, What did these words mean to the people who made them up, in the late first and second century? What issues can have been in their minds? True, much is to be learned from the answers to these questions supplied by the exegetes from the third to the twentieth century. But since, in the main, the supposition of the established exegetical tradition is non-historical and therefore uninterested in what pericopae meant at the outset, the established tradition, without reevaluation, will not serve any longer. That is not to suggest it cannot be drawn upon: the contrary is the case. I know no other road into the heart of a pericope. At the same time, the established agendum — the set of issues, problems, and questions deemed worth consideration — is to be drastically reshaped, even while much that we have received will be reaffirmed, if on grounds quite different from those which motivated the great exegetes.

The classical exegetes faced the task of showing the profound interrelationships, in logic and meaning, of one law to the next, of developing and expanding the subtleties and complexities of law, in the supposition that in hand is a timeless and harmonious, wholly integrated and unitary structure of law and logic. In other words, the established exegetical tradition properly and correctly ignores questions of beginnings and development, regarding these questions as irrelevent to the true meaning of the law under the aspect of eternity. And that is indeed the case — except when we claim to speak about specific, historical personalities, at some one time, who spoke the language of their own day and addressed the issues of their own epoch. URBACH claims to tell us not about 'Talmudic Judaism' in general — organized, as is clear, around various specific topics — but to describe the history and development of 'Talmudic Judaism'. Yet, if that is the case, then the sources adduced in evidence have to be examined with the question in mind, What did the person who made up or formulated this saying mean to tell us? And the answer to that question is not to be located either by repeating the essentially eisegetical results already in hand or by pretending that everything is obvious.

We have to distinguish between the primary issue, present to begin with in a pericope, and secondary problems or considerations only later on attached to the pericope. How do we confidently distinguish between the primary message of a pericope and the secondary *eisegesis* found in the great commentaries? We have to ask, What does the narrator, legislator, or redactor propose to tell us in a particular, distinct pericope? That is to say, through the routine form-analytical and literary-critical techniques already available, we have to isolate the smallest units of tradition, and, removing them from their redactional as well as their exegetical-eisegetical framework, ask about their meaning and original intent. Modes of emphasis and stress, for example, are readily discerned. Important materials will commonly be placed at the beginning of a pericope, or underlined through balanced, contrary allegations. But stylistic considerations and formal traits are helpful primarily in isolating pericopae and establishing their primary units for analysis. What is decisive is the discernment of what the narrator includes or omits, what seems to be his obvious concerns and what he ignores.

Once the importance of a fresh exegesis of rabbinical texts is established, the next problem is to select the documents on which the work should begin. Here URBACH's work illustrates the fateful error of assuming that rabbinical literature is essentially timeless, so that there is "neither early nor late in Torah". Applied to the present work, it results in the notion that whatever is attributed to anyone was really said by the person to whom the saying is attributed, therefore tells us about the period in which he lived — and this without regard to the date at which the document in which said saying occurs was redacted, as I have stressed. Thus side by side in URBACH's compilation are sayings in Mishnah and in late Amoraic and even medieval compilations of materials. In a fresh approach to the problem of the history of Talmudic Judaism, we should, I believe, establish guidelines by which we evalute materials first occurring in late compilations. 'Mishnah-Tosefta' assuredly comes to redaction by ca. 200 A.D. On the face of it, 'Mishnah-Tosefta' therefore constitutes a more reliable testimony to the mind of second century rabbis than does 'Yalquṭ Shime'oni' or 'Yalquṭ Re'uveni'. If that is obvious, then it follows that we have to begin our work with the analysis of the main ideas attributed to authorities in 'Mishnah-Tosefta'. These have clearly to be worked out, and the materials occurring in later compilations, of Amoraic and medieval origin, are to be tested for conceptual and even thematic congruence against the materials occurring in earlier documents.

The question remains. If it is assumed that 'Mishnah-Tosefta' testify to the time in which the document was finally redacted, then how shall we know what layers of thought come before the time of the redaction of the document itself? How shall we know, furthermore, whether a person to whom a saying is attributed really said it? To deal with the latter question, I do not believe we have any way of verifying whether a person to whom a saying is attributed actually said it. Our history of Talmudic Judaism will unfold by periods, may even produce significant differentiation among named authorities within the several periods, but it will, so far as I can see, not supply a definitive answer to the question of whether 'Aqiva really said what he is claimed to have said. While that question — whether we have *ipsissima verba* of a particular historical figure — is deemed terribly pressing in the study of the founder of Christianity, the importance of the question is for theological, not historical reasons. We do not know everything we might like to know; that does not mean what we do know is not worth knowing. Yet the other matter — how we can find out whether anything in 'Mishnah-Tosefta' antedates the redaction of 'Mishnah-Tosefta' — requires more considerable attention. Here we must begin with a working hypothesis and test that hypothesis against the results attained in its application.

The simplest possible hypothesis is that the attributions of sayings to named authorities may be relied upon in assigning those sayings to the period, broadly defined, in which said authorities flourished. We do not and cannot know, for example, whether ʿAqiva actually said what is attributed to him. Are we able to establish criteria by which we may conclude that what is assigned to ʿAqiva likely belongs in the period in which he lived, e. g., to his school or associates (or even to the man himself)? This proposition can indeed be tested. We have laws which interrelate in theme and conception and which also bear attributions to successive authorities, e. g., to a Yavnean, to an Ushan, and to an authority of the time of Rabbi. If we are able to demonstrate that what is assigned to a Yavnean is conceptually earlier than, and not dependent upon, what is assigned to an Ushan, then, on the face of it, the former indeed is an earlier tradition, the latter a later one. The unfolding of the rabbis' ideas on legal and other questions may be shown to take place through sequences of logic, with what is assigned to later masters often depending upon and generated by what is assigned to the earlier ones. When we find a correlation between such logical (not merely thematic) sequences and temporal ones, that is, if what is assigned to a later master does depend in theme, conception, principle, and inner logic upon what is attributed to an earlier master, then we have history: we know what comes earlier, what comes later. We are able therefore to describe ideas probably characteristic of authorities between the disaster of 70 and the Bar Kokhba debacle, and from that time to the period of Rabbi, and in the time of Rabbi. Doubtless work on Amoraic materials will yield the same series of disciplined sequences of correlated attributions and logical developments, showing the general reliability of the attributions by periods and making possible a description of ideals held in a given period by various authorities. On that basis, indeed, we can describe the ideas really characteristic of one period in the historical unfolding of Talmudic Judaism and relate them to ideas characteristic of earlier and later periods. That sort of historical inquiry is virtually not attempted by URBACH, simply because he takes for granted, as I said, that what is assigned to a given authority really was stated by that authority. Having no problems, he obviously is unable to propose solutions and then to test them.

A further descriptive historical task is to be undertaken. When we concentrate attention on the most reliable witnesses to the mind of the earlier rabbis, those of the first and second century, we find ourselves engaged in the analysis primarily of legal texts. 'Mishnah-Tosefta' and related literature focus attention on halakhic problems. Are there underlying unities of conception or definitions of fundamental principles to be discerned within the *halakhah*? No one familiar with the literature and its classical exegesis is in doubt that there are. These are to be spelled out with some care, also correlated and compared to conceptions revealed in writings of other Jews, not solely rabbinic Jews, as well as Christians and 'pagans'. When, for example, we describe primary concerns and perennial issues inherent in laws attributed to Ushans, we find that, in much acute detail, rather fundamental issues of physics are worked out, e. g., the nature of mixtures, which will not have surprised Stoic, natural philosophers (History of the Mishnaic Law of Purities. XII. Tohorot. Commentary [Leiden 1976], pp. 206—209). Again, an enduring interest of Yavnean pericopae is in the relationship between intention and action, an issue both of interest to Paul and those who told stories about Jesus, on the one side, and of concern to philosophers of disaster and rebuilding in the earlier destruction, for instance, Jeremiah. The thought of Yavneh in any event has to be brought into relationship with the context in which the rabbis did their work, the aftermath of the loss of the Temple, just as the work of the Ushans, following the much greater this-worldly catastrophe brought on by Bar Kokhba, must always be seen against the background of crisis. Indeed, the formation of earlier rabbinic Judaism, from its primitive beginnings after 70 to its full and complete expression by the end of Ushan times in 170, is the product of an age of many painful events, events deemed at the time to bear the most profound theological weight. Much of the *halakhah* both can and should be interpreted in this particular context, and many of its issues, not to be reduced to economic or social concerns, express profound thought on the inner meanings of the age itself. It follows that once the exegetical work is complete (if provisionally) and the historical sequences of individual units of law fairly well established, the larger issues emergent in underlying unities of conception and definitions of fundamental principles are to be uncovered, so that the legal materials may produce a history of major ideas and themes, not merely sets of two or three logical-temporal sequences of minor details.

That is how we must answer the question, if Mishnah was redacted in ca. A.D. 200, then how do we know that anything in Mishnah derives from before A.D. 200? Traditionalists in Jewish scholarly circles have different answers. They posit transmission in exact words said by a given authority through oral means. They further hold that what is not assigned to a given authority goes "way way back". But materials not given in the name of a particular master share not only the literary, but also the conceptual, traits of materials assigned to a great many named masters, in particular in the period from 130 to 170. The traditional view in this matter is simply wrong.

In time, when the work outlined here is done, we shall see the outlines of the much larger history of legal, therefore religious, ideas, the unfolding of the world-view of the rabbis who created rabbinic Judaism. These outlines will emerge not merely from discrete sayings, chosen more or less at random, about topics of interest chiefly to us, e. g., was rabbinical ethics theonomous or autonomous? what did 'the rabbis' believe abont life after death, the Messiah, eschaton? and so on. Rather, the morphology of the rabbinic world-view will emerge inductively, differentiated as to its historical stages and as to the distinctive viewpoints and conceptions held by individual authorities or circles, within which that larger world-view originated.

Second, a new approach to the description and interpretation of the world-view of the earlier rabbis should emerge. This proceeds along critical-historical lines, taking account of the problems of dating sayings, of the diversity of the documents which purport to preserve opinions of the earlier masters, and the like. That is important, to be sure. But there are more important aspects of this work.

People do not seem to realize the immense dimensions of the evidence in our hands. We have much more than just a few sayings on this and that. We have a vast law-code, a huge exegetical corpus in respect to the Hebrew Scriptures and their translation, collections of stories about authorities, various kinds of sayings assigned to them — an extraordinarily large mass of materials. Our approach, for the first time, must encompass the totality of the evidence, cope with, take account of, sources of exceptional density and richness. The law, as I said, is the definitive source of the world-view of the earlier rabbis. What is earliest and best attested is 'Mishnah-Tosefta'. Therefore, if we want to know what people were thinking in the first and second centuries, we have to turn, to begin with, to that document, which must serve as criterion in the assessment of whatever first appears in the later compilations of rabbinical sayings and stories. Books on rabbinic Judaism which focus upon non-legal sayings (without regard, even, to the time at which the documents containing those sayings were redacted) simply miss the point of rabbinic Judaism.

But the legal sayings deal with picayune and inconsequential matters. The major problem is to derive, from arcane and trivial details of laws of various sorts, the world-view which forms the foundations of, and is expressed by, these detailed rules. That work must be done in a systematic and comprehensive way. And, in consequence, the definition of the agendum of scholarship is to be revised, not merely in terms of the adaptation and systematic application of methods of literary-critical, form-analytical, and redactional-critical, work hitherto unknown in this field, nor in terms of the introduction of historical-critical considerations, hitherto neglected or introduced in an episodic way and with dismal lack of historical sophistication, — not merely in these aspects, but in terms of its very shape and structure.

Let us now ask, If we do take account of the entire corpus of sayings attributed to a given authority, if we do preserve the critical stance and perspective on their pertinence to the person to whom they are assigned, then what sort of questions are we able to answer? How shall we define, or redefine, the historical agendum? The pages which follow are an effort to exemplify answers to these questions.

III. Definition of Rabbinic Judaism

The central conception of rabbinic Judaism is the belief that the ancient Scriptures constituted divine revelation, but only a part of it[3]. At Sinai, God had handed down a dual revelation: the written part known to one and all, but also the oral part preserved by the great scriptural heroes, passed on by prophets to various ancestors in the obscure past, finally and most openly handed down to the rabbis who created the Palestinian and Babylonian Talmuds. The 'whole Torah' thus consisted of both written and oral parts. The rabbis taught that that 'whole Torah' was studied by David, augmented by Ezekiel, legislated by Ezra, and embodied in the schools and by the sages of every period in Israelite history from Moses to the present. It is a singular, linear conception of a revelation, preserved only by the few, pertaining to the many, and in time capable of bringing salvation to all.

The rabbinic conception of Torah further regards Moses as 'our rabbi', the first and prototypical figure of the ideal Jew. It holds that whoever embodies the teachings of Moses 'our rabbi' thereby conforms to the will of God — and not to God's will alone, but also to his w a y. In heaven God and the angels study Torah just as rabbis do on earth. God dons phylacteries like a Jew. He prays in the rabbinic mode. He carries out the acts of compassion called for by Judaic ethics. He guides the affairs of the world according to the rules of Torah, just as does the rabbi in his court. One exegesis of the creation legend taught that God had looked into the Torah and therefrom had created the world.

The symbol of Torah is multidimensional. It includes the striking detail that whatever the most recent rabbi is destined to discover through proper exegesis of the tradition is as much a part of the Torah revealed to Moses as is a sentence of Scripture itself. It therefore is possible to participate even in the giving of the law by appropriate, logical inquiry into the law. God himself, studying and living by Torah, is believed to subject himself to these same rules of logical inquiry. If an earthly court overrules the testimony, delivered through miracles, of the heavenly one, God would rejoice, crying out, "My sons have conquered me! My sons have conquered me!"

The final element in the rabbinic conception of Torah concerns salvation. It takes many forms. One salvific teaching holds that had Israel not sinned — that is, disobeyed the Torah — the Scriptures would have closed with the story of the conquest of Palestine. From that eschatological time forward, the sacred community would have lived in eternal peace under the

[3] The sources on which the following section is based will be found in J. NEUSNER, History of the Jews in Babylonia (Leiden, 1965—1970), II, 151—240; III, pp. 95—194; IV, pp. 279—402; and V, pp. 133—216. A summary of the matter is in ID., The Way of Torah. An Introduction to Judaism (Encino, 1974) pp. 9—60.

divine law. Keeping the Torah was therefore the veritable guarantee of salvation. The opposite is said in many forms as well. Israel had sinned, therefore God had called the Assyrians, Babylonians, and Romans to destroy the Temple of Jerusalem; but in his mercy he would be equally faithful to restore the fortunes of the people when they, through their suffering and repentance, had expiated the result and the cause of their sin.

So in both negative and positive forms, the rabbinic idea of Torah tells of a necessary connection between the salvation of the people and of the world and the state of Torah among them. For example, if all Israel would properly keep a single Sabbath, the Messiah would come. Of special interest here is the rabbinic saying that the rule of the pagans depends upon the sin of Israel. If Israel would constitute a full and complete replication of 'Torah', that is, of heaven, then pagan rule would come to an end. It would end because all Israel then, like some few rabbis even now, would attain to the creative, theurgical powers inherent in Torah. Just as God had created the world through Torah, so saintly rabbis could now create a sacred community. When Israel makes itself worthy through its embodiment of Torah, that is, through its perfect replication of heaven, then the end will come.

Learning thus finds a central place in the rabbinic tradition because of the belief that God had revealed his will to mankind through the medium of a written revelation, given to Moses at Mount Sinai, accompanied by oral traditions taught in the rabbinical schools and preserved in the Talmuds and related literature. The text without the oral traditions might have led elsewhere than into the academy, for the biblicism of other groups yielded something quite different from Jewish religious intellectualism. But belief in the text was coupled with the belief that oral traditions were also revealed. In the books composed in the rabbinical academies, as much as in the Hebrew Bible itself, was contained God's will for man.

The act of study, memorization, and commentary upon the sacred books is holy. The study of sacred texts therefore assumes a central position in Judaism. Other traditions had their religious virtuosi whose virtuosity consisted in knowledge of a literary tradition; but few held, as does Judaism, that everyone must become such a virtuoso.

Traditional processes of learning are discrete and exegetical. Creativity is expressed not through abstract dissertation, but rather through commentary upon the sacred writings, or, more likely in later times, commentary upon earlier commentaries. One might also prepare a code of the law, but such a code represented little more than an assemblage of authoritative opinions of earlier times, with a decision being offered upon those few questions the centuries had left unanswered.

The chief glory of the commentator is his *hiddush*, 'novelty'. The *hiddush* constitutes a scholastic disquisition upon a supposed contradiction between two earlier authorities, chosen from any period, with no concern for how they might in fact relate historically, and upon a supposed harmonization of their 'contradiction'. Or a new distinction might be read into an ancient law, upon which basis ever more questions might be raised and solved. The focus of interest quite naturally lies upon law, rather than theology, history, philosophy, or other sacred sciences. But within the law it rests upon legal theory, and interest in the practical consequences of the law is decidedly subordinated.

The devotion of the Jews to study of the Torah, as here defined, is held by them to be their chief glory. This sentiment is repeated in song and prayer, and shapes the values of the common society. The important Jew is the learned man. The child many times is blessed, starting at birth, "May he grow in Torah, commandments, good deeds".

The central ritual of the rabbinic tradition, therefore, is study. Study as a natural action entails learning of traditions and executing them — in this context, in school or in court. Study becomes a ritual action when it is endowed with values extrinsic to its ordinary character, when set into a mythic context. When a disciple memorizes his master's traditions and actions, he participates in the rabbinic view of Torah as the organizing principle of reality. His study is thereby endowed with the sanctity that ordinarily pertains to prayer or other cultic matters. Study loses its referent in intellectual attainment. The act of study itself becomes holy, so that its original purpose, which was mastery of particular information, ceases to matter much. What matters is piety, piety expressed through the rites of studying. Repeating the words of the oral revelation, even without comprehending them, might produce reward, just as imitating the master matters, even without really being able to explain the reasons for his actions.

The separation of the value, or sanctity, of the act of study from the natural, cognitive result of learning therefore transforms studying from a natural to a ritual action. That separation is accomplished in part by the rabbis' conception of Torah, and in part by the powerful impact of the academic environment itself.

A striking illustration of the distinction between mere learning and learning as part of ritual life derives from the comment of Mar Zutra, a fifth-century A.D. Babylonian rabbi, on Isaiah 14:5, "The Lord has broken the staff of the wicked, the scepter of rulers." He said, "These are disciples of the sages who teach public laws to boorish judges." The fact that the uncultivated judge would know the law did not matter, for he still was what he had been, a boor, not a disciple of the sages. Mere knowledge of the laws does not transform an ordinary person, however powerful, into a sage. Learning carried with it more than naturalistic valence, as further seen in the saying of Amemar, a contemporary of Mar Zutra: "A sage is superior to a prophet, as Scripture says, 'And a prophet has a heart of wisdom'" (Psalm 90:12). What characterized the prophet was, Amemar said, sagacity. Since the prophet was supposed to reveal the divine will, it was not inconsequential that his revelation depended not upon gifts of the spirit but upon learning.

The rabbi functioned in the Jewish community as judge and administrator. But he lived in a society in some ways quite separate from that of Jewry as a whole. The rabbinical academy was, first, a law school. Some of its graduates served as judges and administrators of the law. The rabbinical school was by no means a center for merely legal study. It was, like the Christian monastery, the locus for a peculiar kind of religious living. Only one of its functions concerned those parts of the Torah to be applied in everyday life through the judiciary.

The school, or *Yeshiva* (literally, 'session') was a council of Judaism, a holy community. In it men learned to live a holy life, to become saints. When they left, sages continued to live by the discipline of the school. They invested great efforts in teaching that discipline by example and precept to ordinary folk. Through the school classical Judaism transformed the Jewish people into its vision of the true replica of Mosaic revelation.

The schools, like other holy communities, imposed their own particular rituals, intended, in the first instance, for the disciples and masters. Later, it was hoped, all Jews would conform to those rituals and so join the circle of master and disciples.

As with study, the schools' discipline transformed other ordinary, natural actions, gestures, and functions into rituals — the rituals of 'being a rabbi'. Everyone ate. Rabbis did so in a 'rabbinic' manner. That is to say, what others regarded as matters of mere etiquette, formalities and conventions intended to render eating aesthetically agreeable, rabbis regarded as matters of 'Torah', something to be learned. It was 'Torah' to do things one way, and it was equally 'ignorance' to do them another (though not heresy, for theology was no issue).

The master of Torah, whether disciple or teacher, would demonstrate his mastery not merely through what he said in the discussion of legal traditions or what he did in court. He would do so by how he sat at the table, by what ritual formulas he recited before eating one or another kind of fruit or vegetable, by how he washed his hands. Everyone had to relieve himself. The sage would do so according to 'Torah'. The personality traits of men might vary. Those expected of, and inculcated into, a sage were of a single fabric.

We must keep in mind the fundamental difference between the way of Torah and ways to salvation explored by other holy men and sacred communities. The rabbi at no point would admit that his particular rites were imposed upon him alone, apart from all Israel. He ardently 'spread Torah' among the Jews at large. He believed he had to, because Torah was revealed to all Israel at Sinai and required of all Israel afterward. If he was right that Moses was 'our rabbi' and even God kept the commandments as he did, then he had to ask of everyone what he demanded of himself: conformity to the *halakhah,* the way of Torah. His task was facilitated by the widespread belief that Moses had indeed revealed the Torah and that some sort of interpretation quite naturally was required to apply it to everyday affairs. The written part of Torah generally shaped the life of ordinary pious folk. What the rabbi had to accomplish was to persuade the outsider that the written part of the Torah was partial and incomplete, requiring further elaboration through the oral traditions he alone possessed and embodied.

IV. The Origins of Rabbinic Judaism

While the rabbinic conception of Torah naturally is believed, by people within rabbinic Judaism, to originate with Moses at Sinai and to constitute nothing other than a statement of historical facts, the beginnings of the rabbinic structure are to be located in the aftermath of the destruction of the Second Temple in 70 C.E.[4] At that time, remnants of various groups in the Judaism of the period before 70 gathered at Yavneh, and, under the leadership of Yohanan ben Zakkai, began to construct the ruins of the old age into a new synthesis.

Before the destruction, there was a common 'Judaism' in the Land of Israel, and it was by no means identical to what we now understand as rabbinic Judaism. The common religion of the country consisted of three main elements, first, the Hebrew Scriptures, second, the Temple, and third, the common and accepted practices of the ordinary folk — their calendar, their mode of living, their everyday practices and rites, based on these first two. In addition we know of a number of peculiar groups, or sects, which took a distinctive position on one or another aspect of the inherited religious culture. Among these sects, the best known are the Pharisees, the Sadducees, and the Essenes; this third group, described chiefly in the writings of Josephus, a historian who wrote at the end of the first century, exhibits traits in common with the group known to us from the so-called Dead Sea Scrolls but cannot have been identical to it in every respect.

When the Temple was destroyed, it is clear, the foundations of the country's religious-cultural life were destroyed. The reason is that the Temple had constituted one of the primary, unifying elements in that common life. The structure not only of political life and of society, but also of the imaginative life of the country, depended upon the Temple and its worship and cult. It was there that people believed they served God. On the Temple the lines of structure — both cosmic and social — converged. The Temple, moreover, served as the basis for those many elements of autonomous self-government and political life left in the Jews' hands by the Romans. Consequently, the destruction of the Temple meant not merely a significant alteration in the cultic or ritual life of the Jewish

[4] This section summarizes the results of J. NEUSNER, A Life of Yohanan ben Zakkai (2nd ed., Leiden, 1970) and ID., Development of a Legend. Studies on the Traditions concerning Yohanan ben Zakkai (Leiden, 1970).

people, but also a profound and far-reaching crisis in their inner and spiritual existence.

The reconstruction of a viable cultural-religious existence is the outcome of the next half-century, for between ca. 70 and ca. 120, we know in retrospect, a number of elements of the religious-cultural structure of the period before 70 were put together into a new synthesis, the synthesis we now call rabbinic Judaism. It was in response to the disaster of the destruction that rabbinic Judaism took shape, and its success was in its capacity to claim things had not changed at all — hence the assertion that even at the start, Moses was 'our rabbi' — while making the very destruction of the Temple itself into the verification and vindication of the new structure. Rabbinic Judaism claimed that it was possible to serve God not only through sacrifice, but also through study of Torah. There is a priest in charge of the life of the community — but a new priest, the rabbi. The old sin-offerings still may be carried out, through deeds of loving kindness. Not only so, but when the whole Jewish people will fully carry out the teachings of the Torah, then the Temple itself will be rebuilt. To be sure, the Temple will be reconstructed along lines laid out in the Torah — that is, in the whole Torah of Moses, the Torah taught by the rabbis. And, like the prophets and historians in the time of the First Destruction, the rabbis further claimed that it was because the people had sinned, that is, had not kept the Torah, that the Temple had been destroyed. So the disaster itself was made to vindicate the rabbinic teaching and to verify its truth.

Now let us stand back from this synthesis and ask, how was it put together? What are its primary elements? What trends or movements before 70 are represented by these elements?

Two primary components in the Yavneh synthesis are to be discerned, first, the emphases of Pharisaism before 70, second, the values of the scribal profession before that time. The former lay stress upon universal keeping of the law, so that every Jew is obligated to do what only the elite — the priests — are normally expected to accomplish. Pre-70 Pharisaism thus contributed the stress on the universal keeping of the law. The second component derives from the scribes, whose professional ideal stressed the study of Torah and the centrality of the learned man in the religious system.

The unpredictable, final element in the synthesis of Pharisaic stress on widespread law — including ritual-law observance, and scribal emphasis on learning — is what makes rabbinic Judaism distinctive, and that is the conviction that the community now stands in the place of the Temple. The ruins of the cult, after all, did not mark the end of the collective life of Israel. What survived was the people. It was the genius of rabbinic Judaism to recognize that the people might reconstitute the Temple in its own collective life. Therefore the people had to be made holy, as the Temple had been holy, and the people's social life had to be sanctified as the surrogate for what had been lost. The rabbinic ideal further maintained that the rabbi served as the new priest, the study of Torah substituted for the Temple sacrifice, and deeds of loving kindness were the social surrogate for the sin-offering, that is, personal sacrifice instead of animal sacrifice.

V. Pharisaism after 70

Pre-70 Pharisaism is clearly defined by the Gospels' Pharisaic pericopes and the rabbinic traditions, about the Pharisees[5]. Both stress the same concerns; first, eating secular food in a state of ritual purity; second, careful tithing and giving of agricultural offerings to the priests, and obedience to the biblical rules and taboos concerning raising crops; third, to a lesser degree, some special laws on keeping the Sabbaths and festivals; and, finally, still less commonly, rules on family affairs. Therefore, late Pharisaism — that which flourished in the last decades of the Temple's existence and which is revealed in the Gospels and in rabbinic traditions — is a cult-centered piety, which proposes to replicate the cult in the home, and thus to effect the Temple's purity laws at the table of the ordinary Jew, and quite literally to turn Israel into a "kingdom of priests and a holy nation". The symbolic structure of Pharisaism depends upon that of the Temple; the ideal is the same as that of the priesthood. The Pharisee was a layman pretending to be priest and making his private home into a model of the Temple. The laws about purity and careful tithing were dietary laws, governing what and how a person should eat. If a person kept those laws, then, when he ate at home, he was like God at the Temple's altar table, on which was arrayed food similarly guarded from impurity and produced in accord with Levitical revelation. By contrast, the rabbi was like God because he studied the Torah on earth, as did God and Moses 'our rabbi' in the heavenly academy.

The best corpus of traditions supplied by the post-70 rabbis concerns the Houses, or disciples, of Shammai and Hillel, circa A.D. 10—70, approximately sixty-five of whose pericopes are attested by early Yavnean comments or continuations or other discussions indicating knowledge of pericopes in pretty much their present state. When we compare the pericopes of Eliezer b. Hyrcanus, attested at Yavneh, with those of the Houses, evidently deriving from the same period, we find that Eliezer stands well within the framework of pre-70 Pharisaism[6]. The subject matter of Eliezer's rulings attested at Yavneh covers much the same

[5] This section summarizes the results of J. Neusner, The Rabbinic Traditions about the Pharisees before 70 (Leiden, 1971). I. The Masters. II. The Houses. III. Conclusions.

[6] This table summarizes the results of a comparison of the traditions attributed to Eliezer b. Hyrcanus, among the earliest authorities of Yavneh, and those assigned to the Houses of Shammai and Hillel. The sources are in J. Neusner, Eliezer ben Hyrcanus. The Tradition and the Man (Leiden, 1973). I. The Tradition. II. The Man.

ground as the Houses' rulings but introduces new issues as well. The two bodies of material compare as follows ("same" = Eliezer rules on or in the same pericope):

HOUSES	ELIEZER
A. Temple Law, Jerusalem, Pilgrimage, and Priestly Dues	
1. Burning unclean with clean meat	1. Same
2. Laying on of hands	2. —
3. Bitter-water ritual	3. . . . . (But Eliezer rules on on other aspects of the ritual; M. Sot. 1:1)
4. Israelites eat first-born animals with priests	4. —
5. Children make pilgrimage	5. —
6. —	6. Cattle given to the Temple are not sacrificed but sold
7. —	7. Liability for lost redemption lamb set aside for firstling of an ass
8. —	8. One may not dedicate all one's property to Temple
9—10. —	9—10. Preparing sin-offering water, two rulings
11. —	11. Whole-offering parts confused with sin-offering parts are burned together
12. —	12. Blood from blemished offerings mixed with blood from unblemished offerings is sprinkled
13. —	13. Wrong intention renders meal offering invalid
B. Agricultural Tithes, Offerings, and Taboos	
1. Unclean heave offering mixed with clean (Eliezer b. Hyrcanus)	1. Same
2. Giving heave offering of grapes, and the remainder is eventually made into raisins (Eliezer b. Hyrcanus)	2. Same

3. Removing old produce at Nisan (Joshua b. Ḥananiah)	3. —
4. *Peah* from olives, carobs — how given (Gamaliel II)	4. —
5. Forgotten-sheaf rules (Eliezer b. Azariah; Joshua b. Ḥananiah)	5.
6. Seventh-year-produce rules (Ṭarfon)	6.
7. Second-tithe money in Jerusalem (Ṭarfon; Ben Zoma; Ben Azzai; Aqiva)	7. —
8. Heave-offering vetches (Aqiva)	8. —
9. Fleece offering (Aqiva)	9. —
10. Date of New Year for trees (Aqiva)	10. —
11. Olive presses in walls of Jerusalem (Aqiva)	11. —
12. Fourth-year-fruit rules (Aqiva)	12. —
13. Mixed seeds in vineyard (Aqiva)	13. —
14. Heave offering from black and white figs (Ilai)	14. Same
15. —	15. Clean heave offering for unclean
16. —	16. Cakes of thank offering of Nazirite exempt from dough offering
17. —	17. *Orlah* laws abroad
18. —	18. Status of *etrog*
19. —	19. Seventh-year oil may be used for anointing hide
20. —	20. Dough offering on 15 Nisan
21. . . . (but cf. M. Shev. 4:2B)	21. First-fruits in garden are guarded, therefore liable
22. —	22. Fruit from abroad is free of liability
23. —	23. Making olives and grapes into oil and wine

C. Sabbath Law

1. *Eruv* in public domain (Ḥananiah, nephew of Joshua)	1. —
2. *Eruv* for separate kinds of food (Ḥananiah, nephew of Joshua)	2. —

3. *Eruv* for alley (Eliezer b. Hyrcanus + Aqiva + disciple of Ishmael)	3. Same
4. Gentile/Sadducee in alley *re eruv* (Gamaliel II = Meir + Judah)	4. . . . (but see no. 7)
5. Work started before Sabbath (Aqiva)	5.
6. —	6. No *eruv* if field has wall
7. . . . (but see no. 4)	7. Failure of partner to participate in *eruv* does not restrict others
8. —	8. Woman may wear tiara on Sabbath
9. —	9. Acquiring a share in the *eruv*

D. Festival Law

1. How much does one drink to be liable on the Day of Atonement (Eliezer b. Hyrcanus)?	1. Same
2. Large cakes re Passover (Gamaliel II)	2. —
3. Pick pulse on festival (Gamaliel II)	3. —
4. Other festival rules (Gamaliel II)	4. —
5. Size of *Sukkah* (Eleazar b. R. Ṣaddoq)	5. —
6. —	6. Hart's tongue on Passover
7—10. —	7—10. Rulings on rite of Atonement
11. . . . (Eliezer attests Houses' dispute; M. Bes. 1:1)	11. Egg born on festival
12. —	12. New millstone on festival week

E. Liturgy

1. Order of blessing: oil versus myrtle (Gamaliel II)	1. —
2. Proper position of saying *Shema* (Eleazar b. Azariah; Ishmael; Ṭarfon)	2. —

3. How far recite *Hallel* at Seder (Ṭarfon; Aqiva)	3. —
4. *Tefillin* in privy (Aqiva)	4. —
5. Where shake *lulav* (Aqiva, re Gamaliel; Joshua)	5. —
6. Limit re *ṣiṣit* (Jonathan b. Batyra)	6. —
7. Circumcision of child born circumcised (Eleazar b. R. Ṣaddoq)	7. —
8. —	8. New Year liturgy (Lev. 23:24)

F. Uncleanness Laws

1. Quarter *qab* on bones in 'tent' (Joshua b. Ḥananiah)	1. —
2. Woman kneading in 'tent' (Aqiva; Joshua b. Ḥananiah)	2. —
3. If man shook tree — preparation for uncleanness by reason of water (Joshua b. Ḥananiah)	3. —
4. Uncleanness of liquids — Yosi b. Yoʿezer (Eliezer b. Hyrcanus + Aqiva)	4. Same
5. Uncleanness of scroll wrappers (Gamaliel II)	5. —
6. When do olives receive uncleanness in harvest (Gamaliel II)	6. —
7. Mustard strainer (Eleazar b. R. Ṣaddoq)	7. —
8. Itch inside itch (cleanness rite) (Aqiva)	8. —
9. Insusceptibility of sheet (Aqiva)	9. —
10. Searching grave area (Aqiva)	10. —
11. Issue of semen in third day (Aqiva)	11. —
12. Uncleanness of fish (Aqiva)	12. —
13. —	13. Partitions in 'tent'
14. —	14. Shoe on the last is incomplete, therefore clean
15. —	15. Even though door is open, house is clean — re 'tents'

16. —	16. Jars tightly covered with bit of corpse inside
17.	17. Dirt from grave area
18. —	18. Leprosy sign deliberately removed
19. —	19. Ritual status of honeycomb

G. Civil Law, Torts, and Damages; Criminal Law

1. Damaged bailment (Aqiva)	1. —
2. —	2. Woman hanged ± naked

H. Family Law and Inheritances

1. Vow not to have intercourse (Eliezer)	1. Same (may not be our Eliezer)
2. Husband's inheritance when wife dies as a minor (Eliezer b. Hyrcanus)	2. Same
3. Signs of adulthood (Eliezer b. Hyrcanus)	3. Same
4. Levirate rules re brothers married to sisters (Eliezer b. Hyrcanus; Eleazar b. Azariah; Abba Saul)	4. Same
5. Levirate rules re co-wives (Ṭarfon; Eleazar b. Azariah; Aqiva; Joshua b. Ḥananiah)	5. —
6. Test rags for each act of intercourse (Joshua b. Ḥananiah)	6. —
7. Sanctifies property and intends to divorce wife (Joshua b. Hananiah + Eliezer b. Hyrcanus)	7. Same
8. Wife remarries on testimony of one witness (Aqiva; Gamaliel II)	8. —
9. Grounds for divorce (Aqiva)	9. —
10. Dividing estate where order of deaths is unclean (Aqiva)	10. —
11. Blood of woman who has given birth and not immersed (Eliezer)	11. Same
12. . . . (but see no. 2)	12. Deed of a female minor is null

13. —	13. Levir refused by minor
14. . . . (but see no. 9)	14. Conditional divorce valid
15. —	15. Minor who has exercised right of refusal still controls usufruct of *melog* (= no. 12)

I. Miscellany

1. Taboo against drinking gentile wine (Gamaliel II)	1. —
2. Eliezer b. Hyrcanus re overturning couch before festival (b. M. Q. 20a) is given by Eleazar b. R. Simeon as Houses dispute (Tos. M. Q. 2:9)	2. Same

Eliezer Alone

1. Releasing vows made easy
2. Gambler may not testify
3. Samaritan bread permitted to Israelites
4. Repent before death
5. Many sinful acts of a single type are punished by an equivalent number of sin offerings
6. Spinning blue wool for fringe

7—9. Nazir who contracts uncleanness on last day of his period — various rulings

The themes of Eliezer's rulings are much the same as those of the Houses, and the proportions seem about right, with one exception. In this stratum, Eliezer is strikingly silent on liturgical matters. This would accord with his ruling that a fixed liturgy is not to be followed; if so, Eliezer would not issue many rulings on the subject.

But the substance in detail of Eliezer's rulings strikingly differs from that of the Houses. Eliezer paid attention to dedications to the Temple; the pericopes of the Houses attested at Yavneh ignore the subject. He has important rulings on the preparation of sin-offering water. The Houses do not rule on the subject. He solves through logic various problems of mixtures of diverse holy materials and how they are to be disposed of. The Houses do not enter those problems at all. He deals with the problem of intention in the cult. The Houses do not. His rulings on the Temple thus concern strikingly fundamental matters. The tendency of those rulings is to figure out the logic and consistent order to be imposed on the Temple cult. What actually was done never enters his framework of discussion. He seems to have attempted to develop a coherent and internally logical set of rules on the Temple cult and its conduct.

While some of the rules on agricultural taboos concern both the Houses and Eliezer, others involve Eliezer alone. These tend to represent striking innovations in antecedent laws. Two themes seem important; first, the status of the produce of foreign countries; second, and of fundamental importance, the easing of the distinctions in produce subject to heave offering. As to Sabbath law, for both the Houses and Eliezer, the *eruv* (Sabbath limit) appears as a predominate concern. In respect to festival law, Eliezer has important new rulings on the rite of the Day of Atonement — appropriate for his agendum for the Temple, which concentrates on the conduct of the cult.

The subject matter of the uncleanness rules is pretty much the same; but the specific rulings of Eliezer are original. Again, his tendency is to solve problems through abstract reasoning rather than through a simple edict or citation of established practice. This would account for the difference between the discrete rules attributed to the Houses on when and whether various objects are susceptible to uncleanness, in contrast with Eliezer's effort on the same themes to give reasons for rulings applying to more than the single case at hand.

Civil and criminal law is virtually ignored by both the Houses and Eliezer. The interest in family law and inheritances is much the same; vows, inheritances, Levirate rules, and divorces concern both parties. But Eliezer's generalization about the nullity of the deed of a female minor and the rule, susceptible to generalization and expansion, about the conditional divorce are unknown to the Houses and constitute far-reaching theoretical innovations.

Entirely new legal themes involve releasing vows, rules of testimony, the law of the Nazirite who has become unclean, and the general principle about liability for various similar sinful acts. These do not yield completely new agenda of legislative legal interest. But they are, individually, quite novel topics on which the Yavnean pericopes of the Houses are silent.

VI. Yoḥanan Ben Zakkai as a Pharisee

Clearly, Eliezer was a post-70 continuator of pre-70 Pharisaism. But what evidence do we have that Yoḥanan b. Zakkai was a Pharisee in pre-70 times?[7] If we examine his legal rulings, we find strikingly few that are pertinent to the predominant agenda of pre-70 Pharisaism:

[7] The source is given above, n. 5.

1. Sifre Num. 123: Heifer sacrifice carried out in white garments.
2. Sifre Shemini 7:12: Loaf unclean in the second degree makes another unclean in the third.
3. Sifra Emor 16:9: *Lulav* taken as a memorial to the Temple.
4. Sifra Emor 16:9: New produce is prohibited on the entire Day of Waving.
5. M. (= Mishnah) Shabbat 16:7: One may cover a scorpion on the Sabbath.
6. M. Shabbat 22:3: One may open a jar to eat dried figs. but one may not pierce the plug of a jar on the Sabbath.
7. M. Sheqalim 1:4: Priests have to pay the *sheqel.*
8. M. Sukkah 2:5: Food must be eaten in the *Sukkah* even for a random meal.
9. M. Rosh HaShanah 1:1: The *shofar* may be sounded on the Sabbath.
10. M. Rosh HaShanah 4:4: Witnesses may testify about the new moon throughout the day.
11. M. Ketuvot 13:1: A woman swears at the end with respect to maintenance.
12. M. Ketuvot 13:2: A person who maintains another man's wife has no claim to recompense.
13. M. Sanhedrin 5:2: Evidence should be carefully tested.
14. M. Eduyyot 8:3, 7: Courts cannot tell the priests whom to marry.
15. M. Kelim 2:2: Broken sides of large jugs are not susceptible to uncleanness.
16. M. Kelim 17:16: A beam of a balance (etc.) is susceptible to uncleanness (not attributed to Yoḥanan).
17. M. Yadaim 4:3: Ammon and Moab give poorman's tithe in the seventh year.
18. M. Yadaim 4:6: Scriptures render the hands unclean (not attributed to Yoḥanan).

The Mishnaic evidence deals, therefore, with the following:

Temple and priesthood: Nos. 1, 7, 14.
Agricultural rules: Nos. 4, 17.
Festival law: Nos. 5,6.
Liturgy: Nos. 3, 8, 9, 10.
Uncleanness laws: Nos. 2, 15, 18.
Civil law, torts, damages, criminal law: Nos. 11,12, 13.
Family law and inheritances: None.

Pre-70 Pharisees and Eliezer tend to rule primarily on agricultural law, Sabbath and festival rules, and uncleanness. Yoḥanan's traditions are scattered; most of those on the festivals have to do with the problems posed by the destruction of the Temple and adoption of its rites in the synagogue. The law in numbers 11, 12, 17, and 18 is not accredited to Yoḥanan; he simply approves what others have done. In all, Yohanan's legal agenda hardly correspond to those of the pre-70 Houses — about which he himself knows nothing — and seem, on the whole, to focus upon the consequence for the liturgy and priesthood of the Temple's destruction, rather than upon any other matter. The greater number of his other rulings has to do with Sabbath and festival laws. To be sure, the whole thing adds up to very little. But while, on the basis of the extant laws, one may reasonably claim Eliezer was a Pharisee, on the same basis one cannot claim the same for Yoḥanan. At best, one may say he might have been a Pharisee. The external evidence does not help; Luke-Acts knows Gamaliel; Josephus knows Simeon b. Gamaliel; but no external source knows about Yoḥanan, despite the decisive role in events of the day claimed for him by the later storytellers.

VII. Eliezer's Pharisaism for the Post-Temple Period

Eliezer legislated, in theory if not in practice, primarily for people subject to Pharisaic discipline and mainly about matters important to Pharisaic piety, so his program for the post-Temple period concerned Pharisaism and little else. We simply do not know what, if anything, he might have had to say to non-Pharisaic Jews at Yavneh and in other parts of the country. Perhaps saying, at that time, to repent before death would have seemed more important than it does now; but it hardly constitutes much of a program for a country which has just lost its autonomous government and capital and for a people suddenly without a sanctuary or a cult.

In the aftermath of the destruction, Eliezer intended to liberalize the application of the Pharisaic discipline. I see no necessary connection between his intent and the recent disaster. Perhaps he simply thought that, by making it easier for large numbers of Jews to take on the Pharisaic way of living, he might win over people who formerly were not Pharisees. Since, moreover, the Pharisaic laws enabled Jews outside of the Temple to participate in its cult in their own homes and so to share in its sanctity, he may have posited the Pharisaic way as a means of preserving both the sanctity and the symbolic presence of the cult during the interim in which they were no more. Hence, it may have seemed wise to formulate the Pharisaic laws in as lenient a way as possible. But if this was Eliezer's intent — and we certainly cannot show that it was — I doubt his motive was purely propagandistic. He gives no evidence that his interest was to win as many Jews as possible to the Pharisaic way and by subterfuge to make it easier for them to undertake the sect's discipline.

The main outlines of his policy for the present age are clear. From the Jews outside of Palestine, obedience to neither the laws of tithing nor the laws of ritual purity nor the agricultural taboos would be required. For the Pharisees among them, the conditions of life in exile were made considerably easier. But this was done by effectively destroying the entire form of their earlier piety. We have no evidence of what, if anything, was offered in its stead. For Pharisees in Palestine, the application of the primarily sectarian laws was to be done in a more lenient way than earlier. Giving heave offering was simplified. One no longer would have to distinguish between clean and unclean produce of the same species in the same state but might give heave offering from the one for the other. Presumably, other distinctions formerly operative in the giving of heave offering would likewise be obscured. The laws of the seventh year similarly would be applied less rigidly than earlier, if the case of the hide anointed by seventh-year oil signifies a broader policy. Hence, greater benefit from the produce of the seventh year would be enjoyed by the pietists. It may be that the more difficult conditions of economic life required some such lenient ruling, but we have not a shred of evidence that economic considerations figured in Eliezer's enactments. The Pharisaic custom of providing an *eruv*, or Sabbath limit, to permit carrying on the Sabbath was extended, so that, first, a fence would be sufficient to establish a single courtyard, however large; second, a person might simply buy a share in an *eruv* from a storekeeper; third, any sort of food, not merely bread, might be used; and fourth, dissenters or forgetful people would not be subject to pressure from their neighbors.

This last point suggests that Eliezer hoped to improve relationships between Pharisees and other Jews, on the one side, and between Jews and Samaritans, on the second. Eliezer allowed Jews to eat with Samaritans. Hence, the *xenophobia* characteristic of the recent war was rejected in favor of a more irenic approach to relationships within the Jewish community, formerly characterized by heated sectarian and civil strife, and between Jewry and its neighbors, earlier marked by Jewish hostility toward closely kindred groups.

The Sabbath rules were set aside in favor of other, equally important religious duties. The tendency to erect ever higher walls around the Sabbath was thus countered by Eliezer's view that the Sabbath was to be no more important than other religious requirements such as circumcision or the Passover. (This corresponds to the Gospels' view that the "son of man is Lord of the Sabbath".) Its sanctity was separate and distinct from, and no greater than, that of the coincident festival. Eliezer may have planned also to liberalize the rules governing work on the intermediate days of a festival.

Vows were to be virtually excluded from the pious life. To be sure, temperamental people would continue to make them. But Eliezer would render the nullification of a vow a routine and simple matter. One might, on any pretext whatever, simply express regret that he had vowed, and the matter was done with. The dedication of one's property to the Temple —

which now would mean its destruction — was limited. An oath to give the whole of one's property to the sanctuary was null. Presumably anyone in sufficient command of his senses to refrain from giving the whole lot would be unlikely to make such a gift to begin with. Likewise, a Nazir, subject to his earlier vow, would not be forced by last-minute accidents into a perpetual renewal of the binding rules. His liability was limited to a few days rather than to the repetition of the whole spell of Naziriteship.

Consistent with his leniency in the giving of tithes and heave offerings, Eliezer may have intended to limit the effect of the uncleanness rules by ruling that uncleanness pertains to no liquids, except (presumably) those specified in Scriptures. Here, matters are less certain; we have a number of conflicting details which seem not wholly in accord with one another or with this basic principle. Certainly, Eliezer wanted to make it easy to neutralize the prohibiting effects of holy materials which have fallen into secular produce or of impaired materials of the cult mixed with acceptable materials. The rules of neutralizing heave offering which has fallen into secular produce are enforced in a lenient way. Mixtures of bowls of blood or of blemished and unblemished sacrificial parts will be readily rendered fit for use on the pretext that one may easily remove the prohibited substance.

Eliezer evidently proposed for the cult to be ruled in accord with an orderly logic, which would settle all manner of details. What may have seemed to him illogical or inconsistent was to be rationalized. I do not see what practical consequences for the Yavnean situation were to be anticipated. Eliezer continued the earlier Pharisaic tendency to apply to the Red-Heifer ceremony a less strict rule as to purity and other questions than was regarded by the Sadducees as proper. But this is not original to him and therefore has nothing to do with his Yavnean program.

One ethical issue seems important. Eliezer held that, faced with a choice of taking affirmative action to prevent a possible violation of the law or of doing nothing at all, a person should assume responsibility and therefore take action. It would not be proper to disclaim responsibility and to stand aside. The contrary view was that one needs do nothing at all, so long as his own hands are not sullied.

In general, therefore, the tendency of Eliezer's own rulings seems to have been in a single direction, and that was toward the rationalization and the liberalization of the application of Pharisaic law. We cannot, to be sure, take for granted that all of even the very best-attested traditions derive from Eliezer and have been formulated in his exact language. Nor is our interpretation of each detail necessarily the only possible way of seeing things. But if this view of Eliezer's own contribution is in the main valid, then it follows that what is asserted by the later tradition is absolutely correct: Eliezer really said nothing he had not heard from his masters. In an exact sense, he was profoundly 'conservative'. By attempting to reform details and to ease the strictness of the Pharisaic law, he hoped to conserve the Pharisaic way of piety substantially unchanged and unimpaired, essentially intact. This must mean that for Eliezer the destruction of the Temple did not mark a significant turning in the history of Judaism. Just as the destruction of the first Temple was followed, in a brief period, by the construction of the second, so he certainly supposed the same would now happen. He would see to it that the third Temple would be different from the second only in the more logical way in which its cult would be carried on, on the one side, and in the slightly simpler requirements of the application of the cult's purity rules to daily life and of the enforcement of the priestly taxes, on the other.

In Eliezer's time, Rome ended its former experiments with the government of the Jews and established direct rule. We know nothing about Eliezer's attitude toward Rome and the new regime in Palestine. Gamaliel had to negotiate with it; Eliezer evidently did not. This must mean that in Yavneh he did not enter into direct relationships with the Roman regime; but we do not know whether other masters of the day, except for Gamaliel, had any more direct contact with the Romans than he evidently did. The larger problems faced by the Jews deprived of their cult and its celebrations, including the observance in the Temple and in Jerusalem of the pilgrim festivals, not to mention the bringing of first fruits and of the second tithes or equivalent funds to the city for consumption — none of these seems to have elicited his attention. He does not legislate about the observance of *Sukkot* after the destruction, as did Yoḥanan b. Zakkai, although we have two rulings pertinent to the festival. He has nothing to say about the New Year or the use of the *shofar* on the Sabbath that coincides with the New Year, as did Yoḥanan; also omitted are the use of new produce and the waving of the *omer*. The various Temple-oriented festival celebrations subject to Yoḥanan's *taqqanot* (ordinances) are ignored in Eliezer's legislation. This is striking, for Eliezer, as an early Yavnean master, ought to have had more to say about the sacred rites now no longer possible to effect than we can discern in respect to these lively issues.

Eliezer certainly did not anticipate that the Temple would never be rebuilt. He had no program for any considerable time before the reconstruction. Perhaps it was hoped that the Romans would not delay in permitting the buildings to be restored. No one in his time could foresee the disastrous Bar Kokhba war or the definitive prohibition of the Jews from Jerusalem in its aftermath.

VIII. Rabbinism at Yavneh

Eliezer's legislation, therefore, suggests he assumed life would soon go on pretty much as it had in the past. Issues important to pre-70 Pharisees predominate in his laws; issues absent in the rabbinic traditions about the Pharisees are — except the cult — mostly absent in his as well. Eliezer therefore comes at the end of the old Pharisaism. He does not inaugurate the new rabbinism, traces of which are quite absent in his historically usable traditions. Indeed, on the basis of his laws and sayings, we can hardly define what this rabbinism might consist of. The centrality of the oral Torah, the view of the rabbi as the new priest and of study of Torah as the new cult, the definition of piety as the imitation of Moses 'our rabbi' and the conception of God as a rabbi, the organization of the Jewish community under rabbinic rule and by rabbinic law, and the goal of turning all Israel into a vast academy for the study of the (rabbinic) Torah — none of these motifs characteristic of later rabbinism occurs at all.

Since by the end of the Yavnean period the main outlines of rabbinism were clear, we may postulate that the transition from Pharisaism to rabbinism, or the union of the two, took place in the time of Eliezer himself. But he does not seem to have been among those who generated the new viewpoints; he appears as a reformer of the old ones. His solution to the problem of the cessation of the cult was not to replace the old piety with a new one but, rather, to preserve and refine the rules governing the old in the certain expectation of its restoration in a better form than ever. Others, who were his contemporaries and successors, developed the rabbinic idea of the (interim) substitution of study for sacrifice, the rabbi for the priest, and the oral Torah of Moses 'our rabbi' for the piety of the old cult.

Eliezer has not been anachronistically 'rabbinized'. To be sure, the transmitters and compilers of traditions later on assumed everyone before them — back to Moses — was a rabbi. But they did not regularly attribute to Eliezer sayings to link him specifically to the rabbinic system of symbols; and this suggests that, just as with the laws a limited agendum defined topics appropriate for attribution to Eliezer, so, with theological matters, ideas originally not within Eliezer's agendum were not commonly added afterward.

If so, we may take seriously the attribution of rabbinic ideas to others of his contemporaries. Where do we first find them? Clearly, Yoḥanan b. Zakkai — whom we could not conclusively show to have been a Pharisee — stands well within the structure of rabbinic symbols and beliefs. It is in his sayings, admittedly first occurring in late compilations, that we find the claim of replacing the cult with something — anything — just as good. He is alleged to have told Joshua that deeds of loving kindness achieve atonement just as satisfactorily as did the cult. He is further made to say that man was created in order to study the Torah. When Israel does the will of its father in heaven — which is contained in the Torah and taught by the rabbi — then no nation or race can rule over it. The cult is hardly central to his teachings and seldom occurs in his laws. The altar, to be sure, serves to make peace between Israel and the father in heaven, but is not so important ("how much the more so") as a man who makes peace among men or is a master of Torah. Yoḥanan's *taqqanot* are even better testimony, for they take account of the end of the cult and provide for the period of its cessation. The Temple rites may be carried on ("as a memorial") outside of the old sanctuary. The old priesthood is subjected to the governance of the rabbi. The priest had to pay the *sheqel* and ideally should marry anyone the rabbi declares to be a fit wife. Eliezer says nothing of the sort; what Yoḥanan has to say about the situation after 70 is either without parallel in Eliezer's sayings or contradicted by their tendency.

To be sure, we are scarcely able to claim that rabbinism begins with Yoḥanan or that Pharisaism ends with Eliezer. But Yoḥanan's tradition certainly reveals the main themes of later rabbinism, although these themes are more reliably attributed to later Yavneans and still more adequately spelled out in their sayings. And Eliezer's laws and theological sayings are strikingly silent about what later on would be the primary concern of the rabbinic authorities, the oral Torah in all its social and political ramifications, and are remarkably narrow in their focus upon the concerns of pre-70 Pharisaism. Further investigation may show that the list of M. Avot 2:1 of Yoḥanan's disciples represents a composite of the five components of the Yavnean group: Eliezer clearly was a Pharisee; Yosi was a priest; Simeon b. Nathaniel was an *am ha'ares*, not observant of the purity laws; Eleazar b. Arakh was a mystic; and Joshua b. Ḥananiah should represent rabbinism. But this remains to be studied.

IX. Rabbinism and Scribism

If Eliezer stands for the old Pharisaism, who stands for the pre-70 scribes? The scribes form a distinct group — not merely a profession — in the Gospels' accounts of Jesus's opposition. Scribes and Pharisees are by no means regarded as one and the same group. To be sure, what scribes say and do not say is not made clear. One cannot derive from the synoptic record a clear picture of scribal doctrine or symbolism, if any, although one certainly finds an account of the Pharisaic law on ritual uncleanness and tithing. Since the materials now found in the synoptics were available in Palestine between 70 and 90, however, they may be presumed accurately to portray the situation of that time, because their picture had to be credible to Christians of the period. (Even the fourth Gospel contains traditions that go back to Palestine before 70, but we concentrate attention on the picture presented by the synoptics.) If so, we have in the synoptics a portrait of two groups at Yavneh in close relationship with one another, but not entirely unified.

Now, having seen in Eliezer an important representative of the old Pharisaism, we find no difficulty in accounting for the Pharisaic component of the Yavnean synthesis. It likewise seems reasonable to locate in the scribes the antecedents of the ideological or symbolic part of the rabbinic component at Yavneh. Admittedly, our information on scribism in the rabbinic literature is indistinguishable from the later sayings produced by rabbinism. But if we consider that scribism goes back to much more ancient times than does Pharisaism, and that its main outlines are clearly represented, for instance, by Ben Sira, we may reasonably suppose that what the scribe regarded as the center of piety was study, interpretation, and application of the Torah. To be sure, what was studied and how it was interpreted are not to be identified with the literature and interpretation of later rabbinism. But the scribal piety and the rabbinic piety are expressed through an identical symbol, study of Torah. And one looks in vain in the rabbinic traditions about the Pharisees before 70 for stress on, or even the presence of the ideal of, the study of Torah. Unless rabbinism begins as the innovation of the early Yavneans — and this seems to me unlikely — it therefore should represent at Yavneh the continuation of pre-70 scribism.

But pre-70 scribism continued with an important difference, for Yavnean and later rabbinism said what cannot be located in pre-70 scribal documents: The Temple cult is to be replaced by study of Torah, the priest by the rabbi (= scribe); and the center of piety was shifted away from cult and sacrifice entirely. So Yavnean scribism made important changes in pre-70 scribal ideas. It responded to the new situation in a more appropriate way than did the Yavnean Pharisaism represented by Eliezer. Eliezer could conceive of no piety outside of that focused upon the Temple. But Yavnean and later scribism-rabbinism was able to construct an expression of piety which did not depend upon the Temple at all. While Eliezer appears as a reformer of old Pharisaism, the proponents of rabbinism do not seem to have reformed the old scribism. What they did was to carry the scribal ideal to its logical conclusion. If study of Torah was central and knowledge of Torah important, then the scribe had authority even in respect to the Temple and the cult; indeed, his knowledge was more important than what the priest knew. This view, known in the sayings of Yoḥanan b. Zakkai, who certainly held that the priest in Yavnean times was subordinate to the rabbi, is not a matter only of theoretical consequence. Yoḥanan also held that he might dispose of Temple practices and take them over for the Yavnean center — and for other places as well — and so both preserve them ("as a memorial") and remove from the Temple and the priests a monopoly over the sacred calendar, festivals, and rites. Earlier scribism thus contained within itself the potentiality to supersede the cult. It did not do so earlier because it had no reason to and because it probably could not. The latter rabbinism, faced with the occasion and the necessity, realized that potentiality. By contrast, earlier Pharisaism invested its best energies in the replication of the cult, not in its replacement. After 70, it could do no more than plan for its restoration.

Scribism as an ideology, not merely a profession, begins with the view that the law given by God to Moses was binding and therefore has to be authoritatively interpreted and applied to daily affairs. That view goes back to the fourth century B.C., by which time Nehemiah's establishment of the Torah of Moses as the constitution of Judea produced important effects in ordinary life. From that time on, those who could apply the completed written Torah constituted an important class or profession. The writings of scribes stress the identification of Torah with wisdom and the importance of learning. Ben Sira's sage travels widely in search of wisdom and consorts with men of power. Into the first century, the scribes continue as an identifiable estate high in the country's administration. Otherwise, the synoptics' view is incomprehensible. Therefore, those who were professionally acquainted with the Scriptures — whether they were priests or not — formed an independent class of biblical teachers, lawyers, administrators, or scribes, alongside the priesthood. We do not know what they actually did in the administration of the country. Perhaps Yoḥanan b. Zakkai's reference to decrees of Jerusalem authorities (M. Ketuvot 13:1ff.) alludes to the work of scribes, who therefore were involved — as the Pharisees certainly were — in the determination of family law and in the settlement of trivial disputes.

The New Testament references support the supposition that the scribes were a separate group, differentiated from Sadducees and Pharisees[8]. The scribes occur in association with the high priests in Matt. 2:4, 16:21, 20:18, 21:15, 27, 27:41; Mark 8:31, 10:33, 11:18, 27, 14:1, 43, 53, 15:1, 31, etc.; with the Pharisees in Matt. 5:20, 12:38, 15:1, 23:2, 13ff.; Mark 2:16, 7:1, 5. But they are not the same as the one or the other. The scribes are called "learned in the law" and jurists (Matt. 22:35; Luke 7:30, 10:25, 11:45, 52, 14:3). They are teachers of the law (Luke 5:17; Acts 5:34).

Mishnaic literature obviously will miss the distinction between Pharisees and scribes, both of whom are regarded as *ḤKMYM*, sages. But we have no reason to suppose all scribes were Pharisees. Schürer points out, "Inasmuch ... as the 'scribes' were merely 'men learned in the law,' there must have been also Sadducaean scribes. For it is not conceivable that the Sadducees, who acknowledged the written law as binding, should have had among them none who made it their profession to study it. In fact those passages of the New Testament, which speak of scribes who were of the Pharisees (Mark 2:16, Luke 5:30, Acts 23:9) point also to the existence of Sadducaean scribes." The scribes therefore represent a class of men learned in Scriptures, perhaps lawyers in charge of the administration of justice. They therefore had to develop legal theories, teach pupils, and apply the law. Naturally, such people would come to the center of the administration of government and law, so they could not have remained aloof from Yavneh. Some of them may, to be sure, have come because they were Pharisees. But others, whatever their original ritual practices, would have come because Yavneh represented the place in which they might carry on their profession.

Josephus — himself a new adherent of the Pharisees — does not confuse the scribes with the Pharisees. In none of his allusions to the Pharisees does he also refer to the scribes (*grammateis*) or call Pharisees scribes. In

[8] E. Schürer, History of the Jewish People in the Time of Jesus Christ (Edinburgh, 1889), I, pt. 2, pp. 319ff.

Life 197—198, he refers to a delegation of Jerusalemites to Galilee. Two were from the lower ranks of society and adherents of the Pharisees, the third was also a Pharisee, but a priest; the fourth was descended from high priests. These were all able to assert that they were not ignorant of the customs of the fathers. To be sure, the Pharisees are referred to as knowledgeable in the Torah; and they have "traditions from the fathers" in addition to those that Moses had revealed. But they are not called scribes. They were (War 1:107—114) exact exponents of the laws. But again they are not called scribes. The long 'philosophical school' account in Antiquities 18:11—17 describes the Pharisees as virtuous and says that "all prayers and sacred rites of divine worship are performed according to their exposition" — but they too are not scribes.

When Josephus does refer to scribes, he does not refer to Pharisees. For example, in War 1:648ff. (= Antiquities 17:152) he refers to two *sophistai* who ordered their disciples to pull down the eagle that Herod had set up in the Temple. They are Judah son of Sepphoraeus and Matthias son of Margalus, men who gave lectures on the laws, attended by a large, youthful audience. If these are scribes, they are not said also to be Pharisees, who do not occur in the account. We find also *hierogrammateis* and *patriōn exegetai nomōn* — but not in the context of the passages about the Pharisees. While, therefore, the Pharisees and the scribes have in common knowledge of the country's laws, the two are treated separately. Josephus does not regard the scribes as wholly within the Pharisaic group; he presents the scribe as a kind of authority or professional teacher of law. Josephus's further references to *grammateis* (singular or plural) are as follows:

Apion 1:290: The sacred scribe Phritobeuates;

Antiquities 6:120: It was reported to the king by the scribes that the host were sinning against God; 7:110: He made Seisa scribe; 7:293 = 7:110; 7:219: Joab took the chiefs of the tribes and scribes and took the census; 7:364: David appointed six thousand Levites as judges of the people and as scribes; 9:164: When the scribe and priest of the treasury had emptied the chest; 10:55: When the money was brought, he gave superintendence of the temple . . . to the governor of the city [and] Sapha the sribe, etc.; 10:94f.: Baruch, scribe of Jeremiah; 10:149: the scribe of Sacchias; 11:22, 26, 29: Semelios the scribe, etc.; 11:128: On the scribes of the sanctuary you will impose no tribute; 12:142: The scribes of the Temple; 11:248, 250, 272, 287: scribes of the Persian kings; 16:319: the scribe Diophantus had imitated his manner of writing; 20:208f.: The *sicarii* kidnapped the secretary of the captain;

War 1:479: village clerks; 5:532: Aristeus, the secretary of the council[9].

[9] H. Thackeray, Josephus Lexicon (Paris 1932), Fasc. 2, pp. 117—118.

It is clear that Josephus does not associate scribes with Pharisees; no scribe is a Pharisee; and no Pharisee is described as a scribe. The two are separate and distinct. One is a sect, the other is a profession.

Since later rabbinism found pre-70 scribism highly congenial to its ideal, it is by no means farfetched to trace the beginnings of Yavnean rabbinism to the presence of representatives of the pre-70 scribal class, to whom the ideal of study of Torah, rather than the piety of the cult and the replication of that cultic piety in one's own home, was central. At Yavneh, therefore, were incorporated these two important strands of pre-70 times — the one the piety of a sect, the other the professional ideal of a class. Among them, as we have seen, Eliezer's teachings made for pre-70 Pharisaism an important place in the Yavnean synthesis.

X. Institutionalized Rabbinism

Thus far, our definition of rabbinism has focused upon its central symbols and ideals. These seem to continue symbols and ideas known, in a general way, from 'scribism' — if not known in detail from individual scribes, who, as I have stressed, formed a profession, not a sect. But what of the later, and essential, singularly characteristic traits of rabbinism: its formation as a well-organized and well-disciplined movement, its development of important institutions for the government of the Jewish communities of Palestine and Babylonia, its aspiration to make use of autonomous political instruments for the transformation of all Jews into rabbis? Of this, we have no knowledge at all in the earliest stratum of the Yavnean period. Clearly, Yoḥanan b. Zakkai worked out the relationship between the synagogue and the Temple. But the nature of the 'gathering' at Yavneh — whether it was some sort of 'academy', or a nascent political institution, or merely an inchoate assembly of various sorts of sectarians, professionals, pre-70 authorities, and whatever — is simply unilluminated. Eliezer's historical record is strikingly silent on this very point. From his materials, we have no evidence on either how he enforced or applied the law outside of his own household or disciple-circle or how anyone else did. We have no hint about the evolution of an institution one might regard as a nascent political authority — a government — in any terms. Eliezer's laws omit reference even to the legal theory behind such an authority. And they are strikingly silent about the whole range of laws to be applied in civil life. Whence such laws reached the Yavneans we do not know. They cannot have come from Eliezer, and, given the nature of the rabbinic traditions about pre-70 Pharisaism, they also do not derive from other Pharisees.

So in all the 'rabbinism' possibly present in Yoḥanan's corpus and remarkably absent in Eliezer's is simply the symbolic and ideological element represented by the study of Torah as the central expression of piety. The political institutions and social expressions of rabbinism make no appearance in the earliest years of the Yavnean period. They emerge, for the first time, in the development of the government under the patriarchate and its associated rabbinical functionaries, beginning with Gamaliel II — circa A.D. 90 — and fully articulated, in the aftermath of the Bar Kokhba debacle, by Simeon b. Gamaliel II, circa A.D. 150. At that point, the rabbinical ideal produced serious effects for the political and social realities of Judaism.

Die Flucht Joḥanan b. Zakkais aus Jerusalem und die Gründung des 'Lehrhauses' in Jabne

von PETER SCHÄFER, Köln

Inhalt

I. Der Text

Die rabbinische Literatur überliefert den Bericht von der Flucht Joḥanan b. Zakkais an verschiedenen Stellen: Abot de Rabbi Natan, Version A, Kap. 4, Ed. Schechter, S. 22f.; Abot deRabbi Natan, Version B, Kap. 6, Ed. Schechter, S. 19; b Gittin 56af.; Midrasch Ekha Rabba, Ed. Wilna 1,31 zu Ekha 1,5 (= Ed. Buber, S. 65ff.); Midrasch Mishle, Parasha 15, Ed. Buber, S. 79f. Im folgenden werden die Versionen in ARNA, ARNB, b Git und EkhR Ed. Wilna jeweils paarweise in Übersetzung dargeboten, um Übereinstimmungen und Unterschiede deutlich werden zu lassen. Vom Druck Wilna abweichende Einzelheiten in EkhR Ed. Buber werden in Fußnoten angegeben; der Fassung im 'Midrasch Mishle' kommt kein selbständiger Quellenwert zu, da sie — bis auf die interpolierte Episode vom geschwollenen Fuß Vespasians — offenkundig von ARNB abhängig ist.

ARNA

Als Vespasian kam, Jerusalem zu zerstören, sagte er zu ihnen: Frevler, warum wollt ihr diese Stadt zerstören und den Tempel verbrennen? Was verlange ich denn von euch anderes, als daß ihr mir einen Bogen oder einen Pfeil schickt,

ARNB

Als Vespasian kam und Jerusalem umzingelte, da lagerte er gegenüber der Mauer Jerusalems [und] sprach zu den Bewohnern Jerusalems: Schickt[1] von ihr[2] (= von der Mauer) einen Bogen und einen Pfeil, und ich gehe in Frieden

Abkürzungen:

Ab — Traktat Abot
AbZa — Traktat Aboda Zara
Ant. — Josephus, Antiquitates
ARNA — Abot deRabbi Natan, Version A
ARNB — Abot deRabbi Natan, Version B
b — babylonischer Talmud
BBa — Traktat Baba Batra
Bell. — Josephus, Bellum
Ber — Traktat Berakhot
EkhR — Midrash Ekha Rabba
Git — Traktat Gittin
j — Jerusalemer Talmud
Jom — Traktat Joma
Kel — Traktat Kelim
Ket — Traktat Ketubot
m — Mischna
Maas — Traktat Ma'aser rishon
Makh — Traktat Makhshirin
Meg — Traktat Megilla
MekhJ — Mekhilta deRabbi Jishma'el
MekhS — Mekhilta deRabbi Shim'on b. Joḥai
MMish — Midrasch Mishle
MTann — Midrasch Tannaim
Ned — Traktat Nedarim
Ohal — Traktat Ohalot
PesK — Midrasch Pesiqta deRab Kahana
PRE — Midrasch Pirqe deRabbi Eli'ezer
QohR — Midrasch Qohelet Rabba
San — Traktat Sanhedrin
Schab — Traktat Schabbat
SiphDt — Midrasch Siphre zu Deuteronomium
t — Tosephta
Taan — Traktat Ta'anit

[1] So (*šgrw*) ist wohl zu lesen statt *šbrw* („zerbrecht"); vgl. auch Schechter, S. 19, Anm. 2.
[2] Statt *mmnw* lies *mmnh*.

ARNA

und ich gehe von euch weg! Sie antworteten: So wie wir gegen die beiden ersten vor dir ausgezogen sind und sie getötet haben, so werden wir gegen dich ausziehen und dich töten!

Als R. Joḥanan b. Zakkai [dies] hörte, ließ er[3] die Bewohner Jerusalems zusammenrufen und sprach zu ihnen: Meine Kinder, warum zerstört ihr diese Stadt und [warum] wollt ihr den Tempel verbrennen?! Was verlangt er denn von euch? Er verlangt doch von euch nichts anderes als einen Bogen oder einen Pfeil und wird von euch weggehen! Sie antworteten ihm: So wie wir gegen die beiden vor ihm ausgezogen sind und sie getötet haben, so werden wir gegen ihn ziehen und ihn töten!

Vespasian hatte Männer, die gegenüber den Mauern Jerusalems lagerten, und jedes Wort, das sie hörten, schrieben sie auf Pfeile und schleuderten [diese] außerhalb der Mauer, um anzuzeigen, daß R. Joḥanan b. Zakkai zu den Freunden des Kaisers gehöre.

Als R. Joḥanan b. Zakkai ihnen [dies] einen, zwei und drei Tage gesagt hatte und sie [es] von ihm nicht annahmen, ließ er seine Schüler R. Eli'ezer und R. Jehoshua' rufen. Er sprach zu ihnen: Meine Kinder, bringt mich fort von hier! Macht mir einen Sarg, und ich werde darin schlafen! R. Eli'ezer hielt sein Haupt, R. Jehoshua' hielt seine

ARNB

von euch weg. Er sprach zu ihnen ein erstes und ein zweites Mal, aber sie nahmen [es] nicht an.

Da sagte R. Joḥanan b. Zakkai zu ihnen: Ihr seid schuld daran, daß diese Stadt zerstört und dieser Tempel verbrannt wird! Sie antworteten ihm: So wie wir gegen die ersten Fürsten ausgezogen sind und sie getötet haben, so werden wir gegen diesen ziehen und ihn töten!

Jedes Wort, das R. Joḥanan b. Zakkai zu ihnen sagte, schrieben sie auf Zettel, banden diese an Pfeile und schleuderten sie außerhalb der Mauer, um anzuzeigen, [daß] Joḥanan b. Zakkai ein Freund des Königs sei.

Als R. Joḥanan b. Zakkai sah, daß sie nicht auf ihn hören wollten, sprach er zu seinen Schülern: Freunde, bringt mich fort von hier! Sie legten ihn in einen hölzernen Sarg. R. Eli'ezer trug [ihn] am Kopfende und R. Jehoshua' am Fußende. So nahmen sie sich seiner an[4] und gingen, bis sie das Stadttor erreichten.

[3] Vielleicht ist mit einer Handschrift statt *šlḥ*: *hlk* („ging er") zu lesen; vgl. SCHECHTER, S. 22, Anm. 46.

[4] *mšmšjn* bzw. (so eine Handschrift) *mštmšjm*; vgl. SCHECHTER, S. 19, Anm. 6. A. SCHALIT (s. unten Anm. 197), S. 308, Anm. 249, verbessert in *mmšmšjn* („sie tasteten sich vorwärts").

ARNA

Füße, und sie trugen ihn, bis sie bei Sonnenuntergang die Tore Jerusalems erreichten.

Da sagten die Torhüter zu ihnen: Wer ist das? Sie antworteten ihnen: Das ist ein Toter. Wißt ihr denn nicht, daß ein Toter nicht über Nacht in Jerusalem bleiben darf? Da gaben ihnen [die Torhüter] zur Antwort: Wenn es ein Toter ist, so bringt ihn hinaus!

Sie brachten ihn hinaus und geleiteten ihn, bis sie zu Vespasian kamen. [Dort] öffneten sie den Sarg, und er stand vor ihm. [Vespasian] sagte zu ihm: Bist du R. Joḥanan b. Zakkai? Wünsche [dir], was ich dir geben soll! Er antwortete ihm: Ich erbitte nichts anderes von dir als Jabne, daß ich gehe und dort meine Schüler unterweise, das Gebet dort festsetze und alle Gebote dort erfülle. [Darauf] sagte [Vespasian] zu ihm: Geh und tu alles, was du tun willst!

ARNB

Als sie zum Stadttor kamen, sprachen sie zu [den Torhütern]: Steht auf und macht uns auf, daß wir hinausgehen und ihn begraben! Da sagten die Torhüter zu ihnen: Wir öffnen nicht, ehe wir ihn nicht vorher mit dem Schwert durchbohrt haben! Sie gaben ihnen zur Antwort: Ihr werdet schuld daran sein, daß man von eurer Stadt schlecht spricht. Morgen wird man sagen[5]: Sogar R. Joḥanan haben sie durchbohrt! Schließlich machten sie ihnen auf.

Als R. Joḥanan b. Zakkai aus dem Tor Jerusalems herauskam, ging er und fragte nach dem Wohlergehen Vespasians, wie man nach dem Wohlergehen eines Königs[6] fragt. Er sagte zu ihm: *Vive domine imperator*[7]! [Vespasian] antwortete ihm: Bist du Ben Zakkai? Er sagte: Ja!

[5] Statt *'wmr* lies *'wmrjm*.
[6] *mlkwt*, wörtlich: „einer Regierung".
[7] *'j rjdwmnj 'jmpwṭrjn*. Der Text ist verderbt. MMish: *rbh djdw mnj plṭwr dmlkwt'*.

ARNA

Da sagte [Joḥanan b. Zakkai] zu [Vespasian]: Willst du, daß ich dir etwas sage? Er antwortete: Sprich! Darauf sagte [Joḥanan b. Zakkai] zu ihm: Du wirst demnächst zur Herrschaft berufen werden! — Woher weißt du dies? Er antwortete ihm: So wurde es uns überliefert, daß der Tempel nicht in die Hand eines gemeinen Mannes (*hdjwṭ*), sondern nur in die Hand eines Königs fallen wird, wie es heißt: 'Das Dickicht des Waldes wird mit dem Eisen niedergehauen werden, und der Libanon wird [nur] durch einen Mächtigen fallen' (Jes 10,34).

Man sagt, daß nicht ein, zwei oder drei Tage vergingen, bis zwei Gesandte aus seiner Stadt zu ihm kamen [und ihm meldeten], daß der Kaiser gestorben sei und man ihn zur Herrschaft berufen habe.

ARNB

Da sagte [Vespasian] zu ihm: Du hast mich betrübt[8]! [Joḥanan b. Zakkai] gab zur Antwort: Fürchte dich nicht, [denn] es steht bei uns geschrieben, daß dieser Tempel nur durch einen König zerstört werden wird, wie es heißt: 'Der Libanon wird [nur] durch einen Mächtigen fallen' (Jes 10,34). Da übergab er ihn zwei Beamten.

Nach drei Tagen kamen Briefe aus Rom zu ihm. Sie berichteten ihm: König Nero ist tot, und die Bewohner Roms haben dich zum König eingesetzt[9].

Da ließ er R. Joḥanan rufen und sagte zu ihm: Erbitte dir einen Wunsch! [Joḥanan b. Zakkai] gab zur Antwort: Ich erbitte von dir Jabne, daß ich dort Torah lerne, dort Ṣiṣit mache und dort alle übrigen Gebote erfülle. Er sprach zu ihm: Es sei dir als Geschenk gegeben!

[8] *hgjtnj*. MMish: *hrgtnj* („du hast mich getötet").
[9] Hier folgt in MMish die Episode vom geschwollenen Fuß Vespasians.

EkhR	b Git
Dreieinhalb Jahre belagerte Vespasian Jerusalem, und er hatte vier Fürsten (*dwksjn* = *duces*) bei sich: den Fürsten von Arabien, den Fürsten von Afrika[10], den Fürsten von Alexandrien und den Fürsten von Palästina[11]. Was den [Namen des] Fürsten von Arabien betrifft, so gibt es darüber zwei unterschiedliche Meinungen: Der eine sagt, er hieß Qilus[12], der andere dagegen meint, sein Name war Pangar[13].	Er sandte gegen sie den Kaiser Vespasian. Der kam und belagerte [Jerusalem] drei Jahre.
In Jerusalem gab es vier Ratsherren (*bwljṭin*)[14] — Ben Ṣiṣit, Ben Gurion, Ben Naqdimon und Ben Kalba Savuaʿ —, von denen jeder einzelne die Ernährung der Stadt für 10 Jahre[15] sicherstellen konnte.	Es befanden sich in [der Stadt] drei reiche Männer: Naqdimon b. Gurion, Ben Kalba Savuaʿ und Ben Ṣiṣit ha-Keset.
(Warum hieß er Naqdimon? Weil die Sonne seinetwegen schien[16]. Ben Kalba Savuaʿ [hieß der zweite], weil jeder, der hungrig wie ein Hund in sein Haus trat, gesättigt wieder herauskam. Ben Ṣiṣit ha-Keset [hieß der Dritte], weil seine Ṣiṣit über Kissen und Polster (*kstwt*) schleiften.	Naqdimon b. Gurion [hieß der eine], weil die Sonne für ihn schien[16]. Ben Kalba Savuaʿ [hieß der zweite], weil jeder, der hungrig wie ein Hund (*klb*) in sein Haus trat, gesättigt (*śbʿ*) wieder herauskam. Ben Ṣiṣit ha-Keset [hieß der Dritte], weil seine Ṣiṣit über Polster schleiften oder, wie manche sagen, weil sein Sitz (*kstw*) sich zwischen den Vornehmen Roms befand.
Der eine sagte: Ich werde Jerusalem 10 Jahre lang mit Weizen und Gerste versorgen. Der andere sagte:	Einer sagte ihnen (= den Bewohnern Jerusalems): Ich werde sie mit Weizen und Gerste versorgen.

[10] Ed. Buber: Phönikien.

[11] Ed. Buber: *sjbjtjnj*. Buber, S. 65, Anm. 246 erwägt die Lesart *sjbstjnj* = Sebaste-Samaria.

[12] Ed. Buber: *'jlm*. Die (vorzuziehende) Lesart *qjlws* bezieht sich möglicherweise auf den Schluß des ‘Midrasch’, wo Pangar/Qilus die Westmauer zum Ruhm (*qlws*; der Text liest allerdings *šbḥ'*) des Vespasian stehen läßt.

[13] Ed. Buber: Abgar (*'bgr*).

[14] Ed. Buber: „drei reiche Männer“ (Ben Ṣiṣit ha-Keset, Ben Kalba Savuaʿ und Naqdimon b. Gurion).

[15] Ed. Buber: „fünf Jahre“. Dies stimmt aber mit dem folgenden Einschub (aus b. Git ?) nicht überein.

[16] Vgl. b Taan 20a.

EkhR

[Ich werde Jerusalem 10 Jahre] mit Wein und Öl [versorgen]. Und der dritte sagte: [Ich werde Jerusalem 10 Jahre] mit Holz [versorgen]. Die Rabbinen lobten den am meisten, der Holz zur Verfügung stellen wollte.)[17]

Es befand sich dort auch Ben Baṭiaḥ, der Neffe Joḥanan b. Zakkais, der die Vorräte beaufsichtigte. Dieser verbrannte alle Vorräte. Als R. Joḥanan b. Zakkai dies hörte, rief er: Wehe (*wj*)! Man ging und hinterbrachte Ben Baṭiaḥ: Dein Onkel hat 'Wehe' ausgerufen! Da ließ er ihn kommen und fragte ihn: Warum hast du 'Wehe' gerufen?! [Joḥanan b. Zakkai] gab zur Antwort: Ich habe nicht 'Wehe' (*wj*)[18], sondern 'Wa' (*wh*)[19] gerufen. Da sagte [Ben Baṭiaḥ]: Du hast also 'Wa' gerufen — und warum dies? Er gab zur Antwort: Weil du alle Vorräte verbrannt hast, denn ich sagte bei mir: Solange die Vorräte vorhanden sind, werden sie ihr Leben nicht im Kampf einsetzen[20]. So wurde R. Joḥanan b. Zakkai zwischen 'Wai' und 'Wa' gerettet, und auf ihn trifft der Schriftvers zu: 'Der Vorteil des Wissens ist, daß die

b Git

Der zweite sagte ihnen: [Ich werde sie] mit Wein, Salz und Öl [versorgen]. Und der dritte sagte ihnen: [Ich werde sie] mit Holz [versorgen]. Die Rabbinen lobten den, der Holz zur Verfügung stellen wollte, denn Rab Ḥisda pflegte seinem Diener alle Schlüssel anzuvertrauen, außer den für das Holz. Rab Ḥisda sagte nämlich: Eine Vorratskammer [voll] Weizen erfordert 60 Vorratskammern [voll] Holz. Sie hatten [genug], um [die Stadt] 21 Jahre zu versorgen.

Unter ihnen befanden sich jene Zeloten (*brjwnj*). Unsere Lehrer sagten zu ihnen: Laßt uns hinausgehen und Frieden mit ihnen (= den Römern) machen! Sie ließen sie aber nicht, [sondern] sagten zu ihnen: Wir wollen hinausgehen und mit ihnen kämpfen! Da sagten unsere Lehrer zu ihnen: Dies wird nicht gelingen! Da standen sie auf und verbrannten die Vorräte an Weizen und Gerste, so daß eine Hungersnot ausbrach. ... (Folgt die Episode von Martha, der Tochter des Boethos).

[17] Dieser eingeklammerte Abschnitt findet sich nur in der Ed. BUBER. Er dürfte von b Git hier eingedrungen sein.

[18] Griech. οὐαί.

[19] Griech. οὐά.

[20] Wörtlich: „werden sie ihre Körper nicht hingeben, den Kampf zu machen". Ed. BUBER ergänzt: „und den Feind zu verfolgen".

EkhR	b Git
Weisheit ihre Besitzer am Leben erhält' (Qoh 7,12).	
Drei Tage später ging R. Joḥanan b. Zakkai aus, um auf dem Markt spazierenzugehen und sah sie (= die Bewohner Jerusalems), wie sie Stroh kochten und das Wasser davon tranken. Da sprach er: Menschen, die Stroh kochen und das Wasser davon trinken, sollen den Truppen Vespasians widerstehen?! Er sagte bei sich: Die Hauptsache von allem ist (= ich muß daraus die Konsequenz ziehen), daß ich von hier weggehe. So ließ er Ben Baṭiaḥ kommen und sagte [zu ihm]: Bring mich hier hinaus! Dieser antwortete ihm: Wir sind übereingekommen, daß niemand hier hinauskommt, es sei denn als Toter. Da sagte [Joḥanan b. Zakkai]: Dann bring mich wie einen Toten hinaus![21]	Abba Siqara, der Anführer der Zeloten (*brjwnj*) in Jerusalem [und] ein Neffe R. Joḥanan b. Zakkais, ließ ihm ausrichten: Komm heimlich zu mir! Als er kam, sagte [Joḥanan b. Zakkai] zu [Abba Siqara]: Wie lange werdet ihr es [noch] so treiben und die Welt durch Hunger töten? [Abba Siqara] antwortete ihm: Was kann ich tun, denn wenn ich ihnen etwas [derartiges] sage, töten sie mich! Da sagte [Joḥanan b. Zakkai] zu ihm: Finde einen Vorwand für mich, daß ich [aus Jerusalem] hinaus kann — vielleicht gibt es eine geringe Aussicht auf Rettung[22]. [Abba Siqara] antwortete ihm: Stell dich krank und laß alle Welt zu dir kommen und sich nach deinem Wohlbefinden erkundigen. Dann laß dir etwas Stinkendes bringen und leg es neben dich, damit man glaubt, du seist gestorben. Doch mögen nur deine Schüler zu dir hineingehen, niemand sonst, damit man dir nicht anmerkt, daß du leicht bist. Jene wissen nämlich, daß ein Lebender leichter ist als ein Toter.
R. Eli'ezer trug das Kopfende [der Bahre] und R. Jehoshua' das Fußende, und Ben Baṭiaḥ ging vor ihm her. Als sie [ans Stadttor] ka-	Er tat so. R. Eli'ezer trat (beim Heraustragen des 'Toten') von der einen Seite an ihn heran und R. Jehoshua' von der anderen Seite.

[21] Ed. Buber: „Da schickte R. Joḥanan zu Bar Siqra'a (= Siqara): Komm im Geheimen zu mir. Er sagte zu ihm: Wie lange wollt ihr es noch so treiben, daß ihr die Welt durch Hunger tötet? Er antwortete: Was ist zu tun? Denn wenn ich ihnen etwas sage, töten sie mich! Er antwortete: Finde einen Vorwand für mich, [daß] ich hinauskann — vielleicht gibt es eine kleine Rettung! Er antwortete: Ich kann dich hier nur wie einen Toten (statt *bdmwmjt* lies mit Buber, S. 67, Anm. 206: *bdmwt mjt*) herausbringen! Er antwortete: Dann bring mich wie einen Toten von hier weg!". — Auch diese Erweiterung dürfte auf b Git zurückgehen; vgl. die plötzliche Erwähnung (Abba) Siqaras statt Ben Baṭiaḥs.

[22] Wörtlich: „ein wenig Rettung", „eine kleine Rettung".

EkhR

men, wollten [die Wachen[23] die Bahre] durchbohren. Da sagte Ben Baṭiaḥ zu ihnen: Wollt ihr, daß man sagt: Ihr Lehrer ist gestorben, und sie haben ihn durchbohrt?![24] Als er dies zu ihnen gesagt hatte, ließen sie ihn [durch].

Als sie aus dem Stadttor hinauskamen, trugen sie ihn, setzten [die Bahre] auf einem Friedhof ab und kehrten dann in die Stadt zurück, während R. Joḥanan b. Zakkai unter den Truppen Vespasians umherspazierte. Er fragte sie: Wo ist der König? Da ging man und meldete Vespasian: Ein Jude [ist gekommen] und möchte dich begrüßen. Er antwortete: Er soll kommen! Als er eintrat, sagte er zu ihm: *Vive domine imperator*![25] Da sagte [Vespasian] zu ihm: Mit dem Gruß des Königs hast du mich begrüßt, aber ich bin nicht König! Wenn der König dies hört, wird er mich töten! [Joḥanan b. Zakkai] gab zur Antwort: Wenn du [jetzt] auch nicht König bist, so wirst du doch König sein, denn dieses Haus (= der Tempel) wird nur durch einen König zerstört werden[26], wie es heißt: 'Der Libanon wird [nur] durch einen Mächtigen fallen' (Jes 10,34).

b Git

Als sie an das [Stadt-]Tor kamen, wollten sie (= die Aufständischen) ihn (= den 'Toten') durchbohren, aber er (= Ben Baṭiaḥ?) sagte zu ihnen: Man wird sagen: Sie durchbohrten ihren Lehrer! Da wollten sie ihn stoßen, aber er sagte zu ihnen: Man wird sagen: Sie stießen ihren Lehrer! Schließlich öffneten sie ihm das Tor, und er kam hinaus.

Als er dorthin (= in das römische Lager) kam, sagte er: Friede über dich, König, Friede über dich, König! Da sagte [Vespasian] zu ihm: Du bist des zweifachen Todes schuldig, einmal, weil ich nicht König bin und du mich König genannt hast, und zum anderen: Wenn ich König bin, warum bist du dann nicht eher zu mir gekommen?! Da antwortete [Joḥanan b. Zakkai]: Wenn du sagst: Ich bin kein König, [so antworte ich dir]: Fürwahr, du bist König! Denn wärst du nicht König, würde Jerusalem nicht in deine Hand fallen, wie geschrieben steht: 'Der Libanon wird [nur] durch einen Mächtigen fallen' (Jes 10,34). 'Mächtiger' bedeutet hier nichts anderes als 'König', wie geschrieben steht: 'Ihr Mächtiger wird aus ihr selbst entstammen usw. [und ihr Herrscher aus ihrer Mitte hervorgehen]' (Jer 30,21); und 'Libanon' bedeutet [hier] nichts anderes als 'Tempel', wie geschrieben steht: 'Dieser schöne Berg und der Libanon' (Dt 3,25).

[23] Ed. Buber: „die Zeloten" (*brjwnj*).
[24] Ed. Buber: „sogar ihren Lehrer haben sie nicht verschont".
[25] *wbjb' m'rj 'plṭwr*. Der Text ist verderbt. Ed. Buber: „Mein Herr König lebe!", eine fast wörtliche Übersetzung der lateinischen Begrüßungsformel; vgl. auch b Git.
[26] Ed. Buber: „Dieses Haus wird nicht durch einen gemeinen Mann (*hdjwṭ*), sondern durch einen König zerstört werden, denn es ist das Haus des Herrn der Welt, und kein gemeiner Mann kann ihm etwas anhaben, sondern nur ein König."

EkhR

Man nahm ihn, setzte ihn inmitten von sieben Zellen und fragte ihn: Wie spät ist es in der Nacht?, und er sagte es ihnen; wie spät ist es am Tage?, und er sagte es ihnen! Woher wußte R. Joḥanan b. Zakkai [dies] denn? Durch sein Studium!

Drei Tage später ging Vespasian in Gophna baden. Nachdem er gebadet und einen seiner Schuhe angezogen hatte, wurde ihm die frohe Nachricht überbracht, daß Nero gestorben sei und die Bewohner Roms ihn zum König eingesetzt hätten. Als er daraufhin den zweiten Schuh anziehen wollte, paßte [der Fuß] nicht hinein. Da ließ er R. Joḥanan b. Zakkai herbeibringen und sprach zu ihm: Was sagst du dazu — jeden Tag zog ich zwei Schuhe an, und sie paßten mir; jetzt aber paßt einer und der andere nicht! [Joḥanan b. Zakkai] antwortete: Eine gute Nachricht wurde dir überbracht und es heißt: 'Eine gute Nachricht läßt das

b Git

Und wenn du sagst: Wenn ich König bin, warum bist du dann nicht eher zu mir gekommen, [so antworte ich dir]: Die Zeloten unter uns ließen mich nicht!

Da sagte [Vespasian]: Würde man nicht, wenn eine Schlange um ein Honigfaß gewunden wäre, das Faß wegen der Schlange zerbrechen?! Da schwieg [Joḥanan b. Zakkai]. R. Joseph — manche sagen auch: R. 'Aqiva — rief über ihn aus: 'Er läßt die Weisen zurücktreten, macht ihr Wissen zur Torheit' (Jes 44,25). Er hätte ihm antworten sollen: Man nehme [besser] eine Zange, entferne die Schlange und töte sie, das Faß aber lasse man!

Währenddessen kam zu ihm ein Kurier aus Rom und sagte zu ihm: Steh auf, der Kaiser ist gestorben, und die Vornehmen Roms sind übereingekommen, dich an die Spitze [des Staates] zu stellen. [Vespasian] hatte gerade einen Schuh angezogen und wollte auch den anderen anziehen, doch ging [der Fuß] nicht hinein; dann wollte er den ersten [wieder] ausziehen, doch ging er nicht [vom Fuß] herunter. Da sagte er: Was hat dies zu bedeuten? [Joḥanan b. Zakkai] antwortete: Sei unbesorgt — du hast eine gute Nachricht erhalten, und es steht geschrieben: 'Eine gute Nachricht läßt das Gebein anschwellen' (Spr

EkhR	b Git
Gebein anschwellen' (Spr 15,30). [Vespasian] fragte: Was machen wir, daß [der Fuß] hineingeht? Da antwortete [Joḥanan b. Zakkai]: Gibt es jemanden, den du haßt oder der dir etwas [Böses] getan hat? Man lasse ihn an dir vorbeigehen, und dein Fleisch wird sich zusammenziehen[27], wie es heißt: 'Ein betrübter Geist dörrt den Körper aus' (Spr 17,22).	15,30). Doch, was ist nun zu tun? Laß jemanden, über den du ungehalten bist, kommen und an dir vorübergehen, denn es heißt: 'Ein betrübter Geist dörrt den Körper aus' (Spr 17,22). Er tat so, und [der Fuß] ging hinein. Da sagte [Vespasian] zu ihm: Wenn ihr alle so weise seid, warum bist du dann nicht [eher] zu mir gekommen? [Joḥanan b. Zakkai] antwortete: Habe ich es dir denn nicht erklärt? — [Vespasian]: Ich habe dir aber auch geantwortet!
Man[28] trug Gleichnisse vor ihm vor: Ein Faß, in dem eine Schlange nistet — was tut man damit? [Joḥanan b. Zakkai] antwortete ihnen: Man bringt einen Zauberer und beschwört die Schlange, aber läßt das Faß[29]! Doch Pangar[30] sagte: Man tötet die Schlange und zerbricht das Faß! Ein Turm, in dem eine Schlange nistet — was tut man damit? [Joḥanan b. Zakkai] antwortete: Man bringt einen Zauberer und beschwört die Schlange[31], aber läßt den Turm. Doch Pangar[30] sagte: Man tötet die Schlange und verbrennt den Turm[32]! Da sagte R. Joḥanan b. Zakkai zu Pangar: Alle Nachbarn, die Böses tun, fügen [dies meist] ihren Nachbarn zu[33]. Statt daß du [uns] vertei-	

[27] Ed. Buber: „Er gehe an dir vorüber, du fühlst dich beengt, dein Gebein geht zurück (schwindet), und [der Fuß] geht hinein! . . . Er tat so und konnte auch den zweiten Schuh anziehen. Dann sagte [Vespasian] zu ihm: Wenn ich König bin, warum bist du dann nicht [eher] zu mir gekommen. [Joḥanan b. Zakkai] antwortete: Die Zeloten (*brjwnj*), die es hier (= in Jerusalem) gibt, ließen mich nicht". Vgl. auch dazu b Git.

[28] Ed. Buber: *hdwkwsjn* (= *duces*).

[29] Ed. Buber: „Man bringt ein Schwert und tötet die Schlange, aber rettet das Faß!".

[30] Ed. Buber: Amgar (*'mgr*).

[31] Ed. Buber: „Man bringt ein Schwert und tötet die Schlange".

[32] Ed. Buber: „Im Gegenteil, man reißt den Turm nieder und tötet die Schlange."

[33] Die Araber den Juden. Dieser Satz fehlt in Ed. Buber.

EkhR

digst, klagst du uns an! [Pangar] antwortete ihm: Ich will nur euer Bestes, denn solange dieses Haus (= der Tempel) besteht, fallen die [anderen] Reiche über euch her; wenn dieses Haus aber zerstört ist, werden sie euch in Ruhe lassen[34]! Darauf antwortete R. Joḥanan b. Zakkai: Das Herz weiß, ob es zum Flechtwerk (in der Kelter) oder zum Ränkespinnen dienen soll[35].

Vespasian[36] sagte zu R. Joḥanan b. Zakkai: Erbitte etwas von mir, und ich werde es tun! Da antwortete dieser: Ich bitte darum, daß du diese Stadt in Ruhe läßt und abziehst. Darauf sagte [Vespasian]: Haben mich die Bewohner Roms deswegen zum König gemacht, daß ich diese Stadt in Ruhe lasse?! Erbitte dir etwas [anderes], und ich werde es tun. Da antwortete [Joḥanan b. Zakkai]: Ich bitte darum, daß du das westliche Tor, das nach Lod geht, unbeaufsichtigt läßt, daß jeder, der innerhalb von vier Stunden[37] hinausgeht, gerettet werde.

Als [Vespasian die Stadt] erobert hatte, sagte er zu [Joḥanan b. Zakkai]: Wenn es jemanden gibt, den du liebst oder dem du nahe stehst, laß ihn kommen, ehe der Haufe hineinstürmt[38]. Da schickte

b Git

Dann sagte er zu ihm: Ich gehe nun weg und schicke einen anderen her. Jedoch, erbitte etwas von mir, und ich werde es dir geben! Da antwortete [Joḥanan b. Zakkai]: Gib mir Jabne, seine Weisen und die Dynastie Rabban Gamliels und Ärzte, die R. Ṣadoq heilen.

R. Joseph — manche sagen auch: R. ʿAqiva — rief über ihn aus: ʿEr läßt die Weisen zurücktreten, macht ihr Wissen zur Torheit' (Jes 44,25). Er hätte ihn besser darum gebeten, sie diesmal zu verschonen. Er aber dachte, all dies würde [Vespasian] nicht gewähren und es gäbe nicht einmal eine geringe Aussicht auf Rettung[22].

[34] Wörtlich: „werden die Reiche nicht mehr über euch herfallen". Der Halbsatz fehlt in Ed. Buber.

[35] Sprichwort; vgl. Resh Laqish in b San 26a und J. Levy, Wörterbuch über die Talmudim und Midraschim, III, Berlin–Wien ²1924 (Nachdruck Darmstadt 1963), S. 684 s. v. *ʿql*.

[36] Ed. Buber: „Als Vespasian kam, die Stadt zu erobern . . ."

[37] Ed. Buber: „drei Stunden".

[38] Ed. Buber: „Da schickte er und ließ alle Rabbinen herausbringen. Er suchte auch R. Ṣadoq und dessen Sohn, fand sie aber nicht. Da schickte er R. Eliʿezer und R. Jehoshuaʿ,

EkhR	b Git
er R. Eli'ezer und R. Jehoshua', R. Ṣadoq herauszubringen. Sie gingen und fanden ihn im Tor der Stadt. Als [R. Ṣadoq] kam, stand R. Joḥanan b. Zakkai vor ihm auf. Da sagte Vespasian zu ihm: Vor diesem hinfälligen Greis stehst du auf?! [Joḥanan b. Zakkai] antwortete: Bei deinem Leben, hätte es noch einen wie diesen gegeben, hättest du [Jerusalem] nicht erobern können, auch wenn du die doppelte Menge [Soldaten] gehabt hättest[39]. [Vespasian] fragte: Worin besteht seine Kraft? [Joḥanan b. Zakkai] gab zur Antwort: Daß er eine Sykomorenfrucht aß und darüber 100 Lehrvorträge halten konnte[40]. [Vespasian] fragte: Und warum ist er so mager? [Joḥanan b. Zakkai] antwortete: Von den Anstrengungen des Fastens und der Kasteiungen. Da ließ [Vespasian] Ärzte holen, die ihn ganz allmählich wieder an Essen und Trinken gewöhnten, bis er wiederhergestellt wurde[41]. Da sprach sein Sohn El'azar zu ihm: Vater, gib ihnen ihren Lohn in dieser Welt, da sie keinen Verdienst haben werden mit dir in der zukünftigen Welt! So gab er ihnen jene Berechnung mit Fingern[42] und jene große Schnellwaage[43].	

R. Ṣadoq und dessen Sohn hinauszubringen. Sie suchten in der Stadt drei Tage lang, fanden sie aber nicht. Nach drei Tagen fanden sie sie in einem der Stadttore . . .."

39 Der letzte Halbsatz fehlt in Ed. Buber.

40 Wörtlich: ,,100 Abschnitte erklärte."

41 Wörtlich: ,,bis sein Körper über ihn zurückkehrte". Ed. Buber: ,,bis seine Seele zu ihm zurückkehrte".

42 *ḥwšbn' d'ṣb'* — Fingerrechner? Vgl. Levy, Wörterbuch, III, S. 121; M. Jastrow, A Dictionary of the Targumin, the Talmud Babli and Yerushalmi, and the Midrashic Literature, I, London–New York 1903 (Repr. 1950), S. 441; Arukh, s. v. *ḥšb* und *krsṭ*.

43 *qrṣṭjwn'*; vgl. Levy, Wörterbuch, II, S. 413 s. v. *krsṭjjt'* und II, S. 457, Nachtrag von H. L. Fleischer zu S. 413, Sp. 1, Z. 10; Arukh, s. v. *krsṭ*; Jastrow, Dictionary, I, S. 667, s. v. *krjsṭjwn'*. Ed. Buber fügt hinzu: ,,R. El'azar b. R. Ṣadoq sagte: So wahr ich den Trost sehen möge — obwohl Vater all die Jahre nach der Zerstörung des Tempels noch

EkhR	b Git
Als er [Jerusalem] erobert hatte, teilte er die vier Stadtgebiete (*ṭksjj'*) unter die vier Fürsten auf, wobei das Westtor[44] an Pangar[30] fiel. Und im Himmel wurde beschlossen, daß es[45] in Ewigkeit nicht zerstört werde. Warum? Weil die Schekhinah im Westen ist[46]! Jene (= die übrigen drei Fürsten) zerstörten ihren [Teil], er jedoch nicht. Da ließ [Vespasian] ihn kommen und fragte ihn: Warum hast du deinen [Teil] nicht zerstört? Er antwortete ihm: Bei deinem Leben, zum Ruhme [deines] Reiches habe ich [dies] getan, denn wenn ich es zerstört hätte, hätte kein Mensch gewußt, was du zerstört hast! Wenn die Menschen es jetzt aber sehen, werden sie sagen: Seht die Macht Vespasians, was er zerstört hat[47]! Da sagte [Vespasian] zu ihm: Bei deinem Leben[48], du hast recht gesprochen! Jedoch, weil du meinen Befehl übertreten hast, sollst du auf die Spitze des Daches[49] steigen und dich selbst herabstürzen — wenn du am Leben bleibst, mögest du leben und wenn du stirbst, mögest du sterben. Er stieg hinauf, stürzte sich herab und starb. So ging an ihm der Fluch R. Joḥanan b. Zakkais in Erfüllung.	

lebte, wurde er doch nicht wiederhergestellt wie in den Jahren vorher, damit in Erfüllung gehe, was geschrieben steht: 'Auf ihrem Gerippe klebt die Haut, trocken ist sie wie Holz' (Ekh 4,8)!". — Zur messianischen Formel „So wahr ich den Trost sehen möge" vgl. F. DEXINGER, Ein 'messianisches Szenarium' als Gemeingut des Judentums in nachherodianischer Zeit?, Kairos 17, 1975, S. 275ff.

44 Ed. BUBER: „der westliche Teil".

45 Ed. BUBER: „die Westmauer" (= Klagemauer).

46 Fehlt in Ed. BUBER.

47 Ed. BUBER: „Wenn ich meinen Teil zerstört hätte, so wie jene ihren Teil zerstört haben, würden die Reiche, die nach dir erstehen, nicht wissen, welch große Pracht du zerstört hast. Da ich ihn aber nicht zerstört habe, werden die Reiche, die nach dir erstehen, sie (= die Westmauer) sehen und sagen: Seht, welch große Pracht er zerstörte!".

48 So mit Ed. BUBER und Ḥidushe ha-Rada"l z. St.

49 Ed. BUBER: „des Berges".

II. Die Versionen

Alle Bearbeiter der verschiedenen Versionen des Berichtes vom Auszug Joḥanan b. Zakkais aus Jerusalem und seiner Flucht zu Vespasian stimmen darin überein, daß — trotz der Unterschiede im einzelnen — jeweils die Versionen ARNA und ARNB auf der einen und EkhR und b Git auf der anderen Seite zusammengehören. Im folgenden seien die wichtigsten Unterschiede in den einzelnen Fassungen genannt[50]:

1. Nach ARNA und B verließ Joḥanan b. Zakkai die Stadt, weil er grundsätzlich gegen den Krieg mit den Römern war und für eine schnelle Beendigung der Kämpfe durch die Übergabe der Stadt. Anders dagegen EkhR: Hier entscheidet sich Joḥanan b. Zakkai erst für die Flucht aus dem belagerten Jerusalem, nachdem die Zeloten die Vorräte verbrannt hatten. Joḥanan b. Zakkai ist also nicht so sehr grundsätzlich gegen den Krieg als vielmehr gegen die unsinnige Politik der Zeloten. b Git scheint beide Traditionen zu kennen und zu harmonisieren: es ist zunächst die Rede davon, daß 'unsere Lehrer' (Rabbanan, also nicht Joḥanan b. Zakkai, doch könnte er eingeschlossen sein) die Aufständischen zum Frieden überreden wollten und dann erst vom Verbrennen der Vorräte und der Entscheidung Joḥanan b. Zakkais, angesichts dieser Entwicklung die Stadt zu verlassen.

2. ARNA und B berichten übereinstimmend, daß Vespasian Spione in der belagerten Stadt hatte und daher über die friedliebende Einstellung Joḥanan b. Zakkais schon vor dessen Flucht unterrichtet war. Dazu passend gelangt Joḥanan b. Zakkai nach seiner Flucht auch direkt vor Vespasian, und dieser scheint ihn zu kennen, denn er fragt ihn: „Bist du Joḥanan b. Zakkai?" (ARNA und B). Nach EkhR dagegen (b Git scheint wieder zu harmonisieren) wird er in seinem Sarg zunächst auf einem Friedhof abgesetzt und muß sich erst zu Vespasian durchschlagen.

3. Nach EkhR und b Git ist Ben Baṭiaḥ bzw. Abba Siqara, der Anführer der Aufständischen, Joḥanan b. Zakkai bei seiner Flucht behilflich; dies fehlt natürlich in ARNA und B, da er dort als Römerfreund und grundsätzlicher Gegner des Krieges porträtiert ist.

4. Nach dem Bericht in EkhR wird Joḥanan b. Zakkai inhaftiert („Man nahm ihn und setzte ihn inmitten von sieben Zellen ..."). Dies fehlt in ARN und b Git, doch könnte ARNB („er übergab ihn zwei Beamten") darauf anspielen. Immerhin empfängt Vespasian Joḥanan b. Zakkai auch in b Git mißtrauisch, wenn er ihn fragt: „Warum bist du nicht eher zu mir gekommen?"

[50] Vgl. dazu vor allem G. ALLON, Māḥqārîm b^etôl^edôt Jiśrā'el, I, [Tel Aviv] 1957, S. 238ff.; E. E. URBACH, Haj-j^ehûdîm b^e'arṣām bitqûphat hat-tannā'îm, B^eḥînôt 4, 1952/53, S. 61ff.; J. NEUSNER, A Life of Yohanan ben Zakkai, Leiden ²1970, S. 157ff.; DERS., Development of a Legend, Leiden 1970, S. 114ff., 147ff., 162ff., 228ff.; A. J. SALDARINI, Johanan ben Zakkai's Escape from Jerusalem, JSJ 6, 1975, S. 189ff.

5. Die Bitte Joḥanan b. Zakkais um Jabne etc. wird in ARNA vor der Prophezeiung geäußert, in den übrigen Versionen erst danach, d. h. als Belohnung für die Erfüllung der Weissagung. Die abweichende Reihenfolge in ARNA ist im Rahmen der Tendenz dieser Version, wonach Vespasian Joḥanan b. Zakkai ja schon als Römerfreund kennt und gewissermaßen als Verbündeten in Empfang nimmt, durchaus konsequent; ARNB dagegen ist trotz der mit ARNA gemeinsamen Tradition von den Spionen Vespasians nicht so einheitlich durchkomponiert. Zur eher zurückhaltenden Tendenz von EkhR/b Git paßt schließlich die keineswegs begeisterte Reaktion des Königs auf die Prophezeiung Joḥanan b. Zakkais (vgl. vor allem b Git: „du bist des zweifachen Todes schuldig!").

6. Die Tradition vom geschwollenen Fuß Vespasians und die Sentenz von der Schlange und dem Faß bzw. dem Turm findet sich nur in EkhR/b Git.

7. Der Wortlaut der Bitte ist in ARNA und B fast identisch: „Ich erbitte von dir nur Jabne, daß ich gehe und dort meine Schüler unterweise, das Gebet dort festsetze und alle Gebote dort erfülle" (ARNA); „Ich erbitte von dir Jabne, daß ich dort Torah lerne, dort Ṣiṣit mache und dort alle übrigen Gebote erfülle" (ARNB). In b Git lautet die Bitte dagegen: „Gib mir Jabne, seine Weisen und die Dynastie Rabban Gamliels und Ärzte, die R. Ṣadoq heilen", und in EkhR schließlich ist Jabne überhaupt nicht erwähnt: Joḥanan b. Zakkai erbittet zuerst die Rettung Jerusalems und darf nur, als ihm diese Bitte nicht gewährt wird, einige ihm nahestehende Personen retten.

Betrachtet man die summarisch aufgezählten Unterschiede in den einzelnen Versionen auf der Ebene der Redaktion, so ergibt sich ein deutlich verschieden akzentuiertes Bild der Fluchtgeschichte in den beiden Fassungen ARNA/B und EkhR/b Git. Beide Versionen in ARN zeichnen das Bild eines offen römerfreundlichen Joḥanan b. Zakkai, der den Krieg grundsätzlich ablehnt, dessen prorömische Einstellung bei Vespasian bekannt ist, der im Lager der Römer entsprechend empfangen wird und der schließlich als Lohn für dieses Wohlverhalten Jabne erhält. Anders dagegen EkhR (und z. T. auch b Git): Hier ist Joḥanan b. Zakkai der Flüchtling, der sich erst nach der Verzweiflungs-Politik der Zeloten zur Flucht entschließt, dem einer der Führer der Aufständischen sogar bei der Flucht behilflich ist, der von den Römern keineswegs übermäßig freundlich empfangen, sondern vielleicht sogar inhaftiert wird (EkhR) und der möglicherweise nach der Eroberung Jerusalems nur seine engsten Freunde retten darf (EkhR; b Git erwähnt wie die anderen Fassungen Jabne). Das Hauptproblem, um das beide Fassungen der Erzählung kreisen, ist ganz offenkundig die Frage nach der Zusammenarbeit Joḥanan b. Zakkais mit den Römern und nach dem Maß dieser Kollaboration. Während ARNA und B unbefangen und fast betont die prorömische Politik Joḥanan b. Zakkais hervorheben, die allein den endgültigen Untergang des Judentums verhindern konnte, ist EkhR (b Git) sehr viel zurückhaltender, ja apologetisch:

der Schritt Joḥanan b. Zakkais war ein Akt der Verzweiflung in höchster Not, der sogar von einem Teil der Zeloten gebilligt wurde. Wir haben es bei beiden Fassungen also mit eindeutig tendenziös gefärbten Erzählungen zu tun, die in verschiedener Weise das Skandalon des aus der Kollaboration mit den Römern in Jabne wiedergeborenen Judentums zu erklären bzw. zu rechtfertigen suchen.

So viel läßt sich — bei aller Vorsicht — mit einiger Wahrscheinlichkeit auf der Ebene der Redaktion ermitteln. Ist dies aber auch bereits die historische Wirklichkeit, d. h. zunächst: läßt sich mit guten Gründen die eine Version der anderen vorziehen und damit eine 'ursprüngliche' Fassung ausmachen, die den tatsächlichen Ereignissen am nächsten kommt? G. ALLON hat aus seiner glänzenden Analyse zwar keine direkten Schlüsse auf das Verhältnis der Fassungen zueinander gezogen, gibt aber deutlich zu erkennen, daß er EkhR (b Git) und damit die apologetische Version der Erzählung favorisiert. Im Unterschied dazu vermutet J. NEUSNER, daß wir in ARN(A) die wahrscheinlich älteste Fassung vor uns haben, die in früher amoräischer Zeit (3. Jh. n. Chr.?) entstanden sein könnte[51]. ARNB kombiniert — so NEUSNER — die Hauptelemente von ARNA und b Git, ist also eine Komposition dieser beiden Fassungen[52]. EkhR dagegen sei die späteste Fassung, die die meisten sekundären Erweiterungen enthalte[53]. Eine mögliche chronologische Reihenfolge der einzelnen Fassungen wäre also nach NEUSNER: ARNA — b Git[54] — ARNB — EkhR. Er kommt damit, vor allem in der Frage der mutmaßlich ältesten bzw. jüngsten Fassung, zum genau entgegengesetzten Ergebnis wie ALLON. Problematisch bei dieser Konstruktion NEUSNERS ist insbesondere die Spätdatierung von EkhR, deren Beweisführung im Grunde auf zwei höchst zweifelhafte Argumente reduziert werden kann, nämlich einmal, daß der kürzere Text (in diesem Fall ARN) die älteste und der am weitesten ausgearbeitete Text (EkhR) die jüngste Fassung bietet und zum anderen, daß die in der Endredaktion ältere Quelle (sehr wahrscheinlich ARN) auch bei der Beurteilung von Einzeltraditionen der in der Endredaktion jüngeren Quelle (EkhR) vorzuziehen ist ("*Thus once again we see that the version appearing in the later document is probably later than the one appearing in the earlier document*"[55]).

Beide Argumente gehen oft Hand in Hand, sind aber alles andere als beweisbar. Was das Verhältnis von längerer und kürzerer Fassung einer Überlieferung betrifft, so gilt heute keineswegs mehr als a priori feststehend, daß etwa — um zwei Beispiele zu nennen — eine kurze Mischna-Sentenz dem dazugehörigen breiter ausgeführten 'Midrasch' unbedingt zeitlich vorangehen muß, sondern die 'Mischna' kann umgekehrt den 'Midrasch' sehr

[51] NEUSNER, Development, S. 117f., 228ff.
[52] NEUSNER, Development, S. 229.
[53] NEUSNER, Development, S. 233; vgl. auch S. 162—167.
[54] Wobei die Priorität hier nicht mehr festzustellen ist: "*We do not know whether ARNa comes before b. Giṭ*" (Development, S. 233).
[55] NEUSNER, Development, S. 232.

wohl voraussetzen; ebensowenig ist die knappe Übersetzung eines Bibelverses etwa im 'Targum Onkelos' in jedem Falle älter als die breit paraphrasierende Wiedergabe desselben Verses im 'Targum Pseudo-Jonathan'. Noch problematischer ist das zweite Argument. Es begibt sich nicht nur auf das Glatteis der Datierung rabbinischer Quellen und der Festlegung einer relativen Chronologie anhand der mutmaßlichen Endredaktion der Texte — ein außerordentlich gefährliches Unterfangen, denn nach welchen Kriterien sollte z. B. EkhR in der Endredaktion später sein als b Git? —, sondern es geht auch von einer weiteren, noch anfechtbareren Prämisse aus, indem es zwischen der Endredaktion eines Textes und dem Alter der jeweiligen Einzeltraditionen nicht unterscheidet. Die Unterscheidung zwischen dem Alter der Einzelüberlieferung und der Endredaktion des ganzen Textes ist aber gerade für die rabbinische Literatur und hier insbesondere für aggadische Überlieferungen von elementarer Bedeutung, da wir es mit Traditionsliteratur und nicht mit Autorenliteratur zu tun haben. Ein in der Endredaktion später Text kann sowohl literarische Überlieferungen verarbeiten, die sich — aus welchen Gründen auch immer — in früheren Quellen nicht finden, als auch mündliche Traditionen aufnehmen, die in frühere Quellen keinen Eingang gefunden haben[56].

Den neuesten Versuch einer Analyse der verschiedenen Fassungen und ihrer historischen Situierung hat J. SALDARINI unternommen[57]. SALDARINI stimmt mit NEUSNER in manchen Einzelheiten überein (so z. B. in der Beurteilung von EkhR als Überarbeitung und Erweiterung von b Git), doch geht er anders als NEUSNER und alle seine Vorgänger davon aus, daß alle vier Fassungen der Erzählung von einer Vorlage, gewissermaßen einem Urtext, abhängig sind: *"I will argue that all four versions of the escape story depend upon a* Vorlage, *a basic, original story which then developed through two traditions into four versions"*[58]. Diese Vorlage, die ursprüngliche Fluchtgeschichte, möchte er anhand der allen Fassungen der Erzählung gemeinsamen Elemente rekonstruieren. Diese Elemente sind (nach SALDARINI[59]):

(1) R. Eli'ezer b. Hyrkanos und R. Jehoshua' b. Ḥananja tragen die Bahre Joḥanan b. Zakkais am Kopf- bzw. Fußende. (2) Die Torhüter stoppen den Leichenzug zunächst, lassen ihn dann aber passieren. (3) Joḥanan b. Zakkai begibt sich sofort zu Vespasian. (4) Er begrüßt Vespasian

[56] Vgl. auch die Kritik von J. HEINEMANN ('Aggādôt weṭôledôtêhān, Jerusalem 1974, S. 44) an NEUSNER: „Aggadot und Traditionen verändern sich ständig im Laufe ihrer Überlieferung. Dies bedeutet jedoch nicht, daß ein Gelehrter oder ein Redaktor im 5. Jh., der eine Erzählung über R. Joḥanan b. Zakkai oder ein Dictum aus seinem Munde bringt, die in keiner früheren Quelle erwähnt werden, diese mit Absicht entsprechend seiner ausgeprägten Phantasie gefälscht hat. Es gibt nichts Widersinnigeres als die Annahme, daß alles, was uns erstmals in Bereshit Rabba, Pesiqta deRab Kahana oder Ekha Rabba begegnet und für das man keine Parallele im Jerusalemer oder im babylonischen Talmud finden kann, daß dies notwendigerweise eine 'Erfindung' oder 'Fälschung' der Redaktoren jener Midraschim sein muß."

[57] S. oben (Anm. 50).

[58] SALDARINI, a.a.O., S. 190.

[59] SALDARINI, a.a.O., S. 191f.

als König. (5) Vespasian weist den Gruß als Hochverrat zurück[60]. (6) Das Zitat aus Jes 10,34. (7) Nach drei Tagen kommt die Nachricht aus Rom, daß der Herrscher (Nero) tot ist und Vespasian zu seinem Nachfolger ernannt wurde. (8) Die Freistellung einer Bitte. (9) Die Bitte Joḥanan b. Zakkais um Jabne (mit Ausnahme von EkhR).

Da diese neun Elemente eine einleuchtende und in sich schlüssige Erzählung ergeben, bildeten sie, so SALDARINI, die Vorlage für die späteren Fassungen. Alle anderen Elemente in den übrigen Fassungen seien Hinzufügungen zu dieser rekonstruierten 'Urfassung', die zeitlich in der Periode zwischen der Zerstörung des Tempels (70 n. Chr.) und dem Bar-Kochba-Aufstand (135 n. Chr.) anzusetzen sei.

Die Rückführung der unterschiedlichen Ausformungen einer Tradition mittels des allen Versionen gemeinsamen Nenners auf eine Art Urfassung, von der dann alle abhängig sein sollen, ist zwar verlockend, aber methodisch nicht weniger bedenklich als die Prämissen, von denen die Analyse NEUSNERS ausgeht; sie bevorzugt mit NEUSNER den kürzeren Text vor dem längeren, nur daß dieser kürzere Text erst rekonstruiert werden muß. Die Tatsache, daß der allen Fassungen gemeinsame Fundus groß ist und eine sinnvolle Geschichte ergibt, ist freilich noch kein Beweis dafür, daß eine solche 'Urfassung' jemals existiert hat. Ebensowenig ergibt sich aus dem Hinweis, daß die meisten der angeblich sekundären Elemente auf Jerusalem bezogen sind, die notwendige Schlußfolgerung, daß *"these added elements help to move the story from its original focus on Jamnia to Jerusalem"*[61]. Schließlich nimmt auch die rekonstruierte Vorlage ihren Ausgang in Jerusalem, und es wäre daher durchaus denkbar, daß auch Einzelheiten der Belagerung Jerusalems zum Kern einer solchen 'ursprünglichen' Geschichte gehörten. Vor allem aber ignoriert der sehr künstliche Rekonstruktionsversuch SALDARINIS die Eigenart aggadischer Überlieferung. Die 'Aggadah' geht in der Regel nicht von festformulierten 'ursprünglichen' Traditionen aus, sei es mündlicher oder schriftlicher Art, die irgendwann einmal entstanden und dann im Laufe der Zeit abweichend von dieser 'Urfassung' geändert wurden, sondern sie ist ständig im Fluß befindliche und sich immer neuen Gegebenheiten anpassende, ursprünglich meist mündliche Überlieferung, die zu verschiedenen Zeiten und unter verschiedenen historischen Umständen unterschiedliche literarische Formen annimmt. Hier nach einem Urtext bzw. nach einer mündlichen Urfassung (SALDARINI geht auf das Problem der mündlichen oder schriftlichen Ausgestaltung seiner Vorlage nicht ein) suchen zu wollen, ist eine im Ansatz schiefe Fragestellung und forschungsgeschichtlich ebenso überholt wie etwa der Versuch, einen Urtext des Achtzehn-Bitten-Gebets zu rekonstruieren[62].

[60] SALDARINI beachtet nicht, daß dieser Aspekt in ARNA ganz fehlt und in ARNB nur anklingt.

[61] SALDARINI, a.a.O., S. 201.

[62] Vgl. z. B. L. FINKELSTEIN, The Development of the Amidah, JQR (N.S.) 16, 1925/26, S. 1—43; 127—170.

Zusammenfassend ergeben die drei wichtigsten Analysen der verschiedenen Fassungen der Fluchtgeschichte höchst unterschiedliche Ergebnisse: die eine bevorzugt die Version in EkhR, die andere die in ARN und die dritte einen rekonstruierten Urtext. Alle sind von nicht unproblematischen methodischen Voraussetzungen abhängig, die den Wert ihrer Ergebnisse schmälern. Bei allen richtigen und wertvollen Beobachtungen im einzelnen ist es daher fraglich, ob ein literarischer Vergleich der verschiedenen Fassungen und die Ermittlung einer mutmaßlich ältesten Version für die historische Frage nach den Ereignissen in Jerusalem und Jabne ca. 68–70 n. Chr. von Belang ist. Mit anderen Worten: Die vier verschiedenen Fassungen bzw. die zwei aufgewiesenen unterschiedlichen Versionen der Fluchtgeschichte geben nur einen Einblick in die verschiedenen Absichten ihrer Redaktoren, nicht aber unbedingt auch in die tatsächlichen Ereignisse der Jahre 68 bis 70 n. Chr. Die Frage, welche Fassung als Ganze vorzuziehen ist, ist irrelevant, da alle Fassungen tendenziös sind (und diesem Problem geht man auch nicht mit der Rekonstruktion einer 'gereinigten' Urfassung aus dem Wege). Wenn es überhaupt möglich ist, jenseits der Ebene der Redaktion etwas über die Flucht Joḥanan b. Zakkais aus Jerusalem und die Gründung des 'Lehrhauses' in Jabne zu ermitteln, bleibt nur der Weg, die wichtigsten Einzelüberlieferungen in allen Fassungen unabhängig von ihrer redaktionellen Zusammenstellung und unabhängig vom angeblichen Alter des jeweiligen Textes auf ihren historischen Wert zu befragen[63]. Dieser Versuch soll im nächsten Abschnitt unternommen werden.

III. Die Einzelüberlieferungen

1. Das Verbrennen der Vorräte

Das Verbrennen der Vorräte wird in den oben übersetzten Parallelversionen der Fluchtgeschichte nur in den Fassungen EkhR/b Git erwähnt. ARN überliefert es zwar nicht in unmittelbarem Zusammenhang mit der Fluchtgeschichte, doch finden sich einige versprengte Stücke, die hier zu berücksichtigen sind (ARNA, Kap. 6, S. 31ff.; ARNB, Kap. 7, S. 20; ARNB, Kap. 13, S. 31); ob sie ursprünglich zur Fluchtgeschichte gehörten und nur durch die Redaktion der ARN an andere Stelle gerieten, ist für unsere Fragestellung nicht von Belang. Hinzuzuziehen ist ferner ein Text im Midrasch Qohelet Rabba (7,11 § 1), der möglicherweise von EkhR abhängig ist[64], sowie der Bericht bei Tacitus (Hist. V,12) und bei Josephus (Bell. V,1,4 § 22ff.).

[63] NEUSNER, Development, S. 233, kommt diesen Überlegungen nahe, führt seine Beobachtung aber nicht weiter aus.

[64] Zu den Quellen des Midrasch Qohelet Rabba vgl. L. ZUNZ, Die gottesdienstlichen Vorträge der Juden, historisch entwickelt, Frankfurt a.M. ²1892, S. 265f. (von Ḥ. ALBECK über-

a) ARNA Kap. 6, S. 31ff.

„Und warum heißt er Ṣiṣit ha-Keset? Weil er sich auf einem Bett von Silber[65] lagerte, an der Spitze aller Großen Israels. . . .
Und warum heißt er Naqdimon b. Gurion? Weil die Sonne um seinetwillen schien. . . .
Und warum heißt er Kalba Savua'? Weil jeder, der hungrig wie ein Hund (*klb*) in sein Haus kam, es gesättigt (*śb'*) wieder verließ.
Als Kaiser Vespasian kam, Jerusalem zu zerstören, da wollten die Zeloten (*qannā'îm*) alle diese Güter in Brand stecken. Da sprach Kalba Savua' zu ihnen: 'Warum zerstört ihr diese Stadt und [warum] wollt ihr alle diese Güter in Brand stecken? Laßt mir Zeit, bis ich hineingegangen bin und sehe, was ich im Hause habe'. Er ging und fand, daß er Nahrung für 22 Jahre hatte, um jedem einzelnen [Bewohner] Jerusalems eine Mahlzeit [pro Tag zukommen zu lassen]. Sofort gab er Befehl, [und] sie häuften auf, sonderten aus, siebten, kneteten und buken und bereiteten Nahrung für 22 Jahre für jeden einzelnen [Bewohner] Jerusalems, aber sie gaben nicht darauf acht[66]. Was taten die Bewohner Jerusalems? Sie brachten Brotlaibe[67], mauerten sie ein[68] und bestrichen sie mit Lehm[69].
Und auch [dies] taten die Bewohner Jerusalems: Sie kochten das Stroh und aßen [es].
Jeder einzelne [Bewohner] Israels lagerte gegenüber den Mauern Jerusalems [und] sprach: Wer gibt mir fünf Datteln, dann gehe ich hinunter und hole fünf Köpfe [der Römer]. Man gab ihm fünf Datteln, und er ging hinunter und holte fünf Köpfe von den Leuten Vespasians. Als Vespasian auf ihren Kot blickte und sah, daß sich darin kein einziges Korn befand, sprach er zu seinen Truppen: 'Wenn jene, die nichts anderes als Stroh essen, so unter euch[70] töten — würden sie[71] all das essen, was ihr eßt und trinkt, um wieviel mehr [wäre dann zu erwarten], daß sie euch töten würden!'"

arbeitete hebräische Ausgabe, Jerusalem ²1954, S. 128f.); L. GRÜNHUT, Kritische Untersuchung des Midrasch Kohelet Rabba, Quellen und Redactionszeit, Frankfurt 1892. Vgl. zu QohR jetzt auch J. WACHTEN, Midrasch-Analyse. Strukturen im Midrasch Qohelet Rabba, Hildesheim 1978 (= Judaistische Texte und Studien, 8).

65 Dieser Deutung liegt der Name Ṣiṣit ha-Keseph (und nicht ha-Keset) zugrunde.

66 D. h. sie bewachten die Vorräte nicht. Oder aber man bezieht *'ālāw* auf Ben Kalba Savua': „Sie achteten (= hörten) nicht auf ihn."

67 *'iggûlîm*? Vgl. JASTROW, Dictionary, II, S. 1066 und J. GOLDIN, The Fathers According to Rabbi Nathan, New Haven 1955, S. 46.

68 So mit einigen Handschriften (vgl. SCHECHTER, S. 33, Anm. 80): *gwdrjn 'wtn bgdrjn*; vgl. dazu GOLDIN, a.a.O., S. 46 mit Anm. 35f. (Verweis auf Ez 42,7, wo *gdr* ebenfalls „Mauer" heißt).

69 Möglich ist (mit einer anderen Lesart in ARN) auch die Übersetzung: „Sie brachten Rinder (*'ᵃgālîm*), zersägten sie mit Sägen (*gwrrjm 'wtm bmgrjm*) und bestrichen sie mit Lehm (zur Konservierung?)."

70 Statt *bhn* lies *bkm*.

71 Statt *hjh* lies *hjw*.

Dieser Bericht erwähnt die drei reichen Männer Jerusalems (Ṣiṣit ha-Keset, Naqdimon b. Gurion und Kalba Savua‘) im Zusammenhang mit der Legende vom Torahstudium Eli‘ezer b. Hyrkanos', eines der fünf Schüler Joḥanan b. Zakkais[72]; dieser Kontext ist sehr wahrscheinlich sekundär[73]. Die Namendeutungen sind allesamt Wortspiele, die aus Bestandteilen der drei Namen abgeleitet sind (*kst/ksp, nqd, klb*), wobei insbesondere die mit der Deutung von Naqdimon b. Gurion verbundene legendarische Erzählung durch auffallende Parallelen mit einer ähnlichen Geschichte über den Wundertäter Ḥoni ha-m^{e}‘aggel[74] begründete Zweifel an ihrer Authentizität aufkommen läßt. Im übrigen macht die Schilderung der Ereignisse in ARNA einen eher fragmentarischen und z. T. bis zur Unkenntlichkeit verstümmelten Eindruck. Zunächst sind es die Zeloten (*qannā'īm*), die „alle diese Güter" verbrennen wollen, ohne daß vorher von den Gütern (= Vorräten) die Rede gewesen wäre. Dann widerspricht Kalba Savua‘ dieser Wahnsinnstat mit dem etwas unmotivierten Einwand, daß er erst seine Vorräte zählen will (worauf er Vorräte für 22 Jahre vorfindet). Das tatsächliche Verbrennen der Vorräte wird schließlich überhaupt nicht erwähnt, statt dessen aber ganz unvermittelt die Hungersnot in Jerusalem (Kochen des Strohs) und die außergewöhnliche Tapferkeit der Bewohner Jerusalems trotz der unzureichenden Ernährung.

b) ARNB Kap. 7, S. 20

„Als Vespasian kam und Jerusalem belagerte, da lagerte er gegenüber dem Osten Jerusalems. Es standen alle Sikarier (*sjqrjn*) auf und verbrannten alle Vorräte, die in Jerusalem waren; sie hatten die Absicht, keine Lebensmittel übrig zu lassen.
Und die Bewohner Jerusalems kochten Stroh und tranken das Wasser davon, und [dennoch] gingen sie hinaus und führten Krieg mit ihnen (= den Römern) und töteten [viele] von ihnen.
Als Vespasian den Kot der Bewohner Jerusalems sah, in dem sich kein einziges Korn befand, rief er alle seine Truppen zusammen und sprach zu ihnen: ‘Kommt und seht — hungrige und durstige Menschen gehen heraus, führen Krieg mit euch und töten [viele] von euch. Würden sie essen und trinken, um wieviel mehr gälte dies (= wie viele von euch würden sie dann erst töten)!'"

Hier sind es die Sikarier, die die Vorräte in Jerusalem verbrennen und damit eine Hungersnot provozieren. Ein Grund für die „Absicht, keine

[72] Vgl. m Ab 2,8.
[73] Vgl. auch den ähnlichen Bericht in den beiden Einleitungskapiteln zu PRE (besonders S. 3a f.), der in Anlehnung an ARN gestaltet sein dürfte. FRIEDLANDER in seiner englischen Übersetzung der PRE (Pirḳê de Rabbi Eliezer, translated and annotated . . . by G. FRIEDLANDER, London 1916, Nachdruck New York 1971), S. 6 mit Anm. 2 beruft sich auf ein Genizafragment, in dem auch (im Unterschied zu den gedruckten Ausgaben) das Verbrennen der Vorräte erwähnt wird.
[74] Vgl. m Taan 3,8f.; b Taan 23a; j Taan 3,10f. fol. 66d f.; Ant. XIV,2,1 § 22.

Lebensmittel übrig zu lassen", wird ebensowenig angegeben wie in ARNA. Die Schilderung der Folgen (Kochen des Strohs) sowie der überraschenden und von Vespasian persönlich bewunderten Tapferkeit ist mit dem Bericht in ARNA nahezu identisch.

c) ARNB Kap. 13, S. 31

„Man erzählte über Ben Kalba Savua', daß er Nahrung für drei Jahre für jeden einzelnen [Bewohner] Jerusalems hatte. Als die Sikarier (*sqrjn*) aufstanden[75], verbrannten sie alle Vorräte, die in Jerusalem waren. Sie maßen alles, was er hatte, und fanden Nahrung für drei Jahre für jeden einzelnen [Bewohner] Jerusalems."

Ein kurzes Fragment, das nur (Ben) Kalba Savua' erwähnt und wie in ARNB, Kap. 7, ebenfalls ohne Angabe eines Grundes, den Sikariern das Verbrennen der Vorräte zuschreibt. Die Vorräte reichen hier (im Unterschied zu ARNA) nur für drei Jahre.

d) b Git 56af. (Text s. oben)

Auch hier sind die drei reichen Männer Jerusalems (ausdrücklich als solche apostrophiert!) mit diversen Namendeutungen erwähnt. Bemerkenswert ist die abweichende Erklärung zu (Ben) Ṣiṣit ha-Keset, die gute Kontakte mit den Römern zu suggerieren scheint. Um eine offensichtlich sekundäre Erweiterung dürfte es sich bei dem edlen Wettstreit der Drei handeln, wessen Vorräte die nützlicheren und wichtigeren sind; die Dauer der Versorgung ist diesmal mit 21 Jahren angegeben. Ganz unvermittelt geht die Schilderung dann zu den Zeloten (*brjwnj*) über, deren Widerpart diesmal (vgl. ARNA) „unsere Lehrer" sind, die mit den Römern Frieden schließen wollen (ein Vorgriff auf Joḥanan b. Zakkai?). Im Streit um die richtige Taktik verbrennen die Zeloten schließlich die gesamten Nahrungsmittel. Trotz der etwas kryptischen Ausdrucksweise ist hier die Deutung möglich oder sogar wahrscheinlich, daß die Zeloten die Vorräte verbrannten, um die Bewohner Jerusalems zum Verzweiflungskampf anzustacheln[76]. Abba Siqara, der anschließend als „Anführer der Zeloten" (*brjwnj*) und Neffe Joḥanan b. Zakkais vorgestellt wird, steht nicht in unmittelbarem Zusammenhang mit dem Verbrennen der Vorräte.

e) EkhR 1,31 = Ed. BUBER S. 65ff. (Text s. oben)

In diesem Bericht sind aus den drei reichen Männern offensichtlich durch sekundäre Teilung des Naqdimon b. Gurion vier Ratsherren geworden

[75] Statt *'md* lies *'mdw*.

[76] Dies gilt keineswegs für alle Versionen der Erzählung, wie J. BAER, Jerûšālajim bîmê ham-märäd hag-gādôl, Zion 36, 1971, S. 177 etwas pauschal schreibt.

(richtig dagegen EkhR Ed. BUBER), die zusammen die Versorgung Jerusalems für 40 Jahre sicherstellen können. Die Vorräte werden hier durch den Neffen Joḥanan b. Zakkais persönlich verbrannt, dem ausdrücklich die Bewachung der Vorräte übertragen ist und der nun Ben Baṭiaḥ heißt. Ein Grund für das Verbrennen der Vorräte ist nicht angegeben, doch könnte sich hinter der Joḥanan b. Zakkai in den Mund gelegten Äußerung („Solange die Vorräte vorhanden sind, werden sie ihr Leben nicht im Kampf einsetzen") in Wirklichkeit die Politik der Zeloten verbergen. Dann entspräche der Grund der auch hinter b Git vermuteten Absicht der Zeloten, die Bewohner Jerusalems zum offenen Kampf mit den Römern zu treiben.

f) QohR 7,11 § 1

„Drei Ratsherren (*bljwṭjn*) waren in Jerusalem: Ben Ṣiṣit ha-Keset, Naqdimon b. Gurion und Ben Kalba Savua', und ein jeder von ihnen war imstande, die Stadt für 10 Jahre zu versorgen und zu ernähren. Es befand sich dort Ben Baṭiaḥ, der Neffe R. Joḥanan b. Zakkais; der war Anführer der Sikarier[77] in Jerusalem und als Aufseher über die Vorräte eingesetzt. Dieser erhob sich und verbrannte die Vorräte.
Als R. Joḥanan b. Zakkai dies hörte, sagte er: 'Wehe!' Man ging und hinterbrachte Ben Baṭiaḥ: Dein Onkel hat 'Wehe, Wehe!' gesagt. Er ließ ihn kommen und fragte ihn: 'Warum hast du Wehe gesagt?' Er antwortete: 'Ich habe nicht Wehe (*wj*), sondern Wa (*wh*) gesagt, denn solange die kostbaren Vorräte vorhanden sind, werden die Leute ihr Leben nicht im Kampf einsetzen.'
Zwischen 'Wai' und 'Wa' wurde R. Joḥanan gerettet. Man bezog auf ihn den Vers: 'Der Vorteil des Wissens ist, daß die Weisheit ihre Besitzer am Leben erhält' (Qoh 7,12)."

Der Bericht deckt sich im wesentlichen mit EkhR. Die Zahl der Ratsherren ist korrekt mit drei angegeben, und Ben Baṭiaḥ wird ausdrücklich als Anführer der Sikarier bezeichnet.

g) Tacitus, Hist. V,12

sed proelia dolus incendia inter ipsos, et magna vis frumenti ambusta.

„aber [es gab] Kämpfe, Betrug und Brände unter ihnen selbst, und eine große Menge Getreide verbrannte."

Tacitus spielt hier auf die drei einander bekämpfenden Parteien in Jerusalem an, von denen die eine (unter Simon b. Giora) die äußersten und umfassendsten Mauern besetzt halte (*extrema et latissima moenium Simo*), die andere (unter Johannes von Gischala) die Mittelstadt (*mediam urbem Joannes*) und die dritte (unter Elazar) den Tempel (*templum Eleazarus*

[77] Statt *qsrjn* lies *sqrjn*.

firmaverat)[78]. Diese drei Parteien, so Tacitus, bekämpften sich gegenseitig, wobei Brände ausbrachen und die Getreidevorräte zum großen Teil verbrannten.

h) Josephus, Bell. V, 1,4 § 22ff.

„Sooft also Johannes von beiden Seiten her angegriffen wurde, setzte er seine Anhänger auf einander entgegengesetzten Fronten ein: die aus der Stadt Heraufstürmenden[79] beschoß er von den Tempelhallen aus, die Schützen, die vom Tempel herab angriffen[80], wehrte er mit den Wurfmaschinen ab: Und wenn er einmal von dem Druck der oberhalb von ihm in Stellung befindlichen Bedränger frei war — diese zwang des öfteren Trunksucht oder Ermüdung zu einer Pause —, so machte er mit stärkeren Kräften einen um so verwegeneren Ausfall auf die Simongruppe. Und im ganzen Stadtgebiet, das er bei solchen Vorstößen erreichen konnte, pflegte er die mit Getreide und mancherlei Vorräten angefüllten Gebäude in Brand zu setzen; zog aber Johannes sich zurück, so griff Simon an und tat das gleiche. Es hatte den Anschein, als wollten sie absichtlich zugunsten der Römer das vernichten, was die Stadt für den Belagerungsfall bereitgestellt hatte und so die Nervenstränge ihrer eigenen Kraft durchschneiden. So geschah es tatsächlich, daß das Wohngebiet um den Tempel völlig niedergebrannt und die Stadt zu einem öden Niemandsland und Schauplatz des Bürgerkrieges wurde, daß ferner bis auf einen kleinen Rest alles Getreide verbrannt war, das sonst den Belagerten für nicht wenige Jahre hätte reichen können. Tatsächlich sind sie durch Hunger bezwungen worden, was am allerwenigsten zu befürchten gewesen wäre, hätten sie dieser Not nicht selbst schon im voraus den Weg bereitet[81]."

Dieser Bericht des Josephus stimmt — unbeschadet der unterschiedlichen Länge — mit der Schilderung des Tacitus in zwei wesentlichen Einzelheiten überein: Wie bei Tacitus sind auch hier die einander bekämpfenden jüdischen Gruppen in Jerusalem (genauer und nicht ganz so pauschal: die Anhänger des Johannes und des Simon) schuld an der Vernichtung der Vorräte, und zwar — dies ist die zweite Übereinstimmung — verbrannte nicht alles Getreide, aber der größte Teil (*magna vis* bei Tacitus; πλὴν ὀλίγου πάντα τὸν σῖτον bei Josephus). Zu den Angaben in der rabbinischen

[78] Auf das Problem der Topographie Jerusalems und des genauen Standortes der einzelnen Gruppen kann in diesem Zusammenhang nicht eingegangen werden; vgl. MICHEL—BAUERNFEIND, in: Flavius Josephus, De Bello Judaico — Der jüdische Krieg, Griechisch-Deutsch, ed. O. MICHEL—O. BAUERNFEIND, II/1, München 1963, S. 241, Anm. 5 und BAER, a.a.O., S. 163 mit Anm. 129.

[79] Also die Truppen Simons.

[80] Die Truppen Elazars.

[81] Die Übersetzung aller Zitate aus Josephus' 'Bellum' folgt der zweisprachigen Ausgabe von O. MICHEL—O. BAUERNFEIND, München 1959—1969.

Literatur paßt die (allerdings vage) Notiz, daß die Vorräte „für nicht wenige Jahre“ (οὐκ ἐπ' ὀλίγα ἔτη) hätten reichen können.

Vergleicht man die verschiedenen Berichte von der Vernichtung der Vorräte in der rabbinischen Literatur, bei Tacitus und bei Josephus miteinander, so ergeben sich beträchtliche Unterschiede (die kaum mit der Bemerkung zu nivellieren sind, daß Josephus „mit der Vernichtung der Lebensmittellager durch die Zeloten eine historisch zutreffende und wichtige Tatsache berichtet, die sowohl von Tacitus ... als auch von den Rabbinen ... bestätigt wird[82]“).

Zunächst einmal erwähnen nur die rabbinischen Quellen im Zusammenhang mit den Vorräten drei reiche Ratsherren (*bwljwṭjn* = βουλευταί)[83], die die Lagerung der Vorräte veranlaßten. Von diesen drei Namen, die auch sonst in der rabbinischen Literatur bezeugt sind[84], nennt Josephus nur einen mit Naqdimon b. Gurion möglicherweise identischen Gorion, Sohn des Nikomedes (Γωρίονά τε Νικομήδους υἱὸν), als einen der drei jüdischen Unterhändler, die mit Metilius verhandelten[85]. Die Zeitangaben über die durch die Lagerung der Vorräte mögliche Versorgung Jerusalems schwanken zwischen drei (ARNB Kap. 13), einundzwanzig (b Git), zweiundzwanzig (ARNA), drei mal zehn (QohR), vier mal zehn (EkhR Ed. Wilna) und „nicht wenigen“ (Josephus) Jahren. Weder aus den sehr uneinheitlichen Zeitangaben vor allem in den rabbinischen Quellen noch aus der Tatsache, daß Josephus (Ben) Ṣiṣit ha-Keset und (Ben) Kalba Savuaʿ nicht kennt und umgekehrt die Rabbinen Johannes von Gischala, Elazar b. Simon und Simon b. Giora, die Hauptakteure im belagerten Jerusalem, nicht erwähnen, kann allerdings mit Bestimmtheit abgeleitet werden, daß die Nachrichten der Aggadah über die drei 'Ratsherren' als unhistorisch zu bewerten sind und daß insbesondere (Ben) Ṣiṣit ha-Keset und (Ben) Kalba Savuaʿ „kein Platz in der wirklichen Geschichte der Zerstörung des zweiten Tempels zukommt[86]“. Weder das eine noch das andere ist zu beweisen, und es ist

[82] MICHEL—BAUERNFEIND, II/1, S. 241, Anm. 10.

[83] Genauer: EkhR Ed. Wilna und QohR nennen „Ratsherren“, b Git und EkhR Ed. BUBER „reiche Männer“, und ARN kennt zwar die drei Namen, erwähnt im Zusammenhang mit der Belagerung Jerusalems aber nur (Ben) Kalba Savuaʿ.

[84] Naqdimon b. Gurion: vgl. b Taan 19b; b AbZa 25a u. ö. (das Regenwunder; vgl. dazu die Erzählung von Ḥoni ha-meʿaggel, oben Anm. 74); Ben Ṣiṣit ha-Keset: vgl. j Taan 4,2, fol. 68a („R. Levi sagte: Eine Abstammungsrolle fand man in Jerusalem und in ihr stand geschrieben: Hillel aus [dem Geschlechte] Davids, ... Ben Ṣiṣit ha-Keset aus [dem Geschlechte] Abners, ... Ben Kalba Savuaʿ aus [dem Geschlechte] Kalebs ...“); Ben Kalba Savuaʿ: vgl. b Ned 50a; b Ket 62bf. (R. ʿAqiva heiratet die Tochter Ben Kalba Savuaʿs: diese legendarische Erzählung spricht nicht unbedingt, wie BAER, a.a.O., S. 176, Anm. 176, vermutet, gegen die Historizität unseres Berichtes von den drei reichen Männern in Jerusalem während des jüdischen Krieges).

[85] Bell. II, 17,10 § 461. Eine ähnliche Namensvertauschung könnte auch Bell. II, 20,3 § 563 und Bell. IV,3,8 § 159 vorliegen; vgl. dazu M. HENGEL, Die Zeloten, Leiden/Köln ²1976, S. 374 mit Anm. 4.

[86] BAER, a.a.O., S. 176, Anm. 176.

jedenfalls durchaus denkbar, daß die Aggadah von den drei reichen 'Ratsherren' in ihrem Kern auf eine historische Begebenheit zurückgeht.

Einheitlicher sind die Antworten der verschiedenen Quellen auf die Frage, wer die Vorräte verbrannt haben soll. Trotz unterschiedlicher Terminologie (ARNA: *qannā'îm*[87]; ARNB: *sîqārîn*[88]; b Git: *barjônê*[89]; EkhR/QohR: Ben Baṭiaḥ, der Anführer der Sikarier[90]) stimmen die 'Aggadah', Tacitus und Josephus darin überein, daß die Zeloten selbst für die Vernichtung der Vorräte verantwortlich zu machen sind.

Die entscheidende Frage ist schließlich, warum die Vorräte verbrannt wurden. Hier geben die Quellen wieder verschiedene Antworten: Die gesamte Tradition von ARN stellt nur das Faktum der Verbrennung fest und nennt keinen Grund. Aus b Git und EkhR/QohR ist möglicherweise indirekt zu erschließen, daß die Zeloten die Vorräte mit Absicht verbrannten, um die Juden zum Kampf gegen die Römer anzutreiben, und nach Tacitus und Josephus ist die Vernichtung der Vorräte eine unbeabsichtigte Folge der internen jüdischen Parteienkämpfe. Die Vermutung von H. GRAETZ, daß nach einer rabbinischen Quelle (b Git) die Zeloten die Vorräte verbrannten, weil die drei reichen Ratsherren Friedens- und Römerfreunde waren[91], hat keinen Anhaltspunkt im Text. Zwar ist die Namensdeutung von Ben Ṣiṣit ha-Keset in b Git auffällig, nach der „sein Sitz (*kistô*) sich unter den Vornehmen Roms befand", doch besagt dies alleine als Argument wenig, zumal an anderer Stelle[92] von den „Großen Israels" die Rede ist. Außerdem sind es gerade nicht, wie GRAETZ behauptet, die „drei Reichen und Buleuten", die b Git „zu Römerfreunden stempelt"[93], sondern die Rabbinen (*rabbānān*). Das Argument schließlich, daß der bei Josephus erwähnte Unterhändler Gorion, Sohn des Nikomedes, „den Römern Vertrauen eingeflößt und demgemäß nicht zu den offenen Zeloten, sondern zu den ganzen oder halben Friedensfreunden gehört haben (müsse)"[94], verkennt völlig die Bell. II,17,10 § 449ff. geschilderte Situation und bedarf kaum der Widerlegung.

Sehr viel skeptischer urteilt J. BAER, der davon ausgeht, daß „der Verfasser der 'Aggadah' von der [Tempel]zerstörung seine Erzählung

[87] Wörtlich: „Eiferer", das hebr. Äquivalent des von Josephus häufig verwendeten griech. Terminus οἱ ζηλωταί; vgl. HENGEL, a.a.O., S. 64ff.

[88] Bei Josephus σικάριοι, von lat. *sicarius* („Meuchelmörder"); die 'Mischna' verwendet *sjqrjn* nur an einer Stelle (Makh 1,6). Zum Ganzen vgl. HENGEL, a.a.O., S. 47ff.

[89] Die Ableitung dieses Terminus und seine genaue Bedeutung ist immer noch nicht mit Sicherheit geklärt. Zu den verschiedenen Erklärungsversuchen vgl. HENGEL, a.a.O., S. 55ff.

[90] Ben Baṭiaḥ ist sonst nur noch in der 'Mischna' erwähnt, vgl. Kel 17,12: *zähû' 'ägrôphô šäl bän Baṭî^{a}ḥ* — „das ist die Gewalt(tat) des Ben Baṭiaḥ". Es ist nicht auszuschließen, daß der Name (nicht jedoch die verwandtschaftliche Beziehung zu Joḥanan b. Zakkai) auf eine historische Reminiszenz zurückgeht; er ist jedenfalls dem „Phantasienamen" (HENGEL, a.a.O., S. 56, Anm. 1) Abba Siqara in b Git vorzuziehen.

[91] H. GRAETZ, Geschichte der Juden, III, Leipzig ^{5}1906, S. 528f. mit Anm. 4.

[92] ARNA, Kap. 6; ARNB, Kap. 13.

[93] GRAETZ, a.a.O., Anm. 4.

[94] GRAETZ, a.a.O.

hauptsächlich auf das gründet, was sich bei Josephus findet — alles übrige oder der größte Teil ist die Schöpfung seiner Phantasie“[95]; darüber hinaus seien Josephus und Tacitus von einer gemeinsamen (römischen) Quelle abhängig, die verlorengegangen sei. Diese Josephus und Tacitus zugrunde liegende römische Quelle habe möglicherweise „mit Absicht die Gegensätze und Kämpfe zwischen den Parteien in Jerusalem gefälscht. Im römischen Lager konnte man die Brände sehen, die von den Getreidespeichern in der Stadt aufstiegen, und es ist möglich, daß sie durch Brandpfeile entfacht wurden, die von den Römern selbst geworfen wurden; es wäre ihnen ein Leichtes gewesen, hinterher zu erzählen, daß die miteinander rivalisierenden Juden dies getan hätten“[96]. Baer bringt hier also eine dritte Möglichkeit ins Spiel, die Vermutung nämlich, daß nicht die Juden, sondern die Römer an der Vernichtung der Vorräte schuld gewesen sein könnten. Diese These ist aber doppelt problematisch. Sie macht sich nicht nur die vor allem auf Weber zurückgehende[97] und bis heute umstrittene[98] Hypothese von einem flavianischen Geschichtswerk, das Josephus für die Bücher III—VII § 162 verwertet haben soll, zu eigen, sondern sie versucht auch, diese hypothetische Quelle in diesem einen Punkt mit ganz unbewiesenen (und unbeweisbaren) Vermutungen und gegen die Angaben der erhaltenen Quellen zu rekonstruieren.

Es bleibt somit bei der Schilderung der Ereignisse in der ‘Aggadah’ und bei Josephus/Tacitus, die in der Schuldfrage grundsätzlich übereinstimmt, aber insofern differiert, als die einen von einer absichtlichen und die anderen von einer unabsichtlichen Vernichtung der Vorräte durch die Zeloten ausgehen. Da die rabbinischen Quellen in ihrer Beurteilung keineswegs einheitlich sind (vgl. ARN) und die absichtliche Verbrennung der Vorräte mit dem Ziel, die Juden zum Kampf anzutreiben, nur indirekt erschlossen werden kann, ist vielleicht der Darstellung bei Josephus/Tacitus vor den rabbinischen Quellen (b Git, EkhR/QohR) der Vorzug zu geben.

2. Verhandlungen und Spione

Auf die mögliche Historizität zweier Details in ARNA und B (oben S. 45) muß kurz in einem eigenen Abschnitt eingegangen werden. Beide Versionen in ARN berichten einmal, daß Vespasian von den Bewohnern Jerusalems ausdrücklich die Übergabe der Stadt verlangt habe mit dem Versprechen, sie dann zu verschonen (d. h. wohl: die Stadt und vor allem den Tempel nicht zu zerstören), und zum anderen, daß Vespasian Spione

[95] Baer, a.a.O., S. 177.

[96] Baer, a.a.O., S. 163f.; vgl. auch S. 177.

[97] W. Weber, Josephus und Vespasian. Untersuchungen zu dem jüdischen Krieg des Flavius Josephus, Berlin–Stuttgart–Leipzig 1921 (Nachdruck Hildesheim–New York 1973), S. 78ff.; für unseren Zusammenhang vgl. S. 103.

[98] Vgl. Michel—Bauernfeind, III, S. XXIff.; Hengel, a.a.O., S. 9 mit Anm. 3.

in der Stadt hatte, die über die römerfreundliche Einstellung Joḥanan b. Zakkais informiert waren.

a) Was den ersten Punkt betrifft, so erwähnt Josephus noch bis in das letzte Stadium des Krieges häufig das Angebot der Römer und des Titus[99], die Stadt zu übergeben und damit die schlimmsten Folgen abzuwenden:

> „Titus aber wußte wohl, was für ihn selbst die Erhaltung wie auch der Untergang der Stadt bedeuten würde. Darum versäumte er es nicht, während er die Belagerungsarbeiten eifrig weiter betrieb, die Juden zur Besinnung aufzurufen, und ließ seine militärischen Vorbereitungen von Friedensvorschlägen begleitet sein. Da er der Ansicht war, daß vielfach mit dem Wort mehr als mit Waffen auszurichten sei, ermahnte er sie wiederholt persönlich, doch die schon so gut wie eingenommene Stadt durch die Übergabe noch zu retten[100]."

Ohne Zweifel sind die bei Josephus so gehäuft auftretenden Friedensbemühungen des Titus verdächtig und im Rahmen der hinlänglich bekannten apologetischen und tendenziösen Bemühungen des Autors zu beurteilen. Dennoch ist die von ARN und Josephus bezeugte Möglichkeit solcher Friedensabsichten weder mit dem Hinweis auf eine Stelle bei Sulpicius Severus aus der Welt geschafft, wonach Titus den belagerten Juden keine Gelegenheit zur Übergabe gegeben hätte[101], noch mit der ironischen Bemerkung: „Ist es denkbar, daß der Verfasser der 'Aggadah' das Abschießen eines Pfeiles mit einem Brief meinte, der die Bereitschaft der Juden, sich zu ergeben, signalisierte — womit die Angelegenheit dann erledigt sein und das römische Heer von dort abziehen sollte?[102]." Sulpicius Severus könnte mit gleichem Recht eine Notiz bei Cassius Dio entgegengehalten werden, daß Titus vor dem Angriff auf Jerusalem die Juden zur Übergabe zu bewegen versuchte[103], und überdies läßt die Antwort der Juden auf das Friedensangebot des 'Vespasian' in ARNA („Ebenso, wie wir gegen

[99] Zur Vertauschung von Vespasian und Titus in den rabbinischen Quellen s. unten S. 86 mit Anm. 176f.

[100] Bell. V,9,2 § 360f. Vgl. auch Bell. V,8,2 § 334; V,9,2 § 356; V,9,4 § 375ff. 406 (Josephus-Rede); VI,2,1 § 95; VI,6,2 § 328ff. 345f. (Titus-Rede).

[101] So Baer, a.a.O., S. 176 mit Verweis auf J. Bernays, Ueber die Chronik des Sulpicius Severus, Berlin 1861, S. 59f. Die Stelle bei Sulpicius Severus (Chron. II,30,3) lautet: *Interea Iudaei obsidione clausi, quia nulla neque pacis neque deditionis copia dabatur, ad extremum fame interibant, passimque uiae oppleri cadaueribus coepere, uicto iam officio humandi: quin omnia nefanda esca super ausi ne humanis quidem corporibus pepercerunt, nisi quae eiusmodi alimentis tabes praeripuerat.*

[102] Baer, ebd.

[103] Cassius Dio 66,4,1: Ὁ δὲ Τίτος τῷ πρὸς Ἰουδαίους πολέμῳ ἐπιταχθεὶς ἐπεχείρησε μὲν αὐτοὺς λόγοις τισὶ καὶ ἐπαγγελίαις προσποιήσασθαι, μὴ πεισθεῖσι δὲ ἐπολέμει.
Vgl. auch 66,5,3: Ὁ οὖν Τίτος κήρυγμα αὖθις, ἄδειαν αὐτοῖς διδούς, ἐποιήσατο, ἐκεῖνοί τε οὖν καὶ ὣς ἐκαρτέρουν, καὶ οἱ ἁλισκόμενοι οἵ τε αὐτομολοῦντές σφων τὸ ὕδωρ τῶν Ῥωμαίων λανθανόντως ἔφθειρον, καὶ τῶν ἀνθρώπων οὓς που μόνους ἀπολάβοιεν ἔσφαζον. ὁ δὲ Τίτος οὐκέτ' οὐδένα αὐτῶν ἐδέχετο.

die beiden ersten ausgezogen sind, die vor dir waren, und sie getötet haben, so werden wir gegen dich ausziehen und dich töten")[104] durchaus eine gute Kenntnis der historischen Situation erkennen. Diese Bemerkung bezieht sich sehr wahrscheinlich auf die Niederlage der Römer unter dem letzten Prokurator Gessius Florus[105] oder dem Kommandanten Metilius[106] und unter dem Statthalter von Syrien Cestius Gallus[107]. Es ist daher nicht auszuschließen, daß der Bericht in ARN über das Friedensangebot des Titus und die ablehnende negative Antwort der Juden auf einen historischen Kern zurückgeht.

b) Von Spionen Vespasians ist über die Notiz in ARN hinaus in anderen Quellen nichts bekannt. Josephus berichtet zwar, daß Vespasian durch Überläufer über die Situation in Jerusalem bestens informiert war[108], erwähnt aber keine Spione Vespasians in Jerusalem. Zudem läßt die Darstellung in ARN eine sehr geschickte literarische Bearbeitung erkennen[109] (ARNA: Angebot Vespasians — Antwort der Juden — Vermittlung Joḥanan b. Zakkais — Antwort der Juden — Spione in Jerusalem; ARNB: Angebot Vespasians — Ablehnung durch die Juden — Vermittlung Joḥanan b. Zakkais — Antwort der Juden — Spione in Jerusalem), und es ist zu erwägen, ob die Pfeile der Spione nicht durch die Aufforderung Vespasians („Schickt mir einen Bogen und einen Pfeil") assoziiert wurden oder umgekehrt. Für die Frage nach dem historischen Wahrheitsgehalt dieses Details kann somit nur festgehalten werden, daß römische Spione (Sympathisanten) im belagerten Jerusalem zwar denkbar sind, die Quellenlage aber eine positive oder negative Entscheidung nicht zuläßt.

3. Die Flucht

a) Gründe und Durchführung

Bei der eigentlichen Darstellung der Flucht Joḥanan b. Zakkais aus Jerusalem ist zwischen den Gründen für diese Flucht und der Durchführung der Flucht zu unterscheiden.

α) Hinsichtlich der Gründe geben die verschiedenen Fassungen der Fluchtgeschichte, wie die oben durchgeführte Analyse gezeigt hat, im wesentlichen zwei unterschiedliche Versionen: Nach der Überlieferung des 'Midrasch' (EkhR/b Git) entscheidet Joḥanan b. Zakkai sich erst angesichts der wahnsinnigen Politik der Zeloten (Verbrennung der Vorräte)

[104] Zu den Unterschieden zwischen ARNA und B s. unten.
[105] Bell. II,15,6 § 330ff.
[106] Bell. II,17,10 § 449ff.
[107] Bell. II,19,7 § 540ff. — Graetz, a.a.O., S. 469 bezieht die Notiz in ARN auf Metilius und Cestius, Hengel, a.a.O., S. 291 auf Florus und Cestius.
[108] Bell. IV,7,3 § 410 (Text s. unten S. 75).
[109] So auch Neusner, Development, S. 116.

zur Flucht, nach ARN ist eher seine grundsätzliche Einstellung gegen den Krieg maßgebend für diesen Entschluß (ARNA: „Als R. Joḥanan b. Zakkai es ihnen einen, zwei und drei Tage gesagt hatte und sie es von ihm nicht annahmen ..."; ARNB: „Als R. Joḥanan b. Zakkai sah, daß sie nicht auf ihn hören wollten ..."). Beide Versionen sind denkbar und nicht von vorneherein auszuschließen. Dennoch ist die Vernichtung der Vorräte als unmittelbarer Fluchtgrund nicht sehr wahrscheinlich. Die Komposition der Erzählung in EkhR/b Git mit ihren anachronistischen Elementen (Ben Baṭiaḥ bzw. Abba Siqara der Neffe Joḥanan b. Zakkais; der Versuch Joḥanan b. Zakkais, dem Zelotenführer mittels der Umdeutung von 'Wai' zu 'Wa' nach dem Munde zu reden und damit sein Leben zu retten; die Hilfe der Zeloten bei der Flucht) macht eher den Eindruck, als sei die Episode vom Verbrennen der Vorräte durch die Zeloten sekundär mit der Erzählung von der Flucht Joḥanan b. Zakkais verbunden worden, um eben einen plausiblen Fluchtgrund zu liefern. Dazu kommt eine schon von NEUSNER[110] vorgetragene Erwägung: Die Vernichtung der Vorräte muß, wenn sie historisch ist, im Winter 69/70 n. Chr. stattgefunden haben. Zu diesem Zeitpunkt war es aber, wie Josephus unmittelbar im Anschluß an die Schilderung vom Brand der Vorratshäuser berichtet, kaum noch möglich, die Stadt zu verlassen:

> „Entsetzliche Niedergeschlagenheit und Furcht befielen die echten Bürger der Stadt; es bot sich weder die Gelegenheit, über eine Änderung der Lage zu beraten, noch bestand die Hoffnung auf eine gütliche Einigung oder, falls jemand das beabsichtigte, auf Flucht. Denn alles wurde scharf bewacht; und die Rädelsführer, die sonst in jeder Hinsicht uneins waren, brachten alle, die nach einem Frieden mit den Römern trachteten oder im Verdacht standen, überlaufen zu wollen, als ihre gemeinsamen Feinde um und waren sich nur in diesem Punkte einig, die zu ermorden, die der Rettung wert gewesen wären[111]."

[110] Life, S. 165. Die Flucht selbst datiert NEUSNER (Life, S. 165f.) auf den Frühling 68 n. Chr. In der neuesten Veröffentlichung zur Flucht Joḥanan b. Zakkais von J. W. DOEVE (The Flight of Rabban Yoḥanan ben Zakkai from Jerusalem — When and Why ?, in: Übersetzung und Deutung. Studien zu dem Alten Testament und seiner Umwelt, Festschrift A. R. Hulst, Nijkerk 1977, S. 50—65), die während der Drucklegung dieses Beitrags erschien, wird gegen NEUSNER die These vertreten, daß Joḥanan b. Zakkai erst zwischen dem 15. Mai und dem 25. Juni 69 n. Chr. aus Jerusalem geflohen sei. Dieses Datum gewinnt DOEVE u. a. aus der Tatsache, daß Vespasian am 3. Juli 69 in Caesarea als Imperator begrüßt wurde; lange davor ergäbe weder die Prophezeiung Joḥanan b. Zakkais noch die Bitte um Jabne einen Sinn. Die Argumentation DOEVES basiert also auf der Historizität der Weissagung und der Bitte Joḥanan b. Zakkais (s. dazu unten) und ist insgesamt ein sehr ausgeprägtes Beispiel für die Rekonstruktion der historischen Wirklichkeit als Kombination aller in den Quellen verfügbaren Daten, ohne daß diese Daten kritisch hinterfragt und die Quellen einer literarkritischen Analyse unterzogen werden. Leider scheint DOEVE auch die neueren Arbeiten zum Thema nicht zu kennen. Er zitiert nur die erste Auflage von NEUSNERS 'Life' und erwähnt weder 'Development of a Legend' noch die Beiträge von ALLON, SALDARINI und SCHALIT.

[111] Bell. V,1,5 § 29ff.

Und wie steht es mit der grundsätzlichen Opposition Joḥanan b. Zakkais gegen den Krieg als Fluchtgrund? Hier gilt es zunächst zu bedenken, daß die Darstellung in ARNA und B auch in diesem Punkt suspekt ist. In ARNA erfolgt die Antwort der Juden doppelt, nämlich einmal auf das Angebot des Vespasian und ein zweites Mal (dort gleichlautend) auf den Vermittlungsversuch Joḥanan b. Zakkais; ARNB entgeht diesem Dilemma, indem die volle Antwort nur Joḥanan b. Zakkai gegeben wird und es zum Vorschlag des Vespasian nur heißt: „aber sie nahmen [ihn] nicht an". Es ist müßig, darüber zu diskutieren, auf wen die Antwort besser paßt, auf Vespasian oder Joḥanan b. Zakkai; die Inkonsequenz bleibt bestehen. Dennoch ist aus dieser Inkonsequenz in der Darstellung der ARN nicht zwangsläufig zu schließen, daß Joḥanan b. Zakkai kein Gegner des Krieges mit Rom war und somit auch keinen Grund zur Flucht hatte. Trotz problematischer Einzelheiten und obwohl ein unmittelbarer und ganz konkreter Anlaß für eine Flucht Joḥanan b. Zakkais sich den Quellen schwerlich entnehmen läßt, kann die grundsätzliche und sehr allgemeine Information von der Opposition Joḥanan b. Zakkais gegen den Krieg und der damit — zumindest in den Augen der Zeloten — verbundenen prorömischen Einstellung auf einen historischen Kern zurückgehen (dazu weiter unten).

β) Bei der konkreten Schilderung der Flucht stimmen alle rabbinischen Quellen darin überein, daß Joḥanan b. Zakkai sich als Toter in einem Sarg aus dem belagerten Jerusalem hinausschmuggeln ließ. Dieses immerhin sehr eindrückliche Motiv findet sich in keiner anderen Quelle im Zusammenhang mit einer Flucht aus dem belagerten Jerusalem des Jahres 69/70 n. Chr. Nun hat A. KAMINKA[112] und im Anschluß an ihn BAER[113] auf eine Erzählung hingewiesen, die sich in der 'Alexias' der byzantinischen Prinzessin Anna Comnena aus dem 12. Jh. n. Chr. findet. Dort wird berichtet[114], daß sich der Kreuzfahrerfürst Boëmundus (Βαϊμοῦντος) nach der Eroberung Antiochias in einem stinkenden Sarg von Antiochia nach Korfu bringen ließ, um dort neues Militär zu sammeln. Dieses Motiv, so BAER in einem kühnen zeitlichen Sprung, gehe auf alte griechische *strategemata*-Literatur zurück (wie z. B. bei Aeneas Tacticus, 4. Jh. v. Chr., in dessen erhaltenen Fragmenten es freilich nicht vorkommt!), die ihrerseits die Grundlage für den Fluchtbericht sowohl der 'Aggadah' als auch der Anna Comnena sei, wobei die 'Aggadah' der gemeinsamen hellenistischen Vorlage näher komme als Anna Comnena. Die Schilderung von der Flucht Joḥanan b. Zakkais sei somit keine ursprünglich mündliche Überlieferung, sondern eine literarische Schöpfung, „die der Verfasser unserer 'Aggadah' von einer literarischen Quelle übernommen hat"[115].

[112] Mäḥqārîm bam-miqrā' ûvat-talmûd ûvas-siphrût hā-rabbānît, II: Mäḥqārîm bat-talmûd, Tel Aviv 1950/51, S. 99f.

[113] A.a.O., S. 179ff.

[114] Vgl. Annae Comnenae Porphyrogenitae Alexias, ed. A. REIFFERSCHEID, Lipsiae 1884, II, S. 140f. (XI,12).

[115] BAER, a.a.O., S. 180.

Diese Rekonstruktion BAERS arbeitet mit zu vielen Unbekannten, als daß sie ernsthaft den Anspruch erheben könnte, unsere Fluchtgeschichte schlüssig zu erklären[116]: Der Sitz im Leben der Schilderung der Flucht mag ebensogut ein wirkliches historischen Ereignis wie ein weiter verbreitetes volkstümliches Motiv sein; zu beweisen ist weder das eine noch das andere. Immerhin berichtet Josephus, daß es Überläufer gab, denen die Flucht zu Vespasian gelang:

„Diese Ereignisse wurden Vespasian von Überläufern berichtet. Denn wenn die Aufständischen auch alle Ausgänge bewachten und jeden umbrachten, der sich ihnen aus irgendeinem Grund näherte, so gelang es doch einigen, unbemerkt durchzukommen und zu den Römern zu fliehen, wo sie in den Feldherrn drangen, der Hauptstadt zu helfen und wenigstens die Reste des Volkes zu retten[117]."

Die hier geschilderte Gefährdung der Flüchtlinge stimmt durchaus mit einigen Einzelheiten in der 'Aggadah' überein (vgl. insbesondere den Versuch der Türhüter in ARNB/EkhR/b Git, die 'Leiche' zu durchbohren), und die Flucht im Sarg paßt somit ohne Zweifel zur historischen Situation. Dennoch ist eine endgültige Entscheidung über die Umstände der Flucht nicht möglich, denn denkbar wäre auch das Gegenteil, daß nämlich der Verfasser der 'Aggadah' unter Zugrundelegung der Schilderung des Josephus und mit Hilfe einiger wie auch immer zu seiner Kenntnis gelangter volkstümlicher Motive seinen Fluchtbericht 'konstruiert' hat.

b) Die Flucht eine Legende?

Die Skepsis gegenüber den in der 'Aggadah' geschilderten Umständen der Flucht führt BAER (zusammen mit einigen anderen Überlegungen) zu dem Ergebnis, daß die ganze Fluchtgeschichte eine Legende und Joḥanan b. Zakkai in Wirklichkeit gar nicht aus dem belagerten Jerusalem geflohen sei[118]. Die positiven Argumente, die BAER für diese These angibt, sind im wesentlichen folgende:

α) Der 'Midrasch' überliefert eine interessante Notiz über das Lehrhaus Joḥanan b. Zakkais in Jerusalem:

„R. Pinḥas sagte im Namen des R. Hosha'ja: 480 Synagogen gab es in Jerusalem, und eine jede hatte eine Schule (*bêt sephär*) und ein Lehrhaus (*bêt talmûd*): die Schule zum [Studium] der Schrift (*miqrā'*)

[116] Treffend bemerkt SALDARINI, a.a.O., S. 196: "*But in the end we are left with the haggadic story of the escape in four versions and a twelfth century Christian story which does not clearly relate to the haggada.*"

[117] Bell. IV,7,3 § 410; vgl. auch die oben zitierte Stelle aus Bell. V,1,5 § 29ff., die sich auf Titus bezieht.

[118] A.a.O., S. 185ff.

und das Lehrhaus zum [Studium] der Mischna (*mišnāh*)[119]. Über alle[120] fiel Vespasian her [und zerstörte sie[121]]. 'Und das ganz große Haus verbrannte er mit Feuer'[122] (2 Kö 25,9) — das ist das Lehrhaus R. Joḥanan b. Zakkais! [Und warum wird es 'großes Haus' genannt][121]? Weil man dort die Größe[123] des Heiligen, er sei gepriesen, lehrte[124]!"

Es ist erstaunlich, wie diese eindeutig legendarische und wahrscheinlich auch relativ späte Erzählung — R. Hosha'ja, der Tradent, lehrte in der ersten Hälfte des 3. Jhs. — einen in seinen Urteilen und gegenüber anderen Forschern so kritischen Historiker[125] wie Baer zu überaus weitreichenden Folgerungen verleitet: „Der Autor dieser Überlieferung wußte also, daß der römische Eroberer das berühmte Lehrhaus des größten Gelehrten in den Tagen der [Tempel]zerstörung verbrannte . . ., und in seinen schlimmsten Träumen hätte R. Hosha'ja sich nicht einfallen lassen, daß R. Joḥanan b. Zakkai schon vor der Eroberung Jerusalems aus seinem Lehrhaus geflohen sei . . . und unterdessen im Lager des römischen Heerführers gesessen habe usw. usw.[126]." Diese Argumentation verkennt völlig den Skopus der 'Aggadah' R. Hosha'jas, der es nur um das Lob Joḥanan b. Zakkais geht und die keine Aussage über die historischen Umstände der Eroberung Jerusalems machen will und sehr wahrscheinlich auch nicht kann. Wie groß das Lehrhaus Joḥanan b. Zakkais in Jerusalem war (wenn es überhaupt eines gab) und ob er als der 'größte Gelehrte' z. Z. der Tempelzerstörung bezeichnet werden kann, sei dahingestellt, mit Sicherheit wuchs das Ansehen Joḥanan b. Zakkais und seines Jerusalemer 'Lehrhauses' jedenfalls entsprechend der zunehmenden Bedeutung Jabnes. Die 'Aggadah' ist daher ohne Zweifel aus der Sicht der späteren Ereignisse formuliert. Baer verläßt hier, wie häufiger bei seinen Schlußfolgerungen, plötzlich die Ebene historisch-kritischer Argumentation zugunsten psychologisierender Deutungen. Der Grund dafür wird offenkundig, wenn Baer seine Überlegungen in dem Satz zusammenfaßt: „Auf jeden Fall scheint es, daß ein Mann wie er (sc. Joḥanan b. Zakkai) nicht imstande war, aus Jerusalem zu fliehen und sich vor einem

[119] Gemeint ist offenbar: das eine zum Erlernen der schriftlichen und das andere zum Erlernen der mündlichen Überlieferung.

[120] Statt *kwlhm* (EkhR: *kwln*) ist wohl zu lesen: *'l kwln*.

[121] So mit EkhR.

[122] So ist im Sinne des 'Midrasch' zu übersetzen. Die übliche (und vom Masoretischen Text intendierte) Übersetzung lautet: „Jedes große Haus verbrannte er mit Feuer."

[123] EkhR: „den Preis" (*šbḥ*), doch ist die Lesart des Jeruschalmi vorzuziehen, da sie unmittelbar an den ausgelegten Bibelvers anknüpft (*gdwl* — *gdwlwt*).

[124] j Meg 3,1 fol. 73d; EkhR Ed. Buber, Petiḥa 12, S. 11f.

[125] Vgl. sein Urteil über Neusner (a.a.O., S. 169, Anm. 145): „Dieser Gelehrte nahm den Kern der Aggadah — das Treffen zwischen R. Joḥanan b. Zakkai und 'Vespasian' — als historische Wahrheit und setzte dessen Zeitpunkt auf das Frühjahr des Jahres 68 n. Chr. fest. Es lohnt sich nicht, mit ihm über Einzelheiten zu diskutieren."

[126] A.a.O., S. 186. Auch J. Goldin (Maššāhû 'al bêt midrāšô šäl Rabbān Jôḥānān bän Zakka'i, Sephär haj-jôvel likhvôd Ṣᵉvî Wolfson, Heläq 'ivrî, Jerusalem 1965, S. 69ff.) hält Zweifel an der Historizität des Midrasch in j Meg/EkhR für unangebracht (ohne allerdings daraus dieselben Schlußfolgerungen zu ziehen wie Baer).

götzendienerischen Heerführer niederzuwerfen . . .“[127]. Hier spricht nicht mehr der Historiker, sondern der jüdische Patriot, dessen Beweisführung sich im Grunde auf das Argument reduziert, daß nicht sein kann, was nicht sein darf, und sich somit jeder kritischen Auseinandersetzung entzieht.

β) Einer der Hauptstreitpunkte in der Forschung zu Joḥanan b. Zakkai ist die Frage, inwieweit Joḥanan b. Zakkai auch unabhängig vom Problem der Fluchtgeschichte pro- oder antirömische Äußerungen zugeschrieben werden können. Baer bemüht sich um den Nachweis, daß „keineswegs alle Aussprüche [Joḥanan b. Zakkais] gegenüber den Weltvölkern[128] milde und friedfertig waren“[129], und stützt sich dabei vor allem auf die bekannte Auslegung Joḥanan b. Zakkais und seiner Schüler zu Spr 14,34[130]:

> Es wird gelehrt: R. Joḥanan b. Zakkai sagte zu seinen Schülern: Meine Kinder, was bedeutet der Schriftvers: ‘Wohltätigkeit (*ṣedāqāh*) erhebt ein Volk, aber die Liebe (*ḥäsäd*) der Völker ist Sünde’ (Spr 14,34)?
> Da antwortete R. Eliʿezer und sagte: ‘Wohltätigkeit erhebt ein Volk’ (Spr) — das bezieht sich auf Israel . . .; ‘aber die Liebe der Völker ist Sünde’ (Spr) — alle Wohltätigkeit und Liebe, die die Völker der Götzendiener tun, ist Sünde für sie, denn sie tun dies nur, um sich damit groß zu machen![131] . . .
> R. Jehoshuaʿ antwortete und sagte: ‘Wohltätigkeit erhebt ein Volk’ (Spr) — das ist Israel . . .; ‘aber die Liebe der Völker ist Sünde’ (Spr) — alle Wohltätigkeit und Liebe, die die Völker der Götzendiener tun, ist Sünde für sie, denn sie tun dies nur, damit ihre Regierung Bestand hat![132] . . .
> R. Gamliel antwortete und sagte: ‘Wohltätigkeit erhebt ein Volk’ (Spr) — das ist Israel . . .; ‘aber die Liebe der Völker ist Sünde’ (Spr) — alle Wohltätigkeit und Liebe, die die Götzendiener tun, ist Sünde für sie, denn sie tun dies nur, um sich damit zu brüsten (*lehitjaher*)[133] . . .
> R. Elʿazar[134] ha-Modiʿi sagte: ‘Wohltätigkeit erhebt ein Volk’ (Spr) — das ist Israel . . .; ‘aber die Liebe der Völker ist Sünde’ (Spr) — alle Wohltätigkeit und Liebe, die die Götzendiener tun, ist Sünde für sie, denn sie tun dies nur, um uns zu beschimpfen . . .

[127] A.a.O., S. 188.

[128] Damit sind in der rabbinischen Literatur gewöhnlich die Römer gemeint.

[129] A.a.O., S. 188.

[130] b BBa 10b; PesK Ed. Mandelbaum, S. 20f. (Ed. Buber, S. 12b). Vgl. dazu auch E. E. Urbach, Megammôt dātijjôt weḥävrātijôt betôrat ha-ṣedāqāh šäl ḤZ"L, Zion 16,3—4, 1950/51, S. 1—27; M. Smith, in: Neusner, Development, S. 103f.; Neusner, Development, S. 240ff.

[131] PesK: „Gunsterweise (*ḥsdjm*) sind Sünde für die Völker der Welt, denn sie brüsten sich mit ihnen (*mtjjhrjn*).“

[132] PesK: „Es ist ein Vorteil für die Völker der Welt, wenn Israel sündigt, weil sie sie dann wieder unterdrücken können.“

[133] PesK: „Die Liebe der Völker der Welt ist Sünde für sie . . .“

[134] So ist zu lesen statt ‘Eliʿezer’.

R. Neḥunja b. Haqana antwortete und sagte: ʻWohltätigkeit erhebt ein Volk, und die Liebeʼ ist für Israel, ʻaber für die Völker ist Sündeʼ (Spr)[135].

Da sagte R. Joḥanan b. Zakkai zu seinen Schülern: Die Worte R. Neḥunja b. Haqanas[136] sind meinen und euren Worten vorzuziehen, weil er Wohltätigkeit und Liebe auf Israel bezieht und den Götzendienern [allein die] Sünde zuteilt. . . .

Es wird gelehrt: R. Joḥanan b. Zakkai sagte zu ihnen: So wie das Sündopfer Israel Sühne bringt, so verschafft die Liebe den Völkern der Welt Sühne[137]."

Diese Auslegung der verschiedenen Rabbinen zu Spr 14,34 ist sehr wahrscheinlich in Anlehnung an den bekannten ʻMidraschʼ in Ab 2,9 entstanden, in dem Joḥanan b. Zakkai seine fünf Schüler (Eliʻezer b. Hyrkanos, Jehoshuaʻ b. Ḥananja, Jose ha-Kohen, Shimʻon b. Netanel und Elʻazar b. ʻArakh) nach dem rechten bzw. schlechten Weg fragt, den der Mensch gehen bzw. vermeiden soll. Auch dort entscheidet Joḥanan b. Zakkai sich beide Male (mit fast denselben Worten wie hier) für die Antwort Elʻazar b. ʻArakhs. Legt man dieses Schema hier zugrunde, dann spricht manches dafür, daß die Antworten des R. Elʻazar ha-Modiʻi und vor allem R. Gamliels (II., des Nachfolgers Joḥanan b. Zakkais als Nasi), die beide keine Schüler Joḥanan b. Zakkais waren, zu emendieren bzw. durch andere Namen zu ersetzen sind und daß bei der entscheidenden Auslegung des Fünften mit PesK statt Neḥunja b. Haqana: Elʻazar b. ʻArakh zu lesen ist. Diese letzte und von Joḥanan b. Zakkai bevorzugte Deutung des Sprücheverses geht insofern über die Auslegung der anderen hinaus, als sie nicht nur die Wohltätigkeit (*ṣᵉdāqāh*) auf Israel bezieht, sondern auch die Liebe (*ḥäsäd*), und für die Völker der Welt somit nur die Sünde übrigbleibt. Dennoch besteht der Unterschied nur in einer Nuance, denn auch die von den übrigen vier Rabbinen den Heidenvölkern (= Rom) zugestandene Wohltätigkeit und Liebe besteht ja in Wirklichkeit aus Sünde.

Fällt es schon aus diesen inhaltlichen Gründen schwer, in dem Votum Joḥanan b. Zakkais für die angeblich extremere Deutung Elʻazar b. ʻArakhs eine prononciert antirömische Einstellung zu sehen, so wird dies durch die Baraita am Schluß vollends problematisch. In der Tat widersprechen sich diese Baraita und die Zustimmung zur Antwort Elʻazar b. ʻArakhs. Urbach möchte dieses Problem so lösen, daß er die ʻprorömischeʼ Aussage Joḥanan b. Zakkais am Schluß in die Zeit vor dem Krieg mit den Römern datiert und die Zustimmung zur ʻantirömischenʼ Auslegung Elʻazar b. ʻArakhs in die Zeit nach dem Krieg[138]; Baer dagegen hält die Baraita für

[135] PesK: „R. Elʻazar b. ʻArakh sagte: ʻWohltätigkeit erhöht ein Volkʼ (Spr) — das ist Israel; aber die Sünde ist für die Völker der Welt."

[136] PesK: „Die Worte R. Elʻazar b. ʻArakhs . . ."

[137] Diese Baraita fehlt in PesK.

[138] A.a.O. (Anm. 130), S. 5ff.

sekundär, da sie dem Kern der vorangehenden Diskussion widerspricht[139]. Letzteres ist sicher richtig — die Frage ist nur, welches die 'authentische' Meinung Joḥanan b. Zakkais ist, die Baraita am Schluß oder die Zustimmung zu El'azar b. 'Arakh (wenn man sich nicht der zwar eleganten, aber etwas konstruierten Lösung des 'sowohl — als auch' bei URBACH anschließt). Denkbar (und m. E. vorzuziehen) ist nämlich auch die umgekehrte Vermutung, daß die Baraita am Schluß einen echten Ausspruch Joḥanan b. Zakkais wiedergibt und die vorangestellte Diskussion als eine tendenziöse 'Umdeutung' zu interpretieren ist, die Joḥanan b. Zakkai in Einklang mit späteren (nachhadrianischen?) antirömischen Strömungen bringen will[140]. Für diese Vermutung spricht auch die sekundäre Anlehnung des ganzen 'Midrasch' an m Ab 2,9 und insbesondere die Einführung von R. Gamliel und R. El'azar ha-Modi'i (letzterer lebte zur Zeit des Bar Kochba-Krieges).

Zusammenfassend läßt sich mit dem zitierten 'Midrasch', dessen komplizierte literarkritische Probleme keineswegs endgültig gelöst sind, sicher kein schlüssiger Beweis dafür erbringen, daß Joḥanan b. Zakkai antirömisch eingestellt war und, wie BAER abschließend formuliert[141], daß seine Lehre in Wirklichkeit ,,die Lehre der 'Zeloten' war und nicht der Weg eines Menschen, der in das Lager der Römer floh, während der Tempel noch an seinem Platz stand''[142]. Auch hier ist der Verdacht nicht ganz von der Hand zu

[139] A.a.O., S. 189.

[140] Ähnlich auch M. SMITH, in: NEUSNER, Development, S. 103f.

[141] Im Anschluß an den ebenfalls keineswegs eindeutigen Ausspruch Joḥanan b. Zakkais in der Mekhilta (Jitro, baḥodäš 1, Ed. HOROVITZ—RABIN, S. 203f.): ,,Ihr wolltet nicht einen halben Scheqel pro Kopf für den Himmel (= für Gott) entrichten — siehe, nun müßt ihr 15 Scheqel für das Reich eurer Feinde entrichten! Ihr wolltet nicht die Wege und Straßen für die Wallfahrer ausbessern — siehe, nun müßt ihr die verschiedenen Stationen für die ausbessern, die in die Städte der Könige ziehen!'' Zu vergleichen sind auch zwei weitere Joḥanan b. Zakkai zugeschriebene Dicta: ,,Beeil dich nicht, die Altäre der Heiden zu zerstören, daß du sie [dann] nicht mit eigenen Händen [wieder] aufbauen mußt! Damit du nicht [Altäre] aus Ziegel zerstörst und man zu dir sagt: Baue [neue] aus Stein! [Oder] aus Stein, und man zu dir sagt: Baue [neue] aus Holz!'' (MTann, S. 58; ARNB, Kap. 31, S. 66); ,,Siehe, die Schrift sagt: 'Mit ganzen (= unbehauenen) Steinen (*'bnjm šlmwt*) sollst du [den Altar des Herrn, deines Gottes] bauen' (Dt 27,6) — Steine, die Frieden (*šlwm*) aufrichten! Diese Worte erlauben den Schluß vom Leichteren auf das Schwerere: Wenn der Heilige, er sei gepriesen, schon bezüglich der Steine des Altares, die nicht sehen, nicht hören und nicht sprechen, gesagt hat: 'Du sollst sie nicht mit Eisen bearbeiten' (Dt 27,5), weil sie [nämlich] Frieden aufrichten zwischen Israel und ihrem Vater im Himmel — um wieviel mehr gilt für den, der Friede aufrichtet zwischen Mensch und Mitmensch, zwischen Mann und Frau, zwischen Stadt und Stadt, zwischen Volk und Volk, zwischen Regierung und Regierung, zwischen Familie und Familie, daß über ihn kein Übel kommt!'' (MekhJ, S. 244; Siphra, S. 92b; MekhS, S. 157). Bei diesen und ähnlichen Aussprüchen ist es freilich eine offene Frage, nach welchen Kriterien man die Authentizität feststellen kann. URBACH (ḤZ"L, Jerusalem 1969, S. 533f. = The Sages, Jerusalem 1975, S. 596f.) hält beide für echt und bezieht den ersten konkret auf die historische Situation nach der Niederlage des Cestius Gallus; NEUSNER dagegen (Development, S. 17ff., 128) möchte nur das zweite Dictum Joḥanan b. Zakkai zuschreiben, weil es eine "*essential idea*" Joḥanan b. Zakkais enthalte: "*The functions performed by the Temple and its instruments can be replaced by human virtues.*"

[142] A.a.O., S. 190.

weisen, daß das historische Geschehen nach einem Idealbild gestaltet wurde, das die Realität eher auf den Kopf stellt.

c) Proromische Einstellung Joḥanan b. Zakkais

Für eine eher proromische Einstellung Joḥanan b. Zakkais während des Krieges und damit für die Historizität der Flucht aus dem belagerten Jerusalem sprechen nicht zuletzt auch die Ereignisse in Jabne selbst nach der Zerstörung Jerusalems. A. BÜCHLER[143] und vor allem G. ALLON[144] haben auf den auffälligen Befund in den rabbinischen Quellen verwiesen, daß offenbar nicht nur die Priester, sondern auch zahlreiche Rabbinen — und vor allem der spätere Rabban Gamliel II., der Nachfolger Joḥanan b. Zakkais — sich von Joḥanan b. Zakkai distanzierten. Während die diversen Auseinandersetzungen mit den Priestern[145] sich notfalls noch mit der alten Rivalität zwischen Sadduzäern und Pharisäern erklären lassen (die den Sadduzäern nahestehende Priesterklasse war von den Neuerungen Joḥanan b. Zakkais und dessen Führungsanspruch sicher nicht begeistert), entfällt ein solches Argument bei den Rabbinen ganz. Von den Rabbinen, die aus der Zeit vor 70 n. Chr. bekannt sind und den Krieg offenbar überlebten, werden auffällig viele und vor allem berühmte Gelehrte niemals im Zusammenhang mit dem Lehrhaus Joḥanan b. Zakkais genannt (so etwa Neḥunja b. Haqana[146], Naḥum aus Gimzo, R. Tarphon, Dosa b. Archinos, Naḥum ha-Medi; manche tauchen dann später im Zusammenhang mit R. Gamliel II. wieder auf), und es spricht daher manches für die Vermutung BÜCHLERS und ALLONS, daß dies auf das Verhalten Joḥanan b. Zakkais im Krieg mit den Römern zurückzuführen ist: „Und wenn wir einen Grund dafür suchen, dann bleibt uns nur die Vermutung, daß diese Gelehrten, zusammen mit vielen anderen von den Besten des Volkes, seinerzeit nicht dem Weggang Joḥanan b. Zakkais aus Jerusalem zustimmten, weil sie darin so etwas wie eine 'Absonderung von der Gemeinschaft' sahen und ein Sich-Gemeinmachen mit den 'Freunden des Kaisers', von denen viele den

143 Die Priester und der Cultus im letzten Jahrzehnt des Jerusalemischen Tempels, Wien 1895, S. 16ff. Vgl. auch J. M. GUTMAN, 'Äräṣ Jiśrā'el bam-midrāš ûvat-talmûd, Breslau 1928/29, S. 97ff.

144 Tôl^{e}dôt haj-j^{e}hûdîm b^{e}'äräṣ-Jiśrā'el bitqûphat ham-mišnāh w^{e}hat-talmûd, I, [Tel Aviv] ^{4}1967, S. 60ff. und sein Aufsatz N^{e}śî'ûtô šäl Rabbān Joḥānān bän Zakka'i, in: Mäḥqārîm, I, S. 253—273. Vgl. auch S. SAFRAI, B^{e}ḥînôt ḥ^{a}dāšôt liv'ājat ma'^{a}mādô ûma'^{a}śāw šäl Rabbān Joḥānān bän Zakka'i l^{e}aḥar ha-ḥûrbān, in: In Memory of Gedaliahu Alon. Essays in Jewish History and Philology, [Tel Aviv] 1970, S. 203—226; DERS., T^{e}qûphat ham-mišnāh w^{e}hat-talmûd (70—640), in: Tôl^{e}dôt 'am Jiśrā'el, ed. H. H. BEN-SASSON, I, Tel Aviv 1969, S. 310.

145 Vgl. ALLON, Tôl^{e}dôt, S. 61f.; DERS., Mäḥqārîm, I, S. 255ff.; J. NEUSNER, Priestly Views of Yochanan ben Zakkai, Kairos 11, 1969, S. 306—312; A. GUTTMANN, The End of the Jewish Sacrificial Cult, HUCA 38, 1967, S. 144ff.; C. ROTH, The Pharisees in the Jewish Revolution of 66—73, JSS 7, 1962, S. 72ff.

146 Neḥunja b. Haqana wird zwar b BBa 10b unter den Schülern Joḥanan b. Zakkais aufgeführt, doch ist diese Tradition äußerst zweifelhaft; s. oben S. 78.

Römern tatkräftige Hilfe leisteten, die kämpfenden Juden zu unterdrücken[147]."

Diese These ALLONS (und BÜCHLERS) wird durch die Beobachtung erhärtet, daß von den 'klassischen' fünf Schülern Joḥanan b. Zakkais nach m Ab 2,9 offenbar nur die in der Fluchtgeschichte erwähnten R. Eli'ezer und R. Jehoshua' mit Sicherheit zum engeren Kreis Joḥanan b. Zakkais in Jabne gehörten, während die Belege für die übrigen drei nur dürftig sind[148]. Es scheint sogar, als hätte der 'Lieblingsschüler' Joḥanan b. Zakkais, El'azar b. 'Arakh, es vorgezogen, ein eigenes Lehrhaus in Emmaus zu gründen:

> „Als sie (= die Schüler Joḥanan b. Zakkais) von ihm weggingen, sagte er (= El'azar b. 'Arakh): 'Ich gehe nach Emmaus[149], einen schönen Ort mit schönen und lieblichen Wassern'. Sie aber (= die anderen Schüler) sagten: 'Wir gehen nach Jabne, wo es zahlreiche Gelehrtenschüler gibt, die die Torah lieben'. Der, welcher nach Emmaus ging, einen schönen Ort mit schönen und lieblichen Wassern, dessen Name wurde gering gemacht in der Torah. Die aber, die nach Jabne gingen, wo es zahlreiche Gelehrtenschüler gibt, die die Torah lieben, deren Name wurde groß gemacht in der Torah[150]."

Zwar wird der Zeitpunkt dieses Weggangs nach Emmaus verschieden angegeben (in ARNA ist der Kontext die Tröstung Joḥanan b. Zakkais, nachdem dessen Sohn gestorben war, nach QohR der Tod Joḥanan b. Zakkais selbst und nur in ARNB die Flucht aus Jerusalem), doch ist die wahrscheinlichere Möglichkeit die, daß El'azar b. 'Arakh sich gleich nach der Eroberung Jerusalems von Joḥanan b. Zakkai getrennt hat. Die Anknüpfung der Episode vom Weggang Ela'zar b. 'Arakhs an die Tröstung Joḥanan b. Zakkais durch seine Schüler in ARNA ist sicher sekundär, und auch QohR deutet auf eine relativ späte Ausgestaltung des Materials hin, so daß von den verschiedenen Fassungen wahrscheinlich ARNB vorzuziehen ist. Dafür spricht vor allem auch die Tatsache, daß El'azar b. 'Arakh in keiner gesicherten Tradition im Zusammenhang mit Joḥanan b. Zakkai in Jabne erwähnt wird[151].

147 ALLON, Mäḥqārîm, I, S. 260; vgl. auch DERS., Tôl^edôt, S. 63; BÜCHLER, a.a.O., S. 18: „In erster Reihe war es ohne Zweifel die zu Mißtrauen berechtigende politische Vergangenheit R. Jochanan b. Sakkai's, an der sehr viele Anstoß nahmen."

148 Vgl. ALLON, Tôl^edôt, S. 63; DERS., Mäḥqārîm, I, S. 261f.

149 *dmsjt*, wahrscheinlich identisch mit *'m'ws*; vgl. JASTROW, Dictionary, I, S. 300 s. v.

150 ARNA, Kap. 14, S. 59. Vgl. auch ARNB, Kap. 29, S. 59: „Warum wurde sein (= El'azar b. 'Arakhs) Name nicht wegen [seiner] Weisheit groß? Als sie Jerusalem verließen, sagte er (= Joḥanan b. Zakkai?): Ich gehe (nach Jabne?). Der aber, der sagte: Wir wollen nach Emmaus (*lm'wm*) gehen . . ., dessen Name wurde nicht durch Weisheit groß. Die aber, die sagten: Wir wollen nach Jabne gehen . . ., deren Name wurde durch Weisheit groß." QohR 7,7 § 2: „R. Joḥanan b. Zakkai hatte fünf Schüler, und solange er lebte, saßen sie vor ihm. Als er starb, gingen sie nach Jabne, aber R. El'azar b. 'Arakh ging zu seiner Frau nach Emmaus (*'m'ws*) . . ."; b Schab 147b.

151 Vgl. auch NEUSNER, Development, S. 126: "*Eleazar's name is elsewhere omitted from Yavnean materials, until Aqiban times. I think it likely he did not go to Yavneh at all.*" So schon ALLON, a.a.O. (Anm. 148).

Ein letztes Argument für die Vermutung, daß die führende Rolle Joḥanan b. Zakkais in Jabne (vom Amt des Nasi im eigentlichen Sinne kann wohl noch nicht gesprochen werden[152]) aus politischen Gründen umstritten war, ist schließlich das Verhältnis zwischen Joḥanan b. Zakkai und R. Gamliel II. Die Quellenlage ist in diesem Punkt zwar äußerst dürftig, doch scheint auch R. Gamliel, der Repräsentant einer eher römerfeindlichen Richtung, dessen Familie offenbar durch die Politik seines Vaters Shim'on b. Gamliel im Kriege zunächst kompromittiert war[153], niemals zum Kreis um Joḥanan b. Zakkai in Jabne gehört, sondern sich erst nach dessen (unfreiwilligem?) Rückzug nach Beror Ḥail[154] dort niedergelassen zu haben.

4. Gefangenschaft in Gophna

Von den verschiedenen Versionen der Fluchtgeschichte erwähnt nur EkhR, daß Vespasian Joḥanan b. Zakkai im Anschluß an seine Prophezeiung „inmitten von sieben Zellen" setzen ließ (s. oben). Der Skopus dieser Episode ist ohne Zweifel die Absicht Vespasians, die Fähigkeiten Joḥanan b. Zakkais als 'Wahrsager' zu prüfen; die Geschichte soll also, wie Urbach mit Recht betont, „die Weisheit Joḥanan b. Zakkais hervorheben"[155]. Ob sie deswegen aber auch, wie Urbach daraus folgert[156], „legendarischen Charakter hat", ist eine andere Frage.

EkhR nennt unmittelbar darauf einen Ort namens Gophna, an dem Vespasian sich zu der Zeit befunden haben soll. Dieser Ort (griech. Γόφνα) liegt in Judäa, nördlich von Jerusalem, und ist erstmals seit der Periode des 2. Tempels bekannt[157]; die rabbinische Literatur erwähnt ihn auch unter dem Namen Beth-Guphnin[158]. Vespasian eroberte Gophna wahrscheinlich 68 n. Chr. und versammelte dort zu ihm übergelaufene Priester und andere wichtige Personen:

> „Es gab aber auch solche, die den rechten Zeitpunkt abpaßten, um sich ohne Gefahr abzusetzen, und die dann zu den Römern flüchteten. Unter ihnen waren die Hohenpriester Josephus und Jesus, von Hohenpriestersöhnen drei des in Kyrene enthaupteten Ismael, vier des Matthias und einer eines anderen Matthias. . . . Gemeinsam mit den Hohenpriestern gingen auch viele der übrigen Vornehmen zu den Römern über. Der Caesar nahm sie durchaus freundlich auf, ja er tat noch ein übriges: da er wußte, daß sie den Aufenthalt bei den Römern wegen der fremden Sitten anstößig finden würden, schickte er sie nach

[152] Vgl. dazu H. Mantel, Studies in the History of the Sanhedrin, Cambridge Mass. 1965, S. 28ff.
[153] Vgl. Allon, Tôl^{e}dôt, S. 63f.; Ders., Māḥqārîm, I, S. 267ff.
[154] Vgl. b San 32b; t Maas 2,1; SiphDt § 144, Ed. Finkelstein, S. 200.
[155] Urbach, a.a.O. (Anm. 50), S. 64.
[156] Ebd.; ihm stimmt Baer, a.a.O., S. 180, zu.
[157] Vgl. Bell. I,1,5 § 45 (Judas Maccabaeus); Bell. III,3,5 § 55 (Gophna als Toparchie).
[158] t Ohal 18,16; vgl. A. Neubauer, La Géographie du Talmud, Paris 1868 (Neudruck Hildesheim 1967), S. 157f.; S. Klein, Sephär haj-jišûv, I, Jerusalem 1939, S. 13, 29.

Gophna und empfahl ihnen, dort einstweilen zu bleiben: er werde einem jeden seinen Besitz zurückgeben, sobald er vom Krieg Ruhe habe. Sie aber waren froh, daß sie sich in aller Sicherheit in das ihnen angewiesene Städtchen zurückziehen konnten[159]."

Streicht man in diesem Bericht die zweifellos tendenziösen Lobpreisungen auf die Großmut des Titus, so bleibt als historische Information die Arretierung jüdischer Überläufer in der bereits eroberten (und befriedeten) Distriktstadt Gophna. Zu dieser Information paßt eine Notiz im j Talmud[160]:

„R. Joḥanan sagte: Achtzig Paare von Priester-Brüdern heirateten achtzig Paare von Priester-Schwestern in einer Nacht in dieser [Stadt] Gophna ..."

Trotz des legendarischen Charakters dieser Tradition könnte hier eine im Kern historische Nachricht vorliegen, die dann in die Zeit während oder unmittelbar nach dem Kriege zu datieren wäre und sich ebenfalls auf geflohene Priesterfamilien bezöge.

Interpretiert man die Episode in EkhR auf dem Hintergrund dieser Berichte bei Josephus und im j Talmud, liegt der Gedanke nahe, den historischen Kern dieser Episode darin zu sehen, daß Vespasian bzw. Titus Joḥanan b. Zakkai nach seiner Flucht zunächst in Gophna inhaftierte[161]. Baer dagegen möchte die historische Nachricht nur darauf beschränkt sehen, daß Gophna ein Zufluchtsort für Priester war; die Einbeziehung Joḥanan b. Zakkais in diesen Kreis dagegen sei spät und „typisch für die Entwicklung von 'historischen Fakten'"[162]. Abgesehen davon, daß unklar bleibt, woher Baer die Bezeichnung dieser Aggadah als 'babylonisch'[163] nimmt — sie findet sich nur in EkhR, nicht aber in der Parallelversion b Git und auch nicht in b Ber 44a, der Parallele zu j Taan fol. 69a —, übersieht Baer, daß auch Josephus neben den Hohenpriestern und Hohenpriestersöhnen ausdrücklich die „übrigen Vornehmen" (πολλοὶ δὲ καὶ τῶν ἄλλων εὐγενῶν) erwähnt, die nach Gophna kamen. Es spricht somit ernsthaft nichts gegen die Vermutung, daß Joḥanan b. Zakkai nach seiner Flucht aus Jerusalem wie auch zahlreiche andere jüdische Überläufer (zunächst) in Gophna arretiert wurde.

5. Weissagung und Bitte

a) Die Weissagung

In allen vier rabbinischen Parallelversionen der Fluchtgeschichte gelangt Joḥanan b. Zakkai unmittelbar nach seiner Flucht zu Vespasian,

[159] Bell. VI,2,2 § 113ff.
[160] j Taan 4,8 fol. 69a unten; b Ber 44a.
[161] So mit Allon, Mäḥqārîm, I, S. 226, 242, Anm. 68, 250.
[162] A.a.O., S. 180.
[163] Ebd.: *'aggādāh bavlît.*

begrüßt diesen mit der lateinischen Begrüßungsformel *Vive domine imperator* als König[164] und prophezeit ihm, daß er bald König werden wird (s. oben). Wie steht es mit dem Wahrheitsgehalt dieses Berichtes, d. h. läßt es sich einigermaßen wahrscheinlich machen, daß der aus Jerusalem geflohene Rabbi Joḥanan b. Zakkai den römischen Feldherrn Vespasian in dessen Lager traf und als zukünftigen Caesar begrüßte?

Zunächst gilt festzuhalten, daß die Weissagung von einem Herrscher, der aus Judäa kommen werde, offenbar weit verbreitet war[165]. Tacitus[166] erwähnt eine solche Prophezeiung ebenso wie Sueton[167] und nicht zuletzt auch Josephus:

> „Was sie aber am meisten zum Krieg aufstachelte, war eine zweideutige Weissagung, die sich ebenfalls in den heiligen Schriften fand, daß in jener Zeit einer aus ihrem (sc. der Juden) Land über die bewohnte Erde herrschen werde. Das bezogen sie auf einen aus ihren Volk, und viele Weise täuschten sich in ihrem Urteil. Der Gottesspruch zeigt vielmehr die Herrscherwürde des Vespasian an, der in Judäa zum Kaiser ausgerufen wurde[168]."

Auf die Probleme dieses Textes und insbesondere auf das Verhältnis der Weissagung des Josephus zu Tacitus kann hier nicht eingegangen werden[169]. Für unseren Zusammenhang von größerem Interesse ist eine weitere Stelle bei Josephus, auf die sich der oben zitierte Text bezieht. Es handelt sich um die berühmte Weissagung, die Josephus nach der Eroberung

[164] Der Text in ARNB und EkhR ist zwar verderbt, doch liegt ohne Zweifel die klassische lateinische Formel zugrunde. Daß sich hinter dem *'j rjdwmnj* in ARNB (MS. H) die Formel *Eris, domine, imperator* verbirgt (so SALDARINI, a.a.O., S. 201, Anm. 42), scheint mir nicht sehr wahrscheinlich.

[165] Vgl. dazu ausführlich SCHALIT (unten, Anm. 197), S. 214ff.

[166] Hist. V,13: *Pluribus persuasio inerat antiquis sacerdotum litteris contineri, eo ipso tempore fore, ut valesceret Oriens profectique Judaea rerum potirentur. Quae ambages Vespasianum ac Titum praedixerat; sed vulgus more humanae cupidinis sibi tantam fatorum magnitudinem interpretati ne adversis quidem ad vera mutabantur.*

[167] Vesp. 4,5: *Percrebruerat Oriente toto uetus et constans opinio esse in fatis ut eo tempore Judaea profecti rerum potirentur. Id de imperatore Romano, quantum postea euentu paruit, praedictum Judaei ad se trahentes rebellarunt.*

[168] Bell. VI,5,4 § 312ff. Die Weissagung des Josephus erwähnen auch Sueton, Vesp. 5,6 (*et unus ex nobilibus captivis Iosephus, cum coiceretur in vincula, constantissime asseveravit fore ut ab eodem brevi solveretur, verum iam imperatore*) und Cassius Dio 66,1,4 ('Ιώσηπος δὲ ἀνὴρ 'Ιουδαῖος ἀχθείς τε ὑπ' αὐτοῦ πρότερον καὶ δεθεὶς ἐγέλασε καὶ ἔφη „νῦν μέν με δήσεις, μετ' ἐνιαυτὸν δὲ λύσεις αὐτοκράτωρ γενόμενος"). Vgl. auch Orosius, Hist. adv. pag. VII,9,3.

[169] Vgl. dazu E. NORDEN, Josephus und Tacitus über Jesus Christus und eine messianische Prophetie, Neue Jahrbücher für das klassische Altertum, Geschichte und deutsche Literatur 31, 1913, S. 636—666 = DERS., Kleine Schriften zum klassischen Altertum, Berlin 1966, S. 241—275; WEBER, a.a.O. (Anm. 97), S. 40ff.; A. Z. AESCOLY, Hat-tᵉnûʿôt hammᵉšîḥijjôt bᵉJiśrā'el, Jerusalem 1956, S. 50; H. SCHRECKENBERG, Die Flavius-Josephus-Tradition in Antike und Mittelalter, Leiden 1972, S. 69; zuletzt SCHALIT (unten, Anm. 197), S. 218, 230ff.

der Festung Jotapata und seiner Gefangennahme durch die Römer an Vespasian richtet:

„Du glaubst, Vespasian, in Josephus lediglich einen Kriegsgefangenen in die Hand bekommen zu haben, ich aber komme zu dir als Künder großer Ereignisse. Denn wäre ich nicht von Gott gesandt, so hätte ich gewußt, was das Gesetz der Juden bestimmt und wie es einem Feldherrn zu sterben geziemt. Zu Nero willst du mich schicken? Wozu denn? Werden denn die Nachfolger Neros bis zu deinem Regierungsantritt lange an der Herrschaft bleiben? Du, Vespasian, wirst Kaiser und Alleinherrscher, sowohl du wie dieser dein Sohn. Laß mich jetzt nur noch fester fesseln und für dich selbst aufbewahren, denn du, Caesar, wirst nicht nur mein Herr sein, sondern der über Erde und Meer und das ganze Menschengeschlecht. Ich bitte aber um eine noch schärfere Bewachung, damit du mich bestrafen kannst, wenn ich die Sache Gottes leichtfertig behandle[170]."

Vergleicht man diese Rede des Josephus mit der 'Aggadah' über Joḥanan b. Zakkai, so ergeben sich überraschende Parallelen: Beide sind Überläufer, die um ihr Leben fürchten müssen (Josephus muß sich schon gegenüber seinen eigenen Leuten gegen den Vorwurf des Verrats wehren: „Wir leihen dir Arm und Schwert: stirbst du freiwillig, dann als Feldherr der Juden, stirbst du unfreiwillig, dann als Verräter! Mit diesen Worten zückten sie ihre Schwerter gegen ihn und drohten, ihn niederzustoßen, falls er sich den Römern ergäbe[171]"), beide prophezeien Vespasian die Herrschaft, beide begrüßen ihn als Caesar (Josephus: σὺ Καῖσαρ), und beide werden zunächst verschont, aber gefangen gehalten[172]. Diese auffallende Parallelität der Schicksale des Josephus und des Joḥanan b. Zakkai legt den Verdacht nahe, daß der eine Bericht nach der Vorlage des anderen gestaltet wurde. Da jedoch Josephus schwerlich von der 'Aggadah' abhängig sein wird — es müßte dann schon eine sehr frühe mündliche Überlieferung vom Schicksal des Joḥanan b. Zakkai vorausgesetzt werden, die Josephus seinem Bericht zugrunde gelegt hätte (eine sicher problematische Konstruktion)[173] —, ist die wahrscheinlichere Möglichkeit die, daß die Prophezeiung des Josephus dem Verfasser bzw. Redaktor der 'Aggadah' als Vorlage

[170] Bell. III,8,9 § 400ff.

[171] Bell. III,8,4 § 359ff.

[172] Josephus wird erst nach dem Eintreffen seiner Weissagung befreit, vgl. Bell. IV,10,7 § 623ff.; dies könnte auch in dem Bericht in EkhR vorausgesetzt sein. — Zur Belohnung beider s. unten.

[173] Wie SCHALIT (unten, Anm. 197) zu der Vermutung kommt, daß der von ihm S. 261, Anm. 107 zitierte Satz von GRAETZ die Deutung zulasse, GRAETZ sei der Meinung gewesen, „daß Josephus sich in lügnerischer Weise eine Prophezeiung angeeignet habe, die der Volksmund ursprünglich dem allgemein verehrten Meister Joḥanan zugeschrieben hatte", ist rätselhaft. GRAETZ, a.a.O., S. 500, erwähnt in diesem Zusammenhang Joḥanan b. Zakkai überhaupt nicht.

gedient hat[174]. Dies bedeutet, daß die Historizität einer Begegnung zwischen Vespasian und Joḥanan b. Zakkai mit einer Prophezeiung Joḥanan b. Zakkais an den zukünftigen Caesar ernsthaft in Zweifel gezogen werden muß[175].

Für diese Interpretation sprechen zwei weitere Überlegungen. Die erste betrifft die vielverhandelte Beobachtung, daß die in den rabbinischen Quellen geschilderten Umstände eher in die Endphase des Krieges passen und daher, wenn überhaupt, eine Begegnung Joḥanan b. Zakkais mit Titus statt mit Vespasian zu erwarten wäre[176]. Gerade die anachronistische Erwähnung Vespasians macht es aber wahrscheinlich, daß die Prophezeiung des Josephus die Vorlage der 'Aggadah' in diesem Punkt der Fluchtgeschichte war, denn bei Josephus ist die Person Vespasians absolut milieugerecht, da es sich dort um den Anfang des Krieges handelt[177].

Hinzu kommt ein inhaltliches Argument. Nach der 'Aggadah' stützt Joḥanan b. Zakkai seine Weissagung auf eine Exegese von Jes 10,34: 'Der Libanon (= Tempel)[178] wird durch einen Mächtigen (= König) fallen'. Diese Interpretation Joḥanan b. Zakkais ist vermutlich messianisch zu verstehen. Die Fortsetzung des Bibeltextes lautet nämlich: 'Doch wird ein Zweig aus der Wurzel des Jesse hervorgehen' (Jes 11,1)[179], und genau diese Kombination von Jes 10,34 und 11,1 verwendet ein eindeutig messianischer 'Midrasch' im j Talmud[180]:

[174] So auch Baer, a.a.O., S. 180. Saldarini, a.a.O., S. 198f. erwägt: "*Could both Josephus and the haggada be examples of a type of story circulating after the Great Revolt concerning the relations of captured Jewish leaders to the victorious and awesome figure of the man who personally and through his son Titus commanded the destruction of Jerusalem?*" Dies ist möglich und spricht auf jeden Fall nicht für die Historizität der Weissagung. Anders jetzt Doeve, a. a. O. (Anm. 110), S. 61f.: "*Josephus tells us, that he himself prophesied to Vespasian his coming emperorship. If this would be true it must have happened in the first day of July 67, and Josephus must have been a real prophet! For those days do belong to the period of the unsuccessful revolts against Nero in the western parts of the empire. It seems, therefore, that Josephus stole by finding what Yoḥanan ben Zakkai did.*"

[175] Gegen Schalit (unten, Anm. 197), S. 264, 316ff., der die meisten Züge der Fluchtgeschichte für historisch hält (zu Schalits Deutung der Bitte s. unten). Allon, Māḥqārîm, I, S. 224 hält zwar grundsätzlich an der Historizität der Flucht Joḥanan b. Zakkais fest, hat aber bezüglich der Weissagung (ebenfalls im Blick auf den Parallelbericht bei Josephus) Zweifel (gegen Dexinger, a.a.O., S. 270 mit Anm. 102, der nicht zwischen der Historizität der Flucht als solcher und der Begegnung mit Vespasian unterscheidet).

[176] Vgl. Allon, Māḥqārîm, I, S. 224; Saldarini, a.a.O., S. 198. Neusner, Life, S. 156, Anm. 2 ist umgekehrt der Meinung, daß Joḥanan b. Zakkai nur zu Vespasian geflohen sein kann, weil seit der Belagerung Jerusalems durch Titus eine Flucht nicht mehr möglich gewesen sei.

[177] Gegen Dexinger, a.a.O., S. 270, Anm. 102: „Gerade diese Betonung der Rolle Vespasians spricht m. E. besonders für die prinzipielle Historizität der Berichte. Im Falle einer späteren Erfindung hätte man sicher Titus in den Vordergrund gestellt." Es geht hier nicht um eine 'Erfindung' der 'Aggadah' (diese Kategorie ist ganz unpassend), sondern um eine mögliche Beeinflussung der rabbinischen Fluchtgeschichte durch den Bericht des Josephus.

[178] Vgl. dazu ausführlich G. Vermes, Lebanon. The Historical Development of an Exegetical Tradition, in: Scripture and Tradition in Judaism, Leiden 1961, S. 26—39.

[179] Dieser Vers bezieht sich auf den Messias.

[180] Darauf hat erstmals Vermes, a.a.O., S. 35 hingewiesen.

„Ein Jude bebaute einst seinen Acker, da brüllte sein Ochse vor ihm. Ein vorübergehender Araber hörte dieses Gebrüll und sagte zu ihm: 'Sohn eines Juden, Sohn eines Juden! Spann deinen Ochsen aus und löse deinen Pflugsterz, denn der Tempel wurde zerstört'.
Als dann der [Ochse] ein zweites Mal brüllte, sagte [der Araber] zu ihm: 'Sohn eines Juden, Sohn eines Juden! Spann deinen Ochsen wieder an und binde deinen Pflugsterz fest, denn der König Messias wurde geboren!' ...
Darauf sagte R. Bun: 'Wozu sollen wir uns von einem Araber belehren lassen, gibt es nicht einen ausführlichen Schriftbeweis [dafür]?' 'Und der Libanon wird durch einen Mächtigen fallen' (Jes 10,34). Was steht gleich danach geschrieben? 'Doch wird ein Zweig aus der Wurzel Jesse hervorgehen' (Jes 11,1)[181]."

Es ist sehr wahrscheinlich, daß Joḥanan b. Zakkai, wie dies später R. Bun[182] ausführlich begründet, mit der Zerstörung des Tempels das Kommen des Messias verbindet[183]. Dies ist eine schriftgelehrte jüdische Tradition, die sich als Botschaft an den Eroberer Jerusalems und Zerstörer des Tempels wenig sinnvoll ausnimmt (es sei denn, man vermute, Joḥanan b. Zakkai habe Vespasian sagen wollen: „Deine Macht nützt dir wenig, denn es wird jetzt ohnehin der Messias kommen" — doch widerspricht dies dem Skopus der ganzen Geschichte, denn Joḥanan b. Zakkai wollte bei Vespasian ja schließlich etwas erreichen!). Die näherliegende Annahme ist daher die, in der Prophezeiung mit Hilfe der Exegese von Jes 10,34 kein historisches Ereignis zu sehen, sondern die (sekundäre) Vermischung zweier verschiedener Traditionen, nämlich einmal die in Anlehnung an Josephus gestaltete Prophezeiung Joḥanan b. Zakkais an Vespasian (die unhistorisch wäre) und zum anderen ein selbständiges und möglicherweise tatsächlich auf Joḥanan b. Zakkai zurückgehendes Dictum, das den Bibelvers Jes 10,34f. messianisch interpretiert[184] und mit der Fluchtgeschichte und der Weis-

[181] j Ber 2,4 fol. 5a.

[182] Abin oder Abun I., palästinischer Amoräer der 4. Generation, ca. 4. Jh. n. Chr.

[183] Auch DEXINGER, a.a.O., S. 271, vermutet einen messianischen Hintergrund der Prophezeiung, doch entnimmt er dies dem (traditionell messianisch gedeuteten) Bileamspruch, der in b Git verarbeitet sei. Woher er diese Information bezieht, ist mir unerfindlich, da der Vers Nu 24,7 in b Git nicht zitiert wird. [Brieflich teilt mir Herr Dr. DEXINGER inzwischen mit, daß er sich auf Nu 24,7 in der messianischen Fassung der LXX beziehen und zwischen Nu 24,7 LXX und Jer 30,21 einen Zusammenhang sehen möchte. Dieser Zusammenhang ist freilich sehr vage und die Erläuterung der Exegese von Jes 10,34 mit Hilfe von Jer 30,21/Dt 3,25 in b Git zudem sicher ein späterer Zusatz. Es genügt völlig, daß schon Jes 10,34f. wahrscheinlich messianisch verstanden wurde.] Bedenkenswert erscheint mir dagegen eine andere Vermutung DEXINGERS (S. 271), daß Joḥanan b. Zakkai nämlich eine Tradition ähnlich der seinem Schüler R. Eli'ezer zugeschriebenen vorschwebt: „R. Eli'ezer sagte zu ihm (= zu seinem Kontrahenten R. Jehoshua'): Der Heilige, er sei gepriesen, setzt über sie (= Israel) einen König, so grausam wie Haman es war, und sofort werden sie Buße tun und erlöst werden" (j Taan 1,1 fol. 63d).

[184] Für diese letzte Vermutung spricht, daß Joḥanan b. Zakkai ein weiterer Ausspruch zugeschrieben wird, in dem er ebenfalls die Zerstörung des Tempels = Libanon voraussagt: „Vierzig Jahre vor der Zerstörung des Tempels ... fand man am frühen Morgen

sagung ursprünglich überhaupt nichts zu tun hat. Bei dieser Deutung erübrigt sich auch die Entrüstung BAERS („Der römische Herrscher, der Götzendiener, ist der 'Mächtige', auf den in den Worten des Propheten angespielt wird!") und seine Vermutung: „Es erhebt sich hier wieder der Verdacht eines Einflusses der Diskussionen zwischen Judentum und Christentum auf die Bildung der 'Aggadah'[185]."

b) Die Bitte um Jabne

Die Historizität der Bitte Joḥanan b. Zakkais um Jabne und der Erlaubnis der Römer, in Jabne ein Lehrhaus zu errichten, ist trotz der engen Verknüpfung in den rabbinischen Quellen nicht unbedingt von der Historizität der Weissagung abhängig. Sie muß daher getrennt von der Weissagung auf ihren möglichen historischen Wahrheitsgehalt untersucht werden.

Jabne (griech. Ἰάμνια) wird bei Josephus mehrmals erwähnt[186]. Vespasian eroberte die Stadt zusammen mit Azotos (Ashdod):

> „Denn in der Zwischenzeit war Titus von Gischala nach Caesarea gerückt, Vespasian nach Jamnia und Azotos marschiert, wobei er beide Städte unterworfen und durch Besatzungen gesichert hatte; darauf kehrte er mit einer großen Menge, die seine Friedensbedingungen angenommen hatte, zurück[187]."

Diese Notiz des Josephus wird so zu verstehen sein, daß Vespasian ganz gezielt den jüdischen Bevölkerungsteil eroberter Städte deportierte und an anderer Stelle wieder ansiedelte[188]. Für diese Interpretation spricht das ähnliche Vorgehen des Placidus[189] und eine weitere, sich ebenfalls auf Jabne beziehende Bemerkung des Josephus:

> „Nachdem er die Umgebung der Toparchie von Thamna unterworfen hatte, rückte er nach Lydda und Jamnia vor; in beiden Städten, die er schon vorher in die Hand bekommen hatte, siedelte er eine beträchtliche Anzahl von Juden, die sich ihm ergeben hatten, als Einwohner an und marschierte dann bis nach Emmaus[190]."

die abends geschlossenen Tore des Heiligtums geöffnet. Da sagte R. Joḥanan b. Zakkai zu ihm (= zum Tempel): Tempel, warum erschreckst du uns? Wir wissen, daß du schließlich zerstört werden wirst, denn es heißt: 'Öffne, Libanon, deine Türen, und Feuer verzehre deine Zedern' (Sach 11,1)" (j Jom 6,3, fol. 43c; b Jom 39b).

185 A.a.O., S. 184.

186 Vgl. Bell. I,2,2 § 50; I,7,7 § 156; I,8,4 § 166; II,6,3 § 98; II,9,1 § 167; II,16,1 § 335; III,3,5 § 56; IV,3,2 § 130; IV,8,1 § 444; IV,11,5 § 663.

187 Bell. IV,3,2 § 130.

188 So auch MICHEL—BAUERNFEIND, II/1, S. 209, Anm. 26; ALLON, Mäḥqārîm, I, S. 225f.

189 Bell. IV,7,6 § 438: „Placidus nutzte sein Kriegsglück aus, griff in Eile die umliegenden kleinen Städtchen und Dörfer an, nahm dabei Abila, Julias, Besimo und alle Orte bis zum Asphaltsee und richtete in jedem von ihnen mit den ihm geeignet erscheinenden Überläufern eine Besatzung ein."

190 Bell. IV,8,1 § 444.

Neben anderen Orten (vgl. das bereits erwähnte Gophna, oben S. 82f.) scheinen also Lydda (Lod) und Jabne Städte gewesen zu sein, in die Vespasian gefangene Juden und Überläufer zwangsweise umsiedelte. Aus diesen Hinweisen bei Josephus zieht ALLON die einleuchtende und naheliegende Folgerung, daß Joḥanan b. Zakkai Jabne nicht gewissermaßen als huldvollen Gunsterweis für seine eingetretene Prophezeiung erhielt, sondern zwangsweise dorthin deportiert wurde (nachdem er zuerst in Gophna inhaftiert war): „R. Joḥanan b. Zakkai und seine Gefährten gingen nicht nach Jabne, weil sie sich diesen Ort erbeten hätten, sondern weil sie, wie viele andere von den Flüchtlingen, dorthin geschickt wurden, und zwar nicht zu ihrem Vorteil . . .[191]."

Gegen diese Deutung hat sich mit Vehemenz NEUSNER ausgesprochen. NEUSNER stellt die prononcierte Frage: "*Did the Romans willingly and knowingly permit Yoḥanan ben Zakkai to establish an academy there*?" und beantwortet sie: "*I think it likely that they did.*"[192] Der historische Kern der Fluchtgeschichte ist für ihn daher: "*Yoḥanan did escape from Jerusalem before its destruction. He did go willingly and with Roman approval to Yavneh. He did begin in an elementary way to reconstitute legitimate Jewish authority there.*"[193]

Der Einwand NEUSNERS gegen ALLONS Interpretation richtet sich vor allem gegen dessen weiterreichende Behauptung, daß die Römer nicht nur die jüdische Bevölkerung aus den eroberten Städten deportierten und umsiedelten, sondern insgesamt einen Unterdrückungs- und Vernichtungskrieg gegen das jüdische Volk geführt hätten[194]. Diese These sei eher vom Verhalten der Deutschen im 2. Weltkrieg inspiriert, denn von der historischen Wirklichkeit der Jahre 68—70 n. Chr. ("*Allon sees the Romans as an earlier incarnation of World War II Germany*") und überhaupt typisch für die israelische Geschichtsschreibung ("*The general tendency of Israeli historians is here most vividly portrayed*")[195]. Ohne hier auf die grundsätzliche Frage nach der Art und dem Ziel der römischen Kriegsführung einzugehen, gilt es doch festzuhalten, daß (trotz der engen Verbindung bei ALLON) die These von der zwangsweisen Umsiedlung jüdischer Bevölkerungsteile und der im Rahmen dieser Politik zu sehenden Niederlassung Joḥanan b. Zakkais in Jabne von dem Argument eines 'ethnischen Vernichtungskrieges' unabhängig ist. Die Belege bei Josephus für die Ansiedlung von Überläufern und Gefangenen in ganz bestimmten Städten werden nicht hinfällig, wenn die Römer keinen Vernichtungskrieg geführt haben. NEUSNER trifft mit seiner Polemik also nicht den Kern der Sache. Im übrigen muß er sich den Vorwurf gefallen lassen, daß seine Darstellung der Vorgänge auf einem nicht minder

[191] Mäḥqārîm, I, S. 237; vgl. auch S. SAFRAI, a.a.O. (Anm. 144), S. 309. Reichlich spekulativ ist dagegen die Vermutung von M. STEIN ('Ten lî Javnäh weḥakhāmāhā', Zion 3, 1938, S. 118—122), daß Joḥanan b. Zakkai Jabne erbeten habe, weil die Stadt zum Privatbesitz der römischen Kaiser (und damit auch Vespasians) gehörte und schon vor 70 n. Chr. ein eigenes Sanhedrin hatte.

[192] Life, S. 166. [193] Life, S. 168f.

[194] Mäḥqārîm, I, S. 227ff.; NEUSNER, Life, S. 243—245. [195] Life, S. 245.

problematischen Klischee gründet, nämlich dem Bild des aus unbeachteten Anfängen glanzvoll wiedergeborenen, friedfertigen und ausschließlich mit der Torah beschäftigten Judentums[196].

Den bisher letzten Versuch, die Historizität der Bitte (und auch der Weissagung) zu beweisen, hat A. SCHALIT unternommen[197]. Ausgehend von der Kritik späterer Rabbinen am Verhalten Joḥanan b. Zakkais[198] und der Tatsache, daß die Bitte in EkhR zunächst ausdrücklich lautet: „Ich bitte darum, daß du diese Stadt in Ruhe läßt und abziehst", vermutet SCHALIT, daß es zunächst Joḥanan b. Zakkais Absicht war, „die materielle Rettung Jerusalems und des Heiligtums beim Träger der römischen Heeresmacht in ungeschmälertem Maße durchzusetzen, um das Volk in Judäa vor dem Untergang zu bewahren"[199]. Joḥanan b. Zakkai habe von den Gerüchten über die bevorstehende Ausrufung Vespasians zum Kaiser gewußt und sich diese sowie die Nachrichten über die Aufstände im Westen des Reiches und die zu erwartende blutige Auseinandersetzung des neuen Kaisers mit dem Gegenkaiser in Rom geschickt zunutze gemacht, um Vespasian gewissermaßen im passenden Moment seine Bitte vorzutragen: „Wohl bist du ein aussichtsreicher Anwärter auf den Kaiserthron, wohl ist der Orient im Begriffe, sich für dich zu erklären, aber die faktische Erreichung des Zieles steht noch weit im Felde. Noch ist der Gegner in Rom nicht niedergerungen, noch sind die gefährlichen Aufstände im Westen im vollen Gange. Das sind weit wichtigere und eines Kaisers würdigere Kampfpreise als die Niederringung einer aufständischen Stadt in einer kleinen Provinz im Osten des Reiches. Ich schlage dir vor, grundsätzlich von Jerusalem abzulassen und

[196] Vgl. Life, S. 172f.: "*A Roman centurion passing through the vineyard where Yoḥanan was reaching (teaching?) his students would have wondered who had made the war, for Jews like those huddled in the shadows obviously had not. If he remembered the same faces in an earlier setting, he would have noted little change. The same serene master sat with the same serious disciples. Once they had studied in the shade of the Temple, now in an arbor. Who is afraid of otherworldly Jews like these? The centurion would have looked for a brief moment, smiled at the thought that here, at least, were no trouble-makers, and moved on to weightier concerns. No wonder this weak people would soon pass and be forgotten in history. Hopelessly divided, they could scarcely endure for another century. They fought one another more than they fought Rome. In Yavneh were Jews who ignored the patriot armies and sold liberty in exchange for life. A people relying on such a remnant as this, unconcerned for honor and for liberty, could not long abide. Rome's victory was the final one.*" Inzwischen ist NEUSNER allerdings von dieser Art der 'Geschichtsschreibung' abgerückt; vgl. die Bemerkung in seinem sehr anregenden und engagierten Beitrag, 'The History of Earlier Rabbinic Judaism: Some New Approaches', History of Religions 16, 1977, S. 222, Anm. 11: "*A good example for the uncritical (or, more kindly, precritical) character of the enterprise of rabbinic biography is my* Life of Yoḥanan ben Zakkai *(Leiden,* 1962*; 2d ed., completely rev.,* 1970*).*" Vgl. auch DERS., The Formation of Rabbinic Judaism: Yavneh (Jamnia) from A.D. 70 to 100, ob. in diesem Band (ANRW II 19,2), 3—42.

[197] Die Erhebung Vespasians nach Flavius Josephus, Talmud und Midrasch. Zur Geschichte einer messianischen Prophetie, in: Aufstieg und Niedergang der römischen Welt (ANRW), II 2, Berlin–New York 1975, S. 316ff.

[198] Vgl. b Git (oben S. 54): R. Joseph oder R. 'Aqiva.

[199] A.a.O., S. 318.

dich mit einer friedlichen Lösung des Problems im Wege ruhiger Verhandlungen mit den Vertretern des Volkes zu begnügen, um dich den brennenden Fragen der Bekämpfung der Gegner in Italien und anderwärts und der Wiederherstellung der Ruhe und Ordnung im auseinanderbrechenden Reich zuzuwenden[200]."

Das hier entworfene Wunschbild des weise lenkenden Staatsmannes Joḥanan b. Zakkai hat mit den Realitäten des jüdisch-römischen Krieges, wie wir sie aus jüdischen und nichtjüdischen Quellen erschließen können, wenig gemein. Es ist überhaupt nur verständlich auf dem Hintergrund der SCHALIT in seinem ganzen Artikel leitenden Absicht, den strahlenden Helden Joḥanan b. Zakkai, dessen Handeln „einzig und allein von seiner tiefen Sorge um das Schicksal der Gemeinschaft getragen" war, von dem Finsterling Josephus abzuheben, „dessen Beweggründe Feigheit und ein völliges Abgehen jeglichen Gemeinschaftssinnes waren. ... Dem Gelehrten gegenüber steht die Gestalt des jerusalemischen Priesters Josephus. Was er von Vespasian verlangte, war wesentlich einfacher. Er wollte sein Leben retten und die Freiheit wiedergewinnen. Ihm — im Gegensatz zum Gelehrten — blieb der Erfolg nicht versagt. Er errang ihn um den Preis seiner Ehre in den Augen seiner Zeitgenossen und der späteren Generationen"[201]. Dieses tendenziöse Schwarz-Weiß-Gemälde ist so sehr von subjektiv-moralisierenden Urteilen geprägt, daß es kaum noch den Anspruch erheben kann, als seriöse Geschichtsschreibung gewertet zu werden[202].

Es bleibt somit bei der begründeten Vermutung, daß nicht nur die Weissagung, sondern auch die Bitte Joḥanan b. Zakkais als unhistorisch zu betrachten ist. Besonders verdächtig sind die beiden Fassungen der Bitte in b Git/EkhR. Daß Joḥanan b. Zakkai ausgerechnet um die Dynastie[203] Gamliels, d. h. die Führung des Volkes durch Gamliel II., gebeten haben soll (b Git), ist angesichts der Rivalität zwischen Joḥanan b. Zakkai und Gamliel II. wenig wahrscheinlich und reflektiert offensichtlich spätere Zustände. Dasselbe gilt für die Rettung R. Ṣadoqs (b Git/EkhR). Mag auch die Notiz in ARNA Kap. 16, S. 63, daß R. Ṣadoq in Rom gefangen gehalten

[200] A.a.O., S. 319f.

[201] A.a.O., S. 320f. Ähnlich, wenn auch nicht ganz so negativ, urteilt DOEVE, a.a.O. (Anm. 110), S. 62: *"But whatever Josephus may have said to Vespasian at what time soever, one thing stands firm: he did not use this to take profit of it for the actual needs of his people, as Yohanan did. But on the other hand he became an apologist for judaism in the greek-roman world."*

[202] Vgl. auch die Kritik von H. R. MOEHRING, Joseph Ben Matthia and Flavius Josephus. The Jewish Prophet and Roman Historian, ANRW II 21, Berlin–New York 1979f.

[203] *šwšjlt'* — genealogische Kette (so mit Raschi z.St. und gegen M. [?] DREIFUSS, Das Verhältniß R' Jochanan b. Sakkaï's zum Hillel'schen Patriarchenhause, MGWJ 19, 1870, S. 568—573, der *šwšjlt'* im Sinne von 'Amtskette' verstehen möchte). — Abwegig ist auch die Vermutung von A. BURSTEIN (Baqqāšat Rabbān Jôḥānān bän Zakka'i me'Ispasjānôs, Bitzaron 24, 1951, S. 34—45), daß die Lesart in b Git (*šôšîltā' d^eRabbān Gamlî'el*) auf eine falsch aufgelöste Abkürzung zurückgehe (*šôšîltā' d^eR''G*) und in Wirklichkeit *šôšîltā' d^erêš galûtā'* („die Dynastie des [babylonischen] Exilarchen") zu lesen sei, daß Joḥanan b. Zakkai also zunächst von Vespasian die Oberherrschaft der (davidischen) Exilarchen auch über Palästina erbeten habe.

wurde, zweifelhaft sein und sich auf seinen gleichnamigen Enkel beziehen[204], so bleibt immerhin die Tatsache, daß der Priester und Rabbi Ṣadoq (I.) nach der Eroberung Jerusalems offenbar keine Beziehungen zu Joḥanan b. Zakkai unterhielt, dafür aber später bei dessen Nachfolger Gamliel II. in hohen Ehren stand[205].

Auffallend ist dann insbesondere eine weitere Parallele bei Josephus, und zwar in der 'Vita' und nicht im 'Bellum':

> „Nach der Einnahme Jerusalems forderte mich Titus oftmals auf, aus den Trümmern meiner Vaterstadt zu nehmen, was mir beliebe; denn gern wolle er mir alles gewähren. Ich aber kannte nach der Niederwerfung meines Vaterlandes in dem Unglück, das mich betroffen, keinen süßeren Trost als die persönliche Freiheit von Mitbürgern, und erbat sie mir demgemäß von Titus. Ferner erhielt ich durch seine Gnade die heiligen Schriften zum Geschenk. Später erlangte ich durch meine Fürbitte die Freilassung meines Bruders und fünfzig anderer Männer, die mir sehr befreundet waren. Mit des Caesars Erlaubnis ging ich auch in den Tempel, wo eine große Menge gefangener Weiber und Kinder eingeschlossen war, und rettete alle, die ich als Angehörige meiner Freunde und Verwandten erkannte, hundertundneunzig an der Zahl. ... Hierauf ward ich von Titus in das Dorf Thekoa gesandt. ... Auf dem Wege von dort sah ich wieder Gefangene, die am Kreuze hingen, und erkannte darunter drei meiner Freunde. Mit tiefem Schmerz begab ich mich zu Titus und erzählte es ihm. Sogleich ließ er sie abnehmen und ihnen die sorgfältigste Behandlung angedeihen. Trotzdem starben zwei von ihnen während der Behandlung, der dritte aber ward gerettet[206]."

Wenn auch nicht so augenfällig und detailliert wie bei der Prophezeiung, finden sich hier deutliche Parallelen zur Bitte Joḥanan b. Zakkais in der Fassung von EkhR[207]. Joḥanan b. Zakkai bittet darum, das westliche (nach Jaffa und Lod führende) Tor[208] unbeaufsichtigt zu lassen, damit sich ein Teil der Bevölkerung retten kann, während Josephus „die persönliche Freiheit von Mitbürgern" zu seiner Sache macht[209]. Joḥanan b. Zakkai erhält nach der Eroberung Jerusalems die Erlaubnis, einen, dem er nahe-

[204] So wird allgemein angenommen; vgl. M. Margalioth, Encyclopedia of Talmudic and Geonic Literature, II, Tel Aviv 1964, Sp. 746; W. Bacher, Die Agada der Tannaiten, I, Straßburg 1884, S. 49f.; anders Allon, Mäḥqārîm, I, S. 252, Anm. 82.

[205] Vgl. Allon, Mäḥqārîm, I, S. 256f.

[206] Vita § 75.

[207] Daher ist die Bemerkung Saldarinis: „*Josephus' War has no parallel to Johanan's request for Jamnia, the climax of the haggadic story*" (a.a.O., S. 198) nur bedingt richtig. Die Bitte um Jabne fehlt auch in EkhR, und genau zu dieser Version bietet Josephus' 'Vita' eine Parallele.

[208] Allon, Mäḥqārîm, I, S. 251, Anm. 81 sieht eine Parallele zu den Zeloten, die um freien Abzug in die Wüste bitten (Bell. VI,6,3 § 351).

[209] Der Unterschied ist hier nur der, daß Joḥanan b. Zakkai vor und Josephus unmittelbar nach der Eroberung spricht.

steht, zu retten, und rettet R. Ṣadoq, den 'Vespasian' durch seine Ärzte heilen läßt[210]; Josephus darf seinen Bruder, Angehörige seiner Freunde und Verwandten und noch einmal drei Freunde retten, denen Titus „sorgfältige Behandlung angedeihen" läßt. Da diese Parallelen kaum zufällig sein werden, legt sich auch hier die Vermutung nahe, daß die Bitte Joḥanan b. Zakkais in den beiden Fassungen b Git/EkhR in Anlehnung an die Schilderung des Josephus von dessen Rettungsaktionen nach der Eroberung Jerusalems gestaltet wurde.

Zusammenfassend ergibt sich für die Darstellung der Bitte in den rabbinischen Quellen: Die Joḥanan b. Zakkai in den Mund gelegte Bitte um Jabne ist die aus späterer Sicht formulierte Gründungslegende des 'Lehrhauses' in Jabne und der Neukonstitution des Judentums nach der Katastrophe des Jahres 70 n. Chr. durch Joḥanan b. Zakkai. Die zusätzlichen Details dieser Bitte in b Git/EkhR sind ebenfalls aus späterer Sicht formuliert und möglicherweise z. T. dem Parallelbericht des Josephus entnommen.

6. Der geschwollene Fuß

Die beiden Versionen in EkhR und b Git erwähnen unmittelbar nach der Nachricht vom Tode Neros und der Ausrufung Vespasians zum Caesar eine merkwürdige Episode: Vespasian habe, als er die Nachricht empfing, gerade gebadet und sei dabei gewesen, den zweiten Schuh anzuziehen, doch paßte ihm dieser nicht mehr. Joḥanan b. Zakkai habe mit Hilfe von Spr 15,30 die Wurzel dieses Übels erkannt und ihn, ebenfalls gestützt auf einen Bibelvers (Spr 17,22), geheilt. Zu dieser Episode findet sich eine deutliche Parallele bei dem mittelalterlichen Schriftsteller Landolfus Sagax (11. Jh.):

> *Itaque cum nuntiatum ei* (sc. *Tito*) *a Roma fuisset, quod pater eius imperium potiretur, ex hilaritate nimia crura eius dextra crementum carnis accepit ita, ut calciamentum non reciperet, quem (quae?) Iosephi duci (ducis?) Iudaeorum consilio ut alia restituta est, qui iusserat ante eum hominem transire, in quem plurimum odio habebat.*[211]
>
> „Als ihm (= Titus) von Rom gemeldet wurde, daß sein Vater die Herrschaft erlangt habe, schwoll wegen der übermäßigen Freude sein rechter Fuß an, so daß er den Schuh nicht annahm. Dieser wurde wiederhergestellt wie der andere durch den Rat des Josephus, des Fürsten der Juden, der ihm empfahl, an sich einen Menschen vorbeigehen zu lassen, gegen den er überaus großen Haß empfinde."

Trotz einiger Unterschiede in Einzelheiten (die handelnden Personen sind in EkhR/b Git Vespasian und Joḥanan b. Zakkai, bei Landolfus Sagax

[210] Nach EkhR Ed. Buber sogar zunächst „alle Rabbinen" (*kl rbnn*) und dann R. Ṣadoq!
[211] Landolfi Sagacis Additamenta ad Pauli Historiam Romanam, ed. H. Droysen, in: Monumenta Germaniae Historica, Auctores Antiquissimi, II, Berolini 1879, S. 304.

dagegen Titus und Josephus) sind die Gemeinsamkeiten zwischen dieser lateinischen Erzählung und der rabbinischen 'Aggadah' im ganzen Ductus der Geschichte so groß, daß der Gedanke der Abhängigkeit der einen von der anderen Erzählung naheliegt. So hat denn auch H. LEWY[212] nach ersten Hinweisen von J. BERNAYS[213] ausführlich die These begründet, daß die Episode vom geschwollenen Fuß über die rabbinische Quelle in die mittelalterliche Literatur bis hin zum 'Sachsenspiegel' und zur 'Legenda aurea' des Jacobus a Voragine gelangt sei: "*It seems, therefore, very likely that a converted Jew, having read in Christian chronicles the story of Josephus' prophecy of Vespasian's succession, enriched it with details which he took from the corresponding Talmudic legend of Johanan ben Saccai* . . .[214]." Dagegen hat sich zuletzt J. BAER gewandt und die umgekehrte Vermutung geäußert, daß der rabbinische Bericht als sekundär anzusehen sei[215]. Die Quelle des Landolfus sei nämlich die 'Historia adversum paganos' des spanischen Priesters Paulus Orosius vom Anfang des 5. Jh.s, von dessen Schilderung der Umstände bei der Eroberung Jerusalems[216] Landolfus' Bericht genommen sei. Zwar findet sich die Episode vom geschwollenen Fuß selbst nicht bei Orosius, doch sei sie eine Interpolation, die „in die Handschrift des Orosius durch diesen selbst oder durch jemanden ihm Nahestehenden eingefügt wurde, jedenfalls nicht durch einen späten mittelalterlichen Schriftsteller (sc. Landolfus), der mit dem Stil des Orosius nicht so vertraut war"[217]. Orosius sei somit die Quelle für die rabbinische Literatur: „Die Aggadah entwickelte sich auf der Grundlage der christlichen (westlich-lateinischen) Tradition, die ihr vorausging[218]."

Mit der offenkundigen Schwäche dieser literarischen Beweisführung BAERS, die wieder mit mehreren Unbekannten arbeitet — eine höchst zweifelhafte Interpolation und vor allem die Frage, wie denn der Bericht bei Orosius seinen Weg in b Git/EkhR gefunden haben soll[219] —, ist freilich das zugrunde liegende historische Problem nicht erledigt. Da in der Tat (mit BAER) einige Details der Erzählung bei Landolfus–Orosius historisch wahrscheinlicher sind als die 'Aggadah' (Titus als Eroberer Jerusalems, Josephus im Lager des Titus), spricht manches für die Priorität der lateinischen Quelle (nicht als literarisches Dokument — über ein mühsam konstruiertes Zwischenglied —, sondern als historische Information).

212 Josephus the Physician. A Mediaeval Legend of the Destruction of Jerusalem, Journal of the Warburg Institute 1, 1937/38, S. 221—242 = J. H. LEVY, 'Ôlāmôt niphgāšîm (Studies in Jewish Hellenism), Jerusalem 1960, S. 266—293. Vgl. auch G. KISCH, A Talmudic Legend as the Source for the Josephus Passage in the *Sachsenspiegel*, Historia Judaica 1, 1938/39, S. 105—118; DERS., Forschungen zur Rechts- und Sozialgeschichte der Juden in Deutschland während des Mittelalters, Stuttgart 1955, S. 72ff.

213 Vgl. M. FRAENKEL, Jacob Bernays. Ein Lebensbild in Briefen, Breslau 1932, S. 161ff.

214 A.a.O., S. 227 (hebr. Fassung, S. 274).

215 A.a.O., S. 180ff.

216 Orosius, Hist. adv. pag. VII,9,1ff.

217 A.a.O., S. 183.

218 A.a.O., S. 183, Anm. 201 Ende.

219 Darauf verweist auch SALDARINI, a.a.O., S. 197.

Literarisch ist neben der Alternative, ob die 'Aggadah' von Landolfus oder Landolfus von der 'Aggadah' abhängig ist, auch noch die dritte (und wahrscheinlichere) Möglichkeit einer verlorengegangenen gemeinsamen Quelle zu erwägen, auf die beide Versionen unabhängig voneinander zurückgehen. Über diese Quelle kann man natürlich nur Vermutungen anstellen, aber es ist m. E. nicht auszuschließen, daß diese Quelle Josephus selbst ist, mit dessen Textüberlieferung es bekanntlich nicht zum Besten steht[220]. Was die 'Aggadah' betrifft, so hätte diese jedenfalls, welche Quelle auch immer zugrunde liegt, wie schon an anderer Stelle ursprünglich mit Josephus verbundene Ereignisse (oder Legenden) auf Joḥanan b. Zakkai übertragen[221].

7. Die Diskussion mit Pangar/Abgar

In der Version der Fluchtgeschichte im Midrasch EkhR werden an verschiedenen Stellen vier Fürsten (*duces*) erwähnt, die Vespasian bei der Belagerung unterstützen. Gleich zu Beginn sind sie als die Fürsten Arabiens, Afrikas bzw. Phönikiens, Alexandriens und Palästinas bezeichnet; der Fürst Arabiens ist sogar mit Namen bekannt: er hieß Qilus oder Pangar/Abgar[222]. Nach der Flucht Joḥanan b. Zakkais diskutieren die vier *duces* in Gleichnissen mit ihm über die Frage, was nach der Eroberung Jerusalems zu geschehen habe: Wie soll man mit einem Turm oder einem Faß (wohl sinnbildlich für Jerusalem und den Tempel), in dem eine Schlange (= die Zeloten) nistet, verfahren?[223] Antwort Joḥanan b. Zakkais: Man töte die Zeloten und rette Stadt und Tempel; dagegen Abgar: Man töte die Zeloten und zerstöre Stadt und Tempel[224]!

Auch diese Beratung der Heerführer über das Schicksal Jerusalems hat eine Parallele bei Josephus:

> „Er selbst (= Titus) berief die Offiziere zu sich. Sechs der obersten römischen Führer kamen zusammen, Tiberius Alexander, der die gesamten Streitkräfte befehligte, Sextus Cerealis, der Anführer der 5. Legion, Larcius Lepidus, der Anführer der 10., Titus Phrygius, der Anführer der 15.; ferner Fronto Haterius, der Befehlshaber der beiden

[220] SCHRECKENBERG, a.a.O. (Anm. 169), S. 133 hält die Tradition bei Landolfus für 'fiktiv' und scheint die Meinung derer zu teilen, die in b Git die Quelle sehen möchten (S. 159).

[221] Diese inzwischen mehrmals beobachtete Übertragung von Motiven des Josephus auf Joḥanan b. Zakkai ist indirekt ein Argument für eine verlorengegangene Josephus-Überlieferung als gemeinsame Quelle der 'Aggadah' und des Landolfus.

[222] EkhR Ed. Wilna: Pangar; Ed. BUBER: Abgar oder Amgar.

[223] In der in diesem Punkt sicher sekundären Fassung b Git stellt Vespasian die Frage, doch Joḥanan b. Zakkai weiß keine Antwort; diese wird durch R. Joseph bzw. R. 'Aqiva nachgeliefert.

[224] In EkhR Ed. Wilna ist die Antwort Joḥanan b. Zakkais bezüglich der Zeloten milder: Man beschwöre die Schlange durch einen Zauberer, d. h. hier sicher: Man überrede die Zeloten zur Übergabe.

Legionen aus Alexandria, und Marcus Antonius Julianus, der Statthalter von Judäa; außer diesen wurden noch weitere Statthalter und Obersten hinzugezogen. Ihnen legte Titus nun die Frage des Tempels zur Beratung vor. Einige waren der Auffassung, daß das Kriegsrecht zur Anwendung kommen solle. Denn niemals würden die Juden davon ablassen, Aufruhr zu stiften, solange der Tempel noch stehe, der ja einen Sammlungspunkt für die Juden aus aller Welt bilde. Andere rieten dazu, man solle den Tempel, falls die Juden ihn räumten ... verschonen; falls sie ihn aber zum Kampf beträten, solle man ihn niederbrennen. ... Demgegenüber erklärte Titus, man solle sich, auch wenn Juden den Tempel bestiegen, um von dort aus zu kämpfen, nicht an den leblosen Dingen anstelle der Menschen rächen und jemals ein so herrliches Bauwerk den Flammen preisgeben. Denn der Schaden würde doch die Römer treffen, ebenso wie der Tempel ein Schmuck ihres Reiches wäre, wenn er noch erhalten bliebe. Freudig schlossen sich dieser Meinung nun auch Fronto, Alexander und Cerealis an[225]."

Ohne daß hier auf die verwickelten und umstrittenen Fragen der Historizität dieses Berichtes bei Josephus eingegangen werden kann[226], sei nur auf Gemeinsamkeiten mit der 'Aggadah' in EkhR verwiesen: Beide stimmen darin überein, daß man sich im Lager des römischen Feldherrn über das Schicksal des Tempels nach der Eroberung Jerusalems berät. Allerdings sind bei Josephus die unterschiedlichen Meinungen ganz auf die römische Seite konzentriert; ein Jude (auch nicht Josephus!) nimmt an den Beratungen nicht teil. Titus selbst schließt sich der Meinung derer an, die den Tempel verschonen wollen[227]. Er übernimmt also den Part Joḥanan b. Zakkais in der 'Aggadah', und zwar mit einem ähnlichen Argument wie dieser („Man solle sich nicht an den leblosen Dingen anstelle der Menschen rächen").

Auffallend in der 'Aggadah' ist die betonte Hervorhebung eines *dux* (Pangar/Abgar) als des Befürworters der Tempelzerstörung (Josephus dagegen: „Einige waren der Auffassung ..."). Nach BAER verbirgt sich hinter dem Namen Abgar einer der Herrscher von Osrhoëne, die unter Abgar IX. (179—216 n. Chr.) zum Christentum konvertierten. Da einem Träger dieses Namens in einer christlich-syrischen Quelle die Bereitschaft nachgesagt wird, nach Jerusalem zu ziehen und die Stadt wegen der Ermordung des Messias (Jesus) zu zerstören[228], vermutet BAER antichristliche

[225] Bell. VI,4,3 § 236ff.

[226] Vgl. dazu ausführlich G. ALLON, Šeʳêphat ham-miqdāš, Māḥqārîm, I, S. 206—218; MICHEL—BAUERNFEIND, II/2, S. 173f., Anm. 108 (mit der älteren Literatur); BAER, a.a.O., S. 173.

[227] Ob in diesem Punkt, wie manche Historiker meinen, der (von Tacitus abhängige ?) Bericht des Sulpicius Severus (Chron. II,30,6) vorzuziehen ist, wonach Titus für die Zerstörung des Tempels war, um sowohl das Judentum wie das Christentum auszurotten (*Christianos ex Judaeis extitisse: radice sublata stirpem facile perituram*), ist kaum mit Sicherheit zu entscheiden. Die Erwähnung der Christen macht diese Notiz zumindest verdächtig.

[228] Vgl. dazu S. LIEBERMAN, Midreše Têmān, Jerusalem ²1970, S. 15 mit Anm. 1; J. DERENBOURG, Le Nom de Fangar, REJ 19, 1889, S. 148f.

Polemik in der 'Aggadah'[229]. Der Zusammenhang dieser christlichen Quelle mit der 'Aggadah' ist freilich so vage — weder bezieht sich die christliche Quelle auf die historische Eroberung Jerusalems noch kam der Wunsch Abgars überhaupt zur Ausführung —, daß BAER (wieder) auf eine verlorene Quelle rekurriert: „Es ist klar, daß die Aggadah von der [Tempel-]Zerstörung in der Fassung des Midrasch Ekha ... eine polemische Schöpfung ist, die sich gegen irgendeine Version der christlichen Abgar-Legende richtet, deren Quelle mir nicht mehr greifbar ist[230]." Wahrscheinlicher als die von BAER postulierte antichristliche Polemik scheint mir die Vermutung, daß die betonte Hervorhebung Pangars/Abgars, des *dux Arabiae* (!), sich gegen den Islam richtet. Dies bedeutet jedoch nicht[231], daß die 'Aggadah' als ganze entsprechend spät anzusetzen ist. Der Kern der 'Aggadah' dürfte auf eine historische Quelle vom Kriegsrat der Römer vor der Eroberung Jerusalems — sei es in der Fassung des Josephus, sei es in einer Josephus zugrunde liegenden Quelle — zurückgehen, die dann entsprechend der jeweiligen Tendenz der rabbinischen Redaktoren ausgestaltet und erweitert wurde, bis sie die heute vorliegende Gestalt erhielt.

Die Abhängigkeit der rabbinischen Pangar/Abgar-Aggadah von Josephus ist schließlich am Schluß der 'Aggadah' in EkhR noch deutlicher. Bei Josephus heißt es:

> „Als aber das Heer weder etwas zu morden noch zu rauben fand, ... da befahl der Caesar, die gesamte Stadt und den Tempel zu schleifen. Die Türme Phasael, Hippikus und Mariamne, die die anderen überragten, sollten sie stehen lassen, ebenso die Mauer, soweit sie im Westen die Stadt umgab. Die Mauer sollte der Besatzung, die zurückgelassen werden mußte, zur Anlage eines Lagers dienen, die Türme dagegen sollten erhalten bleiben, um hinfort zu bezeugen, wie herrlich und wie stark befestigt die Stadt gewesen war, die der Heldenmut der Römer überwunden hatte[232]."

Abzüglich der tendenziösen (antiislamischen?) Zuspitzung auf Pangar/Abgar findet sich in der 'Aggadah' dieselbe historische Information wie bei Josephus: Die Westmauer wurde von der Zerstörung verschont, damit die Nachwelt sieht, welche herrliche und unbezwingbare Stadt 'Vespasian' zerstört hat (die 'Aggadah' kombiniert die bei Josephus erwähnten Türme und die Westmauer, weil ihr die Mauer aus theologischen Gründen sehr viel näher liegt als die Türme). Insgesamt ergibt sich also für die Frage nach den historischen Umständen der Flucht Joḥanan b. Zakkais, daß die Pangar/Abgar-Aggadah in ihrem Kern auf Josephus bzw. eine verwandte Quelle zurückgeht und die Einbeziehung Joḥanan b. Zakkais in diese 'Aggadah' als Werk des rabbinischen Redaktors zu betrachten ist.

[229] A.a.O., S. 172ff.
[230] A.a.O., S. 175.
[231] Gegen NEUSNER, Development, S. 232.
[232] Bell. VII,1,1 § 1ff.; vgl. auch Bell. VI,9,1 § 413.

IV. Zusammenfassung in Thesen

1. Alle erhaltenen rabbinischen Quellen sind von der Tendenz geprägt, die Zusammenarbeit Joḥanan b. Zakkais mit den Römern zu erklären und zu rechtfertigen; der historische Wert der Einzelinformationen muß in jedem einzelnen Fall und unabhängig von der redaktionellen Zusammenstellung geprüft werden.

2. Der Zeitpunkt der Endredaktion der zugrunde gelegten rabbinischen Quellen besagt nichts über den historischen Wert ihrer Einzelinformationen; in der Endredaktion späte Quellen können auch historisch wertvolle Nachrichten enthalten.

3. Die rabbinische Darstellung der Fluchtgeschichte ist in einigen Punkten von Josephus oder einer ihm nahestehenden Quelle abhängig.

4. Die Römer haben sehr wahrscheinlich Übergabeverhandlungen geführt und waren durch Überläufer (und Spione?) über die Verhältnisse in der Stadt informiert.

5. Joḥanan b. Zakkai ist während des jüdisch-römischen Krieges 66—72 n. Chr. aus Jerusalem geflohen und zu den Römern übergegangen; einen genauen Zeitpunkt für diese Flucht festzusetzen, ist nicht möglich.

6. Konkrete Gründe für die Flucht sind nicht namhaft zu machen, doch werden seine grundsätzliche Opposition gegen den Krieg und seine Absicht, sich mit den Römern zu arrangieren, eine Rolle gespielt haben; das Verbrennen der Vorräte als unmittelbarer Fluchtgrund ist wenig wahrscheinlich.

7. Joḥanan b. Zakkai wurde von den Römern zuerst in Gophna inhaftiert und mußte sich dann auf römische Anordnung in Jabne niederlassen.

8. Die Weissagung Joḥanan b. Zakkais an Vespasian ist nicht historisch. Dagegen könnte die messianische Auslegung von Jes 10,34 auf ein echtes Dictum Joḥanan b. Zakkais zurückgehen.

9. Ebenso ist die Bitte um Jabne kein historisches Faktum, sondern die Gründungslegende des rabbinischen Judentums nach der Katastrophe des Jahres 70 n. Chr.

10. Die Episode vom geschwollenen Fuß Vespasians hat mit Joḥanan b. Zakkai ursprünglich nichts zu tun, sondern geht möglicherweise auf Josephus zurück.

11. Dasselbe gilt für die Pangar/Abgar-Aggadah, die erst sekundär mit der Person Joḥanan b. Zakkais verknüpft wurde.

Bibliographie

I. Quellen

1. Rabbinische Literatur

Šiššāh Sidrê Mišnāh, ed. Ḥ. ALBECK, I—VI, Tel Aviv 1958—1959.

Tosephta, based on the Erfurt and Vienna Codices, ed. M. S. ZUCKERMANDEL, Jerusalem ²1937 (Neudruck 1963).

Talmûd Jᵉrûšalmî, Ed. Krotoschin 1865/66 (Neudruck Jerusalem 1959/60).

Der babylonische Talmud, ed. L. GOLDSCHMIDT, I—IX, Leipzig–Berlin 1897—1935.

Mechilta d'Rabbi Ismael, ed. H. S. HOROVITZ—I. A. RABIN, Frankfurt a.M. 1931 (Neudruck Jerusalem 1960).

Mekhilta D'Rabbi Šim'on b. Jochai, ed. J. N. EPSTEIN—E. Z. MELAMED, Jerusalem 1955.

Sifra. Commentar zu Leviticus, ed. J. SCHLOSSBERG, Wien 1862.

Siphre ad Deuteronomium, ed. L. FINKELSTEIN, Berlin 1939 (Neudruck New York 1969).

Midraš Tannā'îm, ed. D. HOFFMANN, Berlin 1908/1909.

Aboth de Rabbi Nathan, ed. S. SCHECHTER, Wien 1887 (Neudruck New York 1967).

'Ekhāh Rabbātî, in: Midrāš Rabbāh, III, Ed. Wilna 1887.

Midrasch Echa Rabbati, ed. S. BUBER, Wilna 1899.

Qohälät Rabbāh, in: Midrāš Rabbāh, III, Ed. Wilna 1887.

Midrasch Mischlé, ed. S. BUBER, Wilna 1893.

Pesikta de Rav Kahana, ed. B. MANDELBAUM, I—II, New York 1962.

Pesikta . . . von Rab Kahana, ed. S. BUBER, Lyck 1868.

Pirqê Rabbî 'Älî'äzär, Ed. Warschau 1851/52 (Neudruck Jerusalem 1962/63).

2. Griechische und lateinische Autoren

Annae Comnenae Porphyrogenitae Alexias, ed. A. REIFFERSCHEID, II, Lipsiae 1884.

Dio's Roman History, ed. E. GRAY, VIII, London–Cambridge/Mass. 1968.

Josephus, with an English Translation, IV—IX: Jewish Antiquities, ed. H. ST. J. THACKERAY et al., London–Cambridge/Mass. 1950—1965.

Flavius Josephus, De Bello Judaico — Der jüdische Krieg, Griechisch-Deutsch, ed. O. MICHEL—O. BAUERNFEIND, I—III, München 1959—1969.

Des Flavius Josephus kleinere Schriften . . ., übers. . . . von H. CLEMENTZ, Köln 1960.

Landolfi Sagacis Additamenta ad Pauli Historiam Romanam, ed. H. DROYSEN, in: Monumenta Germaniae Historica, Auctores Antiquissimi, II, Berolini 1879.

Pauli Orosii Historiarum adversum Paganos Libri VII, ed. C. ZANGEMEISTER, in: Corpus Scriptorum Ecclesiasticorum Latinorum, V, Vindobonae 1882.

C. Suetoni Tranquilli Divus Vespasianus, ed. A. W. BRAITHWAITE, Oxford 1927.

Sulpicii Severi Libri qui supersunt, ed. C. HALM, in: Corpus Scriptorum Ecclesiasticorum, I, Vindobonae 1866.

Cornelii Taciti Historiarum Libri qui supersunt, ed. K. HERAEUS, II, ed. ster., Amsterdam 1966.

II. Sekundärliteratur

G. Allon, Nᵉśî'ûtô šäl Rabbān Jôḥānān bän Zakka'i [Das Patriarchat des R. Joḥanan b. Zakkai], in: Sephär haj-jôvel lᵉ J. Klausner [Festschrift J. Klausner], Tel Aviv 1936/37, S. 154—170 = Ders., Mäḥqārîm bᵉtôlᵉdôt Jiśrā'el [Forschungen zur Geschichte Israels], I, [Tel Aviv] 1957, S. 253—273 = Ders., The Patriarchate of Rabban Joḥanan ben Zakkai, in: Jews, Judaism and the Classical World, Jerusalem 1977, S. 314—343.

G. Allon, Hᵃlîkhatô šäl Rabbān Jôḥānān bän Zakka'i lᵉJavnäh [Der Gang R. Joḥanan b. Zakkais nach Jabne], Zion 3, 1937/38, S. 183—214 = Ders., Mäḥqārîm, I, S. 219—252 = Ders., Rabban Joḥanan B. Zakkai's Removal to Jabneh, in: Jews, Judaism and the Classical World, S. 269—313.

G. Allon, Śᵉrêphat ham-miqdāš [Der Brand des Tempels], Javnäh 1, 1938/39, S. 85—106 = Ders., Mäḥqārîm, I, S. 206—218 = Ders., The Burning of the Temple, in: Jews, Judaism and the Classical World, S. 252—268.

G. Allon, Tôlᵉdôt haj-jᵉhûdîm bᵉ'äräṣ-Jiśrā'el bitqûphat ham-mišnāh wᵉhat-talmûd [Geschichte der Juden im Lande Israel in der Periode der Mishna und des Talmud], I, [Tel Aviv] ⁴1967.

J. Baer, Jᵉrûšālajim bîmê ham-märäd hag-gādôl [Jerusalem in den Tagen des großen Aufstandes], Zion 36, 1971, S. 127—190.

A. Büchler, Die Priester und der Cultus im letzten Jahrzehnt des Jerusalemischen Tempels, Wien 1895.

A. Burstein, Baqqāšat Rabbān Jôḥānān bän Zakka'i me'Ispasjānôs [Die Bitte R. Joḥanan b. Zakkais an Vespasian], Bitzaron 24, 1951, S. 34—45.

F. Dexinger, Ein 'messianisches Szenarium' als Gemeingut des Judentums in nachherodianischer Zeit?, Kairos 17, 1975, S. 249—278.

J. Derenbourg, Le Nom de Fangar, RÉJ 19, 1889, S. 148—149.

J. Derenbourg, Ueber einige dunkle Punkte in der Geschichte der Juden, I: R. Jochanan ben Sakkai und R. Gamliel II., MGWJ 37, 1893, S. 304.

J. W. Doeve, The Flight of Rabban Yohanan ben Zakkai from Jerusalem — When and Why?, in: Übersetzung und Deutung. Studien zu dem Alten Testament und seiner Umwelt, Festschrift A. R. Hulst, Nijkerk 1977, S. 50—65.

M. (?) Dreifuss, Das Verhältniß R' Jochanan b. Sakkaï's zum Hillel'schen Patriarchenhause, MGWJ 19, 1870, S. 568—573.

J. Goldin, Maššähû 'al bêt midrāšô šäl Rabbān Joḥānān bän Zakka'i [Einiges über das Lehrhaus R. Joḥanan b. Zakkais], in: Sephär haj-jôvel likhvôd Ṣᵉvi Wolfson, Ḥeläq 'ivrî, Jerusalem 1965, S. 69—92.

H. Graetz, Geschichte der Juden, III, Leipzig ⁵1906.

M. Hengel, Die Zeloten, Leiden/Köln ²1976.

A. Kaminka, Mäḥqārîm bam-miqrā' ûvat-talmûd ûvas-siphrût hā-rabbānît, II: Mäḥqārîm bat-talmûd [Forschungen zur Bibel, zum Talmud und zur rabbinischen Literatur, II: Forschungen zum Talmud], Tel Aviv 1950/51.

G. Kisch, A Talmudic Legend as a Source for the Josephus Passage in the *Sachsenspiegel*, Historia Judaica 1, 1938/39, S. 105—118.

W. Landau, Bilder aus dem Leben und Wirken der Rabbiner: Rabbi Jochanan ben Saccai, MGWJ 1, 1852, S. 163—176.

H. Lewy, Josephus the Pysician. A Mediaeval Legend of the Destruction of Jerusalem, Journal of the Warburg Institute 1, 1937/38, S. 221—242 = J. H. Levy, 'Ôlāmôt niphgāšîm (Studies in Jewish Hellenism), Jerusalem 1960, S. 266—293.

J. Neusner, In Quest of the Historical Rabban Yohanan ben Zakkai, HThR 59, 1966, S. 391—413.

J. NEUSNER, Priestly Views of Yochanan ben Zakkai, Kairos 11, 1969, S. 306—312.
J. NEUSNER, A Life of Yohanan ben Zakkai, Studia Post-Biblica 6, Leiden ²1970.
J. NEUSNER, Development of a Legend. Studies on the Traditions Concerning Yoḥanan ben Zakkai, Studia Post-Biblica 16, Leiden 1970.

C. ROTH, The Pharisees in the Jewish Revolution of 66—73, JSS 7, 1962, S. 63—80.

A. J. SALDARINI, Johanan ben Zakkai's Escape from Jerusalem. Origin and Development of a Rabbinic Story, JSJ 6, 1975, S. 189—204.
S. SAFRAI, Beḥînôt ḥadāšôt liv'ājat ma'amādô ûma'aśāw šäl Rabbān Jôḥānān bän Zakka'i le'aḥar ha-ḥûrbān [Neue Aspekte zum Problem der Stellung und Wirksamkeit R. Joḥanan b. Zakkais nach der (Tempel)zerstörung], in: In Memory of Gedaliahu Alon. Essays in Jewish History and Philology, [Tel Aviv] 1970, S. 203—226.
A. SCHALIT, Die Erhebung Vespasians nach Flavius Josephus, Talmud und Midrasch. Zur Geschichte einer messianischen Prophetie, in: Aufstieg und Niedergang der römischen Welt, II 2, hrsg. von H. TEMPORINI und W. HAASE, Berlin–New York 1975, S. 208—327.
A. SCHLATTER, Jochanan ben Zakkai, der Zeitgenosse der Apostel, Beiträge zur Förderung christl. Theologie 1,3,4, Gütersloh 1899 (vgl. dazu L. BLAU, MGWJ 43 = N.F. 7, 1899, S. 548—561).
H. SCHRECKENBERG, Die Flavius-Josephus-Tradition in Antike und Mittelalter, Leiden 1972.
D. SPIEGEL, Die Kaiser Titus und Hadrian im Talmud und Midrasch sowie bei den zeitgenössischen Geschichtsschreibern, Wien 1906, S. 10—16.
J. SPITZ, Rabban Jochanan ben Sakkai, Leipzig 1883.
M. STEIN, 'Ten lî Javnäh weḥakhāmähā' ['Gib mir Jabne und seine Weisen'], Zion 3, 1937/38, S. 118—122.

E. E. URBACH, Megammôt dātijjôt weḥävrātijjôt betôrat ha-ṣedāqāh šäl ḤZ"L [Religiöse und soziale Tendenzen in der rabbinischen Lehre von der Wohltätigkeit], Zion 16, 1950/51, S. 1—27.
E. E. URBACH, Haj-jehûdîm be'arṣām bitqûphat hat-tannā'îm [Die Juden in ihrem Land in der Periode der Tannaiten], Beḥînôt 4, 1952/53, S. 61—72.
E. E. URBACH, ḤZ"L, Pirqê 'ämûnôt wede'ôt, Jerusalem 1969 = The Sages — Their Concepts and Beliefs, Jerusalem 1975.

Midrash: Palestinian Jews and the Hebrew Bible in the Greco-Roman Period

by GARY PORTON, Urbana, Ill.

Contents

I. Introduction

The scholarly study of midrash is in its infancy. Until the fourth and fifth decades of this century the studies of ZUNZ[1], GEIGER[2], BACHER[3], and STRACK[4] supplied most of our knowledge of this literature. ISAAC HEINEMANN's classic study of midrash, in which he undertook a philosophical investigation and justification of this literature, first appeared in 1949[5]. This work was directed against the scholars of the previous century who had dismissed midrash as fanciful and unimportant. The studies of RENÉE BLOCH, first published in 1954, drew attention to the literary and historical problems posed by the midrashic literature[6]. Her work was partly responsible for a renewed interest in the midrashic character of some biblical passages and a realization of the importance of targumic and cognate literature for the study of midrash. GEZA VERMES has drawn more attention to numerous non-rabbinic and non-Jewish parallels to many stories found in the exegeses of the rabbis[7]. He has also investigated the 'midrashic' element in the literature from Qumran and in the *targumim*. Most recently ADDISON

[1] L. ZUNZ, Die gottesdienstlichen Vorträge der Juden (Frankfurt-am-Main: 1832). Second edition appeared in 1892. Our references are to the 1966 reprint.

[2] A. GEIGER, Urschrift und Übersetzung der Bibel in ihrer Abhängigkeit von der inneren Entwicklung des Judentums (Breslau: 1857). Reprinted in 1928.

[3] W. BACHER, Die Agada der Tannaiten (Straßburg: 1884—1890), 2 vols. Second edition appeared in 1903. ID., Die Agada der palästinensischen Amoräer (Straßburg: 1892—1899), 3 vols. ID., Die Agada der babylonischen Amoräer (Straßburg: 1878). Second edition appeared in 1913. ID., Die exegetische Terminologie der jüdischen Traditionsliteratur (Leipzig: 1899—1905), 2 vols. Reprinted in one volume in 1965. Our references are to the 1965 reprint.

[4] H. STRACK, Einleitung in Talmud und Midrasch (München: 1887). One should also mention the following works as being important in the formation of modern ideas about midrash: D. HOFFMANN, Zur Einleitung in die halachischen Midraschim (Berlin: 1887). H. ALBECK, Untersuchungen über die halakischen Midraschim (Berlin: 1927).

[5] I. HEINEMANN, The Paths of Agadah [דרכי האגדה] (Jerusalem: 1949). Our references are to the second edition issued in 1954.

[6] R. BLOCH, Écriture et tradition dans le judaïsme — Aperçus à l'origine du Midrash, Cahiers Sioniens VIII (1954), pp. 9—34. ID., Note méthodologique pour l'étude de la littérature rabbinique, Recherches de Science Religieuse XLIII (1955), pp. 194—227. ID., Note sur l'utilisation des fragments de la Géniza du Caire pour l'étude du Targum palestinien, Revue des Etudes Juives XIV (1955), pp. 5—35. ID., Quelques aspects de la figure de Moïse dans la tradition rabbinique, Moïse l'Homme de l'Alliance (Paris: 1955), pp. 93—167. ID., Art. 'Midrash' in: Supplément au Dictionnaire de la Bible, ed. L. PIROT (Paris: 1950), V, cols. 1263—1280.

[7] G. VERMES, A propos des commentaires bibliques découverts à Qumrân, Revue d'Histoire et de Philosophie Religieuses XXXV (1955), pp. 95—103. ID., The Symbolic Interpretation of Lebanon in the Targums, Journal of Jewish Studies IX (1958), pp. 1—12. ID., Bible and Midrash: Early Old Testament Exegesis, The Cambridge History of the Bible, eds. P. ACKROYD ond C. EVANS (Cambridge: 1970) I, pp. 119—231. ID., Scripture and Tradition in Judaism (Leiden: 1961). ID., Post-biblical Jewish Studies (Leiden: 1977).

WRIGHT has investigated midrash from the point of view of a literary genre[8].

While these scholars have made possible important advances in our knowledge and understanding of midrash, many problems still exist. On the one hand, some of the basic assumptions current in the nineteenth century concerning the purpose, nature, *Sitz im Leben*, and origin of midrash have been accepted by modern scholars without criticism. On the other hand, the works of BLOCH, VERMES, WRIGHT, and TOWNER[9] have demonstrated the existence of midrashic prototypes in the Bible and the presence of thematic parallels to rabbinic stories in non-rabbinic and non-Jewish texts. The importance and scope of these parallels still are unclear. In this essay we shall reconsider some basic assumptions about midrash and delineate the distinctive traits of the various types of midrashic activity.

II. דרש*—DRŠ and* מדרש*—MDRŠ*

1. *DRŠ* in the Bible

The Hebrew term for biblical exegesis is *MDRŠ*, a noun derived from the root *DRŠ*. GERTNER writes that "the fundamental notion of *DRŠ* in the Bible is that of inquiring and investigating"[10]. Ezra 7:10[11], however, is the first instance in which *DRŠ* is employed with reference to a written text. Before this time, God[12] or a human king[13] appear as the object of *DRŠ*[14]. "From now [the time of Ezra 7:10] onwards", writes GERTNER, "nothing in the religious and national life of the people could be decided upon without 'inquiring of' the text"[15].

HEINEMANN has attempted to demonstrate that in the Bible *DRŠ* means to make an effort to adopt the laws; that is, it means more than mere inquiry[16]. In support of his hypothesis, HEINEMANN cites Psalm

[8] A. WRIGHT, The Literary Genre Midrash (New York: 1967).

[9] W. TOWNER, The Rabbinic 'Enumeration of Scriptural Examples' (Leiden: 1973).

[10] M. GERTNER, Terms of Scriptural Interpretation: A Study in Hebrew Semantics, Bulletin of the School of Oriental and African Studies XXV, 1 (1962), p. 5.

[11] כי עזרא הכין לבבו לדרוש את תורת יהוה ולעשת וללמד בישראל חק ומשפט. "For Ezra directed his heart to investigate the Torah of Yahweh and to do and to teach in Israel statute[s] and judgment[s]."

[12] For example, Genesis 25:22, Exodus 18:15, I Samuel 9:9, I Kings 22:8, Ezekiel 20:1.

[13] For example, II Chronicles 30:10.

[14] GERTNER, loc. cit.

[15] Ibid.

[16] I. HEINEMANN, The Development of Technical Terms for the Exegesis of Scripture: I: [התפתחות המונחים המקועים לפירוש המקרא א. דרש] Leshonenu XIV, 3—4 (1946), pp. 182—183.

119:155: "Far from the evil ones is salvation, for they do not seek (דרשו—*DRŠW*) your statutes." He argues that in this verse *DRŠW* means to obey the statutes rather than to investigate them. Similarly in Psalm 119:94, "I am yours, save me, for your commandments I have sought (דרשתי—*DRŠTY*)", *DRŠTY* connotes observance of the commandments. HEINEMANN offers I Chronicles 28:8 as further support for his view[17]. However, these few examples do not suffice for the explanation of *DRŠ* throughout the whole of biblical literature. The numerous instances in which God appears as the object of *DRŠ* suggests that the term has a wider range of meaning than HEINEMANN is willing to admit. Apparently, the term most often denoted inquiry or investigation; however, by the end of the biblical period, *DRŠ* had also acquired the sense of "inquiring in order to do"[18].

2. *DRŠ* at Qumran and in Rabbinic Literature

In the documents from the Qumran community, *DRŠ* has a variety of meanings. GERTNER translates the root as searching, inquiring, seeking, visiting, caring for, desiring, wishing, studying, investigating, and interpretating[19]. GERTNER and HEINEMANN agree that in the Tannaitic[20] literature *DRŠ* signifies some type of logical deduction[21]. The latter emphasizes that this meaning does not appear before the Tannaitic period. Even though Shemaiah and Abtalion are called דרשנין—*DRŠNYN* in the Babylonian Talmud[22] because they logically derive laws from Scripture, HEINEMANN astutely notes that the term was probably assigned to them, at the earliest, in the Tannaitic period; therefore, its meaning reflects that age and not the pre-Tannaitic period during which the sages allegedly lived[23]. GERTNER

[17] ועתה לעיני כל ישראל קהל יהוה ובאזני אלהינו שמרו ודרשו כל מצות יהוה אלהיכם למען תירשו את הארץ הטובה והנחלתם לבניכם אחריכם עד עולם. "And now before the eyes of all Israel, the congregation of Yahweh, and in earshot of our God, keep and investigate all the commandments of Yahweh, your God, so that you shall inherit the good land and you shall cause your sons after you to inherit it forever."

[18] The sole important uncontested appearance of דרש in the Apocrypha is Ben Sira 32:18: "He that seeks God will receive discipline, and he who resorts to him diligently will obtain favor. He that seeks the law shall gain her." HEINEMANN, art. cit., pp. 184—185.

[19] GERTNER, art. cit., p. 11.

[20] The first two centuries of our era are designated the Tannaitic period. The documents under discussion are Mishnah, Tosefta, Mekhilta, Sifra, Sifré.

[21] HEINEMANN, art. cit., p. 185.

[22] Pesaḥim 70b: אמר אם יבוא אליהו ויאמר להם לישראל מפני מה לא חגגתם חגיגה בשבת מה הן אומרים לו תמהני על שני גדולי הדור שמעיה ואבטליון שהן חכמים גדולים ודרשנין גדולים ולא אמרו להן לישראל הגיגה דוחה את השבת. "He said: 'If Elijah should come and say to Israel, Why did you not sacrifice the *ḥagigah* on the Sabbath? what would they say to him? I am astonished at the two great men of the generation, Shemaiah and Abtalion, who are great sages and great expositors but have not said to Israel, The *ḥagigah* overrides the Sabbath.'"

[23] Shemaiah and Abtalion are traditionally dated in the first century before our era. H. STRACK, Introduction to the Talmud and Midrash (New York: 1965), p. 108.

stresses that in rabbinic literature *DRŠ* is exclusively connected with Torah; it has lost its more general import which it possessed in the biblical literature[24]:

> "In midrashic literature *DRŠ* does occasionally still occur in the old biblical sense of investigating and inquiring[25]. But its main use there is as a technical term for typical midrashic interpretation. All ways of this interpretation are called *darash*: interpretation by the strict hermeneutical rules, metaphorical or allegorical interpretation, and interpretation by means of all the devices and skill and artifice known and used in midrash[26]."

3. *MDRŠ* in the Bible

The noun *MDRŠ* appears twice in the Bible. II Chronicles 13:22 reads: "And the rest of the things of Abijah and his words and his ways are written in the midrash of the prophet Iddo (במדרש הנביא עדו—*BMDRŠ HNBY' 'DW*)." II Chronicles 24:27 states: "And as for his sons and the many oracles against him and the founding of the house of God, these are written upon the midrash of the book of kings (על מדרש ספר המלכים—*'L MDRŠ SPR HMLKYM*)." Bloch assumes that the term denotes the same idea in 'Chronicles' as it does in rabbinic literature: «*Il est probable que lorsque le Chroniqueur emploie le terme, il fait allusion à des ouvrages historiques qui glosent l'Écriture dans un but d'instruction et d'édification*[27].»

[24] Gertner, art. cit., p. 8.

[25] Mishnah Sanhedrin 4:1: אחד דיני ממונות ואחד דיני נפשות בדרישה. "The laws of money and the laws of persons are the same with regard to examination." Mishnah Baba Metziah 2:7: אמר את האבדה ולא אמר סימניה לא יתן לו והרמאי אף על פי שאמר סימניה לא יתן לו שנאמר עד דרוש אחיך אותו עד שתדרוש את אחיך אם רמאי הוא אם אינו רמאי. "If he named what was lost but could not describe its special marks, it may not be given to him; and it may not be given to a [known] deceiver even though he described its special marks, for it is said: Until thy brother is inquired concerning it (Deut. 22:2) [which means] until you shall inquire of your brother whether he is a deceiver or not a deceiver."

[26] Gertner, art. cit., pp. 6—7. Gertner notes that in Mishnah Sheqalin 1:4 *DRŠ* means to study and infer by analysis: אמר לו יוחנן בן זכאי לא כי אלא כל כהן שאינו שוקל חוט אלא שהכהנים דורשים מקרא זה לעצמן כל כהן כליל תהיה לא תאכל. "Said to him Rabban Yoḥanan b. Zakkai: Not so! Rather, if a priest did not pay the *sheqel* he committed a sin: but the priests used to expound this verse to their advantage: And every meal offering of the priest shall be wholly burnt: it shall not be eaten (Lev. 6:23) . . . ."

[27] R. Bloch, 'Midrash', Dictionnaire de la Bible, Supplément, V, col. 1264. Similarly S. R. Driver writes: "To judge from the title, the book here referred to will have been a work on the Book of Kings, developing such incidents as were adapted to illustrate the didactic import of the history. And this seems in fact to be the motive which prevails in many of the narratives in the Chronicles: they are pointed illustrations of some religious or moral truth . . . ." S. R. Driver, An Introduction to the Literature of the Old Testament (Cleveland and New York: 1963), p. 529.

Bacher suggests that the term means book, essay, or study[28], and Zeitlin describes the midrash mentioned in 'Chronicles' as a book in which were recorded the inquiries of the kings and the answers and the explanations of the prophets[29]. Gertner interprets *MDRŠ* as narrative or account[30]. Lieberman, on the other hand, doubts that the term carries the technical meaning of rabbinic times. He notes that the Septuagint translates *MDRŠ* as βιβλίον or γραφή[31]. Finkelstein claims that the *MDRŠ* of the prophet Iddo was a collection of oracles. The *MDRŠ* of the book of kings was "probably our book of kings". It was called a *MDRŠ* because it was "an authoritative prophetic production". He concludes that *SPR* in II Chronicles 24:27 is a scribal interpolation to make clear to a later generation the obsolete meaning of *MDRŠ*[32]. The obscure nature of these passages leads us to support Wright's conclusion that "none of the theories of the meaning of *MDRŠ* in Chronicles is without at least apparent difficulties, and there is no real basis available yet for deciding between them"[33].

4. *MDRŠ* at Qumran and in Rabbinic Literature

MDRŠ possesses a variety of meanings in the literature from the caves of the Dead Sea. It refers to juridical investigation, study of the law, and interpretation. Wright concludes that although the term denotes interpretation by the time of the Qumran community, it does not of itself connote biblical interpretation. However, when used in connection with Scripture, *MDRŠ* seems to have a more comprehensive meaning than *PYRWŠ* or *PŠR*[34].

In rabbinic literature *MDRŠ* has achieved the status of a technical term. While it still may mean study or inquiring in a general sense, its main use is to designate Scriptural interpretation. The term signifies both the process whereby Scripture is expounded and the product of this exegesis[35].

5. Conclusions

Our review of the linguistic evidence indicates that only in the first centuries of the common era did the terms *DRŠ* and *MDRŠ* attain the

[28] W. Bacher, Die exegetische Terminologie der jüdischen Traditionsliteratur (Leipzig: 1899), I, p. 104: „*Thatsächlich wird beim Chronisten nichts anderes bedeuten als Buch, Schrift* . . . ."

[29] S. Zeitling, Midrash: A Historical Study, Jewish Quarterly Review, XLIV (1953), pp. 24—25.

[30] Gertner, art. cit., pp. 10—11.

[31] S. Lieberman, Hellenism in Jewish Palestine (New York: 1950), p. 48.

[32] L. Finkelstein, The Origin of the Synagogue, American Academy for Jewish Research: Proceedings III (1930), p. 56.

[33] Wright, op. cit., p. 37.

[34] Ibid., pp. 40—41.

[35] Gertner, art. cit., p. 9.

technical meaning of searching Scripture and producing comments upon the Holy Text. In rabbinic literature the terms are intimately connected with the Hebrew Bible and designate the process by which one interprets, explains, corrects, or expounds the text as well as the interpretation, explanation, correction, or exposition itself. We should stress, however, that the terms apply to any interpretation of Scripture and not just to those which are presently contained in our midrashic collections.

III. Definition of Midrash

1. Previous Definitions and their Problems

Many scholars have attempted to construct a concise, accurate description of midrash. However, the majority of these characterizations have been adduced from the supposed purpose of midrash or its function within the context of the Jewish society. For example, SLONIMSKY finds the essence of midrash in its consolation, "that is, [its] feeding of the life-impulse when harassed and threatened by tragic circumstances"[36]. SANDERS writes that midrash "at least means the function of an ancient or canonical tradition in the ongoing life of the community .... When one studies how an ancient tradition functions in relation to the needs of the community, he is studying midrash"[37]. WRIGHT lists BLOCH's various descriptions of midrash, the majority of which refer to the purpose and the function of the literature:

> "Renée Bloch ... has defined rabbinic midrash as a homiletic reflection or meditation on the Bible which seeks to reinterpret or actualize a given text of the past for present circumstances. Then in her discussion of biblical material ... she classifies each of the following as midrash: historical works which gloss Scripture for instruction and edification; a meditation on history, tending to give to this history a relevance for contemporary preoccupations; a re-use of traditional sacred texts with a religious reflection on their content and on the past to which they witness, making them relevant for the contemporary situation ...; the use of Scriptural texts for the purpose of edification in the light of contemporary needs; a work which alludes to earlier history and suppresses, embellishes and rearranges the traditional account and imposes a new meaning on them; a work with

[36] H. SLONIMSKY, The Philosophy Implicit in the Midrash, Hebrew Union College Annual, XXVII (1956), p. 235.

[37] J. SANDERS, Torah and Canon (Philadelphia: 1972), p. xiv.

> Scriptural reminiscences which proceeds entirely from a meditation on Scripture; a development on OT texts . . .[38]"

Since midrash had a variety of purposes[39], the above descriptions are too narrow. The element which unites the various types of midrashic literature has nothing to do with their intended purposes; rather, it is a matter of literary form. WRIGHT notes that

> "the basic midrashic structure, common to all forms that can be labeled midrash down to the smallest independent unit, is merely that one begins with a text of Scripture and proceeds to comment on it in some way. The midrashic unit must be so structured that the material contained therein is placed in the context of a Scriptural text and is presented for the sake of the biblical text"[40].

Some have argued that the Scriptural text need not be explicit. GERTNER draws a distinction between covert midrash in which neither the text, nor the midrashic idea, nor the midrashic technique is defined or mentioned and overt midrash in which the verse, idea, and most often the technique are explicitly stated[41]. Similarly, SANDERS argues that "any definition of midrash which limits its scope to the citation and use of an actual biblical passage is deficient"[42].

The suggestion that midrash does not require a clear reference to a biblical text must be rejected. While the centrality of Scripture in the life of the Palestinian Jewish community from 586 BCE to 70 CE is questionable[43], there is no doubt concerning the importance of the Hebrew Bible after the first centuries of our era[44]. Since virtually everything could be and was connected to Scripture after 70 CE, SANDERS' claim or GERTNER's covert midrash leads to the conclusion that everything was midrash. Either suggestion obliterates all distinctions within the various sorts of midrashic literature, mishnaic literature, liturgical literature[45], and mystical litera-

[38] WRIGHT, op. cit., pp. 19—20.

[39] Infra p. 111.

[40] WRIGHT, op. cit., p. 67.

[41] M. GERTNER, Midrashim in the New Testament, Journal of Semitic Studies, VII, 2 (1962), pp. 268—269.

[42] SANDERS, loc. cit.

[43] Infra p. 112ff.

[44] On the history and thought of the Babylonian Jewish community see J. NEUSNER, A History of the Jews in Babylonia (Leiden: 1969—1970), 5 vols. On the history and thought of the Jewish community in Palestine see E. SCHÜRER, A History of the Jewish People in the Time of Jesus Christ, trans. J. MACPHERSON (New York: 1881). Revised edition of vol. 1 by G. VERMES and F. MILLAR (London: 1973). S. SAFRAI and M. STERN, The Jewish People in the First Century (Philadelphia: 1974). G. F. MOORE, Judaism in the First Centuries of the Christian Era: The Age of the Tannaim (Cambridge: 1927).

[45] The liturgical poetry of the time contain Scriptural references and allusions. The *shema* itself contains three passages from Scripture. See J. HEINEMANN, Prayer in the Period of the Tannaim and the Amoraim [תפילה בתקופת תנאים ואמוראים] (Jerusalem: 1966).

ture[46]. For this reason, the citation of or the clear and unambiguous reference to a biblical text is essential for midrash. Implied midrash, covert midrash, or any other definition which eliminates the explicit reference to the biblical text should be rejected.

2. Midrash and Canon

Midrash is based on a canonical text. For our purposes, canon designates those texts which were accepted as authoritative by the community. As Östborn states: "Canon is authoritative and normative . . . ."[47]. As we shall see, this criterion raises several problems with regard to biblical texts which are described as midrash, for the term is applicable only if the verse to which the midrashic passage refers was considered authoritative by the author and the community[48]. If the original passage is canonical or proto-canonical, its later use is properly designated as midrash. However, if the prior text had not achieved canonical status, the later comment is not midrash.

3. Midrash and Revelation

Östborn convincingly argues that revelation is not a criterion for canon[49]. Revelation is, however, a basic presupposition of Jewish midrash. Jewish midrashic activity assumes that the God who created and rules the world had revealed His will on Sinai[50]. The midrashist further believed that this will was explicit and implicit in the Hebrew Bible which he possessed in a fixed form. Since it is man's task to obey the will of God, it is also his duty to discover this will. This theological presupposition which was common to all midrashists, be they a scribe, a rabbi, an Essene, or any other type of Jew, places midrash within the realm of a religious activity. The impetus for midrash was of a religious nature. Whether the interpretation sought to discover and to elucidate God's will or to validate a certain individual's claim to leadership within the Jewish community or to demonstrate God's concern for His people, it was primarily a religious activity. It was undertaken within a community which accepted as fact that the God who created the world, who made a covenant with Abraham and his descendants, and who led the Hebrews out of Egypt and into the Promised Land also revealed His will to Moses. For a work to be classified

[46] The *hekhalot*-literature is supposedly based on Ezekiel's vision of the chariot. On this literature see G. Scholem, Jewish Gnosticism (New York: 1965).

[47] G. Östborn, Cult and Canon, Uppsala Universitets Arsskrift 1950:10, pp. 16—17.

[48] Infra p. 112.

[49] Östborn, art. cit., p. 19.

[50] Moore, op. cit., I, pp. 3—323. Neusner, op. cit., III, pp. 149—158. J. Neusner, History and Torah (New York: 1965), pp. 7—29.

as midrash, the midrashist and the community must both agree on the revealed nature of the original text. Further, all must view the midrashist's activity as a sacred enterprise. These criteria become important when we attempt to classify a work such as Ezekiel's play concerning the Exodus[51]. If Ezekiel and his audience considered the Biblical text as revealed and if they believed that the play attempted to deal with God's will, we can call the play midrash. However, if Ezekiel or his audience saw the Bible as merely one example of an ancient classical text or if he wrote the play merely to re-create an interesting event of the past, the work is not midrash. It should be clear that what is midrash to one is not necessarily midrash to another. Even if Ezekiel considered the story of the Exodus as revealed and authoritative, the play would be midrash only to a Jewish community who also accepted these views; the play would not be midrash to a non-Jew.

4. Conclusions

For our purposes, midrash is a type of literature, oral or written, which has its starting point in a fixed, canonical text, considered the revealed word of God by the midrashist and his audience, and in which this original verse is explicitly cited or clearly alluded to.

IV. The Bible and Palestinian Judaism in the Hellenistic Period

1. Bible as Constitution

The majority of scholars have maintained that Judaism during the hellenistic period was a religion limited by and intimately connected with the Torah, basically as we possess it today. For this reason, they assume that midrashic activity was widespread at that time. SCHÜRER, after quoting John 7:4, "the people which knoweth not the law is accursed", writes: "Such was the fundamental conviction of post-exilic Judaism ....[52]. Its [the Law's] every requirement was a requirement of God from His people, its most scrupulous observance was therefore, a religious duty, nay the supreme and in truth the sole religious duty .... [53]." McNAMARA claims that during the Babylonian Exile the Law of Moses became "the conscious center of the religious life of the Jews .... After Ezra, the funda-

[51] On Ezekiel see K. ZIEGLER, art. 'Ezekiel', Realencyclopädie der classischen Altertumswissenschaft, ed. PAULY, VI A, 2 (1909), col. 1979. A. LESKY, Geschichte der griechischen Literatur (Bern: 1957—1958), p. 681.

[52] SCHÜRER, op. cit., II, div., 2., p. 44.

[53] Ibid., I, div. 2, p. 306.

mental law of the Jewish people was ... the law of Moses"[54]. VERMES describes the properly interpreted Scripture as "the legal charter of national life"[55], and WRIGHT calls the Law the "organizing principle of the community" after the Babylonian Exile[56].

The Samaritan Pentateuch[57], I Maccabees 1:56[58], the appearance of every biblical book with the exception of Esther at Qumran[59], the importance of the Old Testament for the nascent Christian communities, and the centrality of the Bible in rabbinic Judaism testify to the importance of the Hebrew Bible during the hellenistic period. However, these examples do not justify the claim that the Bible was the charter, constitution, or sole source of inspiration and law for the post-exilic Palestinian Jewish community. References to the centrality of the Torah in the Apocrypha and Pseudepigrapha are ambiguous, for the same word denotes Torah, Jewish tradition, and secular law. While the Torah is important for Ben Sira[60], travel and common sense are equally valued sources of authority and knowledge. Ben Sira seldom if ever mentions those laws which are central to Exodus, Leviticus, Numbers, and Deuteronomy. Books such as 'Enoch' and the 'Wisdom of Solomon' bring to light much inspirational literature which existed alongside the Torah in the intertestamental period. Wisdom literature and Apocalyptic literature have biblical prototypes; however, these do not testify to the centrality of the Torah in any meaningful sense of the word[61].

2. Bible and Priesthood

There is no doubt that Scripture was important to Palestinian Jews during the Hellenistic period; however, it was not necessarily the sole authority upon which all Jews based their lives. It clearly was not the sole authority at Qumran! The evidence indicates that the Temple and the

[54] M. McNAMARA, Targum and Testament (Shannon: 1972), pp. 22—23.

[55] VERMES, Bible and Midrash, p. 201.

[56] WRIGHT, op. cit., p. 49.

[57] On the Samaritan Pentateuch see J. PURVIS, The Samaritan Pentateuch and the Origin of the Samaritan Sect (Cambridge: 1968).

[58] This passage refers to privately owned scrolls of the Law: "And wherever they found the book of the Law, they tore them up and burned them, and if anyone was found to possess a book of agreement or respected the Law, the king's decree condemned him to death." E. GOODSPEED (trans.), The Apocrypha: An American Translation (New York: 1959), p. 378.

[59] F. CROSS, The Ancient Library of Qumran (Garden City: 1961), p. 40.

[60] The best discussions of Ben Sira are found in R. H. PFEIFFER, History of New Testament Times (New York: 1949) and M. HENGEL, Judentum und Hellenismus (Tübingen: 1969). Second edition 1973.

[61] On Apocalyptic literature see P. HANSON, The Dawn of Apocalyptic (Philadelphia: 1975). ID., Jewish Apocalyptic against its Near Eastern Environment, Revue Biblique LXXVIII (1971), pp. 31—58. ID., Old Testament Apocalyptic Re-Examined, Interpretation XXV (1971), pp. 451—479. On Wisdom literature see HENGEL, op. cit.

priesthood along with the Torah served as the authoritative guide for Palestinian Jews. The complete lack of priestly documents prevents our ascertaining the basis for priestly law; however, those portions of the Mishnah which would have been important to priests such as the sections concerning tithes, sacrifices, and purity show little contact with Scripture[62]. Further, Deuteronomy 33:8ff. indicates that the priests had their own legal traditions and their own records of revelation[63]. While these may have been similar to other traditions in Israel, the priestly revisions of earlier materials within the Pentateuch suggests that the priests did possess teachings completely apart from those held by other Jews. We know that the priesthood was the most cosmopolitan element and the least connected with the worship of Yahweh alone within the Palestinian community at the time of Ezra and Nehemiah[64]. Eventually the reforms of Ezra and Nehemiah which attempted to bring the Jewish community into concord with "the Law of Moses" by separating it from other peoples failed, and the priests soon gained control of the population[65]. If priestly law stands behind the legal system of Qumran, as most scholars assume[66], we have further examples of laws different from those found in our present Torah. Qumran also testifies to a variety of legal positions within the priestly families themselves, for the laws of Qumran supposedly are opposed to the priestly traditions current in Jerusalem. For a significant portion of the post-biblical Jewish community in Palestine the Torah was not necessarily 'the constitution'. For the rulers, their own priestly traditions which may have varied from the traditions scholars commonly call 'Torah' were central. For the common people it is likely that the priestly traditions, not the Torah, furnished the rules by which they were governed and according to which they lived. During the intertestamental period there were two possible sources of authority, two parallel but possibly conflicting paths to God: the priesthood/priestly traditions and the Torah. Until the destruction of the Temple in 70 CE, it is likely that the former were the more important.

[62] We only possess careful studies of some of the laws of purity; see infra, n. 77. However, my impression is that the connection between the biblical discussions of tithing and the laws contained in Mishnah *zera'im* as well as the relationship between the laws of sacrifices in the Bible and Mishnah *qodashim* is similar to the relationship between Mishnah *ṭohorot* and the relevant biblical verses.

[63] "And of Levi he said, Give to Levi thy Thummim, and thy Urim to thy godly one, whom thou didst test at Massah, with whom thou didst strive at the waters of Meribah . . . . They shall teach Jacob thy ordinances, and Israel thy law . . . ." וללוי אמר תמיך ואוריך לאיש חסידך אשר נסיתי במסה תריבהו על מי מריבה .... יורו משפטיך ליעקב ותורתך לישראל. R. DEVAUX, Ancient Israel (New York: 1965), II, pp. 345—357. SCHÜRER, op. cit., I, div. 2, p. 313. On the date of these verses see F. CROSS and D. N. FREEDMAN, The Blessing of Moses, Journal of Biblical Literature LXVII (1948), pp. 203—204, n. 28. See also J. BLENKINSUPP, Prophecy and Priesthood in Josephus, Journal of Jewish Studies XXV, 2 (1974) who argues that the priests in the hellenistic period believed they received direct revelations from God.

[64] M. SMITH, Palestinian Parties and Politics that Shaped the Old Testament (New York: 1971), pp. 99—147.

[65] Ibid., pp. 148—192. [66] Infra, n. 142.

One should not conclude that the study of Torah did not occur during this period. Scholars suggest that the scribes, סופרים—*Soferim*, were chiefly concerned with the study and transmission of the Bible. Rabbinic sources state that the *Soferim* added certain diacritical marks to the biblical text to note emendations[67]. LIEBERMAN posits that the scribes made actual changes in the text itself[68]. He describes the *Soferim* as grammarians "who engaged in the same activity which was pursued by the Alexandrian scholars"[69]. The scribes have been credited with delivering sermons in midrashic form and with teaching the Torah to the people[70]. Although we have no direct knowledge concerning the scribes' activity, if anyone during this period did concern himself with the text of Scripture and did engage in midrashic activities, he must have been among the scribes[71].

With the destruction of the Temple, one source of authority and one path to God ended. Now, some held that one could find God only through Torah, by studying its teachings and by observing its commandments[72]. The destruction of the Temple and the appropriation of the Hebrew Bible by the early Christians helped to focus the attention of the Pharisees and the rabbis on the Bible. This point, however, should not be overstated. FRANKEL's assertion that rabbinic literature is concerned "mainly with the exegetical treatment of the Bible and the systematic development of the law derived from it"[73] is false! The Talmud is not "merely interpretation of the Bible"[74]. There is an entire corpus of Tannaitic literature which is not midrash. The major collection of Tannaitic statements, primarily legal, the Mishnah, is not a commentary on the Bible[75]. Its biblical citations are few and far between. It has been shown that in many cases these citations are later additions to the text[76]. NEUSNER has shown that many of the mishnaic laws of purity have little relation to the biblical texts upon which they are supposedly based[77].

[67] LIEBERMAN, op. cit., p. 21. D. DAUBE, Rabbinic Methods of Interpretation and Hellenistic Rhetoric, Hebrew Union College Annual XXII (1949), p. 241.

[68] LIEBERMAN, op. cit., pp. 28—37.

[69] Ibid., p. 47.

[70] I. H. WEISS, The Generations and their Exegetes דור דור ודורשיו (Jerusalem: n. d.), I, p. 52.

[71] One should realize that there were many different types of scribes. Ben Sira was basically a teacher, not a biblical scholar. He wanted to write a biblical book, not study the biblical text. From the Gospels one gains the impression that there were a number of different types of scribes in first century Palestine.

[72] On Jewish responses to the destruction of the Temple see J. NEUSNER, Judaism in Crisis: Four Responses to the Destruction of the Second Temple, Judaism XXI, 3 (1972), pp. 313—327.

[73] I. FRANKEL, Peshaṭ in Talmudic and Midrashic Literature (Toronto: 1956), p. 44.

[74] Ibid., pp. 75—77.

[75] On the Mishnah see J. NEUSNER (ed.), The Modern Study of the Mishnah (Leiden: 1973).

[76] See J. NEUSNER, The Rabbinic Traditions About the Pharisees before 70 (Leiden: 1971), 3 vols. ID., Eliezer b. Hyrcanus: The Traditions and the Man (Leiden: 1973), 2 vols.

[77] J. NEUSNER, The Mishnaic Laws of Purity (Leiden: 1973—1977). The theory that midrash and mishnah are intimately connected and that the former is the basis of the

The Mishnah could have been constructed in the form of a midrash parallel to Mekhilta, Sifré, and Sifra[78]. Its laws could have been directly and unambiguously connected with Scriptural verses. With respect to the importance Sifra finds in connecting laws to Scripture, NEUSNER states:

> "One polemic fundamental to Sifra's purpose . . . is to demonstrate the inadequacy of reason unaided by revelation. Time and again Sifra asks, Does this proposition, offered with a proof-text, really require the stated proof of revelation? Will it not stand firmly upon the basis of autonomous reason unaided by Scripture? Sometimes Scripture will show that the opposite of the conclusion of reason is the result of exegesis. Therefore, the truth is to be discovered solely through exegesis. At other times, Sifra will show that reason by itself is flawed and fallible, not definitive. At important points it will seek to prove not only a given proposition, but also that that proposition is to be demonstrated solely through revelation, through exegesis of Scripture. In all it is difficult to avoid the impression that the primary purpose of the compilers of Sifra is to criticize Mishnah-Tosefta, a document notoriously uninterested in the exegetical foundations of its laws[78a]."

The fact that Mishnah is not a midrash argues against those who would claim that Pharisaic Judaism or hellenistic Judaism out of which the former grew was exclusively centered around the Torah[79].

3. Liturgical use of the Bible

Along with claiming that the Torah formed the legal basis of the Jewish community after the time of Ezra, many scholars argue that the Torah was publicly read as part of the synagogal service during the intertestamental period[80]. They further claim that midrashic activity accom-

latter is unprovable at best. This theory has been expounded most fully by J. LAUTERBACH, Midrash and Mishnah, reprinted in: J. LAUTERBACH, Rabbinic Essays, ed. L. SILBERMAN (Cincinnati: 1951), pp. 163—256. See NEUSNER's discussion of the problems with this theory in vol. VII of his 'Mishnaic Laws', pp. iii—iv, cited infra, note 78a.

78 These documents are considered Tannaitic as is the Mishnah.

78a J. NEUSNER, A History of the Mishnaic Laws of Purities, VII. Negaim Sifra (unpublished manuscript), pp. i—ii.

79 On the Pharisees see J. NEUSNER, The Rabbinic Traditions About the Pharisees before 70 (Leiden: 1971), and ID., From Politics to Piety: The Emergence of Pharisaic Judaism (Englewood Cliffs: 1973).

80 On the history of the synagogue see H. KOHL and C. WATZINGER, Antike Synagogen in Galilaea, Wissenschaftliche Veröffentlichungen der Deutschen Orient-Gesellschaft 29 (Leipzig: 1916). E. R. GOODENOUGH, Jewish Symbols in the Greco-Roman Period (New York: 1953), I, pp. 178—267. G. WRIGHT, American Schools of Oriental Research: Newsletter IX (1973—1974), pp. 7—8. H. MAY, Synagogues in Palestine, The Biblical Archaeologist Reader, eds. G. WRIGHT and D. FREEDMAN (Garden City: 1961), pp. 229—250. F. FILSON, Temple, Synagogue and Church, WRIGHT and FREEDMAN, op. cit., pp. 183—200. J. GUTMANN, The Synagogue (New York: 1975).

panied this regular, public-reading of Scripture. There is little evidence that the Torah had a liturgical function before the first century of the common era. In 'Against Apion' Josephus writes: "He [Moses] appointed the law to be the most excellent and necessary form of instruction, ordaining not that it should be heard once for all or twice or on several occasions, but that every week men should desert their other occupations and assemble to listen to the Law . . . [81]." Josephus is clear enough. The issue which concerns us is the date of the origin of this custom. Was it common before the destruction of the Temple as some scholars suggest[82]? Since Josephus refers to the public and regular reading of Scripture only in a work written at the end of the first century or the beginning of the second century of our era, we cannot assume that the practice was followed much before that time.

Many scholars employ Luke 4:16—30 as proof for the antiquity of the custom of reading the Torah in the synagogues: "And he [Jesus] came to Nazareth . . .; and he went to the synagogue as his custom was on the Sabbath day. And he stood up to read . . . ." CROCKETT claims that this passage reflects the actual practice of the Palestinian synagogues at the time of Jesus, that is, before the destruction of the Temple[83]. BÜCHLER wrote that Luke refers to an established custom[84]. Although Luke's meaning is clear, there is some question concerning the date of this passage. Recent scholarship has shown that this section is a redactional creation of Luke[85]. This means that the passage reflects a custom of Luke's time, after the destruction of the Temple.

While there is ample support for the claim that the Torah was used liturgically in the Palestinian synagogues after 70 CE[86], attempts to date the practice to the time of Ezra lack convincing support. BÜCHLER himself noted that Nehemiah 8:18[87] does not imply that the reading of the Law was to be a permanent practice[88], and WACHOLDER has drawn atten-

81 Josephus, Against Apion 2:175 trans. H. THACKERAY (Cambridge: 1966, The Loeb Classical Library).

82 McNAMARA, op. cit., p. 36.

83 L. CROCKETT, Luke iv:16—30 and the Jewish Lectionary Cycle: A Word of Caution, The Journal of Jewish Studies XVII, 1 (1966), p. 26.

84 A. BÜCHLER, The Reading of the Law and the Prophets in a Triennial Cycle, Contributions to the Scientific Study of Jewish Liturgy, ed. J. PETUCHOWSKI (New York: 1970), pp. 188—189.

85 D. HILL, The Rejection of Jesus at Nazareth, Novum Testamentum XIII (1971), pp. 161—180. H. ANDERSON, Broadening Horizons: The Rejection at Nazareth Pericope of Luke iv:16—30 in Light of Recent Critical Trends, Interpretation XVIII (1964), pp. 259—275. My colleague Professor VERNON K. ROBBINS drew my attention to these articles. Also see C. PERROT, Luc 4, 16—30 et la lecture biblique de l'ancienne Synagogue, Revue des Sciences Religieuses XLVII, 2—4 (1973), pp. 324—337.

86 The archaeological evidence supports this assertion, for the prominence of the Torah niches would indicate the importance of the Torah in the synagogue. B. GOLDMAN, The Sacred Portal (Detroit: 1966).

87 "And day by day, from the first day to the last day, he read from the book of the law of God."

88 BÜCHLER, art. cit., p. 185.

tion to the lack of evidence for the public reading of the Torah from Nehemiah to Luke[89]. The burden of proof rests upon those who would claim that the Torah was regularly read in the synagogues before 70 CE.

4. Conclusions

There was some limited midrashic activity among Palestinian Jews before 70. The supposed work of the Scribes, the earliest parts of the *targumim* and some early material from Qumran fall into this category. However, claims that the Bible as a closed, revealed text was the central force within the Jewish community and that this fact necessitated extensive midrashic activity fail to recognize the importance of the priesthood and its traditions or the wide variety of ideas and sources of authority within the Jewish society. Those who argue that the regular readings of the Torah within the synagogal service gave rise to midrash find little evidence upon which to base their theory. In short, we have little which suggests that the creation of midrash was of central importance for Palestinian Jews before the first century of our era.

V. Types of Midrashic Activity before the Second Century

1. Midrash in the Bible

Many have drawn attention to midrashic activity found within the Bible itself. VERMES suggests that A. ROBERT was the first to place the roots of the midrashic genre in the post-exilic biblical texts. The latter noted that biblical phrases reappear in those books deprived of their original meaning. In their new context a new significance has been found for them[90]. ZUNZ drew attention to the fact that 'Chronicles' is called midrash because it is the "exposition and reworking of Kings"[91]. SCHÜRER described 'Chronicles' as "a very instructive example of the historical midrash"[92]. WEINGREEN has written that rabbinic midrashic methods are parallel to those employed by the writer of 'Chronicles'[93]. ZUNZ further described Ezekiel as a type of midrash, for it contains the oldest traces of modifica-

[89] J. MANN, The Bible as Read and Preached in the Old Synagogue, prolegomenon by B. Z. WACHOLDER (New York: 1971), I, p. xv.
[90] VERMES, Scripture and Tradition, p. 4.
[91] ZUNZ, op. cit., p. 38. Cf. WEISS, op. cit., I, p. 49.
[92] SCHÜRER, op. cit., I, div. 2, p. 340.
[93] J. WEINGREEN, The Rabbinic Approach to the Study of the Old Testament, Bulletin of the John Ryland's Library XXXIV (1951—1952), pp. 186—187.

tion of Pentateuchal law[94]. BRUCE argues that expressions in Ezekiel and Habakkuk call to mind phrases in earlier prophetic texts; therefore, the former can be considered to contain midrashic passages[95]. BRUCE, among others[96], has suggested that some of the titles in the 'Book of Psalms' reflect midrashic activity: "The titles which give 'historical' information about various Psalms belong to the history of early biblical interpretation and the same may be said of some of the titles which attach certain Psalms to specific cultic occasions[97]." VERMES states that Deuteronomy is partly the result of midrashic activity[98].

It is difficult to ascertain if these biblical passages meet the criteria for midrash we have noted above. It is exceedingly hard to determine whether or not the original passage had achieved canonical status and was considered part of God's revelation at the time it was reworked or commented upon. While the Psalm titles appear to meet our criteria, it is unclear whether or not 'Chronicles' does. In any case, TOWNER's warning that the Bible simply does not comment upon itself in the same manner as non-biblical texts do seems correct[99]. If one compares the biblical passages classified as midrash with the following examples, he will see basic differences in outlook between the two sets of writers.

2. *Targumim*

As Ben Sira's grandson implied, translation involves interpretation:

> "You are therefore invited to read it through, with favorable attention and to excuse us for any failures we may seem to have made in phraseology, in what we have labored to translate. For things once expressed in Hebrew do not have the same force in them when put into another language; and not only this book, but the Law itself, and the prophecies, and the rest of the books, differ not a little in translation from the original[100]."

Our interest centers on the *targumim* which were produced in Palestine during the first centuries of our era. We shall discuss the major Aramaic translations of the Pentateuch: Onkelos, Pseudo-Jonathan, and Neofiti I.[101].

94 ZUNZ, op. cit., p. 45.

95 F. F. BRUCE, The Earliest Old Testament Interpretation, Oudtestamentische Studiën XVII (1972), pp. 38—40.

96 Cf. B. CHILDS, Psalm Titles and Midrashic Exegesis, Journal of Semitic Studies XVI (1971), pp. 137—150. My colleague Professor DAVID L. PETERSEN drew my attention to this article.

97 BRUCE, art. cit., pp. 45ff.

98 VERMES, Bible and Midrash, p. 199.

99 TOWNER, op. cit., p. 1.

100 GOODSPEED, op. cit., p. 223.

101 The *targumim* to the prophets and writings are much later. For a bibliography for the study of *targum* see VERMES and MILLAR, op. cit., pp. 99—114.

Onkelos is more or less a literal translation of the text[102]. Most of the paraphrases occur in the poetic passages, such as Genesis 49[103]. The general opinion is that Onkelos originated in Palestine and was completed in Babylonia. KUTSCHER writes: "The eastern elements in the T[argum] O[nkelos] can easily be explained ... by the fact of its transmission in Babylonia. But it would be difficult to account for the presence of western elements if it had originated in the east ... [104]." Since the Babylonians received many of their traditions from Palestine, one could assume that they also received their Targum from the west[105]. KAHLE, on the other hand, believed that Onkelos originated in Babylonia. Since Onkelos is not cited in Palestinian documents and since the former became important late in the rabbinic period when the western academies had already declined, KAHLE concludes that Onkelos is an eastern, Babylonian, document[106]. The exact date at which Onkelos was edited is uncertain. GEIGER suggested the fourth century[107]. DIAZ MACHO argues that since Onkelos is based on the Massoretic text of the Hebrew Bible, the former could not have been composed before the end of the second Jewish commonwealth[108].

Pseudo-Jonathan covers most of the Pentateuch[109]. It is a composite work, at times reproducing Onkelos verbatim and at times following the Palestinian Targum. Pseudo-Jonathan contains a number of unique paraphrases and some interpolations from midrash[110]. We find some late references in this translation such at the names of Mohammed's wife and daughter[111], the names of the six orders of the Mishnah[112], and the name Constantinople[113]. The paraphrases unique to this *targum* form a unit and often presuppose one another[114]. Some scholars believe Pseudo-Jonathan is merely Onkelos revised by the older forms of the Palestinian Targum[115]. DIAZ MACHO suggests that Pseudo-Jonathan is a combination of Onkelos with the Palestinian Targum; the latter formed the basis and was modified

102 ZUNZ, op. cit., p. 66. MCNAMARA, op. cit., p. 173.

103 MCNAMARA, op. cit., p. 175.

104 E. KUTSCHER, The Language of the Genesis Apocryphon, Scripta Hierosolymitana IV (1958), p. 10. For a complete discussion of the age of Onkelos see R. LEDÉAUT, Introduction à la littérature Targumique (Rome: 1966), pp. 78—84.

105 Ibid., pp. 9ff.

106 P. KAHLE, The Cairo Geniza, second edition (Oxford: 1959), pp. 191ff.

107 GEIGER, op. cit., p. 1.

108 DIEZ MACHO, The Recently Discovered Palestinian Targum: Its Antiquity and Relationship with other Targumim, New Testament Studies, Congress Volume (1959), p. 245.

109 For a list of the verses missing from Pseudo-Jonathan see MCNAMARA, op. cit., pp. 177—178. On Pseudo-Jonathan see LEDÉAUT, op. cit., pp. 90—101.

110 The passage on Exodus 14:21 appears to have been taken from Mekhilta.

111 Genesis 21:21.

112 Exodus 26:19.

113 Numbers 24:24.

114 MCNAMARA, op. cit., pp. 178—179.

115 Ibid., p. 180. LEDÉAUT has a number of charts explaining the various theories concerning the relationship of Pseudo-Jonathan to the other *targumim*. LEDÉAUT, op. cit., pp. 98—100.

by the former[116]. VERMES argues that Onkelos depends directly or indirectly on Pseudo-Jonathan[117]. The confusion concerning Pseudo-Jonathan's relationship to the other *targumim* makes the ascertation of its date impossible. McNAMARA writes, however, that portions of this targum reflect the period of John Hyrcanus and Alexander Jannaeus, roughly 134 BCE-76 BCE[118].

Neofiti I is the Palestinian Targum *par excellence*. DIAZ MACHO believes the text belongs to the time after the Greek language had penetrated Palestine. The lack of late references in Neofiti such as we find in Pseudo-Jonathan[119], and the geographical names "point to a rather ancient period"[120]. DIAZ MACHO concludes that the text must be pre-Christian, for it contains a number of paraphrases which favor the Christian interpretation of Scripture. He writes: "It is inconceivable that the Jews would embody in the Targum after the rise of Christianity a Messianic interpretation ... which works ... unambiguously in favor of Christianity[121]." WERNBERG-MØLLER has shown, however, that DIAZ MACHO's text-critical data does not support the latter's early date for Neofiti I[122]. Neofiti contains the entire Palestinian Targum to the Pentateuch apart from a number of verses omitted through homoeoteleuton. It contains innumerable marginal and occasional interlinear glosses. The text is divided according to the liturgical *parashot*[123]. McNAMARA characterizes the paraphrases of Neofiti as "rather sober"; he further notes that it lacks some of the paraphrases found in the other texts of the Palestinian Targum[124].

The following targumic renditions of Exodus 4:24—26 were translated by VERMES:

> Hebrew Bible: "And it came to pass on the road at the lodging place that Yahweh met him and sought to kill him. Then Zipporah took a flint and cut the foreskin of her son and touched it to his feet. Then she said: 'Surely you are the bridegroom of blood to me.' So he left him alone. Then she said: 'You are a bridegroom of blood because of circumcision.'"
>
> Onkelos: "And it came to pass on the way, at the lodging place, that the Angel of the Lord met him and sought to kill him. And Zipporah took a flint and cut off the foreskin of her son and approached him and said: 'May my husband be given to us by the blood of this circum-

116 DIAZ MACHO, art. cit., pp. 239f.

117 McNAMARA, loc. cit.

118 Ibid.

119 DIAZ MACHO, art. cit., pp. 229—230. Cf. LEDÉAUT, op. cit., pp. 114—121.

120 DIAZ MACHO, art. cit., p. 228.

121 Ibid., p. 226.

122 P. WERNBERG-MØLLER, An Inquiry into the Validity of the Text-Critical Argument for an Early Dating of the Recently Discovered Palestinian Targum, Vetus Testamentum XII (1962), pp. 312—330.

123 McNAMARA, op. cit., p. 184.

124 Ibid., p. 186.

cision.' And he desisted from him. Then she said: 'But for the blood of this circumcision, my husband had merited death.'"

Fragmentary Targum[125]: "And she cut off the foreskin of her son and brought it to the feet of the Destroyer, and said: 'My husband wished to circumcise, but his father-in-law did not permit him. Now may the blood of this circumcision atone for the guilt of my husband'. When the Destroyer departed from him, Zipporah gave thanks, and said: 'How beloved is the blood of circumcision which has saved my husband from the hand of the Angel of Death.'"

Pseudo-Jonathan: "And it came to pass on the way, at the lodging place, that the Angel of the Lord met him and sought to kill him because his son Gershom had not been circumcised on account of Jethro, his father-in-law, who did not permit him to circumcise him. But Eliezer had been circumcised by virtue of an agreement they had made between them. And Zipporah took a flint and cut off the foreskin of Gershom, her son, and brought what had been severed to the feet of the Destroying Angel, and said: 'My husband wished to circumcise but his father-in-law prevented him. May now the blood of this circumcision atone for my husband.' And the Destroying Angel desisted from him. Then Zipporah gave thanks, and said: 'How beloved is the blood of this circumcision which has saved my husband from the hand of the Destroying Angel[126].'"

With regard to Neofiti, VERMES writes: "From the standpoint of exegesis, Neof. contains no new element. Apart from its language, which reveals a great affinity to the Geniza fragments[127], verse 24 follows TO, and verses 25—26, notwithstanding a few stylistic differences, agree with 2TJ [Fragmentary Targum][128]."

3. Rewritings of the Biblical Accounts

A second type of midrashic activity current in first century Palestine is the rewriting of the biblical narrative. The most important examples for our purposes are the 'Liber Antiquitatum Biblicarum' [LAB] and the 'Genesis Apocryphon' [GA][129]. LAB is one of the oldest midrashic works in our possession, probably dating from the first or second century of our

[125] On the Fragmentary Targum see McNAMARA, op. cit., pp. 181—182. LEDÉAUT, op. cit., pp. 102—106.

[126] VERMES, Scripture and Tradition, pp. 181—183.

[127] On the Geniza Fragments see McNAMARA, op. cit., pp. 182—183. LEDÉAUT, op. cit., pp. 109—113.

[128] VERMES, Scripture and Tradition, p. 182, note 2.

[129] Jubilees, Philo's Life of Moses, and the early books of Josephus' 'Antiquities' fit into this category.

era[130]. Most scholars believe it was originally composed in Hebrew; however, FELDMAN has expressed some reservations about this suggestion[131]. Concerning the midrashic nature of LAB, FELDMAN writes:

> "There is a parallel between LAB and the Biblical book of 'Chronicles' in its tendency to amplify Biblical genealogies. In the narrative portions there is the same tendency in both works to amplify certain passages while omitting or glossing over others . . . Like 'Chronicles', LAB does have a number of prayers, hymns, and psalms . . . LAB may perhaps be classified as a midrashic type work rather than as a type of work resembling 'Chronicles', which restricts itself to an intensive account of David and Solomon instead of the selective history of the Israelites and which has much less legendary and apocalyptic material. A better parallel to LAB, so far as form is concerned, is that with Josephus' 'Antiquities' and with 'Targumim' . . .[132] Perhaps the most striking recurrent feature is the introduction of names and numbers that are missing from the Biblical text. This would reinforce the view that LAB accords with the talmudic statement that justifies such information in order to answer the sectarians[133]. LAB is much more individual in nature than has hitherto been recognized and is not merely an example of midrashic and targumic writing[134]."

LAB rewrites biblical history. It adds details which are missing and edits the material it reproduces by omitting, shortening, lengthening, or paraphrasing the original text. The verses upon which the comments are based are explicit, and the document arose in a religious setting[135]. According to our definition, LAB is midrash. The following examples are from James' translation. The passages spaced out here appear in the Bible:

> "The beginning of the world. Adam begat three sons and one daughter, Cain, Noaba, Abel, and Seth. And Adam lived after he begat Seth 700 years, and begat 12 sons and 8 daughters. And these are the names of the males: Eliseel, Suris, Elamiel, Brabel, Naat, Zarama, Zasam, Maathal, and Anath. And these are his daughters: Phua, Iectas, Arebica, Sifa, Tecia, Saba, Asin[136].
> And at that time the Lord spake unto his people all these words, saying, I am the Lord thy God which brought thee out of the land of Egypt, out of the house of bondage. Thou

[130] M. JAMES, The Biblical Antiquities of Philo with a prolegomenon by L. FELDMAN (New York: 1971), pp. ix–x.
[131] Ibid., pp. xxvi–xxvii.
[132] Ibid., p. xxxii.
[133] B. Baba Batra 91a: למי נפקא מינה לתשובת המינים.
[134] JAMES, op. cit., p. ixx.
[135] Ibid., pp. xxxiii–xi.
[136] Ibid., pp. 77—76.

shalt not make to thyself graven gods, neither shalt thou make any abominable image of the sun or the moon or any of the ornaments of the heaven, nor the likeness of all things that are upon the earth, nor of such as creeps in the waters or upon the earth. I am the Lord thy God, a jealous God, requiting the sins of them that sleep upon the living children of the ungodly, if they walk in the ways of their fathers, unto the third and fourth generation doing mercy unto 1000 generations to them that love me and keep my commandments. Thou shalt not take the name of the Lord thy God in vain, that my ways be not made vain. For God abominateth him that taketh his name in vain. Keep the sabbath day to sanctify it. Six days do thy work but the seventh day is the sabbath of the Lord. In it thou shalt do no work, thou and all thy labourers, saving that therein ye praise the Lord in the congregation of the elders and glorify the Mighty One in the seat of the aged (Psalm 107:32). For in six days the Lord made heaven and earth, the sea and all that are in them, and all the world, the wilderness that is not inhabited, and all things that do labour, and all the order of the heaven, and God rested the seventh day. Therefore God sanctified the seventh day, because he rested therein . . .[137]"

The 'Genesis Apocryphon', an Aramaic scroll from Qumran, retells the stories of the Patriarchs "in a somewhat stylized fashion . . . The essentials of those stories are generally preserved in this text, even though they are frequently expanded by the addition of details . . . In fact, the scroll presents a free reworking of the biblical stories"[138]. Disagreeing with BLACK's suggestion that GA is a targum, FITZMYER writes:

"It is not surprising that the scroll contains elements similar to the targum and to a midrash, for both genres were already in existence and at least in an early stage of their development, if not yet fully mature in their rabbinical form . . . Though it depends on the biblical text of Genesis and displays at times traits of targumic and midrashic composition, it is in reality a free reworking of the Genesis stories, a retelling of the tales of the Patriarchs. The GA represents then an example of late Jewish narrative writing, strongly inspired by the canonical stories of the Patriarchs, but abundantly enhanced with imaginative details. It is hardly likely that this text was used in the synagogue like a targum, but was most likely composed for a pious and edifying purpose[139]."

[137] Ibid., pp. 107—108.
[138] J. FITZMYER, The Genesis Apocryphon of Qumran Cave 1 (Rome: 1966), pp. 5—6.
[139] Ibid., pp. 9—10.

The following is from FITZMYER's translation; the passages spaced out are literal Aramaic renditions of the Bible:

> "[. . . and I built there an alta]r, [and I called on the name of G]o[d] ther[e . . .], and I said, 'You are indeed to [me the eterna]l [Go]d [. . .]'. Up till now I had not reached the holy mountain; so I set out for [ ] and I kept going southward [ ] until I reached Hebron. At [that time] Hebron was built, and I dwelt [for two ye]ars [there]. Now there was a famine in all this land; but I heard that [there was] gr[ai]n in Egypt. So I set out to [enter] the land of Egypt [ ] which [ ], and I arrived at the Carmon River, one of the heads of the River [ ]. Now we [ ] our land (?), and I [cro]ssed the seven heads of this river which []. Now we crossed (the border of) our land and entered the land of the sons of Ham, the land of Egypt. And I, Abram, had a dream in the night of my entering into the land of Egypt and I saw in my dream [that there wa]s a cedar, and a date-palm (which was) [very beauti]ful; and some men came intending to cut down and uproot the cedar, but leave the date-palm by itself. Now the date-palm cried out and said, 'Do not cut down the cedar, for cursed (?) is he who fells (?) the [cedar]'. So the cedar was spared with the help of the date-palm, and [it was] not [cut down]. (That) night I awoke from my sleep and said to Sarah my wife, 'I have had a dream, [and I] am frightened by this dream'. She said to me, 'Tell me your dream that I may know (it too)'. So I began to tell her this dream; [and I made known] to [her the meaning of this] dream, [and] s[aid], '[ ] who will seek to kill me and to spare you. [No]w this is all the favor [that you must do for me]; whe[rev]er [we shall be, *say*] about me, He is my brother. Then I shall live with your help and my life will be saved because of you'"[140].

4. *Pesher*

The Hebrew Bible was of the utmost importance for the Qumran community. Some have even suggested that the study of Scripture was the focal point of the religious life of the community[141]. How can we explain this phenomenon? The founder of the Qumran sect appears to have been from a priestly family, and the priestly character of the community is clear[142]. The people of Qumran saw themselves as the true priests and their

[140] Ibid., pp. 50—53.

[141] K. STENDAHL, The School of St. Matthew and Its Use of the Old Testament (Philadelphia: 1968), p. 61. Cf. W. BROWNLEE, Biblical Interpretation Among the Sectarians of the Dead Sea Scrolls, Biblical Archaeologist XIV, 3 (1951), p. 56.

[142] CROSS, op. cit., pp. 128ff. G. VERMES, The Dead Sea Scrolls in English (Harmondsworth: 1968), pp. 67ff. J. MILIK, Ten Years of Discovery in the Wilderness of Judea, trans. J. STRUGNELL (London: 1959), pp. 74—80. J. ALLEGRO, The Dead Sea Scrolls: A Reappraisal (Harmondsworth: 1966), pp. 103ff. M. BURROWS, The Dead Sea Scrolls (New

community as the authentic Temple[143]. In order to support their claims, they could not rely on the priestly traditions current in Jerusalem, for these would favor the sect's opponents. For this reason, the writers at Qumran sought proof for their allegations in the remaining source of authority, the Hebrew Bible. Scripture was one of two possible sources of authentication in Palestinian Judaism. With one source, the priestly traditions, removed from its use, the community turned to the Bible. One of the most important characteristics of midrash at Qumran is its effort to show that Scripture, especially the prophets, refers to the history of the sect. The community legitimized itself and its claims to the priesthood by demonstrating that the prophets spoke about it and not the priests reigning in Jerusalem. The midrashic works from Qumran testify to the importance of the Hebrew Bible as a means for authenticating one's claims within the Jewish community. It is important to note, however, that the *pesharim* deal with the history of the sect, and not with its various legal statements.

The commentaries from Qumran are called *pesharim*, for the term פשר is prominent in them. Usually we find a verse followed by פשרו or פשרו על "the explanation of this" or "the explanation of this word is"[144] introducing the interpretation. Consistently, the texts are seen as referring to the sect's history. ALLEGRO notes: "The Qumran commentator is not at all interested in the historical and social context of the biblical prophecy ... It is in its contemporary relevance that the interpreter is interested ...[145]." STENDAHL concurs: "The way in which DSH [commentary to Habakkuk] handles the Habakkuk text presupposes the conviction that prophecy had received its fulfillment in the events which occurred with the Teacher of Righteousness and the community he gathered together and founded around himself[146]." The basic outlook of the *pesher* is eschatological, or even apocalyptic[147]. This point of view of its author distinguishes the *pesher* from other types of midrashim.

BROWNLEE describes some of the important stylistic and literary differences between the *pesher* and the rabbinic midrashim:

> "There are fundamental distinctions of literary style between DSH and the rabbinic midrashim. DSH quotes an entire passage of Scripture and follows it with an interpretation, whose relationship to the individual words or phrases of the Scriptural citation is ascertained only after a very careful study. The *midrash*, however, often cites single words or phrases and presents directly their interpretation; thus the her-

York: 1968), pp. 160—186. For a general bibliography see C. BURCHARD, Bibliographie zu den Handschriften vom Toten Meer, Zeitschrift für die Alttestamentliche Wissenschaft, Beiheft LXXVI, Part II, Beiheft LXXXIX. Cf. H. BIETENHARD, Die Handschriftenfunde vom Toten Meer (Ḫirbet Qumran) und die Essener-Frage. Die Funde in der Wüste Juda (Eine Orientierung), above in this work, ANRW II 19,1, ed. by W. HAASE (1979).

143 CROSS, op. cit., pp. 128—129.

144 MILIK, op. cit., p. 40.

145 ALLEGRO, op. cit., p. 130. Cf. F. F. BRUCE, Second Thoughts on the Dead Sea Scrolls, second edition (Grand Rapids: 1961), pp. 70, 77.

146 STENDAHL, op. cit., p. 190.

147 CROSS, op. cit., pp. 76—78, note 35a, pp. 112—113.

meneutical principles are more easily apprehended than in DSH. The rabbinic *midrashim*, moreover, usually point up the interpretation through a question-and-answer method in which the views of various scholars are cited. . . . DSH, however, cites no authorities; and it dogmatically sets forth its exposition in block, so that the hermeneutic relationships are more elusive and often open to question . . .[148]."

A further difference is that the *pesharim* occur in only one copy, each written by one hand[149]. The multiplicity of versions we have with regard to the *targumim* and the rabbinic *midrashim* does not occur with regard to the midrash of Qumran. The commentaries from Qumran never existed in any other form. While the rabbinic *midrashim* are collections of statements whose original contexts are unknown, the comments in the *pesharim* were constructed originally as commentaries. VERMES translated the following passage from the Habakkuk commentary; the portions spaced out are the biblical verses:

"[But the righteous shall live by faith] (2:4b). Interpreted, this concerns all those who observe the Law in the House of Judah, whom God will deliver from the House of Judgment because of their suffering and because of their faith in the Teacher of Righteousness. Moreover, the arrogant man seizes wealth without halting. He widens his gullet like Hell and like Death he has never enough. All the nations are gathered to him and all the peoples are assembled to him. Will they not all of them taunt him and jeer at him saying, 'Woe to him who amasses that which is not his! How long will he load himself up with pledges?' (2:5—6). Interpreted, this concerns the Wicked Priest who was called by the name of truth when he first arose. But when he ruled over Israel his heart became proud, and he forsook God and betrayed the precepts for the sake of riches. He robbed and amassed the riches of men of violence who rebelled against God, and he took the wealth of the peoples, heaping sinful iniquity upon himself. And he lived in ways of abominations amidst every unclean defilement[150].

5. Conclusions

We have reviewed three major forms of midrashic activity current in Palestine during the first centuries of our era. The *pesher* is unique to

[148] BROWNLEE, art. cit., p. 75. Cf. G. VERMES, A propos des commentaires bibliques découverts à Qumrân, Revue d'Histoire et de Philosophie Religieuses XXXV (1955), pp. 95—103.

[149] CROSS, op. cit., p. 114.

[150] VERMES, The Dead Sea Scrolls, pp. 235—236.

Qumran. Its basic characteristic is the writer's concern with the history of the community. Its comments were clearly intended to be *midrashim*. Each was written by one hand, and each is found in only one copy. The rewritings of the Bible mainly add details missing from the biblical text. They are unified works by single authors[151]. The *targumim* are basically translations of the Hebrew Bible. Some contain elements which are quite old. Each version, however, is a literary whole. All these *midrashim* are anonymous. While the *targumim* were designed for use in the synagogues, the purposes of the other texts are unclear. In their present form, they all date from the first centuries of our era. While they testify to some midrashic activity before the destruction of the Temple, the flourish of this activity as witnessed by the composition of a large variety of complete texts dates to the period after 70 CE. Although many scholars claim that we find midrashic activity in the Hebrew Bible, the Psalm titles, 'Chronicles', and the later prophets reflect a different point of view from the authors of the midrashim we discover in the first century.

VI. Rabbinic Midrash

1. Terminology

Classifications of rabbinic midrash have been imprecise and overlapping. The oldest distinction was between *midrash halakhah* and *midrash haggadah*[152]. The former designates the Mekhilta of Rabbi Ishmael to Exodus, the Mekhilta of Rabbi Simeon b. Yoḥai to Exodus, Sifra to Leviticus, and Sifré to Numbers and Deuteronomy. This nomenclature is imprecise, for these texts contain non-halakhic comments and passages based on non-legal portions of the Bible. *Midrash haggadah* is a tautology, for BACHER has shown that *haggadah* originally meant "the development of the contents of Scripture" and that there was no original distinction between halakhic and haggadic exposition[153]. *Midrash haggadah* would mean midrash midrash. STRACK distinguishes three types of midrashim: Tannaitic, homiletic, and expositional[154]. Included in the first are Mekhilta, Sifré, and Sifra. The middle term refers to the Pesiqta Rabbati and the Pesiqta of Rav Kahana. The last refers to Genesis, Exodus, Leviticus, Numbers, Deuteronomy, Esther, Ruth, Lamentations, Ecclesiastes, and Song of Songs Rabbah. This system is inconsistent, for the first designation indicates a

[151] FITZMYER and FELDMAN do not dispute that the documents they have studied were composed by single individuals.
[152] ZUNZ, op. cit., p. 44.
[153] W. BACHER, The Origin of the Word Haggadah (Agada), Jewish Quarterly Review IV (1892), pp. 416—419.
[154] STRACK, op. cit., pp. 206—224.

period of time, while the latter two are based on literary characteristics. From a literary point of view, there are two types of *midrashim*: Homiletical and expositional. The former designates the Pesiqtot; the latter applies to the rest. The expositional *midrashim* more or less follow the biblical text verse by verse, word by word, or letter by letter. The Pesiqtot, on the other hand, deal with special sections of Scripture appropriate for special Sabbaths, not with given books or consecutive passages. This system is somewhat imprecise, for it applies to the texts as we now possess them. Since these documents are composites of originally discrete sayings and pericopae, our designations do not refer to the original statements in their original context. They are applicable only to the texts as we now have them. This nomenclature should not suggest that the method, language, or style differs between the two types; the terms refer to purely literary and organizational principles.

2. Literary features

Important literary features distinguish rabbinic midrash from the other types we have discussed. First, the rabbinic texts are collections of independent units. The sequential arrangement is the work of the editor(s). It is doubtful that the individual pericopae or statements were originally parts of a consecutive commentary to the Bible. This is in distinction to the GA and LAB which were always intended to be sequential. The fact that the *pesharim* appear in only one copy and that the interpretations would make little sense without the biblical text suggest that the interpretations contained therein originally formed a coherent, sequential work. The situation with regard to the *targumim* is less clear. The literal translations and shorter paraphrases must have been created as a continuous commentary to the text; it is possible, however, that the more expansive sections were not part of an uninterpreted rendering of the Bible in their original form. Second, we often find more than one comment per biblical unit. Several synonymous, complementary, or contradictory remarks may appear in connection with a single verse, word or letter. We find no comparable phenomenen in the other documents. Third, a large number of statements are assigned to a named sage. Unlike the other types of *midrashim*, rabbinic midrashic statements are seldom anonymous. Fourth, the rabbinic comment may be directly connected to the biblical unit or it may be part of a dialogue, a story, or an extended soliloquy. The comment may answer a question which refers to the text but which need not be connected with the text to be comprehensible. In the other forms of midrash, the comments are always directly connected with the text. Fifth, rabbinic midrash atomizes the text to a greater degree than any of the other forms of midrashic activity with the exception of the *targumim* which must of necessity deal with every element within a verse. Each word or letter may serve as the basis for an exegetical remark for the rabbis. Sixth, often the specific method which forms the basis of the comment is explicitly mentioned.

Rabbinic midrash does share some characteristics with the other forms we have investigated. Many of the themes which appear in the rabbinic texts, as well as complete pericopae, also occur in LAB, GA, the *targumim*, the New Testament and other non-Jewish materials[155]. Rabbinic midrash, like LAB, GA, and the *targumim*, often adds details to the biblical text[156], and it often translates difficult words in the manner of the *targumim*[157]. Parallels to the rabbinic methods of exegesis can also be found in the literature from Qumran and in the other literature; however, in these texts the methods are never made explicit[158]. By virtue of the nature of midrash, the rabbinic texts are no more or no less concerned with the literal meaning of the texts than are the other literatures[159].

3. Purpose

The purpose of rabbinic midrash is unclear. We cannot, however, limit ourselves to supplying one reason for all the pericopae. The variety of style suggests a variety of purposes. Many scholars believe that midrash served to relate new laws to Scripture so that the new concepts and practices would be accepted by the community[160]. This theory should not be pushed to far. Many rabbinic efforts to connect Pharisaic-rabbinic law with Scriptural passages seem to have come after the laws had already been 'canonized' in Mishnah, or at least to have developed at the same time that others were stating the laws independent of the biblical text[161]. Also, the act of joining new laws to Scripture served as much to make Scripture relevant and Jewish as it did to give authority to the laws[162]. VERMES notes that midrash was necessary to solve problems within the Scriptural texts, for it was a means of explaining away contradictions and of supplying missing details[163]. Still others have theorized that midrash served to breathe new life into the Jewish community and to keep its spirit alive[164].

155 For example see VERMES, Scripture and Tradition.

156 HEINEMANN, Paths of the Agadah, p. 21.

157 FRANKEL, op. cit., p. 133.

158 BROWNLEE, art. cit., pp. 60ff. STENDAHL, op. cit., 190ff.

159 FRANKEL, op. cit., R. LOEWE, The 'Plain' Meaning of Scripture in Early Jewish Exegesis, Papers of the Institute of Jewish Studies, ed. J. WEISS, I (London 1964), pp. 140—185.

160 BROWNLEE, art. cit., p. 71. ZUNZ, op. cit., pp. 42—43. WEINGREEN, art. cit., p. 190.

161 Supra, note 77.

162 ZUNZ, op. cit., pp. 60—63. I. WEISS, op. cit., I, p. 99. WRIGHT, op. cit., pp. 67—68.

163 VERMES, Bible and Midrash, p. 202.

164 WRIGHT, op. cit., p. 64. VERMES, Scripture and Tradition, pp. 228—229. J. HEINEMANN, Sermons within the Community in the Talmudic Period [דרשות בציבור בתקופת התלמוד] (Jerusalem: 1970), p. 8.

It is generally believed that the *midrashim*, although created by the rabbis, were directed toward the common people. Many feel that we possess actual sermons delivered in the synagogues[165]. This hypothesis is inappropriate for much of our material. First, there is no proof that the rabbis regularly preached in the synagogues; in fact, the evidence from Babylonia suggests otherwise[166]. Second, the *midrashim* are generally brief; it is doubtful that we possess actual sermons. If we have outlines of sermons, it is difficult to envision who made these outlines or under what circumstances they were constructed and transmitted. Third, the *midrashim* are often obscure and elusive. In order to understand them, one would have to have an extremely thorough and sophisticated knowledge of Scripture. Most of the *midrashim* are simply too complex for the common man to comprehend.

It is possible that many of these passages created in the schoolhouses were intended solely for the inhabitants of the schools. They may be simply the productions of holy men dealing with holy texts. We know that one attribute of a rabbi was his extensive knowledge of Scripture[167]. A passage in the Babylonian Talmud states that a judge had to be able to prove that reptiles are clean even though Leviticus clearly states the opposite[168]. To qualify as a judge, a rabbi had to demonstrate his cleverness with regard to Scripture[169]. Maimonides describes some *midrashim* as correct, some as erroneous, and some as rhetorical. He suggests that some of the passages were playful and the products of games[170]. If many of our passages were created for consumption within the schoolhouse and are a result of holy men dealing with a holy text for their own edification and pleasure, we could explain the brevity and sophistication of many of our pericopae. If these comments were all intended to be delivered as sermons to the common people, it is difficult to explain these traits. We thus must have a much broader view of the purposes of rabbinic midrash than we have had to date. Some may have been sermons, some may have been attempts to make Scripture relevent, some may have been intended to make new laws appear old, and some may have been a sort of religious game.

165 J. Heinemann, op. cit., and the opinions cited therein.

166 Neusner, History, III, pp. 234—238; IV, pp. 149—151.

167 Mishnah Avot 5:22: "Turn it and turn it again for everything is in it; and contemplate it and grow grey and old over it, and stir not from it . . ." הפוך בה והפוך בה דכולה בה ובה תחזי וסיב ובלה בה ומינה לא תזוע.

168 Sanhedrin 17a אמר רב יהודה אמר רב אין מושבין בסנהדרין אלא מי שיודע לטהר את השרץ מן התורה. "Said R. Judah, said Rav: They do not cause a person to sit in the Sanhedrin unless he knows [how] to [prove that] a creeping thing is clean from the words of Torah."

169 Lieberman, op. cit., pp. 63—64.

170 I. Heinemann, op. cit., p. 2. Frankel, op. cit., p. 29.

4. Examples

The following examples taken from a variety of *midrashim* should serve to illustrate the traits of rabbinic midrash:

"In the beginning God created... (בראשית—*BR'ŠYT*). R. Yonah in the name of R. Levi said: 'Why was the world created with a ב/*B*? Just as a *B* is closed on all its sides but opened frontward, thus you are not permitted to say: What is below [the world] and what is above [the world]. What is before [creation] and what is behind [creation]. Rather, [you may speak about events] from the day that the world was created and onward.' Bar Kappara said: 'For ask now the days past, which were before you, since the day that God created man upon the earth (Deuteronomy 4:32) [means] you may speculate [concerning things created] from the day that days were created; but you may not speculate on what was before that. And from one end of heaven unto the other (Ibid.) [means] you may investigate [this], but you may not investigate what was before this.' R. Judah b. Pazzi lectured on the Creation Story according to the interpretation of Bar Kappara. Why was it created with a *B*? To teach you that there are two worlds[171]. Another matter: Why with a *B*? Because it connotes a blessing (ברכה—*Berakah*). And why not with an א/*'A*[172]? Because it connotes a curse (ארורה—*Arurah*). Another matter: Why not with an *'A*? In order not to provide a justification for the heretics to plead: 'How can the world endure since it was created with the expression of a curse?' Hence the Holy One, Blessed be He, said: 'Lo, I will create it with the language of blessing, and would that it may stand[173]!'"

"This new moon shall be unto you (Exodus 12:2). R. Ishmael says: 'Moses showed the new moon to Israel and said to them: In this way you shall see and fix the new moon for the generations.' R. Aqiba says: 'This is one of the three things which was difficult for Moses [to understand], and the Omnipresent pointed them out to him with His finger....' R. Simeon b. Yoḥai says: 'Were not all the words spoken with Moses during the day? The new moon He showed him at night! How did He speak with him during the day and show him the new moon at night?' R. Eliezer says: 'He spoke with him during the day near darkness, and He showed him the new moon when [it became] dark[174].'"

"Your lamb shall be without blemish, a male, a year old (Exodus 12:5). [From this verse] I [can] only [learn about a lamb]

[171] ב has the numerical value of two.

[172] Since the א is the first letter of the alphabet it is logical to assume that it should be the first letter of the Bible and the letter with which God began to create the world.

[173] J. Theodor and H. Albeck, Midrash Bereshit Rabba (Jerusalem: 1965), I p. 1f.

[174] H. Horovitz and I. Rabin, Mechilta d'Rabbi Ismael (Jerusalem: 1960), p. 6.

born in this calendar year. From where [can I learn about] the whole first year [of a lamb's life even if it transverses two calendar years]? R. Ishmael used to say: 'It is an a fortiori argument. Just as the Whole Offering, which is a most important offering, is fit to come [as an offering] its entire first year as if it were its first calendar year, how much the more should the Passover-Offering, which is of lesser importance, be declared fit to come [as an offering] its entire first year as if it were its first calendar year!' R. Yosi the Galilean says: 'Just as a ram is not fit at the beginning of [its second calendar year] is fit at the end of it, how much the more should a lamb who is fit at the beginning of [its first twelve months] be fit at the end of it[175]!'"

"And it shall come to pass, that from one New Moon to another, and from one Sabbath to another, shall all flesh come to worship before Me, saith the Lord (Isaiah 66:23). Let our Master instruct us: When a Jew reciting Grace after meals on the New Moon forgets to include the words referring to the New Moon, what should he do? Our Master taught us: If he forgot and did not include the words referring to the New Moon, but at once upon his finishing the Grace remembered them before he diverted his attention from the Grace which he was saying, then he is not required to go back to the beginning of the Grace; instead he makes good the omission by appending to the Grace a short benediction: 'Blessed art Thou, O Lord our God, King of the universe, who hast given New Moons to His people Israel. Blessed art Thou, O Lord, who hallowest Israel and the New Moons.' Now in that part of the Grace which refers to the New Moon — so taught Simeon b. Abba in the name of R. Joḥanan — a man is required to say the prayer 'O Lord our God, bestow upon us the blessing of Thy festal seasons.' Thus we see that New Moons are equal in importance to the festal seasons, in keeping with the verse In the day of your gladness, both in your festal seasons and in your New Moons, ye shall blow with your trumpets (Numbers 10:10). Indeed (insofar as on both days a special prayer for the day is included in the Grace after meals) New Moons are even equal in importance to the Sabbath. So that you may state it as a fact that New Moons are equal in importance to both festal seasons and Sabbaths. And whence do we know that New Moons are regarded as equal in importance to Sabbaths? From the lesson in the prophets prescribed for the New Moon: And it shall come to pass, that from one New Moon to another, and from one Sabbath to another, shall all flesh come to worship . . . [176]."

[175] Ibid., p. 12.

[176] W. Braude, Two Chapters of Pesikta Rabbati in English Translation, Essays in Honor of Solomon B. Freehof (Pittsburgh: 1964), pp. 153—154.

VII. *Summary and Conclusions*

Midrash is a religious activity based on the biblical text. The task was similar to the Alexandrian scholars' works on the ancient Greeks. LIEBERMAN has drawn specific parallels between the text-critical enterprises of the Alexandrian grammarians and the scribes. He has noted, however, that these were independent developments; one did not borrow from the other[177]. The methods and terminology employed by the Tannaim, on the other hand, do suggest dependence on the rhetoricians[178]. DAUBE has shown that HILLEL's exegetical principles are similar in style and nomenclature to those employed by Cicero among others[179]. That the midrashic activity finds parallels in the non-Jewish Greco-Roman world should not surprise us. From the period of Ezra-Nehemiah, if not before, the Palestinians had come into close contact with the Greek world and hellenistic culture[180]. Jews spoke in, wrote in, and thought in Greek forms. As BICKERMAN has shown, the rabbis were similar to the hellenistic philosophers[181]. The rabbis in their schoolhouses discussing, 'correcting', and explaining the Bible were not greatly different from the scholars in the museum in Alexandria[182]. Both groups formed communities which were religious in character. The main difference was that the rabbis were interpreting a text revealed to the Jews by the same God who created the world and who promised a reward to those who faithfully followed His will. There are other contacts between midrash and hellenistic thought. Scholars have consistently noted the stoic, epicurean, platonic, and cynic elements in rabbinic midrash[183].

The parallels between hellenistic works and rabbinic texts should not be overstated, for at their core they are different. Midrash was based on the word of the one and only God. The Bible contained all the secrets of the universe, and midrash was a means of discovering these secrets. The Bible was the guide for human action; it was the standard against which one measured his deeds. The rabbis dealt with only one book, and that book was not of human origin. With the passing of time the study of Torah became the most holy task one could perform. It became the goal of a man's life. Its rewards were found in this world; but, more important, they

177 LIEBERMAN, op. cit., pp. 20—46.

178 Ibid., pp. 55—82.

179 DAUBE, art. cit.

180 HENGEL, op. cit., SMITH, op. cit.

181 E. BICKERMAN, La Chaine de la tradition pharisienne, Revue Biblique LIX (1952), pp. 44—54.

182 R. PFEIFFER, History of Classical Scholarship (Oxford: 1971), pp. 96—99.

183 H. FISCHEL, Studies in Cynicism and the Ancient Near East, Religions in Late Antiquity, ed. J. NEUSNER, (Leiden: 1966) pp. 372—411. H. FISCHEL, Rabbinic Literature and Greco-Roman Philosophy (Leiden: 1973). These are the most recent studies on this problem.

were fully bestowed only the world to come. The interest was not merely historical or antiquarian. The rabbis were not only interested in explaining difficult words or passages, in identifying places, in solving problems within the text. They did these things because it led to salvation, not only of Jews, but of the whole world. Midrash was the product of the rabbi's theology. In all of its forms it was a religious exercise. This was not the case with hellenistic scholarship. We have argued that midrash reached its zenith only after the Temple lay in ruins. We suggested that it was an activity intimately connected with the rabbi's view of God as Creator, Revealer, and Savior. The Torah replaced the Temple as the place where God could be found. The midrashist replaced the priest as the intermediary between God's word and humanity. Midrash replaced the sacrifices as the means of securing God's favor and of joining the upper and the lower worlds[184].

August, 1974

Selected Bibliography

ALLEGRO, J, The Dead Sea Scrolls: A Reappraisal, Harmondsworth: 1966.

BACHER, W., Die Agada der babylonischen Amoräer, Straßburg: 1878.

—, Die Agada der palästinensischen Amoräer, Straßburg: 1892—1899.

—, Die Agada der Tannaiten, Straßburg: 1884—1890.

—, Die exegetische Terminologie der jüdischen Traditionsliteratur, Leipzig: 1899—1905.

—, The Origin of the Word Haggada (Agada), The Jewish Quarterly Review IV (1892), pp. 406—429.

BICKERMANN, ELIAS, The Septuagint as a Translation, American Academy for Jewish Research: Proceedings XXVIII (1959), pp. 1—40.

BLOCH, R., Ecriture et Tradition dans le judaïsme — Aperçus à l'origine du Midrash, Cahiers Sioniens VIII (1954), pp. 9—34.

—, 'Midrash', Dictionnaire de la Bible, Supplément V, Paris: 1950, cols. 1263—1280.

—, Note méthodologique pour l'étude de la littérature rabbinique, Recherches de Science Religieuse XLIII (1955), pp. 194—227.

BROWNLEE, W. H., Biblical Interpretation among the Sectaries of the Dead Sea Scrolls, Biblical Archaeologist XIV, 3 (1951), pp. 54—76.

BRUCE, F. F., The Earliest Old Testament Interpretation, Oudtestamentische Studien XVII (1927), pp. 37—52.

—, Second Thoughts on the Dead Sea Scrolls, 2nd ed. Grand Rapids: 1961.

BÜCHLER, A., The Reading of the Law and Prophets in a Triennial Cycle, in: J. J. PETUCHOWSKI (ed.), Contributions to the Scientific Study of Jewish Liturgy, New York: 1970, pp. 181—302.

BURCHARD, C., Bibliographie zu den Handschriften vom Toten Meer, Zeitschrift für die Alttestamentliche Wissenschaft, Beihefte LXXVI (1956), pp. 1—118.

—, Bibliographie zu den Handschriften vom Toten Meer, Zeitschrift für die Alttestamentliche Wissenschaft, Beihefte LXXXIX (1965), pp. 1—359.

[184] I wish to thank my teachers and colleagues for their help in the preparation of this paper. Professors JACOB NEUSNER, WILLIAM R. SCHOEDEL, WILLIAM S. GREEN, DAVID L. PETERSEN, VERNON K. ROBBINS, and Rabbi STEVEN J. STEINBERG read early drafts of this paper and shared many important insights with me. Much contained herein is a result of the learning of these men. I gratefully acknowledge their help. Errors of judgment and fact are a result of my inabilities and not of their effort.

CHILDS, B., Psalm Titles and Midrashic Exegesis, Journal of Semitic Studies XVI (1971), pp. 137—150.
CROCKETT, L., Luke IV: 16—30 and the Jewish Lectionary Cycle: A Word of Caution, Journal of Jewish Studies XVII, 1, (1966), pp. 13—46.
CROSS, F., The Ancient Library of Qumran, Revised ed. Garden City: 1961.

DAUBE, D., Rabbinic Methods of Interpretation and Hellenistic Rhetoric, Hebrew Union College Annual XXII (1949), pp. 239—264.
DAVIES, W. D., Paul and Rabbinic Judaism, New York: 1948.
DIEZ-MACHO, A., The Recently Discovered Palestinian Targum: Its Antiquity and Relationship with the Other Targums, New Testament Studies: Congress Volume (1959), pp. 222—226.
—, Le Targum Palestinien, Revue des Sciences Religieuses XLVII, 2—4 (1973), pp. 169—231.
DRIVER, S. R., An Introduction to the Literature of the Old Testament, Cleveland: 1963.

FINKELSTEIN, L., The Mekhilta and its Text, American Academy for Jewish Research: Proceedings V (1933—1934), pp. 3—54.
—, The Origin of the Synagogue, American Academy for Jewish Research: Proceedings III (1930), pp. 3—13.
—, The Sources of the Tannaitic Midrashim, Jewish Quarterly Review XXXI, 3 (1941), pp. 211—243.
—, Studies in the Tannaitic Midrashim, American Academy for Jewish Research: Proceedings VI (1934—1935), pp. 189—228.
FISCHEL, H., Rabbinic Literature and Greco-Roman Philosophy, Leiden: 1973.
—, Studies in Cynicism and the Ancient Near East, in: J. NEUSNER (ed.), Religions in Late Antiquity, Leiden: 1966, pp. 372—411.
FITZMYER, J., The Genesis Apocryphon of Cave I: A Commentary, Rome: 1966.
FOHRER, G., Tradition und Interpretation im Alten Testament, Zeitschrift für die Alttestamentliche Wissenschaft LXXIII (1961), pp. 1—29.
FRANKEL, I., Peshaṭ in Talmudic and Midrashic Literature, Toronto: 1956.

GEIGER, A., Urschrift und Uebersetzungen der Bibel in Ihrer Abhängigkeit von innern Entwickelung des Judenthums, Breslau: 1857.
GERTNER, M., Midrashim in the New Testament, Journal of Semitic Studies VII, 2 (1962), pp. 267—292.
—, Terms of Scriptural Interpretation: A Study in Hebrew Semantics, Bulletin of the School of Oriental and African Studies XXV, 1 (1962), pp. 1—27.
GROSSFELD, B., A Bibliography of Targumic Literature, New York: 1972.

HEINEMANN, I., The Development of Technical Terms for the Explanation of Scripture, Leshonenu XIV, 3—4 (1946), pp. 166—181.
—, The Paths of Agadah, 2nd ed. Jerusalem: 1954.
HEINEMANN, J., Sermons in the Community in the Period of the Talmud, Jerusalem: 1970.

JAMES, M. R., The Biblical Antiquities of Philo with a prolegomenon by L. H. FELDMAN, New York: 1971.

KOHLER, K., The Pre-Talmudic Haggada, Jewish Quarterly Review V (1893), pp. 399—419.

LAUTERBACH, J. Z., The Arrangement and the Division of the Mekhilta, Hebrew Union College Annual I (1924), pp. 422—466.
—, Midrash and Mishnah, in: J. LAUTERBACH, Rabbinic Essays, Cincinnati: 1951, pp. 163—256.
LEDÉAUT, R., Introduction à la Littérature Targumique: Première Partie, Rome: 1966.
LIEBERMAN, S., Greek in Jewish Palestine, New York: 1942.
—, Hellenism in Jewish Palestine, New York: 1950.

LOEWE, R., The 'Plain' Meaning of Scripture in Early Jewish Exegesis, Papers of the Institute of Jewish Studies London I (1964), pp. 140—185.

MANN, J., The Bible as Read and Preached in the Old Synagogue with a prolegomenon by B. Z. WACHOLDER, New York: 1971.

MARGOLIOT, E., The Term דרש in the Talmud and the Midrashim, Leshonenu XX, 1 (1959), pp. 50—61.

MARMORSTEIN, A., The Background of the Haggadah, Hebrew Union College Annual VI (1929), pp. 141—204.

McNAMARA, M., Targum and Testament, Shannon: 1972.

MILIK, J. T., Ten Years of Discovery in the Wilderness of Judaea, translated by J. STRUGNELL, London: 1963.

MOORE, G. F., Judaism in the First Centuries of the Christian Era: The Age of the Tannaim, Cambridge: 1927.

NEUSNER, J., Eliezer b. Hyrcanus: The Tradition and the Man, Leiden: 1973.

—, From Politics to Piety: The Emergence of Pharisaic Judaism, Englewood Cliffs: 1973.

—, A History of the Jews in Babylonia, Leiden: 1965—1970.

—, History and Midrash, in: J. NEUSNER (ed.), History and Torah, New York: 1965, pp. 17—29.

—, Judaism in Crisis: Four Responses to the Destruction of the Second Temple, Judaism XXI, 3 (1972), pp. 313—327.

—, The Mishnaic Laws of Purities, Leiden: 1973ff.

—, The Rabbinic Traditions About the Pharisees Before 70, Leiden: 1971.

ÖSTBORN, G., Cult and Canon, Uppsala Universitets Arsskrift, 1950: 10, pp. 7—129.

PFEIFFER, R., History of Classical Scholarship, Oxford: 1971.

SANDERS, J., Torah and Canon, Philadelphia: 1972.

SCHÜRER, E., A History of the Jewish People in the Time of Jesus Christ, translated by J. MACPHERSON, New York: 1891.

—, The History of the Jewish People in the Time of Jesus Christ, Revised and edited by G. VERMES and F. MILLAR, Edinburg: 1973.

SEELIGMANN, I. L., Voraussetzungen der Midraschexegese, Congress Volume, Supplements to Vetus Testamentum I (1953), pp. 150—181.

SLOMOVIC, E., Toward an Understanding of the Exegesis in the Dead Sea Scrolls, Revue de Qumran VII, 1 (= XXV) (1969), pp. 3—15.

SLONIMSKY, H., The Philosophy Implicit in the Midrash, Hebrew Union College Annual XXVII (1956), pp. 235—290.

STEIN, E., Die homiletische Peroratio im Midrash, Hebrew Union College Annual VIII—IX (1931—1932), pp. 353—372.

—, Philo und der Midrash, Zeitschrift für die Alttestamentliche Wissenschaft, Beihefte LVII (Gießen: 1931), pp. 1—51.

STENDAHL, K., The School of St. Matthew and its Use of the Old Testament, Philadelphia: 1968.

STRACK, H., Einleitung in Talmud und Midrasch, München: 1887.

TOWNER, W. S., The Rabbinic 'Enumeration of Scriptural Examples', Leiden: 1973.

TOWNSEND, J., Rabbinic Sources, in: J. NEUSNER (ed.), The Study of Judaism: Bibliographical Essays, New York: 1972, pp. 37—80.

VERMES, G., A propos des commentaires bibliques découverts à Qumrân, Revue d'Histoire et de Philosophie Religieuses XXXV (1955), pp. 95—102.

—, Bible and Midrash: Early Old Testament Exegesis, in: P. R. ACKROYD and G. F. EVANS (eds.), The Cambridge History of the Bible: I, From the Beginnings to Jerome, Cambridge: 1970, I, pp. 199—231.

—, Post-Biblical. Jewish Studies, Leiden: 1977.

—, Scripture and Tradition in Judaism, Leiden: 1961.

WEINGREEN, J., The Rabbinic Approach to the Study of the Old Testament, Bulletin of the John Ryland's Library XXXIV (1951—1952), pp. 166—190.

WEISS, I. H., The Generations and their Exegetes, Jerusalem: n.d.

WERNBERG-MØLLER, P., An Inquiry into the Validity of the Text-Critical Argument for an Early Dating of the Recently Discovered Palestinian Targum, Vetus Testamentum XII (1962), pp. 312—330.

WRIGHT, A., The Literary Genre Midrash, New York: 1967.

ZEITLIN, S., An Historical Study of the Canonization of the Hebrew Scriptures, American Academy for Jewish Research: Proceedings IV (1932), pp. 121—158.

—, Midrash: A Historical Study, Jewish Quarterly Review XLIV (1953), pp. 21—36.

ZUNZ, L., Die gottesdienstlichen Vorträge der Juden, Berlin: 1832.

An Annotated Bibliographical Guide to the Study of the Palestinian Talmud

by BARUCH M. BOKSER, Berkeley, Cal.

Contents

Abbreviations

Arak. = Arakhin
Archive = See Abbreviated Citations
A. Z. = Avodah Zarah
b. = Babylonian Talmud or Bavli; ben or bar.
B.B. = Bava Batra
Bekh. = Bekhorot
Ber. = Berakhot
Bes. = Beṣah
BIA = Bar Ilan Annual
Bik. = Bikurim
B.M. = Bava Mesi'a'
B.Q. = Bava Qamma
BT = Babylonian Talmud
Dem. = Dem'ai
EJ = Encyclopaedia Judaica. Jerusalem, 1972.
Eruv. = ʿEruvin
Git. = Giṭṭin
Hag. = Ḥagigah
Hal. = Ḥallah
Hor. = Horayot
HUCA = Hebrew Union College Annual
Hul. = Ḥullin
JE = Jewish Encyclopedia. New York, 1905, 1907.
JQR = Jewish Quarterly Review
JTSA = Jewish Theological Seminary of America
Ket. = Ketubot
Kil. = Kila'im
KS = Kirjath Sepher
M. = Mishnah
Maas. = Maʿaserot
Mak. = Makot
Meg. = Megillah
Men. = Menaḥot
MGWJ = Monatschrift für die Geschichte und Wissenschaft des Judentums

M.Q.	=	Moʿed Qaṭan
MS	=	Manuscript
M.S.	=	Maʿaser Sheni
Nid.	=	Niddah
Orl.	=	ʿOrlah
PAAJR	=	Proceedings of the American Academy for Jewish Research
Pes.	=	Pesaḥim
PT	=	Palestinian Talmud, Yerushalmi
Qid.	=	Qiddushin
Qod.	=	Qodshin
R.	=	Rav, Rabbi
REJ	=	Revue des Études Juives
R.H.	=	Rosh Hashanah
San.	=	Sanhedrin
Shab.	=	Shabbat
Sheq.	=	Sheqalim
Shev.	=	Sheviʿit
Sot.	=	Soṭah
Suk.	=	Sukah
T.	=	Tosefta
Taan.	=	Taʿanit
Teh.	=	Ṭehorot
Ter.	=	Terumot
Tos.	=	Tosefta
TSJTSA	=	Text(s) and Studies of the Jewish Theological Seminary of America
y.	=	Yerushalmi, Palestinian Talmud
Yev.	=	Yevamot
Zer.	=	Zeraʿim
Zev.	=	Zevaḥim

Abbreviated Citations

The following items are repeatedly cited in the course of the paper. The first and main entry includes full bibliographical information. Thereafter the works are identified by the author's name and the date of publication. In the citation of an article in a journal, the subsequent references delete only the title of the study and are, therefore, not included here. Likewise, I do not, in general, include in the following list abbreviated, second, references within a section when the first instance includes the full bibliographical information.

ABRAMSON (1965) = SHRAGA ABRAMSON, R. Nissim Gaon. Jerusalem, 1965.

ABRAMSON (1974) = SHRAGA ABRAMSON, Inyanot BeŚifrut HaGaonim. Jerusalem, 1974.

ALBECK (1944) = CHANOCH ALBECK, Studies in the Baraita and Tosefta. Jerusalem, 1944.

ALBECK (1967) = CHANOCH ALBECK, Introduction to the Mishnah. Third ed. Jerusalem-Tel Aviv, 1967.

ALBECK (1969) = CHANOCH ALBECK, Introduction to Talmud Babli and Yerushalmi. Tel Aviv, 1969.

APTOWITZER (1938) = (A)VIGDOR APTOWITZER, Introductio ad Sefer Rabiah. Jerusalem, 1938.

Archive I (1972) = Archive of the New Dictionary of Rabbinical Literature. I. Ed. E. Y. KUTSCHER, Ramat Gan, 1972.

Archive II (1974) = Archive ..., II. Ed. M. Z. KEDDARI, Ramat Gan, 1974.

ASSIS (1976) = MOSHE ASSIS, Parallel *sugyot* in the Jerusalem Talmud (In the Tractates: Bikkurim, Shabbath, Soṭah, Makkoth, and Niddah). (Ph. D. Dissertation, Hebrew University, 1976). Jerusalem, 1976.

BARON II—VIII = SALO BARON, A Social and Religious History of the Jews, Vols. II—VIII. New York, 1952—1958. At times cited without the date, just BARON and the volume number.

BOKSER (1975) = BARUCH M. BOKSER, Samuel's Commentary on the Mishnah: Its Nature, Forms, and Content. I. Leiden, 1975.

BOKSER, Two Traditions (1975) = BARUCH M. BOKSER, Two Traditions of Samuel: Evaluating Alternative Versions, Christianity, Judasim and Other Greco Roman Cults. Studies for Morton Smith at Sixty. Ed. J. NEUSNER. Leiden, 1975. IV, 46—55.

EPSTEIN (1948) = JACOB N. EPSTEIN, Introduction to the Text of the Mishnah. Jerusalem, 1948. Indexed second edition, Jerusalem, 1964.

EPSTEIN (1957) = JACOB N. EPSTEIN, Introduction to Tannaitic Literature. Jerusalem, 1957.

EPSTEIN (1962) = JACOB N. EPSTEIN, Introduction to Amoraitic Literature. Jerusalem, 1962.

FELDBLUM (1964) = MEYER S. FELDBLUM, Professor Abraham Weiss: His Approach and Contribution to Talmudic Scholarship, in: The Abraham Weiss Jubilee Volume. New York, 1964. English section, pp. 7—80.

FELDBLUM (1969) = MEYER S. FELDBLUM, Talmudic Law and Literature. Tractate Gittin. New York, 1969.

FRANKEL (1870) = Z. FRANKEL, Mavo HaYerushalmi. Breslau, 1870. Repr. Jerusalem, 1967.

GINZBERG (1909) = LOUIS GINZBERG, Yerushalmi Fragments from the Genizah. I. (Texts and Studies of the Jewish Theological Seminary of America, Vol. III). New York, 1909. Repr. Jerusalem, 1969.

GINZBERG, Geonica I—II (1909) = LOUIS GINZBERG, Geonica I—II. (TSJTSA, Vols. I—II). New York, 1909. Repr. 1968.

GINZBERG (1928—29) = LOUIS GINZBERG, Genizah Studies in Memory of Doctor Solomon Schechter (= Ginze Schechter). I—II. (TSJTSA, Vols. VII—VIII). New York, 1928—1929. Repr. 1969.

GINZBERG (1941) = LOUIS GINZBERG, Commentary on the Palestinian Talmud. 4 vols. (TSJTSA, X, XI, XII, XXI). New York, 1941, 1961. For Vol. I. 1941, Roman numerals refer to the Introduction. Those prefaced by an H = Hebrew introduction. Those without the H = English introduction.

GOODBLATT (1975) = DAVID GOODBLATT, Rabbinic Instruction in Sasanian Babylonia. Leiden, 1975.

GOODBLATT (1979) = DAVID GOODBLATT, The Babylonian Talmud, in: ANRW II, 19.2, pp. 257—336 (= elsewhere in this volume).

HABERMANN (1952) = MEIR HABERMANN, Added chapter, 'HaTalmud HaYerushalmi', to revised ed. of RAPHEL RABBINOVICZ, Ma'amar 'al Hadpaśat HaTalmud. Jerusalem, 1952, pp. 203—222, 252—254.

HIRSCHBERG (1974) = H. Z. HIRSCHBERG, History of the Jews in North Africa. Leiden, 1974.

HOSPERS (1973) = J. H. HOSPERS, A Basic Bibliography for the Study of the Semitic Languages. I. Leiden, 1973.

KAHANA (1972) = KALMAN KAHANA, Maśekhet Shevicjt. Ḥeqer Ve'Iyun. Tel Aviv, 1972.

KASHER (1959) = MENAHEM M. KASHER and JACOB B. MANDELBAUM, Sarei Ha-Elef. A Millenium of Hebrew Authors (500—1500). New York, 1959. Supplemented in Śefer Adam Noah. Ed. ḤAYYIM LIPHSITZ, Jerusalem, 1970, pp. 213—299.

KOHN (1952) = P. JACOB KOHN, Thesaurus of Hebrew Halachic Literature. London, 1952.

KUTSCHER (1972) = See Archive I (1972) and II (1972).

LEVINE (1975) = LEE I. LEVINE, Caesarea Under Roman Rule. Leiden, 1975.

LEWIN (1933) = B. M. LEWIN, Monumenta Gaonica: Methiboth [Śefer Metivot]. Jerusalem, 1933. Repr. 1973.

LEWY (1895—1914) = I. LEWY, Introduction and Commentary to Talmud Yerushalmi. B.Q. I—VI. Jahresbericht des jüdisch-theologischen Seminars Fraenckel'scher Stiftung. 1895—1914. Repr. Jerusalem, 1970.

LIEBERMAN (1929) = SAUL LIEBERMAN, On the Yerushalmi. Jerusalem, 1929.
LIEBERMAN (1931) = SAUL LIEBERMAN, Talmud of Caesarea (Suppl. to Tarbiz, II). Jerusalem, 1931.
LIEBERMAN (1934) = SAUL LIEBERMAN, HaYerushalmi Kiphshuto. Jerusalem, 1934.
LIEBERMAN, TR. (1937—39) = SAUL LIEBERMAN, Tosefeth Rishonim. 4 Vols. Jerusalem, 1937—1939.
LIEBERMAN (1941) = SAUL LIEBERMAN, Greek in Jewish Palestine. N.Y., 1941, 1964².
LIEBERMAN (1947) = SAUL LIEBERMAN, Hilkhoth Ha-Yerushalmi of Rabbi Moses Ben Maimon. (TSJTSA. XIII). New York, 1947.
LIEBERMAN (1950) = SAUL LIEBERMAN, The Old Commentators of the Yerushalmi. Alexander Marx Jubilee Volume. Ed. S. LIEBERMAN, New York, 1950. Hebrew Section, pp. 287—336.
LIEBERMAN (1955ff.) = SAUL LIEBERMAN, Tosefta Ki-fshuṭah Iff. New York, 1955ff.
LIEBERMAN (1963) = SAUL LIEBERMAN, Yerushalmi Horayot. Śefer HaYovel LeRebbi Ḥanockh Albeck. Jerusalem, 1963, pp. 283—305.
LIEBERMAN, SZ (1968) = SAUL LIEBERMAN, Siphre Zutta. New York, 1968.
LIEBERMAN (1971) = SAUL LIEBERMAN, Introduction to the Leiden MS. PT Leiden MS. Cod. Scal. 3. Jerusalem, 1971. I, i—vi.

Makhon-Mishnah (1972) = Makhon HaTalmud. Mishnah. Zeraʿim, I. Ed. YEHOSHUA HUTNER. Jerusalem, 1973.
MARGALIOTH = See MARGULIES.
MARGULIES [or MARGALIOTH] (1960) = MORDECHAI MARGULIES [or MARGALIOTH], Midrash Wayyikra Rabbah. V: Introduction. Jerusalem, 1960.
MARGULIES [or MARGALIOTH] (1962) = MORDECHAI MARGULIES, Hilkhot Hannagid. Jerusalem, 1962.
MARGULIES [or MARGALIOTH] (1973) = MORDECHAI MARGULIES, Hilkhot Ereṣ Yisrael Min HaGenizah, Jerusalem, 1973.
MELAMED (1943) = E. Z. MELAMED, Halachic Midrashim of the Tannaim. In the Talmud Babli. Jerusalem, 1943.
MELAMED [or MELAMMED] (1973) = E. Z. MELAMED [or MELAMMED], An Introduction to Talmudic Literature. Jerusalem, 1973.

NEUSNER (1966—70) = JACOB NEUSNER, A History of the Jews of Babylonia. 5 Vols. Leiden, 1966—70.
NEUSNER (1970) = JACOB NEUSNER. Development of a Legend. Leiden, 1975.
NEUSNER, Formation (1970) = JACOB NEUSNER, Ed. Formation of the Babylonian Talmud. Leiden, 1970.
NEUSNER (1971) = JACOB NEUSNER, The Rabbinic Traditions About the Pharisees Before 70. 3 Vols. Leiden, 1971.
NEUSNER (1973) = JACOB NEUSNER, Eliezer Ben Hyrcanus. 2 Vols. Leiden, 1973.
NEUSNER, Modern Study (1973) = JACOB NEUSNER, Ed. The Modern Study of the Mishnah. Leiden, 1973.
NEUSNER, Purities (1974—1977) = JACOB NEUSNER, History of the Mishnaic Law of Purities. 22 Vols. Leiden, 1974—1977.

POZNANSKI (1907—08) = SAMUEL POZNANSKI, Inyanim Shonim HaNogeʿim LiTequfat HaGeonim. HaKedem I (1907), 48—133; II (1908), 24—54, 91—109, 114—116.

RABINOVITZ (1940) = Z. W. RABINOVITZ, Shaʿare Torath Eretz Israel. Jerusalem, 1940.
RATNER (1901—1917) = B. RATNER, Ahawath Zion We-Jeruscholaim. 11 Vols. Vilna, 1901—1917. Repr. in 10 Vols. Jerusalem, 1967. — Often cited by volume and publication date.

SHAKED (1964) = SHAUL SHAKED, A Tentative Bibliography of Geniza Documents. Paris and The Hague, 1964.
SIMONSOHN (1974) = SHLOMO SIMONSOHN, The Hebrew Revival Among Early Medieval European Jews. Salo Wittmayer Baron Jubilee Volume. Jerusalem, 1974. Hebrew Section. II, pp. 831—858.

SPIEGEL (1965) = S. SPIEGEL, On the Polemic of Pirqoi Ben Baboi. Harry A. Wolfson Jubilee Volume. Ed. S. LIEBERMAN. Jerusalem, 1965. Hebrew Section, pp. 243—274.
STRACK (1931) = HERMAN STRACK, Introduction to the Talmud and Midrash. Philadelphia, 1931.
SUSSMANN (1973—74) = Y. SUSSMANN, A Halakhic Inscription from the Beth-Shean Valley. Tarbiẓ 43 (1973—74), 88—158: and 'Additional Notes', Tarbiẓ 44 (1974—75), 193—195.

TCHERNOWITZ (1946—47) = CHAIM TCHERNOWITZ, Toledoth Ha-Poskim. 3 Vols. New York, 1946—47. Cited by volume and date.
TOWNER (1973) = WAYNE SIBLEY TOWNER, The Rabbinic 'Enumeration of Scriptural Examples'. Leiden, 1973.
TOWNSEND (1972) = JOHN T. TOWNSEND, Rabbinic Sources. Anti-Defamation League of B'nai B'iith. The Study of Judaism: Bibliographical Essays. New York, 1972.

UMANSKI (1952) = YOSEF UMANSKI, Ḥakhme HaTalmud. PT. Jerusalem, 1952.
URBACH (1955) = E. E. URBACH, The Tosaphists: Their History, Writings and Methods. Jerusalem, 1955.
URBACH (1963) = E. E. URBACH, Prolegomena Et Indices Continens. Sefer Arugat HaBosem of R. Abraham b. R. Azriel. Jerusalem 1963.

WEISS (1954) = ABRAHAM WEISS, The Talmud in its Development. New York, 1954.
WEISS (1957) = ABRAHAM WEISS, Court Procedure. New York, 1957.
WEISS (1962) = ABRAHAM WEISS, Studies in the Literature of the Amoraim. New York, 1962.
WEISS (1966) = ABRAHAM WEISS, Studies in the Law of the Talmud on Damages. Jerusalem-New York, 1966.
WEISS, Notes = ABRAHAM WEISS, Notes To Talmudic Pericopae. University Bar Ilan. Ramat Gan, n.d.
WEISS HALIVNI (1968, 1975) = DAVID WEISS HALIVNI, Sources and Traditions, I—II. Jerusalem, 1968, 1975.

Part One

I. Introduction

The present paper provides guidelines and a selected annotated bibliography for the study of the Yerushalmi, the *gemara* produced by Palestinian rabbis in the third to fifth centuries, C. E.*

* I cite the English titles of Hebrew books and articles where they are provided. Where a translation is lacking for an item in a clearly recognizable Israeli Hebrew journal, I generally translate the title. I transliterate the titles of the remaining works.
In several Sections, I star the more important studies.
I owe thanks to the following libraries: the University of California, at Berkeley — Doe Library, Office of Inter-Library Loan, and Robbins Collection, Boalt Law School; Graduate Theological Union, Berkeley; University of California, at Los Angeles — Research Library; and the Jewish Theological Seminary of America, New York. I also thank Profs. MENACHEM SCHMELZER and DAVID WEISS HALIVNI, of the Jewish Theological Seminary of America, Profs. JACOB NEUSNER and RICHARD SARASON, Brown University, and WOLFGANG HAASE, Tübingen, who as editor of this volume offered numerous improvements to the text. I am appreciative, as well, of the substantive improvements and corrections suggested by Profs. JACOB SUSSMANN and LEE LEVINE, Hebrew University, Jerusalem, Prof. MOSHE ASSIS, Hebrew Union College, Cincinnati, and Prof. REUVEN KIMELMAN, Brandeis University, Waltham. I am further grateful to the Committee on Research, UC Berkeley, which provided funds to cover typing and other research expenses.

1. The works and items necessary for the use and study of the text are discussed and representative books or articles cited with suggestions as to how they contribute to or differ in the analysis of a problem. Additional literature is usually cited. Full bibliographical information is provided in the first and/or main entry of a work and recurrently used items are thereafter cited by the author's name and the date of publication. An index to only these items appears at the beginning of the Guide. The format varies, as the problems and the state of the several fields greatly vary. Where there are existing bibliographies, I refer to them and refine my selection. My comments are designed to sensitize the reader to certain problems, draw attention to relevant aids and areas of investigation, and facilitate the critical use of the works and commentaries. On the other hand, in certain basic 'informational' areas a more expository format is followed. The main features of an issue are laid out and footnotes employed accordingly, although annotated lists of the literature are also provided.

My task has not been to pass judgment on every book or study. Moreover, comments generally are limited to a work's relevance to the study of y. and do not deal with its other features. As one cannot sharply distinguish between 'traditional' and 'modern' works I include both. The traditional rabbinic authorities have made important contributions to the study of the Palestinian Talmud in numerous areas in addition to exegesis. As the familiar reader knows or the unfamiliar will soon realize exegetical matters in y. are intimately tied to textual and critical concerns. While I therefore include the serious 'traditional' works and items that cite them, I add as well certain current literature because of its availability on the market. Hopefully my comments will enable one appropriately and fully to use these works.

2. My study does not stand in a vacuum. While there have been no classified, even partial, bibliographies to y., there are three works which are somewhat helpful. M. A. KASHER and J. B. MANDELBAUM, Sarei Ha-Elef, A Millenium of Hebrew Authors (500—1500) (New York, 1959), with its 'Supplement', in ḤAYYIM LIPHSHITZ, ed., Śefer Adam Noah (Jerusalem, 1970), pp. 213—229, contains various lists in which one may find items relevant to y. P. J. KOHN, Thesaurus of Hebrew Halakhic Literature (London, 1952), and JUDAH RUBENSTEIN, Quntriś HaShalem Shel Mefarshe HaYerushalmi (New York, 1949) [published as an appendix to the Shulsinger reprint of the Krotoshin edition of PT (New York, 1949)], each provides a single list of items on y. Likewise there have been several previous introductions to PT. But Z. FRANKEL's Mavo HaYerushalmi (Breslau, 1870, Repr. Jerusalem, 1967) is the only fully comprehensive study and has more or less set the agendum in the later works.*

FRANKEL pointed to the main features of y. and its history and many later writers have but varied in their emphasis, interpretation, or conclusion. Earlier ELIJAH, the Gaon of Vilna, had pointed to the proper exegetical

* For the reception accorded FRANKEL in his own day, see the review of A. GEIGER, Jüdische Zeitschrift für Wissenschaft und Leben 6 (1870), 278—306.

method to analyze y. in its own terms. I. LEWY, 1895—1914, made a methodological breakthrough in his analysis of the editing of y. and careful exegesis of B.Q. I—VI. W. BACHER in his article 'Talmud' in the Jewish Encyclopedia, Vol. 2 (New York, 1905, 1907), made an important contribution as well as excellent review of previous literature.

In the twentieth century, the rise of careful critical Talmudic scholarship, led by JACOB N. EPSTEIN, contributed to an understanding of the y. and its relationship to other bodies of sources. LOUIS GINZBERG published a huge corpus of 'Yerushalmi Fragments from the Genizah' (New York, 1909). Those and subsequently published fragments provided fairly accurate texts, free from many textual and scribal corruptions. Textual studies advanced through these publications and the growing awareness of the importance of the Leiden MS, the only MS to the complete PT and the *Vorlage* to the first printed edition, Venice, 1523.

Further publications from the Geniza indicated that Palestine was the home of creative legal and aggadic activity in the post-Talmudic period. That realization joined the emancipation or freedom from the 'traditional' preference of the BT over the PT and the former's supposed 'authenticity'. While in the nineteenth century this 'turn' may have been related to contemporary religious and intellectual issues, in the twentieth it was tied to a growing historical sophistication.

LIEBERMAN, in a series of publications, squarely faced the main issues in the study of y. He asked refined questions, sought standards in the use of tools, and demonstrated how one should and could employ careful logical evaluation of matters and not mere speculation or unbridled analysis. In 'On the Yerushalmi' (Jerusalem, 1929), he laid down the criteria for textual analysis, cataloged textual problems in the study of y., reviewed previous studies, and set out programs necessary for an adequate resolution. He further carefully analyzed the Vatican MS to 'Soṭah'. [The MS covers 'Zeraʿim' and 'Soṭah'.] In 'Talmud of Caesarea' (Jerusalem, 1931), he produced a systematic study [the only one to date] of the editing of one part of Yerushalmi. He, moreover provided a model how one may and should tackle such questions of higher criticism. In 'HaYerushalmi Kiphshuto: Sabbath, Erubin, Pesahim' (Jerusalem, 1934), in a 30-page introduction and 525-page application to three tractates of y., he further refined and supplemented his earlier introductory remarks. During those and subsequent years he published articles in which he focused on important methodological tools or proper uses of various materials relevant to y., e.g., liturgical poetry (*piyyuṭ*). While all of his subsequent publications illuminate PT, they formally turn away from that document — but only formally. He demonstrates that one must be sensitive to the social, cultural, and political life and linguistic milieu in Late Antiquity, especially in Palestine. Most of these articles appear in 'Greek in Jewish Palestine' (New York, 1941, 1965²), 'Hellenism in Jewish Palestine' (New York, 1950), and collected items in 'Texts and Studies' (New York, 1974). In addition, he turned to the elucidation of 'Tosefta', a corpus whose materials form one of the building blocks of y. He produced a four-volume 'Tosefeth Rishonim' (Jerusalem, 1937—39) to establish the text of 'Tosefta', and in 1955 he issued the first volumes of his monumental edition of Tosefta and comprehensive commentary, 'Tosefta Ki-Fshuṭah' (New York, 1955). There he lays out Tosefta's halakhic and aggadic teachings and modes of thought and indicates how it often forms a 'Palestinian' interpretation of matters, very frequently common to PT but not to BT. He thus enables one to have firm data in the analysis of y.'s content.

J. N. EPSTEIN as well demonstrated the careful philological analysis of texts, and systematically studied the varied knowledge of 'Mishnah' in Amoraic times and how different individuals related to it. His own 'Introduction to PT', in the form of notes, was published posthumously (Jerusalem, 1962). Finally one should mention LOUIS GINZBERG, Commentary on the Palestinian Talmud (New York, 1941—61). Along the lines of the work's subtitle, 'A Study of the Development of the Halakah and Haggadah in Palestine and Babylonia', he analyzed Ber. I—V. He included in Volume I separate long English and Hebrew 'Introductions', wherein he provides a comprehensive review of many of the features of y. and its study. That introduction has become formative in subsequent studies. H. STRACK, Introduction to Talmud and Midrash [= English translation of revised version of fifth and last German edition (Munich, 1921)] (Philadelphia, 1931, variously reprinted), had reviewed or listed the earlier (through about 1920) literature. Z. M. RABINOWITZ, Talmud, Jerusalem, EJ 15 (1972), 772—779 and especially E. Z. MELAMMED, An Introduction to Talmudic Literature (Jerusalem, 1973), review all the aforementioned and other literature. At times, MELAMMED compares the several approaches and adds independent contributions.

3. The present author draws on the above works and even where no reference is made is still often in their debt. From one perspective the paper constitutes an examination of the degree to which LIEBERMAN's program has been acted upon. In addition, however, I try to bring to bear the progress made in numerous areas required in the study of y. Moreover, writers including ABRAHAM WEISS, DAVID WEISS HALIVNI, JACOB NEUSNER, E. S. ROSENTHAL, and others have turned to literary and historical questions, and have attempted to understand rabbinic sources through the history of the materials. For example, they try to elucidate how traditions and pericopae received the shape they presently have. Formally some of these studies are not directly on y. or its problems. But naturally such studies, especially those on BT, also illuminate aspects of y. One of my tasks has been to isolate and indicate those aspects relevant and appropriate to the study of y. With new means, research may thus systematically analyze the problems raised by the earlier works. They may now be first tooled with the historical, literary and philological sophistication laid out in the works of LIEBERMAN and others, and secondly be aware of the modern scholarly agenda of the twentieth century in its study of Late Antique literature, language, religion, and history.

Scholarly circles have unfortunately paid insufficient attention to the study of y. Some interest appears in recent Israeli religious and scholarly circles which are motivated by a concern for the Jewish past in the land of

Israel, particularly in agricultural matters. They tend, though, to limit their studies to 'Zera'im' and related items. On the other hand, many individuals use PT in the study of some other discipline or in the analysis of problems external to y. Hopefully the present study which is formulated and designed to provide a perspective on the problems, issues, and literature will stimulate and facilitate further systematic study of y. and more accurate use of its materials. *

Part Two
The Text of Yerushalmi

II. Title

Sources use several terms to refer to the Yerushalmi. Palestinian circles from the post-Talmudic period refer to y. without naming the work and initially at most cite the name of a tractate. In the land of Israel, the PT undoubtedly was the 'Talmud' par excellence[1].

Elsewhere, however, a distinctive terminology was necessary. Gaonic sources use several terminologies. We find גמרא דארץ ישראל, *GMR' D'RṢ YSR'L*, "the *gemara* of the Land of Israel", or תלמוד ארץ ישראל, *TLMWD 'RṢ YSR'L*, "the Talmud of the Land of Israel". 'Halakhot Gedolot' has *TMLWD DM'RB'*, "the Talmud of the West"[2]. Rabbenu Ḥananel from

* E. S. Rosenthal recently uncovered a heretofore unknown Spanish MS to y. Neziqin, tractates B.Q., B.M., and B.B., and presently, as part of the Project for the Critical Editing of Amoraic Literature, of the Institute for Jewish Studies of the Hebrew University, Jerusalem, is preparing it for publication. The MS's readings are not always identical to those of the L.MS and at times it preserves a separate tradition of the y. text. See Ha'ares, January 28, 1977, p. 16, and below, IV, D. 4. An analysis of the MS is liable to confirm, disprove, or complicate various points discussed in this study, especially as to the history of the y. text, the evaluation of the L. MS, and the theories explaining the differences between y. Neziqin and the rest of the PT. The find makes clear that much work remains and new discoveries may yet appear with significant, if not potentially revolutionary, implications.

[1] See E. S. Rosenthal, Leshonot Śofrim, in: Yuval Shy. A Jubilee Volume Dedicated to S. Y. Agnon. Ed. Baruch Kurzweil (Ramat Gan, 1958), p. 31, as to the practice of the scribe of Vatican MS 30 to Gn. Rabbah. We find the somewhat different unexplicit terms *TLMWD, TLMWD (LWMR) LYMDWNW RBWTYNW*, "the teaching" or "the teaching (says), our rabbis taught us." The latter formula is used to cite Amoraic, including Palestinian, traditions. See Margulies (1973), p. 51, fn. 3 and V. Aptowitzer, Untersuchungen zur Gaonäischen Literatur, HUCA 8—9 (1931—32), 389. Cf. Z. M. Rabinowitz, Sepher HaMa'asim Livnei Erez Yisra'el — New Fragments, Tarbiẓ 41 (1972), 279. Cf. below, Section XVIII. C.

[2] See Louis Ginzberg, Geonica, II: Genizah Studies (New York, 1909, Repr. 1968), index s. v. TLMWD 'RṢ YSR'L, esp. pp. 39, 142, 271, and Id., Genizah Studies, II: Geonic and

Qairawan, sometimes uses the phrase, גרסי במערבא, *GRŚY BM'RB'*, "they read in the West"[3], and R. Nissim of Qairawan, ca. 990—1062 employs a distinctive terminology, גמרא דבני מערבא, *GMR' DBNY M'RB'*, "the *gemara* of the people of the West", and only occasionally *TLMWD 'RṢ YSR'L.* At times R. Nissim names a tractate to which he appends the phrase דבני מערבא, *DBNY M'RB'*[4].

The name ירושלמי, *YRWŠLMY*, Yerushalmi, has few occurrences in Gaonic times, though it is attested. It is used commonly by Ḥananel and perhaps by R. Nissim and clearly occasionally by Alfasi and then frequently by Medieval European authorities[5]. As Jerusalem did not have an Amoraic academy, the term does not fit the historical situation of Talmudic times. Baron has aptly suggested that the term derives from a time after the Moslem conquest of Jerusalem and the subsequent reestablishment of an academy in the city[6].

Scholars have indicated that the word 'Yerushalmi' has also been used so as to refer to certain works other than the PT, a matter which I discuss below[7].

The Venice first edition, 1523—24, and its primary *Vorlage*, Leiden MS Scal. 3[8] both use the term Talmud Yerushalmi, which undoubtedly con-

Early Karaitic Halakah (New York, 1929, Repr. 1969), pp. 328, 324, 287, 335, 337, Samuel Poznanski, 'Inyanim Shonim HaNoge'im LiTequfat HaGeonim [= Variae Relating to the Gaonic Period], HaKedem, 2 (1908), 25, fn. 1, 28, and especially p. 115. J. N. Epstein, Der Gaonäische Kommentar zur Ordnung — Tohoroth (Berlin, 1915), pp. 75f.; Shraga Abramson, R. Nissim Gaon (Jerusalem, 1965), pp. 12, n. 1; 71 n. 3; 212f. Cf. B. M. Lewin, Monumenta Gaonica: Methiboth (Jerusalem, 1933, Repr. 1973), pp. vii—x, and in general, Herman L. Strack, Introduction to the Talmud and Midrash (Philadelphia, 1931), pp. 65, 265.

[3] The use of the word, "in the West", undoubtedly reflects or is a continuation of BT's usage of *BM'RB 'MRY*, "In the West they say", and variations thereof, all of which serve to refer to Palestinian traditions. Cf. J. N. Epstein, Introduction to Amoraitic Literature (Jerusalem, 1962), pp. 292—312.
In the several formulae, the word *GRŚY*, "read", refers to the text of *gemara*; cf. S. Abramson, BeMerkazim UVaTefuṣot (Jerusalem, 1965), p. 125, and Id., 'Inyanot BeSifrut HaGaonim (Jerusalem, 1974), p. 172.

[4] Abramson (1965), loc. cit., and 186f., 186 n. 2, 212—213, 245, and 545f.

[5] Poznanski (1908), p. 115; S. Assaf, Responsa Geonica (Jerusalem, 1942), p. 41, fn. 7; Abramson (1965), p. 212. For the medieval authorities, cf. e.g., the indexes to the several commentaries published in: Harry Fischel Institute Publications Section III. Rishonim. Vol. I [On Tractate Mo'ed Qaṭan] (Jerusalem, 1937); Novellae of Solomon Ben Adret to Tractate Megillah, ed. H. Z. Dimitrovsky (New York, 1956), p. xxx; and Piskei HaRid, The Rulings of Rabbi Isaiah the Elder, I Tractates, Berakhot and Shabbat, ed. Abraham Wortheimer and Abraham Liss (Jerusalem, 1964), Introduction, p. 18. The Tosefot, according to one survey, employ the term *YRWŠLMY* 761 times, and *GMRT 'RṢ YSR'L* 305 times. See Perez Tarshish, The Personalities and Books Referred to in Tosefot, ed. S. A. Neuhausen (New York, 1942), pp. xvii—xviii, fns. 5 and 10.

[6] Salo Baron, A Social and Religious History of the Jews, VI (New York, 1958), p. 331, n. 25. Cf., though, the use of *YRWŠLMY* to refer to Palestine in b. B. Q. 6 b [*MSS* read *YRWŠ-LM'H*; see R. Rabbinovicz, Variae Lectiones in Mischname et in Talmud Babylonicum. Tractate BaBa [Kama] (Monachii, 1882, Repr. Jerusalem, New York, and Montreal,. 1960), p. 8, fn. 3] and in the Vatican MS to y. Orl. 3: 8; 63b.

[7] Section XVIII. F.

[8] See below Section IV. A.

tributed to or caused its subsequent popular usage. Some individuals, of course, used one of the other terms, e.g. Meiri uses תלמוד המערב, *TLMWD HM'RB*, Talmud HaMa'arav, the "Western Talmud"[9].

III. Printed Editions

This section reviews the printed editions of y. Editions that are printed along with commentaries appear in Chapter XX.

The first printed text of the whole PT, is that of DANIEL BOMBERG, Venice, 1523—24.[10] The text without any commentary covers thirty nine of the sixty three tractes of 'Mishnah'. Three of these are incomplete. As indicated below, this text is primarily based on Codex Leiden Scal. 3. All subsequent modern editions are based on the first edition, to which changes have been made, though none on the basis of other MSS.

There are several editions of individual tractates which represent a separate literary tradition. The first complete edition of BT, Venice, 1520—23, contains the text of two PT tractates, y. Sheq. and y. Horayot. As Sheq. lacks a BT tractate, y. Sheq. had been appended to M. Sheq. (1522), following a practice which goes back to Gaonic times. The text is a different type from that of the PT first edition, but it has been contaminated by BT's style and idiom. The inclusion of y. Sheq. with BT likewise accounts for the existence of several medieval commentaries to the tractate. One, the MS which includes the commentary of R. Meshullam, ed., ABRAHAM SCHREIBER, Treatise Shekalim (New York, 1954), contains a text of y. that employed MS(S) different from that used in Ven. p.e. but similar to the one in the supplement in the BT first edition[11]. A list of these MSS appear in Section IV. D.

MOSHE ASSIS is preparing a critical introduction and edition of y. Sheq. which promises systematically to trace and evaluate the readings at each stage of the text. According to his preliminary report[11a], the text of the PT first edition constitutes an eclectic text based upon the L. MS and the BT supplement. The L. MS itself suffered additions of marginal readings

[9] Cf., e. g., ADRET, DIMITROVSKY ed. (1956), ibid., and Menahem HaMeiri, Beit HaBeḥirah to Tractate Berakhot, ed. SOLOMON DAIKMAN (Jerusalem, 1965²), p. 5.

[10] A. M. HABERMANN, HaTalmud HaYerushalmi. An Added Chapter in his Reissue of Raphael Rabbinovicz, Ma'amar 'al Hadpaśat HaTalmud (Jerusalem, 1952), pp. 203—205; ABRAHAM BERLINER, Beit HaDefuś HaIvri Shel Daniel Bomberg, Ketavim Nevḥarim, II, ed. A. M. HABERMANN (Jerusalem, 1949), p. 169; P. KAHLE, Cairo Geniza (Oxford, 1959), pp. 120f.; and especially S. LIEBERMAN, Yerushalmi Horayot, Śefer HaYovel leRebbi Ḥanoh Albeck (Jerusalem, 1963), p. 286.

[11] LIEBERMAN (1963), p. 286, and LIEBERMAN, The Old Commentators of the Yerushalmi, Alexander Marx Jubilee Volume (New York, 1950), Hebrew Section, pp. 295f. and fn. 29; cf. B. RATNER, Ahawath Zion We-Jerusholaim (Vilna, Repr. Jerusalem, 1967), Sheq., pp. 1f.

[11a] MOSHE ASSIS, Concerning the History of the Text of Tractate Sheqalim. Seventh World Congress of Jewish Studies. Jerusalem, Israel, August 8, 1977.

drawn from the BT supplement and readings from another MS. The other extant MS, the Oxford MS published by SCHREIBER, is the most corrupt of all the MSS. Its value, though, is enhanced by the accompanying commentaries.

As b. Horayot lacked the commentaries of the 'Tosefot', the editor (1521) included the y. portion. This text contains important readings. SAUL LIEBERMAN, Yerushalmi Horayot, Śefer HaYovel leRebbi Ḥanoh Albeck (Jerusalem, 1963), pp. 283—305, has shown that this text represents one of the 'other' MSS upon which the Ven. p.e. of the PT purportedly is based, which, however, was not systematically used. Unfortunately each of the two locations of y. Horayot has suffered several series of corruptions by editors who unknowingly successively 'corrected' the text of one on the basis of the previous edition of the other.

y. 'Zera'im', along with that of Sheq. appears in the text and commentary of R. SOLOMON SIRILLO. This edition is discussed in Section IV. C.

Lists of editions include:

Z. FRANKEL (1870), pp. 138b—141b.

STRACK (1931), p. 83, succinct and still useful.

GINZBERG (1941), passim.

*A. M. HABERMANN, HaTalmud HaYerushalmi (Jerusalem, 1952), pp. 203—222 and ns. 252—54, describes contents of editions of the complete y. and of individual tractates and notes the relationship between each of the editions. As the editions common on today's market are reprints of earlier printings, HABERMANN's comments are useful in the evaluation of editions. The listings, with indexes, in 'Kirjath Sepher', published quarterly by Magnes Press, enables one to keep abreast of more recent editions[12].

The editions of note include Krotoschin, 1886, reprinted New York, 1948, and Jerusalem, 1969, which has a brief commentary, based upon that of the Cracow 1609 edition, to which is added corrections and an index to cross references; ZHITOMER, 1860—67, five volume edition with commentaries[13]; especially PETERKOV, 1898—1900 in eight volumes; and Vilna, 1922, with additional commentaries, in 7 volumes, reprinted New York, 1959, and Jerusalem, 1960, 1973.

A. M. LUNCZ issued five volumes of an attempted critical edition, Berakhot through Shev., Jerusalem, 1907—1919, Talmud Hierosolymitanum ad exemplar editionis principis. The text is based upon the Leiden and Vatican MSS, the MS that accompanies the commentary of SIRILLO, and some geniza fragments, and includes cross references and verse indexes, and a succinct commentary.

[12] Of course, one may also consult MENAHEM M. KASHER and JACOB B. MANDELBAUM, Sarei Ha-Elef (New York, 1959) and its 'Supplement', published in ḤAYYIM LIPHSHITZ, ed. Śefer Adam Noah (Jerusalem, 1970), pp. 213—299 [A revised edition is under preparation]; and P. JACOB KOHN, Thesaurus of Hebrew Halachic Literature (London, 1952).

[13] Useful reviews include: Z. FRANKEL, MGWJ 16 (1867), 194—198; P. RITTER, MGWJ 42 (1898), 429f.; JOSEF MIESES, MGWJ 74 (1930), 314f.

While some of the editions, especially the Krotoschin and LUNCZ include cogent emendations, the Venice p.e. still constitutes the best text and the only one that represents a literary tradition. Moreover, the later editions at times changed spellings and incorrectly filled in abbreviations. An offset reprint has made available the first edition; SEFARIM, Berlin, 1924, and in photographic reprint, MEIR and MOSES ROKEAH, New York, ca. 1950.

IV. Manuscripts

The present unsatisfactory state of the y. text requires the use of MSS.

A. The Leiden MS

1. Description and Evaluation. The Leiden Codex Scal. 3, finished in 1334, is the only MS to the complete PT as now extant in print. That is, it contains the text of all portions of y. printed in the Venice first edition. One finds on the margins and the spaces between the lines additions and 'corrections', while in the text itself crossed out or erased and rewritten words and letters. These changes ostensibly are to 'correct' the text, to fill in perceived *lacunae*, to present a reading from a different MS, or to offer a logical connection between two passages. A few corrections are by the same hand as that of the scribe, some of which are introduced by the letters נ"ל, N"L, or נ"א, N"A, the abbreviations for נראה לי, NR'H LY, "it seems to me", and נוסח אחר, *NWŚḤ 'ḤR*, "an alternative reading", but most of the changes are made by a second or even a third hand.

I. ZVI FEINTUCH, The Mishna of the MS Leiden of the Palestinian Talmud, Tarbiẓ 45 (1976), I—II, 178—212, a careful and systematic evaluation of the Mishnah in the L. MS and the practices of the MS's scribe. The scribe often — but not always — copied the Mishnah from Mishnah MS De Rossi 138, Parma.

SCHILLER-SZINESSY, VeHemmah BaKetuvim, Occasional Notices of Hebrew Manuscripts. No. 1: Description of the Leyden MS of the Palestinian Talmud (Cambridge, 1878). Cf. LIEBERMAN (1971), fns. 10 and 12.

FRANKEL (1870), p. 143a.

S. LIEBERMAN, HaYerushalmi Kiphshuto (Jerusalem, 1934), pp. xv—xvi, xx—xxi.

J. N. EPSTEIN, Introduction to Amoraitic Literature (Jerusalem, 1962), pp. 326—327.

Mishnah. Zera'im, I. ed. YEHOSHUA HUTNER (Makhon HaTalmud: Jerusalem, 1972), p. 72, provides a comprehensive recent description of the MS.

BARUCH BOKSER, Samuel's Commentary on the Mishnah (Leiden, 1975), pp. 45, fn. 109; 60, fn. 151; especially 135, fns. 402, 403; and 143, fn. 427, contains examples of 'corrections' entered in the MS.

SCHILLER-SZINESSY (1878), especially, pp. 14, 15, J. N. EPSTEIN[14], Mediqduqe Yerushalmi, I: Leiden MS, Tarbiẓ 5 (1934), 257-272, and 6a (1934), 38—55, and LIEBERMAN (1934), pp. 15—16, and (1963), proved that the L. MS provided the basis for the Venice first edition. LIEBERMAN (1963) showed that, contrary to the colophon, that edition was not systematically based upon three additional MSS, but rather upon just this single one[15]. That is, the copy editor only occasionally consulted a different MS.

LIEBERMAN, Introduction, Palestinian Talmud, Leiden MS, Cod. Scal. 3 (Kedem: Jerusalem, 1971), I, i—vi, reviews the previous evaluations of the L. MS and Ven. p.e. and emphasizes several points with additional examples. The original scribe of the L. MS performed a careful exact work. The emendations which he did on the basis of his own reasoning and which he entered into the text were items blatant to the eye or glaringly necessary and, where verification is possible, are often confirmed. The very few instances of mistakes produce only an insignificant loss. In addition, this scribe often left difficult readings and added, as well, some marginal notes. On the other hand, the copy editor of the Venice p.e. was an unqualified faker whose emendations corrupted the text and often introduced superficially smooth readings which go undetected unless one methodically and carefully employs the L. MS[16]. As already indicated, he did not systematically check other MSS.

E. Z. MELAMMED, An Introduction to Talmudic Literature (Jerusalem, 1973), pp. 508—512.

2. Editions and Use of the Leiden MS. The Leiden MS was recently reprinted in a less than fully adequate facsimile edition, Palestinian Talmud, Leiden MS, Cod. Scal. 3. I—IV (Kedem Publishing: Jerusalem, 1971), with an introduction by SAUL LIEBERMAN[17]. This edition inadequately reproduces

[14] Cf. especially p. 257, fn. 1. EPSTEIN demonstrates that the text of the L. MS contains correct readings, which were corrupted by the Ven. p. e.'s copy editor. Some are emendations of letters and words and others are mistakes in the process of editing or printing; cf. LIEBERMAN (1934), p. xi. Cf. EPSTEIN (1962), p. 337, and GINZBERG (1941), p. H: xxxiii—xxxv, and E. Z. MELAMMED, An Introduction to Talmudic Literature (Jerusalem, 1973), pp. 508ff. FRANKEL, Notizen, MGWJ 6 (1857), 398—400, and (1870), 55a and 141b—143a had seen a relationship between the L. MS and Ven. p. e. but he did not correctly evaluate it. He did point to some systematic changes made by the Ven. p. e., for example, it regularly fills in the abbreviations which appear in the MS.

[15] While even LIEBERMANN had earlier considered the Ven. p. e. an eclectic text, he had emphasized the importance of the readings in the L. MS. Cf. SAUL LIEBERMAN, On the Yerushalmi (Jerusalem, 1929), pp. 46—47, and ID., More on the L. MS, Tarbiẓ 20 (1950) [= J. N. Epstein Jubilee Volume], 107—117. The relationship between the L. MS and Ven. p. e. emerges from any careful comparison of the various readings. Cf. BOKSER (1975), pp. 26, fn. 55; 29, fn. 61; 47, fn. 117; 49, fn. 123; 51, fn. 127; 78, fn. 210; 90, fn. 250; 101, fn. 280; 103, fn. 286; 117, fn. 333; 134, fn. 396; 143, fn. 429; 148, fn. 449; 151, fn. 461; and especially, 126, fn. 362, 363, 365.

[16] LIEBERMAN (1934), p. xvi indicates that the relative number of corruptions varies in each tractate, e. g., few in 'Nezikin', and many in Pes.

[17] The facsimile was originally published in two volumes under the imprint of Makor Publishing Ltd., Jerusalem, but its copies, under suit, were withdrawn and it then

the marginal notes; some are made illegible and some, in handling, are not at all reproduced. Moreover, at times, the text itself is illegible. See P. Sj. van Koningsveld and A. van der Heide, The Pirated Edition of the Leyden Talmud Jerushalmi, Studia Rosenthaliana 8 (1974), 131—137. A new and better edition is being prepared by the firm of Rosenkilde and Bagger.

Additional works which employ or discuss the L. MS include:

Isaak Levy, Der Achte Abschnitt aus dem Tractate 'Sabbath' [ch. 7(8), 10d—11c]. Inaugural-Dissertation der philosophischen Facultät der Kaiser Wilhelms-Universität Strassburg (Breslau, 1891).

I. Lewy, Jerushalmi B.Q. I—VI, Jahresbericht des jüdisch-theologischen Seminars, 1895—1919, Repr. as Mavo UPerush LeTalmud Yerushalmi (Jerusalem, 1970), Ch. V.

B. Ratner, Ahawath Zion We-Jeruscholaim, I—XI (Vilna, 1901—1917, Repr. in 10 vols., Jerusalem, 1967), where available selectively cited readings from L. MS. but did not explain them. See Lieberman (1934), xvi and 397f., and below.

M. Sachs, Diqduqe Śoferim LeTalmud HaYerushalmi: Maśekhet Berakhot (Jerusalem, 1943).

J. N. Epstein, all his works, but especially (1962), 'Notes and Explanations to Chapters of Talmud (Pes. I—II, B.M. X., B.B. I—III)', pp. 147—268, and Id., 'Diqduqe Yerushalmi', pp. 335—606 (supplemented by E. Z. Melammed), a full, but not exhaustive, comparison of readings in Ven. p.e. and L. MS. Epstein's notes run through 'Zera'im'.

Additional articles by Lieberman, see XX. C.

Edward A. Goldman, A Critical Edition of Palestinian Talmud Tractate Rosh HaShanah, [in 4 installments:] HUCA 46—49 (1975—78), provides a 'critical' text that employs the L. MS and geniza fragments. Though Part One discusses the L. MS, it fails to mention and take into account Lieberman's articles.

The editions and commentaries of Luncz, Berakhot-Shev.; Lieberman (1934), Shab., Eruv., Pes., and n.b., p. 526, Ber. I; Ginzberg, Ber. I—V; Shelomoh Goren, HaYerushalmi HaMeforash (Jerusalem, 1961), Ber. I—V (see Section XX. B); Israel Francus, Talmud Yerushalmi, Maśekhet Beṣah (New York, 1967); Yehudah Feliks' editions of chapters on agricultural materials. See XVII. D, and David Weiss Halivni, Sources and Traditions, I—II (Orders Nasihim and Mo'ed, from Yoma to Hagiga), (Jerusalem, 1968, 1975).

B. Vatican MS

1. Talmud Yerushalmi. Codex Vatican 133 (Vat. Ebr. 133), Introduction by Saul Lieberman (= reprint of 'On the Yerushalmi', 1929). Page

appeared, in four volumes, under the name of Kedem Publs., which thus became the publisher of record.

concordance index to the Venice edition by A. P. SHERRY (Jerusalem, 1971). The MS, whose suggested origin is placed at the thirteenth century, contains tractates 'Soṭah' and the Order of 'Zera'im', less 'Bik'. The MS contains many scribal errors though apparently it is based upon a good underlying MS tradition which preserves many fine readings, orthographically, linguistically, and content-wise.

The MS's readings often accord with the citations of y. found in 'Tosefot', cf. LIEBERMAN (1929), p. 54.

2. Study of the MS:

L. GINZBERG, Yerushalmi Fragments from the Genizah (New York, 1909, Repr. Makor: Jerusalem, 1969, and Hildesheim and New York, 1970), appendix, pp. 347—372, presents selected variants, at times inaccurately, copied, from Vat. MS. Cf. GINZBERG (1941), p. lxv.

LIEBERMAN (1929), presents a general study of the MS and its role in an overall textual analysis of y., and a listing with explanatory notes of variants to Sot. Cf. especially pp. 46f. and 53f.

GINZBERG (1941), p. H: xxxv.

EPSTEIN (1962), especially 326—327, notations in the MS for abbreviated pericopae.

SHAMMA FRIEDMAN, Conservative Judaism 26 (1972), 92—94, a fine review of the Makor reprint and a description of the MS in general.

Makhon-Mishnah, I (1972), p. 73, describes the MS.

MELAMMED (1973), pp. 512—514, describes the MS.

ZVI MEIR RABINOVITZ, New Genizah Fragments of the PT, Henoch Yalon Memorial Volume [= Bar Ilan Department Researches, II]. Ed. E. Y. KUTSCHER, et al. (Bar Ilan University, Ramat Gan and Kirjath Sepher, Jerusalem, 1974), p. 500, concerning good readings preserved in the MS.

Y. SUSSMANN, A Halakhic Inscription from the Beth-Shean Valley, Tarbiẓ 43 (1973—74), 107f., fn. 110.

Commentaries and editions that employed the Vat. MS include: LUNCZ (1907—1919), Ber.-Shev.; GINZBERG (1941—61), Ber. I—V; and S. GOREN, (1961), Ber. I—V.

C. 'Yerushalmi Zera'im', and Tractate Sheq. with the Commentary of SOLOMON SIRILLO.

1. The work is found in British Museum MSS 403, 404, and 405 = Or. 2822, 2823, 2824, and in part, in Paris, Bibliotheque Nationale, Supplement Hebreu 1389.

The MSS to the y. text and commentary come from the sixteenth century. According to SUSSMANN (1973—74), p. 108, fn. 110, while the texts of the commentary may represent a first (Paris MS) and a second edition (Brit. Mus.), the y. texts do not substantively vary, excluding mechanical scribal errors.

The text of y. preserves some valuable readings. Often, however, interpolations or 'corrections' were introduced on the basis of BT, *midrashim*, or early rabbinic commentaries. Therefore, one must carefully evaluate the readings. LIEBERMAN (1943), p. xv, however, points out that one can rely upon a reading where in his commentary SIRILLO states that he found it in "exact texts". The readings are particularly valuable as they may derive from MSS and not the Venice 1523 edition of y., a work that did not appear until after SIRILLO had already started his commentary. Only later did he make us of that edition. See LIEBERMAN (1950), pp. 301—302. M. LEHMANN, in an edition of tractate 'Berakhot', 'Meir Netiv' (Mainz, 1875), suggests that volume III of the British Museum MSS, on Hal., Orl., and Bik., is written by SIRILLO himself; cf. Makhon-Mishnah I (1972), p. 74, fn. 9. LEHMANN and G. MARGOLIOUTH, Catalogue of the Hebrew and Samaritan Manuscripts in the British Museum (London, 1905, Repr. 1965), II, 55, suggest that the other two volumes, I—II, were written by a scribe and SIRILLO reviewed and annotated it.

2. The MS has been published:

LEHMANN, Meir Netiv (Mainz, 1875). Tractate 'Berakhot'. Repr. along with Tractate 'Pe'ah' in Vilna ed. of y.

ḤAYYIM YOSEF DINGLAS, ed. of individual tractates of 'Zera'im', including 'Berakhot', I—IX (Jerusalem, 1934—1967). This is a far from perfect edition; cf. KALMAN KAHANA, Maśekhet Shevi'it, Ḥeqer VeIyun I (Bene Brak, 1972), pp. 11f., and SUSSMANN (1973—74), p. 108, fn. 110.

EPHRAIM ZE'EV GERBOZ, ed. to y. Sheq. (Jerusalem, 1958).

KALMAN KAHANA, I—II (1972—73) printed anew from the British Museum MS SIRILLO's text and commentary to y. Shev.

3. Discussion of the text and commentary:

Introductions to edition by LEHMANN (1875), DINGLAS (1934—67), and KAHANA (1972).

MARGOLIOUTH (1905), pp. 54—56.

*LIEBERMAN (1929), p. 47; (1934), p. xv; and (1950), pp. 301—302.

GINZBERG (1941), p. H: cxvii.

*Makhon-Mishnah I (1972), pp. 73—75, excellent remarks.

EJ 14, 1618—1619, s.v. SIRILLO.

*SUSSMANN (1973—74), p. 108, fn. 110.

BOKSER (1975), p. 148, fn. 450, presents an example of an interpolation added into the text.

D. Other MSS

1. As indicated above, y. Sheq. was included with many BT editions. Thus, it is found in Munich Cod. Hebr. 95, written in 1343, reprinted by HERMAN L. STRACK, Der Babylonische Talmud nach der einzigen vollstän-

digen Handschrift München Codex Hebraicus 95 mittels Facsimile-Lichtdrucks vervielfältigt, mit Inhaltsangaben für jede Seite u. einer Einl. versehen (Repr. Sefer: Jerusalem, 1971, I, 218—227). As this formed the basis of RAPHAELO RABINOVICZ's invaluable 'Variae Lectiones', he dealt with y. Sheq., 'Tract. Megillah Et Shekalim' (Munich, 1887, Repr. New York, 1960).

In addition, a text of y. is found in the MS with the commentary of R. Meshullam, ed. ABRAHAM SCHREIBER, Treatise Shekalim (New York, 1954). The y. text, which is somewhat corrupted, is similar to the one in the printed BT's supplement ed. Cf. LIEBERMAN (1950), pp. 295—96, and SCHREIBER's introduction. As to the commentary, see below, Section XIX.I. For the text with SIRILLO, see above, Section C. MOSHE ASSIS's forthcoming critical edition (1979?) will provide a full description of the MSS. See above, Section III, and fn. 11a.

2. ZVI MEIR RABINOVITZ, ed., Qeta' Shel Mishnah ViYerushalmi Shevi'it, Bar Ilan Annual, Studies in Judaica and Humanities, II (= Samuel Bialoblocki Memorial Volume), (Jerusalem, 1964), pp. 125—133. RABINOVITZ provides an introduction and notes to this ca. fourteenth century Yemenite MS to Shev. VII. According to SUSSMANN, however, the fragment actually derives from the Geniza and its continuation is in the Cambridge Library.

3. A. H. FREIMANN, A Fragment of Jerushalmi Baba Kama, Tarbiẓ 6 (1934), 56—63. This fragment of Vatican MS (Vat. Ebr. 530), "not later than fourteenth century", is to B.Q. 2 : 4, 3a[14]—3 : 4, 3c[53]. The text is somewhat carelessly copied, though it contains some good readings and preserves Palestinian orthography; cf. LIEBERMAN (1934), p. xv. It confirms some of the emendations suggested by I. LEWY (1895—1914, Repr. 1970).

The edition includes an introduction and brief notes; Supplementary Comments by S. LIEBERMAN; and an appendix on one pericope by J. N. EPSTEIN, To 'A Fragment of Jerushalmi Baba Kama', pp. 64—65.

4. E. S. ROSENTHAL. Escorial G-1-3, Spanish MS to y. Neziqin, from middle of B.Q. Ch. III to middle of B.B. 9:4, written on the side of a MS to b. B.Q. — B.B. The MS has fewer corruptions than Ashkenazi (European) texts of PT and far fewer textual lacunae than the L. MS. Furthermore, it more accurately preserves Galilean Hebrew and Aramaic. It may serve to explain corrupt texts and evaluate previously proposed emendations. It basically confirms LIEBERMAN's thesis as to the distinct nature and Caesarean origin of Neziqin. But it does not represent a single y. tradition. On the one hand, the readings generally are the same as those of the L. MS and Venice first edition, and its terminology, style, and idioms usually are distinct from those of the rest of PT and characteristic of Caesarea. But, on the other hand, the MS at times lacks the terminology and spelling supposedly distinct to y. Neziqin. Preliminary Report of E. S. ROSENTHAL, Concerning the New MS to PT Neziqin, Seventh World Congress of Jewish Studies, Jerusalem, Israel, August 8, 1977. See also footnote *, at the end of Section I.

5. MOSHE ASSIS, A Fragment of y. Sanhedrin, Tarbiẓ 46 (1977), 29—90, 326—329. The text covers y. San. 5:1, 22c, l. 42 to 6:9, 23c, l. 47. Besides

the introduction and extensive notes, SAUL LIEBERMAN adds important additional comments, 'On the New Fragments of the Palestinian Talmud', ibid., 91—97.

E. Geniza Fragments

These fragments originally found in the so called Cairo Geniza are presently dispersed in libraries throughout the world. One may find an introduction and bibliographical information to the collections in S. D. GOITEIN, A Mediterranean Society, I (Berkeley and Los Angeles, 1967), pp. 1—28, and especially, Involvement in Geniza Research, in: Religion in a Religious Age, ed. S. D. GOITEIN (Association for Jewish Studies, Ktav: New York, 1974), pp. 139f; Article, Genizah Cairo, EJ 16, 1323—44; and MORDECHAI A. FRIEDMAN, 'Introduction', in his forthcoming 'Marriage and Marriage Traditions in Palestinian Tradition as Reflected in the Documents of the Cairo Geniza' (The School of Jewish Studies, Tel Aviv University, 1979). See also SHAUL SHAKED, A Tentative Bibliography of Geniza Documents (Paris and The Hague, 1964).

The fragments constitute brief selections of y. and are not all of the same quality, provenance and date, though scholars have usually dated them to ca. tenth century. SUSSMANN (1973—74), pp. 155f., fn. 497, has questioned this assignment. He believes that the fragments, despite their universally recognized importance, have not been systematically and methodically analyzed as to their date, and may, in fact, come from an earlier period. See below, for ALLONI's edition of fragments. Whether or not he is correct in his suggestion, the fragments deserve further systematic attention. This is especially so since LIEBERMAN's revelation (1963), that the Venice p.e. basically represents the reading of one and not four MSS. This is not to say that earlier scholars have not recognized the importance of these fragments. They have, cf. LIEBERMAN (1934), pp. 14f. and GINZBERG (1951), pp. H: xxxvi—xl. They noted that the fragments accurately preserve Palestinian orthography and assumedly, as well, textual readings, for the texts could not have been revised by European scribes familiar with the more 'popular' and 'authoritative' Babylonian traditions. See below, Section XV. A.

While many fragments have been published, many others have not. These include items from Dropsie College, Philadelphia [see Makhon-Mishnah, I (1972), p. 76 and B. HALPER, Descriptive Catalogue of Genizah Fragments in Philadelphia (Philadelphia, 1924), p. 45, no. 82, y. Dem. 2:1, 22d$^{15-30}$ and l.^{64}—23a^{4}], and (only) a few brief pieces from the Jewish Theological Seminary of America, as I am informed. Forthcoming editions are promised by Makor Publishers, Jerusalem, by ABRAHAM I. KATSH, Mosad HaRav Kook, Jerusalem, and comprehensive, separate, corpora by YAAQOV SUSSMANN, Jerusalem, and by ELIEZER HOROWITZ, Yeshiva University, New York. The more recent editions have included facsimiles, and accordingly at times republish items that had previously appeared. Thus, fragments once published may have appeared a second time or may do so in the future. Therefore, to facilitate identification I include in the following list of published items, the individual fragment's number in its respective collection.

1. Talmudical Fragments in the Bodleian Library, S. SCHECHTER and A. SINGER, ed. (Cambridge, 1896, Repr. Makor: Jerusalem, 1971). Fragments to Ber. $4b^{18-59}$ and $6b^{25-60}$. Description and introduction, p. 6; text, pp. 27—28. Published by LOUIS GINZBERG, in his 'Yerushalmi Fragments' (1909). See next item. Several mistakes in copying are corrected by GINZBERG (1941), I, 238, fn. 8.

2. L. GINZBERG, Yerushalmi Fragments from the Genizah, Vol. I (All published) (= Text and Studies of JTSA) (New York, 1909, Repr. Makor: Jerusalem, 1969, and Hildesheim and New York, 1970).

Fragments to all parts of y. from 'Taylor-Schechter Collection' in Cambridge University Library; Bodleian Library; and from private hands with two supplements, I: 'Extracts from y. found in first edition of Yalqut Shimeoni, Salonica, 1526—27', pp. 309—343; and II: 'Selected variants to Zera'im from Vat. MS number 133', pp. 347—372.

Some texts are incorrectly transcribed. See, e.g., SAUL LIEBERMAN Siphre Zutta (New York, 1968), p. 105 fn. 73, and GINZBERG (1941), I, 238, fn. 8.

On Supplement I, see ARTHUR B. HYMAN, The Sources of the Yalkut Shimeoni, I (Jerusalem, 1974), pp. xxiv—xxv.

Several sections, pp. 29—36, 152—153, 183—184, 230, are not actual y. texts but rather part of a medieval collection which is based upon the y. and which incorporates additions from BT and later sources. See LIEBERMAN (1934), xxv; V. APTOWITZER, Introductio ad Sefer Rabiah (Jerusalem, 1938), p. 276; and EPSTEIN, Ma'asim Livne Ereṣ Yisrael, Tarbiz 1b (1930), 37; and SAUL LIEBERMAN, ed. Hilkhot HaYerushalmi (The Laws of the Palestinian Talmud) of Rabbi Moses Ben Maimon (Text and Studies of JTSA. Vol. XIII) (New York, 1947), preface p. 3. Pp. 29—36 in GINZBERG are part of a book of decisions to be attributed to Maimonides. LIEBERMAN presents a photographic reproduction, and more accurate transcription and thorough annotation of the fragment. See below, and cp. B. Z. BENEDICT, KS 27 (1952), p. 329.

EPSTEIN (1962), p. 327 lists scribal notations for deletions of pericopae.

3. LOUIS GINZBERG, Genizah Studies. In Memory of Doctor Solomon Schechter (= Ginze Schechter), I. Midrash and Haggadah (= Texts and Studies of JTSA, Vol. VII) (New York, 1928, Repr. Hermon Press: New York, 1969).

a. 'Qiṣur Hagadot HaYerushalmi', Abbreviation of y. aggadic material, from the order of Mo'ed., pp. 387—429. Dropsie MS, HALPER, 85.

See LIEBERMAN (1934), p. xxv; EPSTEIN (1930), p. 37; and APTOWITZER (1938), p. 276, who believes that through p. 422 the text is part of 'Śefer Yerushalmi', the medieval compilation based on PT with additions.

b. 'Sheloshah Seride HaYerushalmi', pp. 430–448.
Ber. 7 : 1, 11a–7 : 4, $11c^{29}$.
Shab. 6 : 9, 8d–7 : 1, $9b^{1}$.
Pes. 4 : 9, $31b^{34}$–5 : 1, $31d^{6}$ and 6 : 1, $33a^{20-51}$.

All are from Adler, JTS, 1493.

4. J. N. Epstein, LiSeride HaYerushalmi, Tarbiẓ 3 (1932), 99.

a. A. Z. Ch. II, $41d^{37}$–$42a^{7}$; ch. III, $42c^{2}$ from bottom to $42d^{34}$ = pp. 15–20. Ant. 16.

b. Abbreviated Ket. Ch. I, $25c^{3}$ from bottom – ch. VIII, $32b^{34}$ = pp. 21–26. T.S.F. 17 7a. Cf. Lieberman (1934), p. xxvi.

The passage constitutes explanations glossed into a text. Lieberman (1947), preface p. 3, believes the text is part of Maimonides' work. He presents a photographic reproduction, transcription, and annotated text. See above, on Ginzberg's Yerushalmi Fragments (1909).

c. Hal. Chs. I–IV = pp. 121–136. Ant. 309.

d. Ber. Ch. VIII, 12c = pp. 237–239. Ant. 42.

e. Shab. Ch. XV, 15a–ch. XVI, 15c; ch. XX, 17c–d = pp. 240–245. Ant. 324.

See Lieberman (1934), p. 144.

f. A. Z. Ch. V, 44d–45a = pp. 246–248. Ant. 999.

The several fragments are published with brief textual notes and introductory remarks, especially pp. 15–16 and 121–123, and a supplement on one pericope, pp. 134–136.

5. Solomon Wieder, Qeta' Yerushalmi, Tarbiẓ 18 (1949), 129–136. San. end and Mak. 1 : 1–4; 2 : 7–13 : end. Hungarian Academy of Sciences, Budapest (Kaufmann collection), number 594.

Besides the introduction and notes, Epstein, pp. 136–137, adds a supplementary comment on the importance of the fragment. Of note, the fragment proves that a y. passage existed to Mak. Ch. III and thus confirms the reconstruction of Lieberman (1947), pp. 67–68.

6. D. S. Loewinger, Seridim Ḥadashim, MiYerushalmi Peśaḥim Pereq 5, 6, 7, Alexander Marx Jubilee Volume (New York, 1950), Hebrew Section, pp. 237–283. Pes. Chs. V–VII. Hungarian Academy of Sciences, Kaufmann Collection.

Loewinger provides a brief introduction, slight notes, and an appendix by S. Lieberman, 'LaSeridim HaḤadashim', pp. 284–86. With this new data, Lieberman evaluates the printed edition, readings in MSS, and previously proposed emendations.

7. Nehemya Alloni, Geniza Fragments of Rabbinic Literature, Mishna Talmud, and Midrash with Palestinian vocalization (Jerusalem: Makor, 1973), presents fragments from eight-ninth century, with a careful description and listing (with some misprints) of each fragment, pp. 35–44, 91–93 and full facsimiles, pp. 42–77.

a. Pes. 10 : 2, $37c^{13}$–10 : 9, $37d^{end}$. T.S. 16/328.

b. Taan. 4 : 11, $69c^{43}$–end. } T.S. 12/186–188.
c. Mashqin 1 : 1, $80a^{15}$–3 : 1, $81d^{9}$. }

These items were previously published by C. TAYLOR, Cairo Genizah Palimpsests (Cambridge, 1900), facsimiles III—VIII, and GINZBERG, Yerushalmi Fragments (1909), pp. 191—98.

d. B.Q. 4 : 10, $5a^{15}$—9 : 5, $6d^{5}$. Ms. Georg. c. 1 [2672] and T.S. 12/183, 741.

These were previously published by GINZBERG (1909), pp. 242, 244, 249—250; and P. QURQOVSUV, Zapisok Vostocnie (Pressburg, 1898), pp. 185—205, and analyzed by R. RATNER, HaMelitz (St. Petersburg, 1899), nos. 56, 61, 65, 68, and 72.

e. Shevu. 1: 9,$33c^{12-24}$ [ls. 12—17 = San. 7: 1, $23c^{41-46}$], 1: 9,$33b^{58}$—$33c^{7}$ [= San. 7: 1, $27c^{-5}$—d^{10}]. T.S. 12/749. ALLONI incorrectly identified these fragments and labelled them on the basis of their San. parallel. Accordingly, he mistakenly claimed that ls. 17—24 of the first one was otherwise unattested in texts of y. GINZBERG (1909), pp. 266—267, though, previously published these fragments and correctly labelled them. Prof. SUSSMANN, to whom I owe the above observations, has an additional as yet unpublished fragment to the remaining portion of y. Shevu.

f. Shevu. 1 : 1, $32c^{1}$—d^{43}. T.S. 12/748.

g. A. Z. 2 : 9, $41d^{29}$—$42a^{7}$.
7 : 2, 42c—$42d^{34}$. } Ant. 165.

These fragments were previously published by EPSTEIN, Tarbiẓ 3 (1932), 16—20.

8. ISRAEL FRANCUS, Talmud Yerushalmi, Maśekhet Beṣah (New York, 1967), pp. 259—260. Paris III A35.

In an addendum, FRANCUS describes the fragment and compares it to other readings. The fragment is to be fully published by ELIEZER HOROWITZ.

9. ZVI MEIR RABINOVITZ, New Genizah Fragments of the PT, Henoch Yalon Memorial Volume, ed. E. Y. KUTSCHER, et al. (Bar Ilan University, Ramat Gan and Kirjath Sepher, Jerusalem, 1974) (= Bar Ilan Department Researches, II), pp. 499—511, presents introduction, text of fragments from the Cambridge Taylor Schechter Collection, and notes.

a. Ber. 3 : 4, 6c. NS 329/661.

b. Ber. 3 : 5, 6d. 329/608.

c. Shab. 12 : 3, 13c. 329/578.

d. Qid. 3 : 1, 63c; 3 : 2, 63d; 3 : 3, 64a. NS 171/1.

10. E. A. GOLDMAN, A Critical Edition of Palestinian Talmud Tractate Rosh HaShanah, [in 4 installments:] HUCA 46—49 (1973—78), presents facsimiles of several fragments and fresh transcription and citation of fragments to y. R.H. and to pericopae elsewhere in y. which parallel R.H. Items to Chapter One are:

a. R.H. Ch. 1. T.S.F. 17.9.13.16.24.

b. M.Q. 3: 7. T.S.F. 17.16.

c. Sheq. 3: 1. T.S.F. 17.24.

GINZBERG (1909), 140—147, 152—153, 205^{2-10}, 126^{25-20} and 127^{2-18}, previously published these fragments.

11. S. ABRAMSON, Qeta' Genizah MiYerushalmi Shabbat Pereq Hamaṣni'a, Kobez Al Yad 8 (18) (Jerusalem, 1976), pp. 1—13.

Shab. 10: 2, 12c[5]—10: 3, 12c[30]; 10: 5, 12c[39]—10: 7, 12d[5]. Cambridge fragment without exact box identification.

ABRAMSON provides an introduction, pp. 3—9, to the transcribed and annotated fragments, pp. 10—13.

12. Shev. VII. See Section D. 2. above. According to SUSSMANN this text is a Geniza fragment the second half of which is in the Cambridge Library.

V. Textual Notes to Yerushalmi

The following items focus on the literary history of the text and demonstrate the uses of lower textual criticism which employs MSS. Further works may be found among the commentaries and exegetical articles, presented below in Section XX. C.

1. B. RATNER, Ahawath Zion We-Jerusholaim. 12 vols. (Vilna, 1901—1917, Repr. Jerusalem, 1967), covers Ber. and the Orders of 'Zera'im' and 'Mo'ed', less tractate 'Eruv'.

RATNER realized that early authorities (Rishonim) may have had different literary traditions of y. and he therefore provided citations from these works. At times he adds his own comments. He based the work on the Venice first edition and where available employed Geniza fragments or MSS. Thus once it had appeared he was able to consult GINZBERG's 'Yerushalmi Fragments' (1909). A colleague supplied him with some variants from the Leiden MS.

While the work is enormously helpful, one cannot totally rely on it. He generally gives the early citations only when they diverge from the present text and not where they coincide and therefore confirm it. Moreover, he does not supply the full citations and often fails carefully to isolate the citation of y. from explanatory glosses. Accordingly, one must recheck the sources he lists. Further, RATNER's citations may be inaccurate in that he relied upon later editions of the Rishonim, whose texts are often corrupted, indeed 'corrected' on the basis of the supposed correct text of y. Today one can use first or critical editions of these volumes which are now being published. See below, on Commentaries, Chs. XIX—XX. Finally, RATNER overvalued readings in y. editions that appeared after the Venice first edition. He thought they were based on different MSS. On the other hand, he undervalued the L. MS; cf. 'Introduction' to Ber. A separate issue, which I discuss below, in Section XIX. C, is how to evaluate differences that clearly emerge from the citations, viz., do they represent variants, paraphrases, etc.

The reviews of individual volumes often constitute separate studies. These include: W. BACHER, REJ 43 (1901): 310—317; 46 (1903): 154—159; 50 (1905): 140—144; 52 (1906): 311—314; 53 (1907): 277—280; 57 (1909):

308—311; 60 (1911): 151—154; 62 (1912): 157—159; and 64 (1912): 315—317. S. BUBER, Maaśef 1 (5662) [= 1902], B: 48—62; HaMelitz (1903), #87, 88, 92, 113, 117, 121, 124, 125, 127. S. POZNANSKI, HaṢefirah (1903), #68, 70—72, (1905), #24, (1917), #11, 12; HaOlam (1907), #14; Hed Hazman (1909), #284, 287; HaIvri (5671) [= 1911], #14, 15. V. APTOWITZER, MGWJ 52 (1908): 307—316, 54 (1910): 160—172, 287—288, 417—419, 60 (1916): 107—109.

2. Virtually all the works of SAUL LIEBERMAN, especially: 'Emendations in Jerushalmi' A—F, in Tarbiẓ: A: 2,i (1930), 106—114 (to which cf. EPSTEIN, ibid., pp. 241—243); B: 2, ii (1930), 235—240; a note to A and B: 2, iii (1931), 380; C: 3 (1932), 205—212; D: 337—339; E: 452—457 [to which cf. 4 (1933), 293]; F: 4 (1933), 377—79; and F.b: 5 (1933), 97—110 [to which cf. 6 (1935), 111]. ID., The Uzziahu Inscription and the Torah of the Ancients, Tarbiẓ 4 (1933), 292—293. ID., Jerushalmi Miscellanies, Tarbiẓ 6 (1935), 24—35 (to which cf. EPSTEIN, ibid. pp. 236—37).

3. J. N. EPSTEIN, Jerushalmian Miscellanies, Tarbiẓ 6 (1935), 236—37. ID., Some Varia Lectiones in Jerushalmi, I: The Leiden MS, Tarbiẓ 5 (1934), 257—272, and 6 (1934), 38—55. Note, pp. 39—46 focus on the Ven. p.e.'s copy editor's mistakes in names, first, of masters and their titles and, secondly, of places. ID., Talmudical Miscellanies, Tarbiẓ 3 (1931), 110—111.

VI. Translations

A. Full Text of PT

1. French translation: M. SCHWAB, Le Talmud de Jérusalem. 11 vols. (Paris, 1871, Repr. 1932—33), a generally unreliable rendering.

2. German translation of aggadic portions: AUG. WÜNSCHE, Der Jerusalemische Talmud in seinen haggadischen Bestandtheilen übertragen (Zürich, 1880, Repr. Hildesheim, 1967), with a brief introduction, pp. iii—viii.

B. To Selected Portions of PT

1. Latin translation to twenty tractates: B. UGOLINO, Thesaurus Antiquitatum Sacrarum, Vols. 17—30 (Venice, 1755—65). The texts and translations of *gemara* include: Maas, M.S., Hal., Orl., Bik, in Vol. 20 (1757); Pes., in Vol. 17 (1755); Yoma, Sheq., Suk., R.H., Bes., Tan., Meg., Hag., M.Q., in Vol. 18 (1755); Sot., Ket., Qid., in Vol. 30 (1765); and San., Mak., in Vol. 25 (1762).

2. Ber., in English translation:

a. M. SCHWAB, The Talmud of Jerusalem I: Berakhoth (London, 1886, Repr. N.Y. 1969).

b. Ch. Eight, in English: JACOB NEUSNER, Invitation to the Talmud. A Teaching Book (N.Y., 1973). Besides the translation, which is based on a corrected text, this work includes an introduction to the Yerushalmi and the chapter, and a full commentary on the content and the literary traits of the materials.

3. Bik. The Jerusalem Talmud (Talmud Yerushalmi) Bikkurim. Text, translation, introduction, and commentary, by JOSEPH RABBINOWITZ (London, 1975).

4. Shab., Ch. Seven (Eight), in German: ISAAK LEVY, Der achte Abschnitt aus dem Traktate 'Sabbath'. Inaugural-Dissertation der philosophischen Facultät der Kaiser Wilhelms-Universität Strassburg 1891 (Breslau, n.d.). The translation includes some notes.

5. Suk., in German translation: CHARLES HOROWITZ, Der Palästinische Talmud. Sukkah. Die Felshütte. Bonner Orientalistische Studien (Bonn, 1963). The introduction, pp. 7—13, focuses on motifs and institutions of the tractate and of the holiday of Sukkot. The text, pp. 14—100, contains brief notes.

6. Taan., in English translation: A. W. GREENUP, Taanith From the Palestinian Talmud (London, 1918, 1921). The work lacks an introduction to the translation and tractate and contains only very brief explanatory notes to the text and references to parallels.

7. Ned., in German translation: CHARLES HOROWITZ, Der Palästinische Talmud. Nedarim (Düsseldorf-Benrath, 1957). This work has a one page preface, and brief notes on the bottom of the translation. They are based upon commentaries in the Krotoschin and Vilna editions, and on parallels, and focus, first, on variants and their importance and, secondly, on the exegesis of difficult passages.

8. B.M., Ch. Three, in English translation. A. EHRMAN, ed. The Talmud with English Translation and Commentary (El-Am: Jerusalem, 1965). This work contains an introduction and a modern, though less than fully critical, long commentary and notes. To date, of the several portions published only one part includes a text of y., B.M. 3 : 1, 8b—3 : 9, 9b.

Part Three

Contents and the History of the Materials Incorporated within PT

VII. Scope of Yerushalmi

1. The Venice first edition covers four orders of 'Mishnah' and only several folios in the fifth, of Nid. Traditional authorities and modern scholars have discussed whether this represents the full y. or whether some

part(s) have not been preserved. This includes individual passages; pericopae; the last chapters in three tractates, Mak. 3, Sab. 21—24, Nid. 4—10; and the tractates in 'Qodshin' and 'Ṭehorot'.

There are three possible solutions:

a. The portion was lost at the time of printing or writing of L. MS, or at some earlier, post-Talmudic time.

b. Incomplete compilation. Material other than that extant was never redacted.

c. Further material as unedited sources or in some pre-edited stage never existed.

2. The evidence consists of:

a. Supposed citations by medieval authorities of passages now non-extant or in non-extant portions of y. Cf. the sources and literature listed under 'citations', Section XIX. C.

References to y. may not actually refer to PT, but rather to some midrashic work, qabbalistic tract, or medieval compendium-anthology of y. that consists of material with additions from BT and Gaonic sources, the 'Śefer Yerushalmi'; cf. below, Section XVIII. F. While all the citations cannot be discounted, FRANKEL (1870), pp. 45a—49a, already indicated that a citation in a medieval commentary, even if correctly interpreted, only proves that the authority knew the individual Palestinian tradition and not the whole section or tractate in which the passage supposedly appears.

b. The presence of abbreviated or deleted or whole pericopae that parallel material elsewhere in y. These are scribal deletions; cf. LIEBERMAN (1929), pp. 12—13, 39, and (1949), p. xv. There are also *sugyot* which apparently originate in the missing y. portions (of Shab. and Nid.) and whose extant versions should thus constitute "parallel transferred pericopae". See MOSHE ASSIS, Parallel *sugyot* in the Jerusalem Talmud (In the Tractates: Bikkurim, Shabbath, Soṭah, Makkoth, and Niddah) (Ph. D. Dissertation, Hebrew University, 1976) (Jerusalem, 1976), especially pp. 102, 105—112, 145, 151—157, and Section IX. A. below.

c. Evidence of MSS and geniza fragments. They cover only the already published portions, with the exeception of Mak. Ch. 3, which LIEBERMAN (1947), pp. 67f., had already reconstructed on the basis of parallel *sugyot* elsewhere in y. and of testimonies in medieval authorities. The fragment to Shab. Ch. 20 end, indicates that already at the time of the writing of that fragment the latter chapters of Shab. were missing; EPSTEIN, Tarbiẓ 3 (1931), 245.

d. Fragments of a Palestinian halakhic work on themes contained in the non-extant y. portion, y. Hul.; MORDECHAI MARGULIES [= MARGALIOTH], Hilkhot Ereṣ Yisrael Min HaGenizah (Jerusalem, 1973). Both positions can claim support from this item. It proves that these subjects were studied and therefore assumably preserved in y. Alternatively, as these materials were found in a practical compendium, there was no need for a y. tractate. Cp. LIEBERMAN (1931) and ID., A Few Words on the Book by Julian The Architect of Ascalon 'The Laws of Palestine and its Customs', Tarbiẓ 40 (1971), 409—417.

e. Material on Qod. and Ṭeh. attributed to Palestinians which appears elsewhere in extant portions of y. or in BT.

f. Assumptions of whether or not Palestinians would have studied and taught certain materials, those supposedly halakhicly relevant or practical.

Concerning nos. d—f:

The fact that materials were studied does not logically yield the conclusion that there was an edited y. Indeed BT refers to Palestinian traditions which are appropriate to extant tractates of y. but which are not found there; cf. below, Section XI. 3. Thus y. did not incorporate all traditions. In addition, there existed in Palestine different compilations of materials and *gemarot*; cf. LIEBERMAN (1931) and SZ (1968); GINZBERG (1941), pp. xxxix and H: cxvf. Therefore, one cannot speak of y. in monolithic terms.

g. Publications, supposedly from a lost MS, of an edition of y. Qodshin (Hul., Bekh., Zev., ʿArak.), 1907—09, which today, however, is recognized as a forgery. See, e.g., B. Z. BACHER, Talmud Yerushalmi ʿal Maśekhet Ḥullin UMaśekhet Bekhorot, HaKedem 1 (1907), 20—40, 70—85; V. APTOWITZER, MGWJ 52 (1908), 316—317, 435—436, 625f.; and 54 (1910), 564—570; and HABERMANN (1952), pp. 204 and 253; and SHMUEL HAKOHEN WEINGARTEN, Sinai 32, vol. 62 (1968), 281—287.

h. Supposed testimony by Pirqoi ben Baboi, beginning of ninth century, that Palestinians lack laws of 'Sheḥiṭah' and have forgotten the Orders of 'Qodshin' and 'Ṭehorot'. Pirqoi's testimony, however, is not fully reliable due to his propagandist motives to deemphasize Palestinian tradition, especially in the area of laws of 'Ṭerefah'. See SHALOM SPIEGEL, On the Polemic of Pirqoi Ben Baboi, Harry Wolfson Jubilee Volume (Jerusalem, 1965), Hebrew Section, pp. 243—274, esp. 253—260, MARGULIES (1973), esp. pp. 102—104, and SHLOMO SIMONSOHN, The Hebrew Revival Among Early Medieval European Jews, Salo Baron Jubilee Volume (Jerusalem, 1974), pp. 843—845; and DAVID GOODBLATT, Rabbinic Instruction in Sasanian Babylonia (Leiden 1975), p. 15.

3. Tentative consensus:

The missing chapters in Mak. Shab. and Nid. existed. As to 'Qodshin' and 'Ṭehorot' there is no firm agreement.

4. Literature:

*FRANKEL (1870), pp. 45a—49a, 144a.

MORITZ STEINSCHNEIDER, Handschriften-Verzeichnisse der Königlichen Bibliothek zu Berlin, II: 1 (Berlin, 1878), p. 65.

Z. W. RABINOVITZ, Some Comments on y. Qodshin, Yerushalayim 7 (1907), 177—179; and ID., Shaʿare Torath Eretz Israel (Jerusalem, 1940), pp. 128, 222, 308, 351, 590.

RATNER, Orlah (1971), p. 225.

GINZBERG (1929) II, 560; and (1941), pp. li and H: cxiv–vi.

*LIEBERMAN (1929), pp. 12–13, 39–43 (1947), pp. 67f.

*STRACK (1931⁵), pp. 66–69, 266.

CH. ALBECK, Introduction, Bereschit Rabba (Jerusalem, 1965²).

*EPSTEIN (1962), pp. 330–334.

*SHALOM SPIEGEL, On the Polemic of Pirqoi Ben Baboi, Harry Wolfson Jubilee Volume (Jerusalem, 1965), pp. 253–260.

*JACOB SUSSMANN, Śugyot Bavliot LiŚedarim Zera'im UṬehorot (unpublished Ph.D. dissertation Hebrew University, Jerusalem, 1969), pp. 1–13 [in press: Israeli Academy of Sciences].

MELAMMED (1973), pp. 509–512.

VIII. Arrangement and Contents of Yerushalmi

A. Basic Structure, Contents, and Forms

The *gemara* in y., as in b., basically is structured around 'Mishnah'. One may describe the contents in terms of their formal traits or of their function. *Gemara* consists of: materials formulated as glosses, e.g., to 'Mishnah' or some other teaching or text; autonomous statements; *baraitot*; disputes; debates; questions; answers; lists; biblical exegeses; songs; laments; prayers; stories; and narrative *aggadah*. Items may be unassigned, or attributed to a master, prefaced or unprefaced by the name of a tradent or list of tradents.

The materials serve to: comment upon and analyze the text and content of 'Mishnah' and related sources; present independent teachings and discussion thereon; attack or defend interpretations or statements; cite sources; compare or associate a principle in one text or interpretation with that of another found elsewhere; present cases, stories, and aggadic materials.

Most of the literature deal with a self-defined selection of sources and thus do not cover all the data. Moreover, as generally they do not fully or at all analyze an item's occurrence in y., for comparative purposes I include some works on non-y. sources.

*FRANKEL (1870), pp. 49a–51b, on aggadic materials; 36a–40a, 53b, on attributive formulae that mention a tradent.

*SHMUEL VALDBERG, Śefer Darkhe HaShinuyin (Lemberg, 1870, Repr. Jerusalem, 1970), classifies and analyzes, with lists of instances, methods used in exegesis and expounding of verses.

S. SEKLES, The Poetry of the Talmud (New York, 1880), hardly exhaustive but suggestive.

*LIEBERMAN (1931), pp. 84–108, attributive formulae of traditions in y. Neziqin; ID., Greek in Jewish Palestine (New York, 1941, 1965²), p. 110.

GINZBERG (1941), pp. H: lxxxi–lxxxii.

*Julius Greenstone, Popular Proverbs in the Jerusalem Talmud, Essays in Honor of the Very Rev. Dr. J. Hertz, ed. I. Epstein, et al. (London, 1943), pp. 187—201.

Abraham Weiss, The Babylonian Talmud as a Literary Unit (New York, 1943), and Id., Studies in the Literature of the Amoraim (New York, 1962), for which see David Goodblatt, Abraham Weiss: The Search for Literary Forms, in: The Formation of the Babylonian Talmud, ed. J. Neusner (Leiden, 1970), pp. 95—103.

Dov Noy, HaŚipur Ha'Amami VeTalmud U VaMidrash (Jerusalem, 1960), on folk narratives and stories.

*Joseph Heinemann, Prayer in the Period of the Tannaim and the Amoraim—Its Nature and Patterns (Hebrew), (Jerusalem, 1964). English revised edition (Berlin, 1977).

*Jacob Neusner, Development of a Legend (Leiden, 1970); Id., The Rabbinic Traditions About the Pharisees Before 70, 3 vols. (Leiden, 1971); Id., Eliezer Ben Hyrcanus, 2 vols. (Leiden, 1973); Id., A History of the Mishnaic Law of Purities, I—III: Kelim (Leiden, 1974); IV—V: Ohalot (Leiden, 1975); VI—VIII: Negaim (Leiden, 1975), present systematic study, classification, and analysis of literary forms, patterns, and structures.

*Aaron Mirsky, HaShirah HaIvrit BiTequfat HaTalmud, Yerushalayim, Shenaton LeDivre Śifrut VeHaGut, ed. Gedaliah Algoshe (Jerusalem, 1966), II: 161—179, a suggestive study on literary characteristics and forms of songs and poetry.

*D. Ben-Amos, Narrative Forms in the Haggadah: Structural Analysis, Ph. D. Dissertation, Indiana University, 1967 (University Microfilms, Ann Arbor, 1967, 1975), includes an excellent review of previous treatments of *aggadah*, careful analyses of the traits of legends, tall tale, fable, exemplum, and riddling tale, and a full bibliography.

Benjamin DeVries, Meḥqarim BiŚifrut HaTalmud (Jerusalem, 1968), pp. 284—289, and 290—300, on literary dimensions and types of *aggadah*.

J. Florsheim, Rav Hisda as Exegetor of Tannaitic Sources, Tarbiẓ 40 (1971), 24—48.

Wayne Sibley Towner, The Rabbinic Enumeration of Scriptural Examples (Leiden, 1973). This excellent study includes a discussion and bibliography of earlier works on rabbinic literary patterns.

*Melammed (1973), pp. 275—296, 312—317, and his forthcoming book, 'The Halakhic Midrashim in the Palestinian Talmud'.

*Bokser (1975), by type, formulation, and use analyzes and classifies traditions and attributive formulae of Samuel, some of which appear in y.

Joseph Heinemann and Jakob J. Petuchowski, Literature of the Synagogue (New York, 1975), introductions and selections of prayer and poetry in both Talmuds and in early liturgy, laments, and sermons. Many examples are from y.

*Gary G. Porton, The Legal Traditions of Rabbi Ishmael. I: The Earlier Legal Traditions (Leiden, 1976).

*William S. Green, The Traditions of Joshua ben Hananiah. I: The Earlier Legal Traditions (Leiden, 1979).

Goodblatt (1979), IV. 1: b. ζ and IV. 2.

There are various practical reasons to consider the nature and uses of formulations and patterns. Below, in Section IX. B, I shall discuss the application to exegesis, especially where two or more versions of an item may exist. One should note that the several literary genres may be reflected in variations in grammatical forms. For example, texts of prayers, songs, and public or formal declarations may employ different grammatical forms and usages from passages of colloquial materials. While this has been demonstrated for the BT, it undoubtedly applies, as well, to the PT; Shamma Friedman, Three Studies in Babylonian Grammar, Tarbiẓ 43 (1973—74), 58—69.

As to terms, structured phrasings, and fixed bridging language, all of which may provide or determine the strucutre of a whole pericope, see below, Chapter XVI.

B. Layout

1. Some scholars have tried to describe the layout of the materials. Many have compared y.'s *gemara* to that of b. and have made the obvious observation that PT is briefer, usually with shorter and elliptical or less clear discussions, more to the point and simpler in explaining 'Mishnah' or discussing a tradition. I review the import of these phenomena in the sections on the editing of the text and the role of the scribes, Sections IX and XII. At this point let me say only that much of the greater expansive nature of b. *gemara* unboubtedly comes from the end of the Amoraic period and more so from the Saboraic activity, a process which y. lacked. Cf. Assis (1976), pp. 7f.

The only systematic study of the structure is Lieberman, Talmud of Caesarea (1931), in which he compares the structure of y. 'Neziqin' to that of the rest of y. To my knowledge all other general comments, whatever their merits, are part of research in progress or are not based on a comprehensive and careful study of the data. Moreover, in the formulation of their comments, many works do not sufficiently take into account the diversity of *gemara*, which is the product of different circles. Cf. Lieberman (1931), pp. 23—25; Ginzberg (1941), p. H: lxxxi; and Melammed (1973), pp. 566—567.

Clearly y., like b., presents materials along certain lines. These include:

a. Explanations of 'Mishnah', analyses thereof, and independent teachings related to the theme of 'Mishnah'. Lieberman (1934), p. 215 notes, PT first offers or establishes the reading or simple sense of 'Mishnah' . . ., or cites a *baraita*, and then analyzes and discusses the first part of the text.

b. Series of comments, statements, adages or incidents formally related, one of which is relevant to the context. E.g., *gemara* may contain a series of items attributed to the same master. See FRANKEL (1870), pp. 39a—b, 49a—51b; EPSTEIN, Tarbiẓ 3 (1931), 122; GINZBERG (1941), p. H: lxxvii; and MELAMMED (1973), pp. 565—566, and cp. R. EDELMANN, Some Remarks on the Literary Aspect of the Talmud and Midrashim in their Relation to Hellenistic Civilization, Third World Congress of Jewish Studies, Synopses of Lectures Section: Talmud and Rabbinics (Jerusalem, 1961), pp. IV, 1—7; and A. WEISS (1962).

c. Repetition of a pericope from elsewhere. *Gemara* on the basis of a tangential reference in a pericope elsewhere may include that whole pericope in the referred-to location. Cf. FRANKEL (1870) and LIEBERMAN (1947), pp. 67f. Below I discuss transferred pericopae and to what degree this phenomenon derives from the editors or scribes of the text.

Finally, one should note that Aramaic and Hebrew within y. tend consistently to be used for different purposes. Traditions generally appear in Hebrew while discussions and narratives employ Aramaic. Cf. JULIUS GREENSTONE (1943), esp. p. 187, fn. 2, who indicates that proverbs in contrast to *aggadah* employs Hebrew twice as frequently as Aramaic; E. MARGALIYOT, Ivrit Ve'aramit BaTalmud U VaMidrash, Leshonenu 27—28 (1963—64), 20—33; and MELAMMED (1973), pp. 315—317.

2. Additional literature on the above items include:

FRANKEL (1870), pp. 18b—40a, 47, provides the basic description, though his evaluation does not sufficiently take into account the literary nature of the materials and he unconsciously adopts the Jewish Enlightenment's apologetic that the b. is too long-winded and convoluted.

LEWIN, Methiboth (1933), pp. x—xii.

A. WEISS, The Literary Development of the Babylonian Talmud, 2 vols. (Warsaw, 1937, 1939); (1943); and (1962). Cf. SHAMAI KANTER, Abraham Weiss: Source Criticism, in: NEUSNER, Formation (1970), p. 89.

*ABRAHAM GOLDBERG, The Sources and Development of the Sugya in the Babylonian Talmud, Tarbiẓ 32 (1962—63), 143—152.

B. DEVRIES, Mavo Kelali LeŚifrut HaTalmudit (Tel Aviv, 1966), pp. 108—110.

DAVID WEISS HALIVNI (1968, 1975), passim and for comparative purposes, II: 'Introduction'.

BOKSER (1975), pp. 21—26, 145—157. As to the location of a b. tradition within a y. pericope, see pp. 77—80, and fn. 216; 97—101; and 117—120.

C. 'Mishnah'

1. J. N. EPSTEIN, Introduction to the Text of Mishnah (Jerusalem, 1964[2]), provides a definitive treatment of most matters concerning 'Mishnah', including the text of 'Mishnah' and how later authorities perceived that work. The work is outstanding in both conception of the problem, use of all examples of a phenomenon, analysis, bibliographical comments, laying

out of issues, and usually his conclusions. The relevant portions are pp. 160—508, 673—726, 771—946. See BARUCH M. BOKSER, Jacob N. Epstein's 'Introduction to the Text of the Mishnah', in: The Modern Study of the Mishnah, ed. J. NEUSNER (Leiden, 1973), pp. 13—36.

2. PT originally was one continuous text, without chapter, tractate and *halakhah* 'division'. These are later additions; cf. LIEBERMAN (1929), pp. 11—12; (1934), pp. xxviii—xxix and 238, fn. 1. Later arrangers of y. included certain internal lemmas of 'Mishnah'. Thus the 'Mishnah' presented in the y. MSS or editions and most lemma-citations of 'Mishnah' do not represent the 'Mishnah' used by the Palestinian masters. The passages or citations are added by scribes, who in the process may have placed them in the wrong location. Moreover, the order of *gemara* or its sources may have differed from that of 'Mishnah''s, but scribes arranged the Amoraic material according to 'Mishnah''s order.

Additional literature includes:

Y. H. SHOR, Mishnayot in Talmud Yerushalmi and Bavli, HeḤaluṣ 6 (1862), 32—47.

EPSTEIN, Fragments, Tarbiẓ 3 (1932), pp. 121f.; ID., HaMada' HaTalmudi Uṣerakhov, Proceeding of the Academy of Jewish Studies 2 (Jerusalem, 1935), pp. 5—7; and (1962), pp. 604—606.

RABINOVITZ (1940), p. 636.

MELECH SCHACHTER, The Babylonian and Jerusalem Mishnah: Textually Compared (Jerusalem, 1959) is inexact, unreliable, and conceptually poor.

*MELAMMED (1973), pp. 535—543.

SOLOMON ZEITLIN, HaMishnah SheBiYerushalmi VeHaMishnah SheBeBavli, in: Zer li-Gevurot [= Zalman Shazar Jubilee Volume], ed. B. Z. LURIA (Jerusalem, 1973), pp. 539—548.

FEINTUCH, Tarbiẓ 45 (1976), I—II, 178—212.

S. ABRAMSON, As to Two Terms Used to Cite Mishnah, Sinai 40 (79) (1977), 211—228, especially 228.

3. No single reading or text of 'Mishnah' existed in Amoraic times. Rather masters may have had different recensions and variant individual readings, on the basis of which they taught. EPSTEIN traces how early Amoraim had a 'reliable' text of 'Mishnah', yet taught independent of 'Mishnah'. On the other hand, the later Amoraim read 'Mishnah''s text with greater freedom but tried to base their teachings on it. Reciters or later scribes may alter a text of 'Mishnah' to accord with a given interpretation. EPSTEIN, moreover, historically and philologically classifies modes and terminologies used in citing, explaining, questioning, and ostensibly emending 'Mishnah'.

See also:

FRANKEL (1870), pp. 19a—22a, described many of the phenomena. EPSTEIN besides producing a more systematic and analytical treatment evaluated the assumptions in the study and reformulated the questions.

HANOCH ALBECK, Nuśḥaot BaMishnah Shel Ha'Amoraim, Zvi Chajes Memorial Volume (Vienna, 1933), pp. 1—28.
GINZBERG (1941), pp. H: li—lvi.
LIEBERMAN, SZ (1968).
WEISS HALIVNI (1968 and 1975).
MELAMMED (1973), pp. 535—548.

D. Citation and Use of Sources

1. Y. contains items which ostensibly represent a 'source', i.e., materials which employ some type of a structure, the pattern for which does not depend upon the present context, and which ostensibly represent a teaching from an earlier period. Technically this could include many of the items which I earlier listed under the 'forms' or 'formulations' of the materials, but I presently refer only to *baraitot* and texts of midrashic exegesis.

The major methodological problem in the study of any supposed 'source', whether a *baraita* or even a sermon, is: Does the material represent true 'sources' used or incorporated by the spokesperson-tradent or editor of the pericope or of the PT? Alternatively, is it a literary way in which to arrange and transmit material produced by the one who cited it or edited the pericope? Unfortunately, to my knowledge this issue, in terms of Amoraic material, has not been squarely faced. Cf. DAVID GOODBLATT, Abraham Weiss: The Search for Literary Forms, in: J. NEUSNER, Formation (1970), pp. 96—103, and especially ID. (1979), IV. 1: a, c. Clearly, however, individual material did circulate outside the framework of *gemara*. We find them, whether or not in an earlier or later recension or version, in other literary sources, e.g., 'Tosefta' and 'Bereshit Rabbah', and possibly even in a halakhic mosaic inscription on the pavement of a Beth Shean synagogue. Cf. SUSSMANN (1973—74), and ID., The Boundaries of Eretz-Israel, Tarbiẓ 45 (1976), II—III, 213—257; SAUL LIEBERMAN, The Halakhic Inscription from the Bet-Shean Valley, Tarbiẓ 45 (1976), IV, 54—63, 331; and below, Chapter X, on the *Midrashim*. Cf. Z. SAFRAI, Immanuel 8 (1978), 48—57.

Such texts thus existed; in fact it is the only way to account for the history of materials which appear e. g., in Tos., a 'Midrash Halakhah', and in one or more *baraitot*. But we do not know if every instance of such a text represents a 'source' or a conventional way in which to formulate and present materials. On the other hand, if the text pre-existed outside its present context, irrespective of any revisions, it may include material in addition to or even some that is inconsistent with that which is needed in the present instance. This accords with LIEBERMAN's observation (1934), p. 216, that y. may cite a biblical verse, 'Mishnah', or *baraita* as a metaphoric-idiomatic usage, for such texts were fixed in the mouths of the Amoraim. One must, accordingly, not confuse the issue of form with that of source and must carefully examine each item.

2. Indexes. The reference index in the Krotoschin edition of y. is superior to that in the other editions.

Z. BACHER, Baraitot beTalmud Yerushalmi, Yerushalayim 10 (1913), 59—82, a classified list, with comments, of *baraitot* cited in y.

MICHAEL HIGGER, Oṣar HaBaraitot, 10 vols. (New York, 1938—48), comprehensive, classified collection of *baraitot* in both *gemarot*. He consistently employs MSS and citations of medieval authorities and indicates all the item's versions which appear elsewhere. Vol. 10 includes a page index to *gemara*.

*E. Z. MELAMMED, Halakhic Midrashim in the Talmud. II: Halakhic Midrashim in the Talmud Yerushalmi (Jerusalem, in preparation). A comprehensive classified study. Cf. MELAMMED (1973), pp. 275—296, 312—317, for the tentative results and classifications.

3. Technique of 'citing'. Scholars and commentators describe the ways in which items are cited and the terminologies that are used; they discuss the texts' 'origins' and how they relate to 'Mishnah', *baraitot,* and to other extant versions or corpora of the materials, and they try to account for variations.

I deal here with the modes by which the items are cited, and in the next section with the relationship of a source in y. to its analogue elsewhere.

On the citations of 'Mishnah', see also above, Section C. Of note, differences did not always exist between the modes of citation of 'Mishnah' and *baraita*. A sharp conceptual difference between corpora stems from the latter part of the Amoraic period. Then Rabbi's 'Mishnah' became the 'Mishnah' with a capital M. See EPSTEIN (1948, 1964²) and LIEBERMAN, SZ (1968).

Y. contains fixed terminologies that mark something as a *baraita*, a Tannaitic source, i. e., deriving from a 'known' collection of *baraitot*, or to be more accurate, some type of worked over text.

The classification and usages of such words may be found in:

*HIGGER (1938—48). Besides the full listings, there are introductions.

CHANOCH ALBECK, Studies in the Baraita and Tosefta (Jerusalem, 1944, 1969), examines *baraitot* with the several types of attributive formulae, assigned and unassigned; ID., Introduction to the Talmud, Babli and Yerushalmi (Jerusalem, 1969), Ch. III, esp. pp. 19—43.

*EPSTEIN (1948, 1964²), systematically classifies the items used for 'Mishnah' and *baraitot*. In ID., Introduction to Tannaitic Literature (Jerusalem-Tel Aviv, 1957), pp. 499—746, he focuses on items that correlate with texts in the Tannaitic Midrashim. On p. 501, he refers to the earlier literature.

*MELAMMED (1973), pp. 275—296 and 312—317.

The following phenomena are of note:

a. PT may digest a 'Mishnah', hint at it, and scribes later filled in the rest, and, at times, did so incorrectly; see FRANKEL (1870), pp. 36a—40a;

LIEBERMAN (1934), p. 157; and BOKSER (1975), pp. 101f., fn. 280. This likewise occurred with *baraitot*. Thus LIEBERMAN points out that y. may identify an item with the phrase, ––'מתניתא דר, *MTNYT' DR'*––––––––, "the teaching is that of R. ––––––," and the scribes filled in the referent, אמר ––'דר ..., *DR'*––––––––––*'MR*, ... "For R. –––– said". But they may have erred in this identification.

The fact that originally y. did not always include the citation of the source and that the tendency later was to fill it in would preclude wholesale adoption of RABINOVITZ (1940), pp. 88, fn. 1; 237; 360, who holds that *baraitot* may have been deleted. One thus must evaluate the type and purpose of each citation.

b. PT may paraphrase a *baraita* which, therefore, may not be in its original language; EPSTEIN (1962), p. 254.

c. PT may cite the beginning of a text and refer to its end, and do so even without including, 'וכו, *WKW*, "etc."

d. PT may abbreviate a *baraita*; MELAMMED (1973), pp. 580f.

e. A text may employ some linguistic peculiarities in presenting materials. Thus a, ו, *W*, may represent, הוא, *HW'*, "he" or "that is"; cf. LIEBERMAN, Tarbiẓ 4 (1933), p. 377; BOKSER (1975), p. 27, fn. 56. (The reference to the pages in the article by KUTSCHER should read p. 1602 and not p. 1595.)

A separate issue is, what constitutes a *baraita* or 'true' Tannaitic material? The question responds to the following data:

a. Y. often cites a *baraita* without an introductory term. Writers discuss whether such terms were originally lacking or whether they were subsequently deleted. See LIEBERMAN (1934), pp. 192, 410; and EPSTEIN (1957), pp. 253–255.

b. An Amoraic tradition may be identical to an item in a Tannaitic corpus or to a text in BT, represented as a *baraita*. See EPSTEIN (1957), pp. 253–255; NEUSNER (1973); MELAMMED (1973), pp. 294–296. The Amora may thus represent the teaching as a 'tradition', and not as a 'source'. On the other hand, the individual's contribution may consist in the citation of a given 'source' in a specific context or by the choice of one *baraita* and the rejection of another. See BOKSER (1975), pp. 6–7, and passim.

c. Y. may also introduce disputes or individual teachings of early Amoraim with, תני, *TNY*, "teaches", a term 'normally' associated with a *baraita*, e. g., *TNY ŠMW'L*, "Samuel teaches". See LIEBERMAN (1931), p. 64, fn. 124, and SZ (1968), p. 127; HIGGER (1938–48), esp. Vols. I and IV; RABINOVITZ (1940), p. 68; ALBECK (1944), pp. 15–48; EPSTEIN (1948, 1964[2]), pp. 212–216; GOODBLATT (1975), pp. 77–80, 200–201.

4. The relationship between different versions of *baraitot*. As already indicated, a *baraita* cited in y. may elsewhere have parallels or analogous versions. Commentators and scholars have noticed and tried to account for the variations between the several versions. Too much of the analysis, however, has been prejudiced by a desire to prove or disprove that *gemara*, taken as a monolithic construct, knew or did not know a given

document, also taken as a construct. While evidence may at times support a general conclusion, in fact one can speak of only individual pericopae of a Tannaitic source and of individual *sugyot*. This accords with the existence of different oral reciters who were the depository for the 'sources' and who, when appropriate, would cite individual materials. Moreover, even *sugyot* may be composed of different parts, each of which comes from different circles. See LIEBERMAN (1931), pp. 22—24; GINZBERG (1941), pp. H: lxxx—lxxxi; EPSTEIN (1962), pp. 275—276; ABRAHAM WEISS, Studies in the Literature of the Amoraim (New York, 1962), pp. 166—175, — to which see MEYER FELDBLUM, Professor Abraham Weiss: His Approach and Contribution to Talmudic Scholarship, The Abraham Weiss Jubilee Volume (New York, 1964), English Section, pp. 69—71; and MEYER FELDBLUM, Talmudic Law and Literature: Tractate Gittin (New York, 1969), p. 32; and cp. EJ. s. v. baraita.

In addition, some writers speculate as to the lack, in *gemara*, of a reference to a *baraita* from 'Tosefta' and argue that the failure to cite the source indicates that the document was not known and, therefore, not yet composed. But, as indicated above, the purpose and context of the Amoraic comment and the way in which it circulated may, at times, have made it inappropriate to cite the *baraita*; BOKSER (1975), pp. 6f. Cf. WEISS HALIVNI (1968), p. 295, fn. 6; (1975), pp. 86, 159f., 163f. Moreover, the proposition assumes that everything known was recorded and compiled in *gemara* and that nothing was ever left as a mere allusion—something known to be otherwise, as already indicated; see LIEBERMAN (1947), p. 68, fn. 18.

As to variations, differences between *baraitot* or a *baraita* and passage in a corpus, e. g., 'Tosefta', may reflect divergent attitudes originating in different circles. See LIEBERMAN (1934), pp. 17, 18f.; NEUSNER, Pharisees (1971); Eliezer (1973); and Purities (1974—77), passim. Furthermore, different circles may have had different readings in Tos. A particular *baraita* may accord with such a divergent reading, one that may be preserved in one of the MSS of Tos. See GINZBERG (1941), pp. H: lvi—lxiii; LIEBERMAN, TK (1955ff.), passim and esp. I, 'Introduction', 2—5, 20, and WEISS HALIVNI (1968, 1975), passim,

Recent linguistic and historical studies indicate that one must consider *baraitot* as a separate stratum of materials and not one 'identical' with that of Tannaitic collections. The former employ a separate stratum of Middle Hebrew, which differs from that in 'Mishnah' and 'Tosefta'. In addition, the one who cited the *baraita*, a later Amoraic authority, or the editor of the pericope may gloss the text with explanatory comments, revise it to fit redactional considerations or Palestinian conceptions, or simply to follow a different pattern or structure. Sustained analysis may indicate how these revisions systematically introduce new conceptions into a text or associate new themes with a given-master. Therefore, these *baraitot* must primarily represent 'Amoraic' material. They constitute what an Amora thought, or what was represented as the view of a tannaitic master, or what was considered important to so represent.

Additional literature:

FRANKEL (1870), pp. 22a—28a.

M. S. ZUCKERMANDEL, Tosefta Mishnah und Boraitha (Frankfurt, 1908—1910), includes an index by tractate and page. See H. MALTER, A Talmudic Problem and Proposed Solutions, JQR 2 (1911—12), 75—95.

BOAZ COHEN, Mishnah and Tosefta Shabbat (New York, 1935).

*LIEBERMAN, TR (1938), II: viii—xv; (1947), p. 22, n. 5; TK (1955ff.), passim, esp. I: ii—v, xiv—xxii, III: xiii—xiv, IV: xi—xxiv, V: xiii. See entry ROSENTHAL.

HIGGER (1938—48); and ID., A Yerushalmi View of the Authorship of the Tosefta, PAAJR 11 (1941), 43—46.

RABINOVITZ (1940), pp. 19, 73, 86f., 217, 229, esp. 380f., 482.

ALBECK (1944), pp. 60—185, esp. 89—138; and (1969), esp. pp. 51—78 and 102—143. ALBECK's works contain much useful analysis and do distinguish between our extant text and the item in *gemara* referred to under the same name. But they are flawed by his overly monolithic view of matters and insufficient literary and critical approach. See GARY G. PORTON, Ḥanokh Albeck on the Mishnah, in: The Modern Study of the Mishnah, ed. J. NEUSNER (Leiden, 1975), pp. 209—224; S. C. REIF, Review, Journal of Semitic Studies 19 (1974), 112—117; and ABRAHAM GOLDBERG, Review, KS 47 (1971), 9—19.

EPSTEIN (1948), pp. 1—165, 404—508, 950—970.

A. WEISS (1962), pp. 153—168; 166ff.; and ID., Meḥqarim BaTalmud (Jerusalem, 1975), p. 33, focuses on independent revisions of *baraitot* by separate circles.

ELIEZER ROSENTHAL, HaMoreh, PAAJR (1963), Hebrew, pp. 1—71, esp. 52—57. He reconstructs LIEBERMAN's view on 'Tosefta' and its relationship to y. and summarizes previous views on the matter.

*WEISS HALIVNI (1968, 1975), passim. See Index, s. v. *baraita*.

*NEUSNER, Development (1970), esp. pp. 83—86, 110—111, 133—142, 154—158; Pharisees (1971); Eliezer (1973), esp. II: 236; Purities (1974—77). Besides examining sources for variations in names, details, context, and applying form and tradition criticism, he demonstrates the differences between strata.

DEVRIES, Meḥqarim BeŚifrut HaTalmud (Jerusalem, 1968), pp. 148—160.

FELDBLUM (1969), p. 32.

*TOWNER (1973), passim.

*JOSEPH HEINEMANN, Aggadah and Its Development [Hebrew] (Jerusalem, 1974), esp. 17—47, on divergent versions of aggadic texts.

*MENAḤEM MORESHET, Further Study of the Language of the Hebrew Bārāytot in the Babylonian and Palestinian Talmudim, Archive of the New Dictionary of Rabbinic Literature, II (Ramat-Gan, 1974), pp. English viii—ix, and Hebrew 31—73, esp. 56—73.

BARUCH BOKSER, Two Traditions of Samuel, in: Christianity, Judaism, and Other Greco-Roman Cults, Studies for Morton Smith at Sixty, Part IV, ed. J. NEUSNER (Leiden, 1975), pp. 46—47.

E. E. HALEVY, HaAggadah HaHiśtorit-Biographit (Tel Aviv, 1975), e.g., pp. 129—130.

*GOODBLATT (1979), IV. 1: a, c.

In the analysis of a *baraita* one cannot automatically conclude that a text which ostensibly serves to support or correspond to an immediately preceding Amoraic tradition represents the view of that master or even constitutes material known during his lifetime. Such texts may be introduced by the notation כהדא דתני, *KHD' DTNY*, "Like this it was taught". A later authority may have cited the text and not the author of the tradition, who in fact may even dispute it. See RABINOVITZ (1940), p. 467; G. ALON, Tarbiẓ 12 (1940), 91, 95; and WEISS HALIVNI (1975), p. 540, fn. 7.

IX. Transferred Traditions and Pericopae and Unsmooth Flow of sugyot

A. Transferred Material

1. One finds in y. traditions or complete pericopae which do not seem to fit in their present context. The referrents may be unclear or they may not relate to the preceding or following materials. Moreover one finds in two, three, or four locations analogous traditions or pericopae which show no or slight variations or which present the material in different arrangement. According to ASSIS (1976), p. 1, there are close to one thousand such *sugyot*. These repetitions are the result of transference. The process whereby one duplicates or adapts a tradition or pericope from elsewhere theoretically can occur at several stages in the history of *gemara*; certain types undoubtedly occurred prior to the final compilation of the text and others clearly afterwards, by scribes.

While scholars agree when certain types happened, they disagree as to others. Part of the argument centers on the appropriateness of a comparison with a similar phenomenon of transference found in other texts, e.g., 'Genesis Rabba', 'Sifra', and 'Bavli'.

2. A reciter, tradent or editor of a pericope may apply a comment or tradition to a new context. He may adapt the item's language so as to be appropriate to the issue as formulated in the new context or he may not fully reformulate the material. One may recognize this type of transference when one comes across analogous or identical items which seem to have originated in two separate contexts, or when one notices that the idiom or technical language does not exactly fit in one context.

The more recent literature, which list the earlier studies and traditional authorities who noticed this phenomenon, include:

EPSTEIN (1948), (1957), (1962).

A. WEISS, Court Procedure (New York, 1957), pp. 24, 58—61, 85, 94, 163—165; (1962); ID., Notes to Talmudic Pericopae (Bar Ilan, n.d.), pp. 215--217, esp. fn. 45.

B. DEVRIES, Literary Transfer as a Factor in the Development of Talmudic Law, Bar Ilan Annual I (1963), 156—164, esp. 163f.

WEISS HALIVNI (1968, 1975).

ALBECK (1968), pp. 452—545; 557—576; 657f.; esp. 496—504; 558—560; 657; and cf. 492, fn. 77; 514f.

BOKSER, Two Traditions of Samuel (1975); and (1975), p. 76, fn. 208, and 92, fn. 255.

SHRAGA ABRAMSON, Baale Tosefot ʿal HaTorah (Jerusalem, 1975), pp. 27—43.

3. But the type of transference in y. that creates the greatest problems are those where whole pericopae are repeated and which appear as foreign matter. FRANKEL (1870) and others focused on these materials and LIEBERMAN (1929), (1931), (1933), and (1934) critically analyzed them. EPSTEIN, Tarbiẓ 3 (1932) and (1962), summarized in MELAMMED (1973), also dealt with them. EPSTEIN believes that these items were transferred not only by the earlier scribes but also by the compilers of y. LIEBERMAN holds that they are the results of scribes. See now ASSIS (1976)'s evaluation of the problem and his comprehensive analysis of the phenomenon. See also WEISS HALIVNI (1968, 1975), esp. II: 144, fn. 1; 166, fn. 3; 262, fn. 10; 714, fn. 11; BOKSER (1975), pp. 85—88.

A pericope which contains a tangential reference to a text elsewhere may be transferred to that other context. But this process created problems. As the tradition may not properly fit the context or a whole pericope may not originate in its present location, one must not impose an interpretation upon the item to fit the new context.

The transferences might occur in several stages. Once material was transferred from one place to the second, other material originally from the second place might be transferred to the first. Each of the two locations may thus contain primary and secondary material. At times a reading in a Geniza fragment which lacks the 'second' transference may confirm the process. See BOKSER (1975), p. 126, fn. 362, for an instance where the Gaon ELIJAH of Vilna, in one passage, made such a suggestion, which is confirmed by a Geniza fragment. In general, see ASSIS (1976), passim.

The transferred pericope may have been placed into the wrong location. Where a scribe placed the material in the 'correct' place, he may have juxtaposed disputing *sugyot* deriving from different *yeshivot* and circles. Naturally the inconsistencies create exegetical problems as items may thus not only lack transitional bridging language but may even externally appear to form a single *sugya*.

A scribe may have deleted one or more of the occurrences of the pericopae, as he relied on one of the other instances. But he may delete the original instance. Naturally where the transferred pericope had been incorrectly placed, the deletion of the original instance creates problems.

The MSS and Geniza fragments indicate that at times the scribes made a notation גרש, כו׳, *GRS* or *KW*ʿ, to the effect that material is deleted. The latter term means 'etc.' LIEBERMAN and EPSTEIN differ as to the meaning of the former. LIEBERMAN renders the former as "abbreviated", while EPSTEIN as "[we] learned"; LIEBERMAN (1929), pp. 12—13; and ID., Tarbiẓ 5 (1933), 107—110; and EPSTEIN (1962), pp. 324—330; see MELAMMED (1973), pp. 578—579. E. S. ROSENTHAL, Leshonot Śofrim, in: Yuval Shy, ed. B. KURZWEIL (Ramat Gan, 1958), pp. 294—297, on the other hand argues that this term means "in extenso". Cp. BOKSER, AJSReview 4 (1979).

Subsequent to the deletion, later scribes may have filled in the missing portion and have done so incorrectly. They may have filled in material above or below the proper place and thereby included irrelevant lines. Alternatively, they may have started after the beginning or end before the conclusion of the whole passage and thereby included insufficient material. On the other hand, scribes, relying on the portion preserved before the deletion, may have filled in the deleted sections from a text which has a similar beginning but a different ending, and thus may have supplied the wrong text. EPSTEIN's claim that the scribes would have filled in only on the basis of MSS seems to constitute only an assumption and one which does not sufficiently take into consideration the textual nature of *gemara* and actual scribal practices. See EPSTEIN, Tarbiẓ 3 (1932), 123, fn. 6; (1962), pp. 324—332, and MELAMMED (1973), pp. 580f.

LIEBERMAN proves that one must not automatically conclude that all variations between analogous pericopae are the results of only scribal corruptions. The differences may represent different stages or circles in the redaction of common materials. He demonstrates how the brevity and curtness in 'Neziqin' derive from its earlier compilation and not from deletions of portions found in the parallels elsewhere; LIEBERMAN (1931) and ID., SZ (1968), esp. pp. 125—136. Cf. GOODBLATT (1979), IV. 1:6. g.

B. Examining Out-of-Place Traditions

One has to determine what constitutes the relevant portion of the text. One must isolate each unit of the *sugya* and not impose concepts or issues from one part into the next. One must interpret the passage on the basis of its own content, see if its references are clear and its language appropriate. Where more than one instance is extant one separately examines each part of the pericope. Where 'parallels' do not exist, one must consider if language inappropriate in the present setting makes sense in another one. Where the pericope comments on 'Mishnah', the possibilities are fewer and one can easily employ a concordance to check key terms or matters mentioned in the passage. A similar procedure is necessary for pericopae that do not comment on 'Mishnah'. The forthcoming edition of Kosovsky's 'Concordance to the Palestinian Talmud' will facilitate this.

A further aid is that of form criticism. Certain comments may employ a fixed or stereotyped formulation recurrently used for particular purposes. Thus a B- prefix introducing a brief tradition which for comprehension depends upon some other passage serves to comment and gloss a previous text like 'Mishnah'. See Bokser (1975), pp. 97—101. Once one notices the presence of the form, one can lift the clause out of its context and relate it to its actual referent. Likewise is the case with fixed terminologies, which introduce a structured pericope. Furthermore, the chronology of the masters may be helpful in determining the relationship of the parts of a *sugya*. Finally, one must realize that y. often lacks answers to a question. As a result the material following a question may constitute a separate pericope. See the Sections on Forms and Terminology, VIII, A; and XVI.

One should also consider that the referent to a passage may not be the immediately preceding matter. The referent may have been deleted or interrupted. For the former one must search for the missing deleted pericope or text. In the latter, one must examine the passage penultima to the difficult text. The contiguous text, whether the result of an incorrectly placed transference or inclusion of a marginal addition, may be an interpolation. See Lieberman (1929); (1934), pp. xxv—xxvii, especially p. 27; Epstein, Śefer Ma'asim, Tarbiẓ 1 (1930), 38; A. Weiss, Notes, pp. 44, 46, 127, 217; y. Shev. 1 : 2, 33b, Śefer Nir, loc. cit., and Bokser (1975), pp. 74—77 and cp. 97—101, especially fn. 275; cp. Rabinovitz (1940), pp. 88, 237, and 360. See above on the L. MS, to which add Rabinovitz (1940), p. 28, and A. Weiss, Studies in the Law of the Talmud on Damages (New York, 1966), pp. 67f.

Moreover, as indicated in an earlier section, *gemara* may include an incorrectly filled-in reference; Section VIII. D. See below on interpolations into y. made from post-Talmudic texts.

Thus in examining a text one must be open to the several possibilities and consider if one occurred. See now the additional criteria set out and exemplified in Assis (1976). Other guidelines and tools are presented in the following sections.

C. Additional Literature

Frankel (1870), pp. 36b—40a, 136—139b.

Lewy (1895—1914), Introduction.

I. H. Halevy, Dorot HaRishonim II: Amoraic Period (Frankfurt a.M., 1901. Repr. Jerusalem, 1967), pp. 529—536.

S. Horowitz, Analecten, MGWJ 45 (1901), 310, 314—322, adds examples of transference to those in Frankel.

W. Bacher, Talmud, Jewish Encyclopedia, 12, 6—7, lists of repeated pericopae.

LIEBERMAN (1929), pp. 112—113; (1931), pp. vii, 23f., 26; ID., Miscellanies, Tarbiẓ 5 (1933), 107—110; (1934), pp. xv, 28, fn. 1, 29, 83, 120, 238—239, fn. 1, 479, 523.

EPSTEIN, Additional Fragments, Tarbiẓ 3 (1932), 122—123, 134—136; (1962), pp. 276—279, 322—330.

GINZBERG (1941), pp. H: lxviii—lxxxii.

E. S. ROSENTHAL, Leshonot Śoferim, in: Yuval Shy. A Jubilee Volume Dedicated to S. Y. Agnon, ed. BARUCH KURZWEIL (Ramat Gan, 1958), pp. 293—324.

WEISS HALIVNI (1968, 1975), esp. II: 144, fn. 1; 166, fn. 3; 262, fn. 10; 714, fn. 11.

FELDBLUM (1969), pp. English, 11; Hebrew, 37—41.

MELAMMED (1973), pp. 575—581.

ISRAEL FRANCUS, Additions and Parallels in TB Bava Qamma VII, BIA 12 (1974), pp. ix, 43—63, and the literature cited there, especially S. FRIEDMAN and B. Z. BENEDICT, on transferred pericopae in b.

BOKSER (1975), pp. 76, fn. 208; 85—88; 122—125.

X. Parallels in Midrashic Works

A. Issues and Guidelines

Earlier, under 'Sources', I dealt with items that had parallels in halakhic *midrashim*. Here I consider materials which may have word-for-word parallels of whole pericopae in works nearly contemporaneous or subsequent to the compilation of y., e. g., 'Genesis Rabba'.

Scholars have analyzed the relationship between the y. passages and the parallels in the midrashic works, have tried to account for the variations and have argued the merits of three different propositions: (1) one source knew the other; (2) they both drew from a mutual source; (3) some early version or recension of the one used an early recension or version of the other. Furthermore, some scholars distinguish between the halakhic and aggadic portions in their assertions as to the existence of a 'mutual source' and the rejection of direct borrowing. Some have argued that the midrashic, aggadic materials in y. in toto derive from a midrashic work or source from which the y. editors transposed them into the y. This assumes the unlikely assumption that the aggadic materials do not have an organic place within the y.

One may use the midrashic works and the analogous versions or parallels to (1) establish the reading of a text, which is corrupted in y.; (2) clarify the sequence of the y. text on the basic of the structure in the *midrash*; (3) throw light, in general, on the Palestinian tradition, realia and practices, items which are common to y. and the Palestinian *midrashim*.

Two factors necessitate caution in the use of these materials:

1. Some items in the *midrash*, e. g., Gn. R., may not be integral to the text but additions added into it. Cf. DAVID DAUBE, Collaboration with Tyranny in Jewish and Roman Law (Oxford, 1965), whose insightful comments are partially flawed by his reliance on a scribal interpolation in Gn. R. See THEODOR-ALBECK ed., III, 1184, fn. 5.

2. The *midrash* may have used the passage and adapted and restructured it according to its own purposes. In the process it may add explanatory comments and fill in elliptical or unspecified details. These comments are useful as they serve as commentary to the pericope. But, on the other hand, they may not represent the original meaning of the passage or the one in its context in y.

Thus, as indicated with *baraitot*, one must consider the effect of the history of the tradition. TOWNER has demonstrated the process of standardizing and regularizing a midrashic pattern and how the later use of a text contemporizes the biblical evidence. TOWNER (1973), pp. 124–126; 209–211; cf. 197, 202. See also NEUSNER (1970–77).

B. Indexes

Where y. uses a biblical verse, one should examine the appropriate *midrash* to see if the *midrash* to the work includes the passage. The index in the Krotoschin edition provides a guide to many of the parallels. A. HYMAN, Torah haKetuvah VeHameśurah, 3 vols. (Tel Aviv, 1936, 1965²), is an index to biblical verses in rabbinic literature. In addition, there is an index at the end of Yefeh Mareh, Venice, 1590 commentary and edition to y. *aggadot*.

C. Representative Literature

Items on specific works appear in the appropriate entry below.

FRANKEL (1870), pp. 51b–53b.

BACHER, Talmud, JE, p. 7.

LIEBERMAN (1931), p. vii; (1934), p. xviii, fn. 1; and SZ (1968), p. 130.

L. ZUNZ, HaDrashot BeYisrael, revised. H. ALBECK (Jerusalem, 1957).

M. MARGULIES, Midrash Vayikra Rabbah, V (Jerusalem, 1960), pp. xvii–xxxi.

EPSTEIN (1962), pp. 287–290.

MYRON BIALIK LERNER, The Book of Ruth in Aggadic Literature and Midrash Ruth Rabba, 3 vols. (Ph. D. dissertation, Hebrew University, Jerusalem, 1971), I: 118–131.

MELAMMED (1973), pp. 573–575.

J. HEINEMANN, Aggadah and Its Development (Jerusalem, 1974).

SUSSMANN (1974—75), pp. 127, 141—143 and ID., Tarbiẓ 45 (1976), 218—257, especially 226—227, 252—254.

SAUL LIEBERMAN, On Persecution of the Jewish Religion, Salo Wittmayer Baron Jubilee Volume (Jerusalem, 1974), Hebrew pp. 213—246, demonstrates how to evaluate revisions in aggadic materials.

Z. M. RABINOVITZ, Ginze Midrash (Tel Aviv, 1976), contains fragments to many *midrashim*. See index for specific parallels to y.

D. Specific Works

I include bibliographical items which directly relate to use of y. Additional items may be found in entries in EJ; TOWNSEND, Rabbinic Source, in: Study of Judaism, Bibliographical Essays, Anti-Defamation League (New York, 1972), pp. 37—43; and STRACK (1931).

1. 'Genesis Rabba'.

M. LERNER, Anlage des Bereschith Rabbah und seine Quellen, Magazin für die Wissenschaft des Judentums 7—8 (1880—81) [Reprinted separately: Berlin, 1882], especially 8 (1881), 40—48, 92—107, 130—131.

Ed. J. THEODOR and CH. ALBECK, Bereschit Rabba (Berlin, 1903—1939; Repr. with corrections, Jerusalem, 1965). In the 'Introduction', Vol. III, 66—84, ALBECK discusses the relationship between y. and Gn. R. Pp. 75—84 contain a list of y. materials, arranged in sequence in *gemara*.

See also: LIEBERMAN (1929), p. 39; and SZ (1968), pp. 129—130.

MARGULIES (1960).

EPSTEIN (1962), pp. 287—290, who lists earlier literature. He holds that the y. of Gn. R., like y. 'Neziqin' [sic!] are distinct recensions of y., each different from the extant y. They stem from different *yeshivot*, i. e., places, and not different times.

M. SOKOLOFF, Introduction and index to Midrash Bereshet Rabba, MS Vat. Ebr. 30 (Jerusalem, 1971).

Midrash Bereshet Rabba, Codex Vatican 60 (Jerusalem, 1972).

J. HEINEMANN, Structure and Divisions of Midrash Genesis Rabbah, BIA 9 (1971), 279—289.

LEWIS BARTH, An Analysis of Vatican 30 (Cinn., 1973), esp. pp. 60—65 and fn. 68.

M. D. HERR, Genesis Rabahb, EJ 7, 399—402.

BOKSER, Two Traditions (1975); and AJSReview 4 (1979).

2. Lev. R.

Critical edition, commentary, and indexes by M. MARGULIES, 5 vols. (Jerusalem, 1953—60), esp. V: xxvii—xxxiii.

Albeck, Midrash Vayiqra Rabba, Louis Ginzberg Jubilee Volume (New York, 1945), Hebrew pp. 25—43.

Heinemann, Parshot BeVayiqra Rabbah Shemeqorotehen Mefuqpaqot, Tarbiẓ 37 (1968), 339—354; Id., Profile of a Midrash: The Art of Composition in Leviticus Rabba, Journal of the American Academy of Religion 39 (1971), 141—150, and an expanded version, Id., HaŚifrut 24 (1971), 808—834. Id., Leviticus Rabbah, EJ 15, 152—154.

3. Dt. R.

Saul Lieberman, Midrash Debarim Rabbah (Jerusalem, 1964[2]), Introduction, especially pp. xv—xvii, re use of PT: at times it, like Tanḥumma, summarizes y.

M. D. Herr, Deuteronomy Rabba, EJ 5, 1584—1586.

4. Lam. R.

See Lieberman (1934), p. xii.

5. 'Ruth Rabba'.

Edition, notes, and indexes: Lerner (Jerusalem, 1971). Y. used one of the earlier recensions of R. R. in one of its later editorial stages.

6. Midrash Tehillim

Edition, S. Buber (Vilna, 1891), Introduction, I: xi—xiii, discusses and lists some 117 sources that ostensibly derive from y.

Engl. transl. with notes: W. Braude, The Midrash on Psalms, 2 vols. (New Haven, 1959), I: xxv—xxxi, reviews the literature on the work.

Forthcoming comprehensive critical edition: Shmuel Leiter.

7. 'Pesiqta'

Edition, Meir Friedmann (Vienna, 1880, Tel Aviv, 1963), a fine commentary, but does not sufficiently consider how 'Pesiqta' adapts the materials.

Translation and notes: W. Braude, Pesikta Rabbati, 2 vols. (New Haven, 1968). The introduction, pp. 1—33, reviews the earlier literature, MSS, and editions. The Parma MS and the Prague edition are vital.

M. Zucker, Teguvot Littenu'at 'Avele Ṣiyyon haQara'im BaŚifrut HaRabbanit, Albeck Jubilee Volume (Jerusalem, 1963), pp. 378—385, demonstrates the ninth-century date for the work. In the passage examined and throughout the work a careful reading indicates that the *midrash* reflects a definite point of view and restructures and adapts y. material for its own purposes.

'Pesikta Rabbati', EJ, s. v.

A new critical edition is under preparation by NORMAN COHEN, at Hebrew Union College.

8. 'Pesikta DeRav Kahana'

Critical edition with indexes: B. MANDELBAUM, 2 vols. (New York, 1962).

A. GOLDBERG, Review, KS 43 (1968), 69–79.

Translation and notes: W. BRAUDE and I. KAPSTEIN, Pesiḳta de Rabb Kahana (Philadelphia, 1975), with Introduction and indexes.

9. 'Midrash Shir HaShirim'

Edition, L. GRUENHUT, Midrash Shir HaSchirim (Jerusalem, 1897), Introduction, pp. 19f. discusses the large number of materials parallel to y.

B. M. LERNER, Review, KS 48 (1973), 543–549.

10. 'Yelamdenu Midrashim'

GINZBERG, Genizah Studies (1928), I: 36.

LIEBERMAN (1934), p. 36; ID., Midrash Debarim Rabbah (Jerusalem, 1964[2]), Introduction.

Midrash Tanḥuma, ed. S. BUBER (Levuv and Vilna, Repr. Jerusalem, 1964), Introduction, pp. 5–6.

E. URBACH, Seride Tanḥuma-Yelamdenu, Qoveṣ 'al Yod 16 (1967), 1–54.

Tanḥuma-Yelamdenu, EJ 15, 794–796.

YAAQOV ADLER, Midrash Tanḥuma, Vatican MS 44, in: Kobez Al Yad 8 (18) (Jerusalem, 1976), 15–75, describes the MS and compares its readings to those of the printed edition.

11. 'Midrash Shmuel'

Edition S. BUBER (Vilna, 1925[2]), Introduction, pp. 5–6.

12. 'Avot De R. Nathan'

Ed. SOLOMON SCHECHTER (Vienna, 1887; New York, 1945, 1967[2]).

JUDAH GOLDIN, The Two Versions of Abot DeRabbi Nathan, HUCA 14 (1946), 97–120, demonstrates systematic conceptual adapting of the material; ID., The Fathers According to Rabbi Nathan (New Haven, 1955; New York, 1974). Introduction, translation, notes, and indexes.

ANTHONY SALDARINI, The Fathers According to Rabbi Nathan, Version B (Leiden, 1975). Introduction, translation, notes, and indexes.

XI. Relationship between PT and BT: Mutual Material which may Differ

1. Each *gemara* contains traditions attributed to masters of both Palestine and Babylonia. At times *gemara* may present a whole pericope from the other land. Some traditions or pericopae may be found in both y. and b.; others, though, appear in only one *gemara*, and at times that work is not the one from the master's native land. PT or BT may even specify that a matter comes from 'there' or the 'West', i. e., represents a 'Palestinian' or Babylonian tradition, but the 'native' document lacks that source.

Where both b. and y. contain an item, they may vary in attribution, formulation, context, emphasis, or language. Thus one *gemara* may present a tradition as a statement, while, the other does so as an incident.

Traditional commentators and modern writers have tried to account for the existence of material from the other land and for the variations between common items. The standard explanation focused on the possibility that one *gemara* had seen the completed, or incompleted, work from the other land, a view no longer held. See EPSTEIN (1962), pp. 290—292, and YEQUTIEL GREENWALD, HaRa'u MeŚadre HaBavli et HaYerushalmi? (New York, 1954).

2. FRANKEL (1870), pp. 40a—45a, suggested that on the basis of the 'travelers' who went back and forth between Babylonia and the Land of Israel one can account for the 'foreign' materials. Subsequent scholarship has variously defined the role of these individuals who transmitted traditions between the two countries. Clearly they were not 'official' emissaries (whatever the term 'official' might mean): *Gemara* often indicates that some masters were displeased at their departure. Moreover, many apparently left for economic purposes, as to participate in the silk trade. See NEUSNER, History of the Jews in Babylonia (Leiden, 1969²), I, 94—99; and MOSHE BEER, The Babylonian Amoraim (Ramat Gan, 1974), pp. 158f., 180—191. The part played by the travelers accords with what we know as to how oral reciters in general served to circulate traditions. See, e. g., LIEBERMAN, SZ (1968), pp. 130f. The main travelers include: Ulla, Dimi, and R. Abin, from Israel to Babylonia; and Eleazar, Asi, and Ze'ira, and the return of Dimi, from Babylonia to Israel.

Certain terms, in particular, are used in these contexts: BT uses phrases with the word, **במערבא**, *BM'RB'*, "in the West", e. g., . . . **הכא** . . . **במערבא**, *HK'* . . . *BM'RB'*. . . , "Here . . . [it is said], in the West . . ."; **בעו במערבא**, **הוו במערבא**, **מחכו עליה במערבא**, *B'W BM'RB'*, *HWW BM'RB'*, *MḤKW 'LH BM'RB'*, "They asked in the West," "They discussed in the West", "They laughed concerning it in the West"; and **במערבא מתני/ו**, *BM'RB' MTNY/W*, "They taught in the West"; and **כי אתא**, *KY 'T'*, "When came". In PT one finds **תמן אמרין**, *TMN 'MRYN*, "There they say"; **רבנן דתמן**, *RBNN DTMN*, "Rabbis of there"; or a phrase with the word, **תמן**, *TMN*, "there". For full entries, see C. J. KASOWSKI, Thesaurus Talmudis (Jerusalem, 1954),6, 3047–3050, 30, 1033–1035; YOSEF UMANSKI, Ḥakhme Ha Talmud: Yerushalmi (Jerusalem, 1952), pp. 132, 148. See EPSTEIN (1962), 292–322, who lists and analyzes the usages. See as well TIBOR H. STERN, Composition of the Talmud (New York, 1959), for an uncritical but not unuseful lengthy treatment; LIEBERMAN (1931), pp. 8f, 17; and WEISS HALIVNI (1968), p. 497 and (1975), p. 273, fn. 26.

3. The variations have been explained by the following factors:

a. Mistakes: Transmitters or editors made mistakes which corrupted the materials; FRANKEL (1870), and I. H. WEISS, Dor Dor VeDorshov III (Berlin, 1924), p. 237.

b. Post-compilation corruptions: Scribes through their mistakes produced the corruptions in the text.

c. Transmission and formation: The process of citing and using the tradition yielded variations. This involved: The tradent, the one who cited the item in a specific context, or the editor of a pericope may have adapted it to fit the issue at hand or have revised the tradition on the basis of an interpretation given to it. The differences, as LIEBERMAN emphasizes, may reflect the presence of different sources. The two versions may come from different circles or academies, a fact that accounts for many of the differences between two similar items that are found in different locations in the same *gemara*. See LIEBERMAN (1931), p. viii; ID. (1968), pp. 130f; and A. GOLDBERG, R. Ze'ira and Babylonian Custom in Palestine, Tarbiẓ 36 (1967), 319–341; WEISS HALIVNI (1968, 1975); ALBECK (1969), pp. 559f., and the additional literature, below.

These variations were facilitated by prior differences between: readings or interpretations of mutual sources (*mishnayot* or *baraitot*); overall positions or approaches on a matter through which a tradition is perceived and explained; social, economic, political, and natural realia; language and usage in Middle Hebrew and Aramaic. See above on 'Mishnah' in y., Section VIII. C, and LIEBERMAN (1934), pp. xiii–xiv, ID. (1955ff.), passim; GINZBERG (1941), pp. H: lii–lxxiv; ABBA BENDAVID, Biblical Hebrew and Mishnaic Hebrew (Tel Aviv, 1967), pp. 171–222; WEISS HALIVNI (1968, 1975), e. g., I, 151; S. ABRAMSON, On the Hebrew in the Babylonian Talmud, and M. MORESHET, Further Studies of the Language of the Hebrew Bārāytot in the Babylonian and Palestinian Talmudim, both in: Archive 2 (1974), 9–15, 31–73, and the literature cited there, and English pp. v, viii.

The nature of the compilation itself may have produced differences. BT, and not PT, went through a process which worked over materials and placed them in an expanded literary context. Much of this activity is associated with the anonymous Saboraic masters in Babylonia. As a result, y. items often appear more 'pristine'. See GOLDBERG (1962–63); WEISS HALIVNI (1975), Introduction; BOKSER (1975), p. 236; EPSTEIN (1962), pp. 273–274; and especially S. FRIEDMAN, Glosses and Additions to TB Bava Qamma vii, Tarbiẓ 40 (1971), 418f, and fn. 1, and the literature cited there.

Cf. A. Weiss (1962), pp. 15—23, and (1975), pp. 8—15, and index, s. v. PT, and Feldblum (1964), p. 43, and especially Goodblatt (1979), IV, 1: b. π, 3: c; and S. Friedman, TSJTSA 1 (1977), 275—441.

The compilation process which also entailed the selection of teachings from certain circles and the rejection of those from others may further account for the lack, in y., of a 'Palestinian' tradition, cited in b. The missing item may derive from a circle or academy whose materials were not included within y. See Lieberman (1931); A. Weiss, as cited in Feldblum (1964), p. 43; Albeck, Bereschit Rabba (Jerusalem, 1965²), III, Introduction; and Epstein (1962). This partially explains why b. contains many traditions attributed to Palestinians which deal with M. Ṭehorot while y. lacks a *gemara* on this order. Moreover, even if the items come from the same 'circles', one cannot automatically assume that everything known was included within the compilation of y. See Section XII. 3, on Compilation of y.

4. Additional literature, besides items entered under variations in Baraitot, Section VIII, 4, includes:

Y. H. S., Talmud HaYerushalmi VeTalmud HaBavli, HeḤalutz 6 (1862), pp. 47—55.

Abraham Krochmal, Yerushalayim HaBenuyah (Lemberg, 1867, Repr. Jerusalem, 1971), pp. 6—10.

Frankel (1870), pp. 40a—45a.

I. H. Weiss, Dor Dor VeDorshov III (Vienne, 1871—92, Repr. Berlin, 1924).

Ratner, HaMelitz (St. Petersburg, 1899), nos. 55, 72, 201, 208, 212, 214, 215, 219, 220, 234, 236, 238, 240—242, 244—246, 248, 251, and (1900), nos. 82, 83, 85, 118—120, 128, 198—203.

Halevy (1901), II, 289—293, 297—298; 327—332; 384—391; 455—473; 526—536, 571—573.

Z. W. Rabinovitz, Yerushalayim 10 (1913), 233—254; Id. (1940), p. 519.

W. Bacher, Tradition und Tradenten in den Schulen Palästinas und Babyloniens (Leipzig, 1914, Repr. Berlin, 1966), esp. pp. 506—523 — long, though incomplete, classified lists by master and tradent, including travelers, of occurrences of traditions in *gemara*.

A. S. Rabinovitz, Yerushalayim 13 (1916), 286—292.

A. Weiss (1939), pp. 132ff.; (1943), pp. 169ff.; (1954), pp. 136ff.

Ginzberg (1941), pp. H: xlvii—lxxxiii.

Z. H. Chajes, Students Guide Through the Talmud, trans. and ed. Jacob Schachter (London, 1952, Repr., New York, 1960), pp. 233f., 258ff, 265—270, a comprehensive analytical but not critical study.

Dov Noy, HaŚipur Ha'Amami VaTalmud UvaMidrash (Jerusalem, 1960), e.g., pp. 9, 76, demonstrates how different stories may contain the same motif or similar stories may express different motifs. (Therefore, one must not level differences between diverse versions of an item without asking whether or not the motifs vary. On the other hand, an appreciation of the formal structure and traits of given items may enable one to isolate conflations, additions, or interpolations); and Id., The Jewish Versions of the 'Animal Languages' Folktale (AT 670) — A Typological-Structural Study, Scripta Hierosolymitana 22 (1971), 171—208.

B. DeVries, Review of Abraham Weiss (1962), KS 39 (1964), 197—200, which should be read in the light of Weiss Halivni (1968, 1975).

Steinsaltz, Links Between Babylonia and the Land of Israel, Talpioth 9 (1964), 294—306. Cp. M. Beer (1974) [below].

*Neusner, History of the Jews in Babylonia, 5 vols. (Leiden, 1966—1970), passim, esp. II, 129, 144—145; III, 218—220 — see b. Ber. 24b; and IV, 389.

Feldblum (1969).

*A. Goldberg, Review of Albeck (1969), KS 47 (1971), 9—19.

*Israel Francus, The Original Readings of Three Talmudic Discussions, Tarbiẓ 38 (1969), 338—353, compares b. and y. *sugyot*; Id., Clarification and Explanation in Talmud, Sinai 36 (72) (1971), 32—45, and 37 (73) (1973), 24—49 [= *sugyot* in Ket.]; Id., The Meaning of the Verb PRṬ in Leshon Hakhamim, Sinai 38 (74) (1974), 178—182; Id., Textual Readings and Explanations of the Sugya in TB Yoma 82a [and y. Yoma 8:3, 45a], Tarbiẓ 43 (1973—74), 34—45; and Id., TSJTSA 1 (1977).

*S. Kanter, I. H. Weiss and J. S. Zuri, in: Formation, ed. Neusner (1970), pp. 11—19, analysis of the methods of those named.

*Zwi Moshe Dor, The Teachings of Eretz Israel in Babylon [sic] (Tel Aviv, 1971) [= Bar Ilan Research Monographs 10], on the role of the travelers; they made deliberate changes to harmonize Palestinian *halakhah* with halakhic principles that had crystallized in Babylonian circles. The work includes an index to y. passages and references to other literature.

J. Fraenkel, Bible Verses quoted in Tales of the Sages, Scripta Hierosolymitana 22 (1971), 100—123, while on BT, the literary analysis is also suggestive for PT.

M. D. Herr, The Historical Significance of the Dialogues between Jewish Sages and Roman Dignitaries, Scripta Hierosolymitana 22 (1971), 123—150, includes dialogues found in y.

Z. Kagan, Divergent Tendencies and their Literary Moulding in the Aggadah, Scripta Hierosolymitana 22 (1971), 151—170, from a literary point of view suggestive as to y.

*S. Safrai, Tales of the Sages in the Palestinian Tradition and the Babylonian Talmud, Scripta Hierosolymitana 22 (1971), 209—232, while he claims that divergent and variant episodes contain a historical core, he squarely faces the presence of the variations.

*Robert Goldenberg, The Deposition of Rabban Gamaliel II, An Examination of the Sources, Journal of Jewish Studies 23 (1972), 167—190.

*M. Beer, Nehote, EJ 12, 942—943, and (1974), p. 43, fn. 75.

*J. Fraenkel, Ha Gufa Qashya — Internal Contradictions in Talmudic Literature, Tarbiẓ 42 (1973), 266—301, esp. 288—291, examines how divergent formulations of mutual sources in BT and PT affected the interpretations of *gemara* and the structures of pericopae, and how b. and y. differently formulate certain types of analyses and questions.

*MELAMMED (1973), pp. 597—604, on differences between BT and PT, pp. 442—451, on the travelers. Cf. pp. 461—478.

WILLIAM S. GREEN, The Talmudic Historians: N. Krochmal, H. Graetz, I. H. Weiss, and Z. Jawitz, in: Modern Study, ed. NEUSNER (1973), pp. 107—108, and 114—118, relevant comments on the methods of certain historians.

*LEE LEVINE, Caesarea Under Roman Rule (Leiden, 1975), pp. 89—92, 96, on travelers who come to Caesarea, the city's economic attraction for Babylonians, and the transmission by Caesareans of Palestinian traditions to Babylonia.

S. FRIEDMAN, Qiddushin BeMilvah, Sinai 39 (76) (1975), 47—76, an example of the comparison of b. and y. pericopae.

JACOB N. EPHRATI, Another Meaning of NWH-N'WH, Archive 2 (1974), pp. 16—23.

*BOKSER (1975), pp. 125—128, 219—220, 224—225, 235, on the role of travelers, and ID., Two Traditions (1975).

*WEISS HALIVNI (1975), pp. 253, fn. 4**, 364, fn. 4, 416, fn. 2*.

AMINOAH NOAH, Redaction of the Tractate Qiddushin in the Babylonian Talmud (Tel Aviv, 1977), extensively compares the PT to the BT.

*HENRY A. FISCHEL, Essays in Greco-Roman and Related Talmudic-Midrashic Literature (New York, 1977), and the bibliography there, on literary forms or dimensions which may account for divergent presentation of similar items and varied treatment of the same event or personage. Thus one should not attempt to level differing accounts in order to isolate the 'historical' original.

DAVID ROSENTHAL, Pirqa De'Abbaye (TB Rosh Ha'Shana II), Tarbiẓ 46 (1977), III, 97—109, analyzes an "early [Babylonan] 'Talmud' similar to the Yerushalmi."

BARUCH M. BOKSER, Minor for a Zimun (y. Ber. 7:2, 11c) and Recensions of Yerushalmi, AJSReview 4 (1979), demonstrates how y. may revise a Babylonian tradition to fit its context.

GOODBLATT (1979), IV. 1: a, c, on Palestinian materials in BT.

XII. Compilation of Yerushalmi

1. Classical and modern writers have focused upon the formation of y., an understanding of which is necessary for any study of the work. The scholars take into account the following external (a—b) and internal (c—e) factors:

a. Gaonic and medieval authorities claim that b. knew and rejected y. and its traditions. This statement, however, testifies only to Babylonian propaganda for the supremacy and halakhic preference of BT. See GINZBERG

(1941), pp. H: lxxxiii—vi; MELAMMED (1973), pp. 556—558, and the literature cited in Section XIX. A, especially TWERSKY.

b. Certain post-Talmudic authorities, e.g., Maimonides, attributed y.'s composition to R. Yoḥanan, a second-generation Palestinian Amora. See GERSON COHEN, The Book of Tradition by Abraham ibn Daud (New York, 1967), p. 122, n. to line 18.

c. The present disordered arrangement of the text indicates the absence of any real editing. But this absolute judgment imposes standards based upon the literary character of the b. A refined statement (see paragraph 2) describes the particular nature of the disarray. PT's pericopae are generally briefer and less developed than those of BT. PT's pericopae often run into each other and lack transitional terms and are often out of place.

d. The date indicated, first, by incidents mentioned or not mentioned in y. and, secondly, by the names and number of masters correlated with their chronologies, a point which KROCHMAL (1867), pp. 14—30, had already emphasized. The references end in the fourth century.

e. Evidence of other recensions of y. These include: BT references to supposed Palestinian material not found in our y.; parallels in Gn. R. which do not totally fit the extant y. text.These variations or references may refer to different recensions of y. As to Gn. R.'s references, however, see above Section X. A. In addition, y. in one location, at times, refers to something elsewhere in y. but that reference is not found in the appropriate, supposedly original, place. The reference and the place to which referred apparently come from different recensions. The former's version of the latter location contained the 'missing' citation.

2. The ostensible glaring disarray is such that one writer, YONAH ELIJAH VIEZNER, Givat Yerushalayim, Suppl. to HaShaḥar 2 (Vienne, 1871), was led to claim that the extant y. represents the product of an eighth- or ninth-century incompetent faker, who without understanding collected and combined matter from b. and other sources. This position and the one by HALEVY (1901), II, 528f., that y. is completely unedited, are contradicted by the realization that there existed separate Palestinian traditions which do not agree with those of BT (see above, Sections I. 3. and XI), and by the presence of a certain order within *sugyot* and chapters; LIEBERMAN (1931); GINZBERG (1941); EPSTEIN (1962). Rather, the issue is, What was the nature of the composition and why does it differ from that of BT? In the previous section I partially dealt with the latter problem. I thus turn to a reconstruction of the compilation.

3. FRANKEL suggested a three-stage compilation: (a) Sages orally recited and memorized questions and answers or in lecture notes briefly hinted at them. (b) Individual masters filled out such notes or traditions and edited discrete tractates. Since various individuals independently were active, at times more than one work was produced on the same tractate. (c) In Tiberias the individual tractates were collected and the material therefrom combined. As a result, *gemara* incorporated inconsistent materials from different treatments of the same portions of 'Mishnah'.

Scholars agree that y. contains *sugyot* from different circles or academies and that the bulk of y. received final compilation in Tiberias. See e.g., Z. W. RABINOVITZ, Yerushalayim 8 (1909), 331—334; LIEBERMAN (1931), p. 9, (1934), pp. xii, 471; EPSTEIN (1962); FELDBLUM (1964), p. 43; and SUSSMANN (1973—74), pp. 142, 143, and fn. 394. They have varied, however, as to the reconstruction of the process and the nature of y. B.Q, B.M., and B.B., together called 'Neziqin'.

LEWY (1895—1914), esp. Introduction, pp. 15, 22, n. 1, proved the distinctive nature of 'Neziqin' and suggested that it represents a separate recension. In the process, he indicated how b. and y. contain different versions of the same material.

LIEBERMAN (1931), basing himself on choice of terminology and vocabulary, style, realia, named masters, and differences in construction and content of its pericopae in comparison to those in other tractates, proved that 'Neziqin''s distinctive character reflects a composition earlier (ca. 350) than that of other tractates (ca. 400) and one completed in Caesarea. See HERMAN BLUMBERG, Saul Lieberman on the Talmud of Caesarea, in: Formation, ed. NEUSNER (1970), pp. 114—124. 'Neziqin' is brief, as it represents brief and insufficiently organized and worked over notes (prepared perhaps for judges), in contrast to those of the rest of y., where they were more fully spelled out and expanded. LIEBERMAN goes on to provide a general description of the y. editing. The editor reconstructed notes of students and academies, out of which a later editor selected materials to be in the wider work. The latter also placed pericopae in appropriate places and deleted items inconsistent with views of Palestinian academies. Scribes later further transferred pericopae or disarranged pericopae.

EPSTEIN (1962) [posthumously published] represents EPSTEIN as arguing that, while 'Neziqin' uses Caesarean *gemara*, it does so like *gemarot* of other tractates. It thus represents a different but not chronologically earlier recension of y. and not a Caesarean *gemara*.

LIEBERMAN, SZ (1968), esp. pp. 130f., and ID., A Few Words by Julian the Architect of Ascalon, The Laws of Palestine and its Customs, Tarbiẓ 40 (1971), pp. 409—417, rebuts EPSTEIN's arguments. See also LEE LEVINE (1975), pp. 63f., 86—106; BOKSER, AJS Review 4 (1979), focuses on a recension of y. which is found in Gen. R. and which predates the one in PT; and especially GOODBLATT (1979), IV. 3: a, b, for a possible analogue in redaction of 5½ BT tractates vis-à-vis the rest of BT.

4. Further points include:

The anonymous parts of 'Neziqin' come from Caesarea, while those elsewhere in y. ostensibly derive from Tiberias.

Though y. represents a compilation of expanded reconstructured notes, it still is briefer than b. As indicated in Section XI. 3, this is due to the fact that y. lacked the later Amoraic-Saboraic enrichment and literary expansion. Moreover, as LIEBERMAN indicates, the out-of-place pericopae are those items that have parallels elsewhere in y. and which scribes inexactly transferred. Scribes also brought disorder by incorrectly adding scribal, marginal notations. Moreover, some of the lack of order is due to the later editors or scribes who had a sequence in their 'Mishnah' different from that assumed in the materials and who rearranged the latter to fit the former. Cf. ASSIS (1976), pp. 7f.

Finally, the attribution of editing to Yoḥanan is not a problem. Some writers accept and reinterpret it: The reference refers to a different Yoḥanan or to something associated with Yoḥanan, e.g., his academy: or it implies that he provided only the basic rubric for *gemara*. Alternatively, the attribution is rejected.

5. Additional bibliography:

KROCHMAL (1867), pp. 10—30.

*FRANKEL (1870).

YONAH ELIAHU VIEZNER, Givat Yerushalayim = Suppl. HaShaḥar 2 (Vienna, 1871), covers many of the main features of y. But he sees the text as it is and assumes that b. and y. are a unit, and not compilations of transmitted traditions, and that they and other sources should present a monolithic picture, without variations and differences.

I. H. WEISS, Dor Dor VeDorshov III (Vienna, 1883, Repr. Berlin, 1924), p. 105.

B. RATNER, HaMelitz (St. Petersburg, 1889), nos, 55, 72, 201, 208, 212, 214, 215, 219, 220, 234, 236, 238, 240—242, 244—246, 248, 251; and (1900), nos. 82, 83, 85, 118—120, 128, 198—203.

*BACHER, JE, 13, 5, re relationship of anonymous parts to those assigned.

*Z. W. RABINOVITZ, Yerushalayim 8 (1909), 331—352, and (1940), pp. 61f. and 311, on editing of y. and its location in Tiberias, indicated by ways in which it refers to places and realia of the city. Cf. HIRSCHORN's note, Yerushalayim 9 (1911), 186.

*LIEBERMAN (1931), pp. 5—6.

*GINZBERG (1941), p. H: lxxxiii.

STERN (1959); while he covers many of the problems, he misrepresents FRANKEL and is uncritical from a literary and historical perspective; e.g., for pp. 41—43, re b. Hag. 10a, see 'Diqduqe Śoferim to Hag.', p. 27, n. 3.

*EPSTEIN (1962), pp. 233—279.

M. A. TENENBLATT, Peraqim Ḥadoshim LeToldot Ereṣ Yisrael UBavel BiTqufat HaTalmud (Tel Aviv, 1966); an industrious work marred by an uncritical approach and unfounded assumptions.

*MELAMMED (1973), pp. 555—568.

*WEISS HALIVNI (1968, 1975).

Y. FLORSHEIM, On the Editing of the Palestinian Talmud, Sinai 40 (79) (1976), 30—43.

See also Chapters VII, IX, XVIII.

XIII. The Background to the Compilation of Yerushalmi

A. Locations of Masters

Palestinian masters resided and taught in different locations. Their major centers include: Tiberias, the main center, Sepphoris, Caesarea, and the 'South'. For the last item, only masters from Lud are specified. There, a center existed through the beginning of the Amoraic period. In addition, archaeologists have found a lintel inscription from the Golan that refers to a Bet Midrash, a place of study, בית מדרש, *BYT MDRŠ*.

The literature includes:

FRANKEL (1870), pp. 3b—6b.

*W. BACHER, Zur Geschichte der Schulen Palästina's im 3. und 4. Jahrhundert, MGWJ 43 (1899); ID., Die Gelehrten von Caesarea, MGWJ 45 (1901), 298—310.

S. ZURI, Toldot Darkhe HaLimmud Bishivot Darom, Galil, Sura, VeNeharde'a (Jerusalem, 1914); ID., R. Yose bar Hanina MeQiśrin [of Caesarea] (Jerusalem, 1926).

*LIEBERMAN (1931), especially re Caesarea, p. 9; ID., SZ (1968), pp. 92—94, 122—124, and fn. 173.

BENJAMIN MAZAR, Beth She'arim, Report on the Excavations, 1936—1940 [= I] [Hebrew edition] (Jerusalem, 1957²), pp. 15—20. [English edition, Jerusalem, 1973].

EPHRAIM E. URBACH, The Sages: Their Concepts and Beliefs (Jerusalem, Hebrew edition, 1969. English edition, 1975), Chapter Sixteen.

*DAN ORMAN, Jewish Inscriptions from Dabura in the Golan, Tarbiẓ 40 (1971), 399—408.

NAHMAN AVIGAD, Beth She'arim, Vol. 3, The Archaeological Excavations 1953—1958 (Jerusalem, 1971), pp. 1—6.

*MOSHE BEER, Academies in Babylonia and Erez Israel, EJ 2, 199—205.

M. AVI-YONAH, et al., Sepphoris, EJ, 14, 1177—1178; ID., Tiberias, EJ 15, 1130—1135.

*MELAMMED (1973), pp. 503—507.

*SUSSMANN (1973—74), pp. 88f., concerning places of rabbinic instruction in the Beth Shean area.

*LEVINE (1975), especially pp. 61—106, note 86—97, and fns. 497—523, presents a comprehensive discussion and bibliography on rabbinic circles and institutions in Caesarea and elsewhere.

*GOODBLATT (1975), while focuses on Babylonia provides methodological criteria by which to evaluate the earlier studies and critical guidelines for any inquiry. The work includes a rich bibliography.

REUVEN KIMELMAN, R. Yoḥanan of Tiberias. Aspects of the Social and Religious History of Third Century Palestine. (Unpublished Ph. D. dissertation, Yale University, New Haven, 1977).

See also the literature listed under 'General Historical Background', below, and the additional entries in EJ, s.v. name of the place.

B. Names of Masters and Bibliographical Information

*FRANKEL (1870), pp. 54b—132a.

BENJAMIN W. BACHER, Die Agada der Babylonischen Amoräer (Strassburg, 1878); ID., Die Agada der Tannaiten, 2 vols. (Strassburg, 1890), Hebrew edition, Agadot HaTannaim (Jerusalem, 1920, 1922²); ID., Die Agada der Palästinensischen Amoräer, 3 vols. (Strassburg, 1892—1899), Hebrew edition, Aggadot Amorae Ereṣ Yisrael, 4 vols. (Tel Aviv, 1925—28); = a series of collections of sources attributed to or about different masters subdivided according to subjects, with notes; and (1901).

*AARON HYMAN, Toldot Tannaim Veamoraim, 3 vols. (London, 1909, Repr. Jerusalem, 1964).

ZURI, R. Yose bar Hanina MeQiśrin (Jerusalem, 1926).

*UMANSKY (1952), page index to instances where a name appears in y.

*LIEBERMAN (1931), pp. 6—7, 18, masters' names and their spelling; 84—108, a list of all attributive formulae in 'Neziqin' and the location of each instance.

*EPSTEIN, Tarbiẓ 6 (1934), 39ff.; (1948, 1964²), the second edition includes an index, pp. 1297—1302; (1957); (1962).

RABINOVITZ (1940), especially p. 261 and index, pp. 633—636.

MORDECHAI MARGALIOTH, Encyclopedia of Talmudic and Geonic Literature (Tel Aviv, 1961).

ALBECK (1969), pp. 144—170, 451, 611—622, which must carefully be used, as it does not distinguish between types of sources.

SAMUEL LACHS, R. Abbahu and the Minim, JQR 60 (1970), 197—212.

*MELAMMED (1973), pp. 626—644.

M. BEER, The Babylonian Amoraim (Tel Aviv, 1974), pp. 362—364, on the number of masters. Cf. BARUCH BOKSER, Review, Newsletter, Association for Jewish Studies, 17 (June, 1976), pp. 19, 22.

BOKSER (1975).

*BENIAMIN KOSOVSKY, Otzar Leshon HaTalmud, Yerushalmi (Jerusalem, in press).

LEE LEVINE, R. Abbahu of Caesarea, Christianity, Judaism, and Other Greco-Roman Cults, ed. J. NEUSNER (Leiden, 1975), IV, 56—76, this and LACHS are examples of two recent biographical treatments.

See also ZURI and KIMELMAN, in Section A, and JE and EJ, s.v. name of the individual master for articles with bibliographies.

C. Reasons for the Compilation

Many writers supply the standard reason of 'necessity' to account for the writing down of y. Due to persecution and oppression, the editors of y. worked to preserve 'Torah' from being forgotten. This, as well, explains the supposed disarray of the y. text; in haste the editors did not have an opportunity to orderly arrange the materials. See FRANKEL (1870), pp. 2a—3b, and SUSSMANN (1973—74), pp. 154f. and fn. 494. Two assumptions prompt this 'reason'. The first is the need to find an adequate reason for the writing down of the 'oral' Torah — which assumably would not otherwise have been put into writing (sic!). Further, this approach assumes that Palestine lacked an unbroken tradition of teaching; it thus reflects the gaonic propaganda that Palestine suffered persecutions, a fact which accounts for its 'inferior' Talmud. See Sections VII. 2 and XIX. A. Both of these considerations, however, are not cogent. Moreover, LIEBERMAN denies that in the third and fourth centuries Palestinian Jewry suffered religious persecution and rebelled against the Roman Empire. There was only one insignificant insurrection on the part of Sepphorean Jews; otherwise there was only the general oppression of taxes, which Jews shared with other provincials; SAUL LIEBERMAN, Palestine in the Third and Fourth Centuries, JQR 36 (1946), 329—370; 37 (1946—47), 31—54, and especially 423—424; a popular version of which appears in ID., 'Jewish Life in Eretz Yisrael As Reflected in the Palestinian Talmud', Israel: Its Role in Civilization, ed. MOSHE DAVIS (New York, 1956), pp. 82—91, both reprinted in SAUL LIEBERMAN, Texts and Studies (New York, 1974), pp. 112—189; and BARON IV (Jerusalem, 1954), pp. 234—245. Cf. BARON, II, 295f. and 425, fn. 2, and S. D. GOITEIN, Mediterranean Society II (Berkeley, 1971), p. 197. See JACOB NEUSNER, History IV (1969), 27—35, and the literature cited there, especially pp. 32f.; and S. SIMONSOHN (1974), pp. 831—858, especially 842—846. At this point, we thus do not have an adequate explanation why y. was compiled when it was.

See further literature under 'General Historical Background'.

D. Economic Conditions

F. M. HEICHELHEIM, Roman Syria, in: Economic Survey of Ancient Rome, IV, ed. TENNEY FRANK (Baltimore, 1948), pp. 121—257.

A. KINDLER, ed., Proceedings, International Numismatic Convention. The Pattern of Monetary Development in Phoenicia and Palestine in Antiquity (Jerusalem, 1967), includes various papers on numismatics and economic conditions.

DANIEL SPERBER, Roman Palestine 200—400. Money and Prices (= Bar Ilan Studies in Near Eastern Language and Culture), (Ramat Gan, 1974), especially the Introduction, pp. 15ff., for a review of previous research and their methods. From a textual point of view, this is an excellent work;

see pp. 20f., re Palestinian and Babylonian reinterpretations and revisions of earlier traditions.

LEVINE (1975), especially pp. 48–56 and 68–70.

See Section XVII. B.

E. General Historical Background

I. H. WEISS, Dor Dor VeDorshov III (Vienna, 1883; Repr. Berlin, 1924).

H. GRAETZ, Geschichte der Juden, II[4] (Leipzig, 1897–1911). Hebrew edition, Divre Yime Yisra'el, with additional notes by S. P. RABINOWITZ, II (Warsaw, 1907).

*HALEVY (1901), on the basis of sources critically evaluates often superficial treatments by earlier 'more modern' historians.

A. BUECHLER, The Political and Social Leaders of the Jewish Community of Sepphorus in the Second and Third Century (Oxford, 1909); ID., Studies in Jewish History (London, 1956).

*JEAN JUSTER, Les Juifs dans l'Empire romain, 2 vols. (Paris, 1914). See now R. A. RABELLO, Israel Law Review 11 (1976), 216—287, 391–414, 563–590.

A. S. RABINOWITZ, Attitude of Palestinian Masters to Babylonians, Yerushalayim 13 (1919), 286–292.

ZE'EV JAVITZ, Śefer Toldot Yisra'el, VI–VIII (Tel Aviv, 1934–1935).

*SAMUEL KLEIN, Śefer HaYishuv I (Jerusalem, 1939), a collection of archaeological and literary references to places in Palestine. See S. LIEBERMAN, Review, Sinai, vol. 3, no. 5–6 (30–31) (1939), 462–468. Revisions and additions to entries are appearing in 'Sinai'; e.g., TUVIAH KAHANA, Meqomot Yishuv BeEreṣ Yisrael BaTalmudim UBaMidrashim, Sinai 76 (1975), 134–147.

*SAUL LIEBERMAN, The Martyrs of Caesarea, Annuaire de l'Institute de Philologie et d'Histoire Orientales et Slaves (1939–44), pp. 395–446; ID., Roman Legal Institutions in Early Rabbinics and in the Acta Martyrum, JQR 35 (1944), 1–55, reprinted in Texts and Studies (1974), pp. 57–111.

*GEDALIAH ALON, Toldot HaYehudim BeEreṣ Yisrael Bitqufat HaMishnah VeHaTalmud, 2 vols. (Tel Aviv, 1953, 1955; 1967[4], 1961[2]) [English edition under preparation]; ID., Studies in Jewish History [Hebrew], 2 vols. (Tel Aviv, 1958; I[2], 1967). — More sophisticated studies than earlier works and well indexed, though the 'Toldot', especially volume II, does not represent a finished statement but posthumously published lecture notes.

*MICHAEL AVI-YONAH, In the Days of Rome and Byzantium (Hebrew edition: Jerusalem, 1962, 1970[4]; German edition: [= Studia Judaica, II] Berlin, 1962; English revised edition: [as 'Jews of Palestine'] London 1976).

NEUSNER (1966–1970).

M. A. TENENBLATT, Peraqim Ḥadashim LeToldot Ereṣ Yisrael UBavel BiTqufat HaTalmud (Tel Aviv, 1966), an industrious but uncritical work shaped by incorrect assumptions.

W. Gottlieb, A Messianic Movement in the Third Century as Reflected in the Teachings of R. Johanan and his School at Tiberias, Essays Presented to Chief Rabbi Israel Brodie, ed. H. J. Zimmels, et al. (London, 1967), Hebrew volume, pp. 79—105.

*Benjamin Mazar, M. Avi Yonah, et al., ed., Encyclopaedia of Archaeological Excavations in the Holy Land, Hebrew edition, 2 vols. (Jerusalem, 1970), English revised edition, 4 vols. (1975ff.).

Moshe Beer, Who are the RWBYN [y. Hal. 4 : 4, 60a] ?, Sinai 35 (68) (1971), 144—152, and Id., On the Leaders of the Jews in Sepphoris in the Third Century, Sinai 38 (74) (1974), 133—138.

Israel Konoviṣ, Ma'arakhot Tannaim VeAmoraim: Amoraim (Jerusalem, 1973ff.), a thematically arranged collection of Talmudic sources on individual masters. The texts are completely unreliable.

Y. Brand, Beit She'arim and the Nabateans, Sinai 38 (74) (1974), 139—160.

Lee Levine (1975); Id., Roman Caesarea (An Archaeological-Topographical Study), Qedem, Monographs of the Institute of Archaeology, 2 (Jerusalem, 1975).

E. M. Smallwood, The Jews Under Roman Rule from Pompey to Diocletian (Leiden, 1976).

See also entries throughout this Chapter, in Chapter XVII, below, and in Goodblatt (1979), V. 4: a.

Part Four

Particular Guidelines for Study

XIV. Canons to Establish a Correct Text

A. Types of Mistakes

The text of y., as indicated above in Sections III; IV, A; IX. A, B; and XII. 1, has suffered corruptions by scribes, a fact already recognized by medieval rabbinic authorities. See also Goodblatt (1979), II. 1 and 5. This fact relates to the lack of an unbroken exegetical tradition, and as a result many portions have been incorrectly explained. Frankel (1870), pp. 36a—40a, 136a—138b, focused attention to many of the phenomena and noted that once we are familiar with the usual type of mistakes or what was liable to happen, we can develop procedures to correct readings and offer emendations. Lieberman (1929), (1934) critically analyzed, catalogued and documented the several types, dividing them into (a) standard corruptions that affect any text and (b) those particularly characteristic to y. He did this to set standards for the corrections so that one does not rely just on logic and the context.

(a) Standard corruptions include: 1, exchange of orthographically similar letters; 2, combining two letters into one; 3, division of one letter into two; 4, combining two words into one; 5, division of one word into two; 6, metathesis; 7, homoioteleuton; 8, corruption of foreign words; 9, marginal additions entered into the incorrect place; 10, abbreviations and short forms of words erroneously expanded, especially in the editions subsequent to the Venice first edition, which often incorrectly spelled out words. See especially LOUIS GINZBERG, Some Abbreviations Unrecognized or Misunderstood in the Text of the Jerusalem Talmud, Jewish Theological Seminary of America, Students' Annual (New York, 1914), pp. 138—148.

The second category (b) includes: 1, clauses which have to be inverted; 2, incorrect notation of references to and lemmas of 'Mishnah', see Section VIII. C; 3, presence of 'foreign' items in the text, which do not relate to what precedes or to what follows. LIEBERMAN subdivides this: a, mistakes in boundaries of copied and filled in pericopae; b, scribal mechanical citations; c, mistaken transfers from elsewhere which were not erased. In addition, there are remnants of deleted sections and scribal abbreviations for a deleted middle of a passage, the whole of which is paralleled elsewhere. See above, Section IX. A.

In (1934), pp. xii, xvi—xix, LIEBERMAN adds the following items: 1, incorrect erasures, where the copy editor of a text did not understand the passage or falsely thought there was an apparent duplication; 2, printing mistakes; and 3, general revision of Palestinian orthography or spelling on the basis of that commonly used in the time of scribe; 4, combination of two readings, both of which may be correct: one popular and one literary usage.

See also GINZBERG (1941), pp. H: xvii—xxv, and MELAMMED (1973), pp. 582—594, for further examples, and variations. The several works by LIEBERMAN and EPSTEIN contain many discrete examples of scribal corruptions. See Chapter V.

B. Means to Aid in Textual Reconstruction

1. Fully use parallels in Talmudic literature. With great care one should use the parallel *sugyot*, for as LIEBERMAN warns, the two versions may make up contradictory *sugyot*, deriving from different circles. See, e. g., LIEBERMAN (1931), pp. 2—7. A definitive cross index is still lacking. See above, Sections VIII. D; IX. A; X. A; XI.

2. Readings from MSS. The Geniza fragments are important for they are 'purer' and went through fewer scribal hands. One must rely on the MSS, especially the Leiden MS. See above for a description of these MSS and the guidelines for their use, Chapter IV,

3. Witnesses in medieval authorities and works. With the lack of early commentaries and early witnesses directly to the text, one must fully employ the citations in early authorities, whether in their commentaries on

BT or other works, and the analogous pericopae in midrashic works and other collections. RATNER, 11 vols. (Vilna, 1901—1917), had comprehensively initiated this approach, though his work is incomplete and not totally reliable; see Section XIX. C. Accordingly it is still necessary to collate the readings. To do so, one must know how the medieval authorities had access to y., what type of texts they had, and their methods of citation. See Chapter XIX.

The medieval works contain three types of materials: readings, explanations usually based upon some tradition the authority had received or heard, and filled in lacunae of the text. LIEBERMAN (1929), p. 39, reviews previous attempted collations and the necessary standards required. See GINZBERG (1941), pp. H: xxvi—xxxii, and Section XIX. C.

LIEBERMAN himself provides examples of how one may systematically employ these methods: (1934), and (1947), in which he reconstructs the third chapter of Mak., which found confirmation in a subsequently published Geniza fragment. See also GINZBERG (1941), pp. H: xxv—xxxii, and Sections V, and XX. C.

4. Language of y. Moreover, one must realize the distinctive style and terminology of y. and its usage of Hebrew. See Chapters XV and XVI.

See above, Section IX. B, for suggestions by which to uncover the presence of material out of place in a *sugya* and steps by which to evaluate an unsmooth text.

XV. Language

FRANKEL (1870), chapter Two, esp. 8b—11a, had recognized and described various linguistic peculiarities of the Hebrew and Aramaic in y. These include the fact that the Hebrew and Aramaic differ from those of BT; interchange of certain letters; deletion of certain initial letters; and aspects of orthography. The scientific study of these matters, though, was done in the twentieth century by H. YALON, S. MORAG, J. N. EPSTEIN, E. KUTSCHER, and S. LIEBERMAN who, in particular, tied the textual study of y. with that of its language.

As KUTSCHER, in Archive of the New Hebrew Dictionary of Rabbinical Literature 1 and 2 (Ramat Gan, 1972, 1974), and KUTSCHER and RABIN, in Current Trends in Linguistics 6 (1970), review the history of the research, the characteristics, both strengths and weaknesses, of earlier studies, works, and tools, the major problems, and the ways in which to make use of dialects and languages related to Hebrew and Aramaic, I shall basically confine my remarks to the Hebrew and Aramaic in y. and shall cite the main works. For the dictionaries and grammars of and research relevant in Christian Palestinian Aramaic, Samaritan Aramaic, Syriac, Mandaic, Akkadian, Iranian languages and such, see KUTSCHER and RABIN, and LIEBERMAN (1934), pp. xiii, xviii—xix. For all matters, see the excellent bibliography of DAVID GOODBLATT, The Languages of Rabbinic Literature, in: Understanding Rabbinic Judaism, ed. JACOB NEUSNER (New York, 1974), pp. 396—402, and the somewhat different J. H. HOSPERS, A Basic Bibliography for the Study of the Semitic Languages, I (Leiden, 1973). See also GOODBLATT (1979), III, for literature and an excellent analysis of the state of scholarship.

A. The Nature of PT's Hebrew and Aramaic

1. Hebrew. The Hebrew used and found in y. is part of Middle (or Mishnaic) Hebrew, which exhibits significant differences from that of Biblical Hebrew and later or Medieval and Modern Hebrew. It was a spoken language in the time of the first century. In post-Talmudic times, however, scribes tended, in general, to biblicize the usages found in Talmudic documents and, for those works from Palestine, tended to Babylonianize the forms. The careful study of MSS that preserve the early readings, comparative Semitics, and the like, has enabled scholars in this century to set out the developments and stages of Hebrew. Further research has demonstrated that the Hebrew in y. is to be separately classified from that of 'Mishnah' and 'Tosefta' and thus designated as MH^2.

M. H. SEGAL, Mishnaic Hebrew and Its Relation to Biblical Hebrew and to Aramaic, JQR, O.S. 20 (1907—08), 647—737.

E. BEN YEHUDAH, Thesaurus Totius Hebraitatis, Prolegomena (Jerusalem, 1940, Repr. London and New York, 1960), pp. 83—254.

*E. KUTSCHER, Leshon Ḥazal, Henoch Yalon Jubilee Volume (Jerusalem, 1963), pp. 246—280; ID., The Present State of Research into Mishnaic Hebrew. Some Problems of the Lexicography of Mishnaic Hebrew and Its Comparison with Biblical Hebrew, Archive 1 (1972), pp. 3—82, English summary, iii—xxvii, a revision and expansion of ID., Mittelhebräisch und Jüdisch-Aramäisch im Neuen Köhler—Baumgartner, Festschrift W. Baumgartner (= Suppl. to Vetus Testamentum, 16) (Leiden, 1967), pp. 168—175; ID., Hebrew, Language Mishnaic, EJ 16, 1590—1607, 1659.

H. L. GINSBERG, New Light on Tannaitic Jewry, The Jewish Expression, ed. J. GOLDIN (New York, 1970, and New Haven, 1976), pp. 109—118.

*CHAIM RABIN, Hebrew, Current Trends in Linguistics 6 (1970), pp. 304—346.

*MOSHEH BAR-ASHER, ed., Qoveṣ Maamarim BeLashon Ḥazal (Hebrew University: Jerusalem, 1972), a collection of all the important articles through 1972, many with corrections, and an index; includes KUTSCHER (1963) and MICHAEL SOKOLOFF, HaIvrit Shel Bereshet Rabbah Vat. MS. 30, pp. 257—301, republished from Leshonenu 33 (1965), 25—42, 135—142, 270—279, which isolated the second strata of Middle Hebrew.

M. MORESHET, New and Revived Verbs in the Bārāytot of the Babylonian Talmud, Archive 1 (1972), pp. 117—162, English summary, xxxvi—

xxxix; ID., The Language of the Bārāytot in the Babylonian Talmud is not MH[1], Henoch Yalon Memorial Volume, ed. E. Y. KUTSCHER et al. (Ramat Gan, 1974), pp. xxi—xxii, 275—314, and Archive 2 (1974).

2. a. Aramaic. Galilean Aramaic, as well, has been studied on the basis of uncontaminated texts. Its place within Western Aramaic is clear, though scholars do not all agree as to the sequence and nature of the several dialects.

The following literature includes rich bibliographies:

*KUTSCHER, Studies in Galilean Aramaic, Tarbiẓ 21 (1950), 192—205; 22 (1951), 53—63, 185—192 (English translation with additional notes and bibliography, Bar Ilan Studies in Near Eastern Languages and Culture, 1976), the pioneering study; ID., Aramaic, Current Trends in Linguistics 6 (1970), pp. 347—412, an excellent bibliographical survey of the field and its problems; ID., Aramaic, EJ, 3, pp. 259—287, an excellent exposition and summary, with rich bibliography; ID., Some Problems in the Lexicography of the Jewish Aramaic Dialects, Archive 2 (1974), Hebrew translation of part two of ID., Mittelhebräisch und Jüdisch-Aramäisch im Neuen Köhler-Baumgartner, Festschrift W. Baumgartner (Leiden, 1967), pp. 168—175.

PAUL KAHLE, Cairo Geniza (Oxford, 1959), pp. 200—208, especially 203—205.

*JONAS GREENFIELD, Standard Literary Aramaic, Actes du Premier Congres International De Linguistique Sémitique et Chamito-Sémitique, Paris 16—19, juillet, 1969, réums par ANDRÉ CAQUOT et DAVID COHEN (Paris, 1974), pp. 280—289.

BARRY LEVY, A Grammar of the Neofiti Targum (Leiden, in press), Introduction.

b) Use of Targum: The Targumim may provide help as to the definition of a word or usage. See CHAIM JOSHUA KASOWSKI, Theasurus Aquilae [= Onqelos] Versionis (Jerusalem, 1940).

For the relevant literature, see KUTSCHER, Archive 1 and 2 (1972, 1974); BERNARD GROSSFELD, A Bibliography of Targum Literature, I—II (Cincinnati, 1972, 1977), and the Review of JOSEPH A. FITZMYER, JBL 93 (1974), 135—136; GOODBLATT (1974) and HOSPERS (1973); and the recent studies by ABRAHAM TAL (ROSENTHAL), Ms. Neophyti 1: The Palestinian Targum to the Pentatuech, Israel Oriental Studies 4 (1974), 31ff., on the Aramaic, and ID., The Language of the Targum of the Former Prophets and Its Position within the Aramaic Dialects (Texts and Studies in Hebrew Language and Related Subjects, ed. ARON DOTAN, Vol. 1) (Tel Aviv, 1975), which concludes that the language under study is close to that of PT.

Moreover, y. at times cites a Targumic rendering of a verse. See M. KASHER, Torah Shelemah XXIV (Jerusalem, 1974), pp. 143—154, for a collection and analysis of the instances. (The volume is devoted to a study of the several Targumim and their characteristics.)

B. The Greek and Latin Element

FRANKEL (1870) and others had noticed the large amount of Greek in y. LIEBERMAN's works show how scribes who did not understand the words often corrupted them, a fact that further makes vital the use of MSS.

According to LIEBERMAN, Hellenism in Jewish Palestine (New York, 1950), p. 3:

"Almost every foreign word and phrase have their «*raison d'etre*» in rabbinic literature... all Greek phrases in rabbinic literature are quotations. If a common Greek word is employed by the rabbis only very rarely, whereas they generally use its Aramaic equivalent, some reason must lie behind the rabbinic choice of a Greek term in a particular case."

'Neziqin', in particular, is rich in Greek usage and often uses words in a sense different from that of the rest of rabbinic literature; LIEBERMAN (1931), pp. 13—16, SZ (1968), p. 132, fn. 27.

As to Latin, Palestinian rabbis did not know Latin except for military and judicial terms and names of objects imported from Latin speaking countries, words that usually also were in Syriac and later Greek; LIEBERMAN (1950), p. 17.

S. KRAUSS, Griechische und lateinische Lehnwörter in Talmud, Midrasch und Targum, 2 vols. (Berlin, 1898—99), indicates, whatever the merits of each entry, the large number of Greek and Latin words. See LIEBERMAN (1941), p. 9, and (1950), p. 3; KUTSCHER, Archive 1,2 (1972, 1974), H. ROSEN, Palestinian Koine in Rabbinic Illustration, JSS 8 (1963), 55—72; and D. SPERBER, cited below. The work is highly useful for references to all instances of each entry known to the author and his collaborators.

SAUL LIEBERMAN, virtually all of his works, especially: Greek in Jewish Palestine (New York, 1941, 1965[2]); ID. Hellenism in Jewish Palestine (New York, 1950) — see the reviews of (1941), listed on p. 210, reprinted in (1965[2]), pp. 194f. [especially that of G. ALON, reprinted in his 'Studies in Jewish History', II (Tel Aviv, 1958), pp. 248—277]; TK I ff. (New York, 1955ff.), which includes indexes to foreign words; his collected articles, in 'Texts and Studies' (1974), especially his comments, pp. 1f. (= Esser Millin, in: Eshkoloth (Jerusalem, 1959)] and 59f. [= Roman Legal Institutions, JQR, N.S. 35 (1944), 1—2], that we must make use of Greek sources from Palestine, the coastal area, and Egypt, in particular the works written in popular Greek; and his carefully argued 'How Much Greek in Jewish Palestine', pp. 216—234 [= in: Biblical and Other Studies, ed. A. ALTMANN (Cambridge, 1962), pp. 123—141], wherein he evaluates previous research.

BARON II, 299—300.

J. N. SEVENSTER, Do You Know Greek? (Leiden, 1968), with long bibliography, surveys the sources by which to evaluate the knowledge and use of Greek in various social strata. See the reviews of B. LIFSHITZ. KS 44

(1969), 379—385, whose comments are important, in general; and of D. SPERBER, Leshonenu 34 (1970), 225—227 — while SEVENSTER focuses on the first century, his remarks are (also) relevant to a later period, for many of his literary sources come from a later period, and statements therein even if attributed to an individual from an earlier period may actually reflect the language of the time in which the work was edited or composed.

B. GROSS, To the Etymology of ŠBWRYN (collection of water), Leshonenu 32 (1968), 279—297.

S. SIMONSOHN (1974), pp. 832—834.

D. SPERBER, Greek and Latin Words in Rabbinic Literature, BIA 14—15 (1977), 9—60.

The especially useful Greek dictionaries include:

Hesychius Alexandrinus. Lexicon post IOANNEM ALBERTUM rec. M. SCHMIDT, ed., 5 vols. (Jena, 1858—68, 1966); rec. et emend. K. LATTE, 3 vols. (Kopenhagen, 1953—1966). See LIEBERMAN, SZ (1968), p, 66, fn. 242, and the references cited there.

E. A. SOPHOCLES, Greek Lexicon of the Roman and Byzantine Periods (Cambridge, 1914).

JAMES HOPE MOULTON and GEORGE MILLIGAN, The Vocabulary of the Greek Testament (London, 1930; Grand Rapids, 1974).

WALTER BAUER, WILLIAM F. ARNDT, and F. WILBER GINGRICH, A Greek English Lexicon of the New Testament and Other Early Christian Literature (Chicago and Cambridge, 1957).

C. Comprehensive Dictionaries

KUTSCHER, Archive 1 (1972), pp. 3ff., reviews the dictionaries and related specialized works, cites important reviews, and notes the weaknesses and strengths and thus provides guidelines by which to use the works. As indicated above, I include only the highly important items and secondary literature. For the rest, see KUTSCHER and RABIN (1970).

JACOB LEVY, Wörterbuch über die Talmudim und Midraschim, 4 vols. (Leipzig, 1876—1889, Berlin and Vienna, 1924^2, Repr. Darmstadt, 1963). The second edition contains additions by HEINRICH L. FLEISCHER and LAZARUS GOLDSCHMIDT.

ALEXANDER KOHUT, et al., The Aruch Completum of Nathan b. Yeḥiel, ca. 1030—1106, Italy, an expanded critical version in 8 vols. (Vilna, 1878—1892, 1926^2, Repr. New York, 1957, Jerusalem, 1971). The original work is important for its citations of y., under alphabetical entries. Vol. VIII includes indexes, to y., pp. 100—104. A very important supplement-volume, with notes on Iranian words, by B. GEIGER, appeared, Additamenta ad Librum Aruch Completum, ed. SAMUEL KRAUSS, et al. (= Vol. IX), (Vienna, 1937, Repr. New York, 1957, Jerusalem, 1971). See KRAUSS' introduction and the bibliographical references, iv, n. 1, and LIEBERMAN's Review, KS 14 (1937), 218—228. In general, see BARON VII, 29—32, and

231–232, and especially S. ABRAMSON, On the Aruḳ of R. Nathan, Leshonenu 36 (1972), 122–149; 37 (1973), 26–42, 253–269; 38 (1973–74), 91–117, which analyzes the nature of the work, including the Talmudic texts that it used; e. g., Aruch on the basis of the explanatory sources that it employed may contain different readings of *gemara*. Note, pp. 114–117, an index to entries discussed; and ABRAMSON's additional notes, in his collected articles, Inyanot BeŚifrut HaGaonim (Jerusalem, 1974), pp. 420–421.

I. LOEW, Die Flora der Juden, 4 vols. (Vienna, 1924–34); ID., Fauna und Mineralien der Juden (Hildesheim, 1969), excellent works.

MARCUS JASTROW, A Dictionary of the Targumim, the Talmud Babli and Yerushalmi, and the Midrashic Literature, 2 vols. (New York, 1903, in 1 vol., New York, Berlin, 1926, various subsequent reprints), weak on derivations.

BENJAMIN MAZAR, MOSHE SCHWAB, B. LIFSHITZ, and NAHMAN AVIGAD, Beth She'arim, 3 vols. (Jerusalem, 1957–71), with indexes, is an important source for Hebrew, Aramaic, and Greek inscriptions.

WALTER BAUMGARTNER, B. HARTMANN, and E. Y. KUTSCHER, Hebräisches und Aramäisches Lexicon zum Alten Testament I (Leiden, 1967), KUTSCHER's additions are important.

For collections of inscriptions, see Section XVII. C.

D. Concordances

BENIAMIN KOSOVSKY, Thesaurus to Talmud Yerushalmi, though already finished, has not yet appeared. For earlier attempts, see PAUL KAHLE, Cairo Geniza (Oxford, 1959²), pp. 203–204. Meanwhile the several other concordances to Palestinian texts are highly useful:

CHAIM JOSHUA KOSOWSKI, Thesaurus Thosephthae, 6 vols. (Jerusalem, 1932–1961).

CHAYIM YEHOSHUA KOSOVSKY, Thesaurus Mishnae, corrected edition, 4 vols. (Jerusalem, 1956–60).

BENIAMIN KOSOVSKY, Otzar Leshon HaTanna'im: Concordantiae Verborum Mechilta D' Rabbi Ismael, 4 vols. (Jerusalem, 1965–66); ID., Thesauris Sifra, 4 vols. (Jerusalem, 1967–69); ID., Thesaurus Sifrei, 5 vols. (Jerusalem, 1971–74).

E. Grammars

There are no completely satisfactory grammars. See KUTSCHER, Archive 1 and 2 (1972, 1974).

GUSTAF DALMAN, Grammatik des Jüdisch-Palästinischen Aramäisch (Leipzig, 1905, Repr. Darmstadt, 1960), KUTSCHER: "outdated".

J. T. MARSCHALL, ed. J. BARTON TURNER, Manual of the Aramaic Language of the Palestinian Talmud (Leiden, 1929).

H. ODEBERG, The Aramaic Portions of Bereshit Rabba. II Short Grammar of Galilean Aramaic (Lund, 1939), KUTSCHER: "good for syntax".

W. B. STEVENSON, Grammar of Palestinian Jewish Aramaic, 2nd ed. by J. A. EMERTON (Oxford, 1962²), KUTSCHER, "of little significance".

*E. Y. KUTSCHER, 'Aramaic', and 'Hebrew Language, Mishnaic', EJ 3, 270—274, and 16, 1590—1607, include descriptions of the languages.

F. Additional Bibliography

MOSES SCHLESINGER, Das Aramäische Verbum im Jerusalemischen Talmud, Magazin für die Wissenschaft des Judentums 16 (1899), 1—9.

*SAUL LIEBERMAN, virtually all of his works, especially (1929), (1931), 1ff.; (1934); TR (1937—1939); and TK (1955ff.), which includes long indexes to linguistic and lexicographical comments, though not to all of them. N. B. Introductions, vols. I, III, VI, VIII; and Texts and Studies (1974). See M. Z. KADDARI, Grammatical Notes on Saul Lieberman's Tosefta Kifshutah (Zera'im), Archive 1 (1972), pp. 163—173, xl; and BARUCH BOKSER, Review, Newsletter, Association for Jewish Studies, 12 (November, 1974), pp. 18—19. LIEBERMAN notes that variations in language in different *sugyot* may reflect their different location and time of origin; (1931), pp. 1—2, 16; (1934), pp. xi—xiii.

JACOB N. EPSTEIN, virtually all of his works, especially (1948, 1964²), pp. 1007—1269. See the bibliography to his works, S. ABRAMSON, Tarbiẓ 20 (1950), pp. 7—16. See SHIMON SHARVIT, Studies in the Lexicography and Grammar of Mishnaic Hebrew. Based on the 'Introductions of J. N. EPSTEIN', Archives 2 (1974), pp. 112—124, xv—xvi.

HENOCH YALON, virtually all of his works. See the bibliographies, S. ESH, Henoch Yalon, Bibliography, 1922—1963, Henoch Yalon Jubilee Volume (Jerusalem, 1963), pp. 37—50, to be supplemented by RAPHAEL WEISS, Bibliography, 1963—1970, Henoch Yalon Memorial Volume, ed. E. Y. KUTSCHER, et al. (Ramat Gan, 1974), pp. 1—7. The following three works include much of his important research: ID., Bulletin of Hebrew Language Studies, Wahrman Books, 1963² (corrected reissue, bound together of Jerusalem, 1937—1943); ID., Mavo Leniqud Hamishnah [Introduction to the Vocalization of the Mishna] (Jerusalem, 1964); and especially ID., Studies in the Hebrew Language (Jerusalem, 1971), collected, corrected articles with detailed indexes to words, grammar, and subject.

RABINOVITZ (1940), p. 308.

SIMḤA ASSAF, Tequfat HaGeonim VeŚifrutah (Jerusalem, 1955), p. 172, on the languages of Palestine after the completion of y.

ABBA BENDAVID, Biblical Hebrew and Mishnaic Hebrew Compared, I—II (Tel Aviv, 1967, 1971), points to many changes in usage, grammar, and style. While his individual examples are not always correct, and he insufficiently systematically employed MSS and weighed alternative explanations, he points to many important phenomena and includes useful indexes. See Review, Joshua Blau, KS 44 (1969), 29–35; 46 (1971), 424–428.

M. Sokoloff, Introduction, to Midrash Bereshit Rabba MS. Vat. Ebr. 30 (Makor: Jerusalem, 1971).

James Barr, Linguistic Literature, Hebrew, EJ 16, 1352–1401.

Rabinowitz, Tarbiẓ 41 (1972), 276, re Yerushalmi spelling.

Archive 1, 2 (1972, 1974), the remaining articles not previously cited.

Melammed (1973), pp. 605–620.

Sussmann (1973–74), pp. 138f., 139, 146–152, discusses an inscription of a Talmudic text, some of which is based on y. and which linguistically cannot have been revised, and surveys its spelling, forms, and vocabulary.

S. Friedman, Three Studies in Babylonian Aramaic Grammar, Tarbiẓ 43 (1973–74), 58–69, while on BT undoubtedly also applies to PT: variations in linguistic and grammatical forms may be due to differences in the literary genre of materials.

Shlomo Simonsohn (1974), an excellent critical survey, with bibliography, of the languages of Palestine.

N. B. Indexes to Leshonenu 1–25, 1929–1961 (1967), and Israel Exploration Journal 1–10, 1950–1960, in 11 (1961), 261–264, and 11–20, 1961–1970, in 26 (1976), 271–288, include indexes to words.

XVI. Terms and Fixed Usages

Y. employs a distinctive style, including patterned phrasings and specific terminologies, usages, and words. Aspects of the style and some of the usages are unique to y. while others are found in Palestinian literature in general, and still others have parallels or analogues in Babylonian sources. Sirillo, in his 'Introduction', Part Two, published in his 'Commentary to Berakhot', ed. Dinglas (Jerusalem, 1967), pp. 7–8, already focused on such terms as well as the names of masters in y.

The 'unsmooth' nature of the y. often entails the lack of a term. For example, y. may not contain a term joining sentences or indicating the relationship between two items. See above, Section IX. A. But on the other hand, the presence of a fixed usage may provide a guide to the structure of an ostensibly confused pericope or whole *sugya*.

Various studies have examined the usages of many phrases and terms but a full and exhaustive study of all the relevant items is lacking. Hopefully, the forthcoming concordance to PT will facilitate such a study.

Primary tools to elucidate the fixed language and usage include familiarity with: (a) Palestinian Aramaic and Hebrew, for which see above, Section XV. A; (b) orthographic practices whereby a letter, e. g., *aleph*, א, ', is deleted, or two words are combined, or one is separated into two component parts; and (c) the recurrent patterns in which the words appear.

Methodological guidelines include:

One must not superimpose the Babylonian conception of a term onto its y. parallel or analogue. See e. g., EPSTEIN (1948), pp. 245, 262, and BOKSER (1975), p. 130, fn. 380.

Within y. one must not superimpose one specific usage onto each instance. The terminology may vary in different locations, as pericopae may derive from different circles or places. This is especially so as to 'Neziqin': LIEBERMAN (1931), pp. vii–viii, pp. 1, 6, 7–9, 16, 17. Moreover, the referent or connotation of an item in one place may differ from that elsewhere. Thus, אית אמרין, *'YT 'MRYN*, in 'Neziqin', refers to a Tiberian teaching; LIEBERMAN (1931), p. 17.

A term may often make up the second half of a balanced phrasing. I. e., the word or term is in balance to one in a preceding passage or clause: LIEBERMAN (1934), pp. 17, 254, 453; NEUSNER, Pharisees (1971), and Purities (1974–1977).

A pericope's editor may revise a term in a comment or tradition so as to fit it into its present context. For example, he may replace 'here' in a comment where it originally referred to the location of the spokesperson and where that place differs from that of the place of the editing of the pericope; LIEBERMAN, SZ (1968), p. 131, fn. 22.

Where a term introduces a citation and thereby ostensibly bridges it with a preceding Amoraic statement with which it is compared, the term and citation may be later and or unconnected to the Amoraic tradition; WEISS HALIVNI (1975), p. 540f., fn. 7 and the references there, and BOKSER (1975), p. 95, fn. 263; and 101–102, fn. 280. See above, Section VIII. D, for further related items.

FRANKEL (1870), pp. 13a–17a and chapter Two, focuses on and classifies different usages, in particular patterned phrasing to introduce citations or structured phrases and clauses, and terms. While very useful, the lists are inexhaustive and at times inexact; LIEBERMAN (1929), pp. 47–49. Of note, many of FRANKEL's entries, in abbreviated and at times inexact form, were reprinted in y. Vilna ed., volume one, 'Zera'im'; LIEBERMAN (1929), p. 45.

WILHELM BACHER, Die Exegetische Terminologie der jüdischen Traditionsliteratur, 2 vols. (Leipzig, 1899, Repr. in one vol., Darmstadt, 1965), in Hebrew translation, by A. S. RABINOVITZ, Erchē Midrash, 2 vols. [I = Tannaim; II = Amoraim] (Tel Aviv, 1933, Repr. Jerusalem: Carmiel, 1970[2]), is very important, especially as it differentiates between Palestinian and Babylonian usages; ID., Die Ausdrücke mit denen die Tradition bezeichnet wird, JQR, O. S. 20 (1907–08), 572–596; ID., Tradition und Tradenten in den Schulen Palästinas und Babyloniens (Leipzig, 1914, Repr. Berlin, 1966), while quite useful is marred. See JACOB LAUTERBACH, Bacher's Tradition and Traditionists in the Schools of Palestine and Babylonia, JQR, N. S. 8 (1917), 105–112; the work does not note the significance and usage of each item; the entries are not aptly selected (inexhaustive, lacking significant entries and important instances of included items). LAUTERBACH's article contains important notes on usages.

LIEBERMAN (1929), (1931), (1934), and various articles. Moreover, TK (1955ff.), is replete with notes on y. style and terminology, many of which are indexed, in vols. II, V, VIII, under subject or words. As (1934) lacks an index, I include the following selected items (partial list):

לית כאן . . . אית כאן. *LYT K'N . . . 'YT K'N*, p. 65.
מן מאן, *MN, M'N* (*mān*) = מה, *mah*, pp. 76, 288.
סלקת מתניתא. *ŚLQT MTNYT'*, p. 80. Cf. HY (1948), p. 68 = 'Mishnah', the matter, is finished; henceforth a new topic.
כך אנו אומרים?, *KK 'NW 'WMRYM*, pp. 178–179.
ר׳ — — הורי כההן תנייא., *R — — HWRY KHHN TNYY'*, p. 228.
ר׳ מסתכל ביה., *R MŚTKL BYH*, = in anger, p. 289, and fn. 2.
ומה ופליג., *WHM WPLYG*, p. 316 = A question reacting against 'Mishnah', *baraita*, or an Amora.
חוץ מדעתי., *ḤWṢ MD'TY* = שלא מדעת, *ŠL' MD'T*, p. 497.

See also (1950), pp. 290–292, on כן אנו אמרין (כן אני אומר) *KN 'NW 'MRYN* (*KN 'NY 'WMR*), which is a question.

EPSTEIN, many of his articles. See bibliography, Tarbiẓ 20 (1950). Note, esp. ID., The One Who Taught This Did Not Teach This, Tarbiẓ 7 (1936), pp. 143ff.; (1948, 1964²), the second edition includes a highly useful index; (1954), (1962).

RABINOVITZ (1940). See index, p. 637.

WEISS HALIVNI (1968, 1975), see index. E. g., I: 299, fn. 1, and 360, fn. 11.

'Maftehot' [Indexes] to Leshonenu, Vols. 1–25, 1924–1961 (Jerusalem, 1967).

*MELAMMED (1973), pp. 605–625, esp. 620–625, a long annotated list of usages.

MARGALIOTH (1973), contains a list of Palestinian forms and terms in the Post-Talmudic documents therein published, pp. 23–25, 57–60, 98, 100.

BOKSER (1975), pp. 101–102, fn. 280; 102–105, esp. fn. 289; 133–135, and fns. 380, 393; 135, fn. 400; 144–145; 187–215.

GOODBLATT (1975), an exemplary critical study, demonstrates the necessity and method to distinguish between y. and b. usages. While primarily on BT, it focuses on y. usages of educational institutions and how b. uses fixed language for Palestinian items, e. g., p. 136.

XVII. Aids to the Study of the Yerushalmi

This chapter deals with several subjects and bodies of materials which may greatly illuminate y. They include: geography, archaeology and realia;

inscriptions; history of agriculture; legal studies; and liturgical works. The degree of completeness for each unit varies. The purpose is to bring to the reader's attention the particular area and indicate its importance and relevance to the study of y. Additional items may be found in STRACK (1931), pp. 183–198; MIELZINER (1968), pp. 403–410, 415; EJ, index; and GOODBLATT (1979), V, and Chapter XIII, above.

A. Geography

ADOLPH NEUBAUER, La Géographie du Talmud (Paris, 1968), see the criticisms by ROMANOFF (1935–36), p. 150 (= 4), cited below.

YEḤIEL ṢEVI HIRSCHENSON, Sheva Ḥakhmot (Lemberg, 1883), a helpful dictionary-encyclopedia to places and persons, with notes as to textual variants.

HIRSH HILDESHEIMER, Beiträge zur Geographie Palästinas (Berlin, 1886), Hebrew translation in: Studies in the Geography of Eretz Israel (Jerusalem, 1965).

*Estori ha Parḥi, Kaftor UPeraḥ, ed. A. M. LUNCZ (Jerusalem, 1897[3], Repr. Israel, n. d. [1976?]), critical edition of a thirteenth-century work on geographic and agricultural laws and realia of Palestine. A less adequate edition is Caftor wa-pherach (Berlin, 1852, Repr. Jerusalem, 1959).

SOLOMON J. L. RAPPAPORT, Erek Millin, 2 vols. (Warsaw, 1914–, Repr. Jerusalem, 1970).

ISRAEL S. HOROWITZ, Palestine and the Adjacent Countries (Vienna, 1923, Repr. Jerusalem, 1970,) covers geographical names.

SAMUEL KLEIN, Das Tannaitische Grenzverzeichnis Palaestinas, HUCA 5 (1928), 197–259, Hebrew translation in Studies in the Geography of Eretz Israel (Jerusalem, 1955); ID., Ereṣ Yehudah (Tel Aviv, 1939), includes an index of places and subjects; ID., Ereṣ HaGalil (Jerusalem, 1946). KLEIN's works cite and discuss the texts that mention and describe geographical places.

*PAUL ROMANOFF, Onomasticon of Palestine, PAAJR 7 (1936), 147–227, reprinted with preface, errata, and index (New York, 1937); an exemplary study with attempted complete collection of sources and use of MSS and early editions of texts, including Geniza fragments to y. Note his review of earlier works, pp. 149–150.

*MICHAEL AVI-YONAH, Historical Geography of Ereṣ Yisrael [Hebrew] (Jerusalem, 1951[2]); ID., The Holy Land. From the Persian to the Arab Conquest. A Historical Geography (Grand Rapids, 1966).

MOSHE KOCHAVI, ed., Judah, Samaria, and the Golan. Archaeological Survey (Archaeological Survey of Israel, ed. A. BIRAN, et al. I), (Jerusalem, 1972).

SUSSMANN (1973–74), and Tarbiẓ 45 (1976), 213–252.

B. Archaeological Materials and Realia

*SAMUEL KRAUSS, Talmudische Archäologie, 3 vols. (Leipzig, 1910—12), with indexes, and Hebrew edition, Qadmoniyot HaTalmud, I, i—ii, II, i—ii (Berlin-Wien, n. d. and 1923, Tel Aviv, 1929, 1945). While KRAUSS' method of analysis may need improvement, the work contains a very useful collection of rabbinic and extra-rabbinic sources and discussion; ID., Paraś VeRomi BaTalmud UVamidrashim (Jerusalem, 1948).

GUSTAF HERMANN DALMAN, Arbeit und Sitte in Palästina, 7 vols. in 8 (Gütersloh, 1928—1942, Repr. Hildesheim, 1964).

S. YEIVIN, ed., Trade, Industry, and Crafts in Ancient Palestine (= Library of Palestinology of the Jewish Palestine Exploration Society IX/X), (Jerusalem, 1937).

BARON II, 299—307.

*YEHOSHUA BRAND, Ceramics in Talmudic Literature (Jerusalem, 1953), an excellent study and discussion of rabbinic, archaeological, and classical sources; ID., LeOr Nerot Ḥereś ʿAtiqin, Sinai 73 (1973), 163—167.

ERWIN R. GOODENOUGH, Jewish Symbols in Greco-Roman Period, 13 vols. (Princeton, 1953—1965). Note the list of reviews, 13, 229—230.

MAZAR, et al., Beth Sheʿarim, 3 vols. (Jerusalem, 1956—71), contains numerous items of Palestinian realia.

R. J. FORBES, Studies in Ancient Technology, 9 vols. (Leiden, 1964—1972).

YIGAEL YADIN, ed., Judean Desert Studies: The Finds from the Bar Kokhba Period in the "Cave of Letters" (Jerusalem, Hebrew edition: 1963, English edition: 1963). The finds also throw light on third through sixth-century matters.

*MAZAR, ed., Encyclopaedia of Archaeological Excavations in the Holy Land (Jerusalem, Hebrew 2 vol. edition, 1970, 4 vol. English edition: 1974ff.), includes individual entries with pictures of the sites.

*ELEANOR K. VOGEL, Bibliography of Holy Land Sites, HUCA 42 (1971), 1—96.

*ERIC M. MEYERS, Jewish Ossuaries: Reburial and Rebirth, Biblica et Orientalia, No. 24 (Rome,19 71). ID., The Use of Archaeology in Understanding Rabbinic Materials, in: Texts and Responses. Studies Presented to Nahum N. Glatzer, ed. MICHAEL A. FISHBANE and PAUL R. FLOHR (Leiden, 1975), pp. 28—41. These excellent studies demonstrate how archaeology can help in the interpretation of Palestinian rabbinic sources.

MOSHE KOCHAVI, ed., Judah, Samaria, and the Golan, Archaeological Survey (= Archaeological Survey of Israel, ed. A. BIRAN, et al., I), (Jerusalem, 1972).

SHMUEL SAFRAI, The Synagogues South of Mt. Judah, Immanuel 3 (1973—74), 44—50.

ARYE BEN-DAVID, Talmudische Ökonomie. Die Wirtschaft des jüdischen Palästina zur Zeit der Mischna und des Talmud 1 (Hildesheim und New York, 1974).

C. Inscriptions

Inscriptions in Hebrew, Aramaic, and Greek may shed light on geographical, economic, cultural, political, and textual matters. In general see the excellent bibliographies in EMIL SCHÜRER, The History of the Jewish People in the Age of Jesus Christ. New English Version I, by GEZA VERMES and FERGUS MILLAR (Edinburgh, 1973), pp. 11–16, and, in particular, in CASSUTO–SALZMANN, Hebrew Inscriptions of the End of the Second Temple Period, in: A. M. RABELLO, ed., Studies in Judaism. Jubilee Volume Presented to David Kotlar (Tel Aviv, 1975), pp. 123–144, and the 'Index to Newly Published Documents and Inscriptions' in Israel Exploration Journal 11–20, 1961–1970, printed in 26 (1976), 271–288; and Chapter XV.

S. KRAUSS, et al., SeferHaYishuv, I, i (Jerusalem, 1939).

B. MAZAR, et al., Beith She'arim, 3 vols. (Jerusalem, 1956–71).

H. DONNER, W. RÖLLIG, Kanaanäische und Aramäische Inschriften, 3 vols., 2nd ed. (Wiesbaden, [2]1966–69).

BARUCH LIFSHITZ, Prolegomenon, to Ktav reprint of JEAN B. FREY, Corpus Inscriptionum Judaicarum, 2 vols. [Rome, 1936–52] (New York, 1970).

E. KUTSCHER, Aramaic, EJ 3, 267–270; 283–287.

HOSPERS (1973), especially pp. 319–321.

JOSEPH NAVEH, Corpus of Synagogue Inscriptions (Jerusalem: Israel Exploration Society, in press).

Recent inscriptions include:

An 'En Gedi Inscription: various interpretations thereof in Tarbiẓ 40 (1970), especially that of Saul LIEBERMAN, A Preliminary Remark to the Inscription of 'En Gedi', pp. 24–26, who uses the inscription to throw light on a y. passage.

A. DOTAN, The Secret in the Synagogue Inscription of 'En Gedi, Leshonenu 36 (1971), 211–217, which overly accepts the historicity of Pirqoi ben Baboi's propaganda concerning the historical events in the Holy Land.

DAN ORMAN, Jewish Inscription from Dabura in the Golan, Tarbiẓ 40 (1971), 399–408.

SUSSMANN (1973–74), and ID., Additional Notes, Tarbiẓ 44 (1974–75), 193–195, and Tarbiẓ 45 (1975–76), II–III, 213–257.

FANNO VITTO, Ancient Synagogue At Rehov, Atiqot. Hebrew Series 7 (1974), 100–104, 17*–18*.

LIEBERMAN, Tarbiẓ 45 (1975–76), IV, 53–63, 331.

ELISHA QIMRON, Some Comments to the Tel Reḥov Inscriptions, Tarbiẓ 45 (1975–76), X, 154–156.

Z. SAFRAI, Immanuel 8 (1978), 48–57.

D. Agricultural Matters

Many texts deal with agricultural matters or otherwise require the knowledge of these materials. For general bibliographies, see YEHUDA FELIKS, Mixed Sowing, Breeding, and Grafting (Tel Aviv, 1967) and K. D. WHITE, Bibliography of Roman Agriculture (England, n.d.), a classified detailed index.

The following literature either deals with ancient agriculture in general or in part, or else tries to relate those concerns to Talmudic texts:

*I. LOEW, Aramäische Pflanzennamen (Leipzig, 1881); ID., Die Flora der Juden I—IV, in 5 vols. (Vienna, 1924—34, Repr., in 4 vols., Hildesheim, 1967).

*A. M. LUNCZ, ed. of Estori HaParḥi, Kaftor UPeraḥ (Jerusalem, 1897[3]), a comprehensive collection and study of sources on agricultural matters.

*S. KRAUSS (1910—12) and (1923, 1929, 1945). (See under B, above).

*JULIUS PREUSS, Biblisch-Talmudische Medizin (Berlin, 1911, Repr. London, 1969, and New York, 1970; English ed., New York, 1978).

*A. S. HIRSCHBERG, HaṢemer UPishtah BiTqufat HaMishnah VeHa-Talmud (Jerusalem, 1912).

DALMAN (1928—42). (See under B, above).

*LIEBERMAN, TK Iff. (1955ff.), especially vols. I—II, with an index to flora.

YEHUDAH FELIKS, Plant World of the Bible (Tel Aviv, 1957); *ID., Agriculture in Palestine in the Period of the Mishna and Talmud (Jerusalem, 1963), a systematic study of all facets, with indexes; ID., Rice in Rabbinic Literature, BIA 1 (1963), 177—189; ID., Graft Hybredization of Trees and Vegetables, BIA 3 (1965), 25—45; ID., Mixed Sowing, Breeding, and Grafting (Tel Aviv, 1967), a botanic commentary to Kil. I—II; ID., The Prohibition of Ploughing in the Summer Preceding the Seventh Year, BIA 9 (1972) [= Memorial to H. M. Shapiro, ed. H. Z. HIRSCHBERG (Ramat Gan, 1972], 142—220, and xvii—xviii; ID., Go and Seed in the Seventh Year Because of Arnona, Sinai 37 (1973), 235—249; ID., Pereq Zeraʿim, in: MORDECHAI MARGALIOTH, Hilkhot Ereṣ Yisrael Min HaGenizah (Jerusalem, 1973); ID., The Fifteenth of Shevat, Tarbiẓ 46 (1977), 181—211.

URIAH FELDMAN, Ṣamhe HaMishna (Tel Aviv, n.d.).

FORBES (1964—1972), especially vols. 2, 3, 5. (See under Section B.)

*MICHAEL ZOHARY, Flora Palaestina, 3 vols. (Jerusalem, 1966—75).

*K. D. WHITE, Agricultural Implements of the Roman World (Cambridge, 1967); and ID., Roman Farming (Ithaca, 1970), an excellent introduction and study, with a survey of the ancient literary sources. Although it does not employ Talmudic sources, it throws considerable light on them.

ARMAS SALONEN, Agricultura Mesopotamica (Helsinki, 1968).

ISAAC GILAT, As to the Applicability of the Laws of Ploughing and Seeding and other Labors in the Seventh Year, Sinai 36 (70) (1972), 200—210.

M. E. Kislev, Ḥitta and Kussemet, Notes on Their Interpretation, Leshonenu 37 (1973), 83—95; 242—252, an excellent study.

Sussmann (1973—74).

E. Legal Studies

The knowledge of the legal background of a matter is a prerequisite to the understanding of a text. Naturally, one must not impose a supposed reconstruction of the legal history onto the text, but rather base that reconstruction on the text itself. This is especially so for y. where texts, even analogous ones, may derive from different and disputing circles. Scholars have made different sorts of studies, and have successfully clarified through comparative investigations many oblique matters. They have drawn on the Greek papyrological materials from the Eastern Mediterranean and Egypt, Roman, Syriac, Aramaic, Akkadian, and Biblical materials. See Baron II (1952), pp. 299—302, and Shamma Friedman's Review of Ze'ev Falk, Mavo L'Dine Yisrael, Conservative Judaism 25 (1971), 85—88.

Many studies in 'Jewish Law', however, have not realized the import of historical-literary critical research. Rather they tend to accept attributions at face value, insufficiently to distinguish between the strata of sources, and inadequately to take account of different versions of the same source. See Bernard Jackson, Introduction, Essays in Jewish and Comparative Legal History (Leiden, 1976). For a specific example, the matter of *prozbul*, see Gulak, History of Jewish Law, Talmudic Period I: Law of Obligation and Its Guarantees (Jerusalem, 1939), pp. 31—52, and Menachem Elon, Lien, EJ 11, 227—237, whose pictures of the developments must be reassessed in light of Neusner, Pharisees (1971), I—III; Weiss Halivni (1968), pp. 225—227; and E. Halevy, HaAggadah HaHiṣṭorit-Biographit (Tel Aviv, 1975), pp. 129—130; cf. Bokser (1975), pp. 80—85.

Thus it is vital to pay attention to the date in which conceptual modes emerged and to avoid an anachronistic projection back as if the concepts or principles existed throughout all periods. This is especially so as far as the classification of laws; see, e.g., Yitzhak D. Gilat, From Biblical Severity to Rabbinic Injunction, Benjamin DeVries Memorial Volume, ed. Z. M. Melammed (Jerusalem, 1968), pp. 84—93. Accordingly, one must consider the literary history of the text and the history of the traditions contained therein when one employs the various studies.

Nahum Rakover, A Bibliography of Jewish Law (Jerusalem, 1975), presents a classified and comprehensive listing of Hebrew items. See also Baron II (1952), 299—302.

Major and representative works include:

Asher Gulak, Yeśode HaMishpat HaIvri, 4 vols. (Berlin, 1922, Repr. in 2 vols., Tel Aviv, 1967[2]); Id., σύμφωνον in Betrothal According to the Jerusalem Talmud, Tarbiẓ 5 (1934), 126—133; *Id., Das Urkundenwesen im Talmud (Jerusalem, 1935); *Id., History of Jewish Law, Talmudic Period I: Law of Obligation and Its Guarantees [Hebrew] (Jerusalem, 1939).

Jacob J. Rabinowitz, Jewish Law, Its Influence on the Development of Legal Institutions (New York, 1956).

*Reuven Yaron, Gifts in Contemplation of Death in Jewish and Roman Law (Oxford, 1960), a careful historical study.

Shalom Albeck, General Principles of the Law of Tort in the Talmud [Hebrew] (Tel Aviv, 1965), focuses on B.Q. This and his many articles deal with legal theory and principles, especially in civil matters, e.g., Id., Davar Shlo' Ba' Le'olam, Sinai 38 (1974), 97–119. Id., Dine Mamonot BeTalmud (Tel Aviv, 1976).

Bezalel Porten, Archives from Elephantine (Berkeley, 1968), contains much useful material concerning the nature of documents and procedures used in their writing.

*Boaz Cohen, Jewish and Roman Law: A Comparative Study, 2 vols. (New York, 1966), a collection of various articles previously published in many different places, with an introduction surveying earlier literature, and comprehensive indexes.

*Aaron Kirschenbaum, Self-Incrimination in Jewish Law (New York, 1970).

Dine Israel, An Annual of Jewish Law and Israeli Family Law, ed. Ze'ev W. Falk and Aaron Kirschenbaum Iff. (Tel Aviv, 1970ff.).

S. Lieberman, A Few Words on the Book by Julian the Architect of Ascalon 'The Laws of Palestine and its Customs', Tarbiẓ 40 (1971), 409–417.

Bernard Jackson, Theft in Early Jewish Law (Oxford, 1972), with rich bibliography.

Menachem Elon, Ha-Mishpat Ha-Ivri, 3 vols. (Jerusalem, 1973), a voluminous work which, however, does not sufficiently take into account the critical matters mentioned above. Too often it deals with items as they were perceived in the post-Talmudic times; Id., ed., The Principles of Jewish Law (Jerusalem, 1975), a separate publication of the 'Jewish Law' material from the Encyclopaedia Judaica, with indexes.

Neusner, Purities (1974–1977), though on Mishnaic materials provides examples of careful historical study of the law.

Yochanan Muffs, Joy and Love as Metaphorical Expressions of Willingness and Spontaneity in Cuneiform, Ancient Hebrew, and Related Literatures, in: Christianity, Judaism, and Other Greco-Roman Cults. Srudies for Morton Smith at Sixty, ed. J. Neusner (Leiden, 1975), III, 1–36, especially 1–9, which surveys the field.

Mordechai Friedman, Marriage and Marriage Tradition in Palestinian Tradition as Reflected in Documents of the Cairo Geniza (Tel Aviv, 1979), with bibliography, throws much light on marriage laws and the scribal procedures for documents.

F. Liturgical Works

This section deals with *piyyuṭ* (early liturgical poetry) and other liturgical works.

1. In the study of y. one may make use of early *piyyuṭ* and liturgical texts from Palestine or from lands which drew on Palestinian tradition. They employ biblical, halakhic and aggadic motifs, the themes of which were often coordinated with special Sabbaths or biblical readings. Such works are a continuation of a genre that has roots in Talmudic times; see LIEBERMAN, SZ (1968), pp. 104, 115—116, especially fn. 128, and A. MIRSKY, The Origin of Liturgical Poetry, Studies of the Research Institute for Hebrew Poetry in Jerusalem 7 (1958), 1—129. These works thus form an important resource for liturgical and festival motifs and ideas, midrashic notions, as well as lexicographical and linguistic data. LIEBERMAN, Ḥazanut Yannai, Sinai 9 (22) (1939), 221—250, especially 245—250, demonstrated with numerous examples the importance of these poems for the study of y. Moreover, often an unclear y. passage has been interpreted on the basis of b., especially where the text related to ritual and liturgical matters. Some scholars at times have speculated that a y. text has been doctored to fit a Babylonian tradition. When the matter is employed or reflected in a *piyyuṭ*, we have a reliable text which cannot have been revised and on the basis of which we may evaluate the issue. For examples, see first, LIEBERMAN, TK (1955) I, 322, especially fn. 13 and 360; Z. M. RABINOWITZ, Halakha and Aggada in the Liturgical Poetry of Yannai (Tel Aviv, 1965), pp. 164, fn. 22; and BOKSER (1975), p. 90, fn. 249; and, secondly, LIEBERMAN, TK I (1955), 32—33, on abbreviated forms of the 'Tefillah'. See also the reference to a universal messianic judgement, y. Ber. 4: 3, 8a, as indicated by K. KOHLER, The Origin and Composition of the Eighteen Benedictions, in: Contributions to the Scientific Study of the Liturgy, ed. J. J. PETUCHOWSKI (New York, 1970), pp. 65—66 [= HUCA 1 (1924)], and confirmed by A. M. HABERMANN, Tefillot Meʿen Shemoneh Esreh (Berlin, 1933), p. 46, ls. 4—5.

Scholars have employed the liturgical texts; see especially RABINOVITZ (1965). While they agree that the materials stand within the Palestinian tradition and are exegetically important, they differ as to the date of the early liturgical poets (e.g., LIEBERMAN: fourth century) and whether they directly used the y. and several *midrashim* or drew on those traditions through some other medium or earlier versions of the works. Thus scholars differ whether or not the authors of the *piyyuṭim* cited from a finished or arranged y. Moreover, it has been cogently suggested that the poets would not have examined a written text of y. or such. Rather they would have cited motifs from memory. Naturally this point is important in the evaluation of slight differences between the parallels in *piyyuṭim* and y. In addition, one must note that the poets may have combined several motifs.

A summary of the various positions and lists of sources and literature may be found in EZRA FLEISHER, Piyyut, EJ 13, 573—602; and ID., Shirat

HaQodesh HaIvrit Bime HaBenayim (Jerusalem, 1975). See also references in SHAKED (1964).

2. An important area related to *piyyuṭ* is the history of prayer, its patterns, and practices, JOSEPH HEINEMANN, Prayer in the Period of the Tannaim and Amoraim: Its Forms and Structure (Hebrew: Jerusalem, 1966²; English revised edition: Berlin, 1976), has shown, first, the necessity to recognize the fluidity of prayer-texts and the fallacy of maintaining prior conceptions as to what makes up the required text, and, secondly, how one may use form criticism to understand many aspects of the prayers. Several post-Talmudic works, liturgical halakhic compendia on prayer, like 'Tractate Soferim', ed. M. HIGGER (New York, 1937, Repr. Jerusalem, 1970), and early prayer books provide important information on these matters. These materials and the relevant bibliography are reviewed in ISḤAQ (ISMAR) ELBOGEN, HaTefillah BeYisrael, A Hebrew Revised and Expanded Edition, by YEHOSHUA AMIR, J. HEINEMANN, H. SCHIRMANN, et al. (Tel Aviv, 1972), which includes, as well, important chapters on the triennial cycles, pp. 117ff., and *piyyuṭ*, pp. 210—291.

3. Additional important and representative items on both *piyyuṭ* and prayer include:

ABRAHAM I. SCHECHTER, Studies in Jewish Liturgy (Phil., 1930), especially 21—79, on the 'Palestinian rite', suggested criteria to identify it, its place in certain works, and its role in Italy and elsewhere.

*ABRAHAM M. HABERMANN, Tefillot Me'en Shemoneh Esreh (Berlin, 1933), texts of the *tefillah* in the form of a *piyyuṭ* and a discussion of this genre; ID., Poetry as a Preserver of Forgotten Words and Meanings, P'raqim, ed. E. S. ROSENTHAL, 1 (Jerusalem, 1967—68), 29—35.

*LIEBERMAN (1934), xxi—xxii, on *piyyuṭ* for spelling, usage, exegesis, and readings.

*M. ZULAI, Piyyuṭe Yannai (Berlin, 1938), an important corpus; ID., Linguistic Matters in the Piyyuṭ of Yannai (Hebrew), Studies of the Research Institute for Hebrew Poetry 6 (1946), 161—248.

*JACOB MANN, The Bible as Read and Preached in the Old Synagogue I (Cincinnati, 1940, Repr. Jerusalem, 1970), II (Cincinnati, 1966), Ktav Repr. of Volume I, with Prolegomenon, by BEN ZION WACHOLDER (New York, 1971), especially xx—xxix, xxxvii, which must be carefully used. MANN's work on the Palestinian tradition of the reading of the 'Torah' and the prophetic portions and related laws and customs provides a key to understand many *midrashim* and *piyyuṭim*.

RABINOWITZ (1940), pp. 10—12, 15, 19, 20, 150, 174, 197, 357, 394, on ritual and liturgical matters.

ISRAEL DAVIDSON, et al., Siddur R. Saadja Gaon (Jerusalem, 1941, 1970³), an important early prayer book with notes.

*J. SCHIRMANN, Hebrew Liturgical Poetry and Christian Hymnology, JQR 44 (1953), 123—161, an important study reviewing the evidence for an early date for the beginnings of *piyyuṭ*.

*Rabinowitz (1965), especially p. 65 (on the ways in which Yannai used materials), and pp. 252—262 (on PT), to which cp. B. Z. Wacholder, Prolegomenon, Ktav Reprint of Jacob Mann, The Bible as Read and Preached in the Old Synagogue I [Cincinnati, 1940] (New York, 1971), p. xlix, fn. 64; Id., Interpretation and Sources of Kerovot Yanai, BIA 4—5 (1967), 138—159.

Aaron Mirsky, Reshit HaPiyyuṭ (Jerusalem, 1965); Id., Definitions of Poetry Among Anonymous Liturgical Poets, P'raqim, ed. E. S. Rosenthal, 1 (Jerusalem, 1967—68), 109—113; Id., From Midraš to Piyyuṭ to Jewish Poetry, Leshonenu 32 (1968), 129—139, on the early history of *piyyuṭ*; Id., Śegulot HaPiyyuṭ Shel Yose be Yose, Yerushlayim, Shenaton LeDivre Śifrut Ve'Amanut, 3—4 (1970), 345—362.

*Joseph Heinemann, An Ancient Piyyuṭ Pattern, BIA 4—5 (1967), 132—137; Id., The Triennial Lectionary Cycle, JJS 19 (1968), 41f.

Ezra Fleisher, Maḥzor Piyyuṭ Mitokh Qedushta LeYom Qippur HaMeyuḥeset LeYose be Yose, Kobez al Yad 7 (17), (Jerusalem, 1968), 1—80, especially 1—5 and 14—15; Id., Studies in Piyyuṭ and Medieval Hebrew Poetry, Tarbiẓ 39 (1969), 19—38, how *piyyuṭ* may throw light on y. and Palestinian practices; and Id., Studies in the Problems Relating to the Liturgical Function of the Types of Early Piyyuṭ, Tarbiẓ 50 (1970), 41—63, suggests a relative late date for *piyyuṭ*, post fifth century. Somewhat overly accepts Pirqoi's propaganda. Cf. Sarason (1978), below.

Jacob J. Petuchowski, Contributions to the Scientific Study of Jewish Liturgy (New York, 1950), a collection of important articles by various writers, and an introduction which reviews the field; Id., Theology and Poetry (London, in press), includes translations and commentary to many *piyyuṭim*.

Esther Goldenberg, Hebrew Language, Language of Piyyut, EJ 16, 1609—1612, 1660.

E. S. Rosenthal, Two Comments, Tarbiẓ 41 (1972), 450.

Daniel Goldschmidt, Liturgy, EJ 11, 392—402, especially 395—396; Id., Seder R. Amram Gaon (Jerusalem, 1972), a critical edition of the first extant prayerbook. See below, Section XIX. E.

Y. Tobi, About the Tradition of Mishnaic and Talmudic Hebrew in Medieval Hebrew Poetry, Leshonenu 37 (1973), 137—155.

Y. Rozabi, On the Mishnaic Language Tradition in Spanish Hebrew Poetry, Leshonenu 37 (1973), 311—312.

*Shlomo Simonsohn (1974), 831—888, especially p. 841, reviews the present scholarship as to the date and origin of *piyyuṭ*.

Joseph Heinemann and Jakob J. Petuchowski, Literature of the Synagogue (New York, 1975), includes numerous examples, in English translation, of prayers and *piyyuṭ* from both Talmuds and early liturgical works, and introductions. Petuchowski, in particular, discusses the evidence as to the origin of *piyyuṭ* and the ways in which modern scholars deal with it.

*Richard Sarason, On the Use of Method in the Modern Study of Jewish Liturgy, in: Approaches to Ancient Judaism, ed. William S.

GREEN [= Brown Studies in Judaism, I] (Missoula: Scholars Press, 1977), an important critical review and history of scholarchip, which pays attention to the assumptions that guide the various studies.

Of note, J. SCHIRMANN annually publishes in KS a bibliography on *piyyuṭ*.

G. Miscellaneous Indexes

Aphorism: ABRAHAM ISAAC DZIUBAS, Milin DeYerushalmi (Jerusalem, 1970), non-exhaustive alphabetical index to aphorisms, proverbs, etc. in y.

AARON HYMAN, Oṣar Divre ḤaKhamin UPitgamehem (Tel Aviv, 1956[3]), alphabetical index to idioms in y. and other rabbinic works. See the review (to an earlier edition) of JUDAH FRIES-HOREB, KS 11 (1934), 14, which raises methodological problems in the anthologizing of idioms.

Biblical verses: *AARON HYMAN, Torah HaKetuvah Vehameśurah, 3 vols. (Tel Aviv, 1936—38, Repr. 1965), an index of citations of biblical verses in rabbinic literature.

Index to PT from BT: 'Yefeh Enayim', in back of Romm, Vilna editions of b. See below Section XX. B, s.v. 'Yellin' and 'Kanevski'.

YEHOSHUA HESCHEL ELI ZEEV of Vilna, Ṣion Yehoshua (Vilna, 1869, Repr. Jerusalem, 1970).

Ḥalakhic authorities: ISAAC ARIELE, 'Enayim LeMishpat, III (Jerusalem, 1966). An index to halakhic cross references, supplements and corrections to the 'Ein Mishpat' index in printed editions of y.

XVIII. Post-Talmudic Palestinian Works

There are various works composed or compiled in Ereṣ Yisrael from late or post-Talmudic times and which throw light on the text or content of PT. Somewhat like *piyyuṭ*, they thus represent primary data, though, of course interpretations and practices may have changed since the time of the PT. In general, see ASSAF (1955), pp. 172—179; BARON VI (1958), pp. 62—65; MARGALIOTH (1973), Introduction, pp. 1—16, and passim.

A. Palestinian *midrashim*

As indicated above, these *midrashim* may provide analogues of different versions of materials incorporated in y. From a different perspective, however, they constitute an exegetical resource. For example, they may rework or paraphrase a tradition on the basis of a given interpretation, substitute an unclear word with one which is more common, or preserve the original reading of a text, which in y. has been corrupted. In addition, a *midrash*'s rearrangement of a *sugya* may throw light on its sequence [as already indicated by FRANKEL (1870)] and the setting in which it is used may make clear a referent or content. For these items, see above, Chapter X, and JOHN T. TOWNSEND, Rabbinic Sources, The Study of Judaism, Bibliographical Essays (Anti-Defamation League of B'nai B'rith: New York, 1972), pp. 68—72.

B. Minor Tractates: Halakhic and Ethical Monographs

There is a genre of juridical and ethical collections from Palestine which generally summarize the existing laws in special areas. These non-Talmudic tractates are published in the printed editions of BT, at the end of the order of 'Neziqin'. M. HIGGER provided critical editions, some with English translations. A. COHEN, et al., The Minor Tractates of the Talmud (London, 1965), are not fully critical editions.

Each work varies in its date, nature, and use of y. and/or Palestinian traditions. While some of the material may be based on Talmudic sources, each work is edited after the y. Despite the invariable expansions and developments of the materials, the works serve as a guide to Palestinian practices and traditions, which may enable one to free oneself from superimposing BT's understanding and concepts onto y. At times, moreover, the materials may closely parallel PT sources. HIGGER in his introductions cites all parallel and analogous texts from y.

a) Avot deRabbi Nathan. See above, Section X. D.

b. Treatise Semaḥot (N.Y., 1931, Repr. Jerusalem, 1970—71) on mourning. DOV ZLOTNICK, The Tractate Mourning with a Hebrew text vocalized by E. Y. KUTSCHER (New Haven, 1966), provides a fine English translation, introduction, and notes. Cf. ERIC MEYERS, cited in Section XVII. B.

c) Kallah and Kallah Rabbati (New York, 1936, Repr. Jerusalem, 1970—71).

d) Derekh Ereṣ (New York, 1935, Repr. Jerusalem, 1970), on etiquette.

e) Maśekhtot Zeirot: Yirat Ḥet; Derekh Ereṣ Ze'ira; 'Arayot; Pereq Ma'sim; Pereq Shalom; Pereq Gadol HaShalom (New York, 1928, Repr. Jerusalem, 1970), on various ethical matters.

f) Seven Minor Tractates (Qeṭanot): Sefer Torah; Mezuzah; Tefillin; Ẓiẓit; 'Abadim; Kutim; Gerim; and Treatise Soferim II (New York, 1930, Repr. Jerusalem, 1971).

g) Śoferim (New York, 1937, Repr. Jerusalem, 1970), on scribal and liturgical practices.

Additional bibliography besides KASHER (1959), and EJ, includes:

ASSAF (1955), p. 174.
BARON VI (1958), pp. 62 and 354f.
DEVRIES, Studies in Talmud (Jerusalem, 1968), pp. 259—262.
TOWNSEND (1972), pp. 62—64.

C. 'Ma'asim LiVene Ereṣ Yisrael' = Collection or Digest Recording Court Decisions

The 'Ma'asim' constitute various fragments of Palestinian halakhic works, initially published in Tarbiẓ, by B. Lewin, 1 (1930), 97—101; 2 (1931), 25f., J. N. Epstein, 1 (1930), 33—42, 143—45; 2 (1931), 319—327, and J. Mann, 1 (1930), 1—14. These were collected and reprinted in: 'Śefer HaMa'asim LiVene Ereṣ Yisrael' (Tel Aviv, 1971). An additional fragment was simultaneously published by Z. M. Rabinowitz, Sepher HaMa'asim Livnei Ereṣ Yisra'el — New Fragments, Tarbiẓ 41 (1972), 272—305, and English summary, ii—iii, and by Mordechai Margalioth (1973), pp. ii—vii, and 39—55, which includes facsimiles. One should consult both of the editions, as the text and footnotes may vary, as well as the study of Mordechai Friedmann, Shene Qeta'im MeŚefer HaMa'asim LiVene Yisrael, Sinai 38 (1974), 14—36.

The characteristics of each fragment vary. Apparently, each does not come from the same period. Some represent or are quite close to the original 'Ma'asim', others are abbreviated reworkings of earlier items. They originate clearly at least from the end of the Byzantine period, while the reworkings perhaps from the eight or ninth centuries.

While the texts are somewhat corrupt and the materials therein often, though not always, presented or recorded in an unclear or garbled order, they are very important for the study of y. They indicate the existence of creative legal activity in Palestine in the post-Talmudic period (Byzantine and later), and the acceptance and use of PT in Palestine; much of the materials deal with practical life-matters. See Rabinowitz (1972), pp. 280f, and Margalioth (1973), pp. 2—4. Moreover, the fragments provide witness to many y. texts and exegetical keys to both terminology and passages. See besides the notes of the editors of the texts, Saul Lieberman, LeMa'asim LiVene Ereṣ Yisrael, Tarbiẓ 1 (1930), 137—139; Id., Śefer HaMa'asim — Śefer HaPeśaqim, Tarbiẓ 2 (1931), 377—379; Id., Al HaMa'asim LiVene Ereṣ Yisrael, Ginze Kedem 5 (1934), 177—185; Id., Concerning Sepher HaMa'-'asim, Tarbiẓ 42 (1972—73), 90—96; and M. Friedman (1974). The fragments published by Rabinowitz (1972) and Margalioth (1973) contain, appended to several of the *peśaqim* (decisions), a lenghty selection from *gemara*, mainly from y. 'Yevamot', 'Ketubot', and 'Qiddushim'. Friedman (1974) places the materials in the context of the history of the relevant legal issues; re pp. 32—36, cf. Bokser (1975), pp. 110—115.

Familiarity with the 'Śefer Ma'asim' is also important due to its use in Babylonia where it constituted a source for Palestinian traditions; traces thereof may be found in 'Halakhot Gedolot' (see below, Section XIX. E), 'Responsa', and other works. See Epstein, Tarbiẓ 1 (1930), 36, and Rabinowitz (1972), pp. 275, 278. The isolation of the 'original source' thus better enables one to evaluate the y. references in these Babylonian works.

Reference to y. is found, in part, in Epstein, Tarbiẓ 1 (1930), 33, and with a brief description, in Margalioth (1973), Introduction, pp. 5—7.

The only full index to the y. passages is in MARGALIOTH (1973), pp. 209–210.

Additional bibliography includes:

B. M. LEWIN, Sepher Methiboth (Jerusalem, 1933, Repr. 1973), p. xi.

M. MARGALIOTH/MARGULIES, MaSheu ʿal Śifrut HaHalakhah HaEreṣ Yisraelit BiTequfat HaGeonim, World Congress of Jewish Studies I, Jerusalem, 1947 (Jerusalem, 1952), pp. 255–258; ID. (1973), Introduction, pp. 2–7.

ASSAF (1955), p. 175.

BARON VI (1958), pp. 64–65, 355f.

D. Other Halakhic Works

Several different items including a new edition of 'Hilkhot Ṭerefot Mishel Ereṣ Yisrael', all with introductions and notes are found in MARGALIOTH (1973). Each item reflects Palestinian usages, language, laws, and thus to various degrees illuminates y.

The items deal with ritual slaughter; lists and texts of blessings and other household documents of family matters; family laws; copy of a Palestinian *geṭ*; fragments of laws in a Palestinian Siddur; an agricultural work from various sources — prepared by YEHUDAH FELIKS — that deals with times and duration of seeding, pregnation, and flowering of plants, trees, and animals.

Two indexes facilitate access to y. To the agricultural work: pp. 199–200, to the whole book: pp. 209–210. On the earlier literature see EPSTEIN, Tarbiẓ 2 (1931), 308–320; and ASSAF (1955), p. 175.

E. 'Ḥilukim Sheben Anshe Mizraḥ UVene Ereṣ Yisrael'

This work originates from the beginning of the Gaonic period, ca. eighth century. It consists of a list of fifty-five differences in customs between Babylonians and Palestinians. It enables one to clarify many Palestinian practices and concepts.

Two critical editions exist:

M. MARGULIES [= MARGALIOTH], The Differences Between Babylonian and Palestinian Jews (Jerusalem, 1937), the fullest complete edition with comprehensive introduction, notes, and commentary. MARGULIES dates the work ca. 700; on import for y., see, e. g., pp. 91–94.

B. M. LEWIN, Otzar Hilluf Minhagim Ben Bene Ereṣ Yisrael UVen Bene Bavel (Jerusalem, 1942, Repr. Jerusalem, 1974).

See also ASSAF (1955), p. 179; and ISRAEL SCHEPANSKY, Eretz-Israel in the Respona Literature (Jerusalem, 1966), pp. 50ff.

F. Palestinian *responsa*

Responsa from Palestinian authorities which use the y. text or reflect its conceptions are not extant from the early period (seventh century) and only in few numbers from later. Previously, scholars have attributed this to the fact of Babylonian hegemony such that throughout the Caliphate questions were directed to the Babylonian authorities. Some of the items are preserved in European collections; see Assaf (1955), pp. 173—174, and others in the 'Genizah'. The 'Ma'asim' works indicate that *responsa* were made for use in Palestine and they apparently were not otherwise preserved.

Margalioth (1973), Introduction, pp. 11—13, contains a full list of publications, and comments on the degree to which an item uses y. See also Ginzberg, Geonica I (1909), pp. 90—98.

G. 'Śefer Yerushalmi'

'Śefer Yerushalmi' consists of portions of PT in sequence with chapter and *halakhah* divisions combined with passages from BT and Gaonic additions.

Some unknown authority compiled the work in Palestine after Gaonic teachings spread in the land, ca. eighth century; cf. Margalioth (1973), Introduction.

Various Gaonic and European scholars used the work as if citing y. Aptowitzer reconstructed the work and Epstein, Tarbiẓ 1b (1930), 37, identified various geniza fragments as remnants of the compilation.

Scholars differ as to the relationship of this work and the 'Śefer Ma'asim', and whether Geonim took material from 'Śefer Yerushalmi' or from 'Śefer Ma'asim'.

Literature includes:

B. Ratner (1901—1917), especially Taan., pp. 115—120. See Lieberman's list of references (1929), p. 39.

Ginzberg, Genizah Fragments (1909), pp. 29—36, 152—153; 183—184, 230; Id., Ginze Schechter (1928), I, 390—422. See above, Section IV. E.

Avigdor Aptowitzer, Unechte Jeruschalmizitate, MGWJ 55 (1911), 419—425; Id., Untersuchungen zur Gaonäischen Literatur, HUCA 8—9 (1931—32), 418—421; and Mavo (1938), pp. 275—276.

Lieberman (1934), p. xxv; and (1947), Preface and Introduction.

Urbach (1955), p. 551, and fn. 69.

See also above, Chapter II.

Desideratum

What is needed is a comprehensive index to y. passages and topics for each of the above works. The topic index will help, for the y. passage relevant to the text may not immediately be clear. The student of y. though may be able to make the connection. In the interim, the following two works may be helpful:

Israel Schepansky, Eretz-Israel in the Responsa Literature. I: The Period of the Geonim and the Rishonim (Jerusalem, 1966), an excellent thematically arranged collection of sources with the editor's footnotes. The texts, however, are not critically analyzed to determine if an item constitutes an actual Palestinian practice or something merely attributed to them by non-Palestinians.

Yaaqov Galiś, Minhage Ereṣ Yisrael (Jerusalem, 1968), while it focuses on later 'accepted' Palestinian rituals and customs, as it is arranged by subject matter it provides much useful information on many points.

XIX. Commentaries to Yerushalmi. A: To the Sixteenth Century

A. Introduction

As indicated above, the lack of extant early commentaries to y. and, therefore, a full exegetical tradition to the text, requires one to rely on various sorts of works that in passing comment on y. I first deal with those items, commentaries and works from the middle ages (Chapter XIX), and then turn to the actual commmentaries to PT, which generally come from the sixteenth century and on (Chapter XX. A—B), and finally I survey contemporary works on the y. or works which are relevant to its study (Chapter XX. C). See Goodblatt (1979), II, 3 and 5 and IV, 2, for further introduction to these materials and problems in their use in text criticism and exegesis.

B. The Use of Yerushalmi

Many medieval commentaries to BT and autonomous halakhic and aggadic treatises and codes contain references to y. along with explanations. To make use of the materials one must consider first how and why and to what degree PT was used by the various authorities and the role of the citation or reference. For example, the purpose of an explanation along with a citation may be to support an exegetical or halakhic position and may therefore affect that interpretation; it thus may not represent the simple rendering of y. Alternatively, where the citation is not accompanied by an explicit explanation, one may isolate the implied explanation on the basis of its use. Accordingly, I briefly review the literature which deals with this topic. Secondly, it is important to isolate the technique of citations, viz., what constitutes an actual citation and whether it derives from a y. text or from some intermediate source. I therefore focus on this subject, as well.

1. I. Twersky, Rabad of Posquieres (Harvard Semitic Series, XVIII) (Cambridge, 1962), pp. 104, 107—108, 172, 206—213, 241, 242, 245, presents an excellent comprehensive review of the status and significance of the Yerushalmi in Gaonic and later medieval rabbinic writings. See also Lieberman (1950), pp. 287—289; M. Margalioth, Hilkhot HaNagid (Jerusalem, 1962), Introduction, and Melammed (1973), pp. 515—525.

Traditional authorities through the middle ages and many modern scholars have deemphasized the role and use of the y. As remnants of this attitude may still be found in current works and commentaries, I point to several of the suggested explanations. Some may have actually contributed to the imperfect knowledge, while others may be the result of a prior religious prejudice favoring or accepting the BT as the authoritative halakhic source. The factors include: the supposed inferiority of y., viz. its unedited and unfinished nature; its supposed lack of authority even in Palestine, i. e., the now proven incorrect assumption as to the lack of post-Talmudic Palestinian creativity; the justification that the BT is more inclusive, i. e., the BT is edited after the PT. This assumes the "law follows the last authority" and that the later authority — BT — must have known and selected the valid portions of the earlier, y., or if y.'s logic was correct BT would have grasped and mentioned it. See Twersky; Tchernowitz, Toldot HaPosqim I (New York, 1946), pp. 29—38; Ginzberg (1941), pp. H: xliv—xlv; and Poznanski, HaKedem 1 (1907), 133, 135—148; 2 (1908), 24—54, 114—116; and Spiegel (1965), pp. 243—273; Abramson (1965), p. 550; and Goodblatt (1979), I, end.

2. I now provide guidelines as to the actual use of y.

Babylonian Gaonic authorities, especially in the early period, only briefly and infrequently used the PT. PT initially was widely studied, naturally, in the Holy Land, as proven by the 'Sefer Ma'asim', in Egypt, in North Africa and Southern Italy, though as a result of strong opposition by Babylonian Gaonim the BT received priority. Undoubtedly the success of the b. was greatly enhanced by the fact of the Central Abbasid Caliphate whereby ecumenical law and authority, for all Jewry within the Caliphate, was centralized in Bagdad. Moreover, y. was extensively used in Spain, especially in Provence, and Franco-Germany, particularly from the twelfth century on. In fourteenth and fifteenth century Europe, its use declined. For the later period, see below, Section XX. A.

3. Additional literature includes:

Frankel (1870).

Ratner, HaMelitz (St. Petersburg, 1899), nos. 201, 208, 212, 214, 215, 219, 229, 238, 240—242, 244—246, 248, 251; and (1900), nos. 82, 83, 85, 118—120, 198—203. Id. (1901), preface to 'Berakhot', pp. iv and vi.

*Lewin (1933), pp. xxxix—xlv, on spread of y. and critique of Aptowitzer.

Mordechai Margalioth, Halachoth Kezuboth (Jerusalem, 1942), Introduction, pp. 15, 16; *(1973), pp. 2, 8—16, 102—104.

GINZBERG (1941), pp. xli—l; H: lxxxv, lxxxviii—xc, c—ciii.

TCHERNOWITZ, 3 vols.(1946—47).

B. Z. BENEDICT, On the History of the Torah Centre in Provence, Tarbiz 22 (1951), 85—109, especially p. 93 and fn. 76, "PT studied for its own sake".

*EPHRAIM E. URBACH, The Tosaphists: Their History, Writings and Methods (Jerusalem, 1955), especially pp. 543ff.

*BARON VI (1958), especially pp. 24—26; 330f., fns. 24f.; 346, fn. 57.

H. J. ZIMMELS, Ashkenazim and Sephardim (London, 1958), especially pp. 150—151.

SPIEGEL (1965).

ABRAMSON (1965), pp. 312—313.

S. D. GOITEIN, A Mediterranean Society (1967ff.), especially I, 53, re the tenth century foundation of Qayrawan's academy; ID., Jewish Society and Institutions under Islam, Journal of World History 11 (1968), pp. 170—184 [Reprinted as, Jewish Society Through the Ages, ed. H. BEN-SASSON (New York, 1922)].

ABRAHAM SCHREIBER, ed., Responsa of the Sages of Provence (Jerusalem, 1967), list, p. xxiv, and n. b., p. 433.

HIRSCHBERG (1974), pp. 322—323, 338f.

Specific bibliography for particular individuals appears below.

4. In all the lands and periods where BT was given preference authorities widely used PT to explain a Bavli passage or adjudicate between two explanations of a matter of law. Theoretically the authorities professed the superiority of BT, i.e., not to follow PT when it contradicted BT, a classic statement of which was enunciated by R. Hai Gaon, and then many twelfth-thirteenth century scholars. As a result, masters, especially in Provence, often reinterpreted the PT on the basis of the BT so as not to reject the PT. But they might in fact be swayed by the PT. They in particular did this when certain factors drove them to find a solution differing from that of the plain sense of the BT, e. g., the need to justify a custom. Those who differed with them might then criticize them with the standard charge of relying on the PT. The uses included explanations of words, phrases, or entire passages.

To judge on the basis of the formulation of the extant materials, with very few exceptions, y. did not constitute a subject of independent study. Rather masters explained it when it was cited in the course of an exposition of BT. Thus for the study of y. one must examine relevant parallel or analogous pericopae in b. and consult the commentaries or works thereon and the halakhnic monographs or codes which cite sources from b.

C. Techniques of Citations and Their Collection

Traditional authorities through the ages (see below) as well as modern writers have recognized the importance of employing y. citations found in earlier works. The uses of such citations have basically fallen in two categories. First, individuals have tried to isolate no longer extant portions of y. This assumes that the earlier authorities had texts of y. more complete than the later ones. In Sections VII and XIV. B, I dealt with this literature. See CHAJES, Imre Binah, p. 2; and A. EPSTEIN, Z. W. RABINOWITZ, and S. BUBER, Yerushalayim 7 (1907), 147—179, 229—278. Similarly these citations have been used to fill in *lacunae* in a text. Secondly, writers have sought to establish the correct reading of a text and its explanation; usually the earlier authorities employed exegetical traditions and not mere speculation. RATNER's work represents a serious attempt to gather these citations and explanations. LIEBERMAN (1929), pp. 46f, in his review of these efforts, as indicated above, points to their conceptual flaws. Even RATNER while very useful is marred as well as incomplete. See LIEBERMAN, p. 39, for a list of references in which RATNER discusses the nature of these citations.

LIEBERMAN (1929), pp. 36—46, and (1934), pp. xxiii—xxiv, raised the appropriate methodological questions and suggested guidelines as to what actually constitutes a citation and explanation. I first lay out LIEBERMAN's programmatic principles and then provide a breakdown, drawing as well on individual studies. Unfortunately, to my knowledge a comprehensive systematic examination has not yet been published. [MELAMMED (1973), pp. 515—525, is somewhat helpful.]

The task is threefold. One must determine each authority's characteristic method of citation, his access to y., and the effect of the genre of the work on its citations. An individual may cite exactly, or in a non-exact manner. The latter includes: paraphrase with expansion; digest of content; changed formulation; imposition of one's own style or that more common in the rest of y. [as for pericopae in 'Neziqin'; (1931), p. 2, fn. 1]; brief slice, deleting material irrelevant to the point at hand. But LIEBERMAN notes that even the abridged citation may be helpful so as to reconstruct a text and its meaning, if not the wording, or to choose one of several readings. Below I draw on many of LIEBERMAN's descriptions of individual characteristics.

Secondly, LIEBERMAN focuses on whether or not an individual directly took from y. Earlier other scholars, in particular APTOWITZER, had discussed part of the problem in terms of the circulation of the 'Śefer Yerushalmi' compilation. See Sections II and XVIII. F. LIEBERMAN, though, is concerned whether an individual cites on the basis of a predecessor and not the y. directly. This applies, at times, to even those who frequently cite y. (e. g., Rabiah, Ramban, and Rashba) and who may have employed original texts of y. [See also (1934), pp. 9—8, 89]. This particularly holds for a student who may cite the reading and explanation of his master.

LIEBERMAN likewise points out that two versions or editions of the same work do not represent two separate testimonies (e. g., 'Kol Bo' and 'Orḥot Ḥayyim'), and, further, where different authorities used the same MSS their readings, naturally, constitute only one testimony.

Thirdly, the genre of a work may tend to shape the characteristic types of citations. Codes cite exactly where wording affects *halakhah*, commentaries retrieve explanations of *sugyot*, expounders and moralizers employ aggadic and midrashic materials.

LIEBERMAN turns to the related problem of identifying an actual reference. First, portions of or a whole reference may be to another source ('Śefer Yerushalmi', known to Germans; *Midrash* or Gaonic work; compendia-collections based on PT, like 'Śefer Ma'asim'). He supports CHAJES' observation that an unannotated citation to y. without identifying the tractate and the rest of the pericope may tend to represent a *midrash* or *peśiqta*. Secondly, a reference may constitute a glossed explanation added to the citation. See also (1934), p. 35, fn. 1, and ID., Yemenite Midrashim (Jerusalem, 1940, 1970²), pp. 35—39; and J. N. EPSTEIN, Tarbiẓ 1 (1930), 36—38, and fn. 2, who studies several citation-terminologies, and who suggests a logical criterion by which to isolate non-PT material: "an item not in extant y., and inappropriate on the basis of language and content, and elsewhere attributed to Geonim. Of course, a corruption in the text may have yielded the supposed mention of y". On the other hand, misattributions may occur in reverse. An authority may attribute a y. citation to 'Tosefta'; LIEBERMAN, Tashlum Tosefta (Jerusalem, 1970²), pp. 19, 46—51 (cf. p. 30, fn. 1), 65—66.

D. Medieval Commentaries

1. In the next section I focus on the more important individual commentaries and works and their characteristics. Once a history of rabbinism and medieval Jewish intellectual history is written, we may have a sophisticated comprehensive discussion. Several different sorts of such a study are being undertaken in different locations: Ph. D. dissertations under the guidance of ISADORE TWERSKY, at Harvard, and under E. URBACH and others at the Hebrew University, Jerusalem, and a comprehensive project by HAIM Z. DIMITROVSKY, Jewish Theological Seminary, New York.

2. In the interim the following may be helpful:

P. JACOB KOHN, Thesaurus of Hebrew Halakhic Literature (London, 1952), a comprehensive list, especially useful for items written after 1500, which are not covered in the next work.

M. A. KASHER and J. B. MANDELBAUM, Sarei Ha-Elef. A Millenium of Hebrew Authors (500—1500) (New York, 1959), an excellent guide which includes some references to modern scholarly literature, and its 'Supplement', ID., Quntreś Hashlamah Leśefer Sarei Ha-Elef, in: Śefer Zikaron Adam Noaḥ Baron, ed. ḤAYYIM LIPHSHITZ, et al. (Jerusalem, 1970), pp. 213—299 (a revised edition is under preparation).

Makhon HaTalmud, Yad Harav Herzog, Editions of Mishnah Zera'im (Jerusalem, 1972); ID., b. Ketubot, I (Jerusalem, 1972), contain lists of early authorities, imprintings, and extant MSS.

Aron Freimann and M. Schmelzer, Union Catalog of Hebrew Manuscripts and Their Location, 2 vols. (New York, 1964–73), is a collated index of MSS found in libraries throughout the world.

*N. Rakover, A Bibliography of Jewish Law (Jerusalem, 1975), includes an index to Hebrew studies specifically on individual rabbinic figures and their works.

3. The following studies are especially helpful:

Aptowitzer (1938).

*Ginzberg (1941).

Tchernowitz (1946–47).

B. Z. Benedict, numerous articles, published in KS, Sinai, Tarbiẓ, and Torah SheBe'al Peh.

*Urbach (1955).

*Baron VI (1958), whose notes on these matters are excellent. Besides listing publications, it virtually takes account of all previous literature.

Shaked (1964), highly useful for editions and reviews of Gaonic material.

*Melammed (1973), pp. 515–525, an excellent concise survey that focuses on the use of y.

*EJ articles, many of which I have examined, generally include listing of editions and a summary of scholarly literature.

*I. Ta-Shmah, Ḥiddushei ha-Rishonim — their Order of Publication, KS 50 (1975), 325–336.

4. In my lists below I attempt to confine my comments to introductory remarks concerning a group of works, list the more important individuals and some of their key works, and very selectively refer to the literature which deals with the use of y., the appropriate secondary works and editions. Where a reference to y. is in the analogous pericope in b., access is easy. Most of the recent editions of 'Rishonim' include an index to works 'cited', wherein, if appropriate, are listed y. references. This is especially true of the fine series of critical editions under preparation by Makhon HaTalmud (Yad Harav Herzog) and Mosad HaRav Kook.

5. *Responsa* Literature: The *Responsa* literature which includes many references to y. is being indexed by the Israeli Institute for Jewish Law. Several volumes have so far appeared. These include: M. Elon, ed., Responsa of R. Asher b. Yeḥiel (Jerusalem, 1965), and Id., Responsa of R. Yom Tov Avraham Ashbili and R. Yehudah b. Asher (Jerusalem, 1973). See M. Elon, Responsa and Indices and the Institute for Research in Jewish Law, Proceedings of the Fifth World Congress of Jewish Studies, Jerusalem, 1969, Division V (Jerusalem, 1973), pp. English, 67, and Hebrew, 69–77, on the items completed and under preparation or planned. As to a bibliography of Responsa in addition to Kasher and Kohn, Boaz Cohen, Quntraś HaTeshuvot (Budapest, 1930, Repr. Jerusalem, 1970) is still useful.

I heavily draw on LIEBERMAN's publications. It should be assumed that the items in subsections 2—3, especially the starred ones, include relevant information and I therefore usually do not cite them in the following sections.

E. Gaonic Works

1. POZNANSKI, HaKedem 1 (1907), 136—142, 143, and 2 (1908), 24—40, reviews earlier positions on the use of y., and conveniently lists and evaluates citations of y. in the 'Sheiltot' of Aḥai of Shabḥa, an eighth century homiletical legal-juridical work, 'Seder R. Amram Gaon', 'Halakhot Gedolot', and *Responsa*.

B. M. LEWIN, Oṣar HaGaonim, 13 vols., Berakhot — B.M. (last volume incomplete) (Haifa and Jerusalem, 1938—1943), and ḤAYYIM TAUBES, Oṣar HaGaonim to Sanhedrin (Jerusalem, 1966), presents the Gaonic materials arranged according to the sequence of the b., and is therefore quite useful.

To fully make use of the Gaonic works, besides covering materials not previously used, one should bring up to date the references in POZNANSKI and LEWIN and TAUBES with the literature subsequently published and employ the more recent improved or critical editions of the books.

Concerning, in particular, the Gaonic works, scholars have evaluated the supposed citations. Additional comprehensive literature includes: GINZBERG, Geonica (1909), and ASSAF (1955). See also Y. H. S., HeḤalus 5 (1860), 31—54 (Repr. Jerusalem, 1972), on Gaonic use of y. to explain 'Mishnah' contra b.

2. Individual works:

'Sheiltot': Editions with indexes, ISAIAH BERLIN, 3 vols. (Jerusalem, 1961, Repr. of Vilna), and S. K. MIRSKY, 5 vols. (Jerusalem, 1959—66, 1977), and B. Z. WACHOLDER's Review, JQR, N.S. 53 (1963), 257—61, Geniza fragments (which constitute full and uninterpolated versions), Tarbiẓ 6, 7, 10, 13; EPSTEIN, Tarbiẓ 6 (1935), 460 ff; A. N. Z. ROTH, Gaonic Writings from the Kaufmann Collection, Sura 2 (1955—56), 283f; ABRAMSON (1974), pp. 9—23, 317, 389, 398f.; and cf. A. KAMINKA, Al Divre HaSheiltot DeRAḥai VeYiḥuśan LiYerushalmi, HaKedem 2 (1908), 20—23.

Śeder R. Amran Gaon, ed. DANIEL GOLDSCHMIDT (Jerusalem, 1971); Review, G. L. ORMAN, KS 47 (1972), 361ff.

Halakhot Peśuqot: Śefer Halachot Peśuqot, attributed to R. Jehudai Gaon of the eighth century, ed. S. SASOON (Jerusalem, 1950, Makor Repr. with facsimile, 1969). Cf. p. 14.

Śefer Halakhot Peśuqot O Hilkhot Re'U, ed. A. L. SCHLOSSBERG (Paris, 1886, Repr. Jerusalem, 1967) — a Palestinian Hebrew translation of the previous work. See MARGALIOTH (1973), p. 14; SAMUEL MOREL, edition and study (unpublished Ph. D. dissertation, Jewish Theological Seminary of America).

Halakhot Gedolot, J. HILDESHEIMER, ed. (Berlin, 1888–1892), pp. 10–11, index to y. New edition in press; Vol. I, by EZRIEL HILDESHEIMER (Jerusalem, 1972), who challenges accepted consensus on the relationship of this work to previous two times. See also LEWIN (1933) and A. N. Z. ROTH, Gaonic Writings, Sura 2 (1955–56), 280–283.

*Halakhot Qeṣuvot [Adjudicated Laws], ed. MORDECHAI MARGALIOTH (Jerusalem, 1942), ninth century work that extensively draws on Palestinian customs and 'Sefer Maʿasim'.

F. North African Gaonic-Medieval Works

In general see HIRSCHBERG (1974).

*Śefer Metivot: Monumenta Gaonica, Methoboth to Moʿed, Nashim, and Neziqin, to which is appended Śepher Hefez to Moʿed, Nashim, Neziqin, and Qodashim, ed. B. M. LEWIN (Jerusalem, 1933, Repr. 1973), with notes by SAUL LIEBERMAN, pp. 44–45, 53–55, 115–118, 138–140, a tenth century work most likely from Qairawan, which mediates between Palestinian and Babylonian materials. Arranged in sequence of BT, it abbreviates b. pericopae and focuses on practical law, cites analogous PT pericopae which dispute, supplement, or explicate its law. The work is vital for textual readings and interpretations of y. as it directly lifts pericopae from y. and introduces them usually with the term *GYRŚT YRWŠLMY*, "the reading of the Yerushalmi", or anonymously. Often where b. and y. contain varying formulations of a tradition, the work cites it in y.'s version.

This treatise served as a prototype for several subsequent works, including, probably, 'Śefer Ḥefeṣ', as well as a possible source for indirect citations of y. found in various Rishonim. LEWIN, pp. 134–135, in sequence of PT, collected many citations of y. which employ the Metivot's characteristic formula, *GYRŚ' YRWŠLMY*.

See Review by S. ASSAF, KS 11 (1934), 161–166; V. APTOWITZER, Śefer Ḥefetz and Śefer M'thiboth, Tarbiẓ 4 (1933), 127–152; LIEBERMAN (1934), p. 120, and (1950), pp. 287f.; GINZBERG (1941), p. H: xci; *SAMUEL LOEWINGER, Qetaʿim Ḥadashim MeŚefer Metivot, in: S. LOEWINGER, Genizah Publications in Memory of David Kaufmann (Budapest, 1949, Repr. Jerusalem, 1971), pp. 42–58, and the literature cited there; and MARGALIOTH (1962), pp. 9–11, 18–19.

R. Ḥananel (tenth century). PT is very frequently cited often to decide a *halakhah* in Ḥananel's running commentary-paraphrase of b., and these citations were used by many European scholars including the Tosafists. See B. RATNER, HaMelitz (1899), nos. 208, 212, 214, 215, 219, 220, especially 234; TCHERNOWITZ (1947), II, 4; and ABRAHAM Y. FRIEZLER, Yaḥaso shel Rabenu Ḥananel LiYerushalmi BePherush LeVabli, Niv HaMidrashiyah (1972–1973), pp. 126–134; and cf. MELAMMED (1943), pp. 65–66, 81.

R. Nissim (eleventh century). ABRAMSON (1965), who critically published and analyzed Nissim's works, indicates his great use of y., especially in the

'Megilat Śetarim', which provided or became a 'source' for y. for many later scholars (e.g., Alfasi, Aruch of Nathan, R. Tam). ABRAMSON collects and analyzes their citations, pp. 214—244. Nissim uses the introductory phrase *GMR' DBNY M'RB'*, "*Gemara* of the children of the West", and, occasionally, *TLMWD 'RṢ YSR'L*, "Talmud of the Land of Israel". See pp. iv—v, xxxvii, 12, 17—19, 186, 338f., and also LIEBERMAN (1947), p. xiv. Cf. MELAMMED (1943), pp. 66f, 81.

Isaac Alfasi (b. ca. 1013) Halakhot, frequently cites y., according to ABRAMSON, many of which are from R. Nissim, to explain BT or to derive laws not found in BT. He rejects explicit PT for an implication of the BT. As Alfasi became the main text of study in Spain, his citations were used by many other authorities; LIEBERMAN (1934), p. 267. See TCHERNOWITZ I (1946), pp. 140—149; B. Z. BENEDICT, Books and Fragments on Alfasi and his Method, KS 28 (1952), 210—232, and especially ID., R. Ephraim's Śefer HaTashlum on Alfasi, KS 26 (1950), 322—338, fn. 28; ABRAMSON (1965), pp. 214—222 [cf. RATNER, references under 'R. Ḥananel', to which add nos. 238, 240—242]. YAAQOV SPIEGEL, On the Identity of the Commentary Nemuqe Yosef on Rif's Halakhot, Sinai 37 (72) (1973), 222—227; MARGALIOTH (1973), pp. 40—43; and the very important SHAMMA FRIEDMAN, Introduction, to Halakhot Rabbati of R. Isaac Alfasi MS. JTSA Rab. 692, . . . Facsimile (Jerusalem, 1974), who reviews existings MSS, previous printed editions, their characteristics, and relevant scholarly literature.

Maimonides (Moses b. Maimon, Ramban). Maimonides widely used y. in several works, including the 'Commentary on Mishnah'; 'Śefer Miṣvot'; 'Mishneh Torah', and *Responsa*, while he practically makes it a subject of study in its own right in the Laws of the Palestinian Talmud, ed. SAUL LIEBERMAN (New York, 1947). LIEBERMAN's introduction, esp. pp. v, xv, and notes, in particular to the portion on Ketubot, demonstrate the work's importance for PT's elucidations. As to B. Z. BENEDICT's review, KS 27 (1952), 329—349, cf. BARON VI (1958), p. 370, fn. 100. See also TCHERNOWITZ I (1946), pp. 220—221, on his independent use of y., even as an equal authority to b.; MELAMMED (1973), pp. 522. Cf. H. Y. EHRENREICH, Ozar Hachaim 11 (1935), 152—164, and on the important new edition of the Commentary to the Mishnah, ed. YOSEF QAFIḤ, 7 vols. (Jerusalem, 1963—1968), see J. BLAU's incisive reviews, Leshonenu 30 (1966), 54—60; 31 (1967), 235—239; 32 (1968), 399—401; 35 (1970), 75—78, which indicates that while QAFIḤ's work is highly competent, he does not sufficiently use reference works, especially dictionaries, and, at times, is inaccurate when dealing with variant readings.

G. PT in Spain

MARGALIOTH (1962) reviews the role of y. in Spain.

Palestinian *gemara* and customs had first recognizable influence in the generation prior to that of Shmuel HaNagid. Shmuel HaNagid was the first to use y. His 'Hilkhata Gibarata', partially reconstructed by MARGALIOTH, has some twenty citations of y. (listed p. xiii), some of which are explained, and includes other matters based upon Palestinian customs. The work follows 'Metivot''s pattern and supplements BT decisions with related y. passages and Gaonic materials. According to MARGALIOTH, Shmuel learned y. from his master, R. Ḥanokh who (so MARGALIOTH) came from Italy. Shmuel set an example for Spanish scholars to employ independent judgement by comparing and evaluating sources. Remnants and the influence of his work may be found in those of Iṣḥaq ibn Giat; Judah of Barcelona, Śefer HaItim [see also his 'Book of Documents', ed. HALBERSTAM (Berlin, 1898, Repr. Jerusalem, 1967)]; Avraham b. Isaac Av Bet Din of Narbona, d. 1158 (Śefer HaEshqol, a collection of laws and customs, which fairly accurately preserves material from its sources); and Naḥmanides. See MARGALIOTH (1962), esp. pp. 13, 18f., 21f., 37–51; ABRAMSON (1965), pp. 227–231.

Solomon ben Adret of Barcelona (Rashba): Often cites y., especially in Piśqe Ḥallah (On laws of Ḥallah), ed. ISAKHAR D. BERGMAN (Jerusalem, 1970). Of note, the standard printed editions of *novellae* and *responsa* are abridged. Exemplary critical editions: H. ZALMON DIMITROVSKY, Novellae to Megillah (New York, 1956); ID., Rosh Hashanah (New York, 1961), ID., Responsa, 10 vols. (Jerusalem, in press). His citations often served as the source for Ritba and Meiri; LIEBERMAN (1934), p. 281. DIMITROVSKY (1956) traces how in general various medieval authorities cite from each other. See DIMITROVSKY (in press), vol. 10.

Yom Tob Ashbili: Often cites PT from Rashba; LIEBERMAN (1934), p. 281. In general he cites earlier authorities and then adds his own explanation. *Novellae* to any tractate, may contain passages from many locations, M. Y. BLAU, Commentary of . . . to B.B. (New York, 1954), II, 636–637. Mosad HaRav Kook, Jerusalem, is publishing a critical edition of this important commentary (1974).

Joseph HaLevi ibn Migas: ISRAEL TA-SHMAH, The Literary Work of. . ., KS 46 (1970–71), 136–153, 541–553, 47 (1972), 318–322.

Isaac ibn Giat: In 'Hilkhot Kelulot', he critically uses y.'s analogues to b. A remnant, on most of Mo'ed, arranged by subject, is in 'Sha're Simḥah', ed. ISHAQ BAMBERGER (Fürth, 1861–62, Repr. Israel?, n.d.); MARGALIOTH (1962), pp. 37–40.

Naḥmanides: He clearly cites PT. On his methodology, see S. ABRAMSON, Kelale HaTalmud BeDivre HaRamban (Jerusalem, 1971), and cf. (1965), p. 233. A critical edition is in progress; ID., Makhon HaTalmud I (Jerusalem, 1970ff.).

H. PT in Provence

On the rabbinic and intellectual climate, see I. TWERSKY, Aspects of the Social and Cultural History of Provencal Jewry, Journal of World History 11 (1968) [Reprinted as Jewish Society Through the Ages, ed. H. BEN-

SASSON (New York, 1972)], pp. 185—207, and the literature cited there, especially TWERSKY (1962); and BENEDICT, LeToledotaw shel Merkaz HaTorah BeProvençe, Tarbiz 22 (1951), 85—109; to which add ID., Contributions to a Compendium of Provence Jewish Scholars, KS 27 (1951), 237—248, 392.

R. Abraham b. David (Rabad) of Posquiers. In his commentaries to 'Sifra' and 'Mishnah' and glosses to 'Mishneh Torah', he extensively uses PT, compares its readings with other versions, and explains words, phrases, or entire passages; TWERSKY (1962), pp. 104, 107—108, 211. His pupil, R. Isaac Hakohen, apparently wrote the first commentary to y., now lost. See LIEBERMAN (1950), pp. 289—292.

Isaac b. Abba Maari: Śefer HaIttur (Repr. Jerusalem, 1970), frequently cites y., compares analogous though differing *sugyot* within y. LEWIN (1933), pp. xx, xxiii, isolates sixty citations from Metivot. See LIEBERMAN (1931), p. vii; ID., 'Addenda' to D. S. LOEWINGER's Article, Genizah Publications... Kaufmann 1 (1949), pp. 59—61.

R. Menaḥem HaMe'iri of Perpignan (d. ca. 1315): Beit HaBeḥirah, frequently cites y., at times from another authority, including Rashba; LIEBERMAN (1934), pp. 231, 281. He employs two introductory terminologies: *TLMWD HM'RB*, "the Western Talmud", which is not necessarily an exact quotation and, therefore, must be carefully evaluated, and, at times, *WNWŚḤ DBRYHM*, "and the reading of their words", or *BLŠWN ZH*, "in this language", which are used for exact citations in the original language and style; so ABRAHAM SCHREIBER [SOFER], Beit HaBeḥirah Maśekhet Avodah Zarah (Jerusalem, 1965²), p. x, and to Ketubot (Jerusalem, 1947), pp. xviii—xix. See S. MIRSKY, R. Menachem Hameiri. His Life, Teachings, and Works, Talpioth IV, 1—2 (1943), 42—90.

I. Northern France and Germany

Rashi (1040—1105): His several works, especially the commentary to BT, contain references to y., explicit and non-explicit, which some but not all scholars have identified with actual and direct citations from y. M. HIGGER, The Yerushalmi Quotations in Rashi, Rashi Anniversary Volume (New York, 1941), pp. 119—217, presents a long list in order of their occurrence in the respective works, with notes as to parallels. See also YOSEF HALEV, Yerushalayim 7 (1907), 370—376, citations to y. 'Temurah'; I. BROMBERG, Rashi and the Yerushalmi, Sinai 7—8, 11—12 (94—99) (1945), 62—72, 193—199, 277—290, and 17 (210) (1954), 165—169, 240—244; and especially URBACH (1955), p. 545, and fn. 33; DAVID WEISS HALIVNI, Al Rashi VeHaYerushalmi, HaDoar Year 34, vol. 35, no. 24 (April 29, 1955) (1585), pp. 473—474; BARON VI (1958), 346, fn. 57; and JONAH FRAENKEL, Darko Shel Rashi Beferusho LaTalmud HaBavli (Jerusalem, 1975). There are several compendia of rituals, customs, and liturgy attributed to Rashi and which come from his circle of students. They contain various citations of y.; e.g., 'Śiddur Rashi', 'Śepher HaPardeś', and 'Maḥzor Vitry'.

URBACH (1955), especially pp. 543ff, contra GINZBERG and APTOWITZER demonstrates the not infrequent use of y. among Franco-German Tosafists, led by R. Meir, R. Tam, and Rabiah. Important are not only the commentaries published in the editions of *gemara*, but also those in separate volumes. URBACH traces the presence and uses of y. in the various works. These include: to support an interpretation or to explain and analyze a b. pericope, in the process of which the y. may be explained. The Tosefists generally rely on BT to explain PT; the German ones tend to harmonize b. and y. to remove conflicts, while the French authorities often admit the conflicts. As to texts of y., they often had an incomplete corpus, or did not have the work at hand and cited from memory. They generally do not contain quotations to non-extant portions of y. though their references to y., at times, refer to Palestinian *Midrash-aggadah*. Particular use of y. is found in the works of Samson from Sens, especially his commentary to 'M. Zera'im' in which he systematically cites and explains the appropriate y. pericopae [see Śection K], and in Yehudah b. Qalonymous (see below). See also URBACH, Sefer Arugat HaBosem of R. Abraham b. R. Azriel, IV, Introduction (Jerusalem, 1963), p. 157, 230–234, and the exemplary study of JOSE FAUR, Tosefot HaRosh LeMaśekhet Berakhot, PAAJR 33 (1965), 41–65.

Eliezer b. Nathan (RAbN) of Mainz: Even HaEzer, 2 vols. (Prague, 1610, Repr. N.Y., 1958), frequently cites y. and at times is a source for his grandson, Rabiah; LIEBERMAN (1934), pp. 395, 405, and TCHERNOWITZ II (1947), 46.

Eliezer b. Yoel HaLevi (mid 12th century): 'Śefer Rabiah', in two editions, V. APTOWITZER, incomplete critical edition with separate 'Introductio ad Sefer Rabiah' (Jerusalem, 1938), and second, revised reissued and completed edition by ELIJAH PRISMAN et al., 4 vols. (Jerusalem, 1965), with introduction. He very frequently cites y. and tries to harmonize it with BT; TCHERNOWITZ (1947), p. 54. APTOWITZER (1938), pp. 90, 93–95, 275–277, 468–472, traces the use of y. and employment of actual PT to several tractates and of 'Śefer Yerushalmi', a compilation that included PT and other materials. Thus part of the latter's references to y. may actually derive from such an addition. Moreover, he may present only the content and not the exact wording of y., and he may cite, as well, from Naḥmanides, or may call 'Tosefta', 'Yerushalmi'. See LIEBERMAN (1934), p. 151, 206–207, 405, 420.

Its citations of y. are significant in their own right and because the work served as the source for many authorities including Isaac b. Moses of Vienna, author of 'Or Zarua', MahRam of Routenberg, R. Asher (Rosh), Mordechai, author of 'Hagahot Maimoniot', and Jacob Asheri. On the use in Mordechai see LIEBERMAN (1934), pp. 412–413, and JOEL ROTH and MEIR RABBINOWITZ, Unpublished Ph.D. dissertations, JTSA, critical editions, with introduction, of Mordechai.

The first part of the work, in sequence of BT, presents and evaluates explanations of predecessors and comments in halakhic codes. The second part is made up of decisions and *responsa*. Thus one may consult BT in sequence for analogues to b. pericopae in addition to APTOWITZER's index (1938), pp. 468—472 (which also serves for the second edition, I—III, which maintains the same pagination). The new material in Vol. IV, which remains unindexed, concerns family law. Cf. LIEBERMAN (1934), p. 151; URBACH (1955); (1963), p. 157; ABRAMSON (1965), pp. 545f.

Eleazar b. Judah: 'Śefer Roqeaḥ' uses 'Śefer Yerushalmi'; LIEBERMAN (1929), pp. 36f., APTOWITZER (1938), p. 277, and URBACH (1955), p. 327, fn. 40. His 'Ma'aseh Roqeaḥ' abridges citations; LIEBERMAN (1934), p. 523, and URBACH (1955), pp. 331—334, especially as to the authorship.

Isaac b. Moses of Vienna (13th century): 'Or Zarua', a rearrangement of *gemara* by topic, constitutes an excellent source for y. citations and explanations. Isaac presents an exact citation of the portion which he needed, and often adds explanatory glosses. The work is in 4 vols. (Zhitomir, 1862, and Jerusalem, 1888—1890, Repr. in 2 vols., with additional fragment, New York, n.d.). See LIEBERMAN (1929), pp. 23f.; (1934), pp. 219, 282; and URBACH (1955), pp. 359—370.

Abraham b. R. Azriel: 'Sefer Arugot HaBosem' [Commentary on 'Piyyuṭim'], ed. by E. E. URBACH, 4 vols. (Jerusalem, 1939—1963), employs y., of which he had two texts; (1963), pp. 157, 230—234.

Moses of Quzy (13th century): 'Śefer Miṣvot Gadol', gives content of y., at times with explanations; LIEBERMAN (1929), pp. 23f.

Yehudah BeRebi Qalonymous of Spires: Yiḥuse Tannaim VeAmoraim', ed. YEHUDAH LEB HAKOHEN MAIMON (Jerusalem, 1963), an alphabetical biographical encyclopaedia that cites comments attributed to individual Talmudic rabbis, often from y. He had different texts (MSS) of y., many of which differ from the extant text. He also adds explanations of others or of his own. See pp. xvii, xxix, and URBACH (1955).

R. Meshullam: Commentary on 'Treatise Shekalim', ed. A. SCHREIBER (New York, 1954), thirteenth century. See Section IV.D; especially SCHREIBER's introduction, and LIEBERMAN (1950), pp. 295—297. E. URBACH, KS 31 (1956), 325—328 disputes the attribution and assigns the work to an earlier Tosefist.

A Disciple of R. Samuel Ben R. Sheneur of Evreux: Commentary on 'Treatise Shekalim', ed. A. SCHREIBER (New York, 1954). See LIEBERMAN (1950), pp. 298—300, and URBACH, op. cit.

Unidentified Commentary to y. Shev. Ch. VII. Unpublished JTSA MS, ADLER 3033, pp. 7—8. See S. ABRAMSON, On the 'Aruḳ of R. Naṭan, Leshonenu 36 (1972), 124.

J. Italy

Isaiah the Elder, of Terani, thirteenth century, and the Younger, fourteenth: Rulings of . . . . Critical edition, Makhon HaTalmud, Iff. (Jerusalem, 1964ff.).

K. Collections and Especially Notable Medieval Works

Here I include (1) Collections or Compilations and (2) Works which heavily draw on y. in particular areas, chiefly 'Zera'im'.

1. Collections, Compilations, and Medieval *midrashim*.

Shimeon HaDarshon (13th century): 'Yalqut Shimoni', the largest extant collection of Talmudic-Midrashic sources arranged on the Bible. It contains 199 references in the text and 256 in a special 'addendum', *quntraś*, which appears only in the first edition, in the collections of JELLINEK and EISENSTEIN, and in GINZBERG (1909); ARTHUR B. HYMAN, Meqorot Yalqut Shemeoni, 2 vols. (Jerusalem, 1974, 1975), I, x, xxv. HYMAN contains indexes to y. passages. LIEBERMAN, e.g., (1934), demonstrates the importance of the 'Yalqut' to the study of y. He, however, also notes that at times it did not directly use y., but rather an anthology-collection of y. *aggadot*, like that published in GINZBERG, Genizah Studies (1928), pp. 390ff. Further, we may learn from LIEBERMAN's comments concerning 'Śifre Zutta', SZ (1968), pp. 79f., that while 'Yalqut' does not add anything in the source's style, it apparently, at times, independently replaced and changed an unusual usage with a more common word or deleted difficult words that do not change the content. Moreover, MELAMMED (1943), pp. 68—70, 81f., points out in the process of citation and placement of the sources, 'Yalqut' may make some 'slight' changes or rearrangements. HYMAN reviews the editions and MSS of 'Yalqut'. Of note, the later editions are somewhat corrupt and the citations have often been 'corrected' on the basis of the printed editions of the cited work. LIEBERMAN, SZ (1968), p. 120, fn. 149, notes that the phenomenon earlier demonstrated, as cited above, is especially true in the printed editions. It is therefore important to use the first edition, Salonica, 1501, 1506—07 (Repr. Jerusalem, 1968, 1973), and an Oxford MS, both of which are employed in a new critical edition, ed. HYMAN, LERRER, SHILONE, Iff. (Jerusalem, 1973ff.). See also MORDECHAI MARGULIES [MARGALIOTH], Midrash HaGgadol on the Pentateuch, Genesis (Jerusalem, 1947, 1957²), p. 6, and AARON GREENBAUM, Sinai 76 (1975), 120—133, especially 121, 132.

R. David b. R. Amram of Eden, Midrash HaGgadol, to 'Genesis', ed. M. MARGULIES [MARGALIOTH] (Jerusalem, 1947, 1967²); to 'Exodus', ed. M. MARGULIES [MARGALIOTH] (Jerusalem, 1947, 1967²); to 'Leviticus', ed. E. N. RABINOWITZ (New York, 1932), and ed. STEINSALTZ (Jerusalem, 1976); to 'Numbers', ed. Z. M. RABINOWITZ (Jerusalem, 1967); to 'Deuteronomy', ed. SOLOMON FISCH (Jerusalem, 1972). This fourteenth-century Yemenite midrashic compilation lifts from various sources materials associated with biblical verses and arranges them according to the sequence in the Pentateuch. Occasionally it draws on y. The author combines, rearranges, adds, deletes, and glosses explanations. One must thus carefully examine his references. In particular, he freely constructs the formal arrangement and combination of the sources, formulates materials on the basis of Maimonides, though according to MARGALIOTH, to 'Exodus',

p. 6, he does not change the text of the citation. LIEBERMAN, SZ (1968), p. 79, agrees that difficult words are not replaced or corrupted. On the other hand, Z. M. RABINOWITZ, to 'Numbers', p. xi, found that he changed y. readings, revised them according to b. Aramaic, terminology, forms of names of scholars, language and style, as well as glossed explanations and interpolated at the end or cut off in the middle. Cf. MELAMMED (1943), pp. 70f. See LIEBERMAN, Yemenite Midrashim (Jerusalem, 1940, 1970²), p. 6, and especially MOSHE ZUCKER, Pentateuchal Exegeses of Saadia Gaon and Samuel ben Chofni Incorporated into the Midrash HaGadol, Abraham Weiss Jubilee Volume (New York, 1964), Hebrew Section, pp. 461—462, and fn. 4. On the authorship, see RABINOWITZ to 'Numbers', p. v, fn. 1.

R. Israel ibn al-Nakawa, Menorat Ha-Maor, 4 vols., ed. H. G. ENELOW (New York, 1929—32, Repr. Jerusalem, 1972), an ethical-aggadic compilation. Vol. 4, index, s.v. Talmud, Yerushalmi, lists entries by tractates.

The Mishnah of Rabbi Eliezer or the Midrash of Thirty-Two Hermeneutic Rules, ed. H. G. ENELOW (New York, 1933, Repr. Jerusalem, 1970), a collection of exegetical canons composed by Shmuel b. Ḥofni, a late Suran Gaon. See BARON VI (1958), 406, and especially M. ZUCKER, PAAJR 25 (1956), Hebrew pp. 1ff., pp. 20f. on ENELOW's edition, and fn. 6, there, on the complete free use and alteration of sources. The numerous references to y. are indexed on pp. 390 and 394.

R. Machir bar Abba Mari, Yalqut Makhiri, a ca. fourteenth century collection of talmudic and midrashic sources, to Isaiah, ed. Y. SPIRA (Berlin, 1894), on Proverbs [chs. 18—31], ed. L. GRUENHUT (Jerusalem, 1902), reprinted together (Jerusalem, 1964); on Psalms, ed. S. BUBER (Berdychev, 1899, Repr. Jerusalem, 1964); on Twelve Minor Prophets, ed. ALBERT W. GREENUP, 2 vols. (London, 1909—13, Repr. Jerusalem, 1967); and additions to Proverbs (parts of chs. 2, 3, 14), ed. ISAAC BERDEHAV (Jerusalem, 1927), and to Hosea (1 : 1—14 : 1), ed. A.W. GREENUP, JQR, N.S. 15 (1924—25), 141—212, both republished together as 'Supplement (Hashlamah)' to Hosea and Proverbs (Jerusalem, 1968). Its literal citations of sources are extremely important for textual readings. Wherever a y. pericope contains a verse in toto it is likely to be cited in the 'Yalqut'. Of note, the edition to Proverbs, p.v., contains a list of y. passages. See H. ALBECK, in L. ZUNZ, supplemented Hebrew translation, HaDrashot BeYisrael (Jerusalem, 1954), p. 415, n. 45; GREENUP's Introduction to 'Zephania, Haggai, and Malachi' (London, 1913), and to the Hosea additions, pp. 141—145; LIEBERMAN (1934), p. 72; and MARGALIOTH, Midrash HaGgadol to Genesis (Jerusalem, 1947, 1967²), pp. vi—vii.

R. Samuel be Nissin from Senuth (12th century), Majan-Gannim, Commentary on Job, ed. SOLOMON BUBER (Berlin, 1889, Repr. Jerusalem, 1970), cites many expositions and materials from y. and is thus like a *midrash* on Job, pp. xii—xiv. Wherever y. uses a verse from Job it is thus worth consulting the Commentary, ad loc.

Batei Midrashot, ed. SHLOMO AHARON WERTHEIMER and ABRAHAM JOSEPH WERTHEIMER (Jerusalem, 1968²), a collection of various medieval brief *midrashim*, many of which cite y.; index II, 535. See J. TOWNSEND, Minor Midrashim, in: Anti-Defamation League of B'nai B'rith, Bibliographical Essays in Medieval Jewish Studies: The Study of Judaism, II (New York, 1976).

R. Moseh HaDarshon, Midrash Beresit Rabbati, ed. CHANOCH ALBECK (Jerusalem, 1940, Repr. 1967), various citations, though not exact: combined passages, added items, or only presented the content, p. xxi.

2. Other Especially Notable Works:

Raymond Martini, Pugio Fidei, adversus Mauros et Judaeos (JOHANNES BENEDICTUS CARPZOVUS: Lipsia, 1687, Repr. Gregg, 1967 [1968]), a medieval polemic against Judaism, cites y. passages with Latin translation. See SAUL LIEBERMAN, Shkiin (Jerusalem, 1939, 1970²), pp. 76—77, a list of references, "though they have little value as to the reading of the y." and 89; ID., Texts and Studies (1974), pp. 285—300, especially pp. 293 and 294 [reprinted from Historia Judaica 5 (1943), 88—102, 95—96]; YIṢḤAQ BAER, Hamidrashim Hamezuyafim shel Raymondus Martini UMeqomom Bamilḥemet HaDat shel Yeme HaBenayim, in: Studies in Memory of Asher Gulak and Samuel Klein (Jerusalem, 1942), pp. 28—49, who discusses the passages; and for further literature, REUVEN BONFIL, The Nature of Judaism in Raymundus Martini's *Pugio Fidei*, Tarbiẓ 40 (1971), 360—375, especially pp. 360f., fn. 3, 5. See now C. MERHAVYA, The Hebrew Versions of Pugio Fidei in the Sainte Geneviene MS, KS 51 (1976), 283—288.

Several commentaries to 'M. Zera'im' heavily draw from y. 'Zera'im', as the tractates lack a Babylonian *gemara*. See TWERSKY (1962), pp.107—109; CHANOCH ALBECK, Introduction to the Mishna (1967³), pp. 245—249; and JOEL H. ZAIMAN, The Traditional Study of the Mishnah, in: The Modern Study of the Mishnah, ed JACOB NEUSNER (Leiden, 1973), pp. 5—6; and APTOWITZER (1938), to the named individuals. These include:

Isaac b. Malkiṣedeq of Siponto (first half of 12th century), in his 'Commentary to Mishnah Zera'im', contains numerous citations of y., which many later authorities, e.g., Rashi, Sens, and Meiri, used. He tends to emend his citations. See LIEBERMAN, Tosefeth Rishonim IV (Jerusalem, 1939), pp. xviii—xxi, and ID. (1955), II, 803, fn. 1. Critical annotated edition: NISSAN SACHS (Jerusalem: Yad HaRav Herzog, 1975), based on MSS (Oxford, 392, London OR 6712, but not a third one, JTSA 1304). It was previously available to the end of Bik., in Venice 1522 edition of BT, and to all tractates, in Vilna Romm edition. See the introduction for a list of previous (partial) critical editions; KALMAN KAHANA, ed., Maśekhet Shevi'it, Ḥeqer VeIyyun (Bene Brak, 1972), pp. ii—iii; and especially ISAAC GOTTLIEB, Perush HRYBMṢ, Sinai 39 (77) (1975), 98—109, especially 105f., which demonstrates the importance of evaluating his citations of y. Cf. URBACH (1955), pp. 253f., and BOKSER (1975), passim.

Samson b. Abraham of Sens (ca. 1150—1230), one of the Tosafists. In his 'Commentary to M. Zera'im', in b. editions since Venice, 1522, he presents virtually an analytical commentary on the y. portions that deal with M. He systematically cites and then explains all relevant y. material and compares a *sugya* with its analogues or parallels elsewhere in y. and in b., and its sources with *baraitot* in 'Tosefta' and other works. He, however, does not always exactly cite a source. He employed more than one text of y. and on the basis of an alternative reading, parallel pericopae, and analysis, corrected the text of y. See LIEBERMAN, Tosefeth Rishonim IV (Jerusalem, 1939), pp. xvi—xvii; URBACH (1955), pp. 248, 250f., 253; and KAHANA (1972), pp. i, iii—ix, xii, who emphasized the importance of MS Paris Sorbonne Hebr. 362, which he publishes on Shevicjt, and which is the basis for a new edition, in progress, at Yad HaRav Herzog.

Asher b. Yeḥiel (1250—1328), in his Commentary to M. Zera'im, cites y. The work was first published, in part, in Amsterdam, 1715 ed. of BT, and, in full, Śefer Pi Shenayyim (Altona, 1735) which was reprinted (Bene Brak, 1966/67) with variants from MSS.

Elijah of London (13th century), Commentary to M. Zera'im and Decisions, published in 'The Writings of Rabbi Elijah of London', ed. M. Y. S. SACKS (Jerusalem, 1956), is interspersed with references from y.

XX. Commentaries and Works on Yerushalmi. B: Sixteenth Century On

A. Until the Vilna Gaon

I review both actual commentaries to y. and other works which regularly contain comments or citations of y. FRANKEL (1870), GINZBERG (1941), and MELAMMED (1973), pp. 525—534 (which is most useful when it adds material not found in GINZBERG), review the individuals and provide some characteristics of their work. Editions are listed in: STRACK (1931), pp. 83 and 149; JUDAH RUBINSTEIN, Quntraś HaShalem shel Mefarshe HaYerushalmi [A Complete List (whith author index) of Commentaries to Yerushalmi], (New York, 1949) [published as a supplement to SHULSINGER: New York, 1949, one volume edition of 'Talmud Yerushalmi'] — while not complete, includes most works, among which are items which only tangentially deal with or explain sections of y.; and KOHN (1952). LIEBERMAN (1934), Introduction, and especially (1950) provide a systematic analysis of the important works, those preserved as well as non-extant. As I need not duplicate their efforts, I assume those references and confine myself to a few comments and only cite one of the above for specific critical observations.

YOSEF CORCOS, Commentary on Maimonides' Mishneh Torah, Śefer Zera'im, frequently cites and analyzes y. passages. The commentary appeared in Izmir, 1757, in the SHULSINGER edition of 'Mishneh Torah' (New York, 1957), and in sections, in DINGLAS' edition of SOLOMON SIRILLO (Jerusalem, 1934—67).

Y'AQOV IBN HABIV (ca. 1460—1510), Ein Y'aqov (first ed., Salonica, 1516—1522, with many subsequent editions, some with various commentaries), a collection of *aggadot* from BT and some from PT. According to LIEBERMAN (1950), p. 312, fn. 152, he did not employ MSS of y. LIEBERMAN (1934), xxvii—xxviii, 21, 71, 72, notes that it yet preserves some good readings, though those in the present published editions are corrupt so that one cannot recognize the early text. Moreover, it used an antholog-compendium of *midrash-aggadah* and not necessarily (always?) the PT itself. Cf. GINZBERG (1941), p. H: cviii.

SOLOMON SIRILLO, Commentary to y. Zera'im and Sheqalim (ca. 1530), "one of the best commentaries to y." See LIEBERMAN (1950), pp. 301—302, and above, Section IV.C, for editions and the remaining literature.

YOSEF QARO, Commentary, Kesef Mishneh, to Maimonides' 'Mishneh Torah', cites y., especially on 'Zera'im', and had various y. MSS; LIEBERMAN (1950), p. 313, fn. 157.

MOSEH PIZANTI (1514—1573), 'Commentary to y. Zera'im', only extant in citations in his other work, 'Ner Miṣvah' (Constantinople, 1567) and citations of others; LIEBERMAN (1950), 302—303.

ELEAZAR AZIKRI (1553—1600, Safed), 'Commentary to y. Berakhot', in: Zhitomire, 1860, ed. of PT and reprints; to 'Beṣah', in: ISRAEL FRANCUS, ed. and intro., Talmud Yerushalmi: Maśekhet Beṣah (New York, 1967); and to y. 'Pe'ah', 'Demai', 'Terumot', and 'Pesaḥim', only extant in citations of 'Melekhet Shlomo' of SOLOMON AEDENI. LIEBERMAN (1934), pp. xxvii, 410, and (1950), pp. 304—313, provides a full introduction, which FRANCUS (1967) reproduces with additions, pp. 42—43, as well as a careful analysis of the commentary's characteristics, pp. 53—61.

SAMUEL YAFEH ASHKENAZI, Yefeh Mareh (Venice, 1590), collection of aggadic portions of y. with an extensive commentary. See M. BENAYAHU, R. Samuel Yaffe Ashkenazi and Other Commentators of Midrash Rabba, Tarbiẓ 42 (1973), 419—460, especially 428—430, 444—452, a survey of the various later editions, and excellent observations on the work's characteristics. ASHKENAZI did not employ MSS to PT; LIEBERMAN (1950), pp. 312, fn. 152, 317. Cf. GINZBERG (1941), p. H: cviii. The portion on 'Zera'im' was repeatedly and separately republished, e.g., as 'Aggadot Yerushalmi' (Vilna, 1863), as 'Sefer Ein Yaaqov', ed. ISRAEL SHAPIRO [Warsaw, 1898, Repr. in 'Yerushalmi Zera'im', (Jerusalem, 1972)], and as '(Kol) Aggadot Yerushalmi' (Jerusalem, 1899, Repr. 1964—65). See BENAYAHU, pp. 429f.

SOLOMON AEDENI, 'Melekhet Shelomo', in Venice Romm edition of 'Mishnah' and its reprints. See A. MARX, The Romm Mishnah, JQR 2 (1911—12), 266—270, especially 267—270. The author often cites y. with explanations of 'Rishonim' or of his own, and uses MSS of y. whose variants he notes; LIEBERMAN (1934), pp. xxvii, 128, 129, 155, 367; SZ (1968), p. 100. In general, see E. Z. MELAMMED, Melekhet Shelomo of R. Shelomoh Aedeni, Sinai, vol. 22 (year 44), #5—6 (267—268) (1959), 346—363; and ALBECK (1967), p. 252. KAHANA (1972), p. iii, fn. 6, points to his 'Notes to Śeder Zera'im', a Brit. Mus. MS OR. 5014; see G. MARGALIOUTH, Catalogue of the Hebrew and Samaritan Manuscripts in the British Museum II (London, 1905, 1965), pp. 65—66.

DAVID DARSHAN, author of a brief commentary published in Crocow (1610) edition of y. See LIEBERMAN (1934), p. viii, fn. 1, and especially MELAMMED (1973), pp. 527f.

JOSHUA BENVENISTI (1590?—1665?), Shedeh Yehoshua, A "diffusive and discursive" commentary to I, 'Zera'im' (Ber., 'Peah', 'Hallah, Orlah', 'Bikkurim'), (Constantinople, 1662), reprinted in: Yerushalmi Zera'im (Jerusalem, 1972), II—IV, 'Mo'ed', 'Nashim', and 'Neziqin', parts (Constantinople, 1749), abridged reprint to 'Neziqin', in: Hashlamah LiYerushalmi (= Supplement Volume to Vilna Romm edition, and reprints). See GINZBERG (1941), pp. H: cvxiii—cxix and especially EJ 4: 561f., for a concise description of the commentary's characteristics. The author had only the MS with commentary of SIRILLO; LIEBERMAN (1950), pp. 312, fn. 152, 317.

ELIJAH BEN LOEB FOULDA OF WIZNICIA (Poland, ca. 1650/60—1720), author of an edition with a terse commentary along with separate more lengthy selected notes to y. ,'Zera'im' and Sheq. (Amsterdam, 1710, Repr. Jerusalem, 1971), and B. Q., B. M., and B. B. (Offenbach and Frankfurt, 1725, 1742, Repr. in: HaShlamah LiYerushalmi, Supplement to Romm ed.). GINZBERG (1941), pp. H: cxxi—cxxiii, and especially JACOB HABERMAN, s. v., EJ 6, 648, provide concise descriptions of the work's characteristics. It greatly influenced the study of y. in Germany. LIEBERMAN (1950), pp. 317—318, proves that he did not make use of MSS. His emendations, rather, are based on his own reason, speculation, and readings and interpretations in earlier commentaries, including JOSHUA BENVENISTI.

DAVID OPPENHEIM, of Bohemia (1664—1736), marginal notes to y. (and Foulda), published in Vilna Romm ed.

DAVID FRANKEL of Berlin (1707—1762), author of one of the two basic commentaries to y. (see M. MARGALIOTH, next item), to tractates not covered by Foulda (plus Sheq.), 'Qorban HaEdah', a running commentary that elucidates the text, and 'Shire Qorban', *novellae* reconciling contradiction in *gemara*, textual emendations, with some attention to historical problems, both published in Dessau, 1742, and Berlin, 1757, 1760—62. 'Mo'ed' and 'Nashim' reprinted in Zhitomire ed. and to which 'Neziqin' was added in the Romm Vilna ed. See GINZBERG (1941), p. H: cxxiv, and especially MELAMMED (1973), pp. 528f., and ALEXANDER ALTMANN, Moses Mendelssohn (University, Alabama, and Philadelphia, 1973), pp. 12—13, 180, and fn. 31.

MOSES MARGALIOTH (d. 1780), Pene Moshe, a running commentary, and Mareh HaPannim, additions; in part, Amsterdam and Leghorn, 1754 and 1770, and in full, Zhitomire and subsequent editions. This basic commentary to the entire y. includes textual emendations, draws on spectrum of Talmudic literature, especially 'Tosefta', though at times still follows the practice of introducing b. concepts and issues. The commentaries of FRANKEL and MARGALIOTH provide the pattern for all subsequent work: GINZBERG (1941), pp.lvi—lvii, H: cxxxiv—cxxxv; LIEBERMAN (1934), p. vii, (1950), pp. 318f., and MELAMMED (1973), pp. 529—530.

Elijah, Gaon of Vilna (GRA), produced vital explanations and notes to PT; he interprets a text in its own terms and frequently offers incisive emendations. They are preserved or embedded in his works and those of his students. These include (1) 'Commentary to Shulḥan Arukh', published from an autographed MS; systematically cites y.; (2) 'Shenot Eliyahu', to 'M. Zera'im', published in his lifetime (and variously republished, including Romm 'Mishnah'); (3) 'Commentary to y. Zera'im', in Vilna ed., 1926, in two versions (produced by students); (4) 'Emendations and notes to Śeder Zera'im'; (5) embedded in Israel of Shklov, Taklin Ḥadtin, 'Commentary to y. Sheq'. (Minsk, 1812); (6), cited in Israel of Shklov, Pe'at HaShulḥan (Safed, 1834), from which Ridbaz (in Romm ed. of y.) at times quotes. See Ginzberg (1941), pp. lvii—lx, H: cxxv—cxxx; Tchernowitz III (1947), pp. 212—216; and especially Kalman Kahana, LeḤeqer Be'ure HaGRA LiYerushalmi ULeTosefta (Tel Aviv, 1957), esp. pp. 9f., 32—44, and 54—61, which focuses on the texts used by the GRA, MSS and texts used in the printing of his commentaries, and the relationships between different works and editions; and Yehudah Leib Maimon, Toldot HaGRA (Jerusalem, 1970), especially pp. 176—200 and 252; and Simeon Kohen, R. Yosef Qaro, ed. Iṣḥaq Rafael (Jerusalem, 1969), pp. 258—290, on the 'Commentary to the Shulḥan Arukh'. Cf. I. Joel, A Collection of Hebrew MSS from the Romm Press, KS 13 (1937), 520f., on texts and MSS used in the printed editions; and Jacob Dinstag, R. Elijah of Vilna — Bibliographical List, Talpiot 4 (1959).

B. Nineteenth and Twentieth Centuries: Traditional and Pre-Modern

I now turn to works from the nineteenth and twentieth centuries. The bibliographical lists and works earlier cited also deal with these materials and accordingly I cite only important or representative works or those for which I wish to indicate important secondary literature. I further have expanded my criterion for works published since the nineteen-fifties, as they are not included in the several bibliographies. I separately treat those items which systematically employ MSS or other 'modern scientific' methods, C. This is an arbitrary criterion, for many of the 'traditional' works are highly sophisticated. The former items, however, consciously and systematically make use of the results of the latter group, usually respond to different series of exegetical and historical questions, and, therefore, differently perceive their task and method.

*Hirsch Mendel Pinelis, Darkhah Shel Torah (Vienne, 1861, Repr. Jerusalem, n. d. [1968?]), series of critical analyses of *gemara*. See Weiss Halivni (1968), p. xii, fn. 2, and Joel Gereboff, Hirsch Mendel Pineles: The First Critical Exegete, The Modern Study of the Mishnah, ed. J. Neusner (Leiden, 1973), pp. 90—104.

*Meir Marim of Kobrin (d. 1873), Śefer Nir, Zera'im (Warsaw, 1875, Repr. with Foulda, Jerusalem, 1971); Id., Mo'ed (Vilna, 1890), excellent

incisive commentary, which is aware of the deplacement of materials within the text. Often, though, it is overly elliptical while suggesting several alternative explanations. See LIEBERMAN (1934), pp. vii, and e. g., 11, fn. 1, 53, 66, 76, 82, 157, 229f., 297; and GINZBERG (1941), p. cxxxi.

DOB BERISH ASHKENAZI, Shaare Yerushalmi (Warsaw, 1866).

*JOSHUA ISAAK SHAPIRO of Slonim (1801—1873), Noam Yerushalmi, 4 vols. (Vilna, 1863 and 1869, Repr. in 2 vols., Jerusalem, 1968), excursive and lengthy commentary that often contains insightful comments. It compares b. and y. *sugyot*, points out differences, and refers to relevant pericopae elsewhere in both b. and y. See LIEBERMAN (1934), pp. viii, 80f. It is digested in EFRAYIM DOV HAKOHEN LOF in Gilyone Efrayim, in Vilna ed.

A. KROCHMAL, Yerushalayim HaBenuyah (Lemberg, 1867, Repr. Jerusalem, 1971), on selected passages of y. Ber. to San. with an introduction on the date of y.'s compilation.

ZECHARIAH FRANKEL, Ahavat Ṣion, Talmud Yerushalmi, I: Ber. and Pe'ah (Vienne, 1874, Repr. Jerusalem, 1971); II: Demai (Breslau, 1875), to republished Venice, p. e. text, he adds a brief commentary, with occasional longer notes.

JACOB DAVID of Slotz, 'Perush HaRidbaz', in Vilna Romm ed., contains illuminating explanations, especially on 'Zera'im' and tractate 'Yevamot'; LIEBERMAN (1934), p. viii.

JOSEF H. DUENNER, Commentaries (Hagahot) (Frankfurt am Main, 1897—1923); critical commentary, especially as to flow of materials, and their placement within *gemara*, though insufficiently used 'Rishonim'; WEISS HALIVNI (1968), p. xii, fn. 13.

*ARYEH LEIB YELLIN, 'Yefeh Enayim', published in back of Romm, Vilna b., cites y. and often critically analyzes y. pericopae relevant to b. See LIEBERMAN (1934), p. 226, and RIVKA ZISKIND, Rabbi Aryeh Loeb Yellin Author of 'Yefeh Einayim' (Jerusalem, 1973), especially pp. 21, fn. 30, 63—103, 114—118. For supplements see KANEVSKI, below.

M. S. SIVITZ, Śefer Mashbiaḥ (Jerusalem, 1913, and St. Louis, 1918, Jerusalem, 1929[3]) includes a commentary and a list of words and terms peculiar to y. See RABINOVITZ (1940), pp. 629—634.

*JOSEPH ENGEL, Giljonei HaSchass [on b. and y. Zer.-Neziqin] (Vienne, 1924, and 1929, Repr., n. p., n. d. [Israel, 1972?], and on y. 'Zera'im', in: Yerushalmi Zera'im [Jerusalem, 1972]), of great importance, especially for references to other passages in y. and b. which throw light on a given pericope, and for its citation of medieval authorities.

*ḤAYYIM DAICHES, Netivot Yerushalayim, to 'Neziqin', 3 vols. (Vilna, 1900, London, 1926—27), to y. 'Neziqin', combines depth, erudition, critical sense, and resource to 'Rishonim'; LIEBERMAN (1934), p. vii.

*'Hashlamah LiYerushalmi' (Romm: Vilna, 1928), reprint of numerous important commentaries, variously republished, including as 'Shiṭah Mequbeṣet al Yerushalmi' (Jerusalem, 1971).

DOV MALACHI ENGLENDER, Zehav Ha'Areṣ, I: Ber. Pe'ah, Dem. (Jerusalem, 1944), San. Shev., Mak. (Jerusalem, 1960), lucid explanations of many selected passages, draws on 'Rishonim' and pays attention to the readings of y. upon which their comments are based, and takes account of the peculiar language of y.

Samuel Isaac Hillmann, Or HaYashar, I: Zer. and Mo'ed; II: Nashim and Neziqin (Jerusalem, 1947 and 1948).

Mayyim Efrayim (Boston, 1951).

Mordechai Savitsky, Mareh Esh (Brooklyn, 1956), on 'Sheqalim'.

Joseph Rosen, Ṣafnat Paneaḥ, 3 vols. (Jerusalem, 1959, 1962), on 'Neziqin'.

Ḥayim Kanevski, Tashlum Yefeh Enayim, in: El HaMekorot edition of Vilna Babylonian Talmud (Tel Aviv, 1959), and with additions and corrections in Ḥayim Kanevski, Siaḥ HaSadeh (Bene Brak, 1969), pp. 45a–59b.

Shelomoh Goren, HaYerushalmi HaMeforosh Berakhot (Jerusalem, 1961), projected as a critical edition based on MSS, Geniza fragments, collation of 'Rishonim', and other works with a new commentary. It heavily draws on Ginzberg (1941, 1961) and Lieberman (1947) and (1955) without however giving proper credit. (And this is so even where Ginzberg errs.) The commentary does not capture Palestinian usage, and still has a tendency to introduce concerns not inherent in the text. Moreover, he lets 'Rishonim' set the exegetical alternatives; A. Goldberg, KS 38 (1963), 195–202. On the other hand, at times his comments are of interest and his apparatus helpful, but hardly definitive. His arrangement, though, is an attempt at providing a manageable format for the relevant materials.

Aryeh Pomeranchik, Torat Zera'im (Tel Aviv, 196?), *novellae* to y. 'Zera'im'.

Yosef Sevi Aaronson, ed., Maśekhet Sheqalim min Talmud Yerushalmi VeHaTosefta (Jerusalem, 1964); Id., Pe'ah, Dem., Kil., Shev. (Jerusalem, 1972,) includes various commentaries and the editor's running comments based upon earlier authorities.

Israel Fajgenbaum, Śefer Yad VeShem, II: y. Pe'ah, Shevi'it (Petaḥ Tikvah, 1966), *novellae* and notes.

Mosheh Leiter, Beshuleh Gilyone (Jerusalem, 1967), 724 pp. of brief, and occasionally long, notes to y.

Eliyahu Schlesinger, Yad Eliyahu, I: Yerushalmi-Zera'im (Jerusalem, 1971), especially useful for references to similar phrases and usages elsewhere in *gemara*.

Abraham Karlitz, Ḥazon Ish. Zera'im (Bene Brak, 1973), on Dem., Kel., Shev., Maas., and Orl.

C. Modern Works

I herein include those who consciously employ critical analysis. Aspects of these methods appear in items above or other works, e. g., in different ways, GRA, DUENNUR, PINELIS, and MEIR MARIM. But the following works have tried to take account of the ways in which y. is put together, the history of its text, as well as to some degree general historical and philological considerations, and, at times, literary matters. Where a work still lacks or insufficiently treats one of these matters, the sensitized reader may appropriately revise it. Unfortunately, however, the exegetical and other comments are done in passing, left embedded within the commentary, or are within an article on individual passages. Thus other than brief comments, e. g., the quite different remarks by GINZBERG (1941), pp. H: lxx—lxxx, FRANCUS, Talmud Yerushalmi, Maśekhet Beṣah (New York, 1967), Introduction, and M. S. FELDBLUM. Talmudic Law and Literature, Tractate Gittin (New York, 1969), pp. 37—42, a study to date has not undertaken historical-literary analysis so as to describe systematically and fully the contents of a y. tractate as a whole. NEUSNER, Purities (1974—77), on a different genre of materials, provides one model of what such a commentary could be like. See also the comments by GOODBLATT (1979), IV. 1: c and V. 2, the last two paragraphs.

I do not include the various works which from a specific perspective or discipline, whether, e. g., history, agriculture, or liturgy, explain or deal with y. The items in Chapter XVII provide examples of these approaches. See, as well, Chapters XIII, XIV, and XVIII.

A. M. LUNCZ, Talmud Hieroselymitanum Ad Exemplarin Editiones Principis, I—V (Jerusalem, 1907—1919), text and commentary to y. Ber.-Shev. See Ch. III, above.

ISRAEL LEWY, Commentary to B. Q. I—VI, Jahresbericht des jüdisch-theologischen Seminars (1895—1914, Repr. Jerusalem, 1970), an example of what a critical work can be. See above, Section XII. 3, and E. URBACH, Zechariah Frankel, Israel Lewy, Saul Horowitz, Three Professors of Talmud of the Breslau Seminary, in: Das Breslauer Seminar, The Breslau Seminary, Memorial Volume, ed. G. KISCH (Tübingen, 1963), pp. 177—182.

B. RATNER, Ahawath Zion We-Jerusholaim, 12 vols. (Vilna, 1901—1917, Repr. Jerusalem, 1967), on Ber., Zer.-Mo'ed (less Eruv.), in addition to textual notes includes explanations and comments. See above, Ch. IV. A, and V. 1, and note the list of review-studies by W. BACHER, S. BUBER, S. POZNANSKI, and V. APTOWITZER.

ḤAYYIM HELLER, Concerning a Cross-Reference Index to Yerushalmi, in: Festschrift zum siebzigsten Geburtstage David Hoffmanns, ed. S. EPPENSTEIN (Berlin, 1924), Hebrew section, pp. 55—66; ID., HaM'alot Leshlomon. A Cross-Index and Notes to y. Ter., in: Festschrift zum Vierzigjährigen Amtsjubiläum Dr. Salomon Carlebach, ed. MORITZ STERN (Berlin, 1910), Hebrew section, pp. 246—249. [Reprinted together as 'Shene Quntreśim (Berlin, 1929).]

Z. W. RABINOVITZ (1940), with indexes, incisive notes, comments, and emendations to all of y., employs both early rabbinic works and modern scientific literature available to him, focuses on usage and style of y., and deals with issues stemming from the composition of the text. See the comprehensive review, G. Alon, Tarbiẓ 12 (1940), 88—95.

J. N. Epstein, virtually all his works, especially (1948, 1964²) (1957), and (1962), and, e. g., Id., Owni ('WNY—'NTYKRYS), (y. Git. 4, 46a), Tarbiẓ 8 (1937), 316—318. See the indexed bibliography in Tarbiẓ 20 (1950) — "The father of the study of careful Talmudic scholarship", Lieberman, SZ (1968), p. 135.

Ginzberg, 4 vols. (1941—1961), a voluminous commentary ostensibly to y. Ber. chs. I—V, which analyzes each item in terms of its history in rabbinic literature. It cites medieval authorities and readings from MSS and geniza fragments, pays close attention to y.'s style and terminology, and is invaluable for textual and exegetical purposes. The exposition, though, lacks discipline and systematic arrangement and the comments, at times, have a slight tendency to introduce novel interpretations. One should systematically compare the material to that contained in Lieberman, TK I (1955), on 'Berakhot', which explicitly or without so indicating clarifies, or disagrees, with Ginzberg, or explicitly confirms his suggestions. Moreover, Heinemann's research undermines certain aspects of Ginzberg's attempted historical analysis of liturgical matters. See the reviews of A. Weiss, Jewish Social Studies 5 (1943), 70—73, and A. Goldberg, KS 38 (1963), 195—202, and Melammed (1973), pp. 533f. For his other works, see the 'Bibliography', Louis Ginzberg Jubilee Volume, ed. S. Lieberman, et al. (New York, 1945), English section, pp. 19—47.

Saul Lieberman, virtually all his works, especially (1934), a commentary along his programatic lines to y. Shab., Eruv., and Pes. [cf. H. Y. Ehrenreich, Ozar Hachaim 11 (1935), 85—86, 90—91, 175], (1947) to Ber. and Ket., in which his notes to Maimonides' text actually constitute a commentary in their own right; Id., Tosefeth Rishonim 4 vols. (Jerusalem, 1937—39), to the whole of Tosefta, and TK Iff. (1955ff.) (presently, I—VIII, through the end of 'Nashim'), on which he analyzes practically every y. passage which cites or relates to 'Tosefta'. The indexes to y. passages and usages, vols. II, V, VII, VIII refer to only a fraction of the entries. 'Tosefta' may provide the key to the interpretation of y. as the former often reflects the tradition or approach of Palestine, vis-à-vis that of Babylonia; pp. I: xx, xxi, V: xvii; to which cp. III: xiv. For his other works, see the bibliography, T. Preschel, Dr. Saul Lieberman and his Contribution to Jewish Scholarship, reprint from Hadoar 43, no. 23 (New York 1963); to which add (items not earlier cited): Id., Forgotten Meanings, Tarbiẓ 23 (1967—68), 89—102, and Id., Interpretations in Mishna, Tarbiẓ 40 (1970), 9—17. See now the supplementary bibliography, in: Hadoar 56, no. 15 (2459) (February 11, 1977), 229—231.

A. Weiss, in his books and articles systematically focuses on numerous tractates and pericopae, compares b. and y. *sugyot* and raises historical literary questions, though he does not always sufficiently employ MSS. For a complete listing of his works, see Benjamin Weiss, Annotated Bibliography of the Writings of Dr. Abraham Weiss, Abraham Weiss Jubilee

Volume (New York, 1964), Hebrew section, pp. 5—11, to be supplemented by ID., Meḥqarim BeTalmud (Jerusalem, 1975), pp. 252f. Note in particular the book of collected articles, ID., Notes to Bavli and Yerushalmi Pericopae (Ramat Gan, n. d., 196?).

JACOB BANIEL (Berliner), An Arithmetical Subject in Jerushalmi (y. Shab. 7:1, 9a), Tarbiẓ 15 (1943), 65—70.

S. ABRAMSON, Jerushalmi Shebuoth VI. 2, Tarbiẓ 16 (1944), 53.

HARRY M. ORLINSKY, Studies in Talmudic Philology (y. Ber. 9:3, 13c), HUCA 23 (1950—51), Part One: 499—514.

DAVID WEISS HALIVNI. 2 vols. to date, on 'Nashim' and the second half of 'Mo'ed', (1968, 1975). In his source-critical analysis of b. *sugyot* he systematically employs materials from y. The work makes full use of early and late rabbinic commentaries, MSS, and other literature, and especially focuses on the ways in which the history of a tradition affected its formulation and use. See ROBERT GOLDENBERG, SHAMAI KANTER, and DAVID GOODBLATT, David Weiss Halivni, Meqorot uMeśorot, in: The Formation of the Babylonian Talmud, ed. NEUSNER (Leiden, 1971), pp. 134—173.

JACOB NEUSNER, while his works are not formally an analysis of y. most, in part, if not in whole, are hermeneutically relevant: History of the Jews of Babylonia (Leiden, 1966—70), indicate how to employ Talmudic texts for historical purposes, e. g. dividing between groups of sources; Pharisees (1971) and Eliezer (1973), and Purities, 22 vols. (1974—77), demonstrate the necessity to employ first, form, tradition, and redaction criticism to analyze each discrete text and its pericopae as part of a larger redactional whole, and, secondly, exegetical plain sense to isolate the conception of each version of a text without harmonizing them or introducing absent considerations, and, thirdly, an overview to take stock of the discrete analyses.

MEYER S. FELDBLUM, Talmudic Law and Literature: Tractate Gittin (New York, 1969), includes separate exposition and analysis of y. and then its comparison with b., especially as to their interpretation of M.

I. FRANCUS, Talmud Yerushalmi Maśekhet Beṣah (New York, 1967), a sophisticated introduction to literary aspects of the tractate with notes and addenda on the text in addition to the publication of commentary, along with variants from the Leiden MS.

N. WIEDER, On an Obscure Passage in the Palestinian Talmud (y. Ber. 1 : 8, 3d = Taan. 2 : 3, 65c), Tarbiẓ 43 (1973—74), 46—52.

BOKSER (1975), includes, in English, analyses of y. pericopae, with an attempt to adopt and adapt the best from earlier research and to add considerations as to recurrent formal and literary phenomena.

D. Articles

Various journals, jubilee volumes, and special collections include materials relevant to the study of y. For representative items see the classified listings in STRACK (1931), and in M. MIELZINER, Introduction to the Talmud. With new bibliography, 1925—1967, by ALEXANDER GUTTMANN (New York, 1968[4]), pp. 397—415. For items in Hebrew in numerous fields, see the comprehensive classified index of NAHUM RAKOVER, A Bibliography of Jewish Law (Jerusalem, 1975), specifically on y., pp. 80—82.

Jubilee Volumes: JACOB MARCUS and A. BILGRAY, An Index to Jewish Festschriften (Cincinnati, 1937), to be supplemented by CHARLES BERLIN, Index to Festschriften in Jewish Studies (Cambridge and New York, 1971).

Periodical literature: 1665—1900, MOISE SCHWAB, Répertoire des articles relatifs à l'histoire et à la litterature juives (Paris, 1914—23, Repr. New York, 1970). The following periodical literature frequently have or had materials: 'HaṢofeh LeHakhmat Yisrael'; 'HeḤalus', indexed in the Jerusalem, 1969, reprint; Bet HaMidrash (Vienne, 1865), ed. I. H. WEISS; especially 'Beth Talmud' (Vienne), 1881—1896, indexed in the Jerusalem, 1965, reprint; 'Jerusalem', ed. LUNCZ (Repr. 1972), especially vols. 7—10; 'Ozar Hachaim', ed. EHRENREICH; MGWJ, indexed, in Gesamtregister 1851—1939 (Tübingen, 1966); REJ, which has an index volume following volume 100 (1936), supplemented by vol. 132 (1973); JQR, index 1—20 (1932); 'Sinai', indexed through 1947 (1948); 'Tarbiẓ'; 'Leshonenu'; 'Dine Israel'; and 'Bar Ilan Annual'. The following occasionally have items: HUCA; PAAJR, 'Journal of Jewish Studies'; 'Journal for the Study of Judaism in the Persian, Hellenistic, and Roman Period'; 'Israel Exploration Journal', indexes in vols. 11 (1961), and 26 (1976); 'Bulletin of the Institute for Jewish Studies'; and the 'AJS Review' (New York), 1ff. (1976ff.).

Kirjath Śepher contains classified and indexed listings of books, including full contents of journals and works of collected articles (citations of which were discontinued with the appearance of the next item). The more recent Index of Articles on Jewish Studies, ed. ISSACHAR JOEL, 1 (1966) ff. (Jerusalem, 1969ff.) (to date 12 vols., through 1977), provides an invaluable complete, classified, and indexed list of articles in all languages.

Addendum

(to p. 199, l. 15f.) A. LINDER, The Roman Imperial Government and the Jews under Constantine, Tarbiẓ 44 (1974—75), 95—143. — (to p. 199, l. 20f.) A. OPPENHEIMER, The Am Ha'aretz (Leiden, 1977). — (to p. 203, l. 1) ID., A Lexicon of the Verbs in the Tannaitic Hebrew (Ph.D. dissertation, Hebrew University, Jerusalem, 1972). — (to p. 203, l. 7) See M. SOKOLOFF, The Current State of Research on Galilean Aramaic, JNES 37 (1978), 161—167. — (to p. 203, l. 25) MOSHE BAR-ASHER, Palestinian Syriac Studies (Jerusalem, 1977). — (to p. 206, l. 24) See also I. VINNIKOV, Specimen of a Dictionary and Concordance of the Palestinian Literature (The Letter G), in: Palestinski Sbornik 5 (1960), 151—228. — (to p. 211, l. 38) J. PRESS, Encyclopedia of Eretz Israel, I—IV (Jerusalem, 1951—55), and P. NE'EMAN, Encyclopaedia of Talmudical Geography, I—II (Tel-Aviv, 1972) (Unreliable). — (to p. 212, l. 16) ID., Glass Utensils in Talmudic Literature (Jerusalem, 1978). — (to p. 212, l. 37) ID., et al., Ancient Synagogue Excavations at Khirbet Shema'. Upper Galilee, Israel 1970—1972 [= AOS Annual, XLII] (Durham, 1976). — (to p. 212, end) L. LEVINE, Roman Caesarea. Qedem 2 (Jerusalem, 1975). — (to p. 213, l. 18) *Donateurs et foundateurs dans les synagogues juives (Cahiers de la Revue Biblique, 7) (Paris, 1967). — (to p. 213, l. 23) See now: *On Stone and Mosaic. The Aramaic Hebrew Inscriptions from Ancient Synagogues (Jerusalem, 1978).

Index Nominum

The index includes all entries to names of individuals and places. An asterisk (*) next to a number indicates that the item appears more than once on that page.

The Babylonian Talmud

by David Goodblatt, Haifa

Table of Contents

Abbreviations:

Archive	=	Archive of the New Dictionary of Rabbinic Literature
b.	=	ben
bh	=	Biblical Hebrew
BT	=	Babylonian Talmud
bta	=	Babylonian Talmudic Aramaic
C. E.	=	Common Era
Diq. Sof.	=	Diqduqe Soferim (RABBINOVICZ, FELDBLUM, HIRSHLER)
DTLU	=	Development of the Talmud as a Literary Unit (A. WEISS)
EJ	=	Encyclopedia Judaica
Ex. Term.	=	Die exegetische Terminologie der jüdischen Traditionsliteratur (BACHER)
GQS	=	Gemara Quotations in Sebara, JQR 43 (H. KLEIN)
GS	=	Gemara and Sebara, JQR 38 (H. KLEIN)
HUCA	=	Hebrew Union College Annual
IAL	=	Introduction to Amoraitic Literature (EPSTEIN)
ISG	=	Iggeret R. Sherira Ga'on
ITL	=	Introduction to Tannaitic Literature (EPSTEIN)
ITM	=	Introduction to the Text of the Mishnah (EPSTEIN)
JAOS	=	Journal of the American Oriental Society
JBL	=	Journal of Biblical Literature
JQR	=	Jewish Quarterly Review
JSemSt	=	Journal of Semitic Studies
MGWJ	=	Monatsschrift für die Geschichte und Wissenschaft des Judentums
mh	=	Middle ("Mishnaic") Hebrew
PAAJR	=	Proceedings of the American Academy for Jewish Research
R.	=	Rav, Rabbi
REJ	=	Revue des Études Juives
SGR	=	Some General Results of the Separation of Gemara from Sebara in the Babylonian Talmud, JSemSt 3 (H. KLEIN)
SH	=	Sarei Ha-elef (KASHER and MANDELBAUM)
SLA	=	Studies in the Literature of the Amoraim (A. WEISS)
ST	=	Sources and Traditions (HALIVNI)

STV	=	Seder Tanna'im Ve'amora'im
TD	=	The Talmud in its Development (A. Weiss)
TH	=	Tequfat Hagge'onim (Assaf)
Trad. u. Trad.	=	Tradition und Tradenten (Bacher)
ZDMG	=	Zeitschrift der deutschen morgenländischen Gesellschaft

I. Introduction

Jewish tradition speaks of "the sea of the Talmud"[1]. The metaphor is an apt one for a document as extensive and complex as the Babylonian Talmud (hereafter: BT). It covers 2783 folio pages in the standard editions and treats almost every subject known to man. A Talmudist compiled the following list of topics encountered in BT:

> "Religion and ethics, exegesis and homiletics, jurisprudence and ceremonial laws, ritual and liturgy, philosophy and science, medicine and magic, astronomy and astrology, history and geography, commerce and trade, politics and social problems . . . ."[2]

Despite the heterogeneity of its contents, BT can be characterized as a commentary on the Mishnah of Yehudah the Patriarch, a Palestinian law code published around the year 200 C.E. The Mishnah provides both the external framework and the internal continuity of the Talmud. Following the Mishnah, BT is divided into tractates and chapters. And consecutive commentary on the paragraphs of the Mishnah is the connecting link between the diverse contents of BT. That commentary is composed of pericopae. Generally each pericope relates to a paragraph, sentence, or phrase of the Mishnah. It may record the comments of several generations of masters, usually in chronological order. The earlier masters tend to comment directly on the Mishnah. Later masters may devote more attention to the words of their predecessors than to the Mishnah itself. In the course of the discussion various sources may be cited from elsewhere in the Talmud, the Mishnah, or from cognate literature. Extraneous subjects, suggested by association, are also introduced. Indeed entire pericopae may have nothing to do with the Mishnah.

BT does not contain connected commentary for all 63 tractates of the Mishnah. Only 37 tractates appear in BT. Materials from the remaining 26 are scattered throughout the text. Thus these sections of the Mishnah were studied, but they did not engender composition of separate BT tractates. The following chart summarizes the situation just described.

[1] The earliest attestation of this phrase is from the late middle ages. See E. Ben-Yehudah, Thesaurus totius hebraitatis (London and New York, 1960), Vol. IV, p. 2056. Cf. Midrash Psalms ad 104:25 where the sea metaphor refers to 'the tractates' or to Tannaitic collections.

[2] M. Jastrow, Dictionary of Targumim, the Talmud Babli and Yerushalmi and the Midrashic Literature (New York, 1886—1903), p. V.

Order of Mishnah	Number of Mishnah Tractates in Order	BT Tractates (with abbreviations used in article)
zera'im, 'Seeds' (agricultural laws)	11	1. Berakhot (Ber.)
mo'ed, 'Season' (festival laws)	12	1. Shabbat (Shab.)
		2. 'Eruvin ('Eruv.)
		3. Pesaḥim (Pes.)
		4. Yoma (Yom.)
		5. Sukkah (Suk.)
		6. Beṣah (Beṣ.)
		7. Rosh Hashanah (RH)
		8. Ta'anit (Ta.)
		9. Megillah (Meg.)
		10. Mo'ed Qaṭṭan (MQ)
		11. Ḥagigah (Ḥag.)
nashim, 'Women' (personal status)	7	1. Yevamot (Yev.)
		2. Ketuvot (Ket.)
		3. Nedarim (Ned.)
		4. Nazir (Naz.)
		5. Soṭah (Soṭ.)
		6. Giṭṭin (Giṭ.)
		7. Qiddushin (Qid.)
neziqin, 'Torts' (civil law)	10	1. Bava Qamma (BQ)
		2. Bava Meṣi'a' (BM)
		3. Bava Batra (BB)
		4. Sanhedrin (Sanh.)
		5. Makkot (Mak.)
		6. Shevu'ot (Shev.)
		7. 'Avodah Zarah (AZ)
		8. Horayot (Hor.)
qodashim, 'Holy Things' (sacrificial laws)	11	1. Zevaḥim (Zev.)
		2. Menaḥot (Men.)
		3. Ḥullin (Ḥul.)
		4. Bekhorot (Bekh.)
		5. 'Arakhin ('Arakh.)
		6. Temurah (Tem.)
		7. Keritot (Ker.)
		8. Me'ilah (Me'il.)
		9. Tamid (Tam.)
ṭohorot, 'Purities' (ritual purity)	12	1. Niddah (Nid.)

The masters whose comments appear in the Mishnah and cognate literature are termed *tanna'im,* from the root *tny,* 'repeat'. They flourished in late first and second century Palestine. The later masters cited in the Talmud are designated *'amora'im,* from the root *'mr* which here means 'interpret, explain'. The Amoraim were active in Palestine and in Babylonia during the third through the fifth centuries (= 'the Amoraic era'). The Mishnah commentary composed by the Amoraim is commonly called the Gemara, while Talmud refers to the combination of Mishnah and Gemara[3]. Since a *gemara* was composed in each of the aforementioned countries, we have both a Palestinian and a Babylonian Talmud. Each records views of Amoraim from both countries, but local masters tend to predominate. The sections of the Mishnah covered by each Talmud are not identical. Thus the Palestinian Talmud has tractates for all of Mishnah Order *zera'im,* but none for *qodashim.* Linguistic and stylistic features also distinguish one *gemara* from the other.

The brief description given above of the contents of BT does not hint at the role the document was to play in Jewish history. BT became the constitution of Jewish communities throughout the world. It should be noted that until modern times Jewish communities enjoyed considerable internal autonomy. Most governments did not interfere in issues of personal status and small civil claims between Jews. These matters as well as religious affairs were conducted according to the law of the Talmud. The acceptance of the authority of BT by Jews in Europe, Africa, and Asia raises two questions. First, why was the Talmud of Babylonia preferred to that of Palestine? Second, why should communities far removed from both of the latter countries submit to either Talmud? Answers to the first question can be suggested. Beginning in the eighth century the talmudic academies of Babylonia waged a vigorous campaign to establish the predominance of their Gemara. Fragments of the propaganda they disseminated have survived[4]. The success of their campaign was probably helped by Jewish connections with the Abbasid dynasty which united under its rule a large percentage of the world Jewish population. At this time the Babylonian Talmudic academies were located in Bagdad, the Abbasid capital. Perhaps another reason for the success of BT is its superior literary quality vis-a-vis the Palestinian Talmud. The second question concerns the acceptance of BT outside the Abbasid sphere of influence, for example in the communities of the Rhineland. For the present no convincing explanation exists. In any case, the place of BT in later Jewish history, when it became almost equal to the Bible in holiness and authority, lies beyond the scope of this essay.

[3] It should be stressed that in BT itself *gemara* means 'a tradition', and *talmud* means 'discussion, explication'. See ALBECK, Introduction, pp. 3—7, MELAMMED, Introduction, pp. 323, 326, WEISS, TD, pp. 402—407, and cf. STRACK, Introduction, p. 5.

[4] See S. SPIEGEL, Leparashat Happulmos Shel Pirqoi b. Baboi, H. A. Wolfson Jubilee Volume, Hebrew Section (Jerusalem, 1965), pp. 243—273.

My subject here is BT as a literary document. I shall concentrate on the classical philological issues of language, text-criticism, and source-, form- and redaction-criticism. Other topics relating to the contents of the document, such as law, religion, and folklore, or to its historical background will be discussed briefly in Chapter V below. Throughout I shall limit myself to the scholarship of the past fifty years. For the period before 1925 the reader is referred to H. L. STRACK's classic 'Introduction to the Talmud and Midrash' (Philadelphia, 1925; Reprint in paperback: New York, 1964). This is the English translation of a revised version of the fifth and last German edition (Munich, 1921)[5]. STRACK compiles very full bibliographies on all aspects of Talmudic literature, and I see no reason to repeat what is readily available elsewhere. Moreover, 1925 is not just an arbitrary cut-off point. In the past fifty years the centers of Talmud scholarship shifted from Eastern and Central Europe to the United States and Israel. This shift is reflected in the dominance of English and especially Hebrew in the bibliographies accompanying this essay. Separate bibliographies precede each chapter. The works listed at the head of the chapter are referred to in abbreviated form in the body of the text. A full list of abbreviations appears at the head of the essay.

II. The Text of BT

Bibliography

1. Published Manuscripts

The Babylonian Talmud. Codex Florence. 3 Vols. Jerusalem, 1972.

The Babylonian Talmud. Codex Munich 95. Reprint, Jerusalem, 1971.

The Babylonian Talmud, Seder Nezikin. Codex Hamburg. Facsimile of the Original MS and a Reprint of the Goldschmidt Edition (Berlin, 1914). Jerusalem, 1969.

The Babylonian Talmud, Tractate Hullin, Codex Hamburg 169. Jerusalem, 1972.

Manuscripts of the Babylonian Talmud from the Collection of the Vatican Library, Series A. 3 Vols. Jerusalem, 1972. Series B. 3 Vols. Jerusalem, 1974.

Talmudical Fragments in the Bodleian Library. 1. Fragment of the Talmud Babli, Tractate Keritoth of the year 1123, the oldest dated MS of this Talmud. 2. Fragment of the Talmud Jerushalmi, Tractate Berachoth. Ed. S. SCHECHTER and S. SINGER. Cambridge, 1896. Reprint, Jerusalem, 1971.

Tractate 'Abodah Zarah of the Babylonian Talmud. Ms. Jewish Theological Seminary of America. Ed. S. ABRAMSON. New York, 1957.

The Yemenite MS. of Megilla (In the Library of Columbia University). Toronto, 1916. The Yemenite MS. of Mo'ed Katon (Babylonian Talmud) in the Library of Columbia University. n.p., n.d. Ed. J. J. PRICE. Reprint, Jerusalem, 1970.

ALLONI, N., Geniza Fragments of Rabbinic Literature. Jerusalem, 1973.

HASIDAH, Y., Meginze Yehudah. Daf Gemara Ketav-Yad, Sinai 73 (1973), pp. 224—229.

[5] The bibliography in the English translation contains items as late as 1927. However it is less than complete for the period after 1920.

Katsch, A. I., Ginze Talmud Babli. Jerusalem, 1975.

Id., Massekhet Berakhot Min Haggenizah, Zalman Shazar Jubilee Volume, Jerusalem, 1973, pp. 549—596.

Id., Unpublished Geniza Talmud Fragments, Journal of the Ancient Near Eastern Society of Columbia University 5 (1973), pp. 213—223.

Id., Unpublished Geniza Talmudic Fragments from the Antonin Collection, JQR 58 (1967—68), pp. 297—309.

Id., Unpublished Geniza Talmudic Fragments of Tractate Shabbath in the Antonin Collection in the U.S.S.R., JQR 63 (1972—73), pp. 39—47.

2. Early Witnesses to the Text

ʿEn Yaʿaqov of Yaʿaqov ibn Ḥabib. p. e., Saloniki, 1516.

Haggadot Hattalmud. p. e., Constantinople, 1511. Reprint, Jerusalem, 1961.

Heʿarukh of Natan b. Yeḥiʾel. p. e., Rome, before 1475. Crit. ed. A. Kohut. 8 Vols. Vienna, 1878—1892.

Otzar ha-Gaonim. Thesaurus of the Gaonic Responsa and Commentaries following the order of the Talmudic Tractates. Ed. B. M. Lewin. 13 Vols. Haifa and Jerusalem, 1928—1943.

Otzar ha-Gaonim to Tractate Sanhedrin. Ed. H. Z. Taubes. Jerusalem, 1966.

Sefer Halachot Gedolot. Codex Paris 1402. Introduction by S. Abramson. Jerusalem, 1971.

Sefer Halachot Pesuqot by Rav Yehudah Gaon. Codex Sassoon 263. Introduction by S. Abramson. Jerusalem, 1971.

She'iltot of R. Ahai Gaon. p. e., Venice, 1546. Reprint, Jerusalem, 1971. Crit. ed. (incomplete) S. K. Mirsky. 4 Vols. Jerusalem, 1960—66.

Yalqut Shimʿoni. p. e., Saloniki, 1521—1527. Reprint, Jerusalem, 1968—1973.

3. Critical Editions and Collations of Variant Readings

Feldblum, M. S., Diḳduḳe Sopherim, Tractate Gittin. New York, 1966.

Friedmann, M., Babylonischer Talmud, Tractat Makkoth. Vienna, 1888. Reprint, Jerusalem, 1970.

Hirshler, M., Diqduqe Sofrim Hashalem. Massekhet Ketuvot, I—II. Jerusalem, 1972—1977.

Liss, A., Diqduqe Sofrim Hashalem. Massekhet Soṭah, I. Jerusalem, 1977.

Malter, H., The Treatise Taʿanit of the Babylonian Talmud. New York, 1930. Reprint, Jerusalem, 1973.

Rabbinovicz, R., Diqduqe Sofrim. Variae Lectiones in Mischnam et in Talmud Babylonicum. 12 Vols. Reprint, New York, 1960.

4. Studies

Adler, E. N., Les éditions du Talmud de Pisaro, REJ 89 (1930), pp. 98—103.

Id., Talmud incunables of Spain and Portugal, Jewish Studies in Memory of George A. Kohut, New York, 1935, pp. 1—4.

Id., Talmud manuscripts and editions, Essays in honor of J. H. Hertz, London, 1943, pp. 15—17.

Id., Talmud Printing before Bomberg, Festskrift ... David Simonsen, Kobenhavn, 1923, pp. 81—84.

Aptowitzer, V., Sous quelle forme une édition critique du Talmud est-elle possible et admissible? REJ 91 (1931), pp. 205—217.

Dimitrovsky, H. Z., S'ridei Bavli. Spanish Incunabula Fragments of the Babylonian Talmud. New York, 1978.

Kasher, M. M., ʿAl Devar Hoṣaʾah Ḥadashah Shel Talmud Bavli, Talpioth 3 (1948), pp. 475—496.

Kook, S. H., Dugma'ot Leḥaqirat Girsa'ot 'Al Pi 'Oṣar Hagge'onim, B. M. Lewin Jubilee Volume, Jerusalem, 1939, pp. 127—131.
Marx, A., Pereferkowitsch's Edition of Berakhot, JQR n. s. 2 (1910—11), pp. 279—285.
Prys (Prijs), J., Der Basler Talmuddruck, 1578—1580. Olten–Basel–Lausanne, 1960.
Rabbinovicz, R., Ma'amar 'Al Hadpasat Hattalmud. Ed. M. Haberman. Jerusalem, 1952.
Rosenthal, E. S., Hammoreh, PAAJR 31 (1963), Hebrew Section, pp. 1—71.
Id., Rav, Ben-Aḥi R. Ḥiyyah Gam Ben-Aḥoto? (Peraṭ 'Eḥad Letoldot Hannusaḥ shel Habbavli), H. Yalon Jubilee Volume, Jerusalem, 1963, pp. 281—337.
Zeitlin, S., A Critical Edition of the Talmud. An Appreciation of Malter's Text of Tractate Ta'anit, JQR n.s. 21 (1930—31), pp. 61—73.

1. Introduction

Most documents from late antiquity have come down to us in manuscripts written centuries after the original work was composed. BT is no exception, though it is impossible to pinpoint when it was 'composed'. The latest masters named flourished in the early sixth century. However, major redactional activity and substantive addition continued through the sixth and seventh centuries. Furthermore, extensive materials attributable to authorities of the eighth and ninth centuries found their way into the text. S. Assaf identifies seven such additions in the 18 folios of the first chapter of BM[6]. Glosses and comments continued to move from the margin into the body of BT throughout the middle ages[7]. Finally, the text was freely emended, on the basis of conjecture or variants in manuscripts, until modern times. The printed editions of the nineteenth century, on which all modern printings are based, contain emendations suggested by the commentaries of the sixteenth through the eighteenth centuries. Further changes in the text resulted from censorship. Both Jewish and non-Jewish censors deleted potentially offensive passages and replaced sensitive terms with more neutral ones. The earliest censorship was internal. Passages of a theosophical or magical nature ridiculed by the Qaraites and other anti-rabbinic movements were excised[8]. Later, sections offensive to Christianity were removed either voluntarily or at the insistence of government censors[9].

It turns out that BT reached its present state only in the last century. Thus the point of departure for text criticism must be sought elsewhere. The question is, when did the text achieve a form recognizable as BT, however open to accretion or emendation? According to Assaf the attitude to textual change provides a clue. He notes that through the seventh century there seems to have been no hesitation to add freely to the text. Beginning

[6] S. Assaf, Tequfat Hagge'onim Vesifrutah (Jerusalem, 1955), pp. 135ff.
[7] Writing in the sixteenth century Beṣalel Ashkenazi noted how sections of the eleventh century commentary of Rashi were incorporated into the text of BT in some manuscripts. See page 11 of the preface by S. Y. Zevin to Diqduqe Soferim Hashshalem, Ketuvot I, ed. M. Hirshler (Jerusalem, 1972).
[8] See S. Lieberman, Shkiin[2] (Jerusalem, 1970).
[9] Strack, Introduction, pp. 85f.

in the eighth century conscious substantive changes were no longer made. From then on additions were mainly the result of marginal notes finding their way into the text. Moreover, in the eighth century independent compositions by rabbinic masters began to appear. All this suggests that by the latter date BT was considered a finished work[10]. If we accept the argument of ASSAF, then BT reached its (relatively) final form by the eighth century. Further support for this view comes from the earliest tradition of a written text of BT. A tenth century Talmudist claims that a deposed Babylonian exilarch who arrived in Spain ca. 770 wrote out from memory the complete text of the Talmud[11]. Assuming that BT was 'completed' at this time, our oldest manuscripts are closer to the date when the document was composed than is usually assumed. Nonetheless several centuries separate the more complete manuscripts from the latter date, as we shall see in the following section.

2. Manuscripts

The earliest dated manuscripts extant are from the twelfth century. A Bodleian Library manuscript covering half of Ker. is dated by its colophon to 1123. Of greater importance is Codex Florence from 1177. This text includes Ber., Bekh., Tem., Ker., Me'il., BQ, BM., BB., Sanh., and Shev. (as well as Mishnah Middot and Qinnim) — about a third of BT. Only slightly later is Codex Hamburg of BQ, BM, and BB written in Gerona in 1184. From the following century we have MS JTSA of AZ written towards the end of 1290 in Ubeda, Spain[12]. The earliest manuscript of the entire BT is Codex Munich 95 written in Paris in 1343. Older texts may be found among the undated manuscripts. Most important are the BT texts from the Cairo Genizah some of which predate the year 1000. One of these manuscripts dates from the ninth century according to its editor[13]. This brings us within a century of the completion of BT. Unfortunately the Genizah manuscripts are very fragmentary, and most cover only individual

[10] ASSAF, Tequfat, p. 126.

[11] Quoted in B. M. LEWIN, Otzar ha-Geonim, Vol. I (Haifa, 1938), Responsa, p. 20 ad Ber. 8a, and cf. LEWIN's n. 1 there. See also S. ABRAMSON, Tractate 'Abodah Zarah of the Babylonian Talmud. Ms. Jewish Theological Seminary of America (New York, 1957), p. XIII, n. 1. The Talmudist is the statesman and poet Samuel ibn Nagrela Hannagid, and the deposed exilarch Natronai b. Ḥakinai/Ḥabibai/Zabinai. A passage in Sefer Rabiah, Vol. II (Berlin, 1926), ed. V. APTOWITZER, ‡462, p. 20, refers to "books" from the time of R. Ashi, ca. 400, but it is not clear what they contained. Similarly, a reference to "the Talmud and its interpretation" sent to Spain by Paltoi Gaon in the mid-ninth century need not mean a complete text of BT, cf. ABRAMSON, loc. cit.

[12] ABRAMSON, ibid., pp. XII—XIV, notes that one pericope in this manuscript reflects a *Vorlage* datable to 807! However, it is doubtful whether the *Vorlage* of the manuscript as a whole was so early.

[13] W. H. LOWE, The Fragments of the Talmud Babli Pesachim of the ninth or tenth century in the University Library, Cambridge (Cambridge, 1879).

pages (see the publications of ALLONY, FELDBLUM, HIRSHLER, and KATSCH). KASHER published a list of all extant manuscripts and fragments for each BT tractate in 1948 (Talpioth, cf. STRACK, pp. 81f.). Since then only a few additional Genizah fragments have come to light. The collation of variants for Ket. recently published by HIRSHLER illustrates the amount of material available for one of the important tractates. HIRSHLER had at his disposal seven complete manuscripts and some fifty fragments from the Genizah[14].

The manuscripts of BT are scattered throughout the world. Fortunately photographic technology facilitates textual research. Not only are photographs of the manuscripts widely available, but many of the important ones have been published in reproduction. The aforementioned Codices Munich and Hamburg were printed early in the century. Recently Makor Publishing of Jerusalem reissued them, as well as the collations of variants from the Ker. manuscript by SCHECHTER and SINGER and from a sixteenth century Yemenite manuscript of Meg. and MQ by PRICE. The same firm has also brought out Codex Florence, Codex Hamburg of Ḥul., and a series of Talmud manuscripts from the Vatican Library. The latter include MSS Vat. Ebr. 108 (Shab., MQ), 109 ('Eruv., Beṣ.), 110 (Soṭ., Ned., Naz.), 130 (Ket., Giṭ.), 134 (Yom., RH, Ta., Suk., Beṣ., Meg., Ḥag., MQ), 111 (Yev., Qid., Nid.), 112 (Ket.), 114 (Yev., BM), 118 (Zev., Men.), and 119 (Zev., Tem., 'Arakh., Bekh., Me'il., Ker.). 110 and 111 are actually a single manuscript written in 1381. The other manuscripts lack dates.

3. Witnesses to the Text

Early witnesses to the text of BT or to manuscripts no longer extant supplement the evidence reviewed in the preceding section. The oldest material is the Talmud related literature composed in Babylonia during the early Islamic era. This literature is called 'Geonic' after the heads of the Talmudic academies who bore the title *ga'on*, plural: *ge'onim*. It includes introductions to and commentaries on BT, legal compendia, and responsa to questions of Talmudic law and interpretation. The earliest of these works are the 'She'iltot' and 'Halakhot Pesuqot' from the second half of the eighth century and 'Halakhot Gedolot' from the first half of the ninth century[15]. These documents quote extensively from BT and so constitute

[14] In view of the centrality of BT in Jewish life, we should expect a larger number of manuscripts. The explanation for their relative paucity lies not only in the ravages of time, but in the hand of man. The expulsions and persecutions of Jewish communities in the Muslim and Christian worlds were not conducive to the preservation of old texts. Most serious were the burnings of the Talmud instigated by the Catholic Church. See STRACK, p. 275, n. 2, and on the whole issue of the Church's attitude toward the Talmud see CH. MERCHAVIA, The Church Versus Talmudic and Midrashic Literature, 500—1248 (Jerusalem, 1970) [Hebrew].

[15] See ASSAF, Tequfat, pp. 133—220. She'iltot (p.e., Venice 1546, reprint Jerusalem, 1971); critical edition (incomplete) by S. MIRSKY, 4 Vols. (Jerusalem, 1960—66). Sefer Halachot

a valuable early witness to the text. Frequently they seem to contain not just variant readings, but different recensions of the tractate or pericope under discussion[16]. In either case the three works mentioned are extremely important for text criticism. The Geonic commentaries and responsa are equally important. B. M. LEWIN and H. Z. TAUBES collected these materials (the commentaries are extant in fragmentary form only) and published them according to the order of the tractates. This project is still incomplete, but it does cover about two thirds of BT. Slightly later witnesses appear in the commentaries and legal epitomes of BT compiled by Spanish, North African, Franco-German, and Middle Eastern masters who flourished between the tenth and sixteenth centuries. Jewish tradition calls these authorities *rishonim*, 'the former ones', in distinction to the post-1600 masters who are designated *'aḥaronim*, 'the latter ones'. Two kinds of evidence appear in the work of the *rishonim*. First, they frequently discuss the text and refer to readings in old manuscripts at their disposal. Second, citations of BT in their writings often vary from readings in extant manuscripts and editions. The second category is problematic, for we must allow the possibility of paraphrase or inaccurate quotation from memory. The first category, though, attests to genuine variants.

Other witnesses to the text of BT may be found in compilations of aggadic or non-legal material. Most important are two epitomes of the non-legal sections of BT: 'Haggadot Hattalmud' (p. e. Constantinople, 1511) and ''En Ya'aqov' (sixteenth century). The more general anthologies of aggadic material, such as the Yemenite 'Midrash Haggadol' and the thirteenth century 'Yalqut Shim'oni', may also attest variant readings. In using the latter works one must be careful not to confuse parallel but different sources with variants of the same text. Still another important witness is the ''Arukh', an eleventh century dictionary of rabbinic literature. Its compiler, Natan b. Yeḥi'el of Rome, illustrates his definitions with citations from the sources including BT[17]. Finally, the early printed editions of BT, which of course were based on manuscripts, also preserve valuable variants.

4. Editions

The history of the printing of BT has already been written. R. RABBINOVICZ published an 'Essay on the Printing of the Talmud' in 1866 as an introduction to his 'Diq. Sof.' (A second edition appeared separately in Munich in 1877.) A. M. HABERMAN brought this work up to date in a revised edition which came out in 1952. Those who do not read Hebrew may con-

Pesuqot by Rav Jehudai Gaon. Codex Sassoon 263, Introduction b. S. ABRAMSON (Jerusalem, 1971). Sefer Halachot Gedolot. Codex Paris 1402, Introduction by S. ABRAMSON (Jerusalem, 1971).

[16] Cf. MELAMMED, Introduction, pp. 478—486, summarizing J. N. EPSTEIN.

[17] See ibid., pp. 487—492.

sult the summary in STRACK (pp. 83—85) and the articles by ADLER. The earliest editions appeared within fifteen years of the beginning of Hebrew printing. Incunables of individual tractates are extant from Portugal, Spain, and Italy. DIMITROVSKY has published fragments of the Spanish incunables. In the early sixteenth century tractates were published in Italy and Morocco. The first complete edition of BT was published in Venice between 1520—23 by DANIEL BOMBERG (a non-Jew). Certain features of this edition were adopted by all subsequent printings. The pagination of BOMBERG became standard. He printed the Talmud on numbered folio pages. Each side of the page contained one column of BT text. The column on the obverse side is designated 'a', that on the reverse 'b'. Since all editions follow this system, BT is cited by folio and column. Thus Ber. 33b means tractate 'Berakhot', folio 33, column b (i. e., reverse). Moreover, to this day all editions begin the BT text on page 2, for BOMBERG used page 1 as the title page. Another feature of BOMBERG's edition which became standard is the choice of commentaries printed alongside the text. On the inner edge of each side of the folio he printed the commentary of Rashi (= R. Shelomo Yiṣhaqi of France, died 1105). On the outer edge of each side he printed the Tosafot or 'Supplements'. The latter comprise commentary on BT and supercommentary on Rashi by French and German masters of the twelfth through the fourteenth centuries (including descendants of Rashi). These two commentaries appear in the same location in every subsequent edition of BT. After BOMBERG there were several more sixteenth century printings in Venice, Lublin, Constantinople, and Basel. According to RABBINOVICZ the Frankfurt a. M. edition of 1720—22 became the basis for all future editions. Most twentieth century printings reproduce the Romm edition published in Vilna between 1880—86. Critical editions will be discussed in the following section.

5. Text Criticism

a) The History of Text Criticism

Text criticism of BT is as old as the study of the document. The early commentators achieved a high degree of sophistication in this discipline. For example an eleventh century (?) authority warns of the interpolation into the text of marginal notes:

> "It is common that a reference, explanation, or variant is written in the margin or between the lines. A copyist thinks it is part of the text and writes it all together. He thus leads astray, for [his copy] will fall into the hands of a sage who will treat the matter as a unit and render decisions according to the addition[18]."

[18] Responsen der Geonim, ed. A. HARKAVY (Berlin, 1887), #272 p. 138. See p. 365 for his suggested attribution of this responsum to Hai Gaon.

Indeed it is usually information in the early commentaries which enables us to identify interpolations and late additions to BT. The *rishonim* also devoted considerable attention to variant readings. A good illustration involves a passage at Sanh. 65b. In the eleventh century the *ga'on* Hai reports four different readings of the latter text. He rejects two of them because they were not attested in "our texts". The other two, he claims, are in effect identical[19]. The allusion to "our texts" indicates that the academy of Pumbedita, of which Hai was principal, possessed texts considered authoritative, but other texts also circulated. Incidentally, Hai's contemporary Rashi attests still a fifth reading and appears to know nothing of the four cited by the former. Commentators outside Babylonia, like Rashi, did not have authoritative texts, but many of them placed a high value on Spanish manuscripts of BT. Because of the close connections between Spain and Babylonia during the Geonic period it was felt that these manuscripts contained the most accurate text[20]. We recall the tradition cited above that a deposed Babylonian exilarch wrote out a text of BT in Spain in the late eighth century. In addition to Spanish manuscripts, old manuscripts were highly prized. The *rishonim* frequently allude to "old texts on parchment" which they consulted in order to establish the correct reading[21].

The textual criticism of the early commentators was not limited to collating variants. Many were tempted to emend the text. The aforementioned Hai expressed reservations about this procedure:

> "Some of the 'emenders' (*garsanim*) report this tradition [in the following version]. Certainly this version is easier on the ear than the former [i. e., the unemended version], but it is neither our reading nor that of the early authorities. We must not change Tannaitic sources or the Talmud because of a difficulty we have [in understanding the text], for this is the accepted reading received from our masters upon whom we rely . . .[22]."

Hai thus argues that one should not emend a well attested reading on the basis of conjecture. Other commentators did not share this view. Rashi, for example, suggested many emendations in his commentary based on conjecture as well as variants[23]. In so doing he seems to have initiated a trend among the Franco-German commentators. Soon a reaction set in. A

[19] 'Osar Hagge'onim to Tractate Sanhedrin, ed. H. Z. Taubes (Jerusalem, 1966), p. 68, ad 65b.

[20] See for example, Ramban, Novellae ad BB 134 and 137; Zeraḥyah Hallevi, Hamma'or Haggadol AZ, Chap. I, 2b; Rabad ad Ma'or, Ber. Chapter I end.

[21] For example, Maimonides, Mishneh Torah, Malveh Veloveh 15:2; Ishut, 13:13. B. Ashkenazi, Shiṭṭah Mequbbeṣet ad Ket. 31b, 75b.

[22] Otzar ha-Geonim, ed. B. M. Lewin, Vol. VIII (Jerusalem, 1939), Responsa, p. 207, ad Ket. 68b.

[23] Cf. Melammed, Introduction, pp. 492f.

grandson of Rashi, R. Yaʿaqov b. Me'ir, known as Rabbenu Tam, criticized the excesses of his own brother:

> "May his Lord forgive my brother Samuel, because for every reading R. Shelomo [Rashi] emended, he [Samuel] emended twenty. Not only this, but he erased [readings] in the books[24]."

This passage appears in a tract Yaʿaqov published to correct the textual anarchy, Sefer Hayyashar. In the introduction he set forth the following principles: 1. The existence of variant readings in manuscripts does not justify emendation. 2. One must not emend on the basis of conjecture. 3. One should not emend on the basis of parallel sources[25]. The second principle repeats the opinion of Hai cited above. The third recognizes the distinction between variants of the same text and different though parallel texts. I understand the first principle to mean that variant readings may represent valid text traditions, and therefore we cannot disqualify one in favor of another. All of these principles are accepted by modern students of rabbinic literature. Indeed Urbach notes that the text critical methodology of the Tosafists (the Franco-German school of commentators of the 12th—14th century) is fully compatible with modern philological scholarship[26].

b) Collations of Variants and Critical Editions

The major contribution of modern BT text criticism consists of the systematic collation of variant readings. R. Rabbinovicz was the pioneer in this endeavor. His 'Diqduqē Soferim' compares the readings from Codex Munich 95 with those of the standard printed text. The variants are printed in parallel columns. In the footnotes he discusses variants from other manuscripts as well as those attested in early witnesses. Unfortunately Rabbinovicz did not live to complete his project. His Diq. Sof. does not cover the tractates of Order *nashim*, part of *qodashim*, and tractate Nid. Nor did he manage to record all the variants from Codex Munich. Finally, since the publication of this work, additional manuscript material has come to light. Despite all its shortcomings, Diq. Sof. remains a valuable tool for the study of BT. The project of Rabbinovicz has been continued by M. S. Feldblum in his volume on Giṭ. An advantage in the latter volume is the addition of the standard BT page, in slightly reduced format, opposite the page containing the variants. Feldblum also distinguishes among the variants attested by *ge'onim* and *rishonim*. Only those witnessed by manuscripts of BT are noted among the variants. The rest appear in the footnotes. The footnotes also include 'variants' from parallel sources. Another collation of variants appears in the edition of MS JTSA of AZ by S. Abramson. The most recent development is the projected 'Complete Diqduqē

[24] Sefer Hayyashar, Introduction, cited from a manuscript by E. E. Urbach, The Tosaphists: Their History, Writings, and Methods[2] (Jerusalem, 1955), p. 528.

[25] See Urbach, op. cit., pp. 80—82, 529—533.

[26] Ibid., p. 532.

Soferim' announced by the Complete Israeli Talmud Institute of the Rav Herzog Foundation. This series is a by-product of plans to issue a new edition of BT and its commentaries accompanied by variant readings, full cross and source references, and additional commentaries. Since the collation of variant readings for all of BT is already complete, the editors decided to publish this material immediately rather than wait for the larger project. So far five volumes have appeared. Two contain the Mishnah of order *zera'im*, two cover BT Ket. (edited by HIRSCHLER), and one covers the first part of BT Soṭ. (edited by LISS). In the latter three volumes we find the BT text from the Vilna edition at the top of the page. Below it appear cross references and source references. Below this are variant readings from all known manuscripts, Genizah fragments, and early editions as well as those attested by the *ge'onim* and *rishonim*. Judging by the volumes which have appeared, this series promises to live up to its name and bring to a completion the endeavor initiated by RABBINOVICZ. The value of such a series for all aspects of Talmud scholarship is obvious.

Collations of variants cannot take the place of a critical edition of BT. Unfortunately, little has been done in the latter area during the past fifty years. STRACK listed only one critical edition of a single tractate in his 'Introduction': that of Ber. by N. PEREFERKOWITSCH in 1909. Some twenty years earlier M. FRIEDMANN had published a critical edition of Mak., and in 1913 S. ALBECK brought out a model edition of the first eight folios of Ber. Since STRACK the only attempt at a critical edition was that of MALTER who prepared one of Ta. which appeared posthumously in 1930. FRIEDMANN, PEREFERKOWITSCH, and MALTER all published eclectic texts. (I was unable to obtain a copy of the edition by S. ALBECK). This procedure was sharply criticised by the reviewers. MARX, for example, argues that the project of PEREFERKOWITSCH is premature. Before we can attempt to establish the correct text we must reconstruct the different text types current during the middle ages. Moreover PEREFERKOWITSCH does not establish criteria for choosing one reading over another. Finally, and most basically, MARX doubts whether there ever was a uniform text even in the academies which according to him redacted BT. This doubt is shared by APTOWIZER in his review of MALTER. APTOWITZER argues that even were the critical resources at our disposal reliable — and they are not — the eclectic method would be still inadmissible for a work like BT «*dont la valeur et l'autorité résident dans la tradition*» (p. 208). The adverse criticism had its desired effect, and after MALTER there were no further attempts to produce an eclectic text. Unfortunately no one essayed the more modest task suggested by MARX either. Thus matters stood until the recent work of ROSENTHAL which I shall discuss below.

c) The Principles of BT Text Criticism

If text criticism of BT was neglected by modern scholarship, that of other rabbinic documents was not. The researches of EPSTEIN and LIEBER-

MAN on Tannaitic sources and those of MARGULIES on a Palestinian Amoraic text are especially noteworthy. The principles established in this work should also apply, mutatis mutandis, to BT. EPSTEIN discusses in detail the prerequisites and materials for a scientific edition of the Mishnah. He stresses the difference between *Varianten* and *Versionen* (ITM, pp. 1—7). The former result from errors and changes in the course of oral or scribal transmission of the document. The latter are different versions or recensions of the text. We can legitimately decide that certain *Varianten* are incorrect, but the *Versionen* may have equal textual validity. The application of this distinction to text critical work is illustrated in the best scientific edition of a Tannaitic text we have, that of 'Tosefta' by LIEBERMAN. LIEBERMAN refrains from producing an eclectic text. One of the reasons he gives for this decision is the difficulty in deciding whether a given reading represents a scribal error or a valid alternate version[27]. Given the existence of different versions, an eclectic text would distort the unitary text traditions or text types. Finally, LIEBERMAN notes that we possess few scientific editions of rabbinic texts. Thus we cannot yet adopt the editorial procedures established by classical philology[28]. These considerations lead LIEBERMAN to choose for the body of his edition a manuscript which best represents one text type. He publishes the latter without change together with a full collation of variant readings. Parallel texts from other documents appear in the commentary, not in the critical apparatus[29]. E. S. ROSENTHAL claims that the text critical methods adopted by LIEBERMAN should apply to all of rabbinic literature (Hammoreh, p. 63). And in fact MARGULIES follows the same procedures in his edition of 'Vayyiqra Rabbah', a Palestinian Amoraic *midrash* on Leviticus. He also adds another consideration, deriving from the nature of rabbinic literature. Since these texts are compilations of discrete traditions with only a loose external framework, additions or deletions are not felt by the reader. Thus every copyist can edit the text anew if he so wishes. This makes it almost impossible to recover the *Urtext* as it left the hands of the original editor[30]. LIEBERMAN and MARGULIES thus agree that at present critical editions of rabbinic texts are not possible. For now we must be satisfied with scientific

[27] In his earlier work on the 'Tosefta' readings in the *rishonim* LIEBERMAN writes, "we must take seriously the different readings in the manuscripts and in the *rishonim*. It is not possible to decide that only one of the readings is correct, for in many instances both readings are correct — each one according to the tradition by which it was created. Each one is 'textually true' . . . each text has its own truth." See Tosefet Rishonim, Vol. IV (Jerusalem, 1939), Introduction, p. 15.

[28] ROSENTHAL notes that even some Greek texts do not permit an eclectic edition. 'Traditional' documents composed and edited by generations of savants pose the same problems as rabbinic texts. He quotes REITZENSTEIN on the problems of editing the Poimandres to illustrate this point, see Hammoreh, p. 63.

[29] See ROSENTHAL, Hammoreh, pp. 67—69 for a summary of the text-critical methods of LIEBERMAN in his edition of the 'Tosefta'.

[30] M. MARGULIES, Midrash Wayyikra Rabbah, Part V (Jerusalem, 1960), p. XL.

editions of individual recensions or text types accompanied by a collation of variant readings.

The principles discussed above are applied to BT by ROSENTHAL in the scientific edition of Pes. he is preparing. In a preliminary study of one brief pericope from this tractate he illustrates the problematic of BT text criticism. The text tradition of this passage, which ROSENTHAL believes is representative, turns out to be extremely fluid. This leads him to wonder whether we can overcome even the first hurdle of text criticism: deciding where redaction ends and text tradition begins (see 'Rav' etc.). Whatever the problem, no one is better equipped than ROSENTHAL to overcome it. His edition of Pes. should move BT scholarship beyond the collation of variants to the level of publishing recensions of tractates. However, as ROSENTHAL himself noted with regard to 'Tosefta', it is unlikely that we shall be able to move beyond recensions to the 'original text' in the foreseeable future (Hammoreh, p. 70).

III. The Languages of BT

Bibliography

1. General

BROCKELMANN, C. and BAUMSTARK, A., Aramäisch und Syrisch, Handbuch der Orientalistik, III, 2. ed. B. SPULER. Leiden, 1954.

FRAENKEL, S., Die aramäischen Fremdwörter im Arabischen. Leiden, 1866.

KUTSCHER, E. Y., Aramaic, Current Trends in Linguistics, Vol. 6, The Hague, 1970, pp. 178—183.

ID., Aramaic, Encyclopaedia Judaica, Vol. 3, Jerusalem, 1972, coll. 259—287.

ID., Mittelhebräisch und Jüdisch-Aramäisch im neuen Köhler-Baumgartner, Hebräische Wortforschung. Festschrift W. Baumgartner, Leiden, 1967, pp. 158—175 (= Supplements to Vetus Testamentum, 16).

ID., Some problems of the Lexicography of the Jewish Aramaic Dialects, Archive of the New Dictionary of Rabbinic Literature, II, Ramat Gan, 1974, pp. 96—101, English Summary, pp. XII—XIII.

ID., Studies in Galilean Aramaic. Jerusalem, 1966. = Tarbiz 21 (1951—52), pp. 192—205, 22 (1952—53), pp. 185—192, 23 (1953—54), pp. 36—60 (Hebrew; English edition in press).

ROSENTHAL, F., Die aramaistische Forschung seit Th. Nöldeke's Veröffentlichungen. Leiden, 1939.

ID., An Aramaic Handbook. 2 Vols. Wiesbaden, 1967.

2. Middle Hebrew (especially the Hebrew of BT)

ABRAMSON, S., On the Hebrew in the Babylonian Talmud, Archive of the New Dictionary of Rabbinic Literature, II, Ramat Gan, 1974, pp. 9—15, English Summary, p. V.

BENDAVID, A., Biblical Hebrew and Mishnaic Hebrew². 2 Vols. Tel Aviv, 1967—71.

GINSBERG, H. L., Zu den Dialekten des Talmudisch-Hebräischen, MGWJ 77 (1933), pp. 413—429.

KUTSCHER, E. Y., Hebrew Language: Mishnaic, Encyclopaedia Judaica, Vol. 16, Jerusalem, 1972, coll. 1590—1607.

ID., The Present State of Research into Mishnaic Hebrew (Especially Lexicography) and Its Tasks, Archive of the New Dictionary of Rabbinic Literature, I, Ramat Gan, 1972, pp. 3—28, English Summary pp. III—X.

ID., Some Problems of the Lexicography of Mishnaic Hebrew and its Comparison with Biblical Hebrew, ibid., pp. 29—82, English Summary, pp. XI—XXVII.

MARGALIYOT, E., 'Ivrit Ve'aramit Batalmud Uvamidrash, Lešonenu 27/28 (1963—64), pp. 20—33.

MORESHET, M., Further Studies of the Language of the Hebrew Baraytot in the Babylonian and Palestinian Talmudim, Archive of the New Dictionary of Rabbinic Literature, II, Ramat Gan, 1974, pp. 31—73, English Summary, pp. VIII—IX.

ID., The Language of the Baraytot in the T. B. is not MHe[1], H. Yalon Memorial Volume, Jerusalem, 1974, pp. 275—314, English Summary, pp. XXI—XXII.

ID., A Lexicon of the New Verbs in the Tannaitic Hebrew. Unpublished Ph. D. Dissertation, Jerusalem, 1972. English Summary, pp. I—XIV.

ID., New and Revived Verbs in the Baraytot of the Babylonian Talmud (In Comparison with mh[2] in the Babylonian and Palestinian Talmudim), Archive of the New Dictionary of Rabbinic Literature, I, Ramat Gan, 1972, pp. 117—162, English Summary, pp. XXXVI—XXXIX.

PRIJS, L., Ergänzungen zum talmudisch-hebräischen Wörterbuch, ZDMG 120 (1970), pp. 6—29.

SOKOLOFF, M., The Hebrew of Berešit Rabba According to MS Vat. Ebr. 30, Lešonenu 33 (1968—69), pp. 25—42, 135—149, 270—279.

Midrash Bereshit Rabba. MS Vat. Ebr. 30. Introduction and Index by M. SOKOLOFF. Jerusalem, 1971.

3. Babylonian Talmudic Aramaic and Related Dialects

BEN ASHER, M., The Conjugation of the Verb in 'Halakot Pesuqot', Lešonenu 34 (1969—70), pp. 278—286, 35 (1970—71), pp. 20—35.

EPSTEIN, J. (Y.) N., Babylonisch-Aramäische Studien, Festskrift ... David Simonsen, Kobenhavn, 1923, pp. 290—310.

ID., Glosses babylo-araméennes. I. Les textes magiques araméens de Montgomery, REJ 73 (1921), pp. 27—58, 74 (1922), pp. 40—72.

ID., A Grammar of Babylonian Aramaic. Jerusalem and Tel Aviv, 1960 (Hebrew).

ID., Notes on Post-Talmudic Aramaic Lexicography. I. Linguistic Remarks to Anan's Sepher Ha-Miṣwot, JQR n.s. 5 (1914—15), pp. 233—251. II. Sheeltot, JQR n.s. 12 (1921—22), pp. 299—390.

ID., Zum magischen Text, JAOS 33 (1912), pp. 279—280.

ID., Zur Babylonisch-Aramäischen Lexicographie, Festschrift A. Schwarz, Berlin und Wien, 1917, pp. 317—327.

ID., Studies in Aramaic Philology. Selected with an Introduction and indices by DANIEL BOYARIN. New York 1978.

GINZBERG, L., Beiträge zur Lexicographie des Jüdisch-Aramäischen 1, Festschrift A. Schwarz, Berlin und Wien, 1917, pp. 329—360. 2, MGWJ 78 (1934), pp. 9—33. 3, Essays ... in Memory of Linda Miller, New York, 1938, pp. 57—108.

KAUFMAN, S. A., Akkadian and Babylonian Aramaic — New Examples of Mutual Elucidation, Lešonenu 36 (1971—72), pp. 28—33, 37 (1972—73) pp. 102—104.

ID. The Akkadian Influences on Aramaic. Chicago, 1974.

KUTSCHER, E. Y., Babylonian Aramaic, Encyclopedia Judaica, Vol. 3, Jerusalem, 1972, coll. 277—282.

ID., Babylonian Talmudic, in: An Aramaic Handbook, ed. F. ROSENTHAL, Wiesbaden, 1967, II, 1, pp. 43—45; II, 2, pp. 59—66.

ID., Lemunaḥe Shetarot Batalmud Uvesifrut Ge'onim, Tarbiz 17 (1945—46), pp. 125—127, 19 (1947—48), pp. 53—58, 125—128.

ID., Meḥqar Diqduq Ha'aramit Shel Hattalmud Habbavli, Lešonenu 26 (1962), pp. 149—183.

MALONE, J. L., Observations of Linguistic Similarity between the Babylonian Aramaic of Halakot Pesuqot and Mandaic, Lešonenu 37 (1972—73), pp. 161—164.
MORAG, S., Ha'aramit Habbavlit Bemassoret Teman: Happo'el Hashalem, H. Yalon Jubilee Volume, Jerusalem, 1963, pp. 182—220.
ID., Notes on Phonology of Babylonian Aramaic as Reflected by the Vocalization of Halakot Pesuqot, Lešonenu 32 (1967—68), pp. 67—88, English Summary, pp. IV—V.
ID., On the Yemenite Tradition of Babylonian Aramaic, Tarbiz 30 (1960—61), pp. 120—129, English Summary, p. II.
ID., Some Notes on the Grammar of Babylonian Aramaic as Reflected in the Geniza Manuscripts, Tarbiz 42 (1972—73), pp. 60—78, English Summary, pp. V—VI.
PRIJS, L., Ergänzungen zum talmudisch-aramäischen Wörterbuch, ZDMG 117 (1967), pp. 266—286.
ROSENBERG, J., Das aramäische Pronomen im babylonischen Talmud, MGWJ 77 (1933), pp. 253—265.
ROSSELL, W. H., A Handbook of Aramaic Magical Texts. Ringwood Borough, New Jersey, 1953.
SCHLESINGER, M., Satzlehre der aramäischen Sprache des babylonischen Talmuds. Leipzig, 1928.
TELEGDI, S., Essai sur la phonétique des emprunts iraniens en Araméen, Journal Asiatique 226 (1935), pp. 177—256.
VON SODEN, W., Aramäische Wörter in neuassyrischen und neu- und spätbabylonischen Texten. Ein Vorbericht, Orientalia n.s. 35 (1966), pp. 1—20.
WEISBERG, DAVID B., Some Observations on Late Babylonian Texts and Rabbinic Literature, HUCA 39 (1968), pp. 71—80.

4. Related Eastern Aramaic Dialects

a) Mandaic

DROWER, E. S. and MACUCH, R., A Mandaic Dictionary. Oxford, 1963.
MACUCH, R., Handbook of Classical and Modern Mandaic. Berlin, 1965.

b) Syriac

BROCKELMANN, C., Lexicon Syriacum³. Hildesheim, 1966.
ID., Syrische Grammatik. Berlin, 1899. Reprint, Leipzig, 1965.
PAYNE SMITH, R., Thesaurus Syriacus. 2 Vols. Oxford, 1879—1901. Supplement. Ed. J. P. MARGOLIOUTH, Oxford. 1927.

c) Modern Eastern Aramaic Dialects

GARBELL, I., The Jewish Neo-Aramaic Dialect of Persian Azerbaijan: Linguistic Analysis and Folkloristic Texts. The Hague, 1965.
RITTER, H., Turoyo. Die Volkssprache der Syrischen Christen des Tur ʿAbdin. 2 Vols. Wiesbaden, 1967—69.
RIVLIN, Y. Y., Shirat Yehude Hattargum. Jerusalem, 1959.
SARA, S. L., A Description of Modern Chaldean. The Hague and Paris, 1971.

5. Dictionaries

BEN YEHUDA, E., Thesaurus totius Hebraitatis. 8 Vols. London and New York, 1960.
DALMAN, G., Aramäisch-neuhebräisches Wörterbuch zu Targum, Talmud und Midrasch. Frankfurt, a. M., 1901. 2nd Ed. 1922.
JASTROW, M., A Dictionary of the Targumim, the Talmud Babli and Yerushalmi, and the Midrashic Literature. 2 Vols. London and New York, 1903. Reprint New York, 1950.
KOHUT, A., Aruch Completum. 8 Vols. Vienna, 1878—92.
ID., Additamenta ad Aruch Completum. Ed. S. KRAUSS. Vienna, 1937.

Krauss, S., Griechische und Lateinische Lehnwörter im Talmud, Midrasch und Targum. 2 Vols. Berlin, 1898—1899. Reprint, Hildesheim, 1964.
Levy, J., Wörterbuch über die Talmudim und Midraschim. 4 Vols. Leipzig, 1875—1889. Reprint, Darmstadt, 1963.
Löw, I., Fauna und Mineralien der Juden. Hildesheim, 1969.
Id., Die Flora der Juden. 4 Vols. Wien und Leipzig, 1926—34.

1. Introduction

In reading BT one comes upon no less than four different dialects. They are Biblical Hebrew (bh), the Hebrew of the Tannaim (mh^1 = Middle $Hebrew^1$), the Hebrew of the Amoraim (mh^2 = Middle $Hebrew^2$), and the Aramaic of the Babylonian Amoraim (bta = Babylonian Talmudic Aramaic)[31]. Two of the four may be ignored here. bh occurs only in quotations from the Bible and mh^1 only in quotations from the Mishnah and other Tannaitic sources. Thus I shall concentrate on mh^2 and bta. Although we still do not have adequate grammars and dictionaries of these dialects, research on them has progressed considerably especially in the past 25 years. Much of that progress is connected with E. Y. Kutscher, whose death at 60 was a serious loss to Talmudic scholarship and semitic studies in general. In his own work, in the projects he initiated, and in the students he trained Kutscher laid the foundation for the recovery of the dialects of rabbinic literature. He himself stressed his dependence on the prior work of H. Yalon, Epstein, and Lieberman. These scholars had shown that the current state of our texts severely hinders study of the latter dialects. Older manuscripts of rabbinic documents reveal linguistic features significantly different from those in the common printed texts. It could be demonstrated that during the 1500 years of transmission the original orthography, morphology, syntax, and lexica of the sources had been changed almost beyond recognition. Oral transmitters (*Tradenten*), copyists, and printers, unaware of the true character of the various linguistic strata, 'corrected' the texts in light of what they believed to be the proper forms. This process was both unconscious (especially with the *Tradenten* and coypists) and conscious (especially with the printers). And it affected all of the rabbinic dialects. Let us take bta as an example. Not only the printed texts, but also most manuscripts of BT lack a written vocalization. Nor is there a uniform traditional pronunciation. By contrast, both Biblical Aramaic and the Aramaic of the targums possess written vocalization

[31] For these terms see Kutscher, Baumgartner-Festschr. For the last named dialect Kutscher uses ja^b = Jewish Aramaic, Babylonian. However, this term includes post-Talmudic Geonic Aramaic (see Kutscher, EJ, III), and by rights should also include the Aramaic of the Jewish incantation texts from Nippur and elsewhere. The term bta has the advantage of referring only to the Aramaic of BT.
Additional dialects of Aramaic are found in BT, e.g., in quotations from the Aramaic sections of the Mishnah, from the Bible targums, and possibly in quotations of Palestinian Amoraim. Since this material is very limited, it may be ignored here. I shall also ignore local sub-dialects of bta, the existence of which is noted by Epstein, Grammar, p. 14.

systems. Consequently, bta was 'corrected' so as to conform to the former, better known dialects. Only with the recognition of this problem could the proper direction of research be determined. The study of the dialects of rabbinic literature must be based on old, linguistically reliable manuscripts, on the traditional pronunciation of the various Jewish communities, and, where available, on epigraphic material contemporary with the sources.

2. The Hebrew of BT

The Hebrew of the Tannaim, mh^1, is at present the best known of the rabbinic dialects. A summary in English of the current state of our knowledge can be found in the article by KUTSCHER in EJ, Vol. 16 (coll. 1595 to 1607 with bibliography at 1659f.; cf. KUTSCHER in: Baumgartner-Festschr. and in Archive I). The Amoraim had already recognized the distinction between bh and mh. In the latter half of the third century the Palestinian Yoḥanan b. Nappaḥa distinguished between *leshon torah*, the language of the Pentateuch, and *leshon ḥakhamim*, the language of the sages (see AZ 58b and cf. Ḥul. 137b; note also the Aramaic equivalents *lishana de'oraita* and *lishana derabbanan* at Qid. 2b). The next step was to distinguish between the mh of the Tannaim and that of the Amoraim. This was done by A. GEIGER in the last century (GEIGER, ZDMG 12 [1858], p. 148). KUTSCHER developed this distinction further, but it remained for his student M. SOKOLOFF to work out in detail the difference between mh^1 and mh^2. His study is based on a linguistically reliable manuscript of Bereshit Rabbah, a Palestinian Amoraic midrash on Genesis. SOKOLOFF's conclusions are as follows. mh^1 is a literary language reflecting the Hebrew spoken during the second century C.E. As is now agreed, Hebrew continued as a spoken language, at least in Judah, during the Second Temple period and into the first centuries of the Common Era. This spoken Hebrew appears beneath the surface of the bh of the later books of the Bible and of the Qumran texts, as well as in the Bar Kosiba documents. By contrast, mh^2 (of the Palestinian sources) is a purely literary dialect composed in the Galil during the third through the sixth centuries, at a place and in a time when Hebrew was not the spoken language. As a result, mh^2 was influenced much more than mh^1 by Aramaic, which was the common spoken dialect. Moreover, mh^2 replaced many of the forms unique to mh^1 by forms from bh (SOKOLOFF, Lešonenu, 277f., and cf. 26f.).

As noted above, SOKOLOFF details the differences between mh^1 and mh^2 as reflected in Palestinian sources. KUTSCHER argues that we must further distinguish the mh^2 of Palestinian sources (mh^2p) from that appearing in BT (mh^2b). Structurally the two sub-dialects are identical. The Hebrew of BT also drops mh^1 forms in favor of those from bh, and it also is colored by Aramaic. However the dialects of Aramaic involved are different. mh^2p was influenced by Galilean Aramaic, mh^2b by bta (KUTSCHER, Baumgartner-Festschr., pp. 164—168, cf. H. L. GINSBERG, MGWJ 77, for the distinction between Palestinian and Babylonian mh). Unfortunately we do not yet have a study of mh^{2}b parallel to that of Sokoloff on mh^{2}p. Writing in 1972 Kutscher noted that no linguistically reliable manuscripts of the Hebrew of BT had been identified (EJ 16, col. 1594, cf. 1607; see also Baumgartner-Festschr., pp. 165f. and Archive I, p. 16). Since then the situation has improved. The key so far has been the *baraitot* (singular: *baraita*) appearing in BT. *Baraita*, an abbreviation of *matnita baraita*, 'external Tannaitic tradition', designates all the Tannaitic sources external to the Mishnah of Yehudah the Patriarch. The term thus applies to materials in the Tannaitic collections such as the 'Tosefta' and the halakhic midrashim as well as the apparently Tannaitic sources cited in the two Talmuds. Reversing his earlier position, Kutscher argued that the Hebrew of the BT *baraitot* is significantly different from that found in the Tannaitic collections (Archive I, pp. 40, 45). Another one of his students, M. Moreshet studied this difference. In a series of articles Moreshet compares BT *baraitot* with their parallels in Tannaitic collections and in the Palestinian Talmud. He concludes that while the language of the latter materials is essentially identical to that of the Mishnah, that of the former is not. Thus within mh^{1} also we must differentiate a Babylonian sub-dialect (mh^{1}b) from the Palestinian (mh^{1}p). What distinguishes mh^{1}b is the influence of mh^{2}b. In other words, by listing the unique features of mh^{1}b Moreshet in effect has begun to describe mh^{2}b. It is to be hoped that he will continue with a direct study of the latter. The identification of certain manuscripts of BT as linguistically reliable, such as MS Columbia of Pes., will facilitate such a project. In the meantime the articles of E. Margaliyot and Abramson and the relevant chapters in Bendavid may be consulted. Pending further research, the Hebrew of the Babylonian Amoraim remains the least known of the dialects of rabbinic literature.

3. Babylonian Talmudic Aramaic

The Amoraim recognized that Babylonian Aramaic differs from Palestinian (see, e. g., Ned. 66b). Modern semitic studies agree and locate bta, along with Syriac and Mandaic in the Eastern branch of what Fitzmyer calls "late Aramaic"[32]. Modern study of bta begins in 1865 with the publication of the first grammar of the dialect. Two more grammars appeared in the period covered by Strack's bibliography. The one grammar that has been published since, that by Epstein, is by far the best. Unlike his predecessors, Epstein made extensive use of manuscripts of BT as well as of cognate dialects. The latter include not only Syriac and Mandaic, but also the language of the Jewish incantation texts and of Geonic literature. In a major review (Lešonenu 26, pp. 149—183), Kutscher asserts that Epstein's work is "the only scientific grammar of Babylonian Aramaic

[32] See J. A. Fitzmyer, The Genesis Apocryphon of Qumran Cave I^{2} (Rome, 1971), pp. 22f., n. 60.

that we have", (p. 170, cf. EJ 3, col. 279). Nevertheless, continues KUTSCHER, even this book, composed of posthumously published lecture notes, does not fill the need for a grammar of bta. He lists three major inadequacies in this book. 1. The grammar lacks both a phonology and a syntax, though for the latter we can rely on the excellent study of M. SCHLESINGER. 2. The vocalization is neither systematic nor consistent. 3. The morphology, which comprises the bulk of the book does exploit the manuscript evidence. However, EPSTEIN's use of the latter is sporadic and inconsistent (for all these points see Lešonenu, pp. 151—171). The last point is the most important. KUTSCHER argues that eclectic reliance on the manuscripts is improper. We cannot record forms now from this manuscript, now from that, and then a third time from the printed text — as EPSTEIN does. Rather, we must rely only on those few manuscripts which can be identified as linguistically reliable. This method brought excellent results in research on mh^1 and Galilean Aramaic (cf. 'Baumgartner-Festschr.'). The question is, of course, how do we determine which manuscripts are reliable. For the Palestinian dialects epigraphic evidence provided the key. We have no parallel evidence for bta, for the incantation texts reflect a different dialect. KUTSCHER believes that the solution lies in Geonic texts. These were composed shortly after BT in the same geographical location by native speakers of Aramaic. Although Geonic Aramaic is not identical with bta, it is very close. Moreover, almost all Geonic sources quote extensively from BT. Thus the first step must be to identify linguistically reliable manuscripts of Geonic texts and construct a grammar of the BT quotations appearing there. On the basis of this work we should then be able to identify linguistically reliable manuscripts of BT itself. Eventually, as our results are refined, we shall be able to distinguish bta from the Geonic dialect. Another approach involves studying the traditional pronunciation of bta by various Jewish communities. This method also produced results in the study of mh^1 and Galilean Aramaic. Both of these approaches have been followed. KUTSCHER identified two linguistically reliable manuscripts of Geonic texts. One is MS Sassoon of 'Halakhot Pesuqot'. Apparently based on a *Vorlage* copied by a native speaker of Babylonian Aramaic, it exhibits a full orthography and a grammatical accuracy (e. g. agreement in number and gender of nouns and adjectives, subjects and verbs) lacking in our common printed texts of BT. The second is MS Paris of 'Halakhot Gedolot'. Both of these manuscripts partially vocalize the BT quotations. On the basis of the linguistic picture emerging from the latter KUTSCHER notes that Codex Hamburg Neziqin and MS Columbia Pes. appear to be fairly reliable and may serve for further research. M. BEN-ASHER, another student of KUTSCHER, has begun a study of bta in MS Sassoon, and S. MORAG has begun to research the traditional pronunciation of the Yemenite community. Thus the research program outlined by KUTSCHER is being carried out. Till it is completed, the grammar of EPSTEIN may be consulted, though it should be used together with the review by KUTSCHER. The latter also contributed a short sketch of bta grammar in English in EJ 3 (coll. 279f.).

Examples of texts in bta from linguistically reliable manuscripts together with a glossary compiled by KUTSCHER can be found in ROSENTHAL's 'Aramaic Handbook'.

4. Lexicography

Lexicographical study of rabbinic dialects begins with the Amoraim and continues in the commentaries of the *ge'onim* and *rishonim*. The earliest dictionary of rabbinic literature is the "Arukh' compiled during the eleventh century by Natan b. Yeḥi'el of Rome (p. e. Rome, before 1475; this may be the oldest printed Hebrew book[33]). As KUTSCHER notes (EJ 3, col. 278), the "Arukh' set two trends followed by all later dictionaries. It treats together all the dialects and sources of rabbinic literatures, and it uses a comparative method, adducing Arabic, Persian, Greek, and Latin evidence. In the course of the following centuries several scholars contributed additions and supplements to the "Arukh'. The next independent dictionary to appear was that of LEVY. It is still the best available. A few years later A. KOHUT published a critical edition of the "Arukh' to which he added extensive complementary material. The result is, in effect, a new dictionary, but one with several drawbacks. KOHUT retained the original order of entries. Since the latter was not based on the modern concept of Hebrew grammar, it often is difficult to locate the desired root. A more serious problem results from KOHUT's attempt, in principle praiseworthy, fully to exploit Iranian evidence. Unfortunately, he wrote at a time when modern Iranology was in its early stages. Moreover KOHUT is guilty of a kind of pan-Iranism in that he seeks Iranian etymologies even for obviously semitic words. His limited knowledge of Iranian languages and his farfetched etymologies are largely corrected in the 'Additamenta' to his dictionary edited by S. KRAUSS. A highly competent Iranist, B. GEIGER, was responsible for these corrections as well as for the addition of Akkadian, Arabic, and Mandaic evidence. Shortly after the appearance of KOHUT's work M. JASTROW published his dictionary. The main deficiency in this effort is JASTROW's attempt to find semitic etymologies for words obviously of Greek or Latin origin. The corrective here is to be found in KRAUSS' 'Griechische und lateinische Lehnwörter' and in the many studies of SAUL LIEBERMAN, especially 'Greek in Jewish Palestine' (New York, 1942) and 'Hellenism in Jewish Palestine' (New York, 1950). Finally mention should be made of the specialized lexicographical studies by the brilliant semitist I. Löw[34].

The dates of publication of the dictionaries of LEVY, KOHUT, and JASTROW indicate that these works must be superseded, even were they free

[33] M. MARX, On the Date of the Apearance of the first printed Hebrew Books, A. Marx Jubilee Volume, English Section (New York, 1950), pp. 481—501. MARX dates it to 1469—72.

[34] I have not listed G. DALMAN's 'Aramäisch-neuhebräisches Handwörterbuch zu Targum, Talmud und Midrasch' (Frankfurt a. M., 1901) which is inadequate for use with BT.

from faults. In the past century the study of the dialects of rabbinic literature, of cognate dialects, and of semitic linguistics generally has made great strides. KUTSCHER estimates that the work of his predecessors and older contemporaries, DALMAN, LÖW, YALON, EPSTEIN, and LIEBERMAN, already requires the addition of over 6000 entries to the existing dictionaries. This number constitutes 20% of the lexicon of rabbinic literature according to KUTSCHER (Archive I, pp. 13, 17). The additional lexicographical material which has become available since the publication of the dictionaries may be illustrated for bta. First, many manuscripts and especially Genizah fragments of BT were not available to LEVY, KOHUT, and JASTROW. Second, most of Geonic literature with its closely related dialect has been published only in the last century. Third, while some incantation texts were published in the nineteenth century, only with the appearance of MONTGOMERY's 'Aramaic Incantation Texts from Nippur' could serious study of the language of these texts begin. Fourth, in the past fifty years many new Mandaic texts have been published, and recently a new dictionary and grammar of this closely related dialect appeared. Fifth, further work has been done in this period on modern spoken dialects of Eastern Aramaic. Sixth, Iranology has progressed considerably not only since KOHUT, but also since B. GEIGER and TELEGDI. An up to date study of Iranian influences on bta is a desideratum. Seventh, and finally, study of Akkadian has also advanced. Especially relevant is the increasing recognition of the mutual relation between Akkadian and Aramaic. In bta, spoken in what had been a center of Akkadian culture, we can expect significant Akkadian influence. Recent studies on this issue include those of VON SODEN, S. A. KAUFMAN, and D. B. WEISBERG. The latter two especially deal with bta. Research in all seven of the areas listed will require major revisions in the existing lexica of BT.

The situation described above with regard to bta applies, mutatis mutandis, to the other dialects of rabbinic literature. Clearly the existing dictionaries are out of date and inadequate. KUTSCHER initiated a project aimed at producing a new dictionary of rabbinic literature incorporating recent research and differentiated according to dialects. Completion of this project is obviously not a matter of the immediate future. Its progress and the results of recent lexicographical studies may be followed in the publication of the project, 'Archive of the New Dictionary of Rabbinic Literature'.

IV. Source, Form, and Redaction Criticism

Bibliography

ALBECK, CH. [Ḥ], Introduction to the Talmud, Babli and Yerushalmi. Tel Aviv, 1969.

ID., Le'arikhat Hattalmud Habbavli, Tarbiz 15 (1943/44), pp. 14—26. [= Introduction, Chapter 9.]

ID., Le'arikat Hattalmud Habbavli, Studies in Memory of A. Gulak and S. Klein, Jerusalem, 1942, pp. 1—12.

ID., Leḥeqer Hattalmud: 1. Sugyot Uma'amarim Shenithavu 'Al Yide Ha'ataqot Mimaqom Lemaqom, Tarbiz 3 (1931/32), pp. 1—14. [= Introduction, Chapter 7.]

ID., Leḥeqer Hattalmud: 2. Hishtamshut Bema'amare Ha'amora'im, Tarbiz 9 (1937/38), pp. 163—178.

ID., Nusḥa'ot Bammishnah Shel Ha'amora'im, Abhandlungen zur Erinnerung an H. P. Chajes, Wien, 1933, pp. 1—28.

ID., Sof Hora'ah Visiyyum Hattalmud, Sinai: Sefer Yovel, Jerusalem, 1958, pp. 73—79.

ALBECK, S., Sof Hora'ah Ve'aḥarone Ha'amora'im, Sinai: Sefer Yovel, Jerusalem, 1958, pp. 57—73.

AMINOAH, N., The Redaction of the Tractate Qiddushin in the Babylonian Talmud. Compilation, Redaction, Textual Readings, Parallel Sugyot. Tel Aviv, 1977.

ATLAS, S., On the History of the Sugya, HUCA 24 (1952/53), pp. 1—22.

ID., Leḥeqer Hattalmud, M. Schorr Jubilee Volume, Warsaw, 1935, pp. 9—17.

ID., Some Observations on the Nature of the Amoraic Discussions, Studies in Memory of M. Schorr, New York, 1944, pp. 1—11.

BACHER, W., Die exegetische Terminologie der jüdischen Traditionsliteratur, I—II. Leipzig, 1899—1905. Reprint, Darmstadt, 1965.

ID., Tradition und Tradenten in den Schulen Palästinas und Babyloniens. Leipzig, 1914.

BOKSER, B., Samuel's Commentary on the Mishnah. Its Nature, Forms, and Content. Part One: Mishnayot in the Order of Zeraim. Leiden, 1975.

DE VRIES, B., The form of the Ancient Sugya. (A Chapter from the Problems of the Creation of the Talmud.), Bar Ilan 4—5 (1967) pp. 67—88, English Summary, pp. XXXVII—XXXVIII. [= Studies, Part II, Chapter 1.]

ID., Hamminuaḥ Betalmud Bavli, Lešonenu 29 (1964/65), pp. 160—166. [= Studies, Part II, Chapter 4.]

ID., Literary Transfer as a Factor in the Development of Talmudic Law, Bar Ilan 1 (1963), pp. 156—164, English Summary, p. XXXV.

ID., Meqoman Hammeqori Shel Sugyot Bavliot Messuyyamot, Sinai 58 (1966), pp. 17—24. [= Studies, Part II, Chapter 6.]

ID., The Problem of the Relationship of the Two Talmuds to the Tosefta, Tarbiz 28 (1958/59), pp. 158—170, English Summary, pp. III—IV.

ID., Studies in Talmudic Literature. Jerusalem, 1968.

ID., Ṣuratan Hammeqorit Shel Sugyot Bavliot 'Aḥadot, Y. I. Herzog Memorial Volume, Jerusalem, 1962, pp. 483—492. [= Studies Part II, Chapter 7.]

ID., The Talmudic Formula wtw l' mydy, Tarbiz 37 (1967/68) pp. 30—38, English Summary, p. IV. [= Studies, Part II, Chapter 3.]

ID., The Tractate Me'ila in the Babylonian Talmud, Tarbiz 30 (1960/61), pp. 370—378, English Summary, pp. II—III. [= Studies, Part II, Chapter 5.]

ID., WeHawaynan Ba, Tarbiz 35 (1965/66), pp. 254—268, English Summary, p. IV. [= Studies, Part II, Chapter 2.]

DOR, Z., Hammeqorot Ha'ereṣyisra'eliyyim Bevet Midrasho Shel Rava, Sinai 52 (1962), pp. 128—144, 53 (1963), pp. 31—49. 55 (1964), pp. 306—316. [= Teachings, Chapter 1.]

ID., On the Sources of Gittin in the Babylonian Talmud, Bar Ilan 4—5 (1967), pp. 89—103, English Summary, pp. XXXIX—XLI.

ID., The Palestinian Sources appearing in the Tractate Gittin of the Babylonian Talmud, Bar Ilan 1 (1963), pp. 120—142, English Summary, pp. XXVII—XX. [= Teachings, Appendix II.]

ID., The Teachings of Eretz Israel in Babylon. Tel Aviv, 1971.

EPHRATI, J. E., Contributions of Succeeding Generations to a Sugya in Bava Metzia, Bar Ilan 6 (1968), pp. 75—100, English Summary pp. XVII—XVIII.

ID., The Sevoraic Period and its Literature. Petach-Tikva, 1973.

EPSTEIN, J. [Y.] N., Introduction to Amoraitic Literature. Babylonian Talmud and Yerushalmi. Jerusalem, 1962. [= IAL.]

Id., Introduction to Tannaitic Literature. Mishna, Tosephta and Halakhic Midrashim. Jerusalem, 1957. [= ITL.]
Id., Introduction to the Text of the Mishnah². Jerusalem, 1964. [= ITM.]
Feldblum, M. S., The Impact of the 'Anonymous Sugyah' on Halakic Concepts, PAAJR 38 (1969), pp. 19—28.
Id., Professor Abraham Weiss: His Approach and Contribution to Talmudic Scholarship, A. Weiss Jubilee Volume, New York, 1965, pp. 7—80.
Id., Talmudic Law and Literature, Tractate Gittin. New York, 1969.
Francus, I., Additions and Parallels in T. B. Bava Qamma VII, Bar Ilan 12 (1974), pp. 43—63, English Summary, p. IX.
Friedman, Sh., Glosses and Additions in TB Bava Qamma VIII, Tarbiz 40 (1970), pp. 418—443, English Summary, pp. III—IV.
Id., A Critical Study of Yevamot X with a Methodological Introduction, Meḥqarim Umeqorot. Measef Lemada'e Hayahadut, New York, 1978, pp. 277—441.
Id., Some Structural Patterns of Talmudic Sugyot, Proceedings of the Sixth World Congress of Jewish Studies, Vol. III, Jerusalem, 1977, pp. 389—402.
Gevirtsman, M., ''Ela 'I 'Ittamar Hakhi 'Ittamar' Betalmud Bavli, Sinai 69 (1971), pp. 110—122.
Id., Ṣiṭuṭim Be'ezrat ''Ittamar', Sinai 67 (1970), pp. 43—55.
Ginzberg, L., A Commentary on the Palestinian Talmud, Vol. I. New York, 1941.
Goldberg, A., On the Development of the Sugya in the Babylonian Talmud, H. Albeck Jubilee Volume, Jerusalem, 1963, pp. 101—113.
Id., Palestinian Law in Babylonian Tradition as Revealed in a Study of Perek Arvei Pesahim (Trac. Pesahim Chap. X), Tarbiz, 33 (1963/64), pp. 337—348, English Summary, pp. I—II.
Id., The Sources and Development of the Sugya in the Babylonian Talmud, Tarbiz 32 (1962/63), pp. 143—152, English Summary, pp. III—V.
Id., The use of the Tosefta and the Baraitha of the School of Samuel by the Babylonian Amora Rava for the Interpretation of the Mishnah, Tarbiz 40 (1970/71), pp. 144—157, English Summary, pp. II—III.
Halivni (Weiss), D., Review of 'The Formation of the Babylonian Talmud', JAAR 41 (1973), pp. 260—263.
Id., Sources and Traditions. A Source Critical Commentary on Seder Nashim. Tel Aviv, 1968. [= ST.]
Id., Sources and Traditions. A Source Critical Commentary on the Talmud Seder Moed from Yoma to Hagiga. Jerusalem, 1975. [= ST.]
Id., Talmud: Source Criticism, Encyclopedia Britannica, 1963, Vol. XXI, p. 645 = 1972, Vol. XXI, p. 645.
Jacobs, L., Are There Fictitious Baraitot in the Babylonian Talmud?, HUCA 42 (1971), pp. 185—196.
Id., How Much of the Babylonian Talmud is Pseudepigraphic?, JJS 28 (1977), pp. 46—59.
Kahan, K., Ed., Seder Tannaim we Amoraim. Frankfurt a. M., 1935.
Kahana, I. Z., 'Rules for Decisions' Found in the Babylonian Talmud, Sinai 6 (1939/40), pp. 336—343.
Kaplan, J., The Redaction of the Babylonian Talmud. New York, 1933.
Klein, H., Gemara and Sebara, JQR 38 (1947/48), pp. 67—91. [= GS.]
Id., Gemara Quotations in Sebara, JQR 43 (1952/53), pp. 341—363. [= GQS.]
Id., The Significance of the Technical Expression 'l' 'y 'ytmr hky 'ytmr in the Babylonian Talmud, Tarbiz 31 (1961), pp. 23—42.
Id., Some General Results of the Separation of Gemara from Sebara in the Babylonian Talmud, JSemSt 3 (1958), pp. 363—372. [= SGR.]
Id., Some Methods of Sebara, JQR 50 (1959/60), pp. 124—146. [= SMS.]
Lewin, B. M., Rabbanan Savora'e Vetalmudam. Jerusalem, 1937.
Lewin, B. M., Ed., Iggeret R. Scherira Gaon. Haifa, 1921. Reprint, Jerusalem, 1972.
Lewy, I., Interpretation des 1.—6. Abschnittes des palästinischen Talmud-tractates Nesikin, Jahresbericht des jüdisch-theologischen Seminars. Breslau, 1895—1914.

Melammed, E. Z., An Introduction to Talmudic Literature. Jerusalem, 1973.
Mirsky, S. K. Types of Lectures in the Babylonian Academies, Essays and Studies on Jewish Life and Thought, New York, 1959, pp. 375—402.
Neusner, J., Ed., The Formation of the Babylonian Talmud. Studies in the Achievements of Late Nineteenth and Twentieth Century Historical and Literary-Critical Research. Leiden, 1970.
Rabinowitz, Z. W., Sha'are Torath Babel. Notes and Comments on the Babylonian Talmud. Jerusalem, 1961.
Regensberg, H. D., 'Al 'Arikhat Hattalmudim, Gibbeath Saul: Essays . . . in Honor of Saul Silber, Chicago, 1935, pp. 124—128.
Rosenthal, D., Pirqa De 'Abbaye (TB Rosh Ha' Shana II), Tarbiz 46 (1977), pp. 97—109, English Summary, p. III.
Rosenthal, E. S., Hammoreh, PAAJR 31 (1963), Hebrew Section, pp. 1—71.
Id., Leshemu'at Happetiḥah Shel Bavli Ta'anit, Y. Friedman Memorial Volume, Jerusalem, 1974, pp. 237—248.
Rubinstein, S. M., Leḥeqer Siddur Hattalmud. Kovno, 1932.
Saldarini, A. J., Form Criticism of Rabbinic Literature, JBL 96 (1977), pp. 257—274.
Schachter, M., The Babylonian and Jerusalem Mishnah textually compared. Jerusalem, 1959.
Id., Babylonian-Palestinian Variations in the Mishna, JQR 42 (1951/52) pp. 1—35.
Tennenblatt, M. A., The Formation of the Babylonian Talmud. A Historical and Textual Study. Tel Aviv, 1972.
Weinberg, Y. J., Meḥqarim Battalmud, I. Berlin, 1938.
Weis, P. R., The Controversies of Rab and Samuel and the Tosefta, JSemSt 3 (1958), pp. 288—297.
Weiss, A., The Development of the Talmud as a Literary Unit [Hithavut Hattalmud Bishlemuto]. New York, 1943. [= DTLU.]
Id., Hattalmud Habbavli Behithavuto Hassifrutit. I. Hemmemra. Warsaw, 1937. II. Hassugya. Warsaw, 1939.
Id., Die Herkunft und Entstehungszeit des Talmud-traktats Tamid, MGWJ 83 (1939), pp. 261—276.
Id., The Literary Activities of the Saboraim. A Lecture Held at the Hebrew University, December 31, 1952. Jerusalem, 1953.
Id., Leqorot Hithavut Habbavli. Warsaw, 1929. Reprint, Jerusalem, n. d.
Id., Meḥqarim Battalmud. Jerusalem, 1975.
Id., Meqomah Haqqadum Shel Hammemra, M. Schorr Jubilee Volume, Warsaw, 1935, pp. 39—75.
Id., Notes to Talmudic Pericopae. Bar Ilan University, n. d.
Id., Le problème de la rédaction du Talmud de Babylone par R. Aši à la lumière de la Lettre de Serîra, REJ 102 (1937), pp. 105—114.
Id., Studien zur Redaktion des babylonischen Talmuds, MGWJ 73 (1929), pp. 131—143, 184—211. [= Meḥqarim, Chapter 5.]
Id., Studies in the Literature of the Amoraim ['Al Hayyeṣirah Hassifrutit Shel Ha'amora'im]. New York, 1962. [= SLA.]
Id., The Talmud in its Development [Leḥeqer Hattalmud]. New York, 1954. [= TD.]
Zeitlin, S., Hammishnah Shebayyerushalmi Vehammishnah Shebabbavli, Z. Shazar Jubilee Volume, Jerusalem, 1973, pp. 539—548.
Zussman, J., Babylonian Sugyot to the Order Zera'im and Tehorot. Unpublished Ph. D. Dissertation, Hebrew University, 1961. In press, Israel Academy of Sciences and Humanities.

The terms which appear in the title of this section are borrowed from classical philology and Biblical studies. They have generally not been used by students of rabbinic literature. Conscious application and adaption of these methods to rabbinic documents began only recently[35]. Nevertheless, studies which may be subsumed under these headings have been carried out since the beginning of the study of BT, even by the Amoraim within BT itself. More important, use of these categories should make what follows more accessible to those unfamiliar with Talmud studies. My attempt to impose them on scholarship organized according to different principles results in a certain amount of repetition. Hopefully the gain in clarity outweighs the loss from redundancy.

1. Source Criticism

a) The Palestinian Sources

The Babylonian Talmud, despite its name, contains a large number of sources of Palestinian provenance. These may be subdivided into Tannaitic and Amoraic materials. BT generally, though not always, introduces its Tannaitic sources with special superscriptions. Most of the latter derive from the root *tny*, such as *tenan, tanya, teno rabbanan*, etc. (see ALBECK, Introduction pp. 21—27, 28, 44—47; EPSTEIN, ITM, pp. 74—163, 803—897; MELAMMED Introduction, pp. 258f.; and cf. BACHER, Ex. Term., II, pp. 238—241). Even without superscription Tannaitic material stands out from its context in BT. It is almost entirely in Hebrew while the Amoraic material is often in Aramaic. It mentions only early masters, the Tannaim. Moreover many of the Tannaitic sources cited in BT appear in other documents. The most important of those documents is, of course, the Mishnah of Yehudah the Patriarch. As noted above, BT is primarily a commentary on the Mishnah[36]. Both the manuscripts and printed editions of BT include a complete text of the Mishnah presented chapter by chapter or paragraph by paragraph. However, the appearance of a complete text together with BT is a late phenomenon. This fact emerges from the differences between the text of the Mishnah placed before the Gemara and the

[35] J. N. EPSTEIN inaugurated the application of source criticism to Tannaitic sources and to BT. Form criticism was applied by Y. HEINEMANN to rabbinic liturgical texts and by W. S. TOWNER to one of the halakhic midrashim. The most extensive application and adaptation of these methods in rabbinic scholarship is that by J. NEUSNER, Development of a Legend. Studies on the Traditions Concerning Yoḥanan b. Zakkai (Leiden, 1970), ID., Eliezer Ben Hyrcanus, 2 Vols. (Leiden, 1973), and ID., History of the Mishnaic Law of Purities, Vols I—XXII (Leiden, 1974—78). See now the discussion of SALDARINI.

[36] For the methodology of the Amoraic commentary on the Mishnah see J. FORSHEIM, Rav Ḥisda as Exegetor of Tannaitic Sources, Tarbiz 41 (1971/72) pp. 24—48, English Summary, pp. III—IV; J. FRAENKEL, Ha Gufa Qashya. Internal Contradictions in Talmudic Literature, Tarbiz 42 (72/73), pp. 266—301, English Summary, pp. II—III; S. K. MIRSKY, The Mishnah as Viewed by the Amoraim, Leo Jung Jubilee Volume (New York, 1962), pp. 155—174; J. J. WEINBERG, Studies on Talmudic Commentaries to the Mishnah, Talpioth 6 (1955), pp. 606—636; M. ZUCKER, Ha'Ḥassore Meḥassera' Battalmud, Minḥat Bikkurim ... leAryeh Schwarz (Vienna, 1926), pp. 47—53; MELAMMED, Introduction, pp. 330—394; and EPSTEIN, ITM, pp. 166—672.

citations and rubrics from the Mishnah cited in the body of the Gemara (see EPSTEIN, ITM, pp. 923—927). Originally BT contained only abbreviated citations of the Mishnah paragraph about to be discussed in the Gemara (ibid., pp. 827—921). In addition fuller citations appear where necessary for the discussion (ibid., pp. 771—803 and cf. 803—864; ALBECK, Chajes Mem. Vol.). The study of these rubrics and citations is important primarily for the history of the text of the Mishnah[37]. Still, establishing which text of the latter document lies behind a given pericope of Gemara is often crucial to understanding the BT, as HALIVNI stresses in his commentary. For our purposes it is sufficient to note that the Mishnah, often in a version different from what appears in the separate editions or even from what appears at the head of the Gemara, is a major source of BT.

A second set of Tannaitic sources comprises those traditions not included in the Mishnah of Yehudah the Patriarch. These are the Baraitot. Here some distinctions must be made. We possess several collections of Baraitot: the 'Tosefta', 'Mekhilta Derabbi Yishma''el', 'Mekhilta Derabbi Shim'on b. Yoḥai', 'Sifra', 'Sifre Bemidbar', 'Sifre Zuṭṭa', 'Sifre Devarim', and 'Midrash Tanna'im'[38]. Many BT Baraitot closely parallel texts appearing in these collections. Other BT Baraitot have parallels in the Palestinian Talmud. Finally, some are not paralleled elsewhere. Each group of materials poses a separate set of literary-historical problems. Regarding the first group, the problem is the relation between the BT Baraitot and the extant Tannaitic collections. Were the latter known to the Babylonian Amoraim? Or did the Amoraim cite the Baraitot from other sources? The parallels are often very close, sometimes identical. Yet frequently there are significant differences between the BT version and that in the collection. More striking, BT often ignores sources found in the collections which are relevant to discussions in the Gemara. Complicating the issue is the fact that BT mentions 'Tosefta', 'Sifra', and 'Sifre' by name (e. g., Meg. 28b, Qid. 49b, Sanh. 86a, Shev. 41b; the term *mekhilta* also appears, but not as the name of a book, see EPSTEIN, ITL, p. 545). Does BT refer here to the collections we know by these names? Scholarly opinion is divided on this issue. ALBECK argues that since BT ignores relevant sources in 'Tosefta' and the halakhic midrashim, it could not have known the latter

[37] On the differences between the texts of the Mishnah in BT and in the Palestinian Talmud see EPSTEIN, ITM, pp. 921—923, 932, 1275, and cf. 706—726; M. SCHACHTER, Babylonian-Palestinian Variations in the Mishna, JQR 42 (1951/52), pp. 1—35; S. ZEITLIN, Hammishnah Shebayerushalmi Vehammishnah Shebabavli, Z. Shazar Jubilee Volume (Jerusalem, 1973), pp. 539—548.

[38] Tosefta, ed. M. S. ZUCKERMANDEL, Repr. Jerusalem, 1963; ed. S. LIEBERMAN, Vols. I—V, New York, 1955—1962. Mechilta D'Rabbi Ismael, ed. H. S. HOROVITZ and I. A. RABIN, Jerusalem, 1960. Mekhilta D'Rabbi Šim'on b. Jochai, ed. J. N. EPSTEIN and E. Z. MELAMMED, Jerusalem, 1955. Sifra deve Rav, ed. I. H. WEISS, Vienna, 1862. Siphre D'Be Rab. Siphre ad Numeros adjecto Siphre zutta, ed. H. S. HOROVITZ, Repr. Jerusalem, 1966. Sifre on Deuteronomy, ed. L. FINKELSTEIN, 2nd. edition, New York, 1969. Midrash Tannaim on Deuteronomy, ed. D. S. HOFFMAN, 2 Vols., Repr. Tel Aviv, n.d.

documents. The BT Baraitot are taken from sources other than the extant collections (ALBECK, Introduction, p. 67 re Tosefta, pp. 105—129 re halakhic midrashim). EPSTEIN takes the opposite position. He notes that BT also ignores relevant sections of the Mishnah in its discussions. Obviously this does not mean that the Amoraim did not know the Mishnah. Similarly, ignoring sections of the Tannaitic collections cannot prove BT did not know them. As for the differences between the BT Baraitot and their parallels, EPSTEIN explains that the Amoraim knew the collections in slightly different, earlier recensions (EPSTEIN, ITL, p. 246 re Tosefta, and pp. 547, 609f., 615, 663, 666, 674 re halakhic midrashim; cf. MELAMMED, Introduction, pp. 262, 267). To a certain extent, the debate revolves around semantics. What is the border line between a different recension and a different collection of parallel sources? DE VRIES discusses this issue, and he finally arrives at a position closer to ALBECK than to EPSTEIN (DE VRIES, Tarbiz 30). Other scholars adopt a middle position. With regard to 'Tosefta', P. R. WEIS and A. GOLDBERG suggest that some Amoraim knew these collections and some did not (WEIS, JSemSt, argues that Rava used 'Tosefta', but Samuel did not; GOLDBERG, Tarbiz 40, claims Rava used it). A. WEISS also maintains that the authors of some pericopae knew them, and the authors of others did not (WEISS, SLA, pp. 169—171). S. LIEBERMAN, whose monumental commentary on 'Tosefta' discusses at length the BT parallels to this document, is perhaps best equipped to decide whether the Amoraim used our 'Tosefta'. However, he has yet to express his view on this question[39]. In the last analysis the issue is more relevant to the history of Tannaitic literature than to that of BT. Whether or not the Babylonian Amoraim knew the extant Tannaitic collections, they obviously had at their disposal compilations of Tannaitic sources. Some of those compilations bore the same name as the extant collections; others bore different names, e. g., *tanna deve R. Yishma"el* (cf. ALBECK, Introduction, pp. 36—43; EPSTEIN, ITM, pp. 153—163, ITL, pp. 551, 562—565, 589—597, 630, 705, 708; MELAMMED, Introduction, pp. 258—277).

The second group of BT Baraitot, those with parallels only in the Palestinian Talmud, have attracted less attention (see MELAMMED, Introduction, pp. 258—274). The parallels in the Palestinian Talmud establish the Palestinian provenance of these materials, and they are probably genuine Tannaitic sources. The BT Baraitot without parallel elsewhere are more problematic. Are they of Tannaitic origin? Or are they 'fictitious', i. e., composed by Babylonian Amoraim on the model of the genuine Baraitot? Doubts concerning their provenance arise because many of these sources appear in one place in BT with Baraita superscription and in another place as Amoraic statements (see MELAMMED, Introduction, pp. 407—412; ALBECK, Introduction, pp. 46—49). The suggestion that these Baraitot are 'fictitious' was first advanced by I. H. WEISS in the last century[40].

[39] See ROSENTHAL's attempt to ascertain the position of LIEBERMAN, Hammoreh, pp. 52—56.
[40] I. H. WEISS, Dor Dor Vedorshav (Repr. Tel Aviv, n.d.), Vol. II, pp. 242—244.

Recent opponents of this view include A. WEISS (A. WEISS, TD, pp. 35 to 63). ALBECK and MELAMMED admit that Amoraic interpolations appear in originally Tannaitic sources (ALBECK, Introduction, pp. 28, 34f.; MELAMMED, Introduction, p. 274). ALBECK is willing to go farther. He concedes that some Baraitot are 'new', i. e., post-Tannaitic — but only slightly later than the genuine Baraitot (ALBECK, pp. 47—50). L. JACOBS, after reviewing the various arguments, concludes that "occasionally the redactors [of BT] did use fictitious Baraitot for the purposes of literary device and as a pedagogic means" (JACOBS, HUCA 42, p. 196). The linguistic studies of MORESHET might solve this problem. If certain Baraitot turn out to be entirely in mh²b, rather than merely 'contaminated' by the latter dialect, then it is likely that they are of Babylonian Amoraic provenance. The present writer has argued, also on linguistic grounds, that certain BT Baraitot are not of Palestinian origin[41]. In conclusion, it seems probable that at least some of the unparalleled BT Baraitot are not Tannaitic.

BT also contains Palestinian Amoraic sources. Some of the latter are introduced by special formulae such as *'amri bama'arava*, "they say/explain in the West," *maḥakho 'alah bama'arava*, "they laughed at it in the West," and others. Other formulae refer to scholars, *nāḥotē*, "those who go down", sc. from Palestine to Babylonia. These masters travelled back and forth between the two countries, presumably on business trips, and transmitted traditions from one center to the other. The materials they brought are introduced by *ki 'ata X 'amar*, "when X came, he said". BT also reports on letters exchanged between Palestine and Babylonia (on all these see the sources collected by EPSTEIN, IAL, pp. 293—312, MELAMMED, Introduction, pp. 442—447, 559—561, and BACHER, Trad. u. Trad., pp. 506—520). The largest category of Palestinian Amoraic sources in BT is not set off by special formulae. I refer to the statements of Palestinian masters (see BACHER, Trad. u. Trad., pp. 327—331, 369—394). Finally, scholars note pericopae appearing with minor variations in both Talmuds (EPSTEIN, IAL, loc. cit., MELAMMED, pp. 447—451). The *ge'onim* and *rishonim* explained this phenomenon by asserting that BT knew and used the completed Palestinian Talmud. Today it is recognized that this claim is part of the Babylonian propaganda in favor of the hegemony of BT. Modern scholars agree that at most BT knew earlier recensions of our Palestinian Talmud (for the older claim see EPSTEIN, IAL, pp. 290f., GINZBERG, Commentary, I., pp. 84—86, and MELAMMED, pp. 556—558; in recent times only HALEVY defended this view — for the modern opinion see EPSTEIN, pp. 291f., GINZBERG, pp. 86f., and MELAMMED, pp. 558f.). Recent work concentrates on the detailed study of Palestinian Amoraic materials in BT. The research of A. GOLDBERG (Tarbiz 33) and especially Z. DOR illustrates this trend.

[41] D. GOODBLATT, Rabbinic Instruction in Sasanian Babylonia (Leiden, 1975), p. 73.

b) The Babylonian Sources

Study of the Palestinian sources in BT is facilitated by the existence of other documents containing parallel material. When we turn to the Babylonian sources, we must rely on the traditional methods of source criticism without the help of external sources. Scholars adduce various sorts of evidence indicative of Babylonian sources within BT. Almost all of this evidence derives from intensive analysis of individual pericopae. Most commonly cited are the following items.

α) Variant Versions

Frequently BT records alternate versions of Amoraic statements or pericopae. Several formulae introduce these variants. One such formula is *R. X matni hakhi . . . R. Y. matni hakhi . . .*, "R. X teaches this [version] . . . R. Y teaches this [other version] . . ." Sometimes "R. X" and "R. Y" are replaced by "you . . . we . . .", or "in town X . . . in town Y . . ." (see examples collected by LEWY, Interpretation, pp. 3—14, BACHER, Trad. u. Trad., pp. 578—589). Other formulae introducing variant versions include *'ika de'amri/dematni*, "there are those who say/teach", *lishana aḥarina*, "another version", and *ve'amri lah*, "and [some] say it [in the following version]" (see ALBECK, p. 558 and MELAMMED, pp. 455—457). It is widely agreed that these alternate versions come from sources at the disposal of the editors of the final version of the pericopae (see ALBECK and MELAMMED, loc. cit., and A. WEISS, TD, pp. 179ff., 192—260, 201—349).

β) Quotations

Certain formulae or superscriptions introduce quotations of pericopae. Two of them, *vehavēnan bah*, "and we discussed it", and *velav 'ittamar 'alav*, "and was it not said/explained concerning it", introduce into a pericope discussions whose original context was elsewhere. The fullest study of this phenomenon is by DE VRIES. He shows that the discussions quoted usually relate to a Mishnah paragraph, sometimes to a Baraita, and least frequently to an Amoraic statement. Most of them are found elsewhere in BT, but not all. Even when found elsewhere, the parallel version frequently differs from the quoted version. The disparity between the two versions and especially those discussions not found elsewhere prove that the source of the materials quoted by these formulae is not always our BT (DE VRIES, Studies, pp. 200—214 = Tarbiz 35 [1965—66], pp. 254—268, English Summary, p. IV; cf. ALBECK, pp. 562f. and A. WEISS, DTLU, pp. 14ff.).

A similar phenomenon involves quotations from the Mishnah. While discussing one paragraph of the Mishnah, the Gemara may quote another paragraph. Often that other paragraph is quoted together with its Amoraic commentary. The formula used to introduce these citations is *tenan hatam*, "we learned there"[42]. The Mishnah so cited is frequently from a tractate which lacks Babylonian Gemara. A. WEISS states the common view that "it is almost certain that many of the pericopae introduced by the term *tenan hatam* come from a different source [i. e., other than our BT]" (DTLU, p. 142, cf. pp. 133f., 142—146). WEISS also argues that the term *'ittamar* introduces materials with a fixed literary formulation from some other source (TD, pp. 64—107; cf. GEWIRTSMAN, Sinai 67).

γ) Parallel Pericopae

Many pericopae occur at several places in BT, both in different tractates and within the same tractate. Occasionally the parallel versions are contradictory. Conflicting views are attributed to the same master or statements attributed to two masters are reversed. Sometimes the contradiction is less striking, but it is revealed by close analysis. The medieval commentators, who noticed these passages, called them "inverted" or "transposed" pericopae, *sugyot hafukhot/muḥlafot* (for the medieval sources see EPSTEIN, IAL, p. 12 and ALBECK, pp. 560f.; for examples see EPSTEIN, pp. 24—32, 45—49, 98—101, 107—115 and cf. DOR, Bar Ilan 4—5). Both EPSTEIN and ALBECK agree that the contradictory parallel pericopae evidence different sources (EPSTEIN, IAL, p. 12 and ALBECK, p. 558).

Other parallel pericopae are in effect identical. The difference between them concerns their respective contexts. In one place in BT the passage is directly related to the Mishnah section near which it appears, while in the parallel occurrence it is only peripherally related. Thus the former place seems to be the original context. In the second place the passage is a quotation. The source of the quotation is obviously our BT. Thus the question in the case of identical parallel pericopae is not so much source critical as redaction critical, viz., who is responsible for copying the pericope in its second location? This question will be considered below.

δ) Inconsistencies within a Pericope

ALBECK finds evidence for different sources within individual pericopae. For example, one part of a pericope may ignore a source cited elsewhere in the same passage. Or different sections of the pericope may contradict one another. These phenomena indicate that the pericope is composed of different sources (ALBECK, pp. 569—571). Another indication is the order in which statements of Amoraim are recorded. Usually the order is chronological: first the early masters and then the later ones. Sometimes, though, early masters are cited after later ones. ALBECK explains that the compiler of the original version of the pericope did not know the views of the early masters. The compilers of the present version were able to add the addi-

[42] It was formerly believed that this formula introduces a Mishnah from a different tractate, but EPSTEIN showed that it can introduce a Mishnah from elsewhere in the same tractate, see ITM pp. 814—817.

tional views from some other source. Rather than tamper with the existent, older pericope, they simply attached the new material at the end (ALBECK, pp. 573f.). A. WEISS rejects this second argument. He claims that divergence from the usual chronological order can be explained on logical or thematic grounds (WEISS, Meḥqarim, pp. 160—212). Still, ALBECK's first argument seems beyond question.

ε) The Anonymous Material and Early Redactions of BT

Attributed statements comprise only a part of the Gemara. Almost as numerous are comments not attributed to any named master. Frequently these anonymous materials supply connecting links between attributed statements or serve as a framework for them. Scholars see in this evidence of editing. If a named master comments on or relates to the framework, then the latter must have existed before his time. We thus have evidence of an edited pericope from before the final redaction of BT. This constitutes a fragment of an early redaction of the Gemara which served as a source for our BT. Some of the sources indicated by the evidence noted above may also come from such early editions of Gemara. Z. FRANKEL apparently was the first modern scholar to adopt this argument[43]. It was further developed by Y. I. HALEVY. The latter cited many examples of anonymous material discussed or alluded to by Amoraim. The masters involved belong to every Amoraic generation. This indicates that in every generation material was edited, i. e., given a fixed literary form and arranged according to the order of the Mishnah[44]. HALEVY adds another argument which does not involve the anonymous sections. He shows that some Amoraic comments presuppose a certain order or arrangement of attributed comments. This also indicates that early material had already been edited during the Amoraic era[45]. Finally, HALEVY maintains that in addition to the "Talmud of each generation", there were two major summarizing editions: one in the early fourth century and the second in the early fifth[46]. All of these editions constitute the sources of our BT. KAPLAN reviews the evidence adduced by FRANKEL and HALEVY, and he adds some additional proofs. While admitting that much of the evidence is inconclusive, KAPLAN concludes "enough has been brought to prove the existence of records of Amoraic opinions and discussions, arranged either by subjects or otherwise, before the [final] redaction of the Talmud" (KAPLAN, Redaction, p. 194). These 'records', in some sense early editions of the Gemara, are among the sources of BT.

The most recent proponent of this theory is ALBECK. Like HALEVY he argues that when named masters relate to anonymous sections or

43 Z. FRANKEL, Beiträge zu einer Einleitung in den Talmud, MGWJ (1861), pp. 191—192.
44 Y. I. HALEVY, Dorot Harishonim, Vol. IIa (Frankfurt a. M., 1901 = Vol. V, Jerusalem, 1966), pp. 551—556, Vol. III (Pressburg, 1897 = Vol. VI, Jerusalem, 1966), pp. 117f.
45 HALEVY, op. cit., Vol. II, pp. 557—562.
46 Ibid., p. 480, Vol. III, pp. 116, 120.

presuppose a given order in earlier materials, we have evidence of early redactions of pericopae. He generalizes that "most of the anonymous pericopae arranged in the Talmud after the Mishnah or a Baraita or the words of early Amoraim are early, and not from the time of the late editing" (ALBECK, p. 580 and cf. pp. 578–595). EPSTEIN also appears to accept this line of reasoning, though he does not discuss this issue at length. He states that "we possess fragments of a Talmud edition from the time of R. Naḥman b. Ya'aqov and his disciples, and [from the time of] Abaye and Rava . . ." (IAL, p. 12). Elsewhere he cites what he believes to be early anonymous discussions (ibid., p. 15). He also cites evidence of editorial activity on the part of Naḥman b. Yiṣḥaq (ibid., pp. 21f., 178). Thus EPSTEIN agrees that the sources of BT include early editions of the Gemara.

All of the scholars cited above base their argument on the antiquity of the anonymous sections of BT. Others, including A. WEISS, M. S. FELDBLUM, HALIVNI, and FRIEDMAN, reject the latter assumption. They claim that the anonymous sections are late. Where named masters appear to cite or discuss such sections, this is the work of later editors. Anonymous material was inserted before attributed statements, and comments relating to the former were put in the mouths of the named masters (WEISS, TD, pp. 408–412, and see 295–307 and SLA, pp. 24–58; HALIVNI, ST, II, pp. 2–6; FELDBLUM, PAAJR 38; FRIEDMAN, Critical Study, pp. 294–296, n. 42). Nevertheless, WEISS agrees that there were early editions of the Gemara which constitute sources of our BT. In effect he agrees with HALEVY that every generation, and every center of scholarship, produced its own Talmud. Some of these early editions constitute recognizable strata in our Gemara. WEISS attributes the earliest stratum to the late third century. This is the Talmud of Yehudah b. Yeḥezqel head of the Pumbedita school. This Talmud comprised formulated material from Rav and Samuel, statements of other masters of the first generation of Babylonian Amoraim, and Baraitot. This edition was limited in extent. It did not cover every tractate for which we now have Babylonian Gemara. Even for the tractates this edition did treat, it sometimes was limited to specific chapters only. The second stratum discernable in our BT dates to the early fourth century (cf. HALEVY). This edition of Gemara was equivalent in extent to our BT in the sense that it covered all the tractates for which we now have Gemara. It too originated in Pumbedita, under Abaye. When the latter died, Rava took this edition with him to Meḥoza where it was further supplemented. Later generations continued to add to this edition as it was adopted by the Naresh school under R. Papa and by the school of Sura under R. Ashi. In the latter location material from the Suran Talmud was added. Thus, according to WEISS, the main sources of our BT are the Talmuds of Yehudah b. Yeḥezqel and of Abaye and Rava as supplemented by Papa and Ashi. In addition other early editions of Gemara are cited from time to time, as the formulae discussed above indicate (DTLU, pp. 37–45). Others scholars would reject WEISS' claim that our BT comes from Pumbedita. Epstein, for example, argues that the Gemara before us is essentially that of Sura, while certain tractates come from other centers (IAL, pp. 84, 104). Yet it is almost universally agreed that older editions of the Gemara served as sources for our Talmud.

Still more evidence for an early version of the Gemara is adduced by de Vries. While agreeing that there are early anonymous sections, he asserts that most early pericopae contain attributed material. Fragments of these early sources appear in BT following the superscription *vehavēnan bah.* de Vries notes that many of the pericopae introduced by the latter phrase concern the Mishnah of Orders *zera'im* and *tohorot.* In these Orders there are no BT tractates (except Ber. and Nid.). The pericopae cited are brief and simple. The masters named in them are from the earlier generations of Amoraim. de Vries concudes that materials introduced by *vehavēnan bah* are quotations from an early *gemara* on Orders *zera'im* and *tohorot* which dates to the first half of the fourth century. Thus this early *gemara* constitutes another one of the sources of our BT (de Vries, Studies, pp. 193—202 = Tarbiz 35 [1965—66], pp. 254—268, English Summary, p. IV, and cf. Zussman, Babylonian Sugyot).

A variation on the theme of early editions of the Gemara appears in the work of Epstein. He argues persuasively that each tractate is a separate literary unit with its own redaction history. Some tractates were edited earlier than others. When we find parallel pericopae in different tractates, we can sometimes determine which version is earlier. In these cases the tractate edited earlier served as a source for the tractate edited later. In this way we can explain the 'inverted' or contradictory parallel pericopae. The later tractate modified its source in conformity to its own needs or legal conceptions.

ζ) Form and Subject Matter

A number of scholars discern sources of BT according to criteria of form or subject matter. Kaplan, Klein, Rubinstein, Halivni, Weiss, Feldblum, and Friedman propound what may be called a 'two source' theory. They hypothecate two major blocs of material, each with a unique form, of which BT is composed. However these theories may best be considered under the headings of form criticism and especially redaction criticism. Here I shall briefly treat one aspect of the work of A. Weiss. As will be seen below, Weiss isolates what he believes to be the two main forms of Talmudic literature: the brief independent statement and the discursive discussion. In addition he discovers instances of other forms such as collections of traditions, connected Bible exegesis, and 'treatises' on non-legal topics. Frequently examples of the latter three forms developed by accretion in their present context in the Gemara. That is, they do not represent distinct literary units inserted whole into BT. On the other hand, Weiss argues, in some cases these materials were added to the Gemara as finished units. In such instances we may speak of these units as sources (SLA, pp. 176—294 and cf. NEUSNER, Formation, pp. 100—102; see also FRIEDMAN, Structural Patterns, pp. 396—402).

MIRSKY suggests that the technical, legal discussions and the less technical, primarily non-legal material in the Gemara derive from different sources. The former derive from the daily lectures in the Talmudic academies. The latter originate in sermons of a popular nature delivered in the synagogues of the academies on Sabbaths and holidays. Minutes of both types of lectures were preserved. These minutes were later 'dismantled' and incorporated into the Gemara where thematically appropriate. Fragments of the technical lectures are introduced by superscriptions such as *'ittamar* and *tenan hatam*, those of the sermons by *darash*. Moreover, complete minutes of the two types of lectures survive in post-Talmudic compilations (MIRSKY, Types of Lectures, pp. 375—402). MIRSKY's hypothesis presupposes academic institutions not necessarily attested by our sources, and it thus cannot be accepted[47]. A more modest and much more acceptable theory is argued by B. BOKSER. The latter has begun a study of the Mishnah commentary of Samuel, one of the first Babylonian Amoraim. So far, one volume on material relevant to Order *zera'im* has appeared. On the basis of the evidence assembled there BOKSER believes that a commentary by Samuel circulated as a separate document. This work, and presumably others like it, constitute additional sources of our BT.

η) Post-Amoraic Sources

According to Geonic testimony the last Amoraim died around the year 500 C.E. However, BT contains considerable material from after this date. Some early sixth century masters are mentioned by name in BT. Furthermore, early commentators and some manuscripts identify both comments and entire pericopae as post-Amoraic. These materials are attributed to the 'Savoraic masters', *rabbanan savora'ē*, or the Savoraim. The latter are Babylonian scholars who flourished in the sixth and seventh centuries (see the excellent survey by EPHRATHI). Thus it is universally agreed that among the sources of our BT are Savoraic materials. The extent and nature of the latter are a matter of dispute. Behind this dispute are different theories of the redaction of BT, as we shall see.

The first stage in the research on the Savoraic sources was the collection of all the material attributed to the Savoraim by the early commentators and manuscripts. The characteristics of the material thus assembled enabled scholars to identify still more material as of Savoraic provenance. S. J. RAPAPORT, N. BRÜLL, and others in the nineteenth century and HALEVY, YAVETZ, and YUDELOWITZ in the twentieth carried this work forward[48]. This first phase of research came to a culmination with the

[47] GOODBLATT, Rabbinic Instruction, op. cit., p. 195.

[48] See S. J. RAPAPORT, 'Erekh Millin (Warsaw, 1914), pp. 18—20, cf. Kerem Chemed 6 (1841) Letter 14, pp. 249—256; N. BRÜLL, Die Entstehungsgeschichte des babylonischen Tal-

publication of B. M. LEWIN's 'Rabbanan Savora'e Vetalmudam' in 1937. Despite the extent of Savoraic material revealed by this research, there was a distinct tendency to minimize the Savoraic contribution to BT. This tendency resulted from the widely held view that BT was 'sealed' by the year 500 (see below in the discussion of redaction criticism). If the document was 'sealed', then only insignificant additions were possible. Moreover, poor manuscripts of Geonic sources on the Savoraim and their activity led scholars astray (EPHRATHI, Sevoraic Period, pp. 64—67). Thus from RAPAPORT to LEWIN scholars denied that the Savoraim made any substantive additions to BT. The contribution of the latter was limited to brief glosses, technical terms, and the like (see KAPLAN's summary of the views of RAPAPORT, GRAETZ, FRANKEL, BRÜLL, I. H. WEISS, HALEVY, and YAVETZ in Redaction, pp. 3—27; LEWIN follows the view of HALEVY). Even EPSTEIN repeats the older view. He writes that the Savoraim contributed "merely the external arrangement [sc. of BT, emphasis in the original] without changing anything except for additions and connections between statements and pericopae . . ." (IAL, p. 12, cf. MELAMMED, pp. 473—478).

New theories on the redaction of BT made possible a re-evaluation of the Savoraic contribution. KAPLAN and A. WEISS deny that BT was "sealed" ca. 500. If the Talmud was left 'open', then there is no a priori reason for limiting the Savoraic sources to brief glosses. In fact, both KAPLAN and WEISS, followed by others, assign sizeable portions of BT to the Savoraim. I shall treat the details of their theories below in the discussion of redaction criticism. Here I shall briefly summarize some of the points WEISS made in his lecture on the Savoraim. Following a clue in Geonic sources, BRÜLL had already suggested that the opening pericope of several tractates constitutes a kind of introduction to the tractate composed by the Savoraim. WEISS argues that almost every tractate and many individual chapters begin with Savoraic pericopae. Furthermore, the Savoraim were responsible for what WEISS calls the "literary and stylistic polishing" of the pericopae. This activity included not only the addition of glosses to and connecting links between arguments, but also copying out in full sources alluded to in the original pericope. Here WEISS concurs with EPSTEIN that many parallel pericopae are the result of such *Quellenbeleg* (cf. EPSTEIN, IAL, p. 12). Finally BT contains many Savoraic pericopae. Some of the latter are reworkings of Amoraic material, but others are composed entirely of Savoraic material. WEISS concludes that the Savoraic element in BT is much more extensive than previously assumed (WEISS, Literary Activities, p. 18). Detailed studies of individual chapters of BT by FRANCUS and FRIEDMAN have established the correctness of WEISS' view. Savoraic sources comprise a considerable part of our BT.

muds als Schriftwerk, Jahrbücher für jüdische Geschichte und Literatur II (1876), pp. 16—18, 17, n. 11, 66—73; Y. I. HALVEY, op. cit., Vol. III, pp. 1—63; Z. JAWITZ (YAVETZ), Toldot Yisra'el, Vol. IX (London, 1922), pp. 213—224; M. D. YUDELOWITZ (JUDELOWITZ), Yeshivat Pumbedita Bime Ha'amora' im (Tel Aviv, 1935), pp. 52—54.

c) Summary and Critique

The Palestinian sources of BT include the Mishnah, other Tannaitic materials (the Baraitot), and Palestinian traditions and pericopae. At the base of the Talmud is a recension (or recensions) of the Mishnah of Yehudah the Patriarch. This recension differs from that appearing in the separate editions of the Mishnah and even from that placed at the head of the Gemara. The sources of the Baraitot are disputed. Some come from collections no longer extant. According to EPSTEIN and WEISS others come from earlier recensions of the extant Tannaitic collections such as the 'Tosefta' and the halakhic midrashim. ALBECK and DE VRIES demur. As to the Palestinian Amoraic pericopae, it is now agreed that they do not derive from the Palestinian Talmud now before us, but from the sources thereof or from other editions of the Palestinian Gemara.

The Babylonian sources pose more problems because Babylonian Amoraic documents external to BT do not exist. Nonetheless scholars are unanimous that various Amoraic sources can be discerned within BT. Variant versions of traditions, quotation formulae, contradictory parallel pericopae, and other evidence all point to the existence of such sources. The problem is to delineate and identify the latter and determine their provenance. It is generally agreed that each center of study and each generation had its own Talmud. But which sources belong to which version, and which 'edition' is the forebear of our BT — on these issues there is little agreement. BT also contains post-Amoraic sources, and there is a growing consensus that the extent of this late material is greater than previously believed. As we shall see below, some scholars claim that the Savoraic sources of BT are almost as extensive as the Amoraic ones. Further source critical work on the Savoraic stratum will be difficult. Since this material is almost entirely anonymous, we lack the 'handle' which attribution to named masters gives us in source criticism of Tannaitic and Amoraic materials.

The central stratum of BT, the Babylonian Amoraic material, turns out to be the most problematic. Scholars agree that BT comprises various Amoraic sources and concur on some of the indications thereof. Beyond this there is little agreement. The lack of consensus raises the question, is something wrong with our methodology? A reply may be found in the caveat of E. S. ROSENTHAL regarding source criticism of Tannaitic literature. His comments apply with even greater force to study of BT where we lack the controls provided for Tannaitic literature by the existence of several documents. ROSENTHAL notes LIEBERMAN'S hesitation to treat source-critical issues in his commentary on 'Tosefta'. He infers that the latter feels conditions are not yet ripe for such work. ROSENTHAL goes on to explain why. The source critical techniques of classical philology are possible only after the groundwork has been laid. First, we must firmly establish the philology, lexicography, and historical background of our sources. Once this is accomplished, we may proceed to a scientific exegesis of the latter.

Simultaneously we must carry out detailed text-critical research. Only when all this has been achieved will we be in a position to engage in source criticism (ROSENTHAL, Hammoreh, pp. 34—57). Let us see where we stand with regard to BT. As noted above, much remains to be done in the areas of philology and lexicography. We are in a much better position with respect to the historical background thanks to the recent work of NEUSNER (see below). This work and the 1500 years of traditional exegesis make a scientific exegisis of BT possible, but the latter task has yet to be carried out. As for text criticism, we are now at the stage of a full collation of variants. The real work of text criticism is just beginning. Thus LIEBERMAN's hesitation to engage in source criticism of 'Tosefta' would be all the more justified for BT. And what is true for source criticism is also true for form — and especially redaction criticism.

The nature of the task before us is illustrated by NEUSNER's work on Tannaitic sources. The latter arrived independently at the principles set forth by ROSENTHAL. In his studies on Order *ṭohorot* of 'Mishnah-Tosefta', NEUSNER insists that a detailed, scientific exegesis must precede source and form critical studies. He further demands that such work be systematic, encompassing all the material. Finally, as EPSTEIN suggests, he proceeds tractate by tractate, treating each one as a separate literary unit[49]. It is to be hoped that some of NEUSNER's students will apply his methods to the study of BT. In any event, the clarification of first principles by ROSENTHAL and NEUSNER holds promise for the future of the source criticism of the Talmud as do the detailed literary-critical studies of FRIEDMAN, to be discussed below[50].

2. Form Criticism

a) The Brief Versus the Discursive

Of the three disciplines discussed in this chapter form criticism has been the most neglected by Talmud scholarship. Still, it has not been ignored

[49] See NEUSNER, History of the Mishnaic Law of Purities, op. cit., passim.

[50] I have not discussed HALIVNI's "source critical method" here because this is primarily an exegetical tool. HALIVNI argues that the original form of a statement (= "source") was likely to be changed in the course of transmission from generation to generation and from place to place. The changed form he calls "traditions". Frequently the form of a source on which a given pericope is based differs from the form now before us in the text of the pericope. As a result questions seem pointless, answers irrelevant, discussions forced. By recovering the form which stood before the authors of the pericopae we can resolve these problems. HALIVNI's method is extremely valuable for exegesis of BT, but it does not deal with the classical issues of source criticism. In Vol. II of his 'Sources and Traditions', he does briefly deal with the latter topics and promises a full treatment in a later book. DE VRIES also stresses the changes sources were subject to in the course of transmission as well as the ramifications of these changes, see his 'Literary Transfer as a Factor in the Development of Talmudic Law', Bar Ilan I, pp. 156—164, English Summary, p. XXXV.

entirely. For example, the older work on Savoraic sources devoted considerable attention to the formal characteristics of the latter. Another example is the distinction between attributed and anonymous comments alluded to above. Both of these sets of categories have been subjects of scholarly interest since the last century. However, it is only with the work of KAPLAN and A. WEISS that form criticism, though not by this name, begins to play a major role in research on BT. KAPLAN distinguishes two major forms in the Talmudic material. In essence his distinction is between brief and discursive sources. Other scholars adopt the same formal categories, though they develop them differently. KAPLAN designates the two forms "gemara" and "talmud". "Gemara" consists of "statements of the utmost brevity and simplicity . . . put in simple and concise language, in order to record the final conclusions resulting from previous, sometimes lengthy and complex discussion" (Redaction, p. 196). That discussion constitutes "talmud". In addition to being brief, "gemara" is also "essentially anonymous" (Redaction, p. 227). As noted, it sums up and crystallizes previously existing "talmud". It also gives birth to new "talmud". The "laconic, pithy, often abrupt and ambiguous style", the "vague references" to sources, and the anonymity of "gemara" provoke attempts to resolve the ambiguity, spell out the references, and identify the authors (ibid., pp. 217—227, 233f.). Thus "gemara" and "talmud" engender one another. Each form is introduced by different superscriptions in BT. Those introducing "gemara" are based on the roots *tny* or *qbʿ*; those introducing "talmud" derive from *ʾmr, drš,* and *swm* (ibid., pp. 206—216). KAPLAN stresses that these distinctions are not merely formal. Each form represents a different source. The Talmudic academies possessed "collections of gemara" arranged according to the order of the Mishnah or of the Pentateuch (ibid., pp. 235—249, 270—274). Fragments from these collections appear in BT, though our Talmud is based on one particular collection (see below under redaction criticism). The "talmud" material was added later. While "gemara" and "talmud" thus constitute separate sources, they are first of all formal categories. The former term denotes brief, anonymous material, the latter discursive, attributed material.

Essentially the same distinction appears in the work of H. KLEIN. He names the forms "gemara" and "sebara". KLEIN states that each BT pericope "consists of a central core, which was termed its Gemara, and a discursive explanatory framework termed its Sebara" (KLEIN, GQS, p. 341). There are some differences between KLEIN's categories and those of KAPLAN, aside from the replacement of the term "talmud" by "sebara". One difference stressed by KLEIN concerns the relation between the two forms. He argues that "gemara" always precedes "sebara". The former never follows upon and summarizes the latter (KLEIN, GS, p. 69, n. 7). But KAPLAN admits that the "gemara" now before us in BT preceded the "talmud" before us. More relevant to form criticism is KLEIN's assertion that "gemara" is not always anonymous, but may include attributed statements. However, brevity is not the only characteristic of this form. KLEIN adds that "gemara" is always in Hebrew, while "sebara" is in Aramaic (GS, p. 75). He agrees with KAPLAN that the two categories represent different sources as well as formal types. I shall return to this point below. A third scholar who divided Talmudic sources into brief and discursive was S. M. RUBINSTEIN. Like KAPLAN he lists anonymity as well as brevity as characteristic of the one form, together with absence of source references, proof texts, or argumentation. The second form, which includes the latter three elements, is discursive and attributed. Even more than KAPLAN and KLEIN, RUBINSTEIN stresses the source — and redaction — critical aspects of this formal distinction[51].

The formal distinction between brief and discursive material is also adopted by A. WEISS, though in different terms. WEISS is the only BT scholar who writes extensively on form critical issues. Most of his last book, 'Studies in the Literature of the Amoraim' is devoted to identifying and cataloging the literary genres found in BT. In earlier work, reviewed in the latter volume, he identifies what he believes to be the dominant literary forms used by the Amoraim: the *memra* (plural: *memrot*) and the *sugya* (plural: *sugyot*). The former is a "short Amoraic statement which contains a complete idea, without any dialectics". The *sugya,* on the other hand, is a treatment of some aspect of a topic, generally in dialectical form. In effect we have here the same two categories noted by KAPLAN, KLEIN, and RUBINSTEIN. WEISS goes on to refine and subdivide his distinctions. The *memra,* which may be in either Hebrew or Aramaic, can be "supplementary" or "independent". That is, it may explain or clarify some other source, or it may state a complete idea which stands by itself. Similarly, the *sugya* may be either "explanatory" or "independent". In the former case some older source serves as the point of departure. In the latter the *sugya* is a self-contained discussion (SLA, pp. 1—4, cf. FELDBLUM, Contribution, pp. 13—16). WEISS thus agrees with KAPLAN against KLEIN that there is no necessary connection between brevity and use of Hebrew, but with KLEIN against KAPLAN that the brief material is not always anonymous. Aside from differences in detail and degree of sophistication, all three agree that brevity and discursiveness are the most general formal categories applicable to BT. Further distinctions, such as difference in language, or anonymity versus attribution, are given different valences. Where WEISS stands apart is in his refusal to translate these formal categories into source-critical ones. He does not assert that there were separate sources composed only of *memrot* (= "gemara") or of *sugyot* (= "talmud" or "sebara"). Here WEISS' theory seems preferable, for the source constructs argued by KLEIN, KAPLAN, and RUBINSTEIN are artificial and not substantiated by the evidence.

MELAMMED contributes a detailed description of the features of the *memra* and *sugya* (MELAMMED, Introduction, pp. 395—406, 451—461). He

[51] I was not able to obtain RUBINSTEIN's book. Therefore I rely on the summary in TENNENBLATT, Formation, pp. 81—93.

also discusses at length the halakhic midrashim, i. e., the legalistic exegeses of Biblical verses, attributed to Amoraim (ibid., pp. 296—311). While MELAMMED tends to see these as a separate form, WEISS categorizes them as supplementary *memrot*. Recent research by SH. FRIEDMAN has shed additional light on the *sugya*. In his studies of Chapter X of BT Yev. FRIEDMAN discovers that a tripartite structure is frequent. Thus a statement of an early master will be followed by reactions from three Amoraim. Furthermore, the components of the tripartite *sugya* are themselves often tripartite. This indicates, FRIEDMAN concludes, the contrived literary nature of the *sugya*. This pattern appears particularly in anonymous *sugyot* (FRIEDMAN, 'Some Structural Patterns').

The most promising development in BT form criticism is the recent work of FRIEDMAN. Building on the achievements of his predecessors, especially KAPLAN, KLEIN, and WEISS, he has developed criteria for delineating the various strata in a *sugya*. On the basis of literary (or formal) considerations, FRIEDMAN distinguishes three components (or strata) in most *sugyot*: A- statements of Amoraim; B- anonymous material which provides the framework for A; and C- late glosses. A corresponds more or less to the *gemara* of KAPLAN and KLEIN and to the *memra* of WEISS, and B to the *talmud* of KAPLAN, the *sebara* of KLEIN, and the *sugya* of WEISS. As to the issues in dispute among the latter three scholars, FRIEDMAN asserts that A tends to be brief and in Hebrew, B wordy and in Aramaic, and that in most cases B is chronologically later than A. Where FRIEDMAN goes beyond his predecessors is in his detailed listing and illustration of the criteria for separating the statements of the Amoraim (A) from the anonymous framework (B), even where B has been inserted into A. He lists fourteen such criteria which are then applied in his study of BT Yev. Chapter X. They are as follows. (1) The statements of Amoraim tend to be in Hebrew, the anonymous framework in Aramaic. (2) An explanatory, dependent clause is usually editorial (i.e., from B). Further indications of anonymous 'contamination' of Amoraic statements are (3) clumsy syntax, (4) excessive sentence length, and (5) resumptive repetition. (6) Material which when excluded from the *sugya* leaves a simple, consistent text is likely to be an editorial addition. (7) References to material further on in the *sugya* are likely to be editorial. (8) The appearance of words or phrases used overwhelmingly by late Amoraim or in anonymous sections are likely to be editorial additions when they appear in statements of early Amoraim. (9) Similarly, grammatical forms common in Geonic Aramaic, but rare in BT Aramaic, are signs of editorial additions. (10) A word or phrase which witnesses to the text insert in different places in the *sugya* are likely to be editorial. (11) A clustering of variant readings in a *sugya* may indicate that the text in question is a later insertion, for the text tradition of Amoraic statements is firmer than that of the anonymous sections. (12) The absence of a phrase in the MSS or in parallel passages suggests that it is a later addition. (13) Early commentators (*rishonim*) may reflect a shorter text of the *sugya*, which suggests that the additional material is editorial. (14)

In general, authentic Amoraic statements tend to be brief. FRIEDMAN argues that the probability of separating B from A increases as more of the above criteria appear. The application of the criteria is illustrated in his study of BT Yev., Chapter X, where A and B are graphically distinguished from each other (FRIEDMAN, 'Critical Study'). While I have discussed FRIEDMAN's work under the rubric of form criticism, it obviously has important ramifications for source- and redaction-criticism.

b) Other Forms

In addition to the *memra* and the *sugya* WEISS finds other genres in BT. He groups them into three broad categories: (1) collections (*qevaṣim*, singular: *qoveṣ*), (2) *midrashim* and aggadic compilations, and (3) treatises (*massekhtot*, singular: *massekhet*; the same word means 'tractate', but I translate 'treatise' to avoid confusion). The first category is by far the largest. WEISS lists over 125 instances of this form in BT, and he admits that his catalogue is not exhaustive (SLA, p. 189). He defines a collection as an assemblage of at least three traditions with its own organizational framework. The latter may be topical or formal. The commonest type is the collection of *memrot* all attributed to one master (ibid., pp. 176—208). Occasionally the collection form is obscured by the interpolation of discussions between its components. That is, one or more of the components may have engendered the development of a *sugya*. Moreover, faulty transmission of the text may have corrupted or changed the name of the master in one of the components thereby obliterating the form. Generally, though, the collection form is easy to recognize. Some collections include questions, usually introduced by the verb *b'y*, as well as declarative sentences. Other collections are composed entirely of questions attributed to one master, to several, or unattributed (SLA, pp. 238—246). A related phenomenon is a collection of apparently contradictory sources, introduced by *rmy*, and their resolutions (ibid., pp. 222—224). In some collections the components share more than one feature. For example, the *memrot* in a collection may all be transmitted by the same *Tradent* as well as attributed to the same master, or they may all start with the same formula (ibid., pp. 209—220). Finally some collections are composed of legal decisions (*pisqē halakhah*) either attributed or anonymous (ibid., pp. 247—250). SH. FRIEDMAN notes that many collections have seven components. He calls attention to the Talmudic phrase *shev shema'ata*, 'seven traditions', and he suggests that the later is the name of a literary genre ('Some Structural Patterns').

The second category includes consecutive exegesis of sections of Biblical books and assemblages of aggadic (non-legal) material on a given theme. WEISS lists three instances of the former type involving sections of Esther, Ruth, and Job (Meg. 10b—17a, Shab. 113b—114b, and BB 13b to 17a respectively, see SLA, pp. 276—292, 256—259). Examples of aggadic compilations include units on prayer, the giving of the Torah, the mystical 'works of the chariot' (*ma'asē merkavah*), and legends concerning the destruction of the Second Temple (Ber. 31a—32b, Shab. 86b—89b, Ḥag. 13a—16a, and Giṭ. 55b—58a respectively, see SLA, pp. 251—263). The third category, treatises, includes extended treatments of subjects such as dreams, Ḥannukah, 'wonders and visions', demons, and medicine (Ber. 54a—57b, Shab. 21b—24a, BB 73a—75b, Ber. 6a + Pes. 110a, and Shab. 110a—b + Giṭ. 67b + AZ 28a respectively, see SLA pp. 264—278). The distinction between aggadic compilations and treatises is not clear. Why are units on prayer and mysticism aggadic compilations, while those on dreams and demons treatises? In any event WEISS' threefold division may be retained, for consecutive Bible exegesis should be distinguished from both aggadic compilations and treatises.

MELAMMED suggests an additional formal category: the *ba'aya* or query (MELAMMED, Introduction, pp. 429—441). WEISS prefers to include the latter, together with its answer, in the *sugya* genre (SLA, pp. 238—246). Another sub-category of the *sugya*, the sermonic or midrashic discourse, is also treated separately by MELAMMED under the heading *pirqa*, 'lecture'. This latter form is also discussed at length by MIRSKY. As noted above, MIRSKY argues that this material derives from popular sermons delivered in the synagogues of the Talmudic academies. They included both legal and aggadic topics (MIRSKY, 'Types of Lectures'). FRIEDMAN, as stated above, also discusses the collection form (both collections of *memrot* and of legal decisions), noting the frequency of units containing three or seven members. The recognition of these forms and others is facilitated by the drawing of schematic outlines of the *sugyot* (in: FRIEDMAN, Critical Study). He also treats the query form (which he refers to as the *ba'ē*). According to FRIEDMAN, all these forms are characteristic of the A stratum (statements of Amoraim), rather than the anonymous framework (B). In addition, he briefly describes another Amoraic form which was ignored by his predecessors: the story (*ma'aseh*, *'ovada*). FRIEDMAN lists the following characteristics of the latter form: Aramaic language, brief sentences in asyndetic construction (i.e., without the conjunction *v*), the first sentence begins with a subject, the other sentences begin with a verb. "Contamination" by anonymous, editorial additions may also be discerned in the Amoraic story (FRIEDMAN, Critical Study, pp. 310—312). While the story form has been largely ingnored by talmudists, it has been studied by students of literature and folklore[51a].

[51a] The fullest and most recent treatment, though not devoted only to BT, is O. MEIR, The Acting Characters in the Stories of the Talmud and the Midrash (A Sample), Unpublished Doctoral Dissertation, Hebrew University, 1977. MEIR treats the stories in Tractate Ber. in BT and PT as well as those in two Palestinian midrashim. See also D. BEN-AMOS, Narrative Forms in the Haggadah: Structural Analysis, Unpublished Doctoral Dissertation, University of Indiana 1966; B. DE VRIES Studies, Part I. The Literary Genres of the Aggada; Y. FRAENKEL, Ma'aseh BeRabbi Shila, Tarbiz 40 (1971), pp. 33—40; and A. KARLIN, Darkhe Hassippur Bishne Hattalmudim, Divre Sefer (Tel Aviv, 1952), pp. 5—42.

c) The *Sitz im Leben* of the Forms

It is widely assumed that the *Sitz im Leben* of BT in general is to be found in the Talmudic academies of Babylonia. The latter institutions, which flourished in such towns as Nehardea, Sura, Pumbedita, Naresh, Meḥoza and others from the third century on, composed, preserved, edited, and transmitted the Talmudic materials. The dialectics of the pericopae transcribe or at least reflect the debates during study sessions in the academies. The scholars cited above share this assumption. Most of the forms they isolate are assigned *Sitze im Leben* in the academies. WEISS, for example, claims that the life setting of the *memra* and *sugya* was the Mishnah study of these institutions (SLA, p. 172). KAPLAN argues that the "gemara" form represents formal conclusions of the discussions in the Amoraic academies. The "talmud" before us originated in Savoraic study of the "gemara" collection compiled in the academy of Sura under R. Ashi (Redaction, pp. 235f., 306f.). MIRSKY asserts that BT contains fragments of the minutes of lectures and sermons delivered in the academies ('Types of Lectures'). All these theories presuppose a certain type of institution: the academy. However, it is far from certain that Amoraic instruction was institutionalized in this way. The present writer has argued that disciple circles and apprenticeships rather than academies were the means of instruction during the Amoraic period[52]. If so, then the *Sitze im Leben* suggested for BT in general and the forms in particular must be rejected or revised. Life settings outside the academies are also hypothecated. As noted, WEISS asserts that at least some of the collections (and other forms) are independent literary units inserted into the Gemara. The *Sitze im Leben* he suggests for these units include the collection by disciples of a master's sayings after his death, the exchange of letters or the sending of responsa, and a master's desire to assemble the traditions of an important authority (SLA, pp. 221—225). These suggestions are acceptable, but they account for only a small portion of BT. Thus the question of life settings for the mass of Amoraic sources must await further research on the institutions of the Amoraim.

d) Summary

The form critical study of BT is still at a very preliminary stage. Aside from the contribution of WEISS and of SH. FRIEDMAN, the forms isolated are extremely primitive: attributed versus anonymous, brief versus discursive, Hebrew versus Aramaic. Even WEISS' *memra* and *sugya* are very broad categories. One reason for this state of affairs is that BT scholars have ignored cognate developments in Biblical studies where form criticism has reached a high level of sophistication. Fortunately this situation is changing. NEUSNER, in his work on Tannaitic sources, adapted the achieve-

[52] GOODBLATT, op. cit., pp. 44—59, 263—285.

ment of Biblical form criticism and developed methods appropriate to rabbinic literature. And one of his students, B. BOKSER, applies these methods to the study of BT. BOKSER devotes considerable attention to form-critical issues in his study on the Mishnah commentary of Samuel (BOKSER, Chapter IV—VI). Similarly, FRIEDMAN draws not only on talmudic scholarship, but also on literary and form-critical studies in other literatures. Thus the work of BOKSER and FRIEDMAN, who combine talmudic expertise and knowledge of form-critical methodology, promises further progress in the form criticism of BT. Such progress is bound to enrich other areas of study, including the source and redaction history of BT, Aramaic philology, and the history of the Jews in Sasanian and Islamic Babylonia.

3. Redaction Criticism

a) The Tractates

Unlike form criticism, redaction criticism has received much attention in modern Talmud scholarship. Usually the focus of research is the entire BT. Some scholars also treat the redactional history of individual tractates, and I shall begin with this aspect of the problem. As mentioned, EPSTEIN stresses that each tractate is an independent unit with its own literary history. Thus the proper object of source and redaction criticism should be the tractate. The approach suggested by EPSTEIN has been followed in a few doctoral dissertations submitted by students in the Hebrew University Talmud Department where EPSTEIN taught. In addition the latter composed introductions to individual tractates which appear in his IAL. Most published work, however, concentrates on the so-called 'unusual tractates'. These are Ned., Naz., Me'il., Ker., Tam., and the materials introduced by the superscription *lishana aḥarina* in Tem. The early commentators noted that these five and a half tractates differ from the rest of BT in language and terminology. Geonic sources report that they were not studied in the Babylonian academies of the eighth century (see the sources cited in EPSTEIN, IAL, pp. 55f. and in his 'Grammar of Babylonian Aramaic' [Tel Aviv and Jerusalem, 1960], p. 15, MELAMMED, Introduction, p. 468, and DE VRIES, Studies, p. 230). The significance of the latter fact, and still more the precise nature of the peculiarities of these tractates and their explanation, are a matter of dispute.

I shall begin with the linguistic aspect of the phenomenon. The earlier grammarians of bta, LUZZATTO, LEVIAS, and MARGOLIS, all argued that the language of the 'unusual' tractates is archaic. EPSTEIN argues the opposite. He asserts that their language is closest to the post-Talmudic dialect of the Geonic writing, and it therefore is late (EPSTEIN, IAL, p. 52 and Grammar, p. 16). DE VRIES seems to say the same thing, though the formulation of his conclusion is rather opaque (Studies, p. 231). Since EPSTEIN is the greatest authority on the Geonic dialect, his assessment carries much weight. However, language is not the only, and perhaps not the most important, peculiarity of the 5½ tractates. Scholars also note differences in terminology, style, legal decisions, and even in the roster of masters quoted. Thus the phenomenon cannot be explained merely on linguistic grounds.

One of the earliest attempts at an overall explanation of the 'unusual' tractates is that of HALEVY. He argues that BT as a whole was brought to Palestine in the Savoraic period. Later, when the Babylonian academies neglected the 5½ tractates, the Palestinian schools continued to study them. The peculiarities thus result from the contamination of their text by Palestinian linguistic and terminological traits[53]. However, as RABINOWITZ and EPSTEIN point out, these supposed Palestinian traits do not appear in Palestinian sources such as the Palestinian Talmud (RABINOWITZ, Notes, pp. 299–300, EPSTEIN, IAL, p. 52). A more common view finds the explanation of this phenomenon in the redaction history of these tractates. This had already been suggested in general terms by FRANKEL and BRÜLL. In specific terms LEWY and HOROVITZ argued that the 'unusual' tractates were redacted in Pumbedita while the rest of BT comes from Sura. Thus the peculiarities of the former reflect local dialect and terminology[54]. RABINOWITZ also adopts this explanation (Notes, pp. 299–310). EPSTEIN agrees that the 5½ tractates were edited at a different time and place than the rest of BT. Specifically, they were redacted later than the other tractates, as the similarity of their language to that of the Geonim indicates. Additional evidence of their lateness derives from the comparison of pericopae from the 5½ with their parallels in other tractates. Such a comparison shows that the former depend on the latter. That is, the 'unusual' tractates quote the 'regular' ones and are therefore later (IAL, pp. 54–71 re Ned., 72–83 re Naz., and 131–144 re Tem.). As to the places of redaction, EPSTEIN suggests that Ned. comes from Meḥoza and Naz. from 'Meḥoza-Pumbedita'. The rest of BT was redacted at Sura (ibid., pp. 69f., 82, cf. MELAMMED, Introduction, pp. 468f.).

A different interpretation of the redaction history of the 'unusual' tractates is suggested by A. WEISS and DE VRIES. The school of thought summarized by EPSTEIN stresses that the 5½ differ from the rest of BT not only in external features such as language and style, but also in substantive matters such as methodology and masters cited. WEISS, on the other hand, asserts that the 'unusual' tractates are not so unusual. Their peculiarities are neither extensive nor substantive. For example, the Amoraim who appear are basically identical to those cited in the rest of BT. In essence the 5½ have the same origin as the other tractates. To be sure, some of them, such as Tam., lack the early stratum of Gemara which goes back to Yehudah b. Yeḥezqel. But they all have the middle stratum edited

[53] HALEVY, III, pp. 48f.

[54] Z. FRANKEL, Einleitung in den jerusalemischen Talmud (Leipzig 1859. Rep. Jerusalem, 1967), p. 48a; BRÜLL, Entstehungsgeschichte, op. cit., p. 185; I. LEWY, Interpretation, p. 74; H. S. HOROVITZ, Die Composition des Talmuds, MGWJ 63 (1919), p. 126.

under Abaye and Rava. What, then, is the source of their peculiarities? The answer according to WEISS lies in the post-Amoraic development of these tractates, or rather the lack thereof. Since the 5½ were not studied in the academies, they did not undergo the stylistic revision and supplementation that the rest of BT received in the Savoraic and Geonic era. Consequently the 'unusual' tractates preserve pericopae in their original, unpolished form (WEISS, MGWJ 83, DTLU, pp. 46—128). Thus the peculiarity of these tractates lies in the primitive state of their contents. WEISS does not respond to EPSTEIN's argument that the language of the 5½ is similar to the Geonic dialect. The latter fact would indicate that they were late, or at least were worked over sometime close to the Geonic period. Moreover, the Geonic sources tell us only that these tractates were not studied in the eighth century. They say nothing about the Savoraic period. Until these last two points are clarified, the theory of WEISS remains tentative.

DE VRIES arrives at conclusions similar to those of WEISS. He agrees that the 'unusual' tractates are not late. On the contrary, they preserve the short and rudimentary form of the older Talmudic material. They do so because they did not undergo the stylistic editing that other tractates did. This same fact explains their unusual terminology. In an earlier period Talmudic terminology was fluid. Later it became fixed, and editors standardized the terminology of the 'regular' tractates. This was not done for the 5½ because they were not studied in the academies. As to the quotations from other tractates adduced by EPSTEIN as evidence of lateness, this is not decisive. DE VRIES argues that they represent post redactional additions. In a study of Meʿil. he supplies more details. On the basis of the masters named in this tractate he suggests that it was compiled in the school of R. Papa in the latter part of the fourth century. This school used a terminology different from that current in other academies (Studies, pp. 230—238 re Meʿil., and 188—193, 223—229 on the problem in general, cf. Tarbiz 30 and Lešonenu 29). Here DE VRIES appears to contradict his general position that the unusual terminology reflects the fluid situation of the earlier period. Instead, in the case of Meʿil., it results from the different site of redaction — a position identical to that of EPSTEIN. However, the contradiction is only partial. Had Meʿil. undergone editing later, the standard terminology would have been imposed on it. More problematic is the claim that the 'unusual' tractates received post-Amoraic additions (DE VRIES speaks specifically of Ned. and Naz.). If so, then they were worked over by later editors. Why did they not receive stylistic editing at the same time? Moreover, like WEISS, DE VRIES does not respond to the linguistic argument of EPSTEIN.

To sum up, WEISS and DE VRIES agree that the redactional history of the 5½ tractates differs from that of the rest of BT. They did not undergo the late redactional development found in the 'regular' tractates. Instead they preserve the older, rudimentary form of the pericopae. For the rest of BT redactional activity continued in the post-Amoraic era. This activity included supplementation and stylistic polishing. In contrast to this view EPSTEIN argues that the 'unusual' tractates were redacted later than the rest of BT. Moreover, as earlier scholars had argued, and as DE VRIES himself suggests regarding Me'il., they were redacted at schools other than the one which gave us the 'regular' tractates. The linguistic argument advanced by EPSTEIN, the similarity of the language of the 5½ to the Geonic dialect, is persuasive. But so is the argument from the rudimentary state of the pericopae stressed by WEISS and DE VRIES. And the two arguments lead to mutually exclusive conclusions. As we shall see below, the latter argument is compatible with other data relevant to the redaction history of BT as a whole. However, before we can accept the view of WEISS and DE VRIES we must find an answer to the linguistic phenomenon noted by EPSTEIN. Perhaps as our knowledge of bta and of the Geonic dialect increases, this point will turn out to be less significant[54a]. In any event, study of the 'unusual' tractates suggests the complexities of the larger issue of the redaction of BT as a whole. This issue is our next topic.

b) The Traditional Theory of the Redaction of BT

Since the beginning of modern Jewish studies in the early nineteenth century both Talmudists and historians have felt obliged to present their view on the redaction history of BT. There is no point to review in detail the theories propounded prior to 1925. This has already been done by KAPLAN and in NEUSNER's Formation (see KAPLAN, Redaction, pp. 1—22, 179—194 for the views of GRAETZ, FRANKEL, RAPAPORT, BRÜLL, I. H. WEISS, HALEVY, and JAWITZ; NEUSNER, Formation, pp. 3—47 for GRAETZ, I. H. WEISS, HALEVY, JAWITZ, and ZURI; see also BACHER's view in his article 'Talmud' in the Jewish Encyclopedia, Vol. 12). Moreover, despite differences in details, all these theories are essentially identical. They all repeat the redaction history which crystallized in the middle ages. Thus we may speak of a traditional theory of the redaction of BT, canonized in the writings of the *rishonim*. This theory is based on a few enigmatic passages in BT and in Geonic sources. I shall cite these sources and show how the traditional theory emerged from them. Then I shall indicate why it must be rejected.

[54a] The most recent statement on the language of the $5^1/_2$ tractates is that of S. KAUFMAN, The Akkadian Influences on Aramaic (Chicago, 1974), p. 163. Unfortunately, KAUFMAN ignores the views of WEISS and DE VRIES and asserts that "all agree" that these tractates are late. On the latter assumption, he adresses the question whether the Aramaic of the $5^1/_2$ is colloquial or archaizing. The absence of Akkadian loan words, aside from those common to earlier Aramaic dialects, leads him to conclude that the language of these tractates is not colloquial. Instead, archaization "should be suspected". I wonder whether the negative conclusion of KAUFMAN vitiates the argument of EPSTEIN. If the Aramaic of the $5^1/_2$ tractates is not colloquial Geonic, then perhaps it is archaic, rather than archaizing. In sum, the linguistic evidence may fit in just as well, if not better, with the view of WEISS and DE VRIES that the tractates are early.

BT contains no unequivocal reference to its redaction. Nevertheless two passages are widely believed to allude to such activity. The first appears at BM 86a. Towards the end of 85b we find a story, in bta, about how Samuel Yarḥina'ah healed an eye ailment of Rabbi (Yehudah the Patriarch). The latter sought to ordain the former, but for unexplained reasons he was unable to do so[55]. Samuel Yarḥina'ah then responds,

> "Let the master not be troubled. I myself saw the Book of the First Man, and in it was written, 'Samuel Yarḥina'ah will be called sage, but he will not be called master. And the healing of Rabbi will be by his hand'.
>
> Rabbi and R. Natan are the end of *mishnah*, R. Ashi and Ravina are the end of *hora'ah*. And your sign is, 'until I went into the sanctuary of God (*miqdashe 'ēl*); then I perceived (*'avinah*) their end' (Psalms 73 : 17)."

It is not clear whether what I have set off as a separate paragraph also is quoted from the Book of the First Man. The quotation concerning Samuel Yarḥina'ah is in Aramaic, though the text is too short and the text tradition too uncertain for us to determine which dialect. The section about Rabbi, Natan, Ashi, and Ravina is in Hebrew. As to the sign from Psalms 73, there is agreement that *'avinah* is a play on the name Ravina which is a contraction of Rav 'Avina. Most, but not all, authorities see in the word *miqdashē* an allusion to the name Ashi. Despite the agreement on the former sign, it is not clear which master is meant. Two Amoraim bore the name Ravina. One was a contemporary of Ashi; the other, Ravina b. R. Huna, died over 70 years after Ashi. More problematic are the words left untranslated, *mishnah* and *hora'ah*. The former could be the name of the book Mishnah or an abstract noun meaning '(Tannaitic) teaching'. The second word literally means 'instruction'. I shall return to these issues below. The second passage, from BB 157b, is as follows,

> "Ravina said, 'The first *mahadura* of R. Ashi said to us . . . The latter *mahadura* (of R. Ashi) said to us . . .'"

The words in parentheses are missing in several manuscripts of BT, but they are to be understood. Since Ravina does not quote Ashi directly, but only his *mahadura*, the former need not be the early Ravina. The Aramaic word *mahadura* comes from the root *hdr* which means 'to go round', or 'to return'.

These passages are cited in two important Geonic sources. The later of the two is the more widely quoted. I refer to the responsum of Sherira, *ga'on* of the academy of Pumbedita, to the Jewish community of Qairawan, North Africa from the year 986/7. This responsum is known as 'Iggeret

[55] On this story see NEUSNER, History of the Jews in Babylonia, Vol. II (Leiden, 1966), pp. 135f.

(= Epistle) of R. Sherira Ga'on (hereafter: ISG). The relevant sections are the following[56].

1. "In this way *hora'ah* was added generation after generation until Ravina, when it ceased — as Samuel Yarḥina'ah saw in the Book of the First Man: Ashi and Ravina are the end of *hora'ah*.
   And after this, though there certainly was no *hora'ah*, there were interpretations and explanations (*sevarē*) which are similar to *hora'ah*. And they (?) are called the Savoraic masters (*rabbanan savora'ē*)."
   ISG, ed. LEWIN, p. 66

I note that Sherira assumes the Ashi-Ravina section to be part of the quotation from the Book of the First Man.

2. "On Wednesday, Kislev 13, in the year 811 [Selucid Era = December, 499] Ravina b. R. Huna died, and he is the end of *hora'ah.*"
   ISG, ed. LEWIN, p. 95

3. "In the year 787 [= 475/6] R. Sama son of Rabah died.
   After him R. Assi [Spanish recension: Yosi] presided. In his day was the end of *hora'ah,* and the Talmud *'istetēm.*"
   ISG, ed. LEWIN, p. 97

All manuscripts of the French recension of ISG agree the last word is from the root *stm* in the *'itpe'ēl* verb pattern. The Spanish recension manuscripts have forms from the latter root as well as from the root *swm.* The second root appears in the form *'istayyem,* meaning 'was finished/ completed'. However, the forms from *stm* which appear in all the manuscripts of the superior French recension seem to preserve the original reading. The basic meaning of this root is 'stop up, block, close'. The *'itpe'ēl* verb pattern gives the word a passive force. The question then is, what is meant by the phrase "the Talmud was stopped/blocked/closed"? Another possible interpretation connects the verb with the word *setam,* the Talmudic term for "anonymous, unattributed traditions". The passage would then mean that the Talmud "was made anonymous".

4. "R. Ashi served as principal of the academy for nearly sixty years. This is what Chapter *mi shemet* [of BB, here = 157b] refers to when it mentions the first *mahadura* of R. Ashi and the latter *mahadura* of R. Ashi. For thus the masters instituted: to teach in each semester 12 sections [sc. of BT, *metivata*] whether short or long. Thus he [Ashi] reviewed (*hadar*) his entire learning in 30 years."
   ISG, ed. LEWIN, pp. 93f.

[56] I quote from the critical edition by B. M. LEWIN, Haifa, 1921. LEWIN printed both of the two recognized recensions, the French and the Spanish. I translate the former, following EPSTEIN's view that the French recension is more accurate, see IAL, pp. 610—615.

The second Geonic source cited in connection with the redaction history of BT is Seder Tanna'im Ve'amora'im (hereafter: STV). This is an historical and methodological introduction to BT dated in its present form to the late ninth century[57].

1. "In the year 811 [= 499 C.E.] Ravina, the end of *hora'ah*, died. And the Talmud *nistam*."

STV, ed. KAHAN, p. 6

The Hebrew *nistam*, from the root *stm* in the *nif'al* pattern, is an exact equivalent of the Aramaic *'istetēm*. Variant readings include *nistatam* and *neḥtam*. The former, apparently a *nitaf'al* verb pattern[58], is identical in meaning to *nistam*. The word *neḥtam* means 'was sealed'. I take this to be an explanatory replacement of an original *nistam*.

2. "Rav the elder [or: the Great] was the one who began with *hora'ah*. and from Rav the elder till R. Ashi and Ravina were 204 [variant: 280] years, and they were the end of *hora'ah*."

STV, ed. KAHAN, p. 8

If "Rav the elder" is the famous Amora Rav, then the 204 or 280 years period may begin from 219. That year, when Rav settled in Babylonia according to Geonic tradition, is conventionally considered the beginning of the Amoraic era in Babylonia. 204 years would thus take us to the death of Ashi, dated by STV to 424. 280 years would bring us to 499, the date assigned to the death of Ravina b. R. Huna[59].

Let us now review how the Geonic sources understood the two BT passages quoted above. I begin with BM 86a. ISG 2 and STV 1 identify the Ravina of the latter passage with the later Ravina b. R. Huna rather than with the contemporary of Ashi. This is also implicit in ISG 1 which has the Savoraic era begin immediately after the end of *hora'ah*, and in ISG 3 where *hora'ah* ends during the principalship of Assi which began in 475/6. The reading 280 in STV 2 also suggests this identification. (Even the reading 204 does not rule it out, for the figure could refer only to Ashi.) The Geonic sources also relate to the meaning of the term *hora'ah*. ISG 3 and STV 1 assert that the end of *hora'ah* ca. 500 coincides with the closing/blocking of the Talmud. As variant readings showed, the latter event was understood in the middle ages to refer to the completion or 'sealing' of BT. The second BT passage, BB 157b, is cited only in ISG 4. SHERIRA interprets "the *mahadura* of Ashi" to mean a review of Talmudic traditions by the latter.

57 For both ISG and STV see the excellent form- and source-critical studies by EPHRATHI, Sevoraic Period, pp. 1—32. I quote STV from the critical edition by K. KAHAN, Frankfurt a. M., 1935.

58 For the verb pattern *nitaf'al* see H. YALON, Introduction to the Vocalization of the Mishnah (Jerusalem, 1964), pp. 127—135 = Tarbiz 1 (1930) pp. 118—122.

59 See KAHAN's note ad loc., pp. 32f.

On the basis of the sources just discussed medieval authorities (such as Rashi, R. Nissim, and Maimonides), and after them modern scholars, derived the following conclusions. The BM passage draws a parallel between Rabbi, editor of the Mishnah, and Ashi and Ravina. The point of the parallel is that the latter two did for BT what Rabbi did for the Mishnah. Now according to the Geonic sources the Ravina mentioned is the later master of that name who died in 499, over 70 years after Ashi. Therefore the editing of BT must have been carried out in two phases. The second phase, ca. 500, was the closing or sealing of BT. Following this was the Savoraic era which saw only editorial polishing, but no substantive addition to the now closed text of the Talmud. What was the first phase of the editing in the time of Ashi? This is hinted at by BB 157b. Ashi twice reviewed all the Talmudic material which had accumulated up to his time. While doing so he 'arranged' or 'edited' this material. The great frequency with which Ashi appears in BT and the fact that many pericopae conclude with his comments were seen as confirmation for the latter assumption. The two generations of Amoraim who followed Ashi added some new material and engaged in further editing. Then, with the death of Ravina b. R. Huna in 499, BT was declared closed.

A glance at the summaries of recent scholarly opinion in Kaplan's 'Redaction' or Neusner's 'Formation' will show that there are many variations on this theme. Most of them concern the two phases of editing and what happened between them. For example, the exact nature of Ashi's contribution to the redaction of BT is variously assessed: he composed only the outline or framework of the Gemara, he began the actual redaction but did not finish it, he redacted it orally but did not reduce it to writing, etc. Still the overall picture of the redaction history of BT is identical from the eleventh to the twentieth century. Our BT is the work of Ashi, supplemented by the two following generations. It was completed and 'sealed' by the end of the fifth century. This traditional theory is accepted not only by the pre-1925 scholars, but also by more recent authorities. Among the latter is Epstein. Although he did not write at length on the subject, his position is clear. Thus he alludes to earlier redactions of the Gemara which continued

> "until the time of Ravina [I] and R. Ashi 'the end of hora'ah', and the 'arrangers of the Talmud', who collected all the material which preceded them, generally in its original form; they interpreted it, completed it, and 'arranged' it. But its arrangement was not finished in their day: two generations of Amoraim followed them who completed it and added to it additional interpretations and pericopae until the Savoraim came and 'sealed' it ..."
>
> IAL, p. 12

The attribution of the 'sealing' to the Savoraim is not a departure. Epstein means that they declared BT closed to substantive addition as of the death of Ravina b. R. Huna. After all, Ravina himself could not have done this. Thus his theory is identical to the traditional one described above. On the other hand ALBECK rejects the first phase of editing assumed by the theory, but he accepts the second phase. According to ALBECK BT grew by accretion generation after generation, and there was no final redaction carried out in one time and in one place. Neither BM nor BB refer to such an event. The "end of *hora'ah*" which took place in the time of Ashi and his contemporary Ravina (I) means the cessation of free interpretation of the Mishnah. After the death of these two masters the Amoraim no longer felt competent to derive new laws from the Mishnah. While ALBECK thus rejects the first part of the traditional theory, he retains the second part. He speaks of "the sealing of the Talmud which was finished (*nistayyem*) in the days of Ravina b. R. Huna" (ALBECK, Sinai Jubilee Vol., p. 79). Given the full endorsement by EPSTEIN and the partial one by ALBECK, it is not surprising that the traditional theory of the redaction of BT was then enshrined in recent textbooks and encyclopedia articles (cf. EPHRATHI, Sevoraic Period, pp. 58—62).

If we return to the original sources, we see that they cannot bear the weight of the traditional theory. The key phrases "the end of *hora'ah*" and "the Talmud was closed/blocked" are far from clear. Interpretations are as numerous as the scholars who discuss these phrases. Moreover, BM includes in the parallel it draws not only Rabbi, but also R. Natan who on no account was an editor of the Mishnah. Thus there is no reason to assume that the parallel between Rabbi and Natan on the one hand and Ashi and Ravina on the other refers to editorial activity on their part. As ALBECK stresses, the passage makes no reference to editing at all. No one interprets *hora'ah* to refer to the latter activity. Nor do BB or the Geonic sources attribute editing to Ashi. As noted, ISG explains BB 157b as alluding to Ashi's review of his learning, an activity attributed to other masters also (cf. WEISS, DTLU, p. 245, n. 9). This is certainly the most reasonable interpretation. In sum, the sources cited earlier may have given rise to the traditional theory, but they cannot support it. And aside from these sources, that theory has nothing else on which to rely.

From the methodological standpoint, the weakness of the traditional theory lies in its dependence on a very few, enigmatic passages. HALEVY stressed long ago that only extensive internal analysis could solve the problem of the redaction of BT. However, he himself could not break free of the framework canonized by the medieval commentators who were, for HALEVY, authoritative. What HALEVY could not do was accomplished almost simultaneously by KAPLAN and A. WEISS. Both rely entirely on internal evidence and follow their results through to the end. Each tests the traditional theory against the internal evidence and finds it wanting. I shall begin with the latter aspect of their work. KAPLAN analyzes at length the material attributed to Ashi. While these passages constitute a major stratum within BT, they are no more prominent than material attributed to other masters such as Ashi's older contemporary, Papa (KAPLAN,

Redaction, p. 78). Moreover, the extent of the material produced after Ashi, including reworking of traditions of the latter, "militates against the commonly accepted tradition that he [Ashi] was its [the BT's] editor", (ibid., p. 95, cf. 127 and the intervening discussion, and 192). A study of the material attributed to Ravina I and II yields similar conclusions regarding the latter (ibid., pp. 128—133, 143—147). In sum, there is no evidence in the sources from the last Amoraic century (= the fifth century) for any editing of BT. KAPLAN concludes that at the death of Ravina b. R. Huna in 499 "the editing of the Talmud was still a task to be undertaken and achieved" (ibid., p. 147).

WEISS also rejects the traditional theory. First he shows that the sources on which the latter is based do not support it. For example, he argues that BM 86a originally referred not to Ashi, but to Assi (i. e., *'śy* or *'sy* instead of *'šy*; *ś* and *š* are identical in the Hebrew alphabet). The latter was the contemporary of Ravina b. R. Huna mentioned in ISG 3 above. The passage means that in the time of Ravina II and Assi the Amoraic era came to an end. WEISS also stresses that Sherira never asserts that Ashi edited BT. In fact, the traditional theory is the creation of the *rishonim*. Nor does any internal evidence prove that the redaction of BT was the work of Ashi (WEISS, DTLU, pp. 245—254). After disposing of the traditional theory WEISS goes on to question the very terms in which the redactional issue is discussed. He asks what could we mean by a "final redaction" of BT? There are two possibilities. Either the final editor reworked the material at his disposal into the form he wanted, or he simply compiled the sources and left them in their original form, at most adding transitions and completions. On either alternative the final editing should have left some traces in BT. However we find no such traces. Certainly there is no evidence of an overall reworking of the material. On the contrary, the material is diverse and contradictory. But even signs of a "scissors and paste" editing are absent. We can discern no general principle of arrangement such as we find in the Mishnah, for example. In sum, there is not a single feature of BT attributable to a final redaction carried out at one time and in one place (ibid., pp. 243f., cf. ALBECK above).

In place of a final redaction, WEISS posits a continuous redaction. That is, the editing of Talmudic materials was simultaneous with their creation. Each generation created new Talmudic material which they added to the Talmud received from previous generations. In addition, Baraitot and Amoraic sources not previously included in the older Talmud might be inserted. The newly added material becomes an integral part of the Talmud which is then passed on to the next generation. This process took place in each center of study in Babylonia. Thus there were several local Talmuds, each of which evolved and grew layer by layer (DTLU, p. 256, SLA, pp. 117f.). The claim that BT grew by accretion from generation to generation appears to go back to Sherira. In the last century HALEVY vigorously argued this position, as ALBECK did in this century (Sinai Jub. Vol.). And as noted above in the discussion of source criticism, most modern scholars assume early redactions or editions of the Gemara. These editions are identical to the strata of BT assumed by WEISS. Where WEISS departs from other scholars is in his denial of a final editing or a 'sealing' of BT. His interpretation of the final stages of the evolution of BT will be discussed in the following section.

To sum up, the traditional theory of the redaction of BT is untenable. Neither the few Amoraic and Geonic sources on which the theory is based nor internal evidence support it. In fact, the internal evidence disproves this theory. There is no convincing evidence that either Ashi, Ravina I, or Ravina II edited BT. Nor is there any sign of a 'sealing' or closing of the document around the year 500. Rather than being closed, BT remained open to extensive addition in the post-Amoraic era. The new material includes entire pericopae indistinguishable from older sources. Thus the 'sealing' of BT in 500 is no less a will-of-the-wisp than the redaction by Ashi. Both stages of the traditional redaction history are unhistorical.

c) The Two Source Theories

The rejection of the traditional redaction history of BT is one of the important achievements in the last half-century of Talmud study. No alternate theory has achieved the wide support once enjoyed by the older view. Still it seems to me that a new consensus is emerging. While differing in terms and details, several recent theories share important structural similarities. They all maintain that BT is composed of two major blocs of material, hence my description of them as 'two source' theories. The scholars to whom this view can be attributed include KAPLAN, KLEIN, RUBINSTEIN, HALIVNI, A. WEISS, and FELDBLUM.

KAPLAN and KLEIN propose the most straightforward version of the two source theory. As explained above, each believes that the two forms they isolate, "gemara" and "talmud" or "sebara", derive from separate sources. And these sources provide the key to understanding the redaction of BT. KAPLAN approaches the latter issue by reinterpreting BM 86a. The term *hora'ah*, he argues, must be interpreted in light of a passage at Ber. 5a:

> "'to instruct them' [Exodus 24:12, *lehorotam*, from the same root as *hora'ah*] — this is *gemara*."

The end of *hora'ah* thus means the end of Gemara. And the latter term has the technical sense of "gemara", viz., the brief summaries of "talmud" arrived at and preserved in writing in the Amoraic academies[60]. KAPLAN finds an historical explanation for the end of "gemara". A persecution towards the end of the fifth century closed the academies and put an end to

[60] KAPLAN, p. 289, n. 2, notes that Codex Munich 95 reads *talmud* instead of *gemara* at Ber. 5a. As B. COHEN points out in his review of KAPLAN, JQR 24 (1933/34), p. 264, *talmud* is clearly the correct reading. This destroys a link in KAPLAN's argument. However, his theory does not stand or fall on this point.

the process by which "gemara" was created. This development also affected "talmud". Previously no need was felt to preserve either the old "talmud" summarized by "gemara" or the new "talmud" created while studying the recently composed "gemara". The ongoing activity of the academies and the written collections of "gemara" made preservation of "talmud" unnecessary. The closing of the academies thus affected both "gemara" and "talmud" (KAPLAN, Redaction, pp. 235—296). Even the eventual reopening of the schools could not turn the clock back. KAPLAN describes the new situation as follows:

> "In the deserted halls of the academies, among the wreckage of the old system of oral instruction, the Saboraim came face to face with the danger of losing contact with posterity. They realized the need to preserve at least a minimum of the exposition necessary to compose a Talmud for the elucidation of the Mishnah and of the gemara. This stupendous undertaking was conceived and accomplished by the Saboraim."
>
> Redaction, p. 297

As the basis of their work the Savoraim took the "gemara" collection of Ashi, for "this was the standard work in the literature of gemara . . . the most authoritative . . . the most complete . . ." (ibid., p. 306). This fact explains the medieval tradition which asserted that Ashi was the redactor of BT. In fact he compiled the "gemara" upon which the Savoraim built our Talmud (ibid., p. 289). To be sure, the latter did not preserve Ashi's work intact, but rearranged it (ibid., p. 307). In addition to the "gemara" of Ashi the Savoraim drew on the "gemara" collections of other academies, treatises on special subjects, and "talmud" material which had been preserved orally (loc. cit.). Despite the role played by older material, "the Saboraim are the designers and real builders of the Talmud" (ibid., p. 301). Thus, according to KAPLAN, BT consists of two major sources: an Amoraic source (essentially the "gemara" collection of Ashi) and a Savoraic source (the "talmud" composed for Ashi's "gemara"). In KAPLAN's own words, "the gemara of R. Ashi, accompanied by the Saboraic exposition, make up the bulk of the present Talmud" (ibid., p. 306).

KLEIN arrives at a conclusion identical to that of KAPLAN, though without the historiographical superstructure of persecutions and closed academies[61]. KLEIN simply states that "the compilation of the Gemara was in fact the work of R. Ashi and Rabina [I or II?] . . . Sebara [was] added during the sixth and seventh centuries, the era of Rabbanan Saborai", (KLEIN, SGR, p. 37, cf. GQS, pp. 344f.). Here too we have two sources: the Amoraic "gemara" and the Savoraic "sebara". S. M. RUBINSTEIN also propounds a similar theory. He argues that our BT is composed of two written sources. The earlier source is a Talmud composed of brief, anony-

[61] I do not mean to imply that the persecutions and closing of the schools were not historical. They clearly were. See NEUSNER, History, Vol. V (Leiden, 1970), pp. 60—69.

mous material without source references, proof texts, or argumentation. This description, of course, recalls the "gemara" of KAPLAN and KLEIN. This early Talmud served as the basis of the second source. The latter completed and explicated the early Talmud, adding source citations, proof texts, and argumentation. These last three elements were often put in the mouths of early masters who appeared in the first source. In addition, the compilers of the later Talmud created entire 'artificial' pericopae out of materials from the early one. According to RUBINSTEIN this explains how early masters sometimes comment on the views of later ones as well as the contradictory parallel pericopae. In the latter case one of the 'inverted' pericopae is 'artificial'. The detailed working out of RUBINSTEIN's theory involves further distinctions and complications, but overall he maintains the two source scheme. He does not explicitly date the two Talmuds. So we cannot know whether his second source is of Savoraic provenance[62].

A different version of the two source theory appears in the Introduction to the second volume of HALIVNI's 'Sources and Traditions'. HALIVNI promises to develop his theory in a later book, but for the present we can rely only on the brief outline in that Introduction. He begins by pointing out that almost half of BT consists of anonymous material. Siding with WEISS against ALBECK and EPSTEIN, HALIVNI argues that most of this material is late. (The few early unattributed sources result from *Tradenten* forgetting who the authors were.) We never find named masters quoting or directly commenting upon anonymous traditions. Where they appear to do so, this is the work of later editors. HALIVNI then asserts, "We must see the *gemara* as a composition made up of two books, a book of Amoraim and a book of anonymous material, which differ from each other in language, methodology, and history" (HALIVNI, ST, Vol. II, pp. 7—8). The anonymous material includes additions interpolated into attributed traditions as well as comments deduced from the words of named masters. Here too we have two sources: the "book of Amoraim" and the "book of anonymous material". The former was apparently completed by the time of Ashi, for HALIVNI suggests that the latter dates from the period between Ashi and the Savoraim (the last 70 years of the fifth century). HALIVNI's brief summary leaves many questions unanswered. Most important, what are the differences in "language, methodology, and history" between the two sources? On what basis does he date the "book of anonymous material" to the last three quarters of the fifth century? Yet even at this preliminary stage the parallels with the theories of KAPLAN, KLEIN, and RUBINSTEIN are apparent.

The assignment of A. WEISS to the two source school is not as obvious as was the case with the four scholars just discussed. Still I believe that he belongs here. First of all, his reconstruction of the redaction of BT is, in its original form, almost identical to that of KAPLAN. As we saw, WEISS

[62] TENNENBLATT, Formation, p. 86, n. 12 infers that both of RUBINSTEIN's sources are Amoraic in provenance.

rejects the concept of a final redaction. Instead, he argues that the Gemara evolved from generation to generation as new material was created, edited, and added to the Talmud received from the preceding generation. This process continued until the close of the fifth century. At this point a worsening of the political status of the Jews in Babylonia put an end to it. The deterioration of their position also weakened their creative powers. The persecutions which marked the final decades of the fifth century caused a break in academic activity. After a few years the situation of the Jews improved, and Talmud study resumed. By the time this happened, the older material had achieved a new authority and holiness in the eyes of the people. It was seen as something that could not be created anew. Thus the evolution of Gemara characteristic of the Amoraic period did not resume. However, the received text of the Talmud was not in a finished state. Many pericopae remained without literary polish and explanation. Therefore the sages of the new period saw as their main task the explication of difficult pericopae and the facilitation of the study of the Talmud in general. Their literary activity involved adding glosses and connecting links between arguments, adducing sources, copying out parallel pericopae, and the like (DTLU, pp. 256–257). WEISS here agrees with KAPLAN that a persecution put an end to Amoraic literary activity, and that the Savoraim felt incapable of continuing the latter. He differs by limiting the contribution of the Savoraim to "literary polishing". Yet the Amoraic Talmud he posits, with its unfinished, unpolished pericopae, recalls the first member of the various two source theories discussed above.

WEISS later revised his account of the last stages of the formation of BT. In his final statement on this issue he drops the sharp historical and literary break between the Amoraic and Savoraic eras. He now asserts that the evolution of BT continued through the Savoraic period. The Talmud contains not only redactional material from the Savoraim, but entire pericopae. And "regarding literary form and presentation there is no difference between them [Savoraic sources] and the Amoraic Talmud". Moreover, BT contains more of the late pericopae than is usually assumed (SLA, p. 118). In stressing the continuity between the Amoraic and Savoraic strata WEISS somewhat overstates his case. Elsewhere he makes clear that we can often distinguish Savoraic from earlier material (see 'Literary Activities'). And he continues to maintain that the literary polishing of unfinished Amoraic pericopae was a major part of Savoraic activity. In any event, in the revised version of his theory WEISS attributes to the Savoraim a much larger role in the formation of BT. He asserts that were we able to identify all the post-Amoraic material, "we would find that the Talmud produced by the Amoraim was very different, both in quantity and in quality, from the Talmud before us" (Literary Activities, p. 18).

Implicit in WEISS' account is a distinction between the Talmud of the Amoraim and the Talmud of the Savoraim. The former was briefer, stylistically less polished, abrupt in transitions, and poor in cross references and source citations. These are precisely the traits which distinguish the "gemara" of KAPLAN and KLEIN and the early Talmud of RUBINSTEIN. One wonders whether HALIVNI's "book of Amoraim" will turn out to share these traits also. The same description calls to mind the rudimentary pericopae characteristic of the five and a half 'unusual' tractates. As noted, WEISS and DE VRIES argue that these pericopae are distinguished by the absence of Savoraic editing and supplementation. That is, in these 5½ tractates we see what the Amoraic Talmud looked like before it was supplemented by the Savoraic Talmud. Another illustration of the former may be found in the materials introduced by the formula *vehavēnan bah*. We recall that DE VRIES argued that these sources were simple pericopae which he assigned to an early edition of the Gemara. Still further illustration of the nature of the Amoraic Talmud comes from the Palestinian Talmud. Both RUBINSTEIN and GOLDBERG note that when we separate out the older stratum of BT, we find pericopae identical in form to the simpler, less polished pericopae of the Palestinian Gemara (see GOLDBERG, Tarbiz 32). In any case, WEISS concludes that the Talmud of the Savoraim remedied the deficiencies of the Amoraic Talmud — just as the "talmud" or "sebara" did for the "gemara" of KAPLAN and KLEIN, RUBINSTEIN's later Talmud for his early one, and, in a sense, HALIVNI's "book of anonymous material" for his "book of Amoraim". In connection with HALIVNI, I note that WEISS' student, M. S. FELDBLUM, identifies the anonymous element in BT as post-Amoraic (FELDBLUM, PAAJR 38). FRIEDMAN also argues that the anonymous framework is (in most cases) later than the statements of the Amoraim, though he does not explicitly attribute the later stratum to the Savoraim (FRIEDMAN, 'Critical Study').

Thus a consensus has emerged which recognizes two main sources or strata within BT. The Amoraic stratum contains material, most of it attributed to named masters, from the third through the fifth centuries. The Savoraic stratum dates from the sixth and seventh century and is mostly anonymous. The first element evolved from generation to generation and probably never underwent a final redaction — aside from the editing it received at the hands of the Savoraim. The later element both explicates and expands the older material. That is, it glossed and edited the older stratum, but it also created new material on the model of the older sources. Each stratum of Talmud is itself complex and composed of various sources. Because of its anonymity I doubt that we shall be able to say much about the formation of the Savoraic Talmud. However, more progress in the isolation and identification of this stratum can be expected. Several questions remain to be answered. What caused the change in style from attributed to anonymous traditions? Why did the Savoraic form of literary activity — anonymous additions to BT — cease in the eighth century, when separate books attributed to authors began to appear in rabbinic circles in Babylonia? Nonetheless the redactional history suggested by the new consensus, which is based on extensive internal analysis of BT, is a clear advance over the traditional theory discussed in the previous section. The emergence of this new theory is another important achievement of Talmud scholarship since 1925.

V. Hilfsbücher *and Related Works*

Bibliography

1. Introductions, Methodology, Bibliographies, Encyclopediae, Special Lexica

Albeck, H., Die Entwicklung der Talmudischen Wissenschaft seit Zacharias Frankel, Das Breslauer Seminar. Jüdisch-Theologisches Seminar (Fraenckelscher Stiftung) in Breslau, 1854—1938. Gedächtnisschrift, Tübingen, 1963, pp. 167—174.

Ashkenazi, S. and Yarden, A., Ozar Rashe Tevot. Thesaurus of Hebrew Abbreviations. Jerusalem, 1969.

Assaf, S., Tequfat Hagge'onim Vesifrutah. Jerusalem, 1955. [= TH.]

Bader, G., Cyclopedia of Hebrew Abbreviations. New York, 1951.

Berkovits, E., Talmud, Babylonian, Encyclopedia Judaica, Vol. XV, Jerusalem, 1972, coll. 755—767.

Blidstein, G. J., Method in the Study of Talmud, JAAR 39 (1971), pp. 186—192.

Chajes, Z. H., The Student's Guide through the Talmud by ... Z. H. Chajes, Translated from the Hebrew, Edited and Critically Annoted by J. Schachter. New York, 1960.

Corre, A., ed. Understanding the Talmud. New York, 1975.

De Vries, B., Mavo' Kelali Lasifrut Hattalmudit. Tel Aviv, 1966.

Goldschmidt, L., Oznayim LaTorah. Konkordansiyah leTalmud Bavli lefi Nosim, ed. R. Edelman. Copenhagen, 1959.

Gross, M. B., Oṣar Ha-agadot. 3 Vols. Jerusalem, 1954.

Guttmann, M., Mafteaḥ ha-Talmud. Songrad, Budapest, Wratislaviae, 1906—30. 3 Vols.

Id., Zur wissenschaftlichen Talmudpflege der neueren Zeit, MGWJ 74 (1930), pp. 172—184, 75 (1931), pp. 241—268, 80 (1936) pp. 425—430.

Hasidah, I. I., Oṣar Ma'amare Halakhot. 2 Vols. Jerusalem, 1959.

Hyman, A., Oṣar Divre Ḥakhamim Upitgamehem³. Tel Aviv, 1955.

Id., Toldot Tanna'im Ve'amora'im. 3 Vols. London, 1910. Reprint, Jerusalem, 1964.

Id., Torah Hakketuvah Vehammessurah. 3 Vols. Tel Aviv, 1960.

Jacobs, L., Studies in Talmudic Logic and Methodology. London, 1961.

Jeiteles, B., Oṣar Tanna'im Ve'amora'im. 2 Vols. Manchester, 1961—62.

Joel, I., ed., Index of Articles on Jewish Studies, Vol. 1—5. Jerusalem, 1966—1970.

Kasher, M. M., Torah Shelemah, Vols. 1—5. New York, 1953—1962.

Kasher, M. M. and Mandelbaum, J., eds. Sarei Ha-elef. A Millenium of Hebrew Authors (500—1500 C. E.). New York, 1959. [= SH.]

Kasovsky (Kosowsky), B., Thesaurus Nominum quae in Talmude Babilonico reperiuntur, Vols. 1ff. Jerusalem, 1976ff.

Kasovsky, C. J. and B., Thesaurus Talmudis: Concordantiae verborum quae in Talmude Babilonico reperiuntur. Vols. 1ff. Jerusalem, 1954ff.

Kolatch, A. J., Who's Who in the Talmud. New York, 1964.

Konovitz, Y., Ma'arkhot Ha'amora'im. Ma'amarehem Behalakhah Uva'aggadah Mesuddarim Lefi Ha'inyanim. R. Yoḥanan ve Resh Laqish. Jerusalem, 1973. Rav veShemu'el. Jerusalem, 1974.

Krengel, J., Talmud, Jüdisches Lexikon, Vol. 4, 2, Berlin, 1930, coll. 835—855.

Maged, A., Sefer Bet Aharon, Vols. 1ff. New York, 1962ff.

Maimon, Y. L., Abaye veRava. Jerusalem, 1965.

Margalioth, M., Encyclopedia of Talmudic and Geonic Literature. 2 Vols. Tel Aviv, n. d.

Mayer, R., Zum sachgemäßen Verstehen talmudischer Texte, Abraham Unser Vater. Festschrift Otto Michel, Leiden, 1963, pp. 346—355.

MEISELES, I., Talmud, Recent Research, Encyclopedia Judaica Year Book 1974, pp. 266—270.
MELAMMED, E. Z., Mavo' Lesifrut Hattalmud³. Jerusalem, 1961.
MIELZINER, M., Introduction to the Talmud. With a New Bibliography, 1925—1967 by A. GUTTMANN. New York, 1968.
SCHACHTER, J., Mavo' Lattalmud. Tel Aviv, 1954.
ID., 'Oṣar Hattalmud. Tel Aviv, n.d.
SCHÜRER, E., The History of the Jewish People in the Age of Jesus Christ. A New English Version Revised and Edited by G. VERMES and F. MILLAR. Vol. 1. Edinburgh, 1973.
SEVER, M., Mikhlol Hamma'amarim Vehapitgamim. 3 Vols. Jerusalem, 1961—62.
STEINBERGER, N., Bibliyografiyah Lemore Hattalmud. Jerusalem, 1970.
STEINSALTZ, A., The Essential Talmud. Trans. C. GALAI. New York, 1976.
STERN, A., Handbuch der Hebräischen Abbreviaturen. Sighetul-Marmatiei, 1929.
STRACK, H. L., Introduction to the Talmud and Midrash. Philadelphia, 1931.
TOWNSEND, J. T., Rabbinic Sources, The Study of Judaism: Bibliographical Essays, New York, 1972, pp. 35—80.
UMANSKI, Y., Ḥakhme Hattalmud. Jerusalem, 1949.
WIESENBERG, E., Observations on Method in Talmudic Studies, JSemSt 11 (1966), pp. 16—36.
ZEVIN, S. J., ed. Enṣiklopediyah Talmudit. Vols. 1ff. Jerusalem, 1949ff. English Translation by I. EPSTEIN and H. FREEDMAN, Encyclopedia Talmudica. Vol. 1. Jerusalem, 1969.

2. Commentaries

A. Texts

Abraham of Montpellier. Commentary on the Tractates Nedarim and Nazir composed by Rabenu Abraham of Montpellier. Ed. M. Y. BLAU. New York, 1962.
Abraham b. David of Posquieres. Novellae to Tractate Bava Qamma. Ed. S. ATLAS. New York, 1963.
Asher b. Yeḥi'el (Rosh). Tosfe HaRosh to Tractate Qiddushin. ed. M. S. SHAPIRA. Tel Aviv, 1969. Tosfot HaRosh: Bava Meṣi'a'. M. HIRSHLER and J. D. GORODETZKY. Jerusalem, 1959.
Ashkenazi, Beṣalei, Shiṭṭah Mequbbeṣet. 4 Vols. New York, 1966.
Isaiah the Elder of Trani (Rid). Pisqe HaRid Vepisqe HaRiaq. 2 Vols. Ed. A. J. WORTHEIMER, et al. Jerusalem, 1964—66. Teshuvot HaRid. ed. A. J. WORTHEIMER. Jerusalem, 1967. Tosafot HaRid. New York, 1955.
Me'iri, Menahem. Bet Habbeḥirah.
'Avodah Zarah. Ed. A. SOFER. Jerusalem, 1965.
Bava Batra. ed. A. SOFER, New York, 1957.
Bava Meṣi'a'. ed. K. SCHLESINGER. Jerusalem, 1959.
Bava Qamma. ed. K. SCHLESINGER. Jerusalem, 1950.
Berakhot². ed. S. DICKMAN. Jerusalem, 1965.
Beṣah. ed. K. SCHLESINGER, Jerusalem, 1965.
'Eruvin. ed. B. HIRSHLER. Jerusalem, 1968.
Giṭṭin, ed. K. SCHLESINGER, Jerusalem, 1964.
Ḥagigah. ed. Y. S. LANGE. Jerusalem, 1970.
Ḥallah, Sheqalim, Tamid, Middot. ed. A. SOFER. Jerusalem, 1969.
Horayot, 'Eduyot. ed. A. SOFER, Jerusalem, 1969.
Ḥullin. ed. A. LISS. Jerusalem, 1970.
Ketuvot. ed. A. SOFER. Jerusalem, 1947.
Makkot.² ed. S. STERLITZ. Jerusalem, 1965.
Megillah, Mo'ed Qaṭṭan. ed. M. HIRSHLER et al. Jerusalem, 1968.
Nedarim.² ed. A. LISS. Jerusalem, 1970.
Niddah. ed. A. SOFER. New York, 1949.
Pesaḥim.² ed. Y. KLEIN. Jerusalem, 1967.

Qiddushin.[3] ed. A. SOFER. Jerusalem, 1963.
Sanhedrin.[2] ed. A. SOFER. Jerusalem, 1965. ed. Y. RALBAG. Jerusalem, 1971.
Shabbat. ed. Y. LANGE. Jerusalem, 1968.
Shevu'ot. ed. A. LISS. Jerusalem, 1968.
Sukkah. ed. A. LISS. Jerusalem, 1966.
Ta'anit. ed. A. SOFER. Jerusalem, 1967.
Yevamot. ed. S. DICKMAN. Jerusalem, 1968.
Yoma. Ed. H. B. RABITZ. Bene Beraq, 1966.
Soṭah, Nazir, ed. A. LISS. Jerusalem, 1967.

Moses b. Naḥman (Ramban). Novellae. 3 Vols. Jerusalem, 1928—29. Complete Novellae. Ed. M. HIRSHLER. Vols. 1ff. Jerusalem, 1970ff.

Pereṣ, Rabbenu. Tosafot to Tractate Pesaḥim. ed. S. VILMAN. New York, 1970. Tosafot to Tractate Bava Meṣi'a'. ed. M. HIRSHLER. Jerusalem, 1970.

Qinon, Shimshon. Sefer Keritot. ed. S. SOFER. Jerusalem, 1965.

Solomon b. Adret (Rashba). Novellae. 3 Vols. Jerusalem, 1962.

Yom-Tov b. Abraham of Seville (Ritba). Novellae. 3 Vols. New York, 1964. The New Hiddushey Ritba to Baba Metzia. ed. S. A. HALPERN. London, 1962. Commentary of the Ritva on Baba Bathra. ed. M. Y. BLAU, 2 Vols. New York, 1953—54.

A Digest of Commentaries on the Tractates Babha Kamma, Babha Mesi'a and Babha Bhatera of the Babylonian Talmud. Compiled by Zechariah Ben Judah Aghmati. Reproduced in Facsimile from the Unique Manuscript in the British Museum Or 10 013. Edited by J. LEVEEN. London, 1961.

LEWIN, B. M., ed. Otzar ha-Geonim. Thesaurus of the Gaonic Responsa and Commentaries, following the order of the Talmudic Tractates. 13 Vols. Haifa and Jerusalem, 1928—43.

TAUBES, H. S., ed. Otzar ha-Geonim to Tractate Sanhedrin. Jerusalem, 1966.

KIBLEVITZ, S., ed. Otzar Mefarshei Hatalmud. Bava Metzia. 2 Vols. Jerusalem, 1971—73. Makkoth. Jerusalem, 1975.

SCHREIBER, A., ed. Tosfoth Hachme Anglia on Tractate Betzah, Megillah, Kiddushin. Jerusalem, 1970.

B. Studies

APTOWITZER, A., Letoldot Perushe Rashi Lattalmud, B. Heller Jubilee Volume, Budapest, 1941, pp. 3—17.

FRAENKEL, Y., Darko Shel Rashi Beferusho Lattalmud Habbavli. Jerusalem, 1975.

FREIMANN, A., List of the Early Commentaries on the Talmud, L. Ginzberg Jubilee Volume, Vol. 2, New York, 1945, pp. 323—354.

FRIDMAN, S., Sefer Sha'arei Shalom. Tel Aviv, 1965.

KOHN, N. J., Sefer Osar Haggedolim 'Allufe Ya'aqov. 9 Vols. Haifa, 1966—70.

KOHN, P. J., Osar Ha-Be'urim We-Ha-Perushim. Thesaurus of Hebrew Halakhic Literature. London, 1952.

KRENGEL, J., Talmud-Kommentare, Jüdisches Lexikon, Vol. 4, 2, Berlin, 1930, coll. 858—888.

SHAQED, S., A tentative bibliography of Geniza documents. Paris, 1964.

TA-SHMAH, I., 'Hiddushei ha-Rishonim', — their Order of Publication, Kirjath Sepher 50 (1975), pp. 325—336.

URBACH, E. E., Die Entstehung und Redaktion unserer Tossafot, Jahresberichte des Jüdisch-Theologischen Seminars in Breslau, 1936.

ID., The Tosaphists: Their History, Writings, and Methods[2]. Jerusalem, 1955.

3. Translations and Anthologies

A. English

The Babylonian Talmud. Translated into English with notes, glossary, and indices. ed. I. EPSTEIN. 35 Vols. London, 1935—52.

The Talmud with English Translation and Commentary. ed. A. Ehrman. Fascicles 1ff. Jerusalem and Tel Aviv, 1965ff.
Malter, H., The Treatise Ta'anit of the Babylonian Talmud. Philadelphia, 1928.
Cohen, A., Everyman's Talmud. New York, 1949.
Montefiore, C. G. and Loewe, H. M., A Rabbinic Anthology. Philadelphia, 1960.
Newman, L. I. and Spitz, S., The Talmudic Anthology. New York, 1945.
Neusner, J., Invitation to the Talmud. New York, 1973.

B. German

Der Babylonische Talmud ... herausgegeben ... nach der Bombergschen Ausgabe ... nebst Varianten ... übersetzt und mit kurzen Anmerkungen versehen. L. Goldschmidt. 9 Vols. Berlin, Wien, The Hague, 1897—1935.
Geis, R. R., Vom unbekannten Judentum. Freiburg, 1961.
Mayer, R., Der Babylonische Talmud (Auswahl). München, 1963.
Strack, H. L. and Billerbeck, P., Kommentar zum Neuen Testament aus Talmud und Midrasch. 4 Vols. München, 1922—28.

C. Hebrew

Hattalmud Habbavli. trans. and comm., E. Steinsaltz. Vols. 1ff. Jerusalem, 1969ff.
Talmud Bavli 'Im Targum 'Ivri Uferush Ḥadash. ed. Y. N. Epstein. Bava Batra. trans. and comm., S. Abramson. Jerusalem, 1957. Bava Meṣi'a'. trans. and comm., M. N. Ṣoval and H. Z. Dimitrovsky. Jerusalem, 1960. Bava Qamma. trans. and comm., E. Z. Melammed. Jerusalem, 1952.

4. Related Fields

A. History

Amir, A. S., Mossadot Veto'arim Basifrut Hattalmudit. Jerusalem, 1977.
Beer, M., The Babylonian Amoraim. Aspects of Economic Life. Ramat Gan, 1974.
Id., The Babylonian Exilarchate in the Arsacid and Sassanian Period. Tel Aviv, 1970.
Dimitrovsky, H. Z., ed., Exploring the Talmud. Vol. 1. Education. New York, 1976.
Goodblatt, D., Rabbinic Instruction in Sasanian Babylonia. Leiden, 1975.
Neusner, J., A History of the Jews in Babylonia. 5 Vols. Leiden, 1966—70.
Neusner, J., ed. Soviet Views of Talmudic Judaism. Five Papers by Yu. A. Solodukho in English Translation. Leiden, 1973.
Yudelowitz (Judelowitz), M. D., Ha'ir Naresh (Bebavel) Bezeman Hattalmud, Sinai 14 (1943), pp. 94—99, 15 (1944) pp. 93—98, 226—229.
Id., Ha'ir Sura, Sinai 1 (1937), pp. 168—174, 268—275, 2 (1938), pp. 156—162, 317—324, 418—422, 3 (1939), pp. 130—132.
Id., Ḥayye Hayyehudim Bezeman Hattalmud. Ha'ir Pumbedita Bime Ha'amora'im. Jerusalem, 1928.
Id., Ḥayye Hayyehudim Bezeman Hattalmud. Sefer Nehardea. Vilna, 1905.
Id., Meḥoza. Miḥayye Hayyehudim Bezeman Hattalmud. Jerusalem, 1947.
Id., Yeshivat Pumbedita Bime Ha'amora'im. Tel Aviv, 1935.
Zuri, Y. S., History of Hebrew Public Law. The Reign of the Exilarchate and the Legislative Academies. Period of Rav Nachman bar Jizchak (320—355). Tel Aviv, 1938.

B. Archaeology, Geography, Realia

Ben-David, A., Talmudische Ökonomie. Die Wirtschaft des jüdischen Palästina zur Zeit der Mischna und des Talmud, 1. Hildesheim und New York, 1974.

BRAND, Y., Ceramics in Talmudic Literature. Jerusalem, 1953.
GOODENOUGH, E. R., Jewish Symbols in the Greco-Roman Period, Vols. IX—XI; Symbolism in the Dura Synagogue. New York, 1965.
KRAELING, C. H., The Synagogue (= The Excavations at Dura-Europus. Final Report VIII, 1). New Haven, 1956.
KRAUSS, S., Talmudische Archäologie. 3 Vols. Leipzig, 1910—12.
OBERMEYER, J., Die Landschaft Babylonien im Zeitalter des Talmuds und des Gaonats. Frankfurt a. M., 1929.
MONTGOMERY, J. A., Aramaic Incantation Texts from Nippur. Philadelphia, 1913.
NE'EMAN, P., Enṣiklopediyah Lege'ografiyah Talmudit. 2 Vols. Tel Aviv, 1972.
SMITH, M., Goodenough's Jewish Symbols in Retrospect, JBL 86 (1967), pp. 53—68.

C. Religion

BÜCHLER, A., Studies in Sin and Atonement in Rabbinic Literature of the First Century. London, 1928.
GOLDBERG, A. M., Untersuchungen über die Vorstellung von der Schekhinah in der frühen rabbinischen Literatur. Talmud und Midrasch. Berlin, 1969.
HERFORD, R. T., Talmud and Apocrypha. New York, 1933. Reprint, New York, 1971.
HESCHEL, A. J., The Theology of Ancient Judaism. 2 Vols. London and New York, 1962—65.
HIRSCH, W., Rabbinic Psychology. Beliefs about the Soul in Rabbinic Literature of the Talmudic Period. London, 1947.
KADUSHIN, M., The Rabbinic Mind². New York, 1965.
ID., Worship and Ethics. A Study in Rabbinic Judaism. Evanston, 1964.
MACH, R., Der Zaddik in Talmud und Midrasch. Leiden, 1957.
MARMORSTEIN, A., The Doctrine of Merits in Old Rabbinic Literature. London, 1920.
ID., The Old Rabbinic Doctrine of God. 2 Vols. London, 1927—37.
ID., Studies in Jewish Theology. London, 1950.
SCHOLEM, G., Jewish Gnosticism, Merkabah Mysticism, and Talmudic Tradition. New York, 1960.
URBACH, E. E., The Sages. Their Concepts and Beliefs. Trans. from the the Hebrew by I. ABRAHAMS. 2 Vols. Jerusalem, 1975.

D. Law

ALBECK, S., The Law of Property and Contract in the Talmud. Tel Aviv, 1976.
COHEN, B., Jewish and Roman Law. 2 Vols. New York, 1966.
ID., Law and Tradition. New York, 1959.
ELON, M., Jewish Law. History, Sources, Principles. 2 Vols. Jerusalem, 1973.
FINKELSCHERER, H., Zur Frage fremder Einflüsse auf das rabbinische Recht. Samuel und das sasanidische Recht, MGWJ 79 (1935), pp. 381—398, 431—442.
GERSHFIELD, E. M., ed., Studies in Jewish Jurisprudence, I—II. New York, 1971—1972.
GULAK, A., Das Urkundenwesen im Talmud. Jerusalem, 1935.
ID., Leḥeqer Toldot Hammishpaṭ Ha'ivri Betequfat Hattalmud. Jerusalem, 1939.
ID., Toldot Hammispaṭ Beyisra'el Betequfat Hattalmud. Jerusalem, 1939.
ID., Yesode Hammispaṭ Ha'ivri. 4 Vols. Berlin, 1922.
HIGGER, M., Intention in Talmudic Law. New York, 1927.
KATZ, S., Die Strafe im talmudischen Recht. Berlin, 1936.
KIRSCHENBAUM, A., Self-Incrimination in Jewish Law. New York, 1970.
LEVINE, B. A., On the Origins of Aramaic Legal Formulary at Elephantine, Christianity, Judaism and other Greco-Roman Cults. Studies for Morton Smith at sixty, Vol. 3 (= Studies in Judaism in Late Antiquity 12), Leiden, 1975, pp. 55—71.

MUFFS, Y., Studies in the Aramaic Legal Papyri from Elephantine. Leiden, 1969.
RUBIN, S., Das talmudische Recht ... Sachenrecht ... Vienna, 1938.
YARON, R., Gifts in Contemplation of Death in Jewish and Roman Law. Oxford, 1960.

1. Introductions, Methodology, Bibliographies, Encyclopediae and Special Lexica

a) Introductions and Methodology

Methodological and historical introductions to BT began to appear in the Geonic period (ASSAF, TH, pp. 147—153). The oldest extant introduction is the aforementioned Seder Tanna'im Ve'amora'im from the late ninth century. Since this book is a composite of older material, we must assume that the history of BT introductions goes back still farther. Whatever its origins, this genre became a popular one in rabbinic circles. Several introductions were composed in the medieval and early modern periods (see the lists in STRACK, pp. 135—137, CHAJES-SCHACHTER, pp. xvff., and KASHER, SH, pp. 113—117). Recent introductions include the Hebrew works of EPSTEIN, ALBECK, and MELAMMED (listed in the bibliography to Chapter IV). The latter two are general, systematic introductions to both Tannaitic and Amoraic literature, not just to BT. EPSTEIN's 'Introduction to Amoraitic Literature', published posthumously from lecture notes, is both too technical and too specific to be considered a real introduction. The part devoted to BT contains introductions to nine tractates (Pes., Beṣ., Suk., Ned., Naz., Soṭ., Qid., Bekh., and Tem.) and commentaries on six chapters from three tractates (Chapters I and II of Pes., X of BM, and I—III of BB). Also available in Hebrew are several introductions designed for use in Israeli high schools. These books are of some value for the beginner who can read modern Hebrew (see the list in STEINBERGER, Bibliyographiyah, pp. 39—43; the best of these works are those by DE VRIES, MELAMMED, and SCHACHTER). The best introduction in an European language remains that by STRACK. A revised edition of this classic would be a worthwhile project. The introduction of MIELZINER was recently reprinted with the addition of a new bibliography. The section on Talmudic hermeneutics and the dictionary of technical terms make this work very useful. Further insight into Talmudic methodology may be found in JACOBS' book on the subject. Finally, CORRE anthologizes over 30 important contributions to Talmudic studies by twentieth century scholars.

b) Bibliographies

As noted above, the bibliography of STRACK is outstanding for the period up to ca. 1925. M. GUTTMANN's review of 'recent' literature is helpful for the years between 1925—1930 (Monatsschrift, 74, 75, 80), while MEISELES covers the early 1970's. The recent reprint of MIELZINER's 'Introduction' contains a bibliography for the years 1925–1967 compiled by A. GUTTMANN, STEINBERGER'S 'Bibliyographiyah' contains sections on Introductions and Hilfsbücher, Textbooks, Selections, Anthologies, and Translations and includes short evaluations of each work listed. TOWNSEND lists in his 'Rabbinic Sources' bibliographies on editions, translations, and encyclopediae. He also treats targumic and midrashic literature. Exceptionally full bibliographies are found in each volume of NEUSNER'S 'History of the Jews in Babylonia', though of course they are not limited to BT. Attention should also be called to his essay 'Bibliographical Reflections' which appears as Appendix II of the fourth volume of his 'History'. The revised edition of SCHÜRER'S 'History' contains excellent bibliographies in the section 'Sources: Rabbinic Literature' (pp. 68–118). Finally, recent publications can be followed in 'Kirjath Sepher' and in the invaluable 'Index of Articles on Jewish Studies' edited by I. JOEL (beginning with 1966).

c) Encyclopediae and Special Lexica

I include here thesauri and compilations of various kinds. Perhaps the most important work in this category is the word concordance to BT, now nearing completion, by CH. J. and B. KASOVSKY. The latter has begun publication of a name concordance. These monumental works are based on the standard printed text of BT, an unavoidable decision given the current state of text criticism. In any case, the KASOVSKYS' project is of inestimable value to all aspects of Talmud scholarship. Subject concordances have been compiled by GOLDSCHMIDT and M. GUTTMANN. The entries in that by GOLDSCHMIDT are brief phrases in Hebrew-Aramaic keyed both to his German translation and to the standard pagination of the original text. The 'Mafteaḥ' of GUTTMANN is an alphabetical list of subjects and terms from all of rabbinic literature, not just BT. It covers only the first half of the Hebrew alphabet. The fullest name and subject index appears in the final volume of the English translation of BT edited by I. EPSTEIN. Unfortunately this is keyed only to the pages of the translation.

The 'Encyclopedia Talmudica' appearing under the editorship of ZEVIN is devoted exclusively to legal matters. It includes as much medieval as Talmudic material. An English translation of the first volume has appeared. Another encyclopedia devoted to legal topics is HASIDAH'S 'Oṣar', a compilation of rules from rabbinic literature. The two volumes published so far reach the letter m. Several encyclopediae collect sayings of the Talmudic masters. GROSS (''Oṣar'), HYMAN (''Oṣar'), and SEVER ('Mikhlol') arrange the sayings alphabetically. JEITELES (''Oṣar'), KONOVITZ ('Ma'erkhot'), and MAIMON do so by author. HYMAN ('Torah') and KASHER ('Torah Shelemah') collect rabbinic exegesis according to the order of the Bible. The former merely lists the references in rabbinic literature, the latter cites the comments in full. Biographical encyclopediae of the Talmudic masters include the works of HYMAN ('Toldot'), KOLATCH ('Who's Who'), and MARGALIOTH ('Encyclopedia'). The best list, though the most sparse in biographical detail, appears in ALBECK's 'Introduction'. UMANSKI ('Ḥakhme') lists the masters and the pages in BT where they are mentioned. MAGED ('Sefer') has begun an encyclopedia of 'Talmudic principles and personalities'. Two older special lexica remain useful. They are BACHER's 'Exegetische Terminologie' and the glossary of hermeneutics in MIELZINER's 'Introduction'. Among more recent publications, the ''Oṣar Hattalmud' by SCHACHTER is a handy dictionary of technical terms of great help to the beginner. Several dictionaries of abbreviations, which are so common in rabbinic literature, are available. Those of ASHKENAZI, BADER, and STERN, listed above, are full and reliable.

2. Commentaries

Exegetical work on BT begins within the document itself. Later masters explicate the work of earlier ones, and one source explains another. The Savoraic material, as Geonic sources stressed, frequently takes the form of commentary. Commentaries external to BT begin to appear in the Geonic era, in the form of books, responsa, and legal compendia. Many of these works, especially the books of commentaries, are lost or extant only in fragments, though the Cairo Geniza continues to disclose new material (see the bibliography of SHAQED). A full description of the BT related literature of the Geonim appears in ASSAF's 'Tequfat Hagge'onim' (pp. 137—146 for commentaries, 154—210 for legal compendia, and 211—220 for responsa; cf. KASHER, SH, pp. 246—248). B. M. LEWIN published a thesaurus of this material, arranged according the order of BT, in his 'Otzar ha-Geonim'. LEWIN's work covers Ber., Orders *mo'ed* and *nashim*, BQ, and the first third of BM. A similar work on tractate Sanh. was recently published by H. Z. TAUBES.

The post-Geonic commentaries (I include legal epitomes of BT) are divided by Jewish tradition into those of the *rishonim*, ca. 1000—1600, and those of the *aḥaronim*, ca. 1600 to the present. STRACK publishes a list of the major commentaries composed through the nineteenth century (Introduction, pp. 149—154, cf. BACHER, Talmud Commentaries, Jewish Encyclopedia, 12, pp. 27—30 and J. KRENGEL, Talmud-Kommentare, Jüdisches Lexikon, Vol. 4, 2 [Berlin, 1930], coll. 858—888). A fuller list, but covering only the *rishonim*, was compiled by FREIMAN. He records, tractate by tractate, all known commentaries, both published and unpublished (Marx Jub. Vol.; this is an expanded version of the article cited by STRACK, p. 149). The published commentaries of the *rishonim* are also listed by KASHER (SH, pp. 117—245, and see 248—255 for responsa and 255—279 for legal compendia). TA-SHMAH contributes a history of the publication of the early commentaries (Kirjath Sepher 50). For commentaries published since the appearance of KASHER's list the bibliographical journal 'Kirjath Sepher' may be consulted. Many of the major commentaries appear in the standard editions of BT. As mentioned above, the Complete Israeli

Talmud Institute plans a new edition with improved texts of the classical commentaries together with variant readings from manuscripts thereof. Pending completion of this project, the major achievement of the past half century has been the publication of the commentaries of Menaḥem b. Shelomo Hamme'iri of Perpignan (died 1306). Previously this work was available in manuscript only, and when STRACK wrote only the commentary on Suk. and Mishnah Avot had been published. Another recent project seeks to publish selected commentaries of the *aḥaronim*. So far three volumes have appeared under the general editorship of KIBLEVITZ. My bibliography at the head of this chapter lists the most recent editions of the major commentaries, especially those not printed together with BT. Biographical and bibliographical data on the *rishonim* appear in the encyclopedia of KOHN. Similar information on the Tosafists, the Franco-German commentators of the twelfth through the fourteenth centuries, can be found in the works of FRIDMAN and URBACH. The latter also discusses the methodology of these authorities. The history of the greatest BT commentary, that of Rashi, is sketched by APTOWITZER, while FRAENKEL studies its methodology.

All of the commentaries alluded to above are traditionalist in outlook. They all accept the authority of BT. Moreover, they all assume a consistency of religious and legal principles throughout the document. Within the limitations imposed by these assumptions they achieve a high degree of exegetical sophistication. For example, I have already mentioned that the text-critical work of the *rishonim* is compatible with modern philological method. Thus in areas of 'lower criticism' and in exegesis of individual pericopae the traditionalist commentaries have much to teach the modern student of BT (cf. the remarks of HALIVNI in the Introduction to ST, Vol. 1). However, in questions of 'higher criticism', of source, form, and redaction history, they are inadequate. Indeed these issues hardly exist in the ahistorical world view of the medieval commentators. Moreover, even those few commentators with an interest in realia and the historical background of BT were very poorly informed on these subjects. Thus the traditionalist commentaries, which continue to be composed, leave much for the scientific exegete to accomplish.

Oddly enough, modern Talmud scholarship has neglected the task of exegesis. A systematic, modern commentary on BT does not exist. To be sure, hundreds of pericopae have been explicated in the course of recent literary and historical studies. But we have nothing for BT equivalent to LIEBERMAN's commentary on the 'Tosefta' or that of NEUSNER on 'Mishnah-Tosefta' *ṭohorot*. Aside from annotated translations (to be considered below), the only scientific exegetical studies of BT are EPSTEIN's commentary on six chapters (IAL, pp. 145—270), that of HALIVNI on Orders *mo'ed* and *nashim*, RABINOWITZ' 'Notes', and the articles by WEISS collected in 'Notes' (see bibliography to Chapter IV). The work of HALIVNI, which is projected to cover all of BT, is the fullest. But even he does not claim to supply a complete, systematic commentary, The absence of a full, scientific exegesis of BT is one of the failures of modern Talmud scholarship, especially if such an exegesis must precede other literary studies as ROSENTHAL and NEUSNER argue.

3. Translations and Anthologies

The oldest translations of Aramaic sections of BT appear in a ninth century Hebrew recension of Halakhot Pesuqot known as 'Hilkhot Re'u' (see MELAMMED, Introduction, pp. 482f.). Subsequent translations up till 1925 are listed by STRACK (pp. 144f., 154—159). Translations of the entire BT are available in German and English. Both the German version, by GOLDSCHMIDT, and the English one, by several scholars under the editorship of I. EPSTEIN, are generally reliable. The latter has fuller notes. In addition to these works, translations of individual tractates have appeared since 1925 in English, German, Italian, Spanish, Arabic, and modern Hebrew (see STEINBERGER, Bibliyographiyah, pp. 59—74 and TOWNSEND, Rabbinic Sources, pp. 61f.). Among the English translations, the best is MALTER's fully annotated rendition of Ta. However, he does not translate the standard printed text, but an eclectic text which he prepared. A vocalized edition of BT with English translation and commentary began to appear in 1965, edited by EHRMAN. So far only a few fascicles, covering parts of Ber., Qid., and BM, have come out. The strictures of NEUSNER on this project should be consulted (Invitation, pp. 250f.). Most recent translations have been into Hebrew. The highest scholarly level was achieved in an abortive project initiated by EPSTEIN. Only three tractates appeared: BQ, BB, and BM. They include the original text and Hebrew translation in parallel columns with variant readings, cross references, and brief commentary. The translation is too literal and the commentary too brief for these volumes to be of much help to the beginner. The more advanced student will benefit from the fact that these volumes are the work of such outstanding Talmudists as ABRAMSON, DIMITROVSKY, and MELAMMED. A project of greater benefit to the beginner is the Hebrew translation and commentary by A. STEINSALTZ. The latter has already completed about a third of BT. STEINSALTZ succeeds in bringing the Talmud within reach of anyone who reads modern Hebrew. However, the author's outlook is traditionalist.

Selected BT texts in translation have also appeared in several languages. My bibliography above lists works of this kind which have appeared since 1925 in German and English (for Hebrew anthologies and selections see STEINBERGER, pp. 48—58). Generally these anthologies are organized thematically and include sources from all of rabbinic literature. They also exhibit a tendency to prefer non-legal texts. All these factors prevent the reader from gaining an accurate impression of the character of BT. The major exception is NEUSNER's 'Invitation'. This work contains related legal sections from the Mishnah, Tosefta, Palestinian Talmud, and BT in English translation with a detailed commentary and analysis together with a very instructive introduction and a bibliographical supplement. The commentary and analysis enable the reader to follow the mode of Talmudic argument. This book provides the best entry into Talmudic literature for the English reader.

4. Related Fields

a) History

One of the major achievements of recent Talmud scholarship is J. NEUSNER's 'History of the Jews in Babylonia'. This work supersedes all previous histories. NEUSNER summarizes all modern scholarship on the Sasanian background as well as that on the Jewish community of Babylonia itself. More important, he achieves significant breakthroughs in several areas of research. I shall mention just two which are relevant to the study of BT. NEUSNER is the first to define the socio-political role of the masters cited in BT. Previously scholars viewed the masters as "popular leaders" and "part of the people". NEUSNER proves that they constituted a distinct "estate" often in conflict with the masses. Their influence over the people derived from two sources. In civil law and certain areas of ritual they were able to impose their views because of their status as functionaries of the autonomous Jewish administration headed by the exilarch. In other areas they were limited to moral persuasion based on their reputation as "holy men", a reputation they seem to have cultivated. This distinction results in part from NEUSNER's insight that we must distinguish between actual court cases reported in BT and purely academic discussions. A second breakthrough concerns the religion of the Talmudic masters. For our purposes the most important point is NEUSNER's discovery of the ritualistic aspect of their academic activity, a part of what he calls "the ritual of being a rabbi". Both of these points enrich our understanding of BT passages, and they are only examples. A scientific exegesis of BT will have routinely to consult the source index of NEUSNER's 'History'.

M. BEER has contributed two valuable monographs. His 'Exilarchate' complements NEUSNER's study of the relations between the masters and the exilarchs. The detailed study of the economic status of the masters in his 'Babylonian Amoraim' reinforces NEUSNER's discovery of their class status. BEER's work supersedes the inadequate pamphlet on 'The Commercial Life of the Jews in Babylonia' by J. NEWMAN. The latter's 'The Agricultural Life of the Jews in Babylonia', 200–500 (London, 1932) is at best a preliminary collection of relevant sources. Further contributions to the economic history of the Jews in Babylonia appear in the provocative essays by Y. SOLODUKHO, edited in English translation by NEUSNER (Soviet Views). They are written from the standpoint of an orthodox Marxism-Leninism. A. BEN-DAVID's 'Talmudische Ökonomie' is limited to Palestine as its subtitle indicates: Die Wirtschaft des jüdischen Palästina zur Zeit der Mischna und des Talmud (Band I, Hildesheim and New York, 1974). Still this book is helpful for comparative research. YUDELOWITZ' studies on the various Jewish towns in Babylonia also contain data relevant to economic history. Finally, the academic institutions of the Talmudic masters are studied in YUDELOWITZ' monograph on the Pumbedita academy (Yeshivat Pumbedita) and in the present writer's 'Rabbinic Instruction in Sasanian Babylonia'.

b) Archaeology, Geography and Realia

The only archaeological remains of the Jews in Babylonia from Talmudic times are the incantation texts published by MONTGOMERY and others. These texts are important both for the study of Jewish Babylonian Aramaic and for the history of Judaism in Babylonia. The Dura Europos Synagogue is several hundred kilometers from Babylonia. Nevertheless KRAELING uses Talmudic sources to explicate the synagogue frescoes. GOODENOUGH vigorously rejects this approach (see M. SMITH, JBL 76, for the current state of the question). At the very least, the Dura Europos discovery reveals a Mesopotamian Jewish community contemporary with the early Amoraic era in Babylonia. The dearth of Jewish remains from the latter country is symptomatic of a larger problem. In general the archaeological evidence from the Sasanian sphere is less than that available from the Roman world. While considerable progress has been made during the past 50 years in Sasanian archaeology, it still lags behind that of the Roman empire. And in the Jewish sphere the situation has not improved at all. Iraq remains closed to students of Jewish history. Thus both in general topics and in specifically Jewish ones we must often rely on comparative evidence from outside Babylonia. And specialized monographs, such as BEN-DAVID's 'Ökonomie' and BRAND's 'Ceramics in Talmudic Literature', understandably concentrate on Palestine. The only synthetic study available is S. KRAUSS' 'Talmudische Archaeologie'. Published at the beginning of the century, this work is clearly outdated from the archaeological standpoint. Moreover, KRAUSS fails to differentiate the various chronological strata within rabbinic literature. However, as a collection of the literary evidence from Talmudic sources the work still has value. Until Talmudic scholars are allowed into Iraq, OBERMEYER's 'Landschaft' remains the definitive study of the geography of Jewish Babylonia. For the flora, fauna, and minerals mentioned in BT, the studies of I. Löw, cited in the bibliography to Chapter III (above, p. 276) are invaluable.

c) Religion

The only study devoted entirely to the religion of Babylonian Jews appears in the relevant chapters of NEUSNER's 'History'. All other scholars take as their subject 'rabbinic Judaism', a term which covers both Palestine and Babylonia, both Tannaim and Amoraim. NEUSNER himself finds little in the thought of the Babylonian Amoraim not attested in Tannaitic or Palestinian Amoraic sources, so the common approach may be justified. In any case, the general studies of rabbinic Judaism do treat topics and personalities found in BT. BÜCHLER and MOORE claim to treat an earlier period, but many of their sources are from BT. The fullest compendium of rabbinic religious thought is URBACH's 'The Sages', though here too Babylonian Judaism receives limited attention. In the realm of theosophy (I include magic and mysticism) we do have evidence unique to Babylonia. I refer to the incantation texts from late Sasanian times. The implications of this material for Babylonian Judaism are discussed at length by NEUSNER in his 'History'. Jewish theosophy of the Talmudic period in general is studied by SCHOLEM (especially in 'Jewish Gnosticism'), but he concentrates on Palestine.

d) Law

In this area also little differentiation is made between Palestine and Babylonia. This approach is justifiable, for BT is based on a Palestinian law code, the Mishnah. Most recent work is comparative. A. GULAK pioneered the comparative study of Jewish and Roman law (including that of the papyri). Further contributions were made by B. COHEN. R. YARON also exploits the Elephantine documents in his model study on 'Gifts in Contemplation of Death'. His stress on the development of the law enables him to delineate the contribution of specific Babylonian masters. A recent trend in legal research seeks continuities with the Akkadian legal tradition. MUFFS found such continuities both at Elephantine and in BT. B. LEVINE briefly summarizes the current state of research on this question ('Smith Festschrift'). Since BT comes from what had been a center of Akkadian culture, and since bta is much influenced by Akkadian, we can expect to find many such continuities in BT law. Clearly this topic is a promising one for future research. Treatment of the influence of Iranian legal traditions may be found in the article by FINKELSCHERER (MGWJ 79) and in NEUSNER's 'History'.

Indices

I. Index of Names

II. Index of Places

III. Index of Citations

A. Babylonian Talmud and Amoraic Midrashim

B. Medieval Sources

Die Beurteilung Roms in der rabbinischen Literatur

von GÜNTER STEMBERGER, Wien

Inhalt

I. Vorgeschichte

Die geschichtliche Frage der jüdisch-römischen Beziehungen ist viel bearbeitet worden[1]. Hier geht es jedoch nicht so sehr um historische Fakten, sondern um die subjektive Beurteilung Roms und der Römer in den rab-

[1] Literatur in Auswahl: J. JUSTER, Les Juifs dans l'empire romain, 2 Bände, Paris 1914; M. RADIN, Jews among the Greeks and the Romans, Philadelphia 1915; O. ROTH, Rom und die Hasmonäer, Beiträge zur Wissenschaft vom Alten Testament XVII, Leipzig 1914; M. GRANT, The Jews in the Roman World, London 1973; M. S. GINSBURG, Rome

binischen Quellen[2]. Der besprochene Zeitraum reicht von Nero bis Diokletian. Bevor wir auf die einschlägigen Texte eingehen, sei jedoch kurz die Vorgeschichte skizziert, haben doch die jüdisch-römischen Beziehungen schon mehr als zwei Jahrhunderte vor Nero eingesetzt.

Erstmals in der jüdischen Literatur wird Rom in Dan 11,30 genannt:

„Kittäische Schiffe greifen ihn an und er kehrt eingeschüchtert um. Nun wird er zornig gegen den heiligen Bund . . .“[3].

Dieser Vers beschließt eine Darstellung der Geschichte der hellenistischen Welt von der Perserzeit bis zum Zeitpunkt des Verfassers, der demnach kurz nach 168 v. Chr. geschrieben haben muß. Denn hier ist deutlich vom Auftritt des Popillius Laenas vor Alexandrien die Rede, als Antiochus IV. Ägypten wieder aufgeben mußte. Der Verfasser von Dan 11 ist über die politischen Ereignisse seiner Zeit gut informiert, hat daraus jedoch nicht

Abkürzungen:

ANRW	Aufstieg und Niedergang der römischen Welt
HUCA	Hebrew Union College Annual
JJS	Journal of Jewish Studies
JQR	Jewish Quarterly Review
MGWJ	Monatsschrift für Geschichte und Wissenschaft des Judentums
PEQ	Palestine Exploration Quarterly
REJ	Revue des Études Juives

et la Judée, Paris 1928; A. Giovannini—H. Müller, Die Beziehungen zwischen Rom und den Juden im 2. Jh. v. Chr., Museum Helveticum 28 (1971) 156—172; V. Burr, Rom und Judäa im 1. Jh. v. Chr. (Pompeius und die Juden), ANRW I 1, hrsg. v. H. Temporini, Berlin—New York 1972, 875—886; W. Weber, Josephus und Vespasian, Stuttgart 1921; A. Schlatter, Die Tage Trajans und Hadrians, Beiträge zur Förderung Christlicher Theologie I 3, Gütersloh 1897; H. Bietenhard, Die Freiheitskriege der Juden unter den Kaisern Trajan und Hadrian und der messianische Tempelbau, Judaica 4 (1948) 57—77, 81—108 und 161—185; L. Huteau-Dubois, Les sursauts du nationalisme juif contre l'occupation romaine. De Massada à Bar Kokhba, REJ 127 (1968) 133—209; S. Lieberman, Palestine in the Third and Fourth Centuries, JQR 36 (1945f.) 329—370; 37 (1946f.) 31—54. Zu nennen sind auch eine Reihe wertvoller Artikel von E. M. Smallwood in verschiedenen Zeitschriften sowie ihr Buch: The Jews under Roman Rule from Pompey to Diocletian, Studies in Judaism in Late Antiquity XIX, Leiden 1976 (erst nach Abschluß des Manuskripts erschienen).

[2] Wertvolle Materialsammlungen: I. Ziegler, Die Königsgleichnisse in Talmud und Midrasch beleuchtet durch die römische Kaiserzeit, Breslau 1903; S. Krauss, Monumenta Talmudica Band V, Teil I: Griechen und Römer, Wien 1914. — Bearbeitung der Texte: N. Wasser, Die Stellung der Juden gegenüber den Römern nach der rabbinischen Literatur, Zürich 1933; P. Kieval, The Talmudic View of the Hasmonean and Early Herodian Periods in Jewish History, Diss. Brandeis University 1970; M. D. Herr, Roman Rule in Tannaitic Literature. Its image and conception (hebr.), Diss. Jerusalem 1970 (mir nicht zugänglich; Teile davon sind als Aufsätze veröffentlicht und werden später genannt).

[3] כתים wird in der Septuaginta mit Ῥωμαῖοι wiedergegeben und auch heute von der Mehrzahl auf Rom gedeutet: so z. B. O. Plöger, Das Buch Daniel, Kommentar zum Alten Testament XVIII, Gütersloh 1965, 164. Anders J. Carmignac, Les Kittim dans la «Guerre des Fils de Lumière . . .», NRT 77 (1955) 737—748, p. 746: «des navires étrangers».

geschlossen, daß Rom die kommende Macht sein werde. Er steht Rom neutral gegenüber.

Zum ersten direkten Kontakt ist es dann 164/3 gekommen. Nach 2 Makk 11,34—38[4] haben sich die römischen Legaten Quintus Memmius und Titus Manius schriftlich den Juden angeboten, in Antiochien beim syrischen König für sie zu intervenieren. Trotz mancher Einwände gegen die Echtheit des Briefes und die Geschichtlichkeit des Berichts beurteilt die Mehrheit der Interpreten 2 Makk 11 positiv[5]. Außer dieser Stelle erwähnt 2 Makk Rom nur noch in 4,11. Was die Beurteilung Roms betrifft, ist kaum etwas zu entnehmen. Der Verfasser steht Rom positiv oder zumindest neutral gegenüber[6].

Die ausführlichste Schilderung der neuen Großmacht Rom finden wir in 1 Makk 8,1—16, einem Text, der den „um die Mitte des 2. Jahrhunderts in der Bevölkerung des Ostens allgemeinen Vorstellungen von der Macht und Politik der Römer" entspricht[7]. Trotz mancher Ungenauigkeiten und Übertreibungen[8] verrät der Text im allgemeinen eine gute Kenntnis von den

[4] 2 Makk ist im 1. Jahrh. v. Chr. entstanden; die Schrift ist nach eigenem Zeugnis eine ἐπιτομή eines größeren Werkes des Jason von Cyrene, der wohl knapp nach den geschilderten Ereignissen des 2. Jahrh.s geschrieben hat. Vgl. demnächst R. Doran, The Jewish-Hellenistic Historians before Josephus, ANRW II 21, hrsg. v. W. Haase, Berlin–New York 1979.

[5] Z. B. Th. Liebmann-Frankfort, Rome et le conflit judéo-syrien (164—161 avant notre ère), Antiquité Classique 38 (1969) 101—120, pp. 105—107, gegen O. Mørkholm, Antiochus IV of Syria, Classica et Mediaevalia, Dissertationes VIII, Kopenhagen 1966, 163f. Für die Geschichtlichkeit u. a. auch E. Täubler, Imperium Romanum I, Leipzig 1913, 239; E. Will, Histoire politique du monde hellénistique II, Annales de l'Est, Mémoires XXXII, Nancy 1967, 288; J. Briscoe, Eastern Policy and Senatorial Politics 168—146 B.C., Historia 18 (1969) 49—70; T. R. S. Broughton, The Magistrates of the Roman Republic I, Baltimore 1952, 439f., übernimmt die Namen der Legaten für 164 aus 2 Makk. Ebenso positiv praktisch alle Kommentare zu 2 Makk.

[6] Damit ist 2 Makk jedenfalls vor 63 v. Chr. zu datieren. Die gegenüber 1 Makk seltene Nennung Roms könnte allerdings schon eine gewisse Desillusionierung anzeigen.

[7] So H. Fuchs, Der geistige Widerstand gegen Rom in der antiken Welt, Berlin 1938, 46 (Nachdr. ebd. 1964).

[8] Nach V. 3 sind die Römer schon Herren über ganz Spanien, was sie erst 19 v. Chr. geworden sind, auch wenn sie schon 206 die spanischen Besitzungen Karthagos übernehmen konnten; die „Könige" von den Grenzen der Erde in V. 4 sind wohl Hannibal und Hasdrubal; entgegen V. 7 ist Antiochus III. in der Schlacht von Magnesia 190 v. Chr. nicht „lebendig gefangen" worden, sondern konnte fliehen (Verwechslung mit Perseus?); nach Livius 37,39 betrug die Zahl der Kampfelefanten nur 54, nicht 120, wie in V. 6; Schwierigkeiten machen auch die Namen der Provinzen in V. 8; nach V. 15 kamen die 320 Senatoren täglich zusammen: diese Zahl stimmt nur, wenn man, wie schon A. Gentil vorgeschlagen hat, zu den 300 Senatoren auch die Beamten rechnet, die Zutritt zu den Sitzungen hatten — 2 Konsuln, 2 Prätoren, 2 Quästoren, 4 Ädile und 10 Volkstribune (cf. F.-M. Abel, Les livres des Maccabées, Études Bibliques, Paris 1949, 151). Das „täglich" stimmt natürlich nicht; völlig unverständlich ist schließlich, daß der Text von nur einem Konsul weiß (V. 16). Die Annahme Täublers (Anm. 5), 244, das Mißverständnis sei entstanden, weil nur ein Konsul den Vertrag unterzeichnet habe, ist sehr fraglich.

geschichtlichen Umständen des Aufstiegs Roms. Da in den Versen 9—10 die Niederlage des achäischen Bundes und die Plünderung Korinths im Jahre 146 v. Chr. als bekannt vorausgesetzt werden, ist der Standpunkt des Verfassers dieses Textes jedenfalls nicht der des Makkabäers Judas (gestorben im Monat Nisan 160), wie vorgegeben wird. Der Text spricht von der Kriegstüchtigkeit der Römer, dem Wohlwollen, das sie ihren Freunden entgegenbrächten, und ihren Freundschaftsbündnissen (8,1—2); „allen, die sich auf sie verließen, hielten sie die Freundschaft" (8,12); eine Ratsversammlung unter Führung eines einzigen Mannes herrsche über sie und alle gehorchten dem einen ohne Neid und Eifersucht (8,15—16).

Diese auf den ersten Blick unglaublich naive Darstellung ist wohl nur aus einer bestimmten Tendenz des Verfassers zu verstehen. Nach manchen ist Eupolemos, ein Mitglied der Gesandtschaft des Makkabäers Judas nach Rom (8,17), als der Verfasser von 1 Makk[9] oder zumindest von 1 Makk 8[10] anzusehen; dieser wäre daran interessiert gewesen, den von ihm ausgehandelten Vertrag durch eine entsprechende Präambel ins beste Licht zu rücken. Ist es jedoch wahrscheinlich, daß ein Mitglied der makkabäischen Delegation von nur einem Konsul weiß und den Senat täglich zusammenkommen läßt? Die Datierung des Textes in eine spätere Zeit (auch vor 63) ist ebenfalls problematisch, können doch die römischen Machtkämpfe in Palästina nicht unbekannt geblieben sein. Schon die Geschichte des Makkabäeraufstandes hat übrigens auch klargemacht, daß Rom seine Verträge nicht hielt und politische Splittergruppen (wie die Makkabäer) nur unterstützte, solange es damit wichtigere Gegner schädigte (so hatte Rom ein Freundschaftsbündnis mit den Seleukiden und trotzdem einen Vertrag mit Judas geschlossen, seinen Tod dann aber auch nicht gerächt). 1 Makk 8 ist als bewußte Schönfärbung Roms nur in einer Zeit verständlich, in der die Anlehnung an diese Großmacht schon innerjüdisch fraglich geworden war und deshalb verteidigt werden mußte. Eine genaue Datierung ist allerdings nicht möglich.

Der anschließend berichtete Vertrag des Judas mit Rom (1 Makk 8,17—32) ist vielfach untersucht worden[11] und hier nicht zu besprechen; ebensowenig die Stellen über die Bekräftigung des Vertrages unter Jonatan und Simeon (1 Makk 12,1—4.16; 14,16—24.40; 15,15—24)[12] und die ent-

[9] So K. D. Schunck, Die Quellen des I. und II. Makkabäerbuches, Halle (Saale) 1954, 70—74. Vgl. R. Doran (Anm. 4).

[10] So z. B. B. Z. Wacholder, Eupolemos. A Study of Judaeo-Greek Literature, Monographs of the Hebrew Union College III, Cincinnati 1974, 35, der wohl zu Recht 1 Makk 8 für einen Einschub hält (anders G. O. Neuhaus, Quellen im 1. Makkabäerbuch?, Journal for the Study of Judaism 5 [1974], 162—175).

[11] Neben der in Anm. 1 genannten Literatur besonders E. Täubler (Anm. 5) I 239—254. Seit ihm wird die Echtheit des Vertrags fast allgemein angenommen, auch wenn Einzelheiten problematisch sind: E. Schürer—G. Vermes—F. Millar, The History of the Jewish People in the Age of Jesus Christ, I, Edinburgh 1973, 172.

[12] A. Giovannini—H. Müller (Anm. 1) 170 betonen gegenüber der üblichen Auffassung, die Verträge zwischen Rom und den Juden seien nicht erneuert worden, da sie ewig galten, solange sie nicht gebrochen wurden.

sprechenden Texte des Flavius Josephus[13]. Zu betonen ist lediglich, wie sehr der Verfasser das gute Verhältnis zwischen Rom und den Juden herausstreicht[14], womit natürlich auch die Bedeutung der Hasmonäer ins rechte Licht gerückt wird. Mag auch realpolitisch das Verhältnis der Juden zu Rom sich schon unter Alexander Jannäus oder jedenfalls unter dessen Witwe Salome Alexandra gewandelt haben[15], so hat doch erst das Eingreifen des Pompeius im Jahre 63 einen entsprechenden literarischen Niederschlag gefunden.

Weiß Josephus dem Verhalten des Pompeius in Jerusalem trotz der Tempelschändung positive Seiten abzugewinnen (AJ XIV,4,4 = 69—73), so sind die Verfasser der Psalmen Salomos, die noch unter dem Eindruck der Ereignisse standen, bedeutend kritischer. Ps 8,15—21 sieht das Geschehen als gerechtes Gottesgericht, das mit der Hasmonäerherrschaft abrechnet. Daß Pompeius den Tempel betrat, erwähnt der Verfasser nicht, da er den Römer positiv als Werkzeug Gottes schildern will; viel kritischer ist dagegen schon Ps 17,4—14, der dem Barbaren Pompeius vorwirft, Jerusalem nach heidnischem Kriegsrecht behandelt zu haben. Vollends feindlich gegenüber Rom ist schließlich Ps 2, der den Tod des Pompeius im Jahre 48 als verdientes Gericht wegen seiner Gottlosigkeit deutet[16].

Den Wandel in der jüdischen Einstellung zu Rom nach der Eroberung Jerusalems durch Pompeius reflektiert auch das wohl in der zweiten Hälfte des 1. vorchristlichen Jahrhunderts in der jüdischen Gemeinde von Alexandrien entstandene dritte Buch der Oracula Sibyllina[17], auch wenn die Ereignisse des Jahres 63 nicht explizit erwähnt werden. Antirömisch sind die Verse 46—62; 175—195; 350—366; 464—469; 470—473; 520—535[18].

[13] Die Einstellung des Josephus bespricht O. MICHEL, Die Rettung Israels und die Rolle Roms nach den Reden im 'Bellum Iudaicum' des Josephus, ANRW II 21, hrsg. v. W. HAASE, Berlin–New York 1979f. Siehe auch H. LINDNER, Die Geschichtsauffassung des Flavius Josephus im Bellum Judaicum, Arbeiten zur Geschichte des antiken Judentums und des Urchristentums XII, Leiden 1972. Zur Darstellung der Hasmonäerzeit bei Josephus cf. M. STERN, The Relations between Judaea and Rome during the Rule of John Hyrcanus (hebr.), Zion 26 (1961) 1—22; U. RAPPAPORT, La Judée et Rome pendant le règne d'Alexandre Jannée, REJ 127 (1968) 329—345.

[14] So betont 1 Makk 14,16—19 die Trauer über Jonatans Tod in Rom; aus eigener Initiative Roms wird der Vertrag Simeon bestätigt, und erst 14,24 wird nachträglich erwähnt, daß die Juden dafür einen goldenen Schild gestiftet haben. Cf. dazu E. WILL (Anm. 5) II 342.

[15] U. RAPPAPORT (Anm. 13) vermutet, daß schon Alexander Jannäus eine romfeindliche Politik betrieben habe. Dagegen A. SCHALIT, Die Erhebung Vespasians nach Flavius Josephus, Talmud und Midrasch. Zur Geschichte einer messianischen Prophetie, ANRW II 2, hrsg. v. H. TEMPORINI, Berlin–New York 1975, 208—327, p. 222, Anm. 31.

[16] Ausführlicher zu den Psalmen Salomos V. BURR (Anm. 1) 881f.

[17] V. NIKIPROWETZKY, La Troisième Sybille, Études Juives IX, Paris–La Haye 1970, 216f. Früher wurde die Schrift gewöhnlich ins 2. Jahrh. v. Chr. datiert; die romfeindlichen Texte mußten dann als Nachträge betrachtet oder uminterpretiert werden. Siehe auch den Beitrag von V. NIKIPROWETZKY, La Sibylle Juive et le IIIe livre des pseudo-oracles sibyllins depuis Charles Alexandre, ANRW II 20, hrsg. v. W. HAASE, Berlin–New York 1979f.

[18] Dies sind fast zehn Prozent des Textes: NIKIPROWETZKY, La Troisième Sibylle 201, Anm. 8.

Die Qumrantexte[18a] sprechen vielfach von den Kittim. Dieser Ausdruck ist nicht eindeutig; ursprünglich gilt er von den Einwohnern Kitions auf Zypern, dann allgemein von den Bewohnern des östlichen Mittelmeerraums, den Griechen vor allem und den hellenistischen Reichen, besonders den Seleukiden, später jedoch auch von den Römern. Somit ist die Auslegung vieler Texte von Qumran umstritten; viele von ihnen können jedoch unbesorgt auf Rom gedeutet werden. Im Habakukmidrasch (1QpHab) wird der Prophetentext auf die Kittäer gedeutet,

> „w(eil sie) rasch sind und kraftvoll im Kampfe, so daß sie v(iel)e zugrunde richten (und sie unterwerfen) unter die Herrschaft der Kittäer. Sie nehm(en in Besitz viele Länder (?)) und glauben nicht an die Gesetze (Gottes ...) ... die Kittäer, vor denen Furcht und (Schre)kk(en) auf allen Völkern liegt. Mit Vorsatz ist all ihr Planen (darauf aus), Böses zu tun und (mit Arg)list und Trug verfahren sie mit allen Völkern ... die Herrscher der Kittäer, die da verachten die Festungen der Völker und höhnisch über sie lachen. Mit viel Volk umzingeln sie sie, um sie einzunehmen. Unter Furcht und Schrecken fallen sie in ihre Hand und sie reißen sie nieder wegen des Vergehens ihrer Bewohner (?) ... daß sie ihren Feldzeichen opfern und ihre Kriegsgeräte, sie sind (der Gegenstand) ihre(r) Ehrfurcht" (1QpHab 2—6)[19].

Die nächsten Zeugnisse stammen schon aus der Zeit nach der großen Katastrophe des Jahres 70. In ihnen äußert sich letztmals und in nicht mehr zu übersteigernder Form der Haß der jüdischen Apokalyptiker gegen Rom, während sich gleichzeitig schon das gemäßigtere Denken der Rabbinen abzeichnet. Vor allem drei Schriften sind hier zu nennen: 4 Esra, 2 Baruch und die Offenbarung des Johannes; alle drei sind gegen Ende des 1. Jahrh.s nach Chr. entstanden. Sie wenden das Schema der vier Reiche von Dan 7 für ihre Geschichtsdeutung an, um zu zeigen, daß nach dem vierten Reich

[18a] Vgl. allgemein H. Bietenhard, Die Handschriftenfunde vom Toten Meer (Ḫirbet Qumran) und die Essener-Frage. Die Funde in der Wüste Juda (Eine Orientierung), ob. in diesem Band (ANRW II 19,1).

[19] Übersetzung von J. Maier, Die Texte vom Toten Meer, 2 Bände, München—Basel 1960. G. Vermes, Ancient Rome in Post-Biblical Jewish Literature, in: Id., Post-Biblical Jewish Studies, Studies in Judaism in Late Antiquity VIII, Leiden 1975, 215—224, p. 216, meint, daß der antihasmonäische Verfasser in den Kittäern ein göttliches Werkzeug der Rache sah; die Römer seien grausam geschildert, doch "the Romans are not castigated". Doch ist die Kritik an den gottlosen Römern, die ihren Feldzeichen opfern, unüberhörbar. Zu erwähnen ist hier auch 4QpNah 1,3 und 4QpJes 10,33f. (Texte bei J. M. Allegro, Discoveries in the Judaean Desert of Jordan V: Qumran Cave 4, Oxford 1968, 37 und 13f.; Übersetzung in J. Maier 180. 186f.). Weiters ist ein noch unveröffentlichtes Kalenderfragment aus Höhle 4 zu erwähnen, in dem von einem Massaker durch אמליוס (Aemilius Scaurus, Proquaestor des Pompeius) die Rede ist: J. T. Milik, Ten Years of Discovery in the Wilderness of Judaea, Studies in Biblical Theology XXVI, London 1959, 73. Die Deutung der Kittäer auf die Römer hat G. Jeremias, Der Lehrer der Gerechtigkeit, Studien zur Umwelt des Neuen Testaments II, Göttingen 1963, 10—35, für 1QpHab und 4QpNah ausführlich begründet.

(= Rom) die Herrschaft des Messias kommen werde: so ist die Adlervision von 4 Esra 11—12 klar auf das römische Reich zu deuten, auch wenn Einzelzüge der Auslegung nicht sicher sind[20]; der letzte Kaiser ist offenbar Domitian, auf dessen Tod nur noch zwei kurzlebige Herrscher folgen werden, bevor der Löwe = Messias auftritt. Dasselbe Schema finden wir in 2 Bar 39f sowie in der völlig in jüdischer Tradition stehenden Offenbarung des Johannes, die vom kommenden Untergang der großen Hure Babylon träumt (besonders Offb 17—18)[21].

II. Römische Kaiser und Feldherrn in der rabbinischen Literatur

Das rabbinische Judentum, das nach der Zerstörung Jerusalems durch Titus sich zum Hauptvertreter der jüdischen Geistigkeit entwickelt hat[21a], führte die biblische Tradition der Geschichtsschreibung nicht und die apokalyptische Geschichtsdeutung kaum weiter. Die Unzahl an geschichtlichen Informationen, die wir dem rabbinischen Schrifttum dennoch entnehmen können, sind einerseits eine zufällige Auswahl, während andererseits bestimmte Fakten und Personen wohl bewußt verschwiegen worden sind. Um uns ein richtiges Bild vom sich wandelnden jüdischen Urteil über Rom zu machen, müssen wir einerseits die Chronologie der in rabbinischen Texten erwähnten römischen Führergestalten von der Chronologie der Traditionen trennen, andererseits das Urteil über Personen, die oft bald der Legendenbildung anheimfallen, von den wirklichkeitsbezogeneren Aussagen über die Erfahrungen mit Rom im Alltag scheiden. Beginnen wir also mit den rabbinischen Aussagen über Kaiser und Feldherrn, geordnet nach ihrer Lebenszeit.

Die Zeit vor Nero kommt nur sporadisch in den rabbinischen Texten zur Sprache; die Aussagen seien hier kurz zusammengefaßt.

Augustus kommt nur im späten Text CantZuta zu 1,6 (ed. Buber p. 12) vor (10. Jahrh.): die dem Gesetz ungehorsamen Juden sollen ihre

[20] Dazu H. Gunkel in E. Kautzsch, Die Apokryphen und Pseudepigraphen des Alten Testaments II, Tübingen 1900, 344f.; W. Harnisch, Verhängnis und Verheißung der Geschichte, Forschungen zur Religion und Literatur des Alten und Neuen Testaments XCVII, Göttingen 1969, 250—257; R. A. Kraft, "Ezra" Materials in Judaism and Christianity, ob. in diesem Band (ANRW II 19,1).

[21] Zur Bezeichnung Roms als Babylon und allgemein zu den Decknamen Roms in der jüdischen Literatur C. H. Hunzinger, Babylon als Deckname für Rom und die Datierung des 1. Petrusbriefes, in: Gottes Wort und Gottes Land, Festschrift H.-W. Hertzberg, ed. H. Reventlow, Göttingen 1965, 67—77.

[21a] J. Neusner, The Formation of Rabbinic Judaism: Yavneh (Jamnia) from A.D. 70 to 100, ob. in diesem Band (ANRW II 19,2) 3—42.

Zeitrechnung haben „nach dem Jahr 50 der Regierung des Augustus“[22]. Aus seiner Zeit weiß der Talmud eine Anekdote über Herodes zu berichten, der den Tempel neu errichten möchte, doch — wie er dem von ihm geblendeten Baba ben Buta in einem geheimen Gespräch eingesteht — „Angst vor der Regierung Roms“[23] hat. Auf Babas Rat holt er in Rom die Erlaubnis ein, macht sich jedoch inzwischen schon an die Arbeit. Die Römer ahnen sein Vorgehen und lassen ihm ausrichten: „. . . du bist einer der bösen Knechte, die zuerst handeln und dann um Erlaubnis fragen.“ Spöttisch heißt es weiter: „Du bist nicht König und auch nicht der Sohn eines Königs, sondern Herodes hat sich selbst erst frei gemacht[24].“ Der Text spiegelt natürlich nicht die Einstellung Roms zu Herodes, sondern die der Rabbinen, die auch das Mißtrauen Roms gegenüber dem Vasallenkönig und dessen Hörigkeit entsprechend hervorheben. Nach dem Tode des Herodes kam es in Judäa zu Ausschreitungen, die Varus unterdrückte: darauf spielt wohl der Seder Olam Rabba an (ed. RATNER 145): „Vom Krieg des Varus (so statt Assuerus zu lesen) bis zum Krieg des Vespasian achtzig Jahre[25].“

Tiberius findet ebenfalls keine Erwähnung. Ein Ereignis aus seiner Regierungszeit wird jedoch in der Fastenrolle genannt: „Am 3. Kislew wurden die Bilder aus dem Tempelvorhof entfernt.“ Entgegen der Deutung im Scholion bezieht sich der Text nicht auf die Hasmonäerzeit, sondern auf den Abzug der Feldzeichen, die Pilatus unvorsichtigerweise im Tempel hatte aufstellen lassen[26].

Nicht ganz sicher, doch sehr wahrscheinlich ist die Deutung einiger Stellen auf Caligula. In Tosefta Sota XIII,6 (ed. ZUCKERMANDEL 319) heißt es: „Simeon der Gerechte hörte: Das Werk, von dem der Feind sagte, er werde es in den Tempel bringen, hat aufgehört und Gaius Caligula (Kasgalgas und ähnliche Schreibweisen) wurde getötet; seine Erlässe wurden aufgehoben. Dies hat er in aramäischer Sprache gehört[27].“ Das Problem in der Deutung dieses Textes liegt im argen Anachronismus, hat doch Simeon der Gerechte zur Zeit Alexanders des Großen gelebt. Verschiedene Vor-

[22] Zur Berechnung der Regierungsjahre des Augustus in der jüdischen Chronographie siehe S. KRAUSS (Anm. 2) 63.

[23] דרומי fehlt in den üblichen Talmudausgaben; hier mit S. ABRAMSON, Talmud Babli — Massekhet Baba Batra, Jerusalem 1958, ergänzt.

[24] לא רכא ולא בר רכא הורדוס קלניא מתעביד (רכא = rex); Baba Batra 4a. Cf. P. KIEVAL (Anm. 2) 113.

[25] מפולמוס של אסוירוס עד פולמוס של אספסינוס פ׳ שנים. Die Auslegung auf Varus ist heute allgemein: siehe SCHÜRER—VERMES—MILLAR (Anm. 11) I 332, Anm. 9.

[26] בתלתא בכסלו אתנטילו סימואתא מן דרתא. Siehe H. LICHTENSTEIN, Die Fastenrolle. Eine Untersuchung zur jüdisch-hellenistischen Geschichte, HUCA 8—9 (1931—32) 257—351, 299f.; Text 339.

[27] שמעון הצדיק שמע בטלת עבידתא די אמר סנאה להיתיה להיכלא ונהרג קסגלגס ובטלו גזירותיו ובלשון ארמי שמעו. Parallelstellen: Fastenrolle für den 22. Schebat (LICHTENSTEIN 300f.); jSota IX,14 (24b); Sota 33a. Zur Stelle siehe S. KRAUSS (Anm. 2) 64 und N. WASSER (Anm. 2) 33—35.

schläge eines anderen Simeon, der zeitlich paßt[28], sind nichts als unbelegbare Vermutungen. Ein dem R. Jose (ben Chalafta, Mitte 2. Jahrh.) zugeschriebener Satz im Seder Olam Rabba (ed. RATNER 144) reiht zwar Caligula direkt nach Antiochus IV. Epiphanes ein; doch ist kaum anzunehmen, daß ein bei den Juden so gefürchteter Kaiser, wie es Caligula sein mußte, schon so bald in den Bereich des Ungeschichtlichen abgedrängt werden konnte. Wie unlösbar auch der Anachronismus der Texte ist, beziehen sie sich doch auf den Befehl Caligulas, den Kaiserkult im Jerusalemer Tempel einzuführen, was durch seinen Tod dann gerade noch verhindert wurde.

Von Claudius weiß das rabbinische Schrifttum wieder nichts. Erst mit Nero werden die rabbinischen Texte reichlicher.

1. Nero

Die rabbinische Diskussion über die Ursachen der Zerstörung Jerusalems im Jahre 70 erwähnt Nero in einer eigenartigen Vermischung von Tatsachenkenntnis und Legende. R. Jochanan (bar Nappacha, 2. Hälfte 3. Jahrh.) führt die Zerstörung auf eine tragische Verwechslung zurück. Der irrtümlich statt Qamtsa eingeladene Bar Qamtsa wird vom Gastgeber vor die Tür gesetzt. Aus Ärger über die Rabbanan, die seine Demütigung nicht verhindert haben, beschließt er, sie bei der Regierung (wörtlich „Königshaus", בי מלכא) zu verleumden. Er sagt dem Kaiser, die Juden hätten sich gegen ihn erhoben und brächten die vom Kaiser gestifteten Opfer nicht dar. Ein zur Probe an den Tempel gesandtes Opfertier macht er unterwegs opferuntauglich, und die Priester nehmen es nicht an. So kommt es zur Zerstörung des Tempels[29].

Geschichtliche Erinnerung in diesem Teil der Erzählung ist die Verbindung der Zerstörung Jerusalems mit dem Aufhören des Opfers für den Kaiser (im Jahr 66 als Signal für den Aufstand gegen Rom) sowie die Betonung der innerjüdischen Streitigkeiten als Ursache der Katastrophe[30]. Die größeren Zusammenhänge werden dabei — typisch für viele rabbinische Geschichtserinnerungen — auf die Ebene der Anekdote reduziert.

Die Fortsetzung der Erzählung von Gittin 56a sei wörtlich wiedergegeben:

[28] Siehe die Zusammenstellung bei H. LICHTENSTEIN (Anm. 26) 300f.

[29] Gittin 55b—56a. Ekha Rabbati 4,2 (ed. BUBER 71b.f.) bringt eine nur leicht abweichende Parallele zu diesem ersten Teil der Erzählung. Der Verleumder geht dort zuerst zu einem römischen Befehlshaber (שלטון); dieser gibt ihm als Zeugen einen Eparchen auf dem Weg zum Tempel mit. Der Eparch läßt dem König die Richtigkeit der Anschuldigung bestätigen, worauf dieser sofort aufbricht und das Heiligtum zerstört.

[30] Vielleicht darf man Bar Qamtsa mit dem bei Josephus, Vita 9 (§ 33) genannten Führer der romfreundlichen Partei in Tiberias gleichsetzen: Κομψὸς ὁ τοῦ Κομψοῦ. So N. WASSER (Anm. 2) 45f.; A. SCHALIT, Namenwörterbuch zu Flavius Josephus, A Complete Concordance to Flavius Josephus, Supplement I, Leiden 1968, 76.

„Da sandte er gegen sie den Kaiser Nero. Als dieser kam, schoß er einen Pfeil nach Osten ab und er fiel in Jerusalem nieder, nach Westen und er fiel in Jerusalem nieder, nach den vier Windrichtungen und er fiel in Jerusalem nieder. Da sagte er zu einem Kind: Sag mir deinen Schriftvers auf! Und es sagte ihm: 'Und ich räche mich an Edom durch mein Volk Israel usw.' (Ez 25,14). Da sagte er: Der Heilige, gepriesen sei er, will sein Haus zerstören und seine Hände an mir (wörtlich: an diesem Mann) reinwaschen. Da floh er und bekehrte sich zum Judentum. Von ihm stammt Rabbi Meir ab[31]."

Verschiedene Elemente sind in dieser Legende zu beachten. Vor allem ist es die positive Einstellung zum von der Geschichtsschreibung geächteten Kaiser (den trotz seiner freundlichen Einstellung zum Judentum auch die jüdische Sibylle als Bösewicht zeichnet: OrSib 5,143ff.). Nicht aus eigener Initiative zieht er gegen Jerusalem, sondern aufgestachelt von einem jüdischen Verräter. Nur durch seine Vorsicht kann er der ihm damit gestellten Falle entrinnen. Die Befragung des Orakels erinnert an eine ähnliche Szene in MidrPs 79,27 (ed. Buber 180a). Dort erzählt R. Levi (um 300), achtzehn Jahre lang habe eine göttliche Stimme Nebukadnezzar aufgefordert, nach Jerusalem zu ziehen und den Tempel zu zerstören. Doch Nebukadnezzar hatte Angst; schließlich befragte er einen Wahrsager. Für welche Stadt auch immer er einen Pfeil auswarf, er zerbrach, nur nicht jener für Jerusalem. Da wußte er, daß er Jerusalem zerstören werde.

Beide, Nebukadnezzar wie auch Nero, sind nach dieser jüdischen Deutung Gottes Werkzeug wider ihren eigenen Willen. Beide versichern sich durch ein Orakel, lassen Pfeile schießen, die Jerusalems Untergang anzeigen. Nero geht jedoch noch einen Schritt weiter, befragt nicht nur das heidnische Orakel, sondern auch die Schrift und wird so rechtzeitig gewarnt: letztlich wird Gott sich durch Israel an Rom rächen[32]. Diese

31 שדר עלוייהו לנירון קיסר. כי קאתי, שדא נירא למזרח אתא נפל בירושלים, למערב. אתא נפל בירושלים, לארבע רוחות השמים. אתא נפל בירושלים. א״ל לינוקא: פסוק לי פסוקיך, אמר ליה: ונתתי את נקמתי באדום ביד עמי ישראל וגו׳, אמר: קודשא בריך הוא בעי לחרובי ביתיה, ובעי לכפורי ידיה בההוא גברא. ערק ואזל ואיגייר, ונפק מיניה ר״מ. Meine Übersetzung lehnt sich an die von L. Goldschmidt an; jene von S. Krauss (Anm. 2) 65 ist ein Versuch, den Text den historischen Ereignissen anzupassen: „Er (der Angeber) sandte in Betreff ihrer (der Juden) an Kaiser Nero. Als er (der Bote) angekommen war, warf er (Nero) den Pfeil . . . ." Bezeichnenderweise hat er dann auch die Fortsetzung: „Da sandte er gegen sie Kaiser Vespasianus . . . " in diese Texteinheit aufgenommen. Diese gehört jedoch in einen anderen Traditionszusammenhang als die Legende von Neros Flucht vor dem göttlichen Verhängnis. Der Text setzt die Anwesenheit Neros vor Jerusalem voraus, was Krauss durch seine Übersetzung vermeiden will.

32 Daß der soeben von einem Schulkind gelernte Text als Orakel gilt, ist für die antike Welt vielfach belegt, am bekanntesten im *Tolle, lege* bei Augustinus variiert; für den jüdischen Raum ist der Offenbarungstext natürlich eine Bibelstelle. Es gehört zum literarischen Genus der Stelle, daß Nero nicht nur die talmudische Umschreibung für Gott verwendet, sondern auch „Edom" im Schriftvers sofort als Decknamen für Rom versteht. Hier seien die geläufigsten rabbinischen Namen für Rom kurz zusammengefaßt: auf den Gebrauch der Bezeichnung Kittim für Rom habe ich schon hingewiesen (ob. S. 343); sie

Warnung veranlaßt Nero zur Flucht und letztlich zum Übertritt zum Judentum.

Die Flucht Neros ist auf dem Hintergrund der Nerolegende zu sehen, er sei nach Asien entkommen und werde einst wiederkehren[33]. Tacitus schreibt vom Auftreten falscher Neros in Asien und Achaia (Hist. 2,8), und die Offenbarung des Johannes zeugt schon von einer eschatologischen Deutung dieser Herrschergestalt (Offb 13,11—18). Die Vorstellung vom Nero redivivus ist auch im Judentum schnell bekannt geworden, wie aus dem um 80 entstandenen Text OrSib 4,119—139 hervorgeht: Nero ist demnach aus Italien entkommen und hat bei den Parthern Zuflucht gefunden; von dort wird er einst mit Waffengewalt wiederkehren. Ob man mit S. J. BASTOMSKY behaupten kann, dieser Text *"would have been well known to the Talmudic compilers"*[34], ist äußerst fraglich; daher ist auch die Erklärung, Nero komme in der talmudischen Legende nach Jerusalem, weil man OrSib mißverstanden habe, wo zwischen zwei Passagen über Nero von der Zerstörung Jerusalems die Rede ist, nicht tragfähig. Tatsächlich ist Nero nie in Judäa gewesen und auch keiner der uns bekannten Nero-Prätendenten dort aufgetreten; doch erklärt sich dieser Zug des rabbinischen Textes hinreichend aus den Prinzipien der volkstümlichen Erzählweise.

Neros Bekehrung zum Judentum steht in einer Reihe mit anderen Konversionen bekannter Heiden: *"No notable heathen sovereign escaped conversion in the Jewish legends"*, schreibt M. RADIN[35]. Dennoch ist sie mit diesen nicht ganz gleichzusetzen. Gewöhnlich erzählt man die Bekehrung eines Verfolgers der Juden, um die siegreiche Kraft des Judentums zu demonstrieren: auch die ärgsten Feinde werden schließlich von seiner geistigen Kraft besiegt[36]. In der talmudischen Legende tritt jedoch Nero nicht als Judenfeind auf; daher mag das Motiv der Erzählung hier sehr wohl der antichristlichen Polemik entstammen, wie dies neuerdings N. G.

kommt besonders in den Qumrantexten vor. In der rabbinischen Zeit sind besonders beliebt: Edom oder Esau, seltener Babylon, manchmal Amaleq, am häufigsten jedoch „das frevelhafte Reich" (מלכות הרשעה) oder einfach „das Reich". Dazu ausführlicher C. H. HUNZINGER (Anm. 21). Der Aufsatz von S. ZEITLIN, The Origin of the Term Edom for Rome and the Roman Church, JQR 60 (1969f.) 262—263, leitet den Ausdruck in mittelalterlichen Texten aus dem Osterfeststreit und dem daraus resultierenden Verbot im 4. Jahrh. ab, das Schaltjahr öffentlich durch den jüd. Patriarchen verkünden zu lassen, bietet jedoch nichts zur früheren Verwendung dieses Decknamens für Rom.

33 So W. BACHER, Die Agada der Tannaiten II, Straßburg 1890 (= Berlin 1966) 5; S. J. BASTOMSKY, The Emperor Nero in Talmudic Legend, JQR 59 (1968f.) 321—325; N. G. COHEN, Rabbi Meir, A Descendant of Anatolian Proselytes. New Light on His Name and the Historical Kernel of the Nero Legend in Gittin 56a, JJS 23 (1972) 51—59.

34 S. J. BASTOMSKY (Anm. 33) 323. Zur Datierung von OrSib 4 siehe V. NIKIPROWETZKY, Réflexions sur quelques problèmes du quatrième et du cinquième livre des Oracles Sibyllins, HUCA 43 (1972) 29—76, p. 29f.

35 M. RADIN (Anm. 1) 297. Diese These, daß die Verfolger der Juden Proselyten und ihre Nachfahren jüdische Gesetzeslehrer wurden, ist in Gittin 57b besonders deutlich formuliert.

36 W. BACHER (Anm. 33) II 5, Anm. 6.

COHEN wieder betont hat[37]: im Gegensatz zur christlichen Dämonisierung und Eschatologisierung dieses Herrschers zum Antichrist und zum Tier aus dem Abgrund wird er im Judentum zum tragischen Helden, der auf der Flucht vor dem Schicksal zum Glauben findet.

Daß auch eine andere Fassung der Tradition im Umlauf war, die von Neros Verantwortung für die Belagerung Jerusalems wußte, zeigt die Fortsetzung der Erzählung: „Er sandte gegen Jerusalem Kaiser Vespasian. Dieser kam und belagerte es drei Jahre lang." Sonst wird nur noch Neros Tod im Zusammenhang mit der Ausrufung Vespasians zum Kaiser erwähnt.

2. Vespasian

Die rabbinische Erzählung von der Flucht Jochanan ben Zakkais aus Jerusalem in das Lager Vespasians, dem er die Kaiserwürde vorhersagt (Gittin 56a—b; Abot de Rabbi Natan A 4 und B 6; Ekha Rabbati 1,31), hat A. SCHALIT in diesem Werk ausführlich besprochen, so daß ich nicht mehr darauf eingehen muß[38]. Vespasian, dem die rabbinische Literatur

[37] N. G. COHEN (Anm. 33) 59: *"the Nero legend in Gittin 56a is to be taken as part of the Judaeo-Christian polemic"*, eine implizite Zurückweisung der christlichen Fassung der Legende; R. Meir gelte als sein Nachfahre, weil er aus einer Proselytenfamilie Kleinasiens stamme, wohin einst Nero geflohen sein soll.

[38] A. SCHALIT (Anm. 15) 305—321. In der Beurteilung der rabbinischen Texte kann ich allerdings der sonst so lehrreichen Studie nicht folgen. Vgl. zur Auseinandersetzung mit SCHALIT, op. cit., auch H. R. MOEHRING, Joseph Ben Matthia and Flavius Josephus. The Jewish Prophet and Roman Historian, ANRW II 21, hrsg. v. W. HAASE, Berlin–New York 1979f. Zur Sache ferner P. SCHÄFER, Die Flucht Johanan b. Zakkais aus Jerusalem und die 'Gründung' von Jabne, ob. in diesem Band (ANRW II 19,2) 43—101. Der historische Wert dieser Überlieferung ist sicher viel geringer; auf ihre zahlreichen Probleme ist schon vielfach hingewiesen worden. Vor allem scheint eine Verwechslung Vespasians mit Titus vorzuliegen — oder Jochanan hat die Stadt noch vor Beginn der eigentlichen Belagerung verlassen! Daß die Erwähnung der *duces* in Ekha Rabbati ein Anachronismus ist, der in die Zeit Diokletians verweist, ist klar; doch nicht nur dieses erzählerische Beiwerk ist unhistorisch, sondern auch der Kern der Geschichte äußerst fragwürdig. Y. BAER, Jerusalem in the Times of the Great Revolt, Zion 36 (1971) 127—190 (hebr.), geht zwar zu weit, wenn er die rabbinische Erzählung insgesamt als eine Neufassung des bei Flavius Josephus und in christlichen Quellen Überlieferten versteht und sie auf den Anfang des 5. Jahrh.s datiert (p. 185); jedenfalls ist das Verhältnis der rabbinischen Texte zu Josephus und zu verschiedenen Wandermotiven neu zu überprüfen. Zu dieser Tradition über Jochanan ben Zakkai siehe u. a. G. ALLON, Studies in Jewish History I, Tel Aviv 1957, 219—252 (hebr.); J. NEUSNER, A Life of Rabban Yohanan ben Zakkai, Studia Post-Biblica VI, Leiden 1962, 104—128; ID., Development of a Legend, Studia Post-Biblica XVI, Leiden 1970, 228—234; A. J. SALDARINI, The Fathers According to Rabbi Nathan (Abot de Rabbi Nathan) Version B, Studies in Judaism in Late Antiquity XI, Leiden 1975, 60—64. J. FRAENKEL, Bible Verses Quoted in Tales of the Sages, Scripta Hierosolymitana 22 (1971) 80—99, betrachtet die Erzählung in der Fassung von Gittin rein literarisch von den dort zitierten Schriftversen aus, führt jedoch im Verständnis der Erzählung kaum weiter. Gegen Y. BAER 184, der an der Deu-

auch die Belagerung und Eroberung Jerusalems durch Titus zuschreibt, wird als ein gemäßigter Mann geschildert, der kein Interesse daran hat, den Tempel zu zerstören, sondern sich mit einer symbolischen Unterwerfung der Juden zufrieden geben würde (das Motiv wird dadurch unterstrichen, daß Jochanan die Worte Vespasians wiederholt). Er nimmt Jochanan gnädig auf, gewährt ihm seine Bitte und ermöglicht so dem Judentum das Überleben. Die Tendenz der Erzählung, die wir als 'Gründungslegende' des rabbinischen Judentums bezeichnen können, ist eindeutig ein Votum für die friedliche Koexistenz mit dem heidnischen Kaiserreich.

Ekha Rabbati 1,32 (ed. Buber 35a) erzählt dann, wie Vespasian nach Einnahme Jerusalems seine vier Feldherrn mit der Zerstörung der vier Türme Jerusalems beauftragt; Pangar (auch Amgar oder Abgar geschrieben) bekommt das Westtor zugeteilt, kann dieses aber wegen Gottes Nähe nicht zerstören. Darum sagt er Vespasian, beim Anblick des stehenden Turmes werden alle sagen: „Seht die Macht des Vespasian, was er zerstört hat[39]." Dem stimmt der Kaiser zu; dennoch muß sich Pangar, der *dux Arabiae*, wegen seines Ungehorsams vom Turm stürzen, womit sich Jochanans Fluch an ihm erfüllt.

Diese ganze Erzählung ist offenbar spät und Vespasian darin eine Nebenfigur. Y. Baer könnte durchaus Recht haben, wenn er hier eine jüdische Antwort auf die Abgar-Legende vermutet[40].

Neutral gegenüber Vespasian sind die frühesten Texte, in denen er genannt wird: die Mischna Sota IX,14 sagt, daß im Krieg des Vespasian die Kränze der Bräutigame und die Hochzeitstrommel verboten wurden[41]; da parallele Aussagen über den Krieg des Qitos und den „letzten Krieg" folgen, stammt der Satz aus der 2. Hälfte des 2. Jahrh.s; Sifra Bechuqotai 8

tung von Jes 10,34 „Durch einen Mächtigen wird der Libanon fallen" auf einen heidnischen Fürsten Anstoß nimmt und sie in die spätere jüdisch-christliche Polemik verweist, ist jedoch 4QpJes 10,34 zu nennen: J. M. Allegro (Anm. 19) 13f. A. J. Saldarini, Johanan ben Zakkai's Escape from Jerusalem. Origin and Development of a Rabbinic Story, JSJ 6 (1975) 189—204, bietet eine plausible Rekonstruktion der Vorlage, die den verschiedenen rabbinischen Texten zugrunde liegt, und zeigt ihre Entwicklungsgeschichte gut auf. Auch in der historischen Beurteilung kann ich mit ihm übereinstimmen: wir wissen nur, daß die Rabbinen wußten (oder annahmen), daß Jochanan aus Jerusalem entkommen war und in Jabne seine Schule gegründet hatte. Jabne war wohl das Auffanglager der romfreundlichen Juden. Jochanan hat dort zu lehren begonnen und allmählich offizielle Anerkennung erlangt. "The story of the meeting with Vespasian explains that gradual development by one, crucial meeting" (p. 204).

39 וכדו יחזיין בריאתא אמרין חזו חייליה דאספסיאנוס מה אחרב. Etwas abweichend der Text bei Buber.

40 Y. Baer (Anm. 38) 172. Die Legende von König Abgar von Edessa weiß von dessen früher Bekehrung zum Christentum und seiner Beteiligung an der Belagerung Jerusalems zu erzählen. Näher zur Legende E. Kirsten im Reallexikon für Antike und Christentum, ed. Th. Klauser, IV (1959) 588—593. Vgl. auch kurz H. J. W. Drijvers, Hatra, Palmyra und Edessa. Die Städte der syrisch-mesopotamischen Wüste in politischer, kulturgeschichtlicher und religionshistorischer Beleuchtung, ANRW II 8, hrsg. v. H. Temporini u. W. Haase, Berlin–New York 1978, 895f.

41 בפולמוס של אספסינוס גזרו על עטרות חתנים ועל האירס.

(ed. Weiss 112c) nennt die Tage Vespasians in einem Atem mit der Zeit Jawans (Griechenlands) und jener Hamans — nie hat Gott sein Volk im Stich gelassen (Parallele: Megilla 11a).

Direkt negativ beurteilen Vespasian nur späte Texte und zwar nur, wenn er zusammen mit Titus genannt ist: so wendet MidrPs 17,12 (ed. Buber 67a—b) Ps 17,14 über die Frevler, die in diesem Leben alles haben und sogar ihren Söhnen und Enkeln noch vererben können, auf „Vespasian und seine Gefährten“ (dem Zusammenhang nach seine Söhne) an, die sich am Tempelschatz bereichert haben[42]. Der späte Targum zu Klagelieder 1,19 schließlich ist der einzige Text, der Vespasian einen Frevler nennt: „. . . die Römer, die mit Titus und dem Frevler Vespasian heraufzogen und Wälle gegen Jerusalem bauten[43].“

Somit ist das rabbinische Urteil über Vespasian im allgemeinen neutral bis positiv; auch wenn er als der Eroberer Jerusalems gezeichnet und der jüdische Krieg nach ihm benannt wird, gilt doch der ganze Haß des rabbinischen Judentums dem wirklichen Eroberer Jerusalems, Titus.

3. Titus

Titus, laut Suetonius *amor ac deliciae generis humanae,* durch seine Beziehung zu Berenike auch dem Judentum nicht prinzipiell feindlich[44], gilt in der rabbinischen Literatur, die ihm die Zerstörung des Tempels nie verziehen hat, als der größte Frevler (הרשע, der Frevler, ist sein ständiger

[42] ממתים ידך ה׳. אלו הן גבורי עשו שנטלו המלוכה מתחת ידך. ממתים מחלד. שהשלטת אותם בעולם הזה. חלקם בחיים. שעתידין לחיות בחיי השקט ושלוה בעולם הזה ושלום ועושר. וצפונך תמלא בטנם. שהעשירו ממון של הקדשות הצפונות בלשכות וממונם של ישראל. ישבעו בנים. זה אספסיינוס וחבריו. „Vor diesen Leuten rette mich deine Hand, Herr: das sind die Helden Esaus, die das Königtum deiner Hand entrissen haben. Vor den Leuten der Welt: du hast sie in dieser Welt zu Herrschern gemacht. Ihr Anteil ist im Leben: sie werden ein bequemes und glückliches Leben führen in dieser Welt in Frieden und Reichtum. Mit Gütern füllst du ihren Bauch: Sie sind reich geworden von den Weihegütern, die aufgehäuft waren in den Tempelhallen, und vom Reichtum Israels. Satt sind auch die Söhne: das ist Vespasian mit seinen Gefährten.“ Auch die Fortsetzung des Psalmverses wird auf Rom gedeutet. Ekha Rabbati 1,48 erzählt, „Vespasian, seine Gebeine mögen zermalmt werden“, habe drei Schiffe mit vornehmen Männern und Frauen Jerusalems gefüllt, die er in Rom der gewerblichen Unzucht zuführen wollte. Sie hätten es jedoch vorgezogen, sich ins Meer zu stürzen. Gittin 57b erzählt dasselbe von 400 jüdischen Knaben, ohne daß hier ein Kaiser genannt ist. Der Name Vespasians ist demnach mit dieser Erzählung nur sekundär verbunden worden. Die Stelle ist somit für die rabbinische Bewertung Vespasians kaum heranzuziehen; ebenso verhält es sich mit der Auslegung von Gen 27,22 „Die Stimme ist die Stimme Jakobs, doch die Hände sind die Hände Esaus“ in Gittin 57b. Demnach bezieht sich der Vers auf Hadrian, der in Alexandrien eine Unzahl Juden getötet habe (Verwechslung Hadrians mit Trajan), oder auch auf Vespasian, der so viele in Bet-Ter getötet hat (Verwechslung mit Hadrian).

[43] הינון רומאי דעלו עם טיטוס ואספסינוס רשיעא ובנו כרכומין על ירושלם (ed. Sperber IV A 144).

[44] Nach Josephus, BJ VII,5,2 (§ 100—109) hat er es den Bewohnern von Antiochia auch nicht gestattet, die Juden von dort zu vertreiben.

Beiname), den letztlich auch die geziemende Strafe Gottes trifft[45]. Die stark legendarischen Nachrichten über Titus betreffen 1. sein Verhalten im Tempel, 2. seine Heimreise nach Rom und den baldigen Tod, sowie 3. seinen Nachkommen Onkelos.

a) Titus im Tempel:

Die wohl älteste Fassung dieser Erzählung ist in Abot de Rabbi Natan (= ARN) B 7 (ed. SCHECHTER 10b—11a) überliefert. Dieser Text beginnt mit dem Angriff Vespasians auf Jerusalem; mit einem Katapult schossen die Belagerer einen Schweinskopf auf den Opferaltar und verunreinigten ihn dadurch[46]. Dann heißt es wörtlich weiter:

> „Sie zerstörten ganz Jerusalem, bis sie zum Tempel gelangten. Als sie zum Tempel gelangten, sagten sie zueinander: Wer wird zuerst in den Tempel eintreten? Und dort war ein frevlerischer Mann[47], Titus, der Sohn der Frau Vespasians[48], der frech eintrat, um an sich den Text zu erfüllen: 'Der Frevler zeigt ein freches Gesicht' (Spr 21,29).
> Und nicht nur das: er nahm auch das Schwert und durchstach den Vorhang, um an sich den Text zu erfüllen: 'Halsstarrig rennt er gegen ihn an mit den dicken Buckeln seiner Schilde' (Ijob 15,26).
> Und nicht nur das: er schleppte auch eine Hure in das Allerheiligste und begann gegen Gott zu schmähen, zu lästern, zu fluchen und zu spucken; und er sagte: von ihm habt ihr gesagt, er habe Sisera und Sanherib getötet. Siehe, ich bin in seinem Haus und auf seinem Gebiet. Wenn er Kraft hat, soll er herauskommen und sich mir stellen, um an sich den Text zu erfüllen: 'Und er sagt: wo sind ihre Götter, der Fels ihrer Zuflucht, die das Fett ihrer Opfer essen?' (Dtn 32,37f.).
> Abba Chanan (2. Hälfte 2. Jahrh.) sagte: 'Gott, Herr der Heerscharen, wer ist wie du, mächtiger Herr?' (Ps 89,9). Mächtig bist du, der du die

[45] D. SPIEGEL, Die Kaiser Titus und Hadrian im Talmud und Midrasch, Wien 1906, bietet die wesentlichen Quellen, wenn auch äußerst unkritisch.

[46] Deutlicher ist dies in ARN A4 (ed. SCHECHTER 12a–b) ausgedrückt. Einen ähnlichen Vorfall erwähnt Baba Qamma 82b vom hasmonäischen Bürgerkrieg, der zum Eingreifen des Pompeius führen sollte: die Belagerer sollen den in der Stadt Eingeschlossenen als Opfertier ein Schwein in einem Korb über die Mauer geschickt haben.

[47] Eigenartig ist, daß Titus hier wie ein Unbekannter erst eingeführt werden muß.

[48] Wie schon S. LIEBERMAN, Greek in Jewish Palestine, New York 1942, 164f. betont, ist diese Aussage, Titus sei der Sohn der Frau Vespasians und nicht sein eigener, nicht als geschichtliche Aussage gedacht, sondern verächtlich gemeint: seiner Frau ist ein uneheliches Kind jederzeit zuzutrauen. Cf. auch A. J. SALDARINI (Anm. 38) 68, Anm. 15. Dieselbe Aussage scheint auch in mehreren Parallelen auf. S. ZEITLIN, A Life of Yohanan ben Zakkai, JQR 62 (1971f.) 145—155 (eine Rezension von J. NEUSNER), möchte die Bedeutung des Midrasch Tannaim (den er als mittelalterliches Werk betrachtet) abwerten, indem er auf historische Ungenauigkeiten hinweist, darunter auch die Formulierung „der Frevler Titus, der Sohn der Frau des Vespasianus" (טיטוס הרשע בן אשת של אספסינוס) (p. 153). Damit verkennt er den traditionellen Charakter und die polemische Tendenz dieser Aussage.

Schmähung, die Lästerung und den Fluch dieses Frevlers hörst und schweigst. Morgen, wenn sein Maß voll sein wird, wirst du ihn bestrafen, um die Schrift zu erfüllen: ‘In der Fülle seiner Versorgung kommt er in Not’ (Ijob 20,22). Er (Titus) machte eine Art Behälter und stopfte die Leuchter hinein und sammelte die Tempelgeräte ein und füllte drei Schiffe mit Männern, Frauen und Kindern[49].“

Diese Szene ist in zahlreichen Paralleltexten überliefert, die das Erzählte ausmalen bzw. später als schon bekanntes Predigtbeispiel nur noch kurz andeuten[50]. Auffällig ist die starke Verankerung der Erzählung in der Bibel, wobei jedoch ebenso auffällig der einschlägigste Text nicht genannt wird: „Der König handelt, wie es ihm beliebt. Er wird übermütig und prahlt gegenüber allen Göttern, auch gegenüber dem höchsten Gott führt er unglaubliche Reden. Dabei hat er Erfolg, bis der Zorn (Gottes) zu Ende ist“ (Dan 11,36).

ARN A1 (ed. Schechter 2b) bietet eine interessante Variante der Lästerszene.

„‘Nicht komme über mich der Fuß des Stolzen’ (Ps 36,12). Das ist Titus der Frevler, seine Gebeine mögen zermalmt werden. Einen

49 חרבו את כל ירושלים עד שהגיעו להיכל. כיון שהגיעו להיכל אמרו זה לזה מי יכנס להיכל תחילה. ושם היה אדם רשע בן אשתו של אספסיאנוס העז פניו ונכנס לקיים עליו העז איש רשע בפניו. ולא עוד אלא שנטל את הסייף וגדר את הפרוכת לקיים עליו מה שנאמר ירוץ אליו בצואר בעבי גבי מגיניו. ולא עוד אלא שמשך את הזונה והכניסה לבית קדש הקדשים והתחיל מחרף ומגדף ומנאץ ומרקק כלפי מעלה ואומר זה הוא שאמרתם שהרג את סיסרא ואת סנחריב הרי אני בביתו וברשותו אם יש בו כח יצא ויעמוד כנגדי לקיים עליו מה שנאמר ואמר אי אלהימו צור חסיו בו אשר זבחימו יאכלו. אבא חנן אומר ה׳ אלהי צבאות מי כמוך חסין יה. חסין אתה שאתה שומע חירופו וגידופו וניאוצו של רשע הזה ושותק. למחר כשתמלא הסאה שלו תביא עליו את הפורענות לקיים מה שנאמר במלאת ספקו יצר לו. עשה כמין גדנפא ופרק בה את המנורות ולקט את כלי בית המקדש ומלא ג׳ ספינות אנשים ונשים וטף.

50 Abgesehen von einigen Umstellungen und anderen Varianten ist Gittin 56b die nächste Parallele. Die älteste Kurzfassung ist Sifre Dtn 328 (ed. Horovitz-Finkelstein 378f.): hier wie auch in anderen Texten durchsticht Titus beide Tempelvorhänge. Die anderen Belege sind (zum Teil in Kurzfassung mit der alleinigen Szene des durchbohrten Vorhangs, zum Teil ausführlich inklusive der Rückkehr nach Rom und des Todes des Titus): GenRabba 10, 7 (ed. Theodor-Albeck 82f.); LevRabba 20, 5 und 22, 3 (ed. Margulies 458 und 499—502); NumRabba 18, 22 (ed. Mirkin X 214); DtnRabba 1 (ed. Lieberman 21f.); KohRabba 5, 8; MidrPs 121, 3 (ed. Buber 253b); PRE 49 (ed. Luria 117b); PRK Achare (ed. Mandelbaum 392); Tanchuma Chuqqat 1 (auch Buber) und Achare 4 (Buber 5). Wesentlichere Varianten der Erzählung: nach MidrPs ist „der Sohn der Schwester des Titus“ die handelnde Person (nach einer Handschrift von ARN „der Sohn der Schwester des Vespasian: A. J. Saldarini [Anm. 38] 86, Anm. 15); wie die Vorhänge, so werden auch die Huren gern verdoppelt; der Vorhang selbst dient als Behälter für die Tempelgeräte; sobald Titus in den Vorhang sticht, fließt Blut heraus (Gittin); nach anderen Fassungen beginnt das Schwert (GenRabba) oder auch eine Torarolle (NumRabba) zu bluten; Titus beschläft die Huren auf einer ausgebreiteten Gesetzesrolle (Gittin), die er auf dem Altar ausgebreitet hat (LevRabba). Die Unzucht im Allerheiligsten und das Blutwunder (von Gittin ausdrücklich so bezeichnet) stehen also für einige Zeit im Mittelpunkt der ausmalenden Phantasie, bevor die Sache zu abgedroschen wird, als daß man sie noch ausführlich erzählen möchte.

Zweig[51] in der Hand, schlug er auf den Altar und sagte: Wolf, Wolf (*lykos, lykos*), du bist König und ich bin König. Komm und führe mit mir Krieg! Wieviele Ochsen sind doch auf dir geschlachtet, wieviele Vögel auf dir getötet und wieviele Weine auf dir ausgegossen worden und wieviel Räucherwerk hat man auf dir geräuchert! Du richtest die ganze Welt zugrunde; denn es heißt: 'Weh dir, Ariel, Ariel, die Stadt, wo David gelagert hat. Fügt Jahr zu Jahr, laßt die Feste wiederkehren!' (Jes 29,1)[52]."

Mit dem vorangehenden Text hat diese Stelle in der Lästerszene die Polemik gegen die Verschwendung bei den Opfern im Tempel gemeinsam, ein Motiv, das schlecht in den Mund eines Nichtjuden paßt. Hier scheint mir ein wesentlicher Schlüssel für die Entwicklung zumindest eines Teils der Titussage zu liegen. Die Stelle hat nämlich einige interessante Parallelen, die eindeutig älter sind als die in ARN A1 völlig zusammenhanglos gebrachte Erzählung.

Mischna Sukka VIII heißt es, daß Bilga — eine der Priesterwachen im Tempel — die Schaubrote stets im Süden teilte und ihr Ring zum Aufhängen ihres Anteils am Opferfleisch befestigt und ihr Wandkasten geschlossen war. Diese Benachteiligung einer Priestergruppe bei der Verteilung der Opferanteile wird in Tosefta Sukka IV,28 so erklärt:

„Der Ring Bilgas war immer fest und ihr Kasten geschlossen wegen Mirjam, einer Tochter (Sippenangehörigen) Bilgas. Diese war vom Glauben abgefallen und hatte einen Offizier (στρατιώτης) der griechischen Könige geheiratet. Und als die Griechen in den Tempel kamen, kam Mirjam und schlug auf den Altar und sagte zu ihm: Wolf, Wolf (*lykos, lykos*), du hast die Einkünfte Israels verzehrt und bist in der Zeit ihrer Not nicht für sie aufgestanden[53]."

Der im Mund eines Heiden unpassende Vorwurf gegen den Tempelkult hat in dem hier angedeuteten Milieu den richtigen Sitz im Leben: die

[51] זמורה (bei Schechter im Apparat und im Anhang S. 135) ist statt מורה (Schechter im Text) zu lesen. Mit J. Goldin, The Fathers According to Rabbi Nathan, New Haven 1955, 176, Anm. 38, ist darin ein Euphemismus für das Geschlechtsglied zu sehen.

[52] אל תבואני רגל גאוה. זה טיטוס הרשע שנשחקו עצמותיו שהיה זמורה בידו והיה מכה על גבי המזבח ואומר לקוס לקוס אתה מלך ואני מלך. בוא ועשה עמי מלחמה. כמה שוורים נשחטו עליך כמה עופות נמלקו עליך כמה יינות נסכו עליך. כמה בשמים קטרו עליך. אתה הוא שמחריב את כל העולם כלו שנאמר הוי אריאל אריאל קרית חנה דוד ספו שנה על שנה חגים ינקפו.

[53] בלגה לעולם חולקת בדרום, וטבעתה קבועה, וחלונה סתומה, מפני מרים בת בלגה שנשתמדה, הלכה ונשאת לסרדיוט אחד ממלכי יון, וכשנכנסו גוים להיכל באתה וטפחה על גגו של מזבח, אמרה לו, לוקס, לוקס, אתה החרבת ממונן של ישראל ולא עמדת להם בעת צרתם (ed. Lieberman 277f.; leicht abweichend Zuckermandel 200). Cf. jSukka V, 5 (55d) und Sukka 56b. Nach dem babylonischen Talmud schlägt Mirjam mit einer Sandale auf den Altar: Lieberman, Tosefta Ki-fshutah, Part IV, New York 1962, 909, verweist auf die griechische Sitte, ungezogene Kinder mit Sandalen zu schlagen; die hellenisierte Jüdin behandelt demnach den Altar, wie sie es vom Umgang mit unartigen Kindern weiß.

hellenisierte Priestertochter, die in der Zeit der Seleukiden unter Antiochus III. oder IV., als so viele jüdische Priester die hellenistische Bildung für wichtiger hielten als den Gottesdienst im Tempel (2 Makk 4,14), eine Mischehe eingeht, kommt mit den Truppen Antiochus IV. nach Jerusalem zurück und beteiligt sich selbst an der Entweihung des Heiligtums. Das heißt nicht, daß die Geschichte der Tochter Bilgas als solche historisch sein muß; immerhin dürfte jedoch in ihr zur Seleukidenzeit Geschehenes typisiert und dramatisiert worden sein.

Wenn diese Erzählung später auf Titus übertragen wird, so deshalb, weil man in der rabbinischen Tradition in der Person des Titus alle Tempelschändungen zusammenfaßt: die Tempelzerstörung unter Nebukadnezzar wirkt hier noch nach, viel mehr jedoch die Tempelschändung unter Antiochus IV. Epiphanes, vielleicht auch jene durch Pompeius. Andererseits brauchen die Ereignisse unter Antiochus und Pompeius deshalb keine Erwähnung zu finden, weil sie in den Erzählungen über Titus, den letzten Zerstörer des Tempels, ohnehin genügend verwertet sind. Die rabbinische Tradition über den Tempelschänder Titus lebt also weniger von geschichtlicher Erinnerung als vielmehr von einer zusammenfassenden Typisierung. Der auf den Altar katapultierte Schweinskopf (ARN B 7) hat uns schon in dieselbe Richtung gewiesen. Ebenso ist daran zu erinnern, daß in der Verfolgung unter Antiochus IV. Schweineopfer auf den Altären dargebracht werden sollten (1 Makk 1,47)[54].

b) Heimreise und Tod des Titus

Die Fortsetzung der Erzählung in ARN B 7 und Parallelen schildert dann, wie Titus das Schiff besteigt, um zu seinem Triumph nach Rom zu fahren. Ein aufkommender Sturm läßt ihn glauben, nun räche sich an ihm der Gott Israels, der nur auf dem Wasser Macht habe. Erneut lästert er Gott und fordert ihn zum Kampf auf dem Festland heraus; dieser sendet jedoch eine Mücke, die allein mit dem Frevler fertig wird:

[54] Einige weitere Verbindungspunkte: 1 Makk 1, 56 weiß von der Vernichtung der Torarollen; die Schändung des Altars durch Unzucht hat ihr Gegenstück in 2 Makk 6, 4—5, wonach die Heiden sich im Heiligtum mit Dirnen abgaben und auf den Brandopferaltar verbotene Dinge häuften. Die Anwendung dieses Motivs auf Titus mag in seiner Verbindung mit Berenike einen weiteren Anhalt gefunden haben, wie die talmudische Erzählung ja auch die Beziehung des Herodes zu seiner hasmonäischen Gattin Mariamne zu sexueller Perversion hat werden lassen: Baba Batra 3b (dazu A. Schalit, Das Problem des Rundbaus auf der mittleren Terrasse des Nordpalastes des Herodes auf dem Berge Masada. Versuch einer neuen Deutung, Theokratia II [1970—1972] 45—80, pp. 78f.). Die Tempelplünderung hat ihre Parallele in 1 Makk 1, 21—24 und 2 Makk 5, 15—16. Damit ist die Fassung bei Josephus zu vergleichen, nach dem ein Priester den Vorhang und die Tempelgeräte dem Titus ausliefert: BJ VI, 8, 3 (§ 387—391); Vespasian soll die Torarolle und die Vorhänge des Allerheiligsten in seinem Palast verwahrt haben: BJ VII, 5, 7 (§ 162). Der Tannait El'asar ben Jose (Ende 2. Jahrh.) behauptet, den Tempelvorhang in Rom gesehen zu haben; er sei voll Blut von den Opfern des Versöhnungstages gewesen: Meila 17b und Joma 57a. Cf. auch ARN A 41 (ed. Schechter 67a).

„In Rom verließ er das Schiff und die Römer kamen ihm entgegen und begannen, ihn zu feiern, und riefen ihm zu: Besieger der Barbaren! (νικητὴς βαρβάρων)[55]; als er eingezogen war, ging er ins Bad, und als er herauskam, reichten sie ihm einen großen Weinbecher (διπλοποτήριον); während er trank, kroch eine Mücke in seine Nase und fraß sich ins Gehirn durch. Das sagte man den Ärzten, die sein Gehirn öffneten und eine Mücke von der Größe einer kleinen Taube fanden, die zwei Pfund wog[56]."

Die Parallelen haben die Erzählung weiter ausgemalt; so weiß Gittin, daß die Krankheit sieben Jahre gewährt habe und welche Beruhigungsmittel Titus versucht habe. Besonders die Mücke erregt Interesse: Abbaje (4. Jahrh.) überliefert, sie habe einen Schnabel aus Kupfer und Krallen aus Eisen gehabt (Gittin), während R. Elieser ben Rabbi Jose (Ende 2. Jahrh.) in ARN sogar behauptet, sie selbst in Rom auf der Waagschale gesehen zu haben. Sehen wir von der ausgestaltenden Phantasie ab, haben wir hier ein typisches Beispiel der *mors persecutorum*, angeregt durch den frühen Tod des erst 41jährigen Titus an einer geheimnisvollen Krankheit[57]. Gewöhnlich sterben die Verfolger an Magen- oder Darmkrankheiten: so etwa Antiochus IV. in 2 Makk 9,5ff. oder Herodes laut Josephus, AJ XVII,6,6 (§ 168f.)[58]. Arabische Erzählungen berichten jedoch von Nebukadnezzar, Nimrod und sogar von Kaiser Decius, sie seien genauso wie Titus gestorben[59]. Wenn wir berücksichtigen, daß die rabbinische Tradition Nebukadnezzar und Titus stark parallelisiert[60], dürfen wir mit einer jüdischen Herkunft der arabischen Sage rechnen und auch in der besonderen Krankheit des Titus nicht mehr als einen Topos sehen. Somit ist die gesamte rabbinische Tradition über Leben und Tod des Titus, von wenigen allgemein bekannten Einzelheiten abgesehen, rein aus seiner Typisierung zum Erzverfolger entstanden.

[55] Mit A. J. SALDARINI (Anm. 38) 70, Anm. 27 ist der Lesart von ARN נקיטא בדור jene von LevRabba 22, 3 (ed. MARGULIES 501) vorzuziehen, die einfach den griechischen Ausdruck transkribiert: ניקיטא ברבריה.

[56] ירד מספינה לרומי ויצאו בני רומי לקרתו. התחילו מקלסין אותו ואומר׳ לו ניקיטא ברבריה. וכשנכנס נכנס לבית המרחץ וכשיצא הושיטו לו דיפלי פיטורין וכשהוא שותה נכנס יתוש לחוטמו והיה אוכל בפניו עד שהגיע לתוך מוחו. אמרו לרופאים ופצעו את מוחו ומצאו יתוש כגוזל בר יונה משקל תרין ליטרין (ed. SCHECHTER 11a). Wenn es anschließend heißt, daß beim Entfliegen der Mücke zugleich auch die Seele des Titus weggeht, wird hier der Quälgeist des Prinzeps nun offenbar mit seinem Seelenvogel gleichgesetzt. Gittin 56b fügt an, Titus habe verfügt, daß seine Leiche verbrannt und die Asche auf den sieben Meeren ausgestreut werde, damit ihn der Gott Israels nicht finde.

[57] Gegen N. WASSER (Anm. 2) 57f., der in der Mücke ein Bild für den Liebeskummer des Titus um Berenike sieht (nach anderen ist sie Symbol seiner Gewissensbisse), ist diese Stelle im Rahmen der literarischen Gattung wörtlich aufzufassen.

[58] Siehe dazu A. SCHALIT, König Herodes, Berlin 1969, 637—640. 639, Anm. 198 bringt er weitere Parallelen für diesen Topos.

[59] S. KRAUSS (Anm. 2) 69.

[60] Dazu siehe M. ABERBACH, Art. Nebuchadnezzar, Encyclopaedia Judaica XII, Jerusalem 1971, 914—916.

c) Die Konversion seines Neffen

Als einziger Text setzt Gittin 56b—57a die Erzählung über den Tod des Titus hinaus fort:

„Onkelos, der Sohn des Kalonikos, war ein Sohn der Schwester des Titus. Da er zum Judentum übertreten wollte, ließ er Titus durch Totenbeschwörung erscheinen und fragte ihn: wer ist in jener Welt am bedeutendsten? Israel, antwortete er ihm. Soll man sich ihnen anschließen? Er antwortete: ihre Gebote sind zahlreich und du wirst sie nicht erfüllen können. Geh und bedränge sie in dieser Welt und werde zum Oberhaupt, wie geschrieben steht: 'Ihre Bedränger werden zum Oberhaupt usw.' (Klgl 1,5). Jeder, der Israel bedrängt, wird zum Oberhaupt. Er fragte ihn weiter: worin besteht dein Gericht (wörtlich: das Gericht dieses Mannes)? Dieser antwortete: so wie ich über mich selbst entschieden habe; täglich sammelt man meine Asche, richtet mich, verbrennt mich wieder und streut (die Asche) über die sieben Meere[61]."

Anschließend befragt Onkelos die Totengeister Bileams und Jesu; ob er sich dann tatsächlich bekehrt hat, wird hier nicht gesagt, ist aber aus der sonstigen rabbinischen Tradition vorauszusetzen.

Man hat in dieser Stelle einen Beleg für die Neigung einiger Mitglieder der kaiserlichen Familie zum Judentum und in Parallelstellen einen Hinweis auf die Verfolgung unter Domitian sehen wollen[62]. Dies ist äußerst unsicher, vor allem auch wegen der ständigen Identifizierung der beiden Proselyten Onkelos und Aquila in der rabbinischen Tradition[63]. Die Stelle ist vielmehr typisch für die Tendenz, die Verfolger später zum Judentum übertreten zu lassen: da dies beim Erzfeind Titus nicht gut möglich ist, bekehrt sich zumindest sein Neffe; so stammt von ihm wie auch von Nero ein großer jüdischer Gelehrter ab, und dasselbe wird von Hadrian behauptet. Die Titusgestalt selbst erfährt in dieser wohl späten Ausweitung der Le-

61 אונקלוס בר קלוניקוס בר אחתיה דטיטוס הוה, בעי לאיגיורי, אזל אסקיה לטיטוס בנגידא, אמר ליה: מאן חשיב בההוא עלמא? אמר ליה: ישראל. מהו לאידבוקי בהו? אמר ליה: מילייהו נפישין ולא מצית לקיומינהו, זיל איגרי בהו בההוא עלמא והיית רישא, דכתיב: היו צריה לראש וגו', כל המיצר לישראל נעשה ראש. אמר ליה: דיניה דההוא גברא במאי? א"ל: במאי דפסיק אנפשיה, כל יומא מכנשי ליה לקיטמיה ודייני ליה, וקלו ליה ומבדרו אשב ימי.

62 So E. M. Smallwood, Domitian's Attitude toward the Jews and Judaism, Classical Philology 51 (1956) 1—13, p. 8, die auch auf eine gewisse Ähnlichkeit der Namen Clemens und Kalonikos hinweist. Die Stelle Aboda Zara 11a ist nur bedingt als Parallele heranzuziehen. Dort tritt Onkelos, der Sohn des Kalonimos, tatsächlich zum Judentum über, worauf der Kaiser ihn durch römische Truppen gefangennehmen lassen will. Doch Onkelos bekehrt die Häscher, und das auch bei einer zweiten und dritten Truppe, so daß der Kaiser den Versuch aufgibt. Tanchuma Mischpatim 3 (ed. Buber 41a) weiß von der Bekehrung des „Aquila, des Sohnes der Schwester Hadrians".

63 Cf. L. I. Rabinowitz, Art. Onkelos and Aquila in: Encyclopaedia Judaica XII, Jerusalem 1971, 1405—1406.

gende keine Bereicherung, der Prinzeps ist vielmehr für immer als der Verfolger und Bedränger erstarrt.

Domitian wird in der rabbinischen Literatur namentlich nie erwähnt; seine von Cassius Dio und Suetonius betonte Härte gegenüber den Juden hat in den jüdischen Quellen höchstens indirekten Niederschlag gefunden, wenn wir die noch zu besprechende Romreise der Rabbinen unter Gamaliel sowie einige andere Texte auf diese Zeit beziehen dürfen. Eine direkte Judenverfolgung durch Domitian ist jedenfalls durch die Quellen nicht gedeckt[64]. — Auch die den Juden freundlichere kurze Regierung Nervas[65] hat bei den Rabbinen kein Echo gefunden.

4. Trajan und Quietus

Die rabbinische Tradition über Trajan ist äußerst dürftig. Vor allem sind hier die Stellen zum 'Trajanstag' zu nennen. In der Fastenrolle (die die Freudentage Israels nennt, an denen zu fasten verboten ist) heißt der 12. Adar 'Trajanstag' — so allerdings nur in der späten Textüberlieferung, während die besten Handschriften einen יום טיריון anführen, was man als Tag der τυραννίς oder des τυραννεῖον und ähnlich gedeutet hat. Wie H. Lichtenstein feststellt, sind „alle Versuche, das rätselhafte טיריון zu erklären, ... gescheitert"[66]. Der späte hebräische Kommentar zu dieser Angabe setzt jedenfalls die Lesart 'Trajanstag' voraus. Er verbindet den Tag mit der Ergreifung von Lulianos und Pappos (in der rabbinischen Literatur als die Märtyrer von Lydda bekannt); Trajan bedroht sie mit dem Tode — doch während sie noch miteinander sprechen, „kommt zu ihm eine Gesandtschaft aus Rom und zertrümmert seinen Schädel mit Holzscheiten und Knüppeln"[67]. Diese eigenartige Erzählung von der Ermordung Trajans dürfte wohl eine Umgestaltung der Tradition über die Hinrichtung des Lusius Quietus sein, der unter Trajan den jüdischen Aufstand in der Diaspora niedergeschlagen hatte und dann mit der Verwaltung der Provinz

[64] H. Leon, The Jews of Ancient Rome, The Morris Loeb Series, Philadelphia 1960, betrachtet die Verfolgung von Juden unter Domitian (abgesehen von einigen Adeligen) als unbewiesen.

[65] Die Münzlegende FISCI IUDAICI CALUMNIA SUBLATA wird recht verschieden gedeutet, meist jedoch als Beendigung der ungerechten Eintreibmethoden gesehen: so z. B. E. M. Smallwood (Anm. 62) 4. Cf. auch I. A. F. Bruce, Nerva and the 'Fiscus Judaicus', PEQ 96 (1964) 34—45. P. Petit, Histoire générale de l'empire romain, L'Univers Historique, Paris 1974, 154, hat sicher Unrecht, wenn er von der „*suppression de la taxe personnelle versée par les Juifs au Capitole* (fiscus judaicus)" spricht.

[66] H. Lichtenstein (Anm. 26) 272f. Er datiert die Redaktion der Fastenrolle ins 1. Jahrh., den hebräischen Kommentar (das 'Scholion') in die nachtalmudische Zeit: 257f.

[67] לא נסע משם עד שבאת עליו דיופלי של רומי ופצעו את מוחו בגזירין ובבקעות: ed. Lichtenstein 346. Der Text stammt fast wörtlich aus Taanit 18b. Zu Parallelen siehe M. D. Herr, Persecutions and Martyrdom in Hadrian's Days, Scripta Hierosolymitana 23 (1972) 85—125, p. 107f.

Judäa betraut worden war[68]. Dieses Ereignis könnte tatsächlich von den Juden gefeiert worden sein[69].

Nach R. Jakob bar Acha (1. Hälfte 3. Jahrh.) ist der *tirjon*-Tag an dem Tag aufgehoben worden, als Lulianos und Pappos getötet wurden — wohl in der hadrianischen Verfolgung (jTaanit II,13,66a; Parallele jMegilla I,6,70c). R. Nachman (um 300) begegnet mit demselben Hinweis in Taanit 18b (dort heißt es jedoch „Trajanstag“; die Märtyrerbrüder sind Schemaja und Achija) einem Einwand gegen den von ihm auf den 12. Adar festgelegten Fasttag.

Ausführlicher kommt Trajan, den Ekha Rabbati 1,5 (ed. Buber 33a) als den Feind Israels nennt und dessen Zeit nach EsterRabba Prooemium 4 ebenso wie die Zeit Vespasians eine Zeit der Drangsal war, in Zusammenhang mit dem Aufstand der Juden in Ägypten vor. Mekhilta Beschallach 2 (ed. Horovitz-Rabin 95) sagt anonym, daß Israel trotz dreimaliger Warnung in der Bibel dreimal wieder nach Ägypten gezogen und dabei zu Fall gekommen sei, das letztemal in den Tagen Trajans. In jSukka V,1 (55b) wird diese Tradition R. Schim'on b. Jochai zugeschrieben (Mitte 2. Jahrh.) und näher erklärt:

> „In den Tagen des Frevlers Trajan wurde ihm am 9. Ab (dem Jahrestag der Zerstörung des Tempels) ein Sohn geboren und sie (die Juden) fasteten. Zu Chanukka starb seine Tochter und sie zündeten die Leuchter an. Da ließ seine Frau ihm sagen: bevor du gegen die Barbaren Krieg führst, geh und bekriege die Juden; sie haben sich gegen dich erhoben. Er glaubte, in zehn Tagen hinzugelangen, traf jedoch schon in fünf ein ... und die Legionäre schlossen sie ein und töteten sie. Zu ihren Frauen sagte er: seid meinen Legionären hörig, dann töte ich euch nicht. Sie antworteten ihm: was du denen im Jenseits getan hast, tu auch denen auf Erden. Und ihr Blut vermischte sich mit dem Blut jener, und das Blut floß ins Meer bis Zypern[70].“

[68] So Schürer—Vermes—Millar (Anm. 11) 533, Anm. 91. Cf. N. Wasser (Anm. 2) 82.

[69] A. Schlatter (Anm. 1) 95 wendet dagegen ein, dieses Frühlingsdatum passe nicht zur Abberufung des Quietus, die kurz nach Trajans Tod (August) erfolgte. Doch auch sein eigener Vorschlag (p. 96), der Tag feiere einen jüdischen Sieg über Trajan, läßt sich nicht beweisen; noch weniger ist dies für die Ansicht von L. Finkelstein möglich — zitiert bei H. Bietenhard (Anm. 1) 75 —, der Trajanstag feiere die von Trajan den Juden gegebene Erlaubnis zum Wiederaufbau des Tempels in Jerusalem.

[70] בימי טרוגיינוס הרשע נולד לו בן בתשעה באב והיו מתענין. מתה בתו בחנוכה והדליקו נרות ושלחה אשתו ואמרה לו עד שאת מכבש את הברבריים בוא וכבוש את היהודים שמרדו בך. חשב מיתי לעשרה יומין ואתא לחמשה... והקיפן ליגיונות והרגן. אמר לנשיהן נשמעות אתם לליגיונתי ואין אני הורג אתכם. אמרין ליה מה דעבדת בארעייא עביד בעילווא. ועירב דמן בדמן והלך הדם בים עד קפריס. Der Text ist zum Teil verderbt und nach den Parallelen Ekha Rabbati 1 (ed. Buber 42a) und EsterRabba (Prooemium) zu korrigieren. In der Übersetzung habe ich außer einer Umstellung den Jeruschalmi-Text belassen. A. Schlatter (Anm. 1) 91, Anm. 1 hält diese Stelle für eine späte Hinzufügung, da sie nicht erkläre, warum die Juden nach Ägypten hinabgezogen sind. Eine solche Erklärung ist jedoch bei einem Zeitgenossen der Ereignisse nicht notwendig, auch wenn natürlich eine spätere Überarbeitung der Erzählung nicht auszuschließen ist.

Der Text verharmlost den Kriegsgrund als ein bloßes Mißverständnis, als römische Unkenntnis jüdischer Bräuche. Doch weiß er offensichtlich um die Ausdehnung des jüdischen Aufstandes, seine Zentren in Ägypten und Zypern und seine gewaltsame Niederschlagung. Daß Trajan selbst (und nicht Marcius Turbo) den Aufstand niederschlägt, gehört zum Erzählstil. Kurz zuvor berichtet übrigens derselbe Text (55a—b) die Zerstörung der Synagoge von Alexandrien. R. Jehuda (Mitte 2. Jahrh.) sagt: ,,Wer nicht die doppelte Säulenhalle von Alexandrien gesehen hat, hat nie die Herrlichkeit Israels gesehen.“ Und nach der Beschreibung ihrer Pracht fügt er an: ,,Und wer hat sie zerstört? Trajan der Frevler.“

Im Zusammenhang mit diesen rabbinischen Belegen für die Diaspora-Aufstände unter Trajan ist auch die vieldiskutierte Frage zu stellen, ob auch Judäa sich am Aufstand beteiligt hat. Dabei geht es vor allem um die Texte, die von einem Krieg des Qitos sprechen.

Die schon genannte Stelle Mischna Sota IX,14 nennt den Krieg des Qitos zwischen dem Vespasians und dem letzten Krieg: ,,Im Krieg des Qitos verbot man die Brautkränze und auch, daß jemand seinen Sohn Griechisch lehre[71].“ Laut Seder Olam Rabba 30[72] fand dieser Krieg 52 Jahre nach dem Krieg Vespasians statt. Zwei weitere Stellen könnten sich auf denselben Qitos beziehen, sind jedoch zu zweifelhaft, um das Bild ergänzen zu können[73].

Diese spärlichen Hinweise werden fast allgemein auf die Repression des jüdischen Aufstandes durch Lusius Quietus gedeutet, den Trajan eigens von der parthischen Front zurücksandte. Nach den einen bezieht sich der Ausdruck auf seine Aktionen in der Diaspora[74], während andere, gestützt vor allem auf Ps.-Spartians Aussage in der Vita Hadriani 5,2: *Lybia denique*

[71] בפולמוס של קיטוס גזרו על עטרות הכלה ושלא ילמד אדם את בנו יונית. Manche Handschriften lesen statt Qitos Titus, was die Ausgabe der Mischna von H. Albeck in den Text aufgenommen hat.

[72] So in der von Schürer—Vermes—Millar (Anm. 11) 534, Anm. 92 gebotenen Textfassung. Die Zahl macht genauso Schwierigkeiten wie die der üblichen Ausgaben: 24 Jahre.

[73] S. Krauss (Anm. 2) 82 bezieht auf Qitos auch jSanh I, 19b. Der Name des Hegemon, der dort mit Jochanan ben Zakkai spricht, ist אנגיטוס geschrieben (oder אנג׳יטוס; weitere Varianten auf 19c und in den von Krauss herangezogenen Parallelen); Schürer—Vermes—Millar (Anm. 11) 519 möchten diese Stellen eher mit Claudius Paternus Clementianus verbinden. J. Fürst wieder sieht in den Anmerkungen zur Übersetzung von GenRabba durch A. Wünsche (Der Midrasch Bereschit Rabba, Bibliotheca Rabbinica I, Leipzig 1880, Nachdruck Hildesheim 1967, 540) in GenRabba 76, 6 Macrianus, Quietus und Kyriades genannt; ihm folgt die Textausgabe von Theodor—Albeck 903; ebenso S. Krauss, Griechische und lateinische Lehnwörter im Talmud, Midrasch und Targum II, Berlin 1899 (Nachdruck Hildesheim 1964), 566. Die Schreibweise der drei Namen variiert in den einzelnen Handschriften; Theodor—Albeck hat sie überhaupt nicht in den eigentlichen Text, sondern nur in den Apparat aufgenommen.

[74] So J. Neusner, A History of the Jews in Babylonia I, Studia Post-Biblica IX, Leiden 1965, 71: *"the well-known Talmudic sources on the 'war of Qitus' may refer to Mesopotamian action"*; Schürer—Vermes—Millar (Anm. 11) 533f.; A. Fuks, Aspects of the Jewish Revolt in A.D. 115—117, JRS 51 (1961) 98—104, 98: *"repercussions in Judaea, though actual fighting did not occur there"*.

ac Palaestina rebelles animos efferebant, an die Niederschlagung eines Aufstandes in Judäa selbst denken[75]. Neuerdings hat D. ROKEAH sehr beachtliche Argumente gebracht, den „Krieg des Qitos" überhaupt nicht auf Quietus zu deuten, sondern auf Quintus Marcius Turbo, der den jüdischen Aufstand in Ägypten erstickte[76]: *"the 'War of Kitos' refers to a desaster which occurred in a Greek-speaking diaspora, while the prohibition of the Greek language was a manifestation of solidarity with the destroyed Jewish community*[77]." Ob das Verbot des Griechisch-Unterrichts in Palästina damit hinreichend erklärt ist, bleibe dahingestellt; jedenfalls deckt sich die Erklärung mit der Tatsache, daß römische Kampfaktionen gegen die Juden in dieser Zeit einzig für Ägypten rabbinisch belegt sind; da kein Grund denkbar ist, Kämpfe in Palästina zu verschweigen, werden solche auch kaum stattgefunden haben. Die Entsendung des Quietus nach Judäa war demnach eine reine Vorsichtsmaßnahme.

5. Hadrian

Hadrians Bild in der jüdischen Literatur ist zwiespältig. Einerseits gilt er als der dem Judentum positiv und interessiert gegenüberstehende Gesprächspartner besonders des R. Jehoschua b. Chananja; andererseits ist er wegen des Bar-Kokhba-Krieges neben Titus der meistgehaßte römische Kaiser der rabbinischen Literatur geworden.

a) Das positive Hadriansbild

Das Interesse Hadrians für seine Provinzen und die daraus erwachsende Reisepolitik[78] hat auch in der rabbinischen Literatur ihren Niederschlag gefunden. Der Kaiser, den die jüdische Sibylle in seiner frühen Regierungszeit verherrlicht, er werde „der allerbeste Mann sein und alles kennen"[79], gilt als wißbegieriger Mann, den alles interessiert. Mit seinem Namen spielt MidrPs 93,6 (ed. BUBER 208a—b), wenn es heißt, Hadrian wollte die Tiefe der Adria erforschen und ließ dazu dreieinhalb Jahre lang ein Seil hinab,

[75] So z. B. A. SCHLATTER (Anm. 1) 91: „Judäa hat sich offen am Aufstand beteiligt"; N. WASSER (Anm. 2) 78, der seine rabbinischen Quellen recht phantasievoll verwertet; H. BIETENHARD (Anm. 1) 69; F. A. LEPPER, Trajan's Parthian War, Oxford Classical and Philosophical Monographs, London 1948, 212; E. M. SMALLWOOD, Palestine c. A.D. 115 to 118, Historia 11 (1962) 500—510.

[76] D. ROKEAH, The War of Kitos: Towards the Clarification of a Philological-Historical Problem, Scripta Hierosolymitana 23 (1972) 79—84.

[77] D. ROKEAH (Anm. 76) 83.

[78] Cf. M. K. THORNTON, Hadrian and his Reign, ANRW II 2, ed. H. TEMPORINI, Berlin-New York 1975, 432—476, p. 451ff., sowie ausführlich D. MAGIE, Roman Rule in Asia Minor, Princeton, N.J., 1950, I 612—623.

[79] OrSib V, 48 ἔσται καὶ πανάριστος ἀνὴρ καὶ πάντα νοήσει. Siehe dazu V. NIKIPROWETZKY, Réflexions (Anm. 17) 30—33, der OrSib 5 zwischen 117 und 130 datiert.

bis er von Gott gestoppt wurde; dann wieder soll er Männer in Glaskisten auf den Meeresgrund geschickt haben. Ein ebenfalls später Text, Tanchuma Bereschit 5, erzählt, er habe einst Aqilas gefragt, worauf die Welt steht, und als Antwort bekommen: Luft. Sifre Dtn 357 (ed. HOROVITZ-FINKELSTEIN 429) erzählt außerdem, die kaiserliche Regierung (מלכות בית קיסר) habe zwei Offiziere auf die Suche nach dem Grab Moses geschickt: eine mittelalterliche Quelle bezieht dies auf Hadrian, der ganz Israel durchwanderte, um die Gräber der Könige und Propheten aufzusuchen, das Grab des Mose habe er jedoch nicht entdeckt[80].

Die Einstellung Hadrians zur jüdischen Bevölkerung Palästinas zeichnet eine Anekdote aus dem Midrasch Tannaim (ed. HOFFMANN 262):

> „Als Hadrian die Steigung nach Chammat Gader hinaufzog, traf er auf der Anhöhe von Chammat Gader ein kleines jüdisches Mädchen. Er fragte sie: wer bist du? Sie antwortete ihm: eine Jüdin bin ich. Sofort stieg er von seinem Wagen ab und verneigte sich tief vor ihr. Da ärgerten sich alle Großen des Reiches über ihn und sagten zu ihm: was findest du darin, dich zu erniedrigen und dich vor diesem verächtlichen, unsauberen und schmutzigen Mädchen zu verneigen? Er antwortete ihnen: Toren! Werden sich nicht alle Völker vor ihnen niederwerfen? Es steht doch geschrieben: ‘So spricht der Herr, der Erlöser Israels . . .’“ (Jes 49,7)[81].

M.D.HERR[82] bezieht darauf passend Ps.-Spartianus, Vita Hadriani XX,1: *In conloquiis etiam humillimorum civilissimus fuit, detestans eos qui sibi hanc voluptatem humanitatis quasi servantes fastigium principis inviderent.*

Eine ähnlich positive Einstellung zum Judentum zeigt Hadrian in LevRabba 25,5 (ed. MARGULIES 576—579, dort auch Angabe der Parallelen) in einer Erzählung, deren Grundmotiv auch in der nichtjüdischen Literatur verbreitet ist. Hadrian sah bei Tiberias einen alten Mann beim Baumpflanzen und wies ihn auf die Ziellosigkeit seines Tuns hin; der Alte jedoch meinte, zumindest seine Kinder würden von den Früchten des Baumes

[80] Aqtan de Mar Jakob 6: L. GINZBERG, The Legends of the Jews VI, Philadelphia [4]1959, 410. Die Parallelen zu Sifre, nämlich Sota 14a und Midrasch Tannaim 34, 6 (ed. HOFFMANN 226), sprechen von der „frevelhaften Regierung“, was — wenn die mittelalterliche Deutung auf Hadrian korrekt ist — in die positive Schilderung des wißbegierigen Kaisers nicht paßt. Später besteht ein allgemeiner Trend, zum Namen Hadrians „der Frevler“ oder „seine Knochen mögen zermalmt werden“ automatisch hinzuzufügen, auch wenn der Zusammenhang dem Kaiser ausgesprochen positiv gegenübersteht. Dies gilt vor allem auch von den Stellen über seine Gespräche mit R. Jehoschua b. Chananja.

[81] כשעלה הדרינוס במעלה חמת גדר מצא קטנה אחת בת ישראל על מעלה של חמת גדר אמר לה מה טיבך אמ׳ לו בת ישראל אני מיד ירד מן הקרון שלו והשתחוה לה כעסו עליו כל גדולי מלכות אמ׳ לו מה ראית שבזית עצמך ותשתחוה לבזויה זו שהיא מטונפת ומלוכלכת אמ׳ להן שוטים הלא כל האומות עתידין להשתחות להן שכך כת׳ כה אמ׳ ה׳ גואל ישראל . . .

[82] M. D. HERR, The Historical Significance of the Dialogues between Jewish Sages and Roman Dignitaries, Scripta Hierosolymitana 22 (1971) 123—150, p. 124.

essen. Als der Baum später Frucht trug, brachte der Alte davon dem Kaiser und wurde von diesem reich belohnt. Auf den Protest seiner Höflinge antwortete der Kaiser: „Soll ich den nicht ehren, den sein Schöpfer geehrt hat?“

Den breitesten Raum in der Hadrian positiven Tradition nehmen jedoch seine (oder einfach des Kaisers) Gespräche mit R. Jehoschua b. Chananja ein[83]. Es ist nicht möglich, hier auf diese Gespräche einzugehen, die vor allem religiösen Fragen gewidmet sind. Erwähnt seien nur zwei Stellen: nach KohRabba 2,8 beruft sich Hadrian auf Dtn 8,9 „ein Land ... wo dir nichts fehlt“ und läßt sich von Jehoschua Pfeffer, Rebhühner und feine Seide beschaffen, ist also am reichen Ertrag Israels interessiert; in Berakhot 56a kommt ein politisches Thema zur Sprache: Jehoschua sagt dem Kaiser voraus, er werde träumen, wie ihn die Parther gefangen nehmen und als Hirten einsetzen[84].

In die positive Hadrian-Tradition ist schließlich wohl auch Tanchuma Mischpatim 3 (ed. Buber 41a—b) zu rechnen. Aquila, der Neffe Hadrians, will zum Judentum übertreten, fürchtet sich aber, dies seinem Onkel zu sagen; darum reist er unter dem Vorwand, er wolle Handel betreiben, um so die Leute kennenzulernen, nach Israel; dort läßt er sich beschneiden und studiert die Tora. Später kommt er zu Hadrian zurück und gesteht ihm das Geschehene und begründet es mit Jes 49,7 (jener Stelle, die auch in der zuvor erwähnten Szene zwischen Hadrian und dem jüdischen Mädchen eine Rolle spielt). Da mischt sich der Mitherrscher (סונדוקרוס = συγκάθεδρος) ein, wird jedoch von Hadrian geschlagen und begeht daraufhin Selbstmord[85]. Anschließend meint Hadrian zu Aquila, er hätte doch auch Tora studieren könen, ohne sich beschneiden zu lassen, was dieser jedoch verneint. Hadrian hat demnach nichts gegen eine tiefere Beschäftigung mit dem Judentum und lehnt nur die Beschneidung ab.

[83] M. D. Herr (Anm. 82) 142f. hat die Gesprächsthemen und die Quellen zusammengestellt.

[84] Es schließt sich die parallele Vorhersage des R. Schmuel (Anfang 3. Jahrh.) an Schapur an, er werde von den Römern träumen, die ihn gefangen nehmen und in einer goldenen Mühle harte Kerne werden mahlen lassen. Erwähnt sei hier auch eine legendarische Erzählung von einer Begebenheit zwischen Jehoschua ben Chananja und der Tochter des Kaisers (dem Zusammenhang nach Hadrian): Sie liest aus Ps 104, 3 heraus, der jüdische Gott sei ein Zimmermann, und fordert daher, er möge ihr eine Spindel geben. Auf Jehoschuas Gebet hin wird sie aussätzig, und man gibt ihr eine Spindel in die Hand und setzt sie auf den Marktplatz. In Rom sei es nämlich üblich, Aussätzigen eine Spindel zu geben und sie auf den Markt zu setzen. Wenn sie dort das Garn aufwickeln, erkennen die Vorübergehenden daran ihr Leid und beten für sie. Später trifft Jehoschua die Aussätzige auf der Straße; sie fordert, der Gott Israels möge doch die Spindel wieder von ihr nehmen. Er jedoch antwortet: „Unser Gott gibt nur und nimmt nicht“ (Chullin 60a).

[85] L. I. Rabinowitz (Anm. 63) 1406 versteht die Stelle ganz anders: nach ihm schlägt Hadrian Aquila und nicht den Mitherrscher (dies ist natürlich ein Anachronismus, falls wir den Ausdruck nicht einfach auf einen Thronassistenten deuten sollen), was aber den Selbstmord dieses Mannes völlig unerklärt ließe. So kann er heftige Opposition Hadrians gegen die Bekehrung seines Neffen aus dem Text herauslesen: dieses Verständnis ist jedoch aus den Parallelen über Onkelos hereingetragen.

b) Hadrian und der Bar-Kokhba-Aufstand

Die historische Frage nach den Ursachen des Bar-Kokhba-Aufstandes (132—135) ist noch immer nicht geklärt und kann auch hier nicht wieder aufgerollt werden[86]. Spartian führt ihn auf das von Hadrian erlassene Beschneidungsverbot zurück, Cassius Dio auf den Bau der Aelia Capitolina und die Errichtung eines Zeustempels auf der Stelle des zerstörten jüdischen Heiligtums. Wahrscheinlich hat beides zum Aufstand beigetragen, auch wenn andere in beidem nicht Ursachen, sondern Folgen des Aufstandes sehen.

Nach GenRabba 64,10 (THEODOR-ALBECK 710—712) hatte der Aufstand ein Vorspiel: zur Zeit Jehoschuas b. Chananja dekretierte die Regierung, daß der Tempel wieder aufgebaut werde. Pappus und Lulianos setzten daraufhin Geldwechsler von Akko bis Antiochien ein, die die Leute aus der Diaspora mit allem Notwendigen versorgen sollten (wohl mit den Silbermünzen für die Tempelsteuer). Die Samaritaner denunzierten jedoch die Juden beim Kaiser (im Wortlaut von Esra 4,13), sobald die Stadt gebaut sei, würden die Juden keine Steuern mehr zahlen (vielleicht eine Anspielung darauf, daß der *fiscus Judaicus* dann wieder dem Tempel zufließen werde). Der König wollte seine Erlaubnis nicht direkt zurückziehen, ordnete jedoch auf Anraten der Samaritaner an, der Bauplatz müsse um fünf Ellen verschoben werden, worauf die Juden den Bau einstellten, sich im Granatapfeltal versammelten und einen Aufstand gegen Rom planten. Jehoschua konnte sie davon jedoch mit der an Aesop erinnernden Fabel vom Storch abbringen, der dem Löwen einen Knochen aus dem Rachen zieht und statt eines Lohnes froh sein muß, lebend aus dem Löwenrachen herausgekommen zu sein.

Der geschichtliche Wert dieser Erzählung ist nach Ansicht der Mehrheit gleich null[87], auch wenn vereinzelte nichtjüdische Quellen ebenfalls überliefern, man hätte zur Zeit Hadrians den Wiederaufbau des jüdischen Tempels geplant[88]. Immerhin muß während der Zeit Bar Kokhbas zumindest ein provisorischer Tempel bestanden haben[89].

In diesem Zusammenhang ist auch die eigenartige Notiz in jTaanit IV,8 (69b) zu nennen, wonach Tineius Rufus (ab 132 Statthalter Judäas) den Tempel umgepflügt habe[90]. Damit ist sicher die offizielle Zeremonie der

[86] Siehe dazu besonders H. BIETENHARD (Anm. 1); E. M. SMALLWOOD, The Legislation of Hadrian and Antoninus Pius against Circumcision, Latomus 18 (1959) 334—347 sowie das Addendum, Latomus 20 (1961) 93—96; D. ROKEAH, Comments on the Revolt of Bar Kokhba, Tarbiz 35 (1965f.) 122—131 (hebr.); L. W. BARNARD, Hadrian and Judaism, Journal of Religious History 5 (1969) 285—298 (etwas vereinfachend).

[87] So z. B. H. BIETENHARD (Anm. 1) 93. Positiver beurteilt M. D. HERR (Anm. 67) 91. 93 unter Berufung auf H. GRAETZ die Stelle; ebenso N. WASSER (Anm. 2) 86f.

[88] Cf. H. BIETENHARD (Anm. 1) 85ff., der auch L. FINKELSTEIN's These diskutiert, schon Trajan habe den Wiederaufbau des Tempels gestattet.

[89] Cf. H. BIETENHARD (Anm. 1) 162f.

[90] חרש רופוס שחיק עצמות את ההיכל. Der babylonische Talmud spricht hier einfach von der Zerstörung des Tempels durch „Tyrannus Rufus": Taanit 29a. Tyrannus ist in der rabbinischen Literatur sein üblicher Beiname. Die Texte zeigen ihn öfter in Diskussion mit R. Akiba: cf. M. D. HERR (Anm. 82) 133—135. 145 und (Anm. 67) 112.

Gründung der Aelia Capitolina gemeint, deren Zeitpunkt jedoch aus dem Text nicht hervorgeht. Ebenfalls hierher gehören zwei Texte, die Hadrian mit dem Tempel verbinden. ExRabba 51,5 (ed. Mirkin VI,208f.) sagt R. Schim'on bar Jochai, ein Zeitgenosse der Ereignisse: „Als Hadrian in das Allerheiligste eintrat, gebärdete er sich dort stolz und schmähte Gott[91]." Gelegentlich versucht man Hadrians Namen durch den des Titus zu ersetzen; doch ist die Übertragung eines solchen Motivs von einem Kaiser zu einem anderen nicht ungewöhnlich. In DtnRabba 3,13 (Mirkin XI,65) wendet R. Tanchuma (um 400) Koh 3,5 auf Hadrian an:

> „'eine Zeit, Steine zu werfen', das ist die Zeit, da Hadrian, seine Gebeine mögen zermalmt werden, hinaufzog, um die Steine des Tempels zu zerstreuen[92]."

Tanchuma Bereschit 7 schließlich verbindet die Zerstörung des Tempels durch Hadrian mit seinem Wunsch, als Gott anerkannt zu werden:

> „Als Hadrian, der König von Edom, die ganze Welt erobert hatte, ging er nach Rom und sagte zu seinen Höflingen: ich verlange von euch, daß ihr mich zu Gott macht; denn ich habe die ganze Welt erobert. Sie antworteten ihm: Noch herrschst du nicht über seine Stadt und seinen Tempel. Er ging, war erfolgreich und zerstörte den Tempel, führte Israel in die Verbannung und kehrte nach Rom zurück[93]."

So gering der geschichtliche Wert dieser Texte auch sein mag, zeigen sie jedenfalls, daß für die jüdische Tradition Hadrian als der endgültige Zerstörer des Tempels gilt, wobei sein Streben nach Weltherrschaft und Vergöttlichung die entscheidende Rolle spielten[94].

Nach der Wiedereroberung Jerusalems durch die Römer verschanzten sich die Aufständischen um Bar Kokhba in Bet-Ter, einer Festung etwas südwestlich der Hauptstadt. Die Belagerung und Einnahme dieser Festung im Sommer 135 wird in mehreren Texten in volkstümlicher Form geschildert, wobei — entgegen den Tatsachen, doch der literarischen Gattung entsprechend — Hadrian selbst die Hauptrolle spielt. Der wichtigste Beleg ist jTaanit IV,68d—69a[95]:

91 בשעה שנכנס אנדריאנוס לבית קדשי הקדשים היה מתגאה שם ומחרף לאלוהים.

92 עת שהיא שיעלה אדרינוס שחיק עצמות וינפץ אבני בית המקדש.

93 אנדריאנוס מלך אדום כיון שכבש את העולם כולו הלך לו לרומי אמר לבני פלטרין שלו מבקש אני מכם שתעשו אותי אלוה שהרי כבשתי את כל העולם אמרו לו עדיין לא שלטת בעירו ובביתו. הלך והספיקו בידו והרחיב ביה"מ והגלה את ישראל וחזר לרומי. Die Fortsetzung zeigt Hadrian im Gespräch mit drei Philosophen, die noch immer Einwände gegen seine Vergöttlichung vorbringen.

94 M. K. Thornton (Anm. 78) 458 scheint in moderner Sprache dasselbe zu sagen: "*There is no reason to think that Hadrian introduced emperor-worship for any other purpose than to be a helpful means for unification of the empire*".

95 Die Parallele EkhaRabbati 2, 2 (ed. Buber 51a—62b) ist, wie S. Buber in seiner Einführung 6a—7a betont, von jTaanit abhängig. Gittin 57a—58a bietet eine teilweise Parallele.

„Hadrian tötete in Bet-Ter 80000 Myriaden ... Dreieinhalb Jahre[96] belagerte Hadrian Bet-Ter. R. El'asar von Modiin pflegte in Sack und Asche zu sitzen und täglich zu beten: Herr der Welten, sitz heute nicht zu Gericht ... Da wollte Hadrian abziehen. Aber ein Samaritaner sagte ihm: Geh nicht weg; ich werde sehen, was zu tun ist, um dir die Stadt auszuliefern."

Der Samaritaner ging in die Stadt zu El'asar und tat, als ob er ihm etwas ins Ohr flüsterte. Das wird Bar Kokhba gemeldet; der Samaritaner behauptet, El'asar wolle die Stadt den Römern ausliefern; dieser jedoch leugnet und wird von Bar Kokhba mit einem Fußtritt getötet. „Sofort wurde Bet-Ter eingenommen und Ben Koziba getötet." Seine Leiche wird zu Hadrian gebracht, und es zeigt sich, daß sich eine Schlange um Bar Kokhbas Geschlechtsglied gelegt hat. Daran erkennt der Kaiser, daß nicht er, sondern nur Gott allein den Rebellenführer töten konnte[97].

Die Fortsetzung erzählt dann von den Greueln bei der Einnahme der Stadt: die Pferde wateten im Blut, auf den Steinen klebte das Hirn erschlagener Kinder, und die Toten wurden die längste Zeit nicht bestattet. So übertrieben diese Angaben auch sind, und so sehr sie auch stereotyp wiederholen, was an anderer Stelle von der Einnahme Jerusalems unter Nebukadnezzar gesagt wird, spiegeln sie jedenfalls die besondere Grausamkeit, die die Römer nach der langen Belagerung an den Besiegten walten ließen. Tatsächlich ist der Fall von Bet-Ter den Juden Palästinas ständige und wirksame Warnung vor einem neuen Aufstand geblieben. Beachtlich ist die Tatsache, daß Hadrian in diesem Zusammenhang keine persönlichen Untaten von der Volksphantasie angedichtet werden.

Die Zeit zwischen 135 und dem Tod Hadrians ist als eine Zeit der großen Verfolgungen im jüdischen Gedächtnis hängengeblieben[98]. Hadrian selbst ist nach den rabbinischen Texten aktiv an den Religionsverfolgungen beteiligt und dabei äußerst willkürlich.

„Hadrian, seine Gebeine mögen zermalmt werden, ließ durch einen Herold verkünden: Jeder, der den König nicht grüßt, wird getötet. Ein Jude ging vorbei und grüßte; da sagte er: du als Jude gehst vorbei und grüßt den König? Geht und tötet ihn. Ein anderer ging vorbei und grüßte nicht; da sagte er: geht und tötet ihn. Da sagten seine Rats-

[96] „Dreieinhalb Jahre" dauerte natürlich nicht die Belagerung von Bet-Ter, sondern der gesamte Aufstand (ungefähr); die Zahl ist überhaupt nicht historisch, sondern symbolisch zu verstehen und entspricht der halben Jahrwoche bei Daniel, wie A. Schlatter (Anm. 1) 36 richtig betont. Siehe dazu auch J. Bergmann, Die runden und hyperbolischen Zahlen in der Agada, MGWJ 82 (1938) 361—376.

[97] אדריינוס קיסר הורג בביתר שמונים אלף ריבוא... שלוש שנים ומחצה עשה אדריינוס מקיף על ביתר והוה ר׳ אלעזר המודעי יושב על השק ועל האפר ומתפלל בכל יום ואו׳ רבון העולמים אל תשב בדין היום... בעא אדריינוס מיזל ליה. אמר ליה חד כותיי לא תיזיל לך דאנא חמי מה מיעבד ומשלים לך מדינתא... מיד נלכדה ביתר ונהרג בן כזיבה.

[98] Cf. besonders M. D. Herr (Anm. 67).

herren: wir verstehen nicht, wie du vorgehst! Grüßt einer, tötest du ihn, und grüßt einer nicht, tötest du ihn auch. Er antwortete ihnen: Laßt mich! Ich weiß schon, wie ich meine Feinde töte[99]."

Texte dieser Art[100] sind natürlich keine Tatsachenberichte, als Stimmungsbilder jedoch geschichtlich ernst zu nehmen, insofern sie die Härte der Unterdrückungsmaßnahmen nach dem zweiten gescheiterten Aufstand, der so sehr die Pax Romana gestört hatte, und die daraus erwachsende Hoffnungslosigkeit und Ausweglosigkeit der jüdischen Bevölkerung zeigen. Anders als Titus ist Hadrian nicht nur als Zerstörer Jerusalems, sondern auch als Judenverfolger in die jüdische Geschichtsschreibung eingegangen, darin einzig Antiochus IV. Epiphanes vergleichbar, was die Tradition durch verschiedene Parallelerzählungen deutlich unterstreicht[101].

6. Antoninus und Rabbi

Nach dem Tod Hadrians begann eine Periode bester Beziehungen zwischen Rom und den Juden, nachdem Antoninus Pius die Verfolgungsdekrete aufheben ließ. Die rabbinischen Nachrichten darüber sind nicht einheitlich: eine Baraita (eine tannaitische Lehre, die noch aus dem 2. Jahrhundert stammt) in Taanit 18a erzählt, R. Jehuda b. Schammua habe sich mit einer römischen Matrone beraten und dann eine nächtliche Demonstration organisiert, bei der sich die Juden auf die allgemeine Bruderschaft aller Menschen beriefen: „Sind wir nicht Brüder und Söhne des einen Vaters? Wodurch unterscheiden wir uns von jeglichem Volk oder Stamm?" Diese so sehr dem Zeitgeist entsprechende Argumentation habe Erfolg gehabt (Parallelen: Rosch Haschana 19a; Fastenrolle zum 28. Adar, ed. LICHTENSTEIN 350). Nach Meila 17b hingegen soll R. Schim'on b. Jochai dies zusammen mit El'asar b. Jose erreicht haben, nachdem die Argumentation des als Heiden verkleideten R. Reuben b. Istrobili nichts genutzt hatte. Sie haben, so heißt es, aus der Tochter des Kaisers (dem Zusammenhang nach Antoninus Pius) einen Dämon ausgetrieben. Der Kaiser wollte ihnen darauf jegliche Bitte erfüllen. Auf einem Rundgang in der kaiserlichen Schatzkammer entdeckten sie das Verfolgungsdekret und zerrissen es.

Die zweite Erzählung ist offenkundig eine volkstümliche Überlieferung, auch wenn die Romreise der Rabbinen, um am kaiserlichen Hof zu inter-

---

[99] אדריינוס שחוק עצמות אפיק כרוז ואמר כל דלא שאיל בשלמיה דמלכא יתקטיל, עבר חד יהודאי ושאיל בשלמיה, א״ל את יהודאי עבר קדם מלכא ושאיל בשלמיה, א״ל אזלון קטלון ליה. תוב עבר אוחרן ולא שאיל בשלמיה, אמר להו אזלין קטלון ליה. א״ל בני סנקליטון לית אנן ידעין מהו דרכך, היך מה דלא שאיל בשלמך את קטיל ליה, ודשאיל בשלמך את קטיל ליה. אמר להון הרפוני דאנא ידע היך אקטול שנאי (EkhaRabbati 3, 58, ed. BUBER 69b—70a).

[100] Weitere Beispiele bei H. BIETENHARD (Anm. 1) 176—178 und D. SPIEGEL (Anm. 45) 45f.

[101] Z. B. erzählt Gittin 57b die aus den Makkabäerbüchern bekannte Geschichte von der Mutter und ihren sieben Martyrersöhnen für die Verfolgung unter Hadrian.

venieren, Tatsache sein könnte. Das in der ersten Erzählung genannte Motiv für die Aufhebung der antijüdischen Erlasse hingegen ist nicht nur früher bezeugt, sondern entspricht auch der römischen Mentalität des 2. Jahrhunderts, der die Verfolgung Andersdenkender völlig fremd war.

Nachher soll es zwar nochmals einen jüdischen Aufstand gegeben haben, der allerdings nur in der 'Historia Augusta' belegt ist. Ps.-Capitolinus, Antoninus Pius V,4—5, schreibt vom Kaiser: ... *multas gentes atque Judaeos rebellantes contudit per praesides ac legatos*. Wenn diese Angabe stimmt, kann der Aufstand jedenfalls nur ziemlich unbedeutend gewesen sein[102].

Als Einzelfiguren scheinen Antoninus Pius und seine Nachfolger in der rabbinischen Literatur namentlich nie auf. Doch gibt es zahlreiche Texte über einen gewissen „Antoninus" und Rabbi (d. h. Jehuda Hanasi, der nach der Tradition von 135 bis ins 3. Jahrhundert lebte und dem die Redaktion der Mischna zugeschrieben wird). Bevor wir die Frage nach der Identität des Antoninus stellen, gehen wir auf die Texte selbst ein[103].

In einer Gruppe von Texten, auf die wir nicht näher zu sprechen kommen müssen, stellt Antoninus Rabbi Fragen zu religiösen Themen: wann wird der Mensch beseelt[104]? Von wann an herrscht der böse Trieb in ihm? Wie werden nach dem Tod Leib und Seele zur Verantwortung gezogen[105]? Darf man jederzeit beten? Warum geht die Sonne im Osten auf und im Westen unter? In zwei Fragen zu Stellen aus dem Buch Ijob geht es um Gottes Vorsehung und Güte.

Diese Texte sind von der übrigen Antoninus-Tradition zu trennen, insofern sie einfach die beliebte Fassung religiöser Fragen nach dem Schema: Ein heidnischer Herrscher fragt einen jüdischen Lehrer, sind. Hier ist K. SCHUBERT zuzustimmen, „daß sowohl Antoninus als auch Rabbi Chiffren sind, und daß in Form solcher Gespräche die Auseinandersetzung zwischen dem Rabbinismus und spätantiken Vorstellungen durchgeführt wurde[106]." Die Namen der Gesprächsteilnehmer sind unwesentlich, solange die Grundvoraussetzung stimmt, daß die Genannten mögliche Gesprächspartner sind, daß also auch der heidnische Sprecher an solchen Themen interessiert ist. Da in mehreren der Gespräche eine Auseinandersetzung mit stoischen Vorstellungen vorliegt, die der kaiserliche Philosoph Marcus Aurelius Antoninus vertreten hat, ist es möglich, daß dieser als der imaginäre Gesprächspartner

[102] Cf. E. M. SMALLWOOD (Anm. 86) 341 und die dort angeführte Literatur. Sie rechnet mit einem Aufstand um das Jahr 156.

[103] Sammlung der Quellen: S. KRAUSS, Antoninus und Rabbi, Frankfurt 1910; L. WALLACH, The Colloquy of Marcus Aurelius with the Patriarch Judah I, JQR 31 (1940f.) 259—286.

[104] Cf. dazu E. E. URBACH, The Sages — Their Concepts and Beliefs, Jerusalem 1969, 195. 214 (hebr.).

[105] Zu diesen Texten cf. G. STEMBERGER, Zur Auferstehungslehre in der rabbinischen Literatur, Kairos 15 (1973) 238—266, pp. 250—254.

[106] K. SCHUBERT, Die Kultur der Juden I: Israel im Altertum, Handbuch der Kulturgeschichte, Frankfurt 1970, 236.

Rabbis gedacht ist[107], auch wenn diese Vorstellungen sonst ebenfalls belegt sind[108].

Von diesen religiös-philosophischen Fragen des heidnischen Kaisers an den jüdischen Lehrer zu unterscheiden sind eine Reihe von Anekdoten und schließlich historisch relevantes Material[109], das wohl erst die Benennung der Gesprächspartner der ersten Textgruppe verursacht hat. Zwei Texte sprechen von gegenseitigen Einladungen der beiden (GenRabba 11, ed. THEODOR-ALBECK 90; EstRabba 1,3), ein weiterer schildert ihre reichgedeckte Tafel (Berakhot 57b, Aboda Zara 11a). Konkreter sind die Angaben über ihre wirtschaftlichen Beziehungen: nach jSchebiit VI,1 (36d) hat Antoninus Rabbi 2000 Joch Land in Jiblona verpachtet; nach jJebamot IV,11 (6a) arbeiteten sie in der Rinderzucht zusammen (Antoninus selbst und nicht nur „die Regierung" wird in der Parallele jNidda I,4,49b genannt).

Rabbi, dessen ehrerbietigen Briefstil gegenüber Antoninus GenRabba 75,5 (ed. THEODOR-ALBECK 883) betont, tritt mehrmals als der politische Berater des Antoninus auf. Vor allem ist hier Mekhilta Beschallach 6 (ed. HOROVITZ-RABIN 137) zu nennen:

> „Antoninus fragte unseren heiligen Lehrer: Ich will nach Alexandria gehen; es wird doch nicht ein König auftreten und mich besiegen? Er antwortete ihm: Ich weiß es nicht. Jedenfalls haben wir eine Schriftstelle, daß Ägypten weder einen König noch einen Fürsten hervorbringen kann; denn es heißt: 'Einen Fürsten aus Ägypten wird es nicht mehr geben' (Ez 30,13)[110]."

[107] Dies vertritt vor allem L. WALLACH (Anm. 103), der allerdings weit über das Beweisbare hinausgeht, wenn er schreibt: "*The author of the colloquy was a Jewish Stoic imbued with Hellenism. He used the writings of Poseidonius of Apameia and the 'Self-Contemplations' of Marcus Aurelius. The fragments of the colloquy that have been preserved can be regarded as newly discovered fragments of the lost writings of Poseidonius*" (p. 286). In der Grundthese — der Beziehung dieses kaiserlichen Philosophen zu Mark Aurel — ist ihm jedoch zuzustimmen: cf. E. E. URBACH (Anm. 104) 195 und in: Encyclopaedia Hebraica 19 (1968) 208 (hebr.). M. AVI-YONAH, Geschichte der Juden im Zeitlater des Talmud, Studia Judaica II, Berlin 1962, 38 betrachtet ebenfalls einen Teil der Antoninus-Tradition als Reste eines philosophischen Traktats.

[108] Cf. S. KRAUSS (Anm. 103) 63.

[109] Cf. die Klassifizierung des Materials bei M. AVI-YONAH (Anm. 107) 38.

[110] שאל אנטונינוס את רבינו הקדוש: אני מבקש לילך לאלכסנדריא שמא יעמוד מלך וינצחני. אמר לו: איני יודע מכל מקום כתיב לנו שאין ארץ מצרים יכולה להעמיד לא מלך ולא שר שנ׳ נשיא מארץ מצרים לא יהיה עוד. Zwei weitere Texte verbinden Antoninus ebenfalls mit Ägypten. In Mekhilta Beschallach 1 (ed. HOROVITZ—RABIN 89) heißt es, daß Antoninus die Kriegswagen mit vier Pferden anstelle der drei unter den Pharaonen ausgestattet habe: so zumindest die Deutung von L. FINKELSTEIN, The Sources of the Tannaitic Midrashim, JQR 31 (1940f.) 211—243, pp. 241—243 aufgrund der Parallelstellen. S. KRAUSS (Anm. 103) hingegen verstand den Text von vier Mann Besatzung im Wagen. Sanhedrin 110a (cf. Pesachim 119a) sagt R. Chanina b. Chama, einen der drei von Josef in Ägypten verborgenen Schätze habe Antoninus ben Severus aufgedeckt, was wohl nicht auf ägyptische Silberbergwerke der Römer zu beziehen ist — gegen S. KRAUSS (Anm. 103) 8ff. —, sondern allgemein den hohen Wert dieser Provinz für die römischen Staatsfinanzen betont.

Eine Reihe von Antoninus-Texten findet sich in Aboda Zara 10a—b. Zuerst heißt es, daß kein Sohn eines Königs König werde — eine deutliche Anspielung auf die Adoptivkaiser des 2. Jahrhunderts — ausgenommen nach einer Umfrage (es ist wohl der Senat gemeint). Als Beispiel dafür gilt „Severus, der Sohn des Königs Antoninus. Antoninus sagte zu Rabbi: Ich will, daß mein Sohn Severus nach mir herrsche und auch, daß Tiberias eine Kolonie werde. Bitte ich sie um eines, tun sie es; bitte ich um beides, tun sie es nicht. Er (Rabbi) setzte einen Mann auf die Schulter seines Gefährten, gab dem oberen eine Taube in die Hand und sagte zum unteren Mann: befiehl dem oberen, daß er sie fliegen lasse. Da zog er (Antoninus) den Schluß: er meint, ich soll von ihnen verlangen, daß mein Sohn Severus nach mir herrsche; dieser soll dann Tiberias zur Kolonie erheben[111]".

Die Erhebung der Stadt Tiberias zur Kolonie läßt sich nicht datieren, auch wenn die Nachricht gut zur Tendenz der severischen Kaiser paßt, auch orientalische Städte zu Titularkolonien zu erheben[112]. Die Kombination mit der anderen Frage der Nachfolge durch einen leiblichen Sohn ist natürlich willkürlich und betont nur, daß für Antoninus Tiberias gleichbedeutend war wie sein eigener Sohn. Die Annahme von S. Krauss[113], mit der Erhebung von Tiberias zur Kolonie sei die Steuerbefreiung sämtlicher palästinischer Rabbinen verbunden gewesen und die Maßnahme des Kaisers habe darauf abgezielt, damit die Unterstützung aller Juden zu gewinnen, ist völlig unbelegt. Weder ist, was Krauss voraussetzt, Tiberias als Wohnsitz Rabbis nachzuweisen, noch ist die prinzipielle Steuerfreiheit der Rabbinen mit dem rechtlichen Status von Tiberias verbunden. Tat-

[111] אסוירוס בר אנטונינוס דמלך. א״ל אנטונינוס לרבי: בעינא דימלוך אסוירוס ברי תחותי ותתעביד טבריא קלניא, ואי אימא להו הדא, עבדי, תרי, לא עבדי. אייתי גברא ארכביה אחבריה ויהב ליה יונה לעילאי (בידיה), וא״ל לתתאה: אימר לעילא דלמפרח מן ידיה יונה. אמר, שמע מינה הכי קאמר לי: את בעי מינייהו דאסוירוס ברי ימלוך תחותי, ואימא ליה לאסוירוס דתעביד טבריא קלניא. Die Gleichnishandlung ist hier sekundär aus dem Gleichnis vom Lahmen und Blinden übernommen, mit dem Rabbi dem Antoninus die gemeinsame Verantwortlichkeit von Leib und Seele demonstriert: cf. G. Stemberger (Anm. 105). Dieses Gleichnis wiederum ist erst spät in die Diskussionen zwischen Antoninus und Rabbi aufgenommen worden und ist schon viel früher ohne diesen Rahmen belegt.

Hier seien auch gleich weitere Texte über die Kinder des Antoninus erwähnt: nach Mekhilta Beschallach 1 (ed. Horovitz—Rabin 82) pflegte Antoninus, wenn er von einer Gerichtssitzung spät heimkehrte, persönlich seinen Kindern auf dem Heimweg zu leuchten — ebenso handelte Gott an den Israeliten beim Auszug aus Ägypten, als er ihnen in Form einer Feuersäule voranging. Dieser Text ist ein typisches Königsgleichnis; nur steht anstelle des üblichen „ein König von Fleisch und Blut" hier eben Antoninus, und zwar wohl auch sekundär. Aboda Zara 11b berät sich Antoninus mit Rabbi wegen des unsittlichen Lebenswandels seiner Tochter; dabei verständigen sie sich in einer Geheimsprache, durch Übersendung symbolkräftiger Pflanzen — ebenso wie in einer noch zu nennenden Erzählung (ein Zeichen für das lebendige Wachstum der Antoninus-Tradition). Nidda 45a bezeichnet Justina, die Tochter des Severus und Enkelin des Antoninus, es als Zeitverschwendung, daß sie erst mit sechs Jahren geheiratet hat, wenn das schon mit drei möglich gewesen wäre, wie Rabbi meint.

[112] Cf. P. Petit (Anm. 65) 348.

[113] S. Krauss (Anm. 103) 53—55.

sache bleibt allein a) die Erhebung von Tiberias zur Kolonie (unter den Severern?) und b) die Tendenz, die Kaiserwürde erblich zu machen. Die beiden Erinnerungen sind später erzählerisch miteinander kombiniert worden. Das Prinzip der Erblichkeit dürfte wohl besonders interessiert haben, weil ab Rabbi das Amt des Patriarchen, bisher de facto schon immer in der Familie, nun auch de iure erblich wurde, was wohl nicht die allgemeine Zustimmung der Rabbinen gefunden hat.

Aboda Zara 10a—b fährt dann fort: Antoninus

> „sagte zu ihm (Rabbi): Mich bedrängen die Großen Roms. Rabbi führte ihn in den Garten und riß täglich aus der Reihe vor ihm einen Rettich aus. Da sagte er (Antoninus): Daraus kann ich folgern, was er mir sagen will. Töte sie einzeln und zerkriege dich nicht mit allen auf einmal[114].“

Wie es anschließend heißt, hat Rabbi die Zeichensprache aus Angst vor den Vornehmen Roms verwendet. Die Erzählung gibt die allgemeine Angst vor Verschwörungen wieder, die die Kaiser vor allem des 3. Jahrhunderts stets beherrscht hat[115].

Eine interessante Abwandlung derselben Erzählung finden wir in GenRabba 67,7 (ed. Theodor-Albeck 761). Hier sendet Antoninus einen Boten an Rabbi: was soll er tun? seine Kassen sind leer. Statt einer Antwort reißt Rabbi im Garten große Rettiche aus und pflanzt an ihrer Stelle kleine. Antoninus versteht den Wink und ersetzt gegen Bezahlung Befehlshaber (*duces*) durch neue, bis die Kassen voll sind.

Die bekannte Tatsache der ständigen Geldknappheit der Kaiser und der daraus erwachsenden Gewohnheit, Posten zu verkaufen, hat ihre Parallele in der Praxis der Patriarchen, die in der zweiten Hälfte des 3. Jahrh.s begannen, Richterposten zu verkaufen[116]. Die Stelle (und auch ihre Parallele) ist also nicht eine Verherrlichung der Freundschaft des jüdischen Patriarchen mit dem römischen Kaiser, an dessen Glanz jener teilhat: vielmehr ist sie eine Kritik an der Nachahmung römischer Mißbräuche durch die Patriarchen ab der Mitte des 3. Jahrh.s; sie ist also primär eine innerjüdische Polemik.

Die verschwörerische Gemeinschaft von Antoninus und Rabbi bekommt in anderen Erzählungen den Beigeschmack des gegenseitigen Miß-

114 א״ל: מצערין לי חשובי רומאי. מעייל ליה לגינא, כל יומא עקר ליה פוגלא ממשרא קמיה. אמר, ש״מ הכי קאמר לי: את קטול חד חד מינייהו, ולא תתגרה בהו בכולהו.

115 Diese Verschwörungsangst ist auch der Hintergrund einer Erzählung in Aboda Zara 10b, wonach die Häuser Rabbis und des Antoninus durch einen unterirdischen Gang miteinander verbunden waren und Antoninus jedesmal, wenn er zu Rabbi ging, die zwei Sklaven seiner Begleitung tötete. Wenn es dann heißt, daß bei einer solchen Gelegenheit R. Chanina b. Chama den toten Sklaven wieder belebt, ist dies nur eine dramatische Illustration des jüdischen Glaubens, der Antoninus in den Mund gelegt wird: „Ich weiß, der Geringste unter euch kann Tote erwecken.“

116 Cf. M. Avi-Yonah (Anm. 107) 117—119.

trauens. So ist es schon in Aboda Zara 10b, wo Rabbi das ihm täglich von Antoninus zugesandte, unter Weizen verborgene Gold ablehnt, er brauche es nicht. Dann aber drängt Antoninus es ihm auf: Rabbis Nachkommen würden es brauchen, um es den Nachkommen des Antoninus zurückzugeben. Die Tendenz der Erzählung ist auch hier eine Warnung vor Rom und seinen Gunstbezeugungen — alles muß zurückgezahlt werden; die Landschenkungen an die Patriarchen werden durch hohe Steuern überkompensiert[117].

Schärfer wird diese kritische Haltung in zwei weiteren Texten. Nach Tanchuma Wajjescheb 3 (ed. BUBER) wird Rabbi von Antoninus nach Caesarea zitiert und kommt in Begleitung seines Sohnes Schim'on und des R. Chijja dorthin. Schim'on sieht dort einen großgewachsenen Legionär und sagt zu Chijja: „Wie gemästet sind doch die Kälber Esaus!" Dieser vergleicht ihn mit den Fliegen, die auf dem Markt auf den Trauben- und Feigenkörben sitzen[118]. Rabbi weiß demgegenüber zu bemerken, die Fliegen hätten wenigstens in den ägyptischen Plagen ihre Aufgabe gehabt; „diese Legionäre hingegen sind für nichts bestimmt[119]."

Dasselbe negative Bild malt GenRabba 78,15 (ed. THEODOR-ALBECK 935), ohne Antoninus zu nennen:

„Wenn unser Rabbi zur Regierung zog, dachte er an jenen Schrifttext (Gen 33,15 lehnt Jakob die Begleitmannschaft Esaus ab) und nahm keine Römer mit sich. Einmal dachte er nicht daran und nahm Römer mit sich. Sie waren noch nicht nach Akko gekommen, da mußte er schon seinen Mantel verkaufen[120]."

Der Text spricht wohl von den Bestechungsgeldern, die Bittsteller vor einer Vorsprache bei Regierungsstellen an Mittelsmänner zu zahlen hatten, und entspricht völlig dem uns bekannten Bild von Palästina im 3. Jahrhundert. In allen diesen Texten klingt die Warnung von Abot 2,3 nach: „Seid vorsichtig gegenüber der Obrigkeit. Sie nähern sich dem Menschen nur, wenn sie selbst etwas brauchen."

Völlig positiv und durchaus im Rahmen des historisch Möglichen ist hingegen die in jMegilla III,2 (74a) überlieferte Nachricht[121]:

117 In erster Linie ist hier wohl an das *aurum coronarium* zu denken, über das sich in Baba Batra 8a die Bewohner von Tiberias so bitter vor Jehuda II. (einem Enkel Rabbis) beklagen. Cf. M. AVI-YONAH (Anm. 107) 115f.

118 Weinstock und Feigenbaum sind traditionelle Symbole Israels und des biblischen Gesetzes; das Bild besagt somit die Ausbeutung Israels durch das parasitäre Rom.

119 לגיונים אלו אינם ספונים לכלום.

120 רבנו כד הוה סליק למלכותא הוה מסתכל בהדה פרשתא ולא הוה נסיב עימיה רומאין. חד זמן לא איסתכל בה ונסב עימיה רומאין, לא הגיעו לעכו עד שמכר פינס שלו. Nach einer anderen Lesart mußte Rabbi sein Pferd verkaufen — der Schreiber hat wohl vereinfacht, weil er das lateinische Lehnwort *paenula* nicht mehr verstand.

121 Es geht im Zusammenhang um den Verkauf von Synagogeneigentum. Wenn der Name des Stifters eingraviert ist, darf der Gegenstand nicht weiterverkauft werden.

> ,,Antoninus ließ für die Synagoge einen Leuchter machen. Rabbi hörte dies und sagte: Gepriesen sei Gott, der es ihm ins Herz gelegt hat, einen Leuchter für die Synagoge machen zu lassen[122].“

Dazu ist zu erwähnen, daß es gerade unter den Severern in Palästina eine rege Synagogenbautätigkeit gab. Das Wohlwollen dieser Kaiser gegenüber den Juden ist wohl auch durch die Inschrift von Kitsion in Galiläa bezeugt, die in der dortigen Synagoge gefunden wurde und aus dem Jahr 197 stammt: ὑπὲρ σωτηρίας τῶν κ(υρίων) ἡμῶν αὐτοκρατόρω[ν] καισάρων Λ. Σεπτ. Σεουή[ρου] Εὐσεβ. Περτ. Σεβ. καὶ Μ. Αὐρ. ᾿Α[ντωνε]ίνου [καὶ Λ. Σεπτ. Γ] έτα υἱῶν αὐ[τοῦ ἐξ] εὐχῆς ᾿Ιουδαίων[123].

Dieses römische Wohlwollen führt fast notwendig zur Erzählung, Antoninus sei zum Judentum übergetreten und habe sich beschneiden lassen. Andere Rabbinen bestreiten dies, sprechen ihm aber dennoch einen Anteil an der künftigen Welt zu[124]. Nach Aboda Zara 10b ist Antoninus in dieser Hinsicht eine Ausnahme. Der Satz aus Ez 32,29, in der Unterwelt ,,ist Edom, seine Könige und alle seine Fürsten“ gilt nur von jenen, die nach den Taten Esaus handeln

> — ,,alle seine Könige, ausgenommen Antoninus, der Sohn des Severus“.

Direkt zuvor erzählt derselbe Text:

> ,,Täglich bediente er (Antoninus) Rabbi, brachte ihm zu essen und zu trinken, und wenn er sich ins Bett legen wollte, legte er (Antoninus) sich vor das Bett und sagte zu ihm: Steig über mich auf das Bett . . . Möchte ich dir doch in der künftigen Welt zur Unterlage dienen[125].“

122 כהדא אנטונינוס עשה מנורה לבית הכנסת. שמע ר׳ ואמר: ברוך אלהים אשר נתן בלבו לעשות מנורה לבית הכנסת.

123 J. B. Frey, Corpus Inscriptionum Iudaicarum II. Sussidi allo studio delle antichità cristiane III, Rom 1952, 158. Nicht sicher, jedoch anzunehmen ist, daß die Inschrift schon ursprünglich für die Synagoge bestimmt war. Frey übernimmt die Deutung von E. Renan, daß die Inschrift «*un monument de la terreur laissée par la dureté de cet impérateur vindicatif et rigoreux*» sei. Doch dürften die Juden im Kampf zwischen Septimius Severus und Pescennius Niger sich von vornherein auf die Seite des späteren Siegers geschlagen und so dessen Gunst gewonnen haben: so M. Avi-Yonah (Anm. 107) 77f.

124 jMegilla III, 2 (74a) und die Parallele in I, 13 (72b). Cf. dazu S. Lieberman (Anm. 48) 78—81. Ein später Text, den A. Jellinek, Bet-ha-Midrasch VI, Jerusalem ²1938 (= Leipzig 1877, 130f.), bietet, verlegt die Beziehungen zwischen Antoninus und Rabbi schon in deren früheste Kindheit. Die Mutter Rabbis sei vor den römischen Kaiser gebracht worden, weil sie entgegen dem römischen Verbot ihren Sohn habe beschneiden lassen. Auf dem Weg zur Einvernahme habe sie in einer Herberge übernachten müssen, in der gerade Antoninus geboren wurde. Die beiden Mütter tauschten ihre Kinder aus; so wurde der unbeschnittene Antoninus dem Kaiser vorgeführt und die Mutter daher freigesprochen. Auf dem Rückweg machte die Mutter Rabbis den Kindestausch wieder rückgängig; doch damit war schon der Grundstein der späteren Freundschaft gelegt.

125 כל יומא הוה משמש לרבי, מאכיל ליה, משקי ליה, כי הוה בעי רבי למיסק לפוריא הוה גהין קמי פוריא, א״ל: סק עילואי לפורייך . . . מי ישימני מצע תחתיך לעולם הבא.

Dieser Text führt uns schon wieder in die antirömische Polemik zurück, betont er doch nicht nur die unendliche Gnade, wenn auch ein Nichtjude am ewigen Leben teilhaben darf: er ist wohl eine direkte Anspielung auf die Behandlung des gefangenen Valerian durch Schapur I., der den römischen Kaiser als Fußschemel beim Besteigen des Pferdes benutzt haben soll.

Vom Tod des Antoninus spricht Aboda Zara 10b—11a:

> „Antoninus bediente Rabbi und Artaban bediente Rabh; als Antoninus starb, sagte Rabbi: aufgelöst ist das Band; als Artaban starb, sagte Rabh: aufgelöst ist das Band[126]."

Drei dieser Männer kommen in Jalqut II 579 vor:

> „'Und ich vernichtete die drei Hirten (in einem Monat)' (Sach 11,8): dies sind Rabbi, Antoninus und der Perserkönig Korban (= Artaban), die in einem Monat starben[127]."

Schließlich sei noch Kohelet Rabba 10,7 angeführt, wo Antoninus der Jüngere, der Enkel des älteren Antoninus, Rabbi fragte, wer von ihnen beiden früher sterben werde. Rabbi meint, er selbst, und dies trifft auch zu.

Trotz der so präzise scheinenden Angaben über Antoninus ist er nicht sicher zu identifizieren. Fassen wir zusammen: er ist der Sohn des Severus; ebenso heißt sein eigener Sohn, dessen Kinder wiederum Antoninus und Justina heißen. Außerdem soll er im selben Jahr wie Rabbi und Artaban (V.) gestorben sein. Auch kommt nur ein Judenfreund in Frage, der außerdem Palästina besucht haben muß. Am ehesten kommen wir mit den Angaben zurecht, wenn wir Antoninus mit Caracalla identifizieren. Wenn nach der rabbinischen Tradition der Sohn des Antoninus Severus heißt, muß der Begriff Sohn dann allerdings etwas locker im Sinn von „Nachfolger" verstanden werden, was in diesen Texten durchaus nicht unmöglich ist. Die Sukzessionskette Septimius Severus — Caracalla = Antoninus — Macrinus mit dem selbstverliehenen Beinamen Severus — dessen Sohn Diadumenian (mit dem offiziellen Namen Antoninus) oder Elagabal, ebenfalls ein Antoninus, paßt mit den rabbinischen Angaben zusammen. Allerdings müssen wir auch stets mit der Möglichkeit von Namenverwechslungen oder dem Überspringen eines Gliedes im Stammbaum in rabbinischen Texten rechnen, so daß keine Sicherheit besteht.

A. GUTTMANN hat den zitierten Jalqut-Text verwendet, das Todesjahr Rabbis mit 217, dem Jahr der Ermordung Caracallas, gleichzusetzen,

[126] אנטונינוס שמשיה לרבי, ארטבן שמשיה לרב. כי שכיב אנטונינוס, א"ר: נתפרדה חבילה. כי שכיב ארטבן, אמר רב: נתפרדה חבילה. Die Lesart Artaban (statt des Adrakhan der Drucke, das aber auch immer als Artaban verstanden wird) ist bezeugt in der von S. ABRAMSON publizierten Handschrift: Tractate Aboda Zarah of the Babylonian Talmud. Ms. Jewish Theological Seminary of America, New York 1957.

[127] ואכחיד את שלשת הרועים: זה רבי ואנטונינוס וקרבן מלך פרסי שמתו בירח אחד.

muß dann allerdings in Artaban den Namen eines sonst unbekannten persischen Beamten sehen, was unannehmbar ist[128]. Artaban V., der hier wohl gemeint ist, starb 227. Wenn ein später Text alle drei im selben Jahr sterben läßt, folgt er nur der allgemeinen Tendenz des Midrasch, wichtige Ereignisse in dasselbe Jahr fallen zu lassen.

Da Caracalla Palästina mindestens zweimal besucht hat (199 und 215) und außerdem seine freundliche Einstellung zu den Juden auch anderweitig belegt ist (Historia Augusta, Caracalla 1,6), ist er der wahrscheinlichste Antoninus der rabbinischen Tradition. Dies schließt nicht aus, daß Erzählungen über andere Kaiser der Zeit in seine Legende eingegangen sind, wie dies besonders für die philosophischen Fragen des Kaisers an den jüdischen Lehrer anzunehmen ist; auch die Erzählung von seiner Konversion ist eine reine Legende. So hat das Judentum der Erinnerung an die guten Zeiten unter den Antoninen und Severern gerade in der Person des Kaisers, der sonst eher unrühmlich in Erinnerung geblieben ist, ein bleibendes Denkmal gesetzt. Daß die positive Tradition jedoch nicht so einhellig ist, wie gelegentlich angenommen wird, haben wir hinreichend betont: die Kritik an Rom wie auch an der zu großen Nähe des Patriarchen zur römischen Besatzungsmacht ist in einigen Texten deutlich, die die Situation des ausgehenden dritten Jahrhunderts spiegeln. Die volksnahen Prediger dieser Zeit, auf die diese Texte zurückgehen mögen, haben sich nie so wie das Patriarchenhaus mit der römischen Präsenz in ihrem Land abfinden können.

7. Odenat und Zenobia

Die Militäranarchie des 3. Jahrhunderts hat in der rabbinischen Literatur zahlreiche Spuren hinterlassen, auch wenn die ziemlich kurzlebigen Kaiser kaum einmal namentlich erwähnt werden. Die rabbinischen Texte betonen vor allem die Ausrufung des Kaisers durch die Legionen, die ihm den Purpur zuwerfen und dafür die Schulden erlassen bekommen (ExRabba 15,13 ed. MIRKIN V 176). Das trotzdem meist nur kurze Glück der Kaiser scheint Mekhilta Bachodesch 8 (ed. HOROVITZ-RABIN 233) zu schildern (falls wir diesen Text so spät datieren dürfen):

„Das gleicht einem König von Fleisch und Blut, der in eine Stadt einzieht. Diese stellt ihm Bilder und Standbilder auf und prägt ihm

[128] A. GUTTMANN, The Patriarch Judah I — His Birth and His Death. A Glimpse into the Chronology of the Talmudic Period, HUCA 25 (1954) 239—261, p. 257. J. NEUSNER, A History of the Jews in Babylonia I, Leiden 1965, 85f. wendet sich richtig gegen diese Annahme GUTTMANN's, übernimmt jedoch dessen Datierung des Todes Rabbis auf 217 (82, Anm. 1). Jedoch ist auch dieses Datum alles andere als sicher. Für die anderen Identifizierungsversuche für Antoninus siehe die Zusammenfassung bei L. WALLACH (Anm. 103) 260 sowie S. KRAUSS (Anm. 103), der die ältere Forschungsgeschichte darstellt und selbst für Avidius Cassius plädiert.

Münzen. Nach einiger Zeit stürzen sie die Bilder um, zerbrechen die Standbilder und mindern so das Ansehen (wörtlich: Bild) des Königs[129]."

S. LIEBERMAN sieht in GenRabba 83,3 (ed. THEODOR-ALBECK 998f.) eine Anspielung auf den aus der Gegend von Bostra stammenden Philippus Arabs. R. Abbahu (Ende 3. Jahrh.) sagt dort:

„So spricht der Heilige, gepriesen sei er: schon war das Königtum aus Edom ausgerissen, da kam Bozra und stellte ihm Könige; so befasse ich mich nur noch mit Bozra, wie geschrieben steht: 'Ein Opfer begeht der Herr in Bozra, ein großes Schlachten im Lande Edom' (Jes 34,6)[130]."

Den schon früher auf die *ludi saeculares* gedeuteten eigenartigen Text von Aboda Zara 11b verlegt er ebenfalls in die Regierungszeit des Philippus und sieht darin die Tausendjahrfeier Roms im Jahre 248, wobei der Text durch den persisch-römischen Propagandakrieg jener Jahre verfälscht ist. Es heißt dort, daß Rom alle siebzig Jahre (so in Angleichung an das israelitische Jubeljahr) ein Fest begeht, bei dem ein Lahmer einen Gesunden durch die Straßen führt, der mit den Gewändern des Urmenschen angetan ist. Vor ihm ruft man dabei aus:

„*Sakh qere flstr* (wohl: *socius kyriou falsator*): der Bruder des Herrn ist ein Fälscher; wer es gesehen hat, hat es gesehen, wer es nicht gesehen hat, sieht es nicht mehr (wohl das Jahrhundertfest). Was hat der Betrüger von seinem Betrug und der Fälscher von seiner Fälschung? Und sie leiten daraus ab: Wehe dem einen, wenn der andere sich erhebt[131]."

Tradent ist R. Jehuda (b. Jechezqel, 2. Hälfte 3. Jahrh.) im Namen des R. Schmuel, der knapp nach 250 gestorben ist und mit Schapur in guten

129 משל למלך בשר ודם שנכנס למדינה והעמיד לו איקונות ועשה לו צלמים וטבעו לו מטבעות. לאחר זמן כפו לו איקונותיו שברו לו צלמיו ובטלו לו מטבעותיו ומיעטו בדמותו של מלך. Eine andere Lesart bringt die Verben im Plural: sie machten ihm Bilder usw., während im Singular auch der König die handelnde Person sein kann. Weitere Texte bei M. AVI-YONAH (Anm. 107) 89—92.

130 כך אמר הקב"ה כבר היתה מלכות עקורה מאדום ובאת בצרה וסיפקה לה מלכים. אין לי עסק אלא עם בוצרה הה"ד: כי זבח לי"י בבוצרה וטבח גדול בארץ אדום. S. LIEBERMAN hat seine Deutung zuerst vorgetragen in: The Martyrs of Caesarea, Annuaire de l'Institut de philologie et d'histoire orientales et slaves 7 (1939—1944) (mir nicht zugänglich); I. SONNE, The Use of Rabbinic Literature as Historical Sources, JQR 36 (1945f.) 147—169, pp. 148—150 hingegen bezieht Bozra auf das Ostreich und datiert daher den Text ab Diokletian. In: The Martyrs of Caesarea, JQR 36 (1945f.) 239—253, hat dann S. LIEBERMAN seine Ansicht nochmals verteidigt. Cf. auch S. LIEBERMAN (Anm. 1) 31—33 Übrigens hat schon S. KRAUSS (Anm. 1) 61f. die Deutung des Herrschers aus Bozra auf Philipp vorgetragen (p. 53 ebenso für Jalqut I 133).

131 סך קירי פלסתר, אחוה דמרנא זייפנא, דחמי חמי ודלא חמי לא חמי מאי אהני לרמאה ברמאותיה ולזייפנא בזייפנותיה, ומסיימין בה הכי: ווי לדין כד יקום דין. Cf. S. LIEBERMAN (Anm. 1) 39—41.

Beziehungen stand. Die Identifikationen LIEBERMAN's sind nicht sicher, jedoch erwägenswert. Besonders der zweite Text wirft so gesehen ein bezeichnendes Licht auf diese Zeit.

Größeres Interesse als alle anderen Herrschergestalten dieser Zeit findet der palmyrenische Fürst Odenat, dem es im Kampf Roms gegen Persien nach der Gefangennahme Valerians gelang, sich als Vertreter der römischen Interessen ein halb-offizielles Sonderreich innerhalb des Imperiums aufzubauen[131a]. Zu seinem Herrschaftsgebiet gehörte auch Palästina, dessen Juden anfangs auf ihn große Hoffnungen setzten (Palmyra galt ja den Rabbinen als halbjüdisch). Bald wurden jedoch ihre Hoffnungen bitter enttäuscht, wie einige Texte deutlich zeigen. Hier ist besonders GenRabba 76,6 (ed. THEODOR-ALBECK 903) zu nennen, wo Dan 7,8 auf Odenat gedeutet wird. In Dan 7,8 heißt es, daß dem vierten Tier der Vision (dem endzeitlichen Reich) zwischen seinen zehn Hörnern ein kleines Horn wächst, das drei Hörner ausreißt; dieses kleine Horn hat Menschenaugen und einen großsprecherischen Mund. In Dan 7 ist damit der große Verfolger Antiochus IV. Epiphanes gemeint, der auf die seleukidischen Könige folgt, von denen er drei mögliche Rivalen verdrängt. Für die rabbinische Deutung ist das vierte Tier selbstverständlich Rom (R. Jochanan b. Napacha, gest. 279, deutet anschließend allerdings das kleine Horn auf Rom, die drei ausgerissenen Hörner auf die vorangehenden Reiche); das kleine Horn ist ben Netser (= Odenat), die drei Hörner, die von ihm ausgerissen werden, sind מקרוס וקרוס וקרידוס (viele Varianten): darin sieht man gewöhnlich Macrinus, Kyros und Kyriades[132]; statt des in diesem Zusammenhang unbelegbaren Kyros wird auch Carinus oder — nach der Variante קידוס — Quietus genannt[133]; statt Macrinus kommt auch Macrianus in Frage. Im einzelnen besteht keine Sicherheit, doch müssen hier jedenfalls drei Rivalen um die Herrschaft im Osten nach der Gefangennahme Valerians gemeint sein. Wichtig für uns ist vor allem die Parallelisierung Odenats mit Antiochus IV. Schärfer kann die Ablehnung nicht sein, die auch aus dem Satz klingt, daß der Tag des Falles Tadmors (= Palmyras) für Israel ein Freudentag sein werde (Jebamot 17a). In Ketubot 51b wird Ben Netser übrigens einem Straßenräuber gleichgesetzt.

Zumindest vereinzelt scheinen die Juden auch offen gegen Odenat Stellung genommen zu haben und dafür von ihm bestraft worden zu sein. Dies geht aus jTerumot VIII,10 (46b) hervor, wo R. Ammi und R. Samuel bei Königin Zenobia für den gefangenen R. Zeir(a) b. Chanina Fürbitte leisten. Da bringt ein Sarazene ein Schwert und sagt der Königin, damit habe

131a Vgl. H. J. W. DRIJVERS, Hatra, Palmyra, Edessa. Die Städte der syrisch-mesopotamischen Wüste in politischer, kulturgeschichtlicher und religionshistorischer Beleuchtung, ANRW II 8, hrsg. H. TEMPORINI u. W. HAASE, Berlin–New York 1978, 847f.

132 So S. KRAUSS (Anm. 1) 74f. Cf. die Textausgabe von THEODOR—ALBECK 903 im Kommentar.

133 z. B. S. LIEBERMAN (Anm. 1) 37f., der auf OrSib 13, 162ff. als Parallele verweist. M. BUTTENWIESER, Die hebräische Elias-Apokalypse, Leipzig 1897, 71 möchte statt Kyriades Kallistos lesen.

Bar Natsor den Bruder Zeiras getötet. Darauf verschont die Königin Zeira[134].

8. Diokletian

Diokletian, der in den Jahren 286 und 297 in Palästina war, wird in der rabbinischen Literatur ziemlich oft genannt. Sein Bild ist im Gegensatz zu dem anderer Kaiser kaum von Sagen überwuchert. Die einzige Ausnahme ist die Erzählung von jTerumot VIII,10 (46b–c)[135]. Demnach war Diokles einst Schweinehirt bei Tiberias und wurde von den Schülern des R. Jehuda Nesia verprügelt. Als er dann König wurde und sich in Paneas aufhielt, zitierte er die Rabbinen von Tiberias für den Sabbatausgang zu sich, befahl jedoch dem Boten, das Schreiben erst am Freitagabend zuzustellen. Somit hatten die Rabbinen die Wahl, entweder den Sabbat zu verletzen oder dem Kaiser nicht zu gehorchen. R. Jehuda Nesia und R. Schmuel b. Nachman, die sich gerade im Bade befanden, wurden jedoch vom „Argonauten", einem Geist, der sich in Bädern aufhält[136], aus diesem Dilemma

[134] Hier ist auch auf die aus dem 3. Jahrhundert stammende und später überarbeitete hebräische Elia-Apokalypse zu verweisen. Zur Datierung cf. A.-M. Denis, Introduction aux pseudépigraphes grecs d'Ancien Testament, Studia in Veteris Testamenti Pseudepigrapha I, Leiden 1970, 260. A. Jellinek, Bet-ha-Midrasch III, Jerusalem ²1938 (= Leipzig 1855), p. XVIII setzt den Text viel später an, in die gaonäische Zeit. Den hebräischen Text bringt er pp. 65—68; cf. auch die Ausgabe von M. Buttenwieser (Anm. 133). Die folgenden Zeilen, die auf Zeitereignisse anspielen, sind durchsetzt von messianischen Beschreibungen: „Der letzte König Persiens zieht drei Jahre lang jährlich gegen Rom und breitet sich darin zwölf Monate aus. Und drei Kriegshelden ziehen ihm vom Meer her entgegen und werden in seine Hände überliefert. Der geringste König, der Sohn einer Magd, Gigit ist sein Name, zieht vom Meer herauf ihm entgegen ... An diesem Tage wird er seine Hand ausstrecken gegen ein treues Volk und wird an diesem Tag drei Kriege erregen ... Einen zweiten Krieg führt Demetrius, der Sohn des Poripos und Anpholipos, der Sohn des Panpos ... Einen dritten Krieg führt Mikets Kirtalos, und alle Städte sind mit ihm, ein gar großes Volk von der großen Senke bis nach Jafo und Aschkelon ..." (nach dem hebr. Text bei Buttenwieser 16. 18. 19). M. Buttenwieser betrachtet diesen Text als Parallele zum schon zitierten GenRabba 76, 6. S. 68ff. identifiziert er den persischen König als Schapur I., Gigit als Odenat (beide Wörter können „Weinschlauch" bedeuten); die drei Helden sind Valerian, Kallistos und Macrianus. Die drei Kriege sind der Angriff auf das „treue Volk" Israel (Zerstörung des jüdischen Zentrums Nehardea) sowie die Kämpfe mit Macrianus, Quietus und Kallistos. P. Riessler, Altjüdisches Schrifttum außerhalb der Bibel, Heidelberg ²1966 (= 1928) übernimmt diese Angaben (pp. 1279f.). S. Krauss, Der römisch-persische Krieg in der jüdischen Elia-Apokalypse, JQR 14 (1902) 359—372 — cf. S. Krauss (Anm. 1) 53f. — hat gegen Buttenwieser einige beachtliche Einwände vorgebracht; er selbst möchte die geschilderten Ereignisse einige Jahre früher ansetzen, muß dazu allerdings zu viele Namen abändern, so daß noch immer die Lösung von Buttenwieser die wahrscheinlichere bleibt, auch wenn sie nicht ohne Schwierigkeiten ist. Die Darstellung Odenats als Antichrist paßt jedenfalls zu dem in GenRabba überlieferten Bild.

[135] Leicht abweichende Parallelen: GenRabba 63, 8 (ed. Theodor—Albeck 688—690) und Jalqut I 110.

[136] Der Name ist in verschiedenen Lesarten überliefert: im Talmud אנגיטריס, in GenRabba ארגנטין oder ארגינטין u. ä. M. Schwab liest in seiner Übersetzung des palästinischen Talmuds „Antigoras".

befreit, indem er sie nach Sabbatende wunderbar nach Paneas brachte. Diokletian empfing sie jedoch nicht sofort, sondern ließ sie zuerst in ein seit drei Tagen geheiztes Bad führen. Doch auch aus dieser Gefahr errettete sie der Argonaut. Schließlich wurden sie vom Kaiser zur Rede gestellt:

> „Weil euer Schöpfer an euch Wunder wirkt, verachtet ihr das Königtum. Sie antworteten ihm: den Schweinehirten Dioklet haben wir verachtet; den König Diokletian verachten wir nicht. — Doch auch so sollt ihr einen kleinen Römer ebensowenig wie einen kleinen Talmudschüler bedrängen[137].“

Die Erzählung setzt sich aus mehreren Elementen zusammen. Wie auch Laktanz bezeugt, hieß Diokletian ursprünglich Diokles. Er stammte aus niedrigen Verhältnissen, was die rabbinische Tradition mit der Nachricht, daß er durch die Ermordung des Prätorianerpräfekten Aper = „Eber“ zur Macht kam, zu der Behauptung verbindet, er sei ursprünglich Schweinehirt bei Tiberias gewesen. Zu diesen historischen, jedoch anekdotisch umgeformten Fakten kommt eine erbauliche Belehrung über den Sabbat: wer sich an dieses Gebot hält, kann mit Gottes Hilfe rechnen. Wie die Jünglinge im Feuerofen, so wird auch er vor Feuergefahr errettet. Die Einführung des guten Geistes, der vor Gefahren rettet, weist auf den volkstümlichen Charakter dieses Motivs hin. Von hier auf antijüdische Maßnahmen des Diokletian zu schließen, scheint kaum gerechtfertigt[138]. Interessant ist jedoch die Kombination dieses Verfolgungsthemas mit typischen Motiven der antijüdischen Polemik in der Antike, deren besondere Zielscheibe die Sabbatbräuche der Juden waren. Und daß die Rabbinen ins Bad müssen, bevor sie vor dem Kaiser erscheinen dürfen, ist sicher eine Anspielung auf den den Juden immer vorgeworfenen Schmutz[139]. Schließlich kommt im Gespräch mit Diokletian zum Ausdruck, daß die Juden den Kaiser anerkennen, jedoch mit den kleinen Römern immer Schwierigkeiten haben. Die Parallelisierung des kleinen Römers mit dem kleinen Talmudschüler ist dabei ein beachtliches Zeugnis jüdischer Toleranz.

137 בגין דברייכון עביד לכון ניסין אתון מבזין מלכותא. אמרין ליה: דיקלוט חזירא בזינן. דיקליטיאנוס מלכא לא בזינן. ואפי׳ כן לא מכסי לא ברומי זעיר ולא בחבר זעיר. Statt חבר liest GenRabba גליר = γαλιάριος; auch kommt die Namensform Diokles nur im Talmud vor.

138 Y. Baer, Israel, The Christian Church, and the Roman Empire from the time of Septimius Severus to the Edict of Toleration of A.D. 313, Scripta Hierosolymitana 7 (1961) 79—149 (überarbeitet aus Zion 21, 1956, 1—49 übernommen), p. 128 sieht hier hingegen ein Zeugnis "*that Diocletian carried out actions of coercion and religious compulsion against Jews as well as Christians*". S. Lieberman (Anm. 1) 370 hingegen stellt fest: "*There is no evidence . . . for the persecution of the Jewish religion during the third and fourth centuries*".

139 Siehe dazu M. D. Herr, Anti-Semitism in the Roman Empire viewed in the Light of Rabbinic Literature, Benjamin De Vries Memorial Volume, ed. E. Z. Melamed, Jerusalem 1968, 149—159, sowie in dem Sammelband Hellenistic Views on Jews and Judaism, Issues in Jewish History I, Jerusalem 1974, 33—43 (hebr.).

Die Anwesenheit des Diokletian in Paneas setzt auch jSchebiit IX,2 (38d) voraus. Die Einwohner von Paneas drohen mit Landflucht, da ihnen die Steuern zu hoch sind. Ein Berater (eigentlich „Sophist") hält jedoch Diokletian davon ab, nachzugeben; sie würden schon wieder zurückkommen. Dieser Text handelt wohl nicht von Juden, sondern ist ein allgemeines Bild von der Steuerbelastung jener Zeit[140].

Vom Durchzug des Diokletian in Tyrus weiß jBerakhot III,1 (6a) = jNazir VII,1 (56a) zu berichten. Es geht im Zusammenhang darum, unter welchen Umständen ein Priester ein Reinheitsgebot übertreten darf.

> „R. Jannai sagte: ein Priester verunreinigt sich, um den König zu sehen. Einst kam König Diokletian hierher. Da sah ich den R. Chijja bar Abba, wie er über die Gräber von Tyrus sprang, um ihn zu sehen[141]."

obwohl er als Priester einen Friedhof nicht betreten dürfte. R. Chiskija und R. Jirmeja (4. Jahrh.) fügen im Namen des R. Jochanan (3. Jahrh.) hinzu, man müsse die großen Könige sehen, um von ihnen den davidischen Messiaskönig unterscheiden zu können, wenn dieser endlich kommt.

GenRabba 83,4 (ed. Theodor-Albeck 1000) verbindet ebenfalls die Messiashoffnung mit Diokletian. In Gen 36,43 wird Magdiel als vorletzter Fürst Esaus genannt. Dazu heißt es in der Auslegung, als Diokletian[142] König wurde, erschien er R. Ammi im Traum und sagte: „Heute ist Magdiel König geworden; nur noch ein König muß in Edom kommen." Nach Diokletians Nachfolger erwarteten also manche das messianische Reich, das Ende der römischen Herrschaft.

Ein für die Religionspolitik des Diokletian bedeutendes Zeugnis bietet jAboda Zara I,4 (39d). Demnach soll sich auf dem Markt von Tyrus folgende Inschrift befunden haben:

> „Ich, König Diokletian, habe diesen Markt von Tyrus zu Ehren der Tyche meines Bruders Herakles für acht Tage festgelegt[143]."

Die Gleichsetzung des Mitherrschers Maximian mit Herakles ist ja bekannt, ebenso die religiöse Bedeutung solcher Märkte. Daß gerade Tyrus Sitz eines solchen Herakles-Kultes wurde, versteht sich aus der Tradition, die dort

140 Cf. S. Lieberman (Anm. 1) 350.

141 א״ר ינאי מטמא כהן לראות את המלך. כד סליק דיקליטיינוס מלכא להכא חמון לר׳ חייא בר אבא מיפסע על קיברי דצור בגין מיחמיניה. Vom Durchzug eines kaiserlichen Heeres spricht auch jNedarim III, 2 (37d), wo als Kaiser Julian (לוליינוס) genannt wird. Da jedoch in der Parallelstelle jSchebuot III, 9 (34d) Diokletian genannt wird, möchten manche — so S. Krauss (Anm. 2) 79 — beide Texte auf Diokletian beziehen. Doch siehe dagegen J. N. Epstein, Introduction to Amoraitic Literature, Jerusalem 1962 (hebr.), 274, der an der Lesart Julian festhält und „Diokletian" hier als Fehler betrachtet.

142 Mit W. Bacher, Die Agada der palästinensischen Amoräer II, Hildesheim 1968 (= Straßburg 1896), 310 ist לטינוס als Verstümmelung von Diokletian zu verstehen. Siehe dort auch andere Deutungen: Valentinianus oder Licinius.

143 אנא דיקלטיאנוס מלכא שכנית אהון ירידה דצור בגדיה דארקליס אחי תמניא ימין.

die Verehrung des später mit Herakles gleichgesetzten Moloch hatte[144]. An der Geschichtlichkeit dieses Zeugnisses ist also nicht zu zweifeln.

Die Religionspolitik Diokletians spiegelt sich auch in jAboda Zara V,4 (44d):

> „Einmal zog König Diokletian hierher und verordnete, jedes Volk müsse ein Trankopfer darbringen, ausgenommen die Juden; auch die Samaritaner brachten Libationen dar und daher wurde ihr Wein verboten[145].“

Da eine solche Ausnahme für die Juden nicht belegt ist, nimmt Y. Baer an, es handle sich hier um eine frühere Fassung dieses Ediktes als die bei Eusebius überlieferte. Diese datiert er mit Y. I. Halevy auf das Jahr 286, als Diokletian in Israel war[146].

Die jüdische Tradition über Diokletian ist somit recht sachlich gehalten, was einerseits damit zusammenhängt, daß diese nur in palästinischen Quellen überlieferte Tradition relativ bald nach den Ereignissen festgelegt wurde, andererseits sicher darauf beruht, daß die Juden mit Diokletian keine besonderen Schwierigkeiten hatten, ihn vielmehr aus sicherer Distanz als großen Kaiser anerkannten. Diokletian ist somit der einzige römische Kaiser, zu dem die jüdischen Quellen ein ausgesprochen sachliches Verhältnis haben; die Erinnerungen an alle anderen sind ja, auch wenn sie historische Informationen mitliefern, weitgehend legendarisch umgeformt worden.

III. Die rabbinische Beurteilung Roms im allgemeinen

Die rabbinischen Traditionen über die einzelnen Kaiser sind nur zum geringsten Teil Zeugnis für die Einstellung des Judentums zu Rom während

144 Siehe dazu L. Ginzberg, A Commentary on the Palestinian Talmud I, Texts and Studies of the Jewish Theological Seminary of America X, New York 1971 (= 1941), LXXI.

145 כד סליק דיקליטינוס מלכא להכא גזר ואמר כל אומייא ינסכון בר מן יודאי ונכסון כותייא ונאסר יינן. Der samaritanische Wein wird nun dem Juden verboten, weil er damit in Verdacht käme, an Handlungen des Götzendienstes teilzunehmen. Meist gilt diese Stelle als Beleg für den endgültigen Bruch zwischen Juden und Samaritanern.

146 Y. Baer (Anm. 138) 125. Hier seien zwei weitere Traditionen über Diokletian angefügt. Nach jKilaim IX, 4 (32c) umgeben sieben Meere Israel. Den See von Emesa darf man jedoch nicht mitzählen, denn diesen habe Diokletian durch Zusammenleitung von Flüssen künstlich angelegt. Parallelen dazu finden sich in MidrPsalmen 24, 6 (ed. Buber 103a) und in Baba Batra 74b, in der zweiten Stelle jedoch ohne Erwähnung des Sees von Emesa. NumRabba 12, 4 (ed. Mirkin X 18) spiegelt wohl die Münzpolitik Diokletians, wenn es in einer Diskussion über die sieben Arten Gold heißt, vom gezogenen Gold hatte Hadrian im Gewicht eines Eis, Diokletian im Gewicht eines gordianischen Denars, und Israel gar nichts mehr. Zum gordianischen Denar in der rabbinischen Literatur siehe D. Sperber, Roman Palestine 200—400. Money and Prices, Bar Ilan Studies in Near Eastern Languages and Culture, Ramat Gan 1974, 226.

der Regierungszeit dieser Kaiser. Die große Ausnahme ist Diokletian. Andere Kaiser sind irgenwie Sündenböcke für spätere römische Mißgriffe gegenüber den Juden geworden. Um sie ranken sich immer neue Legenden, gleichsam als Ersatz für die allzu gefährliche Kritik am noch lebenden Herrscher. Diese Legenden haben zum größten Teil ihre endgültige Form wohl im 3. Jahrhundert gefunden, auch wenn die Datierung im einzelnen problematisch ist. Wenn wir hingegen die jüdische Beurteilung Roms in der Zeit zwischen 70 und Diokletian in ihrem geschichtlichen Wandel erfassen wollen, müssen wir auf andere Traditionen zurückgreifen, die wir — jedoch immer mit Vorbehalt — nach ihren Tradenten einordnen können.

1. Zwischen den Aufständen (70—135)

Die rabbinischen Zeugnisse für diese Periode sind aus verständlichen Gründen dürftig. Die Auseinandersetzung mit Rom erfolgte in erster Linie historisch, nämlich als Verarbeitung der Katastrophe des Jahres 70. Geeignetes Organ dafür waren vor allem die Apokalypsen — 4 Esra, 2 Baruch und die Offenbarung des Johannes. Die rabbinischen Lehrer der Periode von Jabne — dort hatte die rabbinische Gelehrsamkeit dieser Jahrzehnte ihr Zentrum — waren hingegen aus Sicherheitsgründen solchen Darstellungen abgeneigt: der Gründer der Schule von Jabne, Jochanan ben Zakkai, gilt vielmehr in der rabbinischen Tradition als Führer der romfreundlichen Partei im von den Römern belagerten Jerusalem; „Rabban Jochanan ben Zakkai gehört zu den Freunden des Kaisers" (ARN A 4, ed. SCHECHHTER 11b und Parallelen)[146a]. Die Schuld an der Zerstörung des Tempels geht nach dieser Tradition zu Lasten der Juden selbst und nicht Vespasians, der gegenüber der aufständischen Stadt eigentlich recht maßvoll handelt. Jochanan ben Zakkai sah nach Mekhilta Bachodesch 1 (ed. HOROVITZ-RABIN 202; cf. Ketubot 66b) in der Unterwerfung unter Rom die göttliche Strafe dafür, daß Israel Gott nicht dienstbar sein wollte. Die römische Herrschaft ist demnach gottgewollt. Wieweit die Rabbinen schon in dieser Periode für das Judentum ihrer Zeit repräsentativ sind, ist schwer zu beurteilen; jedenfalls hat sich diese theologische Begründung der römischen Herrschaft — mit Unterbrechung durch den Bar-Kokhba-Aufstand (132 bis 135) — ständig halten können.

Wie sehr die Rabbinen bereit waren, mit Rom zusammenzuarbeiten, geht auch aus der Nachricht von Edujot VII,7 hervor, daß Rabban Gamliel II. zum Statthalter nach Syrien ging, um von der Behörde bestätigt zu

[146a] Vgl. A. SCHALIT, Die Erhebung Vespasians nach Flavius Josephus, Talmud und Midrasch. Zur Geschichte einer messianischen Prophetie, ANRW II 2, hrsg. v. H. TEMPORINI, Berlin–New York 1975, 208—327, bes. 305ff.; J. NEUSNER, The Formation of Rabbinic Judaism: Yavneh (Jamnia) from A.D. 70 to 100, ob. in diesem Band (ANRW II 19,2) 3—42, bes. 30ff., sowie P. SCHÄFER, Die Flucht Jochanan b. Zakkais aus Jerusalem und die 'Gründung' von Jabne, ob. 43—101, bes. 80ff.

werden. Ebenso heißt es, daß die Familie des Patriarchen vom Verbot, Griechisch zu lernen, ausgenommen ist, weil sie stets mit den Behörden zu tun hat: Baba Qamma 82b–83a[147]. Dieselbe Kompromißbereitschaft Gamliels geht aus jBaba Qamma IV,3 (4b) hervor, wonach die Regierung zwei römische Soldaten sandte, die bei Gamliel studierten und alles für gut befanden, ausgenommen die Vorschrift, daß eine Jüdin einer Heidin keine Geburtshilfe leisten, wohl aber solche von ihr empfangen darf, sowie das Gesetz, daß einem Israeliten geraubtes Gut nicht genossen werden dürfe, das einem Heiden geraubte Gut jedoch ja. „Da bestimmte Rabban Gamliel, auch das einem Heiden Geraubte sei (zum Genuß) verboten, damit der Name Gottes nicht verunehrt werde."

Sicher hat es in dieser Periode genügend Schwierigkeiten mit den römischen Behörden gegeben; doch verdrängen die kooperationsbereiten Rabbinen sie weitgehend aus dem Gedächtnis, so daß nicht einmal der *fiscus judaicus* Erwähnung findet[148]. Von größerem Interesse für die Beurteilung Roms in dieser Zeit sind vor allem die Erzählungen über die Fahrt der vier Rabbinen Gamliel II., El'asar ben Asarja, Jehoschua ben Chananja und Aqiba nach Rom. Die historische Auswertung der zahlreichen rabbinischen Texte[149] ist äußerst schwierig, wie besonders G. Allon hervorgehoben hat[150]. Wir können hier nicht auf die Frage eingehen, ob die Tradition hier mehrere Reisen ineinander verschmolzen hat (meist denkt man an zwei). Dies ist jedenfalls wahrscheinlich, wären doch R. El'asar und R. Aqiba als Vertreter des jüdischen Sanhedrin bei der Reise Gamliels noch sehr jung gewesen, besonders, wenn man diese wie gewöhnlich in die letzten Jahre Domitians datiert[151]. Die Erzählungen sind sagenhaft angereichert — besonders die Seereise (z. B. Baba Batra 74b), die andererseits auch mehrfach als Beispiel bei religionsgesetzlichen Erörterungen zitiert wird (z. B. Erubin IV,1–2) —, und auch die Schilderung Roms gleicht ganz einem antiken Reiseführer, der von der Fremde Wunderdinge zu erzählen weiß. Auch diese Erzählungen sind offenbar lange gewachsen.

Sifre Dtn 43 (ed. Horovitz-Finkelstein 94f.; zahlreiche Parallelen) berichtet von der Ankunft der vier in Rom:

[147] Zum Verbot des Griechischstudiums im rabbinischen Judentum siehe S. Lieberman, Hellenism in Jewish Palestine, Texts and Studies of the Jewish Theological Seminary of America XVIII, New York ²1962, 100–114.

[148] In Mekhilta Bachodesch 1 (ed. Horovitz–Rabin 202f.; cf. Ketubot 66b) sagt Jochanan ben Zakkai, Israel müsse im römischen Reich Steuern zahlen, nachdem es die viel geringere Summe der Tempelsteuer nicht habe zahlen wollen; dies ist nicht als Anspielung auf den *fiscus judaicus* zu verstehen (gegen S. Krauss, Anm. 1, 158, und A. Carlebach, Rabbinic References to the Fiscus Judaicus, JQR 66 [1975f.] 57–61), sondern gilt allgemein von der römischen Besteuerung.

[149] Cf. M. D. Herr (Anm. 82) 138.

[150] G. Allon, Toldot Ha-Jehudim Be-Erets Jisrael Bi-Tqufat Ha-Mischna We-Ha-Talmud, I, Tel Aviv ³1959, 74–77. Cf. N. Wasser (Anm. 1) 65–70 für die ältere Literatur.

[151] So zuletzt E. M. Smallwood (Anm. 62) 10: da die Rabbinen die Seereise im Herbst wagen — nach Tosefta Sukka II, 11 (ed. Lieberman 265) usw. feierten sie das Laubhüttenfest auf dem Schiff —, muß die Reise sehr dringend gewesen sein.

> „Und schon betraten sie Rom; da hörten sie den tosenden Lärm der Stadt, vom Palatin aus 120 Meilen weit[152]."

Angesichts des Treibens Roms weinen die Rabbinen, nur Aqiba lacht. Sie beklagen, daß die Götzendiener in Glück und Sicherheit leben, während der Tempel zerstört und die Wohnstatt wilder Tiere geworden ist; Aqiba hingegen meint: wenn Gott

> „so an denen handelt, die ihn erzürnen, um wieviel mehr an denen, die seinen Willen tun[153]."

Er hofft also auf eine Restauration Israels, wenn es die Tora erfüllt.

Vom Romaufenthalt der Rabbinen erzählt dann DtnRabba 2,24 (ed. Mirkin XI 43), der römische Senat (סנקליטין = σύγκλητος) habe damals beschlossen, binnen dreißig Tagen solle es keinen Juden mehr auf der Welt geben. Ein gottesfürchtiger römischer Senator informierte davon die Rabbinen und beging knapp vor Ablaufen der Frist auf Anraten seiner Frau Selbstmord durch Aussaugen seines Giftringes. Der Senat betrauerte ihn — wie vorhergesehen — dreißig Tage lang und tagte nicht; inzwischen verfiel der Erlaß. Bei einem Kondolenzbesuch erfuhren die Rabbinen dann von der Witwe des Senators, daß dieser beschnitten war. (Variante in Aboda Zara 10b.)

Von diesem Text aus datiert man gewöhnlich die Romreise der Rabbinen in die letzten Tage Domitians. Das ist möglich, doch keineswegs gesichert. Eine geplante Judenvernichtung unter Domitian ist nicht belegt, ebensowenig eine Judenvertreibung. Die Erzählung schematisiert vielmehr eine Bedrohung durch die römische Regierung in Anlehnung an das Buch Ester[154]. Historisch gesichert ist nur eine Romreise Gamliels II. (etwa

[152] וכבר היו... נכנסים לרומי. שמעו קול המיה של מדינה מפיטולים מאה ועשרים מיל. Anstelle der üblichen Deutung auf Puteoli hat schon W. Bacher, Rome dans le Talmud et le Midrasch, REJ 33 (1874) 187—196, 195f. aufgrund der Varianten in den Parallelstellen „Palatin" gelesen. MS London von Sifre פלטיאן stützt diese Deutung. L. Goldschmidt in seiner Talmudübersetzung liest hingegen in der Parallele Makkot 24a „Kapitol", während S. Krauss (Anm. 1) 13 weiterhin auf Puteoli beharrt. „Palatin" dürfte die ursprüngliche Lesart sein; die 120 Meilen sind demnach einfach der Radius der Stadt — Belege für die rabbinischen Vorstellungen von der enormen Ausdehnung der Stadt folgen noch. Die Lesart Puteoli dürfte entstanden sein, als man diesen Zug der Darstellung nicht mehr verstand; allerdings ist auch denkbar, daß einem Schreiber unglaublich schien, daß man den Lärm Roms schon in Puteoli hörte, und er deshalb den Text „korrigierte" (doch warum hätte er dann nicht auch die 120 Meilen ausgelassen?!). Rationalistisch darf man an diese alten Reisebeschreibungen jedenfalls nicht herangehen. Zweifellos will der Bericht das Treiben Roms in seiner unfaßbaren Größe schildern, bietet in orientalischer Übertreibung den Eindruck des Provinzbewohners von der Hauptstadt.

[153] S. Krauss (Anm. 1) 13 übersetzt: „wie erst (einst) mit den Vollstreckern seines Willens". versteht darunter also die Römer und die Rache, die Gott an ihnen vollziehen wird,

[154] Est 3. Vielleicht stammt auch das Motiv des Ringes von dort, übergibt doch 3, 10 der König Haman seinen Siegelring als Zeichen der Vollmacht, er könne mit den Juden tun, was er wolle. In diesem Fall ist das Motiv hier einfach umgedreht worden, ist der Senator das Gegenstück Hamans.

zwischen 85 und 100), eine Bedrohung der Juden sowie die Anwesenheit von Sympathisanten mit dem Judentum im Senat[155].

In Tosefta Aboda Zara VI,7 (ed. ZUCKERMANDEL 469; Parallelen Aboda Zara IV,7 und Aboda Zara 54b) fragen die Philosophen R. Gamliel (bzw. die jüdischen Ältesten in Rom), warum Gott die Götzen nicht zerstöre. Die Antwort lautet, daß die Götzendiener für den Bestand der Welt Notwendiges anbeten — Gestirne und Planeten usw. — und Gott doch nicht wegen dieser Toren die Welt vernichte. Hier wie in anderen Texten ist die apologetische Tendenz deutlich: warum erweisen sich die Anhänger des Heidentums stärker als die Juden? Die Erzählung ist nicht an Rom gebunden. Noch weniger ist dies beim Spottgespräch zwischen Aqiba und einem kaiserlichen Eunuchen in Rom der Fall (KohRabba 10,8), wie die Parallele über Jehoschua ben Qorcha in Schabbat 152a zeigt.

In Rom sollen die vier gepredigt haben, daß Gott nicht wie ein menschlicher König ist, der ein Edikt erläßt und sich selbst nicht daran hält (Ex Rabba 30,9, ed. MIRKIN VI,41), eine Kritik an der Tendenz, den Kaiser über das Gesetz zu stellen.

ARN A16 (ed. SCHECHTER 32b) nennt in einer Kette von Beispielen, wie Israeliten den bösen Trieb überwunden haben, auch R. Zadoq, der nach der Niederlage des Jahres 70 in römische Gefangenschaft kam und dem seine Herrin eine Sklavin zuteilte; er schaute sie jedoch gar nicht an: es zieme sich nicht, daß er mit einer solchen Frau Kinder habe. Daraufhin ließ ihn seine Herrin in Ehren frei (cf. auch Qiduschin 40a)[156]. Als Steigerung dazu heißt es dann in der Fortsetzung, ein römischer Würdenträger habe Aqiba bei dessen Rombesuch gleich zwei schöne Frauen zur Verfügung gestellt und auch er habe sie nicht angeschaut. Darauf stellt ihn der Römer zur Rede: „Sind sie nicht schön? sind sie nicht Menschen wie du? hat nicht der, der dich erschuf, auch sie geschaffen?" — ein typischer Appell also an die allen gemeinsame Menschennatur. Doch Aqiba antwortete: „Was soll ich tun? Ihr Geruch nach Aas und unerlaubtem Fleisch hat mich überwältigt."

In diesen Beispielerzählungen ist die handelnde Person ziemlich gleichgültig. Die Texte kontrastieren den sittenreinen Juden mit der Unmoral der Heiden. Der gesetzesbewußte Jude lehnt jede Mischehe ab — und das besonders in einer Periode der Selbstbesinnung, wie es die Zeit nach 70 gewesen sein muß; andererseits mußte diese Haltung bei Nichtjuden Unverständnis hervorrufen und Angriffe gegen die Juden wecken, die Tacitus so

155 Cf. M. STERN, Sympathy for Judaism in Roman Senatorial Circles in the Period of the Early Empire (hebr.), Zion 29 (1964) 155—167. Ob wir unseren Text, wie es gewöhnlich geschieht, mit den Nachrichten über die Hinrichtung des Flavius Clemens in Zusammenhang bringen dürfen, ist wiederum fraglich.

156 Ekha Rabbati 4, 2 (ed. BUBER 72a) erzählt von einem anderen jüdischen Gefangenen dieser Zeit in Rom, einem hübschen Knaben, den Jehoschua ben Chananja im Kerker fand und an seiner Schriftkenntnis als Juden erkannte. Er weissagte ihm eine Zukunft als Lehrer Israels, und tatsächlich wurde aus dem Knaben der große Rabbi Jischmael.

kennzeichnet: *separati epulis, discreti cubilibus alienarum concubitu abstinent; inter se nihil illicitum*[157].

Ein gutes Beispiel für die verschiedenen Einstellungen des Judentums auch noch am Ende dieser Periode, gerade nach Zusammenbruch des Bar-Kokhba-Aufstandes, ist Aboda Zara 18a, wo Chananja ben Teradion den kranken Jose ben Qisma besucht. Der Kranke will seinen Besucher davon überzeugen, daß es sinnlos ist, gegen die römischen Erlässe weiterhin Tora zu lehren. Die römische Herrschaft stamme von Gott, wie daraus hervorgehe, daß Rom ungestraft den Tempel zerstören und Israeliten töten konnte. Als Jose nach kurzer Zeit starb, wurde er unter großer Beteiligung römischer Würdenträger bestattet. Auf dem Rückweg vom Begräbnis überraschten die Römer Chananja beim Torastudium, wickelten ihn in die Torarolle und verbrannten ihn darin.

Die literarische Verzahnung[157a] der beiden Geschicke läßt ihre Typisierung erkennen; die Grundtendenz der Erzählung ist jedoch sicher historisch: sogar in der Zeit der Religionsverfolgung nach dem zweiten großen Aufstand gab es Rabbinen, die aus theologischen Motiven zur Anerkennung Roms bereit waren. Um so bezeichnender ist, daß nach Sanhedrin 98a—b der romtreue Jose auf dem Sterbebett seine Jünger bat, ihn tief zu begraben: denn in Israel werde es keinen Sarg geben, aus dem nicht ein parthisches Pferd Stroh frißt. Er hoffte demnach auf die Überwindung Roms durch die Parther vor dem Anbruch der messianischen Heilszeit. Diese Hoffnung war allen gemeinsam: nur hatten die einen für kurze Zeit die Übermacht bekommen, die diese Heilszeit mit Waffengewalt herbeizwingen wollten, während die Gemäßigten die Zukunft Gott überließen[158].

2. Von Antoninus Pius bis Caracalla

Die Zeit der Antoninen und Severer war für die Juden im allgemeinen günstig, was sich auch in den Quellen niedergeschlagen hat. Schim'on b. Jochai und El'asar ben Jose sollen nach dem legendarischen Bericht von Meila 17b (cf. p. 27f.) auf einer Romreise die Aufhebung der judenfeindlichen Edikte Hadrians von Antoninus Pius erreicht haben[159]. Nach der

[157] Hist. V, 5. Cf. M. D. HERR (Anm. 82) 136f. Das von HERR gebotene reiche Material über den jüdisch-römischen Dialog in dieser Periode ergänzt das Bild dieser Zeit wesentlich und bezeugt das lebhafte Interesse Roms an jüdischen Vorstellungen und die friedliche Austragung von Meinungsverschiedenheiten. Das setzt jedenfalls — zumindest für bestimmte Kreise — gutnachbarschaftliche Beziehungen voraus.

[157a] Daß die Verknüpfung nur literarisch ist, betont auch J. GUTMAN, The Jewish Wars in the Time of Trajan, Sefer Asaf, Jerusalem 1953, 149—184 (hebr.), p. 174: nach ihm ist Jose ben Qisma zu einer Zeit gestorben, als die Beziehungen zwischen Rom und den Juden noch in Ordnung waren.

[158] Ähnlich zwiespältig ist die Haltung von Rabban Gamliel II., wenn er trotz einer de facto Anerkennung der römischen Regierung in ARN A28 (ed. SCHECHTER 43a) sagt, durch vier Dinge zehre Rom (seine Untertanen) aus: Zölle, Bäder, Theater und Steuern.

[159] Mit W. BACHER, Die Agada der Tannaiten I, Straßburg ²1903 (= Berlin 1965) 381, Anm. 3 ist die Meinung von H. GRAETZ, Geschichte der Juden IV, Leipzig ⁴1908, 191 abzulehnen,

Tradition soll R. El'asar b. Rabbi Jose in Rom den Vorhang des Jerusalemer Tempels gesehen haben (Tosefta Kippurim II,16, ed. LIEBERMAN 239, und öfter), ebenso das goldene Stirnblech des Hohenpriesters (jJoma IV,1,41c), sowie auch die Bruchstücke des salomonischen Thrones (EstRabba 1,2) und die taubengroße Mücke, an der Titus starb (ARN B7, ed. SCHECHTER 11a), was fast an mittelalterliche Pilgerberichte und Reliquienverehrung erinnert. Derselbe R. El'asar erweist sich jedoch Rom gegenüber kritisch, wenn er den Ausdruck Senator als שונא ונוקם ונוטר (*sone wenoqem wenoter*, „Hasser, Rächer, Grollender") deutet: GenRabba 67,8 (ed. THEODOR-ALBECK 763) und jAboda Zara I,2 (39c).

Die verschiedenen Einstellungen der ersten Generation nach Bar Kokhba zu Rom sind in Schabbat 33b typisch zusammengefaßt. R. Jehuda, R. Jose und R. Schim'on sitzen zusammen mit dem Proselytensohn Jehuda. R. Jehuda preist Rom:

> „Wie schön sind die Werke dieses Volkes. Sie haben Märkte, Brücken und Bäder gebaut."

R. Jose schweigt. R. Schim'on antwortet:

> „Dies alles haben sie nur für ihre eigenen Bedürfnisse gebaut — Märkte, um Huren hinzusetzen, Bäder, um sich darin zu vergnügen, Brücken, um Zoll einzuheben."

Der Proselytensohn Jehuda verrät die drei bei der Regierung, worauf Jose nach Sepphoris verbannt wird und Schim'on hingerichtet werden soll.

Die romfeindliche Haltung Schim'ons gründet auf seiner Hoffnung auf die Parther: nach Ekha Rabbati 1,13 (ed. BUBER 39a) soll er gesagt haben, der Messias sei vor der Tür, wenn man ein parthisches Pferd an Israels Gräbern angebunden sieht. Die Mittelposition Joses entspricht seiner Gesprächsbereitschaft[160], während die romfreundliche Haltung

diese Romreise habe erst unter Mark Aurel nach dem Tode des Lucius Verus stattgefunden. Bei einem frühen Ansatz haben wir allerdings Schwierigkeiten mit der Unterbringung der 13 Jahre, die Schim'on bar Jochai vor den Römern in einer Höhle verborgen gelebt haben soll. Die zeitliche Einordnung der Romreisen enthält eine ganze Reihe von Schwierigkeiten. Nach Meila 17a und Joma 53b hat Schim'on bar Jochai in Rom mit Mattia ben Cheresch diskutiert; dieser wird jedoch auch schon bei der Romreise der vier Rabbinen genannt: Joma 86b nennt ihn zusammen mit El'asar ben Asarja, Joma 88a—b mit Jehoschua ben Chananja; das Lehrhaus des Mattia ben Cheresch in Rom wird Sanhedrin 32b genannt. Wir haben schon erwähnt, daß die Reise der vier eine literarische Zusammenziehung mehrerer Romreisen sein muß; somit müssen wir nicht annehmen, Mattia ben Cheresch habe schon zur Zeit Domitians in Rom gelehrt — sonst wäre seine Begegnung mit Schim'on bar Jochai unter Antoninus Pius schon aus zeitlichen Gründen ziemlich unmöglich. Zu Mattia b. Cheresch cf. A. TOAFF, Matia Ben Cheresh e la sua academia rabbinica di Roma, Annuario di Studi Ebraici (Collegio Rabbinico Italiano, Roma) 2 (1964f.) 69—80 (mir nicht zugänglich).

[160] Zu seinen Gesprächen mit der römischen Matrone siehe W. BACHER, Die Agada der Tannaiten II, Straßburg 1890 (= Berlin 1966) 165—170 sowie M. D. HERR (Anm. 82) 145—149. HERR 145 betont "*a slight change in tone*" in den jüdisch-römischen Gesprächen. "*Instead of the respect previously shown, the attitude of the Romans turned into one of contempt.*"

Jehudas darauf beruht, daß er die Erlösung erst in ferner Zukunft erwartet — dann allerdings wird Israel zu den Völkern sagen: „Wo sind eure Präfekten und Statthalter?" (Sifre Dtn 327, ed. HOROVITZ-FINKELSTEIN 378). Pesachim 54b bringt diese Haltung anonym als eine Baraita: sieben Dinge sind verborgen, darunter auch die Ankunft des messianischen Reiches und der Untergang der schuldbeladenen Regierung (cf. KohRabba 11,10).

In Sifre Dtn 37 (ed. HOROVITZ-FINKELSTEIN 72) spricht R. Jehuda aus derselben Einstellung heraus kritiklos davon, daß nun jeder, der etwas auf sich hält, sich in Rom einen Palast baut, wie das einst in Israel gewesen sei. Der etwas später lebende R. Natan sagt ebenso kritiklos, kein Reichtum sei wie der Reichtum Roms[161]. Und R. Schim'on ben Gamliel kann sogar die militärische Macht Roms irgendwie bewundern (Mekhilta Beschallach 1, ed. HOROVITZ-RABIN 89):

„Komm und sieh den Reichtum und die Größe des schuldbeladenen Reiches. Nicht eine seiner Truppen (*numerus*) ist untätig. Sie alle laufen bei Tag und Nacht; jene Ägyptens hingegen standen alle müßig."

Von R. Meir, dem bedeutendsten Mann der Generation nach Bar Kokhba, erzählt Aboda Zara 18b, er habe einmal einen Gefangenen durch List befreit und sei daraufhin steckbrieflich gesucht worden (אתו חקקו לדמותיה דר׳ מאיר אפיתחא דרומי: „Sie kamen und gravierten das Bild des R. Meir auf das Tor Roms"), so daß er nach Babylonien flüchten mußte. In KohRabba 1,28 heißt es, die römische Behörde habe einst von den Rabbinen einen Leuchter angefordert; sie verstanden dies im übertragenen Sinn und sandten R. Meir (dessen Name „Leuchter" bedeutet), der dann mit den Römern eine lange Diskussion führte und auch gefragt wurde:

„Warum heißt das Schwein *chasir*? Weil es einmal Größe und Herrschaft dem Besitzer zurückgeben wird (*mechaseret*)[162]."

Roms (= des Schweines) Herrschaft ist nicht von Dauer.

Anderer Auffassung ist J. G. GAGER, The Dialogue of Paganism with Judaism: Bar Cochba to Julian, HUCA 44 (1973) 89—118, p. 114, Anm. 125, der in nichtjüdischen Quellen diese Behauptung nicht belegt findet.

161 ARN A28 (ed. SCHECHTER 43a). In EsterRabba 1, 15 heißt es im Namen Natans, zehn Teile Reichtum gebe es in der Welt, neun davon in Rom. Doch gibt es auch schon in dieser Zeit Kritik an Roms Reichtum. So wendet sich Sifre Dtn 317 (ed. HOROVITZ—FINKELSTEIN 360) scharf gegen die Habgier der römischen Beamten, die das Land auspressen; für die Legionen, die die Götter Roms sind, muß Israel ständig Steuern zahlen und Naturalien liefern: Midrasch Tannaim zu Dtn 37, 28 (ed. HOFFMANN 202). Sifre Num 131 (ed. HOROVITZ 169) erzählt in einem Königsgleichnis von einem Centurio, der seine Jahre abgedient hat, doch nicht *primipilus* geworden ist; er flieht, wird jedoch wieder gefangen und hingerichtet, während seine Kollegen mit einer hohen Abfindung entlassen werden. Sonst hören wir aus dieser Zeit nichts von entlaufenen Soldaten, noch weniger davon, daß die Bevölkerung dadurch belästigt wird.

162 למה נקרא שמו חזיר? שעתיד להחזיר הגדולה והמלכות לבעליה. Solche Auslegungen sind häufig; cf. z. B. Lev Rabba 13, 5 (ed. MARGULIES 295).

In der zweiten Generation nach dem Aufstand gingen einige in der Annahme Roms so weit, daß sie bei der Ergreifung jüdischer Krimineller mitwirkten. Baba Metsia 83b—84a nennt als solche Kollaborateure R. Jischmael ben Jose und den Sohn des großen Römerfeindes Schim'on bar Jochai, nämlich El'asar ben R. Schim'on. Diesen stellte Jehoschua ben Qorcha deshalb zur Rede:

„Essig, Sohn des Weins, wielange noch lieferst du das Volk unseres Gottes dem Tode aus?"

El'asar verantwortete sich damit, er jäte ja nur die Disteln aus dem Weinberg aus. Ähnlich rechtfertigt sich anschließend R. Jischmael vor dem ihm erschienenen Elia.

Ein gutes Nebeneinander von Juden und Römern ist in dieser Zeit normal, ebenso auch die gegenseitige Hilfe in Notfällen. Das illustrieren zwei legendenhaft ausgemalte Parallelerzählungen in KohRabba 11,1—2. In der ersten Erzählung sieht Bar Kappara (Ende 2. Jahrh.) beim Spaziergang am Strand von Caesarea ein Schiff sinken und einen Prokonsul nackt ans Ufer kommen. Der Rabbi hilft dem Römer und erwirkt später dafür die Freilassung eines jüdischen Gefangenen.

Die zweite Erzählung hat den etwas früheren R. El'asar ben Schammua und einen schiffbrüchigen Römer als Protagonisten. Gegenüber dem ersten Text ist alles gesteigert: El'asar hilft noch großzügiger; der Schiffbrüchige, ein gewöhnlicher Römer, wird nach einiger Zeit Kaiser; er befiehlt, alle Juden zu töten und ihre Frauen gefangen zu nehmen; und auch hier ist natürlich die Fürsprache des Rabbinen erfolgreich.

Die beiden Texte sind in eine Reihe von vier Schiffbrucherzählungen eingefügt, die alle Koh 11,1 illustrieren: „Wirf dein Brot auf das Wasser; noch nach vielen Tagen wirst du es finden" — Wohltun bringt Zinsen. Historisches ist kaum daran, auch wenn dergleichen vorgekommen sein mag. Es ist jedoch für das Römerbild der Zeit typisch, wenn in beiden Erzählungen der Römer zum jüdischen Fürsprecher sagt: „Diese Regierung tut nichts umsonst"; nur in diesem Ausnahmefall ist keine Bestechung notwendig.

Interessant ist auch der Abschluß der zweiten Erzählung. Der Römer wirft den Juden vor, ihr Gesetz nicht zu erfüllen: „Verabscheue nicht den Edomiter, denn er ist dein Bruder (Dtn 23,8). Und bin ich nicht ein Sohn Esaus, eures Bruders? Und ihr habt mir kein Erbarmen erwiesen." Die Juden haben somit die Schrift übertreten und sind des Todes schuldig; doch läßt der Römer Gnade vor Recht ergehen. Dieser wohl nachträglich eingefügte Teil (er hat kein Gegenstück in der Parallelerzählung und paßt auch nicht in den Zusammenhang) betont somit die Pflicht des Juden, den Römer als Bruder zu behandeln, eine sogar in dieser römerfreundlichen Zeit außerordentliche Aussage.

Die Kontakte Rabbis mit Antoninus haben wir schon besprochen. Durch seine Stellung als Patriarch stand er den Römern sicher näher als der

Durchschnitt der jüdischen Bevölkerung; doch ist auch seine im Grunde positive Einstellung durch kritische Distanz begrenzt. Nach R. Abba b. Zabda (2. Hälfte 3. Jahrh.) wollte Rabbi das Fasten am 9. Ab abschaffen, das an die Tempelzerstörung durch die Römer erinnerte und so feindselige Erinnerungen wachhielt. Doch ließen dies die anderen Rabbinen nicht zu. Nach anderer Auffassung hingegen wollte Rabbi nur einmal den 9. Ab nicht als Fasttag halten lassen, weil er auf einen Sabbat fiel (jTaanit IV,9,69c). Wenn die erste Aussage der Wirklichkeit entspricht, war die Absicht Rabbis, unter die Vergangenheit einen Schlußstrich zu ziehen, um mit den Römern ein besseres Verhältnis zu erreichen[163]. Daß es ihm dabei in erster Linie um das Praktische ging, zeigt ein Text in Pesachim 112b: er empfahl demnach seinen Söhnen, den römischen Zoll nicht zu hintergehen; dies begründete er jedoch mit der Möglichkeit, entdeckt zu werden und dabei das ganze Vermögen zu verlieren. Und wie viele andere, so vertrat auch Rabbi trotz seiner Bereitschaft, mit Rom zusammenzuarbeiten, die Hoffnung, Rom werde einst in die Hände Persiens fallen (Joma 10a)[163a]. Somit können wir die Einstellung Rabbis wie wohl auch der Mehrheit der Juden Palästinas zu seiner Zeit so kennzeichnen: Im Praktischen war er auf ein friedliches Zusammenleben bedacht; er akzeptierte die römische Herrschaft, jedoch unter eschatologischem Vorbehalt.

3. Das dritte Jahrhundert

In den Jahren nach dem Patriarchat Rabbis verschlechterte sich das Verhältnis der Juden zu Rom zusehends, auch wenn die Gründe zur Klage nicht spezifisch für die Juden waren, sondern allgemein die Krise des Reiches spiegeln.

Grund besonderer Klage wurde immer mehr die Gerichtsbarkeit Roms. Schim'on b. Laqisch (Mitte 3. Jahrh.) kann zwar Gen 1,13: „Gott sah, daß es sehr gut war" noch auf das römische Reich deuten, das die Rechte der Menschen schützt (GenRabba 9,12, ed. Theodor-Albeck 73); im allgemeinen ist man jedoch davon nicht mehr überzeugt. In LevRabba 13,5 (ed. Margulies 291f.) sagt R. Simon (2. Hälfte 3. Jahrh.) von Rom:

> „Warum wird es mit einem Schwein verglichen? Um dich zu lehren: So wie das Schwein daliegt und seine Klauen vorstreckt und sagt:

[163] Allerdings legt er selbst in jTaanit IV, 8 (68d) Gen 27, 22 „Die Stimme ist die Stimme Jakobs, doch die Hände sind die Hände Esaus" auf die jüdische Niederlage im Bar-Kokhba-Aufstand aus: „Die Stimme Jakobs klagt über das, was ihm die Hände Esaus in Bet-Ter angetan haben."

[163a] Demgegenüber vertritt der Babylonier Rabh die Meinung, Persien werde in die Hände Roms fallen. R. Jehuda (Mitte 3. Jahrhundert) gibt als Begründung Rabhs an, der Sohn Davids werde erst kommen, wenn die frevelhafte Regierung sich neun Monate lang über die ganze Welt ausgedehnt habe (Joma 10a).

siehe, ich bin rein[164], so prahlt diese frevlerische Regierung. Sie ist gewalttätig, raubt und tut, als ob sie den Richterstuhl vorbereitete. Das begab sich mit einem Befehlshaber in Caesarea: er ließ die Diebe, die Ehebrecher und die Zauberer hinrichten und sagte zu seinem Berater, alle drei Verbrechen habe er selbst in einer einzigen Nacht begangen[165].“

MidrPs 80,6 (ed. Buber 182a) bringt dasselbe in leichter Abwandlung:

„So stellt der frevlerische Esau offen den Richterstuhl auf, obwohl er Gewalt übt, stiehlt und raubt; und dabei tun sie, als ob es ein gerechtes Gericht wäre[166].“

Besonders das Gerichtsverfahren mit seinen Fangfragen verärgert die jüdische Bevölkerung. Mehrmals überliefert die jüdische Tradition die typischen Fragen des Richters: „angenommen (ὑπόθεσις), du hast nicht gemordet — womit hast du gemordet? Du hast nicht gestohlen — wer war bei dir, als du gestohlen hast?[167].“

Ebenso erbittert ist die Landbevölkerung über die hohen Steuern und Abgaben an Naturalien, mit denen Rom den Sozialstaat finanziert: „Ist denn Esau ein ‘Wohltäter der Schwachen’ (Spr 28,8)? Doch vielmehr ein Bedrücker der Schwachen! Die Statthalter, *duces* und Eparchen ziehen in die Dörfer und rauben und plündern, und wenn sie zurückkehren, sagen sie: bringt uns die Armen herbei, damit wir sie versorgen![168].“ R. Jakob b. Jose (Variante: Jochai; Daten fraglich) vergleicht in Pesiqta Rabbati 10 (ed. Friedmann 33a) den Steuerzahler mit einem Mann, dessen Kleider sich in den Dornen verfangen haben und der einfach nicht nachkommt, sich freizumachen: „so ist die Herrschaft Esaus. Sie treibt die *annona* ein; noch hat sie die *annona* nicht eingetrieben, kommt schon die Kopfsteuer daher; diese wird noch eingehoben und schon kommt die Rekrutenaushebung[169].“

[164] Die gespaltenen Klauen des Schweins machen es jedoch noch nicht rein: dazu müßte es ja auch ein Wiederkäuer sein (Dtn 14, 8).

[165] למה נמשלה בחזיר, לומר לך מה חזיר הזה בשעה שהוא רבוץ ומוציא טלפיו ואומר ראו שאני טהור, כך היתה מלכות הרשעה הזו מתגאה וחומסת וגוזלת ונראת כילו שהיא מצעת בימה. מעשה בשלטון אחד בקיסרי שהיה הורג את הגנבים ואת המנאפין ואת המנאפין ואת המכשפין ואמר לסנקליטין שלו שלשתן עשה אותו האיש בלילה אחד. Der erste Teil auch in GenRabba 65,1 (ed. Theodor—Albeck 713).

[166] כך עשו הרשע מסייע ליה בימה בפרהסיא מה שהוא חומס וגונב וגוזל ונראין כאלו הן דינין של אמת.

[167] אפותיסיס לא קטלת, ובמה קטלת, לא גנבת, ומן הוה עמך כדגנבת (DtnRabba, ed. Lieberman 18). Cf. GenRabba 37, 2 (ed. Theodor—Albeck 345) und den von S. Lieberman, Roman Legal Institutions in Early Rabbinics and in the Acta Martyrum, JQR 35 (1944f.) 1—57, p. 25 zitierten Jelamdenu-Text aus der Geniza von Kairo.

[168] וכי עשו חונן דלים הוא? והלוא עושק דלים הוא. אלא כגון הגמונים ודכסים ואפרכים שהן יוצאין לעירות וגוזלין ובוזזין וכשהם חוזרים ואומרים: הביאו לנו עניים ונפרנסם. Parallelen bei S. Lieberman (Anm. 1) 357.

[169] כך הוא מלכותו של עשו. גובה את הארנון ועד שלא יגבה את הארנון הרי הגלגולות באה עליהם ועד שזאת ניגבת באים עליהם טירבוס (= טירונים, wie MS Parma liest).

Daß diese Ausbeutung auch vor dem Patriarchen nicht haltmachte, zeigt GenRabba 78,12 (ed. THEODOR-ALBECK 932), wo eine Frau dem Patriarchen in Gegenwart des Resch Laqisch (2. Hälfte 3. Jahrh.) eine Schüssel mit einem Messer präsentiert; der Patriarch nimmt jedoch nur das Messer an. Da kommt ein römischer Kurier, „sah es, fand Gefallen daran und nahm es“ (וחמתה וחמדה ונסבה *wechamta, wechamda, wenasba,* eine offenkundige Parodie auf das *veni, vidi, vici*)[170].

Auf diesem Hintergrund ist es verständlich, daß der vor kurzem noch bewunderte Reichtum Roms jetzt Unzufriedenheit weckt und zu Kritik herausfordert. R. Jehoschua ben Levi (1. Hälfte 3. Jahrh.) sah bei seinem Romaufenthalt mit Teppichen verhüllte Marmorsäulen, die so vor Hitze und Frost geschützt werden sollten. Ein wenig weiter begegnete er am Marktplatz einem Armen in einer groben Decke und schloß daraus, daß Gott beim Geben wie beim Strafen gleich grenzenlos sei[171].

Aus der ersten Hälfte des 3. Jahrhunderts stammt eine Beschreibung Roms (Pesachim 118b), wonach diese große Stadt[172] 365 Märkte besitzt, auf jedem Markt sich 365 Paläste befinden, jeder Palast 365 Aufgänge hat, von denen jeder soviel gekostet hat, daß man davon die ganze Welt ernähren könnte[173]. In die Bewunderung ist wohl schon hier Sozialkritik gemischt; noch deutlicher ist die Kritik, wenn R. Jischmael gegenüber Rabbi, nach anderen gegenüber R. Jischmael b. R. Jose bemerkt, all dieser Reichtum werde einst Israel gehören, wie es in Jes 23,18 heißt: „Sein Gewinn, ihn werde ich als Weihegeschenk dem Herrn geben.“ Ähnlich sagt R. Jose bar Chanina (Mitte 3. Jahrh.) in Megilla 6a, in den Theatern und Zirkussen Edoms würden einst die Fürsten Israels die Menge Tora lehren.

[170] Darauf verweist richtig M. AVI-YONAH (Anm. 107) 115.

[171] GenRabba 33, 1 (ed. THEODOR—ALBECK 300f.); Pesiqta de Rab Kahana 9 (ed. MANDELBAUM 148). Die Parallele LevRabba 27, 1 (ed. MARGULIES 617f.) liest Jehoschua ben Chananja (Mitte 2. Jahrhundert), nur wenige MSS ben Levi.

[172] Der Ausdruck „die große Stadt Roms“ (כרך גדול של רומי) bzw. die ursprünglichere Form „die große Stadt in Rom“ (כרך גדול שברומי) setzt das Verständnis von Rom als Landesnamen voraus. Cf. dazu W. BACHER (Anm. 152) 190f.

[173] Eine ausführliche Beschreibung Roms ohne jedwede Kritik stammt aus der Zeit Diokletians von R. Ulla: אטליא של יון זה כרך גדול של רומי, והויא תלת מאה פרסה על תלת מאה פרסה, ויש בה שס״ה שווקים כמנין ימות החמה, וקטן שבכולם של מוכרי עופות, והויא ששה עשר מיל על ששה עשר מיל, ומלך סועד בכל יום באחד מהן, והדר בה אע״פ שאינו נולד בה, נוטל פרס מבית המלך והנולד בה אע״פ שאינו דר בה, נוטל פרס מבית המלך, ושלשת אלפים בי בני יש בו, וחמש מאות חלונות מעלין עשן חוץ לחומה, צדו אחד ים וצדו אחד הרים וגבעות, צדו אחד מחיצה של ברזל וצדו אחד חולסית ומצולה. „Das Italien Griechenlands, d. h. die große Stadt Rom, mißt 300 zu 300 Parasangen. Es gibt dort 365 Märkte entsprechend den Tagen des Sonnenjahres; der kleinste davon ist der der Geflügelhändler, und sogar der mißt 16 zu 16 Meilen. Der König speist täglich auf einem von diesen. Wer darin wohnt, auch wenn er dort gar nicht geboren ist, erhält seinen Unterhalt vom Königshaus. Ebenso erhält, wer dort geboren ist und nicht dort wohnt, seinen Unterhalt vom Königshaus. Es gibt dort 300 Bäder und 500 Fenster lassen den Rauch über die Mauer abziehen. Auf einer Seite befindet sich das Meer, auf der anderen Berge und Anhöhen, auf der einen Seite eine eiserne Mauer, auf der anderen Dünen und Wassertiefen“ (Megilla 6b). Siehe dazu W. BACHER (Anm. 152) 190—194.

Nach der rabbinischen Fassung der Gründungslegende Roms ist das Geschick Israels mit dem Roms schon von allem Anfang an verflochten. So sagt R. Jitschaq (Ende 3. Jahrh.), an dem Tag, als Salomo die Tochter des Pharao heiratete und damit von den Idealen der mosaischen Religion abwich, steckte der Engel Gabriel ein Schilfrohr ins Meer; dieses wuchs, wurde zu einer Sandbank und darauf wurde später Rom gegründet (Sanhedrin 21b). Ähnlich erzählt der gleichzeitige R. Levi in jAboda Zara I,2 (39c) und fährt fort: als Jerobeam zwei goldene Kälber errichtete, traten Romulus und Remus auf und bauten zwei Schilfhütten in Rom; als Elia entrückt wurde, setzte man in Rom einen König ein[174].

Da Rom demnach nur durch die Sünde Israels großgeworden ist, muß es auch mit der Erlösung Israels wieder untergehen, wie R. Jitschaq in Megilla 6a sagt:

> „Das edomitische Caesarea, die Hauptstadt der Könige. Die einen sagen, in ihr werden Könige aufgezogen, andere, in ihr werden Könige aufgestellt. Caesarea und Jerusalem: wenn dir jemand sagt, beide sind zerstört, glaub es nicht, beide sind bewohnt, glaub es nicht. Sagt einer: Caesarea ist zerstört und Jerusalem bewohnt, Jerusalem ist zerstört und Caesarea ist bewohnt, so glaub es[175].“

Andererseits kann R. Jitschaq in Megilla 6a—b aus der Schicksalsverbundenheit Roms und Jerusalems die Germanen als gemeinsamen Feind fürchten, ein Germanenangriff würde beide vernichten:

> „Wenn das edomitische Germanien loszieht, zerstört es die ganze Welt[176].“

Schon aus der Gründungsgeschichte Roms klingt Verachtung: als Israel schon ein Königreich war, befand sich an der Stelle Roms erst eine

[174] Schabbat 56b und Sifre Dtn 52 (ed. Horovitz—Finkelstein 119), dort in einem späteren Einschub (MS London). Zu Romulus und Remus cf. MidrPs 10, 6 (ed. Buber 48a) und 17, 12 (67b), GenRabba 49, 9 (ed. Theodor—Albeck 511) und öfter. Siehe dazu A. Sulzbach, Die Romulussage im Talmud und Midrasch, Jahrbuch f. jüd. Gesch. u. Lit. 2 (1899) 75—83. In eschatologischen Texten spielt der frevlerische König Armilos eine große Rolle. Mit G. Vermes (Anm. 19) 223 ist er wohl als „Romulus redivivus“ zu verstehen. Er besiegt im Kampf der Endzeit nach 30 Kriegsmonaten den Messias aus dem Hause Ephraim, wird dann aber selbst von davidischen Messias getötet: siehe Targum Jes 11, 4 sowie Targum J I zu Dtn 34, 3 und vor allem die späten Texte bei A. Jellinek, Bet-ha-Midrasch, Jerusalem ²1938, I 56 und II 56f.; 61f.

[175] זו קסרי בת אדום, שהיא היתה מטרופולין של מלכים. איכא דאמרי דמרבי בה מלכי, ואיכא דאמרי דמוקמי מינה מלכי. קסרי וירושלים: אם יאמר לך אדם חרבו שניהן, אל תאמן, ישבו שניהן, אל תאמן. חרבה קסרי וישבה ירושלים, חרבה ירושלים וישבה קסרי, תאמן.

[176] Megilla 6b fügt daran einen Satz des R. Chama bar Chanina (Mitte 3. Jahrh.), der ebenfalls die Germanengefahr beschwört: תלת מאה קטירי תגא איכא בגרמניה של אדום, ותלת מאה ושיתין וחמישה מרזבני איכה ברומי, ובכל יומא נפקי הני לאפי הני ומקטיל חד מינייהו ומיטרדי לאוקמי מלכא: „Im römischen Germanien gibt es 300 Gekrönte und 365 Führer gibt es zu Rom; und täglich ziehen die einen gegen die andern und töten je einen, und sie haben Mühe, einen König einzusetzen.“

armselige Schilfinsel, auf der später zwei Hütten gebaut wurden. In Aussprüchen vom Ende des 3. Jahrhunderts wird diese Verachtung besonders deutlich und die kulturelle Unterlegenheit Roms scharf betont. In Aboda Zara 10a bezieht R. Joseph Obd 1,2 „Du bist tief verachtet" auf Rom; denn „sie haben weder Schrift noch Sprache" (anonym auch in Gittin 80a). Nach Jonatan aus Bet Gubrin ist Latein die Sprache der Kriegsführung (jMegilla I,11,71b); und in jMegilla I,11 (71c) heißt es, die Bibel könne nur ins Griechische entsprechend übersetzt werden: die lateinische Sprache habe ja erst ein Festungssoldat aus der griechischen entwickelt[177].

Die allgemeine Verschlechterung der Lage in der wirtschaftlichen Not des 3. Jahrhunderts[177a] führte nicht nur zu einer immer schärferen Ablehnung Roms, sondern auch zu einem Wiederaufleben des Messianismus. Doch war man weise genug geworden, die messianische Hoffnung nicht durch einen bewaffneten Aufstand verwirklichen zu wollen. R. Jochanan (+279) formuliert diese Haltung in MidrPs 36,6 (ed. BUBER 125b) in einem Gleichnis: wie ein Mann in der Nacht eine Fackel anzündet, die jedoch immer wieder verlischt, bis er es vorzieht, auf das Sonnenlicht zu warten, so ist auch Israel müde geworden, sich von Menschen erlösen zu lassen. Jetzt wartet es nur noch auf die Erlösung durch Gott selbst[178].

Die eigenartige Dialektik im Verhältnis des damaligen Judentums zu Rom führte dazu, daß man immer mehr die Erlösung gerade aus dem verachteten Rom erwartete. So sagt R. Jehoschua b. Levi (1. Hälfte 3. Jahrh.) in jTaanit I,1 (64a):

177 „Aramäisch" steht im Text statt „römisch". Zum Thema siehe W. BACHER (Anm. 152) 189.

177a Vgl. P. CHARANIS, Observations on the Transformation of the Roman World in the Third Century and the Question of the Fall of the Empire, ANRW II 2, hrsg. v. H. TEMPORINI, Berlin New York 1975, 551—559; M. CRAWFORD, Finance, Coinage and Money from the Severans to Constantine, ebd. 560—593; G. WALSER, Die Severer in der Forschung 1960—1972, ebd. 614—656, bes. 639ff.; L. POLVERINI, Da Aureliano a Diocleziano, ebd. 1013—1035, bes. 1032ff. Speziell zur Lage in Palästina s. auch D. SPERBER, Aspects of Agrarian Life in Roman Palestine I: Agricultural Decline in Palestine during the Later Principate, ANRW II 8, hrsg. v. H. TEMPORINI u. W. HAASE, Berlin–New York 1978, 397—443 (mit Bibliographie S. 442f.).

178 Im 3. Jahrhundert gewinnt auch das alte Thema von den vier Reichen, die der Erlösung vorangehen, großen Raum. Zur frühen Ausprägung des Themas und der Verankerung in Dan 2 und 7 siehe M. HENGEL, Judentum und Hellenismus, Tübingen ²1973, 330—336. Das vierte Reich ist jetzt natürlich immer Rom. Typisch für den Fatalismus, der sich nun mit dem Messiasgedanken verbindet, ist die Anwendung des Vier-Reiche-Schemas in der Auslegung von Gen 28, 12 (Jakobsleiter). Nach Schmuel bar Nachman (Ende 3. Jahrh.) sind die auf- und niedersteigenden Engel die Fürsten der Völker der Welt: der von Babel stieg 70 Stufen auf, bevor er fiel, der von Medien 52 und der von Griechenland 180. Edom hingegen steigt und steigt, und man weiß nicht, wie weit, so daß Jakob Gott fragt, ob es für Edom überhaupt einen Abstieg gibt. Gott antwortet mit Obd 1, 4: „Erhebst du dich auch wie der Adler und baust dein Nest zwischen den Sternen, ich stürze dich hinab von dort": LevRabba 29,2 (ed. MARGULIES 670). Für Parallelen siehe G. STEMBERGER, Die Patriarchenbilder der Katakombe in der Via Latina im Lichte der jüdischen Tradition, Kairos 16 (1974) 19—78, p. 38. Im Prinzip hält man zwar an der messianischen Hoffnung fest, rückt sie jedoch in weite Ferne, so daß mehrere Rabbinen in Sanhedrin 98b vom Messias sagen können: „Laß ihn kommen, doch ich will ihn nicht sehen."

„Wenn dich jemand fragt: 'wo ist dein Gott?' (cf. Dtn 32,37), sag ihm: in der großen Stadt Rom[179]."

Er begründet diese Ansicht mit Jes 21,11: „Ausspruch über Edom. Aus Seir ruft man mir zu: Wächter, wie lang noch dauert die Nacht?" (Seir gilt als Synonym für Edom = Rom) und stützt sich auf die Meinung des R. Schim'on bar Jochai, daß die Schekhina (die Wesensgegenwart Gottes) mit Israel in jedes Exil gegangen ist. ExRabba 15,16 (ed. MIRKIN V 181) bringt dieselbe These und wendet daher Jes 63,1 auf Gott an: „Wer ist es, der von Edom kommt?"

So wird dann die Messiashoffnung selbst ebenfalls mit Rom verbunden In Sanhedrin 97b erzählt R. Chanan b. Tachalifa dem R. Joseph von einem Mann, der eine hebräische Schriftrolle über das Kommen des Messias besaß; befragt, woher sie stamme, antwortete er, er habe sich an römische Soldaten verdingt und sie in einem Archiv Roms gefunden. Und nach der bekannten Stelle Sanhedrin 98a erfährt R. Jehoschua b. Levi (1. Hälfte 3. Jahrh.) von Elia, der Messias sitze an den Toren Roms unter den kranken Bettlern, erkennbar daran, daß er den Verband seiner Wunden immer einzeln wechsle, um sofort aufbrechen zu können, wenn er gerufen wird.

Demnach lebt der Messias jetzt schon verborgen in Rom. Diese verborgene Gegenwart im Zentrum des Weltreiches drückt deutlich die Umformung der Erlösungshoffnung aus: die Erlösung ist dort, wo man sie nicht erwartet, sie ist auch völlig anders als erwartet. Das bedeutet gewissermaßen auch den Verzicht auf jegliche innerweltliche Erlösung. Der Kampf gegen Rom wird sinnlos, wenn aus Rom selbst einst der erwartete Erlöser kommen soll[180].

Bibliographie der rabbinischen Quellen

Aboth de Rabbi Nathan, Edited from Manuscripts with an Introduction, Notes and Appendices by S. SCHECHTER, New York ²1967.

Canticum Zuta: Midrasch suta . . ., ed. S. BUBER, Berlin 1894, Nachdruck Tel Aviv o. J.

179 אם יומר לך אדם איכן הוא אלהיך אמור לו בכרך הגדול שברומי. Daß der Messias aus Rom kommt, vertreten auch die Targumim zu Ex 12, 42. Die Angabe fehlt nur in Targum Neofiti, was nach R. LE DÉAUT, La nuit pascale. Essai sur la signification de la Pâque juive à partir du Targum d'Exode XII 42, Analecta Biblica XXII, Rom 1963, 271f., auf ein Versehen des Abschreibers zurückzuführen ist. Siehe auch seine Darstellung der Tradition des Messias aus Rom pp. 359—369. Eine wesentliche Rolle hat in der Entwicklung dieser Vorstellung die Parallelisierung des Messias zu Mose gespielt. Nach ExRabba 1, 26 (ed. MIRKIN V 41) kommt der Messias aus dem Zentrum des Feindes Rom, wie Mose im Palast des unterdrückerischen Pharao großgeworden ist.

180 N. GLATZER, The Attitude toward Rome in Third-Century Judaism, in: Politische Ordnung und menschliche Existenz. Festgabe für E. VÖGELIN, München 1962, 243—257, schreibt p. 257 richtig, daß die Quellen des 3. Jahrhunderts "*show an Israel that has overcome the ancient claim to supersede the fourth kingdom by historical means. She has accepted the fact of Rome's rule of this world and has withdrawn into a realm to which the old Messianic categories no longer apply.*" So habe Israel "*a theology of extra-historical existence*" entwickelt, die dann für das Mittelalter typisch wurde.

Genesis Rabba: Midrash Bereshit Rabba. Critical Edition with Notes and Commentary, ed. J. THEODOR—CH. ALBECK, 3 Bände, Jerusalem ²1965.
Jalqut Schim'oni, 2 Bände, Jerusalem 1967.
Levitikus Rabba: Midrash Wayyikra Rabbah. A Critical Edition Based on Manuscripts and Genizah Fragments with Variants and Notes by M. MARGULIES, 4 Bände, Jerusalem 1953—1958.
Mechilta d'Rabbi Ismael cum variis lectionibus et adnotationibus ed. H. S. HOROVITZ—I. A. RABIN, Jerusalem ²1960.
Midrasch Echa Rabbati. Sammlung agadischer Auslegungen der Klagelieder, ed. S. BUBER, Wilna 1899, Nachdruck Hildesheim 1967.
Midrasch Rabba, 2 Bände, Jerusalem o. J. (für die Zitate von Kohelet Rabba und Ester Rabba).
Midrasch Rabba, ed. M. A. MIRKIN, 11 Bände, Tel Aviv 1956—1967.
Midrasch Psalmen: Midrasch Tehillim, ed. S. BUBER, Wilna 1892, Nachdruck Jerusalem 1966.
Midrasch Tannaim zum Deuteronomium, ed. D. HOFFMANN, Berlin 1908—1909.
Mischna: Schischa Sidre Mischna (Die sechs Ordnungen der Mischna), ed. H. ALBECK—H. YALON, 6 Bände, Jerusalem 1952—1958.
Pesikta Rabbati. Midrasch für den Fest-Cyclus und die ausgezeichneten Sabbathe, ed. M. FRIEDMANN, Wien 1880, Nachdruck Wien 1963.
Pesikta de Rav Kahana. According to an Oxford Manuscript ... by B. MANDELBAUM, 2 Bände, New York 1962.
Pirqe de Rabbi Elieser, ed. D. LURIA, Warschau 1852, Nachdruck Jerusalem 1963.
Seder Olam Rabba. Die große Weltchronik, ed. B. RATNER, Wilna 1897.
Sifra, ed. J. H. WEISS, Wien 1862.
Siphre ad Deuteronomium, ed. H. S. HOROVITZ—L. FINKELSTEIN, Berlin 1939, Nachdruck New York 1969.
Siphre d'be Rab. Fasciculus primus: Siphre ad Numeros adjecto Siphre zutta, ed. H. S. HOROVITZ, Leipzig 1917, Nachdruck Jerusalem 1966.
Talmud Babli, 12 Bände, Wilna 1895—1908.
Talmud Jeruschalmi, Nachdruck der Ausgabe Krotoschin, New York 1948.
Tanchuma: Midrasch Tanchuma, Jerusalem o. J.
Midrasch Tanchuma, ed. S. BUBER, Wilna 1885, Nachdruck Jerusalem 1969.
Targum zu Klagelieder: The Bible in Aramaic, ed. A. SPERBER, Band IV A, Leiden 1968.
Tosephta, ed. M. S. ZUCKERMANDEL, Pasewalk 1880, Nachdruck Jerusalem 1963.
The Tosefta accord. to Codex Vienna ... ed. S. LIEBERMAN: The Order of Moed, New York 1962.

Le paganisme à travers les sources rabbiniques des IIe et IIIe siècles. Contribution à l'étude du syncrétisme dans l'empire romain

par MIREILLE HADAS-LEBEL, Paris

Table des matières

Introduction

Un traité entier du Talmud est consacré au «culte étranger» ('Aboda Zara'), c'est-à-dire à l'idolâtrie. Il ne vise guère comme on pourrait le supposer, l'Israélite suspect de s'adonner au culte des idoles. Le cas de ce dernier relève du droit pénal, aussi est-il explicitement évoqué dans le traité juridique 'Sanhedrin'. Cependant, en raison de la puissance d'un environnement païen qui se fait sentir de manière plus obsédante après les deux guerres juives, les rabbins craignent une contagion plus ou moins consciente pour leurs ouailles. Par leurs mises en garde et leurs interdits, ils veulent donc exercer une médecine préventive. A pareille époque, le christianisme naissant se trouve d'ailleurs dans une situation analogue et réagit de manière comparable. Tertullien, ce contempteur des Juifs, suit à son insu dans le 'De Idolatria' la méthode des rabbins de Palestine: «Il n'est pas de ces moralistes qui supposent que l'esprit seul suffit à tout vivifier. Il aime à tout prévoir pour tout réglementer parce qu'il connaît la faiblesse, la perversité de l'homme et qu'il craint que celui-ci ne s'échappe par le côté où l'on aurait omis de tracer la route à suivre et d'élever des garde-fous»[1]. On ne saurait mieux décrire l'esprit de notre traité.

C'est la valeur documentaire de ce traité et d'autres sources talmudiques qui retiendra ici notre attention. Il est en effet inévitable qu'à travers les listes d'interdits transparaissent les croyances, rites et coutumes, que l'on se proposait d'occulter. Aussi notre traité a-t-il fourni matière dès le début de ce siècle à divers articles ou opuscules se proposant d'élucider soit le caractère romain[2], soit le caractère syrien[3] des cultes décrits. L'édition critique d'ELMSLIE[4] devait bientôt réunir les conclusions de ses prédécesseurs. En 1950, S. LIEBERMAN venait ajouter une contribution de deux chapitres à ce dossier tout en souhaitant[5] voir paraître un ouvrage rassemblant les divers renseignements épars dans la littérature talmudique. Un exemple de la méthode à suivre était plus récemment donné dans un article d'E. URBACH[6] confrontant les passages rabbiniques avec les documents gréco-romains et surtout les découvertes archéologiques. Ainsi parfois les allusions

Abréviations:

CIA — Corpus Inscriptionum Atticarum
C.I.J. — Corpus Inscriptionum Judaicarum
C.I.L. — Corpus Inscriptionum Latinarum
C.N.P. — Corpus Nummorum Palaestinensium
EPHE — Ecole Pratique des Hautes Etudes
H.N. — Histoire Naturelle de Pline l'Ancien
HUCA — Hebrew Union College Annual
IEJ — Israel Exploration Journal
JQR — Jewish Quarterly Review
M. — Mishna
MUSJ — Mélanges de l'Université St. Joseph
QDAP — The Quarterly of the Department of Antiquities in Palestine
REA — Revue des Etudes anciennes
REJ — Revue des Etudes Juives
TB — Talmud de Babylone
TJ — Talmud de Jérusalem
TK — Tosefta Kifšutah, éd. critique de S. LIEBERMAN
Tos. — Tosefta

[1] P. DE LABRIOLLE, Histoire de la littérature latine chrétienne, t. I, Paris 1947[3], p. 126.
[2] H. BLAUFUSS, Römische Feste und Feiertage nach den Traktaten über fremden Dienst, Nürnberg 1909 et ID., Götter, Bilder und Symbole . . ., Nürnberg 1910.
[3] ISIDORE LÉVY, Cultes et rites syriens dans le Talmud, REJ XLIII (1901), pp. 183—205.
[4] The Mishna on Idolatry, Aboda Zara: Texts and Studies, vol. VIII, n° 2, Contributions to Biblical and Patristic Literature, Cambridge Univ. Press 1911, 136 p.
[5] Hellenism in Jewish Palestine, p. 128.
[6] The Rabbinical Laws on Idolatry in the 2nd and 3rd Centuries in the Light of Archaeological and Historical Facts, IEJ IX, n° 3 (1959), p. 149s.

d'un texte qui ne cherche guère à être explicite sur un sujet qu'il anathématise pourront-elles être élucidées.

Au premier rang des documents utilisés s'inscrit la Mishna[7] du traité 'Aboda Zara' accompagnée de la 'Tosefta' correspondante qui tantôt la répète, tantôt la suppose, tantôt la complète. La tradition de cette dernière est d'ailleurs souvent reprise dans la 'Gemara' du Talmud de Jérusalem ou du Talmud de Babylone. La 'Tosefta' d'un autre traité — 'Shabbat' — nous a conservé en ses chapitres VI et VII une énumération de «coutumes amorites» qui mérite également notre attention.

Tels sont les seuls textes suivis que nous possédions sur notre sujet. Le reste se rencontre au hasard de discussions rabbiniques qui en sont parfois fort éloignées.

L'âge de nos sources peut être établi à partir des noms des docteurs cités. Notre Mishna est essentiellement l'œuvre des rabbins du IIème siècle appartenant pour la plupart aux académies galiléennes qui fleurirent après les persécutions d'Hadrien. La 'Tosefta' recouvre cette période mais nous entraîne déjà, pour certaines traditions, dans la première moitié du IIIème siècle.

Malgré les difficultés matérielles que pose l'état du texte, nous espérons pouvoir souligner la valeur documentaire des sources talmudiques à partir desquelles on devrait petit à petit redonner à la Palestine romaine après Flavius Josèphe sa place sur la carte politique, économique, sociale et culturelle du bassin méditerranéen.

I. Divinités et symboles

Les docteurs de la Loi n'avaient qu'une vue toute extérieure du paganisme, à l'inverse de certains polémistes chrétiens, souvent convertis de fraîche date et qui tous étaient imprégnés de la culture gréco-romaine ambiante. Il est donc naturel qu'ils ne nous aient transmis que des données très fragmentaires sur les cultes que les entouraient.

Non seulement leur information était partielle, mais encore, ils répugnaient à mentionner ne fût-ce que le nom d'une idole inclus dans la nouvelle toponymie du pays, et préconisaient volontiers le recours à certains cacophémismes[8], ou conseillaient à tout le moins de s'abstenir de mentionner les idoles, sans prendre la peine de les rabaisser.

Tos. A.Z. VI, 11:

לא יאמר אדם לחבירו המתן לי בצד עבודה זרה פלונית ואני אמתין לך בצד עבודה זרה פלונית שנ׳ ושם אלהים אחרים לא תזכירו.

[7] Pour toute la terminologie talmudique voir HERMANN STRACK, Einleitung in Talmud und Midrasch, München 1921[5], trad. anglaise 1945.

[8] Tos. A.Z. VI, 4; TJ ibid. III, 6; TJ Shab. IX, 1.

«Que nul ne dise à son prochain 'Attends-moi auprès de telle idole' ou 'Je t'attendrai auprès de telle idole', car il est dit: 'vous ne prononcerez pas le nom d'autres dieux'».

Prononcer le nom d'une idole dans de telles conditions, serait en effet avoir l'air de faire du temple païen le propre lieu de résidence du locuteur[9].

Il est intéressant de constater qu'un cas de conscience analogue se pose aux premiers chrétiens. *Deos nationum nominari lex prohibet*, constate Tertullien (Idol. 20), mais dans l'Afrique romanisée, il est amené à admettre, par impuissance plutôt que par indifférence, qu'il n'y a pas de mal à dire «j'habite dans la rue Isis» ou à appeler un homme 'Saturne', si tel est son nom (ibid.). Du moins enjoint-il d'éviter les semi-jurons[10] comme *Mehercule, Medius Fidius* (ibid.), de ne pas se laisser bénir, par un mendiant par exemple, au nom d'une idole (ibid. 22) et de ne pas signer un contrat comprenant le nom d'une idole (ibid. 23).

Un tel état d'esprit, répandu chez les docteurs de la Loi, si ce n'est dans la population juive tout entière, constitue, on s'en doute, un obstacle à notre enquête sur le paganisme local. Fidèles à leurs principes, les rabbins n'auraient dû appeler par son nom aucune divinité païenne. Or des noms de divinités païennes, en nombre réduit certes, se rencontrent dans nos textes. Pourquoi ceux-là plutôt que d'autres ont-ils échappé à l'anathème? Leur mention nous permet-elle de conclure que leur culte était plus répandu? Il paraît bien hasardeux d'en décider sur une telle base.

A côté des cultes expressément désignés, les sources rabbiniques en évoquent bon nombre d'autres qu'il nous incombe d'identifier à travers les symboles décrits.

1. Les divinités païennes nommées

De toutes les idoles honorées dans l'environnement païen de ses rédacteurs, la 'Mishna' ne cite que deux noms: Aphrodite (III, 4) et Mercolis (IV, 1). A cela s'ajoute le culte de l'*ashera* (III, 5) et des hauts-lieux (ibid.). La 'Tosefta', elle, nous fournit un nom supplémentaire en interdisant «la figure de la femme qui allaite et de Serapis» (V, 1).

a) Les divinités gréco-romaines

α) Aphrodite

La présence dans la ville d'Acre-Ptolemaïs de thermes d'Aphrodite où le patriarche Gamaliel II vint un jour se baigner, donne lieu à une savoureuse anecdote dans notre Mishna (III, 4):

[9] Cp. Mekhilta sur Ex. 23, 13, p. 332 éd. Horowitz.

[10] En Sanh. 63b, l'interdiction de donner rendez-vous auprès d'une idole est jointe à celle de jurer ou faire jurer par le nom d'une divinité païenne.

שאל פרוקלוס בן פלוספוס את רבן גמליאל בעכו, שהיה רוחץ במרחץ שלאפרודיטי; אמר לו: כתוב בתורתכם ׳ולא־ידבק בידך מאומה מן־החרם׳, מפני מה אתה רוחץ במרחץ שלאפרודיטי? אמר לו: אין משיבין במרחץ. וכשיצא אמר לו: אני לא באתי בגבולה, היא באת בגבולי. אין אומרים: נעשה מרחץ לאפרודיטי נוי, אלא אומרים: נעשית אפרודיטי נוי למרחץ. דבר אחר, אם נותנין לך ממון הרבה אי אתה נכנס לעבודה זרה שלך ערם ובעל קרי ומשתין בפניה; וזו עומדת על פי הביב וכל העם משתינין לפניה. לא נאמר אלא ׳אלהיהם׳, את שנוהג בו משום אלוה אסור ואת שאינו נוהג בו משום אלוה מתר.

«Proclus, fils de Philosophus (ou plutôt 'le philosophe') interrogea Rabban Gamaliel à Acco tandis qu'il se baignait aux thermes d'Aphrodite. Il lui dit: 'Dans votre Loi, il est écrit: 'que rien de l'anathème ne reste attaché à ta main' (Deut. 13. 18). Pourquoi donc te baignes-tu aux thermes d'Aphrodite?' Gamaliel répliqua: 'On ne répond pas (sur ces matières) dans des thermes'. Quand il sortit, il lui dit: 'Ce n'est pas moi qui suis venu dans son domaine. C'est elle qui est venue dans le mien. On ne dit pas 'faisons des thermes comme ornement à Aphrodite', mais 'faisons une Aphrodite comme ornement pour les thermes'. D'ailleurs, quand bien même, te donnerait-on beaucoup d'argent, tu n'irais pas adorer tes idoles tout nu ou après un incident nocturne, ni uriner devant elles. Or, celle-ci se tient juste devant l'orifice de l'écoulement des eaux et tout le monde vient uriner devant elle. Il n'est question que de 'leurs dieux' (Deut. 12. 3): celui qui est traité comme un dieu est interdit, mais celui qui n'est pas traité comme un dieu est permis».

Un tel texte, de toute évidence, ne nous renseigne guère sur le culte de la déesse puisqu'il vise à démontrer que la présence d'une statue dans les thermes n'a qu'une valeur ornementale. Toutefois, si les thermes d'Acre étaient sous le patronage d'Aphrodite, on peut en inférer que celle-ci jouissait d'un honneur particulier dans la cité. Ceci nous est confirmé par sa représentation sur les monnaies locales. Quelques monnaies du IIIe siècle reproduisant une Aphrodite debout sous une niche et encadrée à droite d'un caducée, à gauche d'un Eros chevauchant un dauphin, sont à rapprocher de notre texte[11].

Cette présence d'Aphrodite est d'autant plus notable qu'elle est rarement attestée dans l'Est du pays[12] du moins sous ce nom. Dans cette région, elle avait en effet à subir la concurrence de l'Astarté sémitique que l'on voit à la même époque représentée sur les monnaies de Césarée[13], et avec laquelle elle est naturellement identifiée[14]. Un peu plus au Nord, Sidon

[11] Cf. L. Kadman, Corpus Nummorum Palestinensium IV, Jérusalem 1961, p. 27 et nos 204, 205, 238, 253, 265.

[12] C'est l'observation que fait L. Kadman, ibid. p. 71, d'après l'étude des monnaies.

[13] Le nom primitif de la cité est sans doute «tour d'Astarté» plutôt que «tour de Straton», cf. L. Kadman, C.N.P. II, p. 52—53.

[14] M.-J. Lagrange, Etudes sur les religions sémites, Paris 1905, p. 456. Astarté, forme phénicienne de la déesse babylonienne Ishtar, n'est autre que l'Ashtoreth, divinité des

possédait un temple d'Astarté, et Byblos un temple d'Aphrodite, au témoignage de Lucien de Samosate, qui visita la région vers le milieu du IIème siècle[15]. L'Aphrodite byblienne, selon son récit, était étroitement associée à Adonis et semble avoir été honorée notamment au moyen de la prostitution sacrée, c'est dire que malgré son nom, elle restait une divinité essentiellement phénicienne. Il est d'ailleurs probable que dans toute la sphère d'influence phénicienne, Aphrodite ait subi l'influence de la «déesse syrienne» dont la renommée avait franchi les frontières[16]. Dans le syncrétisme de l'époque, beaucoup de divinités fusionnent en effet. Ainsi selon Plutarque (Crassus, 17) la déesse syrienne est appelée par les uns Aphrodite, par les autres Héra[17]. Selon Lucien (Dea, 1) c'est l'Héra syrienne, mais elle a des attributs de presque toutes les autres divinités féminines grecques (ibid. 32). La déesse, honorée dans le célèbre temple d'Hiérapolis (Baalbek) comme parèdre du dieu Adad identifié à Zeus[18], porte sur les monnaies de la cité le nom de עתה ou עתרעתה[19] autrement dit Atargatis. Or, il est question dans nos sources talmudiques d'un temple de תרעתא classé parmi les sept temples les plus célèbres du monde, qui ne peut être que celui d'Hiérapolis[20].

Ainsi c'est probablement une Aphrodite très sémitisée qui est raillée par R. Gamaliel dans les thermes d'Acre.

β) 'Mercolis'

Avec une persistance assez rare dans le Talmud où les fantaisies orthographiques sont de règle, revient le nom מרקוליס lu Mercolis ou Marcolis[21] qui correspond visiblement au nom latin du dieu Mercure. Les légères différences phonétiques entre la forme transmise par l'hébreu et le nom latin original de Mercurius ne posent aucun problème: les échanges entre les liquides *l* et *r* sont d'une grande fréquence dans la prononciation, à plus forte raison dans des bouches étrangères: en outre, la forme prise par le «jour de Mercure», notre mercredi, dans les autres langues romanes, *mercoledi* en italien, *miercoles* en espagnol, en confirmant la substitution de

Sidoniens, à laquelle Salomon s'était laissé aller sur ses vieux jours à construire un haut-lieu (I Rois 6. 5. 33), lequel fut plus tard profané par le roi Josias (II Rois 23. 13). Elle représente un aspect de la Déesse-mère.

[15] Cf. Lucien, De Dea Syria 4 et 6. Il signale également un vieux temple d'Aphrodite sur le mont Liban (§ 9).

[16] Néron lui voua pour un temps une adoration exclusive, cf. Suétone, Néron 56.

[17] Sur de telles identifications, voir P.-L. VAN BERG, Corpus cultus deae Syriae II, Etude critique des sources mythographiques.

[18] Les identifications Jupiter—Adad, Vénus—Atargatis sont confirmées par l'archéologie, cf. H. SEYRIG, La triade héliopolitaine et les temples de Baalbek, Syria X (1929).

[19] R. DUSSAUD, Notes de mythologie syrienne II—IX, p. 82—83.

[20] A.Z. 11b: תרעתא שבמפג. Mabog est le nom sémitique de Hiérapolis. Cf. Pline, H.N. V, 19, 81 *Bambycen, quae alio nomine Hierapolis vocatur, Syris vero Mabog — ibi prodigiosa Atargatis Graecis autem Derceto dicta, colitur.*

[21] M. A.Z. IV, 1—2: Tos. ibid. VI, 13—18; TJ. ibid. IV, 1, 43d; TB ibid. 42a, 50a, 51b, 64b, Sanh. 60b, 64a, Ber. 57b.

l à *r*, peut faire supposer que dans la langue populaire on prononçait Merculius[22]. La transcription hébraïque donne une assise supplémentaire à une telle supposition.

La fréquente mention de Mercolis dans la littérature talmudique, laisse supposer que ce culte était particulièrement bien connu des rabbins peut-être parce qu'il était plus facilement observable que d'autres; ainsi que le remarque S. Lieberman[23], Mercolis et עבודה זרה «idolâtrie» apparaissent même parfois comme interchangeables[24]. Plutôt que comme un dieu, Mercolis est traité comme un nom commun désignant un objet familier. Le mercolis est, de toute évidence, exposé en plein air au bord des routes ou dans les champs (TJ A.Z. IV, 1, 43d), visible à tous les passants. Il est susceptible de recevoir des offrandes (M. IV, 2; Tos. VI, 13), mais sa principale caractéristique est d'être entouré de pierres (M. IV, 1; Tos. VI, 14), probablement lancées par les passants qui lui rendent ainsi une forme de culte (Tos. VI, 15—18; Sanh. 60b, 64a).

Cette description est à rapprocher de quelques textes grecs d'époque romaine[25]. Homère ayant mentionné dans l'Odyssée (XVI, 47) un Ἕρμαιος λόφος suscite en effet chez les scholiastes diverses définitions de cette expression. Didyme (Scholies V) donne notamment la définition suivante qui est à mettre en parallèle avec le Mercolis de nos sources talmudiques: ὁ σωρὸς τῶν λίθων ἐν ταῖς ὁδοῖς Ἕρμαιον ὀνομάζεται. D'autres scholies (B, H et Q) nous expliquent que ces tas de pierres échelonnés le long des routes et correspondant aux milliaires romains, sont destinés à rappeler qu'Hermès purifia les routes et marqua d'une pierre chaque endroit purifié: Ἑρμῆς πρῶτος ἐκάθηρε τὰς ὁδοὺς καὶ εἴ που ἐκάθηρε, λίθον ἀπέθετο ἔξω τῆς ὁδοῦ, ὃ σημεῖον ἦν. Ἕρμαιος οὖν λόφος ἀντὶ τοῦ σημεῖον τῆς ὁδοῦ. τὰ γὰρ σημεῖα τῶν Ῥωμαίων μιλίων Ἑρμαίους λόφους καλοῦσιν. La coutume de lancer en passant une pierre à Mercolis décrite à plusieurs reprises dans les sources talmudiques[26], vise selon les scholiastes, à honorer Hermès guide et protecteur des voyageurs: ὅθεν γὰρ τοὺς ἀνθρώπους ἄχρι τοῦ νῦν εἰς τιμὴν Ἑρμοῦ κατὰ τὰς ὁδούς, διὰ τὸ τὸν θεὸν εἶναι τοῦτον καθηγεμόνα καὶ ἐπίτροπον τῶν [ἐκ]δημούντων, σωροὺς ποιεῖν λίθων καὶ διάγοντας προσβάλλειν λίθους καὶ τούτους καλεῖν ἑρμαίους λόφους,. C'est ainsi que se constituent le long des routes ces λίθων συγχώσματα dont les 'Oracles Sibyllins'[27] attestent également l'existence à l'époque romaine. De tels amas de pierres ou les colonnes hermaïques représentant le dieu sans bras ni jambes, servaient également de bornes et délimitaient les propriétés[28].

[22] Cf. H. Lewy, Philologische Streifzüge in den Talmud, Philologus LII (1893), p. 735.
[23] Texts and Studies, New-York 1974, p. 167, art. 'Palestine in the Third and Fourth Centuries', repris de JQR XXXVI (1946), pp. 329—370.
[24] Cp. Ber. 57b et Tos. ibid. VII, 14, 20.
[25] Cf. Lewy, loc. cit., et Elmslie, op. cit., p. 74.
[26] Tos. A.Z. VI, 15—18; Sanh. 60b, 64a.
[27] „Frag." 3, v. 30, p. 231 éd. Geffcken, Leipzig 1902.
[28] Cf. Pausanias II, 38, 7; VIII, 34, 6 et 35, 1.

La tradition qui fait de l'Hermès grec l'inventeur des routes et le patron des voyageurs concerne aussi le Mercure latin[29]. Dans l'Orient hellénisé, les dieux gardèrent généralement leur nom grec, même au temps de la domination romaine: c'est ainsi que notre Mishna (III, 4) mentionne Aphrodite et non Vénus. Comment expliquer dans ces conditions que Mercure ait été honoré en Palestine sous son nom latin?

Or, les faits sont là, et l'archéologie vient confirmer les données talmudiques. Au Liban, dans la région de Baalbek, on connait quelques inscriptions sur bornes, portant les lettres grecques MEP interprétées comme la dédicace MEPKOUPIOU «à Mercure»[30], à côté d'autres faisant apparaître le nom grec ʿEPMOῦ[31]. Une inscription trouvée à Hamm près de Baalbek et datant de + 173 comporte le nom entier en caractères grecs: Μερκουρίῳ Δωμίνῳ κώμης Χάμωνος[32]. Ce Mercure n'est autre que la troisième divinité de la triade héliopolitaine honorée dans les temples de Baalbek. Parfois représenté sous forme de dieu-terme[33], il reste essentiellement une divinité agraire confondue avec Dionysos[34] et un dieu protecteur des troupeaux qui doit beaucoup[35] à l'Adonis phénico-syrien. A travers ces traits syncrétistes, il a pu garder sa vocation de dieu des voyageurs bien qu'il ne soit plus guère représenté avec ses attributs traditionnels: sandales ailées et caducée[36]. C'est sans doute aux légionnaires romains, grands utilisateurs des routes de l'empire qu'il doit d'avoir conservé le nom latin, retranscrit phonétiquement dans le Talmud sous la forme Mercolis.

b) Femme allaitant et Sérapis

Tos. V, 1:

מצא טבעת ועליה צורת חמה צורת לבנה צורת דרקון יוליך לים המלח ואף דמות מניקה וסרפס.

«Si l'on trouve une bague avec l'image de la lune, du soleil ou d'un dragon, qu'on la porte à la Mer Morte; de même pour la figure de la femme qui allaite et de Sérapis.»

[29] Cf. CIL VII, 771 (*vias et semitas commentus est*), III, 5196, V, 4025 (*reducens*), 4249, VI, 3703, VII, 271.

[30] R. MOUTERDE, Le Mercure de la région d'Héliopolis-Baalbek, MUSJ XXIX (1951—52), p. 61.

[31] D. SCHLUMBERGER, Le temple de Mercure à Baalbek-Héliopolis, Bull. Musée Beyrouth III (1939), p. 33 et R. DUSSAUD, Temples et Cultes de la Triade héliopolitaine à Baalbek, Syria XXIII (1942—43), p. 73.

[32] Cf. ibid., p. 74, n. 2 et ID., Notes de mythologie syrienne, p. 26; CLERMONT-GANNEAU, Recueil I, 25; inscription rapprochée de Baal Hammon par I. LEVY, art. cité, REJ XLIII (1901), p. 188.

[33] Voir l'Hermès de Yammouné conservé au Louvre. Cf. P. S. RONZEVALLE, Notes et études d'archéologie orientale, MUSJ XXI (1937—38), pl. XII.

[34] Cf. H. SEYRIG, art. cité Syria X (1929), p. 348s. Ce Mercure est l'objet d'un culte à mystères.

[35] Cf. RONZEVALLE, ibid. p. 39 et 49.

[36] Tout au plus, trouve-t-on sur les monnaies d'Acre un caducée sans doute indépendant de lui, mais Hermès lui-même n'apparaît pas plus sur les monnaies d'Acre que sur celles de Césarée, cf. L. KADMAN, C.N.P. II, p. 58 et IV, p. 81.

Ainsi, le nom de Sérapis ne doit d'avoir été conservé par nos sources qu'au seul fait que le dieu égyptien était alors fréquemment représenté sur le chaton des bagues. La présence de son nom permet d'identifier avec certitude «la femme qui allaite». Il s'agit bien entendu du groupe formé par les deux autres divinités égyptiennes les plus connues hors de l'Egypte: Isis et son fils Horus — en grec Harpocrate —. «Dans l'art, la figure d'Isis allaitant le petit Horus ressemble tellement à la Madone et à l'enfant qu'elle a quelque fois reçu les adorations des Chrétiens ignorants»[37]. Cette représentation qui est en effet courante[38] se rencontre notamment sur des gemmes[39], à côté de diverses représentations de Sérapis seul ou avec Isis, d'Isis seule, ou de la triade égyptienne reconstituée — il est à noter toutefois que dans ce groupe le jeune Harpocrate n'apparaît jamais comme un nourrisson[40].

Toute bague portant de telles effigies doit donc être «jetée à la Mer Morte», formule rabbinique bien connue par laquelle un objet est voué à une irrémédiable destruction.

Cette condamnation s'explique aisément par le caractère idolâtre du motif considéré, mais ce n'est sans doute pas un hasard si elle vise plus particulièrement les divinités égyptiennes. Notre 'Tosefta' nous donne en effet une confirmation éclatante de l'existence en Palestine d'un usage répandu à Rome: *iam vero et Harpocratem statuasque Aegyptiorum numinum in digitis viri quoque portare incipiunt* nous rapporte Pline[41]. La mode de ces bagues venues vraisemblablement d'Egypte, avait pu pénétrer dans le reste du bassin oriental de la Méditerranée bien avant d'envahir Rome même.

Une telle mode répond à l'expansion des cultes égyptiens. Ceux-ci, longtemps pris à Rome entre les proscriptions sénatoriales et l'engouement de la multitude, avaient fini par s'imposer sous Néron[42]. Le cortège triomphal de Titus et Vespasien après leur victoire en Judée était parti du temple romain d'Isis[43]. Les Antonins, plus encore que la dynastie précédente manifestent leur dévotion à des divinités désormais tout à fait romanisées. Elles ont à Rome leurs images, leurs temples, leurs processions. Les dévots d'Isis se rencontrent également chez des écrivains et non des moindres: Plutarque ('Isis et Osiris') ou Apulée (Métamorphoses XI). On assiste au développement d'un véritable syncrétisme isiaque, Isis recouvrant la plupart des grandes divinités féminines de l'Orient et de la Grèce[44].

[37] J. G. Frazer, Atys et Osiris, trad. française, Paris 1926, p. 135.

[38] Cf. H. W. Müller, Isis mit dem Horuskind, Münchn. Jahrb. der bildend. Kunst 3. F. 14, 1963, p. 25—28; V. Tran Tam Tinh, Le Culte d'Isis à Pompéi, Paris 1964, p. 88, note 1.

[39] Cf. G. Lafaye, Histoire du Culte des divinités d'Alexandrie hors de l'Egypte, Paris 1884, Catalogue nos 79 et 80.

[40] Cf. ibid., Catalogue, Section VI.

[41] H.N. XXXIII, 12, 41.

[42] Cf. G. Lafaye, op. cit., p. 59.

[43] Josèphe, B.J. VII, V, 4.

[44] Cf. B. P. Grenfell et A. S. Hunt, Oxyrhynchus Papyri X, 1380 (IIe siècle) où Isis est identifiée à la principale divinité féminine de chaque grande cité, et F. Dunand, Le syncrétisme isiaque, dans: Les syncrétismes dans les religions grecque et romaine (colloque

Quant à Sérapis, il bénéficie d'une faveur toute spéciale sous Hadrien; son culte est même bientôt lié à celui de l'empereur. Comme Isis, il répond aux aspirations hénothéistes de l'époque[45], amalgamant en lui un certain nombre de dieux anciens égyptiens ou grecs[46] devenus de simples émanations de cette divinité suprême. Nombreuses sont les inscriptions portant la formule Εἷς Ζεὺς Σέραπις: «Sérapis seul est Zeus»[47], nombreux les récits des prodiges et guérisons miraculeuses accomplis par lui[48].

Sur le bord oriental de la Méditerranée plus proche de l'Egypte et si accueillant aux divinités nouvelles, les dieux égyptiens durent s'introduire encore plus aisément qu'à Rome. Leur présence est attestée sur la côte syrienne, dès l'époque séleucide[49]. En Palestine proprement dite, l'honneur dans lequel ils sont tenus tous deux — mais surtout Sérapis — est largement confirmé par la numismatique et l'épigraphie, des IIème et IIIème siècles. Isis apparaît notamment sur les monnaies d'Acre-Ptolémaïs, parfois en compagnie du jeune Harpocrate[50]. Quant à Sérapis, il commence à être représenté sur les monnaies à l'époque d'Hadrien et son effigie est reproduite sur les monnaies de la plupart des grandes cités du pays[51]: Césarée, Ptolémaïs, Tibériade, Diospolis, Eleutheropolis, Neapolis de Samarie, ainsi qu'à Aelia Capitolina construite à l'emplacement de Jérusalem. Dans cette même cité, on a retrouvé une inscription provenant d'un monument dédié en 116 par un détachement de la IIIème légion cyrénaïque «à Jupiter, très bon très grand Sérapis»[52]. Un autel dédié sous le règne de Caracalla ou d'Elagabal par un primipile de la *legio VI Ferrata* «au grand dieu Sérapis» a également été découvert à Legio, siège de cette légion[53]. Cela nous confirme, ce que l'on savait par ailleurs, la très grande vogue de Sérapis dans l'armée romaine[54].

Notre texte est un témoignage de plus sur le succès des divinités égyptiennes. Il nous prouve en outre que les Juifs du IIème siècle étaient

de Strasbourg 9—11 juin 1971), Paris 1973, p. 79, hymne d'Isidoros:

«Tous les mortels qui vivent sur la terre infinie,
Thraces et Grecs, et Barbares aussi,
Prononcent ton beau nom que tous honorent,
Chacun dans sa langue, chacun dans son pays.
Les Syriens te nomment Astarté, Artémis, Nanaïa . . .»

45 Cf. LAFAYE, op. cit., p. 88.

46 Cf. Plutarque, Isis et Osiris, § 28, Tacite, Hist. IV, 83.

47 Cf. L. VIDMAN, Sylloge inscriptionum religionis Isiacae et Sarapiacae, Religionsgeschichtliche Versuche u. Vorarbeiten, Berlin 1969, n° 363 et G. LAFAYE, op. cit., p. 88, 252 et Cat. nos 138, 139, 143, 213, 214.

48 Cf. Aristide, Disc. Sacr. 55, Tacite, Hist. IV, 81, Suétone, Vesp. 7, Dion LXV, 8.

49 Cf. P. ROUSSEL, Décret des Péliganes de Laodicée-sur-Mer, Syria XXIII (1942—43), p. 27.

50 Cf. KADMAN, C.N.P. IV, p. 73.

51 Ibid. p. 69.

52 Cf. VIDMAN, op. cit. n° 362 = C.I.L. III 13587e: *[I]ovi o(ptimo) m(aximo) Sarapidi | pro salute et victoria imp(eratoris) Nervae Traiani Caesaris | optumi Aug(usti) Germanici Dacici || Parthici et populi Romani | vexill(atio) leg(ionis) III Cyr(enaicae) fecit.*

53 Cf. VIDMAN, n° 361 et AVI-YONAH, QDAP suppl. XII (1946), pp. 89—91: *Pro salute et incolumitate | domini nostri | [[---]] praesentissimum deum mag(num) Sarapidem || leg(io) VI Ferrat(a) f(idelis) c(onstans) [[Antoniniana]] | Iulius Isidorianus pr(imi)p(ilus).*

54 Cf. G. LAFAYE, op. cit., p. 162.

tout à fait capables de reconnaître leurs effigies, tantôt grâce au groupe formé par Isis et son fils, tantôt grâce aux caractéristiques de Sérapis (barbe, calathos) qui ne nous sont même pas décrites ici, comme si l'identification du dieu allait de soi. Si ces divinités leur étaient si familières, c'est qu'ils n'avaient point besoin d'entrer dans les temples pour les observer; il leur suffisait pour cela de regarder les innombrables pierres taillées les représentant[55].

c) Cultes sémitiques

α) Montagnes et collines

M. III, 5:

הגוים העובדים את ההרים ואת הגבעות — הן מתרין, ומה שעליהם אסורים, שנאמר: ׳לא־תחמד כסף וזהב עליהם ולקחת׳. רבי יוסי הגלילי אומר: אלהיהם ׳על־ההרים׳, ולא ההרים אלהיהם; אלהיהם ׳על־הגבעות׳, ולא הגבעות אלהיהם ומפני מה אשרה אסורה? מפני שיש בה תפיסת ידי אדם, כל שיש בה תפיסת ידי אדם אסור. אמר רבי עקיבא: אני אובין ואדון לפניך: כל מקום שאתה מוצא הר גבוה, וגבעה נשאה, ועץ רענן — דע שיש שם עבודה זרה.

«Dans le cas de montagnes et de collines vénérées par des idolâtres, celles-ci sont permises mais ce qui est sur elles est interdit car il est dit: (Deut. 7. 25) 'Tu ne convoiteras ni l'argent ni l'or qui est sur elles et tu ne le prendras pas pour toi.'
Rabbi José le Galiléen dit: ce sont 'leurs dieux qui sont sur les montagnes' (Deut. 12. 2) mais les montagnes ne sont pas leurs dieux, 'leurs dieux sur les collines' (ibid.) mais les collines ne sont pas leurs dieux.
Rabbi Aqiba dit: 'Je m'en vais te donner un éclaircissement: Sache que tout lieu où tu trouveras une haute montagne, une colline élevée ou un arbre vert (ibid.) est un lieu d'idolâtrie'».

Tos. VI, 8:

הגוים העובדין את ההרים ואת הגבעות אף על פי שהן מותרין עובדיהן בסקילה.

«Si des Gentils rendent un culte aux montagnes et aux collines, ces lieux restent permis mais ceux qui les adoreraient sont passibles de lapidation . . .»

Les montagnes sont à maintes reprises désignées dans la Bible[56] comme étant le siège des hauts-lieux, mais il n'y apparaît pas clairement qu'elles aient été elles-mêmes divinisées. Tel est le sens de la remarque de R. José dans la 'Mishna'. Faut-il, à la lumière de nos texte, considérer que la discussion rabbinique porte sur une question d'actualité ou bien ne doit-on lui attribuer qu'une valeur académique?

[55] Cf. J. Marquardt, Le Culte chez les Romains, p. 130: «Il n'est pas de dieux qui soient plus souvent représentés sur les pierres taillées que Sérapis et Harpocrate.»
[56] Deut. 12, 2; I Rois 14, 23; Jér. 2, 20; 3, 6 etc. . . .

En fait, il semble bien que les anciens lieux de culte cananéens n'aient pas été désertés malgré l'introduction de divinités étrangères. Tout au plus vit-on à l'époque hellénistique, les dieux honorés en ces lieux changer de nom[57]. Sur le Mont Casius des Ougaritains autrefois résidence du Baal du Ṣafon, se poursuivit un culte de Zeus Kasios. Le Mont Thabor devint le séjour de Zeus Atabyrios.

Quant au Carmel, si l'on en croit Tacite (Hist. II, 78) il aurait été lui-même honoré en tant que dieu-montagne[58]; aussi bien n'y voyait-on ni statue, ni temple: *Est Judaeam inter Syriamque Carmelus, ita vocant montem deumque, nec simulacrum deo aut templum.* Ce témoignage pourrait donc confirmer la première partie de notre 'Mishna', étayée également par notre 'Tosefta' et par la 'Mishna' de Hullin (II, 8) mettant en garde quiconque sacrifie aux montagnes ou aux collines (**השוחט לשם הרים או לשם גבעות**). Toutefois, l'inscription du pied dédié à Zeus héliopolitain–Carmel, et retrouvé en ce lieu, laisse planer la même incertitude que notre 'Mishna': Zeus héliopolitain était donc honoré sur ces hauteurs mais était-il pour autant identifié à la montagne[59]?

β) *Ashera*

M. III, 7:

שלש אשרות הן: אילן שנטעו מתחלה לשם עבודה זרה — הרי זה אסור; גדעו ופסלו לשם עבודה זרה, והחליף — נוטל מה שהחליף; העמיד תחתיו עבודה זרה, ובטלה — הרי זה מתר. איזו היא אשרה? כל שיש תחתיה עבודה זרה. רבי שמעון אומר: כל שעובדין אותה. ומעשה בצידן באילן שהיו עובדין אותו, ומצאו תחתיו גל. אמר להן רבי שמעון: בדקו את הגל הזה. ובדקוהו, ומצאו בו צורה. אמר להן: הואיל ולצורה הן עובדין, נתיר להן את האילן.

«Il y a trois sortes d'*asherot*: un arbre planté dès l'origine en l'honneur d'une idole — cet arbre est interdit —; un arbre taillé et émondé en l'honneur d'une idole, mais dont le feuillage s'est renouvelé — on peut prendre les parties nouvelles —; un arbre sous lequel une idole a été placée puis désacralisée — cet arbre est permis.
Qu'est-ce-qu'une *ashera*? Tout (arbre) sous lequel est placée une idole. R. Simeon dit: 'Tout arbre auquel un culte est rendu'. On raconte qu'à Sidon, il y avait un arbre auquel (croyait-on) un culte était rendu, or sous cet arbre, on trouva un monceau. R. Simeon dit: 'Examinez ce monceau'. On l'examina et l'on y trouva une statue. Il conclut: 'Puis-

[57] Cf. A. Caquot, La religion des Sémites occidentaux dans Histoire des religions, t. I, Encyclopédie de la Pléiade, Paris 1970, p. 327.

[58] Elagabal: «dieu-montagne», c'est le nom pris par cet empereur romain d'origine syrienne, et transformé plus tard en Héliogabale.

[59] Caquot, ibid. Même ambiguïté dans la religion des Libyens où «la montagne que sa hauteur rapproche du ciel, source du sacré et même parfois identifiée à lui, devient aisément objet et lieu de culte en même temps», M. Benabou, La résistance africaine à la romanisation, Paris 1976, p. 269.

que c'est la statue qui était honorée, nous autorisons désormais l'arbre'.»

Tos. VI. 8:

איזהו אשרה כל שהגוים עובדין ומשמשין אותה ואין טועמין מפירותיה ר׳ שמעון בן אלעזר אומר שלוש אשרות בארץ ישר׳ חרוב שבכפר קסם (var. פתם) ושבכפר פגשה שקמה שבראני (var. בארני) ושבכרמל.

«Qu'est-ce-qu'une *ashera*? Tout arbre auquel les Gentils rendent des honneurs et des soins sans goûter à ses fruits. R. Simeon ben Eleazar dit: 'Il y a trois *asherot* au pays d'Israël: le caroubier de Kfar Qasem (ou Petem) et de Kfar Pigsha, le sycomore de Rani (ou parmi les pins) au Carmel'.»

La confrontation de ces différents textes permet de nous faire une idée approximative de ce qui était appelé *ashera* à l'époque tannaïtique et qui ne correspond pas nécessairement à l'*ashera* biblique.

L'*ashera* dont le nom provient de la plus grande divinité féminine des Sémites du Nord-Ouest, ainsi que l'a établi le déchiffrement des textes ougaritiques[60], apparaît dans les textes bibliques tantôt comme un arbre vivant (par ex. Deut. 16. 21), tantôt comme un objet fait de main d'homme (ex. I Rois 14—15) qui pourrait être un pieu sacré ou une sorte d'ébauche grossière, de *xoanon*, censée représenter la déesse Ashera[61].

Dans les trois définitions données par notre 'Mishna', ainsi que dans le passage correspondant de la 'Tosefta', l'*ashera* désigne indubitablement un arbre vert. L'*ashera* biblique qui était généralement érigée sous un arbre vert[62] a, semble-t-il, fini par donner son nom à ce dernier. Ainsi, selon notre 'Mishna', l'arbre sous lequel se trouve dressée une idole, porte lui-même le nom d'*ashera*. L'usage de cet arbre, est, de l'avis de R. Simeon, permis, puisqu'il n'est pas lui-même objet d'un culte.

En revanche, les arbres qui sont honorés pour eux-mêmes, tombent sous le coup d'interdictions très strictes: le Juif ne devra en aucun cas tirer profit de son bois, de son feuillage (M. III, 9, Tos. VI, 1 et 8), ni même de son ombre (M. III, 8; Tos. VI, 8). Que l'*ashera* ait été spécialement plantée en vue d'un culte ou que ce soit un arbre soumis à un entretien spécial, il y a en elle **תפיסת ידי אדם** «œuvre de main d'homme» (M. III, 5), ce qui en fait un objet interdit, alors que le reste de la nature même s'il est vénéré par les païens, reste accessible aux Juifs. Il va de soi qu'il est également interdit à l'Israélite d'apporter à l'*ashera* un soin qui s'interprète comme une forme de culte:

[60] Cf. H. Ringgren, Religions of the Ancient Near-East, trad. angl., Londres 1973, p. 140.

[61] Cf. M.-J. Lagrange, Etude sur les religions sémites, Paris 1905, p. 175—176.

[62] Cf. I Rois 14, 23: **ויבנו גם המה להם במות ומצבות ואשרים על כל גביעה גבהה ותחת כל עץ רענן**, «ils se construisirent des hauts-lieux, des stèles, des *asherot* sur toute colline élevée et sous tout arbre vert».

Tos. VI, 9:

ישראל שפיסל את האשרה בין לצרכה בין לצרכו אסור וגוי שפיסל את האשרה לצרכה היא אסורה והוא מותר.

«Si un Israélite élague une *ashera* pour elle-même ou pour son besoin à lui, c'est interdit. Si un Gentil élague une *ashera* pour elle-même, elle est interdite mais lui, est permis».

Selon R. Aqiba, tout arbre vert est suspect d'abriter un culte idolâtre; mais la formule qu'il utilise est directement empruntée à Deut. 12. 2 dont elle constitue une glose:

כל מקום שאתה מוצא הר גבוה וגבעה נשאה ועץ רענן דע שיש שם עבודה זרה.

(M. III, 5)

«Sache que tout lieu où tu trouveras une haute montagne, une colline élevée ou un arbre vert, est un lieu d'idolâtrie».

Il est rappelé par là que tout arbre vert est susceptible d'abriter une idole.

Les trois *asherot* énumérées dans la Tosefta (VI,8) doivent correspondre en revanche à la définition qui les précède: «Tout arbre auquel les Gentils rendent des honneurs et des soins sans goûter à ses fruits». Les deux espèces d'arbres citées: caroubier et sycomore, sont précisément des arbres feuillus toujours verts. Ces deux espèces sont assez fréquemment citées dans le Talmud parfois même conjointement: il est ainsi recommandé de ne faire pousser ni caroubier ni sycomore à moins de 50 coudées d'une ville (B.B. II,7) ou d'une citerne (B.B. II,11), alors que des distances moindres sont admises pour les autres arbres. Cela sans doute, parce que ces arbres ont des racines profondes. Celles du sycomore sont si profondes qu'elles pénètrent «jusqu'aux eaux de l'abîme»[63]. Le sycomore très répandu en Basse Galilée[64] et dans la plaine côtière, attire en outre l'attention par sa haute taille: 8 à 20 m, et sa longévité est proverbiale[65]. Ces raisons ont pu donner au caroubier et au sycomore une place particulière dans le culte local.

Pour être tout à fait complets, il faudrait rappeler le rôle des arbres dans certains cultes alors bien acclimatés dans le pays. Selon la légende, Adonis serait né de Smyrna après qu'elle eut été transformée en arbre à myrrhe. Dans le culte d'Attis, le pin possède un caractère sacré car c'était sous un pin que le dieu s'était mutilé et avait expiré; Cybèle avait ensuite emporté l'arbre pour pleurer sur lui son amant mort. Dionysos est étroite-

[63] T J Taan. I, 3. Cela éclaire la parole bien connue des Evangiles, Luc, 17, 6: «Si vous aviez de la foi comme un grain de sénevé, vous diriez à ce sycomore: déracine-toi et plante-toi dans la mer et il vous obéirait».

[64] Shev. IX, 2: «Là où ne poussent pas les sycomores, c'est la Haute Galilée, (. . .) là où ils poussent, c'est la Basse Galilée».

[65] Cf. Gen. R. 12, 6, p. 105 éd. Albeck: השקמה הזו עושה בארץ שש מאות שנה «le sycomore qui vit 600 ans».

ment associé aux arbres qu'il fait pousser — pin et figuier — et il est même censé les habiter[66]. Le sycomore et surtout le palmier symbolisent en Egypte la source féminine du divin fluide de vie[67]. Il n'est pas exclu que certaines idoles aient été placées sous l'arbre consacré à la divinité qu'elles représentaient[68].

Etant donné les espèces citées à propos du culte de l'*ashera*, il nous paraît infiniment plus probable que les formes revêtues par ce culte à l'époque tannaïtique, dérivent de la vieille tradition cananéenne. Selon ROBERTSON-SMITH (op. cit., p. 186—187) le culte de l'arbre était en Syrie une superstition tenace que le christianisme même ne réussit pas totalement à éliminer; il témoigne avoir observé encore à son époque, des arbres sacrés auxquels étaient suspendues des offrandes. Dans les campagnes, les rites primitifs auraient donc continué à être pratiqués bien longtemps après la chute des grandes divinités du paganisme sémitique, tant il est vrai que la dévotion populaire évolue lentement.

γ) Eau

L'eau a également valeur d'élément sacré dans les religions sémites[69]. Nos textes ne se réfèrent pas explicitement à un culte de l'eau, tel qu'on en pratiquait par exemple à la source du Jourdain, mais le toponyme עין כל 'source de tout' récusé par les rabbins (Tos. A.Z. VI,4), suggère un tel culte. Selon certains[70], le terme de *yerid* habituellement traduit par 'marché' ou 'foire' a pour véritable sens celui de 'descente à un point d'eau' (ainsi s'explique sa parenté avec la racine ירד descendre). Il s'agirait donc en vérité d'une cérémonie caractérisée par une procession dont le but était une nappe d'eau. Un argument intéressant est fourni par la mention dans le Talmud de Babylone (A.Z. 11b) du *Yerid* d'En Baki, identifiable à Baalbek-Hiérapolis. Lucien (Dea, 47—48) atteste que les fidèles s'y baignaient dans un lac et qu'on y célébrait une cérémonie de l'eau. Le *yerid* ne serait rien d'autre étymologiquement que cette κατάβασις ou 'descente', à laquelle aurait pu être annexée une foire. I. LÉVY suppose ainsi, que le *yerid* de Tyr et celui de Botna étaient rattachés à des points d'eau. Ajoutons qu'à Gaza, qui était également le siège d'un *yerid*, se célébrait au bord de la mer la cérémonie religieuse du *maioumas*[71] qui par la suite devait se réduire à des banquets et à des jeux aquatiques et prendre une tournure licencieuse.

[66] Selon Plutarque, Quaestiones Conviviales V, III, 1: «Presque tous les Grecs sacrifient à Dionysos Dendrite».

[67] Cf. E. R. GOODENOUGH, Jewish Symbols VII, New York 1958, p. 95.

[68] Les arbres sacrés sont fréquemment représentés sur les monnaies mais il est généralement difficile de déterminer la divinité à laquelle ils étaient consacrés.

[69] M.-J. LAGRANGE, op. cit., p. 160.

[70] Cf. I. LEVY, Cultes et rites syriens dans le Talmud, REJ XLIII (1901), p. 192 et s., conjecture approuvée par LAGRANGE, p. 168 et SEYRIG, art. cité, Syria X (1929), p. 315 et 340.

[71] Cf. ROSCHER, s. v. Maiumas; ST. A. COOK: The Religion of Ancient Palestine in the light of Archeology, Londres 1930, p. 181.

Un écho de telles pratiques est sensible dans la législation de Hullin II,8: «Si un homme a égorgé un animal en sacrifice à des montagnes, collines, mers, rivières, ou déserts, le sacrifice n'est pas valable.»

δ) Gad

En conseillant de déformer le toponyme Gadaya, notre Tosefta (VI,4) suggère également qu'il renferme le nom d'une divinité. La Bible connaît en effet déjà une divinité cananéenne du nom de Gad, interprétée comme une divinité de la Fortune[72]. Le terme de Gad est d'ailleurs utilisé couramment dans la littérature talmudique avec valeur de nom commun; mais il apparaît clairement à travers certains textes qu'il désigne encore une divinité, une sorte de génie: par exemple, le génie d'une montagne auquel des sacrifices sont offerts (Hul. 40a) ou le génie du foyer en l'honneur duquel un lit[73] pouvait être dressé (Ned. 56a). Ce 'génie' était l'objet d'invocations populaires et prêtait son nom à des formules magiques comme celle que nous cite le Talmud (Shab. 67b) . . . האומר גד גדי, lequel poursuit en affirmant catégoriquement (ibid.): גד אינו אלא לשון עבודת כוכבים «Gad n'est rien d'autre qu'un nom d'idole». Comme tant d'autres noms de divinités païennes, celui de Gad entre dans des toponymes: Baal Gad situé à la source du Jourdain, ou Gadyawan qui semble se placer en Judée (Sanh. 63b).

2. L'interprétation des symboles

Mieux loti que l'archéologue, qui, placé devant telle ou telle figure, peut s'interroger sur sa valeur — symbolique ou purement décorative —, le lecteur du traité 'Aboda Zara' sait immédiatement, grâce à l'interdit rabbinique pesant sur eux, quels sont les symboles les plus fréquemment reproduits en Palestine à l'époque tannaïtique.

Toute décoration n'est point alors proscrite chez les Juifs. Au contraire, le judaïsme semble évoluer vers un certain libéralisme en matière de représentation figurée, libéralisme confirmé par la décoration synagogale des siècles suivants qui atteint sa plus grande audace dans les fresques syriennes de Doura-Europos. Ainsi, à partir du IIIème siècle, les amoraim palestiniens tolèrent officiellement les fresques (TJ A.Z. III,3). Dès le siècle précédent, on voit la maison des patriarches utiliser des sceaux gravés d'un visage humain (Tos. A.Z. V,2 et TJ III,1), alors qu'à l'époque du second Temple, toutes les gravures étaient permises sauf celle du visage humain (ibid. et TB 42b). Les motifs décoratifs utilisés par les artistes juifs sont très souvent semblables aux symboles que reproduisent leurs confrères

[72] Cf. Gen. 30, 11. Lea dit: «Par bonheur!» (בגד) et elle appela son fils Gad. Plus tard, Isaïe vilipende «ceux qui dressent une table pour Gad» (65. 11).

[73] Sur cette coutume, cf. Inscription d'Et-Tayyibé, août 134, dans LAGRANGE, op. cit. p. 508—509: «A Ba'alšamim, seigneur d'éternité, a offert une niche et un lit Agathangelos.»

païens[74]. L'extrême rigorisme excluant toute décoration soupçonnée d'être un symbole païen devient impraticable: il faudrait renoncer aux moindres objets utilitaires, à commencer par les pièces de monnaie. De fait, l'attitude pure et dure de tel sage qui n'avait de sa vie regardé une pièce de monnaie (TJ Meg. I,13; ibid. III,2; Sanh. X,5; TJ A.Z. III,1; TB ibid. 50a; Pes. 104a; Qoh. R. IV,10) est citée comme un rare exemple de sainteté; mais pour la plupart, les nécessités de la vie quotidienne imposent des concessions:

M. III,3:

רבן שמעון בן גמליאל אומר שעל המכבדין אסורין שעל המבזין מתרין.

«Rabban Simeon ben Gamaliel dit que s'il s'agit d'objets de prix, ils sont interdits mais que s'il s'agit d'objets ordinaires, ils sont permis.»

Tos. V,1 = TB 43b:

ועל המכובדין כגון השיריים והנזמים והקטלאות וטבעות הרי אילו אסורות ועל הבזויים כגון היורות מחמי חמין הטיגנין והקוקמסין והספלין והסדינין והמטבע הרי אילו מותרין.

«Les objets recherchés tels que chaînes, boucles d'oreilles, colliers et bagues sont interdits. Les objets dont on fait peu de cas comme les bouilloires pour faire chauffer de l'eau, les poêles à frire, les chaudrons, les bols, les tapis et la monnaie sont permis.»

La distinction ainsi établie entre objets de prix et objets d'utilisation courante dont la matière ne valorise pas le symbole dont ils sont décorés, rencontre quelques difficultés d'application, lorsqu'on se trouve à la démarcation entre le précieux et l'utilitaire. Une autre liste proposée par le Talmud de Jérusalem (III,1) interprète précieux au sens de 'respectable' et en conséquence inclut dans la prohibition le matériel servant à écrire. En fait il semble surtout qu'on ait voulu éviter les amulettes.

Pour les objets de prix ou semi-précieux, reste une porte de sortie: la désacralisation[75]. Ainsi R. Hiyya bar Abba est autorisé à utiliser des coupes portant l'image de la Tyché de Rome, car, pensent ses collègues, l'eau en y coulant désacralise l'objet (TJ A.Z. III,2). Une anecdote rapportée dans les deux Talmuds (TJ ibid. IV,4 et TB, ibid. 43a)[76] illustre le principe

[74] Cf. E. R. Goodenough, Jewish Symbols in the Greco-Roman Period, VII et VIII et Id., The Rabbis and Jewish Art in the Greco-Roman Period, HUCA XXXII (1961), p. 269s.; Urbach, The Rabbinical Laws of Idolatry in the 2nd and 3rd Centuries in the Light of Archaeological and Historical Facts, IEJ IX (1959), p. 238; M. Simon, Verus Israël, p. 34—46.

[75] Certaines cruches de bronze ornées de figures humaines semblent avoir été mutilées intentionnellement par les guerriers de Bar Kosiba (cf. Y. Yadin, Judaean Desert Studies I [1963], pl. 19). Il s'agit moins ici de désacralisation, laquelle ne peut-être opérée par un Israélite, que de réactions hostiles à la représentation de telles figures.

[76] אמר רבי יהושע בן לוי פעם אחת הייתי מהלך אחר ר' אלעזר הקפר בריבי בדרך ומצא שם טבעת ועליה צורת דרקון ומצא עובד כוכבים קטן ולא אמר לא כלום מצא עובד כוכבים גדול ואמר לו בטלה ולא בטלה סטרו ובטלה.

selon lequel un Israélite peut jouir d'un objet idolâtre à condition qu'un païen ait de gré ou de force désacralisé ce dernier, avant qu'il n'en ait pris possession (Tos. V,3).

Devant la richesse inouïe de la symbolique païenne, on aurait pu imaginer que sauf désacralisation, les sages eussent interdit tout motif suspect. Toutefois, seuls certains symboles ont attiré leur anathème[77].

M. III,3:

המוצא כלים ועליהם צורת החמה צורת הלבנה צורת הדרקון יוליכם לים המלח.

«Quiconque trouve des objets avec l'image du soleil ou de la lune, ou celle d'un dragon, qu'il les porte à la Mer Morte.»

Tos. V,1:

מצא טבעת ועליה צורת חמה צורת לבנה צורת דרקון יוליך לים המלח ואף דמות מניקה וסרפס.

«Si l'on trouve une bague avec l'image de la lune, du soleil ou d'un dragon, qu'on la porte à la Mer Morte; de même pour la figure de la femme qui allaite et de Sérapis.»

a) Le symbolisme astral

L'explication qui nous est donnée dans la 'Gemara' (TB 42b) quant à la prohibition particulière concernant les objets ornés d'un soleil ou d'une lune est la suivante: alors que les autres motifs sont purement décoratifs, ceux-là font eux-mêmes l'objet d'un culte. L'idée que les païens rendent un culte aux astres est en effet une constante du point de vue rabbinique sur l'idolâtrie[78], celle-ci n'a-t-elle pas d'ailleurs pour nom עבודת כוכבים ומזלות «culte des étoiles et des planètes», fréquemment réduit au simple sigle עכו"ם?

Une *baraïta* (rapportée ibid. et T J III,3,42d) restreint l'interdiction de la figuration astrale aux seuls «grands luminaires»: soleil et lune, et tolère la représentation des planètes. La 'Mishna' et la 'Tosefta' (cf. supra) se contentent d'interdire les objets marqués d'une lune ou d'un soleil. Ces témoignages convergent pour suggérer que le culte des deux astres avait dû prendre alors une extension particulière.

Le soleil et la lune qui occupent une place importante dans les religions orientales connaissent par leur intermédiaire un succès croissant dans le paganisme romain. La réflexion philosophique de l'époque hellénistique donne au sentiment populaire, appuyé également au départ sur le genre

[77] Goodenough, op. cit. IV, p. 19, suppose qu'ils reçoivent une mention spéciale parce qu'ils étaient plus particulièrement utilisés par les Juifs eux-mêmes; mais la baraïta qui ajoute «la femme qui allaite et Sérapis» n'est pas compatible avec cette supposition.

[78] Cf. Hul. II, 8 repris en A.Z. 42b où il est question de sacrifices faits à toutes les parties de la nature y compris le soleil, la lune, les étoiles et les planètes ce qui équivaut à réduire l'idolâtrie à une sorte de naturisme.

des noms 'soleil' et 'lune', une expression qui implique déjà la divinisation des grands luminaires. Le soleil n'est-il pas appelé par le stoïcien Cléanthe 'maître de l'univers', car il est le plus grand des astres et contribue pour la plus grande part à l'administration de toutes choses[79]; la lune, elle, se voit conférer un rôle nourricier car grâce à ses 'rayons faibles', 'féminins', porteurs de rosée, 'elle allaite à merveille et ainsi nourrit et fait croître'[80].

Ces théories philosophiques, qui privilégient le soleil et la lune par rapport aux autres planètes dont on sait pourtant l'importance dans le système chaldéen, trouvent leur expression dans la religion populaire par l'association du Soleil et de la Lune aux divinités masculines et féminines les plus en vogue dont plusieurs sont en outre l'objet de cultes à mystères liés au calendrier astral et aux saisons.

C'est le cas de Zeus, de Sérapis (cf. supra) et de Mithra[81] présenté tantôt comme distinct de Sol qui lui fait transmettre l'ordre de tuer le taureau, tantôt comme étant lui-même Sol Invictus[82]. Au IVème siècle, Macrobe écrit une dissertation pour prouver qu'Apollon, Mars, Mercure, Esculape, Sérapis, Adonis, Attis, Osiris ne sont que des appellations du Soleil[83]; selon ce qu'il croit savoir, les Syriens adorent à Hiérapolis le Soleil sous le nom d'Apollon[84].

Les études de F. CUMONT ont en outre attiré l'attention sur un processus de solarisation des cultes syriens qui aurait entraîné, à partir de l'époque séleucide, la transformation des Baals locaux en divinités héliaques[85] assimilées au Zeus hellénique[86]. Ses théories ont depuis été remises en question par H. SEYRIG, lequel à la lumière des découvertes archéologiques de Baalbek démontre que dans la triade héliopolitaine, c'est en vérité Mercure qui est assimilé au Soleil[87]. A côté de ce culte syncrétiste, subsistent en Syrie des cultes solaires introduits par les Arabes à l'époque hellénistique dont le plus célèbre est celui d'Emèse auquel Elagabal, avant Aurélien, bâtit un temple à Rome. Sans doute, est-ce un de ces cultes qui est ainsi évoqué par Tacite (Hist. III,24): *Undique clamor et orientem Solem (ita in Syria mos est) tertiani salutavere:* «Un cri s'éleva de toutes parts; le soleil apparut et la troisième légion, comme c'est l'usage en Syrie, salua son lever».

[79] Cf. Stoicorum Veterum Fragmenta I, 499.

[80] Philon, De Providentia II, 77 et n. 3, p. 307 de notre édition (Le Cerf 1973).

[81] Dans la grande salle du Mithraeum des thermes de Caracalla, une inscription votive grecque est dédiée «à Zeus-Hélios, le grand Sérapis, le sauveur et pourvoyeur de richesse, le bienfaisant et invincible Mithra». Cf. M. J. VERMASEREN, Corpus Inscriptionum et Monumentorum Religionis Mithriacae, I, La Haye 1956—1960, p. 190.

[82] Voir ibid. passim, nombreuses inscriptions dédiées à *Deo Soli invicto Mithrae.*

[83] Cf. Saturnales I, 17—23.

[84] Le nom de la cité semble en fait avoir été simplement repris de l'Héliopolis d'Egypte à l'époque de la domination lagide.

[85] F. CUMONT, Théologie solaire du paganisme romain 1909, p. 478.

[86] ID., Etudes syriennes 1917, p. 59.

[87] H. SEYRIG, Le Culte du Soleil en Syrie à l'époque romaine, Syria XLVIII (1971), p. 361s. et p. 367 (médaillons de Mercure héliopolitain avec tête radiée).

Quant à la lune, elle aussi est représentée dans l'iconographie mithraïque, car elle participe au même titre que Sol à l'acte créateur. Le plus souvent, elle n'apparaît qu'en buste, coiffée d'un diadème, avec derrière elle le croissant lunaire[88]. Exceptionnellement, la représentation anthropomorphique fait place au symbole seul. La lune, ce peut être également Isis[89] qui joue «le rôle mystérieux que les Grecs avaient assigné à la Triple Hécate, déesse favorite des sorciers de toute espèce»[90], comme ce peut être Astarté, adorée en tant que déesse de la lune à Sidon[91].

Les archéologues modernes ont constaté la présence de la lune et du Soleil sur de nombreux monuments de la région et au fronton des temples des divinités les plus diverses. Aussi, en sont-ils arrivés à la conclusion que leur fréquente apparition «n'est l'indice ni d'un syncrétisme, ni d'un culte spécifique de ces divinités. C'est un fait de langage symbolique par lequel on veut exprimer le caractère astrologique de la religion. Le Soleil et la Lune sont les plus visibles attributs d'une divinité suprême conçue comme cosmique»[92].

Les docteurs du Talmud nous apprennent qu'à leur époque, ces mêmes motifs étaient répétés sur les bijoux et sur bien d'autres objets plus ou moins précieux. A leurs yeux, il ne s'agit pas de dessins inoffensifs mais de représentations liées à un paganisme abhorré. Le temps n'est pas encore venu où, comme à Beth Alpha et Aïn Douq, on représentera le quadrige solaire sur les mosaïques des synagogues.

b) Le dragon

Ainsi qu'il apparaît dans les textes cités plus haut (M. III,3 et Tos. V,1) la présence de certains symboles dont le 'dragon' sur un objet de prix, et plus particulièrement une bague, condamne cet objet à être jeté à la Mer Morte. Le dragon est même plus directement visé que les autres symboles dans la suite de notre Tosefta (V, 2 fin):

...בלבד הרחוש העשוי כמין הדרקון אסור ושהדרקון תלוי בו נוטלו ומשליכו והשאר הרי זה מותר [...] אם היה חלק הרי זה מותר.

«(Sur des sceaux), n'est interdit que l'ornement en forme de dragon; s'il en est auquel le dragon est simplement attaché, on l'arrache, le jette et tout le reste est permis ... Si le dragon n'apparaît qu'en partie, c'est permis.»

88 Cf. VERMASEREN, op. cit. passim.

89 Elle apparaît chez Apulée (Metam. XI 3 [757] et 4 [759] vêtue d'un manteau étincelant d'étoiles au centre desquelles brille la lune, et le front surmonté d'une plaque circulaire en forme de miroir jetant une lumière blanche, ce qui indiquait que c'était la lune.

90 G. LAFAYE, op. cit. p. 102 et cat. où Isis est souvent décrite le front surmonté d'un croissant ou d'un disque (n°s. 38, 39 et 43).

91 Cf. Lucien, Dea Syria, 4.

92 H. SEYRIG, Le prétendu syncrétisme solaire syrien, dans: Les Syncrétismes dans les religions grecque et romaine (colloque de Strasbourg, 9 et 11 juin 1971), p. 151.

Le Talmud de Jérusalem (III, 3, 42d) insiste également sur ce point:

המוצא דרקון עשוי כמין רחוש אסור רחוש ועליו דרקון נוט' את הרחוש ומשליך את הדרקון.

«Si l'on trouve un dragon utilisé comme ornement, c'est interdit. Si c'est un ornement portant un dragon, on détache l'ornement et l'on jette le dragon.»

Dans tous ces textes, ce n'est pas le vocable hébreu נחש mais le mot grec δράκων qui est utilisé. Ce dernier, à la différence de ὄφις, désigne un serpent de grande taille. Le texte de TJ (ibid.) précise d'ailleurs:

לא שנו אלא דרקון הא כל הנחשים לא.

«ce qui est enseigné ne concerne que le dragon mais non les autres serpents».

De ce dragon, la Tosefta (ibid.) et TJ (ibid.) donnent une description analogue:

איזהו מן הדרקון שאסור ר' שמעון בן אלעזר אומ' כל שהציצין יוצאין מצוארו.

«Quelle est l'espèce de dragon interdite? R. Siméon ben Eléazar[93] dit: 'celui qui a des filaments (ou des écailles) sortant du cou'.»

En grec, le terme de δράκων peut s'utiliser pour désigner des bijoux, colliers ou bracelets, censés reproduire un serpent de grande taille[94]; mais ces bijoux ont moins mérité la sévérité des rabbins que les bagues. Cela se comprend d'autant mieux que, dans l'Antiquité, celles-ci avaient valeur de talismans[95], valeur qui leur était conférée par le motif dont elles étaient ornées. Or, le motif du serpent se retrouve fréquemment sur les anneaux anciens: tantôt le serpent constitue la bague elle-même et s'enroule autour du doigt sur toute la première phalange[96], tantôt il est représenté de manière stylisée et forme un anneau ouvert, terminé à ses deux extrémités par une tête de reptile[97]. Le premier modèle était tout à fait banni par les rabbins, le second était toléré («s'il n'apparaît qu'en partie, c'est permis»). (Tos. VI, 2 et TJ III, 3, 42d); il arrivait également que le dragon fût un ornement rapporté: dans ce cas, il était possible d'utiliser l'anneau servant de support après l'avoir débarrassé de son ornement. C'est sans doute ce à quoi R. Eleazar Hakappar contraignit un païen, dans l'anecdote talmudique (TB A.Z. 43a, TJ ibid. IV, 4) rapportée plus haut.

[93] La définition est attribuée à R. Simeon ben Azaï dans le passage correspondant de TJ. Dans les deux cas, le sens de ציצין n'est pas clair.

[94] Cf. Dict. de Liddell-Scott et de Bailly s. v. δράκων (Lucien, Amores 41).

[95] Cf. E. A. Wallis Budge, Amulets and Superstitions, Oxford 1930, réimpr. New York 1961, Ch. 14.

[96] Cf. Daremberg-Saglio I, 1, illustr. n° 345, p. 294.

[97] Ibid. n° 346.

L'acharnement de nos textes autour de ce motif, n'est certes pas fortuit:

ר׳ חזקיה בשם רב ביני ראה אותן משתחוים לדרקון.

«R. Hizqia dit au nom de Rav Bannaya[98] que celui-ci avait vu (les païens) se prosterner devant le dragon» (TJ ibid.).

Il n'est pas certain qu'à l'époque considérée, le dragon ait déjà été l'emblème des légions romaines[99]. En revanche, le serpent était, à l'époque, associé à toute sorte de divinités d'origines diverses[100]. Il apparaît toujours au bas des monuments de Mithra[101]. Il est lié à Isis et Sérapis représentés couramment sous forme de grosses couleuvres à tête humaine ou même de simples reptiles[102]. Il représente le *genius* de divers lieux et souvent l'Agathodémon dont le culte connut une certaine vogue sous Hadrien qui avait fait représenter son favori Antinoüs comme le 'bon génie'. Il est le compagnon favori d'Esculape qui ne dédaigne pas d'apparaître sous cette forme aux malades venus passer la nuit à l'Asclepeion[103]. A la fin du IIème siècle, sous le règne d'Antonin, on vit même se répandre une de ses incarnations, Glycon, révélée au devin Alexandre d'Abonotichos[104], et pendant un siècle au moins, ce serpent à tête humaine eut son culte, ses prêtres, ses mystères, fut représenté sur des monnaies ou mentionné dans des inscriptions[105]. Zeus Sabazios était quant à lui, caractérisé par un serpent à grosses joues[106]. Si l'on ajoute que le serpent était loin d'être inconnu des cultes sémitiques anciens[107], on trouvera une raison supplémentaire à l'interdit rabbinique et peut-être même son fondement. Le dragon pouvait en effet rappeler le serpent d'airain dont le culte avait été aboli par Ezéchias (II Rois, 18. 4) en tant que survivance de paganisme[108].

A l'époque où se placent nos textes, le serpent représente un talisman particulièrement recherché puisqu'il se rattache aux dieux guérisseurs (Sérapis, Asclépios et sa fille Hygieia). C'est pourquoi, sans doute, on le trouve sur les bagues qui, le plus souvent, servent de sceaux.

[98] Ce nom n'est pas correctement orthographié dans le texte. Nous supposons qu'il s'agit de R. Bannaya, tanna de la 5ème génération, dont les paroles ont pu être rapportées par R. Hizqia, amora palestinien de la 1ère génération (début IIIème siècle).

[99] Ces *signa* barbares venus de Dacie, commencent seulement à s'introduire vers +175 (cf. DAR.-SAGL. IV, 2, p. 1321 s. v. Signa). Cependant, on lit déjà dans les Psaumes de Salomon (fin 1er siècle) II, 29: «Ne tarde pas à les rétribuer sur leur propre tête, à changer l'honneur du dragon en déshonneur», et le texte vise de toute évidence l'empire romain.

[100] Cf. E. KÜSTER, Die Schlange in der griechischen Kunst und Religion, Religionsgeschichtliche Versuche und Vorarbeiten XIII, 2, Gießen 1913.

[101] Cf. VERMASEREN, op. cit. iconographie.

[102] Cf. LAFAYE, cat. nos. 18, 77, 92, 196.

[103] Cf. J. DEFRADAS, La divination en Grèce, dans A. CAQUOT et M. LEIBOVICI, La divination, p. 169.

[104] Cf. Lucien, Alexander sive Pseudomantis.

[105] Cf. DAREMBERG-SAGLIO II, 2, p. 1615 et figure en II, 1, p. 412.

[106] Les mains Votives qui lui sont consacrées portent souvent cet animal, cf. CHR. BLINKENBERG, Archäologische Studien, Copenhague 1904, p. 66—90.

[107] Le Baal Milik phénicien adoré sous cette forme était devenu Zeus Milichios.

[108] Cf. Pes. IV, 8; Ber. 10b.

Le passage suivant de Galien[109] nous paraît être de nature à éclairer tout particulièrement nos sources hébraïques:

Ἰδιότητα δέ τινες ἐνίοις λίθοις μαρτυροῦσι τοιαύτην οἵαν ὄντως ἔχει καὶ ὁ χλωρὸς ἴασπις, ὠφελῶν τόν τε στόμαχον καὶ τὸ τῆς γαστρὸς στόμα περιαπτόμενον. ἐντιθέασί τε καὶ δακτυλίῳ αὐτὸν ἔνιοι καὶ γλύφουσιν ἐν αὐτῷ τὸν τὰς ἀκτῖνας ἔχοντα δράκοντα, καθάπερ καὶ ὁ βασιλεὺς Νεχεψὼς ἔγραψεν ἐν τῇ τεσσερακαιδεκάτῃ βίβλῳ.

«Certains attribuent à quelques pierres une propriété telle que celle que possède en vérité le jaspe vert, lequel porté en sautoir fait du bien à l'estomac et à l'œsophage. Certains le montent en bague et y gravent le serpent radié, comme le roi Nechepsos l'a prescrit dans son quatorzième livre.»

Il pourrait s'agir des amulettes de Khnoubis (variante tardive du nom du dieu égyptien Khnoum) lesquelles toutefois présentent plus fréquemment un serpent radié léontocéphale[110].

Bien d'autres objets étaient également ornés de ce symbole, en particulier les coupes ainsi que nous l'apprend la 'Gemara' palestinienne (ibid.):

שמואל אמר כוס בסיס לדרקון אסור ודרקון בסיס לכוס מותר.

«Samuel[111] dit: 'une coupe servant de base à un dragon est interdite, un dragon servant de base à une coupe est permis'.»

L'intérêt de cette distinction est clair: dans le premier cas, il s'agit d'un objet de culte; dans le second d'une coupe ordinaire à base travaillée en forme de serpent. L'objet cultuel décrit nous paraît correspondre à l'urne symbolisant Isis et dont LAFAYE[112] nous dit que son anse était «surmontée par un aspic aux replis tortueux levant sa tête pleine d'écailles et gonflant son cou traversé de mille raies», description qui concorde on ne peut mieux avec celle du 'dragon' de nos sources.

c) 'Une forme de main ou de pied'

M. III, 2:

המוצא שברי צלמים הרי אלו מותרים מצא תבנית יד או תבנית רגל הרי אלו אסורים מפני שכיוצא בהן נעבד.

[109] De simpl. 10, 19, cité par C. BONNER, Studies in Magical Amulets Chiefly Graeco-Egyptian, Ann Arbor 1950, p. 54.

[110] Cf. BONNER, ibid. Pl. IV et PH. DERCHAIN, Intailles magiques du Musée de Numismatique d'Athènes, Chronique d'Egypte XXXIX (jan.—juil. 1964) Bruxelles, p. 180. Khnoubis aurait été confondu avec l'Agathodémon (ibid. p. 181).

[111] Amora babylonienne de la 1ère génération (1ère moitié IIIème siècle) ayant séjourné en Palestine.

[112] Op. cit. p. 123—124.

«Si l'on trouve des fragments de statues, il sont permis; mais si l'on trouve une forme de main ou une forme de pied, ils sont interdits, car des objets de ce genre font l'objet d'un culte.»

Cette distinction établie par les rabbins montre en eux des observateurs avertis. Il ne semble pas tant que soient visés dans cette mishna les innombrables ex-votos dont se parait tout Asclépeion ou Sérapeion et qui représentaient toutes les parties du corps[113]. Le texte se limite à une «forme de main» ou «une forme de pied» sans apparemment laisser la liste ouverte.

Or, précisément l'archéologie a mis à jour des sculptures du type de celles qui y sont décrites. On connaît bien aujourd'hui ces modèles de mains de bronze portant, fondue à même la paume une figure de Jupiter héliopolitain, et dont un exemplaire se trouve au Musée du Louvre. Cinq de ces mains ont été découvertes dans la région de Saïda, elles sont caractérisées par le geste liturgique des trois premiers doigts ouverts[114].

Des formes de mains sont également associées au culte du dieu phrygien Sabazios répandu dans l'empire romain[115] et grossièrement confondu avec le Dieu des Juifs en raison d'une fausse étymologie le rapprochant de Sabbaot, mais il nous paraît plus naturel, étant donné la proximité géographique d'Héliopolis, de rapporter celles qu'avaient pu observer les docteurs palestiniens au culte de Jupiter Héliopolitain.

Quant aux formes de pied humain, elles sont plutôt en relation avec le culte de Sérapis[116]. Un pied colossal de marbre blanc provenant du temple de Sérapis à Alexandrie est exposé au British Museum. Le pied se retrouve associé à Sérapis sur une monnaie alexandrine d'Antonin Le Pieux où il apparaît surmonté de la tête du dieu[117]. On le voit également au IIIème siècle sur d'autres monnaies de l'empire romain, et notamment à Ptolemaïs-Acre où il est entouré des trois principaux symboles de la cité: foudre ailé, caducée et harpe[118]. Le musée de Beyrouth possède un aigle assis sur un pied humain dédié à Sérapis[119]. On connaît également un buste de Sérapis reposant sur un pied humain[120]. Cependant un pied découvert sur le Carmel est consacré à Zeus héliopolitain.

Ces témoignages archéologiques et numismatiques situent clairement la main et le pied comme des symboles religieux, ce que laissent entendre les sources littéraires talmudiques. Leur signification n'est toutefois pas vraiment élucidée. S'agit-il seulement d'ex-votos (cf. infra p. 447) ou de pieds et de mains symbolisant la puissance de la divinité suprême? Cette

[113] Cf. infra p. 26 et liste des parties du corps représentées, dans CIA II, 835 et 836.
[114] Cf. R. Dussaud op. cit., p. 117.
[115] Chr. Blinkenberg, Archäologische Studien, pp. 66—90 et Goodenough, op. cit. IV, p. 16, n. 65.
[116] Cf. H. Blaufuss, Götter, Bilder und Symbole, pp. 15—19.
[117] BMC Alexandrie, p. 144.
[118] Cf. Kadman, op. cit. IV, p. 75.
[119] Cf. L. Vidman, op. cit., inscription n°. 364 et L. Jalabert, MUSJ II (1907), pp. 309—311.
[120] C'est un marbre grec du Musée des Offices à Florence; cf. Lafaye, catalogue n°. 27.

interprétation a été suggérée[121] à côté de quelques autres, mais aucune n'est absolument certaine.

d) Les symboles du pouvoir et la question du culte impérial

M. III, 1:

כל הצלמים אסורים מפני שהן נעבדין פעם אחת בשנה דברי רבי מאיר וחכמים אומרים אינו אסור אלא כל שיש בידו מקל או צפור או כדור רבן שמעון בן גמליאל אומר כל שיש בידו כל דבר.

«Toutes les statues sont interdites car elles sont adorées une fois dans l'année, tel est l'avis de R. Meir. Les sages disent: 'ne sont interdites que celles qui tiennent à la main un bâton, un oiseau ou un globe'. R. Simeon b. Gamaliel dit: 'toutes celles qui tiennent à la main quoi que ce soit'.»

Tos. V, 1:

וחכמ׳ אומ׳ אין אסור אלא שיש בו מקל או כדור או צפור סייף עטרת וטבעת צלם ונחש.

«Les sages disent: 'n'est interdit que ce qui porte un bâton ou un globe ou un oiseau, un glaive, une couronne, un anneau, une statue et un serpent'.»

Une *baraïta* rapportée dans le Talmud de Babylone (41a) ajoute uniquement à la liste de la 'Mishna', le glaive, la couronne et l'anneau. Le Talmud de Jérusalem (III, 1) énumère également ces six objets et justifie comme suit leur mention: «le bâton est le signe de la domination sur le monde; l'oiseau est un signe important, selon ces mots (Isaïe 10, 14): 'Ma main a trouvé comme un nid la richesse des peuples'; enfin la sphère est le symbole du monde fait selon cette forme . . . l'épée sert à tuer, avec la couronne le roi se pare et avec l'anneau les ordres sont scellés.»

Ces symboles sont de même rapportés à l'idée de domination dans la 'Gemara' babylonienne, qui cite en commençant l'opinion de Samuel, amora de la première génération, selon lequel ce sont les statues des empereurs qui sont visées par cette législation: באנדרטי של מלכים שנינו (40a). Elle poursuit avec explication donnée par une *baraïta* (41a): «Le sceptre parce qu'il exerce son pouvoir sur le monde entier comme avec un sceptre; l'oiseau parce qu'il tient en main le monde entier comme un oiseau; le globe parce qu'il tient en main le monde entier comme un globe.» La Gemara palestinienne confirme une telle interprétation en remarquant (III,1): «A quel cas se réfère la discussion entre R. Meir et les autres docteurs? S'il est notoire que les idoles ont été érigées à l'usage des rois païens, tous doivent s'accorder à en interdire la jouissance.»

[121] Cf. Blinkenberg, op. cit., p. 90: la main du dieu protège et bénit ses fidèles avec les trois premiers doigts levés dans le geste chrétien de la *benedictio latina*.

Les critiques modernes[122] abondent dans cette voie et lisent dans les lignes citées une vigoureuse condamnation du culte impérial. Les emblèmes caractérisant ces statues nous font penser à notre tour que l'interdit en question couvre bel et bien une mise en garde toute particulière contre le culte impérial. L'empereur est en effet couramment représenté en maître du monde avec le sceptre et le globe et accompagné de l'aigle qui symbolise les divinités suprêmes auxquelles il s'identifie mais également l'empire romain. Lorsqu'il n'est pas nu-tête il porte, sur les monnaies notamment, la couronne de lauriers[123] et plus rarement la couronne radiée; il n'est pas rare qu'une Niké ailée (peut-être 'la statue' de la 'Tosefta') lui pose sur le front la couronne du vainqueur[124]. Quant à l'anneau, bien qu'il soit difficilement discernable sur les témoignages iconographiques qui nous sont parvenus, il n'a pas de quoi nous surprendre. Pline qui était en mesure d'en discerner au doigt de deux seulement des anciens rois, Numa et Servius Tullius, atteste qu'à son époque la coutume grecque de porter des bagues était extrêmement répandue[125]: ceux qui se limitaient à une bague la portaient au petit doigt et l'utilisaient comme sceau (H.N. XXXIII 6, 24—25). C'est cet usage — qui n'est donc pas exclusivement impérial — qui est visé ici[126].

Toutefois malgré la très haute probabilité d'une telle interprétation, il ne faut pas perdre de vue le fait que la plupart des divinités dont le culte est attesté localement, sont représentées avec des attributs analogues. 'Le bâton' dont il est question dans nos sources pourrait être aussi bien le sceptre de Zeus ou de Sérapis que le thyrse de Dionysos ou la massue d'Hermès, l'oiseau pourrait être l'aigle symbole de Zeus et des dieux suprêmes ou la colombe d'Aphrodite et de la Derceto ascalonienne, pour ne pas énumérer les autres volatiles consacrés à d'autres divinités. Le globe se rencontre aussi bien dans la main de Mithra, que dans celle de Sérapis[127] ou du Baal du ciel palmyrénien[128]. La couronne peut désigner le calathos de Sérapis, la couronne de tours d'une Tyché, la couronne radiée du Soleil ou la simple couronne tressée portée par tant de personnages mythologiques. L'épée pourrait être celle de Mithra transperçant le taureau. L'anneau orne le doigt de diverses idoles[129].

Les emblèmes énumérés sont toutefois loin d'épuiser la variété des motifs attachés à la représentation des diverses divinités. Sans doute est-ce

[122] Cf. BLAUFUSS, op. cit., p. 10—11; URBACH, art. cité, IEJ IX, p. 239; M. AVI-YONAH, dans: Le rayonnement des civilisations grecques et romaines sur les cultures périphériques, 8ème Congrès international d'archéologie classique, p. 614.

[123] Cf. *baraïta* de TB 41 a citée infra p. 425: «la couronne d'abord simple brin tressé fut interprétée comme étant une couronne royale».

[124] Voir par exemple le célèbre camée de Vienne.

[125] Cp. Juvénal, I, 28; VII, 89; Martial, XI, 50.

[126] Auguste eut successivement trois cachets, l'un portant un sphinx, l'autre l'effigie d'Alexandre, le troisième son propre portrait (Suét. Aug. 4). Sur le sceau de Néron étaient représentés Apollon et Marsyas (Suét., Néron 21).

[127] Cf. ST. COOK, op. cit., p. 192.

[128] Ibid., p. 224.

[129] Cf. Pline, H.N. XXXIII, 6, 24: *etiam in deorum simulacris.*

le sens de l'addition de R. Simeon b. Gamaliel interdisant toute statue tenant à la main quoi que ce soit (M. III, 1).

A cette liste de six emblèmes, la Tosefta (V, 1) ajoute la statue et le serpent. Pour צלם 'statue', on est en droit de se demander s'il ne s'agit pas d'un mot ayant glissé de la ligne précédente (on lirait volontiers אין אסור אלא צלם שיש בו); si tel n'est pas le cas, il pourrait s'agir d'une victoire ailée. Quant au serpent, il accompagne la représentation figurée de plusieurs divinités en particulier celle des dieux guérisseurs Sérapis[130] et Esculape. Lorsque les empereurs se faisaient représenter sous les traits de Sérapis, de Baal Shamim ou du maître de l'Olympe, ils en prenaient tout naturellement les attributs. La représentation de Sérapis se laisse d'autant plus facilement confondre avec celle de l'empereur que le dieu est représenté 'en majesté', assis sur un trône, tenant un long sceptre dans la main gauche[131].

Si depuis le début de leur rencontre avec l'impérialisme romain, les Juifs avaient, en raison des exigences de leur religion, bénéficié d'une dispense de tout acte cultuel pour les dieux de l'empire ou de la cité, celle-ci «ne concernait que les dieux morts et non les dieux vivants qu'étaient les monarques divinisés»[132]. En ce qui concerne le culte impérial, ils devaient en effet un minimum de concessions incluant un serment de fidélité et la célébration des fêtes officielles: anniversaires de l'avènement des victoires, de la naissance des empereurs ou jours de deuil de la famille impériale[133]. Tant que le Temple de Jérusalem subsistait, on y avait offert des holocaustes quotidiens pour le salut de l'Empereur et du peuple romain, cela d'ailleurs sur la cassette impériale[134]. Il reste que, comme le fit durement remarquer Caligula à la délégation de Juifs alexandrins conduite par Philon qui étaient venus intercéder pour leur communauté, les Juifs sacrifiaient 'à un autre' encore que ce fût à l'intention de l'empereur[135]. Les successeurs de Caligula ne prétendirent pas se faire adorer par des hommes aux yeux desquels ce culte était «la plus atroce des impiétés»[136]. Toutefois, après la destruction du Temple, grandit dans certains milieux une hostilité à Rome, qui trouve un aliment supplémentaire dans l'extension du culte impérial: ainsi l'Apocalypse de Jean stigmatise «ceux qui adorent la bête et son image» (ch. 13, 14, 16). Dans un contexte législatif où les métaphores apocalyptiques ne sont pas de mise, les auteurs de notre 'Mishna' anonyme et de la 'Tosefta' correspondante ont fort bien pu préférer une description peu équivoque des statues impériales («celles qui tiennent à la main un bâton, un oiseau ou un globe») à défaut de les désigner nommément, ce qui ne pouvait se faire sans danger.

[130] Cf. Macrobe, Saturn. I, 20 et supra p. 407.
[131] Cf. Lafaye, cat. n°s. 31 et 32.
[132] J. Juster, Les Juifs dans l'empire romain II, p. 338.
[133] Cf. infra p. 433 et Juster, ibid., p. 339.
[134] Cf. Philon, Legatio 157 et Josèphe, B.J. II, 197, Contre Apion II, 77.
[135] Philon, Legatio 357.
[136] Ibid. 118. Cp. Josèphe, Contre Apion II, 73 et 75.

Si la législation rabbinique attire plus particulièrement l'attention sur ce type de statues, c'est sans doute parce que plus que celle de divinités païennes, elles étaient susceptibles d'être honorées par des Juifs craintifs ou moutonniers. Les paroles les plus audacieuses prononcées contre le culte du monarque, diplomatiquement écartées de la 'Mishna', n'ont été sauvées de l'oubli que par une *baraïta* reproduite en TB 41a où malgré le caractère inusité de l'expression, le sens ne nous paraît pas faire de doute[137]: «On a ajouté l'épée, la couronne et l'anneau. L'épée, d'abord considérée simplement comme l'emblème du voleur, fut ensuite interprétée pour marquer qu'il s'arroge le pouvoir de massacrer le monde entier. La couronne, d'abord simple brin tressé, fut ensuite interprétée comme étant une couronne royale. L'anneau d'abord simple marque de distinction[138], fut ensuite interprété pour marquer qu'il s'arroge le pouvoir de sceller la peine de mort pour le monde entier.» Il est clair que ces quelques lignes constituent un acte de résistance politique: d'abord en ne retenant qu'une interprétation dépréciative pour certains emblèmes dont se parent les statues impériales (l'épée, emblème du voleur), ensuite en ne retenant du pouvoir conféré à l'empereur que la force destructrice: celle de massacrer ou de décréter la mort, ce qui est compréhensible pour une nation aussi récemment éprouvée que la nation juive à la fin du IIème siècle.

A la lumière de ces considérations, l'on saisit mieux le fondement de l'admiration vouée à ce saint qui, de toute sa vie, ne regarda une pièce de monnaie (cf. supra p. 414): mieux qu'un autre, en effet, il avait respecté l'interdit lié au culte impérial, puisqu'il avait évité de poser son regard sur les images de l'empereur les plus difficiles à fuir, les effigies marquées sur les monnaies — effigies en relief comme chacun sait, donc déjà amorce de statues[139] — et cela, bien que vivant en un monde où, selon les termes de l'Apocalypse johannique (13.17), «personne ne pouvait acheter ni vendre, sans avoir la marque, le nom de la bête ou le nombre de son nom»[140].

De toute l'analyse qui précède, il nous paraît ressortir que si le tableau des cultes locaux évoqué par les écrits rabbiniques est certainement fort incomplet, ceux-ci ont du moins le mérite d'en dégager les traits les plus saillants. Nous apprenons ainsi qu'aux yeux d'observateurs peu suspects

137 הוסיפו עליהן סייף עטרת וטבעת סייף מעיקרא סבור לסטים בעלמא ולבסוף סבור שהורג את עצמו תחת כל העולם כולו עטרה מעיקרא סבור גדיל כלילי בעלמא ולבסוף סבור כעטרה למלך טבעת מעקרא סבור אישתיימא בעלמא ולבסוף סבור שחותם את כל העולם כולו למיתה. (Texte du ms. espagnol de New York, édité par Shraga Abramson, New-York 1957, p. 192).

138 A Rome, elle permettait en effet de distinguer l'ordre équestre mais, sous l'empire, le droit de le porter fut même accordé à des affranchis. Cf. Pline H.N. XXXIII, 7, 29.

139 C'est ce qu'enseigne notre Tosefta (V, 2) à propos des bagues ornées de motifs idolâtres: «Si le motif est en relief la bague est interdite au profit, s'il est en intaille, elle est permise.»

140 Cp. Matt. 22. 20—21: «Et il leur demanda: 'De qui sont cette effigie et cette inscription ?' 'De César', lui répondirent-ils. Alors il leur dit: 'Rendez donc à César ce qui est à César et à Dieu ce qui est à Dieu'.»

de complaisance, les païens de Palestine étaient de fidèles servants de l'empereur, des adorateurs d'Hermès et des divinités égyptiennes romanisées, Sérapis et Isis, ainsi que de la lune et du soleil, des héritiers des Cananéens qui plaçaient le sacré dans divers aspects de la nature. A cette première esquisse, nos textes sont encore susceptibles d'apporter quelques compléments ou retouches.

II. Fêtes publiques et fêtes privées

Après avoir exprimé l'interdiction frappant tout commerce avec les païens, dès trois jours avant leurs fêtes, la 'Mishna' poursuit ainsi (I, 3):

ואלו אידיהם שלגוים: קלנדא וסטרנורא וקרטסים ויום גנוסיא שלמלכים ויום הלדה ויום המיתה דברי רבי מאיר וחכמים אומרים כל מיתה שיש בה שׂרפה יש בה עבודה זרה ושאין בה שׂרפה אין בה עבודה זרה יום תגלחת זקנו ובלוריתי יום שעלה בו מן הים ויום שיצא בו מבית האסורים וגוי שעשׂה משתה לבנו אינו אסור אלא אותו היום ואותו האיש בלבד.

«Les fêtes des païens sont les suivantes: Calendes, Saturnales, Kratesis, anniversaire des empereurs — jour de naissance et jour de mort, selon R. Meir. Les sages disent: 'chaque mort accompagnée d'incinération comporte de l'idolâtrie, s'il n'y a pas incinération, il n'y a pas idolâtrie. Pour le jour où un païen se rase la barbe et les cheveux, rentre d'un voyage en mer, sort de prison, donne un banquet pour son fils, l'interdiction ne frappe que ce jour et cet homme en particulier'.»

Quant à la 'Tosefta', qui, nous l'avons vu, suppose d'emblée connu l'énoncé de la 'Mishna', elle apporte la distinction suivante (I, 1):

במה דברים אמורים? באידין הקבועין אבל באידין שאינן קבועין אין אסור אלא אותו יום בלבד.

«De quoi s'agit-il? Il s'agit de leurs fêtes fixes, mais en ce qui concerne leurs fêtes mobiles, n'est interdit que le jour même (de la fête).»

Et un peu plus loin (I, 4) elle ajoute deux autres distinctions: l'une entre fêtes locales, nationales ou familiales, l'autre entre fêtes publiques et fêtes privées:

עיר אחת עושה ועיר אחת אינה עושה אומה אחת עושה ואומה אחרת אינה עושה משפחה אחת עושה ומשפחה אחרת אינה עושה העושין אסורין ושאין עושין מותרין קלנדא אף על פי שהכל עושין אין אסור אלא לפולחין בלבד סטרנריא יום שאחזו בו את המלכות קרטיסים יום גנוסיא של מלכים יום של כל מלך ומלך הרי כרבים יחיד אפילו יום המשתה שלו ויום שנעשה בו שלטון ר׳ מאיר או׳ אף יום שעמד בו מחליו אסור.

«Pour les fêtes qu'une cité observe et l'autre non, qu'une nation observe et l'autre non, qu'une famille observe et l'autre non, les rapports avec ceux qui les observent sont interdits et avec ceux qui ne les observent pas, permis. Pour les Calendes, bien que tous les observent, l'interdiction ne concerne que ceux qui y rendent un culte. Saturnales, jour où ils se sont emparés de la royauté, Kratesis, jour anniversaire des empereurs, jour de chaque empereur. Il en est de la collectivité comme des particuliers: cela vaut également pour le jour de son banquet et celui de son entrée en charge. R. Meir dit: 'même le jour où il s'est remis d'une maladie est interdit'.»

Dans ce dernier texte, notre traduction n'a pas cherché à voiler les ambiguités d'une syntaxe corrompue. Elle fait néanmoins apparaître que la liste des fêtes officielles «que tous observent» est, à peu de chose près, identique dans la 'Mishna' et la 'Tosefta'. Bien que la 'Mishna' ne le précise pas, elle distingue elle aussi dans l'ensemble de l'énumération proposée les fêtes publiques et les fêtes privées connues en latin sous le nom de *feriae publicae* (cf. Tos. I, 4 רבים) et *feriae singulorum* (ibid. יחיד)[141]. La 'Tosefta' mentionne également des fêtes locales propres à une nation ou à une cité — en latin *feriae gentium* —, mais n'en donne pas d'exemple. Elle connaît en outre la différence entre *feriae stativae*, fêtes fixes, et *feriae conceptivae*, fêtes mobiles[142], mais n'en donne point d'exemple.

1. Fêtes publiques

M. I, 3	Tos. I, 4
Calendes	Calendes
Saturnales	Saturnales
	Jour où ils se sont emparés de la royauté
Kratésis	Kratésis
anniversaire des empereurs (jour de naissance ou jour de mort)	anniversaire des empereurs (jour de chaque empereur)

a) Les Calendes

Les fêtes énumérées ici sont des fêtes annuelles (Saturnales, anniversaires) à l'exception — toute apparente — des Calendes qui marquent la néoménie chez les Romains. Cependant, les Calendes mensuelles n'étaient pas célébrées avec un grand éclat et n'étaient l'occasion que de quelques rites qui ne dépassaient pas le cadre familial. En revanche, les Calendes de janvier dont tout le monde occidental a hérité, constituaient une grande

[141] Cf. J. Marquardt, Le Culte chez les Romains I, p. 351.
[142] Cf. Ibid., p. 354 et L. Delatte, Recherches sur quelques fêtes mobiles du calendrier romain, Liège 1937.

fête. Ainsi que l'a déjà souligné Blaufuss[143] le commentaire donné dans l'une et l'autre 'Gemara' encourage une telle interprétation.

Le Talmud de Jérusalem cite en effet une *aggada* de Rab (I, 2, 39c) selon laquelle la fête des Calendes aurait été instituée par Adam, qui voyant le jour s'allonger se serait écrié קלון דיאו (καλὸν δία[144], le beau jour?). A cette première *aggada* en répond une autre, rapportée au nom de R. Yohanan (ibid.). Son récit concerne une guerre mythique entre Egyptiens et Romains à laquelle un terme aurait été mis grâce au suicide volontaire du général romain, un vaillant vieillard nommé Januarius et père de douze fils. Lorsqu'il se fut transpercé de son épée, retentit le cri: „*Kalendae Januarii*". On ignore la source de ces deux curieuses traditions qui intéressent notre propos en ce que l'une relie les Calendes au solstice d'hiver et l'autre au nom de Januarius.

Dans la 'Gemara' babylonienne (8a) la date des Calendes est fixée à huit jours après la *Tequfa* et celle des Saturnales à huit avant[145]. Cette expression en elle-même, imprécise, puisqu'elle signifie simplement solstice ou équinoxe, peut être complétée à la lumière des indications de TJ, en *Tequfa* du mois de Tebet ce qui nous place très exactement au solstice d'hiver soit huit jours avant le 1er janvier. La 'Gemara' palestinienne (I, 2, 39c) présente visiblement une erreur textuelle provenant d'une interversion puisqu'elle situe les Calendes huit jours avant le solstice et les Saturnales huit jours après: cette explication étant mise dans la bouche de Rab qui attribuait l'institution des Calendes à l'émerveillement d'Adam devant l'allongement des jours, on peut être certain que l'erreur ne saurait être imputée à Rab lui-même.

Ajoutons à cela le témoignage du 'Midrash Rabba'[146]: «Un Gentil dit un jour à R. Yohanan ben Zakkaï: 'Nous avons nos fêtes et vous avez les vôtres. Nous avons les Calendes, les Saturnales, la Kratesis et vous vous avez la Pâque, la Pentecôte et la fête des Tabernacles. Quel est donc le jour où nous nous réjouissons ensemble'? R. Yohanan b. Zakkaï répondit: 'c'est le jour où tombe la pluie'.» Il apparaît nettement d'après ce passage que les fêtes païennes mises en parallèle avec les trois grandes fêtes de pèlerinage juives sont des solennités importantes, ce qui confirme pour la première d'entre elles, qu'il s'agit bien des Calendes de janvier[147].

[143] Feste, p. 7 et 8.

[144] Peut-être καλὸν δύε 'couche-toi bien', sorte d'adieu au soleil, cf. Lieberman, Hellenism, p. 110.

[145] On a même recours à un moyen mnémotechnique destiné à rappeler que les Calendes citées en premier se placent après le solstice et les Saturnales citées en second se placent avant: c'est le verset de Ps. 139, 5 אחור וקדם צרתני: «Tu me cernes derrière et devant.»

[146] Deut. R. 7. 7 (sur 27. 12) p. 111, éd. Lieberman מעשה בגוי אחד ששאל את רבן יוחנן בן זכאי אמר לו אנו יש לנו מועדות ואתם יש לכם מועדות אנו יש לנו קלנדא סטרנליא וקרטוסיס ואתם יש לכם פסח עצרת וסוכות איזה יום שאנו ואתם שמחים א"ל רבן יוח' ב"ז זה יום ירידת גשמים cp. Esth. R. 7. 12 (sur 3. 8) et Gen. R. 13. 6, p. 116—117 éd. Albeck t. I.

[147] Cf. Tertullien, Idol. 14: *Nimirum Saturnalia et Kalendas Januarias celebrans hominibus placebat?* «Qu'est-ce à dire? que pour plaire aux hommes de son temps, (Saint-Paul) célébrait avec eux les Saturnales et les Calendes de janvier?»

Comme chaque néoménie, la fête des Calendes de janvier était marquée par un culte rendu aux lares domestiques. C'était en même temps un jour de festivités populaires où l'on échangeait des étrennes en argent[148] et des présents de miel[149], figues et dattes en se souhaitant une année douce et prospère (cf. infra p. 449). Lorsque la 'Tosefta' précise: «Pour les Calendes bien que tous les observent, l'interdiction ne concerne que ceux qui y rendent un culte», il nous paraît à peu près certain que l'observance générale qu'elle constate est constituée par l'usage des étrennes. Le patriarche du IIIème s. Judah Nesia se vit un jour lui-même offrir par un *ducenarius* romain un plat plein de deniers; par courtoisie, il accepta une pièce, craignant sans doute de vexer le donateur en refusant le tout; Resh Lakish, plus intransigeant lui conseilla de jeter cette pièce «à la mer Morte» (TJ A.Z. I, 1, 39b). Il y a lieu de penser que le présent refusé constituait des étrennes; son refus s'explique ainsi en raison du lien qui le rattachait à une festivité païenne.

L'usage tout profane des étrennes est, dans la Tosefta (I, 4) nettement distingué du culte, c'est-à-dire surtout du culte public le plus apparent pour un observateur extérieur. Sous le Haut-Empire, les Calendes de janvier, date à laquelle, depuis 153, les consuls entraient en charge, étaient en effet devenues une occasion supplémentaire de marquer son loyalisme à l'égard de la personne de l'empereur. Les anciens vœux hérités de la période républicaine, qui visaient à attirer la protection de Jupiter Optimus Maximus sur l'Etat romain, étaient désormais des *vota publica* pour l'empereur. Cette célébration avait lieu au Capitole de chaque cité[150] et Pline le Jeune[151] nous confirme l'éclat qui lui était conféré dans les provinces. Une *baraïta* de TB (8a) explique que les Calendes concernent la ville où elles sont célébrées et toutes les localités du voisinage mais que les relations avec ceux qui dans ces localités ne prennent pas part aux festivités (sans doute en raison de l'éloignement de la grande cité régionale) sont permises.

C'est donc du culte public et de tous ceux qui l'observent que le Talmud recommande de se tenir à l'écart. Il présentait en effet le double caractère d'idolâtrie et d'allégeance politique et religieuse au monarque divinisé de son vivant.

Les sources talmudiques constituent ainsi un témoignage de première importance sur l'expansion de la fête des Calendes dans cette partie de l'Orient. Jusqu'ici les nombreuses mentions des Calendes chez Tertullien[152] avaient pu faire tirer la conclusion que «c'est en Afrique que la fête se serait

[148] Les pièces d'or constituaient le meilleur des présages, cf. Ovide, Fastes I, 189—226; les empereurs eux-mêmes acceptaient des pièces de monnaie au Nouvel An, cf. Suét., Aug. 57 et 91, Tib. 34, Cal. 42.

[149] Cf. Ovide, ibid. 187—188: *Omen ait, causa est, ut res sapor ille sequatur. Et peragat coeptum dulcis ut annus iter.* Cp. Martial XIII, 27; VIII, 33, 11; Sén. Ep. 87, 3.

[150] Néron 46; Tacite, Annales XVI, 22.

[151] Paneg. 68. 4 et Ep. X, 35—36 et 100—101 où il rend compte de la cérémonie pour 112 et 113.

[152] De Corona 12. 3, Idol. 14, Apolog. 35. 7, où se trouve la formule du vœu: «que Jupiter prenne sur nos années pour ajouter aux tiennes»: *De nostris annis tibi Jupiter augeat annos.*

essentiellement implantée»[153]. Cette fête qui était spécifiquement romaine, dans ses aspects privés comme publics, dut servir de ciment unificateur dans les diverses parties de l'empire: «en raison de sa longue spécificité romaine, elle a dû constituer l'un des éléments de la culture romaine qu'il convenait d'acquérir et de pratiquer si l'on tenait à paraître civilisé»; en outre, «son aspect civique proche du culte impérial en fit un événement à la fois spectaculaire et populaire»[154].

b) Les Saturnales

Les Saturnales viennent toujours en second dans les listes de fêtes païennes reproduites dans la littérature rabbinique (cf. supra p. 426–7). Les déformations du mot sont nombreuses (סטרנוורא סטרנריא), mais la forme la plus proche de l'original סטרנליה[155] émerge aussi quelquefois. Alors que la 'Gemara' des deux Talmuds est fort prolixe en ce qui concerne les Calendes, elle demeure quasiment muette pour tout ce qui touche aux Saturnales. L'unique explication du nom de cette fête donnée en TJ I 2, 39c est fondée sur une étymologie hautement fantaisie[156]: שונא נוקם נוטר היד מה דאת אמר וישטם עשו את יעקב. «Il hait, se venge, tient rancune, ainsi qu'il est dit (Gen. 27. 41): 'Esaü se prit de haine pour Jacob'.» La date de la fête était connue puisque nous avons vu qu'elle était située huit jours avant le solstice d'hiver. De fait, depuis Caligula, les Saturnales donnaient lieu à sept jours fériés — du 17 au 23 décembre —, mais la fête religieuse avec sacrifice et banquet public au bout duquel on se quittait en criant *Io Saturnalia!*[157] ne durait qu'un jour. Seul ce premier jour où la foule répandue dans les rues et festoyant, devait frapper les observateurs juifs, avait un caractère religieux. Les autres n'étaient pas *festi* mais *feriati*[158] et profitaient d'un commerce actif. C'est pourquoi sans doute, il est question en TJ I, 3, 39c d'une petite toile achetée aux Saturnales de Beth Shean. Dans une énumération de la Tosefta (II, 6 = TJ I, 7, 40a = TB 18b) liée aux représentations théâtrales, se rencontre le terme סגלריא que BLAUFUSS[159] s'efforce d'identifier avec les Sigillaria ou fêtes Sigillaires lesquelles constituaient la seconde partie des Saturnales, fêtées dès le 22 décembre en l'honneur du retour du soleil. Cette fête donnait également lieu à des échanges de cadeaux[160] et

153 M. MESLIN, La fête des Kalendes de janvier dans l'empire romain. Etude d'un rituel de Nouvel An, Coll. Latomus, vol. 115, Bruxelles 1970, p. 49.

154 Ibid.

155 Cf. ELMSLIE, op. cit., Ch. I, Excursus 2 et Deut. R. 7. 7, p. 111, éd. LIEBERMAN.

156 Cette étymologie a du moins l'avantage de dépeindre les relations des Juifs avec les Romains, telles qu'elles apparaissaient aux Juifs du IIIème siècle. Rome y est désignée comme dans le 'Midrash' par Esaü dont l'autre nom est Edom.

157 «Ce cri retentissait non pas seulement sur le sol de la patrie mais à l'étranger où il était comme le mot de ralliement auquel se reconnaissaient les Romains», DAREMBERG-SAGLIO IV, 2, p. 1081–1082.

158 Cf. Macrobe, Saturn. I, 10 et 24.

159 Feste 12, p. 25s.

160 Martial leur consacre en 84—85, deux livres d'épigrammes (Xenia et Apophoreta). Cf. aussi Suét., Claude 5, Sén., Ep. XII, 3.

plus particulièrement de statuettes de cire ou d'argile (*sigilla*) d'où elle tirait son nom. Pour notre part, une telle identification nous paraît hasardeuse étant donné la nature du contexte; nous lirons donc plus volontiers sous la transcription hébraïque une référence aux jeux séculaires, en latin, *ludi saeculares* (cf. infra p. 436) — à moins que, comme le suggère en passant BLAUFUSS, le terme discuté soit susceptible de désigner des jeux donnés à l'occasion des Sigillaires, mais une telle coutume n'est pas attestée.

c) *Kratesis* (קרטסים)

Alors que la Mishna (I, 3) énumère ainsi les principales fêtes païennes: «Calendes, Saturnales, Kratesis . . .», la 'Tosefta' intercale entre ces deux derniers noms: יום שאחזו בו את המלכות «le jour où ils se sont emparés de l'empire». Dans le Talmud de Jérusalem (I, 2, 39c) se retrouve une mention comparable qui apparaît assez nettement comme une explication de קרטיסים puisqu'elle se place après ce mot: יום שתפסה בו רומי את המלכות «le jour où Rome s'est emparée de l'empire». Une telle définition légitime la lecture *Kratesis* à partir de la transcription hébraïque, קרטסים[161] puisqu'en effet le mot grec κράτησις se rattache à la racine de κρατέω 'dominer'. Ce terme, inconnu de plusieurs dictionnaires au point que KRAUSS le marque d'un astérisque comme ne se trouvant nulle part ailleurs que dans la littérature rabbinique[162], n'est attesté en grec qu'à une date assez basse et ce plus particulièrement dans la littérature judéo-hellénistique. La Sagesse de Salomon (6. 3) en fournit un exemple qui définit parfaitement son sens: Ὅτι ἐδόθη παρὰ τοῦ κυρίου ἡ κράτησις ὑμῖν καὶ ἡ δυναστεία παρὰ τοῦ ὑψίστου. «Le terme de κράτησις mis en parallèle avec δυνάστεια y a clairement la valeur de 'puissance'.» Dans le passage de Manéthos cité par Flavius Josèphe (Contre Apion I, 26. 248), le mot se retrouve avec le sens de 'domination', mais n'a là encore que valeur de nom commun.

Quelques témoignages papyrologiques connus depuis la fin du siècle dernier apportent un éclairage de première importance sur l'utilisation de ce terme dans nos sources talmudiques. Les papyri égyptiens du Ier siècle sont en effet assez souvent datés suivant τῆς Καίσαρος κρατήσεως[163]. Comme l'a montré WILCKEN[164], il s'agit de l'entrée d'Auguste à Alexandrie, le 1er

[161] C'est ce que lit LEWY dans Philologus LII (1894), p. 733 et tous les autres après lui. L'apparente terminaison de pluriel n'est qu'une erreur de graphie provenant d'une confusion entre les lettres ם et ס dont le tracé est très proche; on connaît d'autres exemples de ce phénomène en hébreu michnique, le plus courant étant לסטים du grec λῃστής 'voleur', qui, en raison de sa transcription erronée est devenu en hébreu un pluriel dépourvu de singulier. C'est pourquoi nous renonçons à la suggestion de BLAUFUSS qui tente de justifier le pluriel par le grand nombre de fêtes instituées pour commémorer les succès du principat ou l'accession au pouvoir des divers empereurs (Feste, § 7).

[162] Cf. Lehnwörter, p. 568 et 667.

[163] Cf. Dict. LIDDELL-SCOTT, réf. à Berliner griechische Urkunden (Ägyptische Urkunden aus den Königlichen Museen zu Berlin), Berlin 1895, p. 174, et GRENFELL, HUNT, HOGARTH, Fayum Towns and their Papyri, Londres 1900, n°. 89.

[164] Cité par LIEBERMAN, Greek in Jewish Palestine, p. 10.

août 30, jour déclaré férié par décret sénatorial et devenu depuis le point de départ d'une nouvelle ère, ainsi que l'atteste Dion Cassius (LI, 19. 6): τήν τε ἡμέραν ἐν ᾗ ἡ 'Αλεξάνδρεια ἑάλω ἀγαθήν τε εἶναι καὶ ἐς τὰ ἔπειτα ἔτη ἀρχὴν τῆς ἀπαριθμήσεως αὐτῶν νομίζεσθαι.

Cette ère n'est autre que l'ère dite actienne[165] qui était assez répandue en Méditerranée orientale. A deux reprises au moins, Flavius Josèphe utilise une telle datation: «après la première Actiade»: μετὰ τὴν πρώτην 'Ακτιάδα (B.J. I, 20. 4) et «la trente-septième année après la défaite d'Antoine par César à Actium» (A.J. XVIII, 2. 1). Son témoignage a le mérite de nous montrer que l'ère actienne était en usage en Palestine.

On conçoit dans ces conditions que la *Kratésis* ait pu être une fête importante dans la région.

Une deuxième définition dérivée de papyri égyptiens du IIIème siècle, nous est proposée par le dictionnaire de LIDDELL et SCOTT, selon laquelle κράτησις désignerait l'accession au pouvoir d'un empereur. Si la formule de la Tosefta (II, 4) יום שאחזו בו מלכות doit s'interpréter comme une explication, elle corrobore cette définition. C'est l'opinion de BLAUFUSS lequel en vient à la suite de KRAUSS[166] à conclure que le terme קרטסים se réfère au *dies imperii* ou *natalis imperii* qui était célébré le 16 avril pour le principat en général ainsi que pour chaque empereur en particulier; et, comme il lit un pluriel, il suggère que le 16 avril était un *natalis imperii* pour chaque empereur ou que chaque empereur célébrait son accession à une date différente „*oder so, daß unter verschiedenen Regierungen verschiedene Tage gefeiert wurden*[167]". Des monnaies déjà signalées par LEWY[168], le confirment dans son interprétation: sur ces monnaies datant des règnes de Galba et d'Othon, la κράτησις est représentée sous la figure d'une femme portant un trophée et une victoire. Nous lui objecterons pour notre part que ce fait n'exclut pas la précédente explication de κράτησις qui nous paraît mieux fondée.

L'explication donnée dans le Talmud de Jérusalem (I, 2, 39c) et reprise dans celui de Babylone (8b): יום שתפשה בו רומי מלכות «le jour où Rome s'est emparée de l'empire» nous paraît aller dans le sens de la première interprétation de κράτησις. La 'Gemara' babylonienne (ibid.) pour autant qu'elle puisse faire autorité en ce qui concerne la Palestine, reproduit avec insistance une tradition rattachant la *Kratesis* à une victoire des Romains sur les Grecs et précise même à une occasion: בימי קלפאטרא מלכתא «du temps de la reine Cléopâtre».

Toutefois, une *baraïta* reproduite par elle distingue la *Kratesis* et «le jour où Rome s'est emparée de l'empire». Cette formulation différente de celle de la 'Tosefta' qui présentait un pluriel sans sujet אחזו, nous oblige-

165 La bataille d'Actium (—31) a permis l'entrée d'Octave à Alexandrie quelques mois plus tard et l'élimination de son rival Antoine.

166 Talmudische Archäologie III, p. 124.

167 Feste § 7, p. 14.

168 Art. cité, p. 733.

rait à envisager pour *Kratesis* un sens autre auquel pourrait convenir la seconde interprétation (accession au pouvoir d'un empereur).

Le cas de *Kratesis* n'est donc pas pleinement élucidé. Le Talmud aura du moins eu le mérite d'attirer notre attention sur ce terme grec mal connu, et de suggérer deux interprétations parallèles[169] à celles des témoignages papyrologiques. Si l'on favorise la première, cela signifierait qu'au IIème siècle encore, l'Orient romanisé fêtait avec éclat le début de l'ère actienne qu'il suivait[170]. Si l'on penche pour la seconde, on fait de κράτησις l'équivalent grec du *dies imperii*.

d) *Genosia* (גנוסיא) des empereurs

La Mishna (I, 3) poursuit ainsi la liste des fêtes païennes:

יום גנוסיא של המלכים ויום הלידה ויום המיתה דברי ר׳ מאיר.

«Le jour de la *genosia* des empereurs et le jour de la naissance et le jour de la mort, selon R. Méir.»

Quant à la Tosefta (I, 4) elle se contente d'ajouter à la *genosia* des empereurs, יום של כל מלך ומלך «le jour de chaque empereur en particulier», sans que là encore, la valeur de cette expression — explication ou suite de l'énumération? — soit claire.

Sous la transcription hébraïque, on s'accorde à reconnaître le mot grec γενέσια. Cet adjectif substantivé pris au neutre, τὰ γενέσια, désigne en grec classique le jour commémorant la naissance d'un défunt, par la suite en grec tardif il se confond avec τὰ γενέθλια 'fête d'anniversaire', et le féminin ἡ γενεσία (ἡμέρα s. e.) s'utilise avec la même valeur que ἡ γενεθλία 'jour anniversaire'; son correspondant latin est *natalis* (*dies* s. e.). Dans l'expression יום גנוסיא l'hébreu se contente donc de traduire 'jour', en laissant tel quel le terme plus technique.

De fait, l'anniversaire des empereurs occupait une place importante dans le calendrier romain, en rapport avec le culte du souverain ou de son *genius*, depuis qu'Auguste avait accepté en —8 d'instituer le sien (le 23 septembre) comme fête régulière[171], accompagnée de jeux de cirque et d'un banquet public. Pour ceux des empereurs qui ne se couvrirent pas d'opprobre, on continua de commémorer leur anniversaire, même après leur mort.

Selon le Talmud de Jérusalem, c'est bien d'anniversaire de naissance qu'il s'agit puisque la *genosia* est reliée à Gen. 40. 20: ויהי ביום השלישי יום

169 Un tout autre sens de κράτησις est discuté par LIEBERMAN, Greek . . ., p. 10—12.

170 Sous Auguste, le 1er août date de son entrée à Alexandrie était la principale fête impériale (cf. L. R. TAYLOR, The Divinity of the Roman Emperor, Middletown 1931, p. 195), aussi bien n'avait-il pas donné le nom d'Augustus au mois de son anniversaire (septembre), mais au 6ème mois Sextilis, où il avait obtenu son premier consulat et vaincu Antoine en 30 (Suétone, Auguste 31). Il est possible que cette fête ait continué d'être célébrée en Orient après Auguste alors qu'elle était éclipsée par d'autres à Rome.

171 Cf. L. R. TAYLOR, op. cit., p. 194.

הלדת את פרעה «le troisième jour, jour de la naissance de Pharaon»; quant au Talmud de Babylone (10a), il interprète גנוסיא comme le jour de l'intronisation des rois chez les païens יום שמעמידים בו עובדי כוכבים את מלכם. Cette interprétation a retenu l'attention de quelques-uns[172] qui rappellent que le jour de l'avènement des empereurs était appelé précisément *dies natalis imperii*, mais ici le témoignage de l'*amora* babylonien nous paraît d'autant plus sujet à caution qu'il est immédiatement suivi d'une *baraïta* où *genosia* et avènement sont distinguées:

והתניא יום גנוסיא ויום שמעמידין בו את מלכם.

La partie de cette *baraïta* concernant l'avènement des empereurs peut être mise en relation avec l'indication de la 'Tosefta' יום שלכל מלך ומלך «le jour de chaque roi», encore que celle-ci soit assez peut explicite.

Une autre difficulté qui n'a pas manqué d'être soulevée dans la 'Gemara' babylonienne provient de la coordination «*genosia* et jour de naissance» dans la 'Mishna'. Pour bien comprendre le texte, il nous paraît important de ne pas couper ce qui suit le terme גנוסיא: «jour de naissance et jour de mort, selon R. Meir. Les sages disent: 'chaque mort accompagnée d'incinération comporte de l'idolâtrie; s'il n'y a pas incinération, il n'y a pas idolâtrie'», puis intervient de manière indubitable une liste de fêtes privées. Rien n'indique en effet qu'il s'agisse de la naissance ou de la mort d'un empereur, il est donc fort possible que les anniversaires en question soient déjà du domaine des fêtes privées; il était en effet de coutume de célébrer les anniversaires de naissance ou de mort[173]. Le Talmud de Jérusalem (I, 2, 39c) nous confirme dans cette impression en commentant:

יום הלידה ויום המיתה עד כאן לצבור מכאן ואילך ליחיד.

«jour de naissance et jour de mort, jusqu'ici il s'agissait de fêtes publiques, à partir d'ici et pour la suite cela concerne les particuliers».

S'agirait-il encore des fêtes impériales, que l'on concevrait fort bien que R. Meir ait jugé bon d'apporter la précision suivante à la suite de la mention de *genosia*, «aussi bien l'anniversaire de la naissance (des empereurs) que celui de leur mort».

e) Apothéose?

La crémation considérée par les sages comme un rite idolâtre, peut également être rapportée soit aux simples particuliers soit aux empereurs. L'on peut être fort tenté notamment d'y voir une allusion à l'apothéose dont la coutume commence à se dessiner dès la mort de César[174] et qui est

[172] Cf. LEWY, art. cité, p. 733—734.

[173] Outre les *parentalia* générales qui se célébraient du 13 au 21 février, il y en avait de particulières à chaque famille dont la date variait suivant les anniversaires et qui comportaient un repas funéraire, cf. MARQUARDT, Culte I, p. 373—374.

[174] Suétone, César 84; Auguste 100; Claude 45.

définitivement institutionnalisée à la fin du 1er siècle à partir de Nerva en même temps que s'accentue la pompe de la cérémonie.

Cette interprétation soutenue successivement par Lewy[175], Blaufuss[176] et Elmslie[177], nous laisse pour notre part fort sceptique. Voudrait-on dire qu'il n'y a pas idolâtrie si l'on commémore la disparition d'un empereur qui n'aurait pas été inciné sur le Champ de Mars avec toute la pompe en usage et, de ce fait, n'aurait pas été proclamé *divus* par le Sénat, après qu'on eut vu s'envoler un aigle portant son âme au ciel[178]. Dans ces conditions, on aurait donc le droit de célébrer l'anniversaire de la mort de Caligula, Néron, Galba, Othon, Vitellius qui n'ont pas été divinisés, mais non celui de la mort de César lors de laquelle, nous dit Suétone[179], «les colonies étrangères prirent le deuil séparément, chacune à sa manière, tout spécialement les Juifs qui allèrent jusqu'à se réunir plusieurs nuits de suite autour de son tombeau».

A ce raisonnement par l'absurde, s'ajoute un autre argument qui n'a pas été jusqu'ici pris en considération, même par Krauss[180] qui pourtant suit de près les sources talmudiques. Il naît de la simple confrontation de notre texte avec un passage de la 'Tosefta' du traité Shabbat ch. VII qui a échappé à l'attention des précédents commentateurs:

שורפין על המלכים ולא מדרכי האמורי שנאמר בשלום תמות ובמשרפות אבותיך הראש׳ וגו׳ וכשם ששורפין על המלכים כן שורפין על הנשיאין אבל לא על הדיוטות מה הן שורפין שורפין עליו מטתו וכל כלי תשמישתו מעשה כשמת רבן גמליאל הזקן ושרף עליו אונקלוס הגר יותר משבעים מנה.

«On fait brûler pour les rois sans que cela soit une coutume amorite, car il est dit (Jer. 34. 5): 'Tu mourras en paix et à l'instar des combustions faites pour tes pères les rois précédents, etc. . . .' et de même que l'on fait brûler pour les rois, on fait brûler pour les patriarches mais cela ne se fait pas pour de simples particuliers. Que fait-on brûler ? Le lit du mort et tous ses effets personnels. On raconte que lorsque mourut Rabban Gamaliel l'Ancien, le prosélyte Onqelos[181] brûla pour lui plus de 70 maneh».

Ce passage est un document important sur les coutumes funéraires locales qui éclaire et corrobore le témoignage du Talmud de Jérusalem (I, 2, 39c) où la même citation de Jérémie est utilisée. Il fait nettement apparaître qu'il ne s'agit pas de crémation du cadavre: l'inhumation était en effet le seul rite admis par les Juifs[182] et le rite funéraire le plus répandu

175 Art. cité, p. 734.
176 Feste § 9, p. 20s.
177 Op. cit., Excursus 2 au ch. I.
178 Cf. Dion, LVI, 42, 3.
179 César 84.
180 Archäologie III, p. 125.
181 Ce dernier est en vérité contemporain de R. Gamaliel II.
182 Le Chroniste racontant la mort de Saül et de ses fils (I Chr. 10. 12) modifie le récit de I Sam. 31. 12 où il était question d'incinération et dit ויקברו את עצמותיהם.

dans le reste de l'empire romain, elle avait à cette époque supplanté largement l'incinération même à Rome[183]. L'interdiction vise uniquement la coutume consistant à faire brûler les objets du mort[184], coutume strictement limitée par les rabbins aux personnages de premier rang, rois ou patriarches, en vertu du verset de Jérémie cité par eux. Pour le reste, elle est considérée comme coutume idolâtre, suivant les termes de notre 'Mishna'.

f) Jeux séculaires

TB A.Z. 11b:

אמ׳ רג יהוד׳ אמ׳ שמואל עוד אחרת יש ברומי אתת לשבעים שנה [...] ומכריזין [...] דחמי חמי ודלא חמי לא חמי...

«Rab Judah dit au nom de Samuel: 'Il est encore une autre fête qui se célèbre à Rome une fois tous les soixante-dix ans' [...] Un héraut crie [...] 'Celui qui a vu cette fête l'a vue, celui qui ne l'a pas vue, ne la verra plus'.»

Soixante-dix ans, c'était environ sous l'empire, la périodicité des *Ludi Saeculares* que semble bien évoquer ici la 'Gemara' babylonienne[185], Aux jeux célébrés avec éclat par Auguste en —17 (an 737 de la fondation de Rome) et pour lesquels Horace avait composé son 'Carmen saeculare', avaient succédé en +47 les jeux donnés par Claude, en 88 ceux de Domitien, en 147 ceux d'Antonin le Pieux, en 204 ceux de Septime Sévère[186]. La 'Gemara' se réfère sans doute à des jeux contemporains de Samuel: ceux qui en 248, sous le règne de Philippe, accompagnèrent la célébration du millième anniversaire de la fondation de Rome[187]. La formule qu'elle attribue au héraut est en tout cas très exactement celle qui était utilisée à l'occasion des jeux séculaires[188].

A défaut de la trouver dans la 'Mishna', il est fort probable que nous possédions une mention de cette fête dans la Tosefta (II, 5—6, p. 462):

העולה לתריטיאות של גוים אסור משום עבודה זרה דברי ר׳ מאיר וחכמ׳ אומ׳ בזמן שמזבחין אסור משום עבודה זרה אם אינם מזבחין אסור משום מושב ליצים. ההולך לאיצטרטיונין ולכרקומין ורואה את הנחשים את החברין בוקיון ומוקיון מוליון סגלריון סגלריא הרי זה מושב לצים...

[183] Cf. F. Cumont, Lux perpetua, Paris 1949, p. 390, et R. Turcan, Origines et sens de l'inhumation à l'époque impériale, REA LX (1958), p. 323—347.

[184] Cf. S. Lieberman, Tosefta Kifshutah III, traité Shabbat, p. 100.

[185] Cf. S. Lieberman, Texts and Studies, p. 162s. art. cité repris de JQR XXXVI (1946). Bien que cette tradition nous vienne de Babylonie, il faut rappeler que Samuel avait vécu en Palestine.

[186] Cf. Blaufuss, Feste § 15, p. 30—31; Dar.-Saglio IV, 2, s. v. ludi saeculares.

[187] Lieberman, ibid., p. 163.

[188] Cp. Suét., Claude 21: *vox praeconis invitantis more sollemni ad ludos quos nec spectasset quisquam nec spectaturus esset*, et Acta augustéens dans: Ephemeris epigraphica VIII, 1., 54—56. Voir Blaufuss, Feste, p. 31, n. 1; Lieberman, Greek, p. 145, n. 7.

«Se rendre au théâtre des païens est interdit pour cause d'idolâtrie, tel est l'avis de R. Méir. Les sages disent: 'lorsqu'on y fait des sacrifices, c'est interdit pour cause d'idolâtrie, sinon cela relève de l'interdit concernant la compagnie des fols' (Ps. I, 1).
Se rendre au stade ou au cirque pour y voir les devins et les magiciens, Bouqion, Moqion, Molion, Seglarion et Seglaria, c'est entrer dans 'la compagnie des fols'[189].»

L'énumération du § 6 (et ses parallèles: TJ A.Z. I, 7 et TB ibid. 18b) a donné lieu à de nombreuses interprétations[190] dont aucune toutefois ne comporte un degré de certitude suffisant. Parmi celles-ci le rapprochement opéré déjà par Perles[191] entre 'Seglarion, Seglaria' et les *Ludi Saeculares* nous paraît tout à fait plausible.

Ces solennités étaient marquées pendant trois jours et trois nuits par des représentations théâtrales et des jeux de cirque précédés de sacrifices (cp. Tos. II, 5), le premier jour étant consacré à Jupiter, le second à Junon et le troisième à Apollon[192].

La mention dans la Tosefta (II, 6) de devins et de magiciens dont s'étonne Blaufuss[193] correspond à un trait bien connu de l'époque impériale où les lieux de spectacles étaient devenus le rendez-vous de tous les diseurs de bonne aventure que le petit peuple venait consulter là[194].

Dans le passage parallèle de A.Z. 18b, l'énumération comporte également le terme de לולין que Blaufuss[195] propose avec raison nous semble-t-il de lire *ludio*, c'est-à-dire acteur. Il est maintenant établi que le personnage à tunique relevée, coiffé d'un casque à crinière, portant un petit bouclier rond au bras gauche et dans la main droite une lance courte, apparaissant sur les monnaies commémoratives des jeux d'Auguste, n'est pas un Salien, mais «le ludion traditionnel des plus vieux jeux romains»[196]. Les *ludiones* sont donc liés aux jeux séculaires.

Dans la 'Gemara' palestinienne (TJ I, 7 40a) apparaissent en outre les mots מלריא, מלרין sous lesquels nous proposons de reconnaître *miliarium, miliaria*. Les monnaies commémoratives du millième anniversaire de la fondation de Rome portent en effet la mention *miliarium saeculum*: siècle de mille années[197]. Si notre 'Tosefta' fait véritablement allusion aux jeux du millénaire célébrés en +248, il se confirme que sa mise au point définitive n'est pas antérieure au milieu du IIIème siècle.

Les *feriae conceptivae* absentes de la 'Mishna', se retrouvent donc en TB et dans la 'Tosefta' sous la forme des jeux séculaires et probablement

189 Sur l'attitude des Juifs vis-à-vis des spectacles, cf. Elmslie, op. cit. p. 26—27.
190 Cf. Krauss, Arch. III, 120, Blaufuss, Feste §§ 11—17.
191 Cit. ap. Blaufuss, ibid. p. 25.
192 Cf. J. Gagé, Recherches sur les jeux séculaires, Paris 1934, p. 47s.
193 Feste § 12, p. 26.
194 Marquardt, Le Culte chez les Romains I, p. 124.
195 Feste p. 28.
196 Gagé, op. cit., p. 66.
197 Ibid. p. 89.

aussi des jeux du millénaire, dont il était impossible de ne pas entendre parler d'un bout à l'autre de l'empire romain, quand bien même on se refusait de prendre part aux fêtes païennes.

2. Fêtes privées

— jour où un païen se rase la barbe et les cheveux;
— retour d'un voyage en mer
— sortie de prison
— banquet pour son fils
— banquet nuptial
— entrée en charge
— fin d'une maladie

Ces fêtes énumérées respectivement par la 'Mishna' et la 'Tosefta', concernent les simples particuliers et non plus les empereurs, contrairement à l'avis de BLAUFUSS[198] qui nous paraît ici insoutenable. S'il en était autrement la 'Mishna' ne conclurait pas l'énumération par «l'interdiction ne frappe que ce jour et cet homme en particulier».

a) Offrande de la barbe et des cheveux

Notre texte fait de toute évidence allusion à une circonstance solennelle où les païens se coupaient la barbe ou les cheveux, accomplissant ainsi un rite religieux.

L'offrande des cheveux, ainsi que l'avait déjà noté WIESELER[199] il y a plus d'un siècle, est une coutume répandue chez plusieurs peuples de l'Antiquité: Egyptiens, Grecs, Romains, auxquels il faut ajouter les Sémites.

Pour nous en tenir à la période considérée, Lucien atteste que de son temps, les jeunes Egyptiens de condition libre gardaient leurs cheveux longs jusqu'a l'âge de l'éphébie: τοῦτο μὲν εὐγενείας σημεῖόν ἐστιν Αἰγυπτίοις ἡ κόμη· ἅπαντες γὰρ αὐτὴν οἱ ἐλεύθεροι παῖδες ἀναπλέκονται ἔστε πρὸς τὸ ἐφηβικόν (Navig., 3). La chevelure faisait ensuite l'objet d'une offrande. Le même Lucien atteste qu'à Trézène en Grèce, il était interdit de se marier avant d'avoir consacré ses boucles à Hippolyte et constate à Hiérapolis une coutume analogue qu'il a lui-même suivie dans sa jeunesse (Dea, 60). Selon Plutarque (Thésée, 4) c'était une vieille coutume que d'offrir les prémices de sa chevelure à Delphes. Cette coutume est d'ailleurs attestée un peu partout dans le monde hellénistique[200]. Elle est parallèle à un usage sémitique ancien qui était sans doute perpétué à Hiérapolis et selon lequel la chevelure de

[198] Feste § 10, p. 23. Son erreur provient d'une mauvaise interprétation de la 'Tosefta' הרי כרבים יחיד traduit par „*Ein König hat auch als Privatperson öffentliches Interesse*"; au lieu de «il en est des fêtes publiques comme des fêtes privées». Un peu plus loin § 18, il envisage pourtant ces mêmes fêtes comme fêtes privées.

[199] Über Haaropfer, Philologus IX (1854), p. 711—715.

[200] Cf. W. ROUSE, Greek votive Offerings, p. 241—242.

l'enfant devait être sacrifiée pour que celui-ci fût admis au statut religieux et social de l'âge adulte[201].

Cependant l'accession à l'âge adulte n'était pas la seule occasion d'offrir solennellement sa chevelure. Le pèlerin de Hiérapolis devait, au témoignage de Lucien (Dea, 55), se raser la tête et les sourcils. La chevelure pouvait également faire l'objet d'une offrande funéraire ou être consacrée après un voeu: l'on voit ainsi l'apôtre Paul se faire raser la tête avant de s'embarquer pour la Syrie (Actes, 18. 18) sans doute afin d'échapper au danger.

En ce qui concerne l'offrande de la barbe, l'on pense immédiatement au rite de la *depositio barbae* bien connu chez les Romains qui l'avaient d'ailleurs emprunté aux Grecs. Les auteurs latins nous signalent l'accomplissement de cette cérémonie par les divers empereurs: Auguste la fêta à l'âge de 24 ans[202], Caligula à 19 ans, le jour où il revêtit ta toge virile[203], Néron choisit de le faire au milieu d'un concours de gymnastique, «dans la pompe d'une hécatombe» et renferma sa barbe «dans une boîte d'or enrichie de perles d'un très grand prix qu'il consacra au Capitole[204]». C'est dans une boîte analogue que l'affranchi Trimalcion conservait la sienne[205].

L'offrande de la barbe est donc spécifiquement un rite de passage à l'âge adulte. En conséquence, l'offrande de la chevelure à laquelle elle est associée doit également être interprétée dans le même sens. Tertullien signale de son côté ce type de cérémonie (Apol., 16) et ne permet au chrétien d'y assister qu'à condition de ne pas participer aux rites idolâtres auxquels il donne lieu, sans doute veut-il parler des libations d'usage.

b) Les fêtes d'actions de grâces[206]

L'on peut, nous semble-t-il, regrouper sous ce titre correspondant au grec εὐχαριστήρια la plupart des fêtes privées énumérées ensuite par la 'Mishna' ou la 'Tosefta': retour d'un voyage en mer, sortie de prison, entrée en charge, fin d'une maladie, chacune de ces circonstances étant en effet susceptible de donner lieu à des sacrifices d'actions de grâces.

Après un heureux débarquement, les Grecs procédaient à des ἐκβατήρια consistant en offrandes de miel, vin, encens, accompagnées parfois du sacrifice d'un porc[207]. Il subsiste des inscriptions commémorant d'heureux retours, certaines remerciant Asclépios, lequel était donc honoré comme

201 Cf. W. Robertson Smith, op. cit., p. 330—331.

202 Dion, XLVIII, 34, 3.

203 Suétone, Caligula 10.

204 Suétone, Néron 12.

205 Pétrone, 29 *et pyxis aurea non pusilla in qua barbam ipsius conditam esse dicebant.*

206 Les *supplicationes* ou *gratulationes* devaient à Rome célébrer les événements heureux de la vie publique ou privée des empereurs (cf. L. Halkin, La supplication d'action de grâces chez les Romains, Paris 1953) mais dans le culte privé devaient exister des supplications d'action de grâces plus ou moins spontanées. Cf. Plaute, Curculio 527: *quando bene gessi rem volo hic in fano supplicare.*

207 Yerkes, op. cit., p. 62. A Rome, on avait célébré une supplication pour le retour d'Octave en août 29, cf. Dion LI, 21, 1.

protecteur d'un péril en général[208]. C'est également lui — ou Sérapis — qui était remercié d'une guérison. Les sacrifices offerts à cette occasion — pas uniquement un coq malgré le célèbre mot de Socrate (Phédon 118 A) —, sont appelés sans doute métaphoriquement par Philostrate (Vie des Sophistes I, 12) ἐκβατήρια τῆς νόσου.

La sortie de prison était également l'occasion d'offrandes aux divinités[209]. Pausanias (II, 13, 4) raconte que les prisonniers libérés suspendaient leurs fers dans un bois sacré.

La coutume de remercier le Ciel en de telles circonstances n'est cependant pas typiquement grecque. On peut la considérer comme la réaction naturelle d'un esprit religieux. Les modalités de l'action de grâces peuvent varier d'une tradition à l'autre mais elles expriment un même fond de piété. De fait, les circonstances que l'on vient d'énumérer doivent, selon la tradition juive, également donner lieu à une célébration:

ארבעה צריכין להודות יורדי הים הולכי המדברות ומי שהיה חולה ונתרפא ומי שהיה חבוש בבית אסורים ויצא.

«En quatre circonstances on doit rendre grâces: lors d'un voyage en mer ou de la traversée d'un désert, à l'occasion d'une guérison ou de sa sortie de prison» (Ber. 54b).

Les rabbins ne récusent donc pas le principe de l'action de grâces, loin de là; ils demandent seulement à leurs fidèles de ne pas favoriser la célébration des rites païens en ces occasions.

Dans la 'Tosefta', nous avons interprété יום שנעשה בו שלטון[210] comme se référant à l'entrée en charge d'un magistrat qui donnait également lieu à des sacrifices[211] et à ce titre était donc une cérémonie prohibée.

c) Le banquet

Dans la 'Tosefta', le terme de 'banquet' peut paraître particulièrement vague, s'agissant d'une société où les occasions de banqueter ne manquaient pas. Du moins est-il clair qu'il ne s'agit pas d'un *epulum publicum* du type de ceux qui accompagnaient les grandes fêtes de l'empire, mais d'un banquet privé.

Dans la Bible, le terme de משתה est utilisé avec une valeur très large et l'on voit entre autres Abraham donner un banquet le jour du sevrage d'Isaac (Gen. 21. 8). Dans la littérature talmudique en revanche, le terme se spécialise au sens de 'banquet nuptial': בית המשתה (Ber. I, 1) désigne la maison de la noce, שבעה ימי המשתה la semaine qui suit le mariage (Ket. 4a). C'est

[208] Cf. ROUSE, op. cit., p. 229—230.
[209] Ibid., p. 233.
[210] Cette expression a conduit BLAUFUSS (Feste, § 10, p. 23) à rattacher à l'empereur les paroles de la 'Tosefta', mais ainsi que nous l'avons vu plus haut, il est clair qu'il ne s'agit plus dans ce passage, de fêtes publiques.
[211] Cf. DAR.-SAGL. III, 2, p. 1534 s. v. magistrats.

d'ailleurs clairement au sens de 'banquet nuptial' que la 'Gemara' palestinienne comprend le משתה de notre 'Mishna'.

Alors que dans la 'Tosefta', il s'agit du propre banquet nuptial du païen considéré: משתה שלו, la 'Mishna' nous parle du banquet donné pour son fils: משתה לבנו. Ce faisant, elle nous découvre un trait de civilisation fort intéressant: les frais de la noce étaient donc à la charge de la famille du jeune homme et non de celle de la jeune épousée.

Or, il semble bien que chez les Grecs[212], comme chez les Romains[213], le banquet nuptial (θοίνη γαμική, *cena*) se tenait en règle générale chez le père de la fiancée. Cependant, on trouve quelques exemples de repas faits dans la maison du père du fiancé[214]. Nos textes supposent la généralisation d'une telle coutume[215], du moins dans cette partie de l'empire. Quoi qu'il en soit, ils n'ignorent pas que ce banquet ne se limitait pas à une simple réjouissance familiale mais qu'il était placé sous le signe de l'idolâtrie. Le repas était en effet toujours précédé d'un sacrifice aux divinités du mariage. Ce que FUSTEL DE COULANGES[216] a dit du Romain est en vérité valable à bien des égards pour l'homme antique en général: «Sa maison est pour lui, ce qu'est pour nous un temple: il y trouve son culte et ses dieux. Chacune de ses actions de chaque jour est un rite; toute sa journée appartient à la religion. Le matin et le soir, il invoque son foyer, ses pénates, ses ancêtres; en sortant de sa maison, en y entrant, il leur adresse une prière. Chaque repas est un acte religieux qu'il partage avec ses divinités domestiques. La naissance, l'initiation, la prise de la toge, le mariage et les anniversaires de tous ces événements, sont les actes solennels de son culte.»

III. Rites

A côté des pratiques à proprement parler religieuses, se rencontrent chez tous les peuples un certain nombre de coutumes qui révèlent la persistance d'une mentalité magique. Quelques-unes de ces coutumes en vigueur dans le pays de la fin du Ier siècle au début du IIIème siècle, se trouvent regroupées dans la 'Tosefta' du traité Shabbat ch. VI et VII sous l'appellation — méprisante, est-il besoin de le préciser — de 'coutumes amorites'. Pour ce qui est des rites religieux en revanche, nous ne disposons

212 Voir la description d'un repas nuptial chez Lucien, Conviv. 8.
213 Cf. Macrobe, Sat. I, 15, 22, Sénèque, Controv. 7. 21.
214 Plaute, Curc. 728, Aul. 262; Cicéron, Ad. Quint. 2, 3, 7; Juvénal, Sat. VI, 202. Voir MARQUARDT, La vie privée des Romains I, p. 62—63.
215 Tel semble être en particulier l'usage juif d'alors puisque le Talmud (Shab. 67b = Tos. ibid. VII, 9) nous parle du banquet donné par R. Aqiba pour son fils, banquet au cours duquel d'ailleurs il ne manqua pas de lever son verre à la santé de ses maîtres et de ses disciples.
216 La Cité antique, Paris 1903[18], p. 254.

d'aucune liste groupée et d'aucune description détaillée. Ajoutons à cette difficulté le fait qu'une pratique à valeur religieuse pour les adeptes de tel culte est fort aisément interprétable en termes de superstition par un observateur étranger.

Bien qu'en règle générale, les rites païens ne soient point décrits, on peut toutefois essayer de les reconstituer grâce à certains interdits énumérés dans le Talmud et qui, de toute évidence, s'y réfèrent. Il s'agit principalement des produits interdits ou réglementés à la vente (M. A.Z. I, 5; Tos. I, 21); pour la plupart des produits interdits à l'achat, l'interdiction se justifie en effet par le contact réel ou probable de ces produits avec du vin dit 'de libation'.

1. Les rites sacrificiels

a) Le choix de la bête

M. I, 5:

ובזמן שהוא בפני עצמו קוטע את אצבעו ומוכרו לו לפי שאין מקריבין חסר לעבודה זרה.

. . . «Lorsque [le coq] est vendu séparément, il faut lui couper un ergot avant de le vendre car l'on ne sacrifie pas d'animal défectueux dans une cérémonie païenne.»

Ibid. I, 6:

ובכל מקום אין מוכרין להם בהמה גסה עגלים וסיחים שלמים ושבורים. רבי יהודה מתיר בשבורה. . .

«Qu'en tout lieu, on ne leur vende pas de gros bétail, de veaux et de poulains, intacts ou non. R. Judah permet les bêtes estropiées . . .»

Tos. II, 1:

מוכר ישר׳ בהמתו לגוי על מנת לשחוט.

«Un Israélite peut vendre à un païen une bête de boucherie.»

Ibid. II, 3:

אין מחליפין להם לא רעים ביפים ולא יפים ברעים לא שבורים בשלימים ולא שלימים בשבורין ר׳ יהודה מתיר בשבורה שאינה יכולה להתרפות.

«On ne doit pas échanger ni laid contre beau ni beau contre laid, ni estropié contre intact ni intact contre estropié. R. Judah permet les bêtes estropiées et inguérissables.»

De la confrontation de ces diverses règlementations il ressort clairement qu'elles visent à empêcher qu'un Juif, volontairement ou non, fournisse à des païens un animal susceptible d'être offert en sacrifice sur l'autel d'une divinité païenne. Le coq mutilé, l'animal estropié ne pourraient en effet subir avec succès l'examen (*probatio*) qui précède normalement tout sacrifice.

L'animal offert en sacrifice à une divinité se doit en effet d'être intact et bien constitué. Pour les Romains, il doit être *purus*[217] et *pulcher*[218] pour les Grecs ἐντελές[219] de même que pour les Juifs, il doit être מובחר 'de premier choix'[220]. Au nombre des défauts qui, selon la Bible (Lev. 22. 21—24; Deut. 15. 21), rendent la bête impropre au sacrifice, viennent à l'époque tannaïtique s'en ajouter d'autres conformément aux prescriptions sacrificielles grecques ou romaines: comment ce qui est jugé impropre pour la table d'une idole serait-il bon pour le culte au Temple[221]? L'on voit ainsi les rabbins requérir exactement comme cela se faisait à Rome[222] que la queue d'un veau destiné au sacrifice atteigne au moins l'articulation de la jambe (Tos. Bekh. IV, 14 et TB ibid. 41a). Cela laisse entendre qu'ils avaient observé sur place les habitudes sacrificielles des païens.

b) La consécration de la victime[223]

Tos. V, 10 (cf. Tos. Tem. IV, 3; TB AZ 44b):

אמר שור זה לעבודה זרה בית זה לעבודה זרה לא אמר כלום לפי שאין הקדש לעבודה זרה.

«Si l'on dit: 'ce bœuf est pour l'idolâtrie, cette maison est pour l'idolâtrie', c'est comme si l'on n'avait rien dit car il n'y a pas de consécration à l'idolâtrie.»

Ibid. 9:

מאמתי נקרא מוקצה משנעשה בו מעשה.

«A partir de quand dit-on de l'animal qu'il est 'réservé'? C'est à partir du moment où l'on a accompli sur lui un rite.»

Selon notre 'Tosefta', la consécration purement verbale à une idole est donc sans valeur aux yeux des rabbins; la victime préalablement soumise à examen, n'est consacrée qu'après l'accomplissement de certains rites. Quels sont donc ces rites? Au terme d'une discussion rabbinique (Tem. 29a), est avancée l'opinion de l'*amora* palestinien du IIIème siècle R. Johanan selon laquelle la consécration est déclarée effective lorsque l'animal est tondu et reçoit des marques de vénération: עד שיגזז ויעבדו בו. L'on reconnaît

217 Cf. G. Wissowa, Religion und Kultus der Römer, p. 351 et note 3.

218 Cf. R. Schilling, The Roman Religion, dans: Historia Religionum I, Leyde 1970, p. 470. passim.

219 Cf. Lucien, De Sacrificiis 12: πρότερον ἐξετάσαντες εἰ ἐντελὲς εἴη.

220 Cf. S. Lieberman, Hellenism . . ., p. 153.

221 Ibid. p. 155.

222 Pline, H.N. VIII, 183 *victimarum probatio in vitulo ut articulum suffraginis contingat: breviore non litant.*

223 Ce point est discuté dans un chapitre spécial par S. Lieberman, Hellenism . . ., p. 147—152.

dans cette brève description un aspect du rituel grec du sacrifice: au cours de l'étape préparatoire, on avait en effet coutume de prélever des poils de la bête et de les jeter au feu[224].

Une autre forme de consécration se trouve décrite dans la 'Gemara' babylonienne de notre traité (A.Z. 54a) par R. Hizqia, contemporain de R. Johanan: כגון שניסך לעבודת כוכבים יין על קרניה. Ainsi que l'a déjà noté Lieberman[225] l'expression hébraïque suit de près ici l'expression latine habituelle: *vinum fundit inter cornua*. Cette libation présacrificielle est en effet un trait bien connu du rite romain[226]. Dès le moment où elle a été effectuée, la victime devient *sacra*. Cette cérémonie qui se passe au temple, n'est pas obligatoirement suivie sur le champ, du sacrifice; ainsi, à Hiérapolis, au témoignage de Lucien (Dea, 57), une fois la libation accomplie, l'animal était ramené pour le sacrifice dans la maison de celui qui l'offrait.

Pour ce qui est des rites sacrificiels païens, certains aspects du culte grec et du culte romain subsistent donc sur cette terre marquée par des influences des dominateurs successifs. A vrai dire, même à Rome les sacrifices peuvent se faire à cette époque *ritu Graeco* ou *ritu Romano*[227].

c) Le sacrifice. Problèmes posés par l'expression עורות לבובין (M. A.Z. II, 3; Tos. ib. IV, 7)

Dans une des listes de produits interdits à la fois à la consommation et au profit, la Mishna (II, 3) cite עורות לביבין. Cette expression énigmatique se trouve expliquée ex abrupto dans la Tosefta (IV, 7) qui donc suppose ici connu le texte de la 'Mishna':

ואילו הן עורות לבובין כל שנקוב כנגד לבו ועשוי כמין ארובה אבל אם היה משוך מותר.

«Quelles sont les peaux dites *levuvin*? Toutes celles qui sont percées à l'endroit du cœur et où est pratiquée une sorte de lucarne, mais s'il y a une fente, c'est permis.»

La dernière partie de ce paragraphe rejoint la suite de la 'Mishna' déjà citée:

רבן שמעון בן גמליאל אומר בזמן שהקרע שלו עגל אסור משוך מתר.

«Rabban Siméon ben Gamaliel dit: 'Lorsque la déchirure est circulaire, c'est interdit, lorsqu'elle se présente comme une fente, c'est permis'.»

Le Talmud de Jérusalem (II, 3, 41a) ajoute de son côté la précision suivante:

[224] Cf. R. Yerkes, Sacrifice in Greek and Roman Religions and Early Judaism, New York 1952, p. 99.
[225] Op. cit. p. 151.
[226] Cicéron, De Divinatione II, 16, 37.
[227] Cf. J. Marquardt, Culte . . . I, p. 223, 226.

כיצד היו עוש׳ קורעה עד שה׳ בחיי׳ ומוצי׳ לבה לעבודה זרה כיצד הוא יודע רבי חונא אמר בשעה שקורעה עד שהוא בחיים הוא נסלל ונעגל לאחר שחיטה הוא נמשך.

«Comment font-ils? Ils déchirent la peau de l'animal encore en vie et extraient son cœur pour l'offrir à l'idole. Comment le sait-on? R. Huna dit: 'si la peau a été déchirée tant que l'animal est encore en vie, l'ouverture se plisse et s'arrondit; si elle l'a été après l'immolation, l'ouverture est une fente'.»

Un des seuls textes grecs qui, selon le dictionnaire de LIDDELL et SCOTT, contienne le verbe καρδιουλκεῖν 'arracher le cœur' est un passage d'un contemporain, Lucien (Sacrif. 13), décrivant un sacrifice:

ὁ δὲ ἱερεὺς αὐτὸς ἕστηκεν ἡμαγμένος καὶ ὥσπερ ὁ Κύκλωψ ἐκεῖνος ἀνατέμνων καὶ τὰ ἔγκατα ἐξαιρῶν καὶ καρδιουλκῶν καὶ τὸ αἷμα τῷ βωμῷ περιχέων καὶ τί γὰρ οὐκ εὐσεβὲς ἐπιτελῶν; ἐπὶ πᾶσι δὲ πῦρ ἀνακαύσας ἐπέθηκε φέρων αὐτῇ δορᾷ τὴν αἶγα καὶ αὐτοῖς ἐρίοις τὸ πρόβατον.

«Le prêtre se tient là tout couvert de sang comme jadis le Cyclope, découpant la victime, retirant les entrailles, arrachant le cœur, versant le sang sur l'autel et accomplissant tous les actes de piété possibles. Pour couronner le tout, il allume un feu et y dépose la chèvre avec sa peau et le mouton avec sa peau.»

Cette opération n'intervient pas du tout avant la mort de l'animal comme le suggèrent nos textes talmudiques. Elle fait partie de la *porrectio* des *exta*. Le cœur est en effet retiré en même temps que le reste des *exta*: foie, vésicule biliaire, péritoine[228]. Son extraction s'appelle en grec καρδιουλκία[229].

Dans quel contexte, s'il est légitime d'ajouter foi au témoignage de l'*amora* palestinien R. Huna, pouvait être réalisée une opération aussi cruelle que l'arrachage du cœur sur une victime vivante? LIEBERMAN[230] suggère qu'il pouvait s'agir des mystères de Déméter, Attis et Cybèle. Nous opterions plutôt, pour notre part, pour ceux de Dionysos. Les fidèles, dans leurs transports frénétiques y déchiraient à belles dents un taureau vivant pour rappeler le cruel festin des Titans[231]. Le dieu, dont ils se pénétraient ainsi était destiné à renaître grâce à la précaution prise par sa sœur Athéna qui avait à la dérobée enfermé son cœur dans une boîte[232]; ils devaient donc, à son exemple prélever le cœur de la victime en vue d'une résurrection du dieu.

Etant donné l'extension des cultes à mystères, à l'époque impériale, on peut se demander si les rites dionysiaques doivent être seuls pris en considération. Le taurobole en particulier était pratiqué tant dans le culte

[228] Cf. DAREMBERG–SAGLIO IV, 2, p. 976 s. v. sacrificium.
[229] Cf. Hésychius s. v., éd. LATTE 1966, vol. II, p. 413 (801).
[230] Hellenism p. 119.
[231] Cf. Arnobe, Adversus Nationes V, 19.
[232] Cf. A. LOISY, Les mystères païens et le mystère chrétien, Paris 1914, p. 32—34.

d'Attis que dans celui de Mithra. Dans le taurobole mithriaque, le sacrificateur devait reproduire le geste de Mithra tauroctone si souvent répété sur les bas-reliefs[233] où l'on voit le dieu enfonçant de la main droite un long coutelas au défaut de l'épaule de la bête. C'est la raison pour laquelle ELMSLIE[234] propose de rattacher «les peaux incisées à la place du cœur» au culte mithriaque. Remarquons toutefois que nous ne possédons aucune indication que l'extraction du cœur ait été pratiquée dans ce culte ou celui d'Attis. Aussi paraît-il préférable de rattacher ce rite aux mystères dionysiaques.

Que les docteurs du Talmud aient pu observer «des peaux percées à l'endroit du cœur», suppose qu'après l'accomplissement des rites, la peau de l'animal sacrifié pouvait sortir de l'enceinte sacrée et par exemple être mise en vente sur le marché. Aucun autre texte ne nous donne de précision sur ce dernier point. Il est en tout cas certain que Dionysos était honoré dans le pays à l'époque romaine et plus particulièrement dans la ville de Beth Shean baptisée Scythopolis qui portait également le nom de Nysa en l'honneur de la nourrice du jeune dieu[235]. La numismatique atteste la persistance de son culte dans cette ville[236] ainsi qu' à Aelia Capitolina[237], à Césarée[238] et au Sud du pays à Rafia[239]. Enfin le Mercure de la triade héliopolitaine a tous les traits d'un Dionysos dont il emprunte même les mystères[240].

2. Le sacrifice du coq blanc

M. I, 5:

מתר למכור לו לבן בין התרנגולין ובזמן שהוא בפני עצמו קוטע את אצבעו ומוכרו לו לפי שאין מקריבין חסר לעבודה זרה.

«Il est permis de vendre un coq blanc au milieu d'un lot, mais lorsque le coq est vendu séparément, il faut lui couper un ergot avant de le vendre, car on ne sacrifie pas d'animal défectueux à une idole.»

Tos. I, 21:

מוכר לו תרנגול לבן בין התרנגולין אמ׳ ר׳ יהודה במה דברים אמורים בזמן שא׳ לו מכור לי תרנגול סתם אבל אם פירש לו מפני שהוא חולה או למשתה בנו הרי זה אסור.

[233] Cf. M. J. VERMASEREN, Corpus Inscriptionum et Monumentorum Religionis Mithriacae II, passim. [234] Op. cit., p. 31.

[235] Pline, H.N. V, 18, 74 *Scythopolim, antea Nysam a Libero Patre sepulta nutrice ibi*. Cf. B. LIFSHITZ, Scythopolis. L'histoire, les institutions et les cultes de la ville à l'époque hellenistique et impériale, ANRW II 8, Berlin–New York 1977, p. 262—294.

[236] Cf. G. F. HILL, Catalogue of the Greek Coins of Palestine in the British Museum, Londres 1914, p. 76s.

[237] Cf. H. COHEN, Description historique des monnaies frappées sous l'empire romain II, Paris 1885, p. 403, n° 1249 (monnaie d'Antonin).

[238] KADMAN, C.N.P. II, p. 56.

[239] Cf. HILL, ibid. p. 174, n° 12. Cette ville prétendait avoir vu coudre (ῥάπτειν) le fils de Sémélé dans la cuisse de son père, Zeus.

[240] SEYRIG, art. cité, Syria X (1929), p. 320s.

«On peut vendre un coq blanc dans un lot d'autres coqs. R. Judah dit: 'Il s'agit du cas où le païen demande tout simplement vends-moi un coq, mais s'il spécifie qu'il est malade ou que c'est pour le banquet de son fils, c'est interdit'.»

Le sacrifice d'un coq à un dieu guérisseur était une pratique extrêmement courante[241] ainsi que l'a noté la 'Tosefta' («s'il spécifie qu'il est malade»). Cependant le coq ne sert pas spécialement à demander la guérison[242]. Il constitue simplement une victime courante parce qu'à la portée de toutes les bourses. Que le coq blanc soit particulièrement recherché s'explique car les victimes blanches étaient consacrées aux divinités supérieures tandis que les victimes noires étaient réservées aux divinités infernales[243].

3. Ex-votos

Dans le passage déjà cité de la Mishna (III. 2), il est permis de se demander si les formes de main ou de pied dont il est question ne sont pas des ex-votos offerts en remerciement à un dieu guérisseur Asclépios ou Sérapis. Nous avons nous-même (supra p. 421) marqué notre préférence pour l'hypothèse de symboles se référant notamment à Sérapis. Cependant en l'absence de certitude absolue, la possibilité que ces 'formes' constituent des ex-votos mérite d'être considérée. Notre hésitation provient en grande partie du caractère très limité de la liste: main ou pied, alors que les ex-votos étaient susceptibles de reproduire tout membre guéri[244]. Il n'est que d'examiner la liste des offrandes votives déposées à l'Asclépeion d'Athènes[245] où presque toutes les parties du corps fondues en or ou en argent, ou bien gravées dans la pierre, se trouvent représentées.

4. Offrandes végétales

M. I, 5:

אילו דברים אסורים למכור לגוים אצטרובלין ובנות שוח ופטוטרותיהן ולבונה [...] ושאר כל הדברים סתמן מתר ופרושן אסור רבי מאיר אומר אף דקל טב וחצב ונקליבס אסור למכור לגוים.

[241] Cf. Hérodas, IV, 12—15; Lucien, Bis Acc. 4; Artémidore, Oneir. V, 9; Plutarque, Pyrrhus 3. 8; Tertullien, Apol. 46; CIG 5890. 66.

[242] Cf. W. Rouse, op. cit., p. 204 et Roscher, I, 630.

[243] Cf. Pline, H.N. X, 156 *ad rem divinam luteo rostro pedibusque purae non videntur, ad opertanea sacra nigrae*. Voir G. Wissowa, op. cit., p. 348.

[244] Cf. Aristide, VI, 69; Clément, Stromates V, 566 D.

[245] Voir Daremberg–Saglio II, 1, p. 375 s. v. donarium et W. Rouse, op. cit., p. 397—398 ainsi que p. 222, fig. 34 (homme tenant un pied votif) et p. 244, fig. 36 (chevelure votive de Thessalie). Cf. C.I.A. II, 403, 756, 1453 (œil) 1482 (mamelles) 766 (ventre, phallus et jambes), 403 (main et cuisse), 1503 (pieds).

«Voici la liste de ce qu'il est interdit de vendre aux païens: des pommes de pin, des figues blanches avec leur pédoncule, de l'encens [...] pour tout le reste, si c'est à usage ordinaire la vente en est permise, si leur destination cultuelle est spécifiée, la vente en est interdite. R. Meir dit: 'il est également interdit de vendre aux païens des dattes de premier choix ainsi que la variété dite de Nicolaos'.»

a) Encens

Tos. I, 21:

ר׳ יהודה בן פתירה אומ׳ בלבונה אין פחות משלשת מנין מוכר לתגר ואין מוכר לבעל הבית.

«R. Judah ben Bathyra dit: 'Pour l'encens on ne vend pas moins de trois manehs à un commerçant et l'on n'en vend pas à un simple particulier'.»

Le Talmud en permettant la vente de l'encens en gros mais non au détail[246], veut éviter au Juif une contribution voyante au culte idolâtre. En effet, l'offrande d'encens aux idoles est un trait trop connu pour qu'on ait besoin d'y insister. Nul n'ignorait que l'encens était brûlé devant les statues des divinités. Ainsi nous lisons dans la 'Gemara' palestinienne (A.Z. III, 1, 39b): «R. Ashian le charpentier dit au nom de R. Johanan 'Pourquoi les images sont-elles interdites? Parce qu'on leur offre de l'encens lorsqu'elles sont érigées'.»

b) Pommes de pin

Les pommes de pin nommées dans notre texte par leur nom grec איסטרובילין de στρόβειλοι avaient un rôle dans divers cultes païens. Ce fruit consacré à Asclépios pour ses propriétés curatives, se retrouve également dans le culte dionysiaque où le thyrse est couronné d'une pomme de pin et dans celui de Sabazios, dont les mains votives sont ornées de pommes de pin[247], mais c'est surtout dans le culte d'Attis qu'apparaît son caractère sacré. Selon la légende, Attis s'était mutilé et avait expiré sous un pin, et c'est sous la forme de cet arbre que Cybèle l'aurait transporté dans la montagne. L'iconographie de ce culte nous présente la déesse tendant à Attis une branche chargée de pommes de pin, rameau mystique qui lui permettra de revenir de l'au-delà[248], car le pin, arbre vivace, concentre en lui les forces vives de la nature pendant la mauvaise saison[249]. A partir

[246] Cp. Tertullien, Idol. 11, où il est demandé au chrétien, de renoncer à tout commerce aidant l'idolâtrie, en particulier au commerce de l'encens.

[247] Cf. Blinkenberg, loc. cit.

[248] Cf. M. J. Vermaseren, The Legend of Attis in Greek and Roman Art, p. 44—45, Pl. XXV, 1.

[249] A. Loisy, op. cit., p. 87.

des pignons, graines très appréciées depuis l'Antiquité sur tout le pourtour de la Méditerranée, on tirait du vin: ceci peut expliquer selon FRAZER[250] les orgies du rite de Cybèle.

Les pommes de pin sont également dans l'Antiquité des symboles de fertilité: «aussi les lançait-on avec des porcs et d'autres agents ou emblèmes de fécondité dans les rondes sacrées de Déméter pour fertiliser le sol et féconder les femmes[251]».

En raison de l'odeur agréable qu'elles dégagent les pommes de pin étaient fréquemment brûlées sur les autels. Peut-être est-ce là une justification suffisante de l'interdit rabbinique.

c) Figues et dattes

L'on conçoit que les figues et les dattes qui constituent le meilleur de la production fruitière locale aient été des fruits fréquemment offerts sur l'autel des diverses divinités. Pour cette destination ne pouvaient être utilisés que des fruits parfaits: figues blanches entières avec leur pédoncule בנות שוח ופטוטרותיהן[252] et dattes de premier choix dont trois espèces nous sont citées: דקל טב (litt. bonne datte), חצב et ניקליבס, celle-ci nommée d'après l'historien Nicolaos de Damas[253] qui avait coutume d'envoyer cette variété (*Phoenix dactylifera*)[254] à l'empereur Auguste[255]. חצב est un hapax interprété généralement comme désignant une espèce de datte[256] et sous lequel LIEBERMAN suggère de lire ἰσχάδας, figues sèches[257].

Les fruits frais étaient offerts aux dieux de la fertilité. La figue en particulier était associée aux cultes de Dionysos et de Cybèle. Les dattes ne faisaient pas l'objet d'offrandes en Italie et en Grèce où elles étaient importées car les palmiers n'y donnent pas de fruits; en Orient où elles sont courantes, il était normal qu'on pensât à les offrir aux dieux.

Figues et dattes sont par nature des fruits sucrés. Au Nouvel An, lorsque venait le temps d'échanger des étrennes, ces fruits constituaient des présents traditionnels destinés à présager une année douce. L'on voit ainsi sur une plaque de cristal offerte à Commode la représentation des étrennes en usage chez les simples particuliers: dattes, figues, ainsi que

250 Atys et Osiris, éd. fçse, p. 11.

251 Ibid.

252 Cf. Löw, Flora I, p. 241s. Le type de figues appelé בנות שוח ne mûrit que tous les trois ans (Sheb. V, 1, Rosh Hashana 15b) R. Johanan traduit ce nom par תאני חיוראתא 'figues blanches' (Ber. 40b, Shab. 14a).

253 Cf. B. WACHOLDER, Nicolaus of Damascus, Berkeley 1962, p. 89. L'identification du terme talmudique fut effectuée pour la première fois au XVIIème siècle par BENJAMIN DE MUSAFIA dans son 'Mosaf ha'arukh'.

254 Cf. Pline, H.N. XIII, 9, 45 qui les décrit comme une variété de *dactyli*, de grande taille: *sicciores ex hoc genere Nicolai, sed amplitudinis praecipuae, quaterni cubitorum longitudinem efficiunt* et Athenaeus XIV, 22.

255 A ce que rapporte Plutarque, Quaest. Conv. VIII, 4, 723 D.

256 Löw, Flora II, p. 321 et 323, qui lit חצד.

257 Texts and Studies p. 175.

laurier (présage de victoire) et monnaie d'or (présage de richesse)[258]. L'interdit rabbinique pourrait donc être motivé par ces pratiques[259]; dans ce cas, il lui suffirait d'être limité à la période des Saturnales et des Calendes.

Selon S. LIEBERMAN[260], בנות שוח ne désignerait guère des figues mais une variété de pin correspondant au grec πίτυς. La preuve lui en paraît fournie par cette définition de TJ Shebi'ith V, 1, 35d: מה היא בנות שוח פטיריה où le dernier mot mis en parallèle avec *benot šuah* est lu par lui πιτύδια. Il devrait donc plutôt s'agir selon lui, de pommes de pin brûlées sur l'autel[261].

A la faveur d'un texte magique[262] rapproché par lui de notre 'Mishna' et énumérant «bois de cyprès, dix pommes de pin, deux coqs blancs et encens», il n'est pas impossible de penser avec LIEBERMAN[263] que notre passage se réfère à des pratiques magiques. Cependant nous avons vu qu'en dehors de telles pratiques, tous ces éléments entraient également dans les rites courants.

5. Le culte du Mercolis

a) Trois pierres

M. IV, 1:

רבי ישמעאל אומר שלוש אבנים זו בצד זו בצד מרקוליס אסורות ושתים מותרות וחכמים אומרים שנראות עמו אסורות ושאין נראות עמו מותרות.

«R. Ismaël dit: 'Trois pierres l'une à côté de l'autre placées près d'un Mercolis sont interdites: deux sont permises'. Les sages disent: 'celles qui paraissent être avec lui sont interdites et celles qui ne paraissent pas être avec lui sont permises'.»

Ainsi que nous l'avons vu, le Mercolis peut être lui-même entièrement constitué d'un tas de pierres. Ici, il s'agit apparemment de pierres n'en faisant pas partie, mais disposées en son honneur. Une *baraïta* (B.M. 25b) nous décrit en effet une sorte de petit dolmen ou *trilithon*[264], appelé par une déformation curieuse בית קוליס 'maison de Qolis':

אלו הן אבני בית קוליס אחת מכאן ואחת מכאן ואחת על גביהן.

«Les pierres du Beth Qolis sont ainsi: une d'un côté, une de l'autre et une troisième par-dessus.»

[258] M. MESLIN, art. cité, p. 35.
[259] Cf. ELMSLIE, op. cit., p. 9.
[260] Texts and Studies, p. 170 s., art. repris de JQR XXXVI (1946).
[261] Cf. Tamid, 29b.
[262] K. PREISENDANZ, Papyri Graecae Magicae II, p. 88.
[263] Art. cité, p. 173—174.
[264] ELMSLIE, op. cit., p. 62.

b) Offrandes

M. IV, 2:

מצא בראשו מעות כסות או כלים הרי אלו מתרין פרכילי ענבים ועטרות שלשבלים ויינות ושמנים וסלתות וכל דבר שכיוצא בו קרב על גבי המזבח אסור.

«Si l'on trouve à sa tête des pièces de monnaie, un vêtement ou des objets, ils sont permis; mais si ce sont des sarments de vigne, des couronnes d'épis, du vin, de l'huile, de la fleur de farine et tout ce qu'il est de coutume d'offrir sur l'autel, c'est interdit.»

Tos. VI, 13:

מרקוליס וכל מה שעליו אסור מצא עליו יינות שמנים וסלתות וכל דבר שכיוצא בו קרב לגבי המזבח אסור מעות וכלים מותרין אחרים אומ׳ אף מעות וכלים שעל גבי אבן העליונה הרי אילו אסורין.

«Mercolis avec tout ce qu'il porte sur lui est interdit. Si l'on trouve sur lui du vin, de l'huile, de la fleur de farine et tout ce qu'il est de coutume d'offrir sur l'autel, c'est interdit; mais les pièces de monnaie et les objets sont permis. D'autres disent que même les pièces et les objets sont interdits, s'ils sont disposés sur la pierre supérieure.»

On voit par la distinction établie dans ces deux textes, que les rabbins avaient conscience que certaines offrandes étaient communes aux rites païens et au cérémonial du temple: vin, huile, fleur de farine[265]. Il fallait donc à leurs yeux d'autant plus s'en tenir à l'écart. Pour les autres, ils reconnaissaient qu'ils pouvaient constituer une tentation lorsqu'ils étaient exposés en plein air sur la pierre supérieure d'un Mercolis et divergeaient quant à l'attitude à observer.

C'est le culte populaire d'Hermès qui nous est décrit ici. Le dieu, sous sa forme de dieu-terme ou de tas de pierres élevé en l'honneur de l'inventeur des routes (cf. supra p. 404), avait en effet droit à de menues offrandes ou ἑρμαῖα dont la plupart nous sont énumérées ici.

Les offrandes végétales étaient destinées à apaiser la faim des voyageurs. En Grèce, la plus courante était constituée de figues sèches d'où l'expression σῦκον ἐφ' Ἑρμῇ[266], mais ce type d'offrande n'est pas mentionné ici. Les rabbins ont interdit plus particulièrement les offrandes susceptibles de faire l'objet de libations comme le vin et l'huile et autres oblations non sanglantes, comme la fleur de farine, ainsi que les épis de blé offerts en tant que prémices des fruits de la terre, ce qui suppose que le dieu honoré ainsi a un caractère agraire, comme le Mercure de Baalbek. En Grèce, les couronnes d'épis étaient souvent remplacées par des guirlandes de fleurs[267]. L'offrande de raisins peut s'expliquer par le caractère

[265] Cf. Mombres 7 passim, 8.8 etc. . .

[266] Cf. Hesychius, s. v. σῦκον.

[267] Cf. Daremberg–Saglio III, 1, p. 131 s. v. Hermae.

de plus en plus nettement bachique pris par les cérémonies célébrées autour des Hermès[268].

Que les hermès aient été également parfois gratifiés de pièces de monnaie et consultés comme des oracles, nous est confirmé par un texte de Pausanias (VII, 22, 2), concernant, il est vrai, l'Achaïe.

Quant aux vêtements, ils constituent une offrande courante dans les cultes sémitiques: offrir un vêtement c'est offrir une partie de soi[269], mais chez les Grecs, ils sont susceptibles d'être offerts aussi bien qu'un simple ustensile à titre d'ἀνάθημα pour remercier la divinité[270].

Pour se concilier la divinité qui préside aux voyages, il existait donc des rites divers: lancer de pierres (cf. supra p. 404), oblations non sanglantes (vin, huile, farine) ou encore consécration de vêtements ou d'objets.

Ce culte probablement très ancien et apparemment d'origine grecque semble, ainsi que nous l'avons vu plus haut (p. 405), avoir été très populaire dans la région où viennent sans doute s'ajouter des éléments syncrétistes empruntés au Mercure héliopolitain.

6. Décoration de boutiques

M. I, 4:

עיר שיש בה עבודה זרה והיו בה חנויות מעטרות ושאינן מעטרות זה היה מעשה בבית שאן ואמרו חכמים המעטרות אסורות ושאינן מעטרות מתרות.

«Dans le cas d'une ville où se tient une fête idolâtre et où certaines boutiques sont décorées de guirlandes et d'autres non, comme cela s'est passé à Beth Shean, les sages ont dit: 'les décorées sont interdites et les non décorées sont permises'.»

Dans la lointaine Carthage, Tertullien met de même en garde les Chrétiens contre la pratique consistant à orner de guirlandes les portes car les Romains ont même des dieux des entrées[271]. Les entrées sont, en l'honneur de ces divinités décorées à l'occasion des grandes festivités publiques[272].

Le Talmud de Jérusalem (I, 4) requiert une précision sur le type d'ornement interdit: «Selon R. Johanan, il s'agit du myrte; selon Resh Lakish quel que soit l'ornement il motive l'interdit.»

[268] Ibid.

[269] W. Robertson Smith, op. cit., p. 335.

[270] Yerkes, op. cit., p. 62. Voir liste d'ustensiles et instruments divers (armes, instruments de métier) dans Daremberg–Saglio II, 1, p. 376—378 s. v. donarium.

[271] Idol. 15: *Cardeam a cardinibus appellatam et Forculum a foribus et Limentinum a limine et ipsum Ianum a ianua . . . . . Etiam apud Graecos Apollinem* θυραῖον *et Antelios daemonas ostiorum praesides legimus.*

[272] Cf. ibid.: un Chrétien est puni car ses esclaves avaient couronné sa porte à l'annonce de telles festivités.

En occident, ces guirlandes étaient le plus souvent faites de laurier[273], mais il est en effet fort possible que le myrte ait rempli le même usage dans ces régions où il est fort abondant.

7. Offrandes de bijoux

M. I, 8:

ואין עושים תכשיטין לעבודה זרה קטלאות ונזמים וטבעות רבי אליעזר אומר בשכר מתר.

«On ne fabrique pas de bijoux destinés à une idole: ni colliers, ni boucles d'oreilles, ni bagues. R. Eliézer dit: ‛contre salaire c'est permis'[274].»

L'addition de R. Eliézer, tellement surprenante au regard de la législation anti-idolâtre, n'est pas commentée dans la ‛Gemara', comme si elle n'avait même pas été formulée. Elle suppose en tout cas que le métier d'orfèvre était alors un gagne-pain courant chez les Juifs. Une inscription grecque de Beth Shearin[275] évoque ainsi «Leontios, père de Rabbi Paregorios et de Julianos, fonctionnaire du palais, orfèvre (ἀπὸ χρυσοχ[ο]ῶν)».

Les artisans juifs étaient donc mis en demeure de refuser toute commande de bijoux destinés à l'ornement d'une idole[276]. Ce type d'offrandes était en effet courant dans tout le monde antique comme l'attestent les listes conservées par les inscriptions[277].

Pline note, à son époque, la coutume de mettre des bagues *etiam in deorum simulacris* (H.N. XXXIII, 6, 24). Les statues recevaient également des couronnes, des diadèmes, des frontaux, des pendants d'oreille, des colliers, des chaînes, des bracelets, des anneaux de jambe, des épingles et broches et autres ornements tels que pierres précieuses, boutons, ceintures, éventails ou miroirs.

Parmi les différents aspects du culte idolâtre les rabbins établissent une hiérarchie. On lit ainsi en M. Sanh. VII, 6 (cp. Tos. ibid. X, 3):

המגפף והמנשק והמחבד והמרבץ והמרחיץ, הסך, המלביש והמנעיל — עובר בלא תעשה.

[273] Cf. ibid.; Pline, H.N. XV, 39, 127: *sola et domos exornat et ante limina excubat* et Tert., Apol. 35, 4: *Cur die laeto non laureis postes obumbramus nec lucernis diem infringimus?* Le laurier en effet purifie et consacre, cf. Marquardt, Culte I, p. 211, n. 2.

[274] κατέλλα = *catella* ‛collier serré', cf. Krauss, Arch. I, p. 203 et Id., Lehnw. II, p. 525. נזמים = boucles d'oreilles. Les deux mots sont fréquemment associés. Cf. Sôta I, 6; Shab. VI, 1; Kel. XI, 8; Me‛ila V, 1; Sifré Nb. 11, p. 5a; Gen. R. 95. 23; Nb. R. 9, 33.

[275] Cf. Frey, C.I.J. II, n° 1006.

[276] Cp. Tertullien, Idol. 8 qui condamne tout art et toute profession au service des idoles.

[277] Cf. inscriptions citées par Daremberg–Saglio II, 1, p. 376, et Lafaye, op. cit., p. 136—137: inventaire du trésor de l'Isium d'Acci — Guadix — et p. 135: objets livrés au temple d'Isis situé à Némi près de Rome.

«Quiconque enlace ou embrasse (une idole), balaye ou arrose (le sol devant elle), la lave, l'oint, la vêt ou la chausse, transgresse un précepte négatif.»

En d'autres termes, il s'agit là pour un Juif de fautes vénielles. (Même le geste licencieux par lequel le dieu cananéen Baal Peor était censé se trouver honoré appartient à cette première catégorie: la pratique consistant à découvrir devant la statue du dieu ses parties les plus intimes est en effet fréquemment mentionnée dans le Talmud[277a], au point qu'on peut se demander si cet usage n'était pas encore en vigueur à l'époque tannaïtique[277b]. Ce fait n'est toutefois guère établi et il est possible que les diverses anecdotes relatives au culte de Baal Peor constituent une variation sur un thème biblique à classer dans le genre satirique de la 'dérision des idoles'.)

L'idolâtrie proprement dite, celle pour laquelle un Juif est théoriquement passible de la peine capitale (Sanh. VII, 6), consiste dans le sacrifice, l'offrande d'encens ou de libations à une divinité païenne ainsi qu'à la prosternation devant elle.

Dans quelle mesure la brève évocation de ces rites résulte-t-elle d'une observation réelle de la part des rabbins? Point n'est besoin de dire qu'ils ne fréquentaient point les temples mais les temples n'étaient pas, et de loin, les seuls lieux où ces rites étaient observables, alors que les 'mercolis' se multipliaient le long des routes, les statues sur les places ou dans les édifices publics. Quant aux sacrifices, ils pouvaient être accomplis dans la demeure d'un simple particulier comme sur la place publique. Un passage tannaïtique (Hul. II, 9) précise à ce sujet qu'il est interdit de sacrifier sur la place publique afin de ne pas paraître suivre les coutumes des *minim*, terme qui, dans ce passage, aurait selon LIEBERMAN[277c], le sens de 'Gentils'. Quoi qu'il en soit, le poids de l'environnement païen était tel que certaines pratiques idolâtres ne pouvaient passer inaperçues, quand bien même eût-on voulu les ignorer.

IV. Coutumes amorites

C'est dans la 'Tosefta' du traité Shabbat (ch. VI—VII) que se trouve une liste de coutumes locales dites 'amorites' contre lesquelles les autorités rabbiniques mettent en garde. Cette liste déjà constituée dans sa majeure partie au début du IIIème siècle est, dès cette époque, couramment désignée sous le nom de 'chapitre amorite' ('פרק האמוראי' TB Shab. 67a).

[277a] Sanh. VII, 6, TJ ibid. X, 28d passim, TB ibid. 64a, 106a; Sifré Deut. I, 131, éd. HOROVITZ, p. 171.

[277b] Cf. Jewish Encyclopedia II, p. 382.

[277c] Greek ..., p. 141, n. 196 et Hellenism ..., p. 135.

Par une telle dénomination, la législation de ce chapitre veut de toute évidence se rattacher à la Bible où les Amorrhéens constituent avec les Cananéens, le peuple préisraélite le plus souvent mentionné. Tous les peuples de Canaan, selon la Bible, s'adonnent à des abominations parmi lesquelles la divination et la sorcellerie[278]. Dans la littérature postbiblique, il est plus particulièrement question des Amorrhéens en relation avec des pratiques magiques comme celles qui nous sont décrites dans la 'Tosefta' de 'Shabbat'. Un texte de l'Apocalypse syriaque de Baruch nous en donne un témoignage frappant: «les eaux noires que tu as vues pleuvoir en cinquième lieu (évoquent) les œuvres des Amorrhéens et les incantations de la magie qu'ils pratiquaient, l'impiété de leurs mystères et la contamination de leur impureté[279]».

L'énumération des 'coutumes amorites' devrait éviter à l'Israélite de se laisser aller à suivre l'exemple de ces peuples dont il est dit (Lév. 18.3): «ce qui se fait au pays de Canaan où je vais vous introduire, vous ne le ferez pas, vous ne marcherez point suivant leurs mœurs». En Deut. 18. 9—11, il est précisé: «Tu n'apprendras pas à commettre des abominations comme celles de ces nations. Qu'on ne trouve chez toi personne qui fasse passer son fils ou sa fille par le feu, qui pratique la divination (ק·סם קסמים), qui observe la nue (מעונן), qui use de charmes (מנחש) ou de sorcellerie (מכשף), qui opère un enchantement (ח·בר חבר), qui consulte un esprit ou un oracle (ושאל אוב וידעני), qui interroge les morts (ודרש אל המתים)[280].»

Dans la couche vraisemblablement la plus ancienne de notre Tosefta (VII, 13 et 14) se trouvent définis deux des termes de la liste deutéronomique: מנחש et מעונן, dont les définitions ne recouvrent pas totalement les pratiques énumérées dans tout le passage précédent (VI, 1—VII, 2). Ces deux termes en effet se réfèrent à la seule divination; or, dans le reste du passage, nous rencontrons des pratiques qui relèvent de la sorcellerie et de la nécromancie. Aux deux définitions de la 'Tosefta' qu'il reprend, le traité Sanhédrin (65a–b) ajoute celles des termes ידעוני et בעל אוב repris de Deut. 18, 10—11.

Pour ces diverses définitions et énumérations, il ne fait aucun doute que les rabbins se réfèrent à des pratiques courantes à une époque où la magie était florissante y compris parmi les Juifs eux-mêmes[281]. Bien mieux, dans l'empire romain, les Juifs ont réputation de magiciens[282]. De fait, grand nombre de formules des documents magiques antiques portent la marque du judaïsme ou bien ressortissent à un syncrétisme judéo-païen[283].

[278] Deut. 18, 10—14; Jer. 10, 2—3; II Rois 21, 2 et 6; II Chron. 33, 2 et 6.

[279] Ap. Bar. LX, 1 trad. P. Bogaert, éd. du Cerf, Paris 1969.

[280] Trad. Dhorme, éd. de la Pléiade.

[281] Le Talmud rapporte de nombreuses anecdotes prouvant que les rabbins étaient capables de la pratiquer en certaines occasions, tout en la réprouvant en principe, ex. Sanh. 65a, 68a.

[282] Cf. Juster, Les Juifs dans l'empire romain II, p. 209 et note 2; M. Simon, Verus Israël, Paris 1964², p. 395s.

[283] Cf. Simon, op. cit., p. 396s. et 407; J. Gager, Moses in Greco-Roman Paganism, New-York 1972, ch. IV Moses and Magic, et textes dans K. Preisendanz, Papyri Graecae Magicae I (1928), II (1931).

Il n'en demeure pas moins qu'aux yeux des rabbins, la magie est proprement du paganisme: le sorcier est passible de mort[284] et quiconque se laisse aller à prononcer des incantations perd sa part du monde futur[285]. Toutefois, l'acharnement même avec lequel ils pourfendent certaines pratiques, prouve qu'elles étaient en usage parmi les fidèles ou du moins constituaient pour eux une tentation non négligeable[286].

Pour la 'Tosefta' du traité 'Shabbat', nous avons la chance de disposer d'une édition critique établie par Saul Lieberman[287] qui recueille toutes les variantes existantes dans les sources rabbiniques et cite un grand nombre de parallèles chez les auteurs grecs et latins, pour la plupart repris de la traduction allemande commentée de Heinrich Lewy[288], relative à nos deux chapitres. C'est donc, bien entendu, à l'édition de Lieberman que nous renvoyons pour l'établissement du texte.

1. Coiffures

Les premières coutumes amorites énumérées dans la 'Tosefta' de Shabbat (VI, 1), n'ont apparemment aucun caractère religieux ni magique, puisqu'elles sont relatives à la coiffure:

אילו דברים מדרכי האמורי המספר קומי והעושה בלורית.

«Telles sont les coutumes amorites: se couper les cheveux et entretenir une houppe.»

Le terme מספר 'couper les cheveux' est en lui-même neutre; il peut toutefois renvoyer à la coutume de se raser les tempes, présentée dans la Bible comme caractéristique de plusieurs nations voisines d'Israël[289] et réactualisée à l'époque de Marc-Aurèle où la tonte rase ἡ κουρὰ ἡ ἐν χρῷ est à la mode[290].

C'est bien le second élément בלורית[291], qui est le plus répréhensible comme le montre ce passage de la 'Tosefta' de A.Z. (III, 6):

ישראל המספר את הגוי כיון שהגיע לבלוריתו שומט את ידו.

«Lorsqu'un Israélite coupe les cheveux d'un Gentil en arrivant à sa houppe, il doit retirer sa main.»

284 Ex. 22, 17; Lev. 20, 27, d'où la législation talmudique de Sanh. 65a.

285 Sanh. XI, 1.

286 *"Halachic negation is a historical affirmation"*, rappelle L. Blau, Early Christian Archaeology, HUCA III (1926), p. 187.

287 Tosefta Kifshutah, vol. III, p. 79—99.

288 Morgenländischer Aberglaube in der römischen Kaiserzeit, Zeitschrift des Vereins für Volkskunde III (1893), p. 24—40 et 130—143.

289 Cf. Jer. 9, 25; 25, 23; 49, 32; Lév. 19, 27.

290 Cf. Marquardt, Vie privée I, p. 248.

291 Cf. TB A.Z. 29a, TJ ibid. II, 1. Voir étymologies proposées pour בלורית dans Krauss, Archäol. I, p. 645, n. 841.

L'explication d'un tel comportement nous est donné dans le Midrash[292]:

העושה בלורית אינו מגדלה אלא לשם עבודה זרה.

«Quiconque entretient une houppe, ne fait pousser celle-ci qu'en l'honneur d'une idole.»

L'usage de laisser croître une mèche de cheveux pour une raison sacrée est connue par des sources grecques et selon Rouse[293], il était assez courant pour donner naissance à un proverbe inspiré du célèbre vers des 'Bacchantes' d'Euripide (v. 494): ἱερὸς ὁ πλόκαμος τῷ θεῷ δ'αὐτὸν τρέφω.

Deux bustes, l'un d'homme l'autre de femme, à la chevelure complètement rasée, sauf une mèche pendant sur l'oreille droite sont inclus par Lafaye dans son catalogue des monuments figurés relatifs aux divinités alexandrines (n°s 83 et 84); cependant, lui-même, rappelle que les prêtres d'Isis avaient souvent la tête entièrement rasée à la mode égyptienne[294] — Juvénal ne les appelait-il pas *grex calvus*[295]: «le troupeau chauve»? Le pèlerin de Hiérapolis est de son côté également tenu de se raser entièrement la chevelure ainsi que les sourcils[296]. Cette coutume n'est donc à rattacher vraisemblablement ni au culte d'Isis ni à celui de la déesse syrienne.

Toutefois, la coiffure n'est pas motivée uniquement par des raisons religieuses; la mode y joue également un rôle. Les deux principales coiffures de l'époque romaine sont le κῆπος et le σκάφιον[297]. Il semble que dans la première, les cheveux aient été portés longs tout autour de la tête et courts sur le dessus du crâne[298] et que dans la seconde, seul le sommet du crâne soit resté chevelu, le reste des cheveux étant tondu circulairement au bord de la tête[299]. Notre texte pourrait viser ce dernier type de coiffure qui est en contravention avec l'injonction biblique (Lév. 19, 27). לא תקפו פאת ראשכם: «vous ne tondrez pas en rond le bord de votre tête», mais l'interdiction de la Tosefta (A.Z. III, 6) ne reçoit d'explication vraiment satisfaisante que si la mèche dont le contact est interdit, est consacrée par un vœu à une divinité païenne.

La suite de l'énumération de Tos. Shabbat VI, 1 comporte une expression d'interprétation difficile pour laquelle plusieurs variantes sont propo-

292 Deut. R. II, 18; cf. Lieberman, TK p. 80—81.

293 Op. cit. p. 242, où il donne une intéressante citation de Diphile ap. Ath. VI 225 B ἐνταῦθα γοῦν ἔστιν τι ὑπερηκοντικῶς, κόμην τρέφων μὲν πρῶτον ἱερὰν τοῦ θεοῦ, ὥς φησίν· οὐ διὰ τοῦτό γ', ἀλλ' ἐστιγμένος πρὸ τοῦ μετώπου παραπέτασμ' αὐτὴν ἔχει.

294 Op. cit., p. 151.

295 Juv. VI, 526.

296 Lucien, Dea 55. Les *galli*, après une période de deuil de 30 jours ne peuvent également rentrer au Temple que s'ils se sont rasé la tête (ibid. 52).

297 Cf. Souda s. v. κῆπος, Pollux II, 29.

298 Selon Lieberman, TK p. 81 המספר קומי pourrait renvoyer à une espèce particulière de cette coiffure dénommée 'Εκτόρειος κόμη, ce qui justifierait l'usage du mot grec κόμη dans la 'Tosefta'.

299 Cf. F. W. Nicolson, Greek and Roman Barbers, Harvard Studies in Classical Philology, II (1891), p. 51.

sées. Si l'on garde la lecture מגבה, elle se réfère à une tonsure sur le sommet du crâne[300] et il pourrait s'agir d'une forme de κῆπος. Telle est l'interprétation de LEWY qui lit לגודגודין au sens de קדקד 'sur le crâne'. D'autres, comme FURST, interprètent גודגדים comme se référant à Gad, dieu de la Fortune[301], mais aucune autre source n'atteste qu'une telle tonsure ait été pratiquée en l'honneur de Gad. Les autres lectures citées par LIEBERMAN[302] לגרגרין ou המנבח לגדגניות «qui aboie après les grillons» ou «après la roquette», nous entraînent loin du domaine de la coiffure.

2. Procédés divinatoires

a) La croyance aux présages

Une liste de présages nous est donnée à propos de la définition du *menaheš*[303].

Tos. Shabbat, VII, 13:

איזהו מנחש האומר נפלה מקלי מידי נפלה פת מפי וקרא איש פלוני מאחריי וקרא לי עורב ונבח בי כלב ועבר נחש לימיני ושועל לשמאלי ופסק צבי את הדרך לפני אל תתחיל בי שהרי שחרית הוא ראש חודש הוא מוצאי שבת הוא.

«Qu'est-ce-que l'interprète des présages? Celui qui dit: 'mon bâton est tombé de ma main, mon pain est tombé de ma bouche, un tel m'a appelé par derrière, un corbeau m'a appelé, un chien a aboyé après moi, un serpent est passé à ma droite, un renard à ma gauche, un cerf m'a coupé la route, ne commence pas par moi car c'est le matin, c'est le premier du mois, c'est la sortie du Sabbat'.»

Le Talmud de Babylone présente à peu de chose près le même texte en Sanhédrin 65b—66a, mais avec le possessif de la troisième personne («Son pain, son bâton») et conclut en citant le verset biblique «'vous ne pratiquerez ni la divination, ni l'astrologie' (Lev. 19, 26), comme ceux qui tirent des présages des belettes[304], des oiseaux et des poissons»: לא תנחשו ולא תעוננו כגון אלו המנחשים בחולדרת בעופות ובדגים.

[300] Tel est le sens technique de גבחת (cf. Nega'im X, 10, B.Q. 83a) par opposition à קרחת tonsure à l'arrière du crâne.

[301] Ap. LEWY, art. cité, p. 25, n. 2.

[302] TK p. 81.

[303] Selon l'étymologie, ce terme renvoie d'abord aux présages tirés des mouvements des serpents (cf. BAUDISSIN, Studien zur Semitischen Religionsgeschichte, Leipzig 1878, I, p. 157s.); dans la LXX, il est rendu (ex Nb. 23, 3) par οἰωνίζομαι, c'est-à-dire qu'il est interprété comme se référant à l'ornithomancie; ici le terme a pris une valeur générique et désigne la divination en général.

[304] Sur les présages fournis par la belette dans le monde grec, cf. textes cités par LEWY, p. 135—136. L'ἰχθυομαντεία ou divination par les poissons (Athén., Deipnosoph. VIII, 8) est peu acclimatée en Grèce et semble venir d'Orient, cf. A. BOUCHÉ-LECLERQ, Histoire da la divination dans l'Antiquité I, Paris 1879, p. 151.

b) Les animaux de présages

Dans cette longue énumération de présages le cri de certains animaux ou l'apparition soudaine de tels autres a son importance. C'est dans une ode d'Horace[305] que nous trouvons, sans doute, la liste la plus similaire: «Que les impies aient pour les conduire le présage d'une orfraie redoublant son cri, d'une chienne pleine ou bien d'une louve gris-fauve qui descend en courant des campagnes de Lanuvium et d'une renarde avec sa portée, que coupant leur route commencée un serpent vienne obliquement pareil à une flèche effrayer leurs bidets gaulois[306].»

Certains animaux paraissent donc plus aptes que d'autres à fournir des omens: les deux listes ont en commun un oiseau, un chien, un renard et un serpent.

Le chien animal sacré chez les Sémites est lié à diverses divinités sémitiques ainsi que l'Hécate grecque[307] qui aime à être invoquée sous le nom de chienne. Ces rapports avec des puissances supérieures, lui valent sans doute quelque pouvoir de divination. L'aboiement du chien est considéré comme un omen dans quelques sources arabes[308], de même d'ailleurs que le hurlement du loup, l'apparition de cet animal sur la droite ou sur la gauche[309] ou encore le glapissement du renard[310]. Chez les Grecs et les Romains, les présages tirés des quadrupèdes étaient généralement de mauvais augure[311]. La façon dont ces animaux se présentent a toutefois son importance: aussi bien dans la civilisation grecque que dans la tradition arabe[312], la gauche est généralement défavorable et la droite favorable.

Le serpent semble s'être prêté très tôt aux spéculations divinatoires, dans le domaine sémitique, ainsi que l'indique son rapport étymologique avec מנחש le devin[313]. Si, dans le texte d'Horace cité plus haut, sa traversée d'une route en oblique apparaît comme un mauvais présage, d'autres passages de notre Tosefta nous montrent au contraire qu'il est susceptible de porter bonheur[314].

Tos. Shab. VI, 16:

נפל נחש על גבי מיטה ואמר עני הוא וסופו להעשיר עברה היא זכר יולדת בתולה היא לאדם גדול נישאת הרי זה מדרכ׳ האמ׳.

[305] Odes III, 27 début: *Impios parrae recinentis omen / ducat et praegnans canis aut ab agro / rava decurrens lupa Lanuvino / fetaque volpes; / rumpit et serpens iter institutum / si per obliquom similis sagittae / terruit mannos . . .*

[306] Trad. Villeneuve, éd. Belles Lettres.

[307] Cf. W. R. Smith, Religion of the Semites, p. 290—292.

[308] Cf. T. Fahd, La divination arabe, Leyde 1966, p. 503—504.

[309] Ibid. p. 514.

[310] Ibid. p. 517—518.

[311] Cf. L. Hopf, Thierorakel und Orakelthiere in alter und neuer Zeit, Stuttgart 1888, p. 20s.

[312] Cf. Fahd, op. cit., p. 443.

[313] Cf. supra, p. 458 n. 303.

[314] Selon Berak. 57 a, l'apparition d'un serpent en songe est de bon augure.

«Dire, lorsqu'un serpent tombe sur un lit[315] que de pauvre on va devenir riche, ou s'il s'agit d'une femme enceinte, qu'elle aura un garçon, ou s'il s'agit d'une jeune fille qu'elle va épouser un homme important, c'est une coutume amorite.»

Cette croyance n'a rien d'étonnant lorsqu'on observe la vénération positive dont fait l'objet le serpent dans l'Orient et la Grèce, si bien que son image sert souvent de talisman[316]. Pour les Romains, l'apparition d'un serpent peut également être interprétée comme étant celle du *genius*[317].

c) Ornithomancie: corbeau et coq

De tous les oiseaux susceptibles de fournir des omens, le corbeau est celui qui sans doute revient le plus fréquemment dans des traditions diverses. C'est son cri, plus que son vol, qui suscite l'attention: n'en distinguait-on pas chez les Grecs soixante quatre variétés[318]? Il fait partie des ᾠδικοί ou *oscines* en compagnie de la corneille du hibou et du pivert.

Dans le texte de notre Tosefta (Shab. VI, 6):

קרא עורב ואמר לו צרח קרא עורב ואמר לו חזור לאחוריך.

«lorsqu'un corbeau croasse lui dire 'crie' ou lorsqu'il croasse lui dire 'retourne-toi'»,

et dans son parallèle du Talmud babylonien (Shab. 67b):

האומר לעורב צרח ולעורבתא שריקי והחזירי זנביך.

«dire à un corbeau mâle 'crie' et à un corbeau femelle 'siffle et tourne ta queue'»,

il est possible que les termes שרק, צרח, קרא se réfèrent à différents cris auxquels étaient attachés pour les uns un bon augure et les autres un mauvais augure. Les Arabes distinguent ainsi *šaḥağa* 'croasser d'une voix rauque' de *na'aba* 'croasser tout court'[319] et opposent au mauvais présage du grand cri *ġâq*, le bon présage du petit cri *ġîq*[320]. Pline[321] signale le cri étouffé du corbeau comme un présage particulièrement funeste.

Une autre version de la 'Tosefta' signalée par LIEBERMAN (p. 86) et qui comporte le simple changement d'une lettre (צרה au lieu de צרח) peut

[315] Les serpents étaient alors des hôtes habituels dans les maisons; cf. l'anecdote rapportée en Shab. 156b à propos de la fille de R. Aqiba sauvée, grâce à ses mérites personnels, de la morsure d'un serpent caché dans sa chambre. Voir aussi Philon, De Providentia II, 105 et Pline, H.N. XXIX, 22, 72.

[316] Cf. supra p. 418.

[317] Cf. LEWY, art. cité, p. 37.

[318] Cf. Pindare, Fr. 285 SNELL.

[319] FAHD, op. cit., p. 449.

[320] Ibid. p. 509.

[321] H.N. X, 15, 33: *pessima eorum significatio cum gluttiunt vocem velut strangulati.*

paraître toutefois préférable. Elle aboutit en effet au sens suivant: quiconque lorsqu'un corbeau croasse dit: «malheur!» ou bien «retourne sur tes pas»[322].

Dans cette version sont mieux explicitées les appréhensions des Anciens liées au cri du corbeau[323] ou de la corneille, les oiseaux noirs: *Nigraque funestum concinit omen avis* écrit le poète Properce (II, 28, 38).

Un autre volatile qui était volontiers crédité d'un instinct divinatoire naturel était le coq[324]. Nous en avons un écho dans nos textes:

Tos. Shab. VI, 5:

האומר סקלו תרנגול זה שקרא בערב[325] תרנגולת זו שקראה כזכר האכילוה כרבלתה שקוראה כזכר.

«Quiconque dit 'Lapidez ce coq qui a chanté le soir ou cette poule qui a chanté comme un coq et faites-lui manger sa crête car elle chante comme un mâle'.»

L'idée que le chant du coq entendu le soir[326] et à des heures extraordinaires constitue un mauvais présage est courante dans l'Antiquité. Pline constate (H.N. X 24, 49): *Habent ostenta et praeposteri eorum vespertinique cantus*, et le Trimalcion de Pétrone (Satiricon, 74) fait, pour se débarrasser d'un tel prophète de malheur, immoler sur le champ un pauvre volatile.

Quant à la poule qui chante comme un coq, elle constitue également une anomalie inquiétante. Il en va de même du coq gloussant comme une poule, selon un proverbe arabe cité par Lewy (p. 31): «Lorsqu'un coq chante comme une poule, il faut l'égorger.»

De semblables traditions se retrouvent également chez les Persans:

«Si un coq chante, dans une maison, avant le moment du chant des coqs, cela sera une tentative de prévenir un malheur qui est sur le point de frapper cette maison.»

«Si une poule chante, dans une maison, comme les coqs, cela sera un avertissement aux gens de cette maison contre un malheur qui est sur le point de s'abattre sur eux[327].»

322 Cf. Horace, Odes III, 27, 15: *teque nec laevus vetet ire picus nec vaga cornix:* «que ni le pivert sinistre ni la corneille vagabonde ne te défende de partir», trad. Villeneuve, éd. Belles Lettres.

323 Cf. Cicéron, Divin. I, 39, 85 et 7, 12; Plaute, Aul. IV, 3, 1, Pline, H.N. X, 15, 33, textes mentionnés par Lewy, art. cité p. 32. Voir E. Massoneau, La magie dans l'Antiquité romaine, Paris 1934, p. 111 et Defradas, La divination en Grèce, dans: Caquot et Leibovici, La divination, p. 167—169. Chez les Arabes également le corbeau est essentiellement un oiseau de mauvais augure, cf. Fahd, op. cit., p. 507.

324 Sur l'alectryomancie, cf. Bouché-Leclercq, Histoire de la divination dans l'Antiquité, I, Paris 1879, p. 144—145.

325 T.B. Shab. 67b: שחטו תרנגול זה שקרא ערבית, voir autres variantes chez Lieb., p. 85.

326 Lewy, art. cité, p. 30 préférerait lire קרא כעורב «il a chanté comme un corbeau».

327 Texte cité ap. Fahd, p. 505—506.

Dans le domaine de l'ornithomancie, nombre de croyances communes se retrouvent donc en Orient et sur le pourtour de la Méditerranée.

d) Faits fortuits

Tout peut servir de présages pour un esprit à l'affût de signes.

Tos. Shab. VI, 2:

נפלו ממנו נצוצות ואמר אורחין לנו.

«Si on laisse tomber des étincelles dire: 'nous aurons des invités'.»

Cette croyance dont nous ne connaissons pas de répondant dans l'Antiquité, a des prolongements en Europe médiévale[328].

Selon une tradition persane ou arabe légèrement différente, «le feu qui s'allume au bas des marmites, annonce des pluies abondantes ou l'arrivée d'un hôte (. . .). Si tu vois que la lampe ou la bougie ou le feu du brasier lancent beaucoup d'étincelles, cela annonce une pluie abondante au même endroit ou dans le voisinage[329]».

Tout acte soustrait à la volonté pouvait également dans l'Antiquité être imputable à l'influence divine. On sait qu'il en était ainsi de divers phénomènes physiologiques[330] (convulsions et palpitations, éternuement, bourdonnements d'oreille). Notre Tosefta (VII, 13) y ajoute certains gestes manqués — tels que faire tomber un bâton de sa main ou un morceau de pain de sa bouche — qui devaient être interprétés comme des avertissements providentiels.

Chez les Romains, ainsi que l'atteste Pline[331], la chute du pain était un incident fâcheux qu'il fallait conjurer. On a un écho d'une tradition parallèle quoique d'inspiration différente en vigueur dans certains milieux juifs.

Tos. Shab. VI, 2:

ניטלה פת הימנו ואמר החזירוה לי שלא תאבד ברכתי.

«Lorsqu'on vous prend du pain dire 'rendez-le moi afin que ma bénédiction ne se perde pas'.»

Toute parole, phrase, exclamation, surprise par hasard a en outre pour celui qui l'entend valeur de κληδών[332]. L'appel de son propre nom par derrière mentionné dans nos sources (ibid.) doit constituer un aspect de cette divination clédonomantique.

[328] Cf. Lewy, art. cité, p. 28.

[329] Cité par Fahd, La divination arabe, p. 476—477.

[330] C'est le principe de la divination palmique, cf. Bouché–Leclercq, Histoire de la divination dans l'Antiquité I, p. 160.

[331] H.N. XXVIII, 5, 27: *Cibus etiam e manu prolapsus reddebatur utique per mensas (. . .) et sunt condita auguria, quid loquenti cogitantive id acciderit, inter execratissima, si pontifici accidat dicis causa epulanti. In mensa utique id reponi adolerique ad Larem piatio est.*

[332] Bouché–Leclercq, ibid. p. 156.

e) Procédés cléromantiques

Tos. Shab. VI, 1:

והמונה ומשליך צרורות לים או לנהר הרי זה מדרכי האמורי.

«Quiconque compte en jetant des cailloux dans la mer ou dans la rivière accomplit une coutume amorite.»

Il s'agit ici d'un présage provoqué, obtenu probablement grâce au chiffre qu'il est possible d'atteindre en comptant jusqu'au moment où les cailloux s'enfoncent dans l'eau[333]. Pausanias (III, 23, 8) rapporte une forme similaire d'hydromancie: à Thalamai, en Laconie, on jetait dans le lac d'Ino des galettes qui fournissaient un présage favorable si elles s'enfonçaient dans l'eau[334].

Toutefois, le jet de cailloux est susceptible de multiples interprétations diverses et constitue en particulier un symbole d'expulsion des esprits malfaisants[335].

Selon une croyance attestée dans la littérature biblique, une baguette magique pouvait rendre des oracles. C'est contre une telle divination que s'indigne le prophète Osée (4. 12): «Mon peuple consulte son bois, et son bâton (מקל) lui apprend l'avenir.» En écho au prophète, notre 'Tosefta' (Shab. VII. 4) classe au nombre des coutumes amorites, le fait de «consulter son bâton pour savoir si l'on partira ou non»: השואל כמקלו ואמ׳ אם אלך אם לא אלך-qui lui paraît être un cas particulier de cette antique coutume.

Mais la rhabdomancie n'est déjà plus du simple ressort du *menaheš* qui se contente d'interpréter ce qui se présente à lui, elle est du ressort du *qosem* plus engagé dans la magie[336].

Ce procédé semble s'être rencontré également en domaine grec[337].

f) Hémérologie et météorologie

Tos. VII, 14:

מעונן איזהו מעונן ר׳ ישמעאל אומר זה מעביר על העין ר׳ עקיבא אומר אילו נותנין עתים כגון אילו אומרין היום יפה לצאת מחר יפה ליקח היום חמה נחפת מחר גשמים יורדין כגון אילו האומ׳ לימודי ערבי שביעיות להיות יפות ועקורות קיטניות להיות רעות וחכמ׳ אומ׳ אילו אוחזי העינים.

«Qu'appelle-t-on *me'onen*? Selon R. Ismaël, c'est celui qui se passe quelque chose sur l'œil[338]. Selon R. Aqiba, ce sont ceux qui fixent des temps en disant par exemple 'aujourd'hui est un bon jour pour se mettre

333 Cf. Lieberman, TK III, p. 82.

334 Cf. Defradas, art. cité, p. 173.

335 Fahd, La divination arabe, p. 189.

336 Cf. Sifré, Deut. 18, p. 218 éd. Finkelstein. Sur *qasama*, cf. W. R. Smith, On the Forms of Divination and Magic enumerated in Deut. XVIII, 10, 11, Journal of Philology XIII (1885), p. 279s.

337 Cf. Nicandre, Theriac. 613 cité par Lewy, p. 131.

338 Cf. TB Sanh. 65b זה המעביר שבעה מיני זכור על העין «celui qui applique la semence de sept espèces mâles sur ses yeux».

en route, demain sera un bon jour pour acheter, aujourd'hui soleil voilé, demain de la pluie' ou en disant: 'le froment est beau mais stérile[339] à la veille des années sabbatiques, tandis que les légumineux sont mauvais'. Selon les sages, ce sont les illusionnistes.»

Selon la définition de R. Aqiba, la prédiction du *me'onen* porte sur les jours ou les années fastes et néfastes. Peuples d'Orient, Grecs, Romains, tous possèdent des calendriers du faste et du néfaste[340]. Ce type de calendrier est inconnu de la Bible où seule compte l'obéissance aux lois divines. En ce qui concerne les veilles d'années sabbatiques, le dicton attribué au *me'onen* va en outre à l'encontre de la promesse: «je vous manderai ma bénédiction dès la sixième année et elle donnera une production pour trois ans» (Lév. 25. 21).

Ce dicton ainsi que les appréhensions exprimées au paragraphe précédent de la Tosefta (VII, 13): «Ne commence pas par moi, car c'est le matin ou le premier du mois, ou la sortie de sabbat», prouvent bien que c'est en milieu juif que les rabbins avaient à combattre les 'coutumes amorites'. Le caractère astrologique de telles prédictions n'est pas souligné dans le texte mais il y a tout lieu de penser qu'elles se rattachaient à l'astrologie.

L'une des prédictions énumérées: «aujourd'hui soleil voilé, demain de la pluie», relève apparemment davantage de la prévision météorologique que de la divination. En cela le *me'onen* est bien, conformément à son étymologie, le scrutateur des nuées (*'anan*). Cette pratique se développe naturellement dans tout pays sec où la pluie est attendue comme une bénédiction. Si elle est ici condamnée, c'est sans doute que la forme de pratique considérée apparaissait alors comme étant liée à la divination[341] plutôt qu'à la science.

g) Oniromancie et nécromancie

Tos. VI, 7:

האומר [...] נשוק בארונו של מת כדי שתראנו אל תישק בארונו של מת שלא תראנו בלילה הפוך את חלוקך שתהא חולם חלומות אל תהפוך את חלוקך שלא תהא חולם חלומות שב על המכבד שתהא חולם חלומות אל תישב על המכבד שלא תהא חולם חלומות הרי זה מדרכי האמורי.

«Dire (...) 'embrasse le cercueil d'un mort pour le revoir en songe la nuit; retourne ta chemise pour faire des rêves, ne la retourne pas pour ne pas en faire; assieds-toi sur le balai pour faire des rêves, ne t'y assieds pas pour ne pas en faire', appartient aux coutumes amorites.»

[339] Cp. Sifré Deut. 18, p. 219 éd. FINKELSTEIN **למודי ערבי שביעיות להיות חטים יפות עקורות**. Nous suivons ici la lecture proposée par S. LIEBERMAN, p. 98 et étayée par une citation de Pline, H.N. XVIII, 54, 195: *semen optimum anniculum, bimum deterius, trimum pessimum, ultra sterile.*

[340] Cf. FAHD, La divination arabe, p. 483, n. 5.

[341] Cf. BOUCHÉ-LECLERCQ, La divination dans l'Antiquité I, p. 199 et FAHD, op. cit., p. 416—417.

1. Monnaie d'Acre-Ptolémaïs, IIe siècle, représentant Aphrodite debout sous une arche

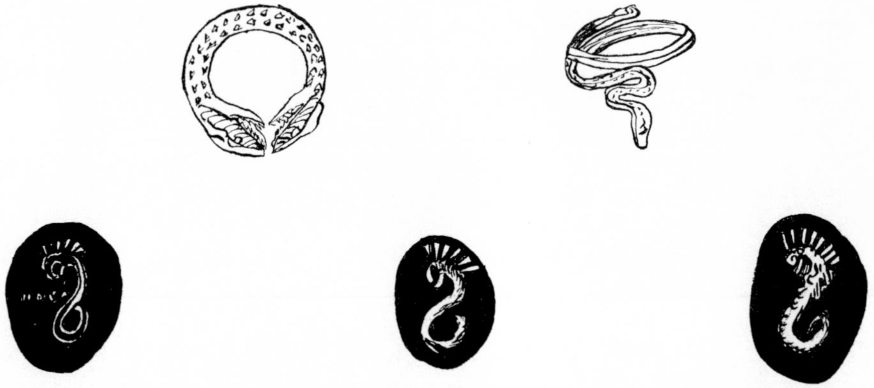

2. Bagues grecques à motif de serpent. Gemmes à motif de Khnoubis

3. Buste de Sérapis reposant sur un pied humain

La foi en l'oniromancie est sans doute une des croyances les plus universellement répandues. Ce n'est pas elle qui est incriminée ici: les rabbins du Talmud ont aussi leurs clefs des songes et telle page talmudique[342] constitue un véritable petit traité d'onirocritique. Ce qui est taxé de 'coutume amorite', c'est la croyance en la production artificielle des songes: vouloir modifier l'avenir en provoquant ou modifiant le songe qui est censé l'annoncer, c'est déjà faire œuvre de magie.

Les croyances rapportées ici ont leurs parallèles dans divers pays d'Europe[343]; pour ce qui est du balai devenu depuis l'accessoire des sorcières, Pythagore défendait déjà d'en enjamber[344].

De l'oniromancie à la nécromancie, il n'y a qu'un pas, lorsque ce sont des morts que l'on cherche à voir en songe. Certains même n'hésitaient pas à aller dormir sur le tombeau du mort auquel ils demandaient de les assister par un songe révélateur[345]. Une *baraïta* du traité Sanhédrin (65b) définit ainsi le nécromant (א״ב):

ודורש אל המתים זה המרעיב עצמו והולך ולן בבה״ק כדי שתשרה עליו רוח טומאה.

«celui qui consulte les morts, c'est celui qui jeûne et passe la nuit dans un cimetière, afin que l'esprit impur entre en lui.»

Dans notre 'Tosefta', il n'est pas question d'une forme aussi caractérisée de sorcellerie, mais seulement d'une femme «qui conduit son fils parmi les morts», המגוררת בנה לבין המתים (VI, 1), afin sans doute d'attirer sur lui la protection de quelque défunt et de le délivrer d'un mal[346].

La nécromancie proprement dite est beaucoup plus violemment condamnée dans le Talmud qui voue à la lapidation le nécromant ventriloque (זה המדבר משחין Sanh. 65a), comme celui qui parle avec sa propre voix (זה המדבר בפיו ibid.). La ventriloquie[347] était en effet couramment utilisée — et pour cause! — par les évocateurs des ombres.

Ainsi que le souligne ce dernier exemple, la divination conduit en fin de compte à la sorcellerie.

3. Talismans

Il n'est sans doute pas de civilisation qui ne connaisse la pratique des talismans destinés à protéger contre la maladie, le mauvais œil ou les esprits malfaisants. La 'Tosefta' en énumère quelques-uns.

[342] Cf. par ex. Berak. 57a. Pourtant le prophète Zacharie (10. 2) avait dit: «les songes prédisent de l'illusion»: והחלומות השוא ידברו.

[343] Cf. Lewy, art. cité, p. 33.

[344] Plutarque, Quaest. Rom. 112: μηδὲ σάρον ὑπερβαίνειν.

[345] Cf. Bouché-Leclercq, op. cit., p. 330—331.

[346] Cf. Lewy, article cité, p. 25.

[347] Cf. Bouché-Leclercq, op. cit., p. 338; Marquardt, Culte I, p. 137.

a) Talismans portés sur soi: un pendule ou un fil rouge

Tos. Shab. VI, 1:

והקושר מטולטלת על יריכו וחוט אדום על אצבעו.

«quiconque attache un pendule à sa hanche et un fil rouge à son doigt».

Le fil rouge ou le morceau d'étoffe de cette couleur sont des moyens prophylactiques bien attestés dans diverses sources antiques citées par LEWY (p. 26) parmi lesquelles ce passage de Dioscoride (III, 95): περιαφθὲν δὲ φοινικῷ ῥάκει θρεμμάτων νόσους ἀπελαύνει: «entouré d'un morceau d'étoffe rouge, il écarte les maladies des nourrissons».

Déjà en Assyrie, une corde de laine rouge éclatante paraissait le meilleur remède contre certaine maladie des yeux: «Ils imaginaient que par un contact plus ou moins prolongé avec la partie malade, le lien s'imprégnait du mal et l'emportait avec lui»[348].

Quant à la coutume de se nouer un fil autour du doigt, elle se rencontre notamment chez les Arabes (sans que la couleur du fil soit spécifiée), le but de ce geste étant de «se rendre attentif et de diminuer, par là, la magie de l'imprévu»[349].

Un peu plus loin, dans notre 'Tosefta' (Shab. VII, 11), il est encore question d'un fil:

הקושר חוט על גבי אדום רבן גמל׳ אומר אינו מדר׳ האמו׳ ר׳ אלעזר בר׳ צדוק אומר הרי זה מדרכי האמ׳.

«attacher un fil à du rouge (ce n'est pas une coutume amorite selon Rabban Gamaliel, c'en est une selon R. Eleazar parlant au nom de R. Ṣadoq)».

La variante par rapport au chapitre précédent où il était question d'un fil de couleur rouge, peut laisser pressentir une altération dans le texte. Aussi, LEWY veut-il lire: על גבי אדם 'à un homme' (p. 134). Il s'agirait alors d'un nœud possédant une vertu prophylactique sans que sa couleur ait une importance particulière.

C'est précisément le cas du 'nœud d'Hercule'[350] qui est crédité chez les Romains d'un pouvoir de guérison ou du moins d'une certaine efficacité[351].

Quant à ce que nous avons traduit par 'pendule' (מטולטלת), il peut s'agir d'une pierre précieuse ou non, suspendue au côté par un fil[352]. Il est

[348] Cf. FOSSEY, La magie assyrienne, Paris 1902, cité par E. MASSONEAU, La magie dans l'Antiquité romaine, p. 117.

[349] FAHD, La divination arabe, p. 475.

[350] Cf. DAREMBERG–SAGLIO IV, 1, fig. 5323, p. 87 s. v. nodus.

[351] Pline, H.N. XXVIII, 17, 63: *Volnera nodo Herculis praeligare mirum quantum ocior medicina est, atque etiam cottidiani cinctus tali nodo vim quandam habere utilem dicuntur.*

[352] Cf. LIEBERMAN, TK III, p. 82.

notoire en effet qu'à chaque pierre précieuse était attribuée, suivant sa couleur, une vertu prophylactique particulière[353]. A moins qu'il ne s'agisse dans notre texte d'un remède ainsi décrit par Pline[354]: «Pour guérir les maux des aines certains détachent un fil d'une toile, y font neuf ou sept nœuds en prononçant à chacun le nom de quelque veuve puis l'attachent à l'aine. Ils prescrivent aussi de porter, attaché avec un fil, un clou ou tout autre objet sur quoi on ait marché pour que le mal ne soit plus douloureux.» Une petite pierre rejetée par un calculeux et attachée au-dessus du pubis était également créditée de maintes guérisons[355].

b) Autres talismans

Tos. VI, 4:

הפוקק את החלון בסירא והקושר ברזל בכרעי המיטה של חיה והעורך לפניה שולחן הרי זה מדרכי האמורי אבל פוקקין את החלון בגלופקרין או בעמיר ונותן לפניה ספל של מים וקושרין לה תרנגולת שתהא לה לצות ולא מדרכי האמורי.

«Boucher la fenêtre avec de l'aubépine, attacher du fer aux montants du lit d'une accouchée[356], dresser devant elle une table, ce sont des coutumes amorites, mais l'on peut boucher la fenêtre avec une couverture ou une gerbe, placer devant elle une tasse d'eau, attacher à son lit une poule pour qu'elle lui tienne compagnie[357], sans que cela soit compté au nombre des coutumes amorites.»

c) L'aubépine

Boucher sa fenêtre avec de l'aubépine visait à écarter toutes les influences maléfiques. Les Grecs pensaient en effet que des branches d'aubépine attachées aux portes et aux fenêtres avaient pour vertu d'écarter les sorcières et de protéger contre les fantômes[358].

d) Le fer et les clous de fer

Attacher du fer au pied du lit d'une accouchée (Tos. Shab. VI, 4 הקושר ברזל בכרעי המיטה של חיה), jeter du fer devant les tombes (ibid. 12 הזורק ברזל מפני הקברים), placer un tisonnier de bois ou de fer sous sa tête (ibid. 13

[353] Voir la liste dans Daremberg–Saglio I, 1, p. 252, s. v. amuletum.
[354] H.N. XXVIII, 12, 48 *Inguinibus medentur aliqui licium telae detractum alligantes novenis septenisve nodis, ad singulos nominantes viduam aliquam atque ita inguini adalligantes. Licio et clavum aliudve quod quis calcaverit, alligatum ipsos iubent gerere, ne sit dolori vulnus*. Trad. Ernout, Belles Lettres.
[355] Ibid. 9, 42.
[356] Cf. infra d).
[357] Cp. Elien, De Nat. Anim. IV, 29: καὶ νῦν ταῖς τικτούσαις ἀλεκτρυὼν πάρεστι.
[358] Cf. J. G. Frazer, Commentaire sur Ovide IV, p. 142 (à propos de Fastes VI, 129) cité par Lieberman, TK p. 84. Voir aussi Lewy, art. cité, p. 29.

(הנותן מקל של אוד וברזל תחת ראשו הרי זה מדרכי האמורי) sont considérés comme autant de 'coutumes amorites' tandis que «mettre des poussins dans un crible et placer du fer entre eux contre le tonnerre ou l'éclair est permis».

Plusieurs sources romaines nous confirment que le fer et plus particulièrement les clous de fer avaient un pouvoir magique aux yeux des Anciens. Déjà à l'époque républicaine, le dictateur devait, selon l'usage, planter un clou pour détourner la peste[359]. Les Romains croyaient également que planter un clou de fer à l'endroit frappé en premier par la tête d'un individu tombant d'épilepsie, pouvait guérir définitivement cette maladie[360]; ou qu'un cercle formé trois fois au moyen d'un morceau de fer autour d'un enfant ou d'un adulte détournait d'eux les maléfices[361]. Placée sous l'oreiller, une pierre à affûter ayant servi à aiguiser beaucoup de fers pouvait provoquer des révélations de la part d'un malade victime d'un empoisonnement[362].

Les clous ayant attaché à la croix un supplicié étaient particulièrement recherchés des magiciens[363]. R. Meir lui-même croyait à leur vertu[364].

En ce qui concerne la protection des poussins et surtout des œufs, contre le tonnerre, l'usage du fer était si répandu qu'il n'était même plus remis en question et apparaissait comme une recette pratique, un vieux procédé de paysan, plus que comme un moyen magique; aussi le traité d'agriculture de Columelle[365] le mentionne-t-il.

En revanche, il est clair qu'attacher du fer au pied du lit d'une accouchée pour écarter de celle-ci les esprits auxquels elle passait pour être particulièrement exposée[366], relève de la magie. Cette pratique et celle de jeter du fer devant les tombes, sans doute pour se protéger des morts malveillants correspondent à la croyance populaire décrite dans une scholie de l'Odyssée[367]: κοινή τις παρὰ ἀνθρώποις ἐστὶν ὑπόληψις ὅτι νεκροὶ καὶ δαίμονες σίδηρον φοβοῦνται. Notre texte ajoute que «jeter du fer aux sorciers est permis» (ibid. מפני חרשן הרי זה מותר) ce qui légitime une sorte de magie défensive. Pline[368] semble lui-même croire au pouvoir de clous arrachés à des tombes et disposés sur le seuil des maisons pour se protéger des cauchemars.

[359] Marquardt, Culte I, p. 130.

[360] Pline, H.N. XXVIII, 17, 63.

[361] Ibid. XXXIV, 44, 151.

[362] Ibid. XXVIII, 12, 47.

[363] Cf. E. Massoneau, op. cit., p. 114. Selon Pline, H.N. XXVIII, 9, 41, ce sont les cheveux d'un tel supplicié qui guérissent de la fièvre quarte.

[364] Le Talmud (Shab. 67a) le justifie partiellement d'avoir permis de sortir le sabbat avec un œuf de locuste, une dent de renard ou le clou d'un gibet en indiquant que ce que l'on fait 'pour raison de santé' (משום רפואה) est permis; mais cette opinion est rejetée par les rabbins.

[365] De re rustica VIII, 5. Cp. Pline, H.N. X, 75, 153: *remedium contra tonitrus clavus ferreus sub stramine ovorum positus.*

[366] Cf. E. Massoneau, op. cit., p. 77.

[367] Schol. Q sur Od. XI, 48, citée par Lewy, p. 29—30.

[368] H.N. XXXIV, 44, 151.

4. Sortilèges

La croyance à la vertu des talismans est en partie un corollaire de la croyance aux sortilèges. Il faut en effet pouvoir se protéger non seulement contre la maladie et les mauvais esprits (qui probablement l'envoient) mais aussi contre les sorts jetés par un sorcier ou provoqués par certaines catégories de gestes.

a) Les 'nœuds' magiques

Tos. Shab. VI, 9:

האומר אל תפשיל ידך לאחוריך שלא תאסר עלינו מלאכה הרי זה מדרכי האמורי.

«Dire 'ne croise pas les mains derrière ton dos afin de ne pas lier notre travail', c'est une coutume amorite.»

'Lier' אסר est le terme utilisé dans les textes magiques et les formules d'incantation[369]. L'idée qu'en croisant les doigts, les mains ou les jambes, l'on crée des 'nœuds magiques' de mauvais augure[370] ou qui paralysent l'action, est très ancienne chez les Romains qui interdisaient de porter les jarrets sur l'un ou l'autre genou dans les assemblées, les sacrifices et les prières publiques[371]. Les doigts entrelacés constituaient à leurs yeux un maléfice pour la femme enceinte ou le malade se tenant à proximité[372].

L'amitié, elle, constitue un nœud à préserver. Aussi, la voix populaire dit-elle.

Tos. Shab. VII, 12:

על תעבור בינותינו שלא תפסיק אהבתינו.

«Ne passe pas entre nous afin de ne pas casser notre amitié»: croyance 'amorite', selon notre 'Tosefta'.

L'attitude consistant à s'asseoir sur une charrue n'entre pas à proprement parler dans la catégorie des nœuds magiques mais elle produit un effet analogue.

Tos. Shab. VI, 8:

האומר אל תשב על המחרישה כדי שלא תכביד עלינו מלאכה הרי זה מדרכי האמורי אל תשב על המחרישה שלא תישבר הרי זה מדר׳ האמורי אם בשביל שלא תשבר ודאי הרי זה מותר.

«Dire: 'Ne t'assieds par sur la charrue afin de ne pas alourdir notre tâche', ou 'ne t'assieds pas sur la charrue afin qu'elle ne se brise pas', c'est une coutume amorite. Si c'est vraiment pour qu'elle ne se brise pas, bien entendu c'est permis.»

369 Cf. S. Lieberman, Greek in Jewish Palestine, p. 120, n. 34.

370 Cf. E. Massoneau, op. cit., p. 196.

371 Pline, H.N. XXVIII, 17, 59. 372 ibid.

b) Pouvoirs bénéfiques (ou maléfiques) de certains individus

Tos. Shab. VI, 3:

היה מתחיל במלאכה ואמר יבוא איש פלוני שידיו קלות ויתחיל בה פלוני שרגליו קלות ויעבור לפנינו הרי זה מדרכי האמורי בחבית או בעיסה אמר יבוא פלוני שידיו מבורכות ויתחיל הרי זה מדרכי האמורי.

«Dire en entreprenant un travail: 'que vienne un tel qui a les mains légères et qu'il commence', ou 'que vienne un tel qui a les pieds légers et qu'il passe devant nous', c'est une coutume amorite. Dire sur une cruche ou sur la pâte 'que vienne un tel qui a les mains bénies et qu'il commence', c'est une coutume amorite.»

La croyance que certains individus sont capables de jeter des sorts bons ou mauvais se retrouve dans toutes les civilisations. Notre principal témoin sur les croyances répandues dans le monde romain au début de l'empire, Pline l'Ancien, mentionne les uns[373] et les autres[374].

Le contraire de l'expression **רגל קלה** est **רגל רעה** littéralement 'mauvais pied' qui équivaut dans certains textes rabbiniques à 'malchance'[375]. L'expression grecque correspondante est κακοποδινός[376]. Inversement on peut dire en latin *boni pedis homo*[377].

c) Vertus des plantes

Tos. VI, 7:

האומר אכול תמרת החזרת זו שתהא זוכרני בה אל תאכלנה מפני ברקות.

«Dire: 'Mange ce pied de laitue, afin de te souvenir de moi' ou 'n'en mange pas par crainte de l'ophtalmie'[378].»

Les vertus attribuées aux plantes sont innombrables[379] mais toutes ne sont pas naturelles et souvent, comme dans le cas cité ici, il n'y a qu'un pas de la médecine à la magie.

d) Cuisson magique

Tos. Shab. VI, 14—15:

המצוות לתנור בשביל שלא תיפל הפת הנותן קיסמין באזני קדירה בשביל שלא תהא מרתעת ושופעת לאחוריה הרי זה מדר׳ האמורי אבל נותנין קיסם של תות וזכוכית לתוך הקדירה בשביל שתבשל מהרה אבל אסרו חכמ׳ בזכוכית מפני סכנת נפשות.

[373] H.N. XVIII, 54, 197: *fit quoque quorundam occulta ratione quod sors genialis atque fecunda est.* [374] H.N. XXVIII, 6, 30 et 32.

[375] Cf. S. Lieberman, Texts and Studies, Roman legal institutions in early rabbinics and in the Acta martyrum, p. 59, repris de JQR XXXV (1944).

[376] Marc le Diacre, Vita S. Porphyrii 19, éd. Grégoire–Kugener, p. 16, cité par Lieberman, ibid.

[377] Augustin, Lettre 44, cité ibid., n. 13. [378] Cf. Pline, H.N. XX, 26, 64 fin.

[379] Voir tous les livres XII à XXVII de l'Histoire Naturelle de Pline.

«Crier après le four pour que le pain ne s'affaisse pas, mettre des copeaux sur les poignées d'une marmite afin qu'elle ne recule pas et ne déborde pas, c'est une coutume amorite (mais l'on peut mettre un copeau de mûrier[380] ou du verre à l'intérieur de la marmite afin de hâter la cuisson; toutefois, nos sages ont interdit le verre en raison du danger).»

השותקת לעדשים והמוצצת לאורז[381] והמטפחת לנר הרי זה מדר׳ האמ׳.

«Faire taire les lentilles, crier après le riz, battre des mains devant la flamme, c'est une coutume amorite.»

A ces diverses 'recettes', la *baraïta* correspondante du Talmud babylonien (Shab. 67b) ajoute l'usage d'uriner devant sa marmite, considéré comme un moyen de hâter la cuisson המשתנת בפני קדירתה בשביל שתתבשל מהרה. Pline qui énumère complaisamment les vertus tant médicinales que magiques de l'urine[382] omet de mentionner celle-là.

Tout le folklore européen est plein de contes de cuissons magiques où les aliments et les ustensiles obéissent aux ordres donnés. On en trouve ici l'esquisse.

5. Rites de conjuration

Dans son édition de la 'Tosefta', ZUCKERMANDEL n'a pas retenu en Shabbat VI, 17, p. 118, 1. 2, la leçon de certains manuscrits qui donnent le texte suivant:

המושבת אפרוחים אמרה איני מושבתן אלא בבתולה איני מושבתן אלא ערומה.

«Installer des poulets en disant je ne les fais mettre que par une vierge et que par une vierge nue.»

LEWY[383] et LIEBERMAN[384] ont en revanche maintenu ce texte et ce d'autant plus volontiers que Pline[385] garantit l'efficacité de certains pansements faits dans de pareilles conditions: *si virgo imponat nuda jejuna jejuno*. La vierge nue est donc créditée du pouvoir de détourner le mal.

L'accomplissement d'une action de la main droite ou gauche a aussi son importance. Le texte de la 'Tosefta' Shab. VI, 17 se poursuit ainsi:

המושבת אפרוחים אמרה [...] איני מושבתן אלא בשמאל איני מושבתן אלא בתרי המקדש בתרי והמשליח בתרי.

380 Pline (H.N. XXIII, 64, 127) signale de même que les tiges des figues sauvages accélèrent la cuisson de la viande de bœuf, permettant ainsi une grande économie de combustible.

381 Voir discussion sur les variantes de cette expression et les divers sens possibles chez LIEBERMAN, p. 88—89. Nous nous rallions au sens retenu par LEWY, art. cité, p. 37.

382 H.N. XXVIII, ch. 18 et 19.

383 Art. cité, p. 38.

384 TK III, p. 89.

385 H.N. XXVI, 60, 93.

«Installer des poulets en disant [...] je ne les mets que de la main gauche, je ne les mets que des deux mains, utiliser les deux mains pour la remise d'un contrat de mariage ou d'un acte de divorce[386].»

Nombreux sont les actes pour lesquels les Mages, selon le témoignage de Pline, conseillent d'utiliser la main gauche[387]. Si la gauche a une valeur ambiguë et éventuellement favorable chez les Romains, en revanche chez les Grecs seule la droite porte chance. C'est sans doute pour n'être en reste avec aucune tradition que certains utilisaient leurs deux mains là où une seule aurait suffit.

Tos. Shab. VI, 18:

הנותנת ביצים[388] ועשבים בכותל וטחה בפניהם והמונה שבעה ואחד הרי זה מדרכי האמ׳.

«Mettre des œufs et de l'herbe dans un mur et les emmurer, compter sept et un c'est une coutume amorite.»

Selon l'explication du *ʿArukh* reproduite par LIEBERMAN, cela se réfère à l'usage de piquer dans un mur au moyen d'un bâtonnet les coquilles d'œufs brisées après l'éclosion. De son côté, Pline rapporte qu'afin de conjurer les envoûtements, il était d'usage après avoir mangé des œufs ou des escargots d'en briser aussitôt les coquilles[389].

Quant au nombre sept la valeur magique qu'on lui attribue dès la plus haute antiquité, s'accroît du fait que le nom de la septième lettre grecque[390] ζῆτα est rattaché par une étymologie populaire à la racine de ζῆν vivre[391]. On conçoit donc que certains aient préféré compter ʿsept et un' au lieu de ʿhuit'[392]. Ajoutons à cela que le nombre impair est en faveur dans l'Antiquité. Virgile[393] ne dit-il pas: *Numero deus impare gaudet.*

Tos. Shab. VI, 2:

המספק והמטפח והמרקד לשלהבת הרי זה מדרכי האמרי.

«Se frapper des hanches, applaudir ou danser devant une flamme c'est une coutume amorite.»

[386] Cf. LIEBERMAN, TK III, p. 90.

[387] H.N. XX, 49, 126; XXI, 83, 143 et 104, 176; XXII, 24, 50; XXIV, 54, 103 etc.

[388] ZUCKERMANDEL, p. 118, l. 4 אפרוחים. La leçon retenue par LIEBERMAN est corroborée notamment par TB Shab. 67b. A la ligne suivante, il garde שבעה ואחד au lieu du simple שבעה.

[389] H.N. XXVIII, 4, 17.

[390] Les lettres grecques servent à compter comme les lettres hébraïques.

[391] Cf. Le jeu de mots sur le grec rapporté au nom de R. Abbahu en Genèse Rabba XIV, 2, interprété dans S. LIEBERMAN, Greek in Jewish Palestine, p. 22—23.

[392] Le texte de TB Shab. 67b précise המרקדת והמונה שבעים ואחד אפרוחים בשביל שלא ימותו «danser et compter soixante-dix (erreur au lieu de sept ?) et un poulets afin qu'ils ne meurent pas».

[393] Bucoliques, Eclogue 8, 75. Cp. Pline, H.N. XXVIII, 5, 23 *Cur impares numeros ad omnia vehementiores credimus?*

Un texte de l'évêque syrien du Vème siècle Théodoret[394] rapproché par LEWY de ce passage, nous rapporte qu'il était de coutume dans certaines cités d'allumer une fois l'an des feux sur les places et de sauter par dessus afin de détourner le mal et de se purifier.

Il est également possible que ce soit une façon de conjurer l'incendie comme dans le passage suivant: Ibid. 10

התוסם אור בכותל ואו' הדא[395] היא הרי זה מדר' האמרי ואם בשביל ניצוצות הרי זה מותר.

«Fixer une torche au mur en disant *hada*, c'est une coutume amorite, mais si c'est à cause des étincelles, c'est permis.»

Ce geste avec la formule qui l'accompagne est sans doute à rapprocher de l'usage de tracer sur les murs des prières pour détourner les incendies, dont parle Pline[396].

La même formule est reprise pour accompagner le geste de jeter de l'eau (Ibid. 11):

השופך מים ברשות ואומ' הדא הרי זה מדר' האמרי ואם אמר מפני עוברים ושבים הרי זה מותר.

«Jeter de l'eau dans la rue en criant *hada*!, c'est une coutume amorite, mais si on précise que c'est pour avertir les passants c'est permis.»

Ce passage nous montre clairement, que l'expression הדא accompagnant l'action de jeter de l'eau dans la rue ne visait pas seulement à avertir les passants[397], mais probablement à écarter quelque esprit malfaisant ou à conjurer un malheur[398]. Pline rapporte que lorsqu'il était question d'incendie dans quelque banquet, on s'empressait de répandre de l'eau sous la table[399].

A la 'barrière d'eau', se substitue dans certains cas la 'barrière de feu'[400]. La bougie déposée à terre était-elle un moyen d'empêcher l'âme du mort de venir hanter les lieux[401]? Cela n'est pas impossible, mais nous ne connaissons pas de parallèle exact à la coutume ainsi décrite (Ibid. 2):

[394] Opera I, 352 éd. SIRMOND, Paris 1642, ap. LEWY, p. 27. Cp. J. GRIMM, Deutsche Mythologie, Aberglaube, n° 918 (cité par LEWY, ibid.): *„Wer übers Johannesfeuer springt, Kriegt dasselbige Jahr das Fieber nicht."*

[395] Voir discussion sur l'orthographe et le sens des deux termes chez LIEBERMAN, TK III, p. 87. LEWY (p. 34) prend l'exclamation au sens de 'gare', comme s'il s'agissait de הלאה mais ce sens fort satisfaisant n'est pas suffisamment fondé.

[396] H.N. XXVIII, 4, 20. Le rite décrit dans la 'Tosefta' est ainsi interprété par L. BLAU, Das Altjüdische Zauberwesen, Budapest 1898, rééd. Graz 1974, p. 65.

[397] Cela se pratiquait en Grèce, cf. Souda s. v. ἀπόνιπτρον· εἰώθασι δὲ οἱ ἀρχαῖοι εἴποτε ἐκχέοιτο ἀπόνιπτρον ἀπὸ τῶν θυρίδων ἵνα μή τις βραχῇ λέγειν τῶν παριόντων, ἐξίτω.

[398] Cf. L. BLAU, op. cit., p. 66.

[399] H.N. XXVIII, 5, 26: *Incendia inter epulas nominata aquis sub mensas profusis abominamur.*

[400] Cf. LEWY, art. cité, p. 27, à propos de πῦρ πρὸ θυρῶν.

[401] Cf. J. G. FRAZER, La crainte des morts dans la religion primitive, 2ème série, Paris 1935, p. 52: chez les Romains, au retour des funérailles on marchait sur le feu sans doute pour empêcher le fantôme d'apparaître.

הניחו נר על הארץ כדי שיצטערו המתים אל תניחו נר על הארץ שלא יצטערו המתים.

«Déposez une bougie par terre afin de tourmenter les morts, n'en déposez pas afin de ne pas tourmenter les morts.»

6. Adjurations ou incantations

Tos. Shab. VII, 1—3:

האומר ממיא וביציא הרי זה מדרכ׳ האמורי ר׳ יהודה אומר יממיא ובוצציא. האומר דגן וקדרון הרי זה מדר׳ האמר׳ ר׳ יהודה אומ׳ דגן על שם עבודה זרה שנ׳ לדגון אלהיהם ולשמחה האמר דני דנו הרי זה מדרכי האמ׳ ר׳ יהודה אומר דן על שם עבו׳ זרה שנ׳ ואמרו חי אלהיך דן.

«Dire *yamia ubeṣia* (mers et marécages?) c'est une coutume amorite; selon R. Judah la formule est *yamia uboṣesia*. Dire *dagan weqidron* c'est une coutume amorite. R. Judah dit: 'Dagan est le nom d'une idole'; ainsi qu'il est écrit (Juges 16. 23): 'à Dagon leur dieu et pour une réjouissance'. Dire *dani danu* c'est une coutume amorite. R. Judah dit: 'Dan est le nom d'une idole'; ainsi qu'il est écrit (Amos 8, 14): 'Vive ton dieu, Dan'».

Ces formules obscures sur lesquelles s'ouvre le chapitre VII de la 'Tosefta' de 'Shabbat' ont déjà suscité maintes conjectures. La troisième se retrouve dans le passage correspondant du Talmud babylonien (Shabbat 67b) qui l'a fait précéder d'une autre formule dont il a déjà été question (supra p. 413) à propos du culte de Gad: גד גדי וסינוק לו אושכי ובושכי, *gad gedi wesinoq lo ushki ubushki*[402].

Il est possible que nous ayons là quelques exemples de ces formules magiques faites de «termes barbares impossibles à prononcer» et «d'étranges mots latins»[403], ou grecs ou araméens. Le point commun de toutes ces formules réside dans une certaine similitude phonétique entre les deux éléments[404] dont elles sont composées.

Les quelques explications avancées n'ont rien de certain de l'avis même de leurs auteurs qui, d'ailleurs, hésitent entre les variantes proposées dans les diverses versions[405].

A propos de דני, Lewy s'autorise de la présence du terme לשמחה dans un manuscrit, pour supposer qu'il recouvre un ἡδονή déformé par aphérèse,

402 Trad. éd. Soncino: *"Be lucky my luck and tire not by day or night* (?)".

403 Pline, H.N. XXVIII, 4, 20 *externa verba atque ineffabilia . . . an latine inopinata.*

404 Pline (ibid.) rapporte que César avait coutume «de répéter trois fois une formule magique afin d'assurer la sécurité de ses déplacements, usage qui, comme on le sait, est maintenant généralisé»: *id quod plerosque nunc facere scimus, carmine ter repetito securitatem itinerum aucupari solitum.*

405 Voir Lieberman, TK III, p. 91—93.

or non seulement *le simha* 'pour une réjouissance' ne correspond qu'approximativement au texte grec, mais en outre, il fait partie de la citation biblique concernant Dagon.

La même formule suscite chez LIEBERMAN[406] quelques suggestions intéressantes sinon totalement convaincantes: ou bien il s'agirait d'une incantation populaire signifiant 'jugez mon cas' et visant à obtenir gain de cause dans un procès, ou bien ce serait la transcription d'une formule grecque présente dans certains papyri magiques: δέννω δέννω ou δένο δένο[407]: «je lie» (par la magie ou par un serment) ou encore δέννω (τὸν) δεῖνα: «je lie un tel».

La présence à côté du mot *dan*, de *gad* et *dagon*, n'interdit pas de penser à notre avis, que, ainsi que le suggèrent les remarques de R. Judah, il y ait effectivement référence ici à quelques-unes des anciennes divinités cananéennes.

Tos. ibid. 5—10:

האמר מרפא הרי זה מדרכי האמורי ר׳ אלעזר בר צדוק לא אמר מרפא מפני בטול תורה, של בית רבן גמליאל לא היו אומ׳ מרפא. האומר יתיר ונותר הרי זה מדר׳ האמ׳ ר׳ יהודה אומר יתיר ונותר אל יהא בביתי. האומר שתו והותירו הרי זה מדר׳ האמ׳ שתו והותירו חמרא לחייכון לא מדרכי האמורי. מעשה בר׳ עקיבא שעשה משתה לבנו ועל כל חבית וחבית שהיה פותח אומר חמרא לחיי רבנן ולחיי תלמידיהון האומר לאו לאו הרי זה מדרכי האמורי ואף על פי שאין ראיה לדבר ויא׳ לאל סור ממנו ודעת דרכיך לא חפצנו.

«Dire *marpé* (guérison) est une coutume amorite. R. Eleazar bar Sadoq, ne disait pas *marpé* car c'est autant de perdu pour l'étude; dans la maison de Rabban Gamaliel, on ne disait pas *marpé*[408]. Dire *yatir venotar* (surplus et reste) c'est une coutume amorite; R. Judah dit 'qu'on n'ait pas de *yatir venotar* dans sa maison'. Dire 'buvez et laissez du vin à votre santé' n'est pas une coutume amorite. On raconte de R. Aqiba que, lors du banquet de son fils, il disait à chaque cruche qu'il ouvrait 'vin à la santé des maîtres et de leurs disciples'. Dire 'non, non' c'est une coutume amorite et bien qu'il n'y ait pas de preuve à cet égard (on peut y rattacher ce verset: Job. 21, 14): or, ils disaient à Dieu: Détourne-toi de nous, nous ne voulons pas connaître tes voies.»

Les formules citées dans ce passage sont très différentes des précédentes en ceci d'abord qu'elles sont en bon hébreu ou araméen et que leur sens obvie se laisse parfaitement circonscrire. **מרפא** de la racine r p ʾ 'guérir'

[406] Cf. Texts and Studies, p. 27—28, trad. de l'article original en hébreu: Some notes on adjurations in Israël, Tarbiz XXVII (1958).

[407] Probablement graphies populaires pour δέω; cf. PREISENDANZ, Papyri Graecae magicae V, 2, p. 154—155.

[408] Cf. Berakhot 53a.

correspond au grec ἴασις. Il s'agit très vraisemblablement d'une formule liée à l'éternuement, laquelle est d'ailleurs autorisée dans d'autres sources rabbiniques[409]. Selon un passage de TJ Berakhot VI, 6, 10d:

דעטיש גו מיכלא אסיר למימ׳ ייס בגין סכנת׳ דנפשא.

«Lorsque quelqu'un éternue au cours d'un repas, on ne doit pas lui dire ἴασις, car on risque [d'avaler de travers].»

Sans doute veut-on d'une manière générale écarter des formules qui attirent la protection d'une divinité étrangère, l'une d'elle relevée par Lewy étant très explicite à cet égard: Ζεῦ σῶσον[410]. Ceux qui considèrent que le lien avec le paganisme est estompé, la trouvent tout simplement superflue comme R. Eleazar bar Sadoq aux yeux duquel elle constitue *bitul Tora*, car les Juifs n'ont aucune raison de croire à l'instar des païens que l'éternuement constitue un mauvais présage[411].

La formule *yatir wenotar* s'éclaire, ainsi que le note Lieberman (p. 95), à la lumière d'un texte de Pline[412] selon lequel la récolte de l'année, est présentée comme 'vieille', c'est-à-dire comme un 'surplus' et un 'reste' de l'année précédente.

La comparaison entre la formule interdite שתו והותירו («buvez et laissez-en») et la formule שתו והותירו חמרא לחייכון[413] («buvez et laissez du vin à votre santé») suggère que dans le premier cas le reste du vin pouvait être consacré à une idole ou à quelque démon, selon Lieberman (ibid.). Il nous paraît plutôt que ce pourrait être une façon de conjurer le mauvais œil et d'attirer la prospérité sur le buveur auquel on souhaite de laisser du vin pour marquer sa satiété.

Dans la répétition לא לא, Lewy (p. 134) voit un écho possible de la formule latine de conjuration *procul a nobis*. Lieberman (p. 96) rapproche ce passage d'une *baraïta* de Pesahim 111a où il est dit qu'il vaut mieux ne pas passer entre deux chiens, deux palmiers ou deux femmes et qu'au cas où cela se produirait, il y aurait lieu de recourir à un verset commençant et se terminant par le nom divin אל ou commençant et se terminant par la négation לא (laquelle est l'anagramme du nom divin). Cela confirme donc qu'il doit s'agir dans notre texte d'une formule de conjuration de la sorcellerie[414], art dans lequel les Anciens reconnaissaient quelque supériorité aux femmes[415].

[409] Cf. Lieberman, TK III, p. 93—94.

[410] Dans une épigramme d'Ammien, Anthol. gr. II, 13, citée par Lewy, p. 132.

[411] Cf. Pline, H.N. XXVIII, 5, 23: *Cur sternumentis salutamus?*

[412] Ibid. *Haec vetera esse dicimus, alia nova optamus.*

[413] TB Shab. 67b אשתה ואותיר אשתה ואותיר יש בו משום דרכי האמורי «que je boive et qu'il en reste que je boive et qu'il en reste», cela fait partie des coutumes amorites.

[414] Cf. Berakhot 62a fin, où une double négation est également utilisée pour se protéger des sorciers.

[415] Cf. Juster, Les Juifs dans l'empire romain II, p. 209.

La liste des 'coutumes amorites' de la 'Tosefta' est une liste ouverte qui ne saurait inclure les innombrables usages plus ou moins teintés de magie qui étaient pratiqués à l'époque. Elle relève probablement ceux par lesquels certains Juifs étaient plus particulièrement attirés en raison du milieu ambiant, et, au nom d'une certaine idée de la piété juive, elle conseille, en écho à la Sibylle alexandrine[416], de ne prendre souci «ni de la courbe circulaire du soleil ou de la lune, ni des prodiges qui se manifestent sur la terre, ni de la profondeur de la glauque mer océane, ni de ce que présagent les éternuements, ni des oiseaux des ornithomanciens, ni des devins, ni des sorciers, ni des conjurateurs, ni des imbéciles supercheries vocales des ventriloques».

V. Conclusion

Les observations éparses recueillies à travers les sources talmudiques nous fournissent une documentation fragmentaire plutôt qu'un tableau cohérent du paganisme local. Cette constatation était prévisible en raison des préoccupations pastorales des rabbins dont elles émanent, préoccupations qui leur interdisaient de s'étendre sur des formes de culte réprouvées, voire de nommer des idoles tenues en abomination.

Beaucoup de ces observations doivent en outre être maniées avec précaution. Bien qu'elles aient été faites en des temps et en des lieux différents, il est impossible d'y démêler les éléments propres au Sud du pays de ceux qui seraient plutôt caractéristiques du Nord; la majorité des autorités citées vivant en Galilée inférieure à la fin du IIème siècle, on peut tout au plus inférer que la réalité la plus largement représentée est la situation religieuse de la Galilée ou du littoral septentrional à cette période. A cette imprécision de localisation et de chronologie, s'ajoute une difficulté provenant des interférences bibliques: les passages bibliques concernant l'idolâtrie sont lus à la lumière de la réalité contemporaine, mais en même temps la situation des temps bibliques est projetée sur l'environnement païen du IIème siècle. L'arbre vert autour duquel un culte est rendu n'a sans doute qu'un rapport lointain avec l'*ashera* du livre des Rois, Baal Peor a probablement disparu, et les Amorrhéens qui donnent leur nom aux 'coutumes amorites' appartiennent à la préhistoire du pays. La langue rab-

[416] Oracles sibyllins III 221—226, éd. Nikiprowetzky, Paris-La Haye 1970:

Οὔτε γὰρ ἠελίου κύκλιον δρόμον οὔτε σελήνης
οὔτε πελώρια ἔργα μεριμνῶσιν κατὰ γαίης·
οὔτε βάθος χαροποῖο θαλάσσης Ὠκεανοῖο,
οὐ πταρμῶν σημεῖ' οἰωνοπόλων τε πετεινά,
οὐ μάντεις, οὐ φαρμακούς, οὐ μὴν ἐπαοιδούς,
οὐ μύθων μωρῶν ἀπάτας ἐγγαστεριμύθων
. . .

binique toute imprégnée de culture biblique, risque ainsi de nous entraîner à des analogies abusives avec le passé lointain.

Lorsque le Talmud apporte des informations qui concernent indéniablement le paganisme contemporain, ses évocations sont trop fugitives pour qu'on puisse opérer à partir de lui seul une reconstitution des pratiques et des cultes locaux. S'il est le témoin unique d'un usage, on ne peut qu'enregistrer son témoignage sans parvenir à la certitude de l'interpréter correctement. En revanche, si son témoignage est parallèle à celui des sources archéologiques et de sources littéraires dont l'immense majorité concerne d'autres régions de l'empire romain, il est alors particulièrement précieux car il fait sortir de l'ombre une religion païenne souvent dissimulée au regard de l'histoire par la forte présence du judaïsme et du christianisme sur la même terre.

De ces considérations méthodologiques, il ressort que l'originalité des formes locales de paganisme — pour tant est qu'il y en ait une — est fort malaisée à dégager. Un fait va de soi: la religion païenne décrite par les rabbins est la religion qui se manifeste hors du temple, celle dont les rapports quotidiens avec l'environnement païen rend le contact inévitable.

Cette religion semble inclure des traits sémitiques qui se manifestent notamment dans des cultes liés à certains lieux: sur une montagne, autour d'un arbre vert ou d'un point d'eau. A côté de ces survivances sémitiques qui doivent concerner essentiellement les campagnes, émergent divers éléments gréco-romains ou du moins très caractéristiques du syncrétisme qui affecte alors le bassin méditerranéen d'un bord à l'autre.

Les fêtes publiques énumérées constituent le trait le plus nettement romain de cette religion. Ce sont des fêtes officielles liées au culte impérial — dont nos sources prononcent une condamnation à peine voilée —, de ces fêtes civiques autant que religieuses par lesquelles Rome s'assurait du loyalisme des populations soumises.

Dans une région où devait se trouver plus encore qu'à Rome «une telle assistance de divinités qu'un dieu s'y rencontrait plus facilement qu'un homme» (Satiricon, 17), bien peu de noms ont été retenus par nos sources. La divinité dont le culte est le plus souvent mentionné est 'Mercolis' en l'honneur duquel les routes sont jalonnées de tas de pierres. Aphrodite dont la statue orne les thermes d'Acre, paraît moins pernicieuse que les dieux égyptiens romanisés: «la femme qui allaite» (Isis) et Sérapis, dont d'innombrables gemmes reproduisent l'effigie. Sans doute, certaines de ces divinités ont-elles au bout d'une longue symbiose avec l'hellénisme, fusionné avec les vieilles divinités locales mais les noms cités empêchent de détecter les divinités sémitiques sous-jacentes. Tout au plus trouve-t-on mentionné en passant Atargatis de Baalbek, Gad sans doute équivalent de Tyché. Sans doute, discerne-t-on çà et là quelques aspects proprement locaux au niveau des fêtes privées et des diverses manifestations de la crédulité populaire, mais on est surpris de constater que tant d'usages connus en Grèce et à Rome ont leur répondant exact sur ces rivages asiatiques. La politique de romanisation ne saurait être pour rien dans de telles croyances ou pratiques. Celles-ci supposent des échanges de longue date entre populations d'Orient et d'Occident, où il est difficile de discerner l'apport de l'un et de l'autre.

Le 'culte étranger' en Palestine présente donc une spécificité mineure dans la civilisation méditerranéenne de l'époque impériale où le syncrétisme entre les religions venues d'Orient et celles de l'Occident est la règle. Dans leur refus des concessions au monde environnant, judaïsme et christianisme primitif devaient apparaître comme d' 'étranges étrangers'.

Bibliographie

I. Sources rabbiniques

A. Pour l'ensemble des sources citées,

Voir la présentation de la littérature rabbinique donnée par CH. TOUATI, art. Talmud, Encyclopaedia Universalis, vol. 15, Paris 1975, pp. 718—721, qui comporte également une liste des traductions du Talmud en anglais, allemand et français.

B. Pour le traité 'Aboda Zara'

Abodah Sarah oder der Götzendienst. Ein Traktat aus dem Talmud. Traduction allemande de F. C. EWALD, Nürnberg 1868².

Fragments de manuscrits de TJ avec accents massorétiques provenant de la 'Geniza' du Caire dans J. N. EPSTEIN, Li-Seridei ha-Yerušalemi, Tarbiz III (1931), 15—26.

S. LIEBERMAN, The Talmud of Caesarea, Yerushalmi, tractate Nezikin, Jerusalem 1931.

SH. ABRAMSON, Tractate "Aboda Zarah" of the Babylonian Talmud. Ms. Jewish Theological Seminary of America (avec fac-similé, pp. 1—132), New-York 1957.

Edition critique de la 'Mishna' par W. L. ELMSLIE, The Mishna on Idolatry Aboda Zara, Texts and Studies, vol. VIII, n° 2. Contributions to Biblical and Patristic Literature, Cambridge University Press 1911.

C. Pour la 'Tosefta' du traité Shabbat, ch. VI et VII

Edition de M. S. ZUCKERMANDEL d'après le ms. d'Erfurt, 1881, reprod. Jérusalem 1937 et 1963.

Edition critique de S. LIEBERMAN avec commentaires, Tosefta Kifshutah, Seder Mo'ed, New-York 1961—62.

Traduction allemande des ch. VI et VII par H. LEWY dans: Morgenländischer Aberglaube in der römischen Kaiserzeit, Zeitschrift des Vereins für Volkskunde III (1893), pp. 24—30 et 130—143.

II. Auteurs anciens

Nos références renvoient généralement aux éditions bilingues de la série Loeb ou des Belles Lettres et, pour Philon, aux éditions du Cerf.

III. Archéologie et numismatique

Actes du 8ème Congrès International d'archéologie classique (Paris 1963): Le rayonnement des civilisations grecques et romaines sur les cultures périphériques, Paris 1965.

AVIGAD, N., Beth Shearim III: The Archeological Excavations during 1953—1958 (héb.), Jérusalem 1971.
AVI-YONAH, M., Mount Carmel and the God of Baalbeck, IEJ II, 1952, n° 2, pp. 118—124;
ID., Scythopolis, IEJ XII (1962), n° 2, pp. 123—134.
ID., Newly discovered Latin and Greek inscriptions, QDAP XII (1946), nos 3—4, pp. 84—102.

BLINKENBERG, CHR., Archäologische Studien, Copenhague 1904.

COHEN, H., Description historique des monnaies frappées sous l'empire romain, communément appelées médailles impériales, 8 vol., 2ème édition, Paris, 1880s.

DAREMBERG, CH. et ED. SAGLIO, Dictionnaire des antiquités grecques et romaines, 5 vols., Paris 1877—1919.
DUSSAUD, R., Temples et Cultes de la triade héliopolitaine à Baalbek, Syria XXIII (1942—43), pp. 32—77.

HAMBURGER, H., Coin Issues from Caesarea Maritima, IEJ XX (1970), nos 1—2, pp. 81—91.
HILL, G. F., Catalogue of the Greek Coins of Phoenicia in the British Museum, Londres 1910.
ID., Catalogue of the Greek Coins of Palestine in the British Museum, Londres 1914.
ID., Some Palestinian Cults in the Graeco-Roman Age. Proceedings of the British Academy 1911—12, pp. 411—427 (étude fondée sur la numismatique).

JALABERT, L. et R. MOUTERDE, Inscriptions grecques et latines de la Syrie, Paris 1929—1953.

KADMAN, L., Corpus Nummorum Palestinensium:
vol. II: The Coins of Caesarea Maritima, Jérusalem 1957;
vol. IV: The Coins of Akko-Ptolemaïs, Jérusalem 1961.

LIFSHITZ, B., L'hellénisation des Juifs de Palestine. A propos des inscriptions de Besara (Beth Shearim), R.B. LXXII (1965), pp. 520—538.

MOUTERDE, R., Antiquités de l'Hermon et de la Beqâ, MUSJ XXIX (1951—52), pp. 19—89.

RONZEVALLE, P. S., Notes et Etudes d'archéologie orientale (3ème série II). Jupiter héliopolitain nova et vetera, MUSJ XXI (1937—38), pp. 3—85.

SAULCY, F. DE, Numismatique de la Terre Sainte, Paris 1874.
SCHLUMBERGER, D., Le Temple de Mercure à Baalbek Héliopolis, Bulletin du Musée de Beyrouth III (1939), pp. 25—36.
SEYRIG, H., La triade héliopolitaine et les temples de Baalbek, Syria X (1929), pp. 314—356.
ID., Le culte du Soleil en Syrie à l'époque romaine, Syria XLVIII (1971), pp. 337—373.

VIDMAN, L., Sylloge inscriptionum religionis Isiacae et Sarapiacae, Berlin 1969.

YADIN, Y., Bar Kokhba, Londres–Jérusalem 1971.

IV. Contexte historique

ALLON, G., A History of the Jews in Palestine during the period of the Mishna and Talmud (hébr.), 2 vols., Tel-Aviv 1961.
ID., On the social History of Palestine in the days of the Mishna (hébr.), Tarbiz XXI (1950), pp. 106—111.
APPLEBAUM, S., The Province of Syria-Palestina as a Province of the Severan Empire (hébr.), Zion XXIII (1958), pp. 35—45.
AVI-YONAH, M., Map of Roman Palestine, QDAP V (1936), n° 4, pp. 139—193.
ID., Geschichte der Juden im Zeitalter des Talmud in den Tagen von Rom und Byzanz, 2 vols., Berlin 1962.
ID., Carta's Atlas of the Period of the Second Temple, the Mishna and the Talmud (hébr.), Jérusalem 1966.
ID., Historical Geography of Palestine, in: The Jewish people in the first century, éd. par S. SAFRAI et M. STERN, vol. I, Assen 1974.

BACHER, W., Rome dans le Talmud et le Midrash, REJ XXXIII (1896), pp. 187—196.
ID., Die Aggada der Tannaiten, 2 vols., Strasbourg 1903, rééd. Berlin 1965.
BAMBERGER, B. J., Proselytism in the Talmudic Period, Cincinnati 1939.
BARON, S. W., Histoire d'Israël, vie sociale et religieuse, trad. V. NIKIPROWETZKY, t. II, Paris 1957.
BEN-DAVID, A., Talmudische Ökonomie, vol. I, Hildesheim 1974.
BOUCHIER, E. S., Syria as a Roman Province, Oxford 1916.
BRAND, J., Ceramics in Talmudic Literature (hébr.), Jérusalem 1953.
ID., Concerning Greek Culture in Palestine during the Talmudic Period (hébr.), Tarbiz XXXVIII (1968), pp. 13—17.
BÜCHLER, A., Les Dosithéens dans le Midrasch, REJ XLIII (1901), pp. 50—71.
ID., Political and Social Leaders of the Jewish Communities of Sepphoris in the 2nd and 3rd Centuries, Oxford 1909.
ID., The economic Condition of Judaea after the Destruction of the Second Temple, Londres 1912.
ID., Studies in Jewish History. The Adolph Büchler Memorial Volume edited by I. BRODIE and J. RABBINOWITZ, Oxford Univ. Press 1956.

DERENBOURG, J., Essai sur l'histoire et la géographie de la Palestine d'après le Talmud et autres sources rabbiniques, Paris 1867.

GOODENOUGH, E. R., Jewish Symbols in the Graeco-Roman Period, Bollingen Series XXXVII, 13 vols., New-York 1953—1968.
ID., The Rabbis and Jewish Art in the Graeco-Roman Period, HUCA XXXII (1961), pp. 269—279.
GRAETZ, H., Histoire des Juifs, t. III, trad. française, Paris 1888.
GUTTMAN, A., The Patriarch Judah I, his Birth and his Death; a Glimpse into the Chronology of the Talmudic Period, HUCA XXV (1954), pp. 239—262.

HENGEL, M., Judentum und Hellenismus, Tübingen 1969, trad. angl.: Judaïsm and Hellenism, 2 vols., Londres 1974.
HERR, M. D., The historical Significance of the Dialogues between Jewish Sages and Roman Dignitaries, Scripta Hierosolymitana XII, Jérusalem 1971.

JONES, A. H. M., The Cities of the Eastern Roman Provinces, Oxford 1937.
ID., The Urbanization of Palestine, Journal of Roman Studies XXI (1931), pp. 78—85.
JUSTER, J., Les Juifs dans l'empire romain, 2 vols., Paris 1914, reprod. 1969.

KLEIN, S., The Land of the Cuttim in Talmudic Times (hébr.), Yerushalayim X (1914),
KRAUSS, S., Griechische und lateinische Lehnwörter in Talmud, Midrasch und Targum, 2 vols., Berlin 1898—99.
ID., Talmudische Archäologie, 3 vols., Leipzig 1910—1911, réimpr. Hildesheim 1966.

LABRIOLLE, P. DE, Histoire de la littérature latine chrétienne, t. I, Paris 1947.
LE BLANT, E., Compte-rendu de la traduction de M. SCHWAB du traité 'Aboda Zara', t. x, du Talmud de Jérusalem (Paris 1889), in: Journal des Savants, mai 1890, pp. 309—320.
LEVINE, L., Caesarea under Roman Rule. Studies in Judaïsm in Late Antiquity, vol. 7, Leyde 1975.
LEWY, H., Philologische Streifzüge in den Talmud, Philologus LII (1893), pp. 733—735.
LIEBERMAN, S., Greek in Jewish Palestine, New-York 1942.
ID., Hellenism in Jewish Palestine, New-York 1950.
ID., Texts and Studies, New-York 1974.
LÖW, I., Die Flora dei Juden, 4 vols., 1926—1934, réimpr. Hildesheim 1967.

NEUBAUER, A., La géographie du Talmud, Paris 1868.
NEUSNER, J., A Life of Rabban Yohanan ben Zakkai, Leyde 1962.

ROSTOVTZEFF, M., The Social and Economic History of the Roman Empire, 3 vols., Oxford 1967⁵.

SAFRAI, S., The Status of Provincia Judaea after the Destruction of the Second Temple (hébr.), Zion XXVII (1962), pp. 216—222.
SCHALIT, A., Roman Administration in Palestine (hébr.), Jérusalem 1937.
ID., Roman Policy in the Orient from Nero to Trajan (hébr.), Tarbiz VII (1936), pp. 159—180.
SCHÜRER, E., Geschichte des Jüdischen Volkes im Zeitalter Jesu Christi, 3 vols., Leipzig 1907—1911[4].
ID., trad. angl. A History of the Jewish People in the Time of Jesus Christ, Edimbourg 1891 et nombreuses rééd.
SCHWABE, M., On the Jewish and Graeco-Roman Schools in the Days of the Mishnah and Talmud (hébr.), Tarbiz XXI (1950), pp. 112—123.
SIMON, M., Verus Israel, Etude sur les relations entre Chrétiens et Juifs dans l'Empire romain (135—425), Paris 1964[2].
SONNE, I., The Use of Rabbinic Literature as Historical Sources, JQR XXXVI, n° 2 (1945), pp. 147—169.
SOREQ, Y., Rabbinical Evidences about the Pagi Vicinales in Israel, JQR LXV, n° 4 (1975), pp. 221—24.

URBACH, E., The Sages, their Concepts and Beliefs (hébr.), Jérusalem 1971.
ID., The Rabbinical Laws on Idolatry in the 2nd and 3rd Centuries in the Light of Archaeological and Historical Facts, IEJ IX (1959), n°s 3 et 4, pp. 149—165 et 229—245.

VERMES, G., Post-Biblical Jewish Studies, Studies in Judaism in Late Antiquity, vol. 8, Leyde 1975.

WACHOLDER, B., Nicolaus of Damascus, Los Angeles 1962.
WALLACH, L., A Palestinian Polemic against Idolatry, HUCA XIX (1945—46), pp. 389—404.

V. Religions sémitiques

BAUDISSIN, W., Studien zur semitischen Religionsgeschichte, Leipzig 1878.

CAQUOT, A., La religion des Sémites occidentaux, dans: Histoire des religions, t. I, Encyclopédie de la Pléiade, Paris 1970, pp. 307—355.
CONDER, C. R., Syrian Stone-lore, Londres 1886.
COOK, ST., The Religion of Ancient Palestine in the Light of Archaeology, Schweich Lectures 1925, Londres 1930, ch. III, The Graeco-Roman Age, pp. 153—230.
CUMONT, F., Les religions orientales dans le paganisme romain, Paris 1929.
ID., Lux Perpetua, Paris 1949.
ID., Théologie solaire du paganisme romain; Extrait des Mémoires présentés par divers savants à l'Académie des Inscriptions et Belles lettres XII, Paris 1909.
ID., Etudes syriennes, Paris 1917.

DUSSAUD, R., Notes de mythologie syrienne II—IX, Paris 1905.

LAGRANGE, M. J., Etudes sur les religions sémitiques, 2e éd., Paris 1905.
LEVY, I., Cultes et rites syriens dans le Talmud, REJ XLIII (1901), pp. 183—205.

RINGGREN, H., Religions of the Ancient Near East, trad. angl., Londres 1973.

SEYRIG, H., La triade héliopolitaine et les temples de Baalbek, Syria XX (1929), pp. 314—356.
ID., Le culte du soleil en Syrie à l'époque romaine, Syria XLVIII (1971), pp. 337—373.
ID., Le prétendu syncrétisme solaire syrien, in: Les syncrétismes dans les religions grecque et romaine (Colloque de Strasbourg 9—11 juin 1971), Paris 1973, pp. 147—151.
SMITH, W. ROBERTSON, Lectures on the Religion of the Semites, Londres 1927[3].

VI. Lec Cultes païens dans l'Empire romain

ALFÖLDI, A., Die alexandrinischen Götter und die Vota publica am Jahresbeginn, Jahrbuch für Antike und Christentum 8—9 (1965—6), pp. 53—87.

Beaujeu, J., La religion romaine à l'apogée de l'empire I. La politique religieuse des Antonins (96—192), Paris 1955.
Benabou, M., La résistance africaine à la romanisation, Paris 1976.
Blaufuss, H., Römische Feste und Feiertage nach den Traktaten über fremden Dienst, Nürnberg 1909.
Id., Götter, Bilder und Symbole nach den Traktaten über fremden Dienst, Nürnberg 1910

Cerfaux, L. et J. Tondriau, Un concurrent du christianisme. Le culte des souverains dans la civilisation gréco-romaine, Bibl. de théologie, série III, Paris–Tournai 1957.

Delatte, L., Recherches sur quelques fêtes mobiles du calendrier romain, Liège 1937.
Dunand, F., Le syncrétisme isiaque à la fin de l'époque hellénistique, dans: Les syncrétismes dans les religions grecque et romaine (colloque de Strasbourg 9—11 juin 1971), Paris 1973, pp. 79—93.
Dumézil, G., Fêtes romaines d'été et d'automne, Paris 1975.

Frazer, J. G., Atys et Osiris, trad. fçse, Paris 1924.

Gagé, J., Recherches sur les jeux séculaires romains, Paris 1934.

Hornbostel, W., Sarapis. Studien zur Überlieferungsgeschichte der Erscheinungsformen und Wandlungen der Gestalt eines Gottes (Etudes préliminaires, n° 32), Leyde 1973.
Halkin, L., La supplication d'action de grâces chez les Romains, Liège 1953.

Jeanmaire, H., Dionysos, histoire du culte de Bacchus, Paris 1951.

Krauss, S., Aegyptische und Syrische Götternamen im Talmud, Semitic Studies in Memory of Rev. Dr. Alexander Kohut, Berlin 1897.
Küster, E., Die Schlange in der griechischen Kunst und Religion, Religionsgeschichtliche Versuche und Vorarbeiten XIII, 2, Gießen 1913.

Lafaye, G., Histoire du culte des divinités d'Alexandrie Sérapis, Isis Harpocrate et Anubis hors de l'Egypte depuis les origines jusqu'à la naissance de l'école néo-platonicienne, Paris 1884.
Latte, K., Römische Religionsgeschichte, Munich 1960.
Loisy, A., Les mystères païens et le mystère chrétien, Paris 1914.

Malaise, M., Les conditions de pénétration et de diffusion des cultes égyptiens en Italie (Etudes préliminaires n° 88), Leyde 1972.
Marquardt, J., Le culte chez les Romains, trad. fçse, 2 vols., Paris 1889.
Id., La vie privée des Romains, trad. fçse, Paris 1892, 2 vols., in: Manuel des Antiquités romaines de Th. Mommsen et J. Marquardt XII—XIII, Paris 1889—90, et XIV—XV, Paris 1892—93.
Meslin, M., La fête des Kalendes de janvier dans l'empire romain. Etude d'un rituel de Nouvel An, Coll. Latomus, vol. 115, Bruxelles 1970.
Mesnil du Buisson, Etudes sur les dieux phéniciens hérités par l'empire romain (Etudes préliminaires, n° 14), Leyde 1970.
Müller, H. W., Isis mit dem Horuskind, Münchn. Jahrb. der bildend. Kunst 3. F. XIV (1963), pp. 7—38.

Nicolson, F. W., Greek and Roman Barbers, Harvard Studies in Classical Philology II (1891), pp. 41—56.
Nilsson, M. P., Geschichte der griechischen Religion, vol. II, Die hellenistische und römische Zeit, München 1968³.

Roscher, W. H., Lexikon der griechischen und römischen Mythologie, 6 vols., Leipzig 1884—1937.
Rouse, W., Greek Votive Offerings, Cambridge 1902.

Schilling, R., The Roman Religion, dans: Historia Religionum, Leyde 1969.

TAYLOR, L. R., The Divinity of the Roman Emperor, Middletown 1931.
TOUTAIN, J., Les cultes païens dans l'empire romain: les provinces latines, 3 vols., Paris 1906—1917.
TRAN TAM TINH, V., Essai sur le culte d'Isis à Pompéi, Paris 1964.
TURCAN, R., Origines et sens de l'inhumation à l'époque impériale, REA LX (1958), pp. 323—347.

VAN BERG, P. L., Corpus Cultus Deae Syriae (Etudes préliminaires, n° 28), 2 vols., Leyde 1972.
VERMASEREN, M. J., The Legend of Attis in Greek and Roman Art, Leyde 1966.
ID., Corpus Inscriptionum et Monumentorum Religionis Mithriacae I et II, La Haye 1956—1960.

WIESLER, FR., Über Haaropfer, Philologus IX (1854), 711—715.
WILL, E., Le relief cultuel gréco-romain, Paris 1955.
WISSOWA, G., Religion und Kultus der Römer, Munich 1912, rééd. 1971.
WITT, R. E., Isis in the Graeco-Roman World, Londres 1971.

YERKES, R. K., Le sacrifice dans les religions grecque et romaine et dans le judaïsme primitif, Paris 1955.

VII. Divination et magie

BAYET, J., La croyance romaine aux présages déterminants. Aspects littéraires et chronologie, Coll. Latomus, vol. II, Bruxelles 1949, pp. 14—30.
BLAU, L., Das altjüdische Zauberwesen, 1ère éd., Budapest 1898, reprod. Graz 1974.
BLOCH, R., Les prodiges dans l'Antiquité classique (coll. «Mythes et Religions»), Paris 1963.
BONNER, C., Studies in Magical Amulets, chiefly Graeco-Egyptian, Ann Arbor, Mich. 1950.
BOUCHÉ-LECLERCQ, A., Histoire de la divination dans l'Antiquité I, Paris 1879.
BUDGE, E. A. WALLIS, Amulets and Talismans, New-York 1961.

CAQUOT, A., La divination dans l'ancien Israël, in: A. CAQUOT et M. LEIBOVICI, La divination I, Paris 1968, pp. 83—113.

DEFRADAS, J., La divination en Grèce, in: A. CAQUOT et M. LEIBOVICI, La divination I, Paris 1968, pp. 157—195.
DERCHAIN, PH., Intailles magiques du Musée de Numismatique d'Athènes, Chronique d'Egypte XXXIX, 1964, pp. 180—182.

FAHD, T., La divination arabe, Leyde 1966.
FLACELIÈRE, R., Devins et oracles grecs, Paris 1961.

GAGER, J. J., Moses in Graeco-Roman Paganism, New-York 1972 (ch. IV: Moses and Magic).

LEWY, HEINRICH, Morgenländischer Aberglaube in der römischen Kaiserzeit, Zeitschrift des Vereins für Volkskunde III (1893), pp. 24—40 et 130—143.

MARQUES-RIVIÈRE, J., Amulettes, talismans et pantacles dans les traditions orientales et occidentales, Paris 1950.
MASSONEAU, E., La magie dans l'Antiquité romaine, Paris 1934.
MOUTERDE, R., Objets magiques. Recueil S. Ayvarz, MUSJ XXV, Fasc. 6 (1942—43), pp. 105—128.

PREISENDANZ, K., Papyri Graecae Magicae I, Leipzig–Berlin 1928, II 1931.

SCHILLING, R., Religion et magie à Rome, dans: Annuaire EPHE, Vème section, 1967—1968, Paris 1967, pp. 31—55.

THOMPSON, R. CAMPBELL, Semitic Magic — its Origins and Development, 1ère éd., Londres 1908, rééd. New-York 1971.

VERNANT, J.-P., et BOTTÉRO, J., Divination et rationalité, Paris 1974.

Liste des illustrations

1. Monnaie d'Acre-Ptolémaïs, IIe siècle, représentant Aphrodite debout sous une arche (Staatliche Museen, Berlin). Photo Collège de France, d'après moulage (voir p. 402).

2. Bagues grecques à motif de serpent (DAREMBERG et SAGLIO I p. 294 nos 345 et 356). Gemmes à motif de Khnoubis (G. BONNER, Studies in Magical Amulets, chiefly Graeco-Egyptian, pl. IV nos 88, 89, 90) (voir p. 418/19).

3. Buste de Sérapis reposant sur un pied humain (Musée des Offices, Florence). Photo ALINARI, Florence (voir p. 421).

Rabbinic Anthropology

by Emero Stiegman, Halifax, Canada

Contents

I. Preliminary Considerations

1. Character of the Sources

The literature which provides the data for a rabbinic anthropology consists of those documents in which the religious oral tradition of the

Jews came eventually to be recorded[1]. The Pharisees' doctrine of a revealed Sinaitic oral Torah, of which they were the custodians and teachers, moves through vast blank spaces of post-exilic history, back to the figure of Ezra the Scribe, who is insistently characterized by the Chronicler as learned

Abbreviations:

1. Journals, Series

AGAJU	Arbeiten zur Geschichte des Antiken Judentums und des Urchristentums.
ANRW	Aufstieg und Niedergang der römischen Welt
BEHESR	Bibliothèque de l'école des hautes études, Sciences religieuses.
BSS	Biblical and Semitic Studies.
BWANT	Beiträge zur Wissenschaft vom Alten (und Neuen) Testament.
BZNW	Beihefte zur Zeitschrift für die neutestamentliche Wissenschaft.
CT	Corpus Tannaiticum.
DSAM	Dictionnaire de spiritualité ascétique et mystique.
HNT	Handbuch zum Neuen Testament, Tübingen
HR	History of Religions.
HTR	Harvard Theological Review.
HTS	Harvard Theological Studies.
HUCA	Hebrew Union College Annual.
JAAR	Journal of the American Academy of Religion.
JBL	Journal of Biblical Literature.
JBR	The Journal of Bible and Religion.
JQR	Jewish Quarterly Review.
JR	Journal of Religion.
LJC	Library of Jewish Classics.
PG	J. P. MIGNE, edit. Patrologia, Series Graeca.
RB	Revue Biblique.
RSR	Recherches de Science Religieuse.
SGFWJ	Schriften der Gesellschaft zur Förderung der Wissenschaft des Judentums.
SGJ	Schriften der Gesellschaft des Judentums.
YJS	Yale Judaica Series.
WUNT	Wissenschaftliche Untersuchungen zum Neuen Testament.
WMANT	Wissenschaftliche Monographien zum Alten und Neuen Testament.

2. Miscellaneous

Antiq.	Flavius Josephus, The Jewish Antiquities
Aram.	Aramaic
edit.	edited by, edition, editor
Enc. Jud.	Encyclopaedia Judaica. Jerusalem, 1971
f.	folio
Heb.	Hebrew
lit.	literally
M.	[as in M. Aboth] Mishnah
No.	Number
par.	paragraph
pl.	plural
Pt.	Part
T.B.	Talmud Babli, Babylonian Talmud
T.P.	Talmud Yerushalmi, Palestinian Talmud
Tos.	[as in Tos. Sanhedrin] Tosefta
trans.	translator, translation

[1] For a brief survey of rabbinic works — editions, translations, and bibliography of scholarship — see EMIL SCHÜRER, The History of the Jewish People in the Age of Jesus Christ (175 B.C.—A.D. 135), A New English Version, revised and edit. by GEZA VERMES

in the law (Ezra 7.6, 11; Neh. 8.1, 4, 13; 12.26, 36), a man whose knowledge of the law accounts for his leadership of the community (Ezra 7.12, 21, 25). Although the evolving Oral Law — both in its specifically juridical form, Halakhah, and in homiletic reflection and comment, Haggadah — was not edited for written publication until the redaction of the Mishnah, about the year A.D. 200, the period of thought-development it expresses begins with the Second Temple era, ca. 520 B.C. The period concludes with the completion of the Babylonian Talmud, ca. A.D. 499[2]. The works included are the Mishnah[3], the Tosefta[4], the two Talmuds[5], and the midrashic collections[6]. When a text from the Jewish Prayer Book can be shown to derive from the rabbinic era, it too becomes an authentic source[7].

The characteristics of this literature which impinge upon the effort to discern a common anthropology in the rabbis may be seen in the following

and FERGUS MILLAR, Vol. 1 (Edinburgh, 1973), pp. 68—118. Regarding SCHÜRER's original 'Geschichte der jüdischen Völker im Zeitalter Jesu Christi', 2 Vols. (Frankfort, 1886—90, third and fourth edit., 3 Vols. and 'Register', Leipzig, 1901—1911), a classic of history as chronicle, see the just strictures of G. F. MOORE, Christian Writers on Judaism, Harvard Theological Review, 14 (1921), 197—254. A comprehensive tabulation of editions, with brief comments, is JOHN T. TOWNSEND, Rabbinic Sources, in: The Study of Judaism: Bibliographical Essays, publication of the Anti-Defamation League of B'Nai B'Rith (New York, 1972), pp. 35—80.

[2] The question of when the Mishnah and the Talmuds were put into writing has long been disputed. According to one view, the Mishnah was not only orally edited, but finally written, ca. A.D. 200, by Rabbi Judah the Patriarch himself; the writing of the Palestinian Gemara, ca. A.D. 400, by Johanan; the Babylonian Gemara, ca. A.D. 499, by Rabina, completing the work of Rab Ashi. This was held generally by the medieval Talmudists of Spain, Italy, and Germany. Another view has it that both Mishnah and Talmud were written down for the first time in the sixth century by the Saboraim, as the successors to the Amoraim are called. So, in particular, the scholars of medieval France. For details, see HERMANN L. STRACK, Introduction to the Talmud and Midrash (New York, 1931; a Temple Book reprint, N. Y., 1972), pp. 18—20. SAUL LIEBERMAN, Hellenism in Jewish Palestine (New York, 1950), p. 87, argues that throughout the age of the Talmud there was no written Mishnah.
Post-Talmudic literature of the Halakhah, its traditions and associated writings through the centuries, is designated by the technical term "Rabbinical Literature". The expression is not restricted to works by rabbis but rather to the subject matter and aim of the teaching of Judaism. See 'Rabbinical Literature', by ISRAEL MOSES TA-SHMA, in: Encyclopaedia Judaica (Jerusalem, 1971). Our sources, instead, will be referred to as rabbinic literature.

[3] שנה Heb., "to repeat"; משנה *Mishnah*, lit. "repetition".

[4] תוספתא *Tosefta*; lit., "addition". The Tosefta is a collection of materials omitted from R. Judah the Patriarch's Mishnah, organized according to the six orders of the Mishnah.

[5] למד Heb., "to study", "learn"; תלמוד *Talmud*, lit. "learning". תלמוד ירושלמי Jerusalem Talmud, spoken of more properly as Palestinian Talmud. תלמוד בבלי Babylonian Talmud. The standard introduction is HERMANN L. STRACK, op. cit. — useful, for example, as a manual for identifying individual rabbis, listed by generations, with bibliography.

[6] דרש Heb., "to expound", "explain"; מדרש *Midrash*, lit. "exposition", "explanation", "interpretation".

[7] See, for example, The Standard Prayer Book, authorized English Translation by the Rev. S. SINGER, Enlarged American Edition (New York, 1915). The standard study of Jewish liturgy is ISMAR ELBOGEN, Der jüdische Gottesdienst in seiner geschichtlichen Entwicklung (Leipzig, 1913). See also ZVI IDELSOHN, Jewish Liturgy and Its Development (New York, 1932), excellent but overly brief in its treatment of historical development (part I).

facts: (1) These works are compilations; a redactor's influence is present in the gathered materials[8]. (2) The textual problems are considerable — e.g., in both Talmuds, where no critical edition is available. (3) The historical setting of much that is reported is unknown, so that (among other things) critical appraisal of the redactors' perspective is limited. (4) The theology of rabbinic authors is in a highly unselfconscious state; even thematic organization receives, in "the sea of the Talmud", extremely low priority. (5) The pastoral concern of these authors frequently prefers prudential considerations to analytic precision. (6) Though these texts are the working documents according to which the community's life was formed, they are also school instruments; they represent more the manner in which the Torah was to be studied than a set of dogmatic conclusions to such study.

2. Method

By the logic of these characteristics, a rabbinic anthropology cannot be securely drawn until after a busy generation of *Vorstudien*. Rabbinic scholarship still struggles to move beyond a state of prolonged adolescence[9]. The present effort is embarrassed in the recurring awareness of a tenuous perceptual link between text and history.

Though the rabbis did not organize their thought around theological themes, an anthropology, however tentative, must proceed from fixed categories. This study begins in the perception of man's historicity as the cardinal category of rabbinic anthropology. In the principal prayer of rabbinic Judaism, the Shema which the devout recited twice daily, the giving of the Torah on Sinai was recalled and relived: "Hear, O Israel: The Lord our God is one Lord", etc. (Deut. 6.4). The central tenet of religion was possessed, not merely as the eternal truth, but as the word of God received historically. This fact establishes the historicity of man, both as basic attribute and theological principle[10]. The rabbis' abiding sense of the

[8] JACOB NEUSNER, Form and Meaning in Mishnah, JAAR, 44, Nr. 1 (March 1977), 27—54, esp. p. 34.

[9] Regarding the present state of scholarship on early rabbinic Judaism, see JACOB NEUSNER, The History of Early Rabbinic Judaism: Some New Approaches, History of Religions, 16, No. 3 (February 1977), 216—236. Also, NEUSNER's Introduction to The Study of Judaism (see n. 1, above), pp. 1—6, esp. p. 2: "The field [history of Judaism] is in a primitive, scarcely cultivated state" — a view which is explained in the more recent article, above (1977). EPHRAIM E. URBACH, The Sages: Their Concepts and Beliefs, 2 vols. (Jerusalem, 1975), I, 5, remarks: "Modern Jewish scholarship (*Wissenschaft des Judentums*) has paid but little attention to our subject." 'The Sages' will be cited as URBACH.

[10] For a bibliography on the historical character of Judaism, see SALO WITTMAYER BARON, A Social and Religious History of the Jews, 2nd edit., revised and enlarged, 15 Vols. (New York, 1952—69), I, 295, n. 6. BARON conceives of a simple dichotomy among religions — nature religions and historical religions. Quoting Deut. 4, 19—20, he concludes, "Here we have it succinctly: Exodus versus astral powers!" I, 15. See the section 'Histori-

human temporal dimension will be preserved if we gather their sayings around the themes of origin, nature-condition, and destiny.

3. The Rabbis

The title rabbi derives from the noun *rav*, meaning "great" in biblical Hebrew; and in Mishnaic Hebrew, a "master" as distinguished from a slave. In the generation of Hillel (1st cen. B.C.) "rabbi" became a title applied to the sages of the Oral Law[11].

In Talmudic times the title was bestowed only upon those properly ordained in Eretz Israel. The Babylonian sages used the alternative title *rav* (We shall abbreviate both titles as R.). When reference is made to "the rabbis" without qualification, the sages of the Oral Law in the period of the formation of the Talmud are meant — the Tannaim[12], whose sayings are compiled in the Mishnah, and the Amoraim (A.D. 200—499)[13], whose judgments and interpretations form the Gemara ("completion")[14]. Given these constrictions and expansions, "the sages" is at times the preferred expression[15].

The rabbinate spoke for a religious option which had been one among several in Jewish Palestine up to the destruction of the Second Temple in A.D. 70. There had been alternative answers to such questions as, how might the Law be understood with respect to new national circumstances? How might it be internalized and universalized? What accommodation should be made with the impressive and expanding sophistication of the thought and culture of the gentiles? What attitude should be taken to the endless sufferings inflicted by the powerful upon the chosen people, particularly its poor and weak ones? To the priestly establishment and its Sadducean allies, all was well, and change was heresy. To sectaries like the

cal Monotheism', I, 4—10. This view is properly qualified by W. F. ALBRIGHT, From the Stone Age to Christianity, 2nd edit. (New York, 1957), p. 318, n. 21.
The influence of events upon the ideas of rabbinic Judaism is exemplified in JACOB NEUSNER, History and Structure: The Case of Mishnah, JAAR, Vol. 45, No. 2 (June 1977), 161—192. The author says, "The history of the ideas of Mishnah . . . works itself out on a grid of vertical and horizontal lines. The vertical is the line of thought . . . the horizontal is the line of events" (p. 162). He studies the Order of Purities in Mishnah as a case in point.

11 See 'Rabbi, Rabbinate', Introductory section, by editorial staff in 'Encyclopaedia Judaica' in loco. GEORGE FOOT MOORE, Judaism in the First Centuries of the Christian Era: The Age of the Tannaim, 3 vols. (Cambridge, Mass., 1927—30), III, 15—17 — to be cited as MOORE.

12 תנא Aram. "to repeat", or "one who repeats" (cf. Heb. שנה); pl., *Tannaim.*

13 אמר *Amora:* lit., "speaker"; pl. *Amoraim.*

14 גמר Heb. "to complete"; גמרא Aram. *Gemara,* lit. "completion", "tradition"; sometimes popularly applied to the Talmud as a whole.

15 See, e.g., URBACH, I, 1; also, URBACH, The Sages, in: Encyclopaedia Judaica, s.v. at col. 636. L. FINKELSTEIN, Ha-Perushim we'Anshe Keneset ha-Gedola (New York, 1950), p. 54, n. 151, would have Aboth 1, 1, read "raise up many sages". Against this, see URBACH, II, 944, n. 86.

Essenes, nothing was well, and the rejection of all institutions was necessary. What stood to be changed in the Law, as Hellenizers like Philo saw it, was its primitive, provincial, unallegorized flatness. As the Judaeo-Christians saw it, the Law had been "fulfilled" and an altogether new covenant had been instituted. Against all these possibilities, the Pharisees claimed a middle course, which they saw as the wisdom of the *sopherim* (the early Scribes, from Ezra) — the principle of the Oral Torah, institutionalized in a scholar class and representing unmeasurable adaptibility within radical continuity[16]. The position is defined as much by the alternatives it rejected as by what it affirmed. The rabbis — the sages mentioned in the literary compilations of the Oral Law — developed the Pharisaic option.

II. Anthropology

1. The Caution against Speculation

As the study of the rabbis was the word of God, the anthropology sought in their texts must be theological. Whether pursued through the methods of theology, philosophy, or the social sciences, anthropology of itself ambitions system; it is "the conscious effort of man to achieve an understanding of himself"[17]. But, we have seen how the character of the rabbinic sources militates against the emergence of a systematic anthropol-

[16] The word Pharisee (Greek, Φαρισαῖος) is from the Aramaic פרישא *Perisha*, derived from the verb פרש *perash*, "to separate". In rabbinic texts it appears only in the Hebrew form פרוש *Parush*. We are not told from what the פרושים, *Perushim*, are separated. ALEXANDER GUTTMANN, Rabbinic Judaism in the Making (Detroit, 1970), p. 130, quotes J. Z. LAUTERBACH, Rabbinic Essays (Cincinnati, 1951), pp. 109—110, saying that the priestly party probably called the lay teachers "Separatists" in a derogatory sense when these were excluded from the Sanhedrin during the reign of John Hyrcanus. For other accounts see MOORE, I, 59—62. On the Pharisees generally, see J. NEUSNER, From Politics to Piety: Pharisaic Judaism in the New Testament Times (Englewood Cliffs, N. J., 1972); ID., The Rabbinic Traditions about the Pharisees Before 70, 3 vols. (Leiden, 1971); E. URBACH, The Sages: Their Concepts and Beliefs; LOUIS FINKELSTEIN, The Pharisees: The Sociological Background of Their Faith, 2 vols. 3rd edit. (Philadelphia, 1966); R. T. HERFORD, The Pharisees (London, 1924); RALPH MARCUS, Pharisees, Essenes and Gnostics, JR, 32 (1952), 153—163; JACOB Z. LAUTERBACH, The Pharisees and Their Teachings (New York, 1930). Regarding H. STRACK and P. BILLERBECK, Kommentar zum Neuen Testament aus Talmud und Midrasch, 4 vols. (München, 1922—28), IV, 334—352, excursus no. 14: 'Die Pharisäer u. Sadduzäer in der altjüdischen Literatur', see the objections of E. P. SANDERS, Paul and Palestinian Judaism (Philadelphia, 1977), pp. 42—43. The late appearance of SANDERS' important work has restricted my use of it to supplying appendages of caution toward some Christian studies; e.g., I concur in its censure of the use of sources in W. BOUSSET, Die Religion des Judentums im späthellenistischen Zeitalter (ed. H. GRESSMANN), HNT 21 (Tübingen, 1966), repr. of 1925 ed.

[17] "Anthropology", in: KARL RAHNER and HERBERT VORGRIMLER, Theological Dictionary, edit. CORNELIUS ERNST (New York, 1965), p. 25.

ogy. Indeed, the caution regarding all theologizing from these sources has been a by-word in Talmudic study. Even slight acquaintance with the history of human speculation would render it unnecessary to labor the idea that the systematizing drive easily overwhelms respect for history and experience. The Jewish philosophers of the Middle Ages, the Cabbalists, and the later Hasidim all wished to ground their systems upon rabbinic literature. But, in force of their systems, we are told, the historical meaning of the rabbis' sayings was either dimmed or altogether obscured[18].

The caution against the search for systems rests upon important facts. First, speculative thinking in its traditional western guise appears only in an unsustained manner in rabbinic texts. When an ethical question leads to discussion of a doctrinal issue, a brilliant axiom may be produced, such as, "Everything is in the hands of Heaven except the fear of Heaven"[19]. But, there is no analytic exposition. The juxtaposing of a demand for completely disinterested worship and obedience to God's Law and of a doctrine of retribution would seem to titillate the intellect to produce the available demonstration of compatibility. We find none[20]. Instead of an intellectual overview, we have "a complicated arrangement of checks and balances"[21].

If we ponder the reasons for this non-speculative mentality, which existed in an era of flourishing speculation, we may find them in the era itself. Both Hellenistic philosophy and Christian theology were seen as menaces to the integrity of the Torah, and their example may have been a deterrent to speculation itself. Then, the few fixities that rabbinic religion insisted upon were more in the nature of experienced realities than of well organized idea-complexes[22]. The sages of the Oral Law were the heirs of the biblical wisdom tradition, and there is where one should look for an explanation of the non-speculative inclination of the rabbis. The unsystematized state of biblical wisdom writing is not so much an evidence of speculative underdevelopment as an affirmation of Israel's vision of things. There is no comprehensive theoretical view of the world and no idealized portrait of man; but, together with spoken caution regarding all-embracing efforts to explain, there is insistence that the truth about man and the world is achieved more in a relationship of trust with things than in the pursuit of theoretical knowledge[23]. Gerhard von Rad believes the inability of the wisdom authors to objectivize certain things speculatively

[18] Urbach, I, 4.

[19] T. B. Berakhot 33b.

[20] J. Guttmann, Philosophies of Judaism, pp. 38—39, offers a list of evidences of the lack of systematic thinking in Talmudic literature.

[21] S. Schechter, Aspects of Rabbinic Theology (New York, 1908; reprint, N. Y., 1961), p. 17. Cited as Schechter.

[22] Id. This undeveloped suggestion serves Schechter better than the facile assertion that the rabbis "felt no need for formulating their dogmas into a creed" (p. 12).

[23] Gerhard von Rad, Wisdom in Israel (London, 1972), p. 318. This is a partial summation of the author's conclusion.

must be sought in the nature of their faith in God: "Did not Israel, in all her attempts to perceive the course of human experience, always come back to Jahweh who comprehended all things in his power"[24]? A comprehensive *logos* about man or the world threatened to come between her and the God of History. Rabbinic literature reproduced this caution and likewise declined to join the great dialogue of the "thinkers". It is plausible to assert that its authors' understanding was similar to that of their immediate forebears.

2. Exaggerated Caution

The attempt of later generations to dissuade readers from seeking underlying speculative content in the doctrine of the Synagogue has not always been free of excess. Complete misunderstanding of the sense of that caution may be seen in RENAN's curious observation that the Jews were wholly deprived of philosophic talent[25]. The speculative vigor that produced the LXX translation and harmonized Jewish and Greek sapiential thinking in the Book of Sirach, when turned to other tasks, issued in the thought of Philo, and Aristobulus (ca. 170 B.C.) before him. To generations of Greeks, the Jews were a race of philosophers[26]. But, even when meanings are not so wide of the mark, it has been easy to lose sight of certain necessarily theological features of rabbinic documents — the fact, for instance, that as compilations they are subject to the theological agendum of their redactors. SCHECHTER reflects that some ideas of the earlier rabbis may have found no place in the Mishnah "through some dogmatic consideration unknown to us"[27]. While one must agree that system must not be seen as a book's content when no system was proposed, it seems excessive to hold that one may not organize the proposed content according to the demands of understanding — on the assumption that the material is not deprived of relationships, however unarticulated, among the parts. Since there are no parts without a whole, a contextual interpretation will always be in force. The unholy systematizer of rabbinic literature may be pardoned for seeking simply the right context.

To proclaim rabbinism impervious to any systematization is to claim more than that the historic meaning of rabbinic dicta, the foundation to further speculation, are difficult to establish; it is to claim perception of something essential and all-conditioning in the teachings of the Synagogue — which is a gnostic-like proclamation of a system even within the very declaration of its impossibility.

[24] Ibid., p. 72.

[25] ERNEST RENAN, Histoire génerale et système comparé des langues sémitiques (Paris, 1855), p. 1.

[26] MARTIN HENGEL, Judaism and Hellinism: Studies of their Encounter in Palestine During the Early Hellenistic Period, 2 vols., WUNT, 10 (London, 1974), pp. 255—261: 'The Jews as Philosophers according to the Earliest Greek Witnesses'.

[27] SCHECHTER, p. 4.

Systematization may be encouraged by the clear presence of speculative elements in rabbinic texts. Of special interest is the discussion on the most important commandment. This attempt to reduce the entire list of biblical commandments to a single principle of conduct produced various versions of Lev. 19.18: "Thou shalt love thy neighbor as thyself"[28]. Elsewhere there is an effort to distinguish between ethical and ritual commandments. Ethical commandments are those that ought to have been written had they not already occurred in Scripture, while ritual commandments lack this self-evident quality[29]. A theological use of angelology can be observed. To avoid excessive anthropomorphism, the rabbis attributed certain functions to the angels; but, when this was misunderstood as a distancing of God, the usage was retired[30]. Possibly the most outstanding example of speculative thinking in rabbinic texts will be found in the Mishnah — not in an assembling of categorical notions or within any of the parts of the work, but in the development of a language system in which an acute formalization of syntactical and rhetorical structures represents the system of relationships that governs the moral cosmos[31]. "The people who memorized conceptions reduced to these particular forms", says NEUSNER, "were capable of extraordinarily abstract perceptions"[32]. The rest of the Talmud, the Gemara, has a systematizing dimension of its own, though with respect to the whole this may be considered minor. The Babylonian Amoraim often reduce the myriad Halakhoth of Mishnah to general principles — e.g., *mukzah*, embraces all objects one did not intend to use during a Sabbath or holy day. Such a formulation represents the distillation of other more particular principles from the Halakhoth in Mishnah, Tosefta, and the *baraita*[33]. The process obviously speaks of systematic analysis.

Implied in these comments is a modest conception of the program of anthropological systematization of rabbinic literature: A reader should strive to establish the intellectual context of the rabbinic sayings about man, aware both of the historical and philological difficulties of the text and of the theological starting point he brings to it[34]. He will, then, eschew the pretention that his product is wholly descriptive and will submit it as *a*

[28] See, e.g., Sifra to Lev. 19.18; T.B. Shabbath 31a.

[29] Sifra to Lev. 18.4, cited by J. GUTTMANN, Philosophies of Judaism, pp. 36—37.

[30] The case involves the interpretation of the Song of Songs and subsequent polemic with Origen, described by URBACH, I, 152—153, with reference to Cant. Rabbah.

[31] JACOB NEUSNER, Form and Meaning in Mishnah, p. 44, contends that the Mishnah is, in encapsulated form, "an account of the inner structure of reality".

[32] Ibid., p. 33.

[33] ELIEZER BERKOVITS and the Editorial Staff, Talmud, Babylonian, Encyclopaedia Judaica, 15, 755—768, at 759.

[34] KAUFMANN KOHLER, Jewish Theology: Systematically and Historically Considered (New York, 1968), p. 4, speaks of theology as "formulating religious truth as it exists in our consciousness today". KOHLER is not remembered as one who advanced the methods of historical theology; but, if historical theology is to escape the delusions of historicism, it can never tolerate a dimmed consciousness, not only of the limitations of textual access to lived reality, but also of its own inevitably present-day point of view.

rabbinic anthropology. The limits of this conception must be respected by those (like myself) for whom the tradition of the Synagogue exists largely as a complex literary artifact. The challenge for those writing from within the tradition is comparable and not substantively different — that of demonstrating that conclusions flow from the text[35].

Also implied in the foregoing remarks is a conviction about the urgency of theological anthropology in itself. "Every historical (*geschichtlich*) understanding of 'the world' has prior to, but inseparably connected with it a corresponding self-understanding of man."[36] This existentialist principle we accept as self-evident. Therefore, the problem, to which we now apply ourselves, is not whether the rabbis had an anthropology, but to what extent their literature gives us access to it and what this literature reveals it to be.

III. Man's Origin

The Gnostics of the Hellenistic world were wont to begin their journey of circular thought with a question: From where do you come, and whither are you going? R. Joshua ben Hanania (ca. 100), in an excess of prudence, would not tolerate the question and despaired of Simeon ben Zoma when this colleague admitted to entertaining it[37]. The question of origin had, of course, been addressed in the Bible: "In the beginning God created heaven and earth" (Gen. 1.1). The idea of creation is the irreducible starting point of biblical religion, and there was much rabbinic reflection upon it[38]. The object of this reflection was God — e.g., as omnipotent and the only power[39], as present everywhere[40]; but the characteristics of God which emerged were not of primarily metaphysical interest. That God is everywhere means that no sin is secret to Him[41] and nothing is beyond His providence[42]. The foolish denial of God was not understood as a position on God's existence

[35] J. M. Chinitz, Judaism, The Elusive Revelation (New York, 1965), pp. 187—204, discusses this problem as one of more than academic correctness. His objections to the theologizing of Abraham J. Heschel, Torah min hashamayin, 2 vols. (New York, 1962—65), and Id., God in Search of Man (New York, 1955), are on this ground. See pp. 198ff.

[36] Rudolf Pesch, Man (Anthropology): II. Biblical, Sacramentum Mundi, 3 (New York, 1969), 361—365, at p. 361.

[37] Gen. Rabbah 2, 4, pp. 17—18; Tos. Hagigah 2, 6; T.P. ibid. 2, 1, p. 77a; T.B. ibid. 15a. S. Lieberman, How Much Greek in Jewish Palestine?, in: A. Altmann, edit., Biblical and Other Studies (Cambridge, Mass., 1963), XXI, 135—139, interprets the episode.

[38] Kaufmann Kohler, Jewish Theology, p. 147, speaks of the "idea" of creation, in what seems a constructive attempt to minimize, provisionally, the supernatural character of the biblical witness.

[39] E.g., The Almighty, Heb. הגבורה, lit. "the power", as in Sifre Deut. par. 9 (on Deut. 1.9).

[40] As in Mekhilta, Bo 1, in edit. M. Friedmann (Vienna, 1870); in edit. J. H. Weiss (Vienna, 1865), f. 2a, below. Baba Batra 25a.

[41] As in Tanhuma, edit. Buber, Naso, par. 6 (f. 14b—15a).

[42] As used in T.P. Berakhoth 13c; Tos. Berakhoth 7,2; Gen. Rabbah 9,3.

but rather on providence and retribution[43]. Even as all things were considered in relation to God, their Creator, statements about God may be considered in reverse perspective as reflecting human self-awareness. Sayings about "the beginning", then, are of intense anthropological interest.

1. In the Beginning

In the Book of Genesis the rabbis studied the Work of Creation. They remained true to it though they broadened the panorama with details unrecorded in it. Remnants of mythical epics that had left more than a trace in the Bible still circulated[44]. Some elements from the cosmogonic myths of the Greeks, Persians, and Gnostic sects turn up occasionally in a Talmudic Text. Nothing, however, which suggests widely shared rabbinic opinion is in contradiction to the religious directions of Genesis[45]. Some texts — such as Gen. Rabbah, 3.4; Tanhuma on Exodus 37.1 (edit. Buber); T.B. Hagigah 12a; Exodus Rabbah, 15.22 — show clear evidence of Gnostic influence; but they show as well an attempt to Jahwehtize the alien element. Beginning with the Amoraim of the third century many mythological flourishes enter the exposition of the Work of Creation. Though materially similar to Iranian sources, their theological point is in accord with the Bible.

Frequently noted is the comment on Prov. 8.22, 30, by the Amora R. Hoshaiah. The biblical text speaks of the preexistence of wisdom: "Then I was beside him like a master workman [*ʿāmôn*]" (v. 30). Since the Book of Sirach (29.8–9), wisdom had been identified with the Torah. R. Hoshaiah, therefore, remarks that in the beginning God looked in the Torah and created the world[46]. Not surprisingly this has suggested an analogue in Philo, where the Torah, as the matrix of creation, represents the Platonic ideas[47]. The differences, however, between Philo's account and the rabbi's leave the latter no more significance than that of a literary embellishment[48]. Of no greater speculative weight is a similar anonymous

[43] E.g., Sifra Behukkotai Perek 3, end (ed. Weiss f. 111c); Tos. Shebuoth 3,6. See W. Bacher, Die Agada der Tannaiten, 2 vols. (Strassburg, 1884—90), II, 384.

[44] See M. Cassuto, Shirat ha-Alita be-Yisra'el, Keneset, 8 (1943—44), 121—142.

[45] The subject is broad and intensely debated. See, e.g., Hengel, I, 153—175, who inclines in several places to a different conclusion. Alexander Altmann, Studies in Religious Philosophy and Mysticism (London, 1969), pp. 128—139, supports an opinion not at all uncommon among scholars — that some rabbinic sayings about creation are from Plato's 'Timaeus' mediated by Philo. Our conclusion is closer to Urbach, I, 184—213; Moore, I, 357—385; and Schechter, pp. 21—45.

[46] כך היה הקב"ה מביט בתורה ובורא את העולם. "Thus the Holy One, blessed be He, was looking in the Torah and creating the world" (Gen. Rabbah 1, 1, p. 2).

[47] De Opificio Mundi, 17—20. See J. Horovitz, Untersuchungen über Philons und Platons Lehre von der Weltschöpfung (Marburg, 1900), p. 80 and n. 2. A survey of the discussion may be found in Hengel I, 169—175.

[48] Wolfson, Philo, Pt. I, 243, noted the major difference. See Urbach, I. 198—200.

midrash, where God is said to have sought workmen for the building of the world, and the Torah answered, "I shall put at your service twenty-two workmen, namely the twenty-two letters of the Torah"[49]. The Work of Creation was accomplished, not with toil, but with an utterance; and understanding of this work would be reached, not through the speculations of aliens, but in the study of the revealed word.

Controversy against sectaries occasioned much of the discussion of the Work of Creation. Some Gnostics explained the evil in man by holding that he was not exclusively God's work. The plural of "Let us make man" (Gen. 1.26) gave the rabbis occasion to discuss this. The earliest Amoraim gave the angels a consultative role[50]. Later even this was denied; God consulted within Himself[51]. Though there was insistance upon creation by utterance[52], there was no hypostatizing of a *logos*.

In all of this the chief preoccupation was that the radical monotheism of Genesis not be compromised. God who created had no collaborators or competitors. By affirming creation in its rabbinic sense, man desacralizes his world. He is not caught up in a cosmic dualism of good and evil. The existence of the things to which he relates is ultimately explained only in the will of God.

2. The World as Environment

In the Work of Creation all the world had preceded man. The rabbis offer many explanations of the Bible texts, and frequently these appear to be religious reflections upon experience rather than mere textual clarifications. The verse "And there was evening and there was morning" (Gen. 1.4) leads R. Judah ben R. Simon (ca. 350)[53] to affirm an order of time before the present one: "From this is to be inferred that the Holy One, blessed be He, created worlds and destroyed them, until He created these, declaring, 'These please me, those did not please me'"[54]. This view opposes the aspiration of the Gnostics — or of other Platonizing currents in religion — to be liberated from the present order and its flaws. It represents an

[49] Tanhuma to Isa. 48.13.

[50] See, e.g. Gen. Rabbah 8,4, p. 59; 17,4, p. 155.

[51] Ibid., pp. 60—61; p. 62 and n. 1. Urbach, I, 207—208, describes various reactions of the Christian Fathers to the rabbinic view that God consulted the Angels, mentioning Justin Martyr, Theophilus of Antioch, Irenaeus, Tertullian, and Basil.

[52] M. Aboth 5,1; Mekhilta, Shira 10, p. 150; Gen. Rabbah 17.1, p. 151.

[53] See W. Bacher, Die Agada der palästinischen Amoräer, 3 vols. (Strassburg, 1892—99), III, 160—220, Proöm. 71—73.

[54] (ט) א׳׳ר אבהו מלאד שהיה בורא עולמות ומחריד̇ן עד שברא את אלו. אמר דין הניין לי יתהון לא הניין לי. "From this is to be inferred that the Holy One, blessed be He, created worlds and destroyed them, until He created these, declaring, 'These please me, those did not please me'" (Gen. Rabbah 3, 7, p. 3). A succession of worlds was held by many Stoics. See H. A. Wolfson, Philo: Foundations of Religious Philosophy in Judaism, Christianity, and Islam (Cambridge, Mass., 1947), Pt. I, p. 195.

optimism which may be constructively contrasted with religious movements generally, at the threshold of the middle ages[55]. (See below, pp. 545–50).

God, who made all things good, made all for a purpose; He uses them all in His service[56]. They are so splendid that, in contemplation of them, the Psalmist asks, "What is man that Thou art mindful of him?" (Ps. 8.4, et passim). The poetry of paradox in this eighth psalm pervades the rabbinic dicta about man's world. On the one hand, the world was made for Israel, or for the righteous[57], and man was given dominion over it (Gen. 1.26); on the other, things have beauty and purpose which man, especially because of his ignorance, must be reminded to respect: "One can say to him: A gnat preceded you in the work of creation"[58]. The creation of all the world before man is seen as evidence of the autonomy of things with respect to man — a truth to be balanced by the affirmation that all was created for man. Since each man is different, each has the duty of saying, "For my sake the world was created"[59].

The first exercise of man's dominion was Adam's display of wisdom in naming the animals[60]. But, man is not the measure of all things. Nature is not measured against him in metaphysical categories. The comprehensive view which the notion "nature" implies is nowhere in evidence. Things were not forced to coalesce; each was seen, not "objectively", but (as we have noted) in its specific, separate relationship to its Maker. While such a view retards systematization, it compels an acceptance of creatures, not according to their supposed nature, but according to their concrete relationships, to God not least. Man also, then, is not seen as an essence, but as related[61]. To enquire about man is, among other things, to enquire about his relationship to his world — "essentially", one may say. Perhaps this explains why the rabbis could affirm man's centrality in creation and his dominion without reducing the world to a mere complex of useful functions. Happily, they lacked the "system". What is certain is that in rabbinic literature there is no such reduction.

To demonstrate this it will be enough to indicate, selecting from a vast wealth of texts, a few attitudes towards animals. The themes are not

[55] The time is roughly the age of St. Augustine (354—430), whose personal religious temperament became a significant influence in medieval Christendom. See Henri-Irénée Marrou, Saint Augustin et la fin de la culture antique (Paris, 1938), pp. iii, 541. F. van der Meer, Augustine the Bishop: Religion and Society at the Dawn of the Middle Ages (New York, 1965), p. 562. The axiomatic pessimism of the middle ages is inherited from reactions to the corruption and decadence of late antiquity.

[56] Gen. Rabbah 10, 7, pp. 79ff.; idem., the indicated parallels.

[57] Sifre Deut. par. 47, on Deut. 11.21.

[58] Tos. Sanhedrin viii, 4—5; T.P. ibid., iv, 12—13, p. 22b; T.B. ibid. 38a. Though the point is not to develop the beauty of gnats, but to remind man of his finitude before God, man's position in the time-sequence of creation is seen also as an evidence of the worth of the world independently of its relation to man.

[59] M. Sanhedrin 4, 5.

[60] Gen. Rabbah 17, 4, p. 155.

[61] Von Rad, Wisdom in Israel, pp. 69, 71—73, 311, 314—315, argues this position from biblical wisdom literature. The rabbis, demonstrably, are heirs to the tradition.

unfamiliar, but they gain special point as qualifications of the anthropocentric characters of the world in one tradition of biblical religion. We read in Josephus that when Herod entertained by offering the spectacle of great beasts struggling to the death, foreigners were delighted, "but to the Jews it was a palpable breaking up of those customs for which they had so great a veneration"[62]. The prohibition of attending the Greco-Roman arenas read, "One who attends the stadium sits in 'the seat of the scornful'" (Ps. 1.1)[63]. The Talmud describes with meticulous care and detail how an animal is to be slaughtered for food; the regulations implement the desire to inflict as painless a death as possible[64]. The story is told of R. Judah that as a calf was being led to slaughter it hid its head in the rabbi's garment, and he said, "Go, since you were created for that purpose!" Heaven afflicted him with great sufferings, which were removed when, in a second episode, he saved two young weasels from harm, saying, "Leave them alone, for it is written, 'His mercies are over all His works' (Ps. 145.9)"[65]. The care of domestic animals and pets is seriously regulated[66]. The character of Moses is illustrated in his humane treatment of animals. A midrash on Exodus offers a legend similar to the parable of the Good Shepherd (Lk. 15.3–7), but the legend centers upon the care of Moses for the animals, literally. Then, "The Holy One, blessed be He, said, 'Since you are merciful to the flock of a human being, you shall be the shepherd of my flock, Israel'"[67].

This empathy with the animals of the earth is never weakened by ineffectual romanticizing. Various species are admired for their habits. Had not the Torah been given for man's guidance, it was said, he could have learned decency and many virtues from several kinds of animals[68]. Yet, the rabbis were clear about the absence of any "moral" life in animals: These had no evil impulse, and so were amoral[69]. Animals, it was agreed, would have no after-life[70].

The world as human environment consists of God's other creatures. They are not understood as an integral non-human cosmos, metaphysically inferior to man, but as creatures which relate primarily to God, who has put all in man's care.

3. Creation of Man

The awe expressed in Psalm eight over man's position in creation becomes wonderment over man himself, God's final creation.

[62] Antiq. XV, 8, 1.
[63] T.B. Abodah Zarah 18b.
[64] T.B. Hullin I, 1; 17b; 9a.
[65] T.B. Baba Metzia 85a.
[66] T.B. Berakhoth 40a.
[67] Ex. Rabbah 2, 2. Composed between the seventh and twelfth centuries.
[68] T.B. Erubin 100b.
[69] Aboth de-R. Nathan 16; an extra-canonical tractate of the third or fourth century.
[70] Midrash to Ps. 19.1; 81b.

A. Microcosm

"One man", R. Nehemiah is reported to have said, "is equal to the entire work of creation"[71]. The sense here regards not only man's prerogative as the only creature of earth who recognizes his maker, but man's marvelous formation. "All that the Holy One, blessed be He, created in the world He created in man", said R. Jose the Galilean[72]. The idea is expanded in detail: The hair corresponds to thickets, the lips to walls, the teeth to doors, the neck to a tower, the fingers to nails. The microcosm image is not original. It may be associated, materially, with the Hellenistic theme of the great cosmic tree. Comparing R. Jose's development of the idea, however, to Philo's we observe that what is extolled in the rabbi's thinking is, not man's spiritual nature, but the complexity of a human body as it grows in the maternal womb. As a human being develops, there forms within him the other creatures over which he will come to marvel. The image corroborates man's understanding of his centrality and leadership in creation; but, unlike its Hellenistic counterpart, it keeps him close to his earthly setting. Adam, therefore, is figured as exhorting all creation over which he is master to join in his song, "The Lord reigns, He is clothed with majesty"[73].

B. Image of God

Beyond being a summation of the world, man's foundational distinction was that he was made in the Image of God (Gen. 1.27; 5.1; 9.6; Ps. 8.5). It is clear that this revelation of man's special relationship to God was the starting point of rabbinic reflection upon humankind. R. Akiba said, "Beloved [to God] is man, in that he was created in the [divine] image; still more beloved in that it is known to him that he was created in the image, as it is said, In the image of God He made the man"[74]. Akiba's colleague and disciple, Simeon ben Azzai, isolated the verse "This is the book of the generations of Adam: In the day that God created man, in the likeness of God made He him", and called it the great principle of the Torah[75]. It was the comprehensive source of all law governing man's dealings with man. It is explicitly invoked in the questions of manslaughter and of

[71] Aboth de-R. Nathan, Version 1, 31, p. 91.

[72] **ויצר בארכל מה שברא בעולם**. "All that the Holy One, blessed be He, created in the world He created in man." R. Eleazar son of R. Jose the Galilean, in Aboth de-R. Nathan, Version 1, 31, 3.

[73] Pirke Rabbi Eliezer, ch. 2, edit. of R. David Loria (Warsaw, 1852).

[74] M. Aboth 3, 14.

[75] Sifra Kiddushin, 4, 12, presents R. Simeon ben Azzai in dialogue with R. Akiba, who had remarked, "To love your fellowman is the basic principle of the Torah"; ben Azzai's rejoinder, given above, is cited from Gen. 5.1: בְּיוֹם בְּרֹא אֱלֹהִים אָדָם בִּדְמוּת אֱלֹהִים עָשָׂה אֹתוֹ.

wishing ill to others[76]. To Hillel is attributed, as we shall see, the conviction that it grounded the obligation to keep the body clean by bathing[77].

That a divine likeness was the common inheritance of mankind was universally agreed by the rabbis, but the question of the nature of this likeness seems not to have arisen. The conclusion of the Wisdom of Solomon, that the image is man's immortality (2.23), finds no echo in their text. It was enough that the reality of divine likeness explained God's love for man (Akiba's saying, above), man's central position in creation, and man's obligation to his fellowman.

The subject was one of great edification and provoked the question whether man was indeed less than the angels. Some held the view, in common with the apocryphal literature and with notions held by Greeks and Iranians, that man was inferior to the angels — not, however, because he was embodied but because he was a sinner[78]. Others are represented by the disciples of R. Akiba, saying, "O Israel, you are more beloved of me than the ministering angels; . . . you are greater in my sight"[79]. In this as in all, Israel is the norm of humanity. Man's position over the angels is not fixed; it depends upon observance of the Torah[80]. God's love for Israel and Israel's response of love is the subject of the homilies that allegorically interpreted the Song of Songs, which R. Akiba had pronounced "most holy"[81]. Israel is God's beloved because she is made in His Image.

C. Macroanthropos

The solidarity of Israel represents the true state of humanity; man is one. The story of Adam and Eve is the story of the race. In the Midrashic expositions of the Tannaim the formation of the child in the womb is emphasized as a miracle without compare[82]. Every child is as much the work of the Creator as was the first man. From the beginning of the third century, however, some of the Amoraim suspected that Adam as parent of the race was physically not the same as God had created him. His sin had diminished him[83]. He had extended from one end of the world to the other. He had also been created hermaphrodite; then God "sawed him

[76] For manslaughter: Mekhilta, Bahodesh 8 (edit. FRIEDMANN f. 70b; ed. WEISS f. 78a); for wishing ill to others: Gen. Rabbah 24, 7.

[77] Lev. Rabbah 34,3 on Gen. 5.1.

[78] See, for example, Tos. Abodah Zarah 1, 17—18, p. 461; Cant. Rabbah 1, 4: Eccles. Rabbah 1,1; T.P. Berakhoth 9, 2, p. 14b.

[79] Aboth de-R. Nathan, Version 2, 44, p. 124. See also T.B. Hullin 91b, an anonymous *baraita*, and its commentary in Gen. Rabbah 45, 21, p. 737.

[80] Sifre to Num., par. 119, p. 143.

[81] M. Yadayim 3, 5.

[82] Mekhilta de-R. Ishmael, Wa-yehi 8, p. 144; Mekhilta de-R. Simeon ben Yohai 15, 11, p. 94; Midrash Samuel 5, 6, p. 59; Midrash Tehillim 18, 26, p. 154. All cited in URBACH II, 790, n. 58.

[83] T.B. Hagigah 12a; T.B. Sanhedrin 38b; Gen. Rabbah 8, 1, p. 55; Aboth de-R. Nathan, Version 1, end of ch. I, p. 8.

asunder and made him with a back on each side"[84]. The presence of such embellishments of the Genesis narrative indicates obvious Gnostic influence. The Amoraim who indulge these fantasies do indeed impose their biblical faith upon the material but compromise, meanwhile, what others sought in dwelling upon man's last place in the sequence of creation; for, all told, in a rabbinic anthropology, the most comprehensive characteristic of the first man and every man is creatureliness.

4. Providence

Even as God continues to create so, in His free will, He governs His creation. R. Akiba meditated upon the order which God maintains in the world[85]. And, his disciple, R. Simeon ben Yohai reflected, "Unless Heaven wills it, a bird is not ensnared; how much more so does this apply to a human being!"[86] Even those things for which a man must strive are to be seen as dispensed finally by the Creator. One must labor to become wise as well as to become rich; yet, both wisdom and riches are the gifts of God[87]. Such examples of Providence in human life uncover a characteristic of man's creatureliness.

The notion of Providence is an inheritance from the Bible[88]. God's Providence has two aspects: one involves the governance of the world, providing for its needs, including those of man; the other consists in scrutinizing the actions of man, to allow the dispensation of justice (Jeremiah 32.19)[89]. The question of the relationship between the two will be taken up later (see below, pp. 523—27). Here we must observe that man understands himself in relation to a God who is provident. Providence is of God's character; it is not predicated of an un-free order of the world.

That man's needs are freely and lovingly supplied by the Creator makes it possible for man to understand himself as son. (The filial relationship, meanwhile, is not exhausted in this.) The fatherly care of God for Israel is a familiar theme in Hebrew Scripture[90]. Characteristic of the piety of the rabbis is that they greatly increased the usage of addressing God as father[91]. When both aspects of Providence are intended, the titles Father and King are used together[92].

[84] Gen. Rabbah 8, 1, p. 55; see also Lev. Rabbah 14, 1, p. 296; T. B. Berakhoth 60A.
[85] Sifra, Shemini, Sec. 5. [86] T.P. Shebiith 9, 1, p. 38a. [87] T.B. Niddah 70b.
[88] השגחה Heb. *Hashgaha*, Providence. See n. 108, below.
[89] URBACH, I, 256.
[90] See Deut. 1, 31; Isa. 63, 8ff.; 46, 3ff; and in Greek, Wisdom 11,10.
[91] M. Aboth 3,14; P.B. Baba Batra 10a; Pesikta Rabbati c. 27 (edit. FRIEDMANN f. 132b) on Jer. 2, 4; T.B. Kiddushin 36a; Sifre Deut. on 14, 1, par. 96 and 308 (ed. FRIEDMANN f. 133a—b); par. 320 (f. 137a). All cited by MOORE, II, 203, notes 2, 3, 4. C. TAYLOR, Sayings of the Jewish Fathers, 2nd edit. (Cambridge, 1897), p. 124, finds the phrases of the Lord's Prayer (Matt. 6. 9–13) in contemporary rabbinic prayers.
[92] T.B. Berakhoth 11b. See S. SINGER, Daily Prayer Book, p. 39ff. and p. 96; pp. 55—57; p. 234. T.B. Taanith 25b.

5. God's Nearness and Distance

The God addressed as Father in Heaven was also near to earth and accessible. The epithet *Shekhinah* expressed the presence of God, with no qualifications. "The angel of God" who went before the camp of Israel, in Exodus 14.19, becomes the *Shekhinah* itself in rabbinic rendering[93]. This understanding of biblical angelology is frequent. The sense was that God was personally and directly involved in Israel's wellbeing. God's "humility" was a theme taken from Psalm 18.36: "Thy humility has made me great"[94]. The Creator's closeness to His world was expressed in a great variety of titles such as Father of the world[95]. Every endearing relationship was invoked to signify His nearness to Israel — e.g., brother, sister, bride, lamb, eye[96]. Their suffering was His suffering, and their subjection His subjection[97]. Expressions of this nearness were not intended as a credal notion but as an exhortation to experience, even as they signaled the religious experience of those who pronounced them. Such faith-experience found its truest expression in the act of prayer, of which the rabbis spoke much. A consciousness of the *Shekhinah* was not achieved through prayer formulas undertaken as a fixed task but in that service of the heart commanded in Deut. 11.13: "Which is the service of the heart? Prayer"[98]. "The Holy One, blessed be He, longs for the prayer of the righteous"[99].

In what sense God was near inevitably developed into a question. In Tannaitic sources a distinction is made through the coordinate terms *Maqom* (place) and *Shamayim* (Heaven), both post-biblical[100]. *Maqom* is used as a metonomy of place, common in Semitic languages (e.g. Gen. 11.1; 21.23; 1 Sam. 5.12), referring to God who reveals Himself in whatever place He wishes, since He is in all places. It expresses God's nearness, for the world is His place[101]. But, lest this closeness to man's earth be misread, a balancing truth had to be affirmed: Man is not God; man is addressed

[93] Mekhilta de-R. Ishmael, Massekhta de-Shira, iii, p. 128, cited in URBACH I, 136, and II, 741, n. 1.

[94] For acts of such "humility" see Tanhuma ed. BUBER, Wayyera 3 (f. 42b); Gen. Rabbah 8, 13; Eccles. Rabbah on Eccles. 7, 2; T.B. Sotah 14a; Tanhuma ed. BUBER, Bereshith 4.

[95] Midrash Prov., ch. 10. SCHECHTER, p. 26, lists titles gathered from the Midrashim.

[96] SCHECHTER, p. 47, assembles references.

[97] Mekhilta 16a.

[98] As, for example, in R. Simeon's saying in M. Aboth 2, 18: קבע *keba*: lit. "a fixed task"; "routine". See also T.B. Taanith 2b; T.B. Berakhoth 29b.

[99] T.B. Yebamoth 64a.

[100] See the clear treatment in 'Nearness and Distance — Omnipresent and Heaven', URBACH, I, ch. 4, 66—79. See also MOORE, I, ch. 5: 'Majesty and Accessibility of God', 423—442.

[101] YITZHAK BAER, On the Problem of Eschatological Doctrine during the Period of the Second Temple, Zion, 23/24 (1958/59), pp. 25ff., reads *Maqom* as one of the earliest signs of the meeting of Israel's religious intuition with Western abstract thinking (pp. 33—34). The word derives, he thinks, from Plato's teaching, and denotes the place beyond the perception of the senses. But such an abstract, transcendental character in *Maqom* accords ill with specific instances in the rabbinic texts. See URBACH, I, 74: II, 715—716, notes 35 and 39.

by God from afar — from "heaven", as the Tannaim read, e.g., in Deut. 4.36; 26.15; 1 Kings 8.30; Jon. 1.9; and Ezra 1.2. This interest was served by the use of the epithet *Shamayim* — "Heaven", for the God of Heaven — which occurs in such phrases as "the fear of Heaven"[102], "the kingdom of Heaven"[103], and "the yoke of Heaven"[104]. The anthropological sense becomes clear when the expression has an obvious antithetical edge, as in "the honor of Heaven" as opposed to "the honor of man"[105], "the laws of Heaven" as different from "the laws of man"[106], "the Father in Heaven" and not "a father of flesh and blood"[107]. From the third century onward the coordinates which spoke both of God's immanence and of His transcendence fall into disuse, probably because *Maqom* lent itself to easy misunderstanding by Jewish Gnostics. The expression "the Holy One, blessed be He" is preferred by the Amoraim[108]. But, despite changing usages, the rabbinic conviction is clear: Man originates in a creation to which God is lovingly present but from which He is simply distinct.

6. Election as Origin

God's nearness to man was understood in His nearness to Israel, His chosen people[109]. In the Bible God is Israel's lover. A Tannaitic Midrash offers an account of Israel's conversation with the peoples: "When they hear her descriptions of God's beauty, they wish to follow her to Him", but the Israelites reply, "You have no part in Him, as it is written, 'I am my lover's and my lover is mine'"[110]. Since, as we have said, what appears of greatest concern in rabbinic literature is, not man as quiddity but related man, the special relationship of Israel to God is a defining element. The divine election is an anthropological determinant. Though man is made in God's image, his understanding of himself (anthropology) may fail to be governed by that reality. R. Akiba declared that the election of man consists in the fact that it was revealed to him that he was made in God's image[111]. They are elected to whom it has been given to know who they are. (Again, though God is intended, human self-awareness is concomitant.)

If election is a constitutive prerogative for Israel, it is that for all mankind, as one reads in rabbinic texts — for example, "Though His good-

[102] M. Aboth 1, 3; 4, 12.
[103] Mekhilta de-R. Ishmael, Ba-hodesh, 5, p. 219.
[104] Tos. Sotah 14, 4; Sifra, Be-har, 5, 109c.
[105] Tos. Yoma 2, 8.
[106] M. Baba Kamma 6, 4.
[107] M. Yoma 8, 9.
[108] קדשא בריך הוא, *Qudsha berekh Hu*: lit (Aram.), "Holiness, blessed be He".
[109] See M. Kaduschin, Aspects of the Rabbinic Concept of Israel, HUCA, 19 (1945—46), 57—96. Buber, Darkô shel Miqrá' (Jerusalem, 1964), pp. 88—89, on the relationship of the Sinai covenant to Israel's election.
[110] Sifre Deut., par. 343 (edit. Friedmann, p. 143a).
[111] חִבָּה יְתֵירָה נוֹדַעַת לוֹ שֶׁנִּבְרָא בְּצֶלֶם: "Still greater was the love that it was made known to him that he was created in the image of God" (M. Aboth 3, 14).

ness, loving-kindness, and mercy are with Israel, His right hand is always stretched forward to receive all those who come into the world, . . . as it is said, 'Unto me every knee shall bow, every tongue shall swear'". (Isa. 45. 23)[112]. To the Synagogue, all men are potentially what, in His mercy, God has made Israel. She claims only the privilege of the first-born. (See below, pp. 559—61.)

Why Israel was chosen to enter a special covenant with God and to receive the Torah was an inevitable question. A midrash on Leviticus has Moses himself present the question to God[113]. Various answers occur. Israel's election was simply predestined[114]. This was, in some accounts, in foresight of the goodness of the Patriarchs[115]. One opinion has it that Israel was chosen when they acclaimed God their king at the Red Sea (Exod. 15.18)[116]. Quite beyond any homiletic conceit, however, is the teaching that election was a two-way encounter; God chose Israel and she chose Him. This two-fold election took place at Sinai, where the entire Torah was presented to all peoples and refused by all except Israel. As the common doctrine of the two second-century schools of R. Ishmael and R. Akiba, it may be presumed to be, as well, the tradition that preceded them. It is frequently evoked, with varying details[117]. At times one reads disclaimers of any merit in election, in easier accord with such biblical teaching as Deut. 9.4: "Do not say in your heart . . . 'It is because of my righteousness that the Lord has brought me in to possess this land'"[118]. But, in an era when their people suffered the bewildering loss of every material blessing and endured from every direction the scorn of the powerful, the rabbis chose to encourage them by representing their election, not only as the mystery of God's freedom, but also as the fact of their forefathers' acceptance. If man as such is offered the Torah, the chosen people are the choosing people.

The anthropological conclusion to this enquiry into human beginnings is as follows: Man explains himself, in some measure, in his origin. To the Jewish sages, man was the creature of the only God, who had lovingly established him as leader in a good world, to which God was present in power and care. Made in the image of God, man was given, in history, a knowledge of this origin and the Law according to which his nature was to develop, in the worship of this loving God.

112 Mekhilta 38b. See also ibid. 102a; Sifre 73a. In the saying of R. Akiba, above, note that man and Israel are combined.

113 Pesikta de-R. Kahana 16a; Lev. Rabbah 2.4. Both texts are from the seventh to the ninth centuries.

114 Gen. Rabbah 1, 4.

115 E.g., Yelamedenu, Num., par. 766; Exod. Rabbah 15, 17; 42, 9. Cf. on the merit of the Patriarchs, M. Aboth 5.1; Gen. Rabbah 3, 8; T. B. Berakhoth 7b.

116 Pesikta de-R. Kahana 16b and 17a and parallels.

117 E.g., Tos. Sotah 8, 6; Sifre Deut. par. 343 (edit. Friedmann f. 142b); T.B. Shabbath 88b.

118 E.g., Midrash Tanhuma 5, 9a (edit. S. Buber). Cf. Schechter, p. 61: "The great majority of the Rabbis are silent about merits, and attribute the election to a mere act of grace (or love) on the part of God."

IV. Man's Nature and Condition

The effort to understand man must centre upon his experience. Although the light shed by human origins is indispensible, it must be focused upon the conscious present. The concept of man's historicity held by the Synagogue — God had spoken to her, she knew, in events — located man in a concrete here and now, which unlike many Hellenistic sectaries, she took with engaged seriousness. Here we shall distinguish *nature* from *condition* in order to isolate what constitutes the human, excising from "human nature" philosophic preconceptions of a static essentialism.

1. Human Nature: The Experience of Dividedness

While assuming personal oneness, individuals assert that they suffer in body but are glad in soul (II Macc. 6.30), or that enemies may injure the body but not the soul (IV Macc. 10.4). The Talmud observes, in this vein, the great difference between bodily needs and spiritual attributes[119]. At the end of the second century R. Simai spoke of a suspended human state, in these terms:

> "All created beings that were created from heaven, their soul and body are from heaven; and all creatures that were created from the earth, their soul and body are from the earth, except man, whose soul is from heaven and his body from the earth. Therefore, if he observed the Torah and did the will of his Father in heaven, he is like the beings above, for Scripture states, 'I said ye are godlike beings and all of you sons of the Most High' (Ps. 82.6). But if he did not observe the Torah nor do the will of his Father in heaven, he is like the creatures of earth below, as it is said, 'Nevertheless ye shall die like men' (Ps. 82.7)[120]".

The Tannaim generally thought of man as composed of various parts, attesting to an experience of dividedness: Every man born is accounted for by partners — "The white is from the male . . . and the red is from the female . . . and the spirit and the life and the soul are from the Holy One, blessed be He"[121]. This sense was sharpened by the fact that death deprived man of speech and movement while leaving the body whole.

[119] T.B. Hagigah 16a. See also Gen. Rabbah 8, 11, p. 64.

[120] לא עשה תורה ולא עשה רצון אביו שבשמים הרי הוא כבריות של מטה שנאמר אכן כאדם תמותון. "But if he did not observe the Torah nor do the will of his Father in heaven, he is like the creatures of earth below, as it is said, 'Nevertheless ye shall die like men'." R. Simai in Sifre, Ha'azinu (edit. FINKELSTEIN), p. 341, par. 306.

[121] T. P. Kilaim 8, 4, p. 31c. See also T. B. Niddah 31a. URBACH, I, 218—219, speaks of the frequent occurrence among the Tannaim of the image of man as meat that is preserved by the salt given by God.

Thought of an after-life — e.g., what form of existence one might have while awaiting the resurrection of the body — occasioned speaking of man in terms of body and soul[122]. The dichotomous view was common among the rabbis. R. Simai, quoted above, obviously felt this had a foundation in Scripture. And R. Simeon ben Lakish (ca. 250) repeats his account[123]. Hillel had asked, "Is not the poor soul a guest within the body? Today it is here and tomorrow it is gone"[124]. R. Johanan ben Zakkai wept as he lay dying because his soul would survive his body and face the judgment of God[125]. R. Judah told a story about a lame man and a blind man who collaborated in stealing figs from an orchard and were punished together. "So will the Holy One, blessed be He, bring the soul, replace it in the body and judge them together"[126]. R. Judah also discusses the time the soul is instilled into the body[127]. The body, we read in the Talmud, is "the scabbard of the soul"[128].

The container-of-the soul notion is seen in the expression *guf*, which is the usual word for body in rabbinic literature from very early in the period[129]. Although a holistic meaning for *guf* ("body, person, self") is assigned by the standard lexicons of rabbinic literature, all the examples offered can be proven dichotomous[130]. As one hears discussion of *guf* and *nephesh* (life, soul) in their different origins, in their separation at death, in the reuniting of body and soul at resurrection, and in the conscious existence of the soul in the interim, it is not possible to interpret these authors' sense of the difference as merely aspectual.

Josephus adds his testimony to what our examples show. For the Essenes, he tells us, soul and body make up the whole man. They resign their souls confident of receiving them back. Souls, they believe, emanate from very fine ether, become enmeshed in the prison of the body, and are released at death[131]. The Pharisees, he goes on, believe each soul is immortal, that the souls of the wicked suffer eternal punishment and the souls of the righteous enjoy reward, and that only the souls of good men go into another

[122] E.g., T.B. Shabbath 152b, ff.

[123] Tanhuma Bereshith 15, edit. Buber.

[124] Lev. Rabbah 34, 3.

[125] T.B. Berakhoth 28b.

[126] T.B. Sanhedrin 91a.

[127] Ibid. 91b. For further examples, see R. Meyer, Hellenistisches in der rabbinischen Anthropologie, BWANT 4, 2 (Stuttgart, 1937), pp. 15—16, 27.

[128] T.B. Sanhedrin 108a.

[129] גוף *gûf*: body. Robert H. Gundry, Sōma in Biblical Theology, With Emphasis on Pauline Anthropology (Cambridge, 1976), p. 71, says "as early as the second century B.C." How the author derives this date is not clear, though he shows that a dichotomous meaning is common in intertestamental writings (pp. 87—90).

[130] Gundry, Sōma, pp. 74—76. The lexicons examined are J. Levy, Wörterbuch über die Talmudim und Midraschim, 2nd ed. (Berlin, 1924), s. v.; and his 'Neuhebräisches und Chaldäisches Wörterbuch über die Talmudim und Midraschim' (Leipzig, 1876), s. v.; M. Jastrow, A Dictionary of the Targumim, the Talmud Babli and Yerushalmi, and the Midrashic Literature (New York 1950), s. v.

[131] Jewish War II, 8, 6, par. 136; II, 8, 10, par. 153; II, 8, 11, par. 154—158; Antiq. XVIII, 1, 5, par. 18.

body[132]. The Sadducees alone believe that souls perish with bodies[133]. The sectarian writings of the Dead Sea Scrolls yield the same body-soul duality that Josephus reported regarding the Essenes[134]. Anthropological duality is the common conception of the age[135].

But, between a body-soul duality and a cosmic dualism of good and evil there is an essential difference; the first need not imply the second. Nor does duality tell us anything about how the relationship of body and soul is conceived; distinctness is neither autonomy nor antagonism[136]. Were one to read that human dignity lay in the spiritual character of the soul, or that the Image of God was borne in the soul and not the body, then one could suspect that more was being affirmed than the fact of duality. It can be said in general that the rabbis assessed the union of body and soul more positively than did their contemporaries[137].

In the second half of the third century the Amoraim began to speculate about the pre-existence of souls and lost something of the earlier positive valuation of man's embodiedness. An analogy explains how the soul is more responsible for evil doing than is the body: It is like the well raised daughter of a priest, from whom more is expected than from the untrained daughter of a common Israelite[138]. A variation states, "The body comes from the village and the soul comes from the court"[139]. Whether or not this is an inevitable evolution from that speculative response to the experience of human dividedness postulating an inner man and his outward container will be settled as much by one's philosophical starting point as by his repossession of a history to which rabbinical documents permit access. For URBACH, "there is a great gulf between the teaching of the Amoraim concerning man and the thought of the early Tannaim"[140]. SCHECHTER, instead,

132 Jewish War II, 8, 14, par. 163; Antiq. XVIII, 1, 3, par. 14.

133 Jewish War II, 8, 14, par. 165; Antiq. XVIII, 1, 4, par. 16.

134 GUNDRY, Sōma, pp. 96—107.

135 R. H. CHARLES, Eschatology (London, 1899; reprint, New York, 1963), p. 288.

136 URBACH, I, 224, speaks of "the antithesis between flesh and spirit in Rabbinic dicta" which is not "the conception of the basic antithesis between spirit and matter" (I, 241). See also p. 248. Accordingly he treats dualism as a matter of degree: The rabbis do not hold the "extreme" dualism of Iranian cosmology, but a "mitigated" dualism. URBACH's thought is not unclear in the large context, but there is the strong implication that an anthropological dualism of body and soul has, in itself, common ground with a cosmic dualism of good and evil, even if the potential error is not realized in the sages.

137 The case of Hellenistic philosophies should be evident. Regarding Philo, cf. De opificio mundi, 27; see WOLFSON, Philo, Pt. I, p. 390. For Josephus, see Jewish War III, 8, 5, on suicide. The Essenes' anti-body attitude is seen in their literature; see D. FLUSSER, The Dualism of 'Flesh and Spirit' in the Dead Sea Scrolls and the New Testament, Tarbiz 27 (1958), 158—165. In the Pauline view, normative to Patristic and medieval Christian spirituality, human embodiedness is the occasion of being divided from the Lord through the preoccupations of marriage, which is the paradign of man's involvement in the passing order of the world. (1 Cor. 7.28–35.)

138 Lev. Rabbah 4, 5, p. 90.

139 Midrash Tanhuma 3, 4a and b (edit. BUBER); Eccles. Rabbah 6, 6.

140 The Sages, I, 248.

wished to establish continuity between the simile of the villager (body) and the cortier (soul), contending that it should be understood in relationship to the texts which cite the Tannaim, where he seems to find no notable difference[141]. Body and soul, and their alternative expressions, are not univocal terms. The content of these ideas and the value judgments they provoke must be derived from the catalogue of specific affirmations made about them. Duality in man does not determine an anthropology. A soul so nearly-self-contained with respect to the body that, as a midrash on Genesis explains, while the body sleeps "it ascends and draws life for him from on high"[142], — for the function of the soul in the body is like that of God in the world[143] — such a concept of soul will eventually commend the ascetical-contemplative approach to life which Platonists, Gnostics, and Stoics advocated, even while the systems and mythologies of these are held reprobate[144]. It is antecedently possible that philosophic ideas coming from outside rabbinic Judaism acted for some as a catalyst in the tapping of resources that lay deep within Rabbinism itself. The rabbinic sage learned from all men; and, like his biblical forebears, he Jahwehtized the cultures of his neighbors. The Amoraic loosening of the body-soul amalgam opens onto the contemplative religion of much medieval Judaism[145]. Clearly, this is not to say that the looser association of body and soul which portends later developments may lay claim to the mainstream of rabbinic religion. Nor is this to say that philosophic ideas which bear in their train associations wholly corrupting of biblical religion should not be virulently mistrusted. Whether the concept of soul and body found in some of the Amoraim was implicit from the beginning of rabbinic tradition or represents a development explainable only as the influence of intellectual currents either novel or alien to the Torah is a historical question of considerable theological significance. Whether what was "implicit" from the standpoint of systematics was in any way operative in an earlier consciousness becomes, of course, a major element of the historical problem. (To assume that the implicit, in this sense, was operative is an intellectualist delusion.) What

[141] Aspects, 261, n. 1. The author mentions the texts we have cited above. There is laconic acknowledgment of a theological problem, however, in the remark that the earlier text to which the Amoraic saying may be tied is missing in four other parallel occurrences of the episode. The problem is not pursued. The problem text is from Mekhilta 36b and Mekhilta of R. Simon, p. 59, the dialogue between Rabbi and Antoninus on the judgment of the body: "Before thou asketh me about the body which is impure, ask me about the soul which is pure".

[142] Gen. Rabbah 14, 9, pp. 133—134: "R. Johanan, in the name of R. Meir"; cited by URBACH, I, 248. Josephus, Jewish War VII, 8, 7, had elaborated the theme, detailing an obviously Gnostic picture of the body-soul relationship, far beyond what this midrash envisions.

[143] Lev. Rabbah 4, 8, p. 96.

[144] URBACH's conclusion, that "even those sages who maintained the dualism 'body-soul' did not draw extremist inferences from it" (I, 250) is well taken; but a statement like "*the* concept of the unity of body and soul" (emphasis mine; IDEM), recalls us to an orthodox anthropology as against a hererodox one constituted of sheer duality.

[145] J. GUTTMANN, Philosophies of Judaism, pp. 35—36.

did the rabbis say about the body and the soul? The answer, detailed through the following units, should justify the conclusion that what some Amoraim may have seen "implied" in earlier rabbinic sayings, supposedly justifying the importation of new anthropological ideas, could not properly ground their view that a loose, near-autonomous association of body and soul was the conception underlying the tradition of the Oral Torah.

A. Duality in the Bible

Before reviewing the conceptions of body and soul in rabbinic writings, we must enquire whether the dichotomous view of man we have just observed is in any way proper of the Bible, the rabbis' written Torah. The common assumption that this cannot be so has forced commentators to explore implausible hypotheses[146]. One is accustomed to hearing that the anthropological duality of the rabbinate comprises "concepts for which there is no biblical authority"[147]. Much has been said about the holistic meaning of anthropological terms in the Bible, particularly by Christian biblical theologians, eager to eliminate post-Cartesian projections from the text or to invalidate the supposed perception of Platonic spiritualities[148]. With respect to the modern misconception to be rectified, this current of scholarship has served us well. "Man became a living soul (*nephesh*)" does not mean, in Gen. 2.7, that man is essentially immaterial. "The breath (*ruah*) of all mankind" (Job 12.10) is not a part of man's psyche, but the

[146] R. MEYER, Hellenistisches, pp. 36ff., surmised that the early Hasidim passed on to the sages a Hellenistic and Iranian dualism incompatible with the religion of Israel and that it profoundly affected Jewish piety.

[147] URBACH, I, 224. These concepts were kept in bounds, the author thinks, by the belief in reward and punishment and by the postulate of free will. "In the Bible a monistic view prevails" (I, 214).

[148] New Testament scholars, in particular, interested in the Hebrew roots of Paul's anthropological thought, had, until very recently, reached a consensus on the holistic meaning of the key term, σῶμα (lit., "body") as the New Testament rendering of a Hebraic concept. W. D. STACEY, The Pauline View of Man (London, 1956), p. 182, writes of "BULTMANN's conclusive treatment of this point". See R. BULTMANN, Theology of the New Testament, I (New York, 1951), 192—203. But there have been qualifications of the point. K. GROBEL, Σῶμα as 'Self, Person' in the LXX, in: Neutestamentliche Studien für Rudolf Bultmann, Beihefte zur Zeitschrift für die neutestamentliche Wissenschaft, 21 (Berlin, 1954), 52—59, considered the holistic meaning to be metonymy. J. BARR, The Semantics of Biblical Language (London, 1961), pp. 89—106, criticized the methods of deriving holistic meanings. H. CONZELMANN, An Outline of the Theology of the New Testament (New York, 1968), p. 176, concluded holistic meanings are aspectual. R. JEWETT, Paul's Anthropological Terms (Leiden, 1971), p. 10, practically abandoned the holistic view and affirmed that Paul's terms often manifest a dichotomous concept, though only because he borrowed the terminology of opponents. R. GUNDRY's 'Sōma in Biblical Theology' (1976) discovers so generally dichotomous an anthropology throughout rabbinic Judaism and early Christianity, grounded in similar usage in Hebrew Scripture, that the need for JEWETT's "borrowing" hypothesis is at least much reduced.

manifestation of human life entire and the power that moves it[149]. Statements about *guf* or *basar* are not statements about mere flesh, but assume the psychosomatic unity of man[150]. But, it is time to become more precise and to allow the question whether the case for anthropological holism in the Bible has not been overstated. That in biblical literature there is no difference among terms which translate as body and soul is not the same perception as that *nephesh*, *guf*, and *ruah* "form an indivisible entity"[151]. What is indivisible is composed. At least different notions are involved. The use of one word for another and the use of a part for the whole are altogether familiar language stratagems; these phenomena in the biblical handling of anthropological terms do not warrant the conclusion that the notions involved are identical[152]. Biblical man is a unity, not a monad.

ROBERT GUNDRY, conscious of the aberrations which the holism thesis has intended to remove, has recently shown that its theological agendum is sounder than its philology[153]. First, he notes the contention that the Hebrews lacked a concept of body as a discrete entity, and concludes that, to the contrary, they did know and frequently use "the same concept as that which is conveyed in the popular meaning of *sōma*"[154]. The usual word is *basar*. Perhaps to formulate the philological problem in terms of body-as-discrete-entity is to saddle it with unnecessarily complicating assumptions. The content of the body-concept — discrete entity, aspect of monadic man, intellectual principle, the matter of the Gnostics, or whatever — will derive from the catalogue of statements made about the body. This is not less true of *sōma* in Greek philosophy, with its complex links to a "popular meaning". That the Bible has no concept of Plato's *sōma* or Descartes' *corpus* would be a significant assertion. That it has no concept akin to anything outside twentieth-century '*bibelwissenschaftlich*' existentialism is another question — the one which GUNDRY addresses with lively irreverence. Meanwhile, nothing in the author's evidence can commit biblical language to so stark an epistemological realism as seems to be implied in the infelicitous body-as-discrete-entity formula. Second, GUNDRY examines the chief tenets of the biblical anthropology derived from holistic meanings of body-soul terminology (pp. 118—122). The problem area is

[149] וַיְהִי הָאָדָם לְנֶפֶשׁ חַיָּה: "Man became a living soul" (Gen. 2.7). וְרוּחַ כָּל־בְּשַׂר־אִישׁ: "The breath of all mankind" (Job 12.10). See J. PEDERSEN, Israel: Its Life and Culture, I (London, 1926; reprint 1946—47), 100, for comment on *ruah*.

[150] See F. BROWN, S. R. DRIVER, and C. A. BRIGGS, Hebrew and English Lexicon of the Old Testament (Oxford, 1959), in loco. On other meanings of *basar*, see J. A. T. ROBINSON, The Body: A Study in Pauline Theology (London, 1952), p. 12.

[151] URBACH, I, 215, makes both statements.

[152] See A. R. JOHNSON, The Vitality of the Individual in the Thought of Ancient Israel, 2nd edit. (Cardiff, 1964), pp. 1—2, 37—87.

[153] Sōma, ch. 11: 'Anthropological Duality in the OT', pp. 117—134. A. R. JOHNSON, The Vitality of the Individual, in a similar vein, has proposed that biblical anthropology is, not holistic, but synthetic.

[154] GUNDRY, p. 118.

the fate of man in death. Sickness, we are told is a weakening, and death is the extremity of weakness. Since soul stands on a continuum with flesh, it does not survive the body. The dead are, not souls, but "shadows, shades", ethereally material, collected in Sheol[155]. GUNDRY reviews the difficulties of such a reading. Since death is not held to be extinction, to where does the soul drain away? Though the shade is pictured as a weak body, it cannot be the earthly body which clearly corrupts. The image seems to be merely an analogy, leaving the soul as the shade, though the term is not used because of its connotation of vitality. Death involves, then, a separation of body and soul. Third, the author offers positive evidence of a dichotomous anthropology in the Hebrew Scriptures. (1) The parallelism of terms for the corporeal and incorporeal, "sometimes by way of contrast, sometimes by way of complement" (p. 123), denotes the whole man[156]. (2) The parallelism of expressions meaning the inner man and the outer man signify a difference of kind[157]. (3) Parallelism of spirit (*ruah*) and flesh refer to human complementarity. In this context the author, strangely, declines to read *ruah* as the divine Spirit[158]. (4) Texts treating of Sheol can be read least problematically by understanding that the soul goes there rather than being "dissipated" in death[159]. (5) Statements about the gathering of the deceased to his ancestors may have originally denoted burial in a family sepulcher but became a euphemism for death; in death, then, something of man immediately leaves the body[160]. (6) The shades in Sheol are pictured as capable of activity, moving and speaking (Isa. 14.9, 18, 19—20; 29.4; Ezek. 32.21; Job 26.5); they are the "knowing ones" (Lev. 19.31; 20.6; Isa. 19.3; 1 Sam 27.3–19). The limitation of their activity is due to their unnatural separation from their bodies. Passages thought of as picturing Sheol as a place of nullity may be explained: Death takes away the reason

[155] See E. KÄSEMANN, Leib und Leib Christi, Beiträge zur historischen Theologie, 9 (Tübingen, 1933), pp. 1—23; and a bibliography on the question in GUNDRY, Sōma, p. 119, n. 1.

[156] Some examples are Job. 13.15; 14.22; Ezek. 44.7, 9: 36.26; Isa. 10.18; Num. 16.22; 27.1.

[157] Examples: Ps. 16.9; 84.3b; 73.26a; 63.2; Prov. 11.17; Jer. 45.5. Cf. Isa. 31.3.

[158] Examples: Eccles. 12.7; cf. 3.21; Job 34.14–15; Eccles. 12.7; Gen. 2.7; Isa. 42.5; Zech. 12.1; Cf. Num. 16.22; 27,16; Gen. 6.3; Ezek 37.1–14. The Spirit-flesh contrast of Scripture involves a meaning different from the body-soul complement which GUNDRY here tries to establish. The author contends, against EICHRODT, that to distinguish between the individual spirit of man and the divine spirit within him is "arbitrary" (p. 125, n. 1). To the contrary, this distinction, noted by many writers, is based, not upon lexical items, but upon the theological sense derived from many Scriptural contexts. See W. EICHRODT, Theology of the Old Testament, II (Philadelphia, 1967), 47—48, 131—134. CLAUDE TRESMONTANT, Etudes de métaphysique biblique (Paris, 1955), p. 146. Since the focus of GUNDRY's study is Paul, this Spirit-flesh contrast should commend itself particularly, for nowhere is it so clear, and so distinct from the complements body-and-soul. See CHARLES HOMER GIBLIN, In Hope of God's Glory: Pauline Theological Perspectives (New York, 1970), pp. 86—88, 391—392. JOSEPH FITZMYER, The Letter to the Romans, The Jerome Biblical Commentary, 2 (Englewood Cliffs, N.J., 1968), art. 53:82.

[159] Sample texts: Job 33.18, 21, 22, 28, 30; Ps. 16.10; 89.49; 30.4; 49.16; Prov. 23.13–14; Ps. 86.13; 49.16; Isa. 38.10, 17. That at death the soul departs, or is breathed forth: Gen. 35.18; Job 11.20; 31.39; Isa. 53.12; Jer. 15.9; Lam. 2.12; Ps. 23.3.

[160] Sample texts: Gen. 15.15; 25.8–9; 49.28; 50.14; 1 Kings 2.10; 16.28; 2 Kings 21.18.

for which the living praise God, i.e., His deliverance of them from death. The dead are cut off from the cultic ritual at the sanctuary (cf. Ps. 6,6; 30.10; 88.11–13; 94.17; 115.17; Isa. 38.18). (7) "The prohibition of necromancy (Exod. 22.18; Lev. 20.27; Deut. 18.10–12) and of offerings to the dead (Deut. 26.14; cf. Ps. 102.28) further show that the people of the O.T. think of the dead as alive, apart from the flesh, which has returned to dust" (p. 131).

The Hebrew Bible offers an anthropological vocabulary which corresponds to that of languages which represent man as a duality. This would constitute presumptive (though obviously not conclusive) evidence that it too viewed man as a duality. The strength of GUNDRY's case lies in its calling attention to the fact that the highly elaborated argumentation to the contrary has not invalidated the presumption. Deriving a metaphysical psychology from religious texts may be beyond the ken of mere scholarship. For the rest, the difference between a biblical anthropology which finds the earth to be man's place and a Hellenistic anthropology which makes man an alien spirit exiled upon the earth is not bodysoul duality but the perception of goodness in the divine will which made man embodied.

There are no records which allow us to move in historical stages from biblical duality to the duality we have observed in rabbinic literature; but there are points of rational convergence. First, it is noteworthy that the Bible conceives the soul as poured out at death and surviving in an unnaturally separated and weakened condition in Sheol, as GUNDRY has shown, and that the Pharisees pass on a tradition (with nebulous beginnings) of belief in a resurrection of the body. A development of doctrine here is highly plausible. Second, in Scripture the closeness of the body-soul bond is such that its unity is exaggerated by many writers as monistic simplicity. This closeness, we may assume, is what governed the highly integrative rabbinic body-soul duality. It is not impossible that the Tannaitic conception was aided in its explicitation by Greek terminology, but its roots are deep in the Torah.

B. Body

a) Birth and Creation

For Philo, pristine man, the first historical man, and the descendants of this first man were different. He does not speak of physical birth in the context of creation. Since man's body is earthly, transient, and given to sin, it can have no connection with God. The great craftsman Nature makes human bodies[161]. For the rabbis, instead, birth continues the creation. It is not possible now for man to propagate without woman, nor woman without man; yet, "it is not possible for both of them without the *Shekhinah*"[162].

[161] De Opificio Mundi, 134—142.
[162] T. P. Berakhoth 9, 1, p. 12d; Gen. Rabbah 22, 2, p. 206; 8, 9, p. 63.

Different, too, from Philo's thinking of bodies independently of souls is the rabbinate's insistence that "it is impossible for the body to be without the soul, and if there is no soul there is no body, and if there is no body there is no soul"[163]. The body which comes into the world, animated by a soul, bears the divine image even as the soul does; for, as R. Akiba said, "Whoever sheds blood destroys the image"; and his disciple Ben Azzai even added, "Whoever does not engage in propagation of the species is deemed by Scripture to diminish, as it were, the likeness"[164].

b) Sexuality

The means of propagating the species was reflected upon by the sages (see below, pp. 546—47) in the manner of biblical wisdom literature, with ambivalence[165]. They did not objectify sexuality, but saw it in its relationship to several realties — to God's creative purpose, to a man and woman's ability effectively to intend that purpose, to pleasure, to human affectivity, and to a child. We observe, therefore, no attempt to work out a logical continuity between some statements which conceptualize experience one way and other statements which uncover a different experience. Sexuality is good and evil, constructive and destructive, a duty and a misfortune, beautiful and shameful. Sexuality in itself is never at issue. Absent from this broad portrayal is both Gnostic scorn of materiality and Ovidian hedonism.

Although the rabbis found a problem in the fact that sexual dynamism moved on an amoral impulse, a representation of their complex attitude must begin with the observation that they canonized the Song of Songs and perpetuated a tradition of reflection upon it[166]. The erotic love of man and woman here portrayed becomes, in tradition, also the appropriate metaphor of the love between Jahweh and Israel, according to the image beloved of the prophets (Hos. 1—3; Isa. 62.5; Jer. 3.1–10; Ezek. 16; 23). In the West, before the twelfth century, literary evidence of the association of sexuality with love is rare. Yet, there is ambivalence. "Come, let us ascribe merit to our ancestors"; one reads in the Talmud, "for, if they had not sinned, we should not have come into the world"[167]. An interpreter's facile removal of "sin" from the act by which man is conceived is not allowed by the text, for the difficult reading is echoed elsewhere with greater explicitness: "How can a man keep himself far from the evil impulse which is within him, since his very birth is the effect of its working?"[168] Its

[163] Midrash Tanhuma 3, 4a and b (edit. BUBER); Eccles. Rabbah 6.6. The context here is different, but the assertion is of validly general character.

[164] Tos. Yebamoth 8, 4, p. 250; Gen. Rabbah 34, 12, p. 326. Cited in URBACH, I, 227. See also Mekhilta to 20, 17; 70b.

[165] VON RAD, Wisdom in Israel, p. 311, n. 27 collects examples of this ambivalent attitude to phenomena in Proverbs — 17.27; 11.4; 10.16; 27.7, 14.

[166] The Song of Songs portion of the Midrash Rabbah is probably from the seventh century.

[167] Γ. B. Abodah Zarah 5a.

[168] Aboth de-R. Nathan 16.

working overrides rational choice. But, starker is the lament of R. Acha that in sexual intercourse even the greatest saint cannot well escape a certain taint of sin, since the act is performed more with the purpose of satisfying animal appetite than with the intention of begetting a child[169]. Also in this homily "its working" as distinct from mutual love is underlined: "When they perform their needs, each one turns his head in a different direction and Thou dost introduce every drop that a man has. This is the meaning of David's words, 'For though my father and my mother have forsaken me, the Lord will take me up' (Ps. 27.10)"[170]. Human action was seen, in point of fact, to fall invariably short of the possibilities celebrated in the Song of Songs.

Sexuality, nevertheless, is good. "The fact is", said R. Samuel bar Nahman, "but for the evil impulse, a man would not build a house, nor take a wife, nor beget children"[171]. R. Tanhum said in the name of R. Hanilai, "A Jew who has no wife abides without joy, blessing or good"[172].

Some Amoraim, as we have seen, believed Adam was created androgynous and that God then divided him into two sexes[173]. A century after R. Samuel bar Nahman (late third century), to whom this speculation is first ascribed, the Christian bishop Gregory of Nyssa proposed a similar idea: Man was made two sexes only in a revision of the creation, when God foresaw man's downfall and his desire for community with lower beings[174]. The rabbinic texts do not develop the Platonic theme explicitly into this dim view of sexuality, though a similar direction is present. Furthermore, they did not become fountainheads of reflection in later tradition as did Gregory's[175].

169 Lev. Rabbah 14.5, p. 308.

170 שמאתר שעשו צרביהן זה היפך פניו לכאן וזו הופכת פניה לכאן ואתה מכנים כל מיפה טיפה ומיפה שיש הו. והוא שדוד אמר (מס כו) כי אבי ואמי עזבוני וה׳ יאספני. "When they perform their needs, each one turns his head in a different direction, and Thou dost introduce every drop that a man has. This is the meaning of David's words: 'For, though my father and my mother have forsaken me, the Lord will take me up' (Ps. 27.10)." Lev. Rabbah 14, 5, p. 308. Schechter, p. 253 and n. 1, citing this passage, remarks, "The sense of the passage is not very clear." See also Yalkut Machiri Ps. to this verse. Before R. Acha, R. Reuben ben Strobilus had said, "Because the first drop that a man injects into a woman is the evil impulse". Aboth de-R. Nathan, version I, 16, p. 63, cited by Urbach, II, 898, n. 53. See Bacher, Die Agada der palästinensischen Amoräer, III, 144.

171 Gen. Rabbah 9, 7, p. 71. See also Aboth de-R. Nathan, version I, 16, the saying of R. Reuben ben Strobilus.

172 T. B. Yebamoth 62b; Gen. Rabbah 17, 1, p. 151. See also T. B. Yoma 67a.

173 Gen. Rabbah 8, 1. Bacher, Die Agada der palästinensischen Amoräer, I, 547, and n. 3, cites the parallels and various attributions. See Plato, Symposium, 189D—190A.

174 De hominis opificio, 16 (PG 44, 177ff.).

175 Regarding Gregory's theory, see Michael Müller, Die Lehre des hl. Augustinus von der Paradiesesehe und ihre Auswirkung in der Sexualethik des 12. und 13. Jahrhunderts bis Thomas von Aquin, Studien zur Geschichte der katholischen Moraltheologie I (Regensburg, 1954), pp. 13—14. Augustine discarded the theory, but it reappears in the Cistercian spirituality of the twelfth century. See Jean Daniélou, Saint Bernard et les Pères grecs, in: Saint Bernard théologien. Analecta Sacri Ordinis Cisterciensis 9, 2 (1953), 43—54, at p. 52.

Is the "evil impulse" which works sexual incitement situated in the body? It is manifested there, in all the members[176]. But it is in the heart; better, in the very soul of man[177]. The Gnostic doctrine which held evil to be in the materiality of the body was clearly perceived as the antithesis of the Torah.

In the consideration of differences between the sexes, are women esteemed equally with men? The rabbinate was a markedly patriarchal society. Many ideas and attitudes of alien provenance were in full vigor: Human conception, for example, was explained as the lodging of the creative male principle, the sperm, in the passive, nurturing womb[178]. Women were not to be students of the Law, and this conditioned the saying, "A man is obliged to offer three benedictions daily: that He has made me an Israelite, that He has not made me a woman, that He has not made me a boor[179]". The Talmud preserves the sense of Ben Sira (42.9) in the remark, "It is written, A daughter is a vain treasure to her father. From anxiety about her he does not sleep at night; during her early years lest she be seduced, in her adolescence lest she go astray, in her marriageable years lest she does not find a husband, when she is married lest she be childless, and when she is old lest she practice witchcraft[180]". With other societies, the Synagogue frequently expressed the fear of occult practices by women[181]. It would be inane to catalogue all the respects in which this society was male-oriented, because little of this distinguished it from its contemporaries. Nevertheless, a rabbinic anthropology will not produce the image of woman as the co-equal partner with man for the building of society. To say, simply, that this is a question of cultural evolution is to evade the question of how religion functions in a culture. But, the attempt to discover what is characteristic of rabbinism in the relationship of the sexes, and therefore what anthropological principle may be isolated for expanded reflection, will find an effective beginning in such phenomena as the sacred character of Jewish family life and the relatively strong legal position of women, with respect to other societies, in matters like divorce[182]. A further question is whether those religious insights which may be thought of as upholding the specifically male-oriented character of rabbinic society must not be

[176] Aboth de-R. Nathan 32a; T. B. Nedarim 32b; Exod. Rabbah 1, 6.

[177] Sifre Num. par. 116, p. 127.

[178] T.B. Sanhedrin 90b, ff.

[179] T.B. Menahoth 34b.

[180] T.B. Sanhedrin 100b.

[181] T.B. Yoma 83b; M. Aboth 2, 8; T.B. Sanhedrin 67a.

[182] On the one hand, there was the formal law: "A woman may be divorced with or without her consent, but a man can only be divorced with his consent" (T.B. Yebamoth 14, 7); on the other hand, there were safeguards to protect the woman from abuse — e.g., the man had to pay a marriage settlement (T.B. Yebamoth 63b); insanity was an obstacle to, not a cause for, divorce (T.B. Yebamoth 14, 7); above all, the woman could present a case to the court, and "the court may bring strong pressure to bear upon the husband until he says, 'I am willing to divorce my wife'" (T.B. Arakhin 5, 6). In specified cases the court would accept a wife's plea and oblige the man to divorce his wife (T.B. Ketuboth 7, 9ff.).

considered — in faith and in criticism — valid, indeed, and divinely given, but, at one stage of history, incompletely possessed or partially realized. Theological anthropology is the intellectual nexus between religious awareness and social evolution.

c) Attitude Toward the Body

What the body was, in the religious awareness of the rabbinic authors, must be seen in a survey of their attitudes towards it. They occasionally used expressions like "things of heaven" and "things of the world", but their "things of heaven" included what others would have pronounced earthly[183]. A rabbi took his son to task for not having attended the homily of R. Chisda. The son apologized, but remarked that he had once heard R. Chisda speak and the subject matter concerned things of the world. The lecture had been on sanitary rules. "He is occupied with the life of God's creatures", answered the angry father, "and do you venture to call such matters 'things of the world'?"[184]

There was much discussion about the body among the rabbis, and the general tenor is one of awe at God's creation. They spoke of anatomy in the manner of an exploration of the divine plan. What was the function of "the two hundred forty-eight limbs?"[185] Why does not the breath of man escape through his several orifices?[186] Why are there many sources of fluid in the face?[187] Which parts control the various emotions?[188] Physical differences and mental ones produce the wondrous phenomenon of individuality[189].

A certain kind of metaphysical evaluation, we may say, in terms of greater and lesser, was brought to the human duality: The parts that originate in the parents are left to decay at death, while the part that is from God returns to Him. "Said R. Papa, 'This is the meaning of the popular saying: Shake off the salt and [you may as well] throw the meat to the dog'[190]." In these accounts the senses are of the soul. The esteem of what is of the parents, however, may be seen in the special emphasis given to the precept to honor father and mother, equated with the precept to honor God. The three are partners in man[191]. But, for the clearest account of how

183 See T.B. Berakhoth 7, b; T.B. Shabbath 33, b.

184 T.B. Shabbath 82, a. See also T.B. Shabbath 150, a.

185 T.B. Oholoth 1.8.

186 Gen. Rabbah 1, 3.

187 Num. Rabbah 18, 22.

188 T.B. Berakhoth 61a, b. See also Gen. Rabbah 68, 3.

189 T.B. Sanhedrin, 38a.

190 T.B. Niddah 31a. Also, T.P. Kilaim 8, 4, p. 31c, quoted above, re. the three parts of man. A similar account attributed to R. Judah the Patriarch, in Eccles. Rabbah 5, 10. The metaphysical dimension of the thought should not be pressed for consequences. It remains primitive because it is felt in this case not to be consequential.

191 Urbach, I, 218—219. Mekhilta de-R. Ishmael, Ba-hodesh, 8, p. 231; T.B. Kiddushin 30b; T.P. Peah 1, 1, p. 15c; T.P. Kiddushin 1, 7, p. 61b.

and why the body was esteemed, metaphysical considerations to the contrary not withstanding, one must look to the oft-repeated story of Hillel's bath.

> His disciples said to him, "Master where are you going?" He replied, "To perform a religious duty." And they said to him, "And what is the religious duty that Hillel is going to perform?" He answered, "To bathe in the bathhouse." They said to him, "Is that a religious duty?" He answered them, "Yes. If in the case of the images of the kings, which are set up in their theaters and circuses, the attendant in charge of them cleanses them and washes them and he is provided with sustenance, how much more so we, who have been created in the divine image and likeness, as it is written, 'In the image of God made He man'!"[192]

Since it is man who is made in the Image, body as well as soul, the care of the body is of religious interest. Its health and majesty were seen as signs of God's good pleasure. "The Holy One, blessed be He, takes pride in them who are tall of stature"[193]. The *Shekhinah* alights on one who is of imposing appearance[194]. The rule was: "We elect to the Sanhedrin only men of tall stature"[195]. If one wished to study, he should cultivate good health. "A disciple of the sages should not reside in a city where there is no physician"[196]. A rabbinic saying has it, "Physical cleanness leads to spiritual purity"[197]; and the cleanness referred to is regular bowel movements. Much stress was placed on such cleanness, because it was understood to have moral implications[198]. Cleanness was for the outside too: "One should wash his face, hands, and feet every day out of respect for his Maker[199]. After the destruction of the Second Temple, many of the laws of ritual purity were given allegorical meanings by the rabbis[200]. This would seem to have facilitated an understanding, beyond the functional, of physical cleanliness. In the care of the body there was much meaning.

Cleanliness was, of course, a matter of health[201]; and health rules abound in the Talmud. We read of the necessity of bathing[202], anointing[203], preventing constipation[204], blood-letting[205], moderation in all things[206],

[192] Lev. Rabbah 34, 3, p. 776.
[193] T.B. Bekhoroth 45b.
[194] T.B. Shabbath 92a.
[195] T.B. Sanhedrin 17a.
[196] T.B. Sanhedrin 17b; T.B. Kiddushin, 66d.
[197] T.B. Abodah Zarah 20b.
[198] T.B. Makkoth 16b; T.B. Sanhedrin 17b; T.B. Berakhoth 15a.
[199] T.B. Shabbath 50b.
[200] See Jacob Neusner, The Idea of Purity in Ancient Judaism (Leiden, 1973), especially pp. 72—107.
[201] T.B. Berakhoth 19a; 47b; 53b; T.B. Sotah 4b; T.B. Tamid 27b.
[202] T.B. Berakhoth 57b; T.B. Kiddushin 66d; T.B. Shabbath 25b; T.B. Gittin 68a; etc.
[203] T.B. Shabbath 41a.
[204] T.B. Berakhoth 25a; 55a; 60b.
[205] Bekhoroth 44b; T.B. Shabbath 129b; T.B. Berakhoth 60a.
[206] T.B. Ketuboth 111a; T.B. Gittin 70a.

proper diet[207], a wholesome environment[208], and staying in good spirits[209]. To understand this concern as tangential to religion is to allow a non-rabbinic evaluation of the body to intrude into the Talmud. The attitude of the rabbis toward the body is best appreciated from the point of view of man made in God's image — body as well as soul.

C. Soul

A midrash on Genesis explains: "The soul is called by five names: *Nephesh, Ruah, Neshamah, Yechidah,* and *Chayyah*. *Nephesh* is the blood; as it is said, 'For the blood is the life (*nephesh*)' (Deut. 12.23). *Ruah* is that which ascends and descends; as it is said, 'Who knoweth the spirit (*ruah*) of man whether it goes upward?' (Eccles. 3.21). *Neshamah* is the disposition. *Chayyah* is so called because all the limbs die but it survives. *Yechidah*, 'the only one', indicates that all the limbs are in pairs, while the soul alone is unique in the body"[210]. The first three terms are in common usage in rabbinic literature, but it is difficult to define their difference. *Nephesh* applies to animals as well as humans, because it indicates life, or the blood. The distinction between a rational and irrational soul is not made by the sages[211]. *Ruah* and *Neshamah* seem to be used interchangeably to mean one man's psyche which is his exclusively. It is the "breath" infused into him by God. The soul is that in man which recognizes God. In a manner of speaking, "An additional soul is given to man on the eve of the Sabbath, which is taken from him at the end of the Sabbath"[212].

a) Moment of Creation

The question of the time when an embryo receives its human soul was settled in the following dialogue between R. Judah the Patriarch and his friend Antoninus[213]:

> "He [Antoninus] further enquired, 'At what stage is the soul instilled in man?' Rabbi said to him, 'As soon as he leaves his mother's womb'. He replied, 'Leave meat without salt for three days, will it not become putrid? The answer must be: From the moment that he (the child) is commanded into existence'. And Rabbi admitted to him that Scripture also supports him: 'And the spirit of God is in my nostrils (Job 27.3) —

[207] T.B. Berakhoth 2b; T.B. Baba Kamma 92b; T.B. Erubin 83b; T.B. Shabbath 152a.
[208] T.B. Baba Bathra 2, 8ff.
[209] T.B. Berakhoth 58b; M. Anoth 2.16; T.B. Gittin 70a.
[210] Gen. Rabbah 14, 9.
[211] Notice, for example, the lack of distinction at Berakhoth 44b.
[212] T.B. Taanith 27b.
[213] Probably the emperor Marcus Aurelius Antoninus (A.D. 121—180), a Stoic philosopher.

> when didst thou give me the soul? From the moment that thou didst command me (cf. Job 10.12)'[214].

Until this time, the Tannaitic view had been: "The embryo is the thigh of its mother[215]."

b) Immortality

The term immortality does not occur in the sayings of the rabbis[215]. And there is no explicit affirmation of this as a teaching. But certain evidences that the idea was generally assumed must be considered. Hillel speaks of the soul as a "guest within the body"[217]; R. Johanan ben Zakkai expects his soul to face judgment after death[218]; and R. Judah the Patriarch asserts that God will replace the soul within the body and judge them together[219]. It is difficult to understand how any of this can be if there is no survival of the soul after death. An old rabbinic prayer reads, "Thou didst breathe it [the soul] into me, thou preservest it within me; and thou will take it from me, but wilt restore it hereafter"[220]. The soul which returns to God who gave it was either the power of God Himself, an undifferentiated psychic energy, or the individual life principle of the man, created and infused by God. The first two present insurmountable theological problems to rabbinic thought. Nevertheless, the sages' hope was not in immortality but in the resurrection of the body. Immortality, in Hellenistic context, might suggest simply the nature of things; resurrection, the power and goodness of God.

c) Pre-existence

To say that God creates immortal souls is to say they begin but do not end. However, as we have said, some of the sages affirmed the pre-existence of souls[221]. The case is easily misrepresented, and attention must be given to what some Talmudic authors, whose interest in philosophical matters may have been neglegible, had in mind with such affirmations. First of

[214] Gen. Rabbah 34, 10, pp. 320—231; T.B. Sanhedrin 91b.

[215] T.B. Gittin 23b; T.P. Baba Bathra 3, 1, p. 13d; T.B. Temurah 30b; T.B. Hullin 58a. Urbach, I, 243, concludes a review of the relevant Halakhah with these words: "Among the Tannaim we do not find anyone who upholds, in the field of Halakhah, the view that the embryo, while still in its mother's womb, is a separate body, and regards it as a living being... It would appear that in the sphere of Halakhah this opinion is not earlier than the time of the Amora R. Johanan [ca. 250]."

[216] אלמות *'almawet*: immortality.

[217] Lev. Rabbah 34, 3.

[218] T.B. Berakhoth, 28b.

[219] T.B. Sanhedrin 91a.

[220] Cited by C. G. Montefiore and H. Lowe, Rabbinic Anthology (1938; reprint, Philadelphia, 1959), p. 312, from the Singer translation of the Jewish Prayer Book.

[221] See, e.g., T.B. Hagigah 12b; T.B. Yebamoth 62a; T.B. Niddah 13b; Gen. Rabbah 8, 7. R. Meyer, Hellenistisches, pp. 49—61, 63—64, 78ff.

all, what has been taken for pre-existence in some regards merely the foreknowledge of God[222]. The pre-existence notion enters rabbinic texts only in the second half of the third century. Some speak of all the souls in *guf*, where no treasure-house-of-souls metaphor need be seen, but merely all the souls predestined for bodies — emphasizing God's foreknowledge[223]. In another instance, where pre-existence is posited, the religious intent is to find all the souls of future Israelites present at the giving of the Torah[224]. The theoretical consequences of the Platonic notion seem not to have been realized, and they were never drawn by other sages.

2. Human Condition

The central reality of the human condition was as we have seen, God — the love which worked man's creation and election. In the light of this divine love, the rabbis reflected upon three elements which powerfully determine human existence: freedom, sinfulness, and suffering.

A. Freedom

a) Providence and Freedom

In the Bible it is consistently assumed that man is left to choose between right and wrong after God has taught him what they are — as He taught Adam and Noah and all the nations at Sinai. At the same time God governs the world and scrutinizes the ways of mortals[225]. This twofold providence which the rabbis acknowledged cannot be ignored when one considers their teaching on freedom. They had no special term for this providence, but the concept was clear[226]. For Josephus, the Essenes, Sadducees, and Pharisees could be represented according to differences in their conception of the tension between freedom and the decrees of God, which (for his Hellenistic audience) he called fate[227]. The Essenes held that all was determined by such "fate"; the Sadducees denied that anything in human

[222] E.g., the instance of the Tanna R. Eleazar of Modiim, in Mekhilta de-R. Ishmael, Massekhta de-Wa-yehi, 3, p. 99. Cf. R. Meyer, Hellenistisches, p. 48, n. 1.

[223] T.B. Yebamoth 62a; 63b; T.B. Abodah Zarah 5a. See also, Gen. Rabbah 24, 4, p. 233; Lev. Rabbah 15, 1, p. 319. Urbach, I, 236—237.

[224] Tanhuma, Nissavim, 3. Urbach, I, 236—237. See also pp. 245—248, for instance of souls forgetting the Torah at birth.

[225] That God governs and provides: Mekhilta de-R. Ishmael, Shirah 3 (edit. Horowitz—Rabin), p. 126. See Bacher, Tannaiten, I, 45. That God examines the deeds of men: e.g., M. Aboth 3.15, commented upon below.

[226] השגחה *hashgahah*: Providence. The word was coined by the Tibbonides translators of the Middle Ages.

[227] Antiq. XIII, 5,9. Moore, I, 457—458, speaks correctly of Josephus' Jewish meaning of εἱμαρμένη "fate", as the decrees of God, or Providence.

affairs was so determined; the Pharisees took a middle course, holding that some things were determined while others were in man's power.

Rabbinic affirmation of human freedom of choice is general. The texts commented upon were Deut. 11, 26—28: "Behold, I have set before you this day a blessing and a curse, etc." and Deut. 30, 15—20: "See, I have set before you this day life and good, and death and evil, in that I command you this day to love the Lord your God . . . therefore, choose life, that thou mayest live"[228]. Man was responsible for his choices. The Halakhah, accordingly, furnished examples of the legislating of prudence[229]. A qualifying of freedom is seen in the strength of habits and circumstances: "He that guards himself against sin three times has the promise that God will henceforth guard him"[230]. "If a man hearkened to one precept, he is enabled to hearken to many precepts"[231]. "The School of R. Ishmael taught: Transgression dulls the heart of man"[232].

With equal firmness Providence was upheld. We have heard the saying of R. Hanina, "Everything is in the power of Heaven, except the fear of Heaven"[233]. Even in the exercise of man's freedom, God is present in power: R. Simeon ben Lakish said, "If a man comes to defile himself the opportunity is given him [by God]; if to purify himself, he is helped to do it"[234]. God's scrutiny is nowhere so graphic as in R. Akiba's saying: "The shop stands open, and the Shopkeeper gives credit, and the account book lies open, and the hand writes; and everyone that wishes to borrow let him come and borrow"[235].

Another remark of R. Akiba's has frequently been accepted either as the solution to the Providence-Freedom question or as the clearest statement of it: "All is seen, but freedom of choice is given; and the world is judged by grace; yet, all is according to the excess of works [good more than evil, or vice versa]"[236]. However, the expression "all is seen" cannot refer to knowledge of the future. The stem *safa* (see) in Tannaitic use refers only to knowledge of the present[237]. R. Akiba, then was not speaking of God's foreknowledge, but simply underlining man's responsibility for

228 See Sifre Deut., par. 53—54; Sifre on Deut. 11, 26, par. 53. BACHER, Tannaiten, II, 302ff.

229 T.B. Shabbath 32a; Sifre Deut., Sect. 229; Mekhilta Mishpatim, par. 4; T.B. Makkoth 10b.

230 T.B. Shabbath 104a; Sifra 91a.

231 Mekhilta de-R. Ishmael (Wa-yassa 1, p. 157).

232 T.B. Yoma 39a.

233 T.B. Berakhoth 33b; T.B. Megillah 25a; T.B. Middoth 16b.

234 T.B. Shabbath 104a, and parallels.

235 M. Aboth 3.17.

236 מִשְׁנָה טו הַכֹּל צָפוּי, וְהָרְשׁוּת נְתוּנָה: וּבְטוֹב הָעוֹלָם נָדוֹן וְהַכֹּל לְפִי רֹגב הַמַּעֲשֶׂה. "All is seen, but freedom of choice is given; and the world is judged by grace; yet, all is according to the excess of works" (M. Aboth 3, 15).

237 URBACH, I, 257: "The use of safa in the signification 'to know beforehand', . . . I found only in Amoraic sayings." This seeming non-concern with the paradoxical character of the issue would corroborate SANDMEL's contention that, because there is little consciousness of a "grace and free-will" conflict in Jewish literature, religious anthropology has not been of central concern. S. SANDMEL, Reflections on the Problem of Theology for Jews, JBR 33 (April 1965), 101—112, at p. 106.

his actions. There is no evidence in rabbinic writings of any attempt to offer a speculative reconciliation between Providence and freedom. Both doctrines are simply upheld.

How the deeds of man affect his life regards the problem of reward and punishment, but to the extent that this deals with human control over events it was conceived as another way of defining the relationship between Providence and free will. An ancient mishnah said, "If a man performs but a single precept, he is granted good and length of days"[238]. But this expectation changed. Although most, it seems, continued to believe right action might in some way favorably affect one's lot in life, they came to lose confidence that hardship represented divine judgment. The key figure in the shift of opinion was R. Akiba. His disciple Ben Azzai stated baldly, "The reward of a precept is a precept, and the reward of a transgression is a transgression"[239]. Omitting significant nuances, the Tanna R. Jacob concluded, "There is no reward for precepts in this world"[240]. Rab (early 3rd. cen.) later emphasized both the teaching and example of Akiba (see below, pp. 531—32)[241].

b) Impulse and Freedom

Man's freedom is challenged by his impulses. The sages read in the Bible, "The imagination of man's heart is evil from his youth" (Gen. 8.21) and "Every imagination of the thoughts of his heart was only evil continually" (Gen. 6.5)[242]. The expression *yeser ha-ra*, "evil imagination", is used in rabbinic literature in a variety of applications, where no one translation fits. We may call the imaginative stimulus an impulse[243]. That this impulse is lamentable, that God made it, that it is simply "the heart of man" we learn in the following saying of R. Abahu (early 4th century) commenting upon Gen. 6.6, "The Lord regretted He had made man on the earth, and He was grieved at his heart": "He mourned only over the heart of man", said the rabbi, "as one does who has made something bad . . . So God: It was I that put the bad leaven in the dough, for 'the devising of man's heart is evil from his youth'. So the words are to be understood: He grieved over the heart of man"[244]. And the paradox is heightened in the words of R. Phineas ben Jair (ca. 200): "My sons, I created for you the evil impulse; I created for you the Law as an antidote. The evil impulse must be very evil, since its creator Himself testifies against it: 'The devising of the heart

238 M. Kiddushin 1, 10; See also T.B. Sanhedrin 101a; T.B. Berakhoth 61b.

239 M. Aboth 4, 2.

240 T.B. Hullin 142a; T.B. Kiddushin 39b.

241 See, e.g., T.B. Menahoth 29b.

242 יֵצֶר לֵב הָאָדָם רַע מִנְּעֻרָיו: "Every imagination of the thoughts of his heart was only evil continually" (Gen. 8.21).

243 See F. C. Porter, The Yeçer Hara: A Study of the Jewish Doctrine of Sin, Biblical and Semitic Studies (n. p., 1902). U. Cassuto, From Adam to Noah (Jerusalem, 1961), p. 303.

244 Tanhuma to Noah, par. 4 (edit. Buber). For "the leaven in the dough", see Gen. Rabbah 34, 10; T.B. Berakhoth 17a; etc.

of man is evil from his youth' (Gen. 8.21)." The theme that balances the evil impulse with the Law is frequent[245].

At times the evil impulse was personified. The context of such passages reveals suggestions, not of any cosmic evil principle, but of a tempter-servant-of-God — an idea which allows the *yeser* a reality extrinsic to human nature[246]. The usual representation, however, kept it quite intrinsic. Even so, it had associations with false gods. By the will of man, this "foolish old king" might compete with the Torah as representation of what man was[247].

That this *yeser ha-ra* entered man as he issued from the womb Rabbi learned from Antoninus[248]. We have associated it with the sex drive, but there is no kind of sin to which it does not push man[249]. Yet, even as all that God made, the evil impulse is good, for by it man performs, at least in inferior motivation, what in any case must be done. R. Samuel ben Nahman quoted Eccles. 4.4 to this effect. He remarked: "Solomon said, 'All labor and all excelling in work is a man's rivalry with his neighbor'[250]." Clearly, then, the evil impulse is not in itself evil. It needs to be directed and controlled[251].

Less is said about a contrary "good impulse". Perhaps it is a later creation, but the Tannaim were already familiar with the expression[252]. It is taken for granted that the evil impulse is stronger than the good[253]; but a man should range the good against the evil. Sometimes it is said that man can rule his evil impulse[254]; at other times that he cannot[255]. Singularly effective was immersing oneself in the study of the Torah[256]. The command, "Thou shalt love the Lord thy God with all thy heart" is interpreted to mean "with both thine impulses, the good impulse and the evil impulse"[257].

245 E.G., Sifre Deut., par. 45, on Deut. 11.18; TB. Kiddushim 30b; T.B. Baba Bathra, 16a.

246 See T.B. Baba Bathra 16a; Sifra, Aharè Perek 13 (ed. WEISS, f. 86a); T.B. Yoma 67b; T.B. Sukkah 52a.

247 For *yeser ha-ra* as pretender to sovereignty and "foolish old king", see T.B. Berakhoth 61b; Cant. Rabbah i, 2; Aboth de-R. Nathan, version I, 16, 32a; Eccles. Rabbah 4, 14; 9, 7; Midrash Tehillin 9, 5, p. 82.

248 T.B. Sanhedrin 91b; Gen. Rabbah 34, 10.

249 Pesikta (edit. BUBER) f. 38b—39a; cf. T.B. Yoma 67b.

250 Gen. Rabbah 9, 9; Eccles. Rabbah on Eccles. 3.11.

251 T.B. Sanhedrin 107b; T.B. Sotah 47a; Pesikta (edit. BUBER), f. 158a; on Ps. 4, 5.

252 SCHECHTER, p. 243, offers these references: M. Berakhoth 9, 5; Sifre 73a; Aboth de-R. Nathan 47a; T.B. Berakhoth 61b.

253 Aboth de-R. Nathan, version I, 16, 32a; Eccles. Rabbah 4; 9, 7; Midrash Tehillin 9, 5, p. 82.

254 Gen. Rabbah 34, 10; Eccles. Rabbah 9, 1; Sifre 74a; Gen. Rabbah 87.5; Lev. Rabbah 23, 11.

255 SCHECHTER, pp. 265—266, cites the following rabbinic prayer: "May it be Thy will, O my God, and the God of my fathers, that thou breakest the yoke of the evil impulse and remove him from our hearts . . . It is revealed and it is known before Thee that we have not the strength to resist him; but may it be Thy will, etc." For a similar prayer, see T.P. Berakhoth 4, 2, 7d, and T.B. Berakhoth 60b.

256 T.B. Berakhoth 5a.

257 Sifre Deut. par. 32, on Deut. 6.5 (edit. FRIEDMANN, f. 73a); M. Berakhoth 9, 5; Tos. Berakhoth 7, 7.

Although the speculation upon the universal experience which is expressed in these terms may seem elemental or non-existent, the fact is, the *yeser ha-ra* theme occasions anthropological conclusions of great significance. First, man is not what his inclinations would lead him to become. Much that is natural and created by God in man may not represent man's proper possibilities, and in this extended sense is evil. Second, to be simply himself, man depends upon God's revelation of the truly human way in the Torah.

B. Sin

In the biblical view and among the rabbis, human evil-doing is conceived primarily in relation to God; it violates Him. This religious, rather than ethical, concept is what is meant by sin[258]. The idea is well communicated in a text which enumerates broad types of sin: "All the iniquities of the children of Israel, and all their transgressions, even all their sins" (Lev. 16.21) are interpreted: "Iniquities are the insolent misdeeds; transgressions are rebellious acts; sins are unwitting offences"[259]. For "sins", the Law had provided the sin-offering in the Temple. The notion of such material sins helps toward an understanding of the sense in which willful transgressions are sins. They are the deliberate rejection of the authority of God, a throwing off of the yoke of the Law[260].

Small sins lead to great ones. The evil impulse pushes a man, "until at last it says, 'Worship other gods, and he goes and does it'"[261]. This bondage is the gravest consequence of sin. Besides this, as we shall see, the social organism is weakened (see pp. 551—61) and an unrepentant sinner is punished in *Gehinnom* (see pp. 531—32).

a) Death and Sin

Nothing in rabbinic literature permits the conclusion that the first sinner passed on to his posterity a wounded nature. Only an unwarranted metaphorical reading of what for some Amoraim was Adam's physical diminution after sin can produce that view. But, many rabbis held that death came into the world with Adam's sin. The specific connection they saw between that sin and death is a vexed question.

R. Akiba taught, against the view of many sages, "If a man is worthy, he is vouchsafed the full period [of his allotted lifespan]; if he is unworthy, his years are reduced"[262]. In another saying he asserted, "And righteousness

[258] See Sifre Num., par. 111ff. (edit. Friedmann, f. 31b—33b), quoting Num. 15.30ff.

[259] Israel's true (deliberate) sins were פשעיהם, "their acts of rebellion" — Sifra, Aharè Perek I (edit. Weiss, f. 80d). See also Tos. Yom ha-Kippurim 2, 1; T.B. Yoma 36b.

[260] Aboth 3, 5; Tos. Sotah 14, 4.

[261] T.B. Shabbath 105b; Tos. Baba Kamma 9, 31.

[262] T.B. Yebamoth 50a. Also, Eccles. Rabbah 3, 4.

delivereth from death — not from death itself, but from violent death"[263]. The issue had to do with whether the course and extent of one's life was determined by one's righteousness or sinfulness. In R. Akiba's view, the existence of death could not be attributed to human sins. All his disciples held to this[264]. Several Tannaitic *baraitoth* discuss the death of Moses in this connection; one of them disassociates even Moses' death from sin: "The Ministering Angels said to the Holy One, blessed be He, 'Sovereign of the universe, why did Adam die?' He replies, 'Because he did not fulfill my commandment'. Said they to him, 'But Moses did fulfill Thy commandments'. He answered them, 'It is my decree, the same for all men, as Scripture states: This is the law — when a man dieth (Num. 19.14)'"[265]. Death as a divine decree makes it unnecessary to link death with an individual's sins.

One view had it that the presence of death was to be explained by the sin of the golden calf at Sinai. Again there had been the opportunity of choosing life, but instead, the people "walked in the footsteps of Adam"[266]. Another way of linking death to sin appeared in the answer of R. Hama ben R. Hanina (first century) to the question: Why did God impose death upon Adam? "Because the Holy one, blessed be He, foresaw that Nabuchadnezzar and Hiram would declare themselves gods"[267] — in foresight therefore, of the sins of history.

In the time of the Amoraim death is more frequently associated with personal sin. R. Ammi (end of third century) said, "There is no death without sin, nor suffering without iniquity"[268]. This saying, however, is part of a Talmudic discussion which concludes with the words, "This proves that there is death without sin and suffering without iniquity, and Rab Ammi stands refuted"[269]. From what we have seen, this conclusion itself constitutes simply another view. Those of R. Ammi's persuasion could point to the teaching that all men, including the Patriarchs, were sinners — though it was not uttered in the context of the controversy[270].

An exceptional opinion was that of R. Meir, expounded by R. Simeon ben R. Eleazar: Since all was made good, death too is good[271]. Death is not a decree, then, but part of the order of creation. The Amora R. Johanan seems influenced by this when he accounts for the death of the righteous

[263] T.B. Shabbath 156b. URBACH, I, 264—265, prefers this reading from 'Haggadot ha-Talmud' (Constantinople, 1511) and 'En Ya'aqov' (editio princeps, Salonica, 1515), over that of the printed edition, where the sense is the reverse.

[264] URBACH, I, 426.

[265] Sifre Deut., par. 339, p. 388. See T.B. Shabbath 55b. For other Baraitoth, see also T.B. Shabbath 55b; Sifre Num., par. 137; T.B. Yoma 87a. Similarly, Mekhilta, Ba-hodesh, 9, p. 237; T.B. Abodah Zarah 2a.

[266] Exod. Rabbah 32, 1; also, Seder Eliahu Zuta, edit. FRIEDMANN (ME'IR ISH-SHALOM), p. 179.

[267] Gen. Rabbah 9, 5, p. 70.

[268] T.B. Shabbath 55a.

[269] T.B. Shabbath 55b.

[270] T.B. Arakhin 17a. See also, T.B. Sanhedrin 46b; 101a.

[271] Gen. Rabbah 62, 2, p. 673.

as a rest granted them[272]. But even here, we cannot see death as merely a physical necessity; much less so in the views we have surveyed, where, though there are different accounts of the association, death is associated with sin.

b) Repentance and Atonement

Man the sinner was not seen as simply fallen; he could atone for his sin. The closest thing to the experience of the very glory of God, one read in Ex. 33.19, was the assurance of His merciful forgiveness. Though the loss of ritual means of atonement proper to the temple cult was to be mourned, the rabbis had always known that Scripture relativized public sacrifice[273]. The following Talmudic passage situates ritual atonement among the possibilities open to the sinner:

> "They asked Wisdom (Hagiographa), 'What is the punishment of the sinner?' Wisdom answered, 'Evil pursues sinners' (Prov. 13.21). They asked Prophecy, 'What is the punishment of the sinner?' Prophecy answered, 'The soul that sinneth, it shall die' (Ezek. 18.4). They asked the Torah, 'What is the punishment of the sinner?' Torah answered, 'Let him bring a guilt-offering and it shall be forgiven unto him, as it is said: And it shall be accepted for him to make atonement for him' (Lev. 1.4). They asked the Holy One, blessed be he, 'What is the punishment of the sinner?' The Holy One, blessed be he, answered, 'Let him do repentance and it shall be forgiven unto him, as it is said: Good and upright is the Lord: Therefore will he teach sinners in the way' (Ps. 25.8) — that is, that he points the sinners the way that they should do repentance"[274].

The reason for ritual atonement was to secure man's compliance with God's will[275]. After A.D. 70, such ritual was virtually reduced to the Day of Atonement (Lev. 16). Atoning power is ascribed also to the Torah and deeds of loving kindness[276], and to death as well[277]. It was not the rituals of the Day of Atonement but the day itself that atoned, though on two conditions — repentance and restitution[278].

In the passage above, regarding the punishment of the sinner, the intention is not to assert that the three sections of Scripture present mutually

[272] Gen. Rabbah 62, 2, p. 71; T.B. Megillah 15a.

[273] See Sifre Deut., par. 43, on Deut. 11.15 (edit. FRIEDMANN, f. 81a); Aboth de-R. Nathan 4, 5. BACHER, Tannaiten, I, 39.

[274] T.P. Makkoth, 31d; Pesikta de-R. Kahana, 158b (edit. BUBER).

[275] Sifre 54a.

[276] T.B. Rosh Hashanah 18a; Aboth de-R. Nathan 11a and b; T.B. Sukkah 49b.

[277] Tos. Yoma 4 (5), 6, p. 251 (edit. LIEBERMAN), where parallel passages are listed; Mekhilta de-R. Ishmael, Ba-hodesh, p. 228; Tos. Yoma 86a.

[278] Sifra 83a; T.P. Yoma 45c. On the conditions, Sifra 102a; T.P. Yoma 45b.

exclusive approaches, but rather that the most God-like aspect of the pursuit of forgiveness is repentance. Only a fool brings sacrifice while unrepentant[279]. Repentance is, of course, the act of man; yet, it manifests the power of God, whose mercy initiates the encounter. He paves the way for man[280]. We read among the rabbis, "Said the Holy One, blessed be He, to Jeremiah, 'Go and bid Israel do repentance'. He went and delivered his message. Thereupon they said to him, 'With what face can we enter before His presence? Have we not made Him angry?' . . . Then God said to him, 'Go back and tell them: If you return to me, is it not to your Father in Heaven to whom you come?'"[281] His right hand of mercy, "the strong hand", represses His strict justice[282]. In this divine power He says, "On the Day of Atonement I will create you a new creation"[283]. The rabbinic expressions of wonderment over the power of repentance are numerous and affecting[284]. In this vein it was forbidden ever to allude to the former sinfulness of a penitent; in his repentance he had been created anew[285].

There was no special word "to repent". The sages coined a phrase ("to do a return") from a biblical root[286]. The sense of repentance is affected also by the Scriptural verb used in such expressions as "God will not repent of His action"[287]. It has to do with a change of purpose as well as with sorrow. Repentance, therefore, begins in thought and inner decision, and its effect is instantaneous — though it is followed by words of confession[288]. God asks no more than that man say, "I have sinned"[289]. Repentance is so indispensable that it was pronounced one of the things that preceded the creation of the world. "When He drew the plan of the world He found it could not stand until He had created repentance"[290]. Even the great moral catastrophes were seen as providential. They afforded examples that no sin is beyond repentance[291]. But, "when an evil man dies [unrepentant], his hope shall perish" (Prov. 11.7)[292].

279 T.B. Berakhoth 23a.
280 Tanhuma 4, 8.
281 Pesikta de-R. Kahana (edit. Buber, 165a.
282 Sifre 50b.
283 Pesikta Rabbati (Edit. Friedmann), 169a.
284 See, e.g., Pesikta Rabbati (edit. Friedmann), f. 185a; Pesikta (edit. Buber), f. 157a—b; T.B. Yoma, 86a, end. See Bacher palästinischen Amoräer, I, 534.
285 T.B. Baba Metzia 58b.
286 שוב *shub*: lit., "to turn"; "to repent". תשובה lit., "a turning round"; "repentance".
287 נחם *nacham*: "to be sorry", "regret", "to change one's mind" (as in Greek μετανοεῖν) — e.g., Num. 23.19; 1 Sam. 15.29; Ezek. 24.14; Jer. 18.8; 3.13.
288 Pesikta Rabbati, 185a (edit. Friedmann); Pesikta de-R. Kahana, 163b; cf. T.B. Kiddushin 49b; T.B. Gittin 57b.
289 T.P. Taanith 65d; Midrash Tanhuma (edit. Buber), 2, 91b; 4, 70a.
290 Pirke Rabbi Eliezer, 11; ibid., 12. Cf. Num. R. 2, 7; Midrash Prov., 10.
291 T.B. Abodah Zarah 4b and 5a; T.B. Shabbath 65a; Num. Rabbah 18. 21.
292 Eccles. Rabbah 7.15; Pesikta Rabbati (edit. Friedmann), 184, a and b; Midrash Prov., ch. 6; Eccles. Rabbah 1, 15, and 7.15; Pirke Rabbi Eliezer, ch. 43. Schechter, 341, n. 1, however, cites later Haggadoth to the effect that some sins may be removed even after death. This, he notes, is not the common view.

Beyond the details of the rabbinic doctrine of repentance is the strong impression of which G. F. MOORE speaks: "In no ancient religion is normal piety so pervaded by the consciousness of sin, the need for repentance, and the conviction that man's sole hope is the forgiving grace of God"[293].

c) Reward and Punishment

The punishment for sin and the reward for observance, as presented in the Bible, is generally linked to the present life. Rabbinic Judaism was well rehearsed in the Decalogue, where one read of the iniquity of the fathers as being visited upon the children, and in the Shema, where goodness was rewarded with length of days and a fertile land. From this awareness to the expectation of a revivification of the dead, to bliss in *Gan Eden* and to misery in *Gehinnom* — to retribution in a future life — there is clearly development. While the Sadducees had scoffed at the idea, the Pharisees, as we shall see ('The End of History and Beyond', below pp. 561 ff.), found no difficulty in the discovery of proof-texts. The doctrine of retribution in another life is an extension of the notion of God's justice, of His unfailing love, and of His faithfulness in fulfilling His promises to His people. One may speculate that the development represents an individualizing of the concept of retribution with respect to the doctrine of the prophets, which spoke in terms of the nation[294].

The later doctrine did not displace the earlier one; it merely extended it. One's accounts are not closed with one's death. It was taught: "If a man says give this sela to charity in order that my children may live, or in order that I may merit thereby life in the world to come, he is a wholly righteous man"[295]. The reward in this life, thought R. Tarfon (ca. 130), preceded that of the world to come[296]. R. Akiba's metaphors are eloquent: "The ledger lies open, and the hand writes, and whoever wishes to borrow may come and borrow, but the collectors regularly make their daily rounds, and exact payment from a man with or without his knowledge, and they have that whereon they can rely in their demand, and the judgment is a judgment of truth, and everything is prepared for the feast"[297]. The collectors are sufferings and tribulations[298]. Sometimes one does not recognize them.

That good and evil befall man in response to his deeds was not left a general rule. Sometimes specific misfortunes are fitted to corresponding sins[299]. "Measure for measure" was the norm. "With what measure a man

[293] II, 214. JOHN BRIGHT, A History of Israel (Philadelphia, 1959), p. 421, speaks of "that keen sense of the burden of sin which postexilic Jews felt".

[294] MOORE, II, 291.

[295] T.B. Rosh Hashanah 4a, and the parallels cited there.

[296] M. Aboth 2, 16; T.P. Shabbath 6, 9, p. 8d; Lev. Rabbah 27, p. 624.

[297] M. Aboth 3, 16.

[298] URBACH, I, 437, alluding to the commentaries on Akiba's saying — those of Maimonides and R. Jonah.

[299] M. Shabbath 2, 6; T.B. Shabbath 32a; 32b; 33a.

metes it shall be meted out to him again"[300]. The generation of the Flood and the men of Sodom received appropriate requitals[301]. Time and again rabbinic sayings offered the reminder that the principle was still in vigor; the observation of Job that the wicked man prospers was to be refuted[302]. Even those who thought "the reward of a precept is a precept" were not unaware of the general view[303].

But, in the generation of the persecution of Hadrian, the conventional doctrine underwent a change. Those who observed the commandments met torture and death. It was still possible to explain such catastrophe as payment for miniscule offenses, but R. Akiba disagreed[304]. He and his colleagues spoke of those to whom sinful commands were given, and who were bound in conscience to resist, as liable to death at the hands of heaven; in their death they made atonement and attained a share in the world to come. R. Akiba explained his own joy in suffering martyrdom: Throughout his life he had loved God with all his might and all his heart, and now he rejoiced to be able to love Him also with all his soul (life)[305]. Such an attitude is emptied of its significance if it is seen as acceptance of punishment for sin[306]. Akiba and his disciples advanced the understanding of adversity: One was to accept it with love, as the means of serving God with one's very life.

C. Suffering

For generations after R. Akiba's death his maxim "suffering is precious" was reflected upon[307]. His disciples repeated it in their sayings. R. Eliezer ben Jacob found a Scriptural text on which to base it. He said, "Scripture declares: My son, do not despise the Lord's discipline . . . Why? 'For the Lord reproveth him whom He loveth' (Prov. 3, 11–12) . . . Which then is the way that leads a man to life in the world to come? You must say, 'It is suffering'[308]". The School of Ishmael agreed. From it we read, "Anyone who for forty days has known no suffering has received his reward in this world"[309]. The association of suffering with love became, among the Tannaim, so secure that the figure of Abraham was interpreted as that of a hero of suffering. R. Eliezer ben Jacob asserted that Abraham had been thrown into the fiery furnace[310]. Before Abraham, an anonymous Tanna tells us,

[300] M. Sotah 1, 7—10.
[301] Tos. Sotah 3, 6—11, p. 296; T.B. Sanhedrin 108a.
[302] Gen. Rabbah 9, 11, p. 73, and parallels cited there.
[303] R. Ben Azzai as cited in M. Aboth 4, 2.
[304] For one such stereotyped explanation, see Mekhilta de-R. Ishmael, Mishpatim, 18, p. 313.
[305] T.P. Berakhoth 9, 7, p. 14b.
[306] URBACH, I, 443.
[307] The words of Akiba are in T.B. Sanhedrin 101a.
[308] Mekhilta, Ba-hodesh, 10, p. 240; T.B. Berakhoth 5a; Tamhuma Tese, 2.
[309] T.B. Arakhin 16b.
[310] Gen. Rabbah 44, 13, p. 435.

God had judged the world ruthlessly, as in the case of the men of the generation of the Flood, the men of the tower of Babel, and the men of Sodom. Then Abraham suffered. Now, "Should you ask: Why does suffering come? On account of God's love for Israel"[311].

But, some continued to look for the sins to be expiated as an explanation for adversity[312]. For the early Amoraim there were two kinds of suffering — suffering of love and suffering due to sin[313]. Some sages even performed acts of self-affliction, not waiting for suffering[314]. But, this was criticized by others on several accounts. Resh Lakish is reported to have thought, "A scholar may not practice fasting, because he diminishes the work of heaven"[315]. Others pointed out that everyone was subjected to petty inconveniences, which should be considered suffering[316].

It should be evident from this type of reflection upon suffering that the rabbis did not speculate upon it in the same way as did others — e. g., the Stoics — who saw a problem of evil. There is evidence of attempts to justify the divine judgments — particularly in the accounts of martyrs, who accept their affliction with an affirmation of trust in God's goodness[317], or in the words of solace offered to the bereaved[318]. Israelite history was at times reviewed from the point of view of theodicy. Why, for example, was not David allowed to build the Temple?[319] But, if theodicy is thought of as calling into question the existence of God because of the existence of evil, the reflections of the sages give no evidence that the question was entertained.

V. Man's Destiny

God's human creature of dual nature and free, moves to the destiny for which he was made. "Whatever the Holy One, blessed be He, created in His world, He created but for His glory"[320]. How man furthers the glory of God in a manner so characteristic as to be defined thereby was a subject of thought for the sages. "When the Holy One, blessed be He, consulted the Torah as to the creation of the world, she answered: 'Master of the world, if there be no host, over whom will the king reign, and if there be no

311 Sifre Deut., par. 311.
312 M. Kiddushin 4, 14; Tos. Baba Metzia 3, 25, p. 378; T.B. Shabbath 33a.
313 T.B. Berakhoth 5a; 5b; Gen. Rabbah 92, 1, p. 1137; Cant. Rabbah 2, 15; T.B. Baba Bathra 116a.
314 T.P. Nedarim 8, 1, p. 40d; T.B. Kiddushin 81b; Tos. Oholoth 4, 2, p. 600; 5, 11—12, p. 603; T.B. Hagigah 22b; T.P. Shabbath 5, 4, p. 7c.
315 T.B. Taanith 11a—b.
316 T.B. Arakhin 16b.
317 See, e.g., Sifre Deut., par. 307, p. 346; T.B. Abodah Zarah 18a.
318 T.P. Sanhedrin 6, 12, p. 32d; See M. Aboth 4, 22.
319 Midrash Tehillim, 62, 4, p. 309.
320 Pirke de-R. Eliezer, ch. 3.

peoples praising Him, where is the glory of the king?' The Lord of the world heard the answer, and it pleased Him"[321]. A creature combining angel and beast would be able to rise or fall and, in his rising, bring recognition to the Creator from the center of His work[322]. Study of human destiny may aptly begin in this recognition (1. The Kingdom of God) — followed by consideration of the divine self-expression which man is to recognize (2. The Torah), the action which this recognition involves (3. Learning and Action), its human context (4. Human Solidarity), and the concept of how this action terminates (5. The End of History and Beyond). In rabbinic thought, man's destiny is received, and man knows himself in it.

1. The Kingdom of God

The biblical expression "I am the Lord" denotes kingly authority[223]. God lays absolute claim to man's obedience. In the Shema one speaks of "the kingdom of God", and rabbinic literature coins the phrase "the kingdom of heaven". The kingdom has invisible and visible aspects.

A. The Invisible Kingdom

The Talmud enjoins upon the worshipper that, when he pronounces God the "only one", he dwell long enough in his mind to declare Him king over all four corners of the world[324]. He who wishes to receive upon himself the yoke of the kingdom of heaven should first prepare himself, read the Shema and pray[325]. The kingdom, then, is an invisible reality within the human heart. To receive the kingdom is to realize within oneself the attitude of total love of God expressed in the Shema, to surrender one's heart to the divine will. "What is the section of the Law where there is to be found the acceptance of the kingdom of heaven? . . . This is the Shema"[326]. The kingdom in this text is distinguished from idols, and all that is not God is an idol. "The Lord, He is God; in heaven above and on the earth beneath, there is none else" (Deut. 4.39)[327].

The love of God, which is internal acceptance of His reign, has a quite specific meaning. "Love God with all thy desires, even with thy evil impulse, so that there may be no corner in thy heart divided against God . . . Love

[321] Idem. On the subject of man's being created for God's glory, see Aboth de-R. Nathan, 67b with notes at end; Exod. Rabbah 17, 1; Gen. Rabbah 5, 1.

[322] See Midrash Tanhuma (edit. Buber), Indroduction, 76a.

[323] It is read this way in Sifre 19b; Mekhilta of R. Simon, p. 30. My treatment of the kingdom theme follows the organization of Schechter, pp. 65—115.

[324] T.B. Berakhoth 13b.

[325] T.B. Berakhoth 14b, 15a.

[326] Sifre 34b; cf. T.B. Berakhoth 13a; Deut. Rabbah, 2. 81; Sifre 80a.

[327] T.B. Rosh Hashanah 32b.

Him under all conditions, both in times of bliss and happiness, and in times of distress and misfortune"[328].

This "yoke" of the kingdom of God was, to the sages, the truest freedom. "If thou hast brought thy neck under the yoke of the Torah, she will watch over thee"[329]. What R. Akiba received with joy as he recited the Shema during his martyrdom was this yoke of the kingdom[330].

The inner disposition by which one receives the kingdom — "And thou shalt love the Lord thy God with all thy heart" (Deut. 6.5) — consists in placing His words upon the heart, "For through them thou wilt learn to know the Holy One, blessed be He, and cleave unto His ways"[331]. The love which obeys is "the fear of Heaven", taught by Antigonus of Sokho: "Be like servants that minister to the master, not for the sake of receiving a reward; and let the fear of Heaven be upon you"[332]. His ways, of course, regard human conduct in the visible kingdom. Even so, such conduct receives its human constitution from the awareness of its conformity to the divine plan for mankind.

B. The Universal, Visible Kingdom

The visible kingdom has a universal aspect. God seeks the tribute of all human freedom. Man, as free, is at the center of creation; in him divine kingship can come to full realization. With man's creation, God became king over the world[333]. The first man invited the whole creation "to clothe God with majesty and strength"[334]. One of the sages exclaimed at the thought, "Beautiful is the world . . . in which the Holy One, blessed be He, is king"[335]. The graceful state was short-lived. The abuse of freedom sullied both man and his world. The sin of the following generations was their assertion that the world was an automaton, with no Lord over it[336]. Violence reigned[337]. Only with Abraham, the first to call God master and concerned in human

328 Sifre 73a. Cf. T.B. Berakhoth 61b, with parallels.

329 T.B. Erubin 54a. Cf. M. Aboth 3, 5: הדבי נהוניא בן הקנה אומר כל המקכל עליו עול תירה(טו). מעבירין ממנו עול מלכות ועול דרך ארץ. וכל הפרק ממנו עול תורה. נותנין עליו עול מלכות ועול ד"א. "R. Nehanya ben Ha-Kanah said: 'He that takes upon himself the yoke of the Torah, from him shall be taken away the yoke of the kingdom [i.e., of those in power over him] and the yoke of worldly care'." T.B. Erubim, 54a. See also Midrash Tehillim (Schocher Tob), edit. Buber, 2, 11; M. Berakhoth 2, 5.

330 T.P. Berakhoth 14b.

331 Sifre 74a.

332 M. Aboth 1, 3. For discussion of the relationship between fear and love in rabbinic literature, in historical development, see Urbach, I, 400—419.

333 T.B. Rosh Hashanah 31a; Aboth de-R. Nathan, Appendix 76b. With this citation Schechter, p. 82, begins an exposition of the nature of the universal, visible kingdom in chronological survey.

334 Pirke Rabbi Eliezer, ch. 11.

335 Gen. Rabbah 9, 4; Exod. Rabbah 15, 22; cf. Num. Rabbah 10, 1.

336 Aboth de-R. Nathan 47b, with parallels.

337 Mekhilta 67b.

action, did the light return[338]. Making God beloved of His creatures, Abraham was the first missionary[339]. God became again the King of the earth[340]. Jacob too taught his children to receive the yoke of the kingdom of heaven[341]. Yet, the kingship was uncertain until a whole people was formed devoted to proclaiming His sovereignty. When they sang to Him at the Red Sea — or more importantly, when at Sinai they affirmed, "All that the Lord hath said we will do and be obedient (Ex. 24.7)" — His kingdom was firmly established[342]. God then found more delight in men than in angels[343]. On the very spot of the establishment of the kingdom, however, Israel worshipped the Golden Calf and followed that rebellion with other acts of rejection[344]. Yet, despite numerous relapses, there now existed a whole people who had once chosen God as their king. A remnant would always be faithful and form the foundation of the spiritual world[345].

Clearly, therefore, for the rabbis the kingdom of God is in this world. It is established by man's awareness of God's closeness to him. This awareness means knowledge of God's ways — an acknowledgment of responsibility to the king who is concerned in human action. Here the kingdom idea is more moral than eschatological. The kingdom is not identical with the Torah, for one receives first the yoke of the kingdom and then, by consequence, the yoke of the commandments[346]. The kingdom is not political; the rabbis recognized every authority as appointed by heaven[347]. In its aims the kingdom of God is universal. This is obvious in traditional kingship prayers — e.g., "Our God and God of Our Fathers, . . . be exalted above all the earth in thine honor . . . that whatever has been made may know that Thou hast made it"[348].

C. The National, Visible Kingdom

A midrash on Exodus speaks of Israel's special connection with the visible kingdom. "As long as Israel is united into one league, the kingdom of heaven is maintained by them"[349]. The kingdom is closely associated with the redemption of Israel from the exile, coming of the Messiah, and the restoration of the Temple; this is its national aspect. The reality was celebrated in legends and myths around chiliastic themes, in which, despite

[338] Gen. Rabbah 3, 8; T. B. Berakhoth 7b.
[339] Sifre 73a, with parallels; Pesikta de-R. Kahana (edit. Buber), 1b; Pesikta Rabbati 18b.
[340] Sifre 134b.
[341] Num. Rabbah 2, 8; Gen. Rabbah 93, 8 and parallels.
[342] At the Red Sea: Exod. Rabbah 23, 1. At Sinai: Pesikta de-R. Kahana (edit. Buber), 17a.
[343] Exod. Rabbah 51, 8, and parallels.
[344] Num. Rabbah 7, 2.
[345] T.B. Yoma 38b.
[346] T.B. Berakhoth 13a.
[347] T.B. Berakhoth 58a; T.B. Abodah Zarah 17a.
[348] Singer edition of the Prayer Book, p. 249; cited by Schechter, pp. 93—94.
[349] Ex. Rabbah 38, 4; Midrash Shemuel, B. 5, 11 and references.

excesses, fixed elements are discernible: The Messiah will restore the kingdom of Israel, which will then extend over the whole world. In one last battle the enemies of Israel will be destroyed. All humanity will then accept the spiritual hegemony of Israel. The Messiah will institute an age of bliss in which the dead will revive and death will disappear (See below, pp. 561—69). The narratives speak of the enemies of God in the biblical terms designating Israel's historical foes, Amalek and Edom[350]. Against the kingdom of God is arrayed the alien kingdom which Israel must strive against until the end of history[351].

The near-identification of the kingdom of God with Israel, to be restored and enlarged by the Messiah, adds specific meanings to the kingdom concept itself: (1) The kingdom of God is in this world. (2) Israel is its depository, not its exclusive possessor[352]. Israel's nationhood, again, was understood as the rule of the Torah rather than as an ethnic unit under a political system[353]. From this nation the kingdom was to be expanded by repentance and proselytism. "Behold, even one of the other nations who fulfills the Torah is as the high priest himself"[354]. (3) The coming of the kingdom is dependent upon Israel's full acceptance of God's sovereignty. "Before we pray for redemption", it was said, "we must first make Him king over us"[355]. (4) Neither corrupt and brutal government nor dehumanizing economic and social conditions are compatible with the kingdom.

Man's destiny, therefore, is the kingdom of God. This means man is created to acknowledge God in full love and obedience, to form the human community under His rule, and to restore the world in accord with His graceful design.

2. The Torah

Acceptance of the Kingdom of God necessitates acceptance of the Torah. "If you have received my kingdom, receive now my decrees"[356]. The term *Torah* means a teaching[357]. The LXX rendering, *nomos* (law), is unfortunate, for it constricts what is a complex notion. When Torah refers

[350] E.g., Pesikta de-R. Kahana (edit. Buber), 28a; 29a; Pesikta Rabbati (edit. Friedmann), 51a and parallels; Mekhilta 56a, 56b; Midrash Tehillin (Schocher Tob), edit. Buber, 97, 1 and 99, 1.

[351] Lev. Rabbah 13, 5 and parallels.

[352] Sifre 72b and notes; Deut. Rabbah 2.

[353] Schechter, p. 105, supports this view with a citation from Saadya Gaon: "Because our nation is only a nation by reason of its Torah." John Bright, A History of Israel, p. 419, remarks of Judaism after the exile, that Ezra's law was not imposed upon a well-defined national community but "served as the constitutive element that defined a new community".

[354] Sifra 86a. Also, Mekhilta 95b and parallels.

[355] Sifre 72b and notes; Deut. Rabbah 2.

[356] Sifra 85d; Mekhilta 67a, 67b.

[357] תורה *Torah*: lit. "teaching", "instruction", "doctrine".

to the Pentateuch, the implication is that the Prophets and the Hagiographa form a kind of Haggadah to it; they too are the Torah[358]. But the entire content of God's word was revealed at Sinai. Narrative parts of the Pentateuch were Torah as well. Ben Azzai said that the account of creation — man's creation in the image of God — taught a greater principle than did the law of loving one's neighbor as oneself[359]. Torah, in its properly broad sense, was complemented by *mitzwoth* (precepts); the two are not infrequently juxtaposed[360]. One of the early Amoraim, R. Simlai, said, "Six hundred and thirteen precepts were delivered unto Moses on Mount Sinai, three hundred and sixty-five of which are prohibitive laws, corresponding to the number of days of the solar year, whilst the remaining two hundred and forty-eight are affirmative injunctions, being as numerous as the limbs constituting the human body"[361]. The point of the homily was that all precepts might be compressed into the principle of seeking God. As in any law code, much of the material had to do with situations that no longer obtained. Even so, the great number of commandments was far from an embarrassment. R. Simlai's number suggested that God's law applied to the whole man through the whole year. For everything God loved He gave a commandment[362]. "To the nations of the earth He gave a few laws; but His love to Israel was particularly manifested by the fulness and completeness of the Torah, which is wholly theirs"[363]. We have seen the opinion that revelation was a greater evidence of divine love than was creation[364]. The corollary to this awareness was that the Law was held to be theonomous rather than autonomous — that is, it stood on the authority of God and not on a perception of the necessary ethical dimension of society. R. Hanina taught: "Greater is he who is commanded and fulfills a precept than he who is not commanded yet fulfills it"[365].

A. Wisdom and Torah

Receiving the law-for-man did not involve, in the view of the sages, merely putting together those insights which the experience of ages might teach. God taught man directly in the Torah. Nothing there was held back[366].

[358] E.g., T.B. Megillah 31a; T.B. Baba Bathra 13b.
[359] Sifra 89b and parallels. BACHER, Tannaiten, I, 720.
[360] E.g., T.B. Berakhoth 31a; T.B. Makkoth 23a; M. Aboth 3, 11.
[361] T.B. Makkoth 23b and parallels. First occurrence of this number is in Mekhilta 67a.
[362] Num. Rabbah 17, 5; cf. Lev. Rabbah 6, 8.
[363] Ex. Rabbah 30, 9, and parallels.
[364] R. Akiba in M. Aboth 3, 14.
[365] T.B. Kiddushin 31a. See URBACH, I, 323—324: Philo (De Abra. 6) was in error saying that the Patriarchs "regarded Nature as the most venerable law". For HENGEL, I, 173, observing the Torah was living "in conformity with the law of the world" — a Stoic attitude flowing from the identification of Torah and Wisdom. This view accords ill with R. Hanina's teaching above.
[366] Deut. Rabbah 8, 6.

The biblical search for wisdom had led to the conclusion that wisdom was the Torah (Prov. 8). This was a statement about the content of that wisdom which all sought. At the same time it was a universalizing of the Torah; for, reflection on how a human life might be shaped, which reflection was wisdom, was the province of everyman. She is "not the Torah of the Israelites, but the Torah of man; her gates are open to receive the righteous nation which keeps the truth"[367]. That fear of the Lord which kept the mind open to mystery and newness was the beginning of wisdom (Prov. 1.7; 9.10; 15.33; Ps. 111.10; Job 28.28)[368]. This condition, necessary for wisdom, was the condition for understanding the Torah. A midrashic comment has David pray, "Make me understand the way of Thy precepts (Ps. 119.27) ... for, if Thou wilt not make me understand them, I shall know nothing"[369].

R. Eliezer ben R. Zadok and R. Akiba spoke of the Torah as "an instrument with which the world was created"[370]. We have observed earlier the difficulty some have found in this conception of the pre-existence of the Torah[371]. But, the pre-existence theme was never consolidated into doctrinal significance. It is an ornate way of speaking of the Law as a manifestation of the eternal will of the Creator. Of more significance, however, is the rabbinic understanding of divine revelation as a matter that deals more with what God demands of man than with what God Himself is. This is the sense of calling the whole of God's word to man Torah; and this is the sense of the conviction that what the nations seek in wisdom God has already given to man in the Torah.

The Torah-wisdom identification must be considered particularly in the perspective of the Pharisaic doctrine that the revelation at Sinai included the content of Jewish oral tradition. Three times in the Mishnah we read of "statutes given by God on Sinai"[372]; in the Gemara the expression is common. In the two oldest traditions about the Oral Law, the word Torah is used with differences of connotation. The Torah around which the sages were to build a fence (M. Aboth, 1, 1) and which went out from the Great Court to all Israel (M. Sanhedrin, 9, 2) was the Halakhoth such as it is found in the Mishnah. Instead, the Torah spoken of by Simon the Just (in M. Aboth, 1, 1) — "Upon three things the world is based, upon the Torah, upon Temple service, and upon deeds of loving-kindness" — is study of the Torah[373]. The Oral Torah, then, is a tradition of reflection upon Sinaitic revelation and the body of precisely articulated conclusions from that study as to how the revelation applies to current circumstances. To underline the living character of this Oral Torah and to distinguish it from mere midrashic exposition of the Bible text, the sages avoided the use

[367] Sifra 86b.
[368] Von Rad, Wisdom in Israel, p. 73.
[369] Midrash Tehillim (Schocher Tob), edit. Buber, 119, 16.
[370] Sifre Deut., par. 48; M. Aboth 3, 14.
[371] Hengel, I, 169—175, 311—312 surveys the problem.
[372] T.B. Peah 2,6; T.B. Eduyoth 8,7; T.B. Yadaim 4,3.
[373] Urbach, I, 286.

of biblical forms in the articulation of the Halakhah. Twice in the Mishnah we meet a prohibition against justifying the Halakhoth merely as extrapolations from the written Torah:

> "Greater stringency applies to the words of the Scribes than to the words of the [written] law." (M. Sanhedrin, 11, 3)
>
> "Ye may infer nothing about the words of the [written] Law from the words of the Scribes, and nothing about the words of the Scribes from the words of the Law, and nothing about the words of the Scribes from [other] words of the Scribes." (M. Yadaim, 3, 2)

The faith that the Jewish people alone possessed the divinely given truth, not only in the scrolls of the Bible, but in the scholar class of the living people itself, fostered the study of this truth, the Law — while others might search for it elsewhere, in vain. This faith produced an effort at popular education probably unique in the ancient world[374]. Human analysis suggests that the success of this effort may account for the preservation of the Jewish community. On the other hand, the question has frequently been asked whether a concept of God's word to man as so once-given and comprehensively given does not forever exclude the divine possibility of the prophetic utterance which nurtured ancient Israel. This is basically the same as the question which asks whether the Pharisaic doctrine preserved in the rabbinate did not render the Torah an "essentially unhistorical entity"[375]. But the rabbis' obedience to the Law once-given was, in an inordinately speculative era, a subjection of the speculative mind to the God of history. All the elect had been present at Sinai.

An anthropological distillation of the doctrine of Oral Torah is necessary. That the dynamic by which a community preserves its identity, while responding developmentally to changing circumstances, is an oral teaching revealed at one point in history and maintained in the study tradition of the leaders of the community — this conviction is an expression of superior confidence in human intellect. The rabbis did not, of course, think of this intellectual effort as unaided. The Oral Torah represents a concept of divine assistance in history altogether characteristic of Pharisaism, and of the rabbinate which took up its heritage.

B. Letter and Spirit

Where all wisdom is the Law the concept of law becomes an anthropological concern. Though Torah was more than *nomos*, its teaching gravitated

[374] HENGEL, I, 175. See also I, 78—83, for the excursus 'The Development of the Jewish School'.

[375] D. RÖSSLER, Gesetz und Geschichte, WMANT, 3, 2nd edit. (Neukirchen, 1962), p. 42. E. P. SANDERS, pp. 48—49, notes RÖSSLER's faulty use of sources. See also JOHN BRIGHT, A History of Israel, p. 420. HENGEL, I, 312. The issue is studied in G. VERMES, Scripture and Tradition in Judaism (Leiden, 1961).

to the statement of God's will for man, His law. A traditional criticism of the Judaism rejected by Christianity is expressed in a common interpretation of Paul. The accusation was that those Jews who had rejected Jesus as Messiah by virtue of their understanding of the Law had preferred the letter of the law to its spirit[376]. Accordingly, it seems to have become unnecessary in Christian literature, to make a case in order to conclude to an "anxious and zealous fixation on the letter of the Torah which we meet in Pharisaism"[377]. In place of confidence in the law, Paul proposed faith[378]. This controversy frames a question for anthropology: According to the rabbis' concept of the Law, does man know himself — i.e., the kind of action proper to him — in precise, fixed formulations, corresponding to the Pauline "letter of the law?" Is what Christians understand by the "spirit of the law" absent from rabbinic literature? In Paul the question is tangential to Christology. Here we broach the matter of early Christian-Jewish polemics only as the historic setting necessary to comprehend an anthropological question.

The answer can be drawn from a series of assertions. (1) In the Pharisaic principle of Oral Torah the letter of the written Law was at times made to cede to the living tradition of the Oral Torah, so that what was conceived as the objective of the Law might be attained[379]. One finds a formula parallel to that of the New Testament "It was said . . . but I say to you". — e.g., regarding how a bill of divorce was to be given: "The Torah said on a 'book', whereas the Halakhah said 'on anything'[280]." Paul, the Pharisee, would have learned of the doctrinal and disciplinary inadequacy of a once-written juridical code even before his conversion to a different option in remedying the inadequacy[381].

(2) Rabbinic tradition preserves a doctrinal dispute over the necessity of specific commandments, in which Shammai maximized their significance and Hillel minimized it. Shammai, for example, cultivated the prescribed dedication to the Sabbath, while Hillel said, "Blessed be the Lord day by day"[382]. It is Hillel's view that finds greater resonance in the Talmud[383]. Jesus' attitude toward specific precepts (Mk. 2.23; 7.1–23; Mt. 23.16–27) can be seen as "in part a radicalization of views held by several of Israel's

376 Paul on the spirit vs. the letter of the law: Rom. 2.29; 7.6; 2 Cor. 3.6.

377 Hengel, I, 313. See D. Rössler, Gesetz und Geschichte, p. 16ff. Moore, I, 235—236, makes so feeble an argument for the inviolable character of law in a "revealed religion" as to appear patronizing, in this instance, with respect to the tradition about which he writes.

378 Rom. 3.21—26.

379 R. Johanan and Resh Lakish, Amoraim of the mid-third century, put this in form of a principle: "Rather let a letter of the Torah be uprooted than the Torah should be forgotten in Israel." T.B. Temurah 14b. A similar formulation is reported of Hillel, in Tos. Berakhoth 8, 22, p. 17.

380 T.P. Kiddushin 1, 2, p. 59d. See also T.B. Rosh Hashanah 18b; Tosefta 6, 6; T.B. Bekhoroth 20a; T.B. Hagigah 19a—b.

381 Cf. "We serve not under the old written code but in the new life of the spirit", Rom. 7.6.

382 T.B. Betzah 16a. Shammai's view reported also in Mekhilta de-R. Simeon ben Yohai, p. 148.

383 See T.B. Shabbath 50b (also Tos. Berakhoth 4, 1, p. 8); T.B. Berakhoth 63a.

sages"[384]. A corollary to the dispute is the prudential principle which Hillel offered his disciples: When the Torah is beloved of all Israel, "scatter it" (do not be tied down to minutiae); when the Torah is forgotten, "draw it in" (hold to particulars)[385].

(3) Rabbinic literature proposes, not confidence in one's righteousness as observer of the commandments, but confidence in God. This confidence in God and fidelity to Him is called faith — the attitude of Abraham which God accounted to him as righteousness (Gen. 15.6)[386], and the disposition of Israel at the Red Sea because of which God parted the waters[387], and the disposition of R. Akiba expressed in the words, "A man should habitually say: All that the Merciful One does is for the best"[388].

(4) The rabbis taught interiorization of the Law rather than merely material observance. This may be noted in their exposition of precepts regarding chastity and of the norms of prayer. The caution against adultery of the eye and of the mind is frequent[389]. The account of interiorization proper to prayer includes a recommendation of silent meditation preceding the utterance of formulae[390], the insistance upon right intention[391], the teaching that prayer effectively replaces the Temple cult[392], the inculcation of freedom in prayer[393], and the prescription of total resignation to God's will[394].

(5) In rabbinic literature one encounters humility rather than complacency in the observance of precepts. An anonymous prayer reads, "The needs of Thy people Israel are great and their wit is small"[395]. The idea is implied in the much-used theme that God should do His good pleasure

[384] Urbach, II, 836, n. 92.

[385] Tos. Berakhoth 6, 24; T.P. Berakhoth 9, 8, p. 14d; T.B. Berakhoth 63a.

[386] אמונה *emunah*: faith, confidence, trust, reliance (see Gen. 15.6). Mekhilta 50c. Cf. Rom. 3.4; 9.20–21; Gal. 3.6; James 2.23.

[387] Mekhilta, Beshallah ,3, on Ex. 14.15 (edit. Friedmann f. 29b; edit. Weiss, f. 35b); Mekhilta de-R. Simeon ben Yohai on Ex. 14.5. Cf. Hebrews 11.29: "By faith they crossed the Red sea as on dry ground."

[388] T.B. Berakhoth 60b.

[389] T.P. Berakhoth 3c; T.B. Niddah 13b; Sifre Num. par. 115 (edit. Friedmann f. 35a); Tanhuma (edit. Buber) Shelah, par. 31; Lev. Rabbah 23, 12; Pesikta Rabbati (edit. Friedmann f. 124b); Mekhilta de-R. Simeon ben Yohai on Ex. 20.14 (edit. Hoffmann, p. 111). Moore, II, 267—268: "When Jesus said: 'You have heard that it was said: Thou shalt not commit adultery. But I say unto you that whoever gazes at a woman with desire has already debauched her in his mind', he was not only uttering a Jewish commonplace, but with a familiar figure, 'adultery of the eyes'."

[390] M. Berakhoth 5, 1; T.P. Berakhoth 8d; T.B. Berakhoth 32b.

[391] Sifre Deut. par. 41 (on Deut. 11.13; edit. Friedmann f. 80a); M. Pesahim 5, 2; Tanhuma (edit. Buber) Naso par. 18.

[392] Pesikta Shubah, end (edit. Buber, p. 165b); Tanhuma Korah, par. 12, near end; Pesikta (edit. Buber f. 181a); Midrash Tehillim on Ps. 102.18 (edit. Buber f. 215b—216a).

[393] T.B. Berakhoth 29b; T.P. Berakhoth 8a; 50c. Tos. Berakhoth 3, 5.

[394] Midrash Tehillim on Ps. 40.1 (edit. Buber f. 129a); Tanhuma (edit. Buber) Toledoth, par. 14.

[395] Tosefta 50c.

rather than attend to a specific request[396]. The prayer of Raba (Amora of 4th cen.) began with the reflection that the petitioner had no more claim upon God than if he had never been created[397]. A traditional theme of prayer at meal time was man's complete dependence upon God[398]. R. Joshua ben Levi (ca. 230) claimed to discover in Scripture (Isa. 61.1) that humility is the greatest of the virtues[399]. Hillel was held up as a model of humility to counter the endemic vanity of scholars. He had said, "My abasement is my exaltation, and my exaltation is my abasement"[400].

From this series of assertions it becomes apparent that legalism was in contradiction to the religious perception of the sages. But, perhaps the clearest insight into rabbinism's conception of the Law is available in the law of holiness — the rabbinic understanding of the commandment to be holy: "Ye shall be unto me a kingdom of priests and a holy nation" (Ex. 19.1)[401]. The highest achievement of the Law was the holiness — i.e., God-likeness — of those who observed it. The kingdom of God, the central idea of rabbinic theology, defined man's relationship to God; logically it preceded the law[402]. The rationale of the Law was to provide man with instructions on how he might be holy and thus suited for close association with the Holy One. With respect to the kingdom, then, the Law had an instrumental value. It would be enough to indicate the broadening of biblical commandments in rabbinic understanding in order to conclude that literalism was not proper of the rabbinate. We have noted an example of broadening in the notion of chastity of the eyes and mind. "Thou shalt not kill" (Ex. 20.13) was seen, not merely as the prohibition of physical violence, but of putting a man to shame in public, "which causes his blood to leave his face"[403]. A principle is enunciated: "Sanctify thyself even in that which is permitted to thee"[404].

Another principle seen as supplementing and correcting the Law was the law of goodness, derived from general commandments such as, "Thou shalt do that which is right and good in the sight of the Lord" (Deut. 16.18)[405]. Nevertheless, in every expanding or loosening of the Law, the

[396] T.B. Berakhoth 29b; Tos. Berakhoth 3, 7. Moore, II, 215, n. 3, cites the example of Maimonides (Hilkhoth Tefillah 4, 19) who added to a traditional prayer, "And what is good in Thy sight do"!

[397] T.B. Berakhoth 17a.

[398] M. Berakhoth 6, 1; T.B. Berakhoth 48b; the Singer edit. of the Authorized Daily Prayer Book, pp. 278—285.

[399] T.B. Abodah Zarah 20b; T.B. Arakhin 16b, where the saying is presented as a general maxim.

[400] Lev. Rabbah 1, 5. See exhortations to humility in T.B. Shabbath 30b; T.P. Sotah 24b; Tos. Sotah 13, 3; T.B. Sotah 48b; Tanhuma (edit. Buber) Wayyikra, par. 2 and 4; Lev. Rabbah 1.5; Aboth de-R. Nathan c. 25.

[401] Mekhilta 63a; Sifra 86d; 93b; Num. Rabbah 9. 6. Cf. Lev. 20.26.

[402] Schechter, p. 199.

[403] T.B. Baba Metzia 59a.

[404] Sifre 95a; T.B. Yebamoth 20a.

[405] See, e.g., Sifre 91a; 94a; T.B. Baba Metzia 13b; 30b; Mekhilta 59b; T.P. Baba Kamma 6c.

sages were aware of a problem which no society escapes: A total dissolution of juridical norms in the name of "the spirit" of the law can be as destructive as the fostering of blindness to objectives in the name of "the letter". The dispute between Hillel and Shammai revolved about this issue. Rabbinism proposed for itself a respect for both letter and spirit. It saw in the Torah man's ultimate possibility (i.e., destiny), principles by which it might be achieved — but also specific norms of conduct, willed by God, transcending human ethical reflection.

3. Learning and Action

The relation between theory and practice within the concrete progress of a man's life has always posed a problem of understanding. The conception of an ideal pattern is an anthropological challenge, because it implies a conception of how man is constituted. Among the rabbis one reads diverse, even contradictory, answers. Raba, for example, extolled the Torah as the supreme value and lamented that a colleague's prolonged prayer infringed upon the time reserved for its study[406]. Yet, he frequently remarked, "The goal of wisdom is repentance and good deeds"[407]. When the question had been debated in a conference of rabbis, R. Tarfon (early 2nd. cen.) supported the supremacy of doing over studying; R. Akiba favored studying. And, the decision was unanimous behind Akiba, for the reason that "study leads to doing"[408]. This reason, which J. Guttmann calls naive, hardly meets the anthropological challenge[409]. The rabbis do not advance the speculative issue further. It remained a problem through the generations. But, the society they formed, as their occasional dicta manifest it, testifies to notable insights in the matter.

A. The Torah as Supreme Value

Some remarks about the study of the Torah straddle the issue, presenting the scholar's activity as the efficacy of the teacher of children

[406] T.B. Shabbath 10a.

[407] T.B. Berakhoth 17a, quoted from the version in MSS by Urbach, The Sages, Enc. Jud., 14, 646.

[408] גדול שהתלמוד מביא לידי מעשה. "Study leads to doing" (T.B. Kiddushin 40b). See also T.B. Megillah 27a; T.B. Baba Kamma 17a; T.P. Pesahim 30b; T.P. Hagigah 76c. Cf. Sifre Deut. par. 41 on 11.13 (edit. Friedmann f. 79a). Bacher, Tannaiten, I, 303. On R. Tarfon, see J. Neusner, History and Torah: Essays on Jewish Learning (New York, 1965), pp. 76—102; esp. 97—98, on the assembly which debated the issue at Lud. On R. Akiba's role in the discussion, see L. Finkelstein, Akiba: Scholar, Saint and Martyr (New York, 1936; reprint, New York, 1970), pp. 257—271; the author describes the circumstances out of which the question arose — the danger of openly observing the Torah in the Hadrianic persecution.

[409] Philosophies of Judaism, p. 40.

or the continuation of the missionary role of Moses[410]. Others opt clearly for study over action. There are many religious duties which engage a man in society, "and the study of Talmud Torah is equal to them all"[411]. What the rabbi studied was, not only Scripture, but the Halakhah, the Haggadah, and the Midrash[412]. He studied them for their own sake, not for any pragmatic end[413]. His study was a duty from which he could not release himself[414]. The Law was forever new; by diligent study one accepted it daily from Sinai[415]. Like one who lived in eternity, the scholar of the Law was already engaged in the activity of the world to come. R. Joseph the son of R. Joshua ben Levi, coming out of a coma, told his father of how in the other world men's present positions with regard to fortune were reversed; but of students of the Torah he said, "We are there the same as here; I heard it stated, 'Happy is he who comes here possessed of learning'"[416]. There is a special reward in Gan Eden for students of the Torah. "The Holy One, blessed be He, will reveal to them its mysteries in the world to come"[417]. Finally, study of the Torah is worship — called by the name of the service of the altar (*abodah*)[418].

B. The Goal of Wisdom

Action some believed, hindered a rabbi in his pursuit of the wisdom of the Torah. Such action was of three types — working to earn a livelihood, exercizing administrative and judicial functions, and directly intervening for the relief of the needy. But many thought otherwise. There was no problem, held R. Hiyya (late 2nd cen.), in the case of one who studied without the intention of observing: "It had been better for him not to have been created"[419]. Raba, for whom the goal of wisdom was repentance and good deeds (see n. 407, above), described a more general position in his comment on a psalm: "'The fear of the Lord is the beginning of wisdom; a good understanding have all they that do accordingly' (ps. 111.10). It does not say 'all that learn' but 'all that do'"[420]. Perhaps this mere underlining entitles one to claim for Raba the most systematic view of the issue. If the Torah is wisdom, its very understanding — as Raba read in the psalm —

410 On teaching children: T.B. Baba Metzia 85b. On the role of Moses: T.B. Sanhedrin 99b; Seder Eliahu Rabbah (edit. FRIEDMANN), pp. 17, 63.

411 M. Peah 1, 1. See also T.P. Peah 15d.

412 Sifre Deut. par. 48 (edit. FRIEDMANN 80a top); Lev. Rabbah 22, 1.

413 T.B. Berakhoth 17a; T.B. Sukkah 49b.

414 T.B. Menahoth 99b. Cf. Mekhilta on Ex. 16.4 (edit. FRIEDMANN f. 47b; edit. WEISS f. 55b).

415 On newness: Sifra Deut. par. 33 (on Deut. 6.6); Pesikta (edit. BUBER f. 102a; 105a; 107a). On reception from Sinai: Tanhuma (edit. BUBER) Yitro, par. 7.

416 T.B. Pesahim 50a.

417 T.B. Hagigah 14a.

418 Sifre on Deut. 11.13 par. 41 (edit. FRIEDMANN f. 80a top).

419 Lev. Rabbah 30, 5, p. 826. See parallel saying by R. Johanan, in T.P. Berakhoth, 1, 5, p. 3b; T.P. Shabbath 1, 5, p. 3b; Ex. Rabbah 40, par. 1.

420 T.B. Berakhoth 17a. Version in MSS, cited by URBACH, The Sages, Enc. Jud. 14.646.

is possessed, not in detached study, but in the doing which the "fear of the Lord" involves. In any case, the practice of a majority of the rabbis did not understand the primacy of study as permitting complete disinvolvement from the community. The love of God which was the motive of Torah study would express itself in love of all who bore His image. R. Akiba, who had gained the decision in favor of study, left his study to visit a sick pupil, while others stayed away. He sprinkled and swept the sick man's floor and heard him say, "Master, you have given me new life!" Akiba went out then and taught: "If one fails to visit the sick, it is as though he shed blood"[421]. Love furnished an understanding of the excellence of action. A comment upon Israel as God's beloved ("Behold thou art fair, my love") ran as follows: "You are fair through the giving of alms and performing acts of loving-kindness; you are my lovers and friends when you walk in my ways. As the Omnipresent is merciful and gracious, long-suffering and abundant in goodness, so be you . . . feeding the hungry, giving drink to the thirsty, clothing the naked, ransoming the captives, and marrying the orphans"[422].

We have called the rabbis a scholar class. Certain connotations of both words must be removed through the consideration of how their practice of the Torah related to their learning.

a) Domestic Life

The rabbis did not, in the name of intellectual or spiritual concentration, "liberate" themselves from the joys and cares of family life. To marry and raise a family was accepted as a divine command (Gen. 1.28). They read Genesis 5.2 as implying that an unmarried person was incomplete: "Male and female He created them, and blessed them, and called their name man"[423]. Without at least a brief catalogue of items culled from their sayings regarding domestic life, one will fail to perceive the closeness of the rabbis' involvement in their families or the religious significance they saw in the phenomenon of family.

Although raising a family was spoken of in terms of religious obligation rather than human right, an outstanding degree of personal freedom chracterized several aspects of marriage. Early marriage was advocated[424]; but, "a man is forbidden to give his daughter in marriage . . . until she is grown up and says: I wish to marry so-and-so"[425]. Though we have no record of rabbis resorting to polygamy, and though it is discountenanced in some ways, polygamy was permitted[426]. Divorce was not made diffi-

[421] T.B. Nedarim 40a.
[422] See S. Schechter, edit. Agadath Shir ha-Shirim (Cambridge, 1896), p. 18. Also, p. 61.
[423] T.B. Yebamoth 63a.
[424] M. Aboth 5, 24; T.B. Kiddushin 30a; T.B. Sanhedrin 76a.
[425] T.B. Kiddushin 41a.
[426] T.B. Yoma 13a forbids the high priest to have more than one wife. T.B. Yebamoth 65a prescribes: "A man must give his wife a divorce if she desires it on his taking an additional wife." Nevertheless, "A man may marry as many wives as he pleases". Idem.

cult[427]. Contraception was, for some situations, advocated[428]. But such freedom was in the view of the sages, in function of good marriages and a wholesome family life. Accordingly, we find the saying, "A man's home is his wife"[429].

Children were thought of as "entrusted" to their parents by God[430]. The Talmud reflects the intense longing for children which distinguished Oriental societies. Children were the future of the community[431]. "A childless person is accounted as dead"[432]. And, in the rabbinate this continuity had special religious significance: The child was both recipient and channel in the inheriting of the Torah[433].

The charge to keep alive the Torah accounted for a unique emphasis upon education as a dimension of domestic life. Early in the first century B.C. an attempt was made at creating a school system in Palestine, and a few years before the destruction of the Temple, Joshua ben Gamala carried out a comprehensive scheme[434]. The euphoric exaggeration of school statistics points to the pride of achievement[435]. Elementary schools taught Hebrew and the Pentateuch. Greek was taught, but interest in Greek philosophy was discouraged[436]. Hebrew literacy itself was considered of religious significance. The construction of Hebrew characters was given moral meaning[437]. Rabbinic writing abounds in advice on child rearing and educational psychology[438]. The teacher was held in reverence and, in some matters, the Halakhah gave him precedence over parents, "because the teacher brings the child to the life of the world to come"[439]. A significant legend gave a contemporary version of Israel's perennial struggle against hostile meighbors. It concludes: "'Tell us how we may successfully contend against the people of Israel'. He [a philosopher] answered: 'Go to their Synagogues and schools, and if you hear there the clamor of children rehearsing their lessons, you cannot prevail against them'"[440]. Clearly, in rabbinic thought, an essential element of man's destiny was building a family which would keep alive the Torah as mankind's divine heritage. This was how man would make God king in His world.

427 See, e.g., T.B. Yebamoth 63b. R. Akiba is reported to have argued, "He may divorce her even if he found another woman more beautiful than she". T.B. Gittin 9, 10. Josephus testifies to the freedom of divorce. Antiq. IV, 8, 23.

428 "A minor, a pregnant woman, and a nursing mother." T.B. Yebamoth 12b.

429 ביתו זו אשתו: "A man's home is his wife" (T.B. Yoma 1, 1). See also T.B. Shabbath 118b.

430 Yalkut Prov., par. 964.

431 T.B. Berakhoth 64a.

432 Gen. Rabbah 71.6.

433 See, e.g., T.B. Shabbath 127a; Gen. Rabbah 59.4; T.B. Berakhoth 21b.

434 T.B. Babah Bathra 21a.

435 E.g., T.B. Gittin 58a; T.B. Ketuboth 105a.

436 Lev. Rabbah 7. 3; T.B. Baba Kamma 82b; 83a; T.B. Megillah 9b; T.B. Peah 15c.

437 T.B. Shabbath 104a.

438 T.B. Shabbath 10b; Ex. Rabbah 1.1; T.B. Moed Katan 17a; T.B. Gittin 6b; T.B. Sukkah 46b; 56b; M. Aboth 4, 25; 4, 26; 5, 24; T.B. Baba Bathra 21a; Aboth de-R. Nathan 24; T.B. Erubin 54a and b; T.B. Hagigah 9b.

439 T.B. Baba Metzia 2, 11. See also M. Aboth 4, 15; T.B. Hagigah 76c.

440 Gen. Rabbah 65, 20.

b) Socio-Economic Life

The studious rabbi was engaged not only in his family but in that society which was the people of Israel. He functioned as jurist, judge, and successor of the prophets. He was concerned, then, with the whole life of the people. If the spiritual leaders of other peoples could disregard everyday matters as banal and not proper of man's true destiny, the rabbi could not. His writings show an involvement in every dimension of human existence.

Symptomatic of the seriousness accorded to social values was the rabbinic attitude to a man's right to a good name. The strongest language is reserved for the offense of slander — e.g., "Whoever speaks slander is as one who denies the fundamental principle [i.e., the existence of God]"; or, "Whoever speaks slander is deserving of being stoned to death"[441]. Serious, too, is the work by which one earns a livelihood. The Talmud glosses Deut. 30.19 in this way: "'Therefore choose life' — i.e., a handicraft"[442]. A legend describes Adam's satisfaction at being distinguished from the beast in the divine decree, "In the sweat of your face you shall eat bread" (Gen. 3.18)[443]. A *baraita* reads, "A blessing only alights upon the work of a man's hands"[444]. Wealth and servants should not remove labor from a man's life, nor from that of his wife, who is told, "Idleness leads to lewdness and to mental instability"[445].

The great number of texts on economic justice shows that the subject was of special concern. Offences are condemned. Speculating with money, resulting in the empoverishment of others, increasing the price of food by shrewd contrivance, giving false measure, lending on interest, holding back corn from the market — the perpetrators of such deeds are classed with blasphemers and hypocrites; God will never forget their work[446]. R. Judah (Amora of mid-2nd cen.) can speak for a majority of the rabbis, articulating a conscience highly attuned to social reality: "Most people are guilty of robbery, a minority of unchastity, and all of slander"[447]. We see no inclination to soften the attack on economic injustice. Cheating the public is grouped with murder and adultery as sins for which repentance was unacceptable — a hyperbole — because reparation was impossible[448]. Later tradition preserved a list of things that prevent repentance — i.e., blind the sinner to his sin; prominent was eating the plunder of the poor[449]. A saying had it that the first question to be asked at the heavenly tribunal

[441] T.B. Arakhin 15b. See also T.B. Pesahim 118a; M. Aboth 2, 15; Aboth de-R. Nathan 15.
[442] T.P. Peah 15c.
[443] T.B. Pesahim 118a.
[444] Tos. Berakhoth 8, 8,.
[445] T.B. Ketuboth 5, 5.
[446] Aboth de-R. Nathan 43b; T.B. Baba Bathra 90a.
[447] T.B. Hullin 89a; see also ibid. 91a.
[448] T.B. Baba Bathra 88b; T.B. Yebamoth 21a. For murder: T.B. Sanhedrin 7a. For adultery: T.B. Hagigah 9a and b; T.B. Yebamoth 22b.
[449] Schechter, p. 330—331, cites Maimonides, תשובה ch. 4.

would be, "Hast thou been honest in thy business transactions"[450]? The concern went beyond what is sometimes meant by humane; it regarded the fact that poverty was demoralizing and occasioned its victim to transgress God's law[451]. The rabbis held the authorities of a community responsible for its poor[452]. A quaint saying ran, "Not the mouse is the thief, but the hole [the ready-made occasion] is the thief"[453].

A secularized age may ask whether religious leaders were correct in governing "the everyday affairs" of their people[454], or whether the Halakhah did not sometimes reflect a utopianism[455]. The rabbis' notion of how religion related to the human was clearly different from that of other, and later, societies. Their notion of the function of law included, beyond that of other peoples, a portrayal of how a creature in the image of God related, in God's plan, to his fellowman. In this sense, the Halakhah constituted a reality principle[456]. Even when their frequent and severe stricture against lending at interest was thought of as impracticable, it represented a statement about the nature of the human community[457].

Of less than utopian vision were the Halakhoth regulating a slave-owner's deportment toward his slaves[458]. A Hebrew slave was conceded so many rights that the Talmud records a popular saying, "Whoever acquires a Hebrew slave acquires a master for himself"[459]. The lot of Gentile slaves under rabbinic masters was, according to law, very near the situation reported of the ancient world generally, though extreme brutality was forbidden[460]. Significantly, a rabbi asked, regarding his slave, "Did not He

[450] T.B. Shabbath 31a.

[451] T.B. Erubin 41b.

[452] T.B. Sotah 38b; T.P. Sotah 23d.

[453] T.B. Arakhin 30a.

[454] SIMON DUBNOV, History of the Jews from the Roman Empire to the Early Medieval Period, 6 vols., 4th rev. edit. (New York, 1967—69), III, 248, objects to rabbinic control of "everyday affairs that had no relation to religion".

[455] MOORE, II, 145—146, sees some impracticable provisions as in the tradition of the Deuteronomic law of war (Deut. 20), the septennial wiping out of all debts (Deut. 15, 1—11), and the law of the monarchy (Deut. 17.14). He explains (correctly, I think) that the scope of the Law was beyond the practicable; it was "a revelation of God's ideal for men's conduct and character" (p. 146).

[456] NEUSNER, Form and Meaning in Mishnah, p. 47, et passim.

[457] See, e.g., T.B. Baba Metzia 61b; 71a; Ex. Rabbah 31, 13.

[458] For details of a slave's existence, see S. KRAUSS, Talmudische Archäologie, 3 vols. (Leipzig, 1910—12), II, 83—100. E. URBACH, The Laws Regarding Slavery as a Source for Social History of the Second Temple, The Mishnah, and the Talmud, Papers of the Institute of Jewish Studies, 1 (London, 1964), 1—95.

[459] T.B. Kiddushin 20a. Regarding Hebrew slaves: T.B. Kiddushin 17a and b; 22b; Sifra to Lev. 25.39; Mekhilta on Lev. 25.39, 75a and b; ibid. on Ex. 21.6, 77b; Sifre on Deut. 15.12, par. 118, 99a.

[460] They were bought, sold, despised, flogged, unmourned, etc. See T.B. Kiddushin 1, 3; 22b; 49b; T.B. Baba Kamma 4, 5; 8, 3; T.B. Gittin 13a; 39b; 86a; 97a; T.B. Yebamoth 48b; T.B. Rosh Hashanah 1, 8; T.B. Hagigah 1.1; T.B. Berakhoth 3, 3; 7, 2; 45b; 47b; etc. The maming or killing of a slave was prohibited, as we read in Mekhilta to Ex. 21.20, 83a; ibid. on Ex. 21.26, 85a.

that made me in the womb make him[461]"? By virtue of the rabbinic doctrine that the entire Law was revealed simultaneously at Sinai, the phenomenon of slavery in the Rabbinate cannot be bypassed in an enquiry into rabbinic anthropology; for the Halakhoth regarding slavery cannot be viewed as an early stage in a progressive revelation. That one man could be another man's slave recalls us to the psychological truth discussed earlier, that man was not seen as holding an inviolable position in a metaphysical hierarchy of the world, but rather as a creature in between angels and beasts, moving up or down according to his conduct. More germane to the present argument, the rabbis did not evade this complex phenomenon which was deeply embedded in the larger civilization of which they were a part, but pronounced upon it. In so doing, they assuaged its human inferiority. They could not stand aloof from it, so deeply involved were they in the whole of the socio-economic order.

The exposition of the Torah involved the rabbis with all classes of society. The judgment they passed upon the people of the land was frequently severe in its disapproval. These *am ha-arez* were ignorant and unobservant, particularly of the precepts of ritual purity. Hillel had said, "No *am ha-arez* is pious"[462]. One cannot isolate such comments and thereby conclude that rabbinic appreciation of humanity did not include the lowly uneducated. Besides these harsh sayings, frankly preserved in tradition, one finds many admiring observations. In several places the scholars remind themselves that, though they would be inclined to assess their work as of greater value than the activity of peasants, they must hold the position that what gives value to human effort is "directing the mind to Heaven"[463]. There grew up among the sages a tradition of stories in which the *am ha-arez* are the teachers of virtue to their teachers[464]. This matter occasions the conclusion that, for all their prizing of study, the rabbis envisioned human perfection as a direct relatedness of man to God. As the goal of wisdom, this was accomplished, said Raba, through repentance and good deeds[465].

[461] Concerning acts of kindness towards his slave, R. Johanan said: הלא בבטן עושני עשהו. "Did not He that made me in the womb make him?" T.P. Baba Kamma 8, 4 (6a).

[462] M. Aboth 2, 5.

[463] T.B. Berakhoth 17a; for other applications, see T.B. Yoma 42a; T.B. Shebuoth 15a; T.B. Shabbath 96a. Jacob Neusner, History and Structure: The Case of Mishnah, p. 185, observes that for second-century rabbinism, "Uncleanness derives from intention and not *ex opere operato* from faulty association of material things". After A.D. 70 the Temple as pivot of a system of analogies was replaced in rabbinic thinking by the people itself: "Temple rules and sex rules and food rules form a single system of analogies . . . The system is made to depend upon the intention of ordinary people living commonplace lives" (Id.). The rabbis do not form a sect of the "Clean", like the Essene community, but include the *am ha-arez* within their system.

[464] T.B. Taanith 20a; Lev. Rabbah 9.3; Gen. Rabbah 32, 10.

[465] T.B. Berakhoth 17a, quoted from the version in MSS by Urbach, The Sages, Enc. Jud. 14, 646.

C. The Question of Asceticism

When discussing human destiny scholars of religion at times distinguish between a religious understanding which takes man's earthly career seriously and an ascetical-mystical understanding. "Ascetic" tendencies are contrasted to the affirmation of the world as good[466]. "The doctrine of asceticism" is set against faith in the created[467]. It is questionable whether such protean categories as asceticism and mysticism are useful in the description of a religious tradition. In the instance of rabbinic religion, the commonplace about the absence of these -isms is seriously confusing. In the rabbis' view of human life, was there no renunciation, no prudence, no moral realism, no acceptance of struggle? Nothing of the kind is, of course, meant. What is intended positively by the remark that the sages did not accept "asceticism" is what we have outlined regarding their attitude to marriage and involvement in the life of the community. What this remark tends to obscure is the vigorous presence of a complex of other attitudes which can reveal the sages' conception of the human lot. We must review these.

(1) The rabbis accepted a negative aspect in the law of holiness. "Be holy, for I am holy" (Lev. 11.44) was paraphrased in accord with the ambiguity of the word *kedushah*, which seems originally to have meant "separation": "As I am separated, so be ye separated"[468]. A withdrawal from all that was defiling cast no aspersion on the metaphysical goodness of creation. The motive for this renunciation lay in obedience.

(2) Everything seen as an auxiliary of the evil impulse was prudently resisted. Several proverbs attest to the conviction that luxury and plenty may endanger a man's soul[469]. The question about what was dangerous did not concern what was in itself good. One was to fear a small offense because "It becomes to him something permitted"[470]. The very notion of building

[466] Julius Guttmann, Philosophies of Judaism, p. 34, makes this contrast. It describes a Gnostic mentality, which rabbinism rejected.

[467] Urbach, I, 251. Urbach's denunciation of religious positions of which he disapproves gets in the way of a clear exposition of rabbinism here. He writes of "extreme asceticism, which means the abolition of sexual life", and then extrapolates a theology to go with the phenomenon. But, similar practices may be supported by radically dissimilar theologies. On this question, the author pushes forward with an orthodoxy more rigid than anything he is able to derive from the rabbis. See also I, 447, 478. In 'The Sages', Enc. Jud. 14.653, he writes that the ascetic practices of some Amoraim were "moderate", that they "were never carried to the extreme point of a total rejection of this world"; they never assumed "unnatural proportions". Further on one reads of "Two basic elements of extreme asceticism — total abstinence from sexual intercourse and a life of solitude". This theology of an abstraction is difficult to gainsay.

[468] וִהְיִיתֶם קְדֹשִׁים כִּי קָדוֹשׁ אָנִי: "Be holy, for I am holy" (Lev. 11.45). Schechter, p. 205, speaks about the uncertainty of the original meaning of *kedushah*.

[469] "A man does not enter upon rebellion but when he is full." Sifre 80b; Cf. 136a. A similar remark at T.B. Berakhoth 31c. Also, T.B. Hagigah 9b.

[470] T.B. Yoma 86b; also, 38b; Sifre Deut. par. 187; 108b; Sifre Num. par. 112; 33a; T.B. Sotah 3a: T.B. Berakhoth 29b.

"a fence around the Torah" grounded the policy of prudence[471]. In all this one observes the pursuit of a psychology of sin, or of the sinner as such.

(3) The numerous reflections upon the evil impulse manifest a lively awareness that there was a false-self which was to be denied. It was said, for instance, "A man should walk behind a lion rather than behind a woman"[472].

(4) Humility in the face of temptation was judged sheer moral realism. In the days of the Messiah, one reads, the evil impulse will be exposed to view. "To the righteous he will appear in the shape of a big mountain . . . ; in the eyes of the wicked he will resemble a thin hair"[473].

(5) A certain degree of psychological contrivance was thought necessary to avoid sin. Torah study was a "medicine"[474]; a fixed time was to be established for it[475]. Ways were plotted for opposing the evil impulse[476]. A clever ruse of R. Eliezer was, "Repent one day before your death"[477].

(6) Man's moral life was accepted as a struggle. The right path was difficult[478]. The evil impulse would always reassert itself[479]; it would not be killed until the coming of Messiah[480]. Yet, man was commanded to rule over it[481]. The picture drawn of the moral victories of the patriarchs and prophets was one of immense effort[482]. The evil impulse had to be goaded as a plough animal[483]. An alternative image was war[484].

(7) Necessary in this moral struggle was prayer. Man was to make efforts, but efficacy would come from God. A huge rock lay in the path, it was said; "Chip it off little by little until the hour comes when I will remove it altogether"[485].

(8) Suffering was to be borne courageously, both as atonement for sin and as proof of love. "There are chastenings which purge all the iniquities of man"[486].

The aggregate meaning of this catalogue of remarks is that the rabbinic understanding of what was required for the successful pursuit of human destiny included, essentially, a complex of negativities. Continually, turning to God involved turning away from something. In the rabbinic concept

[471] M. Anoth 1, 1.
[472] T.B. Berakhoth 61a. Similar sayings at M. Aboth 1, 5; 3, 17.
[473] T.B. Sukkah 52a; Cf. Gen. Rabbah 48, 11; 89, 1; Ex. Rabbah 41, 7; 46, 4; Num. Rabbah 17, 6; Deut. Rabbah 2, 80; 6, 14; Pesikta Rabbati (edit. Friedmann) 29a.
[474] Sifre Deut. par. 45; T.B. Kiddushin 30b.
[475] T.B. Shabbath 31a.
[476] T.B. Berakhoth 5a; T.B. Kiddushin 30b; T.B. Abodah Zarah 5b.
[477] T.B. Shabbath 153a.
[478] Sifre Deut. par. 53, 86a.
[479] Gen. Rabbah 54, 1; 70, 8; Aboth de-R. Nathan 16.
[480] T.B. Sukkah 52a. See n. 154, above.
[481] Gen. Rabbah 22, 6.
[482] Sifre 74a; Gen. Rabbah 87, 5; Lev. Rabbah 23, 11; further references given there.
[483] Lev. Rabbah 29, 17; Eccles. Rabbah 2, 11.
[484] T.B. Berakhoth 5a; Cf. Pesikta de-R. Kahana (edit. Buber) 158a.
[485] Pesikta de-R. Kahana (edit. Buber) 165a. Or, similarly, Num. Rabbah 15, 16.
[486] T.B. Berakhoth 5a.

of the evil impulse, one comes to see what is rejected as, not God's good world, but a drive lodged deep within the human self. All things are good, but in man's choosing all things may be erected into idols[487].

D. The Question of Mysticism

What we have seen of the rabbis' conviction of the necessity for striving and naysaying is simply the acceptance of the dictates of human intelligence in following the commands of the Torah. This has sometimes been called moral asceticism, to distinguish it from a striving which ambitions direct union with God — i. e., mystical asceticism. If in the formative generations of rabbinic Judaism, the sages had to distinguish their notion of the moral struggle from that of the Stoics, they had as well to make clear that their approach to God was not that of Gnostic mysticism. Knowing God and loving Him were not to be differentiated from "clinging to His ways"[488]. When the Torah was immersed in the world of Platonic ideas, the mystical religion of Philo resulted. The Law — for the rabbis, once-given at Sinai — was known, thought Philo, in mystical experience, as in the case of the prophets[489]. That rabbinic literature, to the contrary, is mistrusting of all that we call mysticism is a commonplace observation. The Mishnah placed severe restrictions upon discussion of those parts of the Bible most susceptible of mystical interpretation — Gen. 1.1–3, and Ezek. 1.4ff.[490]

The mysticism which SCHECHTER found to be excluded by the rabbis was linked in his mind to "antinomianism", "egotism", "quietism", "religious epicureanism", and "idle spirituality"[491]. Contemplating the divine

[487] If this comprehension of a negative dimension in human striving is not asceticism, then it were well to relinquish that category in discussions of rabbinic theology, for to those who coined the expression, this is what was envisioned. See J. DEGUIBERT et al., Ascèse, ascétisme, DSAM I (1932—37), cols. 936—1010. EMERO STIEGMAN, The Language of Asceticsim in St. Bernard of Clairvaux's Sermones super Cantica Canticorum (Ann. Arbor, Mich: University Microfilms, 1973), examines the theology behind the monastic practices coinciding with practices noted in URBACH's observations (n. 467, above).

[488] See, e.g., Deut. 11.22: לָלֶכֶת בְּכָל־דְּרָכָיו וּלְדָבְקָה־בוֹ. "To walk in His ways and to cleave to Him." Rashi comments, ad locum: ולרבקה בו. וכי אפשר להדבק בשכינה, אלא כל המשיא בתו לת״ח והעושה פרקמטיא לת״ח והמהנה ת״ח מנכסיו מעלה עליו הכתוב כאלו מתדבק בשכינהסר) [כתובות קי״א ב׳]. "'To walk in all His ways': He is compassionate, be thou compassionate; He acts kindly, do thou act kindly." See also Sifre 74a; T.B. Ketuboth 111b.

[489] Philo, Quis rerum divinarum heres sit, par. 258—265. De vita comtemplativa sees an organic mystical meaning for all the Torah. See WOLFSON, Philo, II, 22ff., 48ff.

[490] M. Hagigah 2, 1; M. Megillah 4, 10.

[491] SCHECHTER, pp. 78—79. "His [the mystic's] tendency toward antinomianism, and to regard law and works as beneath him, is also a sad historic *fact*" (p. 78). Cf. the conclusion of GERSHOM G. SCHOLEM, Major Trends in Jewish Mysticism, 3rd revised edit. (New York, 1971), p. 6: "As EVELYN UNDERHILL has rightly pointed out, the prevailing conception of the mystic as a religious anarchist who owes no allegience to his religion finds little support in *fact*." (Emphasis added in both citations.)

glory, he said, was considered the reward of the next world, while this world was understood as one of activity[492]. On one hand, little more than confusion can be brought to the rabbinic vision of things by excluding "mysticism" from it; this is a notion of indeterminate content[493]. On the other hand, there is sufficient clarity about the kind of religion the rabbis disapproved of. "Whoever gives his mind to four things", we read, "it were better for him if he had not come into the world: What is above? What is beneath? What was before time? And, what will be hereafter?" The Mishnah passage immediately continues with a remark essential to its meaning: "And whosoever takes no thought for the honor of his Maker, it were better for him if he had not come into the world"[494]. The "four things" surround man's here-and-now and exclude it from his thoughts. Ben Sira had made the point explicit (3.21–22): "Seek not what is too difficult for you... Reflect upon what has been assigned to you." One who reflects, instead, upon questions that do not concern learning and doing God's will "takes no thought for the honor of his Maker". That is the hazard of "idle spirituality". Should it be objected that a contemplative orientation is not inevitably idle and self-indulgent, then a social dimension will have to be acknowledged in the rabbis' cautions. During the classical period of rabbinism, when, in a succession of tragic circumstances, a communal way of living and believing was being worked out, it would have been thought a compounding of the tragedy if any of Israel's gifted spirits had followed an inclination to withdraw into a spiritual world unaffected by dire circumstances. The need was for builders of the community.

A mystic trend which did exist among the Tannaim concerned itself with the Work of the Chariot (*Merkabah*), Ezek. 1.4ff. The tradition relating to it was restrained and reserved[495]. Nevertheless, that it did exist and that a necessity should have been found in the Halakhah formally to restrict its spread should qualify doctrinaire stands which would rule out any "mysticism" in the rabbinate. Actually, there has been a tension in Judaism, from early rabbinic times, between the analytic and socially engaged tradition, which clearly prevails in the rabbinate, and a more contemplative one. The two are not incompatible[496]. In sum, the rabbis did not believe man

[492] On contemplating glory, T.B. Berakhoth 17a and parallels.

[493] Opposing a very common usage, GERSHOM SCHOLEM, Major Trends in Jewish Mysticism, pp. 5—6, states: "There is no such thing as mysticism in the abstract... There is no mysticism as such, there is only the mysticism of a particular religious system." It would be enough to reflect upon the necessary differences between the mysticisms of Gnostic cosmic dualism, pantheistic monism, and a biblical dualism of Creator and creature to understand the truth of this remark. Other profound differences, within this grouping, abound. To make mysticism essentially Gnostic (as an example) is not to know concretely the text of those whom some traditions call mystics. This is arbitrary.

[494] M. Hagigah 2, 1.

[495] See GERSHOM SCHOLEM, Jewish Gnosticism, Merkabah Mysticism, and Talmudic Tradition (New York, 1960). EPHRAIM E. URBACH, Ha-Masorot al Torat ha-sod bi-tequfat ha-Tannaim [The Traditions about Merkabah Mysticism in the Tannaitic Period], Studies in Mysticism and Religion, presented to Gershom G. Scholem (Jerusalem, 1969), pp. 1—28.

[496] This is the judgment of GERSHOM SCHOLEM, On Jews and Judaism in Crisis (New York, 1977).

was made to contemplate the vision of eternity in this world; but no statement of their views should overlook elements in continuity with an ascetical-contemplative Judaism which developed in a later era[497].

The tension between learning and action was never resolved at a systematic level. Both sides of the issue are affirmed: Torah study is to be valued above every activity; and, the objective in Torah study is to act out the Law. The rabbinic pursuit of family ideals and of socio-economic justice, however, manifest an emphasis on living the life of the community. Though there was a highly developed, however unsystematic, type of moral asceticism, it was not directed to the experience of union with God.

4. Human Solidarity

"Man", says the Mishnah, "was created a single individual . . . for the sake of peace among men, that one should not say to his fellow: My father was greater than yours"[498]. The development of the thought asserts two truths — the wonder of individuality in every human being and the radical unity of the human race. The theme is well worked in the Talmud, not as village philosophy but as a treasured biblical insight. The phenomenon of human society is celebrated: How much labor Adam must have expended to prepare food and clothing, ploughing, threshing, shearing, spinning! But, "all artisans attend and come to the door of my house, and I get up and find all these things before me"[499]. The studious sages reflected that all classes were interdependent: "If the body is taken away, of what use is the head?"[500] "If the house has fallen, woe to the windows!"[501]

In consequence of this unity the sin of one man injures all men. R. Simeon ben Yohai (end of 3rd cen.) is credited with this striking figure: Several men were sitting in a boat when one of them began boring a hole beneath him. "What business is it of yours", he asked them; "am I not boring under myself?"[502] An offense against any man is an injury to God. The formula in the case of asking forgiveness for damage done a man who died before satisfaction could be given him was, "I have sinned against the Lord, the God of Israel, and against the man I have injured"[503]. The summation of the Law, Hillel had said, was "Do not do to your fellowman what you hate to have done to you"[504]. And in another place, positively, "If I am not for myself, who will be for me? And being for myself, what am

497 J. GUTTMANN, Philosophies of Judaism, p. 36.
498 M. Sanhedrin 4.5.
499 T.B. Berakhoth 58a.
500 Gen. Rabbah 100, 9.
501 Ex. Rabbah 26, 2.
502 Lev. Rabbah 4, 6.
503 T.B. Yoma 87a; M. Baba Kamma 8, 7.
504 T.B. Shabbath 31a. R. Akiba later quotes Lev. 19.18: "Thou shalt love thy neighbor as thyself." Sifra ad loc.; T.P. Nedarim 41c; Gen. 24, with THEODOR's note.

I?"[505] A man should serve the community, and without self-seeking motives. "Where there are no men strive to be a man", Hillel said; and the Gemara commented, "Infer from this that where there is a man, do not be a man"[506]. R. Gamaliel (ca. 220) said, "Let all who occupy themselves with the affairs of the community do so in the name of heaven"[507]. And, the service of the community was not to be performed in sublime disregard of human feelings; there was virtue in a certain popularity. "He in whom the spirit of mankind finds pleasure, in him the spirit of God finds pleasure"[508]. Government as such was esteemed. "Pray for the peace of the ruling powers", said R. Hananiah (probably before A.D. 70), "since but for the fear of it men would swallow each other alive"[509]. Among reflections upon government was, "We must not appoint a leader over the community without first consulting them"[510]. All authority was from God. "Even the superintendent of wells is appointed by Heaven"[511]. And, significantly, forever after: "The law of the land is the law"[512]. Even so, "Seek no intimacy with the ruling power"[513]. As for the powerful of the earth, "They stand not by a man in the hour of his need"[514]. Some of these reflections suggest the special historical situation of the Jewish people in and after the disasters of the first century; but, they manifest, above all, a religious comprehension of human solidarity. The unity and societal character of humanity were God's doing. The rabbis celebrated these truths.

A. Unity of the Chosen People

Within this human unity, God had constituted Israel a special unit (see above, pp. 536–37). She was so much a composite personality, rather than an aggregation, that it was difficult in places to tell whether the Bible spoke to Israel or the individual Israelite. The Talmud instructed the elect to address God explicitly from within the whole people: "Always should a man associate himself with the community when praying. How should he pray? 'May it be Thy will, O Lord our God, to conduct us in peace, etc.'"[515]. The very language of the Mishnah — so stylized as to be virtually a code —

[505] M. Aboth 1, 14.

[506] Hillel's saying, M. Aboth 2, 6: וּבִמְקוֹם שֶׁאֵין אֲנָשִׁים, הִשְׁתַּדֵּל לִהְיוֹת אִישׁ: "Where there are no men, strive to be a man" (M. Aboth 2, 5). Comment upon Hillel's saying is found at T.B. Berakhoth 63a.

[507] M. Aboth 2, 2.

[508] M. Aboth 3, 11. See also T.P. Shekalim 47c, where Prov. 3.4 is cited: "So that thou shalt find favor and understanding in the sight of God and man."

[509] M. Aboth 3, 2. See also T.B. Abodah Zarah 4a.

[510] T.B. Berakhoth 55a.

[511] T.B. Baba Bathra 91b. See also Gen. Rabbah 94, 9; T.B. Sanhedrin 49a; T.B. Zebahim 102a.

[512] T.B. Baba Kamma 113a.

[513] M. Aboth 1, 10.

[514] M. Aboth 2, 3.

[515] T.B. Berakhoth 29b.

operated as a medium of Jewish unity, including few and excluding many[516].

Israel's unity stemmed from the patriarchs. She was not merely descended from them but had been constituted a covenantal people in view of their merits. This is how the rabbis interpreted the words, "He shows mercy unto the thousandth generation of those that love Him" (Ex. 20.6; cf. Deut. 7.9)[517]. The "merits of the Fathers" is much spoken of in rabbinic writings[518]. The Fathers signify, ordinarily, Abraham, Isaac, and Jacob[519]. Because of the merits of the Fathers Israel was delivered out of Egypt[520], and Moses was allowed to ascend Mount Sinai[521]. After Israel's idolatry no prayer of Moses during forty days and forty nights was efficacious, until he said, "Remember Abraham, Isaac, and Jacob, Thy servants" (Ex. 32.13)[522].

From the time of Shemaya and Abtalyon there was disagreement among the rabbis on many elements of this theme. Shemaya held that the Red Sea was parted because of Abraham's faith, while Abtalyon said it was because of the people's faith[523]. The same issue divided R. Joshua and R. Eleazar of Modiim in interpreting the story of the manna[524]. The School of R. Ishmael argued that one could not conclude, from the fact that the faithless gentiles survived by the merit of Noah (Gen. 8.22), that Israel would live because of the merits of the patriarchs; for, "It is the reward of the commandment that gives you life, not the merit of the patriarchs"[525]. This position did not altogether distinguish the School of R. Ishmael from that of R. Akiba, for many in both schools held it, while others insisted upon the merit of the patriarchs, and still others fused both conclusions[526]. At issue was the necessity of affirming both personal responsibility and the free gift of God; and characteristic of the rabbinic approach to the question was the insistence that the individual be strictly associated

516 NEUSNER, Form and Meaning in Mishnah, p. 32.

517 Mekhilta, Bahodesh 6 (edit. FRIEDMANN f. 68b; edit. WEISS f. 75b).

518 זכות אבות *zachuth aboth*: virtue, or merits, of the Fathers. *Zachuth* is not a biblical usage. In rabbinic literature, sometimes as a legal term, lit. acquittal — e.g., T.B. Baba Metzia 107b; M. Baba Metzia 1, 4; M. Sanhedrin 4, 1. See BACHER, Die exegetische Terminologie der jüd. Traditionsliteratur. 2 Vols. (Leipzig, 1899—1905), I, 50. At times, worthiness — e.g., T.B. Sotah 17a; T.B. Hagigah 5b. In our sense, merit or virtue — e.g., T.P. Kiddushin 61d; Pesikta Rabbati (edit. FRIEDMANN), 38b. See MOORE III, 164, n. 249, for a brief discussion of the terms.

519 "They call not Fathers but the three, and they call not mothers but four [Sarah, Rebecca, Rachel, and Leah]." T.B. Berakhoth 16b. There is a reference at times also to the "merits of the Mothers"—e.g., Sifra 112c; T.P. Sanhedrin 27d; Lev. Rabbah 36, 8; Cant. Rabbah 2, 9.

520 Ex. Rabbah 1, 36; Mekhilta 48a.

521 Gen. Rabbah 28, 1 and 2.

522 T.B. Shabbath 42z; cf. Ex. Rabbah 44, 1.

523 Mekhilta de-R. Ishmael, Massekhta de-Wa-Yehi, 3, p. 99.

524 Mekhilta de-R. Ishmael, Massekhta de-Wa-Yissa, 2, p. 160.

525 Midrasch Tannim, edit. D. HOFFMANN (Berlin, 1909), Mekhilta to Deut., p. 62. Cited by URBACH, I, 497; II, 908, n. 56.

526 URBACH. I. 497—498. For a discrimination of various positions on this question and their historical evolution, see URBACH, I, 258, 496—508.

to the nation. One way of eliminating the threat to full responsibility was to indicate that the merit of the Fathers had ceased sometime before King Hezekiah[527].

Motifs in the merit-of-the-Fathers theme were the merit of every man's ancestors[528], the merit of pious contemporaries[529], and the merit of a pious posterity[530]. What one man did, for good or ill, affected the lot of all the nation. Despite its theological problems, the theme offered a way of maintaining consciousness of the historical continuity of a people and of the solidarity of the elect.

B. Evolution of the Individual

The strong feeling of Israel's unity is complemented in rabbinic literature by a growing sense of individuality. One can observe parallels to Hellenistic individualism in Koheleth (mid 3rd cen. B.C.) and Ben Sira[531]. Gradually the individual teacher emerged and received a following. His students quoted him by name as an authoritative tradent of doctrine, in a chain going back to Moses, very much in the manner of the Greek philosophical schools and Roman law schools[532]. The dialectical form of instruction, with questions and their solutions, was a parallel to the tradition of Greek rhetorical schools[533]. These schools affected also Jewish exegetical methods from late in the first century B.C.[534] But, quite aside from Hellenistic influence, a certain individualism is a normal development of the religion of Israel. There is a growing individuality observable in Jeremiah and Ezekiel[535]. In Ezekiel, for example, the prophetic doctrine of retribution, and therefore of repentance, was individualized[536]. As the older idea of a

[527] The time was disputed. See T.B. Shabbath 55a; T.P. Sanhedrin 27d; Lev. Rabbah 39e.

[528] M. Eduyoth 2, 9; cf. Tos. Eduyoth p. 456; Tos. Sanhedrin 4, 32; T.P. Kiddushin 61a, 63c and references.

[529] "Israel is like one body and one soul ... If one of them sins they are all punished." Mekhilta de-R. Simon, p. 95. Cf. Lev. Rabbah 4, 6.

[530] There are instances of prayers offered for the dead. See Gen. Rabbah 98, 2, with references; T.B. Hagigah 15b; T.B. Sotah 10b; T.B. Makkoth 11b. Schechter, p. 198, however, notes that this doctrine did not take root in Jewish consciousness.

[531] See Israel Lévi, L'Ecclésiastique, 2 vols., BEHESR, 10.1, 2 (Paris, 1898—1901), II, lxxxiiiff. R. Pautrel, Ben Sira et le Stoïcisme, RSR, 51 (1963), 535—549, at p. 535. For a trenchant limiting of Hellenistic influence upon Koheleth, see J. Guttmann, Philosophies of Judaism, pp. 18—20.

[532] See E. Bickerman, La Chaîne de la Tradition Pharisienne, RB, 59 (1952), 44—54, passim. J. Neusner, The Rabbinic Traditions about the Parisees before 70, I, 24—183.

[533] See M. Hadas, Hellenistic Culture: Fusion and Diffusion (New York, 1959), pp. 79ff. D. Daube, The New Testament and Rabbinic Judaism (London, 1956), pp. 151ff.

[534] D. Daube, Rabbinic Methods of Interpretation and Hellenistic Rhetoric, HUCA, 22 (1949), 239—264, finds Hellenistic parallels, for example, to Hillel's seven norms of interpretation. R. Meyer, Hellenistisches, p. 81ff.

[535] Moore I, 113ff., 501; 509, 520; II, 248ff., 292.

[536] E.g., "If the wicked man turn away from all his sins that he hath committed, and keep all my statutes ... he shall surely live." Ezek. 18.21.

common fate for all the dead in Sheol gave place to a belief in the separation of the righteous and the wicked at death and to a resurrection of the dead, repentance in a scheme of personal "salvation" was added to the theme of national deliverance[537]. After A.D. 70 more personal forms of atonement replaced the sacrificial cult of the temple[538]. R. Johanan ben Zakkai consoled a disciple weeping over the loss: "We have an atonement which is just as good — namely, deeds of mercy"[539]. The Diaspora condition threw all upon more individual resources than had been called upon previously. In all this, however, the new awareness does not supplant the older feeling of human solidarity and of the unity of the people, as the documentation of these themes in the preceding sections should make clear.

C. Election as Destiny

The two-sided truth that all men are one and that Israel is one becomes, when relating man to God, a problem. Rabbinic literature stated it by way of wonderment over the seeming redundancy of expressions like, "The Lord our God, the Lord is One" (Deut. 6.4; cf. Ex. 34.23; 2 Kings 21.12): "Before the Lord God, the God of Israel" (Ex. 34.23) — Why is this stated? Has it not already been said, "Before the Lord God?" The reflection ends: "I am the God of all people; nevertheless, I have conferred my name specifically on Israel"[540]. Even after the dispersion, the Jews were in their own minds and before Roman law, not followers of a special religion, but members of a nation[541]. The preservation of this nation was a prerequisite for the eventual reign of God over all mankind. The rabbis understood Israel's bearing of the name of God as indication of her special function — bringing recognition of her God to all humanity. Her election represented her destiny. Were the nation to become exclusivist and lose its universalizing vision, it would frustrate the divine plan. Was the rabbinic attitude to proselytism, specifically, in keeping with this conception?

It is a fact that the Diaspora spread Israel's faith throughout the Empire[542]. But with the two wars against Rome, and the rise of Christianity,

537 Moore I, 502; II, 94ff.

538 See E. Bickerman, From Ezra to the Last of the Maccabees: Foundations of Post-biblical Judaism (New York, 1962), pp. 68ff., on the complex significance of the temple in the nation.

539 Aboth de-R. Nathan 4, 5. Bacher, Tannaiten, I, 39.

540 אלהים אני לכל באי העולם, אף על פי כן לא ייחדתי שמי, אלא על עמי ישראל. "I am the God of all people; nevertheless, I have conferred my name specifically on Israel." Mekhilta de-R. Ishmael, Mishpatim, p. 334, and parallels noted there.

541 For the anomalous treatment of Jews by the Emperors and in Roman law, see J. Juster, Les Juifs dans l'empire Romain, leur condition juridique, économique et sociale, 2 vols. (Paris, 1914), II, 20; cf. I, 416. Jewish religious law was accepted by Rome as civil law, their religious leader as civil leader. Even after A.D. 70 they were allowed to levy taxes. Also see A. M. Rabello, The Legal Condition of the Jews in the Roman Empire, in: ANRW vol. II 13, edit. H. Temporini (Berlin—New York, 1979f.).

542 S. Liebermann, How Much Greek in Jewish Palestine?, in: edit. A. Altmann, pp. 68—90. B. J. Bamberger, Proselytism in the Talmudic Period (Cincinnati, 1939).

hardships arose which curtailed the rabbis' efforts to reach out to the stranger while protecting the integrity of a people[543]. What remained was the fundamental belief that all men must be brought to accept the kingdom by becoming part of this people. R. Eleazar (ca. 260) said: "The Holy One, blessed be He, exiled Israel among the nations only to the end that proselytes might join them, as it is said, 'And I will sow her unto Me in the land'" (Hos. 2.25)[544]. Later, in the name of R. Judah the Patriarch, it was said: "There is a kind of pigeon that is fed and its companions smell her and come to her cote. So, too, when the elder sits and delivers his exposition, many proselytes are converted[545]. To encourage an initiative toward the Gentiles it was said: "Beloved are proselytes, for they are everywhere given the same disignations as Israel"[546].

Side by side with the many expressions of this kind must be placed the few which seem to contradict them. R. Johanan (ca. 280) expressed esteem for the Gentiles but said, "A Gentile who studies the Torah is deserving of death ... It is an inheritance for us but not for them"[547]. R. Isaac Nappaha (ca. 280) said, "Evil after evil shall come upon those who accept proselytes"[548]. It must be remembered that the Christians claimed to have inherited the Scriptures and the birthright of Israel. There seemed to be some anxiety in rabbis like Johanan and Isaac lest confusion enter regarding who was a convert to the religion of the patriarchs[549]. It seems R. Johanan did not want Christians to study the Scriptures. R. Isaac's saying must be placed in the context of his bitter struggle against the usurpative claims of the new Church[550]. Later rabbis contradicted the saying[551]. There is no evidence of the development of a more exclusivist attitude among the Amoraim. At the end of the fourth century R. Phinehas said, "The Holy One, blessed be He, said to Israel: 'If you will not declare my Godhead among the nations of the world, I shall exact retribution from you'"[552]. R. Ashi (d. 427) lamented the stubbornness of the inhabitants of

543 HENGEL, I, 313, concludes, "The almost complete fusion of religion and nationalism ... prevented any assimilation ... A universal missionary consciousness could not really develop freely in the face of this elemental impulse toward national self-preservation". The rabbinic sayings which I gather, below, tend to qualify this conclusion severely.

544 T.B. Pesahim 87b. See also Gen. Rabbah 39, 14, p. 378.

545 Cant. Rabbah 4, 1. This dates from the 7th century or later.

546 Mekhilta on Deut. 10.18, p. 312. Also, Sifre Num. par. 80, p. 76.

547 T.B. Sanhedrin 59a. On R. Johanan's esteem for Gentiles: "Whoever says a wise thing among the nations of the world is called a sage" (T.B. Megillah 16a). "Gentiles outside Eretz-Israel are not idolaters; they are merely keeping to their ancestral customs" (T.B. Hullin 13b).

548 T.B. Yebamoth 109b.

549 J. JUSTER, Les Juifs dans l'empire Romain, I, 254ff., notes that with the edict of toleration (ca. A.D. 140) proselytism was virtually forbidden, for only Jews were allowed to be circumcized. But, the Roman authorities did not enforce this.

550 URBACH I, 551; II, 937, nn. 6 and 7, citing Cant. Rabbah 1, 5—6; Lev. Rabbah 5, 7, p. 120; Esther Rabbah 1, 2.

551 See, e.g., R. Berechiah (ca. 340) in Ex. Rabbah 19, 4; 27, 2.

552 Lev. Rabbah 6, 5, p. 142.

his city, "For they see the glory of the Torah twice a year and not one of them is converted"[553].

In the rabbinic concept of human destiny all men as children of Adam were to accept God's reign, led by the winning example of a faithful Israel. In the end all resistence would be broken down as the kingdom of Israel would be restored and enlarged to embrace mankind.

5. The End of History and Beyond

A man's projection of the conclusion of humanity's career can represent his conception of what is ultimately fitting to human nature and destiny. A complex notion of the human condition may be understood in the inevitably simple lines of its dramatic resolution. As one attempts, however, to gather an account of the end which is representative of the rabbis, one is frustrated, not only by a diversity of versions, but by a multiplicity of elements in each of them. The angels and demons, the great battle and the cosmic cataclysm, the vast other worlds assigned to the good and to the wicked — most of the seemingly Zoroastrian machinery which one finds in apocalyptic literature, beginning with the Book of Daniel, are found in rabbinic accounts[554]. Even though rabbinic conceptions are in accord with later apocalypses and many rabbis show a religious temperament close to that of the apocryphal authors, and all of them share the hope in hard times which stimulated these writings, still at the surface rabbinism ignores them. One must distinguish between items consciously or unconsciously borrowed and the theological intention which deploys them. In rabbinic literature, through the diversity and multiplicity we have mentioned, one detects an altogether clear and simple theology of the end: First, human history will conclude with the visible reign of God over all mankind, a consummation brought about through the total triumph of a restored Israel. Second, God will, in the end, requite every man according to his deeds. With this, of course, the area left for disagreement encloses ideas of considerable significance. The rabbis do not seem to have thought it essential to achieve consensus about the scenario of the end, nor even about the meaning of the terms commonly used for the subject. But, if we read the variegated perimeter of their eschatology with reference to the center, we shall not be confused.

553 T.B. Berakhoth 17b. SCHÜRER—VERMES—MILLAR, op. cit., p. 556, regarding the period following A.D. 135: "Jews and Gentiles now joined forces to ensure that the gulf between them remained deep." On the contrary, the rabbis did not in principle desist from proselytising, though in fact the difficulties were overwhelming.

554 For the various writings collected under the name of Enoch, for Fourth Esdras and the Apocalypse of Baruch, see R. H. CHARLES, edit., The Apocrypha and Pseudepigrapha of the Old Testament in English, with introductions and critical and explanatory notes to the several books, 2 vols. 4th edit. (Oxford, 1913).

Many rabbinic utterances about the end are close to passages in Scripture which treat of *ge'ula*, "redemption"[555]. The concept of *ge'ula*, however, is relatively amorphous and gives rise to further terminology, some of which is not biblical. The Jewish sages speak of "the end of days", "end", "days of the Messiah", "resurrection of the dead", "world to come", "future to come" and "new world"[556]. Two eschatological schemata may be discerned. There is an early stage, beginning probably in Daniel's vision and presenting the national hope in eschatological form — judgment upon the wicked and resurrection of the righteous. The Days of the Messiah are represented as the final period of history and called also the World to Come or the Future[557]. In this scheme, the great feast of Leviathan and an idyllic picture of the land are set in the World to Come[558]. A later phase, instead, parallels apocalypses from the end of the first century, where a clearer division is made between the messianic age of Israel and the eschatological phenomena which come after it — the General Resurrection, the Last Judgment, and the World to Come (or the Future)[559]. Utopian projections, in this scheme, regard the Days of the Messiah, before the World to Come. "This World" is sharply distinguished from the "World to Come" ("Future to Come", at times "The Future")[560].

Again, something of the difficulty in rabbinic sayings about the end was present already in the utterances of the prophets, where "the end of days" or "the day of the Lord" is alternately the time of the perfection of the world and of its destruction. Men would be liberated from wickedness, from catastrophe and war, and the spirit of the Lord would be poured upon all flesh (Isa. 4.2–6; 11.6–9; Joel 3.1–4). But "the day of the Lord" would bring darkness and gloom; earth would again be void and without form (Zeph. 1.15; Jer. 4.23). Rabbinic sayings that speak of perfection and destruction address themselves to the ultimate manifestation of that two-sided reality of the visible kingdom of God — its national and its universal dimensions. That God may be king over all, what is unfit will be destroyed. That God may keep His promise to Israel, making her the kernel of His universal reign, her kingdom will be perfected.

555 גאולה, *ge'ula* redemption; from גאל *ga'al* to redeem.

556 Urbach I, 649, M. Zobel, Gottes Gesalbter, der Messias und die Messianische Zeit in Talmud und Midrasch (Berlin, 1938).

557 "World to Come" is from Enoch 71.15.

558 E.g., T.B. Baba Bathra 74b; ibid. 122a; T.B. Ketuboth 111b.

559 E.g., T.B. Zebahim 118b; Sifre Deut. par. 47 (edit. Friedmann f. 83a).

560 עולם הזה *'olam ha-zeh*, "this age" (epoch, world). עולם הבאה *'olam ha-ba*, "coming age" (epoch, world). S. Sandmel, Reflections on the Problem of Theology for Jews, p. 107, speaks of eschatology as "what is to happen within history at the end of history", as distinguished from "a non-historical transcending of history". But, unless one argues from a metaphysical position, according to which the time-bound creature is a priori incapable of transcending history — an improbable thought to attribute to the rabbis — it is difficult to see how the second scheme of eschatology described above purports to represent anything other than an age beyond the last age of history.

A second theological tension is represented in images of the end. The two plans for retribution — one in the messianic age, the other after a universal judgment — meet the necessity of conceiving Israel as a people that will be redeemed together and of acknowledging the requital of the individual according to his personal conduct.

Clearly, then, rabbinic eschatology is in large part a derived doctrine. Its meanings derive from those central ideas which establish man's relationship to God now, in the present order of the world. Its particulars can be understood only within a pattern of theological concepts. We must now review, in abbreviated form, some salient particulars as they occur in the sayings of the rabbis.

A. The Angel of Death

"They say concerning the angel of death", one reads in the Talmud, "that he is full of eyes all over"[561]. A midrash on Ps. 11 speaks of the angel Dumah: "When a person's time comes to depart from the world, the angel of death appears to take away his soul (*neshamah*) . . . Immediately Dumah conducts him to the court of death among the spirits. If he has been righteous, it is proclaimed before him . . . and he proceeds stage by stage until he beholds the *Shekhinah*"[562]. As we have seen, rabbinic angelology serves to describe God's action in creation. God is sovereign over death. Here, in imagery, we are told that at death the soul leaves the body, and that man is judged immediately upon dying. "O my God", a rabbi prays, "the soul which Thou hast given me is pure; Thou didst create is within me, and Thou wilt take it from me, but wilt restore it unto me hereafter. So long as the soul is within me, I will give thanks unto Thee, O Lord my God"[563]. The dead are removed from the possibility of joining Israel's praise of God[564].

B. Messianic Hope

The Talmud has hundreds of allusions to the Messiah and his mission[565]. The complex phenomenon spoken of regards what one may call both the national, this-worldly form of Jewish expectation and the eschatological

[561] T.B. Abodah Zarah 20b.

[562] Midrash to Ps. 11.7, 51b, 52a.

[563] T.B. Berakhoth 60b.

[564] T.B. Shabbath 30a.

[565] For comprehensive approaches to the messianic question, see J. Klausner, The Messianic Idea in Israel (New York, 1955); G. Scholem, Zum Verständnis der messianischen Idee im Judentum, Eranos-Jahrbuch, 28, 1959 (Zürich, 1960), pp. 193—239; reprinted in Id., Judaica (Frankfurt a.M., 1963), pp. 1—74, Bibliothek Suhrkamp, Bd. 106. M. Zobel, Gottes Gesalbter, for a good assembling of sources.

form. Reflection upon the ultimate triumph of Israel was made necessary by the scandal of her oppression under the successive forms of heathen empire. The humiliation of the Jews was a disturbing representation of the defeat of God Himself and of the indefinite postponement of His reign[566]. But, there would come a time when all men would wish to be part of Israel, seeing her glory — "But we will not accept any of them; for, there is a saying of the rabbis, 'No proselytes are to be accepted in the days of the Messiah'"[567]. Impure motivation is to be rejected. Either before or during the great battle led by the Messiah, all sinners in Israel would be killed (Amos 9.10)[568]. The Messiah's victory would usher in a restoration and augmentation of Israel's golden age. Here imagination ran riot. With the return of the people to the Land of Israel its fertility would be phenomenal. "There will not be a grape that will not yield thirty measures of wine"[569]. "Grain will be produced after fifteen days and trees will grow fruit after one month"[570]. Or, "Women will bear children daily and trees will produce fruit daily"[571]. There would be miracles to eclipse those of the escape from Egypt[572]. The utopean vision produced a reaction in some, who taught that man would be heir to various ills until he departed this life: "There is no difference between this world and the days of the Messiah except the servitude of the heathen kingdoms alone; as it is said, 'For the poor shall never cease out of the land' (Deut. 15.11)"[573].

Many sayings attempt to identify the Messiah. The Tannaim made his name one of the things that existed before the creation of the world[574]. Some authorities said he would be David[545]. Some, Hezekiah[576]. Most accepted that Scripture indicated a descendent of the Davidic line. Josephus reports that every now and then someone claimed to be the Messiah[577]. When R. Akiba proclaimed Bar Kochba the Messiah, R. Jochanan ben Torta remarked, "Akiba, grass will grow in your cheeks and still the son of David will not have come"[578]. Nothing in Tannaitic sources suggests that

[566] מלכות שמים *Malkut Shamayim:* Kingdom of Heaven. For references to *Malkut Shamayim* in this vein, see STRACK-BILLERBECK, Kommentar, I. 172ff.

[567] T.B. Abodah Zarah 3b.

[568] See Cant. Rabbah on 2.13 (edit. Vilna f. 17b); Pesikta Rabbati c. 15 (edit. FRIEDMANN f. 74a, 75a); ibid. c. 35 (f. 161a): Ex. Rabbah 14, 3.

[569] T.B. Ketuboth 111b.

[570] T.P. Taanith 64a.

[571] T.B. Shabbath 30b.

[572] T.B. Berakhoth 12b; Mekhilta Bo 7 (edit. FRIEDMANN f. 7b; edit. WEISS 9b); Mekhilta Beshallah (edit. FRIEDMANN f. 25a; edit. WEISS f. 29b—30a).

[573] T.B. Berakhoth 34b.

[574] Note Ps. 72.17: "His name is eternal; before the sun his name flourished". T.B. Pesahim 54a. Later, Pesikta Rabbati 152b.

[575] T.P. Berakhoth 5a; Lament. Rabbah 1, 51.

[576] R. Johanan ben Zakkai in T.B. Berakhoth 28b. Unique is the view of a certain R. Hillel: "Israel has no Messiah; they enjoyed him in the days of Hezekiah" (T.B. Sanhedrin 98b, 99a).

[577] Antiq. XX, 5, 1; 8, 6.

[578] T.P. Taanith 68d.

the Messiah himself existed before the world or that he was superhuman[579]. The Palestinian Talmud emphasizes, in a rejection of Christian claims, that the Messiah would obey the Mosaic Law[580].

There were many opinions about the time of the Messiah's coming. One view, expressed variously, had it that the time depended upon Israel's worthiness[581]. Elijah would precede him (Mal. 3.23), though there was disagreement about Elijah's function[582]. The formula, "The son of man will not come until . . .", seems to have developed into a homiletic device. The duration of the Messiah's kingdom was disputed as well[583]. Agreed was that it would last a limited time. In the newer eschatology, it was to be followed by a general resurrection, Last Judgment, and endless Age-to-Come. As disasters accumulated, the conviction deepened: Only by the direct action of God would Israel be delivered. A unitary view of history, in which all heathen empires were one seemed to force this conclusion. Through all the welter of opinions, one thing was doctrine: Deliverance would come to Israel as to an entire people.

C. Resurrection

Among those who have "no share in the world to come" is "he that says the resurrection of the dead is not from the Torah"[584]. Here the teaching of the Pharisees has become a dogma with its anathema. A long succession of teachers adduce arguments from several proof-texts, such as these: "The Lord said to Moses, 'Thou wilt sleep with thy fathers and wilt rise' (Deut. 31.16)"[585]. "Thy dead shall live, my dead bodies shall rise. O dwellers in the dust, awake and sing for joy! For thy dew is a dew of light, and on the land of the shades thou wilt let it fall" (Isa. 26.19). "That you may live long in the land which the Lord swore to your fathers to give to them and to their descendents" (Deut. 11.9)[586]. The Book of Daniel had said, "Many of those who sleep in the dust of the earth shall awake, some to everlasting life, and some to shame and everlasting contempt" (12.2). The

579 Moore II, 349.

580 E.g., T.P. Berakhoth 3b and parallels, cited by Schechter, p. 123—124, n. 5.

581 T.B. Sanhedrin 97b; 98a; T.B. Yoma 86b; T.P. Taanith 64a; T.B. Shabbath 118b.

582 Cf. T.B. Kiddushin 70b; M. Shekalim 2, 5; T.B. Pesahim 13a, 20b; T.B. Eduyoth 8, 7.

583 T.B. Sanhedrin 99a collects sayings about the duration of the messianic age with the Scriptural texts from which they were drawn.

584 מָאוֹמֵר אֵין תְּחִיַּת הַמֵּתִים מִן־הַתּוֹרָה: "He who says the resurrection of the dead is not from the Torah" (M. Sanhedrin 10,1). See T.B. Sanhedrin 90a.

585 In T.B. Sanhedrin 90b, the Sadducees object and offer a more natural reading (selected as well by the Revised Standard Version): "This people will rise up". Yet, this text is offered as proof also by R. Joshua ben Hananiah and R. Simeon ben Yohai (Idem).

586 Other arguments and texts in T.B. Sanhedrin 90b—92; T.B. Berakhoth 15b; Num. Rabbah 14, 1; Gen. Rabbah 14, 7. See Strack-Billerbeck, Kommentar, I, 892—897.

occasion was the Hellenistic crisis under Antiochus Epiphanes, a generation of martyrs (ca. 165 B.C.). Reflection upon the lot of their martyrs with reference to God's promises was probably the source of the doctrine for the early Hasidim and their heirs, the Pharisees[587]. The teaching was strongly emphasized in rabbinism, as one sees in a prayer like, "Blessed art Thou, O Lord, who restoreth souls unto dead bodies"[588]. It is clearly repugnant to Greek philosophy and is unknown to the Zoroastrianism which parallels other eschatological items of early Judaism.

The question who will rise produces different answers. On the one hand the Mishnah states, "They that are born are destined to die, and the dead to be brought to life again"[589]. On the other, we read, "The resurrection is reserved for Israel"[590]. Here, again, two schemata of eschatology are in operation. In the earlier view, the righteous dead of Israel were to rise in their own land and participate in the messianic age. Those bodies lying outside Eretz Israel would roll through tunnels made for them by God until they reached the "land of the living" (Ps. 116.9), where they would receive souls (Ezek. 37.14)[591]. The later view, in which all men were to rise for judgment after the messianic age, was simply added to the earlier one. Allusions to the resurrection of the dead without specifications usually refer to the general phenomenon before the Last Judgment. All will rise with their bodily defects, then God will heal the righteous, who will never die[592].

D. World to Come

The most problematic expression in rabbinic eschatology is *Olam ha-ba*, the Age (World) to Come. We have discussed the reason for confusion. The after-life was neither a metaphysical nor an esoteric subject among the rabbis. Given its theological foundation in the necessity of divine retribution, all the rabbis would have placed its central significance in these words: "This world is like a vestibule before the World to Come; prepare yourself in the vestibule that you may enter into the hall"[593]. When R. Joseph reported to his father, R. Joshua ben Levi, that he had seen men's fortunes

587 John Bright, History of Israel, pp. 409—410. The author remarks that the writer of the Book of Daniel is probably one of the Hasidim opposing Antiochus.

588 T.B. Berakhoth 60b.

589 M. Aboth 4, 29. See also, in context Midrash upon Lament. 3.23: "Since Thou art He that renewest us every morning, we know that 'Great is Thy faithfulness' refers to the resurrection of the dead'".

590 Gen. Rabbah 13, 6.

591 T.P. Kilaim 32c; T.P. Ketuboth 35b; 111a; Tanhuma (edit. Buber) Wayyehi, par. 6, and parallels in Buber's notes.

592 On healing bodily defects: Eccles. Rabbah on 1, 4; Tanhuma (edit. Buber), Wayyigash, par. 9. On living forever: T.B. Sanhedrin 92a.

593 M. Aboth 4, 21.

reversed on the far side of death, the father replied, "My son, you have seen a corrected world"[594]. A popular adage ran, "Not everyone has the merit of two tables"[595]. It was said, "Three precious gifts did the Holy One, blessed be He, give to Israel, and all of them He gave only through the medium of suffering; They are Torah, the Land of Israel, and the World to Come"[596].

In the next age, "There is neither eating nor drinking nor procreation of children nor business transactions; no envy or hatred or rivalry; but the righteous sit enthroned, their crowns on their heads, and enjoy the lustre of the *Shekhinah*"[597]. Part of this obviously contrasts with conditions in the days of the Messiah. This World is to the World to Come as the days of the week are to the Sabbath; and, "The Sabbath is a sixtieth part of the World to Come"[598]. Nothing will accompany a man there except "Torah and good deeds"[599]. The fate of the Gentiles with respect to the World to Come seems to have been the subject of whimsical homiletic conceits — even as the time of the Messiah's coming. "R. Eliezer declared, 'No Gentiles will have a share in the World to Come'. ... R. Joshua said to him, '... There must be rigtheous men among the nations who will have a share in the World to Come'"[600]. The latter was clearly the common view.

E. Judgment

To envision judgment in the end was necessary, for God was just. Rabbinic literature at times speaks of the judgment of every individual in a manner that signifies a reckoning demanded immediately at death. The clearest text has it, "At the time of a man's departure from the world, all his actions are detailed before him ... He admits the justice of the verdict and says, 'Rightly hast Thou judged me'"[601]. A different occasion of judgment is the condemnation of the gentile nations spoken of by the prophets (Isa. 3.14; 5.16; Hag. 2.22; Dan. 7.9); it was to open the messianic era. "The Holy One, blessed be He, will sit with the Elders of Israel like a President of the court and judge the gentile nations; as it is said, 'The Lord will enter into judgment with the Elders of His people'" (Isa. 3.14)[602]. Later rabbinic conceptions of the end place some of these features in a

594 T.B. Pesahim 50a. See "The Torah as Supreme Value", above, and n. 97.
595 T.B. Berakhoth 5b.
596 T.B. Berakhoth 5a.
597 T.B. Berakhoth 17a.
598 T.B. Berakhoth 57b.
599 M. Aboth 6, 9. See also T.B. Megillah 28b.
600 Tos. Sanhedrin 13, 2.
601 T.B. Taanith 11a. See also T.B. Berakhoth 58b; M. Aboth 4, 22.
602 Tanhuma Kedoshim par. 1. There is an extended description of the trial centering upon the nations' rejection of the Torah at Sinai, in T.B. Abodah Zarah 2a and b. See also Mekhilta on Ex. 15.7, 39a.

great Last Judgment when, at the end of the messianic era, all the dead will have risen for judgment. The question then is not Israel-and-the-Gentiles but the righteous and the wicked as such; and, the response of the judged shows no concern for messianic participation or exclusion. They say only, "Rightly hast Thou instituted *Gehinnom* for the wicked and *Gan Eden* for the righteous"[603].

F. *Gehinnom* and *Gan Eden*

Once judgment will be pronounced upon resurrected men, the wicked will go to *Gehinnom* and the righteous to *Gan Eden* — both immense areas in relation to the world[604]. The only description of *Gehinnom* concerns fire and darkness[605]. "(Ordinary) fire is a sixtieth of (the fire) of *Gehinnom*"[606]. One denial of any special place reserved for punishment makes a suggestive theological point: R. Simeon ben Lakish (ca. 250) declared, "There is no *Gehinnom* in the hereafter; but the Holy One, blessed be He, will remove the sun from its sheath and blacken the world. The wicked will be punished and the righteous healed thereby"[607]. Despite some sayings to the contrary, the rabbis generally held that punishment would be only for a time, after which the sufferers would be, in some cases, destroyed or, in others, given "a share in the World to Come"[608]. Those neither wholly wicked nor righteous would have a brief immersion in *Gehinnom*, said the School of Shammai; God's mercy would incline the balance to prevent their going there, said the School of Hillel[609].

Gan Eden (The Garden of Eden), where the righteous are to be rewarded, was the source of water for Adam's paradise (Gen. 2.10)[610]. In this blessed place, says the Talmud, "Each righteous person will be assigned a dwelling in accordance with the honor due him"[611]. Man's reward will be the presence of God. Rab, who said there will be no eating and drinking there, further

[603] T.B. Erubin 19a. See also Eccles. Rabbah 3, 9; Midrash to Ps. 1, 12b; T.B. Abodah Zarah 18a; T.B. Shabbath 31a.

[604] גיהנום *Gehinnom:* hell. גן־עדן *Gan Eden:* Garden of Eden. T.B. Taanith 10a.

[605] See T.P. Sanhedrin 29b; T.B. Hagigah 15b; T.B. Yebamoth 109b; Tos. Berakhoth 6, 7; Sifre Deut. par. 357, 149b; Gen. Rabbah 33, 1; Ex. Rabbah 51, 7; etc. T.P. Sanhedrin 29b, by exception, describes other physical pains.

[606] T.B. Berakhoth 57b. See also T.B. Hagigah 13b; T.B. Baba Bathra 74a; etc.

[607] T.B. Abodah Zarah 3b.

[608] T.B. Eduyoth 2, 10, reports the opinion of R. Akiba that suffering will be for twelve months; R. Jochanan ben Nuri said for a period of seven weeks. T.B. Rosh Hashanah 16bff. says the School of Shammai held that some men would remain everlastingly in *Gehinnom*, while the School of Hillel thought some would be destroyed after twelve months and others would live in remorse even after *Gehinnom* ceased to exist. Other opinions abound.

[609] Tos. Sanhedrin 13, 3; T.B. Rosh Hashanah 16b—17a.

[610] "A text teaches: 'A river went out of Eden to water the garden' (Gen. 2.10). Hence the garden and Eden are distinct." T.B. Berakhoth 34b.

[611] T.B. Shabbath 152a.

described final blessedness by quoting Ex. 24.11: "They beheld God, and ate and drank"[612]. His presence was food and drink to them. The great eschatological banquet was developed by some into a wedding feast — the situation which imaged forth God's intimate presence to those gathered about Him: "Does a bridegroom prepare a banquet for guests and not sit with them[613]?" A similar image was the dance which God will stage in *Gan Eden* for the righteous. He will sit in their midst — "And each one will point to Him with his finger, exclaiming, 'Lo, this is our God ... this is the Lord; we have waited for Him'" (Isa. 25.9)[614]. Sometimes the earth-bound imagination expressed other needs and the imagery of the messianic era was reverted to: The banquet became a feasting upon Leviathan (Ps. 74.14), and breezes rustled through the aromatic plants of *Gan Eden*[615]. Nevertheless, the central idea generally remained that the unseen God in whom man had hoped and for whom he had waited would be there; and Isaiah 64.4 was cited: "No one has heard or perceived by the ear, no eye has seen a God besides Thee, who works for those who wait for Him"[616].

The fear of *Gehinnom* and the hope for *Gan Eden* must be set beside what was said earlier about (1) the rabbinic understanding of reward, punishment, and suffering (see above, pp. 531—33), and about (2) the rabbis' unambiguous validation of domestic and socio-economic life (see above, pp. 546—50). Though the defeats of today could become victory under the Messiah and in *Gan Eden*, God was forever present in reward and punishment to those who kept His Law. R. Akiba, who said, "Everything is prepared for the feast", said also, "The collectors regularly make their daily rounds"[617]. R. Jacob (ca. 150), who said "The world is like a vestibule before the World to Come", said also, "Better is one hour of repentance and good works in this world than the whole life of the World to Come"[618]. To the rabbis, man's life continues in a resurrected condition.

In man's destiny, the final condition is an altogether happy enjoyment of God's presence. This follows upon man's acknowledgment, in this world, of God's one-ness over all creation. Acknowledgment takes place when man studiously enquires into God's revealed ways and follows them, testifying to his divine Lover's goodness before all his fellowmen. God's ways teach man how to live as leader of the whole beautiful creation. Rabbinic anthropology in binding man to God binds him to his world and to his neighbor.

612 T.B. Berakhoth 17a. Cf. above, at n. 278. Rab's saying is repeated in Aboth de-R. Nathan 1, 8.

613 Num. Rabbah 13, 2.

614 T.B. Taanith 31a.

615 On Leviathan: e.g., T.B. Baba Bathra 74b; 75a; T.B. Berakhoth 34b. On the plants of Gan Eden: Num. Rabbah 13,2.

616 E.g., T.B. Berakhoth 34b.

617 M. Aboth 3, 16.

618 M. Aboth 4, 16—17.

VI. After the Talmud

With the death of Rabina in 499 the rabbinic era came to an end. It was not, however, a definitive ending. The disciples of the last Amoraim, the Saboraim (ponderers) and their immediate successors, to about the middle of the sixth century, continued to add to the Gemara and, generally, to adjust the editing of the Talmud[619]. Meanwhile, the triumph of Christianity in the Empire had brought further humiliation and persecution to the Jews, a fact which in turn assured that the new religion would have no significant influence upon Judaism. Until the time of the Islamic conquest the Gaon of the academy of Sura in Mesopotamia was the leader of Jewery[620]. Jewish learning eventually moved from the East to North Africa and Southern Europe. Soon Cordova eclipsed Sura. In the profound changes of the succeeding centuries the basic attitudes which took shape in Judaism's formative era persisted.

1. New Needs, New Forms

Changed circumstances demanded new literary forms. The Talmud was a massive, leisurely work. As the Diaspora spread further and more sparsely, more popular forms of the Halakhah came into vogue — epitomes of the Talmud, *responsa* of the Geonim, and legal codes[621].

Even so, the ultimate referrant of Jewish tradition remained the Talmud. Acknowledgment of the needs of popular learning was itself in keeping with eminently rabbinic precedents. Later, in the High Middle Ages, the greatest of medieval Jewish philosophers, Maimonides (Moses ben Maimon, 1135—1204), would summarize the credal idea-content of Judaism in thirteen articles of faith obligatory to every believer[622]. The dogmatizing of Jewish faith would be new; the concern which prompted it had flourished in the Jewish elementary schools. As the seige of oppression loosened, a broader culture developed, and outstanding men produced poetry, philosophy, mystical writings, legends, and commentaries on the Bible and the Mishnah. Feelings toward the Gentiles softened. There was nothing new in the prayer of the Geonim, "Our King, our God, assert the unity of Thy name in Thy world"[623]; but there was newness in the expansiveness asserting itself with regard to Christians and Muslims, who

[619] Some lengthy discussions reported in the Gemara are later than Rabina. See T.B. Ketuboth 2b; T.B. Zebahim 102b.

[620] Gaon probably translates *clarissimus* or *illustris*, titles used by the Roman Emperor addressing heads of the provinces.

[621] H. Strack, Introduction, pp. 163—166.

[622] Commentary on the Mishnah, Sanhedrin 10 (11), a.

[623] Seder Rab Amram, p. 9a.

were seen figured in the prophecy of Zechariah (14.8–9): "It shall come to pass on that day that living waters shall go out of Jerusalem, half of them toward the eastern sea and half of them toward the western sea . . . And the Lord shall be King over all the earth." Poets, philosophers, and mystics declared that Christianity and Islam were agencies of Providence, preparing the world for a purer monotheism[624].

The greater tolerance enjoyed under Islamic rule opened medieval Judaism to Muslim influences. When the Arabs turned enthusiastically to Greek philosophy and wrote works of speculative theology, the Jews were stimulated. Their role in transmitting the Arabian commentators to the Schoolmen was significant. In Maimonides, speculative genius was applied for the first time to the categorical systematization of the Law. The 'Mishneh Torah' (Repetition of the Law) served as a basis for all later compilations, including the Shulhan Arukh[625]. Philo's project of reconciling Greek philosophy with Jewish revelation, which rabbinism had so studiously ignored, had been recommenced by Saadya Gaon (882—942). It was magisterially consummated by Maimonides in his 'Guide for the Perplexed' (1190, in Arabic). Both men were administrative officials among their people and wrote with the pastoral concern characteristic of the rabbis.

After the Talmudic centuries, during which a communal way of believing and practicing had been consolidated, new generations rose, secure enough in the achievements of rabbinism to establish a new direction — that of contemplative religion[626]. The medieval Jewish mystics were many and their writings influential. Man's struggle with the evil impulse, about which the rabbis had so much to say, was portrayed in the 'Hovot ha-Levavot' (Duties of the Hearts) of Bahya ibn Pakuda (late 11th. cen.) according to a more organic conceptualization: The ultimate opponent of God's unity is man's self-love. Nahmanides (1194—1270) speaks about the impossibility of legislating for all the complexity of man's relationships and notes that the Torah itself provides for this in the law of goodness (Deut. 6.18)[627]. The mystic passes on the rabbinic tradition (cf. Sifre 91a; 94a). Regularly, however, these contemplative writings assumed a loose body-soul relationship expressed in Platonic or Neo-Platonic imagery, rather than the more unitary relationship which the earlier rabbis received from the Bible. The medieval contemplatives of Islam and Christianity,

[624] K. Kohler, Jewish Theology, p. 426. The author cites Judah Halevi (Cuzari, 4, 23), Maimonides (H. Melakhim 11, 41; Responsa, 58), and Nahmanides (Derashah, edit. Jellinek, 5).

[625] Joseph Karo (1488—1578) compiled the 'Shulhan Arukh' (Prepared Table), published in 1565. It is the standard code of Jewish law and practice.

[626] G. Scholem, Major Trends in Jewish Mysticism, pp. 7—8, speaks of a first stage of religious consciousness in which the divide between God and man is emphatically established, and of a second stage which "proceeds to a quest for the secret that will close it in". The second is mysticism. The theory is especially plausible in accounting for the contrast between rabbinic and medieval approaches in Judaism.

[627] Nahmanides's Commentary on Deut. 6.18, cited by Schechter, pp. 214—215. Nahmanides's name: Moses ben Nahman, called also Ramban.

thriving on a similar anthropology, created a cultural climate[628]. But, before this, many of the Amoraim had pointed the way.

2. Vigor of the Pharisaic Principle

If we speak of the concept and study-tradition of the Oral Torah as the Pharisaic principle, we may say that the centuries following the Talmudic era revealed the principle's effectiveness. Let us consider two of the many possible facets.

First, the notion of an ultimate wisdom, divinely given in the past, residing in the community, to be identified and formulated by its scholars, gave rise, as we have seen, to the discussion process of the *Zugot* (The Pairs), the rabbinic Schools (Hillel and Shammai, etc.), and the classic antagonists of the Talmud. When the Halakhic controversies of the academies were stilled, the dialectic tradition continued. We may witness it in medieval Jewery in the discussion, for example, generation after generation, over the function of reason or of the speculative mind in Jewish faith. There is a continuous balancing of opinions in a self-corrective pursuit of the answer. Reliance is placed, neither upon a centrally constituted authority nor a hereditary office, but upon the scholars of Israel. Reflection shuttles back and forth — from the Geonim, who affirm the classic view that the rabbis of the academies issue the Halakhah, to the Karaites' schism in the name of exclusively biblical sources; from Saadya Gaon's philosophical defense of tradition against the Karaites, to Judah Halevi's rejection of all discursive methods; from Maimonides' principle that all faith is metaphysical understanding, to Cabbalistic irrationalism. Philosophy and mysticism occur as action and reaction, and all the writers rest their case on rabbinic tradition.

Second, Pharisaism, or its antecedent, begins with the ending of prophecy. The prophets committed the Torah to the men of the Great Synagogue[629]. The most generally followed medieval conception of the relation between the rabbis of old (or their scholarly successors) and the prophets was that of Maimonides, virtually repeated by his later antagonist Gersonides (1288—1344)[630]: (1) Man's highest perfection is knowledge — ultimately the knowledge of God. The supreme knowledge of God is the knowledge of His ethical activity by which we are made to imitate this activity[631]. (Here, with systematic acumen, the majority position of the rabbis on the issue of learning and action is vindicated.) (2) Intellectually,

628 Bahya ibn Pakuda's debt to Arabic Neo-Platonism and the works of Muslim mystics is obvious. Nahmanides shared the Neo-Platonic influences present in the Cabbalah.

629 M. Aboth 1, 1.

630 Levi ben Gershon, known as Gersonides or Ralbag, a rationalist, admirer of Averroës. See Menachem Marc Kellner, Maimonides and Gersonides on Mosaic Prophecy, Speculum, 52, 1 (1977), pp. 62—79, at p. 76.

631 Maimonides, Guide for the Perplexed, III, 54; Arabic p. 134bff.; Hebrew, pp. 598—599; cited by J. Guttmann, Philosophies of Judaism, p. 176.

the prophet and the philosopher engage in the same process — though the prophet is superior to the philosopher, even from a purely speculative point of view, in virtue of the superiority of his intuition[632]. (3) The purpose of prophecy has always been legislation, for man can live only in a society where relationships are determined. Perfect legislation requires prophetic inspiration[633]. It cannot be said without qualification that, for Maimonides, every would-be scholar of the Torah is a prophet, for he holds that the divine will can refuse inspiration even to individuals who have the right disposition and qualifications for prophecy[634]. Nevertheless, God willing, the Jewish sage fills the function of the prophets of ancient Israel. The great Talmudist seems, indeed, to offer an anthropological account of certain dimensions of the Pharisaic principle from which rabbinism sprang.

That the rabbis lived in these members of their posterity cannot be doubted. It is a striking phenomenon in the history of religions that, scattered thinly, with no national center, and no senate to articulate directives, nor any secular power to enforce them, the rabbis held the loyalty of their religious nation, presided over its increase, and inspired its organic development.

VII. Conclusion

To the Synagogue man's basic attribute was his creaturely historicity. The historical situation of Israel, from the rebuilding of the Temple to the completion of the Talmud, presents one constant — the precariousness of her existence. Rabbinic anthropology is man's concept of himself when his people are few and continually threatened, when he is oppressed and unesteemed, and when, because of confidence in a divine promise given in history, to be fulfilled in history, he determines to continue as a people. The inner dynamic perceptible in this concept is integrative. Rabbinic man assumes a close unity of body and soul, for the nation cannot be sustained as an aggregate of spirits. He relies upon the unity of man and wife, for the wholeness of the essentially-embodied condition depends upon a joyful complementarity from which increase will spring. He affirms the unity of a people, for neither individual nor family may find an adequacy of human resources outside the people. He postulates the unity of mankind, for the nation knows no reason for permanence outside its mission to humanity. "When I am for myself", asked Hillel, "what am I"? (M. Aboth 1, 14).

[632] Guide, II, 38: Arabic, pp. 82b—83; Hebrew, pp. 333—334; cited by J. Guttmann, op. cit., p. 172. M. M. Kellner, Maimonides and Gersonides on Mosaic Prophecy, p. 64. Cf. Philo's concept of prophecy, above, n. 489.

[633] Guide, II, 40: III, 27; cited by J. Guttmann, op. cit., p. 172.

[634] Guide, II, 32; Arabic, pp. 73aff; Hebrew, pp. 317—318; cited by J. Guttmann, op. cit., p. 172.

Smaller motifs as well were grounded in historical circumstances. The great significance found in economic justice, for example — perhaps unique before the modern era — may be tied to the radical leveling of all Jewish classes after the Roman wars. It is experienced and declared by scholars stripped of the heritage of economic privilege. When the Synagogue interpreted its precarious existence in the light of the Scriptures, it formed itself in a literature which reflected similar historical conditions.

That God spoke in history established man's historicity as theological principle as well. The facts of Israel's circumstances spoke a truth about man. For many the adventitious was in tension with the reality of ideas, the inviolability of the spirit in matter, or the order of the *cosmos*. For the Jew, instead, there was no escaping the order of fact; in that order God addressed man. The complementary human truth represented by Israel's hope was also of the order of fact. Uttered in time, God's promises regarded time and would be fulfilled within time, though His loving kindness would not end with time. For many, man's destiny beckoned a return to where he had been — to a pristine condition. For the Jew, every man was to move on — to making God one in His creation — to where man had never been.

Related to man's historicity is the received character of his humanity. The rabbis' reflection upon experience yielded a perception of self accessible not in those speculative extrapolations from the data of consciousness which tell of the nature of things, but in a listening which arrives as a foundational relationship: Man is to God as His very image, because God willed to make him so. The complex of man's other relationships — man's received position in creation — may be explained in that one. Man is that part of creation which is endowed with the capacity to recognize its Creator. In his uniqueness he may read his destiny, that of awakening creation as a whole to respond, through his acknowledgment, to the Creator. As images of the one God, all men, in their wondrous diversity, are one. As spoken to and elected, Israel too is one, a people chosen to lead the way. The word communicated to man is God's law. The more man values communication with God the more studiously will he seek to know what God has legislated. Through changing times, he must meet the challenge to his intellect of continually rediscovering in the written and oral Torah his true origin, nature, and destiny. Here he will be apprized of God's final gift to his humanity, its complete reconstitution after death.

Although all biblical anthropologies will have much in common, no living religious tradition will merely duplicate the concepts of ancient Israel. For Christianity, the Image of God is hypostatized; it is not man, but the Godman, who as Mediator is the Revelation, the Atoner, Petitioner of the Spirit, and Judge; while man is made in the image. For Islam, what is communicated by way of the human prophet is, not only God's teaching (Torah), but the uncreated, eternal Qur'an, and only in an extended sense does man receive the revealed word. In rabbinic Judaism the assumptions which necessitate a new institutional form of Israelite tradition firmly establish a point of view on the Hebrew Scriptures. Each of these three religious currents represents for the biblical tradition a mutation from which, inevitably, anthropological variation must develop. Although rabbinic anthropology is in large part determined by numerous basic notions which it shares with other sectors of this biblical tradition, the following salient ideas constitute its specific difference: (1) Man's knowledge of ultimate reality is God's communication comprehensively and definitively made in history, received in simple independence of the speculative mind, and preserved and clarified by the scholar class of rabbis. (2) The content of this knowledge regards divine one-ness; it constitutes a radical, voluntaristic monotheism in which, besides simple insistence upon God's ontological uniqueness, all is oriented to the determination of such human conduct as will make Him one in worship. In this knowledge man discovers himself. (3) In his origin, man is altogether defined by relationships — to God as His image, to his fellowman as brother, and to all other creatures as leader and custodian. (4) In his nature and condition, man is a close body-soul unity, blessed in his bodily life, unwounded by the sin of Adam. (5) In his destiny, man is called to full acknowledgment of God's reign, to a kingdom now represented by the People of Israel, who in the days of the Messiah to come will comprise all the elect of mankind.

Bibliography

1. Rabbinic Sources

Aboth de Rabbi Nathan, edit. S. SCHECHTER (Vienna, 1887; reprint, New York, 1945).

The Babylonian Talmud, edit. I. EPSTEIN, English Translation (London, 1935—48).

The Fathers According to Rabbi Nathan, English Translation, J. GOLDIN, YJS, 10 (New Haven, 1955).

Mechilta de-Rabbi Simon b. Jochai, edit. D. HOFFMANN (Frankfurt a. M., 1905; reprint, Tel Aviv, 1967—68).

Mechilta d' Rabbi Ismael, critical edition, H. S. HOROWITZ and A. RABIN (Frankfurt a. M., 1928—31; reprint, Jerusalem, 1960). Edit. M. FRIEDMANN (Vienna, 1870); edit. J. H. WEISS (Vienna 1865).

Mekilta de-Rabbi Ishmael, critical edit. and trans. J. Z. LAUTERBACH, 3 Vols., LJC (Philadelphia, 1933—35; reprint, 1949).

Mekhilta d' Rabbi Simon b. Yochai: Fragmenta in Geniza Cairensi reperta digessit. Apparatu critico, notis, praefatione instruxit (Jerusalem, 1955).

Midrasch Tehillim (Schocher Tob): Sammlung agadischer Abhandlungen über die 150 Psalmen, edit. S. BUBER (Vilna, 1891; reprint, New York, 1947; Jerusalem, 1965—66).

The Midrash on Psalms, trans. W. G. BRAUDE, 2 Vols., YJS, 13 (New Haven, 1959).

Midrash Bereshit Rabba, critical edit. with notes and commentary [in Hebrew], J. THEODOR, 3 Vols. (Jerusalem, 1965).

Midrash Rabbah, edit. and trans. H. FREEDMAN and M. SIMON, 10 Vols. (London, 1939; reprint, 1961).

Midrash Rabbah 'al Hamishah Hummeshe Torah we Hamesh Megillot (Vilna, 1884—87).

Midrash Tanchuma: Ein agadischer Commentar zum Pentateuch von Rabbi Tanchuma ben Rabbi Abba, . . . kritisch bearbeitet . . . , S. BUBER (Vilna, 1885; reprint, 1912—13; New York, 1946; Jerusalem, 1963—64).

The Mishnah, English trans. H. DANBY (Oxford, 1933).

Mishnayoth, Text with annotations and literal translation, P. BLACKMAN, 3rd edit., 6 Vols. (New York, 1965).

Pesikta de Rav Kahana, Critical Edition in Hebrew and English, B. MANDELBAUM, 2 Vols. (New York, 1962).

Pesikta: Die älteste Hagada redigiert in Palästina von Rab Kahana, edit. S. BUBER (Lyck, 1868; reprint, Vilna, 1925; New York, 1948—49; Jerusalem, 1962—63).

Pesikta Rabbati: Discourses for Feasts, Fasts, and Special Sabbaths, English trans., W. G. BRAUDE, 2 Vols. YJS, 18 (New Haven, 1968).

Pesikta Rabbati: Midrasch für den Fest-Cyclus und die ausgezeichneten Sabbathe, edit. M. FRIEDMANN (Vienna, 1880; reprint, Tel Aviv, 1962—63).

Sifra, der älteste Midrasch zu Levitikus. Nach Handschriften neu herausgegeben mit Anmerkungen bis 3:9, edit. M. FRIEDMANN, SGFWJ (Breslau, 1915).

Sifra deve Rav: Hu Sefer Torat Kohanim, edit. J. H. WEISS (Vienna, 1862; reprint, New York, 1946).

Sifra: Halachischer Midrasch zu Leviticus, German trans. J. WINTER, SGJ, 24 (Breslau, 1938).

Sifrè debè Rab: Der älteste halachische und hagadische Midrasch zu Numeri und Deuteronomium, edit. M. FRIEDMANN (Vienna, 1864; reprint, New York, 1968).

Talmud Bavli (Vilna, 1886).

Talmud Yerushalmi, Venice-Cracow-Krotoschin edit. (New York, 1948).

Tosefat Rishonim, critical edit. S. LIEBERMAN, 4 Vols. (Jerusalem, 1936—39).

2. Secondary Literature

ALBRIGHT, W. F., From the Stone Age to Christianity. 2nd edit. New York, 1957.

ALTMANN, ALEXANDER, Studies in Religious Philosophy and Mysticism. London, 1969.

BACHER, W., Die Agada der babylonischen Amoräer. 2nd edit. Frankfurt, 1913.

ID., Die Agada der palästinensischen Amoräer. 3 Vols. Strassburg, 1884—90. Vol. 1, 2nd edit. Strassburg, 1903.

ID., Die Agada der Tannaiten. 2 Vols. Strassburg, 1884—90. Vol. 1, 2nd edit. Strassburg, 1903.

ID., Die exegetische Terminologie der jüdischen Traditionsliteratur. 2 Vols. Leipzig, 1899—1905.

BAER, Y., On the Problem of Eschatological Doctrine during the Period of the Second Temple, Zion, 23/24 (1958/59), 3—34, 141—165.

ID., Israel Among the Nations [Heb.]. Jerusalem, 1955.

BAMBERGER, B. J. Proselytism in the Talmudic Period. Cincinnati, 1939.

BARON, S. W., A Social and Religious History of the Jews. 2nd edit. New York, 1952—69.

BICKERMANN, E., La chaîne de la tradition Pharisienne. RB, 59 (1952), 44—54.

ID., From Ezra to the Last of the Maccabees: Foundadations of Post-Biblical Judaism. New York, 1962.

BLENKINSOPP, J., Prophecy and Canon: A Contribution to the Study of Jewish Origins. London, 1977.

BONSIRVEN, J., Le Judaisme palestinien au temps de Jésus-Christ. Paris, 1934.

BOUSSET, W., Die Religion des Judentums im späthellenistischen Zeitalter (ed. H. GRESSMANN). HNT 21. Tübingen, 1966. Reprint of 1925 ed.

BRIGHT, J., A History of Israel. Philadelphia, 1959.

BUBER, M., Darkô shel Migrā'. Jerusalem, 1964.

CHARLES, R. H., edit. The Apocrypha and Pseudepigrapha of the Old Testament, in English, with introductions and critical and explanatory notes to the several books. In conjunction with many scholars. 2 Vols. 4th edit. Oxford, 1913.

ID., Eschatology. New York, 1963.

CHINITZ, J. M., Judaism, The Elusive Revelation. New York, 1965.

CASSUTO, U., From Adam to Noah. Jerusalem, 1961.

DAUBE, D., The New Testament and Rabbinic Judaism. London, 1956.
ID., Rabbinic Methods of Interpretation and Hellenistic Rhetoric. HUCA, 22 (1949), 239—264.
DUBNOV, S., History of the Jews From the Roman Empire to the Early Medieval Period. 6 Vols. 4th edit. New York, 1967—69.

EDDY, S. K., The King is Dead: Studies in the Near-Eastern Resistance to Hellenism 334—31 B.C. Lincoln, 1961.
ELBOGEN, I., Der jüdische Gottesdienst in seiner geschichtlichen Entwicklung. Leipzig, 1913.
Encyclopaedia Judaica. Ed. in chief C. ROTH, G. WIGODER. 16 Vols. Jerusalem, 1971.

FARMER, W., Maccabees, Zealots, and Josephus. New York, 1956.
FINKELSTEIN, L., Akiba: Scholar, Saint, and Martyr. New York, 1936; reprint, 1970.
ID., Ha-Perushim we-'Anshe Keneset ha-Gedola. New York, 1950.
ID., edit. The Jews: Their History, Culture, and Religion. 2 Vols. 3rd edit. New York, 1960.
ID., The Pharisees: The Sociological Background of Their Faith. 2 Vols. 3rd edit. Philadelphia, 1966.
FRANKEL, Z., Dar'ke ha-Mishnah, Leipzig, 1859.

GEIGER, A., Nachgelassene Schriften. 5 Vols. Breslau, 1885.
GINZBERG, L., Die Haggada bei den Kirchenvätern. Berlin, 1900.
ID., The Legends of the Jews. 6 Vols. Philadelphia, 1913—28.
ID., Some Observations on the Attitude of the Synagogue toward the Apocalyptic Eschatological Writings. JBL, 41 (1922), 115—136.
GOLDSMIDT, L., Subject Concordance to the Babylonian Talmud, edit. R. EDELMANN. Copenhagen, 1959.
GOODENOUGH, E. R., By Light, Light. New Haven, 1935.
GROBEL, K., Σῶμα as 'Self, Person' in the LXX. Neutestamentliche Studien für Rudolf Bultmann. BZNW, 21. Berlin, 1954, 52—59.
GUNDRY, R. H., Sōma in Biblical Theology: With Emphasis on Pauline Anthropology. London, 1976.
GUTTMANN, A., Rabbinic Judaism in the Making: A Chapter in the History of the Halakhah from Ezra to Judah I. Detroit, 1970.
GUTTMANN, J., Philosophies of Judaism. Philadelphia, 1964.

HADAS, M., Hellenistic Culture: Fusion and Diffusion. New York, 1959.
HENGEL, M., Judaism and Hellenism: Studies in their Encounter in Palestine during the Early Hellenistic Period. 2 Vols. London, 1974.
HERFORD, R. T., The Pharisees. London, 1924; reprint, New York, 1962.
HIRSCH, W., Rabbinic Psychology. London, 1947.

IDELSOHN, Z., Jewish Liturgy and Its Development. New York, 1932.

JEWETT, R., Paul's Anthropological Terms: A Study of Their Use in Conflict Settings. AGAJU, 10. Leiden, 1971.
JOHNSON, A. R., The Vitality of the Individual in the Thought of Ancient Israel. 2nd edit. Cardiff, 1964.
JUSTER, J., Les Juifs dans l'empire Romain, leur condition juridique, économique, et sociale. 2 Vols. Paris, 1914.

KADUSCHIN, M., Aspects of the Rabbinic Concept of Israel. HUCA, 19 (1945—46), 57—96·
ID., The Rabbinic Mind. New York, 1952.
KLAUSNER, J., The Messianic Idea in Israel. New York, 1955.
KOHLER, K., Jewish Theology: Systematically and Historically Considered. New York, 1968.
KRAUSS, S., Talmudische Archäologie. 3 Vols. Leipzig, 1910—12.

LAUTERBACH, J. Z., The Pharisees and Their Teachings. New York, 1930.
LÉVI, I., L'Ecclésiastique. 2 Vols. BEHESR, 10. 1, 2. Paris, 1898—1901.
LIEBERMAN, S., Greek in Jewish Palestine. New York, 1942.
ID., Hellenism in Jewish Palestine. 2nd edit. New York, 1962.

Id., How Much Greek in Jewish Palestine? in: A. Altmann, edit. Biblical and Other Studies, Cambridge, Mass., 1963, 123—141.
Id., Some Aspects of After-Life in Early Rabbinic Literature. H. A. Wolfson Jubilee Volume. Jerusalem, 1965.

Mantel, H., Studies in the History of the Sanhedrin. Cambridge, Mass., 1961.
Marcus, R., Pharisees, Essenes, and Gnostics. JBL, 73 (1954), 157—161.
Meyer, R., Hellenistisches in der rabbinischen Anthropologie. BWANT, 4,2. Stuttgart, 1937.
Montefiore, C. G. and H. Lowe. Rabbinic Anthology. 1938; reprint, Philadelphia, 1959.
Moore, G. F., Christian Writers on Judaism. HTR, 14 (1921), 197—254.
Id., Judaism in the First Centuries of the Christian Era, The Age of the Tannaim. 3 Vols. Cambridge, Mass., 1927—30.

Neusner, J., Form and Meaning in Mishnah. JAAR, 45 (1977), 27—54.
Id., edit. The Formation of the Babylonian Talmud: Studies in the Achievements of Late Nineteenth and Twentieth Century Historical and Literary-Critical Research. Leiden, 1970.
Id., The History of Early Rabbinic Judaism: Some New Approaches. HR, 16 (1977), 216—236.
Id., History and Structure: The Case of the Mishnah. JAAR, 45 (1977), 161—192.
Id., The Idea of Purity in Ancient Judaism. With a Critique and Commentary by Mary Douglas. Leiden, 1973.
Id., From Politics to Piety: Pharisaic Judaism in New Testament Times. Englewood Cliffs, N. J., 1972.
Id., History and Torah: Essays on Jewish Learning. New York, 1965.
Id., History of the Jews in Babylonia. 5 Vols. Leiden, 1965—70.
Id., The Rabbinic Tradition about the Pharisees Before 70. 3 Vols. Leiden, 1971.
Nickelsburg, G. W. E., Resurrection, Immortality, and Eternal Life in Intertestamental Judaism. HTS, 26. Cambridge, Mass., 1972.

Oesterley, W. O. E., The Jews and Judaism during the Greek, Period: The Background of Christianity. London, 1970.

Pautrel, R., Ben Sira et le Stoïcisme. RSR, 51 (1963), 535—549.
Porter, F. C., The Yeçer Hara: A Study in the Jewish Doctrine of Sin. Jerusalem, 1902.

Von Rad, G., Wisdom in Israel. London, 1972.
Rahner, K., R. Pesch, and J. Splett, Man (Anthropology). Sacramentum Mundi, 3 (New York, 1968—70), 358—370.
Rössler, D., Gesetz und Geschichte, WMANT 3. 2nd edit. Neukirchen, 1962.
Russell, D. S., Between the Testaments. Philadelphia, 1965.

Sanders, E. P., Paul and Palestinian Judaism: A Comparison of Patterns of Religion. Philadelphia, 1977.
Sandmel, S., Philo's Place in Judaism: A Study of Conceptions of Abraham in Jewish Literature. Cincinnati, 1956.
Id., Reflections on the Problem of Theology for Jews. JBR, 33 (April 1965), 101—112.
Schechter, S., Aspects of Rabbinic Theology. 1909; reprint, New York, 1961.
Schlatter, A., Geschichte Israels von Alexander d. Gr. bis Hadrian. 3rd edit. Stuttgart, 1925.
Scholem, G., Jewish Gnosticism, Merkabah Mysticism, and Talmudic Tradition. New York, 1960.
Id., Major Trends in Jewish Mysticism. 3rd edit. Jerusalem, 1941.
Id., On Jews and Judaism in Crisis. New York, 1977.
Id., Zum Verständnis der messianischen Idee im Judentum. Eranos-Jahrbuch, 28, 1959 (Zürich, 1960), 193—239.
Schubert, K., Einige Beobachtungen zum Verständnis des Logosbegriffs im frührabbinischen Schrifttum. Judaica, 9 (1953), 65—80.
Id., Die Religion des nachbiblischen Judentums. Freiburg–Vienna, 1955.

SCHÜRER, E., Geschichte des jüdischen Volkes im Zeitalter Jesu Christi. 2 Vols. Frankfurt, 1886—90, third and fourth edit., 3 Vols. and 'Register', Leipzig, 1901—1911. Extensively rewritten as following item.

ID., The History of the Jewish People in the Age of Jesus Christ (175 B.C.—A.D. 135). Vol. I. New English version revised and edit. by GEZA VERMES and FERGUS MILLAR. Edinburgh, 1973.

SCHWEITZER, F. M., A History of the Jews Since the First Century A.D. New York, 1971.

SINGER, S., edit. and trans. The Standard Prayer Book. Enlarged American Edition. New York, 1915.

SMITH, M., Palestinian Judaism in the First Century, in: MOSHE DAVIS, edit. Israel: Its Role in Civilization. New York, 1956.

STRACK, H. L., Introduction to the Talmud and Midrash. 1931; reprint, New York, 1972.

STRACK, H. L. and P. Billerbeck, Kommentar zum Neuen Testament aus Talmud und Midrasch. 4 Vols. Munich, 1922—28.

The Study of Judaism: Bibliographical Essays. New York, 1972.

TAYLOR, C., Sayings of the Jewish Fathers. 2nd edit. Cambridge, 1897.

TSCHERIKOWER, V. (TCHERIKOVER, A.), Hellenistic Civilization and the Jews. Philadelphia, 1959.

URBACH, E., Ha-Masorot al Torat ha-sod bi-tequfat ha-Tannaim [The Traditions about Merkabah Mysticism in the Tannaitic Period], in: Studies in Mysticism and Religion presented to Gershom Scholem. Jerusalem, 1969, pp. 1—28.

ID., The Laws Regarding Slavery as a Source for Social History of the Second Temple, the Mishnah, and Talmud, Papers of the Institute of Jewish Studies. Vol. 1. London, 1964, 1—95.

ID., The Sages: Their Concepts and Beliefs. 2 Vols. Jerusalem, 1975.

VERMES, G., Scripture and Tradition in Judaism. Leiden, 1961.

WOLFSON, H. A., Philo: Foundations of Religious Philosophy in Judaism, Christianity, and Islam. Cambridge, Mass., 1947.

ZEITLIN, S., Rashi and the Rabbinate. JQR, 31 (1941), 1—20.

ID., The Rise and Fall of the Judean State. 2 Vols. Philadelphia, 1962—67.

ZOBEL, M., Gottes Gesalbter, der Messias und die Messianische Zeit in Talmud und Midrasch. Berlin, 1938.

Logos-Theologie im Rabbinat.
Ein Beitrag zur Lehre vom Worte Gottes im rabbinischen Schrifttum

von HANS BIETENHARD, Bern

Inhalt

Vorbemerkung

Bei meiner Bearbeitung von Sifre Deuteronomium (SDeut) stieß ich in § 343[1] auf einen Midrasch über den *dibbūr*, d. h. über das Gotteswort (Gottesrede), wie es bei der Offenbarung und Gesetzgebung am Sinai von Gott ausging[2]. Um diese Aussage zu klären und die hinter ihr stehenden Anschauungen zu erfassen, suchte ich den andern rabbinischen Stellen über den *dibbūr* nachzugehen. Es zeigte sich dabei bald, daß der Sprachgebrauch nicht einheitlich ist: In den Texten wechselt oft *dibbūr* mit *dibbēr*. Das ist auch der Fall, wo es bei einzelnen Überlieferungen parallele Rezensionen gibt. Wo kritische Ausgaben rabbinischer Texte greifbar sind, läßt sich dieselbe Feststellung machen: Die Textzeugen wechseln zwischen *dibbūr*

[1] FINKELSTEIN, Siphre ad Deuteronomium, 399, Z. 11—15.
[2] Die Stelle wird hier unten S. 595 zitiert.

und *dibbēr*. Leider gibt es nicht zu allen rabbinischen Schriften Konkordanzen, so daß man allzu oft auf den Zufall angewiesen ist, wenn man einem bestimmten Wort, hier also *dibbūr*, nachgeht[2a].

Ferner zeigte sich, daß zahlreiche Berührungen inhaltlicher Art mit Vokabeln ähnlicher Bedeutung vorliegen (was nicht anders zu erwarten ist!): Neben dem schon erwähnten *dibbēr* wären zu nennen: *memrā, 'amirā, ḳōl, ḥoḵmā, schekinā, rūaḥ* u. a. Ausgehend von *dibbūr* könnte man, allen diesen Begriffen nachgehend, eine umfassende Theologie des Wortes Gottes nach rabbinischer Auffassung schreiben. Das kann hier nicht geschehen. So beschränke ich mich bewußt auf die Vokabel *dibbūr*. Nur gelegentlich konnte auf *dibbēr* und noch seltener auf 'benachbarte' Begriffe eingegangen werden. Aus den oben erwähnten Gründen konnte auch bei solcher Beschränkung keine Vollständigkeit erzielt werden. Deshalb ist die vorliegende Arbeit, wie im Titel bemerkt, ein Beitrag zur Lehre vom Worte Gottes im rabbinischen Schrifttum.

I. Dibbūr *als 'Wort, Reden, Sprechen, Sprache'*[3]

Die erst im rabbinischen Sprachgebrauch feststellbare Vokabel ד(י)בור (*dibbūr*) ist eine Bildung des Intensivstammes von der Wurzel *dbr* = 'sprechen, reden'[4]. Es handelt sich also um eine spezifisch neuhebräische (bzw. mittelhebräische, so der neuere Sprachgebrauch) Wortbildung[5].

In der Bedeutung 'Wort' kommt *dibbūr* z. B. an folgenden Stellen vor:

„Wer lernt von seinem Genossen einen Abschnitt, oder einen Lehrsatz, oder ein Wort (*dibbūr*), oder auch nur einen Buchstaben, muß ihm Ehre erweisen [...]". "[...] um wie viel mehr muß, wer von seinem Genossen einen Abschnitt, oder einen Lehrsatz, oder einen Vers, oder ein Wort (*dibbūr*), oder auch nur einen Buchstaben lernt, ihm Ehre erweisen"[6]. „Wer aber sein bloßes Wort (*dābār* oder *dibbūr*?) hält, erwirbt sich den Beifall der Gelehrten"[7]. In diesem zuletzt angeführten Satz ist *dibbūr* textkritisch nicht gesichert, indem in den Mischna-Ausgaben auch *dābār* erscheint[8].

[2a] Vgl. die Konkordanzen, die KOSOVSKY herausgegeben hat, und die mir verfügbar waren.
[3] Stellen z. T. aus STR.-BI. II 317, kontrolliert jeweils nach dem hebr. oder aram. Grundtext.
[4] BARTH, Die Nominalbildung in den semitischen Sprachen 53. — B. führt *dibbūr* nicht an.
[5] MARTI-BEER, Aḇôṯ, 166 Anm. 3.
[6] Ab VI 3: MARTI-BEER, Aḇôṯ, 166f.
[7] MSchebi X 9.
[8] Allgemein kann gesagt werden, daß *dibbūr* in den Textzeugen häufig mit *dibbēr* wechselt, vgl. die 'Vorbemerkung' dieser Arbeit (S. 580). *Dibbēr* ist at.lich, es begegnet Jer 5, 13; 9, 7.

„Wenn Mose sprach, stand Aaron zu seiner Rechten und Eleazar zu seiner Linken und Ithamar zur Rechten Aarons, und die Rede (*haddibbūr*) ging von ihnen (beiden) aus, wie wenn sie beide gesprochen hätten"[9]. „Der Gedanke wird als Wort (*dibbūr*) angesehen [...] der Gedanke wird nicht als Wort (*dibbūr*) angesehen"[10]. „Dein Reden (*dibbūrḵā*) am Sabbat sei nicht wie dein Reden (*kedibbūrḵā*) am Werktag. Das Reden (*dibbūr*) (ist) verboten, das Nachdenken (ist) erlaubt"[11]. „R. Eli'ezer (um 90 n. Chr.) hat gesagt: Woher (läßt es sich erweisen), daß das Wort (*haddibbūr*) wie eine Tat (anzusehen) ist? (Weil) es heißt: 'Durch das Wort J's sind die Himmel gemacht worden' (Ps 33,6)"[12].

In der Bedeutung 'Ausdruck, Vokabel' findet sich *dibbūr* an der folgenden Stelle: (Zu Jer 8, 19) „R. Joḥanan († 279) sagte: Dieser Ausdruck (*dibbūr*) (scl. *schū'ah*) hat drei Bedeutungen: Geschrei, Wehklage, Aechzen ..."[13].

In der Bedeutung 'Wort, Befehl, Edikt' finden wir *dibbūr* an folgenden Stellen: „'Meine Seele entfloh mir, als er zu mir sprach' (HL 5, 6). Beim Worte (*bedibbūr*) des Kyros, der verfügt hatte: Wer nicht über den Euphrat gegangen ist, darf nicht hinübergehen". — „'Meine Seele entfloh mir, als er zu mir sprach' (HL 5, 6). Bei seiner (Gottes-)Rede (*bedibbūrō*). Wegen der Stimme seiner ersten (Gottes-)Rede (*dibbūrō*), als er sprach: 'Ich bin J', dein Gott' (Ex 20, 2)"[14]. — „Der (Gott), welcher Rechenschaft gefordert hat vom Menschengeschlecht der Sintflut und vom Menschengeschlecht der (Sprach-)Verwirrung, der wird auch in Zukunft Rechenschaft fordern von jedem, der nicht bei seinem (einmal gegebenen) Worte (*bedibbūrō*) bleibt"[15].

Um das Aussprechen eines einzelnen Wortes handelt es sich an der folgenden Stelle: „Und wie viel (Zeit darf höchstens verstreichen, daß man noch sagen kann) 'sofort'? So viel (wie es braucht, um) ein Wort (*dibbūr*) (auszusprechen). R. Simon (um 280) (sagte) im Namen von R. Jehoschu'a b. Levi (um 250): So viel (Zeit, wie es braucht), um einander zu grüßen ..."[16]. — „Da ist ausgeschlossen (der Fall), wo du seine Tochter für deinen Sohn begehrst oder seinen Sohn für deine Tochter. Oder sogar (der Ausdruck des) Begehrens durch einen Ausspruch (*bedibbūr*)? Die Schrift sagt lehrend: (Zitat Deut 7, 25)"[17].

Im Sinne von 'Satz' erscheint *dibbūr* an der folgenden Stelle: „[...] das, was innerhalb (der Zeit), während welcher man einen Satz (*dibbūr*)

[9] Mek Ex Pisḥa 12, 1; der letzte halbe Satz zweimal, beim zweiten Male im Namen von R. Schim'on b. Joḥaj (um 150).

[10] bBer 20b.

[11] bSchabb 113b.

[12] bSchabb 119b.

[13] Eḵa r., prooem. 32.

[14] Schir r. 5, 4, zu HL 5, 6.

[15] MBM IV 2: WINDFUHR, Baba Messia, 48f.

[16] jBer I 1 4b, 27ff.; dasselbe in jMo'ed ḳaṭ III 7, 83c, 37.

[17] Mek Ex Baḥodesch 20, 14.

(aussprechen kann) gesprochen wird, gilt als ein Satz (*kedibbūr*). — Ich will dir sagen: Wenn das, was innerhalb (der Zeit), während welcher man einen Satz (*dibbūr*) (aussprechen kann), ausgesprochen wird, als ein Satz (*kedibbūr)* gälte, so wären alle der Ansicht, daß er rückwirkend unzulässig ist, hierbei aber streiten sie, ob das, was innerhalb (der Zeit), während welcher man einen Satz (*dibbūr*) (aussprechen kann), gesprochen wird, als ein Satz (*kedibbūr*) gilt. Die Rabbanan sind der Ansicht: Was innerhalb (der Zeit), während welcher man einen Satz (*dibbūr*) (aussprechen kann), gesprochen wird, gilt nicht als ein Satz (*kedibbūr*), und R. Jose ist der Ansicht: Was innerhalb (der Zeit), während welcher man einen Satz (*dibbūr*) (aussprechen kann), gesprochen wird, gilt als ein Satz (*kedibbūr*). Ist denn R. Jose der Ansicht, was innerhalb (der Zeit), während welcher man einen Satz (*dibbūr*) (aussprechen kann), gesprochen wird, gelte als ein Satz (*keddibūr*) ...“[18].

Von da aus erweitert sich *dibbūr* zur Bedeutung ‘Reden, Sprechen’: „Und so wird im Namen von R. Me’īr gelehrt: Er sagt zu ihr: Dein Schweigen ist schöner als dein Reden (*middibbūrēḵ*)“[19]. — „Hat sie sich mit einem andern verheiratet, von diesem Kinder bekommen und fordert nun ihre *keṯubbā* (Hochzeitssumme), so kann er, so sagte R. Jehuda, zu ihr sagen: Dein Schweigen wäre für dich besser als dein Reden (*middibbūrēḵ*)“[20]. Die Vorzüge der verschiedenen in Palästina gesprochenen Sprachen werden auf folgende Weise dargelegt: „R. Jonaṯan aus Bet Gubrin (Eleutheropolis, um 270) sagte: Vier Sprachen sind schön, daß die Welt sich ihrer bediene. Diese sind: Die griechische zum Gesang, die römische zum Krieg, die syrische (aramäische) zur Trauerklage, und die hebräische zur Rede (*dibbūr*) [...]“[21]. — „Das lehrt, daß Mose sich nicht zu seinem Geschäft wandte und nicht in sein Haus hinabstieg, sondern vom Berge (aus) zum Volk (sprach). Etwa nur für diese Rede (*ledibbūr*)? (Daß es auch gilt für) den Rest der Worte (*haddebārōṯ*), woher (läßt es sich erweisen)?“[22]. — Zu Deut 33, 2: „Wie das Feuer (bewirkt), daß die sich mit ihm Beschäftigenden unter den Geschöpfen erkannt werden, so sind die Schüler der Weisen auf der Straße bekannt an ihrem Gang und an ihrem Reden (*ubedibbūrām*) und an ihrem Überwurf“[23]. — ‘Reden’ ist nicht immer Reden in gleicher Art und Weise: „‘Mirjam und Aaron aber redeten über Mose’. ‘Reden’ (*dibbēr*, v. l. *dibbūr*) bezeichnet überall eine harte Ausdrucksweise (Zitat Gen 42, 30)“. [...] „‘Reden’ (*dibbēr*) bezeichnet also überall eine harte Ausdrucksweise. ‘Sprechen’ (*’amirā*) dagegen bezeichnet überall die flehentliche Bitte“[24].

[18] bBḲ 73ab; Übers. von Goldschmidt, Babyl. Talm. VII 249.

[19] jGiṭ IV 8, 46a, 75f.

[20] MGiṭ IV 8.

[21] jMeg I 11, 71b, 63ff.; dasselbe jSoṭ VII 2, 21c, 12ff.; Midr Esther 4, zu 1, 22; Str.-Bi. II 451, zu Joh 5, 2.

[22] Mek Ex Baḥodesch 19, 14.

[23] SDeut § 343; S. 400, Z. 4ff. Finkelstein.

[24] SNum § 99; S. 97, Z. 21—25 Horovitz; vgl. Kuhn, SNum 259f.; dasselbe in bMakk 11a; in bSchabb 63a heißt es aber, unter Berufung auf Ps 47, 4(!), daß unter ‘Reden’ (*dibbūr*) ein sanftmütiges Sprechen gemeint sei.

II. Dibbūr *als Gottesspruch, Gottesbefehl, Gottesrede.*

Die folgenden Stellen zeigen, daß *dibbūr* = Wort für das Wort/Reden sowohl des Menschen wie auch Gottes gebraucht werden kann:

„Mit zehn Ausdrücken wird (die Prophetie) benannt: Prophetie (*nebūāh*), Gesicht (*ḥazōn*), prophetische Rede (*haṭṭafa*), (Gottes-)Rede (*dibbūr*), Ausspruch (*'amirā*), Befehl (*ṣiwwuj*), Ausspruch (*massā*, Last), Spruch (*māschāl*), Gleichnisrede (*meliṣāh*), Rätsel (*ḥidāh*). Und welches ist der härteste von allen? [. . .] R. Joḥanan († 279) sagte: Die (Gottes-)Rede (*dibbūr*), denn es heißt (Zitat Gen 42, 30)"[25]. Daß *dibbūr* nach rabbinischer Auffassung eine 'harte Redeweise' bezeichnet, sahen wir oben[26].

An zahlreichen Stellen wird *dibbūr* gebraucht als Bezeichnung des Redens Gottes, das er in seiner Offenbarung hat ergehen lassen: An Abraham, an Mose, an Israel am Sinai und in der Wüste, an Propheten, an David usw. Das Wort *dibbūr* wird in diesem Zusammenhang am besten mit „(Gottes-)Rede" wiedergegeben. Gott tut mit verschiedenen Ausdrücken Israel seine Liebe kund: „R. Abba b. Eljaschib (4. Jh.) fügt noch zwei hinzu: Mit Liebe und mit der (Gottes-)Rede (*bedibbūr*)". Für die (Gottes-)Rede wird als Schriftbeleg auf Jes 40, 2 verwiesen[27]. Hier ist also *dibbūr* nicht Bezeichnung für eine 'harte Redeweise'! — „Alle Israeliten standen vor dem Berge Sinai und sagten: 'Wenn wir noch weiter hören' (Deut 5, 22). Und Mose hörte die Stimme der (Gottes-)Rede (*haddibbūr*) allein und blieb am Leben"[28]. „R. Abin begann im Namen von R. Berekja dem Alten (4. Jh.?): 'Damals redetest du in einem Gesicht mit deinem Frommen' (Ps 89, 20). Sie (die Bibelstelle) redet von Abraham; denn mit ihm wurde geredet in (Gottes-)Rede (*bedibbūr*) und im Gesicht (Zitat Gen 15, 1)"[29]. „Sie redet von David; denn mit ihm wurde im Gesicht geredet und mit der (Gottes-)Rede (*ubedibbūr*) (Zitat 2 Sam 7, 17)"[30]. — „Was für ein Unterschied besteht zwischen den Propheten Israels und den Propheten der Weltvölker? R. Ḥama b. Ḥanina (um 260) und R. Isaḵar von Kefar Mandu (um 360). R. Ḥama b. Ḥanina sagte: Der Heilige, g. s. er! offenbart sich den Weltvölkern nur mit einer halben (Gottes-)Rede (*dibbūr*), wie es heißt (Zitat Num 23, 4). Aber den Propheten Israels mit einer ganzen (Gottes-)Rede (*dibbūr*), wie es heißt: 'Und er rief Mose'"[31]. Dieser Gebrauch des Wortes *dibbūr* ist schon alt und geht in die Zeit der Tannaïten hinauf, wie einige der im folgenden anzuführenden Zitate zeigen: Zu Ex 12, 1. „Das verstehe ich (so), daß die

[25] Gen r. 44, zu 15, 1; vgl. die Parallele in Schir r. 3, 3, zu HL 3, 4.
[26] Vgl. S. 583; vgl. auch bMakk 11a im Vergleich von Gen 42, 30 mit Mal 3, 16.
[27] Gen r. 80, zu 34, 8.
[28] Lev r. 1, 1, zu 1, 1.
[29] Lev r. 1, 4, zu 1, 1.
[30] Ebda.
[31] Lev r. 1, 13, zu 1, 1.

(Gottes-)Rede (*haddibbūr*)[32] (sich richtete) an Mose und Aaron. Wenn es aber heißt (Zitat Ex 6, 28), (dann bedeutet das, daß) die (Gottes-)Rede (*haddibbūr*)[32] (sich) an Mose richtete, aber die (Gottes-)Rede (*haddibbūr*) richtete sich nicht an Aaron"[33].

Anruf Gottes und Offenbarungsrede werden unterschieden: „'Und J' rief ihn' usw. Das zeigt an, daß der Ruf der (Gottes-)Rede (*ledibbūr*) vorangeht"[34]. „'Und er rief und redete' (Lev 1, 1). Das Rufen ging der (Gottes-)Rede (*ledibbūr*) vorauf"[35]. — Wann befahl Gott den Kauf des Passah-Lammes, und wann wurde es gekauft? Um diese Frage geht es im folgenden Text: „Die (Gottes-)Rede (*haddibbūr*) (erging) am ersten (Tage) des Monats, und der Kauf (des Lammes) geschah am zehnten und das Schlachten am vierzehnten. Du sagst: Die (Gottes-)Rede (*haddibbūr*) am ersten (Tage) des Monats und der Kauf am zehnten und das Schlachten am vierzehnten. Oder (doch) nicht (so), vielmehr die (Gottes-)Rede (*haddibbūr*) und der Kauf am zehnten und das Schlachten am vierzehnten? [...] Wann erging die (Gottes-)Rede (*haddibbūr*)?". Die Diskussion geht in diesem Stil weiter, wobei '(Gottes-)Rede' (*dibbūr*) noch sechsmal begegnet[36].

Durfte Elia auf dem Karmel einen Altar errichten? „R. Simlaj (um 250) sagte: Eine (Gottes-)Rede (*dibbērā*) (erlaubte es). Er sprach zu ihm: 'Und auf dein Geheiß (*ubedibbērkā*) habe ich (dies) getan' (1 Kön 18, 36). Und auf deine (Gottes-)Rede (*ubedibbūrkā*) (hin) habe ich (dies) getan"[37].

Gottes Reden bei der Offenbarung am Sinai geschah auf wunderbare Weise. So hatte er es nicht nötig, nach Art der Menschen und menschlicher Rede, ein Wort, bzw. ein Gebot, nach dem andern zu sagen. Er konnte vielmehr alle zehn Gebote auf e i n Mal sagen, ohne daß dadurch ein unverständlicher Schall entstanden wäre. Ja, alle Gebote und Worte überhaupt, die in der Ṯora stehen, wurden in einem einzigen Gottesspruch, in einer einzigen (Gottes-)Rede gesagt:

(Zitat Ps 115, 5) „Diese haben einen Mund und reden nicht, aber der, welcher sprach und es ward die Welt, ist nicht so. Vielmehr spricht er zwei Worte (*debārim*) in e i n e r (Gottes-)Rede (*dibbūr*), was so zu reden Fleisch und Blut nicht möglich ist. (Zitate Ps 62, 12; Jer 23, 29; Hi 37, 2)"[38]. Ähnlich das folgende: „(Das) lehrt, daß der Ort (=Gott) die zehn Worte (*haddebārōṯ*) in einer (einzigen) (Gottes-)Rede (*bedibbūr*) sprach, was so zu sagen Fleisch und Blut nicht möglich ist"[39]. „Allein, das lehrt, daß der Heilige, g. s. er! die zehn Worte in e i n e r (Gottes-)Rede (*bedibbūr*) sagte und später sagte er jeden einzelnen (Gottes-)Spruch (*dibbūr dibbūr*) für sich allein. (Das) verstehe ich (dahin), daß alle übrigen Worte, die in der Ṯora

[32] V. l. *haddibbēr, haddābār*.
[33] Mek Ex Pisḥa 12, 1; vgl. dasselbe, etwas kürzer, in Ṯanḥ Bo 5, 1.
[34] Mek Ex Baḥodesch 19, 3.
[35] SLev I 1, zu 1, 1; Str.-Bi. II 317.
[36] Mek Ex Pisḥa 12, 3.
[37] jṮaan II 8, 65d, 45f.
[38] Mek Ex Schiraṯa 15, 11.
[39] Mek Ex Baḥodesch 20, 1.

(stehen), alle (auch) in einem (einzigen) (Gottes-)Spruch (*bedibbūr*) gesagt wurden. Die Schrift sagt lehrend: 'Alle diese Worte'. Diese Worte wurden in einem (einzigen) (Gottes-)Spruch (*bedibbūr*) gesagt, und alle übrigen Gebote in der Tora wurden Wort für Wort (*dibbūr dibbūr*) für sich allein gesagt"[40].

Diese wunderbare Fähigkeit der (Gottes-)Rede erweist sich vor allem darin, daß sie gleichzeitig Gebote und Vorschriften erlassen kann, die unterschiedliche oder gar widersprüchliche Anordnungen enthalten: „'Gedenke des Sabbattages, daß du ihn heilig haltest' (Ex 20, 8). 'Gedenke' und 'bewahre' (Deut 5, 12) — beide wurden in einem (Gottes-)Spruch (*dibbūr*) gesagt. 'Wer ihn entweiht, soll sterben' (Ex 31, 14). 'Am Sabbat aber zwei Lämmer' usw. (Num 28, 9). Beide (Gebote) wurden in einem (Gottes-)Spruch (*bedibbūr*) gesagt. 'Die Blöße der Frau deines Bruders' (Lev 18, 16). 'Und ihr Schwager soll zu ihr kommen' (Deut 25, 5). Beide (Gebote) wurden in einem (Gottes-)Spruch (*bedibbūr*) gesagt. 'Du sollst nicht Mischgewebe anziehen' (Deut 22, 11). Und 'du sollst dir Quasten machen' (Deut. 22, 12). Beide (Gebote) wurden in einem (Gottes-)Spruch (*dibbūr*) gesagt, was Fleisch und Blut so zu sagen nicht möglich ist, denn es heißt (Zitat Ps 62, 12)"[41].

Das Erschrecken der Israeliten vor den Erscheinungen der Theophanie bei der Gesetzgebung (Ex 20, 18ff.) wird z. B. auf folgende Weise beschrieben: „R. 'Aḳiba sagt: Das ist der Tag der Gesetzgebung. Denn die Israeliten erbebten (und wichen) zwölf Mil zurück und dann rückten sie zwölf Mil vor, 24 Mil auf jedes einzelne (Gottes-)Wort (*dibbūr wedibbūr*) [...]"[42]. „'Und blieb in der Ferne stehen'. Zwölf Mil außerhalb. Das zeigt an, daß die Israeliten zwölf Mil zurückwichen und dann zwölf Mil vorrückten, 24 Mil auf jedes einzelne (Gottes-)Wort (*dibbūr wedibbūr*). Es ergibt sich, daß sie an diesem Tage 240 Mil zurücklegten"[43]. — Anders versteht Rabbi, der Redaktor der Mischna († 219), die Stelle Ex 20, 18: „Rabbi sagt: (Dies ist gesagt), um das Lob Israels bekanntzumachen; denn als sie alle vor dem Berge Sinai standen, um die Tora zu empfangen, hörten sie die (Gottes-)Rede (*haddibbūr*) und legten[44] sie aus, wie es heißt (Zitat Deut 32, 10) [...] Denn als die (Gottes-)Rede (*haddibbūr*) ausging, legten sie sie aus"[45].

„R. Levi (um 300) sagte: [...] so, als der Heilige, g. s. er! redete, sagte jeder einzelne aus Israel: An mich (*'immi*) erging die (Gottes-)Rede (*haddibbūr*)"[46]. — „R. Jose b. Ḥanina (2. Jh.) sagte: Gemäß der Kraft jedes einzelnen sprach die (Gottes-)Rede (*haddibbūr*) mit ihm. Und verwundere

[40] Mek Ex Baḥodesch 21, 1.

[41] Mek Ex Baḥodesch 20, 8; vgl. dieselbe Tradition in jNed III 2, 37d, 60ff.; Ex r. 28, 3, zu 19,10; vgl. auch SNum § 42, zu 6, 26, S. 47f. HOROVITZ; Num r. 11, 14, zu 6, 22; SDeut § 233, S. 265f. FINKELSTEIN.

[42] Mek Ex Baḥodesch 19, 4.

[43] Mek Ex Baḥodesch 20, 18.

[44] *Mephareschim* = sie erklärten, legten aus.

[45] Mek Ex Baḥodesch 20, 18.

[46] Das läßt sich verstehen als: „Mit mir redete J'"; so auch in den folgenden beiden Sätzen.

dich nicht über diese Sache, denn wir finden beim Manna, als es zu Israel herabkam, (da) kostete es jeder einzelne von ihnen gemäß seiner Kraft[47] – die (Gottes-)Rede (*haddibbūr*) um wie viel mehr!"[48].

Alles, was im Pentateuch steht, wurde dem Volk Israel am Sinai offenbart, also auch die Ereignisse und die sie begleitenden und beurteilenden Gottesworte auf dem Zug durch die Wüste nach der Sinaioffenbarung. Nur waren diese Dinge dem Volk am Sinai noch nicht einsichtig, sondern sie wurden es erst, als die betreffenden Ereignisse eintrafen: „Und Mose sagte: Das ist's, was J' gesprochen hat folgendermaßen: 'Die mir nahestehen, an ihnen erweise ich mich als heilig' (Lev 10, 3). Dieser (Gottes-)Spruch (*haddibbūr*) wurde zu Mose am Sinai gesagt, aber sie erkannten es nicht, bis das Ereignis eintraf"[49]. „R. Jiṣḥaḳ begann (Zitat Jer 15, 16). R. Schemuel b. Naḥman (um 260) sagte: Dieser (Gottes-)Spruch (*haddibbūr*) wurde Mose am Sinai gesagt, aber er wurde erst bekannt, als die Veranlassung dazu sich ergab". „'Und Aaron schwieg' (Lev 10, 3). Und woher (läßt sich erweisen), daß er Lohn für sein Schweigen erhielt? Weil er gewürdigt wurde, daß die (Gottes-)Rede (*haddibbūr*) sich an ihn richtete, wie es heißt: 'Und J' redete zu Aaron' (Lev 10, 8)"[50].

Da das offenbarende Reden Gottes sich vor allem am Sinai, bei der Gesetzgebung, ereignete, bekommt *dibbūr* geradezu die Bedeutung 'Gesetzgebung': „Vor der (Gottes-)Rede" (*lifne haddibbūr*) bedeutet also „vor der Gesetzgebung"; „von der (Gottes-)Rede an" (*min haddibbūr*) ist „von der Gesetzgebung an"; „nach der (Gottes-)Rede" (*leaḥar haddibbūr*) ist „nach der Gesetzgebung"[51]. Beschneidung und tägliches Opfer bestanden schon vor der Gesetzgebung (*lifne haddibbūr*)[52]. *Dibbūr* = (Gottes-)Rede in der Bedeutung 'Gesetzgebung' erscheint auch in der folgenden Diskussion über die Wichtigkeit von Erscheinungsopfer (vgl. Deut 16, 16) und Festopfer. „Das Haus Schammaj sagt: Größer ist das Erscheinungsopfer als das Maß des Festopfers. Das Erscheinungsopfer (gehört) ganz dem Höchsten, was so beim Festopfer nicht (der Fall ist). Aber das Haus Hillel sagt: Größer ist das Maß des Festopfers als das Maß des Erscheinungsopfers. Das Festopfer war gebräuchlich vor der (Gottes-)Rede (*haddibbūr*) und nach der (Gottes-)Rede (*haddibbūr*), was so nicht (der Fall ist) beim Erscheinungsopfer" [...] „Und das Festopfer war gebräuchlich vor der (Gottes-)Rede (*haddibbūr*)

[47] „Dem gegenüber speistest du mit Engelkost dein Volk und sandtest ihnen ohne Ermüden zubereitetes Brot vom Himmel herab, das jeglichen Genuß darbot und eines Jeden Geschmack ansprach. Denn dein Wesen (ὑπόστασις) offenbarte deinen Kindern deine Süßigkeit, und indem es dem Begehren des Genießenden entgegenkam, verwandelte es sich in das, was einer wollte" (Sap Sal 16, 20f.).

[48] Ṭanḥ B Jetro § 17; nach bSchabb 88b (Bar) teilte sich jedes Wort (*kōl dibbūr wedibbūr*), das aus dem Munde Gottes ausging, in 70 Sprachen.

[49] SLev Schemini I 36, zu 10, 3.

[50] Lev r. 12, 2, zu 10, 9.

[51] SLev Tazri'a I 4, zu 12, 2; SLev Nega'im 1, 2, zu 13, 2. 9; SLev Meṣor'a I 2, zu 15, 2; IV 1, zu 15, 19; SLev Emor III 2, zu 21, 17.

[52] bJeb 5b; der Ausdruck begegnet im folg. Satz noch einmal.

und nach der (Gottes-)Rede (*haddibbūr*), was so bei den beiden (andern) nicht der Fall ist"[53].

III. Dibbūr *als Umschreibung (Ersatzwort) für Jahwe/Gott*

Das Judentum hat es in den Jahrhunderten um die Zeitwende vermieden, den Eigennamen Gottes, Jahwe, auszusprechen — aus Angst vor Profanierung und Mißbrauch in Zauber und Magie. Man wollte durch das Nichtaussprechen des Jahwe-Namens das Gebot Ex 20, 7 erfüllen. Statt des Jahwe-Namens wurden Ersatzworte verwendet: 'Herr' (*'adonaj*, gr. *kyrios*)[54], der 'Name'[55], 'Himmel'[56], 'Memra da J'J''[57], 'der Ort' (*hammaḳōm*)[58] u. a.

BILLERBECK[59] hat nun Zeugnisse aus dem rabbinischen Schrifttum zusammengestellt, in denen auch das Wort *dibbūr* = (Gottes-)Rede als solche umschreibende Bezeichnung für Jahwe bzw. Gott begegnet. Diesen Zeugnissen wenden wir uns nun zu. Nach BILLERBECK wäre der erste, der (Gottes-) Rede (*dibbūr*) als Ersatz für Jahwe brauchte, R. Jehoschu'a b. Levi (um 250) gewesen: „R. Jehoschu'a b. Levi sagte: [. . .] bevor das Offenbarungszelt aufgestellt war, pflegte die (Gottes-)Rede (*haddibbūr*) in den Zelten der Völker der Welt aus- und einzugehen, und sie waren entsetzt, wie es heißt: 'Denn wo wäre ein sterblicher Mensch, der wie wir die Stimme des lebendigen Gottes aus dem Feuer hätte reden hören und am Leben geblieben wäre' (Deut 5, 23 [26])"[60]. Ähnlich, etwas kürzer, redet folgende Stelle: „R. Jehoschu'a b. Levi sagte: [. . .] du findest, ehe das Offenbarungszelt aufgestellt war, hörten die Völker der Welt die Stimme der (Gottes-)Rede (*haddibbūr*) und waren entsetzt in ihren Palästen"[61].

Man kann sich — vor allem bei der ersten, R. Jehoschu'a b. L. zugeschriebenen, Fassung dieser Tradition — fragen, ob da wirklich *dibbūr* = (Gottes-)Rede Ersatzwort für Jahwe/Gott ist. Denn im Klartext würde in diesem Fall der Ausspruch von R. Jehoschu'a b. L. besagen, daß Gott selbst

[53] TḤag I 4 (S. 232 Z.); STR.-BI. II 143, zu Luk 2, 41; dasselbe SDeut § 138, S. 193 FINKELSTEIN: Auf R. Jose den Galiläer zurückgeführt; SDeut liest *dibbēr*, mit Ausnahme des Textzeugen Rom, der *dibbūr* liest.

[54] ThWbNT III (1938) 1056—1080, Atkl. κύριος (QUELL), 1081ff. (FOERSTER).

[55] ThWbNT V (1954) 268, Atkl. ὄνομα (BIETENHARD).

[56] ThWbNT V (1954) 512, Atkl. οὐρανός (TRAUB).

[57] STR.-BI. II 326—333.

[58] STR.-BI. II 309f.

[59] STR.-BI. II 317f. — BILLERBECKS Aufstellungen haben sich weithin durchgesetzt. Sie trafen aber auch von Anfang an auf Widerspruch, der bis heute nicht verstummt ist, e. g.: BOUSSET–GRESSMANN, Die Religion des Judentums, 342 Anm. 1; 346 Anm. 1; DIEZ MACHO, El Logos, 390ff.; vgl. auch den Abschnitt IV der vorliegenden Arbeit (unten S. 592ff.).

[60] Tanḥ B Ṯerumāh § 8; zu diesem Text vgl. unten, S. 601.

[61] Lev r. 1, 11, zu 1, 1.

in den Zelten der Weltvölker aus- und einging! Das dürfte aber schwerlich der Meinung des Rabbi entsprochen haben. Seiner Meinung dürfte eher die Auffassung entsprechen, daß die Stimme bzw. die (Gottes-)Rede (*dibbūr*) Jahwes sich den Völkern der Welt kundtat. Somit müßte hier zwischen Jahwe/Gott und seiner offenbarenden Rede unterschieden werden.

BILLERBECKS Auffassung dürfte eher folgende Stelle entsprechen: „'Und J' rief Mose' (Lev 1, 1). Aber nicht wie Abraham. Bei Abraham steht geschrieben: 'Es rief der Engel J's Abraham' (Gen 22, 11). Der Engel ruft, und die (Gottes-)Rede (*haddibbūr*)[62] redete. Aber hier — sagte R. Abin (I., um 325, oder II., um 370) — sagte der Heilige, g. s. er!: Ich bin es, der ruft, und ich bin es, der redet, wie es heißt (Zitat Jes 48, 15)"[63]. D. h. bei der Offenbarung an Abraham wird der Ruf des Engels dem Reden Jahwes gegenübergestellt. Das entspricht zwar dem Sinn des Textes von Gen 22, 11 nicht, wo gemeint ist, daß der Engel selbst ruft und dann auch redet! — Folgende Stellen entsprechen ebenfalls der Auffassung BILLERBECKS: „Alle Israeliten standen vor dem Berge Sinai und sagten: 'Wenn wir noch weiter hören' (Deut 5, 22). Wisse, daß es so ist; denn von allen rief die (Gottes-)Rede (*haddibbūr*) nur den Mose, wie es heißt: 'Und er rief Mose'"[64]. — „R. Ṯanḥum b. Ḥanilaj (um 280, Schüler von R. Jehoschu'a b. Levi) sagt: . . . Denn die Israeliten standen vor dem Berg Sinai und vermochten die Stimme der (Gottes-)Rede (*ḳōl haddibbūr*) nicht zu hören, wie es heißt (Zitat Deut 5, 22)"[64a]. — „R. 'Azarja (um 380) sagte: Jene 38 Jahre hindurch, welche die Israeliten in der Wüste gleichsam in den Bann getan waren, hat die (Gottes-)Rede (*haddibbūr*) mit Mose nicht geredet, bis jene ganze Generation aufgerieben war"[65].

Aber schon bei den Parallelstellen, die es zu dieser zuletzt angeführten Tradition gibt, muß man sich fragen, ob (Gottes-)Rede (*dibbūr*) einfach Ersatzwort oder Umschreibung für Gott/Jahwe sein kann: „Es geschah keine (Gottes-)Rede (*dibbūr J'* [sic!]) an (*'im*) Mose"[66]. „Es geschah keine (Gottes-)Rede (*dibbūr*) zu (*'im*) Mose"[67]. Das will besagen, daß sich keine Offenbarungsrede Gottes an Mose ereignete, was aus der Fassung in bṮaan deutlich hervorgeht. Wäre hier *dibbūr* Ersatzwort für Gott, würde der Satz besagen, daß Gott nicht mit Mose war — das aber dürfte kaum die Meinung des Rabbi gewesen sein. — In einem Midrasch, der die beiden Stellen Num 1, 44 und 3, 39 miteinander vergleicht, heißt es: „Das will dich lehren, daß die Fürsten Israels die Leviten nicht auf Befehl der (Gottes-)Rede (*haddibbūr* bzw. *haddibbēr*) gezählt haben, aber Mose zog sie hinzu, um ihnen Ehre zu erweisen"[68]. Die Wendung „auf Befehl der (Gottes-)Rede" (*'al pi haddib-*

[62] Andere Ausgaben: *haddibbēr*.
[63] Lev r. 1, 9, zu 1, 1.
[64] Lev r. 1, 1, zu 1, 1.
[64a] Tanḥ Waijjḳra § 1.
[65] Schir r. 2, 27, zu HL 2, 13.
[66] bṮaan 30b.
[67] bBB 121ab.
[68] Num r. 6, 8, zu 4, 34.

būr) findet sich auch sonst[69]: „Und immer, wenn sie nach dem Befehl der (Gottes-)Rede (*mippi haddibbūr*) gezählt wurden, traf sie keine Plage. Aber immer, wenn sie nicht nach dem Befehl der (Gottes-)Rede (*mippi haddibbūr*) gezählt wurden, traf sie eine Plage. Und wann wurden sie nicht nach dem Befehl der (Gottes-)Rede (*mippi haddibbūr*) gezählt und es traf sie eine Plage? In den Tagen Davids, wie es heißt (Zitat 1 Chron 21, 1)"[70/71]. „Und Elia opferte zur Zeit, da die Höhen verboten waren. R. Simlaj (um 250) sagte: (Es geschah auf göttlichen) Befehl (*dibbērā*). Er sprach zu ihm: 'Und nach deinem Wort habe ich gehandelt' (1 Kön 18, 36). (D. h.) und nach deinem (Gottes-)Spruch (*ubedibbūrkā*) habe ich gehandelt"[72]. — Zu Ex 17, 9 wird bemerkt: „Aber sagte er es ihm etwa aus eigener Einsicht? Nein. Vielmehr auf Befehl der (Gottes-)Rede (*mippi haddibbūr*) vermochte Josua die Nachkommenschaft Amaleks zu vertilgen"[73]

„R. Schim'on b. Joḥaj (um 150) sagte: [. . .] Bevor der erste Mensch sündigte, hörte er die Stimme der (Gottes-)Rede (*ḳōl haddibbūr*) und stellte sich auf seine Füße und konnte gegen sie bestehen. Nachdem er gesündigt hatte, hörte er die Stimme der (Gottes-)Rede (*ḳōl haddibbūr*) und versteckte sich, wie es heißt (Zitat Gen 3, 8)"[74]. — „Und wenn Mose ins Offenbarungszelt ging, um mit Ihm zu reden, hörte er die Stimme der (Gottes-)Rede (*dibbērā*), (die) mit ihm redete von oben her, von der Deckplatte, die über der Lade des Zeugnisses war, zwischen den beiden Keruben hervor. Von da pflegte die (Gottes-)Rede (*dibbērā*) mit ihm zu reden"[75]. „Wenn Mose ins Offenbarungszelt ging, um mit Ihm zu reden, hörte er die S t i m m e d e s G e i s t e s, die mit ihm redete, wenn sie vom Himmel der Himmel herabgekommen war auf die Deckplatte, die über der Lade des Zeugnisses war, zwischen den zwei Keruben hervor. Von dort pflegte die (Gottes-)Rede (*dibbērā*) mit ihm zu reden"[76]. BILLERBECK faßt auch an dieser Stelle — das Tg. Neofiti 1 kannte er noch nicht — (Gottes-)Rede (*dibbērā*) als Ersatzwort für Gott auf. Es scheint aber eher so zu sein, daß (Gottes-)Rede (*dibbērā*) ein Äquivalent ist für 'Geist' (Gottes); denn es heißt ja ausdrücklich, daß

[69] jSchabb VII 2, 10c, 30; dasselbe j'Erub V 22c, 22f. 52f.: Auf dem Zug durch die Wüste lagert sich das Volk, bzw. bricht es auf, nach dem (Gottes-)Spruch (Befehl). — Die Israeliten meinten, daß die (Gottes-)Rede (*haddibbūr*) den Aaron gerufen habe, Jalḳut Num § 764, aus Jelammedenu; STR.-BI. II 319.

[70] Pesiḳt r. 10 (40b).

[71] Nach Befehl, auf Geheiß (*'al pi haddibbūr*), bḤull 5a.

[72] jT̲aan II 8, 65d, 45f.; dasselbe jMeg I 13, 72c, 52f.

[73] Pesiḳt r. 13 (54a).

[74] Num r. 11, 5, zu 6, 22; dieselbe Tradition in Schir r. 3, 14, zu HL 3, 8 im Namen Rabbis († 219); Midr Schemuel 17 § 4 (49a) im Namen von R. Schim'on b. Joḥaj (um 150); Pesiḳt 44b; Pesiḳt r. 15 (68b) im Namen von R. Jischm'ael — diese Angabe wäre nach BILLERBECK richtig, STR.-BI. II 318. Die Stellen Midr Schemuel, Pesiḳt und Pesiḳt r. lesen nur *ḳōl* = Stimme, ohne *dibbūr* = (Gottes-)Rede, was, wieder nach BILLERBECK, ursprünglich wäre: Nach alter Gewohnheit wird die Gottesbezeichnung ganz weggelassen, wo kein Mißverständnis möglich war. So sind die beiden Stellen kein Beleg für den Gebrauch von *dibbūr* als Ersatz für 'Gott' bzw. 'Jahwe' im 2. Jh.

[75] Tg. Neophyti 1 Num 7, 89.

[76] Tg. Jerusch I Num 7, 89; vgl. STR.-Bi. III 175, zu Röm 3, 25.

der Geist Gottes vom höchsten Himmel her in das Offenbarungszelt herabkam und mit Mose redete.

„Die (Gottes-)Rede (*dibbērā*) wollte mit ihm (scl. Jacob) reden“[77]. In Gen r. 68, zu 28, 11 ist die Rede vom „Heiligen, g. s. er!“. Der Vergleich der beiden Stellen zeigt, daß *dibbērā/dibbūrā* Ersatzwort ist für „der Heilige, g. s. er!“.

Ein Midrasch über die Passahnacht (zu Ex 12, 42) lautet im Targum: „Eine Nacht der Beobachtung und bestimmt ist sie für die Erlösung für den Namen J's, wenn die Israeliten befreit aus dem Lande Ägypten ausziehen. Denn vier Nächte sind es, die aufgeschrieben sind im Buche der Erinnerungen. Die erste Nacht: Als J' sich offenbarte über der Welt, um sie zu schaffen. Die Welt war wüst und leer, und die Finsternis war ausgebreitet über dem Abgrund. Und die Rede (*mēmrēh*) J's war das Licht und leuchtete. Und er nannte sie 'erste Nacht'“ [...] „Die vierte Nacht: Wenn die Welt zu ihrem Ende kommt, um erlöst zu werden: Die eisernen Joche werden zerbrochen, und die Geschlechter der Gottlosen werden vernichtet, und Mose wird aus der Steppe heraufsteigen (und der König, der Messias von der Höhe [oder: von Rom ?!]). Dieser wird an der Spitze der Herde führen, und dieser wird an der Spitze der Herde [oder: der Wolke ?!] führen, und sein Wort (*mēmrēh*) wird zwischen den beiden führen. Und ich und sie werden zusammen führen. Das ist die Passah-Nacht für den Namen J's, eine Nacht der Beobachtung, und bestimmt ist sie für die Erlösung von ganz Israel für ihre Geschlechter“[78]. Vgl. dazu das bisher bekannte Targum: „Vier Nächte sind im Buche der Erinnerungen vor dem Herrn der Welt aufgeschrieben. Die erste Nacht, da er sich offenbarte, um die Welt zu schaffen. Die zweite, da er sich Abraham offenbarte. Die dritte, da er sich in Ägypten offenbarte und seine linke Hand jede Erstgeburt der Ägypter tötete und seine rechte Hand die Erstgeborenen Israels errettete. Die vierte, da er sich offenbaren wird, um das Volk, das Haus Israels aus den Völkern heraus zu erlösen. Und sie alle nennt er Nächte, die zu beobachten sind“[79].

„Und Mose stieg hinauf, um Belehrung von J' zu erbitten, und es rief ihn das Wort (*dibbērā*) J's vom Berge folgendermaßen . . .“[80]. „Es redete die (Gottes-)Rede (*dibbērēh*) J's die ganze Pracht dieser Worte folgendermaßen . . .“[81]. — „Die (Gottes-)Rede J's (*dibbūrā de J' J'*) rief den Mose, und der Mēmrā Jahwes redete mit ihm“[82]. Hier ist der „Mēmrā J's“ Gott selbst, bzw. die Umschreibung für Gott, im Gegensatz zur (Gottes-)Rede (*dibbūrā de J' J'*). Es ist zu beachten, daß in den drei zuletzt erwähnten Beispielen *dibbūrā* nicht wie sonst absolut gebraucht wird, sondern in der Genetivkonstruktion *dibbūrā de J' J'*. — In Lev r. 1, 9 steht dem Engel die (Gottes-)

[77] Tg. Jerusch I Gen 28, 10; statt *dibbērā* hat Tg. Jerusch II ad 1c. *dibbūrā*.
[78] Tg. Neophyti 1 Ex 12, 42.
[79] Tg. Jerusch I Ex 12, 42; Str.-Bi. IV 55.
[80] Tg. Neophyti 1 Ex 19, 3; R. Le Déaut ebda. 332 Anm. 1: «Dibberah = *le 'Logos', la 'Parole', le 'Verbe'. D'ordinaire on emploie* Memra».
[81] Tg. Jerusch II Ex 20, 1; Str.-Bi. II 319.
[82] Tg. Jerusch I Lev 1, 1.

Rede (*dibbūr*) gegenüber, also ist hier *dibbūr* = *Mēmrā de J' J'* = Gott[83]. — „Damals rief die (Gottes-)Rede (*dibbērā*) den Mose und J' redete mit ihm aus dem Offenbarungszelt folgendermaßen ...“[84]. — „Wenn sie (scl. die Lebewesen, 'Tiere', *ḥaijjoṯ*) stillstanden, ließen sie ihre Flügel vor der (Gottes-)Rede (*dibbūrā*) schweigen“[85/86].

Wenn auch einige Fragen offen bleiben, bestätigen die meisten der in diesem Abschnitt beigebrachten Stellen die These BILLERBECKS, daß *dibbūr dibbēr*/aram. *dibbūrā, dibbērā* Ersatzwort ist für Jahwe/Gott.

IV. Dibbūr *als selbständige Wesenheit (Hypostase*[87]*)*

Das Rabbinat befaßte sich mit der Ṯora nicht nur in inhaltlicher Hinsicht, sondern es betrachtete, auf Grund des biblischen Berichtes, auch die Umstände, unter denen die Ṯora dem Volke Israel am Sinai gegeben wurde. Hier war — von unserem Zusammenhang aus — vor allem die Stelle Ex 20, 18 wichtig: „Und das ganze Volk sah (*rō'im*) die Stimme (*hakḳōl*) ...“. Moderne Übersetzungen, z. B. die Zürcher-Übersetzung, geben das *rō'im* des Textes mit 'wahrnehmen' wieder. Das Rabbinat hält aber weithin am wörtlichen Sinn und Verständnis des Textes fest: „Das Volk sah die Stimme ...“[88].

Bei solch wörtlichem Verständnis des Satzes erhebt sich aber notwendigerweise die Frage, wie man denn eine Stimme sehen könne. Schon in tannaïtischer Zeit haben sich Gelehrte mit dem Problem der Sichtbarkeit von Gottes Stimme bzw. Reden beschäftigt: „R. 'Akiḇa sagt: Sie sahen und hörten, was sichtbar war: Sie sahen ein Wort (*dābār*) von Feuer ausgehen aus dem Munde der Kraft[89], und es war eingegraben auf die Tafeln, wie es heißt:

[83] STR.-BI. II 318.

[84] Tg. Neophyti 1 Lev 1, 1.

[85] Tg. Ez 1, 25; vgl. bḤag 13b (Bar): Wenn die (Gottes-)Rede (*haddibbūr*) aus dem Munde Gottes ausgeht, schweigen die *ḥaijjoṯ*, wenn sie nicht ausgeht, reden sie.

[86] Nach DOMINGO MUÑOZ ist *dibbērā* jünger als *mēmrā*, vgl. Neophyti 1 III 80*f.

[87] Zum Begriff der Hypostase: „ Die 'Hypostasen' sind wie die Engel Mittelwesen zwischen Gott und Welt, die sein Wirken auf die Welt ermöglichen. Sie sind nur abstrakter, schemenhafter, schwerer zu fassen, als die derben und anschaulichen Gestalten des volkstümlichen Engelglaubens. Sie erscheinen als Mitteldinge zwischen Personen und abstrakten Wesen, nicht so losgelöst von Gott wie die konkreten Engelgestalten, mehr mit seinem Wesen verschmolzen und zu ihm gehörig, und doch wieder gesondert gedacht ...“ (BOUSSET–GRESSMANN, Die Religion des Judentums, 342); „In der modernen Religionswissenschaft hat das Wort H. einen teilweise neuen Sinn bekommen. Es bezeichnet eine oft nur halbselbständige göttliche Wesenheit, die eine mehr oder weniger durchgeführte Personifizierung einer Eigenschaft, einer Wirksamkeit oder irgend eines Attributes einer höheren Gottheit darstellt“ (H. RINGGREN, Atkl. Hypostasen, RGG III³ [1959], Sp. 504).

[88] Auch die LXX lasen den uns heute vorliegenden Ms-Text. Statt 'sah' liest der Samaritanus *schām'a* = „hörte“.

[89] Vgl. Matth 26, 64.

'Die Stimme J's sprüht Feuerflammen' (Ps 29, 7)"[90]. 'Aḳiḇa kombiniert also Ps 29, 7 mit Ex 20, 18 und kommt so zur Aussage, daß das Gotteswort bei der Gesetzgebung sichtbar war. Es ist hier nicht zu untersuchen, inwiefern diese Kombination beweiskräftig ist. — In der Auslegung von Num 12, 8 findet sich folgende Ausführung: „'Von Mund zu Mund rede ich mit ihm' ... 'im Schauen' [במראה]. Das [bezeichnet] das Schauen der Rede (*dibbur*). Oder (bezeichnet es vielleicht) vielmehr das Schauen der Scheḵina? Da ist es eine Belehrung, daß es heißt: 'Und er sprach: Mein Angesicht kannst du nicht schauen, denn es schaut mich kein Mensch und lebt' (Ex 33, 20)"[91]. KUHN bemerkt dazu: „Der Text wird so verstanden: 'Von Mund zu Mund rede ich mit ihm im Schauen', d. h. so, daß er meine Rede auch sieht. Wie man sich das vorstellte, ist nicht mehr deutlich erkennbar"[92]. — Der folgende Ausspruch von R. Jehuḏa lautet ähnlich wie der soeben zitierte Ausspruch von R. 'Aḳiḇa und ist vielleicht von diesem abhängig: „R. Jehuḏa (um 150) sagt: Wenn ein Mensch mit seinem Genossen redet, wird er gesehen, aber seine Stimme wird nicht gesehen. Aber die Israeliten hörten die Stimme (*ḳōlō*) des Heiligen, g. s. er! und sahen auch die Stimme (*haḳḳōl*) ausgehen aus dem Munde der Kraft, und Blitze und Donnerschläge, wie es heißt (Zitat Ex 20, 15)"[93]. — „Bar Ḳappara (um 220) sagte: Der Heilige, g. s. er! machte das Unsichtbare sichtbar und das Unhörbare hörbar, und das, was nicht redet, daß es redete. Wenn du sagst: Das Unsichtbare sichtbar, woher (begründest du diese Behauptung)? (Von da, wo es heißt:) 'Und das ganze Volk sah die Stimmen und die Blitze' (Ex 20, 18)"[94]. — Daß das Wort Jahwes am Sinai sichtbar wurde für das Volk, wird hier auf ein besonderes (wunderbares) Wirken Gottes zurückgeführt.

In seiner Weise hat auch Philon von Alexandreia sich mit diesem Problem der Sichtbarkeit von Gottes Stimme auseinandergesetzt: „Die zehn Worte oder göttlichen Aussprüche [...] hat der Vater des Weltalls vor versammeltem Volke [...] geoffenbart. Also hätte Gott eine Art Stimme gehabt, mit der er selbst sie ausgesprochen? Nicht doch! Solches darf uns gar nicht in den Sinn kommen. Denn nicht wie ein Mensch ist Gott, daß er des Mundes, der Zunge, der Arterien bedürfte, vielmehr scheint er mir zu jener Zeit etwas Hehres und Wunderbares geschaffen zu haben, indem er befahl, daß ein unsichtbarer Schall in der Luft sich bilde, wunderbarer als alle Instrumente der Welt, ausgestattet mit vollkommenen Harmonien, nicht ohne Seele, aber auch nicht wie ein aus Leib und Seele bestehendes Lebewesen, sondern bloß eine vernunftbegabte Seele voll Klarheit und Deutlichkeit; diese Seele, der Luft Gestalt gebend und sie weithin spannend und zur feuerroten Flamme wandelnd, ließ wie ein Lufthauch, der durch die

[90] Mek Ex Baḥodesch 20, 15.

[91] SNum § 103, S. 101, Z. 15 HOROVITZ; KUHN, SNum, 269.

[92] In Anm. 12 bemerkt KUHN: „Demnach kann es sich hier nur um das Schauen der Rede handeln". So auch BILLERBECK, STR.-BI. II 317 z. St.

[93] Pirḳe R. Eli'ezer 41 [98a] (gegen Ende); diese Quelle ist spät, und es erhebt sich die Frage nach der Authentizität des Ausspruchs.

[94] Midr Schemuel 9, 4 (37b); BACHER, Tannaiten II, 520.

Trompete gestoßen wird, eine Stimme mit so artikulierten Lauten ertönen, daß die ganz entfernt Stehenden in gleicher Weise wie die Nächsten sie zu hören glaubten [. . .]"[95]. In derselben Schrift[96] spricht sich Philon noch deutlicher aus und redet von der Sichtbarkeit der göttlichen Stimme: „Eine Stimme ertönte darauf mitten aus dem vom Himmel herabkommenden Feuer, alle mit ehrfurchtsvollem Schrecken erfüllend, indem die Flamme sich zu artikulierten Lauten wandelte, die den Hörenden vertraut waren, wobei das Gesprochene so deutlich klang, daß man es eher zu sehen als zu hören glaubte. Es bestätigt mir meine Behauptung die heilige Schrift, in der es heißt: 'alles Volk sah die Stimme' (2 Mos. 20, 18); höchst bedeutsam, denn Menschenstimme ist zu hören, die Stimme Gottes aber ist in Wahrheit zu sehen; warum? Weil es nicht Worte sind, was Gott redet, sondern Taten, die das Auge besser unterscheidet als das Ohr".

Diese Ansicht von der Sichtbarkeit der göttlichen Stimme steht im Zusammenhang mit der antiken Auffassung, nach welcher alles körperlich konkret vorzustellen ist: „Alles Schaffende ist Leib" (Diogenes VII 56); *quidquid facit corpus est* (Seneca, epist. 117, 2); von den Stoikern berichtet Origenes (c. Cels. VI 71), daß nach ihrer Ansicht das Wort Gottes ein „körperlicher Geist" sei (σῶμα πνευματικόν), was Origenes selbst ablehnt[97].

Die im folgenden angeführte Tradition ist anonym und daher zeitlich nicht genau einzuordnen, da sie aber tannaïtisch ist, dürfte sie nicht später als das 2. (Anf. 3.) Jh. n. Chr. anzusetzen sein:

> „'Er schützte es' (Deut 32, 10). Mit den zehn Geboten. Das lehrt, daß, als die (Gottes-)Rede (*haddibbēr*) aus dem Munde des Heiligen, g. s. er! ausging, sahen die Israeliten sie und achteten auf sie und erkannten, wie viel Auslegung in ihr ist, und wie wiel Halaḵa in ihr ist, und wie viele (Folgerungen) vom Leichteren auf das Schwere in ihr sind. 'Er hütete es wie seinen Augapfel' (ebda.). Sie gingen zwölf Mil und rückten vor zwölf Mil über jedem einzelnen Wort (*dibbūr wedibbūr*), und sie bebten nicht zurück, weder vor den Stimmen noch vor den Blitzen"[98].

Es gibt Traditionen, nach denen die Offenbarungsrede Gottes sich nicht direkt an die Israeliten wandte, sondern daß gesagt wird, Engel hätten sie dem Volke übermittelt. Dabei wird die Vorstellung vom Worte Gottes wieder ganz konkret:

> „Eine andere Auslegung. 'Er küsse mich mit Küssen seines Mundes' (HL 1, 2). R. Joḥanan († um 279) sagte: Ein Engel trug die (Gottes-)Rede (*haddibbūr*) vom Heiligen, g. s.er!, jedes einzelne Wort (*'al ḵōl dibbūr wedibbūr*) und ging zu jedem einzelnen Israeliten und sagte zu ihm: Nimmst du dieses (Gottes-)Wort (*haddibbūr*) auf dich? So und

[95] de decal. 32—35. Philos Werke deutsch, Bd. I 377f. (übers. von L. Treitel).
[96] de decal. 46.f; ebda. S. 381.
[97] Die Stellen bei Dürr, Die Wertung des göttlichen Wortes, 146.f; vgl. auch Sap Sal 7, 24f., ebda.
[98] SDeut § 313, S. 355 Finkelstein.

so viele Rechtssätze sind in ihm, so und so viele Strafarten sind in ihm, so und so viele Entscheidungen sind in ihm, und so und so viele Gebote und so und so viele (Folgerungen vom) Leichteren auf das Schwerere sind in ihm, so und so viele Belohnungen sind in ihm. Und der Israelit sagte zu ihm: Ja! Wiederum fragte er ihn: Nimmst du die Gottheit des Heiligen, g. s. er! an? Und er sagte zu ihm: Ja, ja! Sofort küßte er ihn auf den Mund. Das ist, was geschrieben steht: 'Dir ist es gezeigt worden, um es zu erkennen' (Deut 4, 35), (nämlich) durch einen Boten (Engel). Aber die Rabbinen sagen: Die (Gottes-)Rede (*haddibbūr*) selbst ging zu einem jeden einzelnen aus Israel und sagte zu ihm: Nimmst du mich auf? So und so viele Gebote sind in mir [...]" usw.

(Fortsetzung wie oben, wobei es immer heißt „sind in mir").

„Sofort küßte ihn die (Gottes-)Rede (*haddibbūr*) auf den Mund [...] und sie lernten die Ṯora. Das ist, was geschrieben steht (Zitat Deut 4, 9). Die Worte, die deine Augen gesehen haben. Wie die (Gottes-)Rede (*haddibbūr*) mit dir gesprochen hat. Eine andere Auslegung. 'Dass du die Worte nicht vergessest'. Zwei (Gottes-)Reden (*dibbūrim*) hörten die Israeliten aus dem Munde des Heiligen, g. s. er! R. Jehoschuʿa b. Levi (um 250) sagte: Nach der Meinung der Rabbinen (ist es so): (Erst) nach allen (Gottes-)Reden (*haddebārōṯ*) steht geschrieben: 'Rede du mit uns, und wir wollen hören'"[99].

„'Zu seiner rechten Hand ist ein feuriges Gesetz an sie'[100] (Deut 33, 2). Als die (Gottes-)Rede (*haddibbūr*, v. l., *dibbēr*) ausging aus dem Munde des Heiligen, g. s. er!, ging sie aus zur Rechten des Heiligen, g. s. er! zur Linken Israels und ging um das Lager Israels herum, zwölf auf zwölf Mil, und dann ging sie zur Rechten Israels, zur Linken des Heiligen, g. s. er!, und der Heilige, g. s. er! faßte sie mit seiner Rechten und grub sie auf die Tafel. Und seine Stimme ging von einem Ende der Welt zum andern, wie es heißt (Zitat Ps 29, 7)"[101].

In einer andern Rezension dieses Midrasch lautet die Überlieferung so (sie nennt auch den Autor!):

„Und wie ging die (Gottes-)Rede (*haddibbūr*) aus dem Munde des Heiligen, g. s. er!? R. Schimʿon b. Joḥaj (um 150) und die Rabbinen. R. Schimʿon b. Joḥaj sagt: (Die Schrift) lehrt, daß die (Gottes-)Rede (*haddibbūr*) ausging von der rechten (Seite) des Heiligen, g. s. er!, zur Linken von Israel, und sich umwandte und um das Lager Israels herumging, 18 auf 18 Mil, und zurückkehrte und die rechte (Seite) Israels umgab, zur Linken des Heiligen, g. s. er! Und der Heilige, g. s. er! faßte sie mit seiner Rechten und grub sie auf die Tafel, und seine Stimme ging aus von einem Ende der Welt zum andern, um zu erfüllen, was geschrieben steht (Zitat Ps 29, 7). Aber die Rabbinen sagen: Gibt

99 Schir r. 1, 13, zu HL 1, 2; BACHER, Die Agada der pal. Amoräer I, 313.
100 So versteht der Midrasch die Stelle.
101 SDeut § 343, S. 399, Z. 11—15 FINKELSTEIN; dasselbe in Jalḳuṭ Maḵiri Ps 29 § 25 (94a).

es denn oben eine linke (Seite)?! Steht denn nicht geschrieben: 'Deine Rechte, J', herrlich in Kraft, deine Rechte, J', zerschmettert' usw. (Ex 15, 6). Allein, die (Gottes-)Rede (*haddibbūr*) ging aus dem Munde des Heiligen, g. s. er! von seiner Rechten zur Rechten Israels, und dann ging sie zurück von der Rechten Israels zur Rechten des Heiligen, g. s. er!, und der Heilige, g. s. er! faßte sie mit seiner Rechten und grub sie in die Tafel, und seine Stimme ging aus von einem Ende der Welt zum andern, wie es heißt (Zitat Ps 29, 7)".

Hier endet die Diskussion der Tannaïten; was im folgenden berichtet wird, ist eine Diskussion von Amoräern über eben diese Tradition.

„R. Berekja (um 340) sagte: R. Ḥelbō (um 300) lehrte mich, daß die (Gottes-)Rede (*haddibbūr*) selbst sich von selbst eingrub, und als sie sich eingegraben hatte, ging seine Stimme aus von einem Ende der Welt zum andern, wie es heißt (Zitat Ps 29, 7). Ich sagte zu R. Ḥelbō: Steht denn nicht geschrieben: 'Sie waren beschrieben mit dem Finger Gottes' (Ex 31, 18)? Er sagte zu mir: Du meintest mich (mit diesem Einwand) zu erwürgen?! Ich sagte zu ihm: Und was ist (denn) der Sinn (dessen), was geschrieben steht: 'Steinerne Tafeln, beschrieben mit dem Finger Gottes' (Deut 9, 10)? Er sagte zu mir: Wie ein Schüler, der schreibt, und sein Lehrer zeigt es ihm mit seiner Hand"[102].

Zu diesen Auffassungen vom Ausgang des Wortes aus Gottes Mund ist zu sagen: Es wird aufgefaßt als eine konkrete, selbständige Wesenheit, nicht als bloßer Schall[103]. Es ist aber auch kein Geschöpf Gottes, man muß es vielmehr als eine Emanation bezeichnen, die von Gott ausgeht. Es ist auch nicht eine Folge von einzelnen Wörtern, Sätzen und Aussprüchen, sondern es ist auch hier ein Ganzes, das die Zehn Gebote auf einmal enthält. Ferner geht es selbst und als solches in die Gesetzestafeln ein: Die einzelnen Worte bzw. Laute werden nicht in Buchstaben und Schrift umgesetzt und dann so in die Tafeln eingegraben, sei es von Gott oder von Mose: Gott gräbt die Gottesrede als solche in Stein und Schrift ein, sie wird selbst Stein und Schrift.

Nun haben wir seit einiger Zeit zu diesem Text eine nahe Parallele, die im folgenden anzuführen ist:

„'Und J' sprach die ganze Herrlichkeit dieser Worte folgendermaßen. Das erste (Gottes-)Wort (*dibbūrājjā*, sic!), das aus dem Munde des Heiligen — sein Name sei gepriesen! — hervorging, (war) wie Funken und wie Blitze und wie Feuerfackeln. Eine Feuerfackel aus seiner Rechten und eine Feuerfackel aus seiner Linken flog und erhob sich in die Luft des Himmels und kehrte zurück. Und ganz Israel sah es und fürchtete sich. Es kehrte zurück und grub sich ein auf die zwei Bundestafeln. Und er sprach: Mein Volk (*'ammā*), meine Kinder [...] Und es kehrte

[102] Schir r. 1, 13, zu HL 1, 2; vgl. BACHER, Tannaiten II, 118.
[103] Man wird bei der Schilderung ihrer Wirksamkeit an Jes (9, 7); 55, 10f. erinnert.

um und umkreiste die Lager Israels, und es kehrte zurück und grub sich ein auf die zwei Bundestafeln. Und ganz Israel sah es. Dann rief er und sagte: Mein Volk, Kinder Israels, ich bin J', euer Gott, der ich euch erlöste und aus dem Lande Ägypten, aus dem Sklavenhause herausführte".

Es folgt dasselbe noch einmal (nur ist der Fehler *dibbūrājjā* vermieden, und es steht *dibbērā* im Text) als Einleitung zum Gebot „du sollst keine andern Götter neben mir haben"[104]. — Die Verwandtschaft dieser Paraphrase des Bibeltextes mit SDeut § 343 ist offenkundig, obwohl einige kleinere Differenzen nicht übersehen werden sollen: Hier wird von Feuererscheinungen berichtet, die das Ausgehen der (Gottes-)Rede aus dem Munde Gottes begleiten (vgl. Ex 20, 18); abweichend ist auch der Zug, daß die (Gottes-)Rede sich in die Luft erhob und dahinflog; ferner, daß die (Gottes-) Rede sich selbst in die Bundestafeln eingrub — nach Sifre und den Parallelen gräbt Gott die (Gottes-)Rede in die Tafeln ein. Übereinstimmend aber wird in beiden Texten berichtet, daß die (Gottes-)Rede das, bzw. die, Lager Israels umkreiste und dann in die Tafeln einging bzw. eingegraben wurde. Im ganzen wird man sagen können: Abweichungen und Übereinstimmungen sind von der Art, daß man in SDeut § 343 und Par. einerseits und im Tg. Neophyti 1 anderseits zwei Rezensionen einer und derselben Tradition zu sehen hat. Damit ist aber auch ein Anhaltspunkt gewonnen für den zeitlichen Ansatz dieser Tradition: Wenn Tg. Neophyti 1 ins 2. — ev. sogar ins 1. — Jh. gehört, dann auch die hier erhaltene Tradition. Diese Annahme wird gestützt durch die Rezension in Schir r., wo R. Schim'on b. Joḥaj als Autor genannt wird. Aber je nach der Datierung von Tg. Neophyti 1 kämen wir in zeitlicher Hinsicht noch weiter hinauf, und Schim'on b. Joḥaj wäre der Tradent einer älteren, targumischen, Tradition. Auf alle Fälle ist die (Gottes-)Rede, der *dibbūr* — der Logos! — hier eine relativ selbständige Größe. Man wird noch nicht sagen dürfen, daß sie eine persönliche Wesenheit ist, aber der Schritt zu einer solchen Auffassung ist klein. Er wird denn auch getan, in einer Tradition, die nun anzuführen ist:

„R. 'Azarja (um 380) und R. Aḥa (um 360) (sagten) im Namen von R. Joḥanan († um 279): In der Stunde, da die Israeliten (das Wort) 'Ich' auf dem Sinai hörten, ging ihnen die Seele aus[105]. Die (Gottes-)Rede (*haddibbūr*) kehrte zum Heiligen, g. s. er! zurück (und) sagte vor ihm: Herr der Welten! Du lebst, und deine Ṯora lebt, aber du hast mich zu Toten gesandt! Sie sind (ja) alle tot! In dieser Stunde begann der Heilige, g. s. er! (von neuem) und versüßte ihnen die (Gottes-)Rede (*haddibbūr*), wie es heißt: 'Die Stimme J's erschallt mit Macht, die Stimme J's dröhnt hehr' (Ps 29, 4)"[106].

[104] Tg. Neophyti 1 Ex 20, 1—3.
[105] Im Hintergrund steht HL 5, 6; der Bezug zur Rede Gottes ist nahegelegt durch die allegorische Deutung des Hohen Liedes.
[106] Num r. 10, 3, zu 6, 2; dasselbe Schir r. 6, 3, zu HL 5, 16; Jalḳuṭ Maḵiri Ps 29 § 20(94a).

Es ist ganz klar, daß hier die (Gottes-)Rede (*dibbūr*) eine von Gott selbst deutlich unterschiedene Wesenheit ist, und zwar ist sie hier persönlich aufgefaßt: Sie redet mit Gott, aus dessen Mund sie ausging, von Person zu Person. Man kann sich fragen, ob sie von der Ṯora unterschieden wird, sagt sie doch zu Gott: „Du lebst, und deine Ṯora lebt". Es wäre möglich, daß die (Gottes-)Rede (*dibbūr*) doch mit der Ṯora identisch ist: Wenn die (Gottes-)Rede sagt: „Du lebst, und deine Ṯora lebt", könnte eine indirekte Redeweise vorliegen im Sinne von: „Du lebst, und ich, die Ṯora, lebe auch". Solche indirekte Redeweise ist im semitischen — vor allem im alttestamentlichen und jüdischen — Sprachbereich sehr häufig. Ein solches Verständnis des Satzes ist also durchaus möglich. Die (Gottes-)Rede (*dibbūr*) kann aber auch aufgefaßt werden als 'Trägerin' der Ṯora, als das Mittel und Werkzeug, in und mit dem die Ṯora zum Volke gebracht wird. Aber wie auch immer: Die (Gottes-)Rede (*dibbūr*) ist eine von Gott ausgehende und doch von ihm verschiedene metaphysische Wesenheit persönlicher Art. Wir haben hier ein deutliches Zeugnis von 'Logos'-Theologie vor uns, wenn wir uns geläufige griechische Termini anwenden wollen. Die Aussagen, die wir hier vor uns haben, gehen auch über die at.lichen Aussagen vom 'Wort' (*dābār*) als Hypostase hinaus; denn auch wo im AT *dābār* als Hypostase erscheint, ist der *dābār* nicht in dieser Weise Gott gegenüber verselbständigt, schon gar nicht personalisiert, so daß er mit Gott sprechen könnte. Zugleich ist aber festzustellen, daß hier das Verhältnis von (Gottes-)Rede (*dibbūr*)/Logos und Gott nicht durchreflektiert ist.

Ein Midrasch zu Gen 48 beschäftigt sich mit dem Segen, den Jakob den Söhnen Josephs, Manasse und Ephraim, geben will. Zunächst heißt es da, daß der Hl. Geist nicht auf Jakob zurückkehrte, so daß er nicht segnen konnte. Das schmerzte nun Joseph, und er fiel auf sein Angesicht (vgl. Gen 48, 12) und flehte zu Gott um Erbarmen:

> „. . . und sogleich sagte der Heilige, g. s. er! zum Hl. Geist: Bis wann soll sich Joseph grämen?! Offenbare dich schnell und geh ein in Jakob, daß er sie segnen (kann), denn der Heilige, g. s. er! kann nicht (mit an-)sehen, daß der Stamm auf seinem Angesicht liegt! Auch Josua, sein Enkel, fiel auf sein Angesicht. Sogleich sprang die (Gottes-) Rede (*haddibbūr*) auf ihn und sagte: 'Stehe auf, warum denn liegst du auf deinem Angesicht?' (Jos 7, 10)"[107].

Da nach Jos 7, 10 Jahwe mit Josua redet, könnte man zunächst daran denken, daß auch im vorliegenden Midrasch (Gottes-)Rede (*dibbūr*) Ersatzwort ist für Jahwe/Gott. Dieses Verständnis wäre gegeben, wenn es z. B. hieße: „Die (Gottes-)Rede (*dibbūr*) sprach . . .", oder wenn eine ähnliche Wendung gebraucht würde. Das steht aber nicht da, sondern der Midrasch interpretiert den Bibeltext und führt zur Erklärung eine andere Vorstellung ein: Wenn es heißt, daß die (Gottes-)Rede auf Josua 'sprang', kann damit kaum Gott selbst gemeint sein. Vielmehr ist hier an eine von Gott verschie-

[107] Pesiḳt r. 3 (12a).

dene Wesenheit zu denken, die von ihm ausgeht und in seinem Namen redet und handelt, d. h. auf Josua 'springt'; wir haben es wieder mit einer Hypostase Gottes zu tun. Wir denken im at.lichen Bereich wieder an Jes 54, 10f., aber auch an eine Stelle wie 1 Sam 10, 10, wo es heißt, daß der Geist Gottes über Saul kam. Der Gedanke an den Geist Gottes wird ja durch den ganzen Textzusammenhang des Midrasch nahegelegt. Man würde also eher die (Gottes-)Rede (*dibbūr*) mit dem Geist Gottes in Zusammenhang bringen, als den Ausdruck als Ersatzwort für Jahwe/Gott ansehen: Geist und Wort sind in diesem Midrasch die wirkenden Kräfte Gottes. Zudem ist darauf aufmerksam zu machen, daß hier auch der Hl. Geist eine von Gott unterschiedene und persönliche Wesenheit ist: Gott redet mit dem Geist und gibt ihm Befehle, er läßt ihn nicht einfach als eine unpersönliche Kraft aus sich ausgehen.

Näher bei der Vorstellung von Pesiḳt r. 3 steht folgende Ausführung über das Wirken des Logos für Israel in Ägypten. Der Text zeigt, daß die in Pesiḳt r. 3 vorkommende Vorstellung sehr alt ist und in vorchristliche Zeit hinaufreicht, in den alexandrinischen Bereich:

> „Da sprang dein allmächtiges Wort vom Himmel, vom Königsthron, wie ein wilder Krieger mitten in das dem Verderben geweihte Land herab, als scharfes Schwert tragend deinen ernsten Auftrag, und trat hin, alles mit Tod erfüllend, und berührte den Himmel, und stand doch auf der Erde" (Sap Sal 18, 15f.)[108].

Auch hier handelt es sich nicht um dichterische, bildhafte Redeweise, schon gar nicht um Gott selbst, sondern um die Vorstellung vom Logos als Hypostase[109].

In besonders eigentümlicher Form erscheint die Aussage über die Wirksamkeit der (Gottes-)Rede (*dibbūr*) in einem Midrasch über die Rückkehr Moses aus Midian und sein Zusammentreffen mit Aaron:

> „Als sich ihm (Mose) die (Gottes-)Rede (*haddibbēr*) in Midian offenbarte und zu ihm sagte, daß er nach Ägypten zurückkehren sollte, wie es heißt: 'Und J' sprach zu Mose in Midian: Geh, kehre nach Ägypten zurück' (Ex 4, 19), (da) teilte sich die (Gottes-)Rede (*haddibbūr*) in zwei Stimmen und wurde zu zwei Personen (*dio peraṣōfin* [sic!] = δύο πρό-

[108] Sap Sal 18, 15f. Ὁ παντοδύναμός σου λόγος ἀπ' οὐρανῶν ἐκ θρόνων βασιλείων ἀπότομος πολεμιστὴς εἰς μέσον τῆς ὀλεθρίας ἥλατο γῆς ξίφος ὀξὺ τὴν ἀνυπόκριτον ἐπιταγήν σου φέρων καὶ στὰς ἐπλήρωσεν τὰ πάντα θανάτου καὶ οὐρανοῦ μὲν ἥπτετο, βεβήκει δ'ἐπὶ γῆς.

[109] Bousset-Gressmann, Die Religion des Judentums, 347; Eichrodt, Theologie des Alten Testaments 2, 46; Dürr, Die Wertung des göttlichen Wortes, 126: „Was nach unserer Darlegung zur Hypostase gehört und Jes 55, 10f. noch fehlte, ist hier wirklich vollzogen. Das Wort ist zur selbständigen Macht geworden, die als Krieger (vgl. Ps 19, 6) einherzieht". Nach Dürr liegt der Stelle 1 Chron 21, 16 zugrunde. Zwischen Gottheit und Welt ist „sein Wort als Mittler getreten", „mit denselben Kräften ('allmächtig') ausgestattet wie die Gottheit selbst. Das eben ist Hypostase".

σωπα). Und Mose hörte in Midian: 'Geh, kehre nach Ägypten zurück', und Aaron hörte in Ägypten: 'Geh Mose entgegen nach der Wüste zu' (Ex 4, 27). Aber wer in der Mitte war, hörte überhaupt nichts. Das meint: 'Gott donnert wunderbar mit seiner Stimme' (Hi 37, 5)"[110].

Die Parallele zu dem zitierten Text aus Tanḥ B, die wir in Tanḥ Schemōṯ 26 haben, zeigt, daß die Gottesbezeichnung „der Heilige, g. s. er!" an Stelle von (Gottes-)Rede (*dibbūr* bzw. *dibbēr*) stehen kann. Darauf weist BILLERBECK mit Recht hin: *Dibbēr/dibbūr* ist also Ersatzwort für 'Gott'. BILLERBECK beachtete aber den Fortgang des Midrasch nicht, in welchem (Gottes-)Rede (*dibbūr*) wieder erscheint, wo aber dieses Verständnis des Ausdrucks ausgeschlossen ist; denn der Text sagt ja deutlich, daß sich die (Gottes-)Rede (*dibbūr*) in zwei Personen teilte: Unmöglich kann hier (Gottes-)Rede (*dibbūr*) Ersatzwort für Gott sein, sie ist vielmehr eine von Gott ausgehende Wesenheit, eine Hypostase, die sich sogar in zwei Personen aufteilen kann[111]. Der Midrasch kommt wohl darum zu dieser Ansicht, weil er der Meinung ist, daß der Befehl an Mose und derjenige an Aaron in einem und demselben Augenblick, und d. h. auch in einem und demselben Gotteswort, erteilt wurden. Dazu liegt freilich auf Grund des Bibeltextes keine zwingende Nötigung vor: Man kann ohne weiteres annehmen, daß Gott sein Wort an Mose und an Aaron nacheinander hat ergehen lassen. Aber der Midrasch will das wunderbare Wirken Gottes und seines Wortes in der Geschichte Moses darlegen: Mose und Aaron erhalten je einen korrespondierenden und koordinierten Auftrag, der sie dann zusammentreffen läßt. Und diese Koordination kann und will der Midrasch nur so erklären, daß eben die (Gottes-)Rede sich in zwei Personen aufteilte. Besonders bemerkenswert ist hier, daß zur Beschreibung dieses Vorganges griechische Begrifflichkeit verwendet wird, so daß sogar im hebräischen Text griechische Ausdrücke erscheinen[112]. — Die Vorstellung von den beiden Personen des Offenbarungswortes erscheint aber auch in einem Midrasch über die Gesetzgebung am Sinai:

„Wie ging die Stimme (*haḳḳōl*) aus? R. Ṯanḥuma (bar Abba, um 380) sagte: (In) zwei Personen (*dō peraṣōfin* = δύο πρόσωπα) ging sie aus und

[110] Ṯanḥ B Schemoṯ § 23 (7b); dasselbe Ṯanḥ Schemoṯ 26 (70a), wo am Anfang statt *haddibbēr* steht „der Heilige, g. s. er!"; so auch Ex r. 5, zu 4, 27: Autor ist R. Reuben (um 300); vgl. auch STR.-BI. II 318f.

[111] Mit der bloßen Übersetzung 'Angesicht' für *prosōpon*, was die ursprüngliche Bedeutung des Wortes ist, ergibt der Text keinen Sinn, aber *prosōpon* wird ja oft in der Bedeutung 'Person' gebraucht: LIDDELL und SCOTT, A Greek English Lexicon, 1533 s. v.; KRAUSS, Lehnwörter II, 495 begnügt sich allerdings mit der Bedeutung 'Gesicht, Antlitz', aber auf S. 202 gibt er s. v. *dioparzup* die Bedeutung 'mit doppeltem Gesicht, zweifach geartet' an.

[112] Wenn oben bei der Beschreibung der '(Gottes-)Rede' (*dibbūr*) der griechische Logos-Begriff ausdrücklich angeführt wurde, könnte dies als nachträgliche Interpretation eines alten Textes angesehen werden bzw. als ein 'Hineinlesen' von etwas, das so im Text nicht steht. Ein derartiger Vorwurf kann hier aber nicht mehr gemacht werden, wo der Midrasch selbst griechische Begrifflichkeit verwendet und sie expressis verbis anführt.

erschlug die Götzendiener, welche sie nicht angenommen hatten, aber gab Leben den Israeliten, welche die Ṯora angenommen hatten"[113].

Dazu sei zunächst festgestellt, daß die 'Stimme' wie die (Gottes-)Rede als eine von Gott ausgehende Wesenheit angesehen wird, die wirkt und handelt: Sie tötet die Heiden und gibt den Israeliten Leben. Nach Deut 32, 39 und 1 Sam 2, 6 ist es Jahwe selbst, der tötet und lebendig macht. Nach Hos 6, 5 tötet Jahwe durch die Worte seines Mundes. Aber an der vorliegenden Stelle ist die at.liche Redeweise griechisch interpretiert und aufgefaßt: Die persönlich aufgefaßte 'Stimme' Gottes wirkt Leben und Tod. 'Stimme' und (Gottes-)Rede (*dibbūr*) dürfen wohl als gleichbedeutend angesehen werden; das geht deutlich hervor aus der Fortsetzung des Textes in Tanḥ Schemot 26, der oben (S. 600) zitiert wurde. Wenn wir hier auf das Griechische verweisen, tragen wir nichts in den Text hinein: Griechische Worte stehen im hebräischen Text selbst! In ähnlicher Weise kann Philon von Alexandreia vom Wirken des Logos reden, vgl. de somn. I 86, das unten (S. 607) zitiert wird.

Eine ähnliche Auffassung von der (Gottes-)Rede findet sich im folgenden Midrasch:

„R. Jehoschu'a b. Levi (um 250) sagte: Wenn die Völker der Welt gewußt hätten, wie schön das Offenbarungszelt für sie war, hätten sie es mit Zelten und Lagern umgeben. Denn bevor das Offenbarungszelt stand, pflegten sie die Stimme der (Gottes-)Rede (*haddibbūr*) zu hören und waren entsetzt in ihren Palästen. Das ist, was geschrieben steht: 'Denn wo wäre ein sterblicher Mensch, der wie wir die Stimme des lebendigen Gottes aus dem Feuer hätte reden hören und am Leben geblieben wäre?' (Deut 5, 26). R. Simon (um 280) sagte: Zweigestaltig (*diprospin* = διπρόσωπος) pflegte die (Gottes-)Rede (*haddibbūr*) auszugehen: Als Mittel zum Leben für Israel, aber als Mittel des Todes für die Völker der Welt"[114].

Im ersten Teil dieses Midrasch kann die (Gottes-)Rede aufgefaßt werden als Ersatzwort für 'Gott', aber dieses Verständnis ist im Ausspruch von R. Simon nicht möglich, ja durch den Wortlaut gänzlich ausgeschlossen. Die (Gottes-)Rede ist eine von Gott ausgehende, selbständig handelnde Wesenheit, eine Hypostase. Sie muß hier aber nicht unbedingt aufgefaßt werden als aus zwei Personen bestehend: Man kann das *diprospin* als zwei Aspekte dieser e i n e n Wesenheit ansehen, den lebenspendenden und den tötenden. Wollte man freilich sich das *diprospin* konkret vorstellen — und sowohl vom altorientalischen wie vom spätantiken Denken her ist das nahegelegt —, käme man zu einer Anschauung, wie sie etwa beim römischen

[113] Ex r. 5, 9, zu 4, 27; dasselbe Ṯanḥ Schemoṯ 25 (70a); vgl. BACHER, Agada der paläst. Amoräer III, 473.

[114] Schir r. 2, 11, zu HL 2, 3; dasselbe als Tradition von R. Simon in Lev r. 1, 11, zu 1, 1; vgl. Ṯanḥ B Terumāh § 8 (47a), oben S. 588.

Gott Ianus vorliegt, der zwei Gesichter hat! Es ist in diesem Zusammenhang vielleicht nicht uninteressant, festzustellen, daß zu Beginn des 3. Jhs. Sabellius versuchte, das christologische (Trinitäts-)Problem mit Hilfe des *Prosopon*-Begriffes zu lösen[115]. R. Simon und R. Jehoschu'a b. Levi sind jüngere Zeitgenossen des Sabellius!

Daß bei dem doppelten Ausgang des Wortes, bzw. bei seiner zwiefachen Wirksamkeit als lebenspendend und todbringend, auf Griechisches bzw. Hellenistisches verwiesen wurde, ist auch nahegelegt durch eine Stelle aus Philon von Alexandreia:

> „Besonders schön und trefflich aber wird berichtet, daß die Stimme aus dem Feuer hervorkam; denn geklärt und geläutert sind die Worte Gottes wie Gold im Feuer. Es deutet ferner symbolisch etwa folgendes an. Da die Aufgabe des Feuers eine doppelte ist, zu leuchten und zu brennen, so werden die, die dem Gotteswort gehorsam sein wollen, wie in schattenlosem Licht allezeit wandeln und die Gesetze selbst als leuchtende Sterne in der Brust tragen; die ihm aber ungehorsam sind, werden ewig entflammt und verzehrt werden von den Begierden, die in ihrem Innern, die einem Feuer gleich das ganze Dasein derer, die sie beherrschen, zerstören werden"[116].

Philon psychologisiert hier und verlegt die Wirkung, die das aus dem Feuer kommende Gotteswort hat, in die Seele des Menschen — den einen zum Heil, den andern zum Verderben. Die Brücke zu den Ausführungen der Rabbinen läßt sich aber leicht schlagen, und ein Zusammenhang zwischen beiden — dem Hellenisten Philon und dem palästinischen Rabbi — ist nicht ausgeschlossen. Solcher Zusammenhang braucht nicht notwendig ein literarischer zu sein, es kann sich auch um die (mündliche) Übernahme alexandrinischer exegetischer Traditionen durch das Rabbinat handeln, oder beide können von einer gemeinsamen exegetischen Tradition herkommen. Mit Recht macht der Übersetzer Philons aufmerksam auf die Stelle Mek Ex Baḥodesch 19, 18: Die Ṯora ist Feuer, wurde mitten aus dem Feuer gegeben und ist mit Feuer vergleichbar[117].

Wie Gott nach dem AT mit seinem Wort schafft, so tut er es auch nach der rabbinischen Tradition. Im Segensspruch bei Tisch wird dies bei jeder Mahlzeit bekenntnishaft ausgesprochen: „Durch dessen Wort alles geworden ist"[118]. „Habe ich nicht durch ein Wort (*bedābār*, v. l. *bedibbūr*) die Welt geschaffen ..."[119]. — „Geliebt ist das Heiligtum vor dem, der sprach und es ward die Welt; denn als der Heilige, g. s. er! seine Welt schuf, schuf

[115] Vgl. Hippolytos, Elench. IX 16—19: GCS 26 (1916), 248f.; vgl. Kallistos, ebda. X 3f., S. 283.

[116] de decal. 48f.; Philos Werke deutsch, Bd. I 381 (übers. von L. Treitel).

[117] Vgl. SDeut § 343, S. 399, Z. 16ff. Finkelstein.

[118] MBer VI 2f (dreimal).

[119] Gen r. 28, 2, zu 6, 7.

er sie nur durch das Wort (*bamma'amar*), wie es heißt (Zitat Ps 33, 6)"[120/121]. —

„Drei Geschöpfe gingen der Welt voraus: Das Wasser, und der Wind (*rūaḥ*, Geist) und das Feuer. Das Wasser wurde schwanger und gebar die Finsternis. Das Feuer wurde schwanger und gebar das Licht. Der Wind (Geist) wurde schwanger und gebar die Weisheit. Und durch diese sechs Geschöpfe wird die Welt geleitet: Durch Wind (Geist), durch Weisheit und durch Feuer und durch Licht und durch Finsternis und durch Wasser. Deswegen sagte David (Zitat Ps 104, 1). Ein Mensch sieht eine schöne Säule (und) sagt: Gepriesen sei der Steinbruch, aus dem sie gehauen wurde. Schön ist die Welt — gepriesen sei der Ort (= Gott), der sie gehauen und geschaffen hat mit dem Wort (*bedibbēr*)"[122].

Beachtenswert ist in diesem Text die gnostisierende Interpretation der Schöpfungsgeschichte: Wasser, Wind (Geist) und Feuer sind die Urelemente[122a], schöpferische Kräfte, die 'schwanger' werden und je ein weiteres Element aus sich heraussetzen. Bei diesem Geschehen kann, so wie der Text lautet, auf die schöpferische Tätigkeit Gottes verzichtet werden: Die Urelemente emanieren die nächstfolgenden Kräfte 'Finsternis, Licht und Weisheit', welche mit ihnen zusammen die Welt 'leiten'. Erst mit dem Schlußsatz des kleinen Midrasch lenkt der Gedankengang zur biblischen Aussage der Schöpfung der Welt durch das Wort Gottes zurück.

Im Schöpfungsbericht von Gen 1 sieht Schim'ōn b. Zoma (um 110) eine Schwierigkeit:

„'Und Gott machte die Feste' (Gen 1, 7). Das ist einer von den (Schrift-) Versen, mit denen Ben Zoma die Welt erschütterte. (Es heißt da, sagte er:) 'Und er machte'. Ich verwundere mich! Sind sie (denn) nicht durch das Wort (*bamma'amar*) (geschaffen worden, es heißt ja:) 'Durch das Wort J's sind die Himmel gemacht, durch den Hauch seines Mundes ihr ganzes Heer' (Ps 33, 6)"[123].

Wir führen diese Stelle hier an, obwohl in ihr die Vokabel *dibbūr* nicht vorkommt, wohl aber *ma'amar*, weil behauptet worden ist, „daß in der rabbinischen Literatur das schöpferische Wort Gottes nirgends mehr als 'Hypostase' erscheint"[124]. Wahrscheinlich vermißte Ben Zōma am Schluß

[120] Mek Ex Schiraṭa 15, 17.

[121] Diese Beispiele bei SCHLATTER, Der Evangelist Johannes, 4. Mit Recht macht SCHLATTER auf die sehr häufige Gottesbezeichnung aufmerksam: „Der, der sprach, und es ward die Welt" — der Ausdruck ist eine bekenntnisartige Formulierung (ein Beispiel oben S. 602).

[122] Ex r. 15, 22, zu 12, 12.

[122a] Vgl. FOERSTER, Die Gnosis I. Zeugnisse der Kirchenväter, 315—399: 14. Kapitel: 'Die Drei-Prinzipien-Systeme I-VI'; S. 383f. (aus Hippolytos, Ref. V 19, 1ff.) das System der Sethianer, das die drei Prinzipien „Licht, Geist, Finsternis" kennt. — S. 405: Mythos vom „Mutterschoß", der „Aeonen" hervorbringt (Kainiten ?).

[123] Gen r. 4, 6, zu 1, 7.

[124] So BOUSSET-GRESSMANN, Die Religion des Judentums, 342 Anm. 1.

von Gen 1, 6 die Bemerkung „und es geschah also“[125], während sie an den beiden andern Stellen, wo es heißt „und Gott machte“ (Gen 1, 16. 25), jeweils in den vorhergehenden Versen (Gen 1, 15. 24) steht und ausdrückt, daß dem göttlichen Befehl sofort die Ausführung folgte. Ben Zōma hat wahrscheinlich in Gen 1, 7 einen Hinweis darauf gesehen, daß der Stoff, aus dem die Welt durch Gott geschaffen wurde, dem Schöpfer vorgegeben war: Gott wäre also Demiurg und nicht Schöpfer im üblichen biblischen Sinne gewesen, der mit dem Worte schafft, auch den Stoff, die Materie, als das ‘Material’ der Welt. Hier dagegen wäre eine unbiblische Lehre von der Ewigkeit des Weltstoffes zu erkennen, also eine — vom Umkreis des Rabbinates aus gesehen — griechisch-hellenistische Lehre von der Präexistenz der Materie. Wie Ben Zōma das Problem gelöst hat, erfahren wir leider nicht, denn der Midrasch bricht unvermittelt ab. Vielleicht hatte Ben Zōma eine Geheimlehre zur Verfügung aus den Spekulationen über das ‘Schöpfungswerk’ (*ma‘assē berēschiṯ*)[126].

In den Umkreis der Anschauungen von der schaffenden Kraft der (Gottes-)Rede (*dibbūr*) gehört die folgende Aussage über die Erschaffung von Engeln:

> „Denn R. Schemuel b. Naḥmani (um 260) sagte: R. Jonaṯan (um 220) sagte: Jedes einzelne (Gottes-)Wort (*ḳōl dibbūr wedibbūr*), das aus dem Munde des Heiligen, g. s. er! ausgeht, von dem wird ein Engel geschaffen, wie es heißt (Zitat Ps 33, 6)“[127].

Billerbeck bemerkt dazu: „Da nun jedes göttliche Befehlswort ein Ganzes für sich bildet, so kann sich weder ein Befehlswort in zwei Engeln, noch zwei Befehlsworte in einem Engel verkörpern. Die letzte Konsequenz dieser Theorie war dann natürlich, daß die Engel zugleich mit der Ausführung ihres Auftrages wieder in das Nichts zurücktraten. — Auch diese Schlußfolgerung ist in GnR 78 (49d) gezogen worden [. . .]“. Auf weitere Probleme der Angelologie kann hier nicht eingegangen werden[128].

Zu der Vorstellung, daß aus einem jeden Gotteswort ein Engel geschaffen werde, sei immerhin auf einen analogen Gedanken bei Philon von Alexandreia aufmerksam gemacht (Philon redet von den ‘edelsten Seelen’ und sagt):

> „Diese pflegen die andern Philosophen Dämonen zu nennen, die heilige Schrift aber, die einen passenderen Namen braucht, Engel (ἄγγελοι). Denn sie verkünden (διαγγέλλουσιν) die Befehle des Vaters den Kin-

[125] Diese Bemerkung steht in LXX!

[126] Bacher, Tannaiten I², 423; Weinstein, Zur Genesis der Agada, 199; Str.-Bi. III 671, zu Hebr 1, 2; zur heutigen exegetischen Problematik der Verse Gen 1, 6. 7 vgl. Westermann, Genesis, 162—164.

[127] bḤag 14a; vgl. Str.-Bi. III 815, zu Offb 14, 6—9.

[128] Merkwürdig ist die Stelle 3 Hen 27, 3, wo es heißt, daß der hohe Engel Radweriel mit jedem Wort (*dibbūr wedibbūr*), das er ausspricht, einen Engel schafft. Vgl. dazu Odeberg, 3 Enoch, 96.

dern und die Bedürfnisse der Kinder dem Vater. Darum läßt er sie auch hinauf- und hinabsteigen [...], weil es uns hinfälligen Menschen frommt, uns der vermittelnden und schlichtenden Logoi zu bedienen, weil der Allwaltende und die höchste Stärke seiner Macht Bestürzung und Entsetzen erregt"[129].

Festzuhalten ist hier, daß die Engel von Philon „Logoi" = Worte, scl. Gottes, genannt werden. — Zu Gen 48, 15 erklärt Philon Al.:

„Denn er (scl. Jakob) ist überzeugt, daß die Güter vorzüglicher Art der Seiende in eigener Person gibt, die Güter zweiten Ranges sind seine Engel und Einzelkräfte (λόγους)"[130].

Und an anderer Stelle:

„Denn diejenigen, die die Sonne nicht sehen können, den reflektierten Sonnenstrahl als Sonne ansehen und den Hof um den Mond, als wäre es dieser selbst, so nehmen sie auch das Abbild Gottes wahr, seinen Engel-Logos, als wäre es er selbst"[131].

V. Nachtrag

1. Diskussion einiger Stellen aus Tg. Neophyti 1

A. Diez Macho hat einige Stellen aus Tg. Neophyti 1 zusammengestellt, an denen seiner Meinung nach das 'Wort' von 'Jahwe'/'Gott' unterschieden werden kann oder muß[132]. Wir diskutieren diese Stellen im folgenden.

„Und Henoch diente in Wahrheit vor J'. Und man wußte nicht, wo er war, denn er wurde weggenommen durch das Wort (*bemēmār*) von vor J' (*min ḳodām*)"[133].

In unserem Zusammenhang ist es weniger wichtig, daß es im Ms-Text heißt, „Henoch wandelte mit Gott (*'elohim*)", und daß auch das zweite 'Gott' (*'elohim*) im Targum durch J' (Jahwe) ersetzt ist. Wenn die Wendung „und Gott hatte ihn weggenommen" im Targum wiedergegeben wird durch „er wurde weggenommen durch das (ein) Wort von vor J'", kann 'Wort' als Ersatz für 'Gott' aufgefaßt werden. Man muß sich allerdings sofort

[129] de somn. I 141f.; Philos Werke deutsch, Bd. VI, 201f. (übers. von M. Adler).
[130] leg. alleg. III 177; Philos Werke deutsch, Bd. III 142 (übers. von I. Heinemann).
[131] Philon Al., de somn. I 239; Philos Werke deutsch, Bd. VI 221 (übers. von M. Adler).
[132] Diez Macho, El Logos, 393: „*En diversos pasajes del Targum palestino el Memra de Yahvé aparece como distinto o distinguible de Yahvé*". Dazu in Anm. 48 folgende Stellen aus Tg. Neophyti 1: Gen 5, 24; 9, 13. 16; 18, 17; 19, 24; 28, 10. 15; 38, 7; Ex 6, 7; 29, 45.
[133] Tg. Neophyti 1 Gen 5, 24.

fragen, ob nicht die gewählte Satzkonstruktion diesem Verständnis widerstreitet: Es heißt ja *bemēmār min ḳodām J'* und nicht *bemēmār J'* = ,,durch das Wort J's". D. h.: Wird durch die gewählte Wendung nicht doch das 'Wort' von 'Jahwe' unterschieden? Ist nicht das 'Wort' das Werkzeug oder Mittel, durch das Jahwe den Henoch zu sich nimmt? Muß also nicht doch zwischen Jahwe und seinem ,,Wort" unterschieden werden? Man muß sich zum mindesten diese Fragen stellen. Wir haben demnach in Tg. Neophyti 1 Gen 5, 24 einen Grenzfall vor uns: Das 'Wort' kann als Ersatz für 'Jahwe' aufgefaßt werden, aber auch als selbständige Wesenheit, als Mittel Jahwes, mit dem er in der Welt wirkt[134].

> ,,Meinen Bogen werde ich in die Wolken setzen, und er wird ein Zeichen des Bundes sein zwischen meinem Wort (*mēmri*) und der Erde"[135].

Da das Targum hier ganz dem Ms-Text folgt, ist es eigentlich überraschend, daß es in der Schlußwendung nicht auch heißt ,,zwischen mir und der Erde" — vorher kann ja ohne weiteres ,,ich" gesagt werden, wenn Gott redet! Wenn nun in der abschließenden Wendung ,,mein Wort" gesagt wird, dann doch wohl mit der Absicht, zwischen Gott und seinem 'Wort' zu unterscheiden: Der Bund ist zwischen dem 'Wort' (Gottes) und der Erde geschlossen worden. Entsprechend ist die folgende, auf den Bundesschluß bezogene Formulierung:

> ,,Und mein Bogen wird in den Wolken sein, und ich werde ihn sehen zur Erinnerung an den ewigen Bund zwischen dem Worte (*memrā*) J's und allen lebenden Wesen in allem Fleisch, das auf Erden ist"[136].

Ebenfalls in der folgenden Stelle muß wohl zwischen Jahwe und seinem 'Wort' unterschieden werden:

> ,,Und J' sagte durch sein Wort (*bemēmrēh*): Soll ich vor meinem Freund Abraham verbergen, was ich tun (will)?"[137]

Wäre hier *memrā* Ersatzwort für Jahwe/Gott, wäre doch etwa eine Formulierung zu erwarten wie: ,,Und der *mēmrā* J's sprach . . ." oder dgl. Aber Jahwe redet hier selber, wie im Ms-Text, aber nun im Targum durch ein 'Wort'.

> ,,Und das Wort (*mēmrā*) J's ließ herabkommen auf Sodom und Gomorrha Schwefel und Feuer von vor (*min ḳodām*) J' vom Himmel"[138].

[134] Ähnliche Überlegungen müßten wohl auch in bezug auf folgende Stelle gemacht werden, die Diez Macho nicht anführt: ,,Und J' sagte: Das ist das Zeichen des Bundes, das ich setze zwischen mein Wort (*mēmri*) und euch und allen lebendigen Wesen, die mit euch sind für die Generationen der Erde" (Tg. Neophyti 1 Gen 9, 12).

[135] Tg. Neophyti 1 Gen 9, 13.

[136] Tg. Neophyti 1 Gen 9, 16.

[137] Tg. Neophyti 1 Gen 18, 17.

[138] Tg. Neophyti 1 Gen 19, 24.

Die etwas umständliche Formulierung des Ms-Textes: „Und Jahwe liess regnen [. . .] von Jahwe her aus dem Himmel“, ist im Targum so wiedergegeben, daß das erste ‘Jahwe’ mit ‘Wort J’s’ übersetzt wird: Das kann durchaus als Ersatzwort für ‘Jahwe’ angesehen werden, nur ist dann die Frage, warum bei der zweiten Erwähnung Jahwes nicht auch so übersetzt wurde. So läßt sich hier die Auffassung vertreten, daß auch im ersten Fall zwischen ‘Wort Jahwes’ und ‘Jahwe’ selbst unterschieden wird. Für die Unterscheidung von ‘Wort’ und ‘Jahwe’ spricht vielleicht auch die Interpretation Philons von Alexandreia, der hier ein Wirken des Logos beschrieben sieht:

„Denn wenn Gottes Logos zu unserem irdischen Gebäude kommt, steht er denen bei, die mit der Tugend verwandt sind [. . .], ihren Gegnern aber schickt er Vernichtung und heilloses Verderben“[139].

Der Vergleich der beiden Interpretationen erlaubt die Vermutung, daß sie aus ein und derselben exegetischen Tradition stammen, die an der vorliegenden Stelle ein Wirken des göttlichen ‘Wortes’ (*mēmrā*, Logos) sieht.

„Fünf Zeichen geschahen unserem Vater Jakob, als er aufbrach von Beerseba, um nach Haran zu gehen. Das erste Zeichen: Die Stunden des Tages wurden verkürzt, und die Sonne ging unter vor der Zeit, weil die (Gottes-)Rede (*dibbērā*) mit ihm zu reden begehrte [. . .]“[140].

Der in unserem Zusammenhang entscheidende letzte Satz des Zitates hat im Ms-Text keine Grundlage; er gehört zu dem breit ausgeführten Midrasch über Jakobs Flucht zu Laban. BILLERBECK[141] faßt hier *dibbērā* einfach als Ersatzwort für ‘Gott’ auf: Gott wollte mit Jakob reden[142]. Dieses Verständnis läßt sich vertreten, aber die Frage läßt sich nicht abweisen, ob hier nicht doch *dibbērā* als Hypostase aufgefaßt werden kann: Das ‘Wort’ als die der Welt zugewandte Seite, die Offenbarungsseite, Jahwes.

Eindeutig in dieser Hinsicht erscheint dagegen der folgende Text:

„Und nun, ich bin mit dir mit meinem Wort (*bemēmri*), und ich werde dich überall behüten, wohin du gehst, und ich werde dich in dieses Land zurückführen, denn mein Wort (*mēmri*) wird dich nicht verlassen, bis ich getan habe, was ich dir gesagt habe“[143].

Die Worte „und nun, ich bin mit dir“ entsprechen dem Ms-Text, aber das Targum interpretiert sie und beantwortet gleichsam die Frage, wie denn Gott den Erzvater behüten werde, mit dem Hinweis auf Gottes Wort: Es

139 de somn. I 86; Philos Werke deutsch, Bd. VI, 191 (übers. von M. ADLER).

140 Tg. Neophyti 1 Gen 28, 10; dasselbe Tg. Jerusch I und II ad 1c.; Tg. Jerusch II liest *dibbūrā*.

141 STR.-BI. II 319, zu Tg. Jerusch I!

142 Vgl. Gen r. 68, zu 28, 11: „Der Heilige, gepriesen sei er! ließ die Sonne vor der Zeit untergehen, denn er wollte mit unserem Vater Jakob im Verborgenen reden“.

143 Tg. Neophyti 1 Gen 28, 15.

ist das Mittel und Werkzeug, in und mit dem Gott bei ihm sein wird. Und dieses Wort wird — nach dem letzten zitierten Satz — Jakob auch nicht verlassen[144].

Zu dieser Wiedergabe von Gen 28, 15 durch das Tg. Neophyti 1 kann hingewiesen werden auf die Interpretation, welche Philon der Stelle gibt: Wenn nach LXX Gen 28, 11 Jakob einem 'Ort' begegnet, bedeutet das, daß er weder einen von einem sterblichen Körper erfüllten noch auch dem unsichtbaren ewigen Gott begegnet,

> „sondern dem göttlichen Logos [. . .] Denn Gott selbst hält es für unter seiner Würde, zur Sinnlichkeit zu kommen und schickt seine Logoi den Tugendliebenden zu Hilfe [. . .] Notwendig also begegnet er, als er zur Sinnlichkeit kam, nicht mehr Gott, sondern Gottes Logos [. . .] das Begegnen [. . .] geschieht, damit der göttliche Logos plötzlich erscheine und der einsamen Seele eine unerwartete [. . .] Freude dadurch verheiße, daß er ihr Weggenosse werden will"[145].

Es ist bemerkenswert, daß im Targum wie bei Philon Jakob in Bethel nicht Gott selbst begegnet, sondern seinem 'Wort' (*mēmār*, Logos). Wieder kann auf eine gemeinsame exegetische Tradition geschlossen werden, die sowohl für das Targum wie für Philon bestimmend war. Ein direkter literarischer Zusammenhang wird damit nicht behauptet.

> „Und 'Er, der Erstgeborene Judas, verübte böse Taten vor J', und er starb durch das (ein) Wort (*bemēmār*) von vor (*min ḳodām*) J' "[146].

Im Ms-Text heißt es, daß Jahwe den 'Er tötete. Wieder fragt das Targum, wie das geschah, und es beantwortet die Frage dahin: Jahwe tötete ihn durch sein wirkendes Wort. Ein Wort geht aus von Jahwe und tötet (vgl. Jes 9, 7ff.; 55, 10f.).

Die beiden folgenden Stellen treiben die Vorstellung von der Hypostase des Wortes bis an die Grenze des Ditheismus:

> „Und ich sondere euch aus für meinen Namen, als ein Volk der Heiligen, und mein Wort (*mēmri*) wird euch ein Erlösergott sein, und ihr werdet erkennen, daß ich J' bin, euer Gott, der euch erlöst und herausgeführt hat unter dem Joche, (unter) dem ihr als Sklaven der Ägypter gedient habt"[147].

> „Und ich lasse meine Gegenwart (*schekinti*) ruhen inmitten der Kinder Israels, und mein Wort (*mēmri*) wird für sie ein Erlösergott sein"[148].

[144] Man denkt hier wieder an die Wirkung des 'Wortes' als Hypostase, wie sie in Jes 9, 7f.; 55, 10f. beschrieben ist, aber auch an die Wirkung des 'Namens' Jahwes, wie sie etwa in Ps 54, 3 beschrieben ist: „Jahwe, hilf mir durch deinen Namen".

[145] de somn. I 68—70; Philos Werke deutsch, Bd. VI 187f.; vgl. dieselbe Auslegung von Gen 28, 11 auf den „Logos" in de somn. I 116—119; ebda. S. 197.

[146] Tg. Neophyti 1 Gen 38, 7.

[147] Tg. Neophyti 1 Ex 6, 7.

[148] Tg. Neophyti 1 Ex 29, 45.

Wieder ist — in Tg. Neophyti 1 Ex 6, 7 — das 'Wort' Jahwes Mittel der Erlösung, aber es wird so weit verselbständigt, daß es ein 'Erlösergott' wird. Gleich steht es in Tg. Neophyti 1 Ex 29, 45: Nach dem Ms-Text wohnt Jahwe selbst unter dem Volk und ist sein Gott. Das Targum läßt aber die *schekinā* = Gottesgegenwart unter den Israeliten wohnen, und sein 'Wort' wird ihr 'Erlösergott'. Man vergleiche dazu Tg. Jerusch I ad l c.:

> „Und ich lasse meine Gottesgegenwart (*schekinti*) unter den Kindern Israels wohnen, und ich werde ihnen Gott sein".

Diese Interpretation steht dem Ms-Text näher und vermeidet die übergroße Verselbständigung des 'Wortes' in Richtung auf einen 'Erlösergott' und damit auf den Ditheismus hin.

2. Diskussion dreier Stellen aus den Werken des Origenes

Diese Ansichten über die 'Gottesrede' (*dibbūr*, Logos) konnten aber offenbar im Judentum noch weiter getrieben werden, wie aus einigen Nachrichten erhellt, die nun freilich nicht im rabbinischen Schrifttum zu finden sind, die aber auf jüdische Gewährsleute zurückgeführt werden. Celsus beruft sich in seiner Schrift gegen die Christen auf einen Juden, der behauptet habe, „daß der Sohn Gottes der Logos sei"[149]. Noch weiter führt die Angabe des Celsus, daß sein jüdischer Gewährsmann gesagt habe, daß er, bzw. die Juden, erwarte, daß der Sohn Gottes kommen werde, um die Frommen zu richten und die Ungerechten zu strafen[150]. Origenes selbst ist über diese Behauptungen des Celsus sehr erstaunt und bestreitet sie. Er weist darauf hin, daß er zahlreiche Kontakte mit Juden, auch mit jüdischen Gelehrten, gehabt habe, daß aber kein Jude die von Celsus erwähnte Lehre vom Logos als dem Sohne Gottes geteilt habe: Kein Jude nenne den Logos den Sohn Gottes, keiner erwarte, daß der Sohn Gottes als Richter über Gerechte und Gottlose kommen werde. Wohl aber sei es jüdische Lehre, daß der Messias

[149] Vgl. Origenes, c. Cels. II 31 (Lommatzsch XVIII 185): Μετὰ ταῦτα Χριστιανοῖς ἐγκαλεῖ, ὡς "σοφιζομένοις ἐν τῷ λέγειν τὸν υἱὸν τοῦ θεοῦ εἶναι αὐτολόγον" [. . .] Ἐγὼ δὲ καὶ πολλοῖς Ἰουδαίοις καὶ σοφοῖς γε ἐπαγγελλομένοις εἶναι συμβαλών, οὐδενὸς ἀκήκοα ἐπαινοῦντος τό, λόγον εἶναι τὸν υἱὸν τοῦ θεοῦ, ὡς ὁ Κέλσος εἴρηκε καὶ τοῦτο περιάπτων τῷ τοῦ Ἰουδαίου προσώπῳ λέγοντος "ὡς ἔι γε ὁ λόγος ἐστὶν ὑμῖν υἱὸς τοῦ θεοῦ, καὶ ἡμεῖς ἐπαίνοῦμεν".

[150] Vgl. Origenes, c. Cels. I 49 (Lommatzsch XVIII 92f.): Οὐκ ἂν καταλαβὼν τὰ ὑπὸ Χριστιανῶν λεγόμενα, ὅτι πολλοὶ προφῆται προεῖπον περὶ τῆς τοῦ σωτῆρος ἐπιδημίας, περιέθηκε τῷ τοῦ Ἰουδαίου προσώπῳ, ἃ ἥρμοζε Σαμαρεῖ μᾶλλον εἰπεῖν ἢ Σαδδουκαίῳ· καὶ οὐκ ἂν Ἰουδαῖος ὁ ἐν τῇ προσωποποιΐᾳ ἔφασκεν "ἀλλ' εἶπεν ὁ ἐμὸς προφήτης ἐν Ἱεροσολύμοις ποτέ, ὅτι ἥξει θεοῦ υἱός, τῶν ὁσίων κριτής, καὶ τῶν ἀδίκων κολαστής". [. . .] Ἰουδαῖος δὲ οὐκ ἂν ὁμολογήσαι, ὅτι προφήτης τις εἶπεν ἥξειν θεοῦ υἱόν· ὃ γὰρ λέγουσίν, ἐστίν, ὅτι ἥξει ὁ Χριστὸς τοῦ θεοῦ. Καὶ πολλάκις γε ζητοῦσι πρὸς ἡμᾶς εὐθέως περὶ υἱοῦ θεοῦ ὡς οὐδενὸς ὄντος τοιούτου, οὐδὲ προφητευθέντος. Καὶ οὐ τοῦτό φαμεν, ὅτι οὐχ ἁρμοζόντως τῷ Ἰουδαϊκῷ προσώπῳ, μὴ ὁμολογοῦντι τὸ τοιοῦτο, περιέθηκε τό, "εἶπεν ἐμὸς προφήτης ἐν Ἱεροσολύμοις ποτέ, ὅτι ἥξει θεοῦ υἱός".

Gottes zum Gericht am Ende der Tage kommen werde. Nun wurde aber hier Origenes offensichtlich von seinem sonst stupend funktionierenden Gedächtnis im Stiche gelassen; denn an einer andern Stelle seiner Werke zitiert er einen Juden, welcher ihm zu Jes 6 eine sehr bemerkenswerte Auslegung geboten hatte. Dieser Jude sagte nämlich, daß die zwei(!) Seraphim, die in Jes 6, 2 erwähnt werden (vgl. auch V. 6f.) und die das Trishagion ertönen lassen, Gottes eingeborener Sohn und der Heilige Geist seien[151].

Von der geläufigen jüdischen Lehre aus ist auch diese Exegese von Jes 6, 2f. höchst auffällig und befremdlich. Sie sprengt durchaus den Rahmen dessen, was sonst als jüdische Lehre bekannt ist[152]. Nun hat Origenes sein dogmatisches Werk in Alexandreia in Ägypten verfaßt, so daß anzunehmen ist, daß er diese Exegese von Jes 6 von einem dortigen Juden erfahren hat. Dieser Jude stand damit in einer älteren Tradition: Nach Philon von Alexandreia ist der Logos der 'Erstgeborene' (scl. Gottes)[153]. Der Jude, dem Origenes die Exegese von Jes 6 verdankt, vertrat wohl eine frühere Stufe der alexandrinischen Theologie, in der solche Aussagen über den Logos und über den Heiligen Geist noch möglich waren. In der Auseinandersetzung mit der Christologie der Kirche wurden aber soche und ähnliche Lehren ausgeschieden[154].

Celsus schrieb sein Werk gegen die Christen um das Jahr 180. Er hat dabei sowohl mündlich überlieferte jüdische Argumente gegen die Christen verwendet wie auch die Schrift eines (syrischen?) Juden, welcher — um die Mitte des 2. Jahrhunderts? — literarisch gegen die Judenchristen auftrat. Wenn der zeitliche Ansatz der jüdischen polemischen Schrift richtig angegeben ist (über mehr als eine Vermutung kommen wir nicht hinaus), dann ist ihr Verfasser ein Zeitgenosse von R. Schim'on b. Joḥaj, von dem wir oben (vgl. S. 595f.) höchst bemerkenswerte Aussagen über die (Gottes-)Rede (*dibbūr*, Logos) vernommen haben, die ja ihrerseits auf ältere Lehren zurückgehen, wie sie in Tg. Neophyti 1 faßbar werden. Sie sind nicht nur 'hellenistisch'-alexandrinisch, sondern sie wurden auch im Rabbinat Palästinas von einzelnen Lehrern geteilt. Bei palästinischen Lehrern nicht zu belegen ist (bis jetzt wenigstens) die Lehre, daß das 'Wort' (*dibbūr*, *dibbēr* u. a.)

[151] Vgl. Origenes, de princ. I 4 (Lommatzsch XXI 74f.; GCS V 52f.): *Dicebat autem et Hebraeus magister, quod duo illa Seraphim, quae in Esaia senis alis describuntur clamantia adinvicem, et dicentia: „Sanctus, sanctus, sanctus Dominus Deus Sabaoth": de unigenito Filio Dei, et Spiritu Sancto essent intelligenda.* Von dieser Stelle ist auch der griechische Text erhalten: Ἔλεγε δὲ ὁ Ἑβραῖος τὰ ἐν τῷ Ἠσαΐᾳ δύο Σέραφιμ ἑξαπτέρυγα, κεκραγότα ἕτερον πρὸς ἕτερον, καὶ λέγοντα "ἅγιος, ἅγιος, ἅγιος κύριος Σαβαώθ" τὸν μονογενῆ εἶναι τοῦ θεοῦ, καὶ τὸ πνεῦμα τὸ ἅγιον.

[152] Vgl. dazu meine Schrift 'Caesarea, Origenes und die Juden', 27.

[153] Vgl. Philon Al. de conf.ling. 146; Philos Werke deutsch, Bd. V² 138 (übersetzt von E. Stein): „Wenn aber jemand noch nicht würdig ist, Sohn Gottes zu heißen, so bestrebe er sich, sich zuzuordnen dem Logos, seinem Erstgeborenen, dem ältesten unter den Engeln, da er Erzengel und vielnamig ist. Er heißt nämlich: Anfang, Name und Wort Gottes, der ebenbildliche Mensch und der Schauende, Israel". — Vgl. auch ThWbNT IV (1942) 747, Atkl. μονογενής (Büchsel).

[154] Vgl. Schlatter, Geschichte Israels³, 367f. 450 Anm. 363; Simon, Verus Israel, 208f.

als 'Sohn Gottes' anzusehen sei. Die Aussagen über die (Gottes-)Rede, die wir bei den Rabbinen antrafen, lassen es nicht als ausgeschlossen erscheinen, daß auch dieser Schritt getan werden konnte und tatsächlich auch getan wurde. Daß Origenes, als er ca. 248 seine Schrift gegen Celsus schrieb, unter den Juden keine derartigen Lehren mehr fand, ist nicht verwunderlich: Sie sind in der Auseinandersetzung mit der Kirche vom orthodoxen palästinischen Rabbinat ausgeschieden worden. Freilich sind in den Midraschen — aber so weit ich sehe nicht in den Talmuden! — Aussagen über das 'Wort', die (Gottes-)Rede, als Hypostase erhalten geblieben und so auf uns gekommen. Wer aber in der Weise, wie es in SDeut § 343 geschehen ist, die (Gottes-) Rede (*dibbūr*) aus Gottes Munde hat hervorgehen lassen und ihr damit den Charakter einer Emanation Gottes gab, der konnte sie auch als 'Sohn' Gottes bezeichnen und sie als gleichen Wesens mit Gott auffassen. Ob das geschah, steht dahin — explizite Zeugnisse dafür fehlen m. W. bis jetzt. Aber die Unterschiede zur christlichen Betrachtungsweise des Logos und seines Verhältnisses zu Gott sind bei solcher Auffassung nicht mehr grundsätzlicher, sondern nur mehr terminologischer Art: In der Sache wird hier wie dort weithin das Gleiche oder durchaus Ähnliches und Vergleichbares ausgesagt.

3. Der Geist Gottes (*rūaḥ*) als Hypostase.

Wir sahen oben (vgl. S. 599), daß im rabbinischen Schrifttum auch der Geist Gottes (*rūaḥ*) als selbständige, persönliche Wesenheit aufgefaßt werden kann. Es scheint, daß diese Auffassung noch weniger oft im rabbinischen Schrifttum begegnet als die Auffassung von der (Gottes-)Rede (*dibbūr, dibbēr*) als Hypostase. Angelegt dürfte die Verselbständigung, die Hypostasierung, des Geistes (*rūaḥ*) schon im AT sein: In der bekannten Vision des Micha ben Jimla von der göttlichen Ratsversammlung, in der beschlossen wird, König Ahab zu verderben (1 Kön 22), wird die Frage erörtert, wie das zu bewerkstelligen sei. Da anerbietet sich der Geist (*rūaḥ*), in alle Propheten Israels zu fahren und in ihnen zum Lügengeist zu werden. Die Propheten werden dann alle dem Ahab Heil und Sieg prophezeien, während doch tatsächlich sein Untergang beschlossen ist:

> „Micha sprach: Nicht also! Höre das Wort Jahwes! Ich sah Jahwe auf seinem Thron sitzen und das ganze Heer des Himmels neben ihm zur Rechten und zur Linken stehen. Und Jahwe sprach: 'Wer will Ahab betören, daß er nach Ramot in Gilead zieht und dort fällt?' Der eine sagte dies, der andere jenes. Da trat der Geist vor, stellte sich vor Jahwe und sprach: Ich will hingehen und zum Lügengeist werden im Munde aller seiner Propheten. Er sprach zu ihm: Du magst ihn betören und wirst es auch zustandebringen. Gehe hin und tue also"[155].

[155] 1 Kön 22, 19—22; Übersetzung nach der Zürcher-Bibel.

Der Geist (*rūaḥ*) ist hier eine Jahwe gegenüber selbständige, persönliche Wesenheit: Er redet mit Jahwe und macht konkrete Vorschläge in der himmlischen Ratsversammlung; Jahwe redet mit ihm und gibt ihm Auftrag und Sendung. Der Geist (*rūaḥ*) ist hier eine Hypostase[156]. Stellen, die deutlich in dieselbe Richtung weisen, sind z. B. auch Jes 40, 13; 48, 16; 63, 10, ferner Ps 139, 7[157]. Wir finden die Auffassung vom Geist als Hypostase aber auch in jüdisch-hellenistischen Schriften, wo z. B. die 'Weisheit' (σοφία) und der 'Geist' (πνεῦμα) nebeneinander genannt werden:

„Denn in eine Seele, die Übles sinnt, wird die Weisheit nicht einkehren, und der Heilige Geist der Zucht wird die Falschheit meiden“ (Sap Sal 1, 4f.)[158].

„Der Geist des Herrn erfüllt den Erdkreis, und der das All Umfassende erkennt die Rede (sc. des Menschen)“ (Sap Sal 1, 7)[159].

Bousset-Gressmann (ebda.) bemerken mit Recht, „daß die Weisheit, der heilige Geist der Zucht und der Geist des Herrn sämtlich miteinander identisch sind“[160]. In Sap Sal 1, 7 ist der Geist nicht direkt als Organ der Schöpfung bezeichnet[161], wenn er auch kosmische Bedeutung und Funktion hat. Immerhin wird man zugeben, daß ein Anklang an Gen 1, 2 vorliegt! Deutlich schöpferische Funktion hat der Geist dagegen nach Jud 16, 14:

„Du entsandtest deinen Geist und er baute“[162].

Unmittelbar nachher ist vom „Sprechen“ Gottes bei der Schöpfung die Rede: „Denn du sprachst, und sie wurden“[163]: „Geist“ und „Wort“ als schöpferische Kräfte — Hypostasen — Gottes sind durchaus parallel[164]. Denselben Gedanken vertritt syr Bar 21, 4:

„Du hast die Höhe des Himmels durch den Geist gefestigt“.

Auf die Schöpfung des Menschen bezieht sich syr Bar 23, 5:

„Mein Geist erschafft die Lebendigen“[165].

Das Rabbinat hat offenbar den Geist (*rūaḥ*) nicht mit der Schöpfung in Zusammenhang gebracht, was im Blick auf den Vers Gen 1, 2 als auffällig be-

156 Bousset-Gressmann, Die Religion des Judentums, 347f.; ThWbNT VI (1959) 366, Atkl. πνεῦμα B II 5 (Baumgärtel).

157 Bousset-Gressmann, a. a. O., 348.

158 ὅτι εἰς κακότεχνον ψυχὴν οὐκ εἰσελεύσεται σοφία οὐδὲ κατοικήσει ἐν σώματι κατάχρεῳ ἁμαρτίας. ἅγιον γὰρ πνεῦμα παιδείας φεύξεται δόλον καὶ ἀπαναστήσεται ἀπὸ λογισμῶν ἀσυνέτων ...; vgl. Bousset-Gressmann, ebda.

159 ὅτι πνεῦμα κυρίου πεπλήρωκεν τὴν οἰκουμένην, καὶ τὸ συνέχον τὰ πάντα γνῶσιν ἔχει φωνῆς.

160 Vgl. auch Sap Sal 7, 27; 8, 7ff.; 9, 17.

161 Anders Sjöberg, ThWbNT VI (1959) 384, Atkl. πνεῦμα C IIIf.

162 ἀπέστειλας τὸ πνεῦμά σου, καὶ ᾠκοδόμησεν καὶ οὐκ ἔστιν ὃς ἀντιστήσεται τῇ φωνῇ σου.

163 σοὶ δουλευσάτω πᾶσα ἡ κτίσις σου ὅτι εἶπας, καὶ ἐγενήθησαν.

164 So schon Ps 33, 6f.; 104, 30.

165 Sjöberg, a. a. O., Anm. 304.

zeichnet werden muß[166]. Gelegentlich wird der Geist als Fürsprecher für die Menschen genannt[167]. In Lev r. 6, 1, zu 5, 1 wird Bezug genommen auf das Versprechen des Volkes Israel, Gottes Ṯora halten zu wollen (vgl. Ex 24, 7), aber auch auf die Sünde des goldenen Kalbes, welches die Israeliten als Gott anerkannten (vgl. Ex 32, 4). Unter Bezugnahme auf Prov 24, 28 („Sei nicht ohne Ursache ein Zeuge gegen deinen Nächsten") sagte R. Aḥa (um 320):

> „Dieser heilige Geist (*rūaḥ haḳḳodesch*) hat die Verteidigung geführt nach beiden Seiten. Er sprach zu den Israeliten: Sei nicht ein vergeblicher Zeuge für deinen Nächsten (Freund)! Und darauf sprach er zu Gott: 'Sage nicht: Wie er mir getan hat, also will ich ihm tun; ich will dem Manne vergelten nach seinem Werke' (Prov 24, 29)"[168].

Ganz ähnlich lautet die Tradition in Deut r. 3, 11, zu 9, 1:

> „R. Ḥijja bar Abba (um 280) sagte: Als der Fürsprecher (sc. Mose) aufgehört hatte, nahm der heilige Geist zu Gunsten der Israeliten das Wort und sprach zu ihnen: (Zitat Prov 24, 28). 'Sei nicht ohne Ursache Zeuge wider deinen Nächsten'. Das sind die Israeliten, welche 'Nächste' (Freunde) Gottes genannt werden, wie es heißt: (Zitat Ps 122, 8; 78, 36). Auch das, was ihr am Sinai gesagt habt: 'Wir wollen tun und gehorchen' (Ex 24, 7), habt ihr nicht gehalten. Zu Gott sprach er (sc. der heilige Geist): (Zitat Prov 24, 29), sondern: 'Jahwe, Gott, verdirb nicht dein Volk und dein Erbteil' (Deut 9, 26)".

Wir sehen, daß in diesen beiden Stellen, wo der heilige Geist redend eingeführt wird, er Bibelworte sagt. Und man kann sich fragen, ob er hier noch oder schon als Hypostase aufgefaßt wird. An der überwiegenden Zahl der Stellen in der rabbinischen Literatur, wo der heilige Geist (*rūaḥ*) als redend eingeführt wird, handelt es sich um die Zitierung von Bibelstellen oder um deutliche Reminiszenzen an solche. Man kann dann jeweils sagen statt „der (heilige) Geist spricht, bzw. ruft, seufzt" usw.: „Die Schrift sagt". Da überall ist der Geist Gottes nicht als Hypostase aufgefaßt[169].

VI. Zusammenfassung

Wir stellen etwas Selbstverständliches fest, wenn wir sagen, daß zu den unabdingbaren Voraussetzungen des rabbinischen Denkens und der

[166] Str.-Bi. I 48f.; Sjöberg, a. a. O., 384f.
[167] Auf TJud 20, 5 kann ich in diesem Zusammenhang nicht eingehen, da es sich hier m. E. um die Ḳumran-essenische Lehre von den zwei Geistern handelt. Anders offenbar Sjöberg, a. a. O., 387.
[168] Str.-Bi. II 138; ThWbNT V (1954) 809, Atkl. παράκλητος (Behm).
[169] Vgl. die umfangreichen Nachweise und Belege bei Str.-Bi. II 134—138.

rabbinischen Theologie die Bibel (das Alte Testament der Christen) gehört. (Aber es ist gelegentlich nötig, sich auch selbstverständliche Dinge ins Bewußtsein zurückzurufen!) Für unser Thema bedeutet dies, daß auch die alttestamentlichen Aussagen über das 'Wort' zu den Voraussetzungen des rabbinischen Denkens und Redens gehören. Vor allem aber ist festzuhalten, daß die at.lichen Aussagen über das 'Wort' als Hypostase zu dem gehörten, was dem Rabbinat einfach vorgegeben war. Es ist hier nicht zu wiederholen, was der *dābār* im AT bedeutet: Es ist dafür auf die Arbeiten von GRETHER und DÜRR zu verweisen. Hier ist nur festzuhalten, daß der *dābār* schon im AT als absolute Größe erscheint, d. h. ohne auf Jahwe bezogenes Personalsuffix und ohne Genetivkonstruktion[170].

SDeut § 343 mit seinen Parallelen zeigt, daß die Anschauung vom *dibbūr* als Hypostase in tannaïtische Zeit, und wahrscheinlich ins 1. Jh., hinaufreicht. Die Parallelen aus dem hellenistischen Schrifttum, auf die wir gestoßen sind, legen Zusammenhänge mit alexandrinischer Theologie und Logoslehre nahe: At.liches und Hellenistisches verbinden sich hier. Das bedeutet aber, daß es auch an diesem Punkt wenig sinnvoll ist, 'Hellenistisches' und 'Rabbinisches' zu unterscheiden oder gar zu trennen. Eine solche Unterscheidung oder Trennung bewirkt nur, daß die tatsächlichen Probleme und Zusammenhänge verdeckt werden. Palästina und sein Rabbinat gehört zusammen mit Alexandreia und seiner Theologie in eine geistige Bewegung, womit aber wieder nicht einfach die Identität beider Größen behauptet werden soll.

Zu der oben S. 613 erwähnten Stelle Lev r. 6, 1 sagt BILLERBECK: „Hier erscheint der heilige Geist als Partner Gottes genau so wie an andern Stellen die göttl. Strafgerechtigkeit oder die göttl. Barmherzigkeit. Die Hypostasenvorstellung aber hat der alten Synagoge durchaus fern gelegen"[171]. Ähnlich votiert SJÖBERG: „Eher könnte man ihn [sc. den heiligen Geist] eine Hypostase nennen, wenn man dadurch sein selbständiges Handeln ausdrücken wollte. Aber auch dieser einer unjüdischen Vorstellungswelt entnommene Begriff führt leicht zu falschen Vorstellungen. Durch die persönlichen Kategorien in der Beschreibung der Aktivität des Geistes will man ihn nicht als ein besonderes himmliches Wesen darstellen, wohl aber als eine objektive göttliche Realität, die dem Menschen begegnet und ihn beansprucht"[172]. Wir haben — gegen BILLERBECK! — gesehen, daß die alte Synagoge durchaus die Vorstellung von Hypostasen kennt. Und wenn SJÖBERG vom Geist redet als von einer „objektiven göttlichen Realität, die dem Menschen begegnet", fragt es sich, ob hier nicht doch dasselbe ausgesagt werden soll, was man sonst mit dem Begriff der Hypostase ausdrückt. Wir haben ja gesehen (vgl. S. 594), daß für weite Kreise in der Antike,

[170] „Jes 9, 7 ist die älteste Stelle, an welcher der dabar-Begriff spekulativ verwendet und in die theologische Geschichtsbetrachtung eingeführt wird. Der Ausbau der Theologie des dabar, der sich vom Deuteronomium an beobachten läßt, führt zu dessen fortschreitender Objektivierung und Hypostasierung". GRETHER, Name und Wort Gottes, 153f.

[171] STR.-BI. II 134f.

[172] A. a. O., S. 385f.

auch für rabbinische, auch geistige Wesenheiten 'konkret-real' vorgestellt und beschrieben wurden — die Beschreibung des *dibbūr* in SDeut § 343 läßt da wohl an Deutlichkeit nichts zu wünschen übrig! Es ist z. T. wenigstens richtig, wenn SJÖBERG darauf aufmerksam macht, daß „das Stilmittel der Personifizierung und Dramatisierung für die rabb. Lit. typisch ist — so können die beiden Eigenschaften Gottes, seine Barmherzigkeit u. seine Gerechtigkeit, מִדַּת רַחֲמִים [*middat raḥamim*] u. מִדַּת הַדִּין [*middat haddin*] als vor ihm redend dargestellt werden, obgleich sie keine Hypostasen oder gar persönliche Wesen sind —, zweitens, daß die persönliche Reaktion des Geistes immer an Worte der hl. Schrift angeknüpft ist"[173]. Man kann hier fragen (die Frage richtet sich schon an BILLERBECK!), ob die beiden göttlichen Eigenschaften Barmherzigkeit und Gerechtigkeit, wenn sie in dieser Weise personifiziert dargestellt und redend eingeführt werden, nicht „auf dem Wege" zur Hypostasierung sind. Sind sie durchaus keine Hypostasen, ist damit nichts ausgesagt für andere, nun entschieden hypostasierte Begriffe.

Sicher ist, daß im Rabbinat vom *dibbūr* im absoluten Sinne geredet werden konnte — die Zeugnisse, die dafür beigebracht werden konnten, sind wohl eindeutig. BILLERBECKS Aufstellungen bedürfen in dieser Hinsicht der Ergänzung und Korrektur: Der *dibbūr* kann im Rabbinat durchaus auch als Hypostase angesehen werden. Diese Vorstellung kann dann sehr weit vorangetrieben werden: Die (Gottes-)Rede (*dibbūr*) wurde nicht nur als von Gott ausgehende Kraft oder Wesenheit angesehen, sondern man hat sie auch als Person ansehen können: der *dibbūr* kann mit Gott reden! In ähnlicher Weise kann auch vom Geiste Gottes geredet werden: Er wird von Gott ausgesandt und kehrt zurück, um mit Gott zu sprechen. D. h. daß auch der Geist als Person angesehen wird.

Wir wissen nicht, inwieweit diese Ansichten einzelner Lehrer von ihren Kollegen oder von weiteren Kreisen akzeptiert worden sind. 'Dogma' im Sinne einer allgemein verpflichtenden Lehre sind diese Ansichten nie gewesen. Andererseits sind sie auch nie als heterodox abgewiesen worden: Man hat sie zum mindesten toleriert und auch in die Midrasch-Sammlungen aufgenommen. Man fragt sich weiter, ob und wie diese Lehren durchdacht und durchdiskutiert worden sind: Wie das Verhältnis von (Gottes-)Rede (*dibbūr*) zu Gott gedacht wird, wie das Verhältnis von Geist und Gott, von *dibbūr* und Geist. Man würde erwarten, daß auf diese Weise aus disiectis membris ein Gefüge, ein Lehrgebäude, eine Theologie im eigentlichen Sinne, errichtet wurde. Das ist nicht der Fall gewesen — die disiecta membra blieben als solche an ihrem Ort, und es ist mir keine Stelle bekannt, wo der Versuch gemacht wurde, aus ihnen ein durchdachtes Lehrgebäude zu errichten. Vom Standpunkt des christlichen Forschers aus kann man sagen, daß im Rabbinat die Elemente zu einer Trinitätslehre vorhanden sind, sie selbst aber wurde nirgends formuliert.

SCHLATTER hat die Stelle Tanḥ B Schemoṯ 23 zur Erklärung von Joh 1, 1 herangezogen[174]: „Die Vergleichung des Wortes mit Dingen oder Kräften

[173] SJÖBERG, ebda., S. 386. [174] SCHLATTER, Der Evangelist Johannes, 2.

liegt der Stelle fern; denn sie spricht von Gott. Weil das Wort Gottes Wort ist, ist es 'die Ursache' für alles Entstandene. Diese Ursache ist aber kein Neutrum, auch nicht bloße Kraft, sondern Wille und Gedanke, Bewußtheit, handelnde Person. Damit bleibt Joh. in enger Berührung mit den Jerusalemiten; denn für diese war das Gesetz eine persönliche Macht, die gebietet, richtet, gerecht spricht und verdammt, das Leben nimmt und gibt. Darum sagten die Jerusalemiten von der göttlichen Rede, sie habe sich dem, der sie empfing, geoffenbart als eine wirksame Macht, die in göttlicher Vollmacht an ihm handelte"[175]. Es folgt bei SCHLATTER der erste Satz aus Tanḥ B Schemoṯ § 23[176].

In den rabbinischen Schriften konnte keine Stelle nachgewiesen werden, an welcher der *dibbūr* mit der Schöpfung der Welt in Zusammenhang gebracht wird. Aber sofort ist festzuhalten, daß — nach at.lichem Vorgang — auch im Rabbinat davon gesprochen wird, daß Gott mit seinem 'Wort' schafft, nur daß dabei andere Vokabeln als *dibbūr* verwendet werden. (Vielleicht wird eine genauere Durchmusterung des rabbinischen Schrifttums auch noch Aussagen zu Tage fördern, in denen *dibbūr* und Schöpfung miteinander verbunden sind). Auch ließ sich keine Stelle finden, an der der *dibbūr* als Kraft bzw. Wesen erscheint, das am Ur-Anfang, vor der Schöpfung der Welt, bei Gott war. Dagegen gibt der *dibbūr* auch Leben (und Tod), und er ist das Licht — Aussagen, die vom 'Logos' in Joh 1, 4 gemacht werden. Es fehlt andererseits beim *dibbūr* die Aussage von Joh 1, 14, daß der 'Logos' Fleisch geworden ist. Es ist aber zu erinnern an SDeut § 343 (mit Parallelen), wo das Eingehen des *dibbūr* in die Gesetzestafeln beschrieben wird: Er selbst und als solcher geht in die Tafeln ein, wird Stein und Schrift und so in die Welt der Menschen gebracht.

Nachtrag bei der Korrektur:

Erst nach Abschluß der vorliegenden Arbeit wurde mir bekannt die Dissertation von P. SCHÄFER, Die Vorstellung vom heiligen Geist in der rabbinischen Literatur. SCH. schreibt (S. 16): „Es ergab sich unter anderem, daß der hl. Geist vorwiegend als Mittler der von Gott gewirkten Offenbarung verstanden wird; eine Personifikation geschweige denn Hypostasierung des hl. Geistes ließ sich aus diesen Stellen nicht ableiten." Auf S. 36—38 gibt SCH. den Text von Pesikt r. 3 (12a) wieder, den ich oben (S. 599) diskutiert habe. Dazu bemerkt SCH.

[175] Diese Ausführungen SCHLATTERS sind offensichtlich unbeachtet geblieben. Denn nur so läßt es sich erklären, daß in einem neueren Kommentar zum Johannesevangelium geschrieben werden konnte: „Der absolute Logos-Begriff kommt außerhalb des Prologs im Neuen Testament nicht mehr vor. Er begegnet auch nirgends im Alten Testament, nirgends in der spätjüdischen Apokalyptik, nirgends in der rabbinischen Literatur, und nicht in den bis jetzt bekannten qumranessenischen Schriften aus Palästina". SCHULZ, Das Evangelium nach Johannes, 28. Diese Ausführungen sind erstaunlich schon im Blick auf das AT, um so erstaunlicher aber, als Verf. in der Literaturangabe (a. a. O., S. 12) den Kommentar SCHLATTERS erwähnt – aber nicht beachtet. Daß die zitierten Sätze von SCHULZ nicht haltbar sind wurde in der vorliegenden Arbeit gezeigt: Sowohl das AT wie das rabbinische Schrifttum kennen die Vorstellung vom 'Wort' als Hypostase. Vielleicht geht diese Erkenntnis einmal in einen Johanneskommentar ein ...

[176] Vgl. den ganzen Text oben S. 599f.

auf S. 152: „Der hl. Geist wird als von Gott unterschieden vorgestellt. Gott sendet den hl. Geist mit einem bestimmten (begrenzten) 'Offenbarungsauftrag' aus." Ich würde hier doch dazu neigen, den hl. Geist als Hypostase anzusehen. Doch wird es darauf ankommen, wie man den Begriff der Hypostase auffaßt. Die ganze Frage müßte noch weiter diskutiert werden.

Bibliographie

W. Bacher, Die exegetische Terminologie der jüdischen Traditionsliteratur. Zwei Teile (Leipzig 1899 und 1905; Neudruck Hildesheim, 1965).

Id., Die Agada der Tannaiten I. Von Hillel bis Akiba (Straßburg 1903²; Neudruck Berlin, 1965; II (Straßburg 1890; Neudruck Berlin, 1966).

Id., Die Agada der palästinensischen Amoräer I. (Straßburg 1892; Neudruck Hildesheim, 1965); II. (Straßburg 1890; Neudruck Hildesheim, 1966); III (Straßburg 1899; Neudruck Hildesheim, 1965).

J. Barth, Die Nominalbildung in den semitischen Sprachen (Leipzig 1894; Neudruck Hildesheim, 1967).

H. Bietenhard, Caesarea, Origenes und die Juden. Franz Delitzsch-Vorlesungen 1972 (Stuttgart-Berlin-Köln-Mainz, 1974).

W. Bousset–H. Gressmann, Die Religion des Judentums im späthellenistischen Zeitalter (Tübingen, 1926³).

A. Diez Macho, El Logos y el Espíritu Santo, Atlántida I (1963), 381—396.

Id., Neophyti 1. Targum Palestinense. Ms. de la Biblioteca Vaticana. Tomo I. Genesis (Madrid-Barcelona, 1968); Tomo II. Exodo (1970); Tomo III. Levitico (1971); Tomo IV. Numeros (1974).

L. Duerr, Die Wertung des göttlichen Wortes im Alten Testament und im Alten Orient, Mitteilungen der Vorderasiatisch-Ägyptischen Gesellschaft 42, 1 (Leipzig, 1938).

W. Eichrodt, Theologie des Alten Testaments 2 (5. Aufl., Stuttgart, 1964).

L. Finkelstein, Siphre ad Deuteronomium, Corpus Tannaiticum III. 2 (New York, 1969).

W. Foerster, Die Gnosis. I. Zeugnisse der Kirchenväter (Zürich, 1969).

M. Ginsburger, Pseudo-Jonathan (Thargum Jonathan ben Usiel zum Pentateuch. Nach der Londoner Handschrift Brit. Mus. add. 27031) (Berlin, 1903).

Id., Das Fragmententhargum. Thargum Jeruschalmi zum Pentateuch (Berlin, 1899).

L. Goldschmidt, Der babylonische Talmud. Neu übertragen durch L. G. 12 Bde. (Berlin, 1929—1936).

O. Grether, Name und Wort Gottes im Alten Testament, Zeitschrift für die alttestamentliche Wissenschaft, Beih. 64 (Gießen, 1934).

H. S. Horovitz, Siphre D'Be Rab, Corpus Tannaiticum III 1: Siphre ad Numeros adjecto Siphre zutta (Leipzig, 1917).

J. Jastrow, A Dictionary of the Targumim, the Talmud Babli and Yerushalmi, and the Midrashic Literature (New York, 1958).

Ch. Kasowsky, Thesaurus Mishnae. Concordantiae Verborum quae in sex Mishnae Ordinibus reperiuntur. 4 Bde. (Jerusalem, 1956—1960²).

B. Kosowsky, Otzar Leshon Hatannaim. Concordantiae Verborum quae in Sifre aut Torat Kohanim reperiuntur. II (Jerusalem, 1967).

Id., Otzar Leshon Hatannaim. Concordantiae Verborum quae in Mechilta d'Rabbi Ismael reperiuntur. II (Jerusalem, 1965).

Id., Thesaurus Talmudis. Concordantiae Verborum quae in Talmude Babylonico reperiuntur. I—XXVI (Jerusalem, 1954—1975).

S. Krauss, Griechische und lateinische Lehnwörter im Talmud, Midrasch und Targum. I (Berlin 1898; Neudruck Hildesheim, 1964); II (Berlin 1899; Neudruck Hildesheim, 1964).

K. G. Kuhn, Sifre zu Numeri (Stuttgart, 1933—1959): Rabbinische Texte. II. Reihe: Tannaitische Midraschim, hrsg. von G. Kittel(†) und K. H. Rengstorf.

J. Z. Lauterbach, Mekilta de-Rabbi Ishmael. 3 Bde. (Philadelphia, 1949).

J. Levy, Neuhebräisches und chaldäisches Wörterbuch über die Talmudim und Midraschim. Nebst Beiträgen von H. L. Fleischer und den Nachträgen und Berichtigungen zur zweiten Auflage von L. Goldschmidt. I (Leipzig 1924²; Neudruck Darmstadt, 1963).

H. G. Liddell and R. Scott, A Greek English Lexicon (Oxford, 1973⁹).

K. Marti-G. Beer, Abôt (Väter [Gießener-Mischna IV 9]), (Berlin, 1927).

Midrasch Rabba. 5 Bde. (Jerusalem, o. J.).

H. Odeberg, 3 Enoch or The Hebrew Book of Enoch. Edited and translated for the first time with introduction, commentary and critical notes by H. O. (Cambridge 1928; Repr. New York, 1973).

Philo von Alexandria. Die Werke in deutscher Überstzung. Hrsg. von L. Cohn, I. Heinemann, M. Adler und W. Theiler. I—VI (2. Aufl. Berlin, 1962); VII (Hrsg. von W. Theiler, Berlin, 1964).

S. Pie y Ninot, La Palabra de Dios en los Libros Sapienciales, Colectanea San Paciano, (Barcelona, 1972).

A. Schlatter, Geschichte Israels von Alexander dem Großen bis Hadrian (Stuttgart, 1925³).

Id., Der Evangelist Johannes. Wie er spricht, denkt und glaubt. Ein Kommentar zum vierten Evangelium (Stuttgart, 1930).

S. Schulz, Das Evangelium nach Johannes NTD 4 (Göttingen, 1972).

M. Simon, Verus Israel. Études sur les relations entre Chrétiens et Juifs dans l'empire romain (Paris, 1948).

H. L. Strack und P. Billerbeck, Kommentar zum Neuen Testament aus Talmud und Midrasch. I–IV (München, 1922—1928). — Bd. V: Rabbinischer Index, hrsg. von Joachim Jeremias. Bearbeitet von K. Adolph (München, 1956). – Bd. VI: Verzeichnis der Schriftgelehrten. Geographisches Register, hrsg. von Joachim Jeremias in Verbindung mit K. Adolph (München, 1961).

J. Theodor and Ch. Albeck, Midrasch Bereshit Rabba. Critical Edition with Notes and Commentary. 3 Bde. (Jerusalem, 1965²).

N. I. Weinstein, Zur Genesis der Agada. Beitrag zur Entstehungs- und Entwicklungsgeschichte des talmudischen Schrifttums. II. Teil. Die alexandrinische Agada (Göttingen, 1901).

C. Westermann, Genesis, Biblischer Kommentar. Altes Testament, I (Neukirchen-Vluyn, 1968).

W. Windfuhr, Baba Messia ('Mittlere Pforte' des Civil-Rechts [Gießener-Mischna IV 2]), (Berlin, 1923)

A. Wuensche, Bibliotheca Rabbinica. Eine Sammlung alter Midraschim. 5 Bde. (Leipzig 1880—1885; Neudruck Hildesheim, 1967).

M. S. Zuckermandel, Tosefta (Trier, 1882).

Zum Nachtrag:

P. Schäfer, Die Vorstellung vom Heiligen Geist in der rabbinischen Literatur. Studien zum Alten und Neuen Testament, hrsg. von V. Hamp, J. Schmid, P. Neuenzeit, XXVIII (München, 1972).

Palestinian Holy Men: Charismatic Leadership and Rabbinic Tradition

by WILLIAM SCOTT GREEN, Rochester, N.Y.

Contents

The aim of this study is to examine the rabbinic traditions about Ḥoni the Circle-maker, a first century B.C. Palestinian miracle-worker, as an example of the way rabbinic Judaism dealt with figures known in rabbinic literature solely for their ability to perform supernatural feats. Before turning to a direct analysis of the traditions themselves, it is important to place them in a proper context. The introductory sections which follow are deliberately selective and focus only upon those issues in the study of ancient religion which are directly relevant to the problem of the Ḥoni-tradition.

I. The Greco-Roman Background: Mystery Religion, Philosophy, and 'Divine Men'

Philosophies and mystery cults both promised deliverance from the "anxiety"[1] that afflicted mankind in the first three centuries A.D., but

[1] The term derives from E. R. DODDS, Pagan and Christian in an Age of Anxiety, New York, 1970.

their programs for attaining this common goal were essentially different. The ecstatic and dramatic rituals of the cults revealed to believers esoteric cosmic doctrines and brought both salvation from death and behavioral privileges, often libertine, in the present life[2]. The initiate in the mystery cult acquired immortality through communion with the god, "the substitution of a divine for a human personality, brought about either by a magic ritual or by an act of divine grace, or by some combination of the two"[3]. Greco-Roman philosophy, which largely had abandoned speculation and metaphysics for ethics, also promised immortality of a sort, but the philosophical path to immortality was *homoiosis*, assimilation to, rather than identification with, the god[4]. The immediate objective of philosophy was not freedom from death per se but escape from the pain and unpleasantness of life, achieved through conscious, disciplined living in accord with the 'rational' and proper perception of reality as taught by the founder of the school[5]. A. D. NOCK summarizes the differences between the two systems:

> "A mystery evoked a strong emotional response and touched the soul deeply for a time, but philosophy was able both to turn men from evil and hold before them a good, perhaps never to be obtained, but presenting a permanent object of desire to which one seemed to draw gradually nearer and nearer[6]."

The phenomena of religions in the ancient world certainly are more complex, and the distinction between philosophy and mystery sometimes less sharp, than this dichotomy suggests. Nevertheless, attention to this fundamental difference between these two modes of salvation helps elucidate an important polarization of ideas about divine power which characterized the environment in which early rabbinic Judaism[7] took shape. The mysteries offered instant salvation through the miraculous commutation of the

[2] A. D. NOCK, Conversion, Oxford, 1972, pp. 99—121. Also see FRANZ CUMONT, The Oriental Religions in Roman Paganism, New York, 1956; R. E. WITT, Isis in the Graeco-Roman World, Ithaca, 1971, pp. 153ff.; JOHN H. RANDALL, Jr., Hellenistic Ways of Deliverance and the Making of the Christian Synthesis, New York, 1970.

[3] DODDS, op. cit., pp. 76—77.

[4] Ibid., p. 75.

[5] ELIAS BICKERMAN, La Chaîne de la Tradition Pharisienne, Revue Biblique, LIX, 1952, p. 49. Also see RANDALL, op. cit., pp. 161ff.; DODDS, op. cit., p. 92; NOCK, op. cit., pp. 121 and 164—192; RAMSAY MACMULLEN, Enemies of the Roman Order, Cambridge, Mass., 1966, pp. 46—94; T. R. GLOVER, The Conflict of Religions in the Early Roman Empire, London, 1918, pp. 33—74; JOHN FERGUSON, The Heritage of Hellenism, London, 1973, pp. 73—86, 133—151.

[6] NOCK, op. cit., p. 185.

[7] By early rabbinic Judaism I refer to the Judaism of the Tannaitic period, that is, from 70 to ca. 250 A.D. The distinction is actually a literary one. Tannaitic literature is that literature allegedly produced in the period of Mishnah-Tosefta. Amoraic literature is produced during the period of the two Talmuds. The distinction between early and later rabbinism is thus somewhat artificial and is not useful in all respects. But it is functional for the purposes of this essay.

soul. Philosophy presented a slower and more difficult route, the transformation of the intellect.

One important feature common to ancient religion and philosophy that reflects this polarization is the claim that the founder or leader of the movement is divine[8]. In the 'lives' of such figures divinity usually is manifested in two ways: in the attainment of wisdom and moral perfection, and in the possession of supernatural or magical powers. The earliest popular image of the 'divine man' represents him as both sage and miracle worker. Empedocles, who died ca. 444 B.C., conformed to this image and claimed to possess both sorts of divine power. As E. R. DODDS points out,

> "Empedocles represents not a new but a very old type of personality, the shaman who combines the still undifferentiated functions of a magician and naturalist, poet and philosopher, healer and counselor ... After him these functions fell apart, philosophers henceforth were to be neither poets nor magicians; indeed, such a man was already an anachronism in the fifth century[9]."

DODDS' observation requires some clarification. It is clear that the early image of the 'divine man' retained vitality in the Greco-Roman world, especially in lower-class circles[10]. It is equally clear that the reasons for deification were not everywhere identical[11]. As the functions of philosopher and miracle-worker became specialized, especially in the educated, upper-class circles responsible for most of the extant literature of that period, so did the image of the 'divine man'. Divinity was differently authenticated depending on the religious, philosophical, and social values of a given group, and portrayals of specific figures were recast, sometimes radically, to reflect those diverse values. The philosophical schools regarded their founders and great teachers as divine, but shared a "common consensus that the ideal wise man is divine, not because of his miraculous powers, but because of his moral courage and wisdom[12]." Moses' ability to perform miracles was a basic element of Old Testament narrative, and he was an important figure in the world of magic[13]. But in the writings of Philo and Josephus this specific manifestation of divine power, while not denied outright, is minimized and presented as a secondary result of Moses' possession of virtue, philosophically defined[14]. This reimaging of important figures

8 See MORTON SMITH, Prologomena to a Discussion of Aretalogies, Divine Men, the Gospels, and Jesus, Journal of Biblical Literature, XC, 1971, pp. 174—199; MOSES HADAS and MORTON SMITH, Heroes and Gods, New York, 1965; DAVID L. TIEDE, The Charismatic Figure as Miracle Worker, Missoula, Montanna, 1972.

9 E. R. DODDS, The Greeks and the Irrational, Berkeley, 1971, p. 146.

10 See HADAS and SMITH, op. cit., and SMITH's review of TIEDE, op. cit., in: Interpretation, XXVIII, April, 1974, pp. 238—240.

11 FRANZ CUMONT, Afterlife in Roman Paganism, New York, 1959, pp. 110—124.

12 TIEDE, op. cit., p. 43.

13 JOHN GAGER, Moses in Greco-Roman Paganism, New York, 1972, pp. 134—161.

14 TIEDE, op. cit., pp. 101—240.

sometimes took a subtle form. It seems clear that the earliest picture of Jesus represented him as divine primarily because of his miraculous powers[15], yet the depiction of the precise nature of those powers varies from one Gospel to another. Matthew, for example, generally eliminates magical details from his accounts of Jesus' healings and exorcisms, probably for both theological[16] and apologetic reasons[17]. Emphasis on Jesus' miracles as primary proof of his divinity was later rejected by both Tertullian and Origen partially out of a desire to accommodate Christianity to philosophy and partially because competing groups made similar claims for their own founders[18]. That these divergent ideas about divine power also influenced notions of religious leadership is evidenced by the struggle within early Christianity between 'orthodox' church administrators who based their authority on tradition and those 'heretics' who claimed direct access to the spirit, understood salvation along with Paul[19] as possession by Jesus' spirit effected through baptism, and performed magic[20]. It remains to note that the sharp functional distinction between these different types of authority began to blur as the Roman Empire began to disintegrate, and the terms *magicus*, *philosophus*, and *theurgus*, among others, came to be used almost interchangeably[21]. The appearance beginning with the Antonine age of fully developed literary 'biographies' of 'divine men' which reflect the early synthetic idealization conforms to that development[22]. It will be helpful now to attempt to understand early rabbinic Judaism within the limits of the context just sketched.

II. The Rabbinic Context

The central religious institution of ancient Judaism was the temple in Jerusalem and its cult, and the primary religious leaders were the priests.

15 Hans Dieter Betz, Jesus as Divine Man, in: F. T. Trotter, ed., Jesus and the Historian, Philadelphia, 1968, pp. 114—133, and Tiede, op. cit., pp. 241—292. Also see Geza Vermes, Jesus the Jew, New York, 1973, pp. 58—82.

16 John M. Hull, Hellenistic Magic and the Synoptic Tradition, Naperville, Ill., 1974, pp. 116—141.

17 Magic was criminal offense in the Roman Empire. See Morton Smith, Clement of Alexandria and a Secret Gospel of Mark (hereafter, Clement), Cambridge, Mass., 1973, pp. 220ff.

18 Robert M. Grant, Miracle and Natural Law, Amsterdam, 1952, pp. 188—189.

19 See Smith, Clement, pp. 213—216.

20 See Irenaeus, The Refutation and Overthrow of the Knowledge Falsely So Called, Book I, especially Chapter 21. Also see Hans Lietzmann, A History of the Early Church, Vol. II, B. K. Woolf, trans., Cleveland and New York, 1967, pp. 48—68; Smith, Clement, p. 253.

21 MacMullen, op. cit., p. 110.

22 Smith, art. cit., p. 181. Also see Ch. H. Talbert, Biographies of Philosophers and Rulers as Instruments of Religious Propaganda in Mediterranean Antiquity, ANRW II 16,2, ed. by W. Haase, Berlin–New York, 1978, pp. 1619—1651, and E. I. Bowie, Apollonius of Tyana: Tradition and Reality, ib. pp. 1652—1699.

The temple was the point at which the threads joining heaven to earth were knotted, and although God's power was "produced in heaven", it was "distributed from the temple"[23]. The rituals of the temple cult, when properly performed, certified the availability of that power for Israel's needs[24]. The priests were the managers of the cult, and their authority consequently derived from their role as the guarantors of God's continual presence in Israel's midst. The priests understood the formation of the cult and the appointment of its officers as the culmination of God's revelation to Israel, and the priestly editor(s) of the Pentateuch resorted to sophisticated wordplay to associate, indeed to identify, that institution with the covenant formed at Mount Sinai[25]. BARUCH LEVINE points out, however, that the relationship between the cult and covenant is not so pervasive as the P source suggests.

> "The covenant (or covenants) merely served as the charter, or commission under the terms of which the cult ... operated. The inner dynamic of the sacrificial cult bore its own intrinsic efficacy [spacing supplied] and did not exist for the purpose of sanctifying the covenant[26]."

By preserving and protecting God's presence in the temple, the cultic rites exhibit what MARY DOUGLAS calls "instrumental efficacy"[27]. But she suggests that religious rituals possess another sort of efficacy which "is achieved in the action itself, in the assertions it makes and the experience which bears its imprinting"[28]. Following this analysis, the temple rites assume an added dimension: they reflect, shape, and indeed constitute that which is truly real, or holy. From the priestly perspective it was in the temple that "the cosmic and social lines were clearly defined"[29], and God's command that Israel be a holy people could be fulfilled only in the cult. The temple was a saving institution.

This fundamental levitical perception certainly stands at the core of early rabbinic Judaism. More than half of the materials of Mishnah, the authoritative collection of rabbinic law allegedly produced ca. 200 A.D. by the Palestinian Patriarch, Judah, and its corollary collection, Tosefta, directly pertain to matters of the cult. But as JACOB NEUSNER has established, early rabbinic Judaism claimed that the holy life of the cult, limited by the priests to the confines of the temple, applied everywhere to all Israel.

[23] BARUCH A. LEVINE, On the Presence of God in Biblical Religion, in: J. NEUSNER, ed., Religions in Antiquity: Essays in Memory of Erwin Ramsdell Goodenough, Leiden, 1968, p. 82.

[24] BARUCH A. LEVINE, In the Presence of the Lord, Leiden, 1974, pp. 77—90.

[25] DELBERT HILLERS, Covenant: The History of a Biblical Idea, Baltimore, 1973, pp. 143—168.

[26] LEVINE, op. cit., p. 41.

[27] MARY DOUGLAS, Purity and Danger, London, 1966, p. 84.

[28] Ibid.

[29] JACOB NEUSNER, The Idea of Purity in Ancient Judaism, Leiden, 1973, p. 129.

This idea came from the Pharisees, the sect of whom the rabbis were heirs, and assumed an urgency in the aftermath of the temple's destruction in 70[30]. The concrete realization of this idea engaged the Tannaitic rabbis in substantial theorizing both about the detailed nature of the rituals themselves and about their actual or hypothetical application to everyday life. This largely accounts for the centrality of *halakhah* (law, the "way" of doing things) in rabbinic Judaism. But if the performance of rituals within the temple exposes the lines of God's revealed reality, then thinking and debating about those rituals outside the temple, even without the possibility of performing all of them, has the same effect. As NEUSNER recently has shown in striking detail,

> " . . . the Mishnaic rabbis express their primary cognitive statements, their judgements upon large matters, through ritual law, not through myth or theology, neither of which is articulated at all[31]."

Cosmic order and divine power were indeed manifested in the rites of the cult as the priests had claimed, but early rabbinism provided a new access to that knowledge and power by taking ritual beyond the realm of mere practice and transforming it into the object of speculation and the substance of thought. Study became not only a basic rabbinic activity, but, along with prayer and the observance of rabbinic Sabbath, Festival, food, and purity laws, a principal expression of piety as well. Formally, if not substantively, early rabbinic Judaism thus shared much with Greco-Roman philosophy[32].

We earlier noted a divergence in notions about divine power and observed its reflection in differing perceptions of 'divine men' and religious leadership. Early rabbinic evidence on this question is unambiguous. As SMITH shows, "Tannaitic literature contains almost no stories of miracles performed by Tannaim[33]." NEUSNER's comprehensive studies of the Pharisees before 70[34] and his biographical studies of Yoḥanan b. Zakkai and Eliezer b. Hyrcanus[35] reveal a virtually total absence of such stories, even

[30] JACOB NEUSNER, The Rabbinic Traditions about the Pharisees before 70, 3 Vols. (hereafter, Pharisees I, II, or III), Leiden, 1971 fully documents this assertion. Also see JACOB NEUSNER, A History of the Mishnaic Law of Purities, Part 10, Parah: Literary and Historical Problems, Leiden, 1976, pp. 220—230.

[31] NEUSNER, Parah, p. 230.

[32] See BICKERMAN, art. cit.; SAUL LIEBERMAN, Greek in Jewish Palestine, New York, 1942 and ID., Hellenism in Jewish Palestine, New York, 1962; MORTON SMITH, Palestinian Judaism in the First Century, in: M. DAVIS, ed., Israel: Its Role in Civilization, New York, 1956, pp. 67—81. HENRY FISCHEL, Rabbinic Literature and Greco-Roman Philosophy, Leiden, 1973 offers a different perspective on this matter.

[33] MORTON SMITH, Tannaitic Parallels to the Gospels, Philadelphia, 1951, p. 81 (hereafter, Parallels).

[34] NEUSNER, Pharisees I, II, and III.

[35] JACOB NEUSNER, Development of a Legend, Leiden, 1970; ID., Eliezer b. Hyrcanus: The Tradition and the Man, Leiden, 1973.

in late rabbinic collections where we would expect to find them. In the Mishnah-tractate Avot various Pharisaic and early rabbinic masters are praised for their possession of any number of moral, intellectual, or spiritual virtues, but not for their ability to perform miracles. One might explain this fact with the argument that since most of Tannaitic literature is legal in nature, miracle stories would not appear there in any case. But most of the Babylonian *gemara* also is legal[36], and it does have such stories about the sages of its period, the *'amora'im*. Indeed, with the sole exception of the Ḥoni-tradition, no miracle stories about Tannaim appear in Mishnah, and of the few such stories which do exist, most occur first in the *gemara*-stratum of the two Talmuds[37]. The virtual absence of miracle-stories does not mean that ancient Jews generally disavowed such events. Apocalyptic literature is filled with magic, miracles, and demons. Attempts to ascribe the provenance of that literature to Pharisaic or early rabbinic circles are insupportable. Moreover, in antiquity Jews were regarded by many as magicians; indeed, as MARCEL SIMON observes, «*pour les anciens, la magie est, peut-on-dire, congénitale à Israël*»[38]. Finally, as SMITH stresses, we may not account for this phenomenon with the argument that early rabbis did not believe in miracles or take magic seriously, for other evidence suggests that they did[39]. How, then, shall we assess it? Tannaitic literature is hardly apologetic or propagandistic. This means that it deals with issues and concerns most relevant to the internal life of the rabbinic movement. It therefore is poor evidence for any description of the image or role of the rabbis in Palestinian society at large during the first two centuries[40], but it is appropriate for a description of rabbinic self-conception. As the new masters of holiness the rabbis claimed for themselves and their piety the religious authority which once had belonged to the priests and the cult. Consequently, any Jew who claimed access to God outside the new rabbinic structure would have seemed to them suspect. Charismatic figures who professed supernatural powers — magicians, miracle-workers, or 'prophets' — naturally would have presented a challenge to the emerging rabbinic piety and claims to authority[41]. That the authorities behind Tannaitic literature generally did not ascribe such powers to their rabbinic contemporaries or their Pharisaic predecessors is therefore not too

[36] See JACOB NEUSNER, Invitation to the Talmud, New York 1973.,

[37] See for example, GEZA VERMES, Hanina ben Dosa (I), Journal of Jewish Studies XXIII, 1972, pp. 28—50, and ID., Hanina ben Dosa (II), Journal of Jewish Studies, XXIV, 1973, pp. 51—64.

[38] MARCEL SIMON, Verus Israel, Paris, 1948, p. 395. See especially, pp. 394—431 for a full account of Jewish magic.

[39] SMITH, Parallels, pp. 81—85.

[40] Cf. E. E. URBACH, Class Status and Leadership in the World of the Palestinian Sages, in: Proceedings of the Israel Academy of Sciences and Humanities, Jerusalem, 1968, pp. 38—74.

[41] See VERMES, op. cit., pp. 80—82. His discussion of healings, exorcisms, and Jewish charismatics, especially in pre-rabbinic times (pp. 58—80), is basic to this analysis.

surprising, and the resemblance of this perception of divine power to that of the philosophical schools which rejected miracle-working as an authentication of leadership or divinity is clear.

III. The Mishnaic Account of Ḥoni the Circle-maker

It is against this background that the Mishnaic story about Ḥoni the Circle-maker must be examined. As the following account shows, he represents a charismatic type which hardly conforms to an early rabbinic context.

A. They sound [the *shofar*] on account of any calamity which may befall the community, except for too much rain.

B. Once (*m'śh š*) they said to Ḥoni the Circle-maker, "Pray so that rains will fall".

C. He said to them, "Go out and bring in the Passover ovens so that they will not melt."

D. And he prayed, but (*w*) rains did not fall.

E. He made a circle and stood inside it.

F. And he said, "Master [of the Universe] (Kaufmann[42], Parma[43]: *rbwnw*. Loewe[44]: *rbwny*), your children have turned their faces to me because I am like a son of the house (*bn byt*) before you.

G. "I swear by your Great Name (*nšb' 'ny bšmk hgdwl*) that I am not moving from here until you have mercy on your children."

H. The rains began to drip.

I. He said, "I did not ask for this, but for rains of [sufficient amount to fill] cisterns, ditches, and caves."

J. They fell with vehemence.

K. He said, "I did not ask for this, but for rains of benevolence, blessing, and graciousness."

L. They fell as he ordered them (*yrdw ktqnn*),

M. until Israel went up from Jerusalem to the Temple Mount because of the rains.

N. They said to him, "Just as you prayed for them to fall, so pray for them to cease (lit. go away)."

[42] Georg Beer, Faksimile-Ausgabe des Mischnakodex Kaufmann A 50, Reprint: Jerusalem, 1968.

[43] Sisha Sidré Mischnah. Ketav Yad Parma DeRossi 138, Jerusalem, 1970.

[44] H. Loewe, The Mishnah of the Palestinian Talmud, Jerusalem, 1967.

O. He said to them, "Go out and see if the Stone of Strayers has been washed away."

P. Simeon b. Shetaḥ sent [a message] to him.

Q. He said to him, "You deserve to be excommunicated (*ṣryk 'th lndwt*), but what shall I do to you? For (*w*) you act petulantly before the Omnipresent like a son who acts petulantly before his father, yet (*w*) he does his will.

R. "And concerning you Scripture says, 'Let your father and mother be glad, and let her who bore you rejoice' (Proverbs 23:25)."

Mishnah Ta'anit 3:8

IV. The Definition of the Problem

Before turning to the text, it will be helpful to establish the analytical techniques and presuppositions which differentiate this from previous studies of the Ḥoni-tradition. Other investigators for the most part have supposed that the Mishnaic account has a first century B.C. provenance and either have assumed or attempted to demonstrate its historical veracity. Thus BÜCHLER[45] tried to supply historical details missing from the account, for example, the substance of Ḥoni's prayer for rain (D) and the location of the incident, and SARFATTI[46], on the basis of the "simplicity of the events," among other things, concluded that there is "no doubt that Ḥoni is an historical figure and the event, if not in all its details, is what happened." One wonders if the miraculous fall of rain and the flooding of Jerusalem are 'details' which detract from or contribute to the 'historicity' of the event. The distinguishing feature of this pseudocritical approach is its credulity, and its presuppositions differ little from those of the early New Testament scholarship which naively set out to "prove" what the historical Jesus actually had said, done, or felt. Subsequent New Testament research has shown the weakness of this approach for the study of early Christianity, and NEUSNER[47] has exposed its limitations for research into early rabbinic Judaism. Without evidence there is no reason to adopt those theories which claim that the traditions of Mishnah-Tosefta suddenly appeared in their present form ca. 200—250 A.D. after an extended period of continuous and unbroken transmission. To the contrary, the evidence[48] suggests that this literature underwent a process of selection, revision,

[45] ADOLPH BÜCHLER, Types of Jewish Palestinian Piety, New York, 1968, pp. 205—231.

[46] G. SARFATTI, Pious Men, Men of Deeds, and the Early Prophets (Hebrew with English summary), Tarbiz, XXVI, 1956—57, p. 129.

[47] See most recently, The Study of Religion as the Study of Tradition, History of Religions, XIV, 1975, pp. 191—206.

[48] J. NEUSNER, ed., The Modern Study of the Mishnah, Leiden, 1973.

deletion, and accretion. The historical situation of redacted literature, therefore, is the situation of the redactor(s), not necessarily the situation of the figures who appear in it[49]. We have seen that the power to perform miracles had little place in early rabbinic Judaism. On this criterion the story about Ḥoni should not appear in Mishnah at all. The proper subject of investigation, therefore, is not what Ḥoni actually said or where he performed his miracle, but the way Mishnaic redaction has shaped the account of his activity to justify the inclusion of this alien figure in that literature. This can only be done through careful attention to the discrete elements of the narrative. We earlier observed that other groups in antiquity routinely altered or moulded accounts of important figures to suit their own image. In the following analysis we shall want to see to what extent that same phenomenon is true for rabbinic Judaism.

V. Analysis of the Account in Mishnah: The Beginning of the 'Rabbinization' of Ḥoni the Circle-maker

The Mishnah-tractate 'Ta'anit' contains laws dealing with the imposition of public fasts as a response to some community problem, usually the lack of rain. Our passage, however, does not deal directly with fasts, but with the rules governing the sounding of the ram's horn, the *shofar*, which signalled the existence of a community problem and sometimes accompanied or announced the beginning of a fast.

A provides the legal context: one sounds the *shofar* in response to any calamity except excessive rain. Since the story about Ḥoni follows a legal rule and begins with the standard formula for a precedent, *m'śh š*, it ought to provide either a precedent for not sounding the *shofar* or an explanation of why too much rain is not a calamity. In fact, it does neither. The *shofar* is not mentioned at all, and although M—O deals with excessive rain, it provides no example of how one should respond to it. B—R, therefore, is virtually irrelevant to its context, and we shall have to find other reasons for its presence in Mishnah.

We can identify four stages or components to the narrative. B—D contains the request for rain and Ḥoni's initial response; E—L describes Ḥoni's successful action; M—O treats the implications of the action and the response of the petitioners; and Q—R presents a saying of Simeon b. Shetaḥ. We need to consider each section separately and then assess the result of their combination.

[49] For examples of different redactional procedures, see W. S. Green, Redactional Techniques in the Legal Traditions of Joshua b. Ḥananiah, in: J. Neusner, ed., Christianity, Judaism, and Other Greco-Roman Cults: Studies for Morton Smith at Sixty, Leiden, 1975, Part IV, pp. 1—17.

B assumes that Ḥoni has the power to bring rain and that his method of doing so will be prayer. This is an important detail because within rabbinic piety prayer is an appropriate way of reaching God. Indeed, prayers for rain were a standard element of rabbinic liturgy, and it seems reasonable to suppose that they were recited in the belief that they would be answered. C contributes two details. It suggests Ḥoni's certainty that his prayer would be effective, and it places the time of the incident near the beginning of the Passover festival[50]. This last detail gives the entire account an exceptional quality, for Passover normally marks the end of the Palestinian rainy season[51]. D responds directly to the language of B, and it is for this reason that B—D seem to form a distinct stage in the narrative. Ḥoni is asked to pray, and he prays. Significantly, the prayer fails to produce results. This is confusing. After affirming the priority of prayer, an acceptable access to divine power, the pericope seems to question its efficacy. Indeed, had the pericope been constructed to indicate that Ḥoni's success was the result of prayer, D should have been eliminated, leaving E—L as the sole response to the request for prayer. The presence of D suggests that what follows it is not prayer, but something else, and, in fact, the substance of E—L contains no liturgical elements[52]. This sort

[50] A gloss in the Palestinian Talmud, Ta'anit 3:11 (Venice 66d) asserts that the event occurred on Passover eve.

[51] See Mishnah Ta'anit 1:2 and The Mishnah, H. Danby, trans., Oxford, 1933, p. 194, note 15. Professor Morton Smith pointed out this anomaly to me, and Professor Charles Smith helped to assess its significance.

[52] Joseph Heinemann, Prayer in the Period of the Tanna'im and the Amora'im: Its Nature and Patterns (Hebrew with English Abstract), Second Edition, Jerusalem, 1966, pp. 121—127 argues that F—G of Mishnah is an example of "a special type of prayer of the individual, in which the speaker sees himself as standing before God, the judge, and pleading before him like the accused — or his advocate — in a human court of law." Heinemann suggests that this type of prayer "can be recognized both by its content and form pattern. As regards their function, the prayers in this group can be subdivided into prayers in times of danger or grave emergency, confessions of sin, and prayers of thanksgiving. Basically, all have the same structure: (a) the address (usually the wording is *rbwnw šl 'wlm* or the like) without any added epithets or words of praise, (b) the 'statement of the facts' (usually with the introduction *glwy wydw' lpnk* or *lpny ks' kbwdk*), and the pleading, in which the speaker argues his case and seeks to justify himself, (c) the request (usually introduced by *yhy rṣwn mlpnyk*).
"The special character of this type of prayer stands out in particular in section (b), which is quite different from the type of arguments sometimes used in ordinary prayers or supplication to ensure their acceptance; here the argument precedes the request and is put forward in terms of self-justification, reliance on divine promises, and even of complaint. The 'statement of facts' too, is modelled on the duty of the defendant in court to 'reveal his cause' to the judge. While in the 'confession of sins' this part usually contains only the actual admission of guilt, in 'prayers in time of emergency' the pious man (who intercedes for the community) utters complaints or even accusations against God. Often part (c) is missing, the request being expressed merely by implication. Among the particularities of style we note frequent rhetorical questions."
"This aggressive, even impertinent style of prayer is the result of despair, after ordinary prayers have proved of no avail against the threatening catastrophe (mostly: drought). ... In the pattern under discussion [as opposed to usual types of prayer of supplication],

of inconsistency normally suggests a redactional effort to combine two incompatible sources. An analysis of E—L should help resolve this question.

E—L is the center of the account and probably constitutes the core of the Ḥoni-tradition. Framed by B—D and M—O, it is virtually a complete narrative in itself. This observation finds support in a comparison of our Mishnaic passage with the following pericope from Tosefta:

1. Once (*m'śh b*) they said to one *ḥasid*, "Pray that rains may fall."
2. He prayed, and rains fell.
3. They said to him, "Just as you prayed and they fell, so pray that they should cease (lit. go away)."
4. He said to them, "Go out and see if a man [can] stand on the Qeren Ofel and shake his feet in the Qidron River.
5. "We pray that rains will not fall,
6. "but we are certain that the Omnipresent will not bring a flood on the earth, as it [Scripture] says, 'Never again shall the waters be brought as a flood' (Genesis 9:11)."
7. And it says, 'These days recall for me the days of Noah: as I swore that the waters of Noah's flood should never again pour over the earth,

the element of praise is lacking entirely; the supplicant, instead of asking for favours, is claiming rights and demanding justice (From the English Abstract, pp. IX—X)."
HEINEMANN produces (pp. 131—137) thirty-six examples of this sort of 'prayer', but by his own reckoning only ten of them exhibit all the elements of "form pattern" he describes (# 1, 2, 12, 14, 15, 18, 19, 20, 27, 32). Of the remainder, eighteen contain no independent "request" for action (c) (# 3, 4, 5, 6, 7, 8, 9, 11, 16, 21, 28, 29, 30, 31, 33, 34, 35, 36), four either lack the "address" (a) altogether or have a different formula for it (# 13, 23, 24, 25), three have an atypical formula of address and lack an independent "request" (# 10, 17, 26), and one reverses the order of (b) and (c) (22). All this suggests that HEINEMANN has not identified a rigorous literary form of prayer, or even a formulary pattern (for definitions see JACOB NEUSNER, A History of the Mishnaic Law of Purities, Part Three, Kelim: Literary and Historical Problems, Leiden, 1974, pp. 192—236). Moreover, as HEINEMANN himself observes (p. 126), the various examples do not share a common posture towards the deity, but reflect different, even contradictory attitudes. At times the one who prays apologizes and asks forgiveness or mercy. This hardly illustrates a prayer on the pattern of a Law-court in which "the supplicant . . . is claiming rights and demanding justice." In other places the one who prays stands as God's accuser. Since the substance of the various examples exhibits no consistent formal pattern, and the postures they contain are distinctly different, it is hard to understand how the items HEINEMANN lists illustrate a single phenomenon, much less a particular type of prayer.
This is not to say that HEINEMANN's collection of examples is arbitrary, for most do share a common formula of address to God, *rbwnw šl 'wlm*, and its attachment to such a variety of examples suggests that it had a wide application. But the manuscript evidence is consistent with respect to the Ḥoni-tradition: the whole formula does not appear there. So its appearance in the printed editions probably is the work of later editors or printers. By any reckoning, therefore, HEINEMANN's interpretation of F—G is questionable.

so now I swear to you never again to be angry with you or to reproach you' (Isaiah 54:9).

Tosefta Ta'anit 2:13, ed. LIEBERMAN, pp. 334—335, ls. 80—85

The similarity of the situations depicted in both passages has led some investigators[53] to regard the Toseftan account as an abridgement of the Mishnaic pericope and to identify Ḥoni with the *ḥasidim* (pietists), figures characterized in rabbinic literature by their ethical supererogation and extreme legal practices. This conclusion ignores the fact that the pious qualities which distinguish the *ḥasidim* are not ascribed to Ḥoni and, as the following analysis will suggest, seems to be based on insufficient attention to the nature of the two passages. In the synoptic table below, the components of the Mishnaic account are identified as they were in section III above.

Mishnah	Tosefta
B. Once they said to Ḥoni the Circle-maker, "Pray so that rains will fall."	1. Once they said to one *ḥasid*, "Pray that rains may fall."
C. He said to them, "Go out and bring in the Passover ovens so that they will not melt."	(—). ________
D. He prayed, but rains did not fall	2. He prayed, and rains fell.
E.—L. He drew a circle . . . the rains began to drip . . . they fell with vehemence . . . they fell as he ordered them.	(—). ________
M. Until Israel went up from Jerusalem to the Temple Mount etc.	(—). ________
N. They said to him, "Just as you prayed that they should fall, so pray for them to cease."	3. They said to him, "Just as you prayed and they fell, so pray that they should cease."
O. He said to them, "Go out and see if the Stone of Strayers has been washed away."	4. He said to them, "Go out and see if a man [can] stand on the Qeren Ofel and shake his feet in the Qidron River."
(—). ________	5. "We pray that rains will not fall,
(—). ________	6. but we are certain that the Omnipresent will not bring a flood on the earth, as it says, (Genesis 9:11)."
(—). ________	7. And it says, (Isaiah 54:9).

[53] S. SAFRAI, The Teaching of the Pietists in Mishnaic Literature, Journal of Jewish Studies, XVI, 1965, pp. 15—33, and SARFATTI, art. cit.

We saw that D of Mishnah depicted prayer as an appropriate but ineffective means for producing rain. The Toseftan account contradicts this in 2; the rain falls in response to prayer. This illustrates not abbreviation, but alteration. Tosefta furthermore contains material not present in Mishnah (5—7); this hardly supports the argument that it is an abridgement. Moreover, part of Tosefta's additional material (6—7) is highly appropriate to the legal context of Mishnah for it contains what Mishnah should have supplied, namely, the reason that too much rain is not regarded as a calamity. God has promised never again to flood the earth, so too much rain is a technical impossibility. To pray for rain to cease demonstrates lack of faith in God's guarantee. If the Toseftan passage were merely another version of the Mishnaic account, its additional material should have appeared in Mishnah. Finally, the different geographical details of Mishnah's O and Tosefta's 4 also argue against the supposition that the one is a version of the other. In sum, the two accounts not only differ in detail, but reflect conflicting points of view. So we do not have two versions of the same story, one an abbreviation of the other[54], but two different stories which share a common literary structure that probably derives from another source: B, D, N, O in Mishnah (M merely provides a transition from L to N.) and 1, 2, 3, 4 in Tosefta. The different use of that structure in Tosefta and the fact that in Mishnah it merely frames the core of the Ḥoni-narrative (E—L) but is peripheral to its substance increases the probability that E—L and probably C are part of an independent narrative onto which B, D and M—O have been superimposed. The result of the combination of the two accounts is the confusion in D and the evident impropriety of C. As we shall see, the certainty implied in C but turned into arrogance by D coincides with the attitude of E—L.

It is clear that our characterization of Ḥoni can only derive from the rainmaking technique described in E—L. LUDWIG BLAU observes that,

> „*Die Erzählung ist allerdings streng monotheistisch, der Kreis jedoch, den er zog, der Schwur 'bei dem grossen Gottesnamen' sowie die Eigenschaft als Regenmacher deuten auf fremde Vorstellungen*[55]."

The action which produces the rain consists of self-enclosure in a circle and a declaration of refusal to leave it until rain falls. Since no details are provided about the circle itself, our interpretation of its importance depends on an understanding of G. BÜCHLER characterized G as an oath and regarded the circle as "nothing else but a drastic illustration of his [Ḥoni's] declaration, I shall not move from the spot in which I am standing"[56].

[54] SAUL LIEBERMAN, Tosefta Kifshuṭah, Mo'ed, New York, 1962, pp. 1096—97.

[55] LUDWIG BLAU, Das Altjüdische Zauberwesen, Berlin, 1914, p. 33.

[56] BÜCHLER, op. cit., pp. 246—247. BÜCHLER compared Ḥoni's circle to the one drawn by the Roman general Popilius Laenas around Antiochus Epiphanes to prevent the latter's invasion of Egypt. Popilius' action was deliberately coercive; it forced an immediate decision from Antiochus. If Ḥoni's action is similar, we must understand it as a means

This rationalistic interpretation makes drawing the circle into an arbitrary action; any dramatic illustration of intent would have served just as well. BÜCHLER's explanation will serve only if no other is forthcoming.

G certainly employs the language of an oath (*nšbʿ ʾny*), but its form and substance are problematic. Although oaths made in God's name are commonplace in the Hebrew Bible[57], the exact formula of G appears there only once, in an oath made by God himself[58]; it appears in Mishnah only in this passage. God's "Great Name" apparently is not a usual component of oaths. Oaths usually limit the action only of the person who swears. But Ḥoni's oath also affects God; only rainfall can free him from his vow. So G is other than an ordinary oath, as SAUL LIEBERMAN explains:

> "If a Jew wished to adjure an angel in an incantation, he might instead bind himself by an oath according to which the angel should and will act. If the angel acts differently he causes the swearer to perjure himself, which is not compatible with piety[59]."

In E—G, then, Ḥoni encloses himself in a circle and, invoking God's "Great Name", utters the legal equivalent of an incantation to produce rain. H—L demonstrates the efficacy of the action, but H—K tells us more than we need to know. L alone would have sufficed as an appropriate conclusion to G. Since H—K is superfluous to the main point of the narrative, its purpose evidently is to certify that the rainfall is neither an accident nor a caprice of God, but the direct result of Ḥoni's action. Ḥoni's mastery over the rain is shown in the movement from the extreme of too little rain (H) to that of too much rain (J) to the proper amount between the two. So H—L delineates the extent of Ḥoni's power; he is able to do more than merely produce rain; he also can control its quality. To be sure, in conformity with both biblical and rabbinic theology the narrative depicts God as the source of the rain and attributes to Ḥoni appropriate supplicatory language ("I did not ask . . ."), but this in no way mitigates the fact that Ḥoni, not God, dominates and controls the action. What accounts for Ḥoni's unusual ability? The narrative places him in a special relationship with God; he claims to be "like a son of the house" (*bn byt*) before Him. The precise substance of this term is difficult to determine[60], but its use in F implies

of coercing God. But BÜCHLER insisted (p. 249) that the rain fell as a response to Ḥoni's "humble prayer." He cannot have it both ways. For the sources of the account of Popilius' circle, see now E. SCHÜRER, The History of the Jewish People in the Age of Jesus Christ, Revised and edited by GEZA VERMES and FERGUS MILLAR, Edinburgh, 1973, pp. 151—52.

57 See the entry of MOSHE GREENBERG, Encyclopedia Judaica, Jerusalem, 1971, Vol. 12, s. v. Oath, cols. 1295—1298.

58 Jeremiah 44:26.

59 SAUL LIEBERMAN, Greek in Jewish Palestine, p. 108, note 85.

60 BÜCHLER, op. cit., p. 203 suggested that it means "an intimate slave who enjoys his master's confidence . . .," and compared this passage to the story of Ḥaninah b. Dosa who announced the healing of the son of Yoḥanan b. Zakkai (Babylonian Talmud,

a greater than familial intimacy with the deity: the "son of the house" is closer to the "father" than are the "children" since they turn to him for help. He has access to the "father" when the "children" do not. Interestingly, the basis for such intimacy is nowhere stated; its assertion is a sufficient explanation of Ḥoni's power. The metaphorical use of the term ("like a son of the house") in no way alters the structure of the relationship. In sum, C and E—L constitute an account of a figure who, as a result of his intimacy with the deity, exercises extraordinary control over the weather. Through the performance of an unusual rite and the utterance of an incantation he can, at the end of the rainy season, produce rain and even determine its quality.

This combination of elements gives the entire account a decidedly magical character, and all the elements of Ḥoni's technique in fact have counterparts in either ancient or Greco-Roman magic. The circle is an "ancient and universal magical symbol"[61]. Circles were solar symbols in Hellenistic magic, especially in magical rites practiced by members of the mystery cults[62]. In the magical rainmaking competition with the priests of Baal described in I Kings 18, Elijah produces rain in a time of drought by digging a circular trench around the altar on Mount Carmel[63]. JOSHUA TRACTENBERG describes the function of the circle in Ḥoni's rite:

Berakhot 34b). But the single other instance of the term in Tannaitic literature does not suggest the connotation of slave. The passage occurs in Sifré on Numbers, Balaq, p. 131, ed. HOROVITZ, pp. 170, ls. 22—25 and 171, ls. 1ff. It is translated below.
"At that time the Ammonites and Moabites arose and built enclosures for them [the Israelites] . . . and they placed there women who sold them all sorts of sweetmeats, and Israel ate and drank. At the same time a man went out to stroll in the market and asked to purchase an object from an old woman. She was prepared to sell it to him for its value, but a young woman called out to him. And she said to him from inside [the house], 'Come and take it for less.' And he bought from her the first day and the second day. And on the third day she said to him, 'Enter and decide (*brwr*) for yourself whether you are a *bn byt*.' And he entered her house, and the stone vessel was filled with Ammonite wine . . . she said to him, 'Do you want a drink of wine?' And he drank and the wine burned within him. And he said to her, 'Submit to me.' And she found an image of Pe'or . . . and said to him, 'Rabbi, you want me to submit to you. Bow down to this . . ."

61 JOSHUA TRACTENBERG, Jewish Magic and Superstition, New York, 1970, p. 121.

62 A. DELATTE, Études sur la magie grecque: I. Sphère magique du Musée d'Athènes, Bulletin de Correspondance Hellénique, XXXVII, 1913, pp. 247—278.

63 For an interpretation of the magical elements of Elijah's rite, see RAPHAEL PATAI, The 'Control of Rain' in Ancient Palestine, Hebrew Union College Annual, XIV, 1939, pp. 251—286.
SARFATTI, art. cit. compares Ḥoni's rain-making rite to Elijah's: " . . . they both utter oaths ('As the Lord, the God of Israel liveth . . . .' I Kings 17:1); 'I swear by thy Name . . . .'); they both give advance notice, in the form of advice, of God's response, ('Get thee up, eat and drink; for there is the sound of abundance of rain,' I Kings 18:41; 'Go out and bring in the Passover ovens . . . .'). Essentially the miraculous event is carried out in three stages in the case of both of these figures: firstly there is an act indicating the understanding of the event about to transpire (Elijah's building of an altar, Ḥoni's baking the cake [sic!]); secondly, there are prayers on behalf of Israel and of the protagonists themselves ('Let it be known this day that Thou art God in Israel, and that I am thy servant in the words of Elijah,' I Kings 18:36; 'Thy children have turned their

"The invocation of demons is a dangerous business, and the magician must take steps to protect himself in the event that his spirit adjutants get out of hand. What simpler or more obvious device than to exclude them from his immediate environment? ... By this magic act [of enclosing oneself in a circle] the ground and atmosphere surrounding the magician become a private, forbidden precinct[64]."

Knowing the name of a diety or demon was one way to gain control over it, and the use of such names or titles is typical in adjurations and magical incantations throughout the ancient world[65]. Finally, Greco-Roman magicians commonly based their powers on their alleged intimacy with a god; some claimed to be gods, or sons of gods[66]. In short, in the ancient world magicians claimed to be able to do what Ḥoni is alleged to have done[67], and they utilized methods similar to his to do so. It is important to point out that no exact parallel to Ḥoni's rite appears in either primary or secondary sources on ancient magic, so this theory necessarily is more suggestive than probative. The absence of such a parallel, however, will not serve to deny the magical character of Ḥoni's activity. Since this theory accounts for all the details of Ḥoni's action within a coherent, integrated, and historically accurate framework, it seems reasonable to suggest that the root of E—L, the core of the Ḥoni-narrative, is an account of an ancient Jewish magical rite.

As our previous analysis of the relationship of M—O to E—L has suggested, it serves only to confuse the movement of the narrative. H—L

faces to me, for that I am like a son of the house before Thee ... have pity on thy children [sic!],' in the words of Ḥoni); and thirdly, there is God's answer ('Then the fire of the Lord fell,' I Kings 18:38; 'Rains began falling drop by drop .... ')." SARFATTI then compares the activities of Ḥanina b. Dosa to those of Elijah and Elisha and concludes that "these 'men of deeds' represented a later development of the early prophetic type." (Quotations are from the English Summary, pp. II—III.)

It is difficult to know how to assess this claim. First, as we saw, the identification of Ḥoni as a *ḥasid* or "man of deed" depends in large measure on the assumption that Tosefta Ta'anit 2:13 is an abridged version of our Mishnah-passage. That assumption is almost certainly incorrect. Second, since SARFATTI regards the account of Ḥoni's miracle as essentially true, the comparison is not drawn between literary images, but actual miracles! Third, as SARFATTI himself observes, while Elijah is depicted as speaking the word of God and proving God's power to the people (In I Kings 18:1 God promises to send rain, so Elijah is merely the vehicle for the fulfillment of the promise.), Ḥoni is not so depicted. In short, the very characteristics which distinguish Elijah as a prophet are absent from the Ḥoni-narrative. The precise sense in which the figure of Ḥoni is a "development" of the prophetic type is thus unclear.

64 TRACTENBERG, op. cit., p. 121.

65 The evidence may be found in: KARL PREISENDANZ, ed., Papyri Graecae Magicae, 2 Vols., Leipzig, Berlin, 1928; W. S. MCCULLOUGH, ed., Jewish and Mandaean Incantation Bowls in the Royal Ontario Museum, Toronto, 1967; E. M. YAMAUCHI, ed., Mandaic Incantation Texts, New Haven, 1970. Also see SAUL LIEBERMAN, Texts and Studies, New York, 1974, pp. 21—28.

66 SMITH, Clement, pp. 220—221.

67 BLAU, op. cit., pp. 33—34. Also see J. G. FRAZER, The Golden Bough, New York, 1956, pp. 72—89.

represented Ḥoni's power over rain in terms of his ability to moderate between two extremes, insufficient rain and excessive rain. But in M the rain of "benevolence, blessing, and graciousness" produced by Ḥoni is itself threatening, a curious reversal, and in N the people ask him to pray for it to stop. The language of their request is significant. We observed that B—D seemed to reject prayer as the means for bringing rain. N directly contradicts this and specifically labels Ḥoni's activity as prayer. The inconsistency is the result of redaction, and in its new context N effectively removes any ambiguity about Ḥoni's behavior; it recasts his magic ritual into an acceptable image and brings it within the limits of appropriate piety. It remains to observe that O is a pointlessly abrupt ending to the narrative. It ought to be followed by a conclusion which draws on the reference to the Stone of Strayers[68], but since it is part of the structure which derives from a source outside the Ḥoni-narrative, it is difficult to suggest what that conclusion might have been. We saw that the Toseftan passage did supply an ending to the structure, but it cannot have been part of the original. If it had been, it would have appeared in Mishnah. In any case, in its present form O suggests that Ḥoni's power, shown to be considerable in E—L, is limited; he can cause rain, but he cannot make it stop.

We now turn to the lemma of Simeon b. Shetaḥ, P—R. In the present context it certainly is hostile to Ḥoni, thus confirming our earlier contention about the relationship of miracle-working to early rabbinism. It appropriates Ḥoni's metaphor of 'sonship' and interprets it negatively. Ḥoni is indeed a 'son', but an arrogant one who is indulged by the 'father' despite his improper behavior. The hostility is evident too in Simeon's charge that Ḥoni deserves excommunication. This is a curious claim. The technical term for excommunication, *ndh*, is postbiblical and is used elsewhere in Mishnah to denote expulsion from the Pharisaic group on account of transgression of sectarian teachings[69]. But here the action which war-

[68] The Palestinian Talmud, Ta'anit 3:11 (Venice 66d) explains the Stone of Strayers as follows:

"What was the purpose of the Stone of Strayers ? Everyone who had lost something would take it from there, and everyone who had found something would bring it there.
He [Ḥoni] said to them, 'Just as it is impossible for that Stone to be eliminated from the world, so it is impossible to pray that the rains will stop.'"

Neusner (Pharisees I, p. 177) concludes that this, along with other elements of the Palestinian Talmud's version of the Ḥoni-narrative, "certainly come later than the Mishnah and augment it . . . . " The need of later editors to provide both an explanation and interpretation of the Stone of Strayers suggests that its meaning was not clear from the context of Mishnah. Had the above material been part of the original Mishnah version, it is hard to see why it was dropped since, like the additions to Tosefta (6—7), it certainly conforms to Mishnah's legal context. It is worth noting that the Toseftan passage also fails explicitly to refer to the geographical detail of 4, the Qeren Ofel.

[69] Mishnah 'Eduyyot 5:6. The entry in Encyclopedia Judaica, Vol. 6, s. v. 'Excommunication' argues that our Mishnah passage is evidence that *nidduy* was applied outside of the Pharisaic sect. To make this argument, one must regard the entire passage as a unity, which it is not. The argument also assumes that it was routine for Pharisees to excom-

rants such a penalty is nowhere specified[70]. Indeed, as the following expanded version of Simeon's lemma shows, later tradents also had difficulty making sense of the charge.

> "You should be excommunicated, for if a decree had been decreed like the decree [against rain] in the days of Elijah, would you not be found bringing the public to the profanation of the Name [of God]? For anyone who brings the public to the profanation of the Name deserves excommunication."
>
> Palestinian Talmud, Ta'anit 3:11 (Venice 67a) = Palestinian Talmud, Mo'ed Qatan 3:1 (Venice 81d)

The reference is to God's decree of drought in I Kings 17 which was ended by Elijah with the ritual mentioned above. The passage suggests that if the conditions of Elijah's time had been operative in Ḥoni's day, he would have been liable to excommunication for causing the people to transgress God's ordinance. No claim for the similarity of the two cases is made, however, so Ḥoni's transgression is merely potential, not actual. This interpretation is a far cry from the plain sense of Simeon's lemma in Mishnah. All of this suggests that P—R is not integral to the Ḥoni-tradition, and it confirms NEUSNER's judgement that P—R "circulated separately and was probably an independent pericope"[71]. Its inclusion here, therefore, is highly significant. The rabbinic traditions about Simeon b. Shetaḥ allege that he was a key figure in early Pharisaism. In Mishnah Avot. 1:1—8 he is an important link in the chain of Pharisaic masters, and Mishnah Sanhedrin 6:4 attributes to him sufficient political power to hang eighty women, identified as witches in later versions, in a single day. Other traditions assert that he was either President or Vice-president of the Jerusalem Sanhedrin[72]. The issue of the veracity of these claims is irrelevant here. The important point is that the post-70 rabbis, descendants of the Pharisees, regarded Simeon as a founding father, and he consequently served, anachronistically to be sure[73], as the representative of rabbinism in traditions about the pre-

municate individuals not of their sect and that they had sufficient political power to make such an action meaningful. Although Josephus alleges the latter half of this statement, its reliability is questionable. See SMITH, Palestinian Judaism in the First Century. For a convenient summary of the variety of views on this question, see HUGO MANTEL, Studies in the History of the Sanhedrin, Cambridge, Mass., 1961.

[70] A similar saying of Simeon's appears in the Babylonian Talmud, Berakhot 19a. It also threatens excommunication, but provides a reason for the threat. "R. Joseph learned: Thaddeus of Rome accustomed the Romans to eat kids roasted whole on the eve of Passover. Simeon b. Shetaḥ sent [a message] to him and said, 'Were you not Thaddeus, I should decree excommunication against you, because you make Israel eat Holy Things outside the precincts of the Temple." See NEUSNER, Pharisees I, pp. 103—104.

[71] Pharisees I, p. 92.

[72] Pharisees I, pp. 86—141.

[73] Pharisaism and rabbinism are not identical. See JACOB NEUSNER, Pharisaic-Rabbinic Judaism: A Clarification, History of Religions, XII, 1973, pp. 250—270.

Destruction era. The attachment of his lemma to the Ḥoni-tradition, therefore, is a vehicle for bringing that tradition within the limits of early rabbinism. Indeed, although P—R is hostile to the Ḥoni-tradition, certain elements of the passage seem to offer an unwilling confirmation. The notion that Ḥoni is subject to *nidduy*, a sectarian penalty, assumes that he is a member of the Pharisaic, and by extension, the rabbinic group. This suggestion is reinforced by the fact that excommunication is merely threatened, but not executed. Finally, the addition of the verse from Proverbs (R) suggests that Ḥoni has in some sense fulfilled a teaching of Scripture[74].

A rapid review of the salient features of the components of the narrative will show how each has affected the final Mishnaic characterization of Ḥoni. The core of the tradition unquestionably is C and E—L, and it comes first in the redactional process. It contains all the details distinctive to Ḥoni, and in their present form the other sections of the narrative are pointless without it. We observed that it is the description of a magical rite for rain. But a key element of that rite, the incantation (I), is presented in legally proper language and thus is formally consistent with early rabbinic piety. B, D and M—O provide the framework for the whole and derive from a different source. D asserts that before performing his magic ritual Ḥoni turned to prayer, thereby establishing at least his pious intent. N identifies the rain-producing rite as prayer, despite the absence from E—L of any liturgical elements. Thus both sections share the common theme of prayer and function to diminish the magical character of E—L[75]. The lemma of Simeon b. Shetaḥ has been appended to this structure. It denigrates Ḥoni's claim of special intimacy with God but implicitly affirms his membership within the rabbinic group. Finally, R legitimizes the entire account by suggesting that Ḥoni fulfills a teaching of Scripture. It is

[74] Vermes, op. cit., p. 71.

[75] Heinemann's argument (See note 52) that F—G of Mishnah are an example of prayer on the pattern of the "law court" produces the following equivocation on the question of magic:

"In a few of the prayers discussed, semi-magical elements are found (*'lmntym m'gyym lmḥṣh*), for example, the oath of Ḥoni which resembles an adjuration, the drawing of the circle, and his declaration, 'I am not moving from here'; . . . . It appears that there is no essential connection between these acts and the prayer in the patterns of the 'Law-court.' To the contrary, there is something of a contradiction between the prayer of the *ḥasid* and the use of magical means which, as it were, can force man's will on God, . . . but the same situation — a desperate state of misfortune from which there is no rescuer — begets both phenomena as one: the use of a strong prayer, and attempts to influence the deity with means which border on magic. This is the case with respect to those prayers [like Ḥoni's] which contain a kind of 'threat' against God." (Heinemann, op. cit., p. 129, note 12).

In Heinemann's view the "request" element (c) of the prayer in the pattern of a "Law-court" is found in Mishnah's G. But G, Ḥoni's "oath," is senseless without the detail of the circle, which, according to Heinemann, is surely magical. So if F—G is a type of prayer, then such prayer is not contrary to magic, as Heinemann suggests, but integral to it. If F—G is a kind of incantation, then it will not serve as an example of Heinemann's type of prayer. Either way his interpretation seems unlikely.

through these devices that the alien figure of Ḥoni has been brought into the ranks of early rabbinism. As we shall see, this is the first step in the 'rabbinization' of Ḥoni the Circle-maker[76].

VI. The Reason for Including Ḥoni in Mishnah: The Temple and the Power to Bring Rain

We have seen that the basic account of Ḥoni's rain-making rite has undergone considerable redaction to make it conform to early rabbinism. We now need to ask why the authorities behind Mishnah made an exception in the case of Ḥoni and included his tradition in that document. We earlier observed that it was not included to make a point of law. To answer this question we shall have to examine one last piece of evidence. A story in the 'Antiquities' of Josephus apparently refers to Ḥoni. The context of Josephus' account is the civil war between Hyrcanus II and Aristobulus II after the death of Alexandra Salome.

> "Now there was a certain Onias, who, being a righteous man and dear to God, had once in a rainless period prayed to God to end the drought, and God had heard his prayer and sent rain; this man hid himself when he saw that the civil war continued to rage, but he was taken to the camp of the Jews and was asked to place a curse on Aristobulus and his fellow rebels [who had retreated to the temple for safety and were beseiged there], just as he had, by his prayers, put an end to the rainless period. But when in spite of his refusals and excuses he was forced to speak by the mob, he stood up in their midst and said, 'O God, King of the Universe, since these men standing beside me are thy people, and those who are beseiged are thy priests, I beseech thee not to hearken to these men against them, not to bring to pass what these men ask thee to do to others.' And when he had prayed in this manner the villains among the Jews who stood round him stoned him to death[77]."

The point of Josephus' account is political: the righteous man refuses to engage in internecine strife. It is not the story of a miracle-worker who per-

[76] For other views of Ḥoni see E. E. Urbach, The Sages (Hebrew), Jerusalem, 1969, pp. 53, 82—102, 104, 397, 510—11; G. Alon, The History of the Jews in Palestine in the Period of the Mishnah and the Talmud (Hebrew), Vol. I, Tel-Aviv, 1967, p. 124; Martin Hengel, Judaism and Hellenism, 2 Vols., Philadelphia, 1974, Vol. I, p. 207; Alexander Guttmann, Rabbinic Judaism in the Making, Detroit, 1970, pp. 47, 57; Encyclopedia Judaica, Vol. 8, s. v. Honi Hameaggel.

[77] Josephus, Antiquities 14, ii, ls. 22—25, Loeb Edition, Cambridge, Mass., 1966, Ralph Marcus, trans., pp. 459—461. Also see Schürer, op. cit., p. 235 and Vermes, op. cit., pp. 70—72.

forms a miracle, but the story of one who does not. So we cannot assume that Josephus here refers to the Mishnaic account of Ḥoni's rain-making. It is important to point out that Josephus' representation of Ḥoni as "righteous" not only serves the ends of his narrative but also conforms to his tendency to depict the miraculous as "part of the normal process by which God governs the world"[78], and thereby make his picture of Judaism palatable to the Roman audience for which he wrote. We observed this same phenomenon earlier with respect to his representation of Moses. The account contributes to our analysis because it establishes that a figure named Onias, a Greek form of Ḥoni, was known for the effectiveness of his curses and for his ability to bring rain. If such stories were well-known among the Jews of Palestine, it would help to account for Ḥoni's appearance in Mishnah.

But popularity alone is not sufficient justification. A more significant reason emerges from the substance of the Mishnaic story itself. Ḥoni's power enables him to bring rain. The physical well-being of the residents of Palestine depended solely on the regular, annual rainfall, and both biblical and rabbinic sources equate rain with life. As RAPHAEL PATAI observes, there is an intimate connection between the fall of rain and the temple cult.

> "As in the whole Near Eastern area the welfare of the people ultimately depended on an adequate natural water supply, the great temple rituals of those countries were obviously performed with the same purpose in view, namely, to secure the annual water supply by bringing about either the fall of rain, as in Jerusalem and Hierapolis, or the rise of rivers, as in Egypt and Mesopotamia[79]."

Since, as we saw, it was believed that divine power was distributed from the temple, it is not surprising that the life-giving power to bring rain also was localized there. Indeed, Mishnah Sukkah 5:1—5 presents a detailed description of the annual ritual of water-libation which was designed to bring the annual rainfall. The ritual, conducted by priests, took place during the Festival of Sukkot, and belief in its efficacy is suggested by the following saying:

> "Said R. 'Aqiva, "The Torah said . . . 'Bring a water-libation on the Festival [of Sukkot] so that the waters of the rains shall be a blessing for you.' . . ."
>
> Tosefta Sukkah, ed. LIEBERMAN,
> p. 271, ls. 71, 74

[78] G. MACRAE, S. J., Miracles in the Antiquities of Josephus, in: C. F. D. MOULE, ed., Miracles: Cambridge Studies in Their Philosophy and History, London, 1965, p. 132.

[79] RAPHAEL PATAI, Man and Temple, New York, 1947, p. 72. For an interpretation of the ritual of water-libation see pp. 24—53.

Since the power to bring rain depended on the temple[80], its destruction endangered the continuation of regular rainfall, as the following suggests:

> "Rabban Simeon b. Gamaliel says in the name of R. Joshua, 'Since the temple was destroyed there has been no day without its curse and dew has not fallen in blessing'. . . ."
>
> Mishnah Soṭah 9:12

We earlier observed that in the aftermath of the temple's destruction the rabbis claimed that prayer, pious deeds, and the study of Torah had replaced the cult and that they had replaced the priests. This means that the power to bring rain, formerly the prerogative of the priests and the cult, now became the function of the rabbi and his Torah. Indeed, later rabbinical figures assumed an integral relationship between the study of Torah and the ability to produce rain[81]. From this perspective, the inclusion in Mishnah of the account of a popular rain-maker and the transformation of him into a rabbi would have been one way of documenting the claim that the new religion of the rabbis had superseded the old religion of the priests. The rabbinic appropriation of Ḥoni the Circle-maker, then, is part of the larger rabbinic enterprise: the application of the holy life of the temple everywhere to all Israel.

VII. The Talmudic Accounts of Ḥoni the Circle-maker: The Completion of the Process of 'Rabbinization'

We have seen that the general absence of stories about miracle-workers from Tannaitic literature corresponds to the typological specialization of religious leadership characteristic of the Greco-Roman world in the early centuries of our era. We also have observed that the literary evidence of the late second and third centuries reflected a breakdown of those functional distinctions and the emergence of a synthetic image of the religious leader. The Babylonian Talmud documents a similar phenomenon for Talmudic Judaism. The following description is accurate, though in different degrees, for Talmudic rabbis from the third to the seventh centuries:

> "The rabbi was the authority on theology, . . . on the structure and order of the supernatural world. He knew the secret names of God and the secrets of the divine 'chariot' — the heavens — and of crea-

[80] The association of the temple with rainfall continued in rabbinic Judaism long after the Destruction. See PATAI, op. cit., pp. 118ff.

[81] JACOB NEUSNER, A History of the Jews in Babylonia, Vol. III, Leiden, 1968, pp. 119—121, Vol. V, Leiden, 1970, pp. 178—180.

tion . . . The rabbi was therefore a holy man, overcame the evil impulse which dominated ordinary men, was consequently less liable to suffering, misfortune, and sickness. He knew the proper times and forms of prayer, and could therefore pray more effectively. Moreover, the efficacy of his prayers was heightened by his purity, holiness, and merits, which in turn derived from his knowledge of the secrets of Torah . . . . . . He could bring rain or cause drought. His blessings brought fertility, and his curses death. He was apt to be visited by angels and to receive communication from them. He could see demons and talk with them and could also communicate with the dead. He was an authority on the interpretation of omens and dreams, . . . and the manufacture and use of amulets. He was, in anthropological terms, a medicine man[82]."

It must be stressed that while the rabbis claimed such powers for themselves, they regarded them as derived from their devotion to and study of Torah, God's revelation, given once and for all to Moses at Mount Sinai. Torah was revealed in two forms: the Written Torah, preserved in the Scriptures, and the Oral Torah, contained in rabbinic tradition. Torah was preserved exclusively in the rabbinical schools and transmitted from master to disciple as it had been from God to Moses. So supernatural powers were, from the rabbinical perspective, the entirely natural result of the possession and mastery of Torah. Miracles performed without Torah were the work of demons and were regarded by the rabbis as magic.

In the following Talmudic accounts of Ḥoni the Circle-maker, the intrusions of distinctly rabbinic elements are relatively easy to discern.

(a)

A. Our rabbis have taught:
B. Once most of the month of Adar had passed and rain had not fallen.
C. They sent [a message] to Ḥoni the Circle-maker, "Pray so that rains will fall".
D. He prayed, but rains did not fall.
E. He made a circle and stood inside it,
F. as the prophet Habbakuk had done, as it is said, "I will stand at my post, and I will take up my position at the watch tower" (Habbakuk 2:1).
G. He said before Him, "Master of the Universe, your children turned their faces to me because I am like a son of the house before you.
H. I swear by your Great Name that I am not moving from here until you have mercy on your children."

[82] Jacob Neusner, A History of the Jews in Babylonia, Vol. IV, Leiden, 1969, p. 253.

I. The rain began to drip.

J. They said to him, "Rabbi (*rby*), we see you and we will not die. [But] it seems to us that the rain falls only to free you from your vow."

K. He said to them, "You see me, you will not die."

L. He said [to God], "I did not ask for this, but for rains [to fill] cisterns, ditches, and caves."

M. It fell with vehemence.

N. Each and every drop was as big as the opening of a barrel, and the sages estimated that no drop was less than a *log*.

O. They said to him, "Rabbi, we see you and we will not die. [But] it seems to us that the rain falls only to destroy the world."

P. He said to them, "You see me, you will not die."

Q. He said [to God], "I did not ask for this, but for rain of benevolence, blessing, and graciousness."

R. The rains fell as he ordered them,

S. until Israel went up from Jerusalem to the Temple Mount because of the rain.

T. They said to him, "Just as you prayed for it to fall, so pray that it should go away."

U. He said to them, "I have received a tradition that they do not pray on account of too much good.

V. Nevertheless, bring me a bull of confession (*pr hwd'h*)."

W. They brought him a bull of confession, he placed his two hands upon it, and said,

X. "Master of the Universe, your people Israel whom you brought out from Egypt cannot stand either too much good or too much retribution.

Y. You were angry at them, and they could not stand it. You showered goodness upon them, and they could not stand it. May it be your will that there be rest in the world."

Z. Immediately the wind blew, the clouds dispersed, and the sun shone, and the people went out into the field and collected morsils and truffles.

AA. Simeon b. Shetaḥ, sent [a message] to him:

BB. "If you were not Ḥoni, I would excommunicate you,

CC. "for if these years were like the years of Elijah, would not the Name of Heaven be profaned by you?

DD. "But what shall I do, for you act petulantly before the Omnipresent like a son who acts petulantly before his father, and he does his will.

EE. "He says to him, 'Bathe me in warm water'. He bathes him. 'Wash me in cold water'. He washes him. 'Give me nuts, peaches, almonds, and pomegranates'. He gives him.

FF. "Concerning you Scripture says, 'Let your father and mother be glad, and let her who bore you rejoice'. (Proverbs 23:25)."

Babylonian Talmud, Ta'anit 23a

This is an obvious expansion of the Mishnaic account and must be regarded as a later version. It draws Ḥoni further into rabbinism and legitimizes his activity in a number of ways. B drops the detail of the Passover ovens and pushes the incident back one month, thereby diminishing its magical character. Ḥoni now prays for rain in the midst of the rainy season. F provides a prophetic precedent for Ḥoni's action, giving it a kind of Scriptural warrant[83]. G applies the title 'Rabbi' to Ḥoni, and some printed versions suggest that he had disciples[84]. The notion that his ability to bring rain will save the people from death confirms our earlier notion about the importance of rain and rainmakers. The detail about the Stone of Strayers is dropped and replaced by U. This is significant. The claim that Ḥoni is the recipient of tradition casts him in a distinctly rabbinical image. V has Ḥoni offer a sacrifice, thereby associating him with the temple, an appropriate anachronism stressing his proper relationship with the divine. Since the rain stops as the result of the acceptance of the sacrifice and the request which accompanies it, the magical element is further diminished, and the focus of the action shifts from Ḥoni to God. It is now clearly God's will, not Ḥoni's, which controls the rain. Finally, X—Y revise the thrust of the story into a homily about the 'golden mean', giving the whole account a moralizing purpose. In short, this later version of the Mishnaic account has reshaped Ḥoni into an unmistakeably rabbinic image and restructured the account of his rain-making to make it serve different purposes.

(b)

The following account legitimizes Ḥoni in another way:

A. R. Naḥman b. R. Ḥisda discoursed, "What message did the members of the Chamber of Hewn Stone [the Sanhedrin] send to Ḥoni the Circle-maker?

B. "You shall decree a thing and it shall be established for you, and a light shall shine upon your ways. When they cast you down, you shall say, 'There is lifting up', for he saves the humble person. He shall deliver him who is innocent, and you shall be delivered through the cleanness of your hands" (Job 22:28—30).

[83] The analogy with Habbakuk is based not on the verse itself, but its Targumic interpretation. BÜCHLER, op. cit., p. 246, note 2, felt that the Targum was based on Mishnah.

[84] R. RABBINOVICZ, Diqduqé Sofrim, New York, 1960 reprint, Vol. 6, p. 133.

C. You shall decree a thing and it shall be established for you — You decreed from below, and the Holy One, Blessed be He, established your decree from above.

D. And light shall shine upon your ways — A generation was in darkness, you have brightened it by your prayer.

E. When they cast you down, you shall say, 'there is lifting up' — A generation was cast down, you have lifted it up by your prayer.

F. For he saves the humble person — A generation which was humbled, you have saved it by your prayer.

G. He shall deliver him who is innocent — A generation was not innocent, you have delivered it by your prayer.

H. You shall be delivered by the cleanness of your hands — by the work of your innocent hands.

Babylonian Talmud Ta'anit 23a

In the Palestinian Talmud Ta'anit 3:11 (Venice 67a) the same exegesis is attributed to a series of third century rabbis, so its attribution here to the members of the Jerusalem Sanhedrin cannot help but be artificial and serve a polemic purpose. The alleged confirmation by the Sanhedrin serves to condone the legality of Ḥoni's action and certainly transforms him into a pious figure. We should note that the exegesis consistently identifies Ḥoni's act as prayer, thereby demonstrating the effectiveness of Mishnaic redaction.

(c)

The following example, which completes the Talmudic corpus of Ḥoni-stories, adds a final detail to the reshaping of his image.

A. Said R. Yoḥanan, "All his life this righteous man [Ḥoni] was troubled by this verse of Scripture, 'When the Lord returned the dwellers of Zion we were as dreamers' (Psalms 126:1)."

B. "He said, 'Is it possible for a man to dream [continuously] for seventy years?'

C. "One day, while he was walking along the road, he saw a man planting a carob tree. He said to him, 'Since it takes seventy years for a carob tree to bear fruit, are you sure that you will live seventy years to eat from it?' He said to him, 'I found carob trees in the world. As my forefathers planted these trees for me, so I plant them for my children.' He [Ḥoni] sat down to eat and fell asleep. As he slept a grotto formed around him so that he was hidden from view, and he continued to sleep for seventy years. When he awoke, he saw a man gathering carobs from a carob tree and eating them. He said to him, 'Do you know who planted this tree?' He said to him, 'My grandfather'. He said, 'I must have slept for seventy years'. He went to his house. He said to them,

'Is the son of Ḥoni the Circle-maker still alive?' They said to him, 'His son is not alive, but his grandson is'. He said to them, 'I am Ḥoni'. But they did not believe him.

D. "He went to the House of Study. He heard the rabbis say, 'Our studies are as clear to us today as they were in the times of Ḥoni the Circle-maker, for when he came to the House of Study he would explain to the rabbis all their difficulties'.

E. "He said to them, 'I am Ḥoni'. But they did not believe him, and they did not treat him with the respect which was owed him.

F. "He prayed for mercy, and he died."

G. Said Rava, "Hence the proverb, 'Either a companion or death'.

Babylonian Talmud Ta'anit 23a

The significant detail in this account, which is otherwise a version of a popular ancient legend[85], occurs in D where Ḥoni is depicted as a master of rabbinic law, the greatest sage of his generation.

VIII. Conclusion: The Rabbinic Manipulation of Charisma

It is clear that leadership in rabbinic Judaism changed and developed in conformity to the general Greco-Roman background. In accord with its Pharisaic heritage, early rabbinic leadership was specialized. The bulk of the evidence from the first two centuries shows that charismatic types who claimed miraculous powers were antithetical to and played little role in early rabbinism. God might work miracles, but early rabbis could not. Their religious authority was based on mastery of other, less dramatic but no less sacred skills. By the middle of the third century the picture had changed, and supernatural powers were a standard element of rabbinic leadership. Although these two different types of religious authority were combined, the fusion was not balanced. Rabbinic Judaism dealt with the charisma of miracle-working by making its validity depend on knowledge of Torah and controlled it by making it a function of the rabbinic system. The process is illustrated by the traditions of Ḥoni the Circle-maker. Neither healer nor exorcist, he was a relatively easy figure for Tannaitic authorities to 'rabbinize', and the powers attributed to him were appropriate and necessary to the new rabbinic religion. The Mishnaic redaction of his tradition represents the beginning of the change in rabbinism from one type of religious leadership to the other. The alteration is completed

[85] SARFATTI, art. cit., pp. 148—153.

in the Talmudic accounts. Ḥoni the Circle-maker, first century B.C. Palestinian magician, has become 'Rabbi' Ḥoni whose miraculous powers are the result of his piety and mastery of Torah[86].

[86] Thanks are due to my teacher, Professor JACOB NEUSNER of Brown University, for suggesting the undertaking of this study and for his willingness to read and comment on the typescript. Professors MORTON SMITH, Columbia University, GARY G. PORTON, University of Illinois, DEAN A. MILLER, MARY YOUNG, and HARMON R. HOLCOMB, University of Rochester also read or discussed portions of the paper in detail. An early draft of this paper was read at the Biblical Studies Seminar of the Colgate-Rochester Divinity School. The members of that Seminar, Professors RICHARD HENSHAW, WERNER LEMKE, CHARLES SMITH, PAUL HAMMER, DARRELL LANCE, and CHARLES NIELSEN offered several constructive suggestions. For deficiencies in judgement, taste, and interpretation, I have myself to thank.

The Jewish Patriarch (Nasi) in Third Century Palestine

by LEE I. LEVINE, Jerusalem

Table of Contents

I. Introduction

Traditionally both Jewish and Christian historiography have viewed the two devastating wars against Rome as marking the political demise of the Jewish people in antiquity. These events supposedly led to the loss of autonomy through the destruction of Jerusalem and its Temple, and the obliteration of most leadership groups within Jewish society. This

Abbreviations:

ANRW	Aufstieg und Niedergang der römischen Welt, ed. H. TEMPORINI and W. HAASE (Berlin—New York, 1972ff.)
AZ	ʿAvoda Zara
B	Babylonian Talmud
BM	Bava Meziʿa
BB	Bava Batra

stereotype, at times motivated by religious prejudice or ideological presuppositions, is only partially true. Without the necessary qualifications, it represents a serious distortion of historical reality.

The fact is that soon after the first revolt against Rome, the beginnings of a new political organization, the Patriarchate[1], began to emerge among the Jews of Palestine. With the tacit approval, if not outright support, of the Roman government, it began to reorganize the social, religious, and communal life of the Jewish community. Suffering a serious setback as a result of the Bar-Kokhba rebellion of 132—135 and the ensuing religious persecutions, the Patriarchate lost whatever political clout it had. Nevertheless, by the turn of the third century this institution had again succeeded in making notable headway, owing in part to the vigorous and unrivalled leadership of R. Judah I, and in part to the sympathetic attitude of the Roman authorities during the Severan period.

The fortunes of the Patriarchate during the third century are more difficult to assess, and will be explored in depth in the present essay. By the mid-fourth century it is clear that the office had achieved first rank importance within the Roman Imperial system generally, and within the Jewish world in particular. Granted the honorific titles of *spectabilis* and *illustris*[2], holding a *praefectura honoraria*[3], described in one synagogue in-

CII	Corpus Inscriptionem Iudaicarum, ed. J. B. FREY, Sussidi allo Studio delle Antichità cristiane, I. III (2 vols.; Città del Vaticano, 1936—1952)
CJ	Codex Justinianus
CT	Codex Theodosianus
DS	Diqduqei Sofrim, ed. R. RABBINOVICZ (12 vols.; Jerusalem, 1960)
GR	Genesis Rabba, ed. THEODOR ALBECK (3 vols.; Jerusalem, 1965)
HUCA	Hebrew Union College Annual
IEJ	Israel Exploration Journal
J	Jerusalem (Palestinian) Talmud
JESHO	Journal for the Economic and Social History of the Orient
JQR	Jewish Quarterly Review
JSJ	Journal for the Study of Judaism
LR	Leviticus Rabba, ed. M. MARGOLIOT (5 vols.; Jerusalem, 1953—60)
M	Mishna
MGWJ	Monatsschrift für Geschichte und Wissenschaft des Judentums
MQ	Mo'ed Qatan
PG	Patrologia Graeca
PL	Patrologia Latina
REJ	Revue des études juives
RH	Rosh Hashana
SHA	Scriptores Historiae Augustae
T	Tosefta, Zera'im — Nashim, ed. S. LIEBERMAN (New York, 1955—1973) Nezikin — Tohorot, ed. S. ZUCKERMANDEL (Pasewalk, 1881)
TK	S. LIEBERMAN, Tosefta Ki-Fshutah (8 vols.; New York, 1955—1973)
ZNW	Zeitschrift für die Neutestamentliche Wissenschaft

[1] The person holding this office is referred to in rabbinic literature as the Nasi, in Latin as the Patriarch and in Greek (by Origen) as the Ethnarch. Since all these terms refer to the same person, the terms Nasi and Patriarch will be used interchangeably.

[2] CT, XVI, 8,8; 8,11; 8,13; 8,15.

[3] Ibid., XVI, 8,22.

scription as λαμπρότατος[4], by Julian as αἰδεσιμώτατος[5] and by CT as *clarissimus*[6], the Patriarch enjoyed far-reaching prerogatives vis-à-vis Jewish communities throughout the Empire. He was responsible for the synagogues, courts, communal organizations and educational systems, as well as the collection of taxes for the maintenance of his bureaucratic apparatus. In some respects, the authority of the Patriarch in the fourth century was far more extensive than anything wielded earlier by the Hasmonean and Herodian rulers. The Patriarchate came to an abrupt end in the early fifth century with the death of Gamaliel VI (425) and the abolition of the office by the Roman authorities (429).

Strange as it may seem, despite the importance of this office, very little has been written about it. There exists no work of serious proportions devoted to the subject in its entirety. At best the Patriarchate has been treated as part of a larger work on Jewish history, or only with respect to a particular period or source[7]. While a rich collection of material treating the title Nasi and his activities has been presented by MANTEL[8], it is only in the works of G. ALON that this subject has been pursued most intensively from a historical perspective. Unfortunately ALON's history only reaches the Severan period; thus the last two centuries of this office are not dealt with by him[9].

Before addressing the topic itself, a number of comments are in order regarding the sources at our disposal. In the first place, the sources stemming from different periods pose a serious problem of continuity. For the last century of the Patriarchate there is Roman and Christian material attesting to the office and its functions. Most important in this regard is the Codex Theodosianus, whose section on the Jews is dominated by legislation relating to the Patriarch and his appointees[10]. A number of Church Fathers (including Epiphanius, Jerome, and John Chrysostom) mention the Patriarchal office, often in a derogatory fashion[11]. Correspondence between

[4] B. LIFSHITZ, L'ancienne synagogue de Tibériade, sa mosaïque et ses inscriptions, JSJ, IV (1973), pp. 51—52.

[5] Julian, Epistle XXV.

[6] CT, XVI, 8,8.

[7] Under Diocletian, on the basis of a rescript; cf. B. DINBURG, The Diocletian Rescript to Judah from 293 and the Struggle Between the Patriarchate and Sanhedrin in Palestine, Festschrift to A. Gulak and S. Klein (Jerusalem, 1942; Hebrew), pp. 76—93; under Constantine on the basis of CT; cf. A. LINDER, The Roman Imperial Government and the Jews under Constantine (Hebrew), Tarbiz, XLIV (1974—75), pp. 118—126; the later fourth century on the basis of Libanius' correspondence; M. SCHWABE, Libanius' Correspondence to the Nasi in Palestine (Hebrew), Tarbiz, I, 2 (1930), pp. 1—26; IDEM, A New Document on Fourth Century Jewish History, ibid., I, 3 (1930), pp. 1—15.

[8] H. MANTEL, Studies in the History of the Sanhedrin (Cambridge, 1965), Chaps. I, V.

[9] G. ALON, A History of the Jews in Palestine during the Mishnaic-Talmudic Period (2 vols.; Tel-Aviv, 1961; Hebrew); IDEM, Jews, Judaism and the Classical World (Jerusalem, 1977), pp. 374—435. Several aspects of this later period are treated in this last-named book.

[10] CT, XVI, 8.

[11] Cf. J. JUSTER, Les juifs dans l'empire romain (2 vols.; Paris, 1914), I, p. 394, n. 4; ALON, Jews, Judaism (above, n. 9), p. 380, n. 19.

Libanius and the Patriarch has been preserved, and provides precious information regarding the relations between this Jewish official on the one hand, and the Roman authorities, intellectuals of Libanius' caliber, and the Antioch Jewish community on the other[12]. Finally Julian's letter to the Patriarch, if authentic, provides a further glimpse of the status and prestige accruing to this office[13]. However, for this same fourth century, rabbinic literature has almost nothing to say about the Nasi. This absence of material may be significant, although it may, at least in part, reflect the fact that remarkably little material dating from this century has been preserved in rabbinic literature generally, the overwhelming bulk being associated with second and third century sages.

In contrast to this deployment of sources from the fourth century, the situation as regards the third century presents quite the opposite picture. Rabbinic sources from this earlier period are rich in material relating to the Patriarch and the Patriarchal office, while non-Jewish sources are almost non-existent. Apart from several statements in Origen[14], and a cryptic reference in a Diocletian rescript (whose authenticity is disputed[15]), nothing is known about the office from either pagan or Christian writings.

Thus the likelihood of gaining a comprehensive picture of the history of the office is incredibly complicated by this gap in the sources. The break, moreover, is not only chronological, between the second and third century material on the one hand and the fourth on the other, but is also manifest in the very different types of sources represented by each group. Each emphasizes different aspects of the Patriarchate and brings its own assumptions and attitudes to bear on the selection and presentation of material. To trace the continuity between these sources is a challenge of the first order. Do the relations, attitudes and tensions recorded in the third century rabbinic material continue into the fourth, or were there changes and further developments? Conversely, did the prerogatives and authority of the fourth century Patriarchs stem from the period of Diocletian and Constantine, or were they a continuation of the privileges already enjoyed in the third, and even second, century? Or, perhaps neither alternative is correct, and the truth lies somewhere in between: the fourth century Patriarchal prerogatives are indeed new, although based on already extensive privileges rooted in the third century[16].

[12] Cf. above, n. 7.

[13] Cf. above, n. 5. On the authenticity of this letter, cf. S. BARON, The Jewish Community (3 vols.; Philadelphia, 1942), III, p. 29, n. 26.

[14] Ep. ad Afric., XIV; Sel. in Ps. (PG, XII, 1056B); De Princip. IV, 1, 3 (PG, XI, 348).

[15] CJ, III, 13,3. On authenticity, cf. DINBURG (above n. 7); ALON, Jews, Judaism (above, n. 9), pp. 433—435.

[16] Similar considerations apply to the problem of the Babylonian Exilarchate who is mentioned in the sources for the first time around the turn of the third century. The question arises whether the Sassanians were merely continuing an earlier Parthian institution, created something basically new, or continued an already existing institution, while developing it in a wholly unprecedented manner; cf. J. NEUSNER, A History of the Jews in Babylonia, Studia post-biblica, IX. XI. XII. XIV. XV (5 vols.; Leiden, 1965—70),

As regards third century rabbinic sources, with which we will be dealing in extenso, we must note at the outset that the problems involved are formidable. They may be summarized under four headings:

1. Textual — Only a small percentage of rabbinic material is available in a reliable critical edition, with textual variants conveniently and accurately listed. Given the variety of manuscripts available and the long and often complicated manuscript tradition of the Middle Ages, the veracity of any one particular text is open to question.

2. Historical accuracy — It is well known that the rabbis were not historians, and only utilized historical or anecdotal accounts when the latter served their religious interests. Most of the preserved material deals with other rabbis (or Pharisees), events touching upon religious institutions (Temple, academy or synagogue), religious practices (purity, tithes, marriage) or beliefs (charity, study, etc.). Traditions are preserved owing to their religious and moral implications, and the 'facts' involved are often forgotten, blurred over, exaggerated beyond recognition or simply filled in as needed. Names and titles may be used indiscriminately, and applied to persons living decades, if not a century or more, apart[17].

3. Selectivity — Rabbinic literature is far from being a complete corpus of traditions, even regarding issues important to the rabbis. Much has been lost, and what has been preserved has been so for reasons extraneous to the material itself. Valuable historical material might be embedded in a particular interpretation given a Biblical verse. Its preservation usually has nothing to do with that information per se, but only because the accompanying interpretation was valued. Or, for example, we know a great deal more about the rabbis of Tiberias and the life of that particular city because it was there that most Palestinian rabbinic compilations were edited. Of rabbis in other locales, particularly outside the main Galilean centers of Tiberias and Sepphoris, relatively little is known[18].

4. Tendance — The central figures in rabbinic literature are, of course, the sages themselves. They are the main actors and the editors of these collections. Besides constituting a religious elite, the sages were also a well-defined social group, naturally, with its own political interests. Thus rab-

I (1965), pp. 56—58; II (1966), pp. 92—108; M. BEER, The Babylonian Exilarchate in the Arsacid and Sassanian Periods (Tel-Aviv, 1976; Hebrew), pp. 11—32.

17 For example, the title 'Rabbi' (with no personal name) is most often associated with R. Judah I (ca. 175—225), but is also used in connection with R. Simeon b. Gamaliel I (ca. 45—70) — Sifre Deuteronomy XXXVIII, pp. 74—75; R. Simeon b. Gamaliel II (ca. 145—175) — J Nedarim VI, 13,40a; J Sanhedrin I, 2,19a; R. Judah II (ca. 235—260) — B AZ 35b—37a; GR LXXX, 1, p. 950; R. Judah III (ca. 275—305) — ibid., LXIII, 5, p. 689. Similarly, the term רבותינו — 'our rabbi' — might refer to R. Gamaliel III (as is usually the case), R. Judah II (B AZ 37a), or Rabbi Judah I (T Shevi'it IV, 16, p. 183; TK, pp. 541—542).

18 No more striking example of the Galilean-Tiberian orientation of rabbinic literature is available than Sifre Zuta. Composed in Lydda, numerous rabbis are mentioned therein who are not known from other rabbinic works; cf. S. LIEBERMAN, Sifre Zuta (New York, 1968; Hebrew), p. 81.

binic literature is not merely a compendium of Jewish religious traditions. Whatever has been preserved reflects (with few exceptions) the attitudes, interests and prejudices of the rabbis generally, and the particular compilers of this literature in particular. This prism often distorts the picture. Does rabbinic approval necessarily imply general Jewish approval? Or conversely, does their criticism and disdain reflect widespread attitudes, or only their own? With regard to the Patriarchate, these questions will be particularly relevant.

Despite these obstacles, and they are indeed formidable, there is little question that the attempt to utilize rabbinic sources for historical purposes is well-worth the effort. With all their pitfalls as historical documents, rabbinic traditions are a veritable mine of information regarding Jewish and provincial history generally, and the Patriarchate in particular. Whatever the attitudes to a given Patriarch may have been, the various sources have preserved enough data to enable us to reconstruct something of the history of this office throughout the third century. Particularly rich in sources relating to that century, rabbinic material gains in importance precisely owing to the dearth of general information from the period. The oft-heard lament of historians about the lack of data when approaching the critical third century is well taken; it is here that rabbinic literature fills an important desideratum.

Turning to the third century, we find the office of the Patriarch dominated by three men, each named Judah: R. Judah I (ca. 175—225), R. Judah II (ca. 235—260), and R. Judah III (ca. 275—305). If our proposed reconstruction is correct[19], then these men controlled the office for about 75 years of the century. Between their tenures of office, two other figures served, each bearing the name Gamaliel. The careers of the latter, judging from the meager literary remains, were briefer, and undoubtedly less significant.

II. On the Threshold of the Third Century

The prestige enjoyed by the third century Patriarchs was indeed unprecedented. Neither R. Gamaliel II of Yavne nor his son R. Simeon had achieved such a level of official recognition. R. Gamaliel's standing vis-à-vis his colleagues was mixed. On the one hand he was respected and followed, on the other there was great resentment over what was perceived as high-handed measures in imposing his authority over the community of sages. The confrontations with R. Joshua, the excommunication of R. Eliezer and Gamaliel's temporary deposition in favor of R. Elazar b. ʿAzariah, all served to mitigate any favorable sentiment towards him. Little is known of his relations with the wealthy sector of the community. R. Gamaliel's

[19] Cf. Appendix.

standing in the eyes of Rome is unclear. Some sort of recognition was presumably extended; its nature and extent, however, are unknown. One gains the impression that his ministry marks the beginning of an office which was to fully flourish only a century later, but which at this time was still largely inchoate, undefined and untested[20].

The contrast between the Patriarchate of the third century and the tenure of R. Simeon b. Gamaliel (fl. 145—175) is even more striking. Absolutely nothing is known about the political dimensions of R. Simeon's ministry. Contacts with various Jewish communities and leaders are never mentioned, and even accounts of his relationships with other sages are rare. He was missing from some important rabbinic conclaves following the Bar Kokhba revolt and the Hadrianic persecutions[21]. The only extended report of his ministry describes an abortive attempt to depose him as head of the academy[22]. In light of the plethora of traditions about his father and his son, it is unlikely that this paucity of material is coincidental. Rather, it would seem to reflect a nadir in Jewish political fortunes in the mid-second century as a result of the upheavals caused by the second revolt against Rome[23]. All the more amazing, therefore, is the meteoric rise to prominence of the Nasi, R. Judah I, in the following generation. How and why did this take place?

The Severan era was clearly a period of rapprochement between the Jewish community of Palestine and the Roman imperial government. While some in Palestine opted in 193 for Pescennius Niger in his struggle against Severus (and subsequently paid dearly for having backed the losing side[24]), others, including the Jews, supported Severus, and were subsequently rewarded. On his way to Alexandria in 201, Severus bestowed a series of grants on a number of Palestinian communities, and sought to heal old wounds by revoking previously issued punishments[25]. The enigmatic reference by Jerome to a Jewish-Samaritan war (*Judaicum et Samariticum bellum*

[20] The best treatments of the period of R. Gamaliel include: H. Graetz, Geschichte der Juden von den ältesten Zeiten bis auf die Gegenwart (11 vols.; Leipzig, 1897—1911), IV, (1908), pp. 27—40; Alon, above, n. 9, I, pp. 114—192; A. Guttmann, Rabbinic Judaism in the Making (Detroit, 1970), pp. 200—221.

[21] At Usha, for example (Song of Songs Rabba II, 5,3) and at Bik'at Rimon (J Hagiga III, 1,78d).

[22] B Horayot 13b.

[23] Herein we take exception to the oft-held opinion that Jewish political fortunes remained steady, and even were enhanced, under R. Simeon b. Gamaliel II. Cf., for example, H. Zucker, Studien zur jüdischen Selbstverwaltung im Altertum (Berlin, 1936), pp. 153—154; Baron, above, n. 13, p. 141; Mantel, above, n. 8, pp. 36—39.
Often this claim is bolstered by reference to the Stobi synagogue inscription which refers to enormous fines that must be paid to the Patriarchs for breach of agreement. The inscription had been dated to 163 C.E. However, Hengel has clearly demonstrated that the details point to a third century setting (Die Synagogeninschrift von Stobi, ZNW, LVII [1966], pp. 145—183).

[24] Neapolis is specifically singled out for its disobedience, and was severely punished (SHA — Severus, IX, 5).

[25] Ibid., XIV, 6—7; XVII, 1.

motum) may reflect one of the divisions within the country at this time[26]. Severus, for his part, allowed Jews to become members of the decurionate[27], and Alexander Severus, it is claimed, renewed all privileges of the Jews[28]. The latter emperor, said to have kept a statue of Abraham in his private chapel[29], was referred to as an 'archisynagogus' by the pagans of Alexandria and Antioch[30], and alluded to Jewish and Christian practices and sayings in seeking precedents for his own actions[31].

Jewish institutions appear to have benefitted enormously from this newfound sympathy. Few Jewish inscriptions from late antiquity carry dedications to contemporary rulers, but of those that do, several date from this period. Inscriptions from the Galilee[32] as well as Pannonia[33], and perhaps Ostia[34], praise Severan rule and pray for the well-being of the Imperial family. If indeed the earliest Galilean synagogues date from this period, a claim which admittedly has come under serious attack of late, then the newly-won status of the Jews would have demonstrable archeological confirmation[35]. Jewish courts also appear to have gained in stature during this period as support from Roman authorities was now forthcoming. In several instances Roman courts actually enforced decisions of a Jewish tribunal[36]. Finally, the right of the Jews to adjudicate cases involving capital punishment, as stated by Origen (cf. below), undoubtedly originated in this period.

The major beneficiary of this change in attitude on the part of Rome was the office of the Patriarch. Even without Origen's claim that the Nasi enjoyed royal-like powers, this newly found status is well-attested through-

[26] Eusebius, Chronicorum libri duo, ed. A. SCHOENE (Berlin, 1866), p. 177. For a discussion of this and other references to events of these years; cf. L. LEVINE, Caesarea under Roman Rule, Studies in Judaism in Late Antiquity, VII (Leiden, 1975), pp. 64—66.

[27] Digest L, 2,3,3. Several centuries later, Jerome claimed that "Severus and his son Antoninus greatly favored the Jews" — In Daniel, XI, 34—35 (PL, XXV, 570a).

[28] SHA — Alexander Severus, XXII, 4.

[29] Ibid., XXIX, 2.

[30] Ibid., XXVIII, 7.

[31] Ibid., XLV, 6—7; LI, 6—8. Cf. also S. LIEBERMAN, Palestine in the Third and Fourth Centuries, JQR, XXXVI (1946), p. 364; A. MOMIGLIANO, Severo Alessandro Archisynagogus, Athenaeum, XII (1934), pp. 151—153. On Elagabalus' purported sympathies towards Judaism; cf. SHA — Elagabalus, III, 5.

[32] CII, II, 157—158, ‡ 972.

[33] Ibid., I, 489, ‡ 677.

[34] M. FLORIANI SQUARCIAPINO, The Synagogue at Ostia, Archeology, XVI (1963), p. 203. On the 'Severus' synagogue in Rome as reported by the medieval midrash, Genesis Rabbati, ed. ALBECK, p. 209.

[35] H. KOHL, C. WATZINGER, Antike Synagogen in Galilaea, Wissenschaftliche Veröffentlichungen der Deutschen Orient-Gesellschaft, XXIX (Leipzig, 1916), pp. 204—218. Serious reservations have been raised against this dating on the basis of recent excavations at Kfar Nahum; cf. V. CORBO, Cafarnao I (Jerusalem, 1975), pp. 163—169. Cf. also G. FOERSTER, Notes on Recent Excavations at Capernaum (Review Article), IEJ, XXI (1971), pp. 207—209; M. AVI-YONAH, ibid., XXIII (1973), pp. 43—45.

[36] T Yevamot XII, 13, p. 44; J Gittin IX, 10, 50d. Cf. ALON, above, n. 9, II, pp. 112—113; S. APPLEBAUM, The Province of Syria-Palaestina as a Province of the Severan Empire (Hebrew), Zion, XXIII (1958), p. 36.

out rabbinic literature. Perhaps the most dramatic expression is contained in the series of traditions associating Rabbi Judah I with the emperor Antoninus[37]. The relationship between these two men became legendary in Jewish literature. Grants of land[38], increased civic rights for Tiberias[39], and donations to synagogues were allegedly bestowed by the emperor[40], and letters were exchanged between them[41]. It appears quite likely that these two men met on at least one occasion[42]. The enthusiasm of later generations even went so far as to claim that Antoninus converted to Judaism[43]. Whatever the historical worth of these legends — and while most cannot be taken literally, they assuredly must not be summarily dismissed as mere literary devices[44] — it is certain that R. Judah succeeded in striking up a uniquely successful relationship with this important personage. The results of the contact proved beneficial, for both the Patriarchate and the Jewish community at large. The ties between these men were not only an expression of the new attitudes of the era, but undoubtedly contributed mightily to fostering and enhancing them.

Several legal decisions of R. Judah — not all of which became normative — are a further indication of the newly-forged alliance and changing attitudes. R. Judah tried to minimize, if not totally abolish, the severity of days set aside for the commemoration of the destruction of the Temple — the 17th of Tammuz and 9th of Av[45]. If the permission granted a bride to

[37] Cf. the sources collected by S. Krauss, Antoninus und Rabbi (Wien, 1910). The identification of this emperor has been debated for generations, and arguments have been offered for almost every ruler from Antoninus Pius to Severus Alexander, depending in part on the chronology assigned to R. Judah I (cf. A. Guttmann, The Patriarch Judah I, His Birth and His Death: A Glimpse into the Chronology of the Talmudic Period, HUCA, XXV [1954], pp. 239—261). Since we would date Rabbi Judah's death to ca. 225 (cf. below, Appendix), it is certain that the Antoninus named was one of the Severan dynasty. The name was popular at the time (SHA — Caracalla, IX, 1—2; Geta, II, 2), and was adopted by many emperors (ibid., Severus X, 5; Caracalla I, 1; Geta I; Elagabalus IX, 2; Macrinus, III, 4—9). The most plausible candidate is Caracalla; cf. Alon, above, n. 9, II, p. 94; M. Avi-Yonah, The Jews of Palestine (New York, 1976), pp. 39—42.

[38] S. Klein, The Estates of R. Judah Ha-Nasi and the Jewish Community of the Trans-Jordanic Region, JQR, II (1911—12), pp. 545—556; Applebaum, above, n. 36, p. 41.

[39] B AZ 10a.

[40] J Megilla III, 2,72a.

[41] GR LXXV, 5, p. 883; Deuteronomy Rabba, II, ed. Lieberman, p. 64; Midrash Tanhuma — Vayeshev, III, 44a.

[42] Ibid.; GR, LXXVII, 15, p. 935; Mantel, above, n. 8, p. 241.

[43] J Megilla I, 13,72b; III, 2,74a; B AZ 10b; Cf. S. Lieberman, On the Leiden Manuscript of the Yerushalmi (Hebrew), J. Epstein Festschrift (Jerusalem, 1950) (= Tarbiz, XX), pp. 110—111; Idem, Greek in Jewish Palestine (New York, 1942), pp. 78—81.

[44] Cf. L. Wallach, The Colloquy of Marcus Aurelius with the Patriarch Judah I, JQR, XXXI (1941), pp. 259—286.

[45] J Megilla I, 1,70b—c; B Megilla 5a—b. Cf. also J Yevamot VI, 6, 7d; J Ta'anit IV, 69c. Several sages, recorded in these sources, suggest that the proposed change was only a question of whether the 9th of Av which falls on a Sabbath should be commemorated on the following day, or whether it should simply be abolished for that particular year. However, the wording of the report (וביקש לעקור תשעה באב — "he attempted to uproot the 9th of Av'") suggests a far more extreme measure; cf. Alon, above, n. 9, II, 117.

use a litter, prohibited following the Bar Kokhba revolt, indeed refers to Rabbi Judah I, then we have still another case of his eliminating the vestiges of mourning, originally intended as reminders of the tragedies suffered by the Jews at the hands of Rome[46]. Finally, in a series of decisions R. Judah succeeded in granting many of the large Greco-Roman cities of Palestine preferred status in the eyes of Jewish law[47]. They were declared part of Palestine as regards purity (and thus a Jewish priest would not be defiled by entering, as in the case of 'gentile' land), yet the produce of these cities was declared exempt from the obligations associated with Jewish Palestine (tithes, offerings to priests, Sabbatical year requirements, etc.). These cities, which included Caesarea, Ascalon, Bet Guvrin and Bet Shean, thus enjoyed the benefits of Jewish law accruing to both Palestinian and non-Palestinian cities with the liabilities of neither. Undoubtedly Rabbi Judah hoped that these cities would now attract more Jews, and thus enhance the economic, political and social position of the people. Such a move, reflecting the drive towards normalization of relations now characterizing Patriarchal circles, would have been utterly unthinkable a generation earlier.

Thus the eminence of the third century Patriarchate already came into full bloom at the very turn of the century. A series of factors combined to allow, even encourage, such an office to fully crystallize: Severan sympathy and political indebtedness towards Palestinian Jewry, and the dominant personality of R. Judah I, who appears to have controlled Jewish life — politically, economically, socially, intellectually and religiously — for well nigh a half century. This particular confluence of factors was reinforced by the broader policy goals pursued by the Severan dynasty: encouraging local customs, particularly of oriental origin, and a far-reaching attempt to unite the Greek and Latin parts of the Empire, an attempt which climaxed in the incorporation and enfranchisement of the various provinces and populations.

Patriarchal prominence was thus inextricably bound with the power and backing of Imperial Rome. This had been the case already at the time of Gamaliel II of Yavne, but now both sides seemed more willing than ever to nurture this relationship far beyond that of earlier generations. Whatever contemporaries might think of their religious and communal behavior — and there were critics in every generation (cf. below) — the Patriarchs were the undisputed representatives of the people to the authorities. Each important third-century Patriarch is mentioned in connection with Roman officials. We have already taken note of R. Judah I in this regard. With respect to R. Judah II, these ties are reflected in a story of a gift given him by a Roman official on the occasion of a pagan festival[48], and R. Judah III is

[46] M Sota IX, 14. That the term רבותינו might apply to any number of Patriarchs, including Judah I; cf. above, n. 17.

[47] A. Büchler, Studies in Jewish History (London, 1956), pp. 179—244; Levine, above, n. 26, pp. 67—68.

[48] J AZ I, 1, 39b; B AZ 6b. Cf. Lieberman, above, n. 43, p. 141; G. Blidstein, A Roman Gift of Strenae to the Patriarch Judah II, IEJ, XXII (1972), pp. 150—152.

said to have met Diocletian when the latter was visiting Caesarea Paneas[49]. The Patriarchal role as representative of the Jews to Rome is the subject of a homily in which Israel is compared to a vine. Just as the fruit of the vine is introduced at each course of a meal, so Israel has survived every ruling power, always with the help of outstanding representatives: Hanania and his friends under Babylonia, Mordecai under Persia, Simon the Just under Greek rule, and the house of Hillel (i.e. the Patriarchs) in the time of Rome[50].

For their part, the Patriarchs now capped this rise to power with a claim not often used by Jews since the early Second Temple period. They traced their lineage back to King David. For only now, in the third century, the claim appears that Hillel was of Davidic descent[51]. Whether there were any messianic overtones to this assertion is debatable, but connotations of royalty were certainly present, and have found expression in numerous rabbinic sources[52].

III. The Third Century Patriarchate — General Considerations

Thus by the third century, the Patriarchate had clearly become the most prestigious office within Jewish society. When R. Judah I is referred to as 'our holy teacher'[53] and his grandson R. Judah II as 'a great man'[54], it is clear that the Nasi was highly regarded, even among the sages. This fact must be properly appreciated, for many rabbis of the late third and fourth centuries had little sympathy or concern with this office. If then rabbinic sources do preserve unequivocal statements of respect and veneration, such evidence must be considered of the first order.

Patriarchal priority was institutionalized in a series of laws. Mourning practices associated with the death of a Nasi are indicative of his status:

> "Our sages taught: The following rends (of a garment) may never be mended: He who rends for his father, for his mother, for his teacher who taught him Torah, for the Nasi, for the Av Bet Din . . .[55]"

Several traditions go even further in designating the precedence of the Nasi over all other sages, including the Av Bet Din[56]. On hearing of the death

[49] GR LXIII, 25, pp. 688—690; J Terumot VIII, 46b—c.

[50] L. Ginzberg, Geniza Studies I (New York, 1928), pp. 92—93.

[51] GR XCVII, 9, p. 1219 (also pp. 1258—1259); J Ta'anit IV, 2, 68a. Cf. I. Lévi, De l'origine davidique de Hillel, REJ, XXXI (1895), pp. 202—211.

[52] Cf. Juster, above, n. 11, I, pp. 395—396.

[53] B Shabbat 118b.

[54] J AZ I, 1, 39b.

[55] B MQ 26a. Cf. the parallel tradition in Semaḥot IX, 19, ed. Zlotnick, p. 28, as well as B MQ 22b.

[56] Ibid., where the Nasi is singled out above all others, and likened to a parent with regard to mourning practices. Cf. also Deuteronomy Rabba II, 19.

of a Hakham one is to bare his right shoulder, for an Av Bet Din his left, for the Nasi, both[57]. Moreover, there were clearly prescribed procedures of mourning in various institutions depending upon who passed away:

> "Our sages taught: When a Hakham dies, his academy is closed. When an Av Bet Din dies, all academies in his city are closed, and people gather in synagogues altering their (usual) place of sitting . . . A Nasi who dies, all academies are closed, and the people of the synagogue gather in the synagogue, read seven portions (from the Torah) and leave. R. Joshua b. Korha said: They ought not (then) go and stroll about the marketplace, but should sit (at home) in silence[58]."

Indeed the tradition told about the funeral of Rabbi Judah I and the ensuing general mourning is probably indicative of the response of the masses[59].

From the mid-third century similar evidence of prominence emerges, quoted, in fact, in the name of the leading sages of the period. Commenting on the verse: "And he (Jacob) blessed Joseph saying: 'May the God before whom my fathers walked . . .'" (Gen. 48:15): R. Yohanan said: This may be compared to a shepherd who stood and watched his sheep: Resh Lakish (referred this) to the Nasi who went along, with elders preceding him[60]. On several occasions, leading sages urged the Nasi to dress in clothes befitting his high rank[61].

There is no more poignant indication of the esteem in which the Nasi was held throughout this period than the various traditions telling of his court life, especially of the machinations and intrigues on the part of different groups to gain more ready access. Interestingly, each of the three preserved accounts refers to the three leading Patriarchal figures of this third century:

1) R. Judah I

Samuel and those of the house of Shila used to greet the Nasi daily. Those of the house of Shila were wont to go out[62] and enter first, and were seated first. They (once) honored Samuel and allowed him to be seated first. Rav entered there and (similarly) honored Samuel, and allowed him to be seated first[63]. Thereupon those of the house of Shila said: Are we to be considered (of) secondary (importance)? And Samuel agreed to be seated third[64].

[57] B MQ 22b.

[58] Ibid., 22b—23a. Cf. the variant tradition in Semaḥot X, 13, ed. Zlotnick, p. 31, where it is added: "They should sit in grief and in silence like men who have no leader (פרנס)."

[59] J Kilaim IX, 4,32b; J Ketubot XII, 3,35a; B Ketubot 103b.

[60] GR XXX, 10, p. 277.

[61] J Sanhedrin II, 6, 20c.

[62] Cf. Leiden ms.

[63] The dating of each of these accounts is based on the names of the sages mentioned therein. Rav and Samuel were active in Palestine during the lifetime of R. Judah I. Cf. ISG, p. 78.

[64] J Ta'anit IV, 2,68a. Cf. also the tradition in B Ketubot 103b on the fuller who was accustomed to visit R. Judah daily. There was also a custom to visit this Nasi at the begin-

2) R. Judah II

Two leading groups were in Sepphoris, the Bouleteri and Pagani[65]. They went to greet the Nasi daily, and the Bouleteri used to enter and leave first. The Pagani went and learned Torah. They (then) came and demanded to enter first. The question was brought before R. Simeon b. Lakish. R. Simeon b. Lakish asked R. Yohanan . . . who entered the academy of R. Benaia and preached: "In the case of a bastard sage and an ignorant high priest, even the bastard sage has preference over the ignorant high priest[66]."

3) R. Judah III

Those (members of the families) of R. Hoshaya and bar Pazi were wont to greet the Nasi daily[67]. And those of R. Hoshaya used to enter and leave first. Those of bar Pazi went and married into the Patriarchal family, (and) then came demanding to enter first. The question came before R. Ami. R. Ami said to them: "And I will erect the Tabernacle according to its judgement (or rule)" (Exodus 26 : 30). Is there a 'judgement' for wood? Rather whichever board is designated for the north (part of the building) will be placed in the north, for the south will be placed in the south[68].

The above traditions contain a wealth of historical information. For our immediate purpose, however, they attest to the continuing esteem accorded the Nasi throughout the century. Wealthy families vied for attention and favor[69], and bonds of marriage were formed to secure and

ning of the month. When R. Simeon b. Halafta once failed to make his customary appearance, he reputedly incurred the wrath of R. Judah (LR XVIII, 1, p. 395 and parallels). On the custom of visiting one's teacher on a festival, B Sukka 27b.

65 Probably not specific families as below, but rather two well-crystallized interest groups: a city elite and rural landowners.

66 J Shabbat XII, 3 13c; J Horayot III, 48c. Cf. S. Lieberman, Ha-Yerushalmi Ki-Fshuto (Jerusalem, 1935), pp. 175—176.

67 On the prominence of these families: Hoshaya — J Shabbat VI, 2,8a; J Ta'anit I, 2,64a; J Megilla III, 8,74b; b. Pazi — J Shabbat XVII, 1,16a.

68 Cf. above, n. 66. Cf. also Esther Rabba IV, 4, where much the same account is recorded, albeit with some significant variations:
"Two families were wont to visit Rabbi, one of R. Hoshaya and one of the house of R. Judah b. Pazi. When (the house of) R. Judah b. Pazi married (into the house of) Rabbi (Judah III), they demanded to enter first, but R. Ami would not allow it. He said to them: It is written . . . They requested to be ordained. On what basis (did they make such a request)? R. Simon from the South said to them: It is written: 'And God said — Judah will go up' (Judges 1: 2). R. Mani said: This refers to war, however, as regards ordination, 'Those who see the king's face' (Esther 1: 14) — those sitting in the front. Here, too (the appointment goes to) 'those who see the king's face'."

69 The Nasi for his part might grant favors in the form of appointments (J Ta'anit IV, 2, 68a; B Ketubot 103b), presents (J Berakhot VI, 5,10c) or honorary recognition (J MQ III, 1,81c).

strengthen these ties[70]. It is interesting that not only the rich were concerned about such relations. A number of sages, and families closely associated with rabbinic circles, also competed for the good-will of the Patriarch, and mastery of the Torah is mentioned as a means of ingratiating oneself with the Nasi. As might be suspected, more was at stake than first meets the eye; significant rewards were to be gained by winning the favor of the Patriarch. According to at least one source, albeit late but nevertheless accurately reflecting third century conditions, precedence in these situations had a direct bearing on the judicial and communal appointments made by the Nasi, and these in turn carried with them substantial financial benefits[71]. This is never a mean factor, and certainly not in times of heavy taxation and onerous civic levies[72].

The role of the leading sages of the times, as reflected in these accounts, is likewise most revealing. They apparently were only peripherally involved with these intrigues. They might be consulted (and presumably were), but their response was either a sermon delivered in a local academy (R. Yohanan), or some 'sage' advice (R. Ami). Even among the rabbis, the questions posed might seem baffling (Resh Lakish), or suggest very different courses of action (compare the advice of R. Yohanan and Resh Lakish[73]). Whether the advice of the rabbis was heeded by any of the parties concerned is not noted.

It would seem, therefore, that the position of the Patriarch during much of this period was accurately summarized by Origen (who would have been well informed of the situation, living as he did in Caesarea for some twenty years) in his letter to Africanus:

> "Now, for instance, that the Romans rule, and the Jews pay the half-shekel to them, how great is the power wielded by the ethnarch[74], granted by Caesar. We who have experienced it know that he differs in no way from a king of a nation. Secret trials are held according to the law, and some people are condemned to death[75]. And though there is not full licence for this, still it is not done without the knowledge of

[70] The case of a member of the b. Pazi family refusing a marriage with one of the Nasi's house would seem to be unusual, and probably reflects very different historical circumstances (J AZ III, 1,42c; J Sota IX, 17,24c).

[71] Cf. above, n. 68.

[72] With regard to the account relating to R. Judah II, the Talmud has added a brief discussion on the benefits accruing to those who are 'first'. According to one opinion these include priority with regard to redemption from captivity, and receiving clothes and food in time of need. A second opinion includes priority for ordination as well.

[73] Or that of R. Simeon and R. Mani in Esther Rabba IV, 4 (cf. above, n. 68).

[74] On several occasions Origen uses this term for the Nasi, although he also makes reference to the 'Patriarch'; cf. Juster, above, n. 11, I, p. 394, n. 4.

[75] In another place, however, Origen seems to indicate that Jews did not have the right to execute: "They may not punish a murderer or stone an adultress", Ad. Rom. VI, 7 (PG, XIV, 1073). Whether this applied to his own day as well is not altogether clear.

the ruler, as we learned and were convinced of when we spent much time in the country of that people[76]."

IV. Powers and Prerogatives of the Patriarch

What were the powers and prerogatives associated with the office of the Patriarchate in the third century? Here we will treat only those sources which relate to this particular century, using earlier or later material only for purposes of verification or contrast. Such a control is essential. On the one hand there has been a tendency on the part of some to assume that the Patriarchate was essentially a stable and static office throughout most of its history. Thus whatever the sources attribute to one Nasi can be applied to the others as well[77]. On the other hand, there are some who, following the tendentious views of rabbinic literature, have posited a serious decline in the office commencing with the mid-third century. Admittedly, there is some truth to both claims; each taken alone to the exclusion of the other misses the mark. Throughout the third century much remained constant. However, in most spheres there were changes, some of minor importance, others more significant.

1. Declaring Fast Days

The presence of the Nasi was indispensable for conducting propitiatory prayers for rain. Already the Mishna accords the Patriarch a central role in such ceremonies[78]. In the late third century statements by two sages reflect the continuing importance of the Nasi on these occasions:

> "R. Helbo said to R. Judah (III) Nesiah: Come out with us (to the city plaza for prayers) and our trouble will pass. R. Yose said: . . . those fasts which we perform are not considered (valid) fasts. Why? Because the Nasi is not with us[79]."

Indeed there are sources relating to each of the three important Patriarchs of this period which substantiate this claim. On one occasion Rabbi Judah I is said to have played a central role in declaring a fast day[80]; on another he

[76] Ep. ad. Afric. XIV.

[77] This line of reasoning is most clearly spelled out by MANTEL, above, n. 8, p. 175: "Unless we have reason to believe otherwise, we may assume that any function which our sources attribute to one Nasi was also performed by all the Nesi'im." Although subsequently somewhat modified, this assumption clearly informs MANTEL's chapter on the office of the Nasi. Cf. also, ALON, above, n. 9, pp. 374f., 425f.

[78] M Ta'anit II, 1.

[79] J Ta'anit II, 1,65a.

[80] B Ta'anit 24a.

answered a query from the people of Nave regarding fast-day prayers during the summer months[81]. Similarly with regard to the ministry of R. Judah II:

> "The Patriarchal house declared a fast, but failed to inform R. Yohanan and Resh Lakish. In the morning (however) they were informed. Resh Lakish said to R. Yohanan: 'How can we observe it since we have not taken it upon ourselves last night?' He (R. Yohanan) said to him: 'We must follow them' (i.e. the decrees of the Nasi)[82].

The Patriarchal prerogative to declare such fasts is nowhere more poignantly expressed. Note the reactions of these two leading sages. Having had nothing to do with the declaration about which they were belatedly informed, their response was neither antagonistic nor resentful. Resh Lakish's question only related to whether such a decree was binding on him since he had not embarked on the fast at the proper time. R. Yohanan, for his part, responded with total compliance, almost resignation.

In this regard a further tradition, this time from the days of R. Judah III, is most enlightening:

> "The Patriarchal house declared a fast. They prayed but no rain fell. Oshaya the younger of the Hevraya[83] then quoted to them (the verse): 'And if it be done in error, hidden from the eyes of the congregation' (Numb. 15:24) and compared it to a bride who, as long as her eyes are beautiful, requires no bodily inspection. If her eyes are not beautiful, her whole body requires inspection. The servants (of the Nasi) thereupon came and twisted a scarf around his neck and tortured him. Some of the local people said: Leave him alone, Although he bothers us as well, since we see that his intentions are good (lit. — his deeds are for the sake of Heaven), we ignore him[84]."

Here too the Patriarchal prerogative remains unquestioned, for it is he who declares these fasts[85]. However, when rain failed to materialize criticism

[81] Ibid., 14b.

[82] Ibid., 24a. Cf. also the immediately preceding tradition which speaks of a fast declared by R. Judah, and probably also refers to Judah II.

[83] An enigmatic term, probably referring to a Tiberian rabbinic association. Cf. W. Bacher, Zur Geschichte der Schulen Palästinas im 3. und 4. Jahrhundert, MGWJ, XLIII (1899), pp. 345—360; Levine, above, n. 26, pp. 95—97.

[84] B Ta'anit 24a. About the same time a similar incident of torturing a sage by wrapping a scarf around his neck is told of R. Safra in connection with R. Abbahu and the *agoranomoi* of Caesarea; cf. B AZ 4a; S. Lieberman, Martyrs of Palestine, Annuaire de l'Institut de philologie et d'histoire orientales et slaves, VII (1939—44), pp. 399ff.

[85] Compare this to the numerous accounts from Babylonia where the sages are the ones who declare fast days: Rav, R. Nahman, Rava, R. Papa (B Ta'anit 24a—b). In Palestine as well, there are several cases noted of leading sages (R. Hanina b. Hama, R. Joshua b. Levi and Levi b. Sisi) who declared fasts (ibid.). However, each of these men was closely associated with the Nasi, and might well have been functioning with authority invested by the latter. Alternatively, it is possible that these sages had prerogatives for local fasts.

was expressed, from at least one rabbinic quarter. The criticism voiced was trenchant; the fault is that of the Nasi himself. He is clearly unworthy of being the "eyes" (i.e. the leader) of the community. The Patriarch's response was swift, and decisive — even somewhat heavy-handed — so much so that the townspeople intervened (and not out of any great love for the afflicted). Thus the prerogative of the Nasi formally remained the same under Judah III. The criticism to which he was subjected contrasts sharply with the resignation and recognition expressed by R. Yohanan a generation earlier.

2. Declaring and Annulling Bans

The stature and authority of the Nasi is equally evident with regard to bans. Should one be banned from the Nasi, the ban would be binding on Jews everywhere:

> "Our sages have taught: One who has been put under a ban by a teacher is automatically banned to the pupil, but one banned from a pupil is not banned from the teacher. If one is banned from the Av Bet Din he is banned from the Hakham. If he is banned from the Hakham he is not (automatically) banned from the Av Bet Din. One who is banned from the Nasi is banned to everyone[86]."

Not only was the ban on the Patriarch the most severe imaginable, but he alone was able to release bans that were otherwise unabsolvable. On one occasion a case was referred to R. Judah III from Babylonia, it being reported that "there is no man here of the standing of R. Judah who can absolve you[87]." In another case involving Resh Lakish the sages advised him that only the Nasi could be of help[88]. This prerogative remained with the Nasi down through the fourth century[89].

3. Appointment of Judges

Control over the judiciary was an indispensable instrument for exercising control over Jewish society. Over and above their immediate judiciary functions, judges would often serve in a variety of areas in the religious-educational sphere. Levi b. Sisi, for example, was hired by the people of Simonias as a judge, preacher, teacher, hazan, scribe and one who "would fulfill all other needs"[90]. Thus the institution which granted

[86] J MQ III, 1,81d.; B MQ 16a

[87] Ibid., 17a.

[88] Ibid.

[89] CT, XVI, 8,8.

[90] J Yevamot XII, 7,13a; GR LXXXI, 1, p. 969 and parallels. A similar job definition was given by the people of Bostra in asking Resh Lakish for such an appointment; cf. J Shevi'it VI, 1, 36d; Deuteronomy Rabba, ed. LIEBERMAN, pp. 60—61.

such ordinations became a leading factor in determining the direction and course of Jewish communal and religious life. A source of unparalleled import has been preserved with regard to the history and development of ordination:

> "R. Abba (fl. late third century) said: At first each (of the sages) would appoint his own students. For example, R. Yohanan b. Zakkai appointed R. Eliezer and R. Joshua, R. Joshua (appointed) R. ʿAkiva, R. ʿAkiva (appointed) R. Meir and R. Simeon . . . They then bestowed honor on this house (i.e. the Patriarchate) saying: If the court makes an appointment without the consent of the Nasi, then the appointment is of no validity; but if the Nasi makes an appointment without the consent of the court, then the appointment is valid. They subsequently decreed that the court can only make an appointment with the consent of the Nasi, and the Nasi only with the consent of the court[91]."

We thus have a tradition which sets forth a three-stage historical development. In the first period (reflecting the period from 80—130), leading sages appointed students irrespective of the Nasi[92]. The above source presents but one chain of tradition, from R. Yohanan through R. Meir and R. Simeon. There were others as well. The status and rights of such appointees are difficult to assess. An appointment seems to have carried with it participation in the deliberations of the academy. Judicially, however, there seems to have been little more involved than moral and religious suasion. At the same time, we do learn elsewhere of extensive Patriarchal prerogatives in this area. R. Gamaliel II is reported to have appointed sages to "sit in the Yeshivah"[93], and to have removed from office the head (?) of Gadara[94].

The second period delineated reflects a period when Patriarchal dominance was unchallenged, most likely around the turn of the third century under R. Judah I[95]. The best example of such Patriarchal prerogatives is found in the testament of R. Judah wherein he advised his son and successor, R. Gamaliel, regarding judicial appointments[96]. It was

[91] J Sanhedrin I, 2, 19a.

[92] Cf. however ALON, above, n. 9, I, pp. 142—143 who opines that the Nasi's consent was required even here.

[93] Sifre-Deuteronomy XVI, p. 26; B Horayot 10a. The phrase used here להושיב בישיבה (or the variant — להושיב בראש) refers to ordination and applies to some sort of judiciary post. On this whole question and a summary of related literature, cf. MANTEL, above, n. 8, pp. 208—212.

[94] J RH I, 6, 57b; B RH 22a. The identification of this site has been debated. Aside from the obvious Hamat Gader, Gadara of the Shephela and Gezer have been suggested, having the advantage of being near Yavne and the center of rabbinic activity; cf. ALON, above, n. 9, p. 426, n. 137.

[95] The period of R. Simeon b. Gamaliel is ignored in this tradition owing to the very limited prerogatives of this Nasi; cf. above.

[96] J Taʿanit IV, 2,68a. Cf. LIEBERMAN, above, n. 31, p. 361.

this same R. Judah who recommended Levi b. Sisi for the multifaceted post in Simonias[97].

Control of these judiciary posts remained firmly in the hands of the Nasi through the middle of the third century. This is clearly attested in a series of rabbinic polemics from the days of R. Judah II, the purpose of which was to castigate the wealthy judicial appointees for their incompetence, and the Patriarchs for making such selections[98].

Returning once again to the above-quoted source, we find that sometime in the third century another significant change took place in the system of appointments. The Nasi was no longer the sole authority in this matter, but now shared power with the court. Clearly we are witness here to some sort of decline in the prestige and power of the Patriarchate. The extent of this decline will depend, among other things, on our interpretation of the term 'court' (בית דין). If a court of sages more or less independent of the Nasi is intended, then the change must indeed be considered abrupt and far-reaching. If, however, the court of the Nasi himself is meant, then the change, while undeniable and indicative of a reshuffling among certain forces, was far less significant. The former option appears far less likely. The very existence of a central court (be it called a 'court' or Sanhedrin) in the late Roman period remains an open question. In terms of the third century such a supreme independent rabbinical tribunal seems doubtful[98a]; thus it is most probable that the court referred to here is that of the Nasi himself.

While even this kind of re-division of responsibilities within the Patriarchal framework requires explanation, we unfortunately have no explicit data in this regard. Much depends on the date assigned to this development. If, indeed, it occurred already under R. Judah II, then it may have stemmed from the desire of the Nasi to accord the sages, particularly a figure such as R. Yohanan, a more central role in the administration of Jewish communal life. The change, then, would reflect less a diminution of Patriarchal prerogatives than a concern to increase rabbinic participation (although these two phenomena can never be fully separated in such circumstances). If, however, this change took place several decades later, from when we have other evidence of Patriarchal decline (cf. below), then this development would probably reflect a reassertion of rabbinic involvement at the expense of the Nasi's prerogatives. Cogent arguments can be mustered for each alternative, and a definite answer is all but impossible.

One factor, however, which argues for an earlier date (ca. 250) for this change has to do with the activity of several sages who actually seem to

[97] Cf. above, n. 90.

[98] B Sanhedrin 7b; Midrash Samuel VII, 6, 34b; J Bikkurim III, 3,65d. Cf. also Sifre-Deuteronomy XVII, pp. 27—28. On Patriarchal ties to the wealthy, cf. B 'Eruvin 86a; B BM 85b—86a; B Ketubot 103b.

[98a] This rather complex issue has not received adequate attention. We hope to deal with it in another context.

have made such appointments. R. Joshua b. Levi was wont to ordain students[99], and R. Yohanan is said to have ordained sages[100]. Only these two rabbis are associated with such appointments, and it seems more than coincidental that both had strong ties with the Patriarch. R. Yohanan is explicitly referred to on one occasion as being "from the house of the Nasi" (i.e. associated with him or in his service)[101], while R. Joshua's connection stems, in part at least, from the marriage of his son into Patriarchal circles[102]. Thus the fact that these two sages granted ordination is probably not an instance of independent rabbinic activity, but rather of increased participation in Patriarchal operations[103]. If this be granted then we are probably on safe grounds in assuming that stage three of R. Abba's historical reconstruction has been reached by the mid-third century.

A prerogative intimately linked with ordination has to do with firstlings. According to Jewish law, first-born animals are to be consecrated to God. However, certain blemishes or other defects can disqualify animals from such a designation, and the nature of such blemishes would then determine whether the animal could be used for ordinary purposes. Determining the nature of such blemishes became an important task. Indeed it was just such an issue which led to a major confrontation between R. Gamaliel II and his opponents among the rabbis[104]. The fact that by the turn of the third century full ordination included the right to make such decisions (יתיר בכורות) as well as teaching (יורה) and adjudicating (ידין), attests to their frequency and significance[105].

Under R. Judah I, it is clear that the authority controlling one area controlled the other as well. Thus it is little wonder that by the late third century, with the readjustment of Patriarchal authority regarding ordination, the question of authority in this matter also arose. That the issue was a real and difficult one is reflected in a tradition in which the following

99 J Hagiga I, 8, 76c; J Nedarim X. 10, 42b.

100 B Sanhedrin 14a; 30b. Cf. also J Sanhedrin II, 6,20c—d where the discussion between R. Yohanan and R. Hanina bar Sisi makes reference to qualifications for ordination. The assumption here is that R. Yohanan was able to make such appointments, or at least could be influential with the Nasi. Mention should be made of the ordination in Bostra carried out by Resh Lakish with the consent of R. Yohanan (J Shevi'it VI, 1, 36d).

101 B Sota 21a.

102 B Qiddushin 33b and Rashi loc. cit. On ties of marriage between other 'southern' families and the Nasi, cf. J Shabbat XII, 3,13c; J Horayot III, 48c. Such a connection with the Patriarchal operation would explain some of the apparently political activity of R. Joshua. His trips to Rome and Caesarea may have been as an emissary of the Patriarch (GR LXXVIII, 21, p. 923; J Berakhot V, 1,9a).

103 Resh Lakish, a close associate of R. Yohanan, has also been associated with the Nasi on the basis of B Nazir 20b ("Resh Lakish sat before R. Judah [II] Nesiah"), and the fact that on several occasions he reversed the decision of no less an authority than R. Yohanan (B Ketubot 54b; 84b). If indeed R. Yohanan enjoyed Patriarchal backing, then Resh Lakish must have also. R. Yohanan, for his part, had a decision of R. Isaac reversed by reporting it to the Nasi. The latter then dispatched gendarmes to enforce R. Yohanan's ruling (B Nidda 52a).

104 B Bekhorot 36a.

105 B Sanhedrin 5a. Cf. also J Hagiga I, 8,76c; J Nedarim X, 10,42b.

question was raised: is a sage of the academy required to ask permission of the Nasi in such matters or not[106]? While no clear-cut answer is offered, a number of sages stated unreservedly that such a prerogative rested squarely with the Patriarch[107].

4. Calendrical Authority

The right to intercalate the year or the month was far more consequential than might, at first, be assumed. Controlling the Jewish calendar and thus deciding which days would be holy was of cardinal importance for anyone with aspirations to religious leadership. Calendar controversies were not unknown in Jewish history, and very often involved issues of political significance as well. Calendrical issues appear to have played an important role in secessionist movements, be they the breakaway of the northern tribes in the tenth century or of the Essenes in the second. These movements were motivated in part by, and expressed their opposition through, calendrical issues[108]. Later on, in the Middle Ages, the Saadia-Ben-Meir controversy similarly focussed on a calendar question[109].

Already at the outset of the Patriarchate, under Gamaliel II, the authority in such matters passed into the hands of the Nasi. In a dramatic confrontation with a leading sage, R. Joshua, Gamaliel gained his objective and was acknowledged the final determiner of the calendar[110]. This prerogative was transmitted from generation to generation down to the end of the Patriarchate. R. Simeon b. Gamaliel exercised similar authority[111], as did his son R. Judah I. Regarding the latter we read of twenty-four carriages (?) of scholars who came to Lydda under Patriarchal auspices to intercalate the year. When a tragedy befell them, it was decided

106 Here it may be suggested that the term יושב בישיבה may reflect later Palestinian usage, and thus refer to a school or academy rather than to a court; cf. D. Goodblatt, Rabbinic Instruction in Sassanian Babylonia, Studies in Judaism in Late Antiquity, IX (Leiden, 1975), pp. 74—75.

107 B Yoma 78a—b. Cf. the account of R. Ami of Werdina who presumably was in charge of inspecting Patriarchal firstlings (B Beza 27a—b).

108 S. Talmon, Divergencies in Calendar-Reckoning in Ephraim and Judah, VT, VIII (1958), 48—74; Idem, The Calendar Reckoning of the Sect from the Judaean Desert, Aspects of the Dead Sea Scrolls, Scripta Hierosolymitana, IV, ed. C. Rabin, Y. Yadin (Jerusalem, 1976), pp. 162—199.

109 Cf. S. Baron, A Social and Religious History of the Jews (16 vols.; Philadelphia, 1952—1976), V (1957), p. 30.

110 M RH II, 8—9. Perhaps an example of this newly-won authority in practice is to be found in the account of R. ʿAkiva in Nehardea (M Yevamot XVI, 7). However, details surrounding this incident are unclear and therefore no firm conclusions are warranted; cf. Graetz, above, n. 20, IV, pp. 442—443; L. Ginzberg, A Commentary on the Palestinian Talmud, Texts and Studies of the Jewish Theological Seminary of America, X. XI. XII. XXI (4 vols.; New York, 1941—61; Hebrew), III (1941), p. 131, n. 143; Alon, above, n. 9, I, pp. 151—152.

111 J Nedarim VI, 13, 40a; J Sanhedrin I, 2,19a; B Berakhot 63a.

to move the site from Judea to the Galilee[112]. On another occasion, R. Judah sent R. Hiyya to 'Ein Tov to sanctify the new moon[113].

From the time of R. Judah II we have no explicit evidence of the Nasi's activity in this regard. However, there are a number of sources which provide negative evidence, i.e. that authority in this area was not in the hands of sages. For example, the following:

> "R. Yohanan would enter the synagogue in the morning, gather up some scraps of food and eat. And he said: Let this be my portion with those who sanctified the moon here last night[114]."

This account, albeit short, is fascinating for a number of reasons. It attests to regular gatherings in the third century for sanctifying the new moon, an accompanying meal, and the synagogue as the venue for such occasions. For our purposes, however, the interesting fact is that even one of R. Yohanan's stature was not involved in this process. Similarly, his disparaging reference to those who once fixed the calendar, calling them cattle-herders (רועי בקר), reflects a deep antagonism towards those participating in these ceremonies[115]. In what may be a fuller account of this incident, we are told that Resh Lakish was consciously excluded by two other sages from joining the proceedings. When he complained of this to R. Yohanan the latter merely responded that there was little that could be done[116]. In another instance we are told that Resh Lakish was abruptly excluded from such calendrical meetings, in this case because an elder "arrived there first"[117]. Finally a series of traditions from the mid-third century indicate that the privilege of intercalation was restricted to those ordained. Since the latter office was still in the hands of the Nasi, it would seem that the former was also[118].

As for the ministry of R. Judah III, the only evidence available is his query to R. Ami regarding the type of testimony acceptable from witnesses[119]. Nevertheless, despite this absence of sources, there is no doubt that this remained a Patriarchal prerogative. From the fourth century, we have a letter sent from the Nasi complaining of the difficulty in informing Babylonian Jewry of calendrical decisions due to the interference of the Roman government[120]. Soon after, in 358, the Patriarch Hillel II promul-

112 J Sanhedrin I, 2,18c. Cf. also B Hullin 56b. Cf. S. Safrai, The Localities of the Sanctification of Lunar Months and the Intercalation of Years in Palestine After 70 C.E. (Hebrew), Tarbiz, XXXV (1966), pp. 27—38.

113 B RH 25a. R. Hoshaya was probably on a similar mission on behalf of his very close friend, R. Judah II (J Nedarim VI, 13,40a).

114 J Sanhedrin VIII, 2,26b.

115 Ibid., I, 2,18c.

116 B Sanhedrin 26a.

117 J Sanhedrin I, 2,18c.

118 Ibid.

119 B RH 20a.

120 B Sanhedrin 12a. Cf. Lieberman, above n. 31, pp. 331—334.

gated a permanent calendar[121]. In summary, therefore, the evidence appears incontrovertable that the Nasi retained this prerogative throughout the course of late antiquity.

5. Communal Supervision and Taxation

Another important area of Patriarchal activity concerned the Jewish community per se, both in Palestine and throughout the Roman world. Roman law clearly acknowledges the existence of such far-reaching Patriarchal authority throughout the fourth century[122], and rabbinic literature, while concentrating more specifically on Palestine and its immediate surroundings, corroborates this view[123]. Here, too, we are faced with the dilemma of our sources. From the time of R. Gamaliel II and from the fourth century, we have some idea of the extent and nature of such activity. Focussing on the third century, however, the picture is less clear.

One such instance dates from the days of R. Judah I. Upon request, the Nasi sent Levi b. Sisi to Simonias to serve as judge, teacher, etc. The inhabitants of Simonias, however, were not pleased with this selection and summarily dismissed him[124].

Two other sources which deal with this aspect of Patriarchal activity stem from the period of R. Judah III. In one instance R. Hiyya b. Abba asked the Patriarch (via R. Eliezer) for a letter of recommendation (איגרא דאיקר — 'a letter of recommendation') when he travelled abroad[125]. The letter included the phrase: "We have sent you a great man. He is our emissary and is to be regarded as ourselves (i.e. he should be accorded the same privileges) until he returns to us". As it stands the letter itself might conceivably be nothing more than a personal letter of introduction. Nevertheless, it does seem to constitute a formal letter to be borne by an emissary on official business. Thus the Talmud understands it, as an example of a short-term appointment to an official capacity.

The second instance refers to a specific case where the Patriarch R. Judah III sent R. Ami, R. Asi and R. Hiyya to visit various Palestinian communities in order to check on local teachers[126]. It is clear from this that the educational system of Palestinian Jewish communities at least, were

[121] R. Hai Gaon as quoted by R. Abraham b. Hiyya, Sefer Ha'ibbur; cf. GRAETZ, above, n. 20, p. 456, n. 31.

[122] CT, XVI, 8, 14.

[123] J Bikkurim III, 3,65d.

[124] Cf. above, n. 90. On similar instances of communities dismissing candidates, protesting appointments, etc., J. Megilla IV, 5,75b; J Ta'anit IV, 2,68a; B Ketubot 103b; B Berakhot 55a.

[125] J Hagiga I, 7,76d; J Nedarim X, 8,42b. For a similar letter requested by R. Simeon b. Abba from R. Hanina, cf. J MQ III, 1,81c.

[126] J Hagiga I, 7,76c. Cf. also the enigmatic reference to R. Abbahu on a Patriarchal mission to southern Palestine (B 'Eruvin 53b).

subject to Patriarchal control. Whether R. Hiyya was on a similar mission when travelling alone is unknown.

As regards the geographical extent of Patriarchal jurisdiction in the third century, little is known. The Stobi synagogue inscription, dated to 279, would seem to suggest that he enjoyed some official capacity vis-à-vis Diaspora synagogues[127]. From the inscription, however, little is learned about the nature of this association, other than the fact that he is the beneficiary should someone break the dedicatory agreement.

Interestingly, apart from Gamaliel II, almost nothing is recorded about the Nasi himself visiting different Jewish communities. Rarely is he found abroad[128], and even within Palestine, his journeys are infrequent. To assume that travelling third century sages were in the service of the Nasi is unwarranted. Since GRAETZ it has been fashionable to assign all sorts of motives to such rabbinic journeys. The classic example from the second century is R. ʿAkiva's travels, which are taken as an indication of the extensive preparations for the Bar Kokhba revolt[129]. However, unless there is an explicit reference to some such purpose (which there is not in the case of R. ʿAkiva) all such assumptions are best avoided. Rabbis might travel for any one of a number of reasons: for personal or business visits[130], or in connection with the needs of the academy (such as fund-raising)[131].

Fourth century sources regarding Patriarchal contact and control over far-flung communities[132] make it a reasonable assumption that such ties existed in one form or another in the third century as well. However, in the absence of explicit references, this point should not be pressed.

Another area of Patriarchal responsibility involved taxation. Here, too, sources referring to each of the third and fourth centuries tend to emphasize different aspects of this phenomenon. The latter are replete with references to the taxes collected by the Nasi in the Diaspora[133]; of such activity within fourth century Palestine we know practically nothing. Conversely, rabbinic accounts relating to the third century reveal a range of taxes associated with the Patriarch.

First, there were taxes in the form of religious obligations which the Nasi could lessen, redefine or abolish, as deemed necessary. Tithing and sabbatical year obligations were drastically changed in certain locales under the initiative of R. Judah I[134]. Then there were taxes affecting Tiberias.

[127] Cf. above, n. 23.

[128] On one occasion, R. Judah II visited Laodicea (J Yevamot VIII, 1,8d), as had R. Judah I some years earlier (Sifre Deuteronomy 335, p. 385).

[129] GRAETZ, above, n. 20, IV, 135.

[130] Cf., for example, the visits of the Babylonian R. Safra to Caesarea (B AZ 4a).

[131] Cf. Deuteronomy Rabba IV, 8; LR, V, 4, p. 113.

[132] S. KRAUSS, Die jüdischen Apostel, JQR, XVII (1904—05), pp. 370—383; H. VOGELSTEIN, Die Entstehung und Entwicklung des Apostolats im Judentum, MGWJ, XLIX (1905), pp. 427—449.

[133] CT XVI, 8,14 and 17; Epiphanius, Panarion, XXX, 3, 4 and 11; PG, XLI, 409—411, 423.

[134] T Ohalot XVIII, 16—18, p. 617; J Demai II, 1, 22c.

In one case the inhabitants of the city complained to R. Judah I that the sages were no less obligated to contribute to the *aurum coronarium* than they[135]. Was the Patriarch actually in charge of collecting this tax among the Jewish population? Or might this reflect a special relationship between the Nasi and Tiberias, as attested by R. Judah's reported request to the emperor for colonial status for the city[136]? If so, the local residents, for whatever reason, wished to circumvent their local Tiberian authorities.

A second Tiberian tax under Patriarchal control (probably after the Nasi had moved there) was a levy for building (or repairing) the city-walls[137]. The Patriarch demanded that the sages pay as well; the latter protested that they themselves had no need of such protection (and thus should be exempt from paying). Thus, in both the above-mentioned Tiberian cases the issue involved was whether the sages were obligated to contribute. In the earlier incident, Judah I upheld the rabbinic exemption, even when faced with widespread dissatisfaction. In the latter instance, there is no indication that R. Judah II relented in his demand to include the sages in the wall-levy (if he had, it probably would have been mentioned as a rabbinic victory).

In addition to these specific instances, the Nasi was also responsible for other taxes, which presumably became an unbearable burden by the mid-century. This seems to be the background for a truculent sermon against R. Judah II delivered by Yosi of Ma'on in a Tiberian synagogue:

> "Yose of Ma'on expounded in a Tiberian synagogue: 'Hear this, priests' (Hosea 5 : 1) — Why are you not studying Torah? Have you not been given the 24 priestly dues? They replied: They have given us nothing. 'Pay attention, house of Israel' (ibid.) — Why have you not given the twenty-four priestly dues which you were commanded on Sinai? They replied: The king (i.e. the Patriarch) has taken everything. 'Give ear, house of the king, for upon you judgement will come' (ibid.) — Was I referring to you when I spoke of 'The judgement (i.e. dues) of priests'? (Deut. 18 : 3). In the future I will judge you, condemn you and destroy you from the face of the earth. R. Judah (II) Nesiah heard (about this) and became enraged. (Yosi) panicked and fled . . .[138]"

The Nasi is here accused of exacting an exorbitant amount of taxes from the people. Despite the obvious polemical tones of this sermon (for Yose was also complaining here of the loss of income due the sages as the current guardians of the Torah!), the charges are not at all unbelievable, given the horrendous economic situation of the Empire. It is clear from this account that the Nasi played a central role in the tax system of Tiberias, if not of all Palestine.

135 B BB 8a.
136 B AZ 10a.
137 B BB 7b.
138 GR LXXX, 1, pp. 950—953; J Sanhedrin II, 6,20d.

One area involving taxes which assuredly was controlled by the Nasi was the exemptions which accompanied ordination. Those appointed were assured tax benefits, as was the case with other such officials of the realm. Thus such posts became desirable, in addition to whatever social prestige and professional recognition they bore. Since the Nasi retained either absolute or partial control over the process of ordination throughout this period, his influence was always important in allocating these privileges.

6. Legislative Acts[139]

The third century Patriarchs are associated with the following legislative acts:

R. Judah I:

a) Permitting the use of produce immediately following the termination of the sabbatical year[140].
b) Permitting the import of produce to Eretz Israel[141].
c) Permitting acquisition of land from a *siqariqon*, provided that a prescribed sum be set aside for the original Jewish owner[142].
d) Defining the grave impurity of Palestinian Greco-Roman cities[143].
e) Releasing a number of Palestinian Greco-Roman cities from levitical impurity[144].
f) Releasing several cities from tithing and sabbatical year obligations[145].
g) An abortive attempt to abolish sabbatical year laws, and perhaps even the 9th of Av and 17th of Tammuz commemorations[146].

[139] We have confined ourselves as much as possible to official decrees of the Patriarch. For this purpose we have included only those references which 1. speak of the Nasi and his court; 2. refer to "our rabbis", or 3. use the term נמנו ("they were polled") — all of which indicate some sort of official decision. This would exclude, for example, several enactments of Rabbi Judah I taken in connection with the New Moon, allowing the testimony of a murderer or second-hand testimony (J RH II, 1, 58a). In any case some of these latter decisions were only a formalization of an already long-accepted practice; cf. ALON, above, n. 9, II, 154.

[140] M Shevi'it VI, 4; T Shevi'it IV, 17, p. 183. On this and other sabbatical year rulings listed below; cf. S. SAFRAI, The Practical Implementation of the Sabbatical Year After the Destruction of the Second Temple, (Hebrew), Tarbiz, XXXVI (1967), pp. 1—21.

[141] T Shevi'it IV, 16 and 19, pp. 183—184 and TK, p. 542, n. 77. Cf. also J Shevi'it VII, 2,37b.

[142] M Gittin XVIII, 9. On the term *siqariqon*, cf. S. SAFRAI, Siqariqon (Hebrew), Zion, XVII (1952), 56—64; M. GIL, Land Ownership in Palestine under Roman Rule, Revue internationale des droits de l'antiquité, XVII (1970), pp. 45—53.

[143] M Ohalot XVIII, 10, ed. GOLDBERG, p. 135.

[144] T Ohalot XVIII, 17, p. 617. The 24 sages mentioned here are undoubtedly part of R. Judah's court (J Sanhedrin I, 2,18c).

[145] T Ohalot XVIII, 18, p. 617; J Demai II, 1,22c; B. Hullin 6b.

[146] J Demai I, 20a; J Ta'anit II, 66c; III, 66b—c.

R. Gamaliel III:

h) Permission to cultivate fields up to the New Year holiday of the sabbatical year[147].

i) An abortive attempt to apply the rules of tithing to Syria[148].

j) Refinement of an earlier law pertaining to a "rebellious" wife[149].

R. Judah II:

k) Permitting the use of pagan oil[150].

l) Determining the sort of discharge that will make a woman impure[151].

m) Conditions of a divorce decree (*get*) which do not render it invalid[152].

n) An apparently abortive attempt to release the area of Har-Hamelekh[153] from tithing obligations[154].

This list is informative on several counts. Of the fourteen different items (including the abortive attempts), eight deal with agricultural questions: permission to use hitherto forbidden produce (a, b, k), release of produce from various religious obligations, such as tithing (f, g, h, n), and in one case an attempt to extend the tithing laws to Syria. Three enactments deal with the land, problems of acquisition and of purity (c, d, e). The three other instances deal with laws relating to women: impurity, divorce and relations with a spouse. Although the social significance of these last-named acts remains obscure, there is little question that the issues involved in the others were of the utmost importance in the third century. Enormous tax burdens made agriculture a precarious enterprise, with the result that a movement towards urban centers gained momentum[155]. The Patriarchs

147 T Shevi'it I, 1, p. 165; J Shevi'it I, 33a; B MQ 3b. Cf. D. Sperber, Drought, Famine and Pestilence in Amoraic Palestine, JESHO, XVII (1974), pp. 290—293.

148 J Halla IV, 7,60a.

149 T Ketubot, V, 7, pp. 73—74. It is not clear to whom the term רבותינו refers. We have identified it with the court of R. Gamaliel III.

150 M AZ II, 6; T AZ IV, 11, p. 467; J AZ II, 8,41d; B AZ 37a. This ruling is especially remarkable as it reflects a revolutionary change from the normative practice of Second Temple days — total prohibition on use of gentile oil; cf. Josephus, Antiquities, XII, 3,1,120; idem, War, II, 21,2,590—594; idem, Life, XIII, 74—76.
R. Judah II was urged by R. Simlai to allow use of gentile bread, even over rabbinic opposition (B AZ 37a). There is also a report that R. Judah I had already considered such a move, but this tradition is problematic (ibid., 35b; cf. J AZ II, 9,41d).

151 J Nidda III, 4,50d; B Nidda 25b.

152 J Gittin VII, 3,48d.

153 An area in northern Judea; cf. S. Klein, Har-Hamelek (Hebrew), Tarbiz, I (1929), pp. 136—144; I. S. Horowitz, Palestine and Adjacent Countries (Vienna, 1923; Hebrew), pp. 240—241.

154 J Demai V, 9,24d.

155 SHA — Niger, VII, 9; Avi-Yonah, above, n. 37, pp. 89—114; D. Sperber, Trends in Third Century Palestinian Agriculture, JESHO, XV (1972), pp. 227—255; Id., Aspects of Agrarian Life in Roman Palestine I: Agricultural Decline in Palestine during the Later Principate, ANRW II 8 (Berlin—New York, 1978), pp. 397—443.

thus addressed themselves in these enactments to the exigencies of the times. The economic burden of religious obligations was lessened, and certain restrictions on settlement were removed. One decree relaxed the restrictions in acquiring former Jewish land now in the hands of a non-Jew (c). This, too, was clearly an attempt to counter a growing and (for the Jews, at least) undesirable trend, namely the gradual acquisition of Jewish land by a growing pagan population[156].

The Patriarchs were not alone in these attempts to alleviate the burdens of third century Palestinian life. There are a number of sources indicating that the sages operated in a similar vein[157]. Nevertheless, the consistency reflected in these acts is noteworthy, so much so that in one case a Patriarchal court was labelled "permissive"[158].

It is likewise noteworthy that such legislation ceases in the midthird century. During the first half century, each Nasi is associated with at least one such decision. Of the two Patriarchs who functioned during the last half of the century, nothing is known. This might be merely coincidental. Or, in light of the other developments we have noted, it might indeed reflect a certain diminution of Patriarchal prestige and influence (cf. below).

V. The Patriarch and Jewish Society

At this stage it might be helpful to note the kinds of things which the Nasi did not do, at least according to our sources. He was not involved, for example, in building, as the Herodians had been several centuries earlier. Even as central an institution as the synagogue, over which the Patriarch had extensive jurisdiction in the fourth century, bears little trace of Patriarchal involvement in the third. With the exception of the Stobi inscription, few literary or archeological sources connected with synagogues make mention of the Nasi[159]. No public buildings are known to have been erected under Patriarchal auspices nor were gifts bestowed on cities (be they pagan or Jewish) by his office. With regard to cities, the Nasi legislated questions of a religious nature for the Jewish community. With but one exception, we know of nothing which associates the Nasi with the overall political, economic, social or physical aspects of urban life, nor of his relationship with municipal authorities, even in cities where he resided. His

[156] IDEM, On the Transfer of Property from Jew to Non-Jew in Amoraic Palestine (200—400), Diné Israel, IV (1973), XVII—XXXIV.

[157] Cf., for example, E. E. URBACH, The Rabbinical Laws of Idolatry in the Second and Third Centuries in the Light of Archaeological and Historical Facts, IEJ, IX (1959), pp. 149—165, 229—245.

[158] J Shabbat I, 4, 3d and parallels; B AZ 37a.

[159] HENGEL, above, n. 23, pp. 145—183. For one of the few sources speaking of the Nasi in the synagogue, cf. Deuteronomy Rabba VII, 8.

ties to provincial and Imperial officialdom likewise remain obscure, as does his relationship to rabbinic institutions: rabbinic tribunals, the various academies or any other rabbinic organizations[160]. For that matter, we know little about the Patriarchs themselves, their families, daily activities, associates, administrative operations, beliefs, religious practices or cultural proclivities.

In this respect Epiphanius' account of Patriarchal life is a most important corrective[161]. Suddenly we are given a glimpse — albeit fleeting and distorted — of the Patriarchal court in action. The Nasi studies, legislates and administrates. We read of his library, as well as contacts with the world around. Epiphanius provides us with one of those rare opportunities to put rabbinic sources in perspective. As noted, this literature is so overwhelmingly concerned with the rabbis themselves, their beliefs, halakhic discussions and activities, that the Nasi, who by the third and fourth centuries stood at best on the periphery of rabbinic life, is only casually mentioned. But standing on the periphery of rabbinic life does not mean that he was on the periphery of Jewish life as well. And here the limitations of rabbinic literature become most apparent. Epiphanius' story alerts us to the fact that much is ignored, and that diligent efforts are required to counterbalance the decided rabbinic tilt of these sources. The danger of distortion is two-fold: the almost total focus on certain kinds of issues and personalities within Jewish society, and the fact that all is seen through rabbinic eyes and judged according to rabbinic standards. This latter tendency can at least be partially corrected. Efforts can be made to see a tendentious statement in some perspective. The former deficiency, however, is almost insurmountable. How much can we assume is left out? How indicative is the partial picture which we do get? In this sense, the omissions noted above are unfair. For they reveal more about the limitations of the sources than they do about the limitations of the office.

Unfortunately, the sources relating to the Patriarchate of the fourth century cannot provide the necessary corrective. This is not because they are any more objective; indeed they are no less tendentious. The problem is that these sources deal with a wholly new historical era. No one can minimize today the far-reaching changes which took place in the Constantinian and post-Constantinian period, particularly as regards Jewish life. Whereas it was always assumed that this era marked the beginning of the Middle Ages for the Jew (i.e. a period of discrimination and persecution), it has become clear of late that Jewish life was far less adversely affected than imagined. In many cases Jews benefitted from Christian rule, and the privileges extended to Christian clergy applied to Jewish officials as well. Thus, it is entirely conceivable that some (or many?) of the rights and privileges of the fourth century Patriarchate were granted then, and not earlier.

[160] Cf. J Sanhedrin II, 1,19d for one of the few instances explicitly referring to a Patriarch in an academy.

[161] Panarion, XXX, 3—12, PG XLI, 410—428.

Once again we are faced with the problem of limited sources and the issue of continuity.

There is one area, however, where a relatively clear picture is available, and that is with regard to rabbinic attitudes towards the Nasi. As might be imagined, these attitudes were far from monolithic. There were rabbis who fully supported the Patriarch; some were even in his service. Thus R. Efes served as a secretary to R. Judah I[162]; R. Yohanan and R. Joshua b. Levi were associated with R. Judah II[163]. From the days of R. Judah III, the families of Pazi and Hoshaya as well as such rabbinic leaders as R. Ami, R. Asi and R. Hiyya, were on close terms with the Nasi[164]. Several sages such as Resh Lakish or R. Simlai attended the Nasi when on a walk or journey[165]. The personal relationships between R. Hoshaya on the one hand, and R. Gamaliel III and R. Judah II on the other, appear to have been remarkably close[166]. Of the elders constituting the Patriarchal court, who are referred to as "our rabbis" or who preceded the Nasi in his processionals, we know nothing.

Together with this evidence of harmony, there is no lack of discordant notes in rabbinic literature towards the Nasi. R. Judah I was criticized for his decrees regarding tithing[167], declaring certain areas pure[168], and attempting to abolish the sabbatical year restrictions[169]. His rulings were openly flaunted by R. Hiyya[170] who demonstrably refused to acknowledge Patriarchal prerogatives[171], and whose son explicitly downgraded the Davidic lineage claimed by the Nasi[172].

R. Gamaliel III also met with rabbinic opposition, which presumably neutralized his attempts at extending tithing requirements to Syria. His personal behavior as well was subject to rabbinic criticism[173].

R. Judah II was upbraided for his choice of judges who, according to Resh Lakish, were distinctly unqualified for the job. Their appointment, he claimed, was due solely to their wealth[174]. The prestige of the office came under more serious attack when this same Resh Lakish claimed that according to Jewish law the Nasi himself was liable to punishment by

[162] GR LXXV, 5, p. 883.
[163] Cf. above, nn. 99—100.
[164] Cf. above, nn. 66, 126.
[165] J Berakhot II, 1,4b; B AZ 37a. Cf. also B AZ 6b; J AZ I, 1,39b.
[166] A. Hyman, Toldot Tannaim Ve Amoraim (3 vols.; Jerusalem, 1964), I, p. 112. The ties between Hoshaya and Gamaliel were so strong that the former was able to criticize the latter without any apparent adverse reaction; cf. J Shabbat VI, 8a; J Halla IV, 7,60a.
[167] T Ohalot XVIII, 16—18, p. 617; J Demai II, 1,22c.
[168] B Hullin 6b.
[169] J Demai I, 20a; J Ta'anit II, 66c; III, 66b—c.
[170] B MQ 16a—b.
[171] B Qiddushin 33a.
[172] B Sanhedrin 38a.
[173] J Shabbat VI, 8a; J Halla IV, 7,60a.
[174] B Sanhedrin 7b. Similar criticism, dating a generation later, was offered by Jacob of Kfar Nevoraya (J Bikkurim III, 3,65d; Midrash Samuel VII, 6,34b). Cf. also A. Marmorstein, L'opposition contre le Patriarche Juda II, REJ, LXIV (1912), pp. 59—66.

stripes[175]. We have also taken note of Yosi of Ma'on's scathing condemnation of Patriarchal fiscal greed at the expense of other segments of the Jewish population. If that virulent attack was not enough, this same Yosi did not hesitate to predict the imminent demise of the Patriarchal dynasty[176]. Finally the many acts of R. Judah's court — especially that regarding pagan oil — drew the criticism of excessive permissiveness[177].

Rabbinic criticism — or rather disdain — for R. Judah III is expressed in a variety of ways. When R. Judah II died, R. Yannai closed the academy as a sign of mourning. However, when R. Zeira learned of the death of R. Judah III he ignored the news, and was only moved to respond by the prodding of R. Hiyya b. Abba[178]. It was about this time that the b. Pazi family was reported to have spurned an offer of marriage with the Patriarchal house[179]. Not so long before, this same family was counted among the leading supporters of the Patriarchate[180].

Even a cursory perusal of the above-noted allegations is enough to indicate that the list is far from uniform. There is a distinct difference in the charges leveled in the different periods. R. Judah I was criticized for moving too quickly, doing too much, treading in areas for which there was no precedent. There was also the charge that he assumed too much power and too many prerogatives. The proclaimed Davidic tie only capped a tendency which some viewed as an unwarranted and pretentious claim. R. Judah's reaction was interesting. His anger, when expressed, was usually of short duration; he knew when to pull back and not press too far. So, for example, he quickly sensed the extensive objections to the idea of abolishing the sabbatical year agricultural restrictions (and perhaps even the 9th of Av as well), and did not insist on his proposals.

Tensions had exacerbated greatly by the time of R. Judah II. The charges brought against him were far more serious. He was allegedly wreaking havoc with the court system and with people's livelihood. The judges he chose were incompetent, and the people were being bled by onerous taxation. His court was permissive, and he incurred rabbinic opposition by an attempt to include them in a wall-tax. R. Judah's reaction to this criticism was far more severe than his grandfather's. On several occasions he sent out gendarmes to apprehend his critics. In both cases they fled, and it was only due to the mediation efforts of several sages that a rapprochement was achieved. It is noteworthy that in one of these instances Resh Lakish was among the mediators, in the other he was the arch-critic. This should be enough to caution one against delineating too neatly opponents and supporters. Attitudes and relationships changed, if not overnight then at

175 J Sanhedrin II, 1,19d; J Horayot III, 2,47a.

176 GR LXXX, 1, pp. 950—953; J Sanhedrin II, 6,20d.

177 B AZ 37a.

178 J Nazir VII, 1,56a.

179 J AZ III, 1,42c.

180 The following Patriarch, Gamaliel V, is referred to by the Talmud as "an insignificant (lit.-small) person" (J AZ I, 1,39b).

least over months and years. One and the same rabbi might adopt different political stances over a period of time, or even at the same time over different issues. Reality then was no less complex than it is today.

Several other interesting patterns emerge from the list of Patriarchal critics and supporters. Almost without exception the Nasi succeeded in co-opting the leading sages of his generation. Relatively little criticism is directed at R. Judah I from R. Hanina b. Hama, R. Yonatan or R. Ishmael b. Yose. R. Hoshaya, R. Yannai, R. Joshua b. Levi and R. Yohanan were all on excellent terms with R. Judah II, as were R. Ami, R. Asi, and R. Hiyya with R. Judah III. The major criticism came from one of two kinds of groups. The first included sages like Yosi of Ma'on, Oshaya the Younger and, a generation later, one Jacob of Kfar Nevoraia. What unites this group is that they are on the periphery of rabbinic society, sages of minor importance (in terms of extant sources, at least), who lived for the most part outside the main centers of rabbinic activity.

A second group of critics did indeed include more central figures of rabbinic society. Among the detractors of R. Judah I were to be numbered R. Hiyya[181], Bar Kappara[182] and R. Phineas b. Yair[183], and of R. Judah II, Resh Lakish. Common to all these sages is that they lived in (or hailed from) cities other than where the Nasi resided. R. Phineas and Bar Kappara were from the south, R. Hiyya from Tiberias. In fact, Tiberias appears to have been a main center of criticism vis-à-vis the Patriarch, who then lived in Sepphoris. Under R. Judah II the main critics of the Nasi, Yosi of Ma'on and Resh Lakish, were Tiberians. When this Nasi travelled to Hamat Gader, and he seems to have visited that particular place quite frequently (as against Hamat Tiberias?)[184], he was invariably in the company of Sepphoran (and sometimes sourthern) rabbis, rarely with a Tiberian, and never with R. Yohanan. Thus, in addition to other factors motivating criticism or support, geographical considerations may have been at play as well[185]. Competition between the leading Galilean cities of Tiberias and Sepphoris may at times have found expression in the attitudes of certain rabbis towards the Nasi.

VI. The Third Century Patriarchate in Historical Perspective

In summing-up our evaluation of the place of the Nasi within Jewish society throughout the third century, we begin with a general

181 B MQ 16a—b; B Qiddushin 33a.
182 B MQ 16a; B Nedarim 50b—51a; J MQ III, 1,81c.
183 J Demai I, 3,22a. Cf. also J Ketubot I, 1, 25a; T Ohalot XVIII, 18, p. 617.
184 S. Zuri, The Rule of the Patriarch and the Va'ad (London, 1933; Hebrew), pp. 113—115.
185 Cf. L. Levine, R. Simeon b. Yohai and the Purification of Tiberias: History and Tradition, HUCA, XLIX (1978).

observation. The Nasi was both a religious as well as a political figure. Any attempt to see Jewish leadership in this period as a dyarchy, with the Patriarch in charge of political affairs and the sages the religious, misses the mark. That is, of course, not to deny that the Patriarchs enjoyed the political backing of the government or exhibited the political trappings of a court life. Essentially, however, they were heads of a national-religious community, and functioned as teachers and judges no less than political figures. They employed gendarmes[186], but no army; collected taxes, but nowhere near the amounts that were due the Roman government. Free of municipal responsibility and defense requirements, they devoted most of their time to the religious affairs of the community, which of necessity touched upon social, economic, and political issues as well. Their standing was more akin to that of the high priests in Jerusalem in the pre-175 B.C.E. or post-6 C.E. periods, than to Hasmonean or Herodian rulers.

Turning to the various types of prerogatives enumerated above, an interesting pattern is evident. In three areas Patriarchal authority seems to have continued largely unabated: fast days, bans, and the calendar. It is true that R. Judah III was criticized for failing to bring on the rain, but this criticism seems to have been a reflection more of rabbinic attitudes than of Patriarchal prerogatives.

In other areas the standing of the Nasi appears to have taken a turn for the worse. The statement of R. Abba tracing the history of the ordination procedure clearly points to a decline (whatever its significance — cf. above) in Patriarchal authority. It may not be coincidental that towards the end of the third century several rabbis were appointing communal officials (archons and *parnasim*)[187]. While at least one may have indeed been working under Patriarchal auspices (R. Hiyya b. Abba), another clearly was not. The charge which R. Haggai gave to the appointees had a decidedly anti-Patriarchal slant:

> "Whenever R. Haggai would appoint parnasim, he would lift up a Torah and say: All authority which you have comes from the Torah, 'By me kings rule . . . by me princes reign'" (Prov. 8:15—16).

The fact that after R. Judah II no ordinance (Takanah) is attributed to a Nasi, may also be indicative of a declining religious and political status[188].

[186] They might accompany him on a journey (GR LXXVIII, 15, p. 935), enforce decisions by collecting debts (J Shabbat VI, 9,8c) or confiscate property (J Ketubot IX, 2,33a; cf. also B Nidda 52a; B Ketubot 84b) and apprehend detractors (J Sanhedrin II, 1,19d).

[187] J Peah VIII, 7,21a.

[188] Here we are assuming some correlation between the treatment of a Nasi in our sources and his importance in Jewish society generally. This is not always the case. As we have noted, Patriarchs are rarely mentioned in fourth century rabbinic literature, yet we know from non-Jewish sources that their rank and authority were supreme. Nevertheless, rabbinic sources, scanty in general for the fourth, are particularly rich in third century material. This holds true for the entire century. Therefore the absence of certain kinds of

What, then, can be made of these developments? It would seem that the first category — areas of relatively undiminished power — deals basically with the strictly religious prerogatives of the Nasi. There he seems to have maintained, by and large intact, the authority enjoyed earlier. Where the office seems to have suffered, and this brings us to the second category, is in areas which have direct communal and institutional implications. It is regarding the judiciary system, communal organization and legislative acts, that some decline in the Patriarchate is evident.

A number of developments of the late third century would seem to confirm this impression of a partial eclipse. It was at this time that R. Abbahu reached a peak of political prominence hitherto unattained by any rabbinic sage. He was a frequent visitor to the governor's palace in Caesarea[189], and was accorded a variety of privileges by his colleagues because of what was termed 'the honor due the house of Caesar'[190]. Such recognition is *sui generis* in rabbinic literature, and can best be explained on the assumption that the Nasi was not the all-dominant political personality at the time[191]. Had the Patriarchate been flourishing, the cultivation of a Caesarean rabbi as a Jewish political figure by the Roman government would have defied explanation.

A changed status of the Patriarch vis-à-vis Rome is likewise indicated by the none-too-friendly encounter between the Nasi and the emperor Diocletian. When visiting Caesarea Paneas the emperor ordered Judah III to visit him, immediately following the Sabbath. However, he had the orders delivered only immediately preceding the Sabbath so as to force the Nasi to desecrate the holy day. Having miraculously arrived at the meeting without the necessity of travelling on the Sabbath, Judah was subject to a series of indignities by the emperor[192]. How much of this account is historical is difficult to say. The legendary accretions and the discrepancies between the two preserved accounts make any guess in this regard hazardous. What is safe to conclude, however, is that, at the very least, this tradition reflects a strained relation between the Nasi and the Roman authorities. One has just to compare this account with the cycle of stories focussing on R. Judah I and Antoninus to realize the enormous change that had taken place in the interim. The Nasi was clearly not the stronger for it.

One final piece of evidence also involves R. Judah III and Diocletian, this time, however, in a supportive rather than an antagonistic vein. In 293 a rescript was issued by the emperor to one Judah, wherein he asserts the need to follow the recognized and official court channels, as against

data for R. Judah III — available for earlier Patriarchs — may well be indicative. This will be particularly so, when the evidence is cumulative, as in this instance. These are the considerations informing our deliberations.

189 B Sanhedrin 14a; B Ketubot 17a.

190 B Yevamot 65a; B Yoma 73a; B Sota 40a.

191 L. Levine, R. Abbahu of Caesarea, Christianity, Judaism and Other Greco-Roman Cults: Studies for Morton Smith at Sixty, ed. J. Neusner. Studies in Judaism in Late Antiquity, XII (4 vols.; Leiden, 1975), IV, pp. 67—76.

192 GR LXIII, 8, pp. 688—690; J Terumot VIII, 11,46b—c.

all other kinds of judicial arrangements[193]. If indeed the personage addressed is R. Judah III[194], then it is clear that the government was attempting to bolster the flagging political fortunes of the Nasi.

How, then, is one to explain this decline? Can any factors be singled out as contributing to this change? Of necessity our suggestions will be tentative since the sources themselves never address these questions. Nevertheless, the issue is too central to avoid attempting some sort of explanation.

Undoubtedly a central factor in determining the fortunes of the Patriarchate — positively and negatively — was the power, prestige and influence of the Roman government. If not actually a creation of Rome at the time of R.Gamaliel, the Patriarchate at least owed some of its standing to the support and recognition offered by the Imperial government. The Mishna states that R. Gamaliel received *reshut* ('authority') from the governor of Syria[195]. This right is probably equivalent to the Latin *facultas iudicandi*, but in Jewish society it carried with it educational and instructional prerogatives as well[196]. The prominence achieved during the days of R. Judah I was likewise related to Roman political patronage. Patriarchal influence within the community was determined to a large extent by the authority vested in the office by Rome. By the mid-third century, however, Roman political fortunes in the east were at a low ebb. The prolonged and unsuccessful campaigns against Persia culminating in the capture of the emperor Valerian were indeed a blow to Roman political prestige. Moreover, the expansion of Palmyra under Odenathus and Zenobia eliminated any Roman political presence from the area for almost a decade[197]. It is inconceivable that the Patriarchate did not suffer as a result of these traumatic upheavals.

A second factor contributing to this decline was the desperate economic situation of the mid-third century. This crisis affected the Nasi in a variety of ways. In the first place it was certainly more difficult for the Nasi to raise the funds necessary for maintaining his operation. More monies had to be extracted from ever diminishing sources, a demand which surely would not endear him to the people (witness Yosi's virulent diatribe). Secondly, Rome, for its part, was making ever more burdensome demands in the form of taxation, and this, together with the rampant inflationary spiral,

Judae. Privatorum consensus iudicem non facit eum, qui nulli praeest iudicio, nec quod is statuit rei iudicatae continet auctoritatem.

193 CJ, III, 13,3: *Judae. Privatorum consensus iudicem non facit eum, qui nulli praeest iudicio, nec quod is statuit rei iudicatae continet auctoritatem.* Cf. DINBURG, above, n. 7.

194 Reservations regarding this identification have been registered by JUSTER, above, n. 11, II, 104—105; ALON, above, n. 9, pp. 433—435.

195 M 'Eduyot VII, 7.

196 As was the case with the priests in the days of the first Temple, and then under Ezra (7:25—26).

197 GRAETZ, above, n. 20, IV, pp. 269—274; H. J. W. DRIJVERS, Hatra, Palmyra und Edessa. Die Städte der syrisch-mesopotamischen Wüste in politischer, kulturgeschichtlicher und religionsgeschichtlicher Beleuchtung, ANRW II 8, above, n. 155, pp. 799—906, 837ff.

undermined government credibility with the masses. By association, the Patriarch almost surely suffered as a result. Moreover, a second important support of the Patriarchate was also adversely affected by these unstable economic circumstances. Since the beginning of the third century, the Nasi consciously and systematically sought the political alliance and social-communal partnership of the wealthy classes. This had been the Roman provincial policy for centuries, and for the Nasi was the natural result of his newly-gained status. Retention of authority required the assiduous cultivation of the important leadership sectors within Jewish society. The importance of this class was almost unequalled as long as they retained their wealth and social prominence. But with the deepening economic crisis and the erosion of this base of power, the Patriarchate suffered as well.

A third factor influencing the course of the Patriarchate was the crystallization by the mid-third century of an institutionalized rabbinic class whose involvement in and concern for communal Jewish life was markedly on the upswing. The establishment of permanent academies in the main cities during this century set the stage for a more communally-oriented rabbinic leadership[198]. The attitude of the sages towards the *ʿam ha-aretz,* the common people, while antagonistic earlier, likewise changed significantly as a result of this new rabbinic perspective[199]. Similarly, with regard to the sages' view of other Jewish authorities. The Nasi was now challenged on issues directly affecting Jewish communal life. Social and economic policy, and not just strictly religious issues, were subject to scrutiny. This is a far cry from the Patriarchal-rabbinic disputes of earlier generations which, in the main, revolved around internal issues of the academy[200].

However, with all this, the decline which ensued must not be overstated. The office continued throughout this period and, as noted, there are not a few sources attesting to its continued resiliency. R. Hiyya still found it desirable, even necessary, to acquire a letter of introduction from the Nasi, and probably served as his emissary. It is certain that the three leading sages of that generation — R. Ami, R. Asi and R. Hiyya — functioned under Patriarchal auspices when inspecting the educational system of various Palestinian communities[201]. The prestige of the Patriarchal court continued unabated, with leading families vying for priority, and no less a person than R. Abbahu was once accused of favoring Patriarchal interests when adjudicating a case involving a servant of the Nasi[202].

Thus, the picture that emerges is rather different from the usual sketches of the history of this office. The Nasi is often depicted as a weak

[198] Cf. LEVINE, above, n. 26, pp. 92—93.

[199] Cf. A. OPPENHEIMER, The ʿAm Ha-Aretz. A Study in the Social History of the Jewish People in the Hellenistic-Roman Period, Arbeiten zur Literatur und Geschichte des hellenistischen Judentums, XIII (Leiden, 1977), pp. 188—195.

[200] B Berakhot 27b—28a; B Horayot 13b.

[201] Cf. above, nn. 125—126.

[202] B Ketubot 84b.

religious and spiritual figure (a conclusion closely following the judgement of rabbinic literature, consciously or not), while at the same time remaining a powerful political figure. We have found the opposite to be true. Religiously the Patriarchs appear to have maintained a venerated status within Jewish society. Where they did suffer was in certain areas of social and communal prerogatives. The political base of the Nasi was so weakened by events of the third century that their hold on Jewish communal institutions was affected. This political decline undoubtedly had an effect on the Nasi's religious status; the extent, however, is almost impossible to determine. Nevertheless, the Patriarchate succeeded in weathering the storm, and was soon to enjoy more propitious political circumstances. Ironically, it was with the advent of Christian Rome that the office reached a peak of prominence and influence. With the backing of Christian emperors, extensive political leverage was once again added to religious authority. From all indications the last century of the Patriarchate, which coincided with the advent of Byzantine rule, was one of the most flourishing in the history of the office.

Appendix: The Problem of Chronology

One of the critical and vexing problems concerning Jewish history of late antiquity, and the Patriarchate in particular, is that of chronology. For the entire third and fourth centuries there are only two fixed dates regarding events in Roman Palestine and even they are to be found in a source dating from the end of the first millenium. The responsum of R. Sherira Gaon (ed. B. Lewin — henceforth ISG), from the year 986, is one of the first and the most famous of medieval attempts at outlining the ancient period. Aside from these two references, all of R. Sherira's dates apply to the history of the Babylonian rabbinate, and thus are of little value for our purposes. Palestinian Jewish history, for better or for worse, has been forced to make do with this data, and of necessity these two dates have become the anchors around which the chronology of the period is organized.

The first date refers to Rav's departure to Babylonia in the days of R. Judah I. The date given is 530 of the Seleucid era, or 219 C.E.[203] (Another medieval tradition gives the year 500 [= 189 C.E.] as the date of Rav's departure, of the redaction of the Mishna, and sometimes even of R. Judah's death. A number of modern historians have been inclined to follow this.)[204] However, the 219 date is undoubtedly correct, and R. Judah's death probably occurred around the year 225. This would place him squarely in the Severan period, which is the most suitable for explaining the unusually

[203] ISG, p. 78, 5—6.

[204] Cf. G. D. Cohen, ed., Sefer Ha-Qabbalah (Philadelphia, 1967), p. 211; S. Safrai, The Nesiut in the Second and Third Centuries and its Chronological Problems (Hebrew), Proceedings of the Sixth World Congress of Jewish Studies (Jerusalem, 1975), pp. 52—53; Guttmann, above, n. 37, pp. 239f.

good relations between Jewish authorities and the Imperial government. Moreover, the rabbinic account of R. Judah's abolishment of the *aurum coronarium*[205] is a striking parallel to similar actions taken in the days of Alexander Severus[206], and indeed may have been occasioned by them[207].

R. Judah was followed by his son R. Gamaliel III (Berebbi)[208]. However, the sources relating to R. Gamaliel are relatively few in number and, with but one exception[209], the events associated with him are of minor importance. It is, therefore, most unlikely that his term of office was of long duration and probably extended for but a decade or so.

The second date of ISG, equally pivotal for our purposes, refers to the death of R. Yohanan, the leading Palestinian sage of the Amoraic period. According to ISG, R. Yohanan died in the year 590 or 279 C.E.[210], having headed the academy for 80 years (sic!)[211]. While longevity appears to have been a trait of this sage, the claim of an 80 year ministry as head of the academy is clearly legendary. Besides the obviously symbolic nature of the number, such an extended period of activity would have had to have begun already in the days of R. Judah. However, apart from one isolated reference to R. Yohanan at R. Judah's academy[212], nothing is known about contacts between the two. And this for good reason: there probably were none.

We do know, however, that R. Yohanan and others of his generation (Resh Lakish, R. Yonatan, R. Eliezer, and R. Joshua b. Levi) were in continual contact with R. Judah II (Nesiah). Even the leading figures of the previous generation (those who had been the younger colleagues of R. Judah I), such as R. Hoshaya, R. Hanina b. Hama and R. Yannai were often found in his company. That R. Judah II could have bridged these two generations of sages and maintained intimate relations with individuals in each of these groups is quite imaginable. Thus we can assume that Judah II flourished in the second third of the third century.

As regards the latter part of the century, there is an impressive array of sources which describe R. Yohanan's students in contact with a R. Judah Nesiah. This latter generation of sages flourished during the last decades of the third and into the fourth century as well. Thus it is clear that we are dealing here with another R. Judah, the son, or far more likely the grandson, of the above-mentioned R. Judah II Nesiah. There were thus two men by the name of R. Judah who bore the title Nesiah. The first flourished during

205 B BB 8a and DS VIII, 15b.

206 SHA — Alexander Severus, XXXII; Selected Papyri — Loeb, II, 216; LEVINE, above, n. 26, p. 212, n. 279.

207 SAFRAI, above, n. 204, pp. 56—57.

208 B Ketubot 103b.

209 J Halla IV, 7, 60a.

210 ISG, p. 84, 4—5.

211 Ibid., p. 83, 16—17.

212 B Hullin 137b. Cf. also the legendary accounts of R. Judah predicting an illustrious career for R. Yohanan 1) before he was born (B Yoma 82b), and 2) while he was but a student (B Pesahim 3b).

the second third of the century, the other at the end of the third and at the very beginning of the fourth[213].

The question remains as to whether R. Judah III directly followed Judah II, or whether someone else served as Patriarch in between. Jewish aversion to naming a child after a living parent, as well as one specific source (probably referring to R. Judah III and his grandfather, Rabbi — in this case R. Judah II; cf. above, n. 17, on the generic use of the term 'Rabbi' in connection with a number of Patriarchs) indicate that there was indeed another generation between these two men:

> "When R. Judah (III) Nesiah the grandson of R. Judah Nesiah died, R. Hiyya b. Abba (fl. ca. 260—300) pushed R. Zeira in the Gofna synagogue of Sepphoris and defiled him[214]."

Several sources refer to one R. Gamaliel Zuga. We find him together with R. Yohanan[215], Resh Lakish[216] and members of the school of Yannai[217]. Since there was a Patriarch named R. Gamaliel before R. Judah II and another after R. Judah III, there is no difficulty in positing a Gamaliel IV, son of Judah II and father of Judah III. This might well be Gamaliel Zuga. However, the very paucity of reports about him, as well as the above-cited source which does not even name him, point to the fact that this Gamaliel served only a relatively short time, and probably without any significant achievements. This may be due in part to his personality, but may also be a result of the radically altered historical circumstances of the 260's. Roman might was then at a low ebb, as was Patriarchal authority. The fact that Gamaliel Zuga is mentioned only in connection with R. Yohanan and Resh Lakish (died ca. 279), and not with any of the following generation of sages is also noteworthy. The latter had already taken over communal leadership (within rabbinic circles at least) during the last decade of R. Yohanan's life, ca. 270, during Zenobia's invasion[218]. Thus a short period somewhere around 260 would seem to be the most likely date for Gamaliel Zuga's ministry.

The brevity of this Gamaliel's term of office and his relative innocuousness would account for his being ignored in the above-quoted tradition relating to rabbinic reactions to the death of R. Judah III. Moreover, the brevity of his ministry has one other possible implication, namely, that R.

[213] The terminus ad quem for the death of Judah III is 309 C.E. In that year R. Hisda died (ISG, p. 85, 10—11), the same R. Hisda who announced the Nesiah's death (B MQ 22b). The Nesiah referred to can only be R. Judah III. The terminus post quem is 299. In that year, R. Judah of Babylonia died (ISG, p. 85, 9—10), and subsequent to his death the rabbis referred someone to R. Judah III in order to absolve a ban (B MQ 17a). Therefore R. Judah III died between 299 and 309.

[214] J Berakhot III, 1,6a. Cf. also B Yoma 78a.

[215] J Halla IV, 6,60a.

[216] J Berakhot II, 1,4b; J AZ III, 13,43b.

[217] J Berakhot VI, 4,10c.

[218] J Terumot VIII, 10,46b.

Gamaliel's son, Judah III, may have been too young to take over the reins of office immediately. He may have done so only some years later, and the resultant interregnum was dominated by the leading active members of the rabbinic class — R. Ami, R. Asi and R. Hiyya.

Our conclusions regarding the chronological order of the third century Patriarchate are thus as follows:

R. Judah I	ca. 175—225
R. Gamaliel III	ca. 225—235
R. Judah II Nesiah	ca. 235—260
R. Gamaliel IV Zuga	ca. 260—265
Interregnum	ca. 265—275
R. Judah III Nesiah	ca. 275—305
R. Gamaliel V	ca. 305—320

Bibliography

ALON, G., A History of the Jews in Palestine during the Mishnaic-Talmudic Period (2 vols.; Tel-Aviv, 1961; Hebrew).

ID., Jews, Judaism and the Classical World (Jerusalem, 1977).

AVI-YONAH, M., The Jews of Palestine (New York, 1976).

BÜCHLER, A., Studies in Jewish History (London, 1956).

DINBURG, B., The Diocletian Rescript to Judah from 293 and the Struggle Between the Patriarchate and Sanhedrin in Palestine, Festschrift to A. Gulak and S. Klein (Jerusalem, 1942; Hebrew), pp. 76—93.

JUSTER, J., Les juifs dans l'empire romain, leur condition juridique, économique et sociale (2 vols; Paris, 1914).

KRAUSS, S., Antoninus und Rabbi (Wien, 1910).

ID., Die jüdischen Apostel, JQR, XVII (1904—05), pp. 370—383.

LIEBERMAN, S., Greek in Jewish Palestine (New York, 1942).

ID., Palestine in the Third and Fourth Centuries, JQR, XXXVI (1946), pp. 329—370.

LINDER, A., The Roman Imperial Government and the Jews under Constantine (Hebrew), Tarbiz, XLIV (1974—75), pp. 118—126.

MANTEL, H., Studies in the History of the Sanhedrin, Harvard Semitic series, XVII (Cambridge, 1965).

SAFRAI, S., The Practical Implementation of the Sabbatical Year after the Destruction of the Second Temple (Hebrew), Tarbiz, XXXVI (1967), pp. 1—21.

ZUCKER, H., Studien zur jüdischen Selbstverwaltung im Altertum (Diss. Berlin, 1936).